Novell IntranetWare

Professional Reference

Fifth Edition

Karanjit Siyan
Joshua Ball
Jason Ehrhart
Jim Henderson
Blaine Homer
Brian L. Miller
Thomas Oldroyd
Cynthia M. Parker
Danny Partain
Tim Petru
Paul Roberts
Jason Werner
Dennis Williams

New Riders Publishing, Indianapolis, IN

Novell IntranetWare Professional Reference

By Karanjit Siyan

Published by:
New Riders Publishing
201 West 103rd Street
Indianapolis, IN 46290 USA

Printed in the United States of America 1 2 3 4 5 6 7 8 9 0

Library of Congress Cataloging-in-Publication Data

CIP data available upon request

Warning and Disclaimer

This book is designed to provide information about Novell IntranetWare. Every effort has been made to make this book as complete and as accurate as possible, but no warranty or fitness is implied.

The information is provided on an "as is" basis. The authors and New Riders Publishing shall have neither liability nor responsibility to any person or entity with respect to any loss or damages arising from the information contained in this book or from the use of the disks or programs that may accompany it.

Publisher	Don Fowley
Associate Publisher	David Dwyer
Publishing Manager	Julie Fairweather
Marketing Manager	Mary Foote
Managing Editor	Carla Hall
Director of Development	Kezia Endsley

Product Development Specialist
Linda Barron

Acquisitions Editor
Linda Barron

Senior Editors
Sarah Kearns, Suzanne Snyder

Development Editor
John Sleeva

Project Editor
Molly Warnes

Copy Editor
Molly Warnes

Technical Editors
Wendy Johnson, Tim Petru, Jack Belbot

Software Specialist
Steve Flatt

Assistant Marketing Manager
Gretchen Schlesinger

Acquisitions Coordinator
Julie Fairweather

Administrative Coordinator
Karen Opal

Manufacturing Coordinator
Brook Farling

Cover Designer
Sandra Schroeder

Cover Illustrator
©Keith D. Skeen/SIS

Cover Production
Aren Howell

Book Designer
Sandra Schroeder

Director of Production
Larry Klein

Production Team Supervisors
Laurie Casey, Joe Millay

Graphics Specialists/Illustration
Kevin Cliburn, Wil Cruz, Laura Robbins, Bryan Towse

Production Analysts
Dan Harris, Erich J. Richter

Production Team
Lori Cliburn, Kim Cofer, Mary Hunt, Malinda Kuhn, Megan Wade

Indexer
Chris Barrick

About the Authors

Joshua Ball is currently working on cryptology and C2 security for Novell's Network Security R&D department. His experience includes over eight years in software development, six years of networking design and implementation, and three years in computer and network security. He received a Bacholor of Science from the Florida Institute of Technology and has had technical training in system and network security, auditing, intruder detection, network management, and programming of B3 TCBs. He has been active in teaching technological issues including CNE classes. His current interests and research include issues in cryptology, Rating and Maintenance Phase of the C2 evaluation, and security issues within Java.

Jim Henderson began working with NetWare networks in the fall of 1989, when he joined a team that was implementing an academic network at his university which used NetWare 2.15, and eventually upgraded to 3/11. He wrote several special-purpose utilities using only an interrupt debugger, a C compiler, and a copy of Barry Nance's *Network Programming in C,* writing his own interface for the NetWare API as needed. He currently works for a manufacturer of painting equipment in the Minneapolis area, serving a dual role of Network Administrator and PC Specialist, troubleshooting any problems that may come up in a mixed NetWare 4.02 / AS/400 environment.

His current network implementation consists of two NetWare 4/02 servers; one is located in the Minneapolis area, and the other is located in the Chicago area. He also works with an AS/400 system and a Sun Sparc 5 that are on his network.

In his spare time, he is the forum leader for the NetWare 4 forum on NetWire (r), Novell's online information service, provided through CompuServe.

When he is not reading NetWare-related material, he enjoys listening to music (classical and new age), playing soccer, and operating his amateur radio station (call KD4LDO/WO). He is involved in a group that is currently implementing a wireless connection to the Internet, and is also an avid fan of Douglas Adams' *The Hitchhiker's Guide to the Galaxy,* from which most of his improbable sense of humor derives.

Blaine Homer is a technical editor for *LAN Times.* He writes previews, reviews, and product comparisons for the publication. His technical beats include: network hardware, Novell products, network management applications and tools, and network security. Before joining the *LAN Times* Testing Center, Blaine worked for Novell's internal network management team. He also worked for Novell's IS department repairing hardware and surrporting the end user. Blaine also does private network installation and consulting. He has a Bachleor of Science degree from Brigham Young University's Marriott School of Management, with an emphasis in Information Systems.

Brian L. Miller is currently a Senior Network Engineer at KeyLabs, Inc., a full-service Network Testing Lab in Provo, Utah.

Prior to joining Key Labs, Brian was on the staff of *LAN Times* magazine as a Reviews Editor in the *LAN Times* Testing Center, specializing in Unix systems and products, video servers and video-conferencing systems, the Internet and TCP/IP-products, and network security products.

Before joining *LAN Times,* Brian worked at Phillips-Broadcast Television Systems (BTS) Inc., a developer of leading edge network-based Broadcast Video Servers. Brian also spent seven years with Unisys in the Unix Systems Group developing LAN & Communications products for Unix servers, and another four years with Unisys developing

Miniaturized Microwave Data Links in the Defense Systems Division. Brian started his career as a Microwave Radio Systems Repairman in the U.S. Army.

Brian also performs work as a Network and Internet consultant for small business installations and contributes as a freelance writer to several networking publications. Brian received his Bachelor of Science in Electrical Engineering Technology from Weber State University in 1989.

Thomas Oldroyd has worked at the core of the computer networking world for six years. His accomplishments include: marketing network clients, building and managing a 16-member engineering team, providing support for major networking sites such as Disney, the U.S. Navy, and IBM, earning his Certified NetWare Instructor (CNI) credentials, and being a co-inventor on the patent for "Method and Apparatus for Managing Applications in a Network." Thomas graduated from Brigham Young University in 1990 with a degree in Information Management. He is currently working on a Masters of Business Administration at Westminster College.

Cynthia M. Parker is a certified Novell Instructor and an Authorized Certified Novell Engineer in both NetWare 3 and NetWare 4 operating systems. She is a full-time staff Instructor at LANTech of America, Inc., a Novell Authorized Education Center, where she teaches both NetWare 3 and NetWare 4 courses. Cynthia has worked with NetWare since 1989 when she acquired the position of LAN Manager for a major medical practice at the Indiana University Medical Center. As LAN Manager and sole technical support for a rapidly growing and technically evolving network, Cynthia's expertise in LAN/WAN design, implementation, and management was gained through years of hands-on experience working with the product daily. Her talent in relating highly technical information in an articulate manner to educate and support users provided a smooth transition into technical instruction. Cynthia looks forward to working with NetWare for many years to come and plans to stay on the leading edge of technology.

Danny Partain has been involved with NetWare since 1989. He is a Systems Specialist for Raytheon Engineers & Constructors. He is a member of the Adjunct Faculty at Gwinnett Technical Institute in the Business Information Sciences Department. He teaches the following courses: "Introduction to Networking (NetWare)" and "Advanced Networking (NetWare)." He is a Certified NetWare Engineer (CNE). He is a graduate of Southern Polytechnic State University and Gwinnett Technical Institute. He is a member of NetWare Users International and 3COM user groups.

Tim Petru graduated with a Bachelor of Science degree from Brigham Young University in 1991. He has been working in the computer industry for 15 years, and in the networking industry for 10 years. At present, Tim is employed by a large networking software company and has done work in installation, support, and development of networking products. His areas of specialty include networking operating systems, directory services, and security services.

Karanjit S. Siyan is president of Kinetics Corporation. He has authored international seminars on Solaris & SunOS, TCP/IP networks, PC Network Integration, Windows NT, Novell networks, and Expert Systems using Fuzzy Logic. He teaches advanced technology seminars in the United States, Canada, Europe, and the Far East. Dr. Siyan has published articles in *Dr. Dobbs Journal, The C Users Journal, Databased Advisor,* research journals, and is actively involved in Internet research. Karanjit has worked with computer languages such as C/C++, Pascal, LISP, Algol, Ada, MSL, CMS-2, Jovial, Java, and other languages for many years and has written compilers for a number of these languages. Karanjit holds a Ph. D. in Computer

Science. Before working as an independent consultant, Karanjit worked as a senior member of the technical staff at ROLM Corporation and as a software developer and technical manager on numerous projects. As part of his consulting work, Karanjit has written a number of custom compiler and operating system development tools. His interests include Unix-based, NetWare-based, Windows NT–based, and OS/2 networks. He is actively involved in the application of many computer science disciplines, such as networks, operating systems, programming languages, databases, expert systems, and computer security. Dr. Siyan holds certification credentials for Windows NT and holds a Master CNE and ECNE certification for Novell-based networks. He has written numerous books. Karanjit Siyan is based in Montana, where he lives with his wife.

Dennis Williams is an Senior Reviews Editor for *LAN Times* magazine, specializing in WAN and remote communications, network hardware, and Novell and Microsoft products such as IntranetWare and Microsoft Windows NT. Before starting at *LAN Times*, he was Vice President of Ospar Corporation, a high-tech investment firm located in Newport Beach, Califormia, where he directed the MIS Department. He graduated from Brigham Young University with a Bachelor of Science in Information Management. To support his schooling, he worked at several ComputerLand stores installing and maintaining network systems. In addition to his duties at *LAN Times*, he owns a private consulting company, Enterprise Network Solutions, which supports and consults for a number of businesses, colleges, and municipalities. He is also a contributing editor for *NetWare Technical Journal* and has co-authored several books on NetWare. Dennis can be reached by email at dennis_williams@lantimes.com.

Trademark Acknowledgments

All terms mentioned in this book that are known to be trademarks or service marks have been appropriately capitalized. New Riders Publishing cannot attest to the accuracy of this information. Use of a term in this book should not be regarded as affecting the validity of any trademark or service mark.

Contents at a Glance

On the CD

Table of Contents

Part II: The NetWare Network Environment

On the CD

INTRODUCTION

The world is ever changing....

In its day, the Pony Express was a phenomenon—an unusual, significant, occurrence; a marvel. It was a marvel that lead to the postal service, the radio, the television...the Internet. The advances in our abilities to communicate with one another are astounding. And for those who understand today's technology, virtually limitless.

IntranetWare is today's technology. With IntranetWare you can build a comprehensive business communication infrastructure that is flexible enough to answer the communication demands of the future. IntranetWare gives you all the services of a full-service platform—from file, print, directory, messaging, Web publishing, security, and connectivity, to management. It includes high-performance Web and FTP servers as well as other software you need to provide your business and users of your network with access to Internet services and a corporate intranet.

The backbone of IntranetWare is NetWare 4; and the heart of NetWare 4 is Novell's Directory Services (NDS). NDS is built on a platform-independent directory strategy based on open standards. NDS provides a single point of access and management, increasing user productivity, which reduces network administration costs and eases application development. NDS is years ahead of other directory offerings and provides you with a platform on which you can build a limitless communication infrastructure.

IntranetWare offers an excellent foundation upon which you can build your corporate network and intranet, as well as the ability to securely connect to the Internet. In addition to NetWare 4.11—Novell's latest Network Operating System (NOS)—IntranetWare includes software with these unprecedented capabilities:

- NetWare Web Server
- Novell Intranet Access Server
- Novell IPX/IP Gateway
- Multiprotocol routing
- Dynamic Host Control Protocol (DHCP) support
- File Transfer Protocol (FTP) and Unix Print Services
- Netscape Navigator browser
- Developer tools
- Connectivity services
- WAN support

In today's fast-paced world, companies must take advantage of the intranet paradigm. This paradigm will enable you to leverage existing LANs, communication lines, and applications. Your intranet can provide employees with vital company information, training, data, and a connection to the Internet.

Covered In This Book

If you think the world is ever-changing, try getting your arms around technology. The *NetWare Professional Reference* series has established a unique status as some of the most authoritative NetWare books available. This is the 5th edition of this book; and in the tradition of the NetWare books, it offers thorough IntranetWare coverage. Some of features covered are as follows:

- Novell Directory Services
- NetWare 4 installation

- Client support for DOS, Windows, Windows NT, and Windows 95
- NetWare Web Server and related technologies
- TCP/IP with DHCP (Dynamic Host Configuration Protocol) support
- NetWare SMP (Symmetric Multiprocessing)
- C2-level security
- Network auditing
- Enhanced NWAdmin utility, as well as improved installation, management, and migration utilities
- Netscape Navigator
- Novell's IPX/SPX-to-TCP/IP gateway
- FTP services
- NetWare Multiprotocol Router (MPR), with WAN extensions
- And much more

As an added bonus, the CD-ROM includes a Windows-based online command reference for NetWare 2.x through IntranetWare, and some of the latest tools and utilities for administering an IntranetWare network.

Who Should Read This Book?

If you need to understand the technology behind today's Internet and intranets, business communications, or if you have a mixed networking environment and are looking for ways to extend and preserve your investments you should read this book.

Companies are installing corporate intranets at a feverish pace. An intranet is an internal network that employs Internet technology, but is only accessible to those directly involved with the corporation or business. Intranets provide unprecedented communication abilities between employees and partners. Although intranets are internal, most organizations want to connect their intranets to the Internet. There is a variety of reasons for this:

- Link geographically dispersed sites
- Disperse up-to-the-minute information
- Access Internet services from an intranet

Linking Geographically Dispersed Sites

The demand to have access to information from anyplace and at anytime is growing. This demand will continue to escalate as more and more information becomes available on companies through their intranets. Outlined in this book, you will find ways to create links from two diverse worlds—the inside world and the outside world. Links that are secure are links that can be trusted with business-critical information. This book provides procedures to create a trusted network environment based on IntranetWare's Enhanced Security, which has been designed to meet the Controlled Access implementation (Class C2) requirements. IntranetWare is the first general purpose network operating system to receive this C2 rating. Security features that are covered in this book consist of the following:

- **Creating IPX/IP gateways.** Provides access to the Internet from standard IPX by simply loading a Web. This gateway also enables TCP/IP programs to function as if TCP/IP were configured at their desktops—without having to deploy IP to individual workstations. Because there is only one IP address on the network, the IP/IPX gateway can act as a natural IP firewall. This occurs because workstations on the network are invisible to potential intruders.

- **NetWare's C2-compliant auditing.** Enables individuals, acting as independent representatives, to monitor network supervisors and users, as well as network transactions. This level of auditing provides security beyond traditional access rights.

- **Traditional securities.** These include: password protection, file rights, directory trustee assignments, and so on.

The in-depth discussion on security is not limited to the preceding topics. This book will also discuss how to set up multiple levels of access control; including host control, application level control, content control, and so on.

When building a secure system, you must always consider multiple-level access control, authentication, and end-to-end information encryption. This book will help you build such a system using IntranetWare and its components.

Dispersing Up-to-the-Minute Information

Information is not knowledge until it is consumed. This is one of the reasons behind the feverish pace of intranet installation. Today's fast-paced society and market place requires individuals to consume an ever-increasing amount of information—some call it information overload.

The technologies discussed in this book will help you create an information infrastructure that will enable your employees to turn corporate information into useable knowledge, without overloading them.

It will provide you with an understanding of the technology necessary to publish corporate-wide, up-to-the-minute information—information that is timely, relevant, easy to use and access, and secure.

Accessing Internet Services from an Intranet

The World Wide Web (WWW) and Internet have the ability to deliver a limitless amount of information to the desktop, but only to those who are connected. You will need to know how to quickly and efficiently provide your users with access to that outside world, as well as how to manage this huge consumption of bandwidth as information is delivered to each and every desktop in your organization. Creating an efficient, integrated Internet solution makes up part of the scope of this book.

The IntranetWare Web Server enables users to publish their own content through NDS. Using NDS, each user may create content in their home directory and have it published. This will open new doors and break down communication barriers. Because NDS is global, this information is easily managed and controlled network-wide from a single administrative location.

The Internet uses TCP/IP as its network protocol; NetWare uses IPX/SPX. Combining these two worlds used to be difficult. This book will explain how to take advantage of IntranetWare's IPX/IP Gateway, which will provide your users access to both Internet and intranet services. This solution does not demand that you first upgrade each client with a TCP/IP protocol stack. You can simply use your IPX-designed network, which eliminates the time it takes to implement and manage TCP/IP workstations.

Conclusion

Recent studies show that NetWare maintains a commanding lead as the network operating system of choice among all classes of business users. IntranetWare will likely maintain this lead. With IntranetWare, a company gains new options and flexibility in the way it provides employees access to computing resources, information, and the Internet.

With IntranetWare, a corporation can protect its investments in NetWare and extend its Novell network to meet its evolving Internet\intranet needs.

This book includes in-depth information on how to employ and install NetWare 4 features, such as directory services, messaging services, print services, file services, auditing, and security. After reading this book, you will be better prepared to take advantage of NetWare's services as well as how to use the services IntranetWare provides, enabling you to construct a full-service computing environment.

New Riders Publishing

The staff of New Riders Publishing is committed to bringing you the very best in computer reference material. Each New Riders book is the result of months of work by authors and staff who research and refine the information contained within its covers.

As part of this commitment to you, New Riders invites your input. Please let us know if you enjoy this book, if you have trouble with the information and examples presented, or if you have a suggestion for the next edition.

Please note, however: New Riders staff cannot serve as a technical resource for Novell IntranetWare or for questions about software- or hardware-related problems. Please refer to the documentation that accompanies your software or to the application's Help systems.

If you have a question or comment about any New Riders book, there are several ways to contact New Riders Publishing. We will respond to as many readers as we can. Your name, address, or phone number will never become part of a mailing list or be used for any purpose other than to help us continue to bring you the best books possible.

You can write us at the following address:

New Riders Publishing
Attn: Publisher
201 W. 103rd Street
Indianapolis, IN 46290

If you prefer, you can fax New Riders Publishing at:

317-817-7448

You can also send electronic mail to New Riders at the following Internet address:

`jfairweather@newriders.mcp.com`

New Riders Publishing is an imprint of Macmillan Computer Publishing. To obtain a catalog or information, or to purchase any Macmillan Computer Publishing book, call 800-428-5331 or visit our Web site at `http://www.mcp.com`.

Thank you for selecting *Novell IntranetWare Professional Reference*!

PART PART PART PART PART PART PART PART PART PART

I

NetWare 4/IntranetWare

CHAPTER 1

Features of NetWare 4 and IntranetWare

IntranetWare, Novell's latest Network Operating System, is comprised of a combination of product offerings tailored for today's market of heterogeneous networks connected via the public network, the Internet. This chapter provides a general overview of the new features in NetWare 4 and IntranetWare.

NetWare 4 is the fifth generation of Novell's popular network operating system. It is a high-performance server operating environment that provides its users with powerful, reliable processing for file, print, directory, security, and management services—NetWare 4 is the foundation of IntranetWare.

This chapter discusses the enhancements made to NetWare 4 and the new features that constitute IntranetWare. Understanding these features will help you better understand how to build secure, large-scale, enterprise-wide networks and Internets using IntranetWare.

IntranetWare

IntranetWare includes all the functionality of the core operating system NetWare 4 and then adds additional technologies that enable you to build intranets and Internet services on NetWare.

With IntranetWare you not only get NetWare 4, but also several of Novell's intranet\Internet products, including the following:

- **The NetWare Web Server.** The NetWare Web Server tightly integrates with NDS, making the IntranetWare solution the only product offering that lets you browse a global directory, locate information, or find a network resource, regardless of where it is on your intranet.
- **A Multiprotocol router.** The Multiprotocol router enables you to set up a WAN connection to your Internet service provider using leased lines, ISDN or frame relay, eliminating the need for an external expensive hardware router.
- **An IP-IPX gateway.** The IP-IPX gateway lets standard IPX users surf the Internet with their Web browser as well as allowing other TCP programs to function as if TCP/IP were configured at their desktops—without having to deploy IP to individual workstations. And with only one actual IP address on the network, the IP-IPX gateway can act as a natural IP firewall, because workstations on the network are invisible to potential intruders.
- **FTP Services.**
- **New IntranetWare Clients.**
- **Netscape browser.** IntranetWare ships with Netscape's 16-bit (Windows 3.11) and 32-bit (Windows 95 and NT) World Wide Web browsers. The inclusion of these browsers provides you with the license to use the browsers on all of your workstations. Netscape's browser provides a graphical interface and pop-up menus, enabling you to view HTML documents on your internal or external Web sites. Netscape supports Java, and its browser includes the Java Class Loader and the Java Applet Security Manager. Other features of Netscape's browser include integrated e-mail and news reader, a bookmark facility, and a plug-in architecture that can be used to integrate third-party utilities that will extend the browser's abilities and functionality.

NetWare 4 is the core, or backbone, of IntranetWare, and has several enhancements worth noting. These enhancements are discussed in more depth later in this chapter, but for a quick reference to the improvements, see the following table.

Table 1.1 compares the most significant features in NetWare 4.1 and IntranetWare with NetWare 3.12. When reading this chapter remember that IntranetWare includes NetWare 4 and all its features.

Table 1.1
NetWare Features Comparison

Feature/Product	NetWare 3.12	NetWare 4.1	IntranetWare
	Internet/Intranet Feature or Product		
Browser included	no	no	yes
DHCP support	add-on	add-on	yes
FTP	extra charge	extra charge	yes
IP/IPX Gateway	no	extra charge	yes
Java Support	no	no	yes
NetBasic scripting tools	no	no	yes
Multiprotocol Routing	extra charge	extra charge	PPP, ISDN, Frame Relay, AT, X.25
TCP/IP	add-on	add-on	yes
Web Server	no	no	yes
Internet service provider connectivity	no	no	leased lines, Frame Relay, ISDN
	Installation		
Hardware autodetect	no	no	yes
Dynamic device driver selection/configuration	no	no	yes
Integrated install with other Novell products	no	no	yes
	Migration Utilities		
DS Migrate for modeling directory trees	no	no	yes

continues

Table 1.1, Continued
NetWare Features Comparison

Feature/Product	NetWare 3.12	NetWare 4.1	IntranetWare
File Migration from within NWAdmin	no	no	yes
Directory Services			
Browse multiple NDS trees at once	n/a	with update NDS	yes
Directory partition management utilities	n/a	Partition Manager	NDS Manager
Custom views of NDS through object filtering	n/a	with updated NDS	yes
Symmetric Multi-processing available from (SMP) support	no	OEM only	yes
Additive Licensing	no	yes	yes
Licensing Service	no	no	yes
Security			
NetWare Enhanced Security	no	no	yes
RSA public key/ private key	no	yes	yes
Network Auditing	no	yes	improved
Abend Recovery	no	no	yes
NetWare Application Launcher (NAL)	no	yes	yes
Printing			
Print management utilities	bindery-based	Directory-based	Directory-based with new utilities
Number of printers per server supported	16 per server	256 per server	256 per server

Feature/Product	NetWare 3.12	NetWare 4.1	IntranetWare
File Services			
Automatic file compression	no	yes	yes
Block suballocation	no	yes	yes
High-Capacity Storage System (HCSS)	no	yes	yes
Directory entries per volume supported	2 million	2 million	16 million
Long name space supported	OS2.NAM	OS2.NAM	LONG.NAM
Connectivity Services			
Protocol management	limited	yes	yes
Load/bind multiple protocols at installation	no	TCP/IP and AppleTalk in addition to IPX	TCP/IP and Apple-Talk in addition to IPX

Management Advantages of IntranetWare and NetWare 4

Typical networks consist of several LANs tied together using local or wide area links, as shown in figure 1.1. Before you can use a networked printer, hard drive, or other network resources, you (the client) needs to know the location of the resources. In figure 1.1, a user of earlier versions of NetWare had to know the names and the locations of the file servers to which the printer and volume resources are attached. Likewise, before you can access a resource on a server, you must log in to that server. If you need to access a volume resource on another server, you must attach to that server and then create a separate drive mapping. Attaching to a server implies that you need accounts on each server to which you need access. This approach works well in small networks, but is not very practical for large networks with many servers and resources—the demands on management are too great. Remembering what resources are available on which server is not easy. A logical view of the network that hides the network's nonessential, physical details is much easier for the user. Figure 1.2 shows a logical view of the network depicted in figure 1.1.

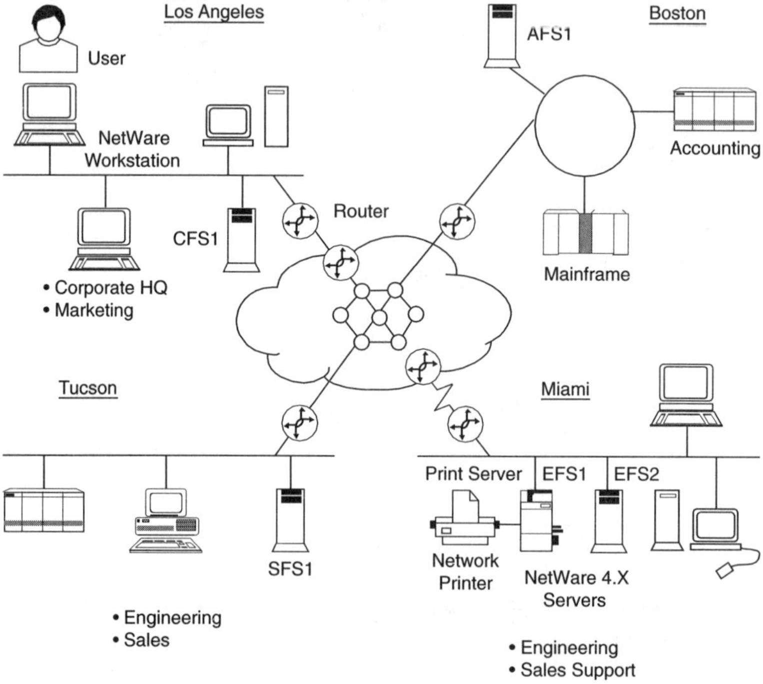

Figure 1.1
Example of a NetWare-based network.

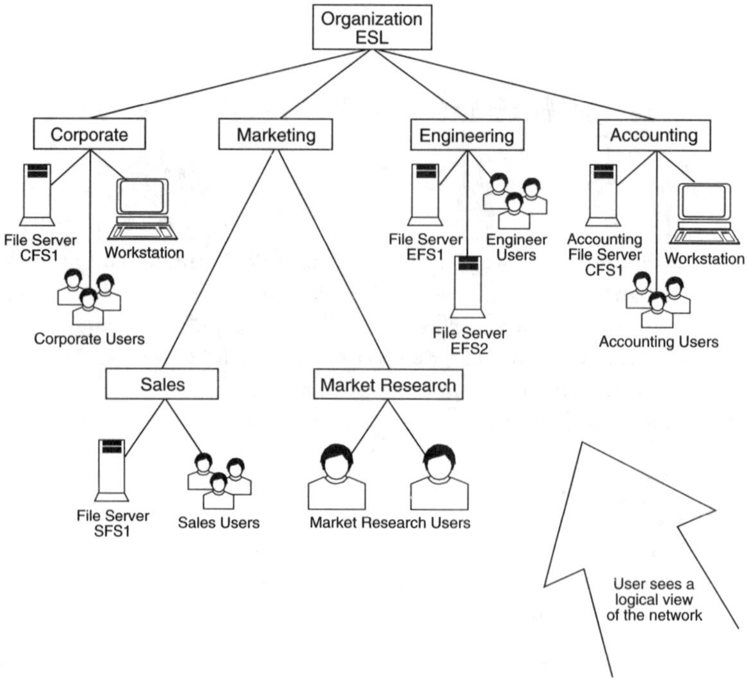

Figure 1.2
Logical view of network shown in figure 1.1.

With NetWare 4, resources are organized in the logical view of the network into groups with a hierarchy that reflects usage, function, or geographical location. If you want to use the resources on this network, you log in to the logical view of the network. Security mechanisms that are global in scope and apply to the entire network enable control of access to resources on the network. In previous versions of NetWare, security mechanisms local to each server (called the *bindery*) controlled access to resources. The bindery does not have network-wide significance. Bindery-based services are, therefore, *server-centric*. To provide a single access to the network, the designers of NetWare 4 created a global database called the Novell Directory Service (NDS). The *Novell Directory Service* is the mechanism in NetWare 4 that provides a logical view of the network.

The Novell Directory Service provides a *global database* service not confined to a single server *and* represents network-wide resources. The NDS is the single most important management difference between NetWare 4 and other Network Operating Systems on the market.

With NWAdmin, IntranetWare's 32-bit network administration utility (NWADMIN), the network administrator can manage all IntranetWare resources centrally, from a Windows 95 workstation or Windows NT workstation. This centralized management can dramatically lower administration time and thus, administration costs. Furthermore, the point-and-click interface of NWADMIN simplifies tasks such as creating users and groups, assigning rights in the directory tree and file system, and browsing and manipulating directory objects (including user profiles, printers, File system objects, Application objects, Directory Map objects, and Alias objects).

Note

> The 32-bit NWAdmin utility has been designed specifically for the 32-bit environment—it takes advantage of the high-performance Windows 95 environment to speed the execution of administrative tasks and increase administrator productivity.
>
> An older version of the administration client also ships with IntranetWare, and can be used with DOS or Windows 3.x.

Other IntranetWare and NetWare 4 Improvements

The following section discusses in more depth some of the more significant inclusions, enhancements, and changes to the feature set of IntranetWare and NetWare 4:

- Novell Directory Services (NDS) enhancements
- Support for C2 network auditing
- Simplified and more efficient memory management architecture

- Improvements in client networking services
- Integrated Storage Management Services (SMS)
- Improvements in network print services architecture
- Multiple language support (internationalization)
- Simplified installation and upgrade procedures
- OnLine DynaText NetWare manuals from Electronic Book Technologies, Inc.
- Enterprise tools, such as NLSP for service advertisement and merging directories
- Bindery synchronizer for central administration of a mixed NetWare 3 and 4 network

Understanding Novell Directory Services

Novell Directory Services is perhaps the most distinct feature of NetWare 4. It provides the network administrator and the user with a logical view of the network that conceals the sometimes bewildering complexity of the actual physical topology and configuration. The logical view of the network can be organized into what makes sense and is easily recognizable. For example, in figure 1.3, the view of the network is hierarchical and reflects the organization chart of the company, which users in that organization can recognize. The physical details of the network, such as the type of cabling, and interconnecting devices, such as routers and bridges, are absent from figure 1.3. In other words, the network administrator and the user do not need to be aware of the physical nature of the network to use it.

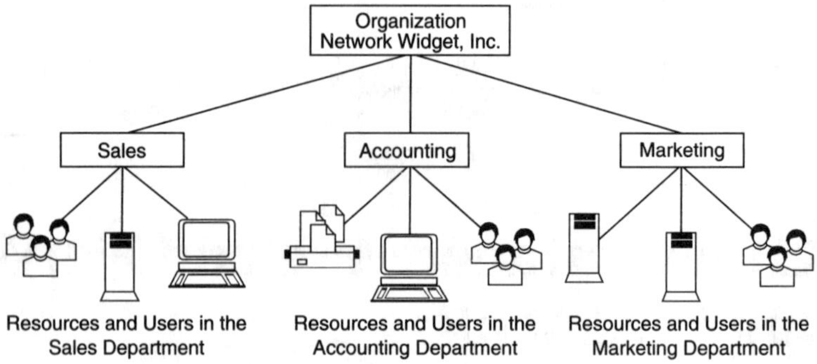

Figure 1.3
Logical network view, reflecting hierarchy of organization.

The Novell Directory Service is what makes the logical view possible. NDS provides a *distributed database* (does not physically reside on any single server on the network) that can serve as a repository of information on all the shared resources on the network. The database is also *hierarchical* because it conveniently groups resources by function, location, or organizational structure.

NDS is essentially a replacement for the *bindery* services that were part of the pre-NetWare 4 product line. The bindery in earlier NetWare releases also served for organizing resources, but the resources were specific to the server on which the bindery resided. The bindery could not easily support information on other nodes on the network, and because it was organized as a *flat database*, as opposed to a *hierarchical database*, it did not offer any natural way to represent usage or organizational relationships between resources.

Some benefits of using NDS are as follows:

- Provides logical organization of the network
- Requires single login to the network
- Offers global network management view
- Provides independence from physical location of resources

With IntranetWare, some new utilities and features that will aid in simplifying your network administration have been added. These improvements include: Merge Tree, Rename Tree, Move subtree, Rename container, NETSYNC, DSMAINT, and DUPGRADE.

Logical Organization of the Network

The logical organization of the network is a benefit derived directly from the way resources can be grouped in a hierarchical fashion in the NDS representation for an organization (refer to figure 1.3). This grouping reflects the way users want to use the network and makes it easy for users and network Administrators to find network resources without knowing the physical details of network connectivity. A user who needs to use a network resource has a *logical pointer* to the NDS database. These pointers are called *objects* and contain information on the resource. In NetWare 4, objects represent all network resources a NetWare user can access.

A file server is an example of a network resource that you can model as a file server object. This file server object contains information such as the file server name, network address, location, and so on (see fig. 1.4). Information about the file server is called *properties* of the file server object.

Figure 1.4
File server represented as an object.

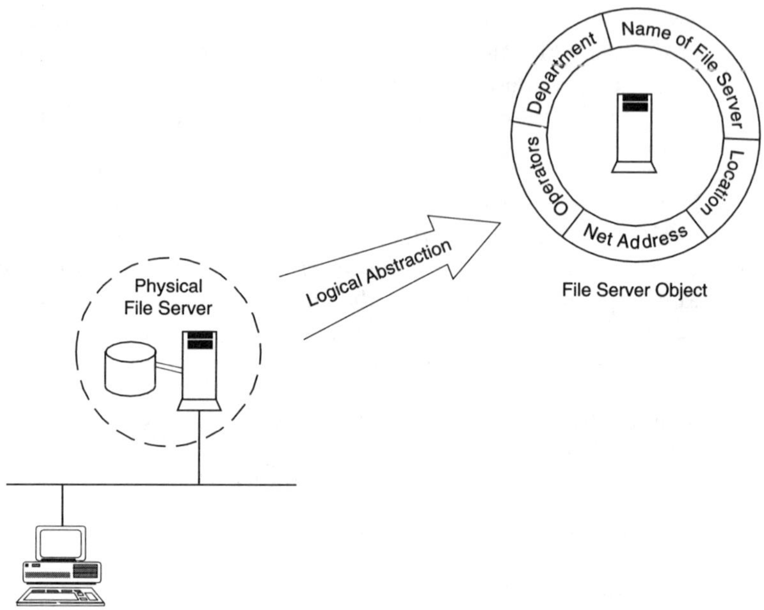

Single Login to the Network

A *single login* to a network (see fig. 1.5) authenticates a user to access all the resources on the network just once. After a user logs in, the network Administrator can limit access to resources on the network. For example, all users can see the structure of an organization's directory by default, even though they cannot access all the objects in this directory unless a network Administrator explicitly gives them access. A single login to a network also simplifies the use of the network because a user does not have to perform separate logins to multiple servers on the network.

Prior to NetWare 4, you had to log in (or attach) explicitly by supplying a user name and password for every server you wanted to access. The number of such concurrent connections was limited to eight. In addition, the network Administrator had to create separate accounts on each server to which you needed access. This easily became burdensome on a large network.

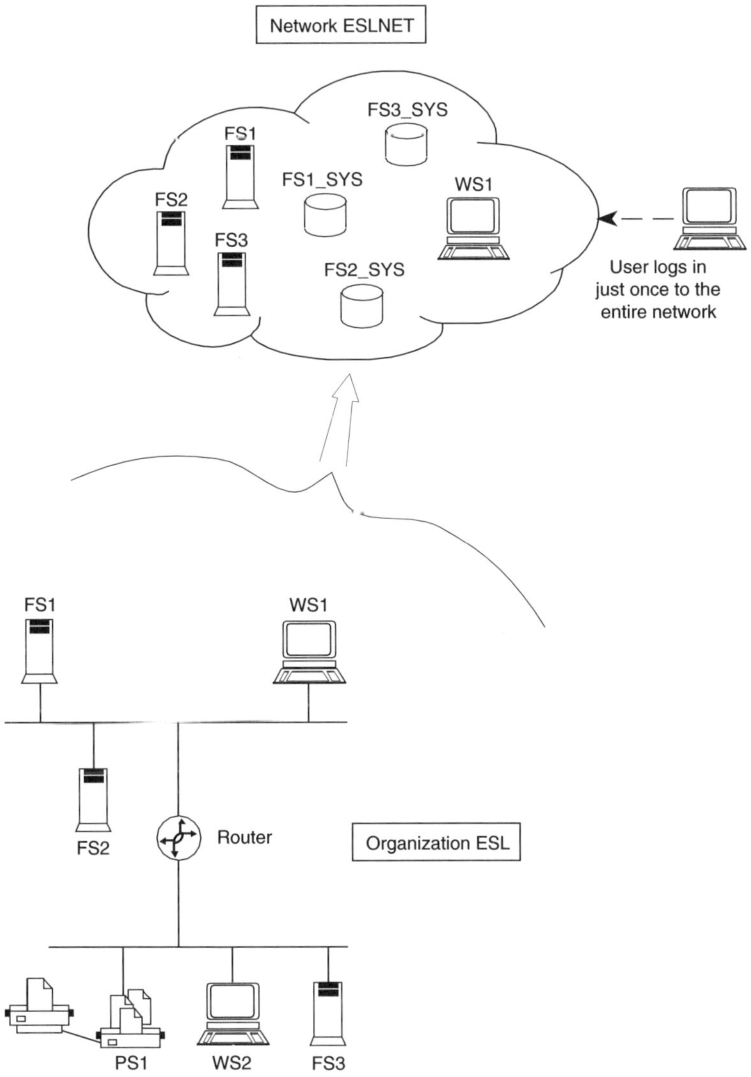

Figure 1.5
A single login to the network.

Single login to a network is possible because the user authentication takes place against a global network directory that is not specific to any server. In figure 1.6, you can see that the first step of a login to a network is authenticating the user against information in the global directory. After authentication of the user is successful, the user is granted access to any resource on the network.

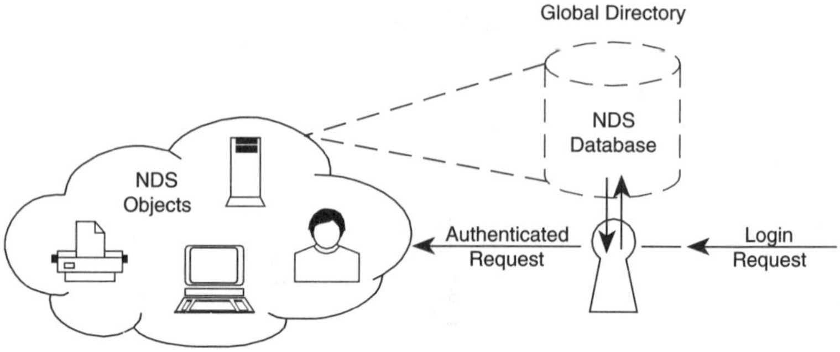

Figure 1.6
User authentication to the network.

Global Network Management

Before NetWare 4, network management tasks had to be performed separately on each NetWare server because network management usually resulted in a modification of the bindery, and the bindery was specific to each server.

Because the NDS is a global database, *global network management,* in which the network administrator can change network resources from anywhere on the network, is possible (see fig. 1.7). The network Administrator can delegate responsibility to other users who serve as network Administrators.

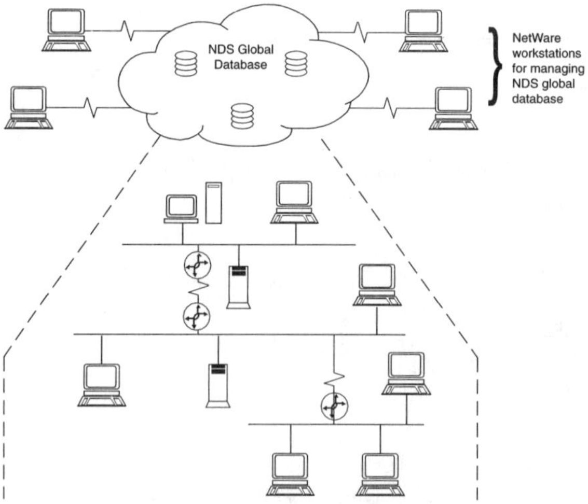

Figure 1.7
Global network management.

Prior to NetWare 4, the Administrator could delegate responsibility to a fixed number of user account managers, workgroup managers, and other operators; whereas NetWare 4 can have many levels of network Administrators who have varying degrees of responsibilities.

Independence from Physical Location of Resources

In pre-NetWare 4 networks, the resources were described in a server bindery and depended on that server. A classic example would be the NetWare printer definitions tied to a specific server. If you had to relocate the printer to another server, you had to move the bindery representation of the printer to another server (see fig. 1.8). In a large network that is in a state of constant change, relocating the printer would become a major task.

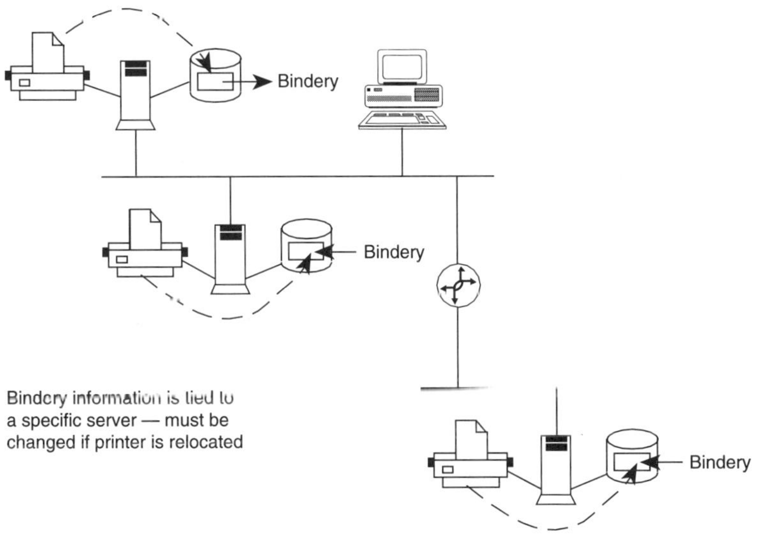

Figure 1.8
Bindery representations of printer definitions.

In NetWare 4, the resource definitions are not tied to any specific server or physical location on the network, which means that you can access a resource without having to worry about the physical location of the resource and figuring out how to reach it. Changes to network resources are made to the NDS object that is part of a global database. You can access the NDS object from any station on the network, provided you are granted security permission for the resource.

Exploring Improvements in the NetWare File System

One of NetWare's strengths is its fast and efficient file system, which has always been central to its popularity and capability to act as a file server. In NetWare 4 the file system is even better. Some improvements are as follows: *block suballocation*, *compression*, and *migration*, and are covered in the following sections.

Block Suballocation

When you install NetWare 4, you can select a disk block size of 4 KB, 8 KB, 12 KB, 16 KB, or 64 KB (1 KB is 1,024 bytes). This capability also exists in NetWare 3; but in NetWare 3, if you create a 200-byte file on a volume that has a disk block size of 4 KB, NetWare allocates a 4 KB block of storage and the remaining 3,896 bytes (4,096–200) are not available for use—a waste of space that exceeds 95 percent. If the disk block size is 64 KB, the waste of space is even greater. Figure 1.9 shows how block suballocation in NetWare 4 works.

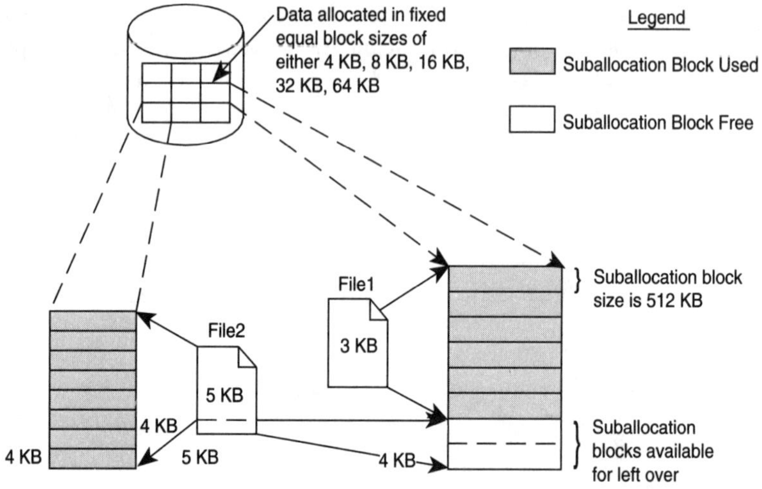

Figure 1.9
Disk suballocation.

NetWare 4 uses the unused disk block space in 512-byte suballocation units. If you create a 200-byte file, for example, NetWare 4 uses a 512-byte suballocation within the 4 KB disk block and the remaining seven 512-byte suballocation blocks are available for sharing by leftover fragments of other files. If all these suballocation blocks were used, then, in the preceding example, only 312 (512–200) bytes would be wasted out of a total of 4,096 bytes—just eight percent. If the disk block size is 64 KB, an even smaller percentage of space is wasted (about 0.5 percent). If the file sizes and leftover fragments are multiples of 512 bytes, no space is wasted.

Block suballocation allows small files and files that are not multiples of the disk block size to share space in a disk block that otherwise would go unused. The improved disk space utilization is accompanied by the extra overhead in the operating system to maintain status of disk blocks that have been suballocated, but because disk writes occur in the background, the impact of the overhead is minimal.

Disk suballocation is enabled by default during a NetWare volumes installation. You can explicitly disable disk allocation during installation. Always allocate a disk block size of 64 KB for maximum gain in server disk performance because at this block size, the software and disk subsystems perform optimally.

NetWare File System Compression

Studies show that the processor utilization of many NetWare servers in real-life networks does not often exceed 70 percent. In heavily loaded servers, processor utilization higher than 90 percent is not uncommon, but such situations are relatively rare. The designers of NetWare 4 decided to use this typically under-utilized processor bandwidth for useful background tasks, such as file system compression. Today, many disk compression utilities are available for DOS. These utilities decompress disk blocks as they are read and recompress them when they are written, which causes the disk to appear slow because of the compression operation that accompanies each read or write operation. In NetWare 4, file compression occurs in the background, which means compression will only take place during times of server under-utilization.

When a file is retrieved, in NetWare 4 it is automatically read into memory and instantly decompressed. This method of decompression actually increases performance—the file can be read into memory more efficiently. After the file blocks are decompressed they are available for use, even as the rest of the file is being decompressed by special *decompression threads* (see fig. 1.10).

In NetWare 4 files remain in the decompressed state for a user-specified period of time. This enables you to better manage your working set of files, or those files that you use most often. For instance, you may want to specify that files should only be compressed after 30 days. When the time does come for a file to be compressed, NetWare will wait for the best time to perform the compression routine. This is known as a background task and is only performed if it will not interrupt current server performance.

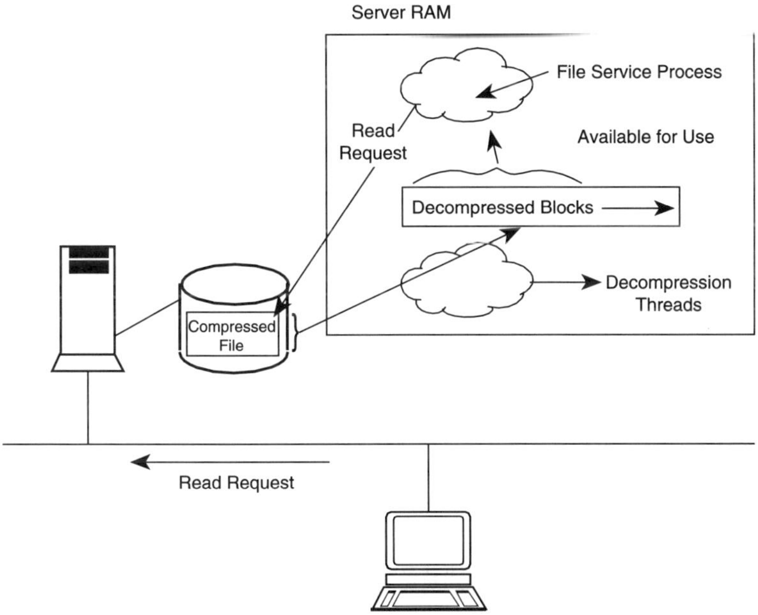

Figure 1.10
A read of a compressed file.

Using the file compression feature, you can increase effective disk space without adding new server drives. The amount of disk space savings depends on the nature of repeated characters or binary patterns in the file and is very high for text files. Savings of up to 63 percent or more is not uncommon, which means that 500 MB of files can take as little as 185 MB of disk space. Such disk space savings are a great advantage because disk space is perennially at a premium on file servers.

NetWare's compression is said to be intelligent; that is, it does not compress a file unless it sees a certain gain in disk space. Furthermore, the network Administrator can explicitly control compression by flagging specific files and directories to compress immediately or to never compress.

The only time you can disable or enable compression is during server installation or creation of the server's volumes. The default setting for compression is enabled, which means that NetWare tries to compress a file if it has not been used for some time, as long as a minimum savings in disk space can be achieved. This minimum disk space savings can be set by the server.

Data Migration

Data migration allows infrequently used files to be moved to a *near-line* or *off-line* storage medium. An example of near-line storage would be *optical disc libraries* (also known as *juke-boxes*), and an example of off-line storage would be a *tape backup device.* When data migration occurs, NetWare 4 still sees the data on the NetWare volumes because the directory entries for the migrated files are still on the NetWare volume. If you access a migrated file, the file is brought back in (*demigrated*) to the NetWare volume by the NetWare operating system (see fig. 1.11). Essentially, data migration frees valuable disk space. Data migration combined with compression is a very effective way to save disk space.

Figure 1.11
Data migration.

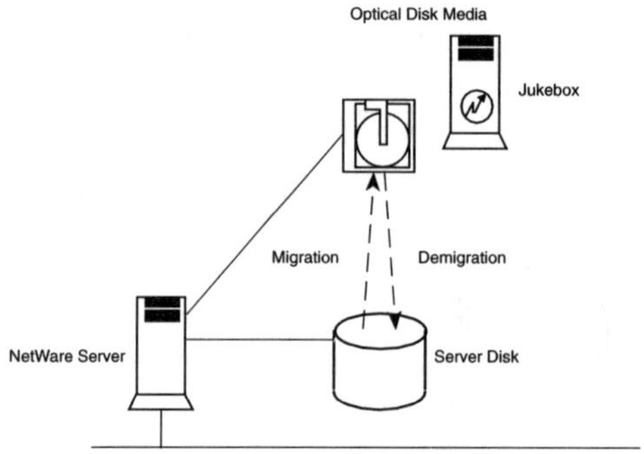

Some of the earlier Control Data Corporation's super computers used data migration, but NetWare 4 is the first to popularize its use among PC-based network operating systems (NOSs).

You can enable or disable data migration during installation of the NetWare volume, and you can use the NetWare utilities to mark files for migration.

You can use the *high-capacity storage system* (HCSS) to implement data migration. The HCSS is a storage and retrieval system that can extend the capacity of a NetWare server by integrating optical libraries into the NetWare file system. HCSS can work in conjunction with data migration so that NetWare can move migrated files from the faster but lower-capacity NetWare volumes to the slower but higher-capacity media that comprise the HCSS.

The operation of data migration and HCSS is transparent to the user. Users use the same commands to access files migrated to the HCSS as to access files that reside on the NetWare volume. If a user accesses a migrated file, it is automatically demigrated by the NetWare operating system.

Migration is performed on an individual file basis, depending on the last time the file was accessed, called the *least recently used* criteria, and the current volume usage. Least recently used criteria for files refers to the least-active files or files that have not been accessed for the longest period of time. If the current volume usage exceeds a *capacity threshold* (the percentage of the server's disk used before data migration begins), data migration occurs.

Long File Name Support

With IntranetWare, LONG.NAM provides the extended name space support needed to use Windows 95, Windows NT, and OS/2 workstation platforms on a NetWare volume. LONG.NAM is a Namespace NetWare Loadable Module that enables non-DOS file names to be stored on a NetWare volume. Because of the popularity of long file names, LONG.NAM is now loaded by default. (LONG.NAM replaces OS2.NAM.)

To store any non-DOS file types on a NetWare volume, you must first load the name space NLM and then add the name space to the volume. After the name space NLM is loaded, you can use the ADD NAME SPACE console command to configure the volumes so you can store other types of file names.

You only add a name space to a volume once by using the ADD NAME SPACE command. You don't need to add a name space to a volume each time the server comes up, so the ADD NAME SPACE command does not need to be placed in your AUTOEXEC.NCF file.

Each time you mount a volume configured for additional name space support (for example, each time you bring up the server), the corresponding name space will automatically be loaded.

When name space support is added to a volume, another entry is created in the directory table for the directory and file naming conventions of that name space (file system). For example, a volume that supports Macintosh files has the following for each Macintosh file: a DOS file name in the DOS name space, and a Macintosh file name in the Macintosh name space.

Because the server must cache the additional name space types, each volume assigned to support an additional name space requires twice as much server memory.

After a name space is added to a volume, the name space can be removed from the volume only by deleting the volume and re-creating it, or by using "VREPAIR."

Increased Directory Entries for Volume Capacity

With IntranetWare, each NetWare server volume can support 16 million directory entries by default and up to 16 million directory entries on volumes that use only the DOS name space. With previous versions of NetWare 4, the limit was 2 million entries per volume.

However, each additional name space requires an additional entry per file. For example, using only the DOS name space requires one directory entry per file. With the DOS and long name spaces loaded, two directory entries are required.

Increased Speed when Mounting Volumes

The software responsible for mounting NetWare volumes has been enhanced. Volumes mount much faster now, sometimes more than twice as fast as with previous versions of NetWare 4.

Proactive File Purging

IntranetWare's file system monitors NetWare volume space that is being used and proactively purges deleted files, which frees up volume space. The file system has also been enhanced to respond more efficiently to clients that are using the new 32-bit IntranetWare client architecture, which means a higher level of performance.

Improved File System Security and Management

Access to the NetWare 4 is established when the user logs in to NetWare 4's Directory Service. This process is known as *authentication.* When a user authenticates to the Directory the user then has access to the areas of the directory and to those files, for which they have been given rights.

The beauty of a hierarchical directory structure is that network administrators can model the logical network after an organizational structure, or after geographical locations of an organization. This enables the administrator to assign certain rights to all network users that are in the accounting department, or all users that are located in Washington. On a more global scale, this means that each organization can have its own network directory tree that reflects the usage and security needs of its network users. This becomes relevant when you start to consider the concept of a global directory—relevant because you could easily restrict others from gaining access to your network, while providing access to geographically dispersed portions of your business.

Also, as part of implementing network security, explicit trustee assignments control access to parts of the network directory tree. Figure 1.12 shows the steps that must occur before a user is granted access to a file on a volume, including login authentication, NDS security, and NetWare file system security.

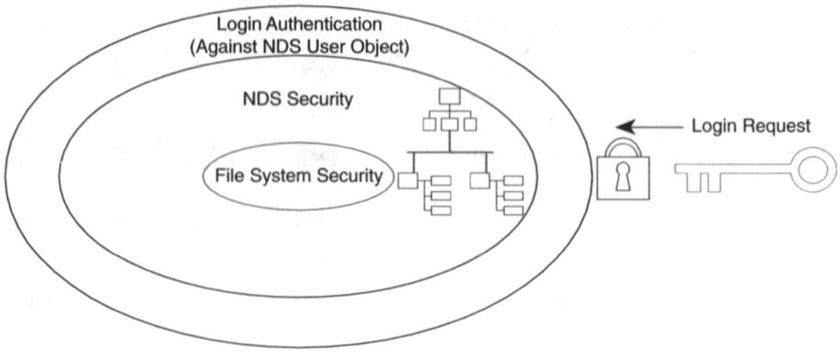

Figure 1.12
NetWare 4 security.

When a user logs in to the network, the user specifies the name of the NDS object that represents the user account. The user's login name and password are used to build a personalized key used to authenticate a user's right to access the network. The actual algorithm used to build the personalized key is RSA, which stands for *Rivest, Shamir, and Adelman*, the original creators of a public encryption key algorithm. Novell licensed this technology from RSA, Inc. to use with NetWare 4.

After the user is authenticated on the network, the user must have rights to directory objects that represent resources on the network. In figure 1.12, a user must pass through the Novell Directory Services security. To access files on a volume, for example, the user must have certain rights to the volume object in the directory tree.

After the user passes through the Novell Directory Services, the File and Directory Trustee rights control the user's access to a file. These rights match those for the NetWare 3 servers.

The network Administrator performs network management. An initial user account called ADMIN is created when a directory tree is first established. This is equivalent to the SUPERVISOR user in versions before NetWare 4, except that the ADMIN user has network-wide responsibility.

The ADMIN user can create other user objects anywhere in the directory tree, and usually does so in such a manner to enable easy access to resources in the directory tree and ease in implementing security on the network.

The network Administrator can delegate different levels of network responsibility to users. For example, the network Administrator can delegate a user the authority to create but not delete other user objects, or assign a user the responsibility of managing part of a directory tree, but not accessing the information represented by the objects. This makes it possible to have multiple levels of network Administrators in a more flexible manner than does the NetWare 3 approach of workgroup and user account managers.

Security in NetWare 4 can be more accurately controlled by creating assistant supervisors who can administer network resources, but do not have access to data that needs to be protected from view, such as payroll data or other financial data.

Exploring Support for Network Auditing

In NetWare 4, you can set up a class of users called *auditors* that can act independently of the network Administrator to audit critical activities on the network. The auditors also can audit past and present transactions on the network for any security breaches (see fig. 1.13). It is important to understand why network auditors need to be independent of the network Administrator. The network Administrator of the directory tree, unless specifically restricted, has unrestricted access to data and resources on the network. As a result, an organization places great trust in the network Administrator. If this trust is betrayed, the network Administrator can cause a great deal of damage to an organization's data and privacy of data.

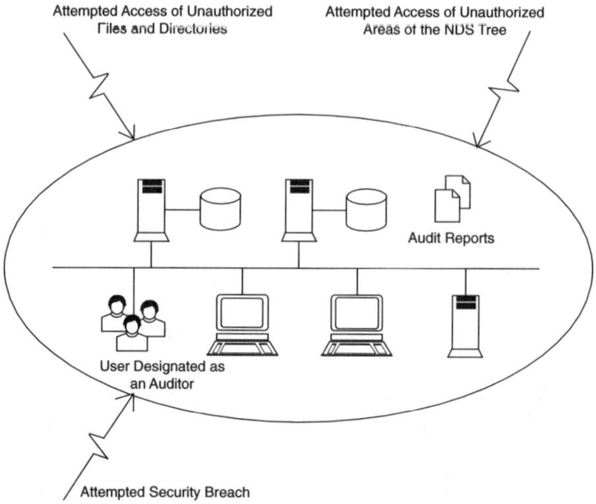

Figure 1.13
Auditing in NetWare 4.

Auditing enables auditor users to monitor actions on the network, including those of the network Administrator. For this reason, auditors should not have Supervisor rights or the equivalent. The auditors' main function is to track events on the network, but they cannot modify data on the network, other than the Audit Data and the Audit History files.

Auditing should not be confused with accounting features of earlier NetWare versions. Accounting allows the tracking of resource usage on the networks, such as disk blocks read and written, storage charges, and service requests. This accounting capability is still available in NetWare 4.

Auditing allows the monitoring of critical events on the network, such as logins and logouts, file operations, directory services object operations (creations, deletions, reads and writes), directory object events, user events, and trustee modifications. To audit files, auditing is enabled at the volume level. For directory objects, auditing must be enabled at the container object level. Container objects are used in the NDS tree for organizational purposes and are discussed in the next chapter. When enabled, log files are created to track audited operations. AUDITCON is the primary utility for implementing auditing. For more on auditing see Chapter 10, "Novell Directory Services Auditing."

Understanding Improvements in Memory Management

In NetWare 3, memory is managed in five pools, each pool serving a different purpose. The pools are for purposes such as permanent memory, cache movable, cache nonmovable, temporary allocated memory, and semipermanent memory. To meet temporary high demands, memory pools can borrow memory from the file cache buffer memory; but after this memory is borrowed, it is not returned. Under certain conditions, memory leakage can occur to the point that the file cache buffer memory is severely depleted, which results in a severe degradation of server performance. To reset the memory pools, you must restart the server (see fig. 1.14).

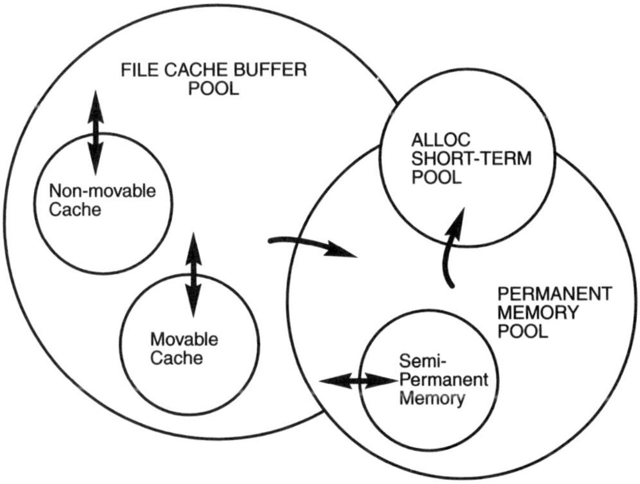

Figure 1.14
NetWare 3 memory management.

NetWare 4 improves considerably upon NetWare 3 memory management. First, NetWare 4 uses no separate memory pools (see fig. 1.15); only one main pool exists—file cache memory. All memory used by processes running on the server are borrowed against this pool and completely returned to it after the given process terminates. Other processes can then reuse the memory returned to the file cache. Consequently, memory management is simpler; memory management also is accomplished in fewer processor cycles, which makes memory allocation faster. The effects of fragmentation are minimized in NetWare 4 because NLMs treat memory as logically continuous. The processor memory management hardware translates the logically continuous address space to physical memory pages that are 4 KB in size.

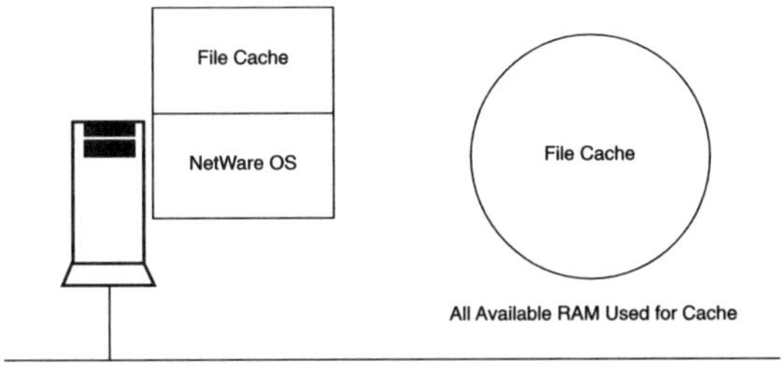

Figure 1.15
NetWare 4 memory management.

Some features of NetWare 4 memory management are as follows:

- Improved server performance because memory management is an important resource for server processes
- Integration with the paged memory architecture of the Intel processors
- Ring protection to control damage caused by misbehaved NLMs
- Ease of writing applications for the NLM developer because memory management is simpler

A controversial aspect of NetWare 3 memory usage is that all programs—the kernel and applications—run in Ring 0 of the Intel 80386 architecture. The Intel 80386 architecture defines four rings—rings 0 to 3 (see fig. 1.16). The idea is to have the operating system kernel run at ring 0, and other programs at one of the outer rings. Programs that run at ring 3, for example, can access the RAM used by programs running in ring 3, but cannot *directly* access RAM for programs running at rings 2, 1, and 0. Therefore, if the operating system kernel runs in ring 0, a program at ring 3 must make an *inter-ring gate call* to make service requests from the operating system kernel. If the program crashes, it cannot affect the operating system kernel. Keeping applications NLMs in a separate ring from the NetWare kernel makes the system more reliable, but the inter-ring call overhead reduces speed.

Figure 1.16
Intel 80386 processor ring architecture.

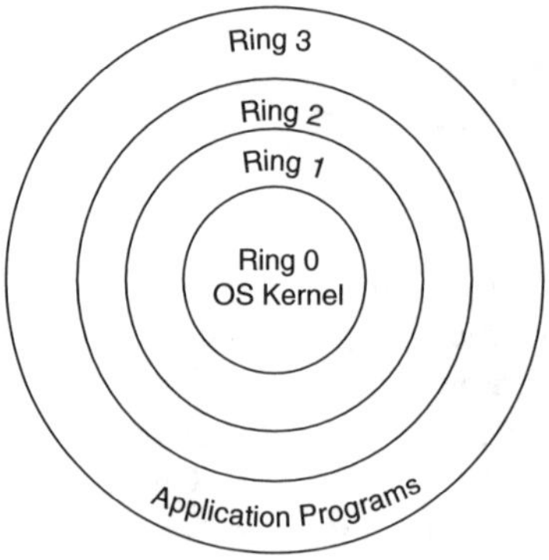

In NetWare 4, all NLMs run in ring 0 by default. The network Administrator, however, can configure the server to run NLMs in an outer ring so that offending programs cannot cause the operating system kernel that runs in ring 0 to crash. As new NLMs are added to the server, they can be loaded in an outer ring for a trial period. They run a little slower here because they must make an inter-ring call. If the NLMs prove to be reliable, they can be added to ring 0, in which they can run faster.

When you purchase NLMs from third parties, check with the vendor to see if they are designed to run in an outer ring of the Intel processor (80386 and higher). Not all NLMs can run in an outer ring.

Understanding Improvements in Client Networking Services

IntranetWare offers in-depth support for a variety of client operating systems, which include:

- DOS/Windows 3.x
- Windows 95
- Windows NT

- MAC
- OS/2
- Unix

DOS and Windows now have the option to use a DOS requester, ODI support, and packet burst protocol support or the Client 32 for DOS\Windows architecture.

The DOS requester allows the redirector capability of later releases of DOS to be used by using the interrupt mechanism INT 2F (hex). The earlier NetWare shell used the DOS INT 21 (hex) mechanism and a software multiplexor mechanism to direct the request to appropriate system services. The additional overhead of the software multiplexor mechanism made that NetWare shell slightly less efficient. In NetWare 4, the DOS requester actually consists of a number of smaller components, called *virtual loadable modules* (VLMs), which the VLM Manager (VLM.EXE) loads and manages only if necessary. VLMs give you the flexibility to selectively load only the necessary services. VLMs are designed to understand NDS, and a VLM component (NETX.VLM) can even be used to communicate with bindery-based servers.

The ODI support is the *open data-link interface* that provides an interface for protocol stacks to talk to network boards that represent layer 2 (data-link layer) of the OSI model. The ODI interface was also available in earlier NetWare client software.

The packet burst protocol allows transmission of multiple packet requests and packet replies, which is an improvement over the single packet request/response behavior of the earlier NCP packet transmissions, and is similar to the window flow control mechanism used in other protocol suites. The packet burst protocol was added to later releases of NetWare 3 and also is available for NetWare 4. The packet burst protocol is particularly useful for multiple NCP packet requests and packet replies in which a single acknowledgment packet can acknowledge a number of requests or replies, which eliminates some of the overhead of the round-trip delay when a sender must wait for the last packet sent to be acknowledged before transmitting the next packet. In addition, fewer packets are sent, which results in reduced network traffic and time for processing packets. Although packet burst protocol comes bundled with NetWare 4, it is an option in NetWare 3.11, involving the PBURST.NLM on the server and the new client shell called BNETX.

DOS/Windows 3.x Client 32

IntranetWare now includes a 32-bit Client for DOS/Windows; providing users with a powerful connection between legacy desktop operating systems and latest network operating system, IntranetWare.

This Client fully supports IntranetWare services and utilities, including Novell Directory Services (NDS), integrated messaging, multiprotocol support, management, security, file, and print. It also brings with it ease of use, manageability, and the security of IntranetWare to older DOS and Windows workstations.

The client for DOS/Windows is based on the Client 32 architecture, but it still provides users with the ability to use all of the features they have been using with 16-bit NetWare Clients. In addition, users can take advantage of a variety of advanced features only available through this new 32-bit client architecture.

Several features are only available through the new client, one of the most significant being for users to authenticate on multiple NDS trees with a single login. This is especially useful if users need to access additional resources that are located on different NDS trees. This multi-tree authentication will enable the user to map drives, capture printers, and access files from any NDS tree they are authorized to use.

32-bit Technology

The IntranetWare Client runs in the 32-bit protected mode environment and uses NetWare Loadable Module (NLM) technology. As a result, it is memory-efficient, dynamic, modular, and portable. This NLM-based client fulfills the dream of having an almost conventional memory-less network client—it uses less than 4 KB of conventional or UMB memory, and uses 32-bit ODI drivers to maximize network performance.

Application Management

The IntranetWare Client for DOS/Windows permits network administrators to use the Novell Application Launcher to create and deploy applications on the network—right from their desk. This makes managing network access to applications simple and straightforward.

With the Novell Application Launcher, administrators can create a custom Windows program group for each Windows user on the network, and then place icons pointing to all the applications that the user is authorized to access. To launch an application, the user then simply double-clicks the application icon in the group. The Application Launcher does the rest, mapping all drives and automatically setting paths.

Flexible Installation and Upgrades

The IntranetWare Client for DOS/Windows can be installed locally at the workstation or over the network from an administrator's location. Network installation and updates eliminate the need for the administrator to travel to each workstation.

Easy-to-follow installation prompts guide the user through the local installation process. The setup program automatically determines the settings for the currently installed client, and uses those settings to configure the IntranetWare Client. The automatic configuration capability of the setup program ensures that the IntranetWare Client takes full advantage of available resources to optimize network performance without user or administrator intervention. Both a DOS-based and a Windows-based setup program are included.

Administrators can install and update the IntranetWare Client over the network using the Auto Client Update utility. ACU operates through network-based login scripts or through the Novell Application Launcher. Whenever a user logs in to the network or clicks on the NAL-installed update icon, the update mechanism checks the current client to see if an update is required. For example, if the IntranetWare Client is already installed, it checks the version of the Client, and upgrades older client software automatically. The administrator can custom-configure the installation and update for each user.

Note With the IntranetWare Client for DOS/Windows, the Auto Client Update utility operates through DOS login only.

A major advantage of the 32-bit client for DOS/Windows is that it can take advantage of features such as 32-bit drivers and client-side caching. Both of these factors increase the performance and decrease network traffic.

For more information on the IntranetWare Client 32 for DOS\Windows refer to Chapter 15, "Supporting DOS, Windows 3.1x, and Windows 95 Workstations."

IntranetWare Client for Mac

For the first time Novell's new IntranetWare Client for Mac OS enables Macintosh workstations to connect to and communicate with an IntranetWare network without using the AppleTalk protocol. It is the first Mac OS Client that allows the client to use either the native IPX protocol or TCP/IP to provide connectivity. With a complete IPX stack for Macintosh workstations, they can now function as a full NDS Client. This means that they can browse a Novell Directory Services tree and log in to Novell Directory services, change passwords, log out, and manage Directory connections.

To fully support the new IntranetWare Client for Mac, you need to complete the following tasks:

1. Install the IntranetWare Client for Mac OS server components on each NetWare 4 server that will support IntranetWare Client for Mac clients.

2. Add the Macintosh name space to all volumes that will supply file services to workstations using the NetWare Client for Mac OS software.

The NetWare Client for Mac OS will provide you with the following features:

- The NetWare Client for Mac OS software fully supports simultaneous connections to multiple Directory trees and NetWare IP networks.

- The software communicates via the AppleTalk, IPX TM, or TCP/IP transports. You can use AppleTalk, IPX, and TCP/IP at the same time.

- Mac workstations will be able to access NetWare file server volumes that do not have the Mac name space loaded. However, without the Mac name space, file names will be limited to the DOS 8.3 naming convention.
- Mac workstations will finally be able to create and place a drive mapping (pointing to a NetWare volume) on its desktop.
- NetWare print queues and printers will be natively available to Mac workstations.
- Mac workstations will be able to open one or more remote connections to one or more NetWare server consoles.

Novell's Windows 95 Client

Like the Client 32 for DOS\Windows, the IntranetWare Client for Windows 95 (Client 32) can be installed locally at the workstation or over the network from an administrator's location, eliminating the need for the administrator to travel to each workstation.

Installation prompts guide you through the local installation process. The setup program automatically determines the settings for the currently installed client, and uses those settings to configure the IntranetWare Client. The automatic configuration capability of the setup program ensures that the IntranetWare Client takes full advantage of available resources to optimize network performance without user or administrator intervention.

Administrators can install Windows 95, using MSBATCH setup. They can also install and update the IntranetWare Client over the network using the Novell Auto Client Update (ACU). ACU operates through network-based login scripts or through the Novell Application Launcher. Whenever a user logs in to the network or clicks on the NAL-installed update icon, the update mechanism checks the version of the IntranetWare Client and upgrades older client software automatically. The administrator can custom-configure the installation and update for each user.

The IntranetWare Client for Windows 95 fully supports all IntranetWare services and utilities, including Novell Directory Services, integrated messaging, multiprotocol support, management, security, file, and print.

The IntranetWare Client is tightly integrated with the Windows 95 operating system so that users can access and manipulate network resources transparently. Users can navigate and access network resources through Windows 95's My Computer, Explorer, and Network Neighborhood. The Client also supports Windows 95 user profiles and system policies, and allows profile and policy information to be stored on IntranetWare servers.

Application Deployment

With the Novell Application Launcher, network administrators can create a custom Windows program group for each Windows user on the network. The program group contains all the applications that the user is authorized to access. To launch an application, the user simply double-clicks the application icon in the group. The Application Launcher does the rest, mapping drives and paths automatically. So network access to applications is simple and straightforward.

Remote Access

The IntranetWare Client for Windows 95 gives users the ability to dial out to remote IntranetWare servers. Remote access allows mobile users to take advantage of full network functionality even when they are away from their offices.

For more information on the IntranetWare Windows 95 Client refer to Chapter 15.

NT Client

The IntranetWare Client for Windows NT seamlessly combines IntranetWare with Windows NT. It currently only operates on Intel-based platforms, but provides several advantages over other NT\NetWare Client offerings. The IntranetWare Client is tightly integrated with the Windows NT operating system providing access to IntranetWare and Windows NT resources transparently. As with the IntranetWare Client for Windows 95, users navigate and access IntranetWare resources through the native Windows NT interfaces of My Computer, Explorer, and Network Neighborhood. The NT also supports Windows NT user profiles and system policies. It also allows profile and policy information to be stored on IntranetWare servers, as well as allowing users the capability to run NetWare login scripts.

This client provides unequaled support to IntranetWare services and utilities, including Novell Directory Services, integrated messaging, multiprotocol support, management, security, file, and print. The IntranetWare Client brings the full power, ease of use, manageability, and security of IntranetWare to Windows NT workstations.

Single Network Login

With a single login, users can be synchronized to their Windows NT workstation as well as to all authorized NetWare and NT network resources. This means that administrators do not have to worry about users remembering multiple names and passwords. Yet, because users gain access to all NetWare services including stored files, printing, and applications, through NDS, security is not compromised.

Client Components

The IntranetWare Client for Windows NT includes the Novell Application Launcher (NAL). NAL enables network administrators to create and deploy applications across the network, reducing the complexity and cost of managing and administering the deployment of network and desktop applications.

The IntranetWare Client for Windows NT also includes the 32-bit NWAdmin utility, which centrally manages all NetWare resources.

Automatic Updates

The IntranetWare Client for Windows NT is integrated into the native Windows NT network installation process, so it's easy to install and update.

Updating the IntranetWare Client for Windows NT is easy. The Auto Client Update part of setup enables administrators to update workstations through network-based login scripts or through the Novell Application Launcher. Whenever a user logs in to the network or clicks on the NAL-installed update icon, the update mechanism checks the version of the IntranetWare Client and upgrades older client software automatically. The administrator can custom-configure the installation and update for each user.

NT workstation users can fully utilize the power, security, and network manageability offered by available NCPs. The strategic advantage is that NT workstation users can take advantage of new IntranetWare services as they become available.

Protocol and Remote Boot Support

The IntranetWare Client for Windows NT can also be used to simultaneously attach to a Windows NT server, meaning it can coexist with the Microsoft peer-to-peer service that allows users to access Windows NT servers. With both the Novell Client and the Microsoft Client installed, users can access all their network resources—IntranetWare and NT.

Full NetWare IP capabilities are included with this client, so sites can run TCP/IP exclusively if they require. Novell leverages the TCP/IP stack included with Windows NT. The IntranetWare Client can also coexist with the Microsoft NetBIOS stack.

The IntranetWare Client for Windows NT can coexist with Remote Access Server (RAS). This means that users can dial in to a NetWare server that is running a version of NetWare Connect 2.1 or higher. It also means that they can also dial in to Windows NT Remote Access Servers. However, the IntranetWare client for Windows NT cannot support Remote Boot (RIPL) because the Windows NT operating system does not support such functions.

Look for future releases of the IntranetWare Client for Windows NT to replicate and synchronization between Novell's Directory Services and Microsoft's Windows NT Primary Domain controllers. For more information on the IntranetWare Client for Windows NT, refer to Chapter 16, "Supporting Non-DOS Workstations."

Introduction to Workstation Manager

Novell's Workstation Manager ships with the IntranetWare client for NT. To use Workstation Manager you must be sure that you are running Novell's IntranetWare client for Windows NT. Novell Administrator component is a snap-in DLL to the Novell Administrator utility

(NWAdmin). It enables administrators to manage both Windows NT workstation user accounts and IntranetWare user accounts from a single point of control—Novell Directory Services (NDS). This however, does not mean that you give up the support of NT features such as user profiles and system policies. Using Workstation Manager together with NT's features enables administrators to configure and maintain better control of user desktops from a central location.

When using Workstation Manager, a user logs into IntranetWare from a Windows NT workstation. Workstation Manager then automatically generates an NT user account on that workstation; taking advantage of the IntranetWare Client's desktop administrative privileges to dynamically create the account during the login process with no user intervention.

Workstation Manager also simplifies the management of roaming users who need to log in to multiple NT workstations as well as simplifying the management of NT workstations that are shared by multiple users. Without Workstation manager, roaming users have to have an NT workstation user account on every workstation to which they need access. Likewise, if multiple users need to share a single NT workstation, every user must have an account on that workstation. Workstation Manager simplifies the management of roaming users because the administrator does not have to create a separate account for those users on every desktop. In addition, the administrator does not have to maintain separate accounts for all potential users on a shared NT workstation.

Workstation Manager creates accounts for roaming and shared users automatically when the users log in. The administrator can specify that the automatically created user accounts are either nonvolatile or volatile. A nonvolatile user account remains resident in the local Windows NT Security Accounts Manager (SAM) after the user logs out. It can be used later, independently of Workstation Manager. A volatile user account is deleted automatically when the user logs out.

Using Workstation Manager, the administrator can enter Windows NT workstation configuration information into NDS and associate this information with users and user groups. The administrator can also associate different workstation configurations with different users and groups, allowing customization of the desktop environment. After the administrator has associated configuration information with a user in NDS, Workstation Manager can automatically create a reconfigured user account on the NT workstation when that user logs in.

In addition, the administrator can use the Novell Application Launcher to create a customized network application group on the workstation. The result: each user sees the same, consistent desktop, no matter which workstation they log in to or how many users share that workstation. And administrators control all user configurations from a central location, so management is easy.

Because the IntranetWare Client runs with administrator privileges, the Workstation Manager component can create and delete NT user accounts dynamically.

Introduction to Novell Application Launcher (NAL)

Network administrators can currently install applications for network users in two ways: They can install applications stand-alone on each user's hard drive and/or install them as shared applications on the network. Installing applications on each hard drive requires the administrator to install, upgrade, and support the application individually for each user. Installing shared network applications is easier, but it still has drawbacks—the administrator must install the Windows icon for the application on each user's desktop. Any upgrade or other change to the application requires additional visits to the desktop, not to mention that users commonly delete icons and may need administrative help to re-create them for shared applications.

The Novell Application Launcher architecture technology is based on three factors:

- Objects can be added to the NDS Schema
- Snap-in capabilities of (NWAdmin)
- The Novell Application Launcher itself

Novell Directory Services (NDS) allows independent software developers to extend the schema and add new objects or properties to the directory services database. In the case of the application launching technology, these new objects are "application objects" that have properties defining how applications are to be managed.

After the application objects are created and the properties defined, they are managed by NWADMIN. This is made possible because NWADMIN allows third-party vendors to place (snap-in) application modules directly into NWADMIN. NWADMIN thus becomes the utility used by the network administrator to customize the system to meet the needs of the installation and provide access to the users.

The Application Launcher itself is run as an application on the Windows desktop. Using a shell technology allows a single executable file to be called, regardless of the type of Windows running. The application then adjusts to the type of Windows (Windows 3.1x, Windows 95, or Windows NT) and executes accordingly. For users who move among different workstations that have different Windows operating systems, this shell technology simplifies the system for both administrators and users.

With NDS, you can create and store application objects right in the directory tree. These application objects are used as pointers to point to the actual location of a network application. Therefore, users are no longer forced to know the exact location of the application to establish drive mappings. Rather, drive mappings can be created by directing the drive mapping command to the application object. Drive mappings that point to an application object, rather than an actual location on the disk, are still established through login scripts or path statements, but the advantage is that network administrators can change the location of the application without having to redo all login scripts and path statements. Application objects can also be configured to store login script-like subroutines that map additional drives and capture printers when users launch specific applications. Thus, when an application is exited, drive mappings, search mappings, and printer ports are automatically removed. Automatically removing connections can help resolve the issue of insufficient server license connections. Using application objects also provides a way to load balance the use of network applications.

Large Internet Packet

Another enhancement in IntranetWare's operating system (an enhancement to NetWare 4) is support for the large Internet packet (LIP). In previous versions of NetWare all packets that were sent through a router were automatically reduced to 512 bytes. With IntranetWare, file servers, workstations, and routers between these components will negotiate and decide on the largest sized packet that can be handled. By using larger packets, more information can be sent over the same "pipe" faster. Common packet sizes are: Token-Ring (4 KB to 16 KB) and Ethernet networks (13.5 KB).

Understanding Integrated Storage Management Services (SMS)

Storage Management Services (SMS) in IntranetWare allows data on the network to be backed up or restored in a common data format and in a hardware- and software-independent manner by using backup utilities. A *target service agent* (TSA) program is run on each device that needs to be backed up and is the target for the SBACKUP program. IntranetWare contains several enhancements, or additional TSAs. It now ships with a Windows 95 TSA that is used to back up and restore information on workstations on the Windows 95 operating system and the IntranetWare Client for Windows 95. IntranetWare also ships with a new Macintosh TSA that can be used to backup and restore Mac clients, if they are running the IntranetWare Client for Mac OS. These targets include workstations as well as NetWare 3 and NetWare 4 servers (see fig. 1.17).

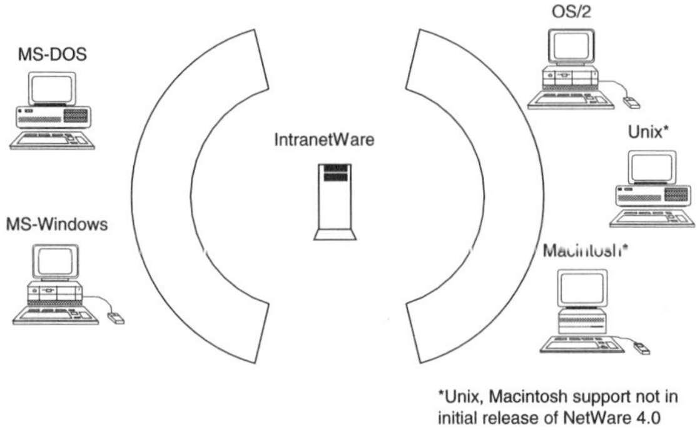

Figure 1.17
SMS and TSAs.

In SMS, the SBACKUP program is responsible for backup and restore operations. SBACKUP is an NLM that runs on a NetWare server. SBACKUP consolidates the NBACKUP functionality of earlier NetWare releases.

SMS consists of a number of other modules, such as the *storage management data requester* (SMDR) used to pass commands between the SBACKUP and the TSAs, and device drivers that use the *Storage Device Interface* (SDI) to communicate between the SBACKUP program and the storage devices (see fig. 1.18).

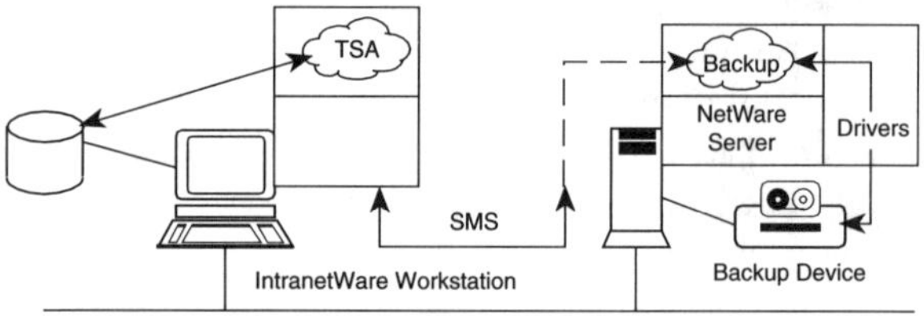

Figure 1.18
SMS architecture.

In IntranetWare SBACKUP uses the NDS TSA to provide a more complete backup of NDS. This includes the ability to backup and restore extensions to the NDS schema. It also does a better job of maintaining the trustee assignments from the Directory and the ability to restore the server's private key. User objects IDs and file trustee assignments, and replica information are also maintained throughout the backup and restore process.

Besides SBACKUP, you might want to consider a number of third-party backup schemes that use SMS. These provide a simpler, streamlined user interface and many advanced backup options.

Novell's Web Server

IntranetWare includes Novell's secure, high-performance, intranet software. This Web software engine enables organizations to publish Web pages internally as well as externally.

Internal Web sites enable organizations to have more efficient interaction between employees, as well as with the business' partners. For instance, your corporate communications department could create an area on the network discussing current issues, partnerships, press releases, and upcoming events. Your human resources department could externally publish benefit packages, job postings, and so on.

The Novell Web Server is integrated with Novell Directory Services (NDS), which provides strong security through NDS authentication and multiple-level access control. This protects you from break-ins both inside and outside your organization. For maximum flexibility, the administrator can tailor each security level to specific users or user groups.

Novell's Web Server includes Novell QuickFinder, a search engine that automatically indexes over 20 types of files. QuickFinder uses very little processor overhead, less than 10 percent overhead for its index. Other major enhancements made to Novell's Web Server are:

- SSL 2.0 and 3.0 (Secure Sockets Layer)
- More performance enhancements
- Native Oracle connectivity
- Virtual directories
- Multihoming support
- PERL 5 support

SSL 2.0 and 3.0 Support

The Novell Web Server supports Secure Sockets Layer (SSL), SSL 2.0, and SSL 3.0 technologies. SSL Technology uses public key/private key encryption technology, resulting in the entire dialogue between the browser and the server being encrypted. Each browser and server has a pair of private and public keys or certificates that are used to lock and unlock the transmitted information. Besides transferring sensitive information, SSL can also authenticate the identity of the browser and the server, and ensure data integrity of the encrypted information. The Novell Web Server further enhances security by combining the encryption technology with the combination NDS authentication. With this combination of technologies your sensitive information is secure.

Performance Enhancements

The NetWare Web Server is now twice as fast as Novell Web Server 2.5, reaching over 700 cps (connections per second) on a 128-client network. NWS is also extremely processor-efficient, and can easily share resources with more CPU-intensive applications.

Native Oracle Connectivity

The NetWare Web Server now supports native connectivity to Oracle 7 databases, accessible through NetBasic programs. Web pages become more meaningful with the ability to publish corporate information dynamically.

Virtual Directories

Virtual directories turn any IntranetWare or NetWare file server into a virtual Web server—the Web pages can reside anywhere on your Novell network, not just on the Web server; full NDS integration ensures you of complete control of your intranet. Virtual directories also remove the need to install and manage multiple Web servers.

Multihoming Support

Multihoming allows a single Web server to host multiple domains, instead of having each server dedicated to a specific domain. For example, `http://company.pr.com and http://`

`company.hr.com` can reside on the same server. NWS supports an unlimited number of domains. With multihoming, Webmasters can reduce the number of Web servers on their intranet, making it easier to manage.

PERL 5

PERL (Practical Extraction and Report Language) is the most popular language used to create CGI (Common Gateway Interface) programs. NWS now supports the newest version of Perl.

Improvements in Network Print Services Architecture

In earlier versions of NetWare print services are defined as part of the print server definition, and the only way to do a network print job is to submit the print job to a print queue. In IntranetWare, you can still send the network print jobs to the network print queue, but in addition, you can send print jobs to the printer object in the NDS tree.

Other improvements in IntranetWare printing include the following:

- Simpler installation of printing services through quick setup options
- Support for a larger number of printers (up to 256) on a single print server
- Remote printers can be set up on NetWare servers
- NPRINTER runs on DOS, Windows, and OS/2 and replaces PSERVER.EXE
- The printer is now an NDS object, which allows a print job to be sent directly to a printer without having to know the print queue

Multiple Language Support (Internationalization)

Because the character of NetWare has become international in scope, NetWare 4 introduces support for international languages to NLMs and network utilities, which means that you can set messages and options associated with utilities in your own language. The default language is English, but other languages can be supported during installation when you run the SERVER.EXE program. After installation, you can use the INSTALL.NLM to configure date, time, and number formats.

You even can have different language NLMs running on the server at the same time; or have one user using the system utility NETADMIN in French and another user using the same utility in Italian. The language support does not mean that NetWare can translate messages between users using different languages. For example, if the SEND utility is used by a French language user to send a message in French to another user who is set up to use Italian, NetWare cannot translate the message from French to Italian.

Although the language might be the same, differences can exist in the way that date, time, and numbers are formatted. A classic example of this is English, which is spoken in both the United States and the United Kingdom. The default format for representing dates in the United States is *mm/dd/yy* (example: 10/16/97). In the United Kingdom, the default date format is *dd/mm/yy* (example: 16/10/97). The formatting does not depend only on the language, but can change across different locales for the same language.

Table 1.2 shows examples of the date, time, and number formats for the United States, United Kingdom, France, and Germany.

Table 1.2
Format Differences for Countries

Country	Number Format	Time Format	Date Format
U.S.A.	355,113.22	11:55:00 p.m.	10/16/97
U.K.	355,113.22	23:55:00	16/10/97
Germany	355.113,22	23:55:00	16.10.97
France	355 113,22	23:55:00	16.10.97

The capability to support differences in language and format representations is called *internationalization.* Internationalization in NetWare is supported through *unicode* representation, which is a standard for representing data in 16-bit rather than the familiar 8-bit ASCII.

Understanding Simplified Installation and Upgrade Procedures

IntranetWare 4 distribution comes on four CD-ROMs. Because of the size of IntranetWare, distribution on high-density floppy disks is no longer an option.

You can attach the CD-ROM drive to the server being installed, or attach it to a remote workstation. Figure 1.19 shows these possibilities; the CD-ROM drive is shown as an external unit to the workstation or server. Internal CD-ROMs are also possible.

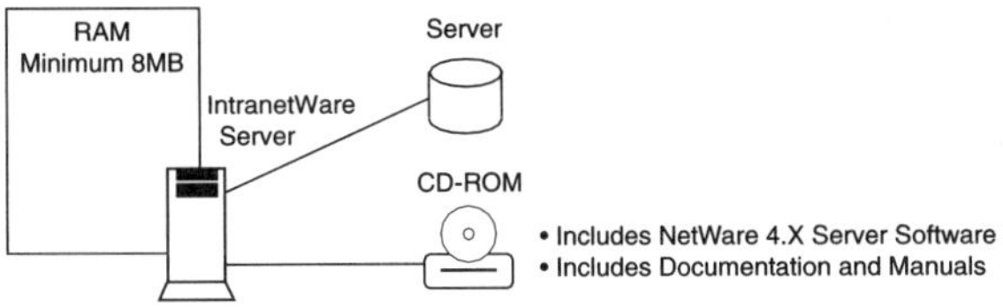

Figure 1.19
IntranetWare installation using CD-ROM distribution.

Note For detailed information on installing IntranetWare, see Chapter 3, "Installing IntranetWare."

Online NetWare Manuals Through DynaText

Prior to NetWare 4.1, Novell manuals were available online by using the Electro Text utility. Electro Text is a graphical utility that worked with Windows 3.1 (or higher) and on OS/2 clients. Beginning in NetWare 4.1, DynaText, from Electronic Book Technologies, Inc., has replaced Electro Text. Figure 1.20 shows a sample DynaText screen.

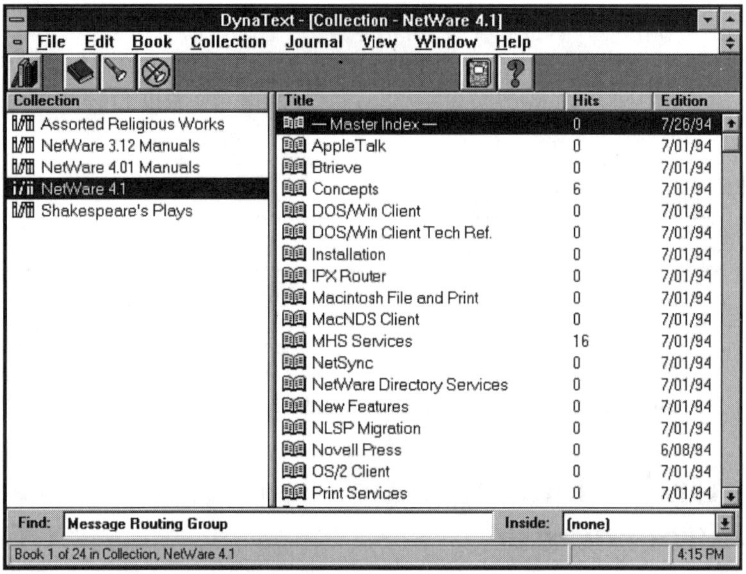

Figure 1.20
Sample DynaText screen.

All the NetWare manuals are available in DynaText format. The following list describes briefly the contents of each of these manuals:

- **Master Index.** The index links to all places in the manuals. Click on a link marker to go to a place in the manual in which to find a term or topic.
- **AppleTalk Reference.** This reference provides the information you need to understand the AppleTalk protocol stack for NetWare servers, and describes configuration parameters for the AppleTalk protocol stack.
- **Btrieve Installation and Reference Manual.** Btrieve is a popular and efficient record manager bundled as an NLM in NetWare servers, and contains information on installing, configuring, executing, and monitoring the Btrieve record management system for NetWare servers.

- **Concepts.** This is an alphabetically arranged glossary of NetWare-related terms and provides a tutorial description of what each term means.
- **NetWare Client for DOS and MS Windows User Guide.** This manual helps you set up and install your client software, introducing you to the client tools for managing your client on a NetWare network. The manual covers concepts and procedures for installing and using NetWare Client software on NetWare 2.x, 3.x, and 4.x networks.
- **NetWare Client for DOS and MS Windows Technical Reference.** This manual describes the parameters you need to configure NetWare workstation software on NetWare 2.x, 3.x, and 4.x networks.
- **Installation.** This manual contains information on how to install a new NetWare 4.x server.
- **NetWare IPX Router Reference.** This manual provides the information you need to understand the IPX protocol for the router, and describes the IPX configuration parameters.
- **Macintosh File and Print Services.** This manual explains how to install, configure, and maintain the NetWare for Macintosh software.
- **Using MacNDS Client for NetWare 4.** This manual describes the NetWare for Macintosh MacNDS Client software. The MacNDS Client software allows access to NetWare 4 NDS services from Macintosh workstations.
- **MHS Services for NetWare.** This manual explains the NetWare MHS (Message Handling Service), and explains how to install and manage it, as well as describes how to use the FirstMail Client software.
- **Installing and Using NetSync.** This manual explains how to install and use the NetSync utility. NetSync is a management utility that enables you to manage NetWare 3.x servers from the NetWare Directory Services.
- **Introduction to NetWare Directory Services.** This manual introduces you to the basics of NDS, and helps you plan the NDS tree.
- **New Features.** This manual introduces you to features that are unique to NetWare 4.x.
- **NetWare Client for OS/2.** This manual describes the installation and configuration of NetWare Client software for OS/2 workstations. This client software can be used for both NetWare 3.x and NetWare 4.x. The manual contains information on accessing network services form Virtual DOS machines, and setting up Named Pipes and NetBIOS protocol support.
- **Print Services.** This helps you with NetWare 4.x printing concepts and explains how you can set up, load, and use network printing utilities. It contains some troubleshooting tips and guidelines for network print services.

- **Supervising the Network.** This helps you set up and administer the network after you complete the NetWare 4.x installation, and covers issues such as managing NDS, NetWare files and directories, creating login scripts, NetWare server maintenance, network auditing, and backing up and restoring data.
- **Utilities Reference.** This contains information on how to use NetWare utilities, such as Text workstation utilities, server utilities, and GUI-based utilities, and contains information on NDS bindery objects and their properties.
- **Upgrade and Migration.** This manual describes upgrading to NetWare 4.x from other NetWare servers, such as NetWare 2.x or 3.x and IBM LAN Server.
- **TCP/IP Reference.** TCP/IP is a de facto protocol for connecting heterogeneous systems together. This manual discusses how TCP/IP can be configured and managed on the NetWare 4.x server and explains the concepts in relationship to NetWare's implementation of TCP/IP.
- **Building and Auditing a Trusted Network Environment with NetWare 4.** This manual provides an overview of the security requirements for large networks and how you can use NetWare 4 auditing to meet these requirements.
- **System Messages.** This is a list of all possible system and warning messages that you might encounter when you configure NetWare 4.x, including the messages according to the modules that generate them, and there are over 150 modules. It explains the possible cause of the error message and the action you can perform to fix it.

The command-line utilities now have a /? switch that gives additional help information on how to use these utilities. This switch is very convenient, providing help from the command line without invoking any other online documentation. Typing illegal command-line parameters actually also results in help screens being displayed.

You also press F1 to access Help in the menu utilities. This help is context-sensitive. The menu utilities such as FILER and PCONSOLE use the familiar C-Worthy menu interface. Unlike previous versions of NetWare, pressing F1 twice (F1,F1) does not display extended help information.

Examining NetWare 4 Utilities

Many people discover when they upgrade from NetWare 3 to NetWare 4 that some familiar utilities, such as SYSCON, are no longer present. SYSCON was a bindery-based network administration tool and has been replaced by the more powerful NETADMIN tool, which is based on NDS.

Some utilities have disappeared or have been consolidated into a more functional utility. For example, the utilities VOLINFO, SALVAGE, and PURGE have been consolidated into FILER. Table 1.3 lists some of these changes.

Table 1.3
NetWare 4 Utility Changes

NetWare 4 Utility	Description
NETADMIN.EXE	Menu-driven text utility used to create NDS objects. Also can be used to assign property values and rights. Consolidates some of the features of pre-NetWare 4 utilities, such as SYSCON, SECURITY, USERDEF, and DSPACE.
NWADMIN.EXE	MS Windows and OS/2 graphical utility to manage NDS tree and perform operations on it. Is a consolidated graphical tool for network management.
UIMPORT.NLM	Text utility for batch creation of users. Replaces the function of the pre-NetWare 4 MAKEUSER utility.
DOMAIN.NLM	Enables the creation of protected domains that allow NLMs to run in rings 1, 2, or 3 of the Intel processors. Runs as a server NLM.
MONITOR.NLM	General purpose server monitor utility for monitoring the server. Runs as a server NLM and consolidates the functions of the pre-NetWare 4 MONITOR and FCONSOLE.
SERVMAN.NLM	Facilitates the easy viewing and changing of the many server SET parameters. Allows these changes to be stored in AUTOEXEC .NCF and STARTUP.NCF files. Runs as a server NLM.
RCONSOLE.EXE	RCONSOLE also performs the function of ACONSOLE REMOTE.NLM (asynchronous console). Used for remote management of server.
NWSNUT.NLM	Library interface for C-Worthy style graphical functions used by server-based graphical tools, such as MONITOR and SERVMAN.
PARTMGR.EXE	Text utility for managing partitions and their replicas.
Partition Manager.GUI	Equivalent of the PARTMGR utility.
DSREPAIR.NLM	Repairs inconsistencies and problems in the NDS database. Provides the functionality of the BINDFIX and BINDREST utilities used to repair the bindery.
DSMERGE.NLM	Used for combining separate NDS trees.

continues

Table 1.3, Continued
NetWare 4 Utility Changes

NetWare 4 Utility	Description
TIMESYNC.NLM	Performs time synchronization. Is set up to load through AUTOEXEC.NCF during NetWare 4 server installation.
CDROM.NLM	CD-ROM support for CD drives attached to the NetWare 4 server.
RTDM.NLM	Real-Time Data Migration utility that runs at the server.
LIST DEVICES	Server console command. Lists device information.
SCAN FOR NEW DEVICES	Server console command. Scans for any new devices added to the server.
MEDIA	Server console command. Used to confirm if requests to insert/remove media on the server were performed.
MAGAZINE	Server console command. Used to confirm if requests to insert/remove magazine on the server were performed.
MIRROR STATUS	Server console command. Used to display status of mirrored partitions.
ABORT REMIRROR	Server console command. Used to stop mirroring of partitions.
REMIRROR PARTITION	Server console command. Used to remirror partitions.
AUDITCON.EXE	Allows independent users to act as auditors. Is a superset of the pre-NetWare 4 ATOTAL and PAUDIT.
RIGHTS.EXE	Consolidates functions of pre-NetWare 4 RIGHTS, GRANT, REVOKE, REMOVE, and ALLOW utilities.
FLAG.EXE	Consolidates functions of pre-NetWare 4 FLAG, FLAGDIR, and SMODE utilities.
FILER	Consolidates functions of pre-NetWare 4 FILER, SALVAGE, PURGE, DSPACE, and VOLINFO utilities.
NPRINTER.EXE	Allows a printer attached to a workstation (DOS or OS/2) or a server to be used as a network printer.
SBACKUP.NLM	Used to perform backup across the network. Consolidates the pre-NetWare 4 SBACKUP and NBACKUP.

NetWare 4 Utility	Description
RPL.NLM	Allows remote booting for diskless workstations (PCs).
KEYB	Server console command. Allows the selection of a nationality or language for the keyboard device.
LANGUAGE	Server console command. Sets up the use of the specified language at the server.
CX.EXE	Allows users to navigate the NDS tree by changing the context. Does for NDS directory what the CD command does for file directories.
LOGIN.EXE	Used to log in or attach to a server. Uses NDS objects and consolidates pre-NetWare 4 LOGIN and ATTACH utilities.
NMENU.BAT	NMENU is the batch utility; MENUMAKE is the menu compiler utility; MENUMAKE.EXE, and MENUCNVT is the menu conversion utility. Menus are based on MENUCNVT.EXE Saber menus.
NDIR.EXE	Consolidates the pre-NetWare 4 NDIR, LISTDIR, CHKDIR, and CHKVOL utilities.
NETUSER.EXE	Replaces pre-NetWare 4 SESSION. Text graphical tool for performing drive mappings, printing, and network attachments.
SEND.EXE	Consolidates the pre-NetWare 4 SEND, CASTON, and CASTOFF utilities.
NLIST.EXE	Consolidates the pre-NetWare 4 USERLIST and SLIST utilities.

Operating System Enhancements

With NetWare 4.11, the NetWare operating system has been enhanced and improved in several ways. The most important changes are as follows:

- Clib Enhancements
- Improved Abend Recovery Options
- NetWare Symmetric MultiProcessing
- SFT III Enhancements

- UPS Connection through a Serial Port
- Platform-Related Improvements

Clib Enhancements

With IntranetWare the CLIB.NLM file has been modularized into several NetWare Loadable Module (NLM) programs. In addition, the functions of MATHLIB.NLM and MATHLIBC.NLM have been included in the CLIB.NLM. Accordingly, MATHLIB.NLM and MATHLIBC.NLM are not included in NetWare 4.11. The functionality of the previous CLIB.NLM is now available in the following NLMs:

- **CLIB.NLM.** An ANSI-compliant runtime interface for the old CLIB functions.
- **FPSM.NLM.** Floating point support library.
- **THREADS.NLM.** NetWare standard NLM threads package.
- **REQUESTR.NLM.** The standard requester package.
- **NLMLIB.NLM.** POSIX and other basic NLM runtime support.
- **NIT.NLM.** The old NetWare interface tools which are being replaced by interfaces in CALNLM32.NLM.

The new set of modules is more efficient and uses 80 percent less dynamic memory than the old CLIB module.

Abend Recovery

With NetWare 4.11, the server operating system has improved recovery options for handling an abnormal end (abend). These improvements include the following features and capabilities:

- Additional information about the source of the abend is displayed on the server console. This information identifies the NLM or hardware problem that caused the abend so an administrator can take corrective actions.
- When an abend occurs, information about the abend is automatically written to a text file, ABEND.LOG. This file is initially written to the DOS partition.

  Then, when the SYS: volume is remounted, the information is appended to the ABEND.LOG file in the SYS:SYSTEM directory and removed from the DOS partition.
- When you enter the "Secure Console" command, DOS is not removed from memory automatically. To remove DOS from memory, you have to explicitly use the "Remove DOS" command. This enables abend logging and the "Auto Restart After Abend" functionality when the console is secured.

- "Auto Restart After Abend" is a new SET parameter that enables the server to automatically recover from an abend in various ways. This parameter is set to ON by default.
- "Auto Restart After Abend Delay Time" is a new set parameter that enables you to specify how long after an abend the server waits before going down to reinitialize itself.

NetWare Symmetric MultiProcessing

The NetWare Symmetric MultiProcessing (SMP) technology enables the NetWare 4.11 operating system to run on a multiprocessor server. NetWare SMP enables a server to run resource-intensive services, such as large databases, document management software, and multimedia applications on a NetWare server.

NetWare SMP provides the following:

- Increased processing power and better network performance.
- Support for up to 32 processors, depending on the hardware platform.
- Support for Advanced Programmable Interrupt Controllers (APICs).

SFT III Enhancements

With IntranetWare, the NetWare SFT III system has been enhanced with two new set parameters and improvements in the PROTOCOLS command.

The "SFT III Error Wait Time" set parameter enables you to adjust all SFT III wait times at once. SFT III wait times include: MSL Error Wait Time, Secondary Take Over Wait Time, IPX Internet Down Wait Time, MSL Deadlock Wait Time, and Check LAN Extra Wait Time.

The default values for each of these parameters is usually sufficient. The "SFT III Error Wait Time" set parameter should be used only for troubleshooting the system.

The "Turbo Memory Synch" set parameter enables you to speed up memory synchronization between a pair of SFT III servers.

In previous versions of NetWare, the PROTOCOLS command did not work with the MSEngine in the SFT III system. With NetWare 4.11, the PROTOCOLS command works identically with the MSEngine, the IOEngine, and non-SFT III servers.

UPS Connection Through a Serial Port

With NetWare 4, the NetWare operating system now supports an uninterruptible power supply (UPS) connection through a serial port.

This functionality is provided by the UPS_AIO.NLM in conjunction with an AIO device driver. In addition, to use UPS_AIO, the serial cable between the server and the UPS device must be designed for use with the UPS device.

UPS.NLM, which is still provided with NetWare 4, enables a UPS connection through a server's mouse port or third-party card and does not require an AIO device driver.

Platform-Related Improvements

With NetWare 4, the server operating system includes some significant internal enhancements that will increase performance. The following is a brief description of hardware/platform-related enhancements:

- The server memory management routines have been enhanced to take advantage of the Global Page attribute in the Intel Pentium Pro microprocessor, which means it will run faster on a Pentium Pro machine than it will on a Pentium machine.
- The high-resolution timer routines have been enhanced to take advantage of the internal clock in Intel's Pentium and Pentium Pro microprocessors. This improves the reliability and performance of NetWare 4's Packet Burst feature.
- The NetWare operating system more fully supports the Peripheral Component Interface (PCI) bus architecture.

Summary

In this chapter, you examined the features of IntranetWare. NetWare 4.11 is the backbone of IntranetWare and represents an exciting change in the way large enterprise-wide area networks can be supported. The principal change is the abilities found in Novell Directory Services, which enables you to superimpose a logical structure or view on a physical network, making the network easier to use and administer.

Because NDS is central to accessing resources on the network, security is integrated into NDS. When a user logs in, that user is authenticated at the NDS level. Auditing can be used to further monitor activity on the network.

Other improvements are found in the client support, including but not limited to Windows 95, Windows NT, DOS, Windows 3.11, and Macintosh clients. Features in each of these client technologies focus on simplifying client management and improving performance.

IntranetWare includes Novell's Web Server, which has many new enhancements, such as support for Oracle databases, virtual directories, multihoming, and SSL 2.0 and 3.0 support, as well as support for PERL 5.

The NetWare OS has been enhanced by a modular CLIB, automatic file purging, serial port ups connectivity, and other platform-related enhancements.

Other areas of enhancement can be found in Storage Management Services, Enhanced and Integrated utilities, and better online documentation.

CHAPTER 2

Understanding Novell Directory Services

Novell Directory Services (NDS) is an information name service in NetWare that organizes devices in hierarchical fashion. These services are network resources such as users, groups, printers, servers, volumes, and other physical and logical network devices.

NDS is perhaps the single most important feature of NetWare 4.x. It enables physical network resources to be managed and displayed as a single view. It also enables you to treat a network that consists of many servers as a single network, allowing for single login; directory services provide much more than single-login authentication. A directory service is a hierarchical, distributed, fault-tolerant database that provides powerful facilities for storing, accessing, managing, and using diverse information about users and resources in computing environments.

NDS replaces the bindery found in NetWare 3 networks. One of the major differentiating factors between the bindery and NDS is that NDS is a distributed database, meaning it can be replicated across the network to multiple servers. This increases fault tolerance as well as improves performance, especially in a wide area network.

The resources stored in the bindery of NetWare 3 are stored in a flat structure and belong to a single server. NDS however, enables you to treat network resources as logical resources. The logical resources are grouped within NDS, to represent their logical relationship to the network as a whole.

This chapter covers basic NDS concepts and how you can use NDS to access and manage network resources. Understanding NDS services is fundamental to managing NetWare 4.x, because access of network resources revolves around how you represent, access, and manage NDS.

Understanding Novell Directory Services

NDS is a distributed global database of services and resources available on the network. The term *global* implies a single database shared by all servers on the network and available to users from any point on the network. Most resources of importance to network management on the network have an entry in this global database.

Conceptually, the global database exists when you install NDS, and is not tied to a physical resource, such as a server. In practice, because NDS is implemented as a database, it must be stored on storage devices on the network, such as physical volumes that are associated with physical servers. Because the NDS database can become very large, it is not stored at any central site (except in very small networks). Another reason for not storing the NDS database at a central site is because you want to improve availability of the NDS in case of a single point of failure. Portions of the NDS database are subdivided and distributed on volume storage devices at strategic locations on the network. These subdivided elements of the NDS are called *partitions.*

NDS Resources

NDS objects are the entities that store the information or data about a network and its resources. They are called *NDS objects* because of their association with NDS. In other words, NDS is simply a collection of objects that follow a given set of rules that govern how they are created and stored. Familiarity with NDS objects is vital in the pursuit to understand and administer a NetWare 4 network. NDS objects can represent both physical as well as logical entities on the network. For example, a physical entity would be an item such as a printer, server, volume, or workstation. A logical NDS object might be user, print queue, group, and so on.

You can think of NDS objects as records in a global database (see fig. 2.1). Because there is an unlimited number of possible NDS objects, they are organized into a hierarchical structure called an *NDS tree.* This allows for a more manageable structure.

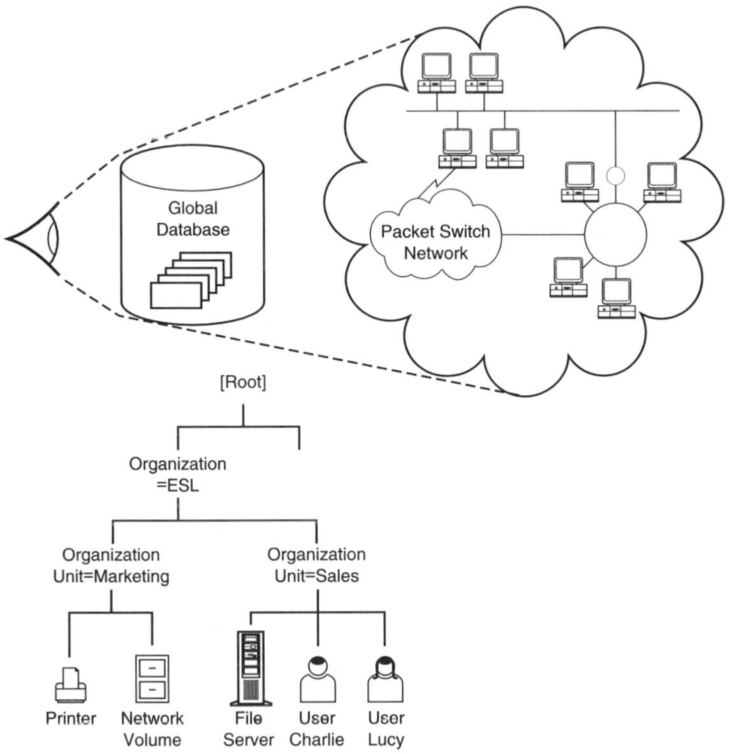

Figure 2.1
NDS global database.

Each NDS object holds information about the resource it represents. Information about a particular object is stored as *properties* of that object. Properties are similar to the fields of a record (see fig. 2.2). For example, the properties of a user object are the user's login name, last name, groups to which the user belongs, the user's telephone number, and so on. Figure 2.3 shows examples of NDS resource objects and their properties. The figure shows some of the properties of a user object and an IntranetWare server object.

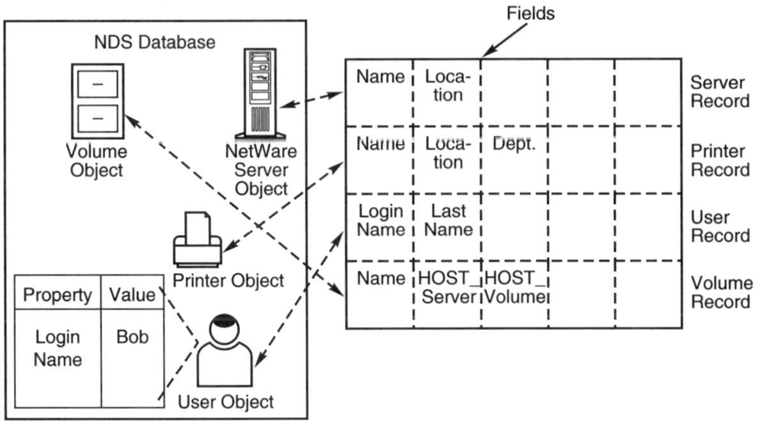

Figure 2.2
Properties of objects.

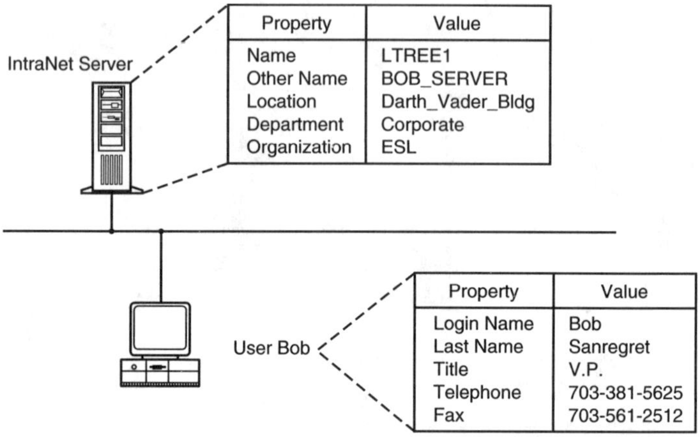

IntraNet Server
Property
Value
Name
Other Name
Location
Department
Organization
LTREE1
BOB_SERVER
Darth_Vader_Bldg
Corporate
ESL
User Bob
Property
Value
Login Name
Last Name
Title
Telephone
Fax
Bob
Sanregret
V.P.
703-381-5625
703-561-2512

Figure 2.3
Example NDS objects and property values.

The properties are listed in the property column and represent the *categories* or *type* of information that can be stored in the object. The actual information stored in a property is listed in the Value column and is called a *property value.* Some properties are crucial, called *mandatory* or *required* properties, and must have a value associated with them. An example of a mandatory property for all NDS objects is the name property, called the *common name.* If an object's name property is not defined, you cannot reference that object. All mandatory properties are vital to correct operation and are thus taken care of by the Novell utilities.

Note

The property of the object specifies the type of information that the object can store, the terms *property* and *attribute* are often used interchangeably.

Some of the NetWare server object's properties are shown in figure 2.4. You can use the NetWare Administrator (NWADMIN) tool to view these properties. Figure 2.4 shows that you can specify the *Department* and *Organization* properties for the server object. The administrator cannot change the properties *Net Address, Status,* and *Version*—they represent the current status of the physical file server.

In NetWare 3.x, the *full name* property for user accounts was optional. But in NetWare 4.x, the last name property is mandatory. This might seem strange, because the last name property does not seem to serve any crucial technical function in the NDS database. The answer to this mystery lies with X.500, on which the NDS is based. In X.500, certain properties are explicitly defined as mandatory while others are optional. Many of the properties defined in NDS user objects are taken directly from the X.500 definition. In X.500, the last name property for user objects is called the *surname* property and is mandatory. NDS defines the last name property as mandatory to comply with X.500.

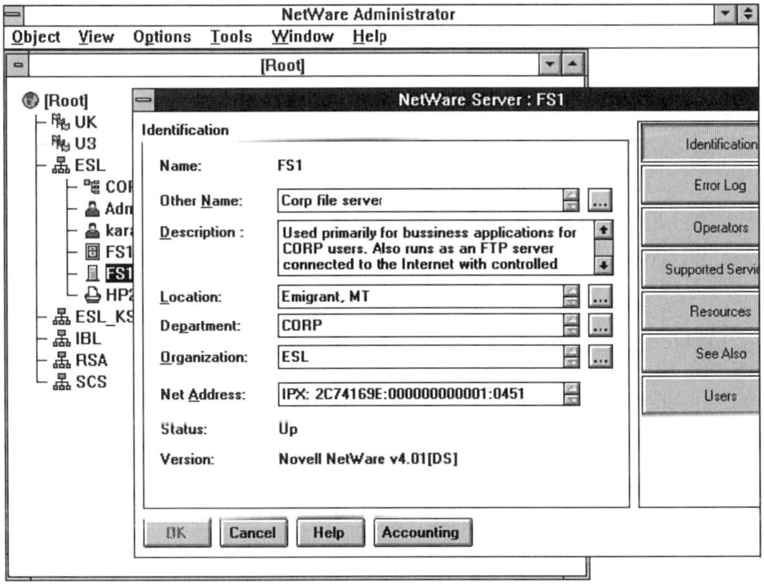

Figure 2.4
NetWare server properties.

Certain properties in NDS are defined for informational purposes and are *optional* properties, such as a user's telephone number, fax number, a title, or electronic mail address. Many objects have an optional See Also property.

Property values can be single- or multi-valued. You can define no more than one value for a single-valued property, such as the network address property of a NetWare File Server object. You can define more than one value for multi-valued properties, such as the telephone number property for user objects; thus, you can define multiple telephone numbers for a single user object.

Property values can be a numeric value, a string, or some special format, as in the case of a network address on an IPX network (4-byte network address, 6-byte node address, 2-byte socket number).

For your organization, decide for which of the optional properties you want to define values. Generally, you should define the optional properties for informational purposes, so that querying the NDS database for information on these property values is possible. However, certain organizations might not want to give out users' telephone numbers or other information regarding the users; in which case, you might just not define certain properties, or you might use NDS security to limit what object property values a user can view.

Comparing NDS to the NetWare Bindery

NDS treats all resources on the network as objects that belong to a global database (directory) that represents the network and has a structure that corresponds to a logical view of the network. NDS does not keep the directory in a centralized location, but rather, distributes portions of it (partitions) across servers on the network—a *distributed database.* The approach used in NDS differs from that used in pre-NetWare 4.0-based networks, in which the resources on a server were centrally located in a flat database, called the *bindery.* The bindery, because it did serve as a centralized database, was subject to being a single point of failure.

The directory database in NDS is organized hierarchically. This enables it to be used to map an organization, representing the relationship between the structure of the organizations and its relationships to network resources.

Contrasting the differences between the NDS and the NetWare 3.x bindery provides an insight into the improved manner in which NetWare 4.x manages network resources. Table 2.1 summarizes the differences between the NDS and the NetWare 3.x bindery.

Table 2.1
NDS versus Bindery

Attribute/Feature	NDS	Bindery
Structure	Hierarchical	Flat
Users	Network-wide	Server-centric
Login	Network-wide	Server-centric
Passwords	Single password	Password per server
Groups	Network-wide	Server-centric
Location	Distributed	Server-centric

Earlier versions of NetWare used the bindery to keep information on network resources in a flat database, which did not represent the logical relationship between network resources. The bindery was server-centric, and was used to store information on resources available at a NetWare server rather than the entire network. So, you had to perform tasks like creating user accounts, establishing groups, and assigning passwords for every server on the network.

Comparing NDS to Microsoft Domains

Microsoft Windows NT Server uses the LAN Manager domain as its basic unit of security and centralized administration. A LAN Manager/Windows NT domain consists of five basic administrative objects: user accounts, local groups, global groups, computers, and printers.

Microsoft Domains are typically created around a workgroup or geographical location. Domains can be replicated across multiple Windows NT servers. Every Windows NT server that contains a copy of the domain is known as a domain controller. There are two types of domain controllers: the *Primary Domain Controller* (PDC) and the *Backup Domain Controller* (BDC). Each Domain must have at least one PDC and may have multiple BDCs. Each Windows NT server may participate as a domain controller in a single domain.

The PDC is responsible for synchronizing across the domain; it does this by periodically communicating with all of the BDCs, to exchange account information and ensure the integrity of the domain database. Although users may use either the PDC or a BDC for login authentication, all changes to the domain occur on the PDC. If the PDC is down or unreachable, changes to the domain cannot occur, making the PDC a single point of failure. However, a Backup Domain Controller can manually be promoted from a BDC to a PDC.

NDS, because it can be replicated, does not have this limitation; it can be partitioned and replicated among many different NetWare 4.1 file servers. Administration of NDS—deleting users, groups, profiles, file servers, printers, print servers, message servers, and organizational units—can be performed on any replica of the database. All updates will be automatically replicated to the NDS database throughout the entire network.

In NT, trust relationships between domains permit cross-domain administration, enabling users and groups in one domain to be assigned rights to resources in a trusted domain. *Trust relationships* provide users a "single login" to their home domain and access to resources in other domains that "trust" the user's home domain. A trust relationship doesn't grant users access to resources in trusting domains; rather, it permits an administrator in the trusted domain to grant access rights to resources in the trusting domain. Only after a trust relationship is established between domains can an administrator grant rights to resources in the trusting domain.

Much more can be said about the differences between Domain relationships and directory services, but it is beyond the scope of this chapter.

Understanding the NetWare Directory Database

NDS is a global, distributed database that keeps information on network resources in a hierarchical manner. The distributed nature of NDS enables it to store information on many types of objects, such as users, printers, servers, and volumes of interest to the network user community (see fig. 2.5). NDS stores the distributed information on NetWare servers throughout the network, transparent to the user. It uses a directory synchronization mechanism, so that directory changes on any part of the NDS database propagate throughout the network. In other words, NDS synchronizes itself to present a consistent view of itself to the rest of the network. Directory synchronization takes place automatically without user intervention. The network administrator can set certain parameters to minimize the effect of directory synchronization on network traffic.

Figure 2.5
NDS database.

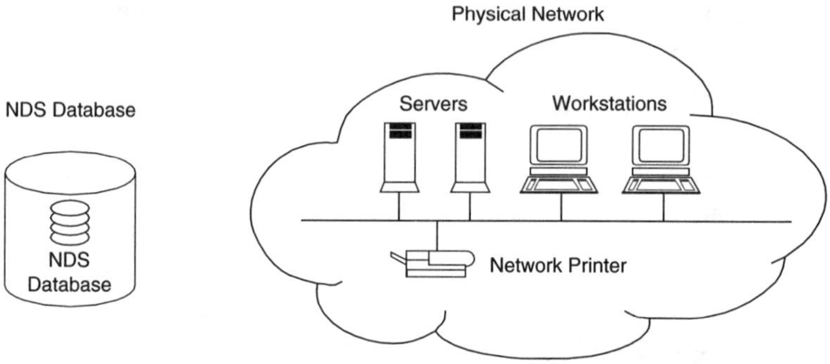

NDS is kept as a hidden data area on a storage volume for security purposes. The NDS presents a hierarchical view of itself to the rest of the world. A new set of *object trustee assignments* made on NDS objects controls access to any portion of the NDS.

The hierarchical relationship in NDS is often described in terms of a directory tree, such as the one shown in figure 2.6.

Figure 2.6
Hierarchical NDS tree for Network Widgets, Inc.

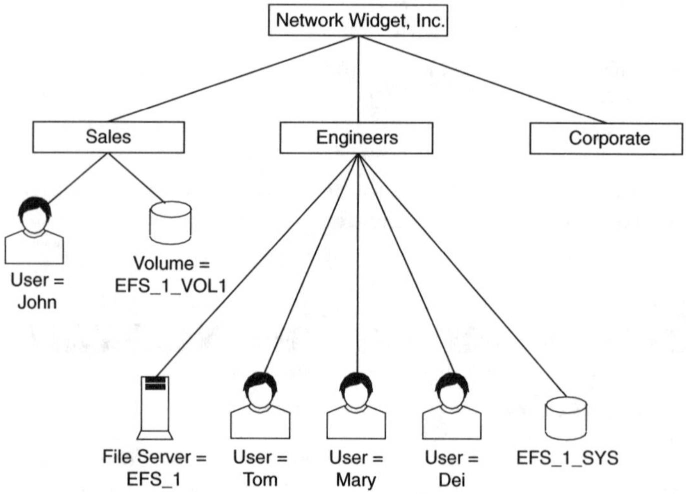

NDS's hierarchical relationship enables you to organize network resources so that they reflect network usage rather than the network's physical topology and connectivity. You can make the directory organization more closely match the user's view of the network. For example, in figure 2.6, engineers Tom, Mary, and Dei, of the organization Network Widget, Inc., have user accounts defined under the departmental unit (*organizational unit,* in NDS terminology)

Engineers. Figure 2.7 shows that the users are not in the same physical location—Tom and Mary are in Dallas, whereas Dei is in Los Angeles—but, because they all belong to the group Engineers, they have similar needs to access network resources. Under these circumstances, grouping them in an organizational unit called Engineers makes sense, regardless of their physical location.

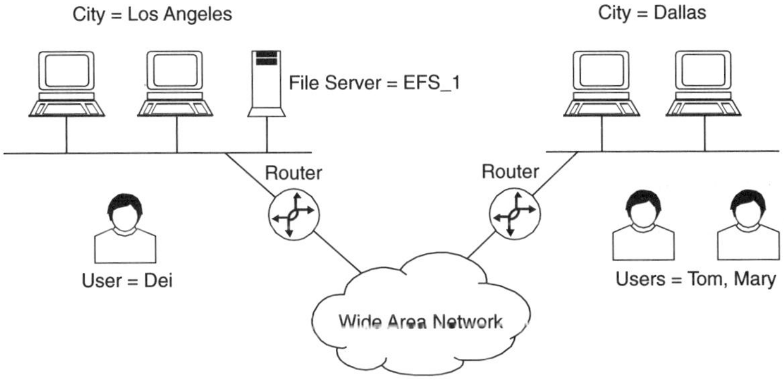

Figure 2.7
Physical network for Network Widgets, Inc.

The file server for the engineers of Network Widget, Inc. is currently defined in Los Angeles. Should you need to physically move the server to Dallas in the future, you can move the file server without changing the NDS view of the network. The file server EFS_1 still is under the organizational unit of Engineers in the NDS tree. In figure 2.6, you can see that volume EFS_1_SYS, physically attached to the server EFS_1, is in the organizational unit Engineers, because the engineers of the company are its primary users. Another volume, EFS_1_VOL1, also is physically attached to the server EFS_1, but its NDS representation is kept in the organizational unit SALES, because members of the sales team are its primary users. One reason that volume EFS_1_VOL1 is kept in the SALES organizational unit might be that the group SALES does not yet have its own file server. You can place network resources in the NDS tree according to use and the user's view of the network rather than physical location of the resource.

The NDS is based on the CCITT X.500 standard. CCITT stands for the Consultative Committee for International Telephone and Telegraphy—now called the ITU (International Telecommunications Union), but the standard is still referred to as that by the CCITT. The ITU is an international body that develops standards in data communications. Many of its members are the standards-making bodies of countries. ITU publishes standards and updates to existing standards at periodic intervals of four years.

NDS does not comply entirely with X.500, but is largely based on the 1988 X.500 recommendations. The X.500 standard has further evolved into the 1992 X.500 and 1994 X.500 specifications, but this was not available to the designers of NDS, as they began work on NDS before 1992.

You can expect Novell's implementation of NDS to comply with the international consensus on X.500, for strategic reasons, although initially this compliance will occur through NDS-to-X.500 gateways. Another area expected to change is the protocol mechanisms for updating the

NDS database when changes occur to it (*directory synchronization*). Novell, like many other X.500 vendors (DEC, Retix, and so on), had to design their own directory services synchronization protocol to deal with directory synchronization, because protocol mechanisms for updating NDS had not been completely specified in the X.500 standards at the time that NDS was designed. Many X.500 vendors, including Novell, are seeking common ways to implement X.500-compliant synchronization methods and services. Novell does provide an API for exchanging data between other name services, which makes possible building name service gateways to other name services.

As mentioned before, NDS complies closely with the X.500 recommendations. The details of the kind of objects that make up the directory are specific to NetWare-based networks. You can use the NDS programming APIs to add other general non-Novell specific classes of objects to the NDS directory, which enables you to integrate the NDS directory with other vendors' X.500 directory implementations.

NDS Components

NDS has a hierarchical structure and uses specific terminology to describe its components. Some of the terms derive from the X.500 recommendations, while others are Novell-specific. Before you can have a working understanding of NDS, you must understand the vocabulary and terms that describe NDS.

Tree Structure of NDS

The NDS database is organized as a hierarchical tree. A tree describes a way of representing data that begins at a single source, traditionally called the *root.* The root, in keeping with the tree metaphor, has *branches,* which can in turn branch off to other branches, or branch off to *leaves.* Figure 2.8 illustrates the tree concept, along with a picture of the NDS tree. The root and leaves of the tree, and the start of a tree branch, are called *nodes* of the tree.

Figure 2.8

NDS tree components.

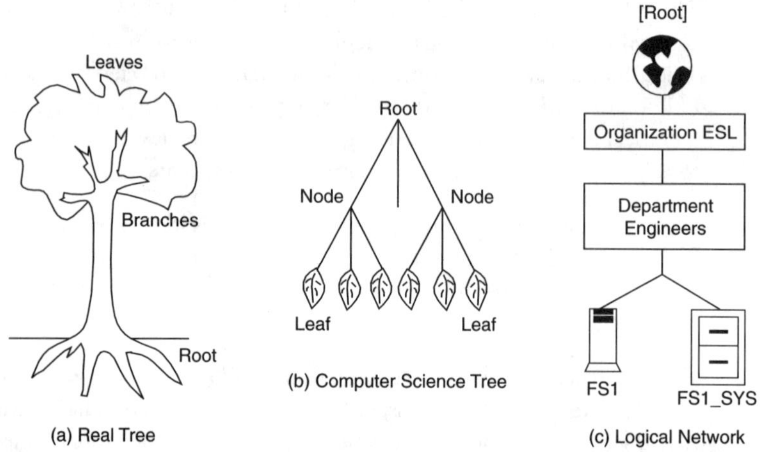

The tree has a single root (refer to figure 2.8), as does the NDS database. If several NDS databases are constructed separately, they have separate roots. Tools exist for combining several separate NDS trees (each with its own root) into a single larger NDS tree; for example, DSMERGE, which enables you to merge two NDS trees.

The root of a tree is the first level of the tree, and describes the entire tree. The root object is created when you install a NetWare 4.x server. Subsequent servers can either be installed in to the same tree (under the same root), or can be given placed in its own tree (own root object).

All objects in NDS are classified as one of two types of objects: a container object or a leaf object. *Container objects* are analogous to subdirectories in the file system, in that they contain other objects (refer to figure 2.8). Whereas *leaf objects* are analogous to files, that is, they do not contain other objects.

Container Objects

A *container object* in the NDS is an object that is allowed to contain other subordinate objects. Container objects provide a practical way to organize objects by departments, geographic location, work groups, projects, common usage of network resources, or other criteria that make the network easier to use and administrate.

The container objects provide a convenient way to organize other nodes into *groups* (see fig. 2.9), which is a key advantage of NDS. Besides using container objects to facilitate logical organization of the NDS tree, you can use container objects as groups to which you can assign certain security rights that affect the security rights of all nodes in the container.

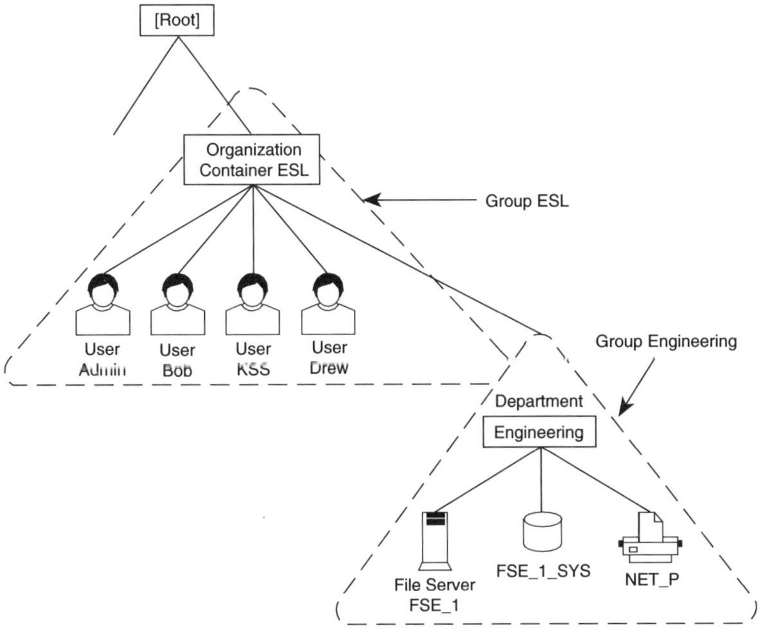

Figure 2.9
Container objects as groups.

NDS defines the following container objects :

- Root
- Country (C=)
- Organization (O=)
- Organizational Unit (OU=)
- Locality and State (L=),(S=)

Although NDS defines the above five container objects, the current NetWare utilities support only the O=Organization, OU=Organizational Unit, and C=Country. The Root class is supported but only the NDS system can create it. Future release of the NetWare utilities will probably implement the L=Locality and S=State.

The type of a container is referred to as *object class*. Each container type in the preceding list has a separate object class definition. An object class definition explains the rules that govern the object's existence in the NDS tree. The Country container's object definition, for example, includes a rule that states that the Country container can exist directly underneath the [Root] object, but cannot be contained in the Organization or Organizational Unit containers. This rule is described by the *Containment Classes* structure rules for NDS objects, which describes the classes of object that are permissible underneath different types of containers.

Leaf Objects

A node in the tree that does not (and cannot) contain any other nodes is called a *leaf object.* A leaf object resembles the leaves of a real tree, in that it does not contain any branches or other leaves. A leaf object is a terminal point in the tree and represents a network resource or service (see fig. 2.10). A leaf object can exist only inside a container object.

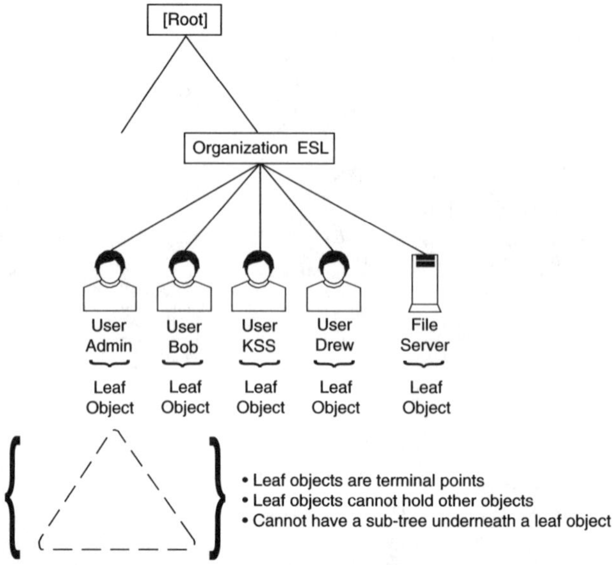

Figure 2.10
Leaf objects.

Object Class and Schema

A NetWare 4.x-based network can have many different types of network resources and services, each of which is described by a special type of leaf object. File server and print server objects are examples of leaf objects. The object definition (also called object type) for an object in the NDS database is called its *object class*. In database technology terms, the collection of the different object definitions possible in the database, and their scope and rules of existence and operation within the database, is called the *schema*.

Note

> The types of NDS objects, their properties, and the rules that govern their creation and existence are called the *directory schema*. The schema defines which objects are in the directories' database, and how objects can inherit properties and trustee rights of other container objects above it. In other words, the schema defines how the directory tree is structured. In NDS, the schema can be expanded or changed by identifying new classes of objects.

Database terms are sometimes used to describe the NDS tree because the NDS tree is a global distributed database, and you should be familiar with them. The NDS schema, therefore, is a collection of object class definitions for objects such as file servers, computers, printers, print servers, and so on (see fig. 2.11). When you create an object of a type that can exist in the NDS schema, you have *instantiated* the object class. The object class implies a potential (not the existence) for an object of that class to exist in the database. You must instantiate (create) the object class before an object belonging to that category can exist.

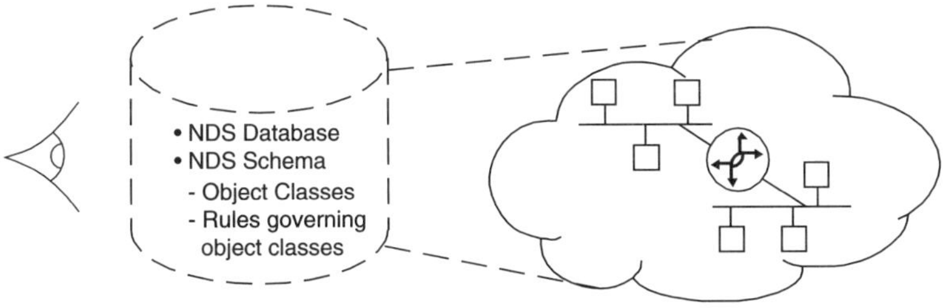

• NDS Database
• NDS Schema
- Object Classes
- Rules governing object classes

Figure 2.11
NDS schema.

In figure 2.8, the nodes ESL and Engineers are container objects, because they can contain other objects. The leaves FS1 and FS1_SYS are examples of leaf objects, because they are the terminal points in the tree and cannot contain other objects.

A container in which objects are defined is a *parent container* to the objects that it contains. Some object classes can contain other objects and some object classes cannot. Leaf object classes, for instance, cannot contain any other object classes. Container object classes can contain other object classes, but rules govern what container class objects can exist in other container class objects. These structural rules are called *Containment Class rules*. An object can exist in or *be subordinate to* only the objects listed among the object's containment classes. Table 2.2 shows the containment class rules for container objects.

Table 2.2
Containment Class Rules for Container Objects

Container Object	Containment Classes (can exist in)	Can Contain
[Root]	*Cannot* exist under any object. Parent to all objects.	Country *Alias* (Alias can be to another country object only)
Country	[Root]	Organization Organizational Unit *Alias* (Alias can be to an Organization or Organizational Unit object only)
Organization	[Root]	Country Organizational Unit Leaf objects
Organizational Unit	Organization Organizational Unit	Organizational Unit Leaf objects

Containers and Directories in File Systems

Containers are similar to directories in a file system. A directory in a file system can contain other subdirectories and files, and similarly, a container in NDS contains other subcontainers and leaf objects (network resources and services), as shown in figure 2.12. You use a directory in a file system to organize files, and similarly, you use containers in NDS to organize network resources. An NDS tree differs from a file system directory tree, in that limitations apply to where container and leaf objects can occur.

NDS tree depth is unlimited. You might want to limit the depth, however, for practical reasons of NDS tree management.

The container typically represents an organization, department within an organization, work group center, responsibility center, geographical location, shared information, or network usage. You should plan with care the container and its relationship to other objects in the tree structure; however, tools now exist that will enable you to restructure the organization of the tree. After you construct the NDS tree, making changes is done with a migrate.exe utility that ships with most versions of NetWare 4.x.

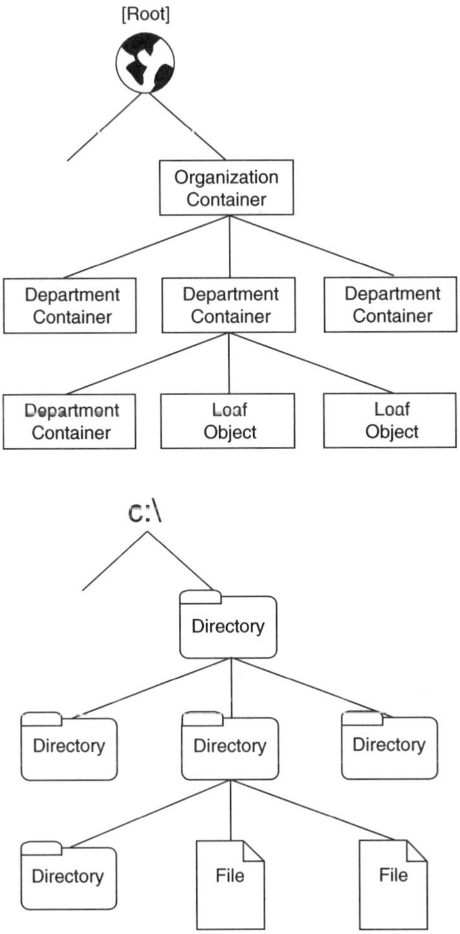

Figure 2.12
Containers versus directories for file system.

Since the release of NetWare 4.x, there have been many migration issues, resulting in updates and patches to the migrate.exe utility. The migration tool was designed specifically to help system administrators who wanted to move platforms within NetWare but keep the same user rights, login access, and data files. In 1992, Novell introduced migrate.exe to help with this problem.

Now, however, there is also a newer, more feature-rich utility, called DS Migrate, that ships with IntranetWare. In order to use this utility you need the latest version of NDS on all of your NetWare 4 servers (in the case of merging trees) and (if you are upgrading older versions of NetWare) you need to be using the latest version of the client and NWAdmin utility. DS Migrate is a migration and modeling solution that resulted from a partnered agreement between Preferred Systems Inc., the makers of DS Standard (the utility on which DS Migrate is based) and Novell, Inc. According to Novell, using DS Migrate is the recommended way of migrating a NetWare server across-the-wire, rather than using MIGRATE.EXE. This recommendation applies for both bindery and file migration.

Object Names

All nodes of the NDS tree must have a unique name, called an *object name*. The root of the tree has the fixed object name of [Root]. Object names are not *case-sensitive*, which means that two objects with the names, NW4CS_SYS and nw4Cs_sYs, respectively, share the same object name. Therefore, [root] and [Root] refer to the same object—the root of the directory tree. Objects directly in the same container cannot share a name. Therefore, in figure 2.13, the container ENGINEERS cannot have two volume objects that have the names NW4CS_SYS and nw4Cs_sYs. Even two objects that have different object classes cannot have the same name. Container ENGINEERS, therefore, cannot have a file server object named ZAPHOD and a user object named ZAPHOD. The two objects can, however, exist in different containers (see fig. 2.14).

Figure 2.13
Object names in a container.

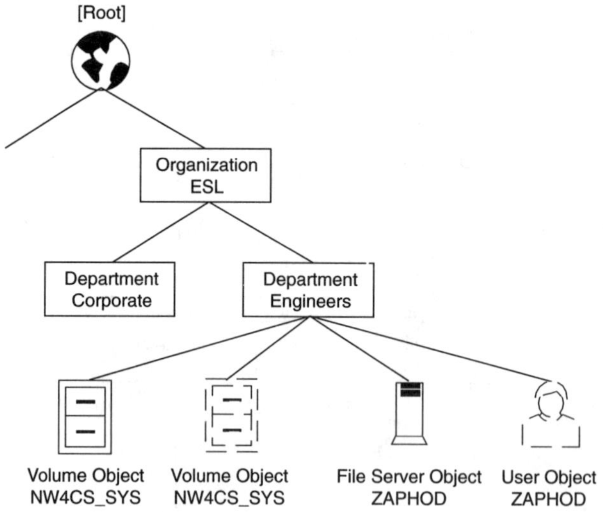

Figure 2.14
The same object names in different containers.

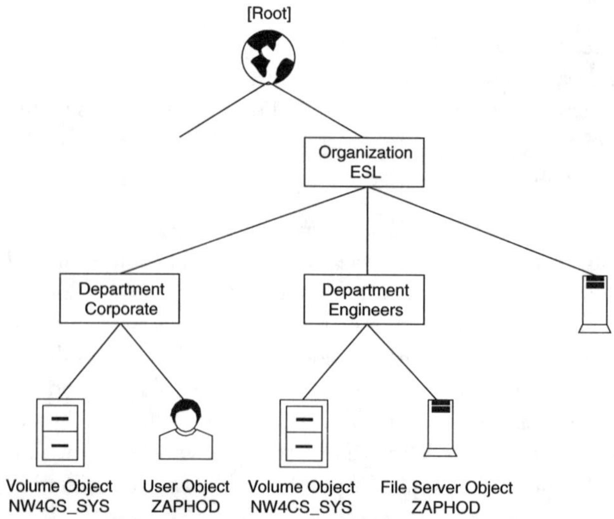

Even though object names are not case-sensitive, NDS preserves the case of the name at the time you create the object for display purposes. So, if you create an object named mY_worKstation, it appears in the case with which the object name was originally created. You can, however, rename objects, except special objects, such as the [Root] object, in the {Public} implicit group object.

To make object names consistent and more readily understandable, an organization should establish object naming conventions.

An object name technically can consist of as many as 64 characters (alphanumeric characters, dashes, underscores, parenthesis, and even spaces). If you use spaces, you must enclose the object name in quotation marks ("") before command line utilities and login scripts can recognize it. You might want to avoid using spaces in object names, if for no other reason than for the sake of simplicity. You actually can create an object name that consists merely of a single blank. Figure 2.15 shows an interesting example of an NDS tree that has two objects that have blank names. The first container object under ESL and the user object underneath the second object both have blank object names. Although blank names might be permitted, avoiding them is well worth your while, because the utilities that query NDS do not handle them consistently.

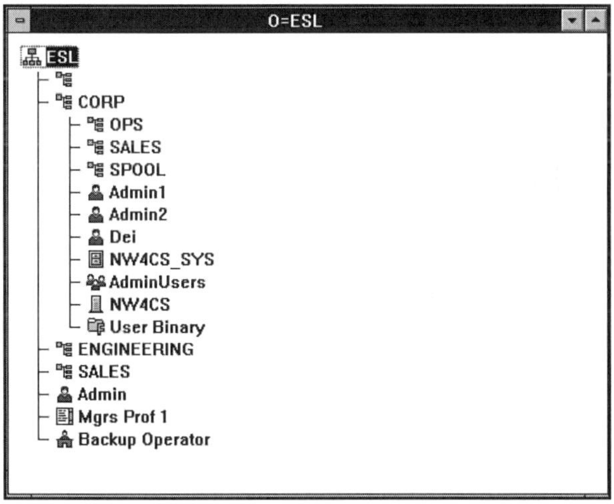

Figure 2.15
Blank name objects.

Object names cannot contain brackets, periods, or percent signs. You can use a few special characters, such as plus (+), period (.), or equals (=), as long as you precede them with a backslash (\). Generally, you should avoid special characters in object names, because they make the names confusing and difficult to use and remember.

NDS might even let you to use characters designated as illegal in the documentation for creating names of objects. Even so, such names are not guaranteed to function consistently in NDS-based commands and utilities, so your best bet is simply to avoid them.

Types of Container Objects

NDS supports four types of container objects:

- The [Root] object
- The Country object
- The Organization object
- The Organizational Unit object

Figure 2.16 shows the icons that represent the different types of container objects. NDS displays these icons when you use the Windows-based network administration tools. The US container, in this figure, represents the Country object. The containers AT&T, DEC, ESL, ESL_KSS, LG, LTREE, MITEL, RSA, SCS, WELFLEET, and WIDGET all represent Organization container objects. The containers ACCOUNTING, CORP, R&D, and SALES represent Organizational Unit container objects.

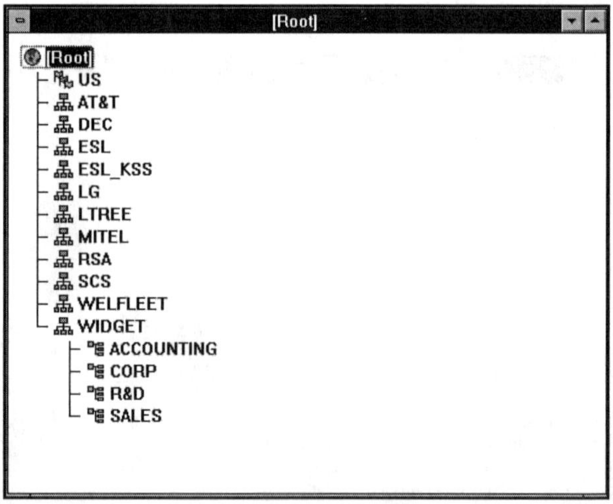

Figure 2.16
Symbolic representations of container objects.

The [Root] Container Object

The most frequently used container objects are the Organization object and the Organizational Unit object. Any one NDS tree can have only one [Root] object, which you cannot rename or delete. In this sense, it is different from the other container objects. The [Root] object can have rights to other objects, and other objects can have rights to it.

You can install NetWare 4.x on separate networks, each with their own [Root] object—easily if the network was built in different segments, and final connectivity of the separate network segments was done later. Under such circumstances, several [Root] objects can exist, each describing a different tree. Now, if you connect the network segments together, the networks represented by the different [Root] objects cannot use normal NDS mechanisms to communicate (see fig. 2.17).

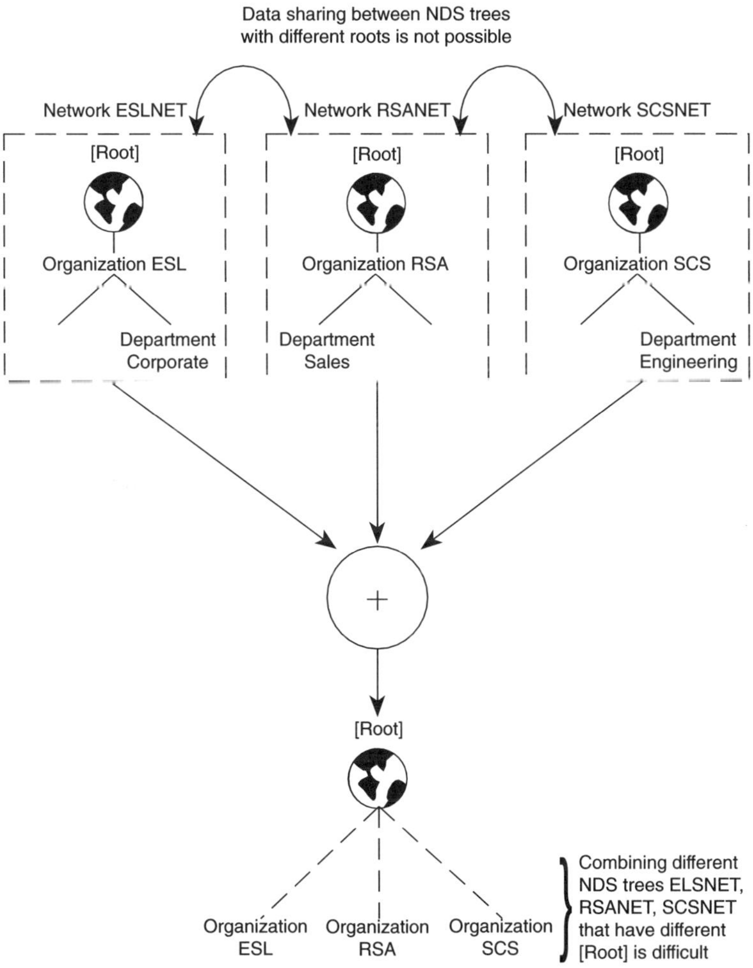

Figure 2.17
Multiple [Root] objects and sharing of data.

You can, however, have two servers, FS1 and FS2, each defined in its own unique tree, TREE1 and TREE2, respectively. You could log in to FS1 under TREE1 as a valid NDS user. If you were to use NetWare 3.x syntax to map a drive to a volume on FS2, NetWare would automatically switch to bindery emulation mode and attempt to connect you. You could then have access to the FS2 object, despite the fact that it is in a separate NDS tree.

1. Log in to TREE1 as a valid NDS user.

2. MAP[]FS2/SYS:

MAP[]FS2/SYS: is the NetWare 3.x syntax that causes NetWare to switch to bindery emulation mode.

When you install a NetWare 4.x server other than *the first server* installed, you should have physical connectivity from this NetWare 4.x server to the rest of the network, so that you could install the server as part of the NDS tree.

In very high-security environments, you might want separate [Root] objects to ensure that users in a directory tree under one [Root] cannot use NDS to access or communicate with users under another [Root]. If you want to merge separate NDS trees, you can use the DSMERGE tool.

The [Root] object can contain only Country, Organization, and Alias objects. Of these, Country and Organization are container objects, and Alias is a leaf object.

The Country Container Object

The Country object is part of the X.500 recommendations, but seldom used in commercial networks based on NetWare 4.x, because many organizations are multi-national in character and are not organized along country boundaries. Also, if an organization uses a Country object, that branch of the NDS tree cannot easily use simplified object names. Country object names are limited to two characters—any two characters, but you should use the ITU's two-letter designations for countries. Figure 2.18 shows an NDS tree that has the two-letter designations for several countries. You can see that you must place the Country object directly below the [Root] object. The Country object is optional. If you use it, it must occur directly under the [Root] object.

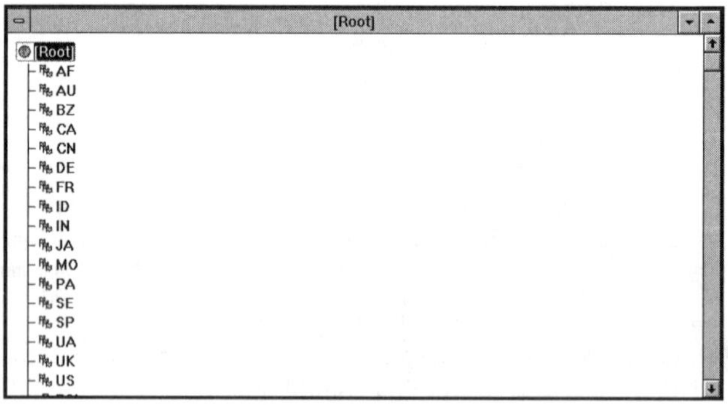

Figure 2.18
Country objects in an NDS tree.

The Organization Object

The Organization object represents the name of the organization. Figure 2.19 shows an NDS tree that has the Organization objects. Notice the special icon used to represent the Organization object. At least one Organization object must be used in an NDS tree, directly below the [Root] object or a Country object. The NDS schema allows you to place an organization object only in these places. In figure 2.19, the organization objects CISCO, HP, IBL, IBM, MS, and NOVELL are placed directly underneath the Country object US. Also, organizations AT&T, DEC, ESL, ESL_KSS, LG, LTREE, MITEL, RSA, SCS, WELFLEET, and WIDGET are placed directly underneath the [Root] object.

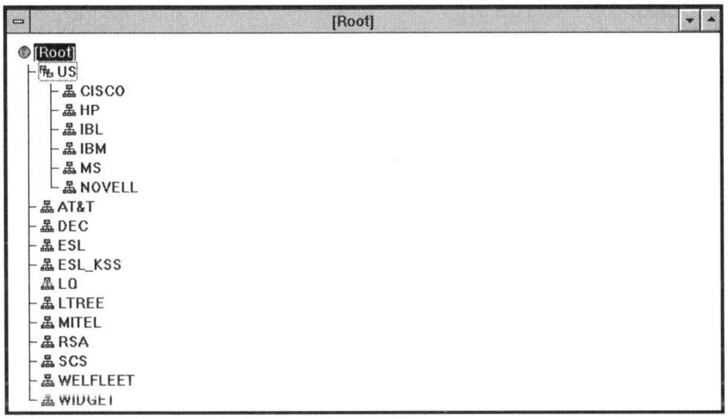

Figure 2.19
Organization objects.

The Organization object can contain any leaf object and Organizational Unit object, but it cannot contain another Organization object.

The Organizational Unit Object

Because an organization is usually subdivided into specialized functions (such as by department, network usage, common jobs, location, work groups, responsibility centers, and so on) the Organizational Unit object can be used to represent the organization's subdivision. The Organizational Unit must occur under an Organization object or another Organizational Unit object. An Organizational Unit cannot occur directly under the [Root] object or Country Object.

Figure 2.20 shows examples of an Organizational Unit object and the different locations in the NDS tree in which it can occur. The organizations HP, MS, and NOVELL in the Country container object have organizational units such as CORP, ENGINEERING, MARKETING, and DISTRIBUTION directly underneath them. The organization ESL_KSS that is directly underneath the [Root] has organizational units CORP, ENG, and SALES underneath it. CORP is used as an Organizational Unit name in more than one organization. The object naming rules require an object name to be unique only within the same *level* of the container, which enables you to use the same object names in different containers.

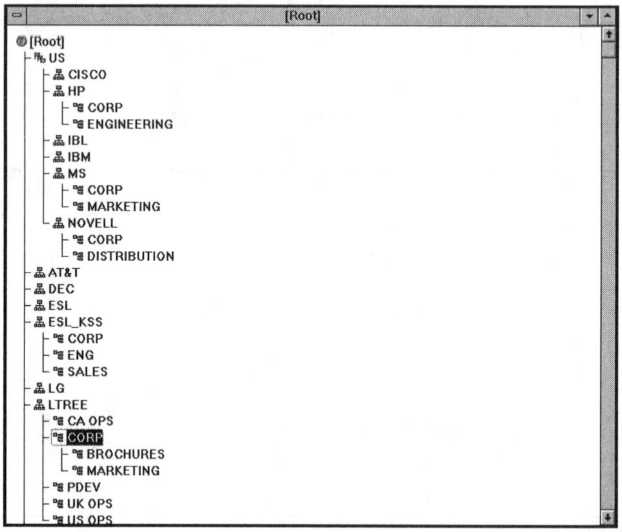

Figure 2.20
Organizational Unit objects.

In figure 2.20, organization LTREE has an Organizational Unit object, CORP, underneath it. CORP has two other Organizational Unit objects directly underneath it, BROCHURES and MARKETING. This is typical of many organizations that can be expected to have subdivisions within a department of an organization.

An Organizational Unit object can contain any leaf object and Organizational Unit object.

Attribute Types

As part of the X.500 scheme of naming objects, an attribute designator represents each object type. For example, the attribute type C represents Country objects, so, for example, the Country object US is represented as follows:

```
C=US
```

The attribute types O and OU represent the other container object types, Organization and Organizational Unit, respectively. The organization IBM, for example, is represented as follows:

```
O=IBM
```

An Organizational Unit object called SALES would be represented as follows:

```
OU=SALES
```

The attribute type designator CN (Common Name) represents a leaf object that represents a resource or a service, so a file server named NW4CS would be represented as follows:

```
CN=NW4CS
```

The different attribute types are summarized in table 2.3. All attribute types, aside from the one for [Root], are part of the X.500 recommendations.

Table 2.3
Attribute Type Designators

Object	Container/Leaf	Attribute Type
[Root]	Container	No special attribute type. Designated by [Root] itself.
Country	Container	C
Organization	Container	O
Organizational Unit	Container	OU
Leaf Object	Leaf	CN

Types of Leaf Objects

Leaf objects are the actual representations of network resources. The other objects ([Root], Country, Organization, and Organizational Unit) are logical in nature and used for organizational purposes.

The NDS schema permits only the following leaf objects by default:

- AFP Server
- Alias
- Computer
- Directory Map
- Group
- NetWare Server
- Organizational Role
- Print Server
- Print Queue
- Printer
- Profile
- User

- Volume
- Bindery
- Bindery Queue
- Distribution List
- Message Routing Group
- External Entity
- Unknown

The preceding standard leaf objects are the only ones currently available. The following sections discuss each of the preceding leaf objects in turn.

AFP Server Object

The *AFP Server leaf object* is currently used for informational purposes only. It represents an *AppleTalk Filing Protocol* (AFP) server that is on your network—perhaps a Macintosh computer running the AFP protocols, or even a VAX server emulating AFP protocols. You can use the AFP server to store information, such as the network address, users, and operators. One of the benefits of NDS is that you can query it for information as you would query in databases. If you have an AFP Server object for each AppleTalk server on your network (see fig. 2.21), you can make general queries such as: "Show me all AppleTalk servers in container O=ESL."

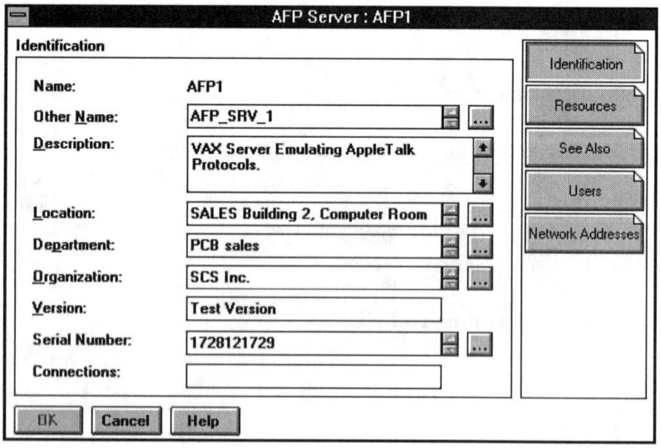

Figure 2.21
AFP Server object.

Alias Object

The NDS system is hierarchical in nature, and the object naming syntax (as you learn later in this chapter) consists of enumerating the NDS objects beginning at the leaf and progressing all the way up to the top of the tree. If you try to reference an object that is not in the container, the naming syntax becomes a little complicated, especially for end users who do not have the training to understand the NDS naming convention (see fig. 2.22).

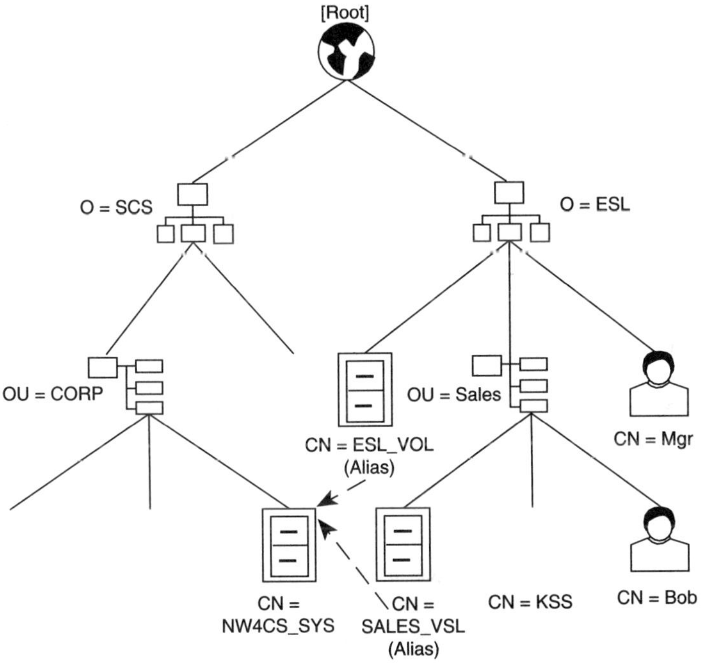

Figure 2.22
Accessing another object via alias.

NDS permits you to define an object called the *Alias object.* An Alias object can point to a leaf or a container object, not unlike the symbolic links used in operating systems such as Unix, except that Unix symbolic links apply to file systems, whereas Alias objects are links to leaf objects in the NDS tree. Figure 2.23 shows the information that you need to supply when you create an Alias object. In this dialog box, alternate_name will be the name of the Alias object being created. You can enter the value for the Aliased object directly or select the browse icon next to this field, which activates the Select Object dialog box. An alias can point to either a container object (an object that holds other containers), or a non-container object (one that does not have any other containers). You can distinguish Alias objects by the "*Lone Ranger*" mask icon that appears next to them.

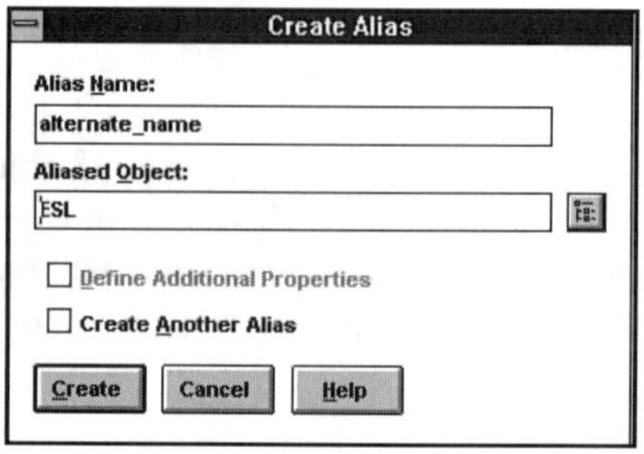

Figure 2.23
Alias object creation.

An alias is a name containing at least one Relative Distinguished Name. This can be a very useful tool for the network administrator who wants to grant users in one container access or rights to resources contained in another OU (this is often used for providing access to printers that are outside the Organizational Unit). In other words, the alias can be viewed as a means of accessing a specific object or set of objects that reside in a different part of the tree.

It is also possible to use the Alias object to point one OU to another OU. This gives the Alias OU access to all of the network resources stored in the other OU. In fact, it appears that alias places the alias's container inside of the other container. When the alias is used in this fashion the object being aliased is known as the *primary object.*

It is best if the Alias object is only used to access a few network resources, during times of migration, or during tree manipulation. Overuse of this object can make tree management difficult.

Computer Object

You use a *Computer object* to represent a non-server computer, such as a workstation, minicomputer, or mainframe, or even to represent a router. You can think of a router as a specialized computer that has multiple network boards and routing logic implemented in firmware or software. A Computer object can contain information such as network address, computer serial number, computer operator, and so on (see fig. 2.24).

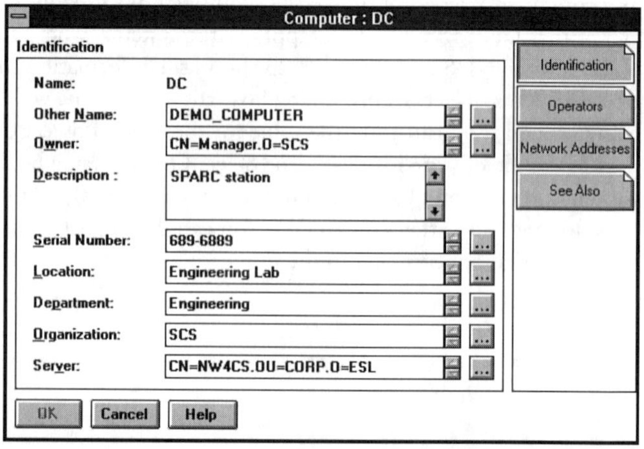

Figure 2.24
A Computer object.

Another key use of the Computer object is to document the user or group that is responsible for its day-to-day maintenance or use.

Directory Map Object

A *Directory Map object* contains a reference or pointer to a directory on a Volume object anywhere in the NDS tree. Currently, Directory Map objects are used only in the MAP command, which lets you use a workstation drive letter to refer to a network directory on a server. Using Directory Map objects can simplify using the MAP command to point to volume objects in other containers.

An important use of the MAP command is in login scripts. *Login scripts* are a sequence of instructions that NDS executes during user login, primarily geared toward setting up a user's network environment. Consider a situation in which a login script that contains the MAP command to map the drive letter G is mapped to a directory in the Volume object FS1_VOL in container O=ESL. If someone later were to move the Volume object to another container, or change the directory path, the mapping would become invalid and it would be necessary to modify all references to the former location of the Volume object and directory. If you use the Directory Map object to do the mapping in the login script, however, you need only change the directory map reference to the new volume/directory location. Figure 2.25 shows a Directory Map object in an NDS tree with some of its properties.

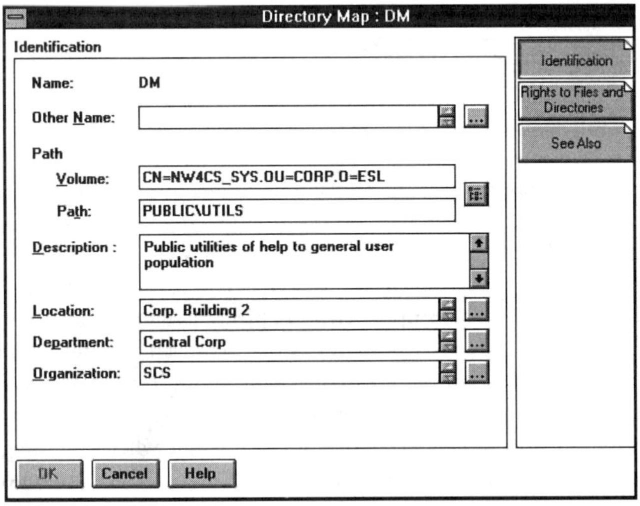

Figure 2.25
A Directory Map object.

Group Object

You use a *Group object* to refer to a collection of users in the NDS tree. A Group object can refer only to a collection of User objects. You use it as a convenience for assigning a number of users the same security rights. Figure 2.26 illustrates the concept of groups. In figure 2.27, the users belong to the same container, which is the most common use of groups. The Group object permits users from other containers to belong to the same group.

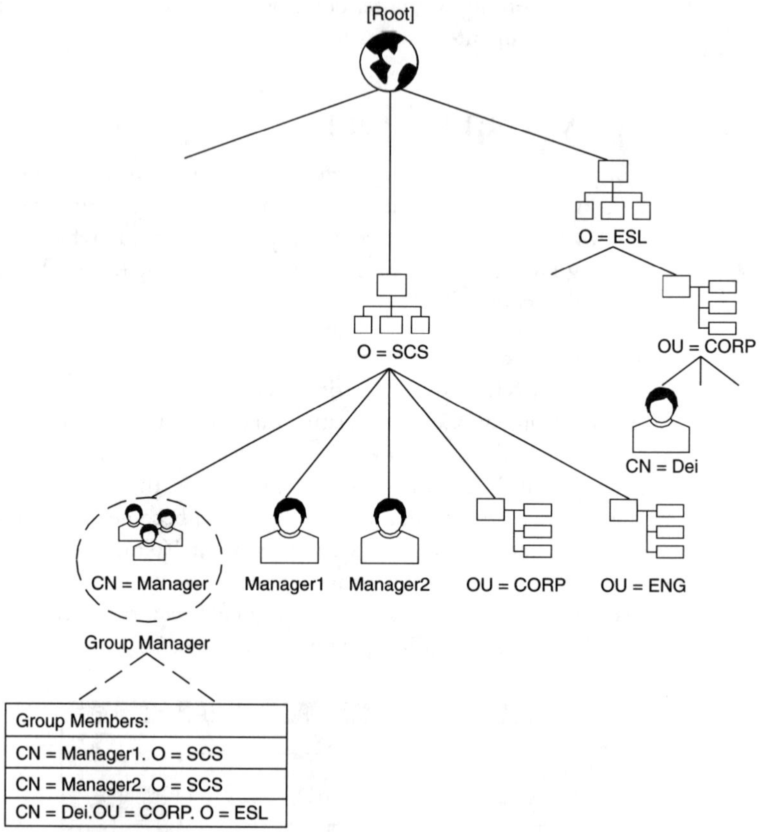

Figure 2.26
The concept of groups.

The Group object is similar in concept to groups in NetWare 3.x, except that Group is an NDS object, not a bindery object. Also, NetWare 4.x does not have a default group, such as group EVERYONE, that, by default, contains all users created on the server. You can use container objects to achieve the effect of a "group EVERYONE." You use the container name to treat all objects created in a container as a group. A Group object has a group membership property, a list of User objects defined anywhere in the NDS tree. You can use members of a Group object only as User objects, but you can use container objects as groups, and members of a container object can be any leaf object or other container objects. You can use container groups to provide a hierarchical relationship between groups not possible when you use group objects and NetWare 3.x groups. In NetWare 3.x, for example, a group cannot contain other groups, which means the subset relationship between groups does not exist. Subset relationships between groups is possible if you use containers that have a natural hierarchical relationship between them.

Figure 2.27 shows the Group object membership property.

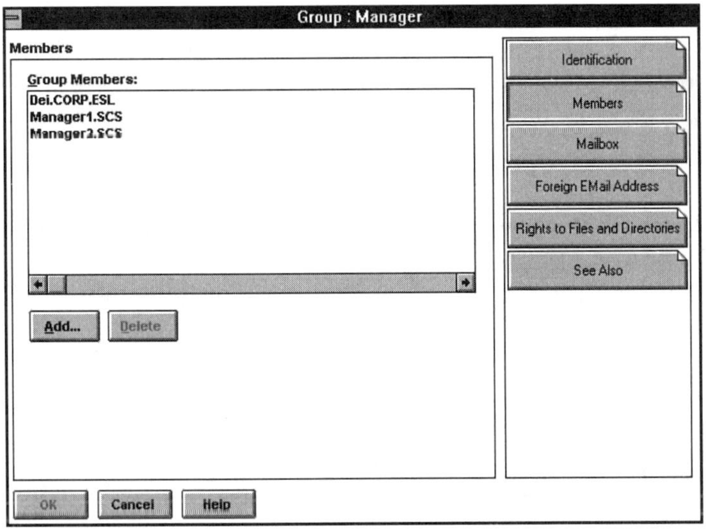

Figure 2.27
Group object membership property.

NetWare Server Object

The *NetWare Server object* represents the physical NetWare Server on a network and provides *NetWare Core Protocol* (NCP) services. Some of the services that this object provides are represented in the NDS tree as special objects that reference the NetWare server. The volume object, for example, might be part of the physical NetWare server, but be represented as a separate volume object.

The NetWare Server object is created during installation. One of the parameters that you specify during installation is the container in which NDS should place the NetWare server. The NetWare Server object contains information such as the physical location of the server object, its network address, the service it provides, and so on.

The NetWare Server object is referenced by other objects in the NDS tree. An example of this is the Volume object that references the NetWare server that acts as its host server. Without the NetWare Server object you could not reference the volume object, and hence the files on the volume.

Figure 2.28 shows a NetWare Server object in an NDS tree and some of its properties. The status of the server is shown as being Up, and its IPX address is IPX:F0004100: 000000000001:0451. The F0004100 refers to the eight-hexadecimal digit internal number of the NetWare server; 000000000001 refers to the 12-hexadecimal digit node number; and 0451 refers to the four-hexadecimal digit socket number for receiving NCP requests. The 000000000001 is a 12-hexadecimal digit node number and is different from the hardware address of the board (sometimes called the node address or the MAC [Media Access Control] address). The version number of the server is reported as well. The DS stands for Directory Services.

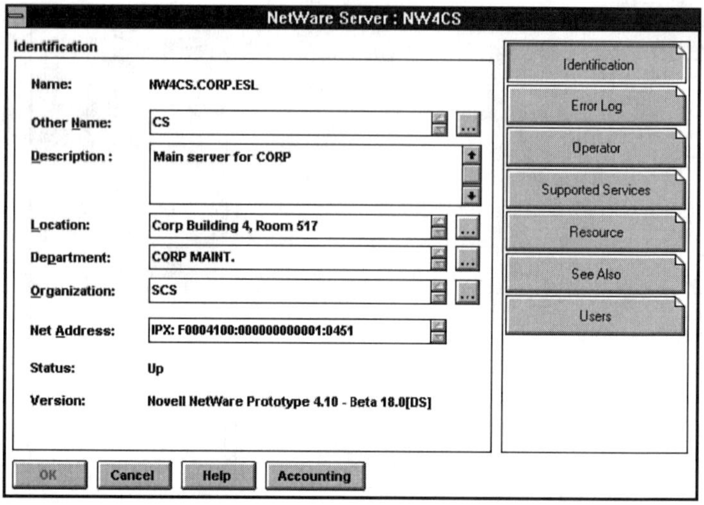

Figure 2.28
The NetWare Server object.

Organizational Role Object

Organizational Role refers to a position or role within a department or organization, a role to which usually a set of responsibilities and tasks is associated. The backup operator who needs access to certain volumes to perform the backup operation would be an example of such a position. The print server operator would be another. You can assign a User object to be an occupant of the Organizational Role object. If you do so, the user object inherits all rights that are assigned to the Organizational Role object (see fig. 2.29). If the responsibility for performing the task is passed on to another user, you can change the user occupant of the Organizational Role object accordingly.

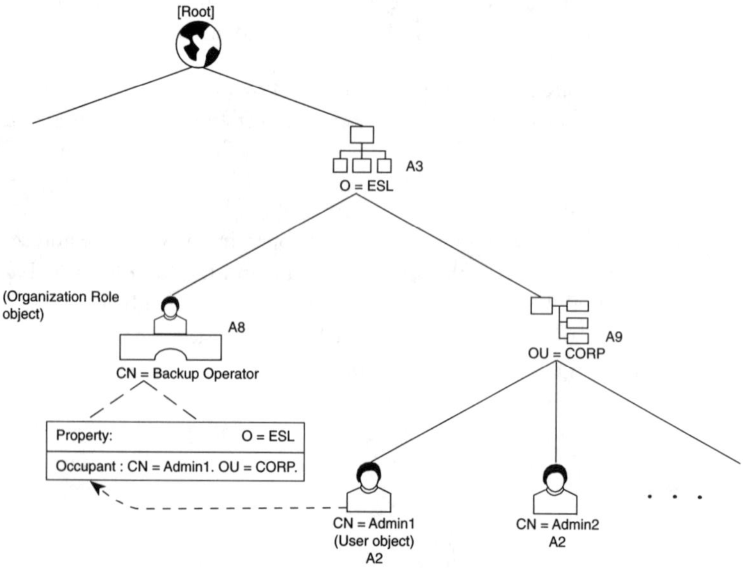

Figure 2.29
The relationship between a User object and an Organizational Role object.

The Organizational Role object is useful when the task the organizational role performs generally does not change, but the person who fulfills that role does change. For example, the person assigned to perform backup tasks could change, depending on the workload of individuals in an organization. Rather than change the rights of the user just to do a certain task, you can assign these rights just once to the Organizational Role object. The occupant of the Organizational Role object then can change, and the assigned occupant still has sufficient rights to perform the organizational role's task. You also can use the Organizational Role object to test the security rights of a user by making the user an occupant of the Organizational Role object and testing the Organizational Role object. Before you can do so, you need to know the password for the Organizational Role object but not the "occupant" user.

Figure 2.30 shows the Organizational Role object and the individual occupying that role at the moment. Only user objects can be assigned to the property Occupant. Figure 2.30 indicates that the occupant of the organization role is the User object Admin1.CORP.ESL

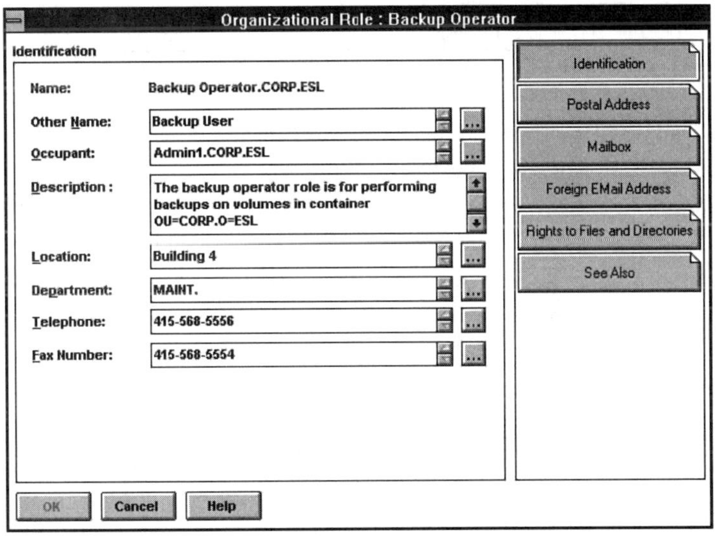

Figure 2.30
An Organizational Role object.

Print Server Object

A *Print Server object* describes the services that the NetWare Print Server provides. You use PCONSOLE and NWADMIN (*NetWare Administrator Tool*) to create the Print Server object. It contains a reference to all the Printer objects it services.

Figure 2.31 shows the Print Server object and some of its properties in the NDS tree. The print server has a property called the Advertising Name, which the print server uses to advertise its services that use Service Advertising Protocol (SAP). The status of the print server in figure 2.31 indicates that it is down.

Figure 2.31

A Print Server object.

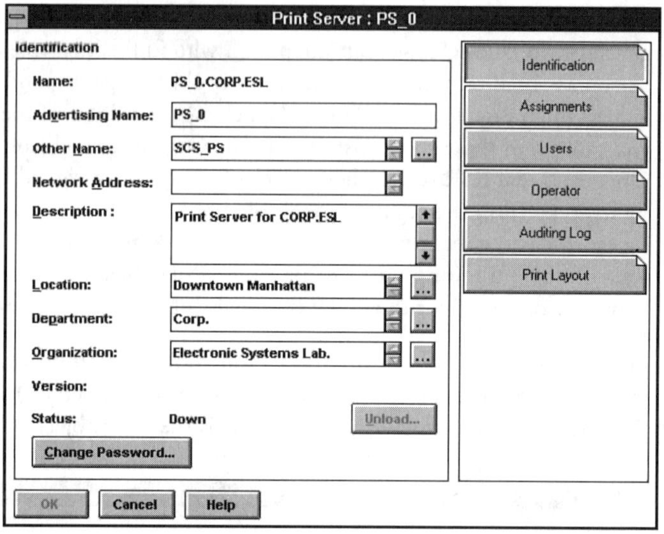

Print Queue Object

The *Print Queue object* serves to describe the network print queues. The print queue has a reference to the Volume object on which the print jobs are stored and it is assigned to a Printer object. Any print job a user sends to the Printer object goes to the associated print queue.

Figure 2.32 shows the Print Queue object in the NDS tree. The Volume property indicates the volume object that supports the print queue. Print queues are stored in the QUEUES directory on the specified volume. The operator flags, at the bottom of the screen, indicate the type of operations that the queue operator permits.

Figure 2.32

A Print Queue object.

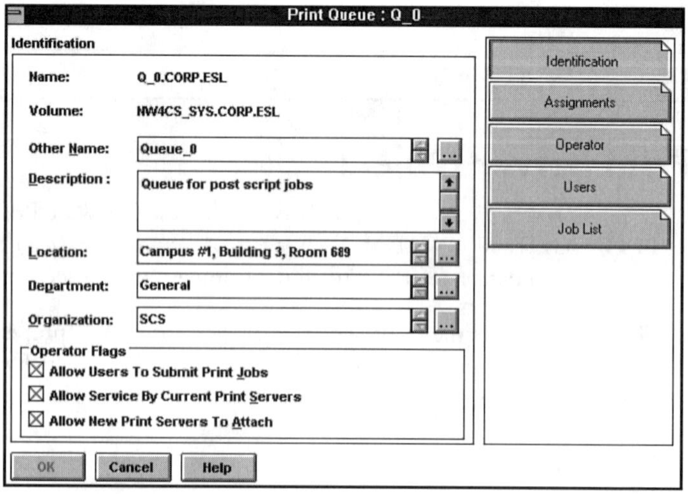

Tip

> It is good practice to place Printer and Print Queue objects at the highest level possible; this will service the most users possible. It is also a good idea to place print queues on volumes other than the SYS volume. This offers greater fault tolerance of the server.

Printer Object

The *Printer object* serves to describe the physical network printer device. Any print job that a user sends to the Printer object goes to the associated print queue.

Currently, more restrictions apply to sending jobs to Printer objects, including the following:

1. You must be a user of *all* the queues assigned to the Printer object.
2. You must have Browse NDS rights to the Printer object and all assigned Print Queue objects.
3. You must designate a default queue for the Printer object.

Figure 2.33 shows a Printer object in the NDS tree and the properties of the Print object that contain references to other printer-related objects. In figure 2.33, only one Queue object is assigned to the Print Queue's property list, at a priority of 1 (highest), so any print jobs sent to the Printer object go to the queue represented by the object: Q_0.CORP.ESL, which also is the default print queue for the Printer object. The print server that this printer services is PS_0.CORP.ESL.

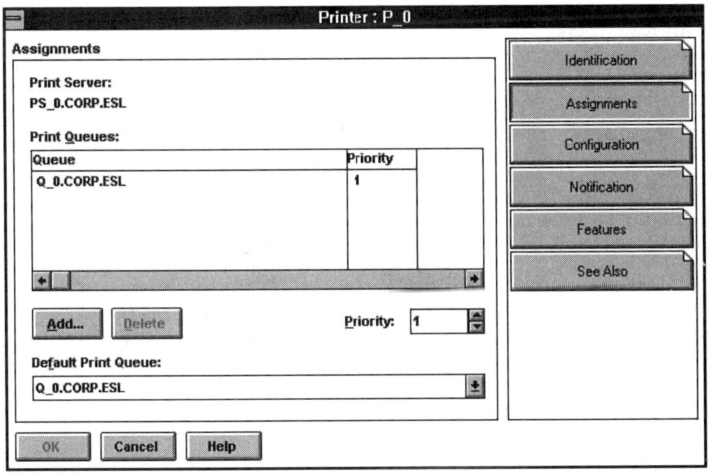

Figure 2.33
A Printer object and the assignment properties.

Profile Object

The *Profile object* is used as a special-purpose scripting object, that is executed by LOGIN.EXE (after the execution of your container login script). It is often used to place special drive mappings or environment settings that you want to apply to a specific group of users. The Profile object is the only login script type that can exist as an independent NDS object. (The user objects that share the login script can be in different containers.)

Figure 2.34 shows a Profile object in an NDS tree and the login script it contains.

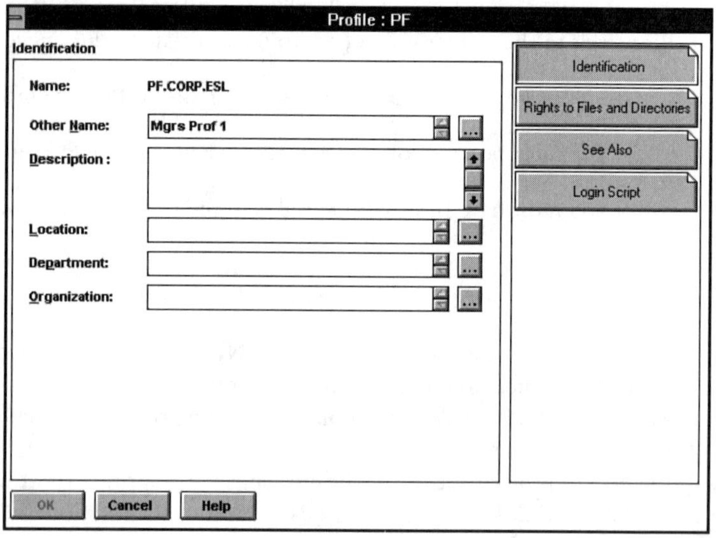

Figure 2.34
A Profile object.

There are three uses for profile scripts.

- Creating a global login script
- Creating a location login script
- Creating a special function login script

In previous versions of NetWare, a System login script contained all of the setting that applied unconditionally to each user. In NetWare 4 however, there is no global system login script. Each Organizational Unit that is created will have its own login script, which is referred to as the OU login script. In NetWare 4, the login scripts are executed in the following order:

- OU login script
- Profile login script, when applicable
- User login script
- Default login script if no other script is available

Because of the order of execution it makes most sense to place the most global settings in the OU login scripts. You can then use the profile scripts to determine access and resources that may based on geographical locations. You may also use the profile login scripts to make specific printer captures. Finally, you can use the personal scripts to assign resources at an individual level.

Note

> The Profile object script executes from one container, even though user objects can be located in other containers. This can cause performance issues while the script is executing, especially when employed on a wide area environment—NDS will have to search the tree to locate a particular object.

When creating users, the NWADNIN utility will enable you to specify that the user be part of a profile. If a user is already created, you can change the user's object properties and assign a User object to a specific profile.

User Object

A *User object* represents the user account of the individual that logs in to the network, and is the user's most important object. Changes to this object have a direct effect on the user. Any user who might need to log in to the network needs the user object. The User object is defined in the NDS tree, which differs from NetWare 3.x, in which User objects are defined on a server. An individual can use this single User object to access all the servers and other network resources to which he or she has rights.

Attributes—*properties,* in NDS terms—of the User object include a home directory on a Volume object to which the user has rights, login restrictions, enabling/disabling intruder lock out mechanism, and so on.

Figure 2.35 shows a user object defined in the NDS tree and some of its properties.

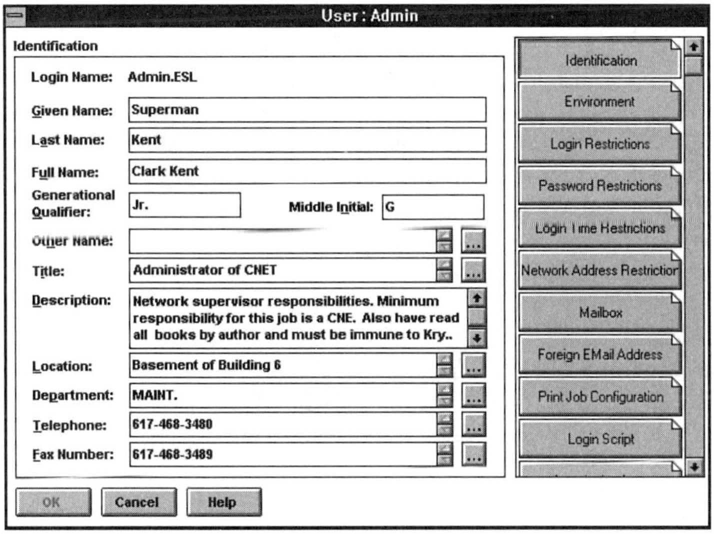

Figure 2.35
A User object.

You can use a user object that has the special name USER_TEMPLATE as a template to create default property values for User objects within that container. You can have only one USER_TEMPLATE object within a container (Organization, Organizational Unit containers) that enables the creation of such objects.

Volume Object

The *Volume object* represents the physical volume that is attached to the server. It represents data storage on the network and is used to represent the file system on the network and for storing print jobs associated with a network queue.

Although the Volume object appears to be independent of the NetWare server, it has a logical connection to the NetWare Server object, to which it is attached. Volume objects, therefore, have a property called the *host server,* which associates the volume with its host NetWare server (see fig. 2.36).

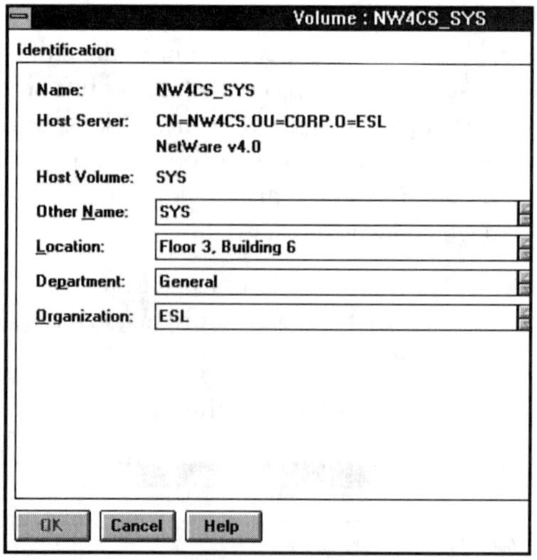

Figure 2.36
A Volume object.

The Volume object is created during initial installation of the NetWare 4.x server in a container, and given a default NDS name that consists of the name of the NetWare 4.x server, followed by an underscore, followed by the name of the physical volume, such as SYS, VOL, and so on. A volume's physical name is the name it received when it was first initialized as part of the installation process using the INSTALL NLM.

```
NDS volume object name = ObjectNameofServer_PhysicalVolumeName
```

If the NetWare server object name is NW4CS, for example, the first physical volume on it, which has the name SYS, would have an NDS name of NW4CS_SYS. If the server has a second volume named VOL1, its NDS name would be NW4CS_VOL1.

If you were to bring a server down, and bring it up with a different name, the new Volume object names based on the new name of the server would appear. The old volume names would become unknown objects.

Bindery Object

The *Bindery object* is created when placing a NetWare 3.x server/service in the NDS tree as part of the upgrade or migration utility. The internals of this object cannot be managed by NDS. The Bindery object is used to provide bindery emulation services, which enable a NetWare 4.x server to be accessed by NetWare 3.x client software that expects to see a bindery-based server.

For NetWare 4.x servers to be accessed by NetWare 3.x client software, the SET BINDERY CONTEXT parameter needs to be set at the NetWare server. This parameter is set by default during the NetWare server installation. Certain utilities such as SBACKUP.NLM and AUDITCON.EXE use bindery emulation. These will not work correctly if BINDERY CONTEXT is not set.

Bindery Queue Object

The *Bindery Queue object* represents a queue placed in the NDS tree as part of the upgrade or migration process. It represents a NetWare 3.x print queue and is used to provide compatibility with bindery-based utilities and applications.

Distribution List Object

The *Distribution List object* was new in NetWare 4.1. A Distribution List object represents a collection of objects that have mailboxes. You can assign objects, such as the Organizational Unit, Group, or User objects, to a distribution list, which enables you to send the same message to many different recipients.

You can nest distribution lists, or, in other words, a distribution list can have other distribution lists as members. However, members of distribution lists do not have security equivalence to the Distribution List object.

Figure 2.37 shows the Create Distribution List dialog box, which you use to create a distribution list. You use Distribution List Name edit box to assign a name to the distribution list object and you use the Mailbox Location edit box to assign a name to the messaging server that contains the mail boxes, which is a property of Organization, Organizational Role, Organizational Unit, Distribution List, Group, and User objects in NDS.

Figure 2.37
The Create Distribution List dialog box for a Distribution List object.

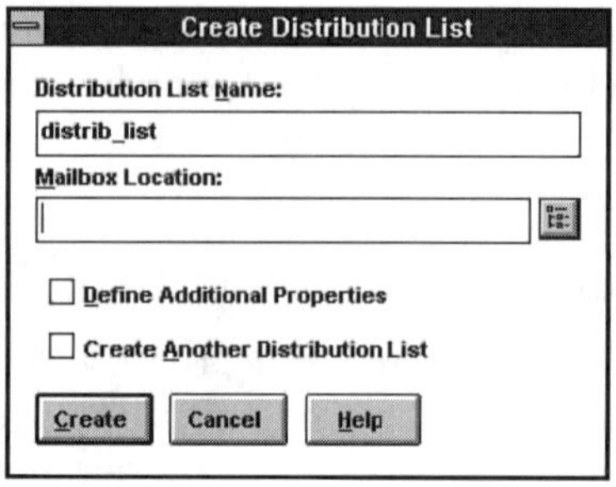

Message Routing Group Object

The *Message Routing Group object* was new in NetWare 4.1. A Message Routing Group object represents a cluster of messaging servers in the NDS tree. Because the messaging servers do frequently synchronize amongst themselves, you should try to avoid connecting message servers in a message routing group through expensive or low speed remote links. All messaging servers connected to the same message routing group send messages directly among themselves.

Figure 2.38 shows the Create Message Routing Group dialog box, which enables you to create a message routing group. You use the Message Routing Group Name edit box to name the message routing group object and the Postmaster General edit box to name the User object who owns and administers the message routing group. The Postmaster General user can modify the Message Routing Group object and its attributes—that is, has the Supervisor object rights to the message routing group.

Figure 2.38
The Create Message Routing Group dialog box for a Message Routing Group object.

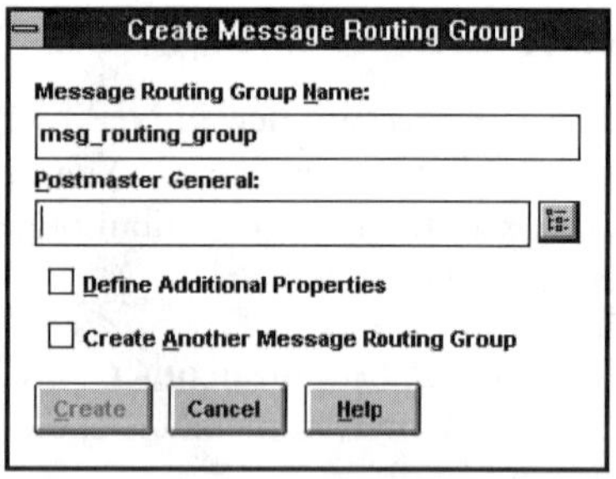

A user who has the following rights is called a *postmaster*:

- Supervisor access to the MHS (message handling system) Messaging Server object.
- Supervisor access to the mailbox location, mailbox ID, and e-mail address properties of users of the MHS messaging server.
- Read access to the message routing group that contains the MHS messaging server.

External Entity Object

The *External Entity object* also was new in NetWare 4.1. An External Entity Object represents a non-native NDS object or service that is imported into NDS or registered with NDS, for example, a non-MHS e-mail address. By importing the non-MHS e-mail address into NDS, you can build an integrated address book for sending mail.

External entities are particularly useful if your messaging environment contains non-MHS Messaging Servers, such as SMTP (Simple Mail Transfer Protocol) hosts, SNADS (Systems Network Architecture Distribution Services) nodes, or X.400 MTAs (Message Transfer Agents). You then can add e-mail addresses for users as well as distribution lists for the non-MHS servers to the NDS. You add non-NDS objects as external entities, but afterward, you cannot use the native NDS messaging applications to access the non-MHS addresses. This enables MHS users to select non-MHS users and lists from a directory list.

An External Entity object has an External Name property, which specifies it's the NDS name, and a Foreign E-mail Address property, which specifies the user's mailbox in a foreign messaging system. Figure 2.39 shows that the foreign e-mail address is an SMTP mailbox, at the e-mail address "SMTP:karanjit@siyan.com," which adheres to the format for SMTP (Internet e-mail) addresses. You can deliver messages sent to this user to an SMTP gateway.

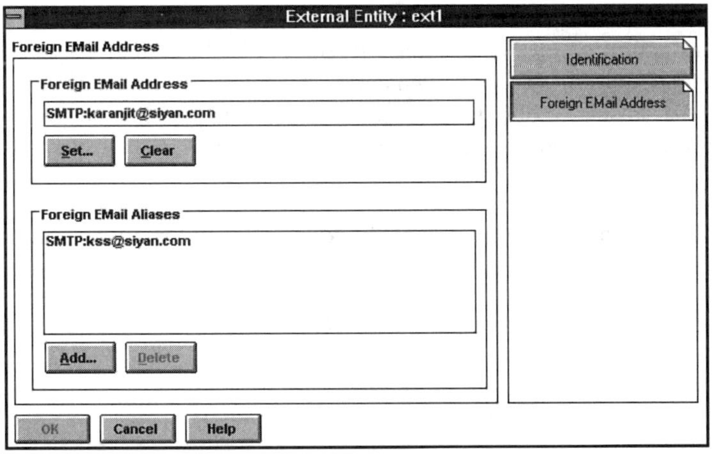

Figure 2.39
External Entity object.

An NDS object can have a mailbox property or a foreign e-mail address property, but not both. You can assign these e-mail property values when you create an object, or later.

Unknown Object

The *Unknown object* represents an NDS object whose object class cannot be determined because its NDS information has been corrupted. Figure 2.40 shows an object of unknown type under the container O=ESL. The Unknown object is the first one listed under O=ESL, and has the question mark (?) icon next to it.

Figure 2.40
An Unknown object.

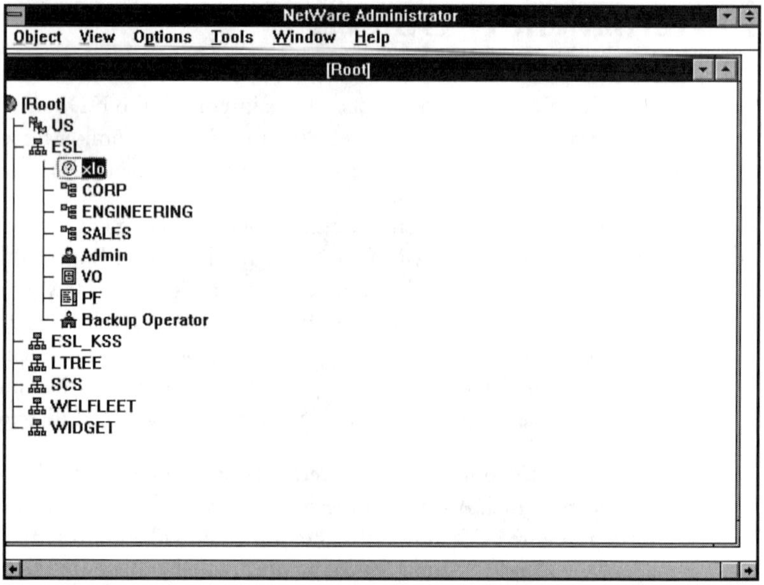

An Unknown object can appear if you bring the server down and then up again specifying a different server name. The new volume names appear, and the old volume names become Unknown objects. In releases prior to NetWare 4.1, if you remove the object to which an alias object points, the Alias object appears as an Unknown object. NetWare 4.1 resolved this problem, so that if you delete an aliased object, NDS removes all alias names that reference the aliased object (including any chain of aliases—alias to an alias to an alias...) when it synchronizes itself.

Too many Unknown objects in an NDS tree can signal an NDS directory corruption problem. You can run the DSREPAIR utility to fix the problem.

Table 2.4 summarizes the preceding discussion and gives a brief description of each type of leaf object.

Table 2.4
Leaf Object Descriptions

Leaf Object Class	Meaning
AFP Server	AppleTalk File Protocol Server; used for informational purposes.
Alias	Link to another object; a substitute name for an object that points to another object in the NDS tree.
Computer	Object that represents a computer: workstation, minicomputer, mainframe, and so on; used for informational purposes.

Leaf Object Class	Meaning
Directory Map	Object that makes simple drive mapping to another container possible and maintaining login scripts easier.
Group	Object that has members that can be other objects; similar to groups in NetWare 3.x, except that Group is an NDS object rather than a Bindery object.
NetWare Server	(Represents a NetWare server on a network) Object that provides NetWare Core Protocol (NCP) services, some of which are represented as special objects in the NDS tree that references the NetWare server.
Organizational Role	Represents a position that has a certain set of defined tasks and responsibilities, and that a user assigned that role can perform.
Print Server	Represents the Print Server service.
Print Queue	Represents the network print queue that holds the print jobs before they are printed.
Printer	Represents a network printer that can accept print jobs.
Profile	Represents an object you can use to share common actions performed during the login processing, regardless of whether they are in the same container.
User	Object that represents the user account; used to contain information on the users who use the network.
Volume	Object that represents data storage on the network; used to represent the file system on the network and used for storing files and print jobs associated with a network queue.
Bindery Object	Object you create when you place a NetWare 3.x server/service in the NDS tree as part of the upgrade process (NDS cannot manage internals of this object); used to provide bindery emulation services.
Bindery Queue	Object created during the upgrade process; represents a NetWare 3.x print queue.
Distribution List	Represents a list of mail boxes or other distribution lists; simplifies sending the same e-mail to a group of users; can contain other distribution lists.
Message Routing Group	Represents a group of messaging servers that can transfer messages directly among themselves.

continues

Table 2.4, Continued
Leaf Object Descriptions

Leaf Object Class	Meaning
External Entity	Represents a non-native NDS object/service imported into NDS or registered in NDS; MHS services, for example, can use External Entity objects to represent users from non-NDS directories such as SMTP, SNADS, X.400, and so on, which enables MHS to provide an integrated address book for sending mail.
Unknown	Object whose object class cannot be determined because its NDS information has been corrupted; you can fix by running DSREPAIR.

Object Properties

An object has attributes, called *properties*, which represent the types of information you can store in the object. In this sense, an NDS object is similar to a record in a database; and the properties of the object are similar to the different field types that can be in a record.

Figure 2.41 shows the file server object. The file server object in figure 2.41 shows the properties Name, Network Address, and Location. The actual values assigned to each of these properties is called the *property value*. A property value is an instance of the property type. Some of the properties of an object are mandatory and critical for proper use of the object. Other properties are descriptive and serve informational and documentation purposes, which enables you to use the NDS as a database of management information. The network administrator fills out the critical values during creation of the object. The network supervisor, who has *write* access to these properties, can fill out the values used for information and documentation later. Examples of properties for the user object that serve informational purposes include the list of telephone and fax numbers for that user, the postal address, and the job title of the user. The name property for a user object is mandatory.

Fill out as many property values for an object as you can with the information you have, because you can use the NDS tree as a database of information that can be queried by using tools such as NLIST.

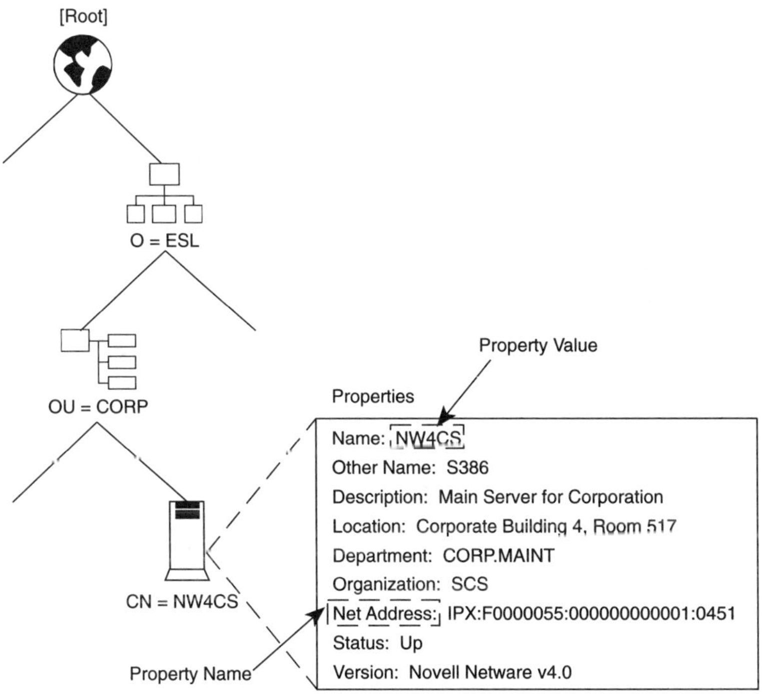

Figure 2.41
An NDS object and properties.

NDS Tree Case Study

Consider the hypothetical organization MICROCOMM, which produces advanced semiconductor devices. Its manufacturing plants and research labs are in San Jose, but its marketing and sales department is in New York. The San Jose facility has a VAX computer, a NetWare 4.x file server used for manufacturing and testing, and another NetWare 4.x server for Research and Development. The R & D engineers are Rick and James; the manufacturing engineers are Tom and Bill. Ed is the network administrator of the entire network.

The New York facility has two file servers, NY_FS1 and NY_FS2, which all users at the facility share. Kirk is the overall network administrator. The SALES department is contained within the MARKETING group. Currently, the salespeople are Janice, Jane, and John. Ron works in the Marketing department, which is currently understaffed.

Figure 2.42 shows a diagram of the physical network for MICROCOMM. Figure 2.43 shows the NDS tree structure. Notice that Ed and Kirk's user objects are defined directly under the container OU=ENGINEERING and OU=MARKETING, because each of them has network administrator responsibility. Shared Resources that all users of the San Jose and New York networks share also are assigned directly within these containers, for example, the printer FS1_PRT and the file servers NY_FS1 and NY_FS2. File servers FS1 and FS2 are placed in the containers OU=MANUFACTURING and OU=R&D. The SALES division is defined as a subcontainer of OU=MARKETING. The salespeople user objects are defined in the OU=SALES container.

Figure 2.42
The MICROCOMM physical network.

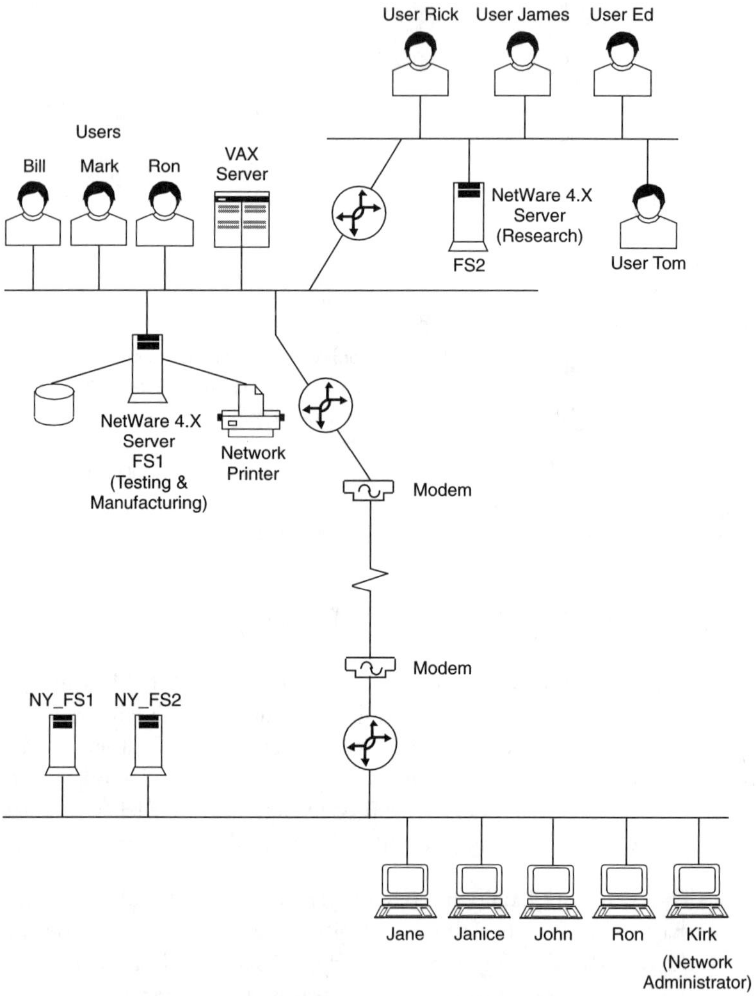

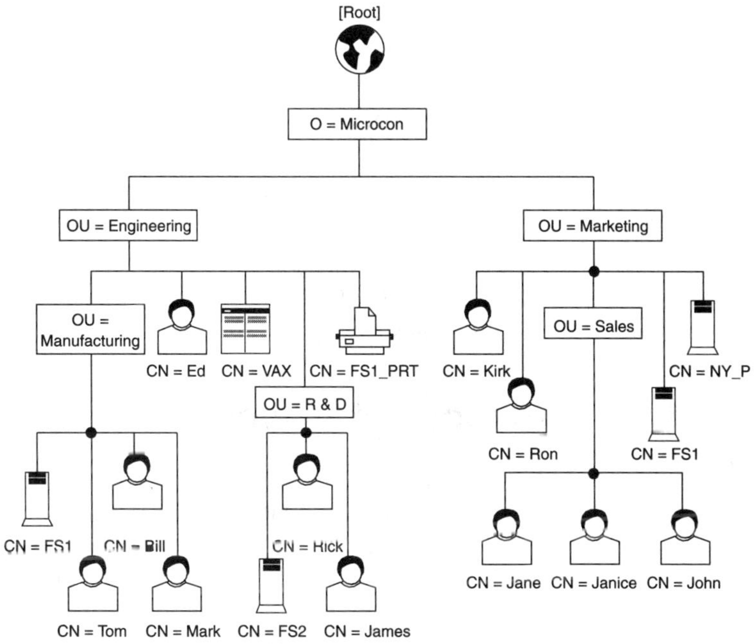

Figure 2.43
The MICROCOMM NDS tree.

Using the preceding example, draw a physical network and an NDS tree for the hypothetical organization, *Electronic Systems Lab* (ESL), based in London, and having facilities in Toronto, New York, and Paris. Research labs are located in Paris and Toronto, marketing in New York, and administration and sales in London. A support staff of network administrators in London manages the entire network. Local contractors perform network services and hardware support at the other sites. Each location has its own servers and printers. London and New York have two file servers and three network printers each, while other locations have a single file server and two network printers attached to the file server. As the company grows, it expects to need to add additional servers. All locations have print servers. The locations are connected by communications links that run at 1.544 Mbps. Each site uses Ethernet-based local networks.

You can make reasonable assumptions for data not provided. You might need to invent names for users at each of the locations, for instance, as well as decide which of the users are network administrators.

When you design the NDS tree for ESL, consider the following issues:

- Depth of the tree. How many container levels do you need?
- All container objects you need. Justify your need for each container.
- Appropriate names for container objects. Should they correspond to departments or geographical location?
- Number of organizational units. Do you need one, or more?

NDS Tools

The two primary tools for creating, deleting, and moving NDS objects are the Network Administrator Tool (NWADMIN.EXE) and NETADMIN.EXE.

UIMPORT is another tool for user batch creation, and is similar to the NetWare 3.*x* tool MAKEUSER.

The Network Administrator Tool is a Windows and OS/2 *Graphical User Interface* (GUI) tool that you can use to manage NDS objects, whereas the NETADMIN tool is a text utility you can use to create NDS objects that use C-Worthy menus.

Setting Up the Network Administrator Tool (NWADMIN.EXE)

To set up the NWADMIN.EXE tool, NetWare 4.x server and the DOS/Windows client software must be installed. The following steps outline how to set up the NWADMIN tool for MS Windows.

Within Windows 3.11 or Windows for WorkGroups

From within Windows 3.11 or Windows for WorkGroups, perform the following:

1. If the NetWare group does not exist, continue on to step 2; otherwise, skip to step 3.

2. Make sure that you are logged in to the NetWare 4.x network.

   Create a new program group called NetWare (or any other name you prefer) by doing the following:

- Select the `File` menu from Program Manager.
- Select `File`, `New`.
- Select Program `Group` from the New Program Object dialog box and choose OK.
- In the Program Group Properties box, enter the following information, then choose OK.

  `Description:` **`NetWare`**

  `GroupFile:`**`C:\WINDOWS\NWUTILS.GRP`** (use the name of your Windows directory if it is not C:\WINDOWS)

3. If a program item is already set for the NetWare Administrator Tool, skip this step. Otherwise, continue on to the following steps to create a program item for NetWare Administrator Tool.

- Highlight the NetWare program group.
- Select the File menu from the Program Manager.
- Select File, New.
- Select the Program `Item` from the New Program Object dialog box and choose OK.
- In the Program Item Properties box, enter the following information, then choose OK.

```
Description: NetWare Administrator Tool
Command Line: Z:\PUBLIC\NWADMIN
Working Directory: Z:\PUBLIC
```

- Answer Yes to the question `The specified path points to a file that may not be available during later Windows sessions. Do you want to continue?`. This message appears because the path is a network drive, and if you are not logged in to the network, the network drive is not available.

  Also, you can specify a network drive other than Z. Z is used because you are likely to have at least one search drive, which will be mapped to search drive Z. You need to make sure that this search drive is not root mapped, though.

- The program item for NWADMIN should appear in the program group.

Within Windows 95

If you are using Windows 95, make sure that you have loaded Novell's Client 32. The Microsoft client that ships with Windows 95 uses outdated NetWare calls and APIs that will not allow it to run the new NWADMIN32. For more information on installing Client 32 please refer to Chapter 15, "Supporting DOS, Windows 3.1x, and Windows 95 Workstations."

If you have already installed Novell's Client 32, use the right mouse button and click on your Windows 95 desktop. This will bring up a utility box with the option for creating a shortcut.

From there, complete the following steps:

1. Highlight new and right-click on shortcut.
2. The Windows 95 Create Shortcut screen will appear. Click on the browse button.
3. This will bring up the Browse screen. Use the look in box to locate the network drive that contains the SYS volume. When you locate this volume, select the volume by clicking on it with the right mouse button.
4. Locate the Public directory and double-click on the directory designation using the right mouse button.
5. Locate the WIN95 directory and double-click on it with the right mouse button.

6. Locate the file, NWADMIN952.EXE and use the right mouse button to double-click on the file.
7. The Create Shortcut screen will appear with the file location and file name correctly entered in the Command line box.
8. Use the right mouse button and click on the Next button.
9. The Create Shortcut screen will appear. Here you can type in the name that you want to use for the new shortcut. NWADMIN95 will be used by default.
10. Use the right mouse button and click on the Finish button.

You will now have an icon located on your Windows 95 Desktop that if clicked will launch the NWADMIN95 utility. For more information on using the NWADNIN95 utility, refer to Chapter 15, "Supporting DOS, Windows 3.1x, and Windows 95 Workstations".

Using the NetWare Administrator Tool

This section gives you a guided tour of using the NetWare Administrator Tool to create the NDS tree structure shown in figure 2.44.

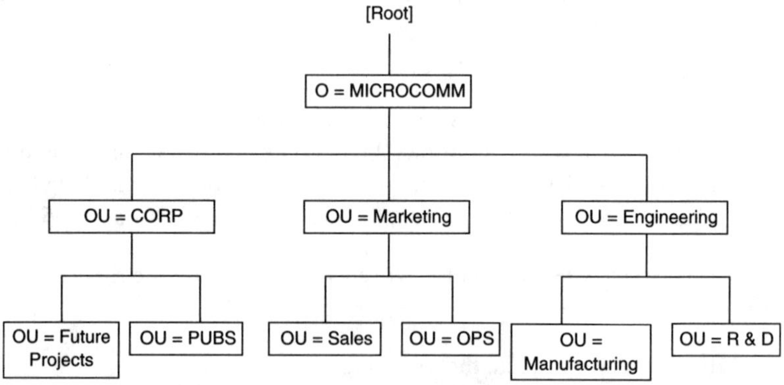

Figure 2.44
A sample NDS tree.

1. Log in to the network as an Administrator account.

   During the initial NDS services installation (when the NetWare 4.x server was first installed), NDS creates a default network administrator user object Admin, which has supervisor privileges to the entire NDS tree. You can use the Admin user object to log in to the network.

2. Activate the NetWare Group and launch the NetWare Administrator Tool program item (double-click on the NetWare Administrator icon).

   You should see a screen similar to that shown in figure 2.45.

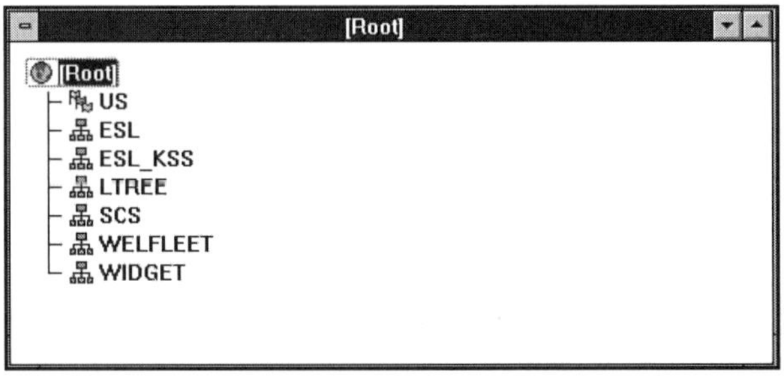

Figure 2.45
The NetWare Administrator menu.

The NDS tree in figure 2.45 shows the NDS tree starting from the current container. To see the NDS tree starting from the [Root], perform the following steps:

- Select the View menu.
- Select the Set Context option. Set the current context to [Root]. You can enter **[Root]** or use the browse icon to browse through the NDS tree and select the context that you want to set as the current context.

3. Highlight the [Root] object. You can do this by clicking on it once.

   Right-click on the [Root] object to see a list of operations that you can perform under the [Root].

   Select Create.

   You should see a list of objects that you can create under the [Root] object (see fig. 2.46).

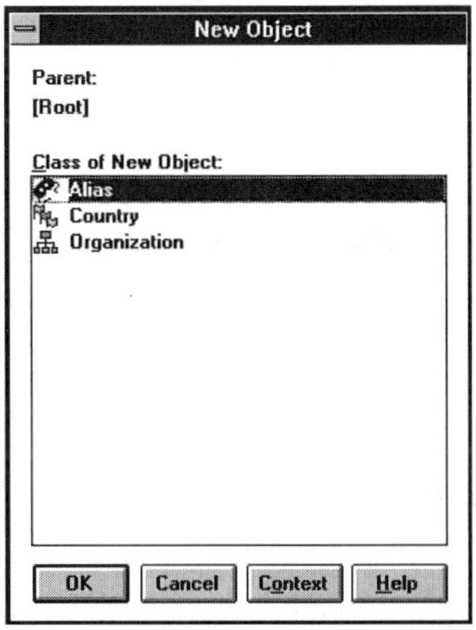

Figure 2.46
New objects under [Root] container.

4. Select the organization object and choose OK.

The Create Organization dialog box, which you use to create the organization object, should appear (see fig. 2.47).

Figure 2.47
The dialog box for creating an organization container.

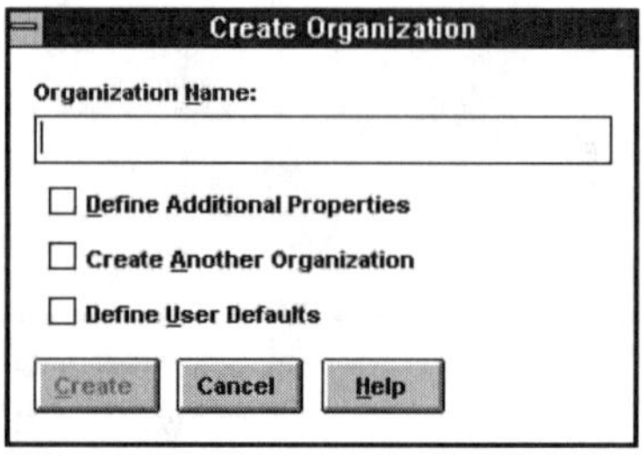

Enter the name of the organization as shown in figure 2.47, then click on the Create button.

The name of the newly created organization, MICROCOMM, should appear in the NDS tree.

5. Highlight MICROCOMM and right-click.

   Select Create.

   A list of objects that you can create under the organization object should appear (see fig. 2.48). Compare figure 2.48 with figure 2.46. The list of objects that you can create under an organization object is much larger.

Figure 2.48
New objects under an organization container.

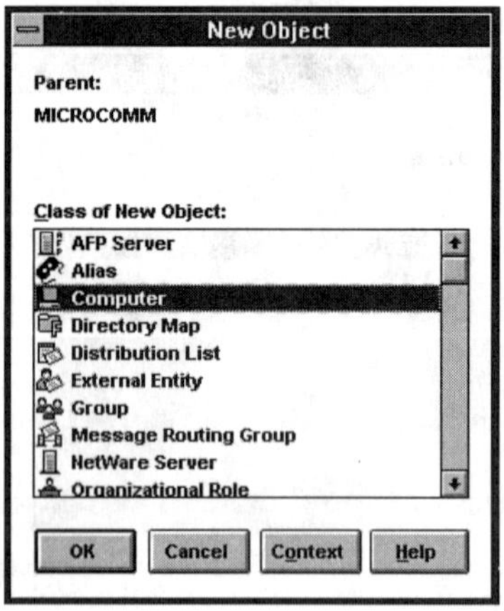

6. Select the organizational unit object and click on OK.

   The Create Organizational Unit dialog box should appear (see fig. 2.49).

```
┌─────────────────────────────────────┐
│ ▬        Create Organizational Unit  │
│ Organizational Unit Name:            │
│ ┌─────────────────────────────────┐  │
│ │                                 │  │
│ └─────────────────────────────────┘  │
│  ☐ Define Additional Properties      │
│  ☐ Create Another Organizational Unit│
│  ☐ Define User Defaults              │
│ ┌────────┐ ┌────────┐ ┌────────┐     │
│ │ Create │ │ Cancel │ │  Help  │     │
│ └────────┘ └────────┘ └────────┘     │
└─────────────────────────────────────┘
```

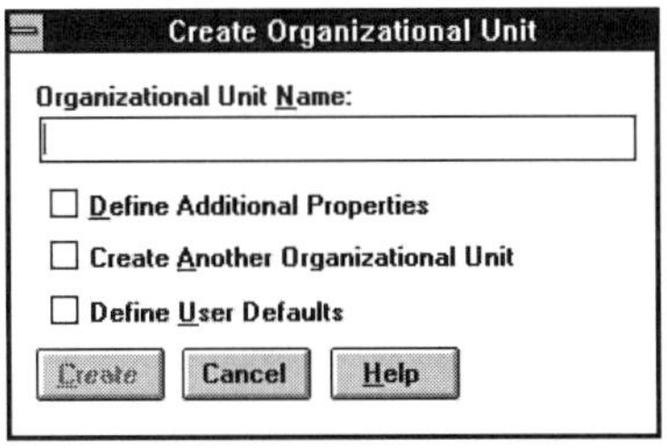

Figure 2.49

The dialog box for creating an organizational unit container.

Enter the name of the organizational unit CORP (refer to figure 2.44), then click on the Create button.

If you double-click on MICROCOMM, the name of the newly created organizational unit CORP should appear in the NDS tree.

7. Repeat steps 5 and 6 to create organizational unit container objects for MARKETING and ENGINEERING (refer to figure 2.44).

8. Repeat preceding steps to create the rest of the organization, as shown in figure 2.44.

9. Delete the NDS tree you just created. You cannot delete a container object that has objects defined in it, so you must delete the bottom-most objects first and proceed from there.

To delete an object, right-click on the object and select the Delete operation. Alternatively, highlight the object, select the Object menu, and choose the Delete operation from the menu.

To delete a group of objects, you can perform the following:

1. Double-click on the container to open it.

2. Highlight the first object you want to delete. Click on the last object to delete and press Shift. The objects between the first and the last object should be highlighted.

3. Press Del.

Using the NETADMIN Utility

This section gives you a guided tour of using the NETADMIN Tool to create the NDS tree structure shown in figure 2.44. NETADMIN is a text-based utility that provides similar functionality to the NetWare Administrator Tool. If you are a system administrator, being able to use NETADMIN to perform NDS operations is very useful, because MS Windows is not always installed at a NetWare workstation and NETADMIN does not require MS Windows, but rather, can work directly on top of DOS.

The goal of the guided tour in this section is to accomplish the same objectives as in the previous section, so that you can compare the differences between using NetWare Administrator and the NETADMIN tools.

1. Log in to the network as an Administrator account.

   During the initial NDS services installation (when the NetWare 4.x server was first installed), NDS creates a default network administrator user object Admin, which has supervisor privileges to the entire NDS tree. You can use the Admin User object to log in to the network.

2. Invoke the program NETADMIN, by typing its name:

   `NETADMIN`

   The NETADMIN screen appears.

   The NETADMIN utility is located in the directory SYS:PUBLIC, and you must have a search path to that directory before NETADMIN works correctly.

   Find the current context, which is at the top of the screen, under `Context`. If not set to [Root], perform the following steps to set it to [Root].

   - Select `Change context`.
   - Enter [**`Root`**] when NDS prompts `Enter context:`.
   - Press Enter to return to the NETADMIN main menu.

3. Select `Manage objects`.

   A list of objects and their class under the [Root] container should appear.

4. Press Ins.

   You should see a list of objects that you can create under [Root].

5. Select `Organization` to create an organization object.

   The Create Organization dialog box should appear (refer to fig. 2.47).

   Enter the name of the organization shown in figure 2.44. You can create a user template for the organization object now or do it later. If a message server is defined for the organization, you can enter its name in the Mailbox location field.

6. Press F10 to save changes and perform the create operation.

When NDS prompts whether you want to create another organization object, answer No.

The name of the newly created organization appears in the Object, Class list.

7. Highlight the newly created organization and press Enter. Your context has now changed to the organization.

8. Press Ins to create an object.

   You should see a list of objects that you can create under the Organization object.

9. Select `Organizational Unit` to create an organization object.

   The Create object Organizational Unit dialog box appears.

   Enter the name of the Organizational Unit shown in figure 2.44. You can create a User Template for the organization object now, or later. If a message server is defined for the organizational unit, you can enter its name in the Mailbox location field.

10. Press F10 to save changes and perform the create operation.

11. When NDS asks if you want to create another organizational unit object, answer Yes and repeat the preceding steps to create all the other organizational unit objects.

12. Review figure 2.44 and repeat the preceding steps to create the rest of the organization.

13. Delete the NDS tree you just created. You cannot delete a container object in which objects are defined, so you must first delete the bottom-most objects and work up from them.

    To delete an object, highlight it from the Object, Class list and press Del. NDS asks you to confirm your delete operations.

NDS Context

NDS context refers to the position of an object in the NDS tree, as described in terms of the container that contains the object. For example, in figure 2.50, the context of object Admin is container ESL, and the context of the file server object FS1 is in container CORP.

Figure 2.50
Referencing objects in another context.

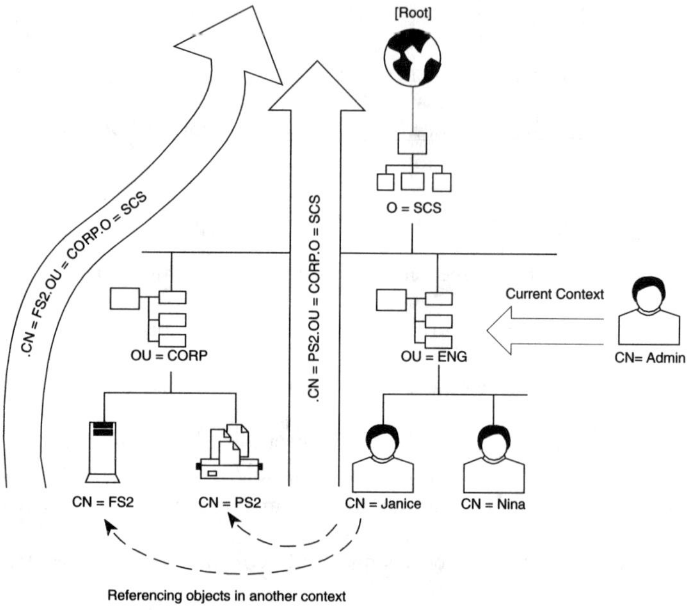

The context of an object is important because some NDS utilities require you to know the position (or location) of the object in the NDS tree. In general, you must know the object's position (context) before you can find it. (You can use certain commands, such as the NLIST command, to help find the object's position in the NDS tree, if you know the object's name. These are discussed later in this chapter.) The context of an object affects how the object is referenced.

Another way you can think of the context is as a *pointer* that locates the object's position in the NDS tree, described in terms of listing, from left to right, the NDS names of the container objects, separated by periods (.). The listing order for the container objects is beginning at the immediate container and working up to the root. Therefore, the context of object Admin in figure 2.55 is `ESL` or `O=ESL`, because there is only one container. The [Root] container object is not listed, because the topmost container [Root] is automatically implied. The second form of representing the NDS context uses the object type designator, such as O (Organization). Both forms are valid, and the second form uses attribute type designators.

Another example is the context of object FS2 in figure 2.50.

```
CORP.ESL
```

or

```
OU=CORP.O=ESL
```

A special type of context, called the *current context,* is the current position of the attached workstation in the NDS tree. An *attached workstation* is one that is connected (logically speaking) to the NDS tree through the network.

The network client software connects to the NDS tree when it loads. If you use DOS as the workstation software, NDS can maintain only one current context for each DOS session. You can set the workstation's current context only to container objects, not leaf objects, because a context is defined as the position of the immediate container that contains the object in the NDS tree.

The current context is the default reference point that the workstation uses to find other objects in the NDS tree. Current context serves in a manner equivalent to the *current directory* in a file system. Just as you cannot set the current directory to a file name, you cannot set the current context to a leaf object.

You can reference objects in the current context of a workstation by leaf object name. For instance, in figure 2.50, assuming a workstation has current context of CORP.ESL, you could reference the objects FS2 and PS2 by their common names:

```
FS2
```

or

```
CN=FS2
PS2
```

or

```
CN=PS2
```

Using the full NDS name of the object is not essential here, which is a great convenience to the user of the workstation. You cannot reference resources not in the current context by leaf name only; you must specify the NDS path name of the object. You would have to use the full NDS path name to reference objects FS2 and PS2 in figure 2.50.

NDS Naming

The NDS structure is closely tied to the concept of naming. In fact, it is fundamental to the directory because the name of the object defines its relationship to other objects in the tree.

In the previous section, you observed that you must use the full NDS path name to define objects not in the current context of a workstation. You can specify NDS path names in three ways, listed below and explained in the sections that follow:

- Complete name
- Typeless name
- Partial name

Complete Name

A *complete name* is the name of an NDS object that includes the leaf name and the names of the containers that contain the leaf object, beginning at the leaf object and proceeding through the tree to the [Root] object. The object names are specified with their attribute name abbreviation (attribute type). The complete name must always begin with a period. Periods are used as separators between object names that comprise the NDS name. *Important:* The leading period has a different meaning than other periods in the NDS object name; it signifies that the name is a complete name, and that you can reference the object by *enumerating* (writing the object names from the NDS object all the way to [Root]) its path all the way to the root.

The general syntax of the complete name of an object is shown in listing 2.1.

Listing 2.1

```
.CN=leaf_object.[OU=org_unit_.{OU=org_unit}].O=organization.[C=country]
Bottom of tree > Top of tree
```

In the preceding syntax, the [] brackets and the {} braces are *meta characters* that have special meaning. The [] indicate that the contents between the [] are optional. The {} indicate that there can be zero or more occurrences. The leading period is required for complete names. Without the leading period, the complete name is just a partial name.

To summarize some of the rules of a complete name: The syntax for a complete name always begins with a period, followed by the NDS path of the object all the way up to the root. Because an NDS tree can have only one [Root], the [Root] object is not listed as part of the NDS tree. If you use an attribute type to qualify the object name in the NDS path, you use the following form:

```
attribute_type_abbreviation=object_name
```

The `attribute_type_abbreviation` will be CN for leaf object, OU for Organizational Units, O for Organization, and C for Country. After the name of the object, the list of containers is enumerated, beginning with the most immediate container and continuing to the [Root] container. The root object is not listed because an NDS tree can have only one [Root]. The square brackets around the Organizational Unit list indicate that the OUs are optional. Examples of types of complete names are listed as follows:

```
.CN=leaf_object.O=organization.C=country
```

or

```
.CN=leaf_object.O=organization
```

or

```
.leaf_object.org_unit (typeless complete name that does not have the attribute
types)
```

`C=country` does not appear in the last two syntax examples of the complete name, because the topmost container is the organization container.

An example of the complete name that lists the organizational units, a single organization, and a country name follows:

```
.CN=leaf_object.OU=org_unit.OU=org_unit.O=organization.C=country
```

The preceding example includes only two Organizational Unit objects, but it could include any number of these objects.

In figure 2.51, the complete names of the objects FS1, PS1, PRINT_1, PRINT_2, and PS2 are shown as follows:

```
.CN=FS1.OU=REGION_A.O=HAL

.CN=PS1.OU=REGION_A.O=HAL

.CN=PRINT_1.OU=OPS.OU=SALES.O=HAL

.CN=PRINT_2.OU=SALES.O=HAL

.CN=PS2.O=HAL
```

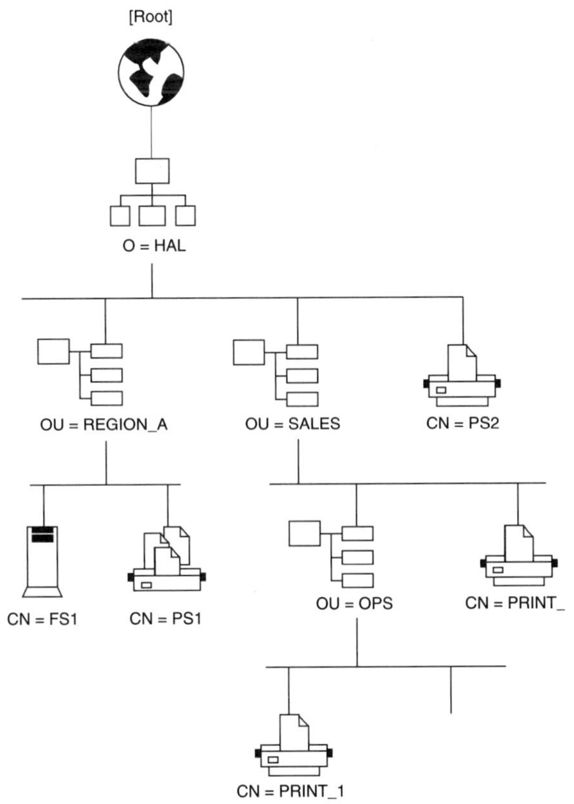

Figure 2.51
The NDS tree for complete name examples.

Partial Name

A *partial name* for an NDS object is its NDS path relative to the current context. A partial name is similar to specifying the name of a file relative to the current directory, whereas a complete name is similar to specifying the name of a file, using its complete path name listing all the directories starting from the root.

Resolving a Partial Name

NDS must resolve the partial name to a complete name by appending the current context to the partial name and adding a period at the beginning to indicate a complete name, as in the following:

```
Complete Name = .Partial Name.Current Context
```

An example, shown in listing 2.2, should help clarify the preceding rule.

Listing 2.2

```
Current Context is  OU=CORP.O=ESL
Partial Name is     CN=HP_PR1
Complete Name is:   . concatenated with CN=HP_PR1 concatenated with OU=CORP.O=ESL
```

If the current context is OU=CORP.O=ESL, the partial name for object HP_PR1 in the current context is CN=HP_PR1. NDS forms the complete name by appending the current context OU=CORP.O=ESL to the partial name CN=HP_PR1 and adding a period at the beginning.

The main purpose of a partial name is to simplify the names for NDS objects in the current context or in the vicinity of the current context.

The examples so far have been of objects in the current context. In figure 2.52, the object FSP_1 is not in the same context as the current context that is set to O=ESL. Here, the partial name of FSP_1 is the object name plus the list of all the containers leading up to the current context O=ESL.

```
CN=FSP_1.OU=CORP
```

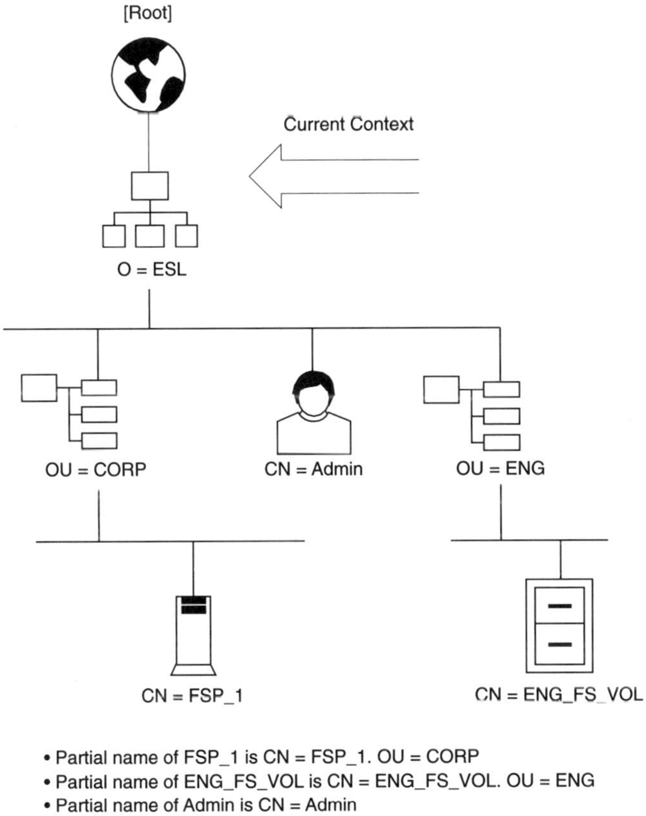
[Root]
Current Context
O = ESL
OU = CORP
CN = Admin
OU = ENG
CN = FSP_1
CN = ENG_FS_VOL
• Partial name of FSP_1 is CN = FSP_1. OU = CORP
• Partial name of ENG_FS_VOL is CN = ENG_FS_VOL. OU = ENG
• Partial name of Admin is CN = Admin

Figure 2.52
The partial name for objects not in the current context, but in the same tree branch.

Similarly, the partial name of ENG_FS_VOL, if current context is O=ESL is the following:

```
CN=ENG_FS_VOL.OU=ENG
```

The partial name of Admin, if current context is O=ESL, is as follows:

```
CN=Admin
```

If the current context is not set to a container that is part of the complete name leading up to the root, appending a period (.) at the end of the NDS name refers to the container above. In figure 2.53, the current context is OU=ENG.O=SCS. If you want to reference the object DEI_FS in OU=CORP, you can use the following partial name:

```
CN=DEI_FS.OU=CORP.
```

Figure 2.53
The partial name for an object when its current context is in a different branch of the NDS tree.

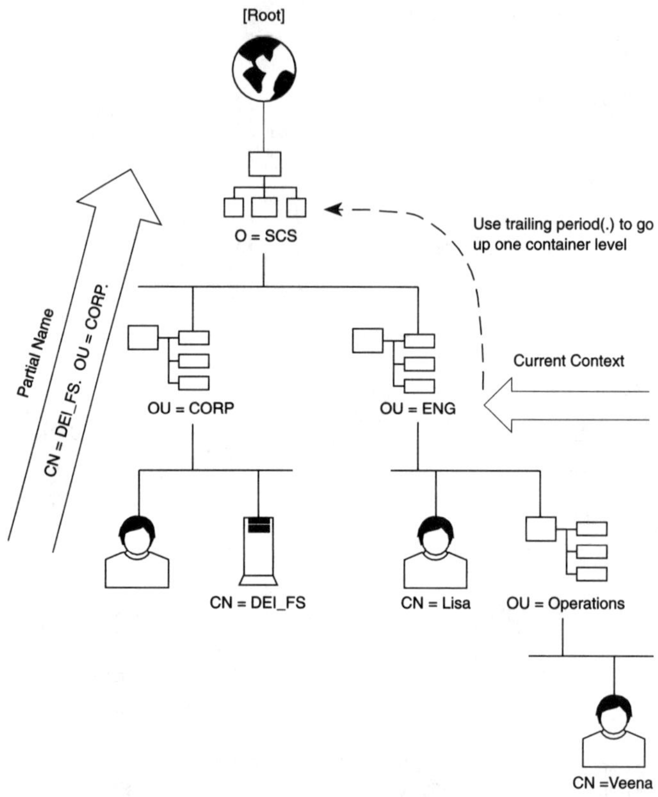

The trailing period (.) refers to the parent container of the current context, which here is O=SCS. The partial name of the object DEI_FS, with respect to the container O=SCS, is CN=DEI_FS.OU=CORP. But because the current context is in a different tree branch (current context is OU=ENG.O=SCS, not O=SCS), you must add a trailing period.

If the current context in figure 2.53 was OU=OPERATIONS.OU=ENG.O=SCS, you could use the following partial name to reference the same object CN=DEI_FS:

```
CN=DEI_FS.OU=CORP..
```

Two trailing periods indicate two parent containers above the current context. The current context is OU=OPERATIONS.OU=ENG.O=SCS, so the two trailing periods refer to the container O=SCS.

The trailing period can occur only in partial names.

The trailing period rules can be summarized as follows:

- **Rule 1.** A single trailing period rule at the end of the NDS partial name removes a single object name from the left of the current context.

- **Rule 2.** NDS appends the name you form by removing a leftmost object from the current context to the partial name.
- **Rule 3.** You add a leading period to form a complete name.

Figure 2.54 shows a partial name that has a trailing period:

```
CN=LUCY.
```

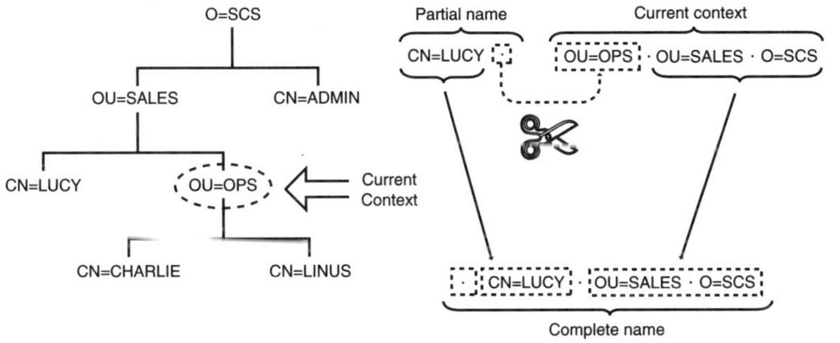

Figure 2.54
Trailing period rules.

The partial name in figure 2.54 has the following current context value:

```
OU=OPS.OU=SALES.O=SCS
```

When you apply the trailing period rule, the trailing period (.) results in the removal of the leftmost OU=OPS from the current context, so that the following name results:

```
OU=SALES.O=SCS
```

According to the second rule, NDS appends the resulting name to the partial name, which forms the following:

```
CN=LUCY.OU=SALES.O=SCS
```

Then, according to the third rule, you add a leading period to form the resolved complete name:

```
.CN=LUCY.OU=SALES.O=SCS
```

Partial Name Example Exercise

The partial names for objects HP_PR1, FS1, VOL1, FS2, and BOB in figure 2.55 are listed in table 2.5 for different current context settings.

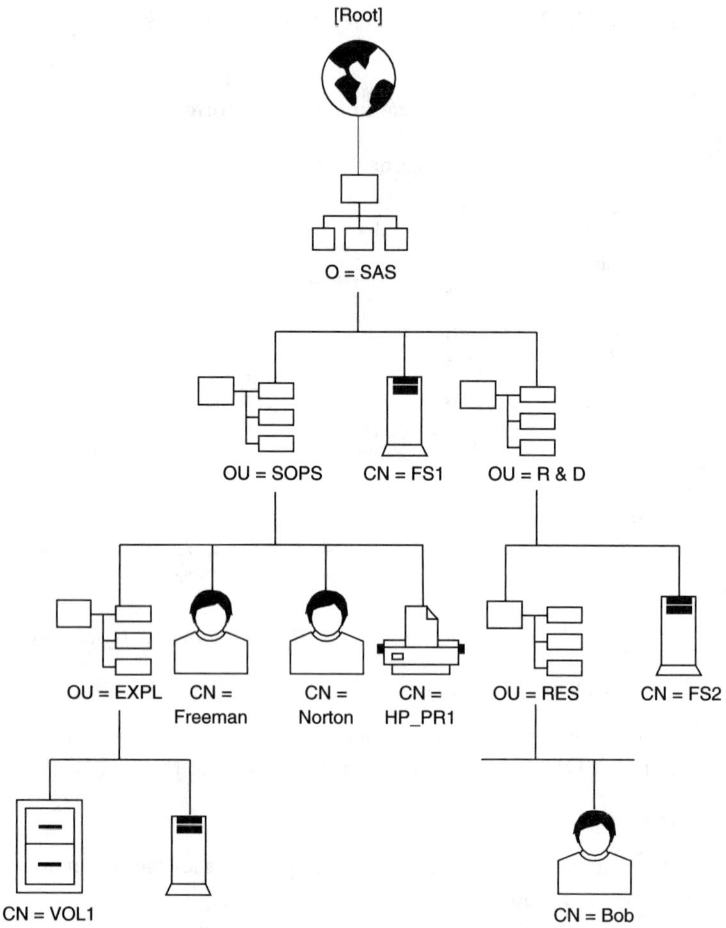

Figure 2.55
The NDS tree for partial name examples.

Table 2.5
Partial Name Examples

NDS Object Name	Current Context	Partial Name
HP_PR1	O=SAS	CN=HP_PR1.OU=SOPS
HP_PR1	[Root]	CN=HP_PR1.OU =SOPS.O=SAS
HP_PR1	OU=SOPS.O=SAS	CN=HP_PR1
HP_PR1	OU=R&D.O=SAS	CN=HP_PR1.OU=SOPS.
HP_PR1	OU=RES.OU=R&D.O=SAS	CN=HP_PR1.OU= SOPS..
HP_PR1	OU=EXPL.OU=SOPS.O=SAS	CN=HP_PR1.

NDS Object Name	Current Context	Partial Name
FS1	[Root]	CN=FS1.O=SAS
FS1	O=SAS	CN=FS1
FS1	OU=SOPS.O=SAS	CN=FS1.
FS1	OU=EXPL.OU=SOPS.O=SAS	CN=FS1..
FS1	OU=R&D.O=SAS	CN=FS1.
FS1	OU=RES.OU=R&D.O=SAS	CN=FS1..
FS1_VOL1	[Root]	CN=FS1_VOL1.OU =EXPL.OU=SOPS.O= SAS
FS1_VOL1	O=SAS	CN=FS1_VOL1.OU =EXPL.OU=SOPS
FS1_VOL1	OU=SOPS.O=SAS	CN=FS1_VOL1.OU= EXPL
FS1_VOL1	OU=EXPL.OU=SOPS.O=SAS	CN=FS1_VOL1
FS1_VOL1	OU=R&D.O=SAS	CN=FS1_VOL1.OU =EXPL.OU=SOPS.
FS1_VOL1	OU=RES.OU=R&D.O=SAS	CN=FS1_VOL1.OU =EXPL.OU=SOPS..
FS2	[Root]	CN=FS2.OU=R&D.O= SAS
FS2	O=SAS	CN=FS2.OU=R&D
FS2	OU=SOPS.O=SAS	CN=FS2.OU=R&D.
FS2	OU=EXPL.OU=SOPS.O=SAS	CN=FS2.OU=R&D..
FS2	OU=R&D.O=SAS	CN=FS2
FS2	OU=RES.OU=R&D.O=SAS	CN=FS2..
BOB	[Root]	CN=BOB.OU=RES.OU =R&D.O=SAS
BOB	O=SAS	CN=BOB.OU=RES.OU= R&D
BOB	OU=SOPS.O=SAS	CN=BOB.OU=RES.OU= R&D

continues

Table 2.5, Continued
Partial Name Examples

NDS Object Name	Current Context	Partial Name
BOB	OU=EXPL.OU=SOPS.O=SAS	CN=BOB.OU=RES.OU=R&D..
BOB	OU=R&D.O=SAS	CN=BOB.OU=RES
BOB	OU=RES.OU=R&D.O=SAS	CN=BOB

NDS Naming Rules

This section summarizes the naming rules that have been discussed in many of the examples in this chapter. Three important concepts involving NDS Path, typeless naming, and period rules are discussed next.

NDS Path

The NDS Path name consists of a list of object names, written left to right, beginning with the referenced object, and leading up to the [Root] object or to the current context. If the object name is preceded with a period (.), the object names refer to the complete name and must lead up to the [Root]. If the NDS path name does not have a leading period, then it refers to a partial name.

Typeless Names and Period Rules

The complete name of the object, in addition to beginning with a period, uses the attribute type names CN, OU, O, and C to designate the type of the object as being a Common Name, Organizational Unit, Organization, and Country object, respectively.

If you make certain assumptions about the type of names, you do not need to specify the attribute names. For instance, if you assume that the leftmost name is a Common Name and the rightmost name is an Organization name, then the intervening objects must be Organizational Units. This is a safe assumption, because all leaf objects must have a common name, and the Organization container is mandatory for an NDS tree, so object names have the following syntax:

```
CN.OU.OU .... .O
```

OU objects are optional, though in actual practice most NDS trees have at least one OU object.

Keeping with the preceding assumptions, you can specify the object name without using the CN=, OU=, and O= attribute names to precede the object name, which simplifies the name. Such names are called *typeless names*, and typeless names do not have attribute names.

Therefore, you can express the following complete name,

```
.CN=DEI.OU=CORP.O=ESL
```

as a typeless complete name by using

```
.DEI.CORP.ESL
```

When NDS encounters a typeless complete name that has a different number of object names than the object names in the current context, it must use the following default typing rule to resolve it into a complete name that has attribute specifiers:

1. The leftmost object is type CN.
2. The rightmost object is type O.
3. All intervening objects are type OU.

Under special conditions, you can use typeless names when the Country object is part of the NDS path. You can use mixed typeless and typed names to specify NDS objects. For instance, you could express the complete name .CN=FS1.O=ESL.C=US as follows:

```
.FS1.ESL.C=US
```

NetWare has a number of utilities for recognizing the type of object being worked on. For example, utilities such as CX and NETADMIN work on container objects when you are changing NDS context because you cannot change your context to that of a leaf object. These utilities do not assume that the leftmost object is a leaf object (attribute type CN) when they see a typeless name. They assume that the leftmost object is type OU or O and attempt complete name resolution accordingly. In general, NetWare utilities are aware of the type of objects on which they should work and can override any default typing rules.

The default typing rule stated earlier applies to NDS names that have a different number of objects than the objects in the current context. Suppose that the current context is as follows:

```
OU=CORP.O=SCS
```

If you submit a typeless name, such as .FS1.MKTG.SCS, it has three NDS objects: OPS, MKTG, and SCS. The default typing rule applies, and the leftmost object is treated as type CN and the rightmost as type O. The intervening objects are type OU. Therefore, NDS resolves the typeless name .FS1.MKTG.SCS to the following:

```
.CN=FS1.OU=MKTG.O=SCS
```

Consider the same example, except the typeless name .FS1.MKTG.SCS is used with the CX command, as follows:

```
CX .FS1.MKTG.SCS
```

CX would assume that the leftmost object is type OU or O (here, OU is the only possibility):

```
.OU=FS1.OU=MKTG.O=SCS
```

If no container accompanies the complete name .OU=FS1.OU=MKTG.O=SCS, the CX command fails.

If NDS encounters a typeless complete name that has the same number of object names as the current context, it must use the attribute specifiers of the current context to resolve it into a complete name.

Consider the same example, in which the current context is as follows:

```
OU=CORP.O=SCS
```

If you submit a typeless name, such as .MKTG.SCS, it has two NDS objects—the same as the number of NDS objects in the current context. Here, NDS resolves the leftmost name to type OU because the leftmost name in the current context is type OU, and resolves the rightmost name to type O, because the rightmost name in the current context is type O. Therefore, the typeless name .MKTG.SCS resolves to the following:

```
OU=MKTG.O=SCS
```

Consider the same example, in which the current context is as follows:

```
O=ESL.C=MX
```

If you submit a typeless name, such as .NTE.SC, it has two NDS objects—again, the same as the number of NDS objects in the current context. Here, NDS resolves the leftmost name to type O because the leftmost name in the current context is type O, and resolves the rightmost name to type C because the rightmost name in the current context is type C. Therefore, NDS resolves the typeless name .NTE.SC to the following:

```
.O=NTE.C=MX
```

If the object does not exist, NDS cannot resolve the name and reports it as an incorrect NDS object.

If your current context is in a Country container and you submit a name that has the same number of NDS objects as the current context but is in an Organization container, NDS resolves it according to the previously stated rule as an object in the Country container. Similarly, if your current context is in an Organization container and you submit a name that has the same number of NDS objects as the current context but the object is in a Country container, NDS resolves it according to the previously stated rule as an object in the organization container. In both these cases, the resolution to complete names is incorrect. You can resolve the problem by specifying the type of the rightmost object, such as that shown in the following examples:

```
.ESL.C=US
.CORP.O=SCS
```

Also, if the NDS utilities expect the typeless NDS names to be leaf objects, they override the previously stated rule and assume that the leftmost object is type CN. Examples of utilities that expect to work on leaf objects are LOGIN, MAP, and CAPTURE.

You can resolve typeless names that are under the Country object, when the current context includes a Country object and the typeless name has the same number of objects as the current object. If the previously stated conditions are not true, resolving typeless names under the Country container can be problematic, because you do not know if the rightmost object is type C or O. You can, in theory, come up with a general scheme along the following lines: Country names can only be two letters, so if the rightmost object name exceeds two letters, it must be an Organization object. The problem is that Organization objects can be two letters, so any name longer than two letters is definitely an Organization object, but a name that has exactly two letters can be a Country object or an Organization object. One solution would be to restrict Organization object names to consist of a minimum of three letters, which would enable you to distinguish between Country and Organization objects based on name length. Another solution would be to use the ITU abbreviations for country codes (recommended two-letter codes for all known countries, which ITU updates regularly). You could have these two-letter country codes in a standard *country file* that comes with NetWare, and if you make it an ASCII text file, you could easily edit it as geo-political boundaries of countries change. The rule then would be that if the rightmost name in a typeless name is listed in this country file, it must indicate a Country object. If the Country object is in the typeless name, the second rightmost name must be an Organization object. However, current releases of NetWare 4.*x* do not implement this solution.

Name Context at Workstation

Novell's client software provides the capability to set the current context before a user logs into the workstation—the Name Context configuration setting is found in different locations, depending on which client you are using. The following sections contain information for the two most popular clients, Windows and Windows 95.

Windows 3.11 Running VLMs

If you are using the older VLM clients, you will place the Name Context in the NET.CFG file. The NET.CFG file is processed when you start the NetWare client software drivers and the network requester software.

The format of the name context follows:

```
NAME CONTEXT = "NDS Path of Context"
```

NET.CFG statements are case-insensitive, so you can enter them as upper- or lowercase.

Suppose you want to set the current context at the time of login for user Bob to

```
OU=CORP.O=SCS
```

You can do this by including the following statement in the NET.CFG file:

```
Name Context = "OU=CORP.O=SCS"
```

You cannot enter a leading period (.) in the name context parameter. For example, the following is illegal:

```
NAME CONTEXT = ".OU=CORP.O=SCS"
```

A sample NET.CFG file that has the name context set to OU=CORP.O=ESL follows. The Name Context specification must occur in the *NetWare DOS Requester* section.

```
LINK DRIVER SMC8000
     FRAME ETHERNET_802.2
     INT    3
     PORT 280
     MEM  D0000
NetWare DOS Requester
     FIRST NETWORK DRIVE = F
     NAME CONTEXT = "OU=CORP.O=SCS"
```

Before you log in to the network, you can use the CX command to explicitly change the name context. Placing the name context statement in the NET.CFG benefits the user, because it can simplify access to the network resources the user uses most frequently. Therefore, for this reason, you should place the name context to the container of the resources a user is most likely to use. If you set the name context of a user to the container of the user object, the user can use the following command to log in to the network:

```
LOGIN UserLoginName
```

User BOB, then, would log in as follows:

```
LOGIN BOB
```

If you set the name context to a context other than the location of the user object, the user has to use the NDS path to the user object, as follows:

```
LOGIN NDSPathToUserObject
```

User BOB, whose user object is defined in OU=CORP.O=SCS, then would have to log in as follows:

```
LOGIN .CN=BOB.OU=CORP.O=SCS
```

or

```
LOGIN .BOB.CORP.SCS
```

The second form demonstrates the use of the typeless complete name, whereas the first form shows the user object being referenced by its complete name with attribute type designators (also called *typed complete name*).

Client 32 for Windows 95

For Windows 95 users, the issues and procedures for setting the name context have been greatly simplified. Simply load Novell's Client 32 software and complete the following steps.

1. Click on the Network icon in the Windows control panel.
2. Highlight the line "Novell NetWare Client 32."
3. Click on the properties tab.
4. Set the name context in "Name Context" field.

For more information on the using Client 32 see Chapter 16, "Supporting Non-DOS Workstations."

NDS Queries from the Command Line

The two primary command line utilities for browsing the NDS tree are as follows:

- Change Context (CX)
- Network List (NLIST)

Used together, the CX and NLIST utilities provide a flexible and powerful way to browse and search NDS object names and properties.

The CX Command

You use the CX utility to change the current context. You can use it alone, without any parameters and options, to find out the current context. Thus, using CX at the DOS prompt, as shown below, displays that the current context is set to O=ESL.

```
F> CX
ESL
F> CD
F:\SYSTEM
```

The CX command is very similar to the CD command, which enables a user to display the current directory or change the current directory for a file system. Keep in mind that CX operates on the NDS directory, not the file system directory. Changing NDS directory context does not change the current file system directory. Therefore, in the preceding example, the CX command reveals that the current context is O=ESL and the CD command reveals that the current directory is F:\SYSTEM. Changing the current context does not affect the current directory setting, and changing the current directory does not affect the current context setting.

The commands that follow refer to the NDS tree in figure 2.56 to make them easier to understand.

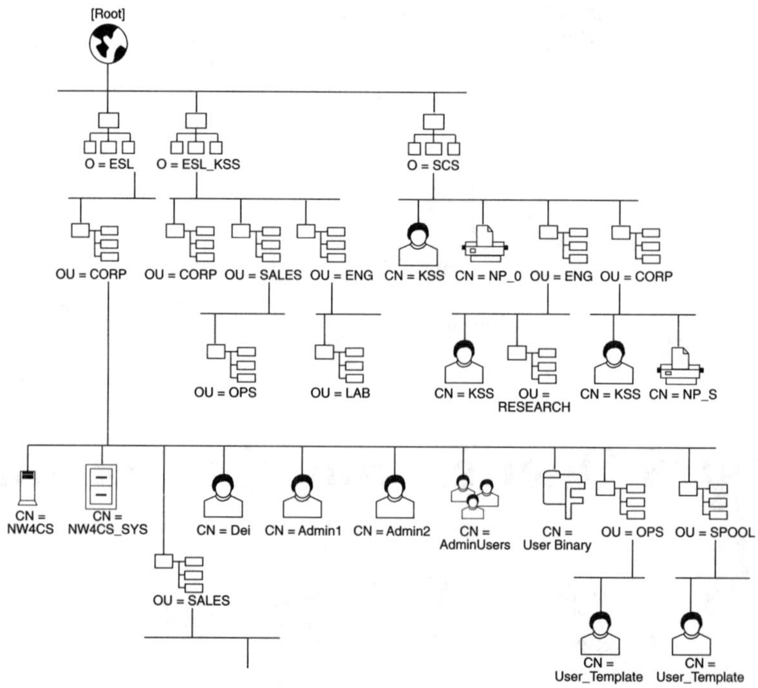

Figure 2.56
An NDS tree example for CX commands.

To change the current context to OU=CORP.O= ESL, you can issue the following command:

```
F> CX .OU=CORP.O=ESL
CORP.ESL
```

The CX command always returns the current context, so this is a quick check to make sure that your CX command functions correctly.

The preceding command used the complete name .OU=CORP.O=ESL. Typeless names can also be used, because the NDS tree does not contain a Country object. For instance, the following command has the same effect as the preceding command.

```
F> CX .CORP.ESL
CORP.ESL
```

To go back one container level above, you can issue the following command:

```
F> CX  .
ESL
```

The period (.) that follows the CX command means that you want to change your context to the parent container. You can combine periods to go up several container levels, as illustrated by the following example:

```
F> CX
CORP.ESL
F> CX ..
 [Root]
```

In the preceding example, the current container is OU=CORP.O=ESL. Using the command `CX ..` goes two container levels up, which in this case is the [Root] container.

What would happen if you tried to go three container levels above if your current context is OU=CORP.O=ESL (see listing 2.3)?

Listing 2.3

```
F> CX
CORP.ESL
F> CX ...
CX-4.19-260: An internal system error occurred during CX's attempt to canonicalize
➥the context: (...)
```

If you try to change the context to a location that does not exist in the NDS tree, an error message appears. In the preceding error message, `attempt to canonicalize the context` refers to the attempt NDS made to transform the user's input into a standard X.500 naming syntax form. *Canonical form* refers to a uniform or standard form.

To change the context to the [Root], you can use the /R option, as follows:

```
F> CX /R
 [Root]
```

To view all container objects (tree structure) below your current context or specified context you can use the /T option, as follows:

```
F> CX /R
 [Root]
F> CX /T
```

Figure 2.57 shows the output of the CX /T command issued from the [Root].

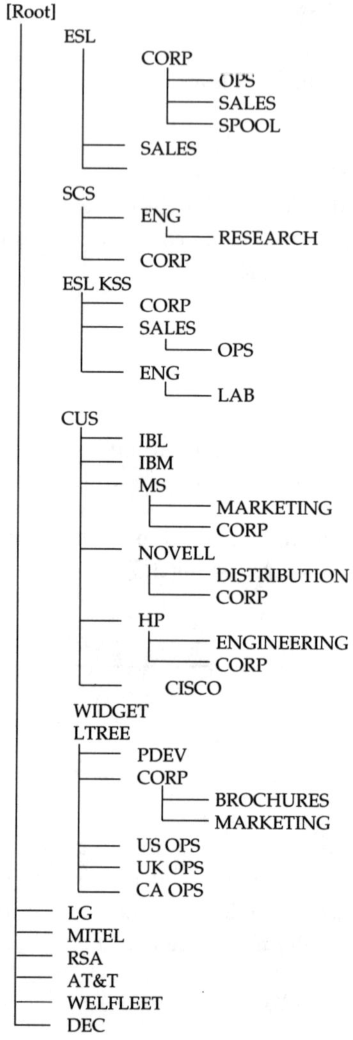

Figure 2.57
The CX /T command issued from the [Root] context.

You can combine /R with other options, such as /T. If you combine /R with /T, the CX /T command is issued from the root of the tree, but the context is not changed. Type the following:

```
F> CX
CORP.ESL
F> CX /T /R
F> CX
CORP.ESL
```

The command CX /T /R (or CX /R /T) produces the output shown in figure 2.58; the context before and after you execute the command remains the same (OU=CORP.O=ESL).

```
CORP.O=ESL
     |— NW4CS
     |— NW4CS_SYS
     |— Dei
     |— Admin1
     |— Admin2
     |— AdminUsers
     |— User Binary
     |— OPS
     |       └— USER_TEMPLATE
     |— SALES
     |       └— USER_TEMPLATE
     └— SPOOL
             └— USER_TEMPLATE
```

Figure 2.58
The CX /T /A command issued from the OU=CORP.O=ESL context.

The /A (or /ALL) option enables you to view all objects at or below the current context. It is meant to be used in conjunction with options like the /T option.

```
F> CX
CORP.ESL
F> CX /T /A
```

The command CX /T /A produces an output that is shown in figure 2.58.

You can combine the CX /T /A command with the /R option, as follows:

```
F> CX
CORP.ESL
F> CX /T /A /R
F> CX
CORP.ESL
```

CX /T /A /R shows all objects starting from the [Root], but the context remains the same (OU=CORP.O=ESL) before and after executing the commands.

To view only container objects at a specified level, you can use the /CONT option, as follows:

```
F> CX
CORP.ESL
F> CX /CONT
```

You can combine the /CONT command with /A to see all objects within the container only, as follows:

```
F> CX
CORP.ESL
F> CX /CONT /A
```

Figure 2.59 shows the output of using the CX /CONT /A command in the current context OU=CORP.O=ESL.

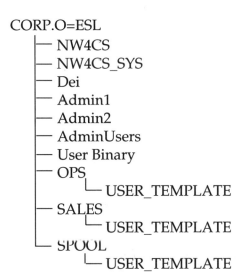

Figure 2.59
The CX /CONT /A command issued from the OU=CORP.O=ESL context.

```
CORP.O=ESL
 ├── NW4CS
 ├── NW4CS_SYS
 ├── Dei
 ├── Admin1
 ├── Admin2
 ├── AdminUsers
 ├── User Binary
 ├── OPS
 ├── SALES
 └── SPOOL
```

What is the difference between CX /CONT /A and CX /T /A? Compare figure 2.59 with figure 2.58. The CX /CONT /A displays all objects in the current context only, whereas the CX /T /A displays all objects in the current context and in the containers below the current context.

If you combine the CX /CONT /A with the /R option, what output will be displayed?

```
F> CX
CORP.ESL
F> CX /CONT /A /R
F> CX
CORP.ESL
```

Figure 2.60 shows the output of using the CX /CONT /A /R command in the current context OU=CORP.O=ESL. The current context before and after executing this command does not change, even though the /R option starts displaying the tree from the [Root] object.

Figure 2.60
The CX /CONT /A /R command issued from the OU=CORP.O=ESL context.

```
[Root]
 ├──── ESL
 ├──── SCS
 ├──── ESL KSS
 ├──── US
 ├──── WIDGET
 ├──── LTREE
 ├──── LG
 ├──── MITEL
 ├──── RSA
 ├──── AT&T
 ├──── WELFLEET
 └──── DEC
```

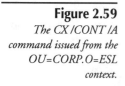

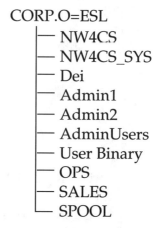

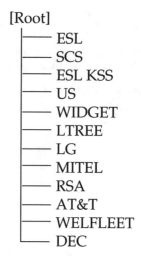

You can use the CX command with typeless and partial names. If the current context in figure 2.56 is O=ESL, for instance, to change the context to OU=CORP.O=ESL, you would use the following partial typeless name:

```
F> CX
ESL
F> CX CORP
CORP.ESL
```

If current context is O=ESL, to change the context to OU=SALES.OU=CORP.O=ESL, you would use the following partial typeless name:

```
F> CX
ESL
F> CX SALES.CORP
SALES.CORP.ESL
```

If the current context is [Root], to change the context to O=SCS, you would use the following partial typeless name:

```
F> CX
 [Root]
F> CX SCS
SCS
```

If the current context is O=SCS, to change the context to O=ESL (refer to fig. 2.56), you would use the following partial typeless name:

```
F> CX
SCS
F> CX ESL.
ESL
```

The preceding example uses the trailing period rule to go one container above the current context.

If the current context is OU=CORP.O=SCS, to change context to OU=SALES.OU=CORP. O=ESL (refer to fig. 2.56), you would use the following partial typeless name:

```
F> CX
CORP.SCS
F> CX SALES.CORP.ESL..
ESL
```

The preceding example uses the trailing period rule to go two containers above the current context.

To view additional help on using the CX command, type the following command:

```
CX /?
```

The following screens (listing 2.4) show the two help screens that appear when you use CX /?. Table 2.6 also summarizes many of the common CX options.

Listing 2.4

```
3 CX                              Options Help                          4.19 3

3 Syntax:  CX [new context ¦ /VER] [/R] [/[T ¦ CONT] [/A]] [/C] [/?]         3

3 To:                                                                    Use:3
3   View all container objects below the                 /T                  3
3     current or specified context.                                          3
3   View container objects at the current                /CONT               3
3     or specified level.                                                    3
3   Modify /T or /CONT to view All objects               /A                  3
3     at or below the context                                                3
3   Change context or view objects relative to root      /R                  3
3   Display version information                          /VER                3
3   Scroll continuously                                  /C                  3

3 For example, to: Type: 3
3   View directory tree below the current context    CX /T                   3
3   View containers within a specific context        CX .O=Novell /CONT      3



3 CX                           General Usage Help                       4.19 3

3 Purpose: View and set current context.                                     3
3 Syntax:  CX [new context ¦ /VER] [/R] [/[T ¦ CONT] [/A]] [/C] [/?]         3

3 New context:                                                               3
3   A context can be entered either relative to your current context or      3
3   as a distinguished name relative to the directory root.                  3
3   Use trailing periods (.) to change to a context relative to a higher     3
3   level of your current context.                                           3
3   To change to a context relative to the root of the directory put a period 3
3   at the beginning of the new context or use the /Root flag.               3

3 To view your current context type CX                                       3
3 Current context is OU=Engineering.O=Novell                                 3
3                                                                            3
3 For example, to change context:                      Type:                 3
3   O=Novell                                             CX .                3
3   OU=Testing.OU=Engineering.O=Novell                   CX OU=Testing       3
3   OU=Marketing.O=Novell                                CX OU=Marketing.    3
```

Table 2.6
Common CX Options

Command (Use)	Description (To)
CX .	Change context to one container above current context

Command (Use)	Description (To)
CX	Display current context
CX /R	Change context to root of NDS tree
CX /T	View all container objects below current or specified context
CX /T /A	View all objects in current context and below
CX /CONT	View container objects at current or specified context only
CX /CONT /A	View all objects at current context or specified context only
CX new_context	Change context to specified context
CX /VER	Display version number of CX and file dependencies
CX /?	Obtain CX help screens

The NLIST Command

The NLIST command enables you to view information concerning different object classes in a convenient tabular format on-screen. NLIST is the fundamental command-line utility for extracting information on NDS objects. You can use it to set up general-purpose queries that search NDS objects based on a number of search criteria, such as the following:

- Property values
- Existence of properties
- Specific branch of the NDS tree

If you want to search for all active users connected to the network, use the /A option, as in listing 2.5.

Listing 2.5

```
F> NLIST USER /A
Object Class: User
Current context: ESL
Conn            = The server connection number
*               = The asterisk means this is your connection
User Name       = The login name of the user
Address         = The network address
Node            = The network node
Login time      = The time when the user logged in
User Name                                         Address         Node
*Admin                                           [    E8022][      C024282D]
One user object was found in this context.
One user object was found.
```

The output of all NLIST commands produces a legend that describes the columns for the tabular information displayed.

The asterisk next to a connection indicates your connection to the server. The output of this command is equivalent to the USERLIST /A command in NetWare 3.x.

To see all user objects defined in the current context and subcontainers, use the /S option, as in listing 2.6.

Listing 2.6

```
F> CX
CORP.ESL
F> NLIST USER /S
Object Class: User
Current context: CORP.ESL
User name= The name of the user
Dis           = Login disabled
Log exp   = The login expiration date, 0 if no expiration date
Pwd         = Yes if passwords are required
Pwd exp  = The password expiration date, 0 if no expiration date
Uni          = Yes if unique passwords are required
Min         = The minimum password length, 0 if no minimum
User Name                                     Dis  Log Exp Pwd  Pwd Exp Uni Min
----------------
Dei                                           No   0-00-00 No   0-00-00 No   0
Admin1                                        Yes  0-00-00 Yes  0-00-00 No   8
Admin2                                        No   9-01-99 No   0-00-00 No   5
A total of 3 USER objects was found in this context.
Object Class: User
Current context: SPOOL.CORP.ESL
User Name                                     Dis  Log Exp Pwd  Pwd Exp Uni Min
----------------
USER_TEMPLATE                                 No   0-00-00 No   0-00-00 No   0
One USER object was found in this context.
Object Class: User
Current context: SALES.CORP.ESL
User Name                Dis  Log Exp Pwd  Pwd Exp Uni Min
----------------
USER_TEMPLATE            No   0-00-00 No   0-00-00 No   0
One USER object was found in this context.
Object Class: User
Current context: OPS.CORP.ESL
User Name                Dis  Log Exp Pwd  Pwd Exp Uni Min
----------------
USER_TEMPLATE            No   0-00-00 No   0-00-00 No   0
One USER object was found in this context.
A total of 6 USER objects was found.
```

NLIST output always begins with the specified Object Class, followed by current context, then the information NLIST returns for the current context.

The NLIST USER /S command, which lists all the users found in the context OU=CORP. O=ESL and all users defined in subcontainers below the context, was issued from the context OU=CORP.O=ESL. Three user objects were defined in the context OU=CORP.O=ESL. User Dei was not disabled and had no login expiration dates. Also, user Dei did not have any restrictions of unique passwords or minimum password length. User Admin1, on the other hand, was disabled, and had the restrictions of a password being required, and passwords being unique and having a minimum of eight characters. User Admin2 was not disabled, but the login account would expire on 9-1-99, and although no password uniqueness is enforced for this user, the minimum password length is five characters. The subcontainers OU=SPOOL.OU=CORP.O=ESL, OU=SALES.OU=CORP.O=ESL, and OU= OPS.OU= CORP.O=ESL were searched next. Each search revealed a user object that had the name USER_TEMPLATE and no restrictions, like user Dei in the container above. You learn later that you can use the user's USER_TEMPLATE in a container as a model for other users you create within that container.

To see property details for a specific user, such as user DEI, refer to listing 2.7.

Listing 2.7

```
F> NLIST USER=DEI  /D
Object Class: User
Current context: CORP.ESL
User: Dei
     Name: Dei
     Object Trustees (ACL):
          Subject: Dei
          Property:  [All Properties Rights]
          Property Rights: [ R   ]
     Object Trustees (ACL):
          Subject: Dei
          Property: Login Script
          Property Rights: [ RW  ]
     Object Trustees (ACL):
          Subject: [Public]
          Property: Default Server
          Property Rights: [ R   ]
     Object Trustees (ACL):
          Subject: [Root]
          Property: Group Membership
          Property Rights: [ R   ]
     Object Trustees (ACL):
          Subject: Dei
          Property: Print Job Configuration
          Property Rights: [ RW  ]
     Object Trustees (ACL):
          Subject: [Root]
          Property: Network Address
          Property Rights: [ R   ]
```

continues

```
     Full Name: Dei Siyan
     Given Name: Dei
     Group Membership: Manager.SCS..
     Home Directory:
          Volume Name: NW4CS_SYS
          Path: USERS\Dei
          Name Space Type: DOS
     Middle Initial: G
     Language:
          English
     Default Server: NW4CS
     Object Class: User
     Object Class: Organizational Person
     Object Class: Person
     Object Class: Top
     Revision: 5
     Security Equal To: Manager.SCS..
     Last Name: Siyan
     Title: Finance Controller
- - - - - - - - - - - - - - - - - - - - - - - - - - - - - - - - - - - -

One User object was found in this context.

One User object was found.
```

The output of the NLIST USER=Dei /D command provides detailed information on the properties for that object. The properties listed for the user are [All Properties Rights], Login Script, Default Server, Group Membership, Printer Job Configuration, Network Address, Home Directory, Language, Full Name, Given Name, Middle Initial, Group Membership, Language, Title, and Last Name.

In the NLIST USER=Dei /D command, the following lines appear at the end:

Object Class: User

Object Class: Organization Person

Object Class: Person

Object Class: Top

The preceding lines reveal the derivation hierarchy for user object Dei. The base class for user object Dei is User class, derived from the Organizational Person super class, derived in turn from the super class Person, derived in turn from super class Top.

To search for user KSS in the current container and all subcontainers, see listing 2.8.

Listing 2.8

```
F> CX
SCS
F> NLIST USER=KSS /S
Object Class: User
Current context: SCS
User name= The name of the user
Dis          = Login disabled
Log exp      = The login expiration date, 0 if no expiration date
Pwd          = Yes if passwords are required
Pwd exp  = The password expiration date, 0 if no expiration date
Uni          = Yes if unique passwords are required
Min          = The minimum password length, 0 if no minimum
User Name                                  Dis  Log Exp Pwd  Pwd Exp Uni Min
KSS                                        No   0-00-00 No   0-00-00 No   0
One USER object was found in this context.
Object Class: User
Current context: CORP.SCS
User Name                                  Dis  Log Exp Pwd  Pwd Exp Uni Min
_ _ _ _ _ _ _ _ _ _ _ _ _ _ _ _
KSS                                       No   0-00-00 No   0-00-00 No   0
One USER object was found in this context.
Object Class: User
Current context: ENG.SCS
User Name                                  Dis  Log Exp Pwd  Pwd Exp Uni Min
KSS                                        No   0-00-00 No   0-00-00 No   0
One USER object was found in this context.
```

The NLIST USER=KSS /S command finds all occurrences of user object KSS in the current context and all subcontainers.

To see all printer objects within the current context and all subcontainers, refer to listing 2.9.

Listing 2.9

```
F>CX
SCS
F> NLIST PRINTER /S
Current context: SCS
Partial Name                                          Object Class
_ _ _ _ _ _ _ _ _ _ _ _ _ _ _ _
NP_0                                                  Printer
One PRINTER object was found in this context.
Current context: CORP.SCS
Partial Name                                          Object Class
NP_0                                                  Printer
One PRINTER object was found in this context.
A total of 2 PRINTER objects was found.
```

To search for a specific property value for an object class such as the user object class, in the current context and all subcontainers, see listing 2.10.

Listing 2.10

```
F> CX
SCS
F> NLIST USER SHOW "Telephone Number"  /S
Object Class: User
Current context: scs
User: Manager1
     Telephone: 310-434-3344
User: Manager2
     Telephone: 310-444-4435
User: KSS
     Telephone: 415-333-4655
A total of 3 User objects was found in this context.

Object Class: User
Current context: ENG.scs
User: AMY
     Telephone: 310-444-4354
One User object was found in this context.

Object Class: User
Current context: CORP.scs
User: Linda
     Telephone: 510-233-3432
One User object was found in this context.

A total of 5 User objects was found.
```

If you left the /S option out in the preceding command (NLIST USER SHOW "Telephone Number"), only the phone numbers for users in the current context of OU=CORP.O=SCS would appear.

To see a specific value for a specific object, refer to listing 2.11.

Listing 2.11

```
F> CX
CORP.ESL
F> NLIST SERVER=NW4CS SHOW "Network Address"
Object Class: Server
Current context: CORP.ESL
Server: NW4CS
IPX/SPX Network Address
Network: F0000055
Node: 1
Socket: 451
One SERVER object was found in this context.
One SERVER object was found.
F> CX .O=SCS
SCS
F> NLIST PRINTER="NP_0" SHOW "Location" /S
```

```
Current context: SCS
Printer: NP_0
Location: Building 6, Room 404
------------------
One PRINTER object was found in this context.
Current context: CORP.SCS
Printer: NP_0
Location: Engineering Lab Bldg, Printer Room 5
------------------
One PRINTER object was found in this context.
A total of 2 PRINTER objects was found.
```

When you use the NLIST SERVER command, you query the network address of server NW4CS. The network address that NDS reports is the internal software address of the server that consists of the *internal network number*, the *socket number*, and the *node number*, which is always set to 1. The internal network number is selected during installation, and the socket number identifies the file service process that handles incoming requests. The NLIST PRINTER command shows the location of the printer object NP_0. The /S option helps find this printer object in the current context of O=SCS and all subcontainers. If you do not use the /S option, NDS finds only the printer object in Building 6, Room 404, and does not find the printer object in Engineering Lab Bldg, Printer Room 5.

To search for all objects possessing a specific property value, use the WHERE option in conjunction with the NLIST command, as shown in listing 2.12.

Listing 2.12

```
F> CX
SCS
F> NLIST USER WHERE "Title" EQ ENGINEER
Object Class: User
Current context: SCS
User name= The name of the user
Dis          = Login disabled
Log exp   = The login expiration date, 0 if no expiration date
Pwd          = Yes if passwords are required
Pwd exp  = The password expiration date, 0 if no expiration date
Uni          = Yes if unique passwords are required
Min          = The minimum password length, 0 if no minimum
User Name                                    Dis  Log Exp Pwd  Pwd Exp Uni Min
------------------
KSS                                          No  0-00-00   No   0-00-00   No  0
One USER object was found in this context.
One USER object was found.
F> NLIST USER=KSS SHOW TITLE
Object Class: User
Current context: SCS
User: KSS
Title: Engineer
One USER object was found in this context.
One USER object was found.
```

In the preceding commands, quotes ("") are placed around property names and values that have spaces around them; otherwise, they are optional. You also can use the equal symbol (=) to replace the EQ comparison operator. Each of the following commands are equivalent and produce the same result:

```
NLIST USER WHERE "Title" EQ ENGINEER

NLIST USER WHERE "Title" = ENGINEER

NLIST USER WHERE "Title" = "ENGINEER"

NLIST USER WHERE Title = "ENGINEER"

NLIST USER WHERE Title = ENGINEER
```

The common NLIST options are summarized in table 2.7.

Table 2.7
Common NLIST Options

Command (Use)	Description (To)
NLIST USER /A	Display active users logged on to the network
NLIST VOLUME /S	Display all volumes in the current context and subcontainers
NLIST USER=Dei /D	Show detail property values for a user
NLIST USER=KSS /S	Search for a specific object in current context and all subcontainers
NLIST SERVER=FS1 SHOW "Network Address"	Show a specific property for a specific server object
NLIST PRINTER WHERE "LOCATION"=LAB	Search for objects that have a specific property value
NLIST /VER	Show version number of NLIST and its file dependencies
NLIST /?	Display top level help screen for NLIST

Figures 2.61 through 2.65 show the help screens that you can obtain by using the NLIST /? command. Figure 2.62 is the top-level help screen, and the other figures are the specific help screens described in the top-level help screen.

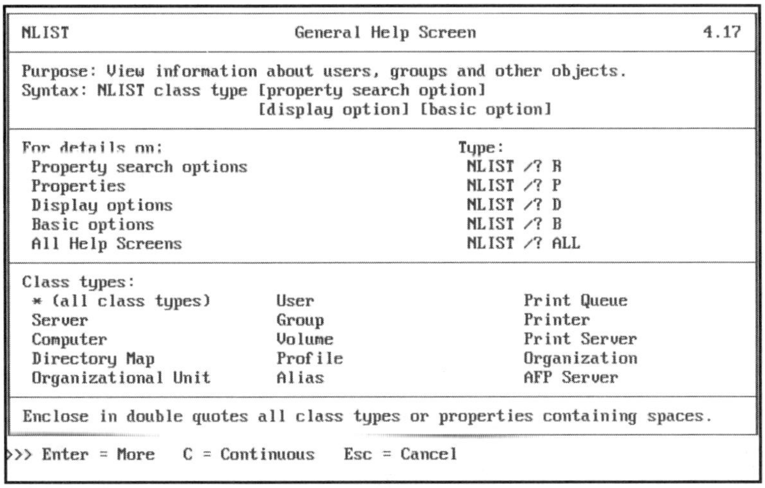

NLIST General Help Screen 4.17
Purpose: View information about users, groups and other objects.
Syntax: NLIST class type [property search option]
[display option] [basic option]
For details on: Type:
Property search options NLIST /? R
Properties NLIST /? P
Display options NLIST /? D
Basic options NLIST /? B
All Help Screens NLIST /? ALL
Class types:
* (all class types) User Print Queue
Server Group Printer
Computer Volume Print Server
Directory Map Profile Organization
Organizational Unit Alias AFP Server
Enclose in double quotes all class types or properties containing spaces.
>>> Enter = More C = Continuous Esc = Cancel

Figure 2.61

The top-level help screen for NLIST.

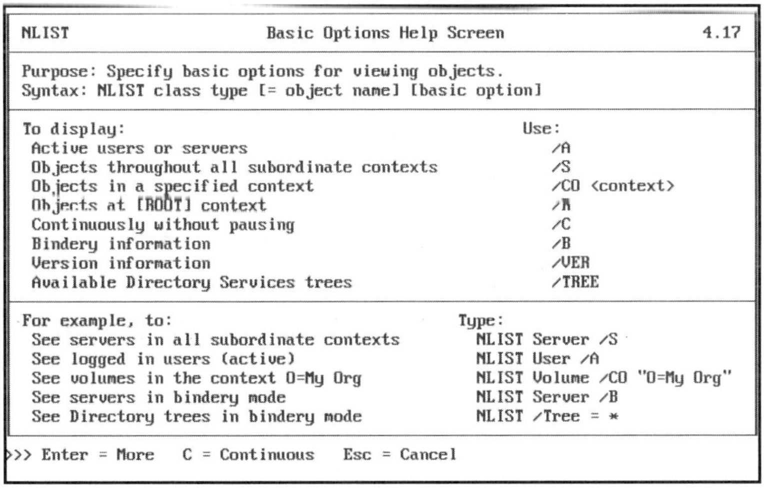

NLIST Basic Options Help Screen 4.17
Purpose: Specify basic options for viewing objects.
Syntax: NLIST class type [= object name] [basic option]
To display: Use:
Active users or servers /A
Objects throughout all subordinate contexts /S
Objects in a specified context /CO <context>
Objects at [ROOT] context /R
Continuously without pausing /C
Bindery information /B
Version information /VER
Available Directory Services trees /TREE
For example, to: Type:
See servers in all subordinate contexts NLIST Server /S
See logged in users (active) NLIST User /A
See volumes in the context O=My Org NLIST Volume /CO "O=My Org"
See servers in bindery mode NLIST Server /B
See Directory trees in bindery mode NLIST /Tree = *
>>> Enter = More C = Continuous Esc = Cancel

Figure 2.62

NLIST /? B: Basic options help screen.

Figure 2.63
NLIST /? D: Display options help screen.

```
NLIST                       Display Options Help Screen                    4.17

Purpose: Select how data is to be displayed.
Syntax: NLIST class type [= object name] [display option]

To display:                                Use:
 Detailed information                       /D
 Only the object name                       /N
 Specific properties                        SHOW property [, property ...]

For example, to:                           Type:
 See detailed information for
  group ADMIN                               NLIST Group = Admin /D
 See the telephone numbers and street
  addresses of all users                    NLIST User SHOW "Telephone",
                                            "Street Address"
 See only the names of the queues in
  current and all subordinate contexts      NLIST Print Queue /N /S

>>> Enter = More   C = Continuous   Esc = Cancel
```

Figure 2.64
NLIST /? R: Property search options help screen.

```
NLIST                       Property Search Help Screen                    4.17

Purpose: Search for objects by property value
Syntax: NLIST object class [ = object name]
           WHERE property <operator> value

Operators:
 EQ = Equal                         LE = Less than or equal
 NE = Not Equal                     GT = Greater than
 LT = Less than                     GE = Greater than or equal
 EXISTS = property exists           NEXISTS = property does not exist

For example, to:                       Type:
 See all users whose
  Login Grace Limit is greater          NLIST User WHERE
  than 0                                      "Grace Logins Allowed" GT 0
 See all users whose
  telephone number begins               NLIST User WHERE
  with 801                                    "Telephone" EQ 801*
 See all queues which have
  an operator                           NLIST Print Queue WHERE Operator EXISTS

>>> Enter = More   C = Continuous   Esc = Cancel
```

Figure 2.65
NLIST /? P: Properties help screen.

```
NLIST                       Properties Help Screen                         4.17

Purpose: Show examples of some properties

Properties for class type User include:
 Email Address
 Group Membership
 Login Script
 Default Server

Properties for class type Server include:
 Network Address
 Organization Name
 Department
 Version

Refer to "Utilities Document" for complete list of properties
  and class types.

C:\HJPRO>
```

NDS Queries Using the NetWare Administrator Tool

You also can use a Graphical User Interface tool, such as the NetWare Administrator Tool, to generate NDS queries.

Perform the following steps to issue the Search option:

1. Launch NetWare Administrator Tool.
2. Highlight the container object from which to carry out the search. If you want to search the entire NDS tree, highlight the [Root] object.
3. Select the Object menu.
4. Select the Search option from the Object menu.

After you perform the preceding steps, a Search dialog box should appear (see fig. 2.66). You use the Start From edit box to indicate the starting point of the search, which can be any container object in the NDS tree. You can use the Browse icon, next to this value, to browse for an appropriate container (see fig. 2.67). The default is to search the entire subtree, as indicated by a default check mark on the Search Entire Subtree check box.

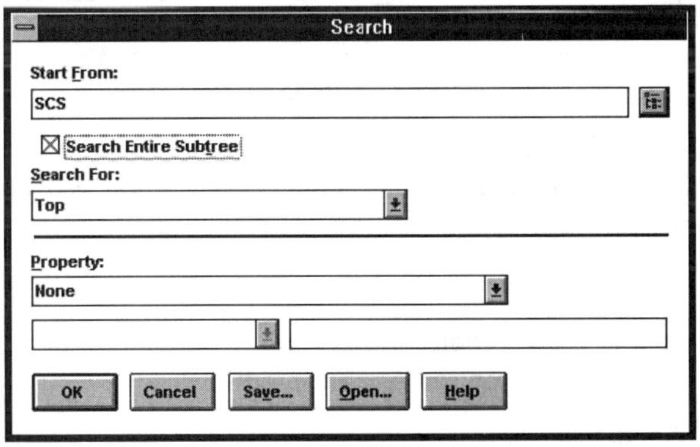

Figure 2.66
The Search option in the NetWare Administrator Tool.

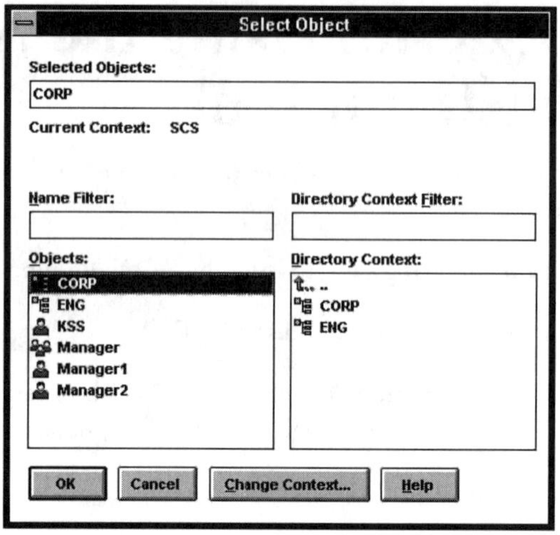

Figure 2.67
The Select Object panel used for browsing to set the value of Start From in the Search option.

Several other object classes are listed in the Search For files. In addition to the standard object classes, additional classifications can be used to aid in finding the objects. These additional classifications are listed in table 2.8.

Table 2.8
Additional Object Classifications for Search Option

Object Classification	Description
Device	Includes all computer and printer objects
Locality	Currently not used by NDS, but can be used by third-party products and tools Locality is used for describing geographical locations such as towns, cities, counties, and so forth
Organizational Person	Lists all users
Partition	Used by the Partition Manager tool to indicate containers that are on the top of a separate partition
Person	Includes all users
Resource	Includes Printer Queue and Volume Objects
Server	Includes NetWare Server, Print Server, and AFP server
Top	Includes every object in the container that is being searched

The Properties list box enables you to select from the different properties that you want to search for. The comparison operators include Equal, Not Equal To, Not Present, and Present. You enter the actual property value for which you want to search in a field.

Figure 2.68 shows the results of searching all Organizational Unit objects in the container O=SCS and its subcontainers. Three Organizational Unit objects were found, as follows:

```
OU=CORP.O=SCS

OU-ENG.O-SCS

OU=RESEARCH.OU=ENG.O=SCS
```

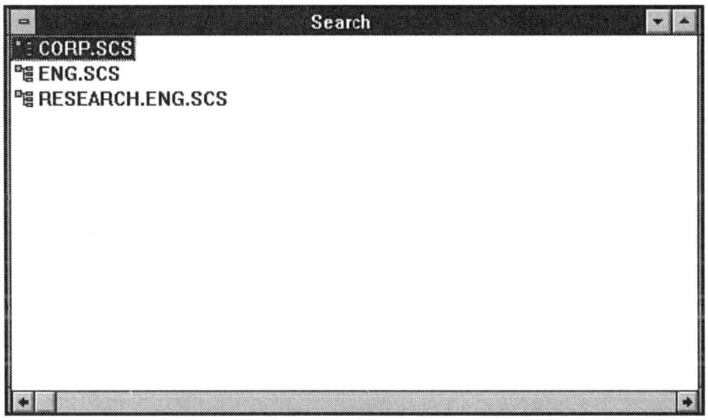

Figure 2.68
The Search results for all Organizational Unit objects in O=SCS NDS database.

The Volume Object

One object is both an NDS object and a file system object: the Volume object. It has characteristics of both a file system object and an NDS object. As an NDS object, the volume is managed by NDS, but its components consist of directories and files.

Summary

In this chapter, you have learned the basics of Novell Directory Services. The NDS represents an exciting way of managing the network as a logical entity. Because NDS is a key service in IntranetWare, many details of its operations were provided in this chapter. One of the concepts covered was NDS as a global database for network management. This global database is accessible from any point on the network. The nature of the NDS objects was examined, and each of the different type of leaf and container objects were described in detail. The NDS naming rules were described with respect to several examples. Among the key concepts that were covered were current context, complete names, typeless names, partial names, and period rules.

The NDS commands CX and NLIST and their most important options were discussed, and numerous examples of how they could be used were provided. The chapter concluded with a discussion on partitioning, replication, and using some of the NDS utilities.

CHAPTER 3

Installing IntranetWare

In this chapter, you learn about installing and upgrading IntranetWare. Normally, you can install software without considering serious design issues. IntranetWare is a powerful and complex operating system, and you should apply some careful consideration before installing it. A very important aspect of the design of an IntranetWare-based network is the NDS tree structure. During the installation, you make decisions about the NDS tree structure for your network. Possessing a good understanding of the NDS directory tree for your organization, therefore, is essential. Remember that making changes after you choose the basic NDS tree structure requires extra effort. You can save considerable time and effort by doing things right the first time.

This chapter not only teaches you how to install IntranetWare, but also covers how to upgrade NetWare 3.x or NetWare 4.x to IntranetWare. Several options are available for migrating to IntranetWare. Preplanning and proper design are key factors to migrating efficiently.

Note

> The remainder of this chapter will refer to "IntranetWare" when talking about the product as a whole. It will refer to "NetWare 4.x" when talking specifically about the network operating system.

Installation Changes

Some earlier versions of NetWare, such as NetWare 3.x and 2.x, were distributed on disks. The number of disks and time required to install NetWare is inconveniently excessive, owing to its complex software programming. A fundamental change in NetWare 4.x is its distribution on CD-ROM disks. Here, IntranetWare follows a path set by some popular versions of Unix, which also are distributed on CD-ROM. IntranetWare comes with four CD-ROM disks and a license disk that has a serial number and a code for the maximum number of users supported by the NetWare OS.

In NetWare 3.x, you had to partition and format the server disk for DOS. You had to load the DOS system before you could load the NetWare server program (SERVER.EXE). To continue the installation, you needed to run the INSTALL.NLM to create a NetWare partition and a NetWare volume.

NetWare 4.x also requires a DOS partition, on hard disk or floppy disk, to start the server (SERVER.EXE) program. If you do not have the server disk prepared, however, the NetWare 4.x installation does it for you. You can use the NetWare 4.x installation program to create a DOS partition and install DOS. The installation program installs a version of DOS called *Novell DOS.*

NetWare 4.1 (and above) installation creates a directory called NWSERVER in the DOS partition and copies the minimum set of programs necessary for starting the SERVER.EXE program and continuing the installation. The NetWare 4.x installation program starts the SERVER.EXE program, loads the INSTALL.NLM, and guides you through the appropriate options for completing the installation.

Despite automated installation steps, and no need to copy numerous floppy disks onto the server, you still must make key decisions to complete a successful installation.

You can still apply experience and knowledge you might have gained from installing earlier version of NetWare. As you go through this chapter, you might recognize many tasks and concepts as being similar to those in NetWare 3.x; for example, NLMs as extensions to the NetWare OS. Other similarities include the following:

- Installation uses the same file extension conventions to indicate different types of NLMs.
- All NLMs, by default, load from the SYSTEM directory.
- PUBLIC directory has the same meaning as for NetWare 3.x.

Installation Requirements

The installation requirements for NetWare 4.x fall into two categories: hardware and software.

Hardware Requirements

The server must be an Intel 80386 or higher processor with at least 20 MB of RAM, and an internal or external hard disk of at least 100 MB partitioned for NetWare. If you plan to install the additional products offered with IntranetWare you should plan on at least 150 MB for your NetWare volume.

Note The minimum configuration with most computers purchased today will have at least a 1 GB hard drive and 16 MB of RAM. The cost of hardware has dropped significantly making this a relatively minor issue.

The server must also have at least one Network Interface Card (NIC) with the correct driver. One of the areas of improvement in NetWare 4.x is that the distribution comes with a longer list of network drivers. Table 3.1 shows the initial list of drivers supported for NetWare 4.x. This list should grow as newer network boards become available. If you cannot find support for the NIC of your choice in the list, consult with the NIC vendor. You can also check the Novell home page on the Internet to see if your driver is tested and certified with NetWare. If you want the most updated list from Novell Labs certification bulletins, point your browser to `http://labs.novell.com/infosys/bulletn.htm`. Drivers downloaded from *Bulletin Board Systems* (BBSs) contain instructions on how to use them in the NetWare 4.x installation. Other optional pieces of hardware are tape backups and optical jukeboxes for data migration.

Table 3.1
Partial List of NetWare 4.x-Supported LAN Drivers for the Server

LAN Driver File Name	Description
3C503.LAN	3COM 3C503 EtherLink II Driver 3COM 3C503 EtherLink II TP Driver 3COM 3C503 EtherLink II/16 Driver 3COM 3C503 EtherLink II/16 TP Driver
3C509.LAN	3COM EtherLink III Family Driver
3C523.LAN	3COM 3C523 EtherLink II Driver/MC Driver 3COM 3C523 EtherLink II Driver/MC TP Driver
3NW391R.LAN	Proteon p1391 RapiDriver
3NW392R.LAN	Proteon p1392 RapiDriver
3NW89XR.LAN	Proteon p189x RapiDriver

continues

Table 3.1, Continued
Partial List of NetWare 4.x-Supported LAN Drivers for the Server

LAN Driver File Name	Description
E21N4X.LAN	Cabletron Ethernet E21xx (ISA/EISA) ODI Server Driver
EXP16.LAN	Intel EtherExpress ISA Family Intel EtherExpress MCA Family
HP386A16.LAN	Hewlett-Packard PC LAN/AT 16
HP386A32.LAN	Hewlett-Packard PC LAN Adapter/16 Plus
IBMETHR.LAN	IBM Personal System/2 Adapter for Ethernet Networks
INTEL593.COM	Intel LAN593 Driver
IPTUNNEL.LAN	IP Tunnel Driver
MADGEODI.LAN	MADGE Hardware Support Module
NCRWL06.LAN	NCR WaveLAN AT/MC
NE1000.LAN	Novell Ethernet NE1000
NE1500T.LAN	Ansel M1500 All-In-One-Networking Novell Ethernet NE1500T
NE2.LAN	Novell Ethernet NE/2
NE2000.LAN	Novell Ethernet NE2000
NE2100.LAN	Ansel M2100 All-In-One-Networking EXOS 105 Novell Ethernet NE2100 Wearness 2110T or Wearness 2107C
NE2_32.LAN	Novell Ethernet NE/2-32
NE3200.LAN	INTEL EtherExpress32 Microdyne EXOS235T Novell Ethernet NE3200
NE32HUB.LAN	Novell Ethernet NE32HUB
NI9210.LAN	Racal-Datacom NI9210
NTR2000.LAN	Novell Token-Ring
PCN2L.LAN	Novell PCN II and PCN Baseband Driver
SMC8000.LAN	SMC EtherCard PLUS Family Server Driver
SMCARC.LAN	Standard Microsystems Corp. ISA or MCA ARCNET Driver
T20N4X.LAN	Cabletron Token-Ring T20XX (ISA/EISA) ODI Server Driver
TCARCH.LAN	Thomas-Conrad ARCNet/TCNS Server Lan Driver
TCE16ATH.LAN	Thomas-Conrad TC5045 Server Lan Drive
TCE16MCH.LAN	Thomas-Conrad TC5045 16-bit Server Lan Driver

LAN Driver File Name	Description
TCE32MCH.LAN	Thomas-Conrad TC5045 32-bit Server Lan Driver
TCNSH.LAN	Thomas-Conrad TCNS Server Lan Driver
TCTOKH.LAN	Thomas-Conrad Token-Ring Server Lan Driver
TOKEN.LAN	Token-Ring
TOKENDMA.LAN	IBM Token-Ring Busmaster
TRXNET.LAN	Novell Turbo RX-Net
UBPCETP.LAN	Ungermann-Bass MIUpc/EOTP MicroChannel adapter
UBPSETP.LAN	Ungermann-Bass MicroChannel adapter

If you ever have server problems, you will need to copy files to the DOS partition for troubleshooting. A good rule of thumb is to increase the DOS partition 1 MB for every 1 MB of server RAM. For example, if your server has 32 MB of RAM, you might want to increase the DOS partition from 15 MB to 47 MB (15 MB + 32 MB = 47 MB).

Minimum hardware requirements for NetWare 4.x follow:

- Intel 80386 processor (or better)
- 20 MB of RAM
- Minimum of 15 MB DOS partition for storing server start up files
- Server disk size of at least 115 MB (15 MB for the DOS partition and 100 MB for the NetWare volume)
- Supported Network Interface Card (NIC)
- CD-ROM drive, if NetWare 4.x is on CD-ROM media

An important but often overlooked attribute is that the server should have an accurate time clock, especially if it is going to act as a Single Reference Time Server, Primary Time Server, or Reference Time Server. Reference Time Servers should, by definition, have accurate time clocks. The Single Reference Time Server and the Reference Time Server are usually ordinary computers, but should have reasonably accurate clocks.

Tip

> See `http://labs.novell.com/infosys/bulletn.htm` for the most up-to-date list of drivers that have passed Novell Labs certification and are supported by NetWare 4.x.

Hardware Requirements for the Root Server

The first NetWare 4.x server that you install defines the initial NDS partition, which also contains the [Root] object of the NDS tree. Therefore, the first NetWare 4.x server that you install is called the *root server.*

Tip

> Although NetWare 4.x will run on an Intel 80386 based computer, it is recommended that a 133 MHz Pentium based computer (at least) be used for the root server.

You want to use a faster machine for the root server, because the root server contains the master replica of the NDS root partition. A user who logs on to a subpartition (see fig. 3.1) and needs to access an object on another subpartition needs access (albeit transparently) to the root server, which contains the linkage information to other partitions. You can contact the object in another subpartition transparently, but a fast root server minimizes access time to other subpartitions.

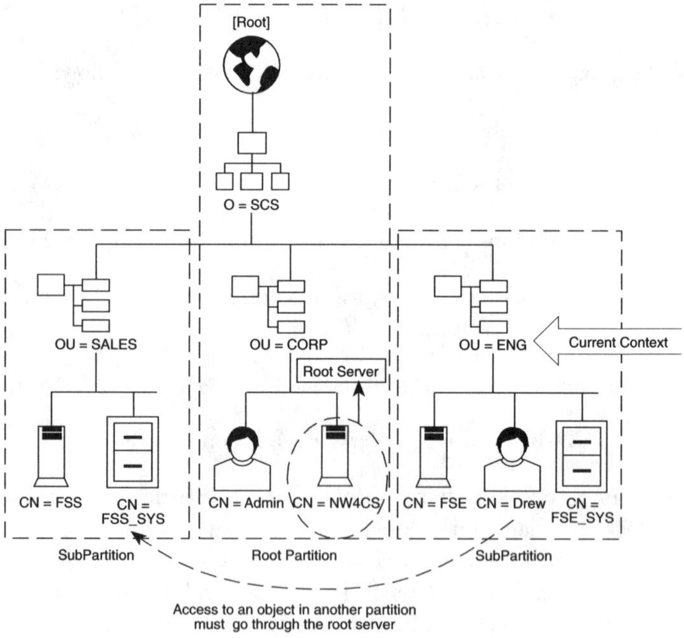

Figure 3.1
Accessing objects in other subpartitions.

Software Requirements for NetWare 4.x

The software requirements for NetWare 4.x include DOS for the initial loading of the server software. The versions of DOS that are supported are DOS 3.1 and higher for a standard Intel platform with an *Industry Standard Architecture* (ISA) or *Enhanced Industry Standard*

Architecture (EISA) bus. *Micro Channel Adapter* (MCA) or *Peripheral Component Interconnect* (PCI) computers must use DOS 3.3 or higher. In most cases you will also need to get the DOS drivers for the CD-ROM drive in the computer. Most CD-ROM manufacturers have DOS drivers they can send to you or can be downloaded from a bulletin board or the Internet.

Tip

> If you plan to install many NetWare servers, you might want to get a generic CD-ROM driver that will work for a large variety of CD-ROM drives.

The other requirement is the NetWare 4.x software and license disk. A registration disk (different from the license disk) is also included, for copying registration information on the installed NetWare 4.x software. To register, send the completed registration disk to Novell. Registration is recommended, but not required.

NetWare 4.x requires DOS for initial loading of the server:

- ISA/EISA bus servers need DOS version 3.1 or higher
- MCA/PCI bus servers need DOS version 3.3 or higher

The NetWare 4.x software comes on CD-ROM, but you can get it on floppy disks. NetWare 4.0 used 36 high-density disks, 25 for the operating system and client, 9 for documentation, 1 for the server license, and 1 for registration. Since then, each version of NetWare has grown larger than its predecessor. If you ordered IntranetWare on floppy diskette from Novell, it would require about 250 high-density diskettes per language to include every product that ships on the four CDs in the IntranetWare box.

If you are installing NetWare 4.x from across the network, you need to have the client software installed on the new server to enable the computer to make a client connection to the existing server.

The hardware and software requirements are shown in figures 3.2 and 3.3.

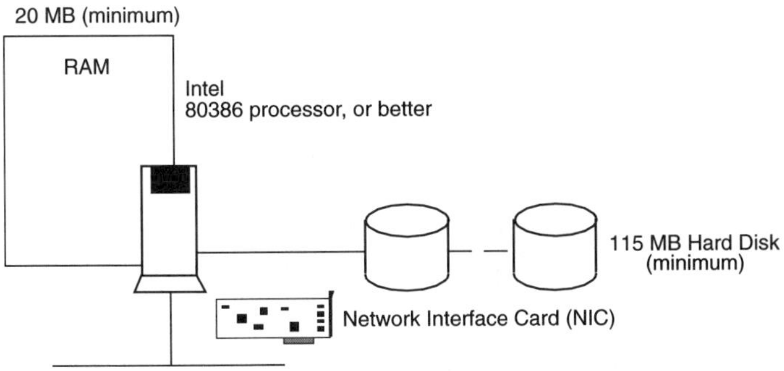

Figure 3.2
The hardware requirements for NetWare 4.x.

Figure 3.3
The software requirements for NetWare 4.x.

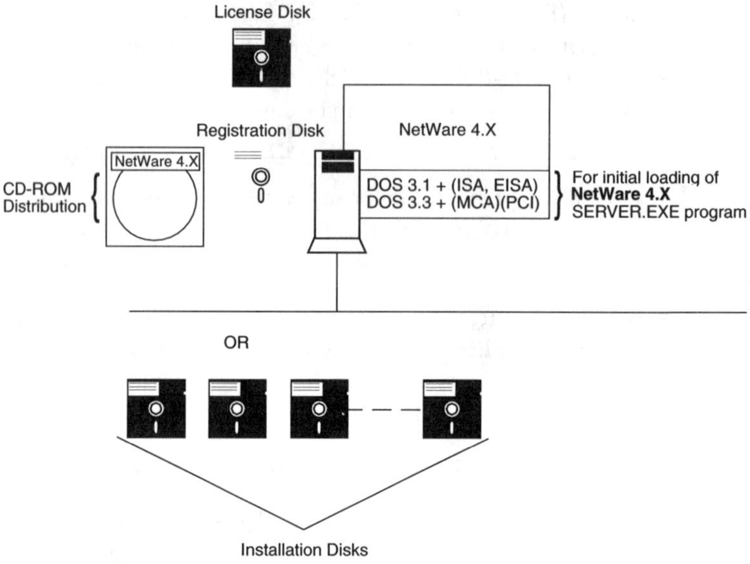

Computing Server Memory Requirements

NetWare documentation contains two ways of computing memory requirements. The first method is documented in the *NetWare Application Notes*, April 1993, and in the *NetWare 4 Installation* manual. The second method is also documented in the *NetWare 4 Installation* manual. The first method is a simplified formula, and the second method is more detailed. This section presents both methods.

Simplified Method for Estimating Server Memory Requirements

You can estimate NetWare 4.x server memory requirements based on the following factors:

1. Disk space supported on the NetWare server.

   Amount of server RAM needed equals 0.008 times the disk space in megabytes.

2. Number of files that have a name space entry other than DOS name space.

   If you add, for instance, the Long, Macintosh, NFS, or FTAM name space to a volume, NDS adds additional directory entries, which contain the filename and attributes for that name space, to the directory entry table.

   Amount of server RAM needed is 20/1048576 multiplied by the number of files that have an additional name space entry and the number of additional name spaces.

   DOS name space, which is the default name space, is not used in the above calculations.

3. Cache memory needed for increased server performance.

   Allocating server RAM for caching can have a dramatic effect in improving server performance.

   In general, a cache size of at least 1 MB should be added, but 4 MB or more will greatly enhance server performance.

4. Memory used by the operating system software.

   Allocate 20 MB to 24 MB for loading the NetWare operating system, directory services, LAN and disk drivers, and the INSTALL.NLM.

5. Memory for CLIB or BTRIEVE.NLM.

   If you are running an application that uses CLIB or BTRIEVE.NLM, you need to add 2 MB to the server RAM. An example of an application that needs these NLMs is PSERVER.NLM (implements printer server on the NetWare server).

6. Any additional NLMs that you want to run on the server.

   Add an estimated memory requirement for these NLMs.

   You can use the preceding factors to arrive at an equation that estimates server RAM. The following equation takes into account the six factors listed previously:

   $E = D \times 0.008 + F \times N \times 20/1048576 + C + S + 2 \times A + O$

   E = Estimated server RAM in megabytes

   D = Disk space in megabytes

   F = Number of files that will be stored on volumes with LONG.NAM or other name spaces. The DOS name space is not included in this calculation.

   N = Number of additional name spaces per file. (LONG, FTAM, etc.) Do not include DOS name space in the calculation.

   C = Cache size (1 MB Minimum, 4 MB or more is better)

   S = Minimum memory required for server. 20 MB as stated in the Novell Installation Manual.

   A = 1 if an application uses CLIB or BTRIEVE.NLM; 0 otherwise

   O = Estimated memory for other NLMs you will load on the server.

The following hypothetical scenario might help clarify use of the preceding equation.

SCS has decided to install a NetWare 4.x server on an Intel Pentium 133 MHz computer that has a 2048 MB (2 GB) hard disk. They plan to run NetWare for Macintosh on the server, so the server must be able to support the Macintosh name space in addition to the default DOS name space. The server volume will hold an estimated 1,500 files. SCS also uses the NetWare server as a print server, but does not run any other application servers. SCS has decided to use 2 MB for caching for improved server performance.

The preceding example's parameters are as follows:

D = Disk space in megabytes = 2048

F = Number of files that have a name space = 1500

N = Number of name spaces per file = 1

C = Cache size = 2

S = Memory needed for server = 20

A = 1 if an application uses CLIB or BTRIEVE.NLM = 1

O = Memory for other NLMs loaded on the server = 0

You can use the following formula to estimate NetWare 4.x server memory requirements. Using the preceding parameters in the equation for estimated server RAM:

$$E = D\times0.008 + F\times N\times20/1048576 + C + S + 2\times A + O$$

$$= 2048\times0.008 + 1500\times1\times20/1048576 + 2 + 20 + 2\times1 + 0$$

$$= 16.4 + 0.028 + 2 + 20 + 2 + 0$$

$$= 40.428 \text{ MB}$$

A server RAM of 41 MB, accordingly, should meet the preceding needs.

Detailed Method for Estimating Server Memory Requirements

You also can use the following detailed factors to estimate NetWare 4.x server memory requirements:

1. Core operating system requirement is 20 MB.

2. Cache memory needed for increased server performance:

   1 MB + (D×5) KB

   in which D = online disk space in MB.

Allocating server RAM for caching can have a dramatic effect in improving server performance.

This formula is based on the assumption that the number of users accessing the server increase with disk space. It is designed to give reasonable performance per user.

3. Memory used by the media manager:

   150 KB + (0.2×D) KB

   in which D = online disk space in MB.

4. Memory for connection in use:

   (2×U) KB

   in which U = number of user connections.

   If the server is already installed, you can use the MONITOR.NLM to get a more accurate value.

   The 2 KB per user is used for holding connection state information for the user.

5. Memory for packet receive buffers:

   (2.3×R) KB

   in which R = number of packet receive buffers.

   If the server is already installed, you can use the MONITOR.NLM to get a more accurate value.

6. Memory for directory cache buffers:

   (4.3×Db) KB

   in which Db = number of directory cache buffers.

   If the server is already installed, you can use the MONITOR.NLM to get a more accurate value.

7. Memory for service processes:

   (9×P) KB

   in which P = number of service processes.

   If the server is already installed, you can use the MONITOR.NLM to get a more accurate value.

8. Memory needed to support file compression, if it is enabled on any volume:

   250 KB

9. Volume requirements:

   a. File Allocation Table:

      (8.2×Vb) Bytes

      in which Vb = Volume Blocks.

      Volume Blocks can be computed by dividing the size of a volume by the block size in use for that volume. Thus:

      Vb = V / B in which V = Volume size and B = Block size.

   b. Block suballocation (if enabled):

      ((B×2 –1) ′ 4096 + 5×Nf) bytes

      in which B = Block size

      Nf = Number of files and Nf can be estimated by dividing the volume size by average file size.

   c. Directory Entry Tables:

      10×Nf bytes

      in which Nf = Number of files.

      10 NLM Requirements.

      Add up all the NLMs that are needed at the server. The following table can be used to estimate memory requirements for some common NLMs.

      If the server is already installed, you can use the MONITOR.NLM to get a more accurate estimate for memory used by NLMs.

NLM	Function	RAM Usage
BTRIEVE.NLM	Needed by database and NetWare NFS, NetWare for Macintosh	700 KB managers
CLIB.NLM	Needed by PSERVER.NLM and other NLMs	500 KB

NLM	Function	RAM Usage
INSTALL.NLM	For installation and maintenance	600 KB
PSERVER.NLM	Implements the print	200 KB server

Using the preceding factors, you can come up with an equation for estimating server RAM. The following equation takes into account the nine factors listed previously:

$$E = S + (1\ MB + (D\times5)\ KB) + (150\ KB + (0.2\times D)\ KB) + (2\times U)\ KB$$
$$+ (2.3\times R)\ KB + (4.3\times Db)\ KB + (9\times P)\ KB + 250\times Fc\ KB$$
$$+ (8.2\times Vb) + ((B\times2-1)\times4096 + 5\times Nf) + 10\times Nf$$
$$+ O$$

E = Estimated Server RAM in megabytes

S = Core operating system requirements = 20 MB

D = Online disk space in MB

U = Number of user connections

R = Number of packet receive buffers

Db= Number of directory cache buffers

P = Number of service processes

Fc = 1 if file compression enabled on a volume; 0, otherwise

Vb = Volume Blocks

B = Block size

Nf = Number of files

O = Memory for other NLMs loaded on the server

The same example applies to the detailed memory estimation.

SCS has decided to install a NetWare 4.x server on an Intel Pentium 133 MHz computer that has a 2000 MB hard disk. The server volume contains an estimated 1,500 files and file compression on the volume is enabled. SCS also uses the NetWare server as a print server, but does not run any other application servers. The server has an estimated 50 users. Assume that the media manager is active, the number of packet receive buffers is 50, directory cache buffers is 50, and number of service processes is 10.

The parameters for this example follow:

S = Core operating system requirements = 20 MB

D = Online disk space in MB = 2000

U = Number of user connections = 50

R = Number of packet receive buffers = 50 (assumption)

Db= Number of directory cache buffers = 50 (assumption)

P = Number of service processes = 10 (assumption)

Fc = 1

Vb = Volume Blocks = 2000 MB / 4 KB = 500,000

B = Block size = 4 KB

Nf = Number of files = 1,500

O = Memory for other NLMs loaded on the server = 200 KB (from table of NLM memory usage)

You can use the following formula to estimate NetWare 4.x server memory requirements. Using the preceding parameters in the equation for estimated server RAM:

$$
\begin{aligned}
E &= S + (1\text{ MB} + (D\times 5)\text{ KB}) + (150\text{ KB} + (0.2\times D)\text{ KB}) + (2\times U)\text{ KB} \\
&\quad + (2.3\times R)\text{ KB} + (4.3\times Db)\text{ KB} + (9\times P)\text{ KB} + 250\times Fc\text{ KB} \\
&\quad + (8.2\times Vb) + ((B\times 2-1)\times 4096 + 5\times Nf) + 10\times Nf \\
&\quad + O \\
&= 20\text{ MB} + (1\text{ MB} + 2000\times 5\text{ KB}) + (150\text{ KB} + 0.2\times 2000\text{ KB}) + 2\times 50\text{ KB} \\
&\quad + 2.3\times 50\text{ KB} + 4.3\times 50\text{ KB} + 9\times 10\text{ KB} + 250\times 1\text{ KB} \\
&\quad + 8.2\times 500000 + ((4\times 2-1)\times 4096 + 5\times 1500) + 10\times 1500 \\
&\quad + 200\text{ KB}
\end{aligned}
$$

= 20 MB + 11 MB + 550 KB + 100 KB

+ 115 KB + 215 KB + 90 KB + 250 KB

+ 4100000 B + 28672 B + 7500 B + 15000 B

+ 200 KB

= 31.65 MB

+ 0.65 MB

+ 3.95 MB (assuming 1024 KB=1 MB and 1024 bytes =1 KB)

+ 0.2 MB

= 36.44 MB

Therefore, a server RAM of 40 MB or more should meet the preceding needs and leave plenty of space for normal file caching needs.

Computing Server Disk Requirements

A NetWare 4.x server needs DOS before you can load its SERVER.EXE program. You can load DOS from a floppy disk or from a DOS partition on the server disk. Launching NetWare 4.x from a DOS partition on the server disk is much more convenient and faster, so you should plan to have at least a 15 MB partition to store SERVER.EXE, STARTUP.NCF, Disk drivers, Name Space NLMs, DOS system files, and COMMAND.COM, as well as other useful utilities (VREPAIR.NLM, and so on).

Typical disk space requirements for NetWare 4.x are represented in figure 3.4 and described in the following table:

NetWare utilities (SYS:PUBLIC)	=	35	MB	(24%)
System files and programs (SYS:SYSTEM)	=	35	MB	(24%)
Login utilities (SYS:LOGIN)	=	2	MB	(2%)
Online help & Viewer	=	60	MB	(40%)
DOS/Windows Client software	=	15	MB	(10%)
Total	=	147	MB	(100%)

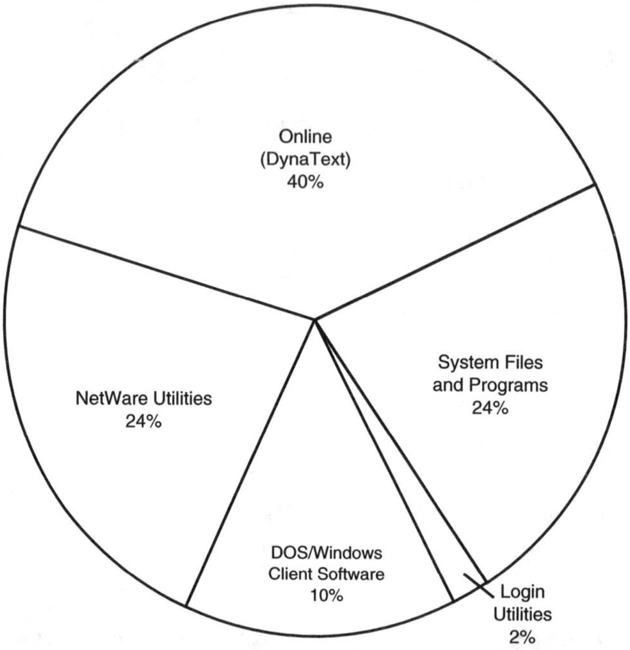

Figure 3.4
Typical NetWare 4.x. disk space requirements.

If you use OS/2 workstations, you should add another 9 MB for the OS/2 client installation and software programs.

The On-line help takes up the largest amount of disk space (40 percent).

These figures are for NetWare 4.x configured for English language support. You can expect disk space requirements to increase as additional language modules are installed.

To save disk space in a multiple server network, install NetWare documentation on a single server. However, if all users on the network access this single server for online documentation, you might need to change to a larger user license version of NetWare 4.x. You might want to split the documentation between two servers to keep the server license cost down and increase availability of the documentation when one of the documentation servers is down.

Determining the Installation Method

NetWare 4.x provides the installer with a number of choices for performing server installation. You can install from the following:

- CD-ROM attached to the server being installed
- CD-ROM mounted as a volume on an existing NetWare server

- Network drive
- Remote installation through Rconsole
- Floppy disks

The INSTALL program is generally the same, regardless of the preceding method that you use—the difference is in time and cost.

Table 3.2 shows rough estimates of the installation times. The figures are not exact because of the large number of variables that need to be considered in such an equation. For example, the installation time varies depending on which type of install you select—simple or custom. Install time also depends on network speeds, CD-ROM data transfer rate, and the fact that floppy disk installation requires close attention from the installer. Most of the time is spent copying the online documentation and the public utilities and files.

> **Note** The times listed in table 3.2 vary significantly from someone installing NetWare for the very first time and someone who has installed NetWare several times before.

Table 3.2
Estimated Installation Time

Network Installation Method	Installation Time (Minutes)
Network drive	30
CD-ROM	45
Rconsole	60
Floppy disk	120

The fastest method is to use a network drive (which assumes Ethernet speeds), but this implies that an already installed server is available. Also, before you can use the network drive method, you need to make sure the files on the NetWare 4.x operating system CD-ROM are copied on an existing server; if copying it is necessary, doing so is time-consuming.

Although the time estimate for the floppy-disk method is only three times as long as the CD-ROM method, you might want to take into account the annoyance factor of inserting hundreds of installation disks. The floppy count for IntranetWare is near 250 floppy diskettes.

Before you can install over the network, you must have a logical connection from the server machine to the network source that has a copy of the network operating system software (see fig. 3.5). You can establish such a connection by installing the network client software on the server machine being installed and making a network connection to the NetWare server that has a copy of the NetWare 4.x CD-ROM. Then you need to map a drive to the exact location of the root directory of the CD-ROM image. Figure 3.5 shows that you use the network drive F to access the NetWare 4.x CD-ROM image. You can use any network driver other than F for this purpose as well. The operating system software can reside on a server disk or on a CD-ROM. Before you can read the CD-ROM, you must have a CD-ROM reader that can read ISO 9660 formatted CD-ROM discs.

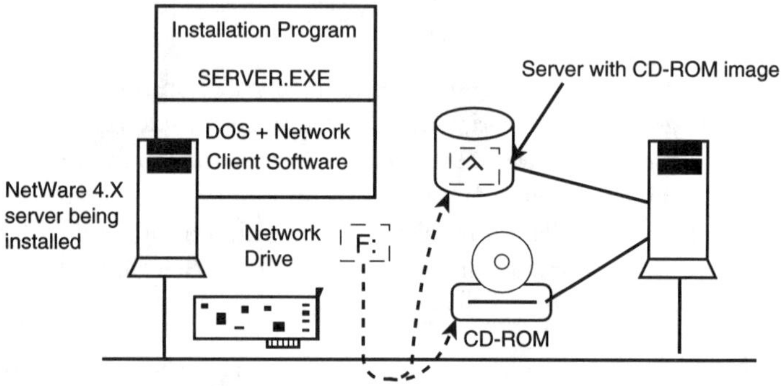

Figure 3.5
Installing over a network.

Do not use memory managers such as HIMEM, 386MAX, or QEMM on the server being installed because they conflict with NetWare's use of the server's extended memory.

When you use the network method to install, there is a potential problem with the network card. To start the installation process you load the DOS LAN driver as part of the client software. This allows you to connect to a server to gain access to the CD-ROM image. The problem arises when the NetWare installation tries to load the network driver for the network card that has the DOS driver currently loaded. Novell resolved this problem for most network cards by allowing a server-to-server connection during the install. You will notice this when the install asks for the user name and password to authenticate to the source server with the CD-ROM image. At this point the install has loaded the network driver and is ready to continue after the the user has authenticated to the source server. It is common during a network drive installation to complete the install without any problems, at which time the new server is brought down to reboot. It is then that the network LAN driver is unloaded and the computer looks for the DOS driver to bring the computer back to its known state before starting the NetWare install. Since the computer will not be able to find the DOS driver, it will not return to the DOS prompt. This will make you think your computer has quit working because it will never return to the DOS prompt. When this happens, do not be concerned. Just turn the computer off and then back on to restart NetWare.

NetWare 4.x Installation

This section reviews the installation procedure and then presents you with the details of performing the installation. Figure 3.6 shows an overview of the NetWare 4.x installation.

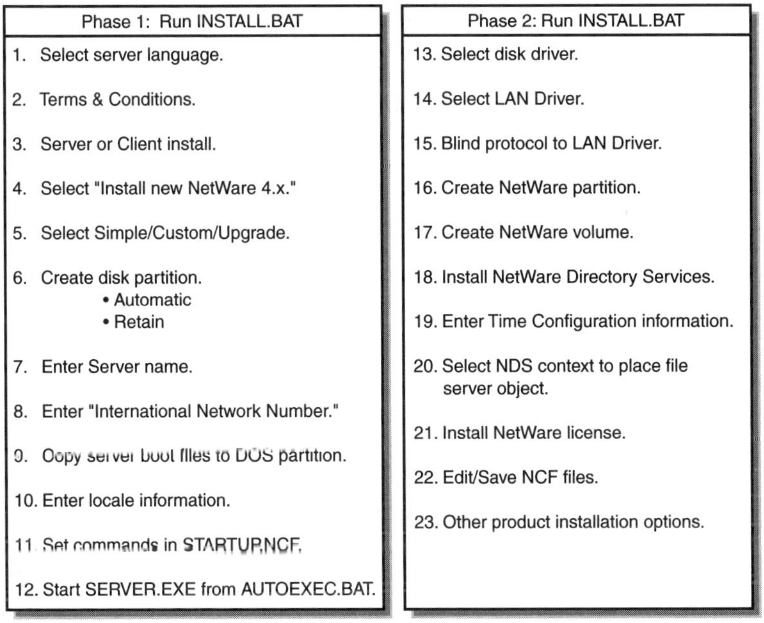
Phase 1: Run INSTALL.BAT
1. Select server language.
2. Terms & Conditions.
3. Server or Client install.
4. Select "Install new NetWare 4.x."
5. Select Simple/Custom/Upgrade.
6. Create disk partition.
• Automatic
• Retain
7. Enter Server name.
8. Enter "International Network Number."
9. Copy server boot files to DOS partition.
10. Enter locale information.
11. Set commands in STARTUP.NCF.
12. Start SERVER.EXE from AUTOEXEC.BAT.
Phase 2: Run INSTALL.BAT
13. Select disk driver.
14. Select LAN Driver.
15. Blind protocol to LAN Driver.
16. Create NetWare partition.
17. Create NetWare volume.
18. Install NetWare Directory Services.
19. Enter Time Configuration information.
20. Select NDS context to place file server object.
21. Install NetWare license.
22. Edit/Save NCF files.
23. Other product installation options.

Figure 3.6
An overview of a NetWare 4.x installation.

The following steps comprise a guided tour of the NetWare 4.x installation.

1. If you use the floppy disk method, you use the INSTALL disk to boot.

   If you use the CD-ROM method, you can run INSTALL from the root directory on your CD-ROM device.

   The CD-ROM must be recognizable by DOS, meaning you must load all the essential drivers to recognize the CD-ROM device. Because each CD-ROM manufacturer has a different set of installation procedures and CD-ROM drivers, you should follow their individual instructions.

   CD-ROM installation users should follow these steps:

   a. Change your directory to the CD-ROM drive.

   b. From the root, run the INSTALL.BAT program.

2. Select the language that you want to be installed and configured for the NetWare 4.x server.

3. The Novell terms and conditions is displayed on the screen. Read through this while pressing "any key" to continue.

4. Select the type of installation desired from the following options list:

- NetWare Server Installation

  Select NetWare Server Installation to install one of the following NetWare 4.x products:

  - NetWare 4.11
  - NetWare 4.11 SFT III

- Client Installation

  Selecting the Client Installation option allows you to install one of the following client products offered by Novell:

  - Client 32 for Windows 95
  - Client 32 for DOS/Windows 3.1x
  - NetWare Client for OS/2
  - NetWare DOS/Windows Client (VLM)
  - NetWare DOS/Windows Client (VLM) for IP

- Diskette Creation

  This option allows you to create diskettes for any of the following Novell products:

  - NetWare Client 32 for Windows 95
  - NetWare Client 32 for DOS and Windows 3.1x
  - NetWare Administration Utility for Client 32
  - NetWare Client for OS/2
  - NetWare DOS/WINDOWS Client (VLM)
  - NetWare DOS/WINDOWS Client (VLM) for IP
  - NetWare for Macintosh (DOS format)
  - NetWare Migration Utility

- Readme Files

  This option will allow you to view the README for one of the following Novell products:

  - ENGLISH Global Readme
  - NetWare 4.11 Readme
  - Application Launcher v1.00
  - Client 32 for DOS and Windows 3.1x
  - Client 32 for Windows 95
  - NetWare/IP 2.2
  - OS/2 Client 2.12
  - VLM Client
  - Web Server 2.51
  - Upgrade Preparation for NetWare 4.0x
  - Upgrade Preparation for NetWare 4.10
  - Installing NetWare Server on Windows 95

  The remaining steps in this section assume that you select NetWare Server Installation from this menu.

5. You should see a screen that has the following options:

   - NetWare 4.11
   - NetWare 4.11 SFT III
   - Display Information (README) File

   Browse through the README files (select the Display Information (README) File option) for tips on resolving installation problems.

6. Select the NetWare 4.11 option to install a new NetWare 4.x server.

   You have the following choices:

   - Simple Installation of NetWare 4.11
   - Custom Installation of NetWare 4.11
   - Upgrade NetWare 3.1x or 4.x

The Simple Installation option allows the installation program to make most of the choices. It assumes the following:

- An existing DOS partition on the server of at least 15 MB with DOS already installed on the partition.
- The server boots from the DOS partition, not a floppy disk.
- All remaining free disk space not used for the DOS partition is used for a NetWare partition.
- Each disk can have only one NetWare volume.
- IPX numbers are randomly generated.
- No changes are made to STARTUP.NCF or AUTOEXEC.NCF file.
- A U.S. keyboard mapping.
- The NDS tree has a single container for all objects.
- Only the IPX protocol will be installed initially.

If the previously stated assumptions are not true, you must select the Custom Installation option.

If you select the Upgrade NetWare 3.1x or 4.x option, back up your data before you upgrade, even if no existing data files are deleted.

The Simple Installation is a subset of the Custom Installation. Therefore, the remainder of the installation procedure describes the custom installation procedure.

7. Select the Custom Installation. You are prompted for the server name.

   Enter a server name, which can be from 2–47 characters and include alphanumeric characters (A–Z, 0–9), hyphens, and underscores. You cannot use a period as the first character.

   After installation, the server name is saved in the AUTOEXEC.NCF file. When the SERVER.EXE program loads during normal startup of the NetWare server, the server name is read from this file.

8. You are prompted for an Internal network number (see fig 3.7). The installation program generates a random number. You can select this internal network number because it is not likely to conflict with an existing internal network number, or you can select your own unique internal network number. Your internal network number can use any combination of hexadecimal numbers 0–9 and letters A–F. It can range from 1–8 digits long with two exceptions. It cannot be 0 or FFFFFFFF.

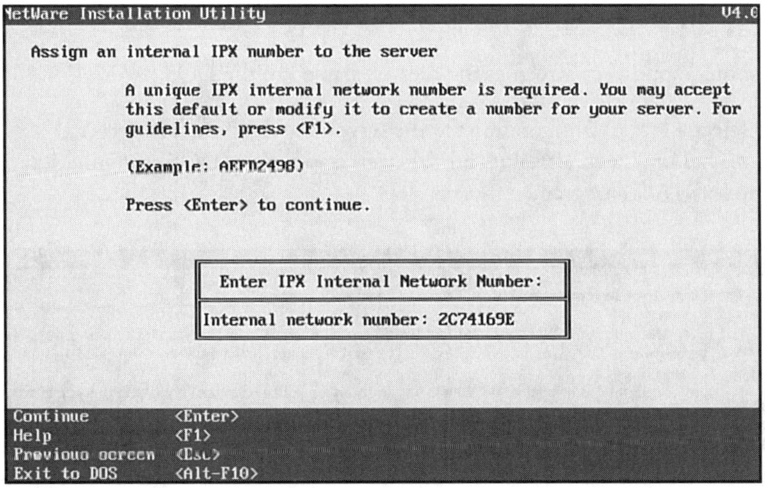

Figure 3.7
NetWare 4.x Installation: Internal Network Number.

You should select your own internal network number according to your own scheme, or use Novell's IPX Registry. Novell is creating an IPX number registry in which you can reserve a range of network numbers to allow the creation of a global IPX network, similar to the existing Internet (global network based primarily on TCP/IP).

Internal network numbers must be different from other internal network numbers and the network numbers used to identify the cable segments.

The internal network number is a logical network that uniquely identifies the NCP (NetWare Core Protocol) processing engine at the heart of the NetWare server. Novell introduced internal network numbers in NetWare 3.0 to solve routing anomalies common in NetWare 2.x networks, in which the NCP processing engine had a network number that matched that of the network installed on LAN_A (the first network adapter on the server).

9. You must now copy the server boot files to the DOS partition. If you do not have a DOS partition yet, the installation program guides you through creating one.

   You are asked to verify the source and destination paths for copying the server boot files. Use F2 to change the source path; use F4 to change the destination path.

   The default source path is the drive from which you initiated the server install. Normally, you should not have to change the source path to a different location.

   The default destination is C:\NWSERVER, and unless you have your own standard for where you copy the server files, you should accept it.

   This initial copy puts the files needed to complete the installation process into the C:\NWSERVER directory on the DOS partition. These files include SERVER.EXE, drivers for disk and network cards, message and help files, and other important NLMs that are loaded during the install process.

10. Press Enter to verify the source and destination paths.

    A status display should appear on-screen as the files are copied to the DOS partition.

11. You are asked to select a locale configuration for the server (see fig. 3.8). The server's configuration appears, but its default values are taken from whatever DOS configuration you use to run the INSTALL program.

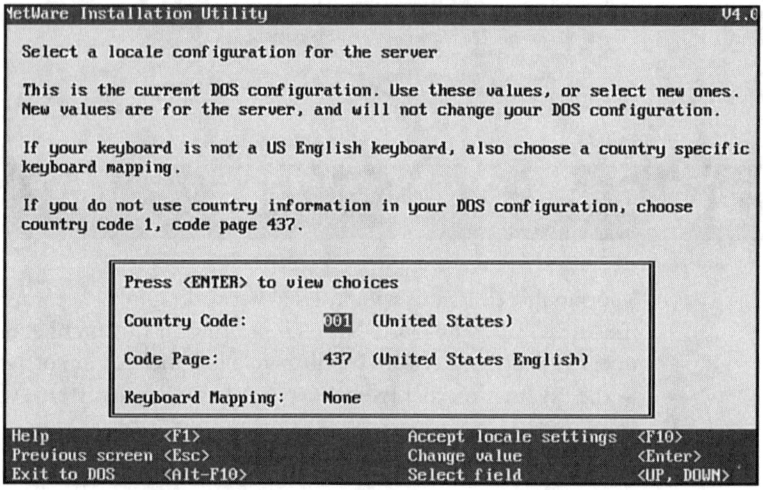
NetWare Installation Utility
V4.0
Select a locale configuration for the server
This is the current DOS configuration. Use these values, or select new ones. New values are for the server, and will not change your DOS configuration.
If your keyboard is not a US English keyboard, also choose a country specific keyboard mapping.
If you do not use country information in your DOS configuration, choose country code 1, code page 437.
Press <ENTER> to view choices
Country Code: 001 (United States)
Code Page: 437 (United States English)
Keyboard Mapping: None
Help <F1>
Previous screen <Esc>
Exit to DOS <Alt-F10>
Accept locale settings <F10>
Change value <Enter>
Select field <UP, DOWN>

Figure 3.8
NetWare 4.x: locale information.

Previous versions of NetWare did not support country-specific conventions, such as differences in keyboard layout. NetWare 4.x supports internationalization and allows other keyboard layouts. The fields in figure 3.8 have the following meanings:

- **Country Code.** Three-digit country code. Consult the COUNTRY.SYS entry in your DOS manual for the applicable country code. The U.S. country code is 001. There are 25 different country codes to choose from.

- **Code Page.** Country-dependent three-digit page code. For U.S. English, the code page value is 437. This defines the character sets that are used for screen display.

- **Keyboard Mapping.** Supports keyboard layout differences specific to a language. The Keyboard Mapping values supported are Belgium, Brazil, Canadian French, Denmark, France, Germany, Italy, Japan, Latin America, Netherlands, Norway, Portugal, Russia, Spain, Sweden, Swiss French, Swiss German, United Kingdom, United States, and U.S. International.

To change any of the locale values, use the arrow keys to highlight the field and press Enter to see the list of supported values. Highlight the desired value and press Enter to select it. This also returns you to the main locale configuration screen. After you make all desired changes, highlight continue and press Enter to accept locale changes.

12. You are asked if you want to specify any special startup SET commands.

    Several SET commands can be placed only in the STARTUP.NCF file. The STARTUP.NCF file resides on the DOS partition and in the directory where SERVER.EXE program was copied. It contains commands to load disk drivers and name spaces, and special commands, such as SET AUTO REGISTER MEMORY ABOVE 16 MEGABYTES=OFF. (Set to ON to automatically add memory above 16 MB for EISA bus server machines.) In NetWare 4.02 and higher, set Reserved Buffers below 16 MB to 200 if the server has devices that use the ASPI interface.

    Select Yes only if your server configuration demands that you set special parameters in the STARTUP.NCF file. Otherwise, select No. You can always edit the STARTUP.NCF file later.

13. You are asked if you want AUTOEXEC.BAT to load SERVER.EXE. If you answer Yes, your AUTOEXEC.BAT is modified to contain the following commands to start the server automatically every time the machine is booted:

    ```
    REM The following lines were created by the _server installation program.
    REM They will cause the server to come up _whenever this computer is booted.
    :BEGIN_SERVER
    C:
    cd C:\NWSERVER
    SERVER
    :END_SERVER
    ```

    If you select No, you must manually start the SERVER.EXE program each time you boot your computer.

    Select No, which is the default. If you are having problems with your server, you cannot reboot the computer and get back to the DOS prompt without using a boot floppy or pressing <Ctrl Break> to cancel out of the AUTOEXEC.BAT process. It is an inconvenience that can be very annoying if you are trying to troubleshoot your hardware. It is a lot easier to manually change to the C:\NWSERVER directory and type server each time you want to load NetWare.

Tip

> If you want to automate the loading of NetWare from your AUTOEXEC.BAT file you can use common IF/THEN logic and query the user at boot time as to if they want to load NetWare. If they respond with a Yes, then execute a batch file created just for that purpose. Then, if the user is trying to troubleshoot the hardware, they can simply respond with a No and not automatically load server each time.

14. If you selected Yes to have the install program add SERVER.EXE to the AUTOEXEC.BAT file, you are asked to verify the location of the AUTOEXEC.BAT file.

15. The SERVER.EXE program loads at this point.

16. NetWare 4.11 includes a new feature that will detect the presence of a multiprocessor computer. If your server is a uniprocessor computer, the install will continue with the next step. If it is a multiprocessor computer, the install will prompt you with the following question:

```
Do you want to install Symmetrical Multi-processing NetWare (SMP)?
```

Enter Yes or No.

If you enter No, you can install SMP later by using the maintenance mode of INSTALL.NLM. Entering Yes adds the following SET command to your AUTOEXEC.NCF file:

```
Set upgrade low priority threads = ON
```

A Yes response also attempts to find the *Platform Support Module* (PSM) files to load. If found, the PSM drivers are displayed in a list for the user to choose from. When the PSM is selected, the install adds the following lines to the STARTUP.NCF and then continues:

```
Load [name of your Platform Support Module (PSM)] (All PSM's will have a .PSM
➥extension.)
Load SMP.NLM
Load MPDRIVER.NLM ALL
```

17. NetWare 4.11 includes a new feature that will autodetect the hardware in the server and load the corresponding drivers for hard disk, CD-ROM drives, or LAN cards, etc. You are presented with information that NetWare is scanning for available drivers.

This feature is supported by computers with advanced bus architectures (PCI, EISA, MCA, PnP ISA). If your server doesn't have an advanced bus architecture, the install will not autodetect the devices; instead, it will present the complete list of disk and network drivers from which to choose.

If the server has an advanced bus architecture, the install will first detect the disk devices and then the network devices. After the devices are detected, the install will attempt to match the devices with a driver. If the matching driver ships with NetWare, the install will display the driver that matches the detected device and only ask the user for confirmation before loading the driver. Occasionally, more than one driver will work for a device. In this case, the install will show only the list of drivers that match or support the detected hardware, and you are expected to choose the driver from the abbreviated driver list. If the supporting driver does not ship with NetWare the complete list of drivers will be displayed for a manual selection. For a detailed explanation of the detection see the section "NetWare Bus Interface" later in this chapter.

a. When install matches the device and driver, it will go directly to the Summary screen and prompt to continue the installation. Press Enter to continue.

b. If multiple drivers are matched with the detected device the install will present only the drivers found that will work with the disk device found in the computer. Highlight the desired driver and press Enter to go to the summary screen. Then press Enter to continue the installation.

c. If the detection does not match a driver with the device the install will present the complete list of shipping disk drivers. Select the disk driver that matches the server disk controller. If the driver you want to use is not listed, press Ins to load the disk driver from a distribution media, probably a floppy disk in the A drive.

You are presented with a screen for selecting the parameter settings for your disk controller, which includes Port value, Interrupt number, DMA value, ABOVE16 (Y for Yes, N for No), and so on.

Make any corrections and verify that the parameter settings match disk controller settings.

To save changes and continue the installation, select the Save parameters and continue option. Follow these instructions to load additional disk drivers and continue the installation.

If the detection does not match a driver with the network device the install will present the complete list of shipping network drivers. Select the network driver that matches the server network card. If the driver you want to use is not listed, press Ins to load the disk driver from a distribution media.

A default set of parameter values for your driver will appear, which shows the following:

- Port value
- Memory address
- Interrupt number
- DMA value (if your NIC uses Direct Memory Access)
- Frame types

The port value, memory address, interrupt number, and DMA values should match the hardware settings on the network card. If not, you must change the default settings on the screen to match those of the network card by selecting Select/Modify driver parameters and protocols.

If the network card parameters match those on-screen, select Save parameters and continue. Repeat this procedure to add any additional drivers.

The frame type values supported are shown in table 3.3.

Table 3.3
Server Frame Types Supported

Frame	Frame Parameter Name	Default Logical Name	Description
IEEE 802.3	ETHERNET _802.3 _	*boardname* _1E_802.3	Novell's raw Ethernet frame type. Does not include an LLC (IEEE 802.2).
IEEE 802.2	ETHERNET 802.2 _	*boardname* _1E_802.2	Default frame type for NetWare 4.x. Essentially IEEE 802.3 frame with an LLC (IEEE 802.2) sublayer.
IEEE 802.3 with SNAP extension	ETHERNET _SNAP	*boardname* _1E_SNAP	Used for Appletalk networks. Essential-ly an IEEE 802.2 frame with an additional 3-octet Organization Unit Identifier(OUI) and a 2-byte Ether Type field.
Ethernet II	ETHERNET _II	*boardname* _1E_II	Ethernet II frame, which differs from IEEE 802.3. Main distinction is the presence of a 2-octet Ether Type field instead of a 2-octet length field (IEEE 802.3).
IEEE 802.5	TOKEN-RING	*boardname* 1T_RING	Standard IEEE 802.5 frame.
IEEE 802.5 with SNAP extension	TOKEN-RING _SNAP	*boardname* _1T_SNAP	Used for Appletalk networks. Essential-ly an IEEE 802.5 frame with an additional 3-octet Organizational Unit Identifier (OUI) and a 2-byte Ether Type field.

Frame	Frame Parameter Name	Default Logical Name	Description
ARCnet	RX-NET	*boardname* _RX-NET	There is only one frame type that is used with ARCnet.

For Token-Ring frames, you can specify a local address that overrides the *Media Access Control* (MAC) address of the Token-Ring that is on the board (each IEEE specification LAN board has a unique 6-octet address). Normally, you should not have to override this address, unless interacting with other networks (such as SNA networks).

The default order of Token-Ring frame transmission calls for the *Most Significant Bit* (MSB) to be transmitted first. Normally, you should not need to change this, unless the board vendor recommends it. To change this value to an *Least Significant Bit* (LSB) order, use the toggle key F4 on the highlighted frame in the Frame Type List. You can get to the Frame Type List by selecting the field Frame Types.

If you decide to change the bit order of address transmission, you also must specify that the order of node (MAC) address transmission is MSB or LSB. The default is MSB. You change the node address transmission order by selecting the value in the Node Address field.

You can change a frame's default logical name by highlighting it in the Frame Type List and using F3. Alternatively, you can edit the LOAD *BoardDriver* statement in the AUTOEXEC.NCF file after the installation.

For Ethernet, the default frame types loaded are ETHERNET_802.3 and ETHERNET_802.2. Although ETHERNET_802.2 is the default frame type for NetWare 4.x, the ETHERNET_802.3 frame type also is loaded for compatibility with existing NetWare 3.x clients.

For Token-Ring, the default frame type is TOKEN-RING.

18. NetWare 4.11 includes a new feature that will autodetect the protocol information available on the network. After you press Enter to continue from the hardware device driver summary list, the install loads the drivers and starts to load and bind protocols and frame types. You are presented with several messages indicating that NetWare is loading Appletalk, IPX, etc. and scanning for network conflicts.

    For each protocol, the install loads all frame types and then sends out packets for each frame type. If there is a return from the packet, the install pulls out the address, and uses that information to know what to bind the driver to. On an existing network, only the protocols and frame types detected are bound to the network card.

Obviously, if the installation is the first server in the network, the install will not find anything to which to bind. In this case, the install will load and bind all 4 frame types for IPX, each with a random generated network address.

If you want to change the detected settings, highlight View/Modify Protocol Settings from the Protocol Selection summary screen and press Enter. You will then need to select which network driver you want to change the settings for and press Enter again. This takes you into the Driver Protocol Settings screen. You can use the arrow keys to choose which protocol and frame type you want to change, and then press Enter to toggle the selection on/off. When selecting a frame type, you are given the option to type in a specific address or have the install generate a random number. If the install has already detected an address for a given frame type, you are not allowed to type in a different address. When you are finished selecting the protocols and frame types press F10 or ESC to return to the summary screen and Continue with installation.

19. You are given a choice of creating disk partitions Manually or Automatically. Manually allows you to specify partition sizes, volume sizes, Hot Fix, and mirroring. Automatically allows you to create an unmirrored NetWare partition in the disk space available. Please note that Automatically destroys any existing data on a NetWare partition.
20. Choose Manually, and follow the directions on-screen to create your NetWare partition.

Note You can only have one NetWare partition per hard disk, but you can have up to eight volume segments per partition.

21. Choose the Create, delete, and modify disk partitions option.
22. Choose the device on which you want to create a partition.
23. Choose Create NetWare disk partition.
24. The disk partition information screen will then display the remainder of the free space to be used as the NetWare Partition. If you do not want to use all the free space, you can press Enter and change the size of the partition. When you are finished changing the partition size press F10 or ESC to save the partition information. A confirmation dialog then prompt you to Create NetWare Partition Yes/No. Choose Yes.
25. Use the Disk Partition Options screen to modify the Hot Fix size or redirection area.
26. Choose Return to previous menu.
27. Choose Continue with installation.
28. An informational dialog box tells you how much free space is available for new volumes. The dialog box also shows you the default volume names that have been given to each of the devices with free space. The first volume for all NetWare servers is called SYS. This is

a default name that is given and cannot be changed. After volume SYS, the default names start with VOL1 and are named consecutively VOL2, VOL3, etc. for each device found with a NetWare partition having free space. All volume names other than SYS can be changed. After reading the dialog, press Enter to continue.

29. After you create the NetWare partition, the Manage NetWare Volumes screen appears, showing a summary of all the proposed volume changes. The volume SYS is always the first volume created. It is created automatically on device 0, and must have a minimum size of 100 MB.

    You can modify the volume parameters (see fig. 3.9), and you can change all volume names, except the volume name SYS.

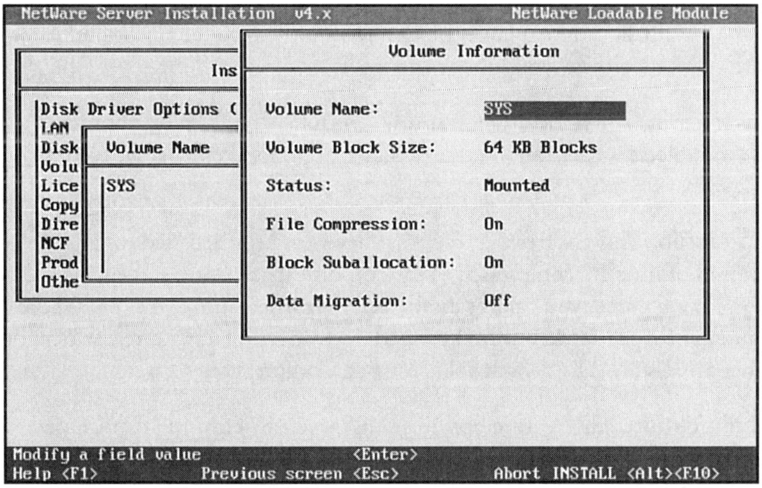

Figure 3.9
Volume Information.

Tip

> You can only modify File Compression and Block Suballocation when you initially create the volume. After the volume has been saved, you have to delete the volume and recreate it to change these settings.

Other parameters you can change on a volume are as follows:

a. **Volume Block Size.** You can set the volume block size to multiples of 4 KB, up to 64 KB (4 KB, 8 KB, 16 KB, 32 KB, 64 KB).

   The volume block size has a default value set according to the size of the volume. Table 3.4 shows the default volume size that is selected.

Table 3.4
Default Block Size versus Volume Size

Default Block Size (KB)	Volume Size (Range is in MB)
4	0 to 31
8	32 to 149
16	150 to 499
32	500 to 1,999
64	2,000 and above

Because of block suballocation, a larger block size is not wasted for small files. After you select the disk block size, you cannot change it.

Select a block size of 64 KB, because most disk controllers perform best at this block size. Also, block suballocation ensures that space is used efficiently, even for larger block sizes.

b. **File Compression.** This ensures that files that have not been accessed for a specified period of time are compressed to save on disk space. After you enable file compression for a volume, you cannot disable it. After installation, you can use the FLAG command (or the FILER utility) to mark individual files and directories with or without compression. The default value for File Compression is On.

c. **Block Suballocation.** This feature optimizes disk space by ensuring that unused fragments of disk blocks are not wasted. Actual disk space is used in 512-byte sizes. Left over space in a block is shared by other files. The default value for Block Suballocation is On.

d. **Data Migration.** This allows automatic movement of files to a near-line storage device, such as an optical jukebox. The default value for Data Migration is Off. Unless a *High-Capacity Storage System* (HCSS) is installed, leave Data Migration set to Off.

30. After you make volume changes, use F10 to save them, then continue the installation. A confirmation dialog asks if you want to Save Volume Changes Yes/No. Choose Yes.

    The volumes you create are mounted.

Note

If you are installing from CD-ROM you might notice that the CD-ROM is mounted automatically as a NetWare volume at the same time as the SYS volume. This will allow the install to continue reading from the CD-ROM.

31. A screen appears, informing you of the path from which NetWare files will be installed. If the path is incorrect, use F3 to change it. Press Enter to continue.

32. The NetWare server then searches the network for a directory tree. If it finds one or more trees, it displays the names of the directory trees. You can select one of the listed trees, or press Ins if you want to create a new tree.

    If this server cannot see any other networks, you are asked if you want to connect to an existing NetWare 4 network. If you choose to connect to an existing network, you can either have the install check again, or you can specify the network name and number to which you want to connect.

    If this is the first server on the network you must enter a name for the new directory tree.

    If you are installing on an existing network, make sure that your server is connected to the network. If you unintentionally create a new [Root] and directory tree, you must allocate time to use the DSMERGE tool to integrate it with an existing network.

    If you attempt to create a new tree when one already exists, a warning message appears, informing you of some of the consequences of your actions.

    New in NetWare 4.02, you can select either a simple NDS installation, or custom NDS installation. The simple NDS installation creates a single-level NDS tree that has a single organization container. In NetWare 4.11, the simple NDS installation is only available in the Simple Installation process. The custom NDS installation is the only option available during the Custom Installation process. If you are using the Simple Installation process you will use the simple NDS installation. Just follow the screen instructions. The remaining numbered instructions describe the custom NDS installation.

33. You are prompted to select a time zone. Selecting the correct time zone is important if you are going to connect to networks in other time zones.

34. You are presented with a form for entering time configuration information for the installed server:

    For *Time Server Type*, enter either a Single Reference Time Server, Reference Time Server, Primary Time Server, or Secondary Time Server. If you select the Single Reference Time Server, you cannot have a Primary Time Server or another Reference Time server. With Single Reference Time Server, only the Secondary Time Servers can exist.

Note

> A Single Reference server establishes the absolute time for all servers in the directory tree.
>
> A Primary server votes with other Primary servers and the Reference server to determin the time.
>
> A Secondary server gets its time from the nearest Primary or Reference server.

For *Standard time zone abbreviation*, enter the abbreviation code for your time zone. This string is for display purposes only. You can enter any value, but it is best to enter a value that is standard for your time zone. The important parameter to set for time zone offset is *Standard time offset from UTC*. The standard time zone abbreviation can also be changed in the AUTOEXEC.NCF file.

For Standard time offset from UTC, verify that the time-offset for your zone is correct. You can set the time-offset in the format *hh:mm:ss* (hours:minutes:seconds) behind or after UTC.

Many areas of the world have daylight savings time, but several others do not. NetWare 4.x offers the flexibility to change the daylight savings time criteria, or disable it altogether.

To enable daylight savings time, answer Yes to `Does your area have daylight savings time (DST)?`; otherwise (to disable), answer No.

The DST time zone abbreviation specifies a string for daylight savings time that is used for display purposes only. The daylight savings rules are set by the DST offset from standard time, DST Start, and DST End parameters. You also can change the DST time zone abbreviation in the AUTOEXEC.NCF file.

The DST offset from standard time is a parameter that represents the time difference between daylight savings time and standard time. This can have the value *hh:mm:ss* and can be set to be *ahead* or *behind* the standard time.

The DST Start and the DST End times indicate the start and end of daylight savings time. You can program the values for these parameters to be on a weekday of a specified month at a specific time, or on a specific day of the month at a specific time. For example, in the U.S.A., in areas that use daylight savings time, the daylight savings time commences at 2:00 a.m. on the first Sunday of the month of April and ends at 2:00 a.m. on the last Sunday of the month of October. If the laws change to a different daylight savings start and end, NetWare 4.x provides the flexibility to provide for these changes from the server console.

The time settings are recorded in the AUTOEXEC.NCF file. The listing that follows shows a sample AUTOEXEC.NCF file containing the time settings. The commands dealing with time settings have been highlighted.

```
set Time Zone = MST7MDT
set Daylight Savings Time Offset = 1:00:00
set Start Of Daylight Savings Time = (APRIL SUNDAY FIRST  2:00:00 AM)
set End Of Daylight Savings Time = (OCTOBER SUNDAY LAST 2:00:00 AM)
set Default Time Server Type = SINGLE
set Bindery Context = O=ESL
file server name FS1
ipx internal net 2C74169E
```

```
load SMC8000 mem=D0000 int=3 PORT=280 FRAME=Ethernet_802.3
➥NAME=SMC8000_1E_802.3
bind IPX to SMC8000_1E_802.3 net=255
load SMC8000 mem=D0000 int=3 PORT=280 FRAME=Ethernet_802.2  NAME=SMC8000
➥1E_802.2
bind IPX to SMC8000_1E_802.2 net=E8022
```

Press F10 to save changes in the time configuration information for the server. Verify that you want to save the time configuration.

35. You should see a screen that asks you to specify a context in which to place this server.

    In the Company or Organization field, enter the name for your primary organization. This should be a name that is readily recognizable by the users of the network. For instance, the company International Business Machines can simply use the abbreviation IBM for the organization name.

    You are given the option to specify three sub-organization units:

    Level 1 Sub-Organizational Unit (optional)

    Level 2 Sub-Organizational Unit (optional)

    Level 3 Sub-Organizational Unit (optional)

    The organizational unit levels are optional because a minimal NDS tree can consist of only the organization container. Before you create the context in which to place the newly installed server, you should consult your NDS tree design.

    After you install the server, you cannot use INSTALL.NLM to change the server context. If you want to change its context , you must use the NETADMIN or NetWare Administrator utilities.

    The server object is created during installation. INSTALL.NLM creates the server object for you but it cannot be used for general NDS management. You can use the NETADMIN and the NetWare Administrator utilities for managing the NDS tree.

    The first server installed in a container gets a Master replica of that partition if the container does not exist. Other servers installed in the same context receive a Read/Write replica of that partition. If the container that holds the server already exists, all servers installed in that container get a Read/Write replica of the partition holding the container. You can use the PARTMGR utility or the Partition Manager tool to modify these partitions further.

    As you enter the values for the organizational unit levels, the Server Context value changes to reflect the names of the organizational unit levels that you enter.

    If you want to place the server in a tree branch containing the country object, you can modify the server context fields by adding .c=xx at the end of the server context, in which *xx* is the two-letter country code.

The Administrator Name field describes the Common Name (CN) for the administrator of the network. It is set to Admin by default, and is placed in the organization container. You can rename, move, and even delete the Admin user object.

Tip

> If you are concerned about leaving a user named Admin available on the network, you should rename the user. Do not delete the Admin user object.

Before you delete the Admin user object, you must make sure that other user objects have Supervisor rights so that the NDS tree can be maintained.

When you design the directory tree, you must know the context of the Admin user, and decide on the initial Admin password.

The Password field is for the Admin user object password. Setting a password is a requirement for completing the installation. If you forget to enter a password and try to continue, the install will prompt you with a message telling you a valid password must be entered before you can continue. You can use the NETADMIN or NetWare Administrator Tool if you want to change the password for the Admin object.

Type the password for the Admin user object and press Enter. You will be prompted to Retype the password for verification. Retype the password and press Enter again.

You are then asked if you want to Save Directory Information and continue. Choose Yes and press Enter.

36. You will now see a message informing you that NDS services are being installed. Another message indicates that the NDS schema is being modified. This is to accommodate your organization and organizational unit entries.

    You are asked to note the following information:

    ```
    Directory tree name

    Directory context

    Administrator name
    ```

    The Directory Context is the NDS context in which the server was placed.

    Press Enter to continue.

37. Insert the NetWare License disk into the server floppy drive and press Enter. The default location is drive A. You can change the path to a different location by pressing F3.

38. The STARTUP.NCF file is displayed (see fig 3.10). This file includes the SMP drivers (PSM), disk drivers (DSK, HAM, CDM), some SET commands, and name space support. Edit this file as necessary and press F10 to save changes and continue.

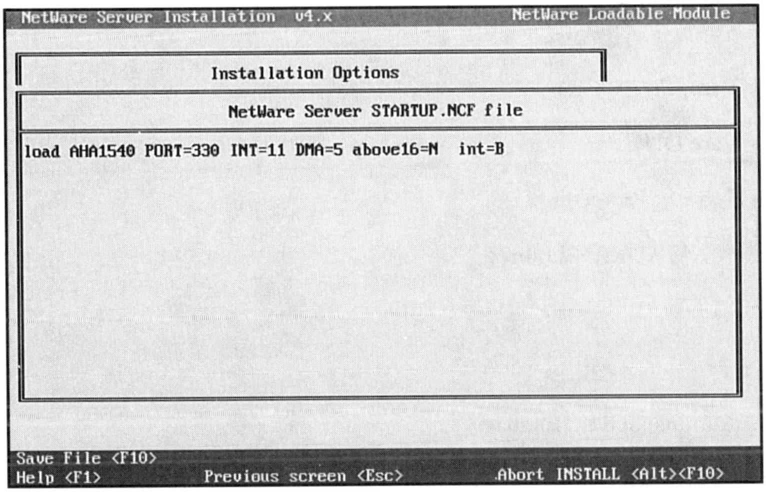

Figure 3.10
The STARTUP.NCF file displayed during INSTALL.

39. The AUTOEXEC.NCF file is displayed (see fig. 3.11). This file includes the commands you want to execute when the NetWare server is booted. Things like time synchronization, bindery context, server name, internal IPX number, SET commands, NLMs to load, and mounting volumes can be included in the AUTOEXEC.NCF. Edit this file as necessary and press F10 to save changes and continue.

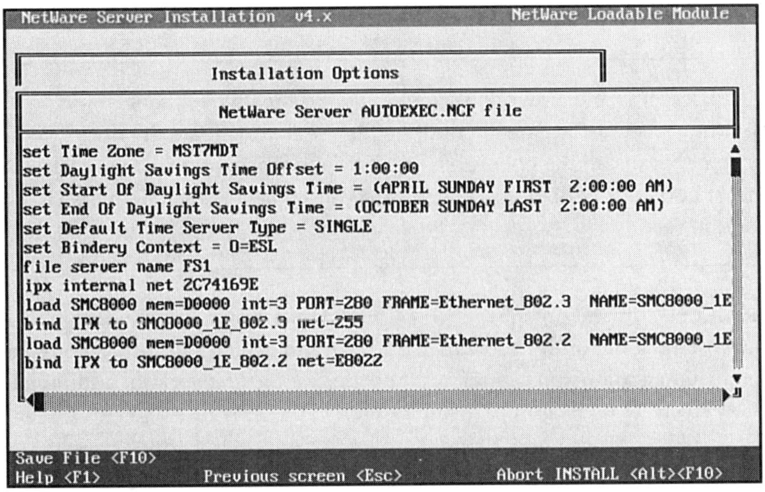

Figure 3.11
The AUTOEXEC.NCF file displayed during INSTALL.

40. You are presented with the Other Installation Options screen. The following options are available:

    - Create Client Installation Directories on Server
    - Make Diskettes
    - Install NetWare IP
    - Install NetWare DHCP
    - Configure Network Protocols
    - Install Legacy NWADMIN Utility
    - Install NetWare WEB Server v2.51
    - Upgrade v3.1x Print Services
    - Install an Additional Server Language
    - Change Server Language
    - Install NetWare for Macintosh
    - Install NetWare Client for Mac OS
    - Configure NetWare Licensing Service (NLS)

    To install one of the additional products select Choose and item or product listed above. Then, highlight the product you want to install and follow the prompts for each product.

Tip

> If this is the first server in the network, you will want to create the client directories on the server and create client diskettes. After you create the diskettes, you can either install the client software on each workstation, or you can create a generic boot disk with enough client software to access the client install directories on the server.

41. Choose Continue Installation and press Enter. The final installation screen contains information about installing the on-line documentation and the client software. After you install the on-line documentation you can refer to Supervising the Network for additional information on how to create users, groups, printers, etc.

42. Press Enter to exit to system console screen.

43. Bring the server down and then up to verify your installation. To down the server, type DOWN and press Enter at the console screen. To exit to the DOS prompt, type EXIT and press Enter.

44. Reboot the computer and execute SERVER.EXE from the DOS prompt.

NetWare Bus Interface

NetWare Bus Interface (NBI) is a new addition to NetWare 4.x that was introduced with the availability of NetWare 4.10 SMP. NBI is a hardware abstraction layer that provides network drivers with an interface that enables them to talk to hardware in a generic way. NBI performs as the guts to the new hardware detection feature found in NetWare 4.11.

The following is a description of how the hardware detection works in NetWare 4.11. The NetWare 4.11 installation first probes the computer to obtain the hardware-specific identification that is available for each card inserted into the motherboard. This is a process supported by most hardware found in advanced bus architectures (PCI, EISA, MCA, PnP ISA).

For each card found, the install tries to match the card ID with the identification strings available in the *LAN driver information* (LDI) and *Disk driver information* (DDI) files. If a match is found in a *X*DI file, then it knows which driver to load for the detected card. The *X*DI file also includes the range of settings available to choose from when loading the driver. If the install identifies multiple drivers that will support a detected card, it will present the list of detected drivers for the user to select a driver from—not the whole list.

If the install doesn't find any hardware ID information or any matches between the ID and *X*DI strings, then the user will have to select the appropriate drivers manually from the complete drivers list.

NetWare Peripheral Architecture™ (NWPA)

In previous versions of NetWare 4.x you had two types of drivers available to support the hardware found in servers. One type is disk (DSK) drivers that were used to support both disk controllers and the devices connected to the controller. The other type is the network card (LAN) drivers that were used to support the network cards needed to connect the computer to the network cabling. This method worked but created problems as the disk devices became more and more intelligent. The disk drivers were too generic to be able to intelligently interface between the NetWare operating system, the controller, and the multiple devices attached to the controller.

NetWare 4.11 introduces *NetWare Peripheral Architecture* (NWPA), which divides the disk driver interface responsibilities into two new modules: a *Host Adapter Module* (HAM) and a *Custom Device Module* (CDM). The HAM is responsible for providing the interface between the NOS and the disk controller. The CDM is responsible for providing the interface between the NOS and the myriad of devices connected to the controller. The benefit is that CDMs are intelligent drivers that are written specifically to support a certain type of device. This means that a hardware vendor can provide a new feature with their tape backup drive and then write a CDM driver that will allow the tape backup software to interact with the drive and provide support for the new feature.

You can install your NetWare 4.11 server using either the traditional drivers (which uses the .DSK drivers) or the NWPA drivers (HAMs and CDMs).

Tip

> If you have a SCSI controller and devices in your server, you would load the HAM driver for the SCSI host bus adapter and a CDM for each SCSI device connected to the adapter. Then, when you need to add another SCSI device to the adapter, you only need to load the CDM for the new device.

Installing from a CD-ROM Mounted as a NetWare Volume

One of the nicer features of NetWare 4.x is that you can install it from a CD-ROM. Many of the CD-ROMs use the Small Computer Systems Interface (SCSI) interface. The advantages of using a SCSI interface are not only faster speeds, but the capability of the SCSI bus to allow several devices to be daisy-chained. This installation assumes that you already have a NetWare server to which you can attach a CD-ROM drive. The following is an outline of the steps for mounting a CD-ROM as a NetWare volume.

1. Copy the CD-ROM drivers (you can find these drivers in the Products\NW411\IBM\411\DISKDRV directory on the CD-ROM) to the server boot directory. The names of the drivers that you need should be in the documentation that accompanies your CD-ROM drive. The following drivers work for most CD-ROM drives:

   ASPITRAN.DSK

   ASPICD.DSK

2. Start the server program from the server boot directory:

```
C:\NWSERVER
SERVER
```

3. Load the CD-ROM drivers from the console or the INSTALL NLM.

   For the ASPICD drivers, you can use the following from the console:

```
SEARCH ADD C:\NWSERVER
LOAD ASPITRAN
LOAD ASPICD
If you use INSTALL.NLM, use the following:
LOAD INSTALL
Select Driver Options from Installation Options
Select Configure disk and storage device drivers from Driver Options
Select Discover and load additional drivers

Select the CD-ROM drivers from the Select driver: list
```

Tip

> If you are planning on mounting the CD-ROM on a regular basis, it is a lot easier to put the load and mount commands into the AUTOEXEC.NCF.

4. Load the CD-ROM driver:

```
LOAD NWPA    (Autoloaded by CDROM.NLM)
LOAD CDROM
CD MOUNT NW411
```

5. Log in to the server on which the CD-ROM drive is mounted from a workstation, and map a drive to the CD-ROM. For example:

```
MAP N:=NW411:
```

6. From the root directory, run the INSTALL.BAT program:

```
N:
Install
```

7. Continue the installation as outlined in the previous section.

Resolving Conflicts with CD-ROM DOS Drivers and NetWare Drivers for NetWare Installation

This section is intended to help those who experience problems with their CD-ROM drives. Most of the time the SCSI CD-ROM drives work properly as the install transitions from the DOS driver to the NetWare driver. First, try the installation process to see if you experience driver conflicts with your hardware. If you do, the solution in this section should help.

If you use a CD-ROM attached to the SCSI controller on the server and want to install the server software directly from the CD-ROM, you need DOS CD-ROM drivers to initially go to the root directory on the NetWare 4.11 operating system CD-ROM. The DOS CD-ROM drivers, however, create conflicts with the NetWare CD-ROM drivers. You can use the following method to avoid this conflict. This scheme also is an educational tool on how you can avoid such conflicts in a similar circumstance.

Consider the situation in which a CD-ROM and the server hard disk are daisy-chained and share the same SCSI controller (see fig. 3.12). One would expect the scheme to work, but it actually produces a problem during the installation. While copying the files from the CD-ROM to the server disk, the installation process freezes, owing to a conflict among the NetWare SCSI driver, DOS SCSI hard disk driver, DOS CD-ROM driver, and DOS BIOS routines when they try to access the same SCSI controller. This conflict is detected when an attempt is made to copy PUBLIC and SYSTEM, or any other files, from the CD-ROM.

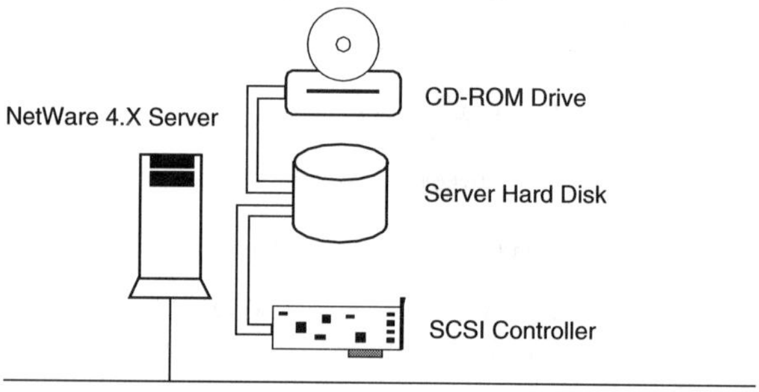

Figure 3.12
A shared SCSI controller problem during installation.

The real problem here is that NetWare relies on DOS for its initial load and access to the CD-ROM during installation. And DOS SCSI drivers conflict with NetWare's use of the SCSI controller.

One way to avoid the problem is not to share the SCSI controller between the server disk and the CD-ROM (see fig. 3.13). This can be done by attaching the CD-ROM through a parallel port using a device such as Trantor's Mini-SCSI parallel port cable. Another way is to use a separate controller for the CD-ROM during the installation. The CD-ROM could be connected to another SCSI controller, or if you are using a non-SCSI CD-ROM, you would attach it to the non-SCSI controller card. In either case, conflict is avoided. Yet another way is to follow the procedure described as follows that allows installation even if the CD-ROM and server disk share the same SCSI controller.

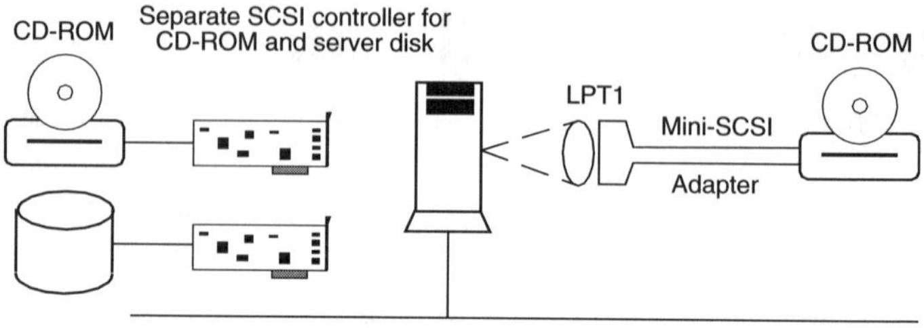

Figure 3.13
Avoiding a shared SCSI controller problem during installation.

1. Go through the following normal NetWare 4.x installation procedure:

   a. Create a small DOS partition on the server disk and format it.

   b. Install the DOS drivers to support the CD-ROM device, so that it is installed as a DOS device. This may involve adding CD-ROM device driver configuration in the CONFIG.SYS and the AUTOEXEC.BAT file in the DOS partition on the server.

   An example of such statements is shown as follows (the actual statements depend on the vendor-specific drivers):

   ```
   File CONFIG.SYS:
   DEVICE=ASPI4DOS.SYS
   DEVICE=ASWCDSNY.SYS /D:ASPICD0
   File AUTOEXEC.BAT:
   MSCDEX /D:ASPICD0 /l:D /m:20
   ```

   In the last example, drive letter D is assigned to the CD-ROM drive.

   c. Ensure that you have a NetWare 4.x disk driver that supports CD-ROM media as a mounted NetWare volume. The disk drivers are in the Products\NW411\IBM\411\DISKDRV directory on the CD-ROM.

2. Go to the root of the CD-ROM drive D:\.

3. Start INSTALL by typing its name.

4. Select the following:

   - Select this line to install in English (choose your preferred language)
   - Read the Novell Terms and Conditions, pressing Enter until finished
   - Select NetWare Server Installation
   - Select NetWare 4.11
   - Select Custom Install

   Use the details in the previous section on NetWare 4.x installation as a guide.

5. Enter the server name and IPX number.

6. Verify the source and destination paths in the Copy server boot files to the DOS partition screen.

7. Enter the correct Country Code, Code Page, and Keyboard Setting.

8. Optionally add SET commands to the STARTUP.NCF file.

9. Make a choice to have the server installation program modify the AUTOEXEC.BAT file on the DOS partition.
10. Select the correct disk drivers.
11. Select the correct protocols and frame types.
12. Select the choice to create NetWare partitions "Automatically."
13. You are warned about having the CD-ROM and server disk on the same controller. Ignore these warning messages because this is the problem you are attempting to solve.
14. Create the server volumes.
15. Insert the license disk when prompted.
16. When the Copy NetWare Files screen appears, DO NOT PRESS F10 to save changes and continue. Use Alt+F10 to break out of the install. Down the server and exit to DOS.
17. Copy NetWare CD-ROM drivers to the server boot directory.
18. Remove DOS CD-ROM drivers that conflict with NetWare CD-ROM drivers:
    a. Remove ASPI driver from CONFIG.SYS.
    b. Remove MSCDEX program from AUTOEXEC.BAT.
19. Reboot the server, and start SERVER.EXE:
    a. CD \NWSERVER
    b. SERVER -NA
    c. SEARCH ADD C:\NWSERVER (to search C:\NWSERVER)
    d. LOAD AHA1540 (use your SCSI disk driver)
    e. MOUNT SYS
20. Load the ASPI CD-ROM driver if CD-ROM is attached via an ASPI controller. Otherwise, go to the next step.

    ```
    LOAD driver
    ```

    in which *driver* is ASPICD or CDNASPI.DOS.
21. Load the CDROM NLM:

    ```
    LOAD CDROM
    ```

22. Run the command:

```
CD DEVICE LIST
```

You should see the CD device displayed.

23. Mount the CD-ROM device:

```
CD MOUNT volumename
```

or

```
CD MOUNT volumenumber
```

The *volumename* and *volumenumber* can be obtained from:

```
CD DEVICE LIST
```

or

```
CD VOLUME LIST
```

Ignore error messages during the mounting of the CD volume.

You should see messages similar to the following:

```
**  Reading in FAT
**  Verifying Directory FAT chain
**  Scanning the Directory
**  Checking Subdirectories
**  Scanning Files with Trustee Nodes
**  Scanning Deleted Files
**  Linking the Name Spaces
```

Some of the messages appear because the CD-ROM is a read-only volume. The mounting process appears to be slow, so please be patient. If your server hangs, try the preceding steps again.

24. Unload INSTALL and then reload it:

```
UNLOAD INSTALL
LOAD INSTALL
```

25. Select Install a New 4.11 Server to start the installation again.

26. Press F3 to specify a different path.

    Enter the name of the directory that contains the distribution software. This is the directory that contains the file NETMAIN.ILS.

27. For *volumename* use NW411.

    Wait for the file to be copied.

28. Press F10 and proceed with the installation as outlined earlier.

Setting File Name Format

In NetWare 4.11, both the simple and custom installation procedures install the DOS file format. It is still important to understand this section because you can start the install with a command line switch that will allow you to choose the filename format (DOS or NetWare). At the root of the CD-ROM drive, type **INSTALL/file_sys** and press Enter. Follow the instruction found earlier in this chapter and select the file format desired. The remainder of this section explains the difference between the two file formats.

Among the NetWare 4.x locale-specific format settings such as date and time, currency, sorting tables, uppercase tables, and so on, are the legal filename characters that you can use to store files on the server. The filename format setting can be done during installation process. During installation, you are asked to choose between DOS format filenames and NetWare format filenames.

A little bit of background might help clarify the ramifications of using this option. NetWare has always allowed extended ASCII codes from 128 to 255 to be included as part of filenames. These characters include many of the line drawing characters and characters in non-English languages (such as accent marks). This allowed NetWare to support filenames that have special characters.

In NetWare 4.x, the installer can conform to DOS legal filename characters or retain the original NetWare legal filename characters that are allowed, including characters with codes from 128 to 255. Your choice determines only the legal character names NetWare 4.x uses, not the legal character names used by an application program running under the NETX shell or the DOS Requester implemented by VLMs.

The NetWare DOS Requester used by NetWare 4.x is fundamentally different from the NETX shell. NETX intercepts DOS function calls (by trapping the software interrupts such as INT 21 hex). NETX examines the commands to see if DOS or the network should handle them. Commands passed to DOS undergo the DOS validation process for legal filename characters. However, commands sent to the network bypass the DOS validation process for legal character names. DOS never sees these "invalid" filenames. So if an application issues a command to create a filename on a network drive, the server would create the file according to its own rules of what was legal and illegal. Because NetWare 3.x allowed characters between 128 to 255 as legal, an application could create a network filename with special codes.

The DOS Requester does not trap the commands first. It lets DOS decide whether the function being invoked should be sent locally or transmitted across the network. This feature is possible with DOS versions 3.x and higher, and is called the DOS redirector function. (Unfortunately, it is often confused with the DOS Requester.) The DOS redirector decides whether DOS or the network should handle the requested function. DOS sees all commands first, so it decides whether the command is valid and verifies the filename before passing the file on the DOS Requester (implemented by VLMs).

If DOS Filename Format was selected at the NetWare server, lowercase and accented characters are converted to uppercase characters. Filename character translation would be done at the server. If the filename request originated from a station running VLMs, the character translation would have been done at the workstation. If the filename request originated from a station running the NETX shell, character translation would not be done at the workstation, but would be handled by the server because the DOS filename format was selected at the server.

If NetWare Filename Format was selected at the NetWare server, lowercase and accented characters are not converted to uppercase characters at the server. It would be up to the workstation to do the character translation. If the filename request originated from a station running VLMs, the character translation would have been done at the workstation. But, if the filename request originated from a station running the NETX shell, character translation would not be done at the workstation, and because the server does not handle character translation (a result of the NetWare Filename Format being selected at the server), the accented characters are not converted, and are left as lowercase.

The preceding discussion implies that there is a potential problem with networks running a mix of NETX and VLM software at the workstations. If the behavior of NetWare 4.x was the same as NetWare 3.x, then only the NetWare Filename Format would exist at the server. Workstations running NETX could then create filenames that would not be recognizable by workstations running VLMs. This is why the DOS Filename Format was created in NetWare 4.x. DOS Filename Format gives greater assurance that the behavior at the server for filenames would be the same for NETX or VLM workstations.

You might be tempted to think that the problem previously discussed could be avoided if all workstations just ran NETX (and used bindery emulation to access NetWare 4.x server) and the NetWare server was configured for NetWare Filename Format. However, not all versions of DOS perform file-name validation identically. DOS versions obtained from different OEM vendors use different rules for valid file-name characters. In this situation, a workstation running DOS from a different vendor can create files on a NetWare server (configured with NetWare Filename Format) that another workstation cannot access.

Interestingly enough, this problem always existed in NetWare 3.x (set to NetWare Filename Format), but most sites never saw it because they ran the same version of DOS. Sites that support DOS from different vendors can run into this same problem.

DOS 3.3 and above can do filename character validation based on the language-specific configuration information given to it. If two workstations on the same network are configured for different languages, they use different code page tables, meaning that workstations can potentially create files on the server that another workstation configured with a different code page cannot understand. If the DOS Filename Format has been selected at the server, the server can remap certain filename characters. If workstations are set to different language configurations, therefore, you might find it preferable to select the NetWare Filename Format so that the server does not try to remap characters in the 128 to 255 range.

The preceding issues become important when you try to upgrade a NetWare 3.x or 2.x server that can have filenames that contain characters in the 128 to 255 range. If the NetWare 4.x server is selected with DOS Filename Format, some of the filename characters become illegal. The server, in this case, remaps the illegal filename character the first time the volume mounts. In NetWare 4.x, VREPAIR is automatically invoked when the illegal characters are detected during the volume mount. VREPAIR translates any lowercase accented characters to uppercase accented characters, according to the rules for the country code and code page the server has installed. Name collisions after character translation are handled by substituting a number for the last character in the filename. Be aware that you need to reconfigure program files that reference these renamed files.

If NetWare Filename Format was selected during the upgrade process, no files are renamed, but you still have the potential problems mentioned earlier: A NetWare format filename at the server and different workstation configurations could produce filenames other workstations might not understand.

Upgrading to NetWare 4.x

You can upgrade to NetWare 4.x from the following:

- NetWare 4.x
- NetWare 3.x
- NetWare 2.x
- Another network operating system

Of the preceding choices, only the NetWare 3.x option is within the scope of this training guide, so most of this section is devoted to that option.

If you are upgrading from NetWare 2.x or NetWare 4.x you should refer to the Upgrade manual in the on-line documentation included with IntranetWare. You can also refer to Novell's home page on the Internet for additional information referring to upgrades. Point your browser to the Consulting Services Online Tool Kit page located at `http://www.novell.com/corp/programs/ncs/toolkit/main.html`.

To upgrade from NetWare 3.x to 4.x, you must take into account the following actions and considerations:

1. Run BINDFIX to clean up and repair any bindery errors. Next, perform a full backup of server data as a precautionary measure.

2. Use SALVAGE to restore any deleted files that you want to retain as part of the upgrade process.

3. Perform any maintenance tasks such as the following:

    a. Rename user accounts to be consistent. If you are upgrading user accounts to a single container, you must make sure that user login names are unique—NDS rules require that objects in the same context have unique Common Names.

       If name collisions do occur (user accounts with the same name on two different servers), the first user account that is created takes precedence. For this reason it is best to start upgrading a NetWare 3.x server that has the largest number of user accounts and other settings.

    b. If a new NetWare 4.x server is to be added to a new branch, create the NDS branch. You can use NETADMIN or NetWare Administrator to perform this task.

4. If you are upgrading an *NetWare Name Service* (NNS) based network, upgrade all servers in a domain at the same time. Servers in the same domain should be placed in the same container. The domain in NNS roughly corresponds to the grouping of objects in a single container. When the first NNS server is upgraded, the installation adds a directory property called `NNS_Domain` to the upgraded bindery object's container.

Translation of Bindery in Upgrade Process

When a NetWare 3.x server is upgraded, bindery objects are placed in a container as part of the upgrade process. Certain rules are applied to ensure the greatest compatibility between the NetWare 3.x setup and the new way of managing resources with NetWare 4.x.

User accounts in NetWare 3.x are translated to NDS user objects. User account information such as login scripts, login restrictions, and passwords become properties of the user objects.

The File and Directory Trustee assignments (for the NetWare file system, and *not* NDS trustee assignments) are retained. There is no difference between the file system rights of NetWare 3.x and NetWare 4.x, except for certain name changes. Inherited Rights Mask (IRM) is called Inherited Rights Filter (IRF) and the Supervisory rights of NetWare 3.x are called Supervisor rights.

NetWare 3.11 groups are converted to NDS group objects. The members of the group become a property of the NDS group object. The security equivalence and file system trustee assignments for groups are retained.

The default account restrictions and print queue objects are carried over from NetWare 3.x. The NetWare 3.x print queue becomes the Bindery Queue object under NetWare 4.x.

The NetWare 3.x console operator becomes an operator property of the server object, and Security Equivalence becomes the Security Equivalence property of the user object.

A utility called PUPGRADE.NLM is available that allows NetWare 3.x print servers, print definitions, and print job configurations as objects and properties of objects. For instance, the printer definition can be converted to an NDS print object, but the print job configuration is assigned as a property of a container object.

Table 3.5 summarizes the translation of bindery information to NetWare 4.x.

Table 3.5
Bindery Translation Summary

Bindery Information	Translated To
User accounts	NDS user objects. NetWare 3.x login scripts, login restrictions, and passwords become properties of user objects.
Group accounts	NDS group objects. Group membership, file and directory trustee assignments, and security equivalencies become properties of user objects.
File System Trustee	Remain the same for NetWare 4.x. There are minor changes in Assignments terminology; for example, IRM becomes IRF, and Supervisory right becomes Supervisor right.
Security Equivalence	Becomes a property of the user object. Property is also called Security Equivalence.
Console Operator	Becomes a property of the server object. Property is called the Operator property.
Print Queues	Become Bindery Queue object that allows their function to be retained.
Default Account	Are carried over from NetWare 3.x. Restrictions.

The Upgrade Process

The NetWare 4.x INSTALL NLM has an option called Upgrade NetWare 3.1x or 4.x Server. This allows a NetWare 3.x server to be upgraded to a NetWare 4.x server using the NetWare 3.x server hardware only (see fig. 3.14).

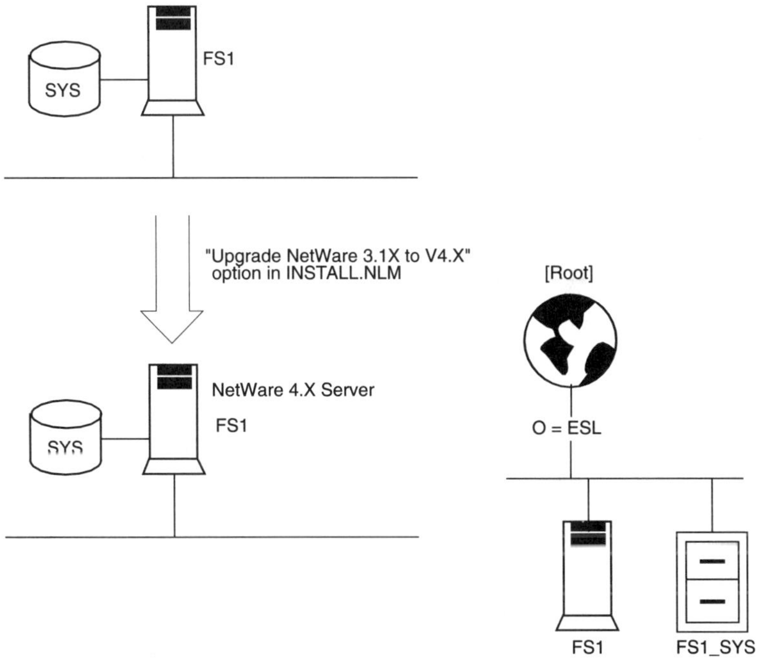

Figure 3.14
Upgrade 3.1x to NetWare 4.x option in INSTALL.NLM.

The following is a guided tour of the installation process. Many similarities exist between the upgrade process and installing a new NetWare 4.x server. The procedure is presented here for your reference and review. Detailed commentary on some of the steps was presented on the NetWare 4.x Installation section earlier in the chapter.

1. You can begin the upgrade by booting with the INSTALL disk if you are using the floppy disk method.

   If you are using the CD-ROM method, the CD-ROM must be recognizable by DOS, which means that you must load all the drivers that are essential for recognizing the CD-ROM device. Because each CD-ROM manufacturer has a different set of installation procedures and CD-ROM drivers, you should follow their instructions.

   CD-ROM installation users should follow the following steps:

   a. Change to the root directory on the CD-ROM drive.

   b. Run the INSTALL.BAT file.

   c. Select the language.

   d. Read the Novell Terms and Conditions.

   e. Select NetWare Server Installation.

   f. Select NetWare 4.11.

2. You should see the screen that says Select the type of installation you are performing. The upgrade option is Upgrade NetWare 3.1x or 4.x.

   Select the Upgrade option.

   You should see a screen (see fig. 3.15) for copying server boot files to a directory on the server's DOS partition. Use F4 to enter a destination directory, such as C:\NWSERVER. If you need to change the source directory, use F3. NetWare creates the boot directory, if it does not exist.

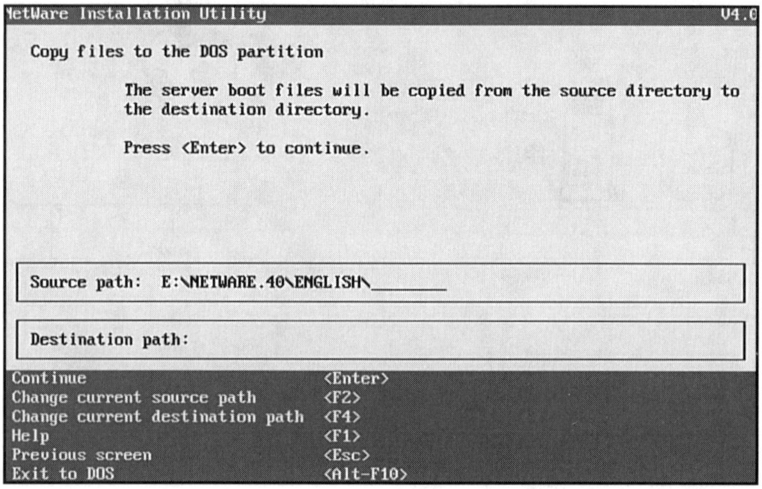
NetWare Installation Utility
V4.0
Copy files to the DOS partition
The server boot files will be copied from the source directory to the destination directory.
Press <Enter> to continue.
Source path: E:\NETWARE.40\ENGLISH\
Destination path:
Continue <Enter>
Change current source path <F2>
Change current destination path <F4>
Help <F1>
Previous screen <Esc>
Exit to DOS <Alt-F10>

Figure 3.15
Copying server boot files.

   Press Enter to begin copying the files.

   If you specified a boot directory that does not contain your existing SERVER.EXE, you are prompted to enter its name.

   You should see a status message of files that are being copied. The files that are copied include the following:

   SERVER.EXE

   INSTALL.NLM

   NWSNUT.NLM (Graphical interface utility for running certain NLMs)

   LAN and disk drivers (*.LAN, *.DSK)

   Message and help files

   Older drivers found on the DOS partition cannot be upgraded. The Upgrade process reports this to you.

3. You should see a locale configuration screen (see fig. 3.16). Select the values for the appropriate locale.

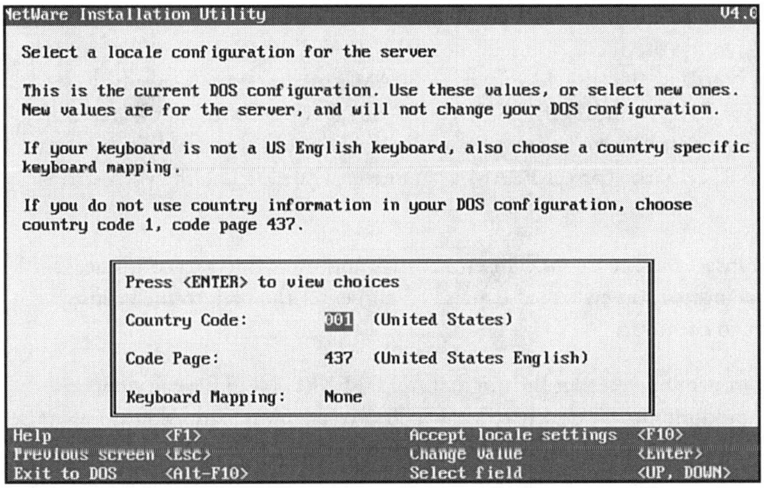
NetWare Installation Utility V4.0
Select a locale configuration for the server
This is the current DOS configuration. Use these values, or select new ones.
New values are for the server, and will not change your DOS configuration.
If your keyboard is not a US English keyboard, also choose a country specific keyboard mapping.
If you do not use country information in your DOS configuration, choose country code 1, code page 437.
Press <ENTER> to view choices
Country Code: 001 (United States)
Code Page: 437 (United States English)
Keyboard Mapping: None
Help <F1>
Previous screen <Esc>
Exit to DOS <Alt-F10>
Accept locale settings <F10>
Change value <Enter>
Select field <UP, DOWN>

Figure 3.16
NetWare 4.x Upgrade: Locale Information.

After making changes, press Enter to save choices and continue.

4. You are informed of the path from which NetWare loads. If you wish to change this (by specifying a network drive, for example), you must use F3 to select a different path.

   Press Enter to select the default path.

5. The INSTALL.NLM autodetection function detects the server hardware and should load the drives without any user input or information. If the device drivers are not auto-detected and loaded automatically, a screen will display the device drivers currently loaded on your server.

6. If the correct disk driver is not loaded, select the disk driver that matches the server disk controller. If the driver you want is not listed, press Ins to load disk driver from a distribution medium.

   Press Enter to continue.

7. You are asked to verify the NetWare 4.x source path. Modify the path, if necessary, by using F3, and press Enter.

8. When file copying is completed, you see a message on the screen informing you of the drivers that were not updated. If these drivers are important to you, you should get their latest versions that work with NetWare 4.x.

   Press Enter to continue.

9. A message appears that the AUTOEXEC.NCF file is being scanned for LAN drivers that have no frame specified.

LOAD statements for loading the LAN driver that do not have an explicit FRAME parameter default to use the IEEE 802.2 frame (FRAME=ETHERNET_802.2) under NetWare 4.x. In NetWare 3.x, the default, if no FRAME parameter was specified, was Novell's raw ETHERNET_802.3. If ETHERNET_802.3 is used with NetWare 4.x, workstations would be unable to log in to the network. To avoid this problem, make sure that you explicitly specify the correct FRAME parameter while loading the LAN driver from the AUTOEXEC.NCF file.

10. You are asked to insert the license disk. Insert the disk and press Enter to continue. If your license file is located somewhere else, press F3 and enter the path to the license file. Then press Enter to continue.

11. You see a screen informing you that the original AUTOEXEC.NCF file can now be executed. You should monitor it closely to see which drivers fail to load. Alternatively, you can edit the AUTOEXEC.NCF file by pressing F3 before AUTOEXEC.NCF runs.

    To continue without executing the AUTOEXEC.NCF file, press F4.

    To execute the AUTOEXEC.NCF file, press Enter.

12. The message `Scanning for available drivers` should appear, and then you are presented with a list of LAN drivers.

13. Scroll through the list and select the correct LAN driver for your NIC. If your driver is not listed, press Ins to load a driver from a floppy disk. If the driver is different from floppy drive A, use F3 to specify an alternate source.

14. If this is an upgrade from NetWare 4.x, the install will prompt for the Admin password. When the password is entered correctly the install will not install Directory Services again. It will update Directory Services and the schema.

15. The Upgrade process searches the network for the existence of a directory tree. If it finds one, it displays the name of the directory tree. You can select this tree or create a new tree by pressing Ins.

    If this is the first server on the network, you must select a name for the directory tree. If you attempt to create a new tree when one already exists, a warning message is displayed informing you of some of the consequences of your actions.

16. You are presented with a form for entering time configuration information for the installed server:

    For Time Server Type, enter either a Single Reference Time Server, Reference Time Server, Primary Time Server, or Secondary Time Server. If you select the Single Reference Time Server, you cannot have a Primary Time Server or another Reference Time server. With a Single Reference Time Server, only the Secondary Time Servers can exist.

For Standard time zone abbreviation, enter the abbreviation code for your time zone. This string is for display purposes only. You can enter any value, but it is best to enter a value that is standard for your time zone. The important parameter to set for time zone offset is Standard time offset from UTC. The standard time zone abbreviation also can be changed in the AUTOEXEC.NCF file.

For Standard time offset from UTC, verify that the time-offset for your zone is correct. You can set the time offset in the format *hh:mm:ss* (hours:minutes:seconds) behind or after UTC.

Many areas of the world have daylight savings time, and several others do not. NetWare 4.x gives you the flexibility of changing the daylight savings time criteria, or disabling it altogether.

To enable daylight savings time, answer Yes to `Does your area have daylight savings time (DST)?` To disable daylight savings time, answer No to this parameter.

The DST time zone abbreviation specifies a string for daylight savings time that is used for display purposes only. The daylight savings rules are set by the DST offset from standard time, DST Start, and DST End parameters. The DST time zone abbreviation can also be changed in the AUTOEXEC.NCF file.

The DST offset from standard time is a parameter that represents the time difference between daylight savings time and standard time. This can have the value *hh:mm:ss* and can be set to be *ahead* or *behind* the standard time.

The DST Start and the DST End time indicate the start and end of daylight savings time. The values for these parameters can be programmed to be on a weekday of a specified month at a specific time, or on a specific day of the month at a specific time. For example, in areas in the U.S. that use daylight savings time, the daylight savings time commences at 2:00 a.m. on the first Sunday of the month of April and ends at 2:00 a.m. on the last Sunday of the month of October. Should the laws change to a different daylight savings start and end, NetWare 4.x provides the flexibility to provide for these changes from the server console.

The time settings are recorded in the AUTOEXEC.NCF file.

17. Press F10 to save any changes in the time configuration information for the server. Verify that you want to save time configuration.

18. You should see a screen that asks you to specify a context in which this server should be placed.

    In the Company or Organization field, enter the name for your primary organization. This should be a name that is readily recognizable by the users of the network. For instance, the company International Business Machines can simply use the abbreviation IBM for the organization name.

You are given the option to specify three suborganization units:

Level 1 Sub-Organizational Unit (optional)

Level 2 Sub-Organizational Unit (optional)

Level 3 Sub-Organizational Unit (optional)

The organizational unit levels are optional because a minimal NDS tree can consist of only the organization container. To create the context in which the newly installed server should be placed, you should consult your NDS tree design.

You are building a partial tree here only. The full directory tree can be built using the NETADMIN or the NetWare Administrator tool. If you have created a new directory tree, the root partition is installed on the NetWare server that you have just installed.

The Administrator Name field describes the *Common Name* (CN) for the administrator of the network. It is by default set to Admin, and is placed in the organization container. The Admin user object can be renamed, moved, and even deleted. Before deleting the Admin user object, you must make sure that there are other user objects that have Supervisor rights so that the NDS tree can be maintained.

You must know the context of the Admin user, and decide on the initial Admin password, when designing the directory tree.

The Password field is for the Admin user object password. Setting a password is not a requirement for completing the installation, even though it is highly recommended that a password be set as early as possible. The password for the Admin object can be set using the NETADMIN or NetWare Administrator Tool.

19. After making the changes, press F10 to save changes. You see a message informing you that NDS services are being installed.

    You should see a status screen informing you of the bindery objects that are converted to equivalent NDS objects.

    The Upgrade process reports the number of volume objects installed in the directory. The volume objects are installed with a Common Name that consists of the file server name and the physical volume name:

    ```
    servername_volumename
    ```

    If the server name is NW4CS, its first volume name (SYS) has the Common Name of

    ```
    CN=NW4CS_SYS
    ```

20. Press Enter to continue. You are asked to note the following information:

    Directory tree name

Directory context

Administrator name

The Directory Context is the NDS context in which the server was placed.

Press Enter to continue.

21. The AUTOEXEC.NCF file is scanned to verify that the Ethernet 802.2 frame type is loaded for Ethernet drivers. AUTOEXEC.NCF also is scanned for time and directory context information. It makes changes to the AUTOEXEC.NCF file. You can make further edits to these changes.

22. Press Enter to continue. You are shown the old AUTOEXEC.NCF and the new AUTOEXEC.NCF, side-by-side. Make any edits you want, and press F10 to save changes and continue.

23. You are presented with the Other Installation Options.

    You might want to create a Registration disk and mail it to Novell.

24. Press F10 to go to the final installation screen, which contains advice on the manuals to which to refer for managing the network.

25. Press Enter to exit to system console screen.

26. Bring the server down and up, to verify your installation.

The Migration Utility

This section discusses the migration of NetWare 2.x and 3.x servers to NetWare 4.x. This is different from the Upgrade process discussed in the previous section; that is done by selecting the Upgrade NetWare 3.1x or 4.x option from the INSTALL NLM. In some of the Novell documentation this is called the *In-Place method.* The In-Place method uses the existing hardware and installs NetWare 4.11 over the top of the existing server software. If you purchase new hardware to install NetWare 4.11, you will probably use the migration feature. Migration allows you to install the new server to transfer the bindery information (users, groups, passwords, queues) while you still have the old server running. This allows you to keep working from the old server until the new server is up and running with all the users and files migrated. This method of migration is called *Across-the-Wire.* The Migrate utilities require that they be run from a workstation. They can be used to upgrade a NetWare 2.x, 3.x, or IBM LAN Server to a NetWare 4.x server.

NetWare 4.11 ships with a pair of new utilities that have simplified the Across-the-Wire migration process. The first utility is DS Migrate. DS Migrate is written by *Preferred Systems Inc.* (PSI). It is a graphical utility that moves the bindery information into NDS. The second utility is File Migration which is written by Novell. It moves the file system information and data such as the trustees, attributes, and restrictions to the new server. To access DS Migrate and File Migration you must select the Tools menu from within the NetWare Administrator utility (NWADMIN).

Note

> If you have a competitive network product such as Microsoft Windows NT or Banyan VINES, you can download utilities for upgrading them to NetWare from the Novell web site.
>
> For additional information on Migration refer to the online documentation that ships with IntranetWare or turn to the Internet and look at the Consulting Services online migration tools.
>
> `http://www.novell.com/corp/programs/ncs/toolkit/migrate.htm`

There is a lot of information available from Novell on how to use the different migration methods. For example the October 1996 issue of Novell Application Notes published "Migrating to NetWare 4.11 Using the Across-the-Wire Method." This article explains the basics for using the new DS Migrate and File Migrate tools. This article and many others can be found on the internet from Novell's home page, WWW.Novell.com. This section will talk about the Across-the-Wire method of migration using the MIGRATE utility. The following two methods can be used to upgrade servers using the MIGRATE utility:

- Across-the-Wire migration
- Same-Server migration

Across-the-Wire Migration

Figure 3.17 shows how the Across-the-Wire migration technique works. The hardware requirements for this technique are the following:

1. A source server that needs to be converted. This could be a NetWare 2.x, 3.x, or an IBM LAN server.
2. A destination server is an existing NetWare 4.x server that has already been installed (using the methods described earlier).
3. A workstation with sufficient disk storage to hold the migrated bindery information, and for running the MIGRATE.EXE utility.

Across-the-Wire migration assumes you already have a NetWare 4.x server installed, and that you wish to migrate data files, user account, and other setup information from a source server (NetWare 2.x, 3.x, or IBM LAN server) to the NetWare 4.x server.

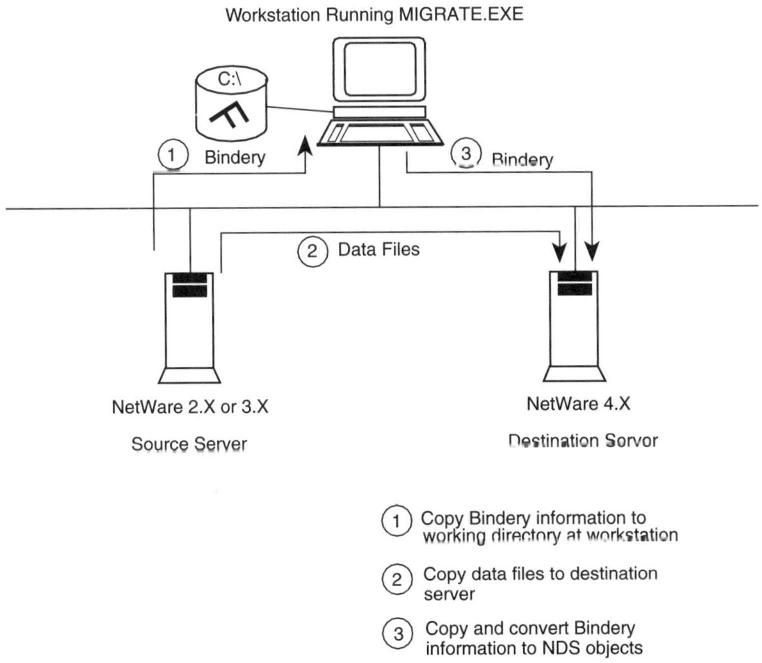

Workstation Running MIGRATE.EXE
C:\
1 Bindery
3 Bindery
2 Data Files
NetWare 2.X or 3.X
Source Server
NetWare 4.X
Destination Server
1 Copy Bindery information to working directory at workstation
2 Copy data files to destination server
3 Copy and convert Bindery information to NDS objects

Figure 3.17
Across-the-Wire migration.

Across-the-Wire migration involves a three-step process:

1. The bindery and/or setup information is copied from the source server to a working directory on the workstation running MIGRATE.
2. The data files are copied directly accross-the-wire from the source server to the destination server.
3. The bindery information is migrated to the NetWare 4.x server from the working directory on the workstation to which it was copied in step one.

Across-the-Wire migration allows you to preserve your data files and your user environment. User accounts are translated to user objects. Default account restrictions, accounting methods, print queues, and print servers are preserved, but passwords are not. The installer has the choice of allowing users to log in to the new system without a password, or assigning passwords that are generated randomly (stored in SYS:SYSTEM\NEW.PWD).

User login scripts are migrated but not modified to match the new environment. These are placed in the SYS:SYSTEM\UIMPORT.DAT file. A corresponding SYS:SYSTEM\UIMPORT.CTL file is also created. You can place the login scripts in the NDS by using the following command from SYS:SYSTEM:

```
UIMPORT UIMPORT.CTL UIMPORT.DAT.
```

The bindery emulation feature of NetWare 4.x allows NDS to emulate a "flat" bindery structure for objects within an Organization or Organization Unit container. This allows compatibility with existing workstations.

Because the Across-the-Wire migration does not modify the source server, it is a very safe method for doing an upgrade.

Same-Server Migration

Figure 3.18 shows how the Same-Server migration technique works. The hardware requirements for this technique are as follows:

1. A source server that needs to be converted. This could be a NetWare 2.x, 3.x, or an IBM LAN Server. There is no separate destination server.

2. A workstation with sufficient disk storage and a backup device to hold the migrated bindery information and the data files. The MIGRATE utility runs at the workstation.

Figure 3.18
Same-Server migration.

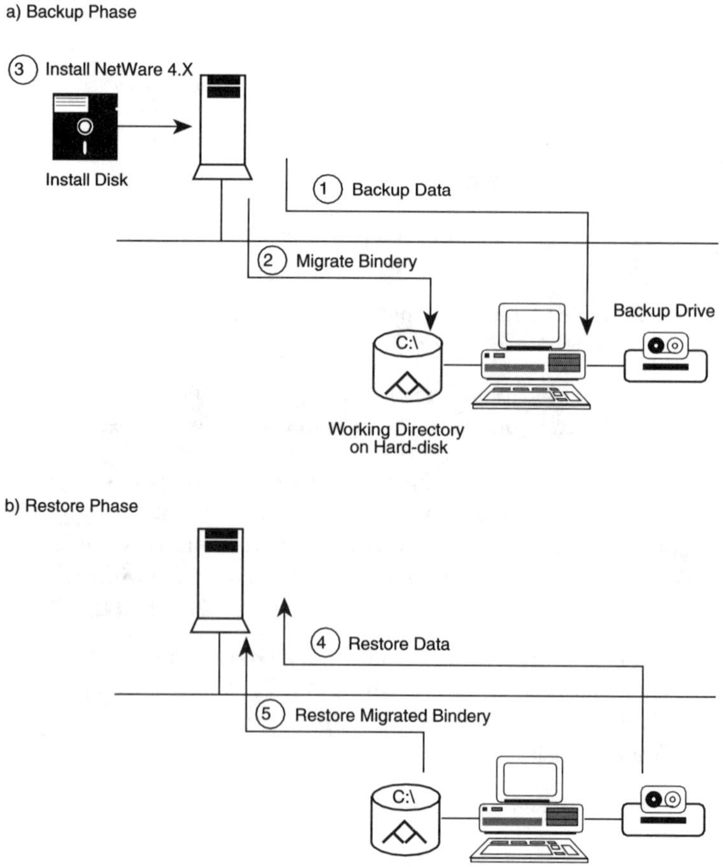

As you can see from the preceding, unlike the Across-the-Wire migration, Same-Server does not assume that you already have a NetWare 4.x server installed. You can use only a single server that is to be converted and a workstation for running MIGRATE. This workstation is also used for backing up and restoring data and the Bindery.

Same-Server migration involves a five-step process:

1. The data files are backed up to the backup device attached to the workstation.

2. The bindery and/or setup information is copied from the source server to a working directory on the workstation.

3. The NetWare 4.x server needs to be installed on the server. Note that to do this, for a NetWare v2.x server upgrade, any prior information on the server disk is lost. This is why doing steps 1 and 2 reliably is very important. NetWare 3.x uses the same partition/ volume structure as NetWare 4.x.

4. Restore backed-up data files from the backup device to the newly installed NetWare 4.x server.

5. Run the MIGRATE utility to migrate bindery information to the NetWare 4.x server. The bindery information was stored in the working directory in step 2.

The Same-Server migration allows you to preserve your data files and your user environment. User accounts are translated to user objects. Default account restrictions, accounting methods, print queues, and print servers are preserved, but passwords are not. The installer has the choice of allowing users to log in to the new system without a password, or assigning passwords that are generated randomly (stored in SYS:SYSTEM\NEW.PWD).

The bindery emulation feature of NetWare 4.x, allows NDS to emulate a "flat" bindery structure for objects within an Organization or Organization Unit container. This allows compatibility with existing workstations.

Because the Same-Server migration modifies the source server, this method has a small risk that data could be lost. The risk is minimized by making sure a good backup of the data and bindery is done in steps 1 and 2.

Other Migration Issues

There are several things you should consider that will help simplify your upgrade to NetWare 4.x. If you are planning to use the migration utilities, you should first clean up your existing servers. This means you should delete old users accounts and directories that are no longer in use. The same goes for old print queues, groups, etc. Anything that you don't intend to use on the new server should be archived instead of migrated.

If you migrate a data file that has the same name as a file that already exists on the destination server, the file is not copied. Instead, an error message appears and is written to a migration report. If you migrate a directory that has the same name as a directory that already exists on the destination server, the files from both directories are merged under the destination directory.

The system login script is not migrated, but user login scripts are migrated.

You might want to use the UIMPORT utility to migrate user accounts. This is similar to the MAKEUSER utility in NetWare 3.x. If you have a CD-ROM disc, you can create the MIGRATE disk by performing the following:

1. Go to the directory \CLIENT\UPGRADE in the NetWare 4.x distribution.

2. Run the MAKEDISK command:

   MAKEDISK A: *language*

   in which *language* is one of the following:

   ENGLISH

   FRENCH or FRANCAIS

   ITALIAN or ITALIANO

   GERMAN or DEUTSCH

   SPANISH or ESPANOL

You must have two formatted disks. One of them should be DOS bootable and should have the FDISK.COM and FORMAT.COM programs on it. You should also have the DOS utilities on the search path. The MAKEDISK batch file uses the DOS LABEL command to label the disks that you produce. The DOS bootable disk that you produce is the "NetWare In-Place Upgrade" disk and the other disk is the "NetWare Migration Utility."

Summary

In this chapter, you have learned the basics of NetWare 4.x installation and how to upgrade from NetWare 3.x to 4.x. Before commencing an installation or an upgrade, you should have a design of the NDS tree. If the server is to be installed in an existing NDS tree, you must make the decision if the server should be installed in a new container or an existing container.

You were shown how to estimate server memory and disk requirements. A guided tour was presented to install a NetWare 4.x server, and many of the installation choices were discussed in detail. Toward the end of the chapter you were presented with a brief look at migration techniques and issues.

CHAPTER 4

Novell Directory Services Security

Novell Directory Services provides a logical view of the network resources and provides access to these resources in a uniform manner. The user needs to log in to the network just once. After the user is logged in, access to network resources is controlled by NDS security.

In this chapter you learn how NDS security is implemented and how it can be used to provide access to only those parts of the NDS tree to which the user should have access. You learn about the default security assignments for many NDS objects. You need to understand the default security assignments to NDS objects before you can further enhance and customize NetWare security.

The rules for computing effective rights are presented, along with the different ways rights can be acquired. You also learn how to implement a network administration strategy by delegating network responsibility.

Overview of Network Security

IntranetWare security includes the traditional NetWare 3.x security dealing with login security and file system security. IntranetWare adds an additional component called the NDS security. The three elements of IntranetWare 11 security are as follows:

- Login security
- NDS security
- File system security

Figures 4.1 and 4.2 show the NetWare 3.x and IntranetWare security. At each of the levels (or elements) of security, a number of tools and options exist. Before you can effectively implement security on a network, you need to understand how to implement the different options at each level, and what tools IntranetWare provides for doing so.

Figure 4.1
NetWare 3.x network security.

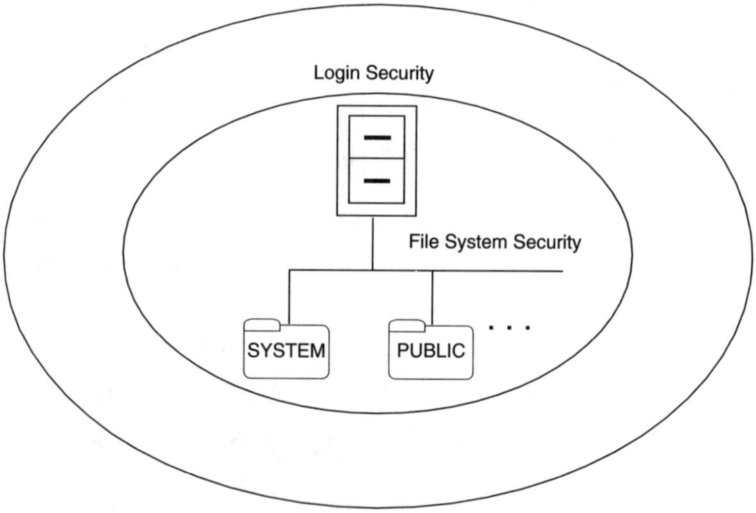

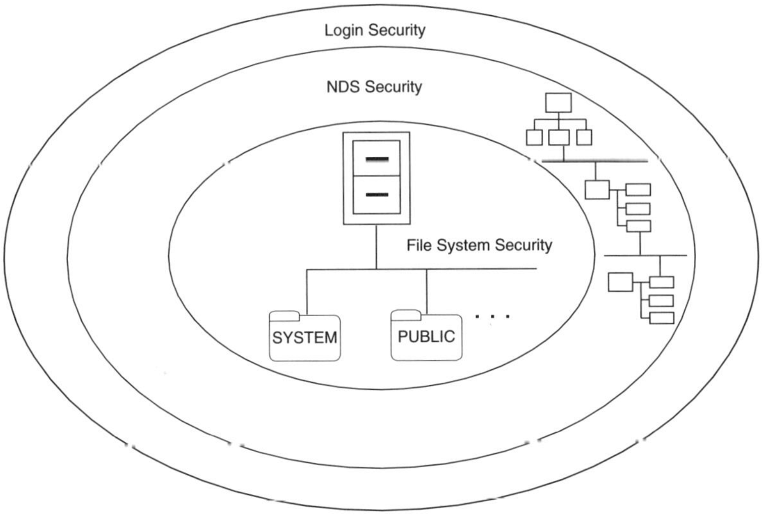

Figure 4.2
IntranetWare network security.

Login Security

The login security in figures 4.1 and 4.2 has a number of components. Login security controls who can gain initial entry into the network. The login authentication of a user must be done against the user object stored in the global NDS database. For instance, a user logging in as an object CN=KARANJIT in container O=ESL must, after initial attachment to the network, type the following command:

```
LOGIN .CN=KARANJIT.O=ESL
```

or

```
LOGIN .KARANJIT.ESL
```

The first login command specifies the complete name of the user object. The second form uses the typeless complete name. This assures that the user can log in from any context in the NDS tree. The context is the location (pointer) in the NDS tree. A user also can use partial names to log in to the network. For example, if the current context is [Root], the following commands would be valid:

```
LOGIN CN=KARANJIT.O=ESL
```

or

```
LOGIN KARANJIT.ESL
```

If the current context is O=ESL, the container that holds the user object being logged into, the following commands could be used:

```
LOGIN CN=KARANJIT
```

or

```
LOGIN KARANJIT
```

Before a user can successfully log in, the user has to pass through several login restriction checks (see fig. 4.3).

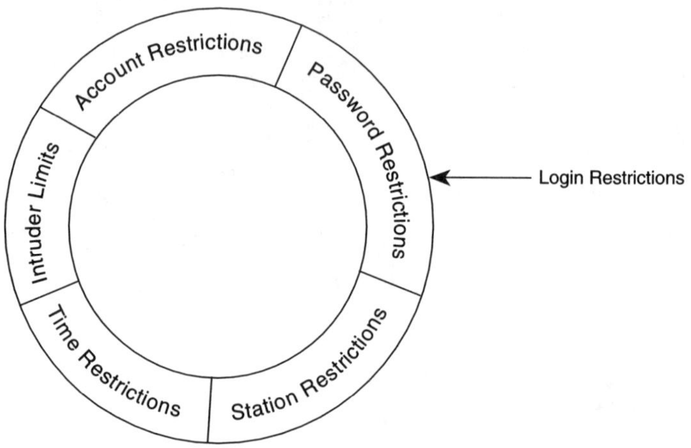

Figure 4.3
Login restrictions.

The login restrictions in figure 4.3 are done on NDS objects, by using the NetWare Administrator and the NETADMIN tool.

The procedure for setting these restrictions is briefly described in the following sections. There are five types of login restrictions in IntranetWare:

- Account Restrictions
- Password Restrictions
- Station Restrictions
- Time Restrictions
- Intruder Limits

Account Restrictions

You can control Account Restrictions by changing the account restriction properties for a user object. Account restrictions includes the ability to restrict a user object in the following ways:

- Disabling the user account

- Setting an expiration date on the user account
- Limiting Concurrent Connections

Figure 4.4 shows the Account Restriction properties for a user object. In this figure the account is enabled, indicated by the absence of the check box on Account Disabled. The Account Has Expiration Date shows that the expiration date on the account is 8/22/99 at 2:00:00 AM. Also, the concurrent connections are limited to 3, which means that the user CN=KARANJIT.O=ESL can log in on no more than three stations at the same time.

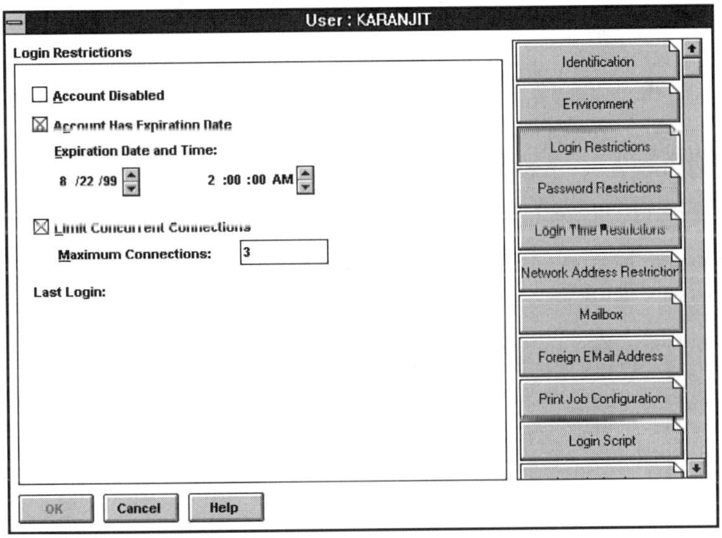

Figure 4.4
Account Restrictions dialog box.

To get to figure 4.4, you need to perform the following actions:

1. Log in to the network with Administrator privileges to at least a portion of the NDS tree that has user objects defined.
2. Start the NetWare Administrator Tool. You should see a screen similar to figure 4.5.

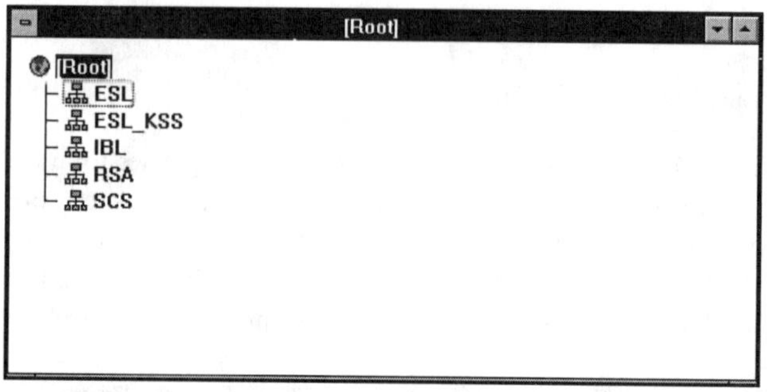

Figure 4.5
NetWare Administrator showing NDS tree.

Set the context of the NDS tree so you can see the entire NDS tree. You can set the context by performing the following:

a. Select View menu

b. Select Set Context from the View menu

3. Examine a container that has user objects defined. Figure 4.6 shows part of the NDS tree in which several users are defined.

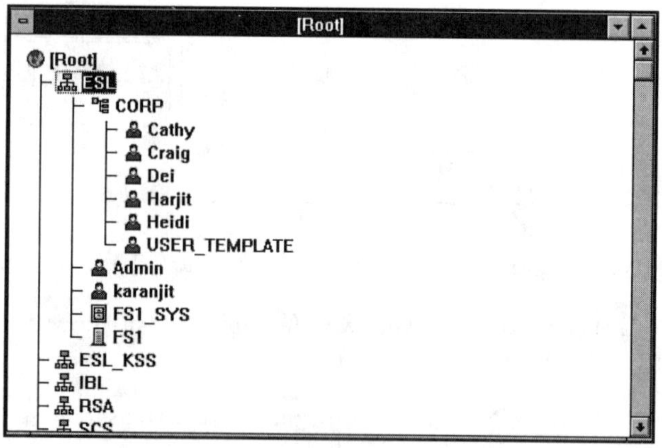

Figure 4.6
NDS Tree with several user objects defined.

Highlight a user object and examine its properties (double-click on the user object, or right-click on the user object and select the Details option).

Figure 4.7 shows the properties of the user object.

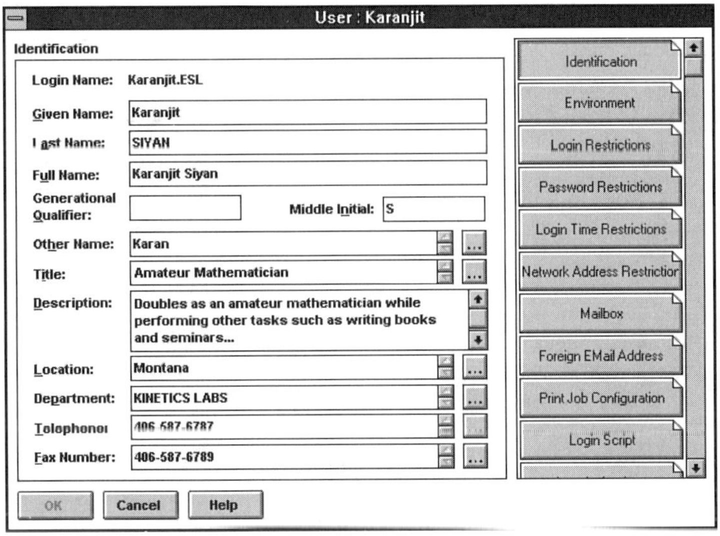

Figure 4.7
Properties of user object CN=KARANJIT.OU=CORP.O=ESL.

4. Click on the Login Restrictions page button, and a dialog box appears in which you can set Account Restrictions.

Password Restrictions

Password Restrictions is a property of a user object. Password restrictions includes the ability to restrict a user's password in the following ways:

- Allow user to change (or not change) the user password.
- Require that a password always be set, or disable this requirement.
- Enforce a minimum password length, or have no control on the minimum password length.
- Force (or do not force) users to change passwords periodically. The periodicity of change can be set from 1 to 999 days, and can be set to start at any date and time.
- Force (or do not force) users to set unique passwords.
- Limit grace logins to a specific number 0 to 999.

Figure 4.8 shows the Password Restriction properties for a user object. In this figure, the user is allowed to change his password. A password is required, and its minimum length is 5 characters. The user is forced to change passwords periodically starting from 11/1/99 at 2:00:00 AM, and intervals of 40 days after that. The password that a user enters must be unique from previous passwords the user may have used. The user is allowed a limit of six grace logins after the password expires, and currently five grace logins are left. If the user does not change the password in the specified number of logins, the account is disabled, after which, an Administrator can re-enable it.

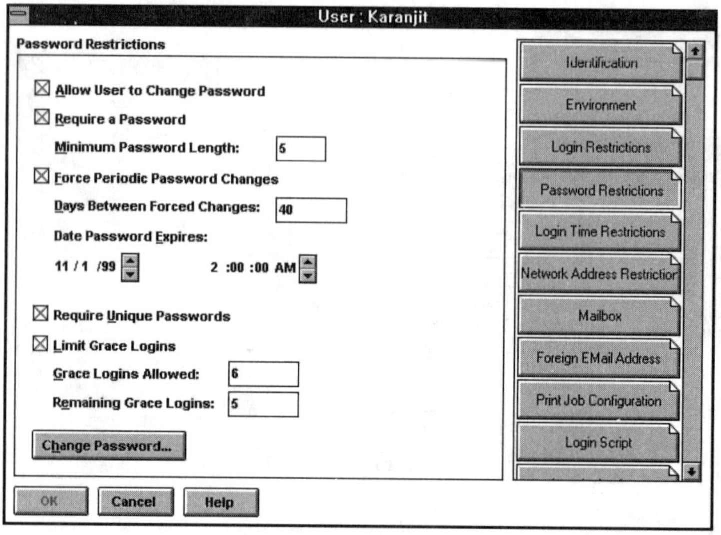

Figure 4.8
Password Restrictions dialog box.

To get to figure 4.8, perform the following actions:

1. Log in to the network with Administrator privileges to at least a portion of the NDS tree that has user objects defined.
2. Start the NetWare Administrator Tool.
3. Examine a container in which user objects are defined.
4. Highlight a user object and examine its properties (double-click on the user object or right-click on the user object and select the Details option).
5. Select the Password Restrictions page button, and a dialog box appears in which you can set Password Restrictions (refer to figure 4.8).

Time Restrictions

Time Restrictions is a property of a user object. Time restrictions includes the capability to restrict a user's ability to log in in the following ways:

- The user can log in during specific days of the week only.
- The user can be restricted to log in at specific times only.
- The granularity of time interval that can be set for logging in is 30 minutes.

Figure 4.9 shows the Login Time Restriction properties for a user object. In this figure the user is allowed to log in on weekdays only. Access on Sunday and Saturday is denied by the times during those days shaded in gray. On weekdays, the user is not allowed to log in from 10 p.m. to 12 a.m., and from 12 a.m. to 4 a.m. This means that the user can only log in from Monday to Friday between 4 a.m. and 10 p.m.

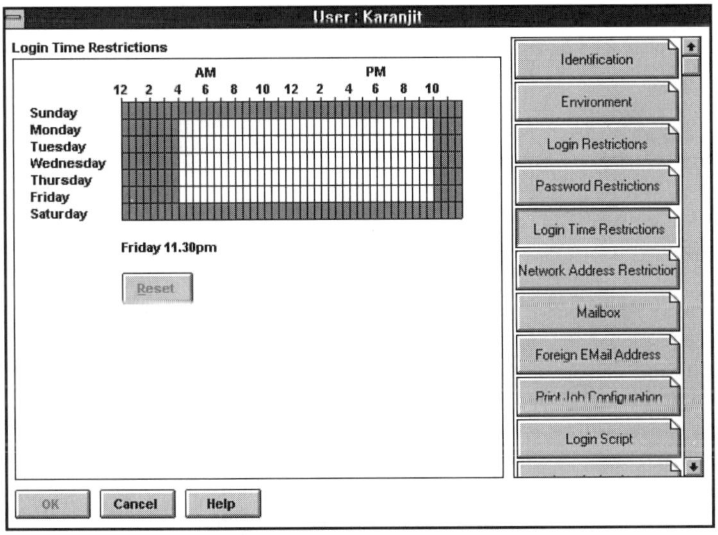

Figure 4.9
Login Time Restrictions dialog box.

To get to figure 4.9, perform the following actions:

1. Log in to the network with Administrator privileges to at least a portion of the NDS tree that has user objects defined.

2. Start the NetWare Administrator Tool.

3. Examine a container that has user objects defined.

4. Highlight a user object and examine its properties. You can do this by double-clicking on the user object, or right-click on the user object and select the Details option.

5. Select the Login Time Restrictions page button, and you see the dialog box for setting Time Restrictions (refer to figure 4.9).

Station Restrictions

Station restrictions (also called Network Address restrictions) includes the capability to restrict a user's ability to log in from specific workstations. In IntranetWare, station restrictions is more powerful and general than NetWare 3.x. Station restrictions in NetWare 3.x could only be done on the hardware address (MAC address) of the workstation's network board. In IntranetWare, station restrictions includes the capability to restrict based on a protocol address. For this reason, the station restriction is also called Network Address Restriction in

IntranetWare. Network Address Restrictions is a property of a user object and enables you to restrict logins based on Network Addresses such as:

- IPX/SPX
- SDLC
- AppleTalk
- OSI
- TCP/IP
- Ethernet/Token Ring

The Network Address formats for some of the address formats are shown in figures 4.10 through 4.12.

IPX/SPX Address format (see fig. 4.10) consists of a 4-byte network number and a 6-byte hardware address. The hardware address is the MAC (Media Access Control) address of the network board.

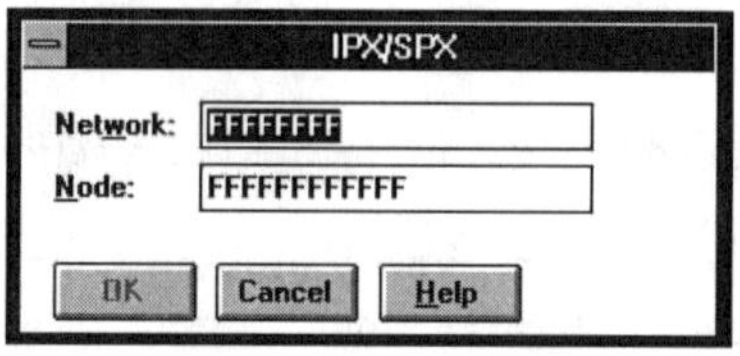

Figure 4.10
IPX/SPX Address Restriction.

The TCP/IP Address format (see fig. 4.11) is the IP address and consists of a 4-byte logical address that is expressed in a dotted-decimal notation. Each of the 4 bytes that make up the IP address are expressed in their equivalent decimal number (range 0 to 255) and separated by the dot (.).

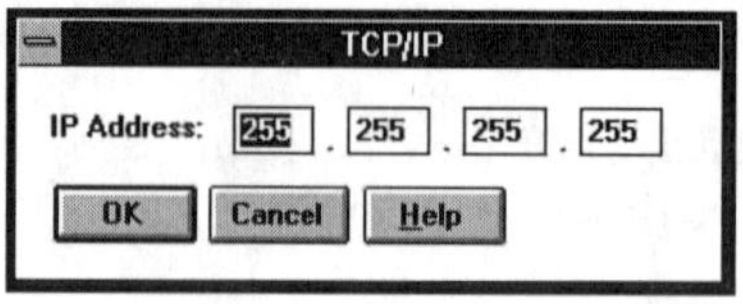

Figure 4.11
TCP/IP Address Restriction.

The Ethernet/Token Ring address format shows the SAP (Service Access Point) address and a 6-byte MAC address. The SAP is a 2-byte field that is part of the *Logical Link Control* (LLC, also called IEEE 802.2) that could be used with frame types such as ETHERNET_802.2, ETHERNET_SNAP, TOKEN-RING, and TOKEN-RING_SNAP. The 6-byte MAC address is broken down into a 3-byte BLOCKID and a 5-byte *Physical Unit ID* (PUID). The terms BLOCKID and PUID are used with IBM's SNA or SAA networks. For LAN usage, these fields can be considered to be one long field that can be used to code the station's MAC address.

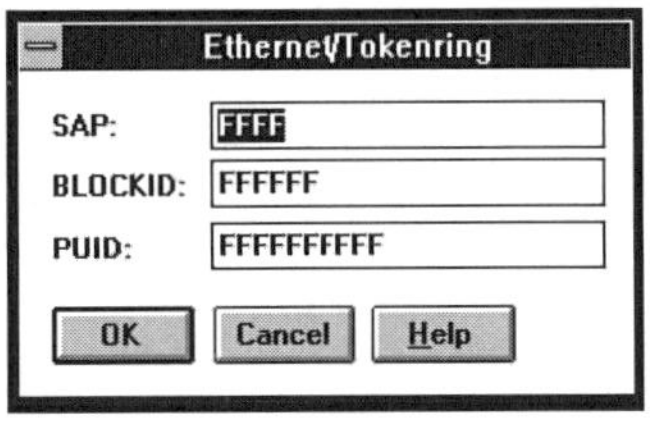

Figure 4.12
Ethernet/Tokenring Address Restriction.

To see the Network Address restriction screens shown in figures 4.10 through 4.12, perform the following actions:

1. Log in to the network with Administrator privileges to at least a portion of the NDS tree that has user objects defined.
2. Start the NetWare Administrator Tool.
3. Examine a container that has user objects defined.
4. Highlight a user object and examine its properties (double-click on the user object or right-click on the user object and select the Details option).
5. Click on the Network Address Restrictions page button, which should bring up a dialog box in which you can set Address Restrictions.

Intruder Limits

Intruder Limits is set in a container object and applies to all user objects within the container. It limits the user's access to the network if an incorrect password was typed in too many times. The account is then locked, and you can use the screen in figure 4.9 to see the number of incorrect login attempts and the station address that was used by the intruder. To enable login for a locked user, select the Account Locked check box.

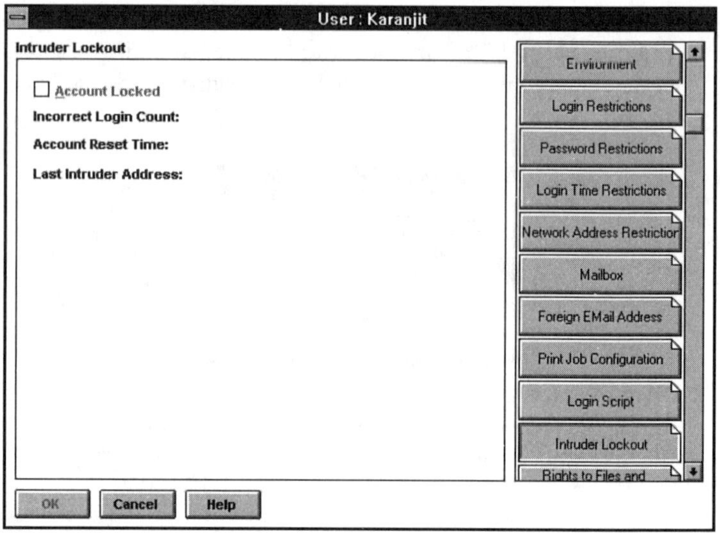

Figure 4.13
Intruder Lockout page.

To get to figure 4.13, perform the following actions:

1. Log in to the network with Administrator privileges to at least a portion of the NDS tree that has user objects defined.
2. Start the NetWare Administrator Tool.
3. Examine a container that has user objects defined.
4. Highlight a user object and examine its properties. You can do this by double-clicking on the user object, or right-click on the user object and select the Details option.
5. Select Intruder Lockout page button, and you see the dialog box for accessing the Intruder Lockout screen (see fig. 4.9).

Login Authentication

When a user first logs in to the network, the network authenticates the user against the information stored in the user's object, such as the user's login name and password. Once authenticated, further requests are validated to ensure that the requests originate from the user's workstation, and that they have not been illegally altered in transit across the network. IntranetWare's authentication mechanism takes place in the background, with no more direct user involvement once the user types in the object and password correctly. In other words, further authentication takes place in the background and is transparent to the user. The authentication of a user is done on each session basis. If the user were to log out of the network, background authentication ceases until the user attempts to log in to the network again.

Authentication is used to ensure that only a valid user could have sent the message, and that the message came from the workstation where the initial authentication data was created. It validates that only the sender could have built the message, and that the message has not been illegally modified during transit across the network. It also guarantees that the message is for the current session only, thus eliminating the threat from play-back attacks, where an attempt is made to capture a valid session and play it back on the network.

IntranetWare authentication is based on the RSA (Rivest, Shamir, Adleman) algorithm. This is a public key encryption algorithm that is extremely difficult to break. The public and private key are strings of numbers that are independent of each other. The independence means that one cannot derive one key from the other. Prime numbers (numbers divisible only by 1 and themselves) have this property, so they are typically used for public and private keys. One of the keys is kept private, which means only a designated user knows about it, and the other key is public which means that all users on the network can have access to it. If a message is encrypted with a private key, it can be decrypted with a public key. And, if a message is encrypted with a public key, it can be decrypted with a private key. This means that a workstation can encrypt its name M, with a private key Kp to form an encrypted message. Any entity on the network, such as a NetWare server, can decode this message with the public key (Kg), using the decryption algorithm (such as RSA), and discover that only the user M could have sent it (because the message contains a coding for the user name).

This relationship can be expressed mathematically as:

Message M, encrypted with private key Kp, using encryption algorithm E = E(M,Kp)

Decrypting message N using public key Kg, using decryption algorithm D = D(N, Kg)

If message N is an encrypted message; that is, N = E(M,Kp), it follows that

D(E(M,Kp), Kg) = M

In step 1 of figure 4.14, the client agent (on behalf of the user) requests authentication. The authentication services on the network return the private key for the user encrypted with the user's password (Pu). This is shown as step 2 in figure 4.14.

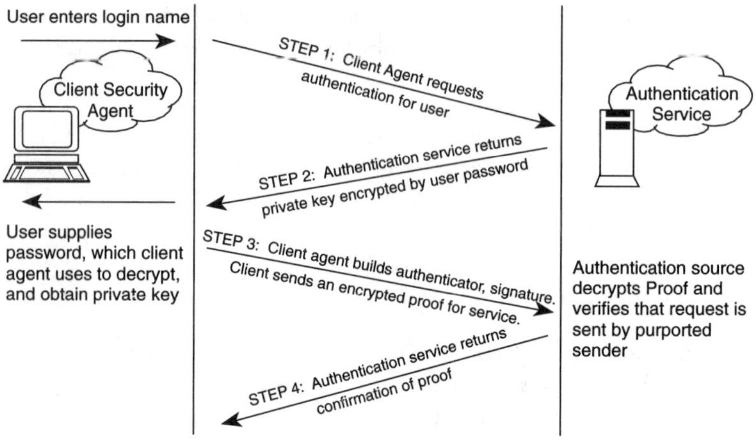

Figure 4.14
IntranetWare Login Authentication.

That is, authentication services return:

```
E(Kp, Pu)
```

The user types in the password and the client agent uses the password supplied by the user (Pu) to decrypt the message. That is, the private key is known to the user, by using:

```
D(E(Kp,Pu), Pu)  = Kp
```

The password is then erased from memory to prevent a hacker (correctly speaking, cracker) from illegally obtaining it. With the private key, the client agent creates a credential (also called an authenticator). The authenticator contains the user's complete name, the workstation's address, and a validity period which is the duration of time the authenticator can expect to be valid. There are other undocumented values that make up the authenticator also. In other words, the authenticator (A) is a mathematical function having the following named values:

A = f(Complete Name of user, Workstation's Address, Validity Period, ...)

The client then creates a signature (S), by encrypting the Authenticator (A) with its private key Kp.

S = E(A, Kp)

A proof (P) is then constructed that contains values derived from the Signature (S), the request for authentication (Rq), a random number generated value (Rn), and is further encrypted by the user's public key (Kg).

P = E (f(S, Rq, Rn), Kg)

The (S, Rq, Rn) in the preceding equation is a mathematical combination of the Signature (S), request for authentication (Rq), and a random number generated value (Rn).

The proof is then sent across the network, instead of the signature (S). This prevents anyone from illegally obtaining the signature. The proof (P) accompanies each authentication request, and is unique for a request, or a session. The random number generator makes it different for each message.

The final request for service (see step 3 in fig. 4.14) contains the request for authentication, the authenticator, and the proof.

```
Final Request = Rq+A+P
```

The authentication services check that the proof contains the signature and the message request. They can do this by decoding the proof with the private key (Kp).

```
D (P, Kp)  = D (E(f(S, Rq, Rn),Kg), Kp) = f(S,Rq,Rn)
```

After S has been obtained, it can decode S with a public key (Kg). Remember that,

```
S = E(A, Kp)
```

So decoding S would give back the Authenticator.

```
D(S, Kg) = D(E(A,Kp), Kg) = A
```

The Authenticator (A) was as follows:

```
A = f(Complete Name of user, Workstation's Address, Validity Period, ...)
```

From the preceding equation, the authentication services can discover the complete name of the user, its workstation address, the validity period, and any other parameters that were encoded. It would be extremely difficult for any other workstation to spoof another workstation's identity.

The proof assures the authentication service that the message has not been modified.

As you can see, the scheme is clever and sufficiently complicated and makes breaking the authentication security a daunting task.

IntranetWare provides a scheme for continual background authentication, once the initial authentication is complete. This makes it difficult to assume the identity of a legitimate user connection.

NDS Security Concepts

After the user is validated for network services, the NDS security is used to determine what network resources (NDS objects) the user is allowed access to. The kind of operations a user is permitted to perform on an NDS object (and files and directories in volumes on the network) are called *rights*. The operations permissible on NDS objects are called *NDS object rights*, and the operations permissible on a NetWare file system are the *file system rights*.

There are several examples of how an NDS object right could be useful. Suppose a user wants to view the structure of a tree. Should the user be allowed to view the directory structure? Viewing the structure (also called browsing) of a tree would be very valuable for a user, if the user is to find out what network resources are available on the network. One of the object rights is called Browse, which enables the user to view the directory structure. Other types of rights are useful to Create, Delete, or Rename objects. You would not want an ordinary user to have these rights. An administrator user should have a special right called the Supervisor right that would grant the administrator all privileges to a directory object.

Figure 4.15 shows that if object rights could not be inherited, explicit rights would have to be assigned at each directory and container level. This would involve greater security administration than is needed in most cases. Using inheritance can simplify the assignment of rights, as seen in figures 4.16 and 4.17.

Figure 4.15
If object rights could not be inherited.

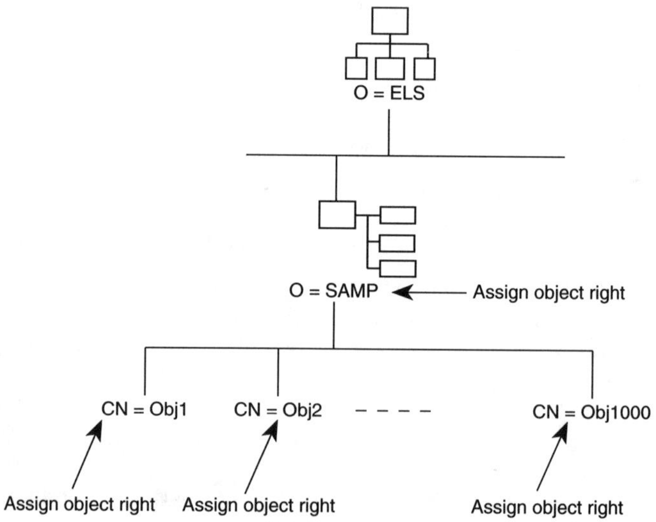

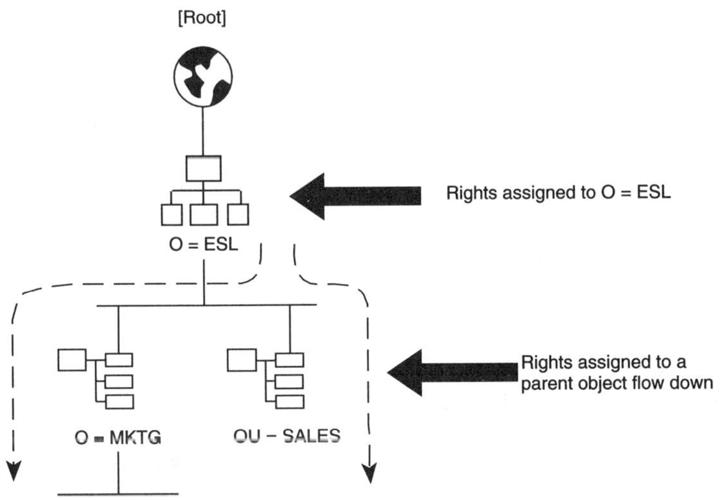

Figure 4.16
Inheritance in object rights for IntranetWare.

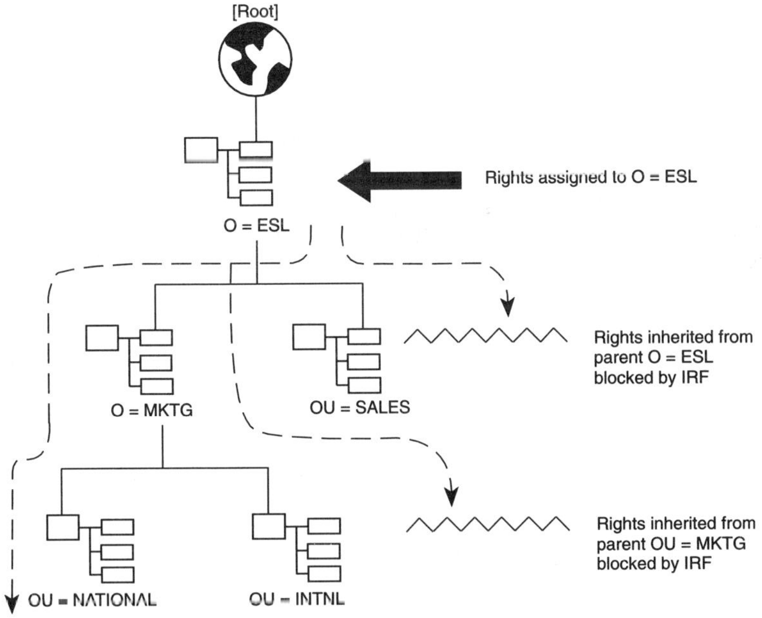

Figure 4.17
Blocking inheritance of object rights in IntranetWare.

When a right is assigned to a container directory object, should all objects in that container get those rights? Objects in a container that receive rights from a parent (superior object) container are said to inherit rights. Inheritance is a very important property and is used in object rights to simplify the assignment of rights. Consider the situation of an organization unit container that has 1,000 objects underneath it (refer to figure 4.16). For the most part, a user/group needs the same right to all the objects in that container. If objects could not inherit rights from their parent container, each one of the 1,000 objects would have to be granted a right individually! Most administrators would not appreciate performing such a task. If, on the other hand, objects could inherit rights, the desired object right could be granted just once for the organization unit container (refer to figure 4.16). What if some objects in the container needed a different set of rights (refer to figure 4.17)? In this case, there needs to be a mechanism to block the flow of rights below a certain container. This mechanism is called the *Inherited Rights Filter* (IRF) and is discussed in greater detail in another section.

Another important question is: Do you want any network administrator to have complete control over the NDS tree for the entire organization? Such control would give this user access to all network resources. Many large organizations are reluctant to do this. NDS object rights give the ability to restrict access to portions of the NDS tree, even to administrator users. Care should be used to prevent a situation in which no one has administrative rights to a portion of the NDS tree.

NDS Rights

NDS provides for two types of rights—the rights to perform operations on the NDS tree structure, and the rights to perform operations on properties of an object (see fig. 4.18). These two rights are quite different.

Figure 4.18
Object versus Property rights.

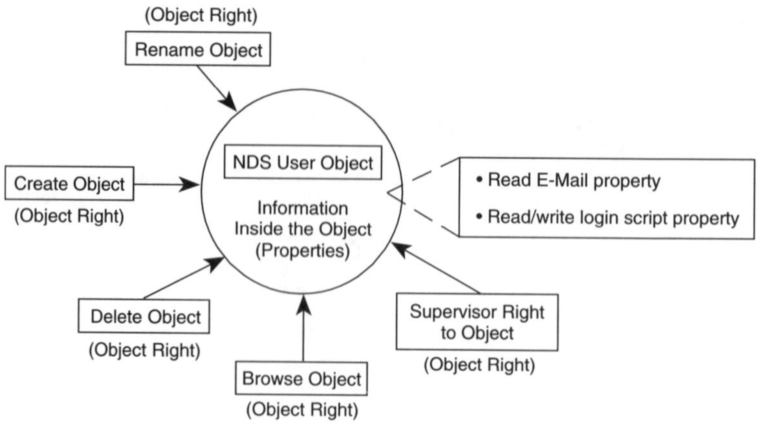

For instance, when working with the NDS structure, you might want to browse the tree, or rename an object. When you are examining the properties of an object, the browse right is not meaningful. You would typically want to be able to read the value of a property or write to it. An example of this would be that you might want a user to have Read access to their E-mail address property, but you may not want users to change their E-mail address. You may, on the other hand, allow a user to modify their login scripts. In this case they need to have Write access to the login script property for the user object.

NDS rights that deal with the structure of objects in the NDS tree are called Object rights. These are used to view and manage objects in the NDS tree.

NDS rights concerning access to the values stored in the properties of an object are called Property rights. Property rights deal with what a user can do with the values of a property.

An NDS object that is granted a specific right is called the trustee of the object (see fig. 4.19). The trustee can be any object in the NDS tree. It is easy to understand that user objects and group objects can be trustees, because they all deal with users. But it may seem strange, at first, to think of a container object as a trustee to another object. Container objects can be considered as groups where the members of the container are the NDS objects in the container. Making a container a trustee to another object gives all user objects in that container rights to the designated object. Moreover, these rights flow down to other containers and objects, unless explicitly blocked at a tree level.

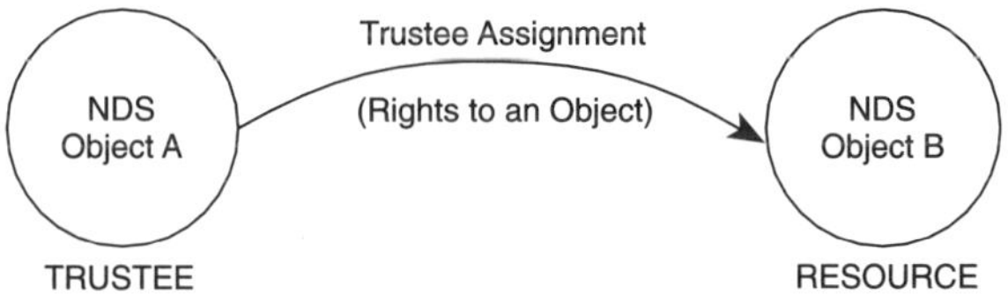

Figure 4.19
Trustee of an Object and Rights to an Object.

In summary, there are two types of NDS rights:

1. Object rights
2. Property rights

The next few sections discuss object rights, then property rights.

Clarifying Terminology

When a right is assigned to an object A for another object B, the object A is called a trustee of object B. The process of granting this right is called a trustee assignment. Oftentimes, the object that has been granted the right, and the right that has been granted, are called a trustee assignment. A trustee can be any other object. In NetWare 3.x, a trustee could be a user account or a group account. In IntranetWare, other leaf objects and container objects can also be made trustees.

When a user object is a trustee, the user who is logged in as the user object can perform the operations allowed by the trustee assignment. When a container is made a trustee of an object, all objects in that container can perform the operations allowed by the trustee assignment. Similarly, when a group object is made a trustee for an object, all user objects that are listed in the group object's Group Membership property can perform the operations allowed by the trustee assignment.

Object Rights

Object rights are assigned to an object in the NDS tree and control the operations that can be performed on the object as a whole. They do not control access to information within the object, but for one important exception. This is a situation in which a Supervisor object right has been granted to an NDS object. Granting the Supervisor object right gives full control over the information inside the object, but the Supervisor right, like any other right, can be blocked by an *Inherited Rights Filter* (IRF).

Property rights control information kept inside the object (property).

Table 4.1 shows the possible object rights.

Table 4.1
Object Rights

Object Right	Abbreviation	Meaning
Supervisor	S	Grants all rights. Assigning this right automatically gives Supervisor rights to the objects All Properties (discussed in a later section).
Browse	B	Grants the right to see an object in the NDS tree. When a request is made to search for an object, its name is returned.
Create	C	Applies to container objects only. Gives the right to create a new directory object within the container. Cannot be given to leaf objects, because they cannot contain subordinate objects.
Delete	D	Grants right to delete an NDS object. Only leaf objects and empty container objects can be deleted.
Rename	R	Grants right to rename object. Applies to leaf and container objects.

Supervisor Object Right

The Supervisor object right grants all possible rights to the user object. An object with Supervisor rights has full access to the information inside the object. This is an exception. Normally, the object rights do not affect access to the contents of the object.

A special right called the All Properties property is used to describe all the properties. When a Supervisor right is assigned, a Supervisor property right is also assigned to All Properties. For this reason, all access to the information inside the object is given if an object has the Supervisor right. Needless to say, this right must be given with care. If you find it necessary, you can block the Supervisor right to branches of an NDS tree by removing this right from the Inheritance Rights Filter for the top-level container for a tree branch.

Browse Object Right

The Browse object right is perhaps the most common right which is given. For readers familiar with NetWare file system security, the browse object right is similar to the File Scan right for file systems. A browse right for an object gives the trustee the ability to see the object's name in the NDS tree. Without this right (if a Supervisor right is not given), the object is hidden from the user's view.

If a browse right is not granted to a trustee for a container, the trustee is denied access to all containers and objects within that tree branch. The default is to give everyone the Browse right to the [Root] object. Because all objects in a directory tree are under the [Root] object, the Browse right is inherited (it also can be said that it flows down) by all objects in the NDS tree.

If you want to deny access to users in a specific part of the NDS tree for security reasons, you can do this by blocking the Browse right (using the IRF) for the container that represents the tree branch.

Create Object Right

The Create object right gives the trustee the capability to create subordinate objects underneath the container. Because leaf objects cannot have subordinate objects beneath them, the create right is not assignable to leaf objects. Figure 4.20 shows an attempt to assign an object right to a leaf object, such as the User1.CORP.ESL_XXX. Notice that the object right Create is not shown as an option for this user.

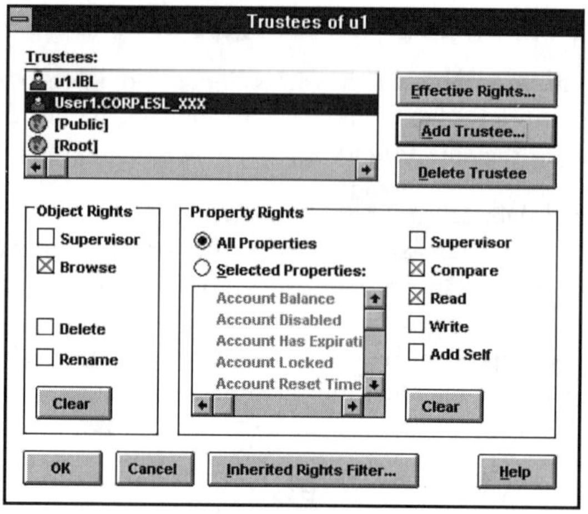

Figure 4.20
Create right not possible for leaf objects.

You must also have Browse rights in addition to Create rights to a container before you can create an object underneath the container using a tool such as the NetWare Administrator. The Browse right is usually inherited, because [Public] is assigned the Browse right to [Root]. You do not need the Browse right to change to a context using the CX command.

Delete Object Right

This grants the trustee the right to delete an object. A container object can be deleted only if it has no other objects beneath it. You must delete the leaf and subcontainer objects before you can delete a container. This rule is primarily there to prevent inadvertent damage to the NDS tree.

If a file server is active, you cannot delete its object—again, for security purposes, so that access to the file server is not lost while users are connected to it.

You can, however, delete a file server's volume object, even while users are logged in to it. This can have disastrous consequences, because users cannot access the volume using NDS. Don't try this on a production system! If someone does manage to delete the volume object, try the following fix:

1. Use NetWare Administrator or NET-ADMIN to create a volume object.

2. If an error message is generated, reboot the server and connect to the server using VLM /PS=*servername*, where you replace *servername* with the name of the server that has the physical volume whose volume object representation was deleted.

3. Log in to the server and create a volume object.

4. Specify the Host Server property to be the NDS name of server, and Host Volume to be SYS.

Alternatively, you can try the following:

1. LOAD INSTALL.NLM at the server.
2. Select Maintenance/Selective Install option.
3. Select Directory Options.
4. Select Install/Reinstall mounted volumes into the directory. You are asked to log in to the NDS as Admin. INSTALL then prompts you to add deleted volumes back into the NDS structure. The volume is placed in the current server context.

Rename Object Right

The Rename object right enables the trustee to change the Name property for the object. In pre-NetWare 4.1, you could rename only leaf objects. In NetWare 4.1, you can rename both leaf and container object names.

In general, you should try to come up with names for container objects that you are not likely to change. What would happen to all the references to NDS container names in scripts if a container name were to change? The scripts and commands that reference the old name must also change, which can create difficult problems on a large, geographically dispersed network. You can use Directory Map objects to minimize the changes you need to make to login scripts.

Use great care when you decide on the names of the container objects. You might want to take into account how easily the container name is recognized by users of the network. Don't make the name too long, and consider how it would appear in the NDS tree (lowercase, uppercase, or combination of both).

The [Public] Trustee

Everyone is given the [Browse] right. Readers familiar with NetWare 3.x might recall that almost everyone was given the Read File scan (RF) rights to SYS:PUBLIC, using the group called EVERYONE. IntranetWare doesn't have default groups called EVERYONE (or a similar name). The problem, then, is how to assign the Browse right to everyone.

The problem is compounded further by the fact that the Browse right would be nice to have for users who are not logged in to the network, but merely attached.

The difference is that users who are logged in to the network have been authenticated by NDS. Users who are attached have a connection to the SYS:LOGIN directory of a NetWare file server. This gives them access to the LOGIN.EXE, CX.EXE, NLIST.EXE, and other programs, that they can use to log in to the network, or search the NDS tree for the name of a resource. Network security usually is not threatened if a user can see the names of network resources. In extremely secure environments, you can revoke the Browse right from any part of the NDS tree. Another advantage of a Browse right available for attached users/workstations is that it permits the NDS to interface with third-party tools or other X.500 implementations that might want to search Novell's implementation of NDS (DIB—Directory Information Base, in X.500 terms) for names of resources and its tree structure.

To solve this problem, the designers of NDS created an implicit group called [Public]. An *implicit group* is different from other groups, called *explicit groups* (such as group objects), in the sense that it does not have an explicit membership. Membership to an implicit group is implied by other means. In the case of the group [Public], all workstations attached (connected to but not logged in as yet) to an IntranetWare network, automatically are members of the group [Public], which makes possible assigning rights to workstations not authenticated by IntranetWare. You must take care to assign to [Public] a minimal set of rights. Otherwise, nonauthenticated connections to the network can have excessive rights to the network. Other operating systems, such as Windows NT, also have the concept of an implicit group, where membership to certain groups is implied when users access a Windows NT station across a network.

When the system is first installed, the group [Public] is made a trustee of [Root] and given the Browse object right to the root object [Root]. Figure 4.21 illustrates this trustee assignment, and figure 4.22 shows the NetWare Administrator screen that shows the assignment of these rights. The Browse object right is inherited by all containers and their subcontainers, down to the individual leaf objects. This enables a user to browse the directory tree.

Figure 4.21

Browse right to trustee [Public] on [Root] object.

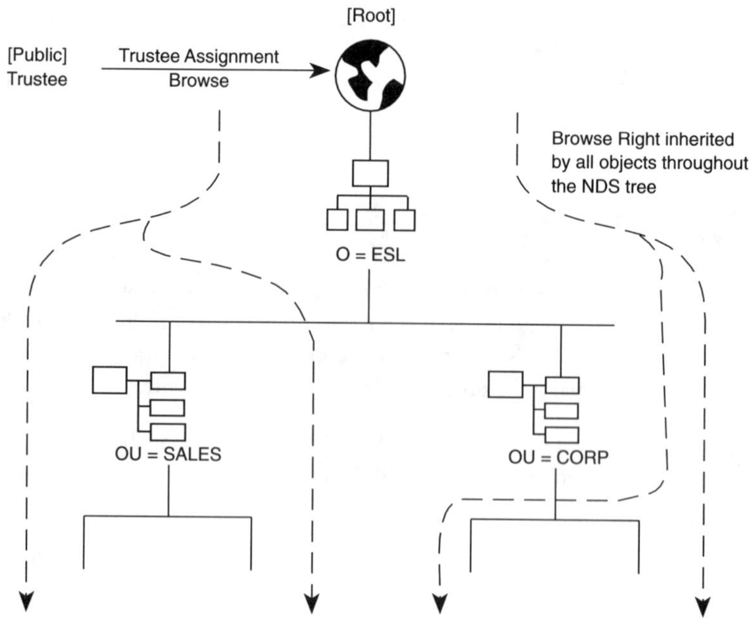

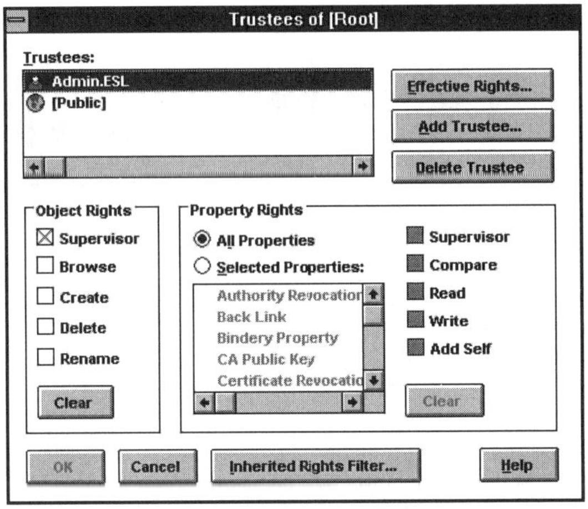

Figure 4.22
NetWare Administrator showing default trustee assignments to [Root] object.

You sometimes might want users to be able to browse only portions of the NDS tree, rather than the entire NDS tree. You can remove the default trustee assignment of Browse for [Public] to [Root] object, and reassign it to the root container (top of tree branch) for which the user needs to see directory resources (see figs. 4.23 and 4.24). These figures show that you can grant the Browse right to all connected users to a specific tree branch. In figures 4.23 and 4.24, the root of this tree branch is at the organization object level O=ESL; it also could be at a lower level in the tree, such as at an Organization Unit level.

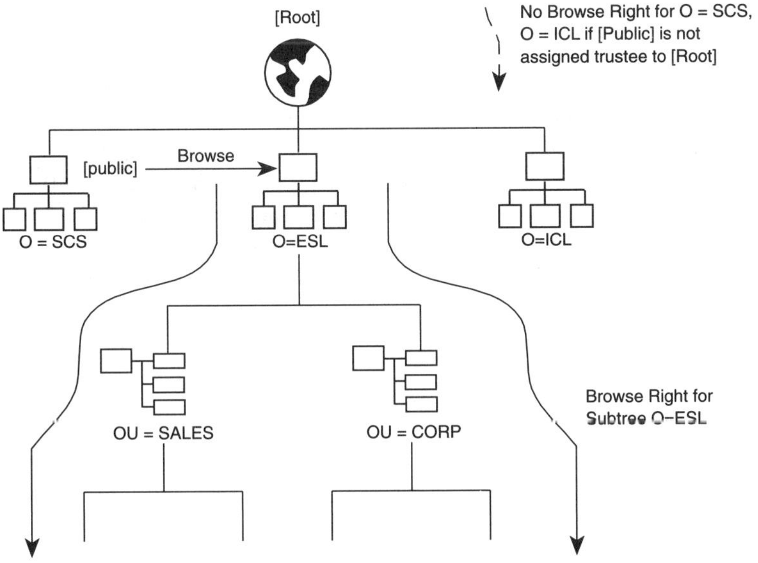

Figure 4.23
Browse right to trustee [Public] for container O=ESL.

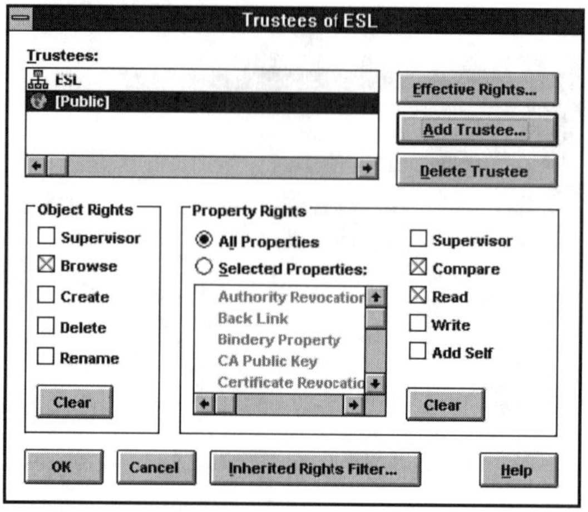

Figure 4.24
NetWare Administrator showing Browse right to [Public] for container O=ESL.

Default Object Rights

IntranetWare sets certain default system rights to simplify the number of administration tasks that would otherwise have to be performed. One of these default rights was the Browse right that the [Public] trustee was given to the [Root] object. Some of the other default rights are discussed in the following sections.

The container object that contains the SYS volume object is given the Read and File Scan (RF) rights to the SYS:PUBLIC directory of the volume object. This is shown in figure 4.25. This figure shows that the CORP.ESL container, which is the parent container of the Server Volume object, is given the Access Rights of Read and File Scan. This allows all objects, such as user and group objects, defined in that container to inherit these rights. In essence, this is equivalent to assigning Read and File scan rights to group EVERYONE in NetWare 3.x. If you have upgraded your server from NetWare 3.x to IntranetWare, and if the group EVERYONE had Read and File scan rights to SYS:PUBLIC, you see the group object EVERYONE in the container where the upgraded IntranetWare server and volume objects are installed. You should also see the group object EVERYONE as a trustee to SYS:PUBLIC with Read and File scan rights.

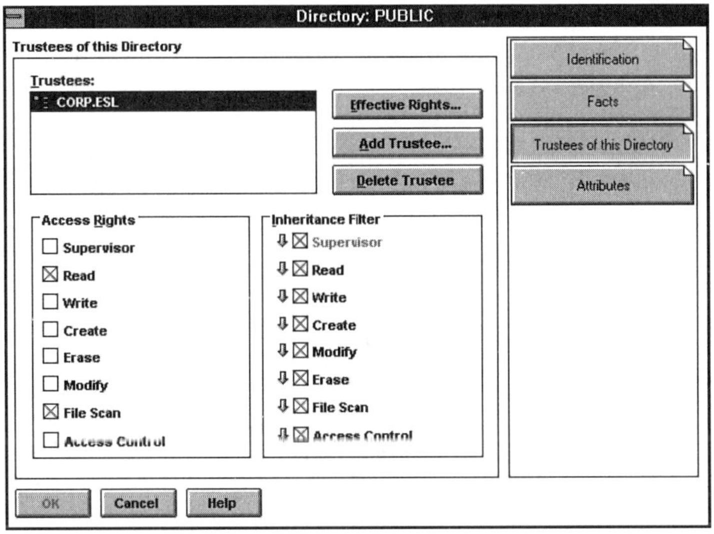

Figure 4.25
Rights to SYS:PUBLIC.

The initial user Admin is by default given the Supervisor object right to [Root]. This means that the Admin user inherits Supervisor object rights to all objects and their contents in the NDS tree. For this reason the password to the initial Admin user must be guarded with care. The Admin user by default is placed in the Organization object container and is named Admin. For security reasons, it might be advisable to rename this user object and move it to another context.

The user object, by default, has the following object trustees assigned to it:

1. The [Root] object is made a trustee to the user object and given the Browse object right (see fig. 4.26). This means that any NDS object can browse the user object.
2. If the creator of the user object is not the Admin user, who has Supervisor rights, the creator is made a trustee with Supervisor rights to the newly created object.

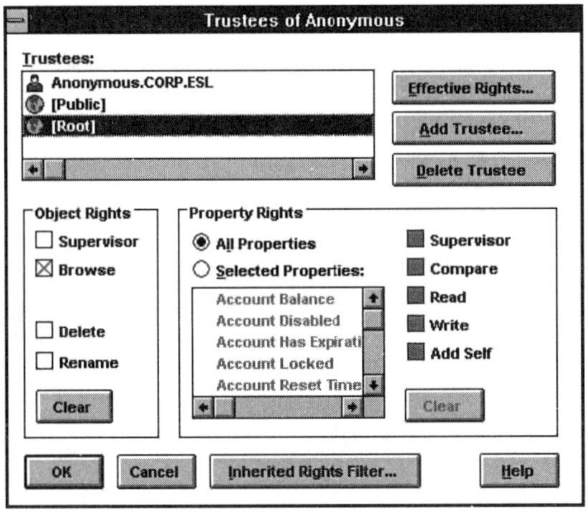

Figure 4.26
Default [Root] trustee assignment for user object.

Another default right is that the creator of the server object is given the Supervisor object right to the server object. Assigning Supervisor right to the server object also gives Supervisor rights to All Properties of the supervisor object. Supervisor All Properties right also implies Write property right to the ACL property of the server object. Anyone who has the Write property right to the ACL property of the server object is given the Supervisor right to the root of the server's volumes. This implies that assigning the Supervisor right to a server object gives *all* file system rights to volumes attached to that server.

Inheritance of Object Rights

When an object trustee assignment is made, the right granted to the trustee is inherited by all objects that are subordinate to it. In the case of container objects, this means that all leaf objects in the container, and all subcontainers, inherit this right. This inheritance of rights is sometimes called *flowing down of rights.* If an object is given an explicit trustee assignment at a lower level in the tree, any object rights that were inherited from above are overwritten.

Figure 4.27 shows an example of an NDS tree, where user object KSS is made a trustee of the organization container O=ESL. The trustee assignment that has been given is the [B C D] rights. This is the right to Browse, Create, and Delete objects. The container O=ESL has two subcontainers: the organization units OU=CORP and OU=ENG. The rights assigned to user KSS for O=ESL flow to these subcontainers. The subcontainer objects inherit the [B C D] right. The [B C D] right for trustee KSS, in turn, flows down to the subcontainers below OU=CORP and OU=ENG. It is important to realize that the [B C D] right is only for a specific trustee; in this case, the trustee is the user object. The rights assigned to Organization Unit container OU=ENG flow to its two subcontainers OU=OPS and OU=LAB. The rights inherited by the OU=LAB container flow further down the tree, but the OU=R&D subcontainer has an explicit trustee assignment of [B] for user object KSS. This explicit trustee assignment overrides the trustee assignment user KSS inherits for OU=R&D from the parent container OU=LAB. The trustee assignment for user object KSS then becomes the new right of [B]. This new right flows down to subordinate containers below OU=R&D. In figure 4.27, these subordinate containers are OU=LASER and OU=NNET. User object KSS inherits the rights of [B] to these containers.

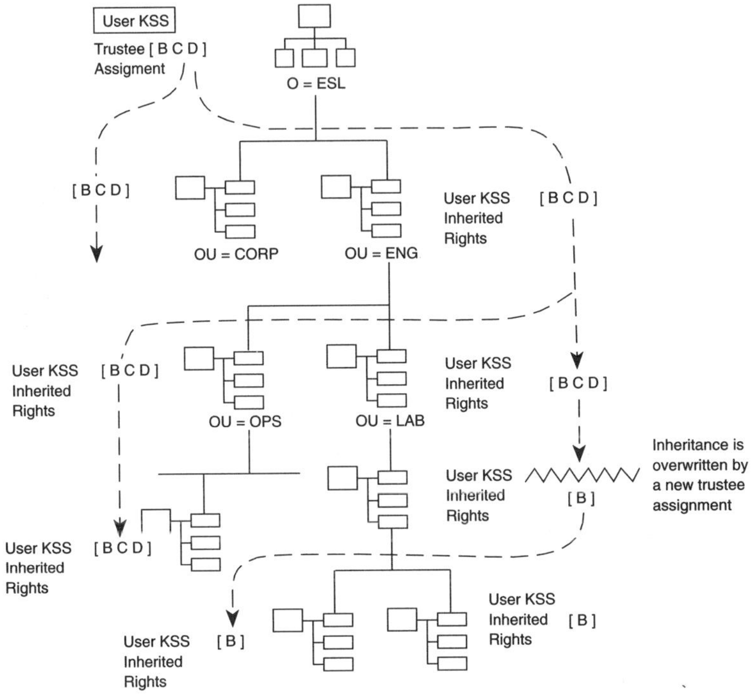

Figure 4.27
Example of Inheritance of Object Rights.

It is also interesting to see that in OU=OPS underneath the OU=ENG container, no explicit trustee assignment was given to user KSS. In this case, the trustee assignment [B C D] flows down and is inherited by the OU=MAINT container subordinate to OU=OPS.

Besides an explicit trustee assignment that overrides any inherited rights, inheritance can also be controlled by using the Inheritance Rights Filter, discussed next.

Inherited Rights Filter

The Inherited Rights Filter is a part of a property of the object, called the ACL property (also called the Object Trustees property). You can use it to control what inherited rights are allowed to be received from above.

Every NDS object has an *Inherited Rights Filter* (IRF). The default value of the IRF is all object rights [S B C D R]. This means that an NDS object has the potential to inherit all rights. The IRF is often confused with the actual object right. The sole purpose of the IRF is to block a right from flowing further down. The IRF cannot be used to block an explicit trustee assignment. The explicit trustee assignment overrides any Inherited rights received from above, and causes the IRF to be ignored.

The IRF functions in a manner similar to the Inherited Rights Filter for IntranetWare file system (same as NetWare 3.x, Inherited Rights Mask, except for the name change). The important difference is that you can remove the Supervisor right for IRF for NDS. In the NetWare file system, you could not remove the Supervisor right from the IRF for a file or directory.

When the Supervisor right is removed from the IRF for an NDS object, the Supervisor right is essentially blocked from that tree branch. Before removing a Supervisor right from the IRF of an NDS object, you must make another object a trustee with Supervisor rights for that object.

In the first NetWare 4.0 release, you were given a warning message when you attempted to remove the Supervisor object right from an IRF. You could, however, override this warning and remove the Supervisor right from the IRF anyway. This essentially produced a black hole in the tree that no one could have access to. Starting with NetWare 4.01, the warning was changed to an error message. If you attempt to remove the Supervisor right from an IRF, an error message is produced instead. This error message informs you that:

```
You cannot filter the Supervisor object right because no User has explicit
Supervisor object right to this object.
```

Figure 4.28 shows an attempt to remove the Supervisor right for an NDS object. The trustee CORP.ESL is highlighted in the Trustees box, which means that the operations that are performed are in relationship to this trustee object. An attempt was made to remove the Supervisor right from the IRF. Figure 4.28 shows the Supervisor box still checked, but the error message that you see in the figure was produced when an unsuccessful attempt was made to clear this box.

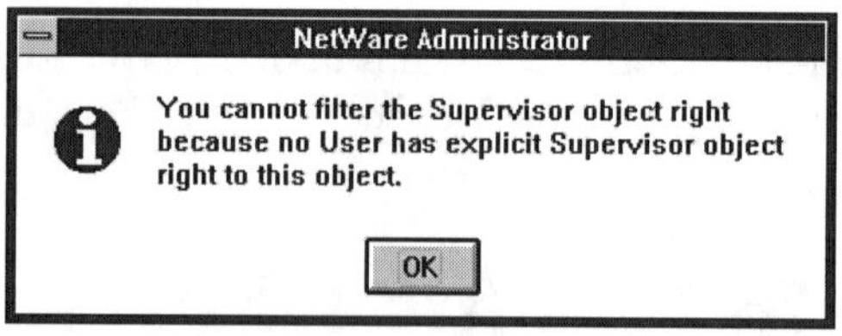

Figure 4.28
An attempt to remove Supervisor right from an IRF for a container object.

The reader who is interested in experimenting with this should try the following:

1. Log in as an Admin user and start the NetWare Administrator.

2. Right-click on a container and select Trustees of this Object. You should see a screen similar to figure 4.29.

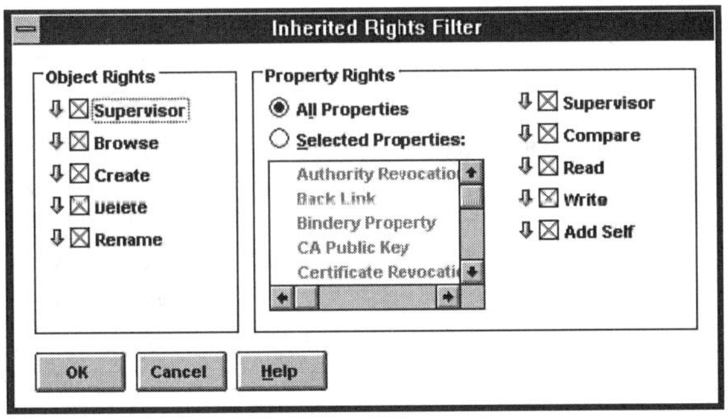

Figure 4.29
The Inherited Rights filter screen.

3. Highlight the container in the Trustee List box and select the Inherited Rights Filter button.

4. You should see the Inherited Rights Filter screen.

5. Click on any of the object rights in the Filter panel. The rights should be exposed for your view.

6. Try to remove the Supervisor object right by clicking on the box next to it. You should see the error message shown in figure 4.28.

If at least one Supervisor trustee assignment to an object exists, you can remove the Supervisory object right from the IRF. In this case, though the Supervisor right is blocked, there is at least one object that can manage the object and its subordinate objects.

Though the Supervisor right can allow a trustee to perform all operations on an object, it is a good practice to assign other rights, in case the Supervisor right is accidentally removed. From the above discussion, you can see that NetWare 4.01 (and higher) checks to see if there exists at least one trustee that has a Supervisor right before allowing the Supervisor right to be removed; but you may still want to assign other rights as a precautionary measure, in case of failures or bugs in an NDS release.

Security Equivalence

You can grant a user object all the security rights of another NDS object, which is called *security equivalence*, and is a property of the user object. Figure 4.30 shows that user Dei is made security equivalent to the user CN=Admin1.OU=CORP.O=ESL and the Organization Unit OU=CORP.O= ESL_XXX. This means that Dei inherits by the definition of security equivalence, whatever rights the user object CN=Admin1.OU=CORP.O=ESL has, plus the rights the container object OU=CORP.O=ESL_XXX has. These rights are in addition to the rights that user Dei already has.

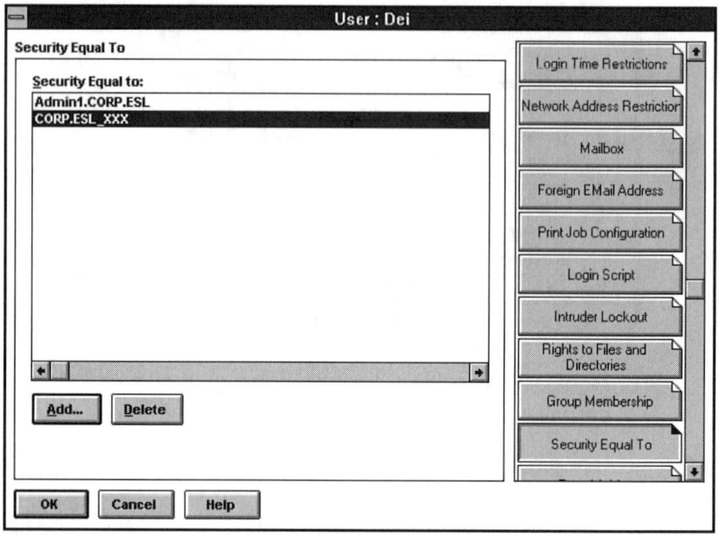

Figure 4.30
Security Equivalence Property of a user object.

Because Security Equivalence is a property of the user object, care should be taken that the user does not have the right to make changes to this property. If a user does have the Write property right to the security equivalance property and the Write property right to the ACL property of an Admin user object, the user could assign an Admin user object as one of the values for the security equivalence property. This would give the user all the rights the Admin user has. The default for a newly created user is that a user can read his security equivalence property, and you should not normally have to change this value.

One situation where security equivalence may be particularly useful is when a user in an organization needs access to files and directories of another user. This user could be made security equivalent to the user whose files and directories need to be accessed. To perform this task, you need to have the Write property right for the user object (property rights are discussed later in this chapter).

Object Effective Rights

An object's *Effective rights* are the rights that a user actually has to the object. The Effective right is not the same as the rights inherited from a parent container because these could be blocked by the IRF. Also, a user may have a right blocked for it, but may inherit a right because a group that the user belongs to, has an explicit or inherited trustee assignment for the object. By the same token, an Effective right is not the same as an explicit trustee assignment, because a user can inherit other rights because a group that the user belongs to has an explicit or inherited trustee assignment for the object.

The Effective rights need to be calculated for each situation. Because of the hierarchical structure of the NDS tree, a right may be inherited from a number of sources. This makes the determination of NDS rights an interesting and challenging task.

Consider the following example. To compute the effective rights of user KSS to the printer object HP_PRINTER, you must consider effective rights that come from any of the following sources:

1. Explicit trustee assignment: This includes the trustee assignment on HP_PRINTER that lists user KSS as a trustee (see fig. 4.31).

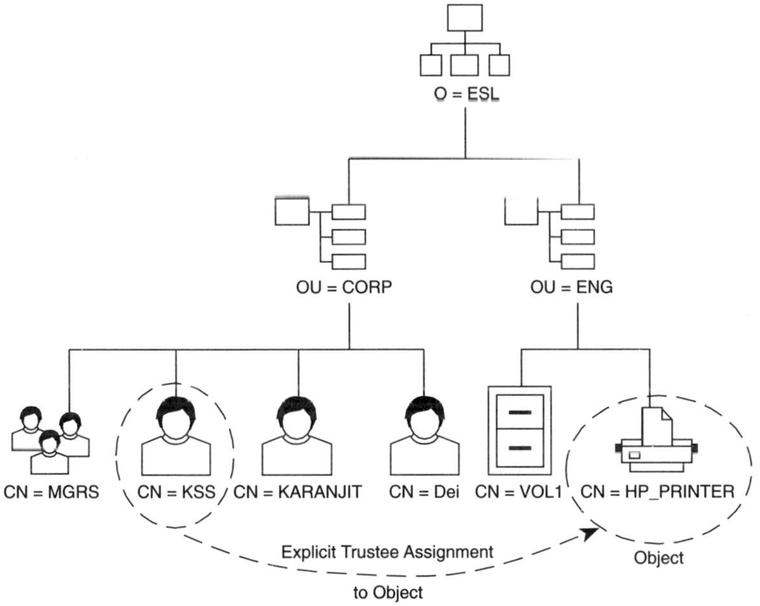

Figure 4.31
Effective Object Rights: Explicit trustee assignment.

2. Inherited from trustee's parent container: Trustee assignment on HP_PRINTER that lists OU=CORP as a trustee. This also includes trustee assignment on HP_PRINTER that lists other parent containers such as O=ESL and [Root] as trustees, since the user KSS is in the tree branch with these objects as roots of the tree branch (see fig.4.32).

Figure 4.32
Effective Object Rights: Inherited from trustee's parent container.

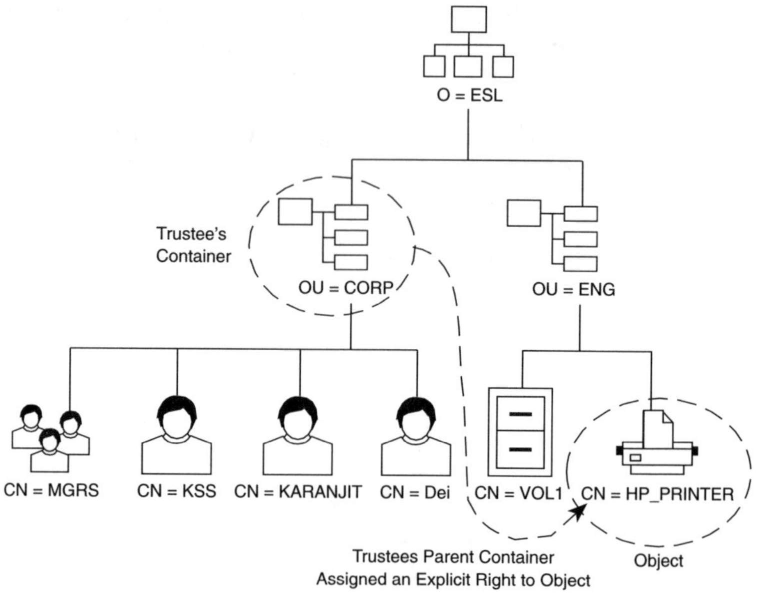

3. Inherited from direct assignment to object's container: Trustee assignment on the container OU=ENG that lists user KSS as a trustee (see fig. 4.33). The rights so assigned must pass through the object HP_PRINTER's IRF.

Figure 4.33
Effective Object Rights: Inherited from direct assignment to object's container.

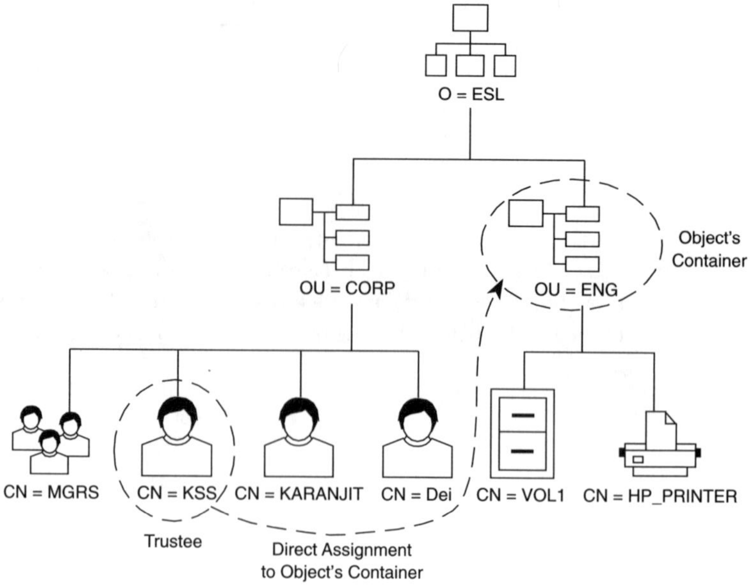

4. Inherited from assignment of trustee's container to object's container: Trustee assignment on the container OU=ENG that lists user object KSS's parent containers such as OU=CORP, O=ESL and [Root] as a trustee (see fig. 4.34). The rights so assigned must pass through the object HP_PRINTER's IRF.

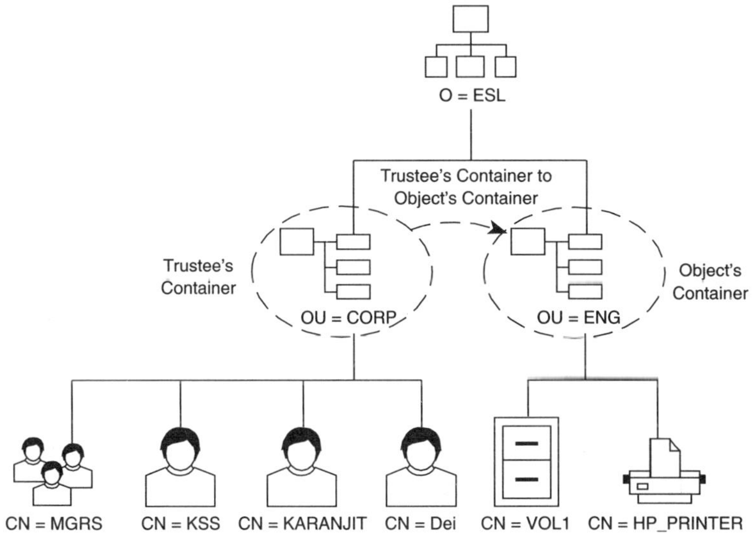

Figure 4.34
Effective Object Rights: Inherited from assignment of trustee's container to object's container.

5. Trustee assignment to a group object: Any trustee assignment made to the group object MGRS which the user KSS is a member of (see fig. 4.35).

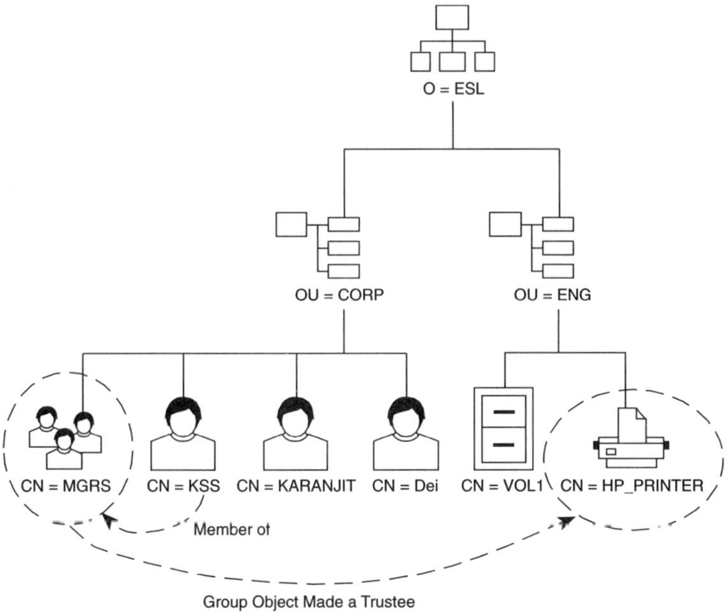

Figure 4.35
Effective Object Rights: Trustee assignment to a group object.

6. Trustee assignment to a security equivalent object: If user KSS is made a security equivalent to object KARANJIT, any right that the user KARANJIT has to HP_PRINTER is automatically inherited by user KSS (see fig. 4.36).

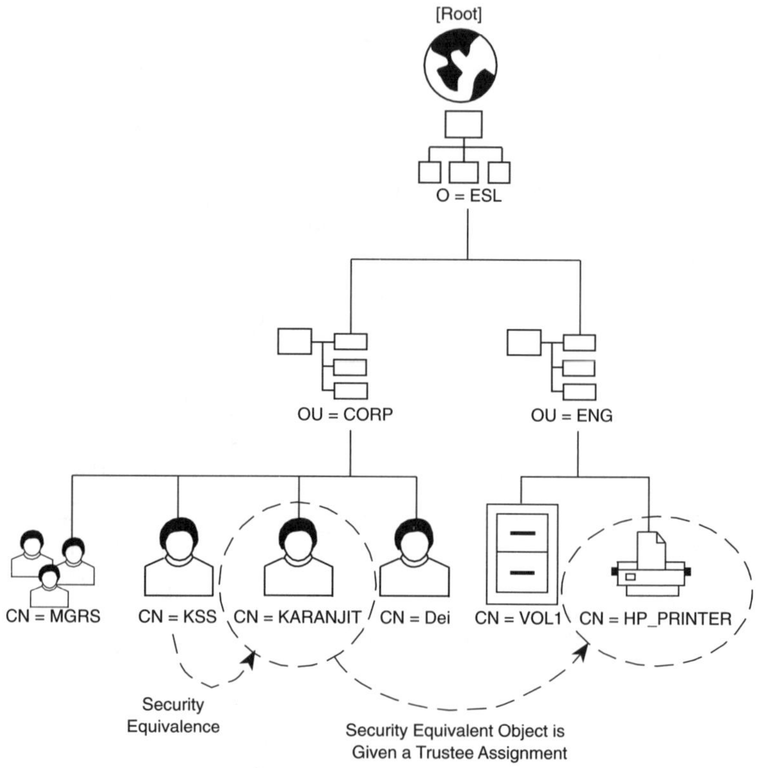

Figure 4.36
Effective Object Rights: Trustee assignment to a security equivalent object.

Calculating Object Effective Rights

Understanding how Effective rights are computed for an object in the NDS tree is extremely important for IntranetWare administration. For this reason, a number of case studies are presented that help you understand how Effective rights work in IntranetWare.

Figure 4.37 shows a worksheet that you can use to compute Effective rights. The figure also shows a partial directory tree that has the containers O=ESL, OU=CORP, and OU=ACCTG. The worksheet for computing Effective rights shows the entries for each of these containers. Each container has entries for the following:

- Inherited Rights Filter (IRF)
- Inherited Rights
- Trustee Assignment
- Effective Rights

O = ESL		
	IRF	
	Inherited Rights	
	Trustee Assignment	
	Effective Rights	
O = CORP		
	IRF	
	Inherited Rights	
	Trustee Assignment	
	Effective Rights	
O = ACCTG		
	IRF	
	Inherited Rights	
	Trustee Assignment	
	Effective Rights	

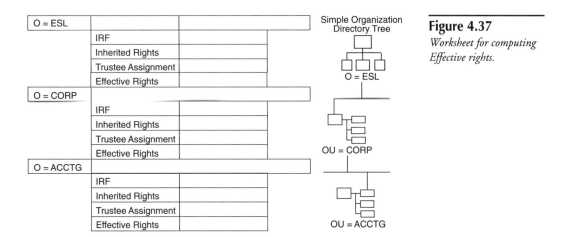

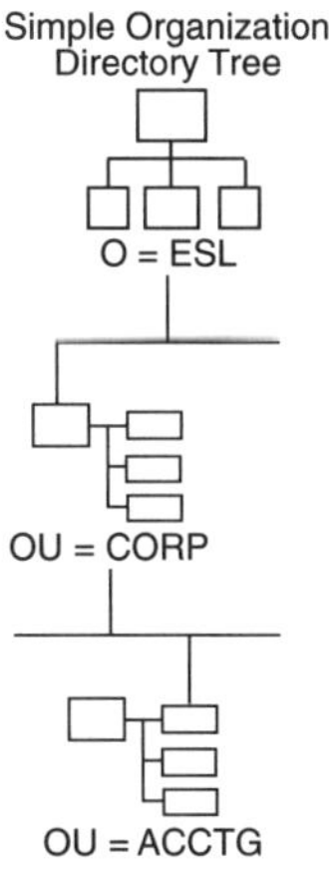

Figure 4.37
Worksheet for computing Effective rights.

While practicing how to compute Effective rights, the worksheet is an invaluable aid, as it systematically shows the rights at each level. With more experience and practice in computing effective rights, you may be able to dispense with the use of a worksheet, and be able to compute effective rights more directly.

Computing NDS Effective Rights

To compute Effective rights for an NDS object, you must consider the following:

- The rights explicitly granted to a user object.
- The rights inherited from above minus the rights revoked by the IRF. If an explicit trustee assignment exists, it overrides any inherited rights for that particular trustee.
- The rights granted to container objects between the object and the [Root]. This applies to container objects that are between the object and the [Root] and the trustee and the [Root].
- The rights granted through security equivalence.

The next few sections present case studies that further explain the rules for computing effective rights.

Effect of Making an Explicit Trustee Assignment

Figure 4.38 shows an NDS tree where user Sean has [B C D R] rights to O=ESL. The IRF for O=ESL, OU=CORP and OU=OPS is [S B C D R]. User Sean is given an explicit assignment of [BR] to OU=OPS.

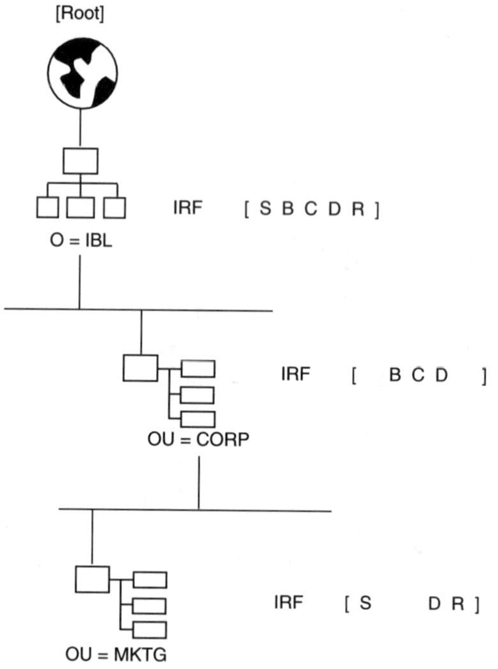

Figure 4.38
Example NDS tree—Explicit trustee assignment.

Figure 4.39 shows the completed worksheet containing the answers and the effect of the explicit trustee assignment to OU=OPS. The explanations for entries in the worksheet are presented next.

Figure 4.39
Worksheet for case study—Explicit trustee assignment.

Container		S	B	C	D	R	
O=ESL							
	IRF	S	B	C	D	R	
	Inherited Rights	None					
	Trustee Assignment		B	C	D	R	User Sean
	Effective Rights		B	C	D	R	User Sean
OU=CORP							
	IRF	S	B	C	D	R	
	Inherited Rights		B	C	D	R	User Sean
	Trustee Assignment						
	Effective Rights		B	C	D	R	User Sean
OU=OPS							
	IRF	S	B	C	D	R	
	Inherited Rights		B	C	D	R	User Sean
	Trustee Assignment		B			R	User Sean
	Effective Rights		B			R	User Sean

Entries for O=ESL

According to the case study, the IRF is [S B C D R]. There are no rights inherited from above, and therefore the entry for Inherited rights is None. An explicit trustee assignment of [B C D R] has been given to the user. The explicit trustee assignment overrides any other Inherited rights, so the Effective rights for the user in container O=ESL are the same as the explicit trustee assignment. That is, Effective rights of the user for O=ESL are [B C D R].

Entries for OU=CORP

According to the case study, the IRF is [S B C D R]. The rights inherited from this are the Effective rights of the parent container masked with the IRF for this container as shown in listing 4.1.

Listing 4.1

```
IRF                           [S B C D R ]
Effective rights of parent    [  B C D R ]

Inherited rights              [  B C D R ]
```

The Inherited rights for OU=CORP are [B C D R]. Since no trustee assignment is made in OU=CORP, the Effective rights are the same as the Inherited rights. That is, Effective rights for OU=CORP are [B C D R].

Entries for OU=OPS

According to the case study, the IRF is [S B C D R]. The rights inherited from this are the Effective rights of the parent container masked with the IRF for this container as shown in listing 4.2.

Listing 4.2

```
IRF                           [S  B C D R ]
Effective rights of parent    [   B C D R ]

Inherited rights              [   B C D R ]
```

The Inherited rights for OU=SOPS are [B C D R] for the user Sean. An explicit trustee assignment of [B R] has been made to OU=OPS for user Sean. This explicit trustee assignment overrides any Inherited rights for user Sean. That is, Effective rights for OU=OPS are [B R], the same as the explicit trustee assignment.

Explicit Trustee Assignment and Security Equivalent Assignments

Figure 4.40 shows an NDS tree where user Sean has [C D R] rights to O=ESL. The IRF for O=ESL, OU=CORP, and OU=OPS is [S B C D R]. User Sean is given an explicit assignment of [R] to OU=OPS. User Sean is made security equivalent to user James who is a member of group Agents. Group Agents has been given an explicit trustee assignment of [C D] to OU=OPS. The [Public] group has been given [B] rights to [Root].

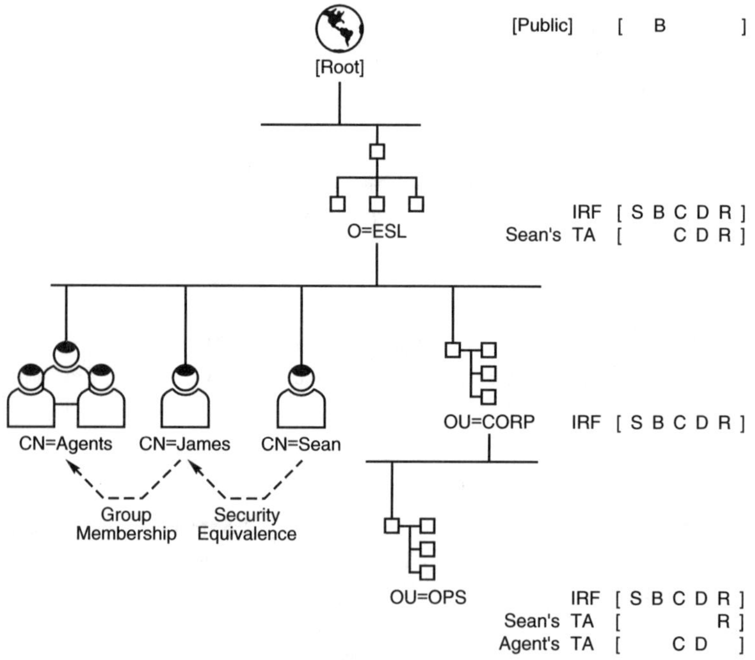

Figure 4.40
Example NDS tree—Explicit trustee assignment and security equivalents.

Figure 4.41 shows the completed worksheet containing the answers and the effect of the explicit trustee assignments and security equivalents for OU=OPS. The explanations for entries in the worksheet are presented next.

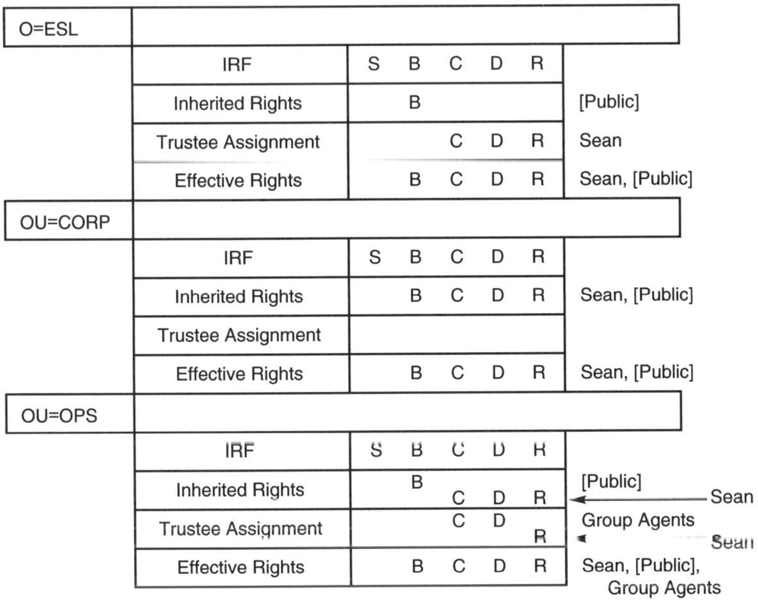
O=ESL
IRF
S B C D R
Inherited Rights
B
[Public]
Trustee Assignment
C D R
Sean
Effective Rights
B C D R
Sean, [Public]
OU=CORP
IRF
S B C D R
Inherited Rights
B C D R
Sean, [Public]
Trustee Assignment
Effective Rights
B C D R
Sean, [Public]
OU=OPS
IRF
S B C D R
Inherited Rights
B
C D R
[Public]
Sean
Trustee Assignment
C D
R
Group Agents
Sean
Effective Rights
B C D R
Sean, [Public],
Group Agents

Figure 4.41
Worksheet for case study—Explicit trustee assignment and security equivalencies.

Entries for O=ESL

The IRF, according to the case study, is [S B C D R]. [Public] has Browse object right to [Root], and therefore the rights inherited from [Root] are computed as shown in listing 4.3.

Listing 4.3

```
IRF                          [S  B C D R ]
Inherited rights from [Root] [   B       ]

Inherited rights             [   B      ]
```

Inherited rights from security equivalence to [public] are [B].

An explicit trustee assignment of [C D R] has been given to the user Sean. The explicit trustee assignment overrides any other Inherited rights for user Sean. Notice that the Inherited rights are through [Public] and there are no Inherited rights for user Sean. So the Effective rights for the user Sean in container O=ESL are the explicit trustee assignment plus any Inherited rights through other sources, such as through [public].

Effective rights of the user for O=ESL are [B C D R]. The [B] rights are from [public] and the [C D R] rights are through an explicit assignment.

Entries for OU=CORP

The IRF, according to the case study, is [S B C D R]. The rights inherited from this are the Effective rights of the parent container masked with the IRF for this container as shown in listing 4.4.

Listing 4.4

```
IRF                          [S B C D R ]
Effective rights of parent   [  B C D R ]

Inherited rights             [  B C D R ]
```

The Inherited rights for OU=CORP are [B C D R]. The [B] rights are inherited from [public] and the [C D R] rights are Inherited rights for user Sean.

Since no trustee assignment is made in OU=CORP, the Effective rights are the same as the Inherited rights. That is, Effective rights for OU=CORP are [B C D R].

Entries for OU=OPS

According to the case study, the IRF is [S B C D R]. The rights inherited from this are the Effective rights of the parent container masked with the IRF for this container as shown in listing 4.5.

Listing 4.5

```
IRF                          [S B C D R ]
Effective rights of parent   [  B C D R ]

Inherited rights             [  B C D R ]
```

The Inherited rights for OU=OPS are [B C D R] for the user Sean. The [B] rights are inherited from [public] and the [C D R] rights are Inherited rights for user Sean.

An explicit trustee assignment of [R] has been made to OU=OPS for user Sean. This explicit trustee assignment overrides any inherited rights for user Sean. This means that the Inherited rights of [C D R] are overridden by the explicit assignment of [R] for user Sean. The [B] right is not overridden, because it is inherited from [public].

User Sean acquires the rights given to group Agents because user Sean is security equivalent to user James, and James is a member of group Agents. The rights acquired through security equivalence are the [C D] rights.

The Effective rights for OU=OPS are as follows:

- The explicit trustee assignment of [R] for user Sean *plus*
- The Inherited rights of [B] from security equivalence to [public] *plus*
- The explicit rights assignment of [C D] assigned through security equivalence to user James

Therefore, the Effective rights for OU=OPS are [B C D R].

Using IRF to Restrict Rights

Figure 4.42 shows an NDS tree where user Sean has [S B C D] explicit rights to O=ESL. The IRF for O=ESL is [S B C D R], for OU=CORP it is [S B], and for OU=OPS it is [B C D R].

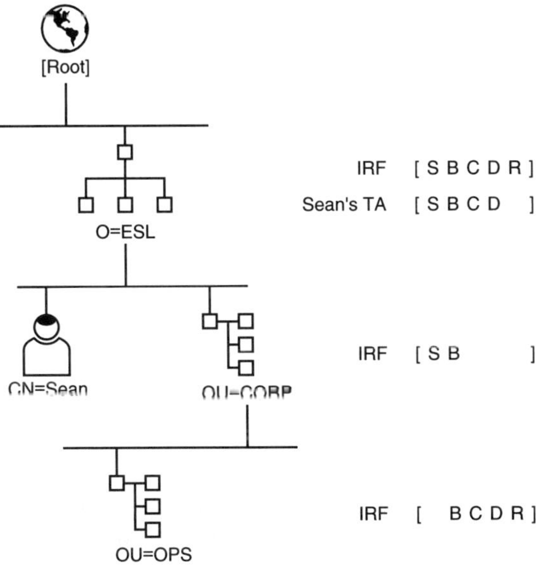

Figure 4.42
Example NDS tree—Using IRF to restrict trustee assignment.

Figure 4.43 shows the completed worksheet containing the answers and the effect of the blocking of rights using IRF. The explanations for entries in the worksheet are presented next.

O=ESL							
	IRF	S	B	C	D	R	
	Inherited Rights	None					
	Trustee Assignment	S	B	C	D		User Sean
	Effective Rights	S	B	C	D	(R)	User Sean
OU=CORP							
	IRF	S	B				
	Inherited Rights	S	B	(C	D	R)	User Sean
	Trustee Assignment						
	Effective Rights	S	B	(C	D	R)	User Sean
OU=OPS							
	IRF		B	C	D	R	
	Inherited Rights		B				User Sean
	Trustee Assignment						
	Effective Rights		B				User Sean

Figure 4.43
Worksheet for case study—Blocking rights through IRF.

Entries for O=ESL

According to the case study, the IRF is [S B C D R]. No rights are inherited from above, and therefore the entry for Inherited rights is None. An explicit trustee assignment of [S B C D] has been given to the user. The explicit trustee assignment overrides any other Inherited rights, so the Effective rights for the user in container O=ESL are the same as the explicit trustee assignment. That is, Effective rights of the user for O=ESL are [S B C D (R)]. The R right is shown in parentheses to remind you that this right was not explicitly granted, but is implied from the Supervisor right.

Entries for OU=CORP

According to the case study, the IRF is [S B]. The rights inherited from this are the Effective rights of the parent container masked with the IRF for this container as shown in listing 4.6.

Listing 4.6

```
IRF                          [S B           ]
Effective rights of parent   [S B C D (R) ]

Inherited rights             [S B (C D R) ]
```

The Inherited rights for OU=CORP are [S B (C D R)]. The actual Inherited rights are [S B], but the (C D R) rights are implied from the Supervisor right. Since no trustee assignment is made in OU=CORP, the Effective rights are the same as the Inherited rights. That is, Effective rights for OU=CORP are [S B (C D R)].

Entries for OU=OPS

According to the case study, the IRF is [B C D R]. The rights inherited from this are the Effective rights of the parent container masked with the IRF for this container as shown in listing 4.7.

Listing 4.7

```
IRF                          [  B  C D R  ]
Effective rights of parent   [S B (C D R) ]

Inherited rights             [  B         ]
```

The Inherited rights for OU=OPS are [B] for the user Sean. Notice that because the [S] right was blocked, the (C D R) rights that were implied because of the presence of the [S] right are removed from the Inherited rights. Since no trustee assignment is made in OU=OPS, the Effective rights are the same as the Inherited rights. That is, Effective rights for OU=OPS are [B].

Using Containers to Assign Rights

Figure 4.44 shows an NDS tree where OU=CORP.O=ESL has [B C D] Explicit rights to OU=SALES.O=ESL. The IRF for O=ESL is [S B C D R]; for OU=CORP it is [S B C D R]; for OU=SALES it is [ ]; and for OU=OPS it is [B]. User objects Nina and Janice are defined in the context OU=CORP.O=ESL. User Nina has an explicit trustee assignment of [S B] to O=ESL and an explicit trustee assignment of [D R] for OU=OPS. What are the rights for user object Nina in container OU=OPS.OU=SALES.O=ESL?

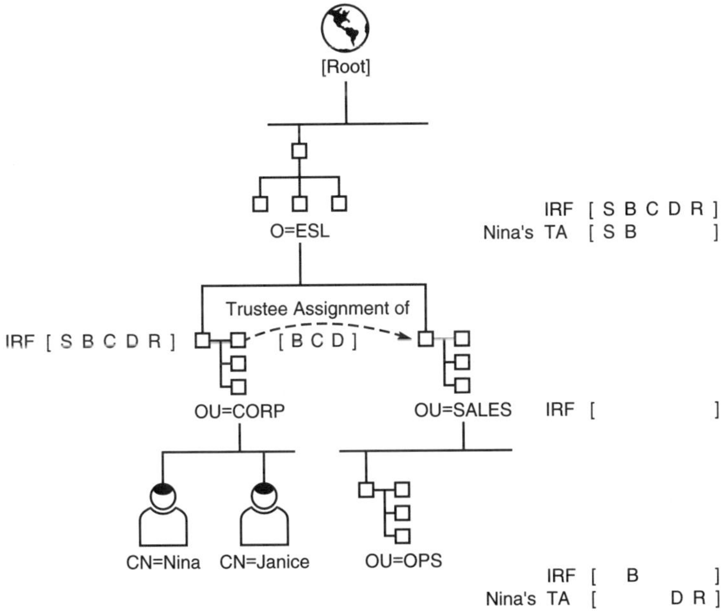

Figure 4.44
Example NDS tree—Assigning rights through containers.

Figure 4.45 shows the completed worksheet containing the answers and the effect of the blocking of rights using IRF. The explanations for entries in the worksheet are presented next.

Figure 4.45
Worksheet for case study—assigning rights through containers.

Container	Entry	Rights	Trustee
O=ESL			
	IRF	S B C D R	
	Inherited Rights	None	
	Trustee Assignment	S B	User Nina
	Effective Rights	S B (C D R)	User Nina
OU=SALES			
	IRF		
	Inherited Rights	No Rights	
	Trustee Assignment	B C D	Container OU=CORP
	Effective Rights	B C D	Container OU=CORP
OU=OPS			
	IRF	B	
	Inherited Rights	B	Container OU=CORP
	Trustee Assignment	D R	User Nina
	Effective Rights	B D R	User Nina

Entries for O=ESL

According to the case study, the IRF is [S B C D R]. There are no rights inherited from above, and therefore the entry for Inherited rights is None. An explicit trustee assignment of [S B] has been given to the user Nina. The explicit trustee assignment overrides any other inherited rights, so the Effective rights for the user in container O=ESL are the same as the explicit trustee assignment. That is, Effective rights of the user for O=ESL are [S B (C D R)]. The (C D R) rights are shown in parentheses to remind you that these rights are not explicitly granted, but are implied from the Supervisor right.

Entries for OU=SALES

The IRF, according to the case study is [ ]. The rights inherited from this are the Effective rights of the parent container masked with the IRF for this container as shown in listing 4.8.

Listing 4.8

```
IRF                           [               ]
Effective rights of parent    [S  B C  D (R) ]

Inherited rights              [               ]
```

The Inherited rights for Nina in OU=SALES are [ ]; that is, no rights.

The container OU=CORP is given an explicit trustee assignment of [B C D] to OU=SALES. The Effective rights of OU=CORP in OU=SALES are the same as the explicit trustee assignment, that is [B C D].

Entries for OU=OPS

According to the case study, the IRF is [B]. The rights inherited from this are the Effective rights of the parent container masked with the IRF for this container as shown in listing 4.9.

Listing 4.9

```
IRF                          [   B       ]
Effective rights of parent   [   B C D   ]

Inherited rights             [   B       ]
```

The Inherited rights for OU=OPS are [B] for the container OU=CORP. User Nina has an explicit trustee assignment of [D R] for OU=OPS. Therefore, the Effective rights of Nina are the Inherited rights via OU=CORP *plus* the Explicit rights to OU=OPS as shown in listing 4.10.

Listing 4.10

```
Inherited Rights from CORP   [   B         ]
Explicit TA                  [         D R ]

Effective rights             [    B    D R ]
```

Nina's Effective rights are [B D R] in OU=OPS.OU=SALES.O=ESL.

Property Rights

Property rights are used to control access to information inside an NDS object. All objects have properties, since all objects are used to store information. An object can have many properties, and you can expect different objects to have different properties. For example, a volume object has a host server property, whose value is the name of the NetWare server the volume is associated with. But this property does not exist for a user object. Similarly, a user has a group membership property that does not exist for a volume object. The group membership is an example of a property that is multi-valued. Another example is the telephone number property. A user can have several phone numbers, so the telephone property for the user has the characteristic of accommodating multiple values. The location property of an object is single-valued, because an object can have only one location.

The X.500 term for a property is an attribute. An attribute can consist of a type and one or more values. In NDS these are termed property values. The attribute type determines the characteristic of the attribute, such as its syntax, number of values allowed, how the values can be tested for comparison, and so on. An attribute value that can contribute to the name of an object is called a *distinguished attribute value*; for example, the name attribute of an object.

Table 4.2 lists the Property rights defined for an NDS object.

Table 4.2
Property Rights Summary

Property Right	Abbreviation	Meaning
Supervisor	S	Grants all rights to All properties.
Compare	C	Grants the right to compare the value to a property. Does not allow you to see the value.
Read	R	Grants right to read the value of a property. Read includes the Compare right, even if the Compare is not explicitly given.
Write	W	Grants the right to add, remove, or change any values of the property.
Add or Delete Self	A	Applies to list property values such as group membership. Grants the trustee the right to add or remove itself from the property value. The trustee cannot add or delete other values of the property. Useful for mailing lists, group lists.

The Supervisor property right grants all rights to a property. You can use the Inherited Rights Filter to block this property.

The Compare property right grants the right to compare the value of a property. A trustee with the Compare property right allows a trustee to compare the property value to any value. The result of this comparison is a logical True if there is a match, and a logical False if there is no match. This property right would be useful for NDS tools that need to check for the existence of a specific value. The Compare right does not give you the right to read a property value. This right is granted by a special property value.

The Read property right grants the right to read a value for a property. This property right would be useful for NDS tools that need to display selected property values of an NDS object. If a trustee can read the value, it follows that the trustee should be able to compare the property value against another value. For this reason, a Read property right includes the Compare property right.

The Write property right allows the property value to be changed. Some property values are multi-valued. In this case, the Write property allows the trustee to remove from or add values to the property.

The Add or Delete Self property right allows the addition of a new property value or the removal of an existing property value. This right applies to multi-valued properties such as group memberships, mailing lists, or the Access Control List (ACL). The Add or Delete Self property right cannot be used to change the value of a property other than itself.

The Write property right includes the Add or Delete Self property.

All Properties Right versus Selective Property Right

You can assign the property rights selectively to specific properties, or apply them to all the properties of an object. Assigning a property right to all the properties of an object is called the *All Properties right.* A property right that refers to an individual or selected property is called a *Selected Property right.* An example of property right assignment is when a user object is created in a container. The user object is given the Read property right to all of its properties (All Properties). It is also given a Read/Write property right to its login script property and the Print Job Configuration property. Users then can modify their user login scripts and print job configurations. If you want to prevent a user from performing these activities, you must restrict these property rights.

The All Properties right is a convenient way of assigning default property rights to all properties. If there are some exceptions to this default, you can use the Selected Property right to individually set the property right of any property. The Selected Property right overrides the property right set by the All Properties right.

The Access Control List Property

Every object has an *Access Control List* (ACL) property, also called the Object Trustees property. This property contains a list of all trustees that have a trustee assignment to the object or its property. It does not list other objects this object may have a right to. Because of this, to grant a right you must go to the object, and then assign a trustee. You cannot go to the trustee and add objects that this trustee may have rights to.

You can use the ACL property value to specify any of the following:

- An object right, such as the [S B C D R] rights
- A right to all properties of the object, called the "All Properties right"
- A right to a specific property

Since an ACL is a property of the object that describes the trustee assignments to the object, it can include a trustee assignment to itself. This trustee assignment to the ACL property would describe which of the operations described by the property rights [S C R W A] a trustee could perform.

Consider what would happen if a trustee had a Write property right to the ACL. Such a trustee could then modify the ACL, and grant and revoke privileges by changing the ACL value. To do this a trustee would in addition need the Read property right and the Browse object right to the object. The trustee could grant itself Supervisor rights to the object. And this would give the trustee complete control over the object and its subordinates (unless blocked by an IRF or explicit assignment).

In actual practice, it is unlikely that you would want to give an Admin user just the Write right to the ACL property. You would probably want to give the Admin user Supervisor object right. This would give complete control over the object and its subordinates, unless as noted earlier, you block the Supervisor right.

Normally, you would probably not single out the ACL property (appears as Object Trustee property in the NetWare Administrator Tool) to give property rights to. But you could inadvertently grant the Write right to All Properties. This in turn would grant the Write right to the ACL property, and then the problem described earlier would exist.

NDS Rights and the File System

A trustee who has the Write property right to the NetWare server's ACL property is granted the Supervisor file system right to the root of each server's volume. It is therefore important that you do not inadvertently assign the Write right to the server's ACL property, or the Write right to the server object (All Properties of the server object).

Normally, the NDS rights are independent from the file system rights. The only exception is the one mentioned above. Actually, the exception is necessary to provide an easy way for a trustee with Supervisor rights to access files and directories in volume objects.

Consider the Admin user, who is normally given the Supervisor object right to the root container of the tree branch that user is expected to manage. This user would then have Supervisor rights to all objects in the tree branch, unless the Supervisor right is explicitly blocked. The Supervisor object right would grant to the user the Supervisor property right to All Properties for all objects, including the server object. If the user has the Write property right to the server object, the user then inherits the Supervisor NetWare File System right to the root of all volumes for which the server is a host.

The Admin user could be explicitly granted the Supervisor NetWare File System right to a volume object also. In general, you can grant any NDS object an explicit NetWare File System right to a file or directory in any volume object, even though you usually grant an NDS object NDS security rights. Figure 4.46 shows a situation in which the user Admin1.CORP.ESL has been granted Supervisor, Read, and File Scan rights to the SYSTEM directory of a volume. Figure 4.47 shows that the NDS group object NETMGRS.CORP.ESL_XXX has been granted Read and File Scan rights.

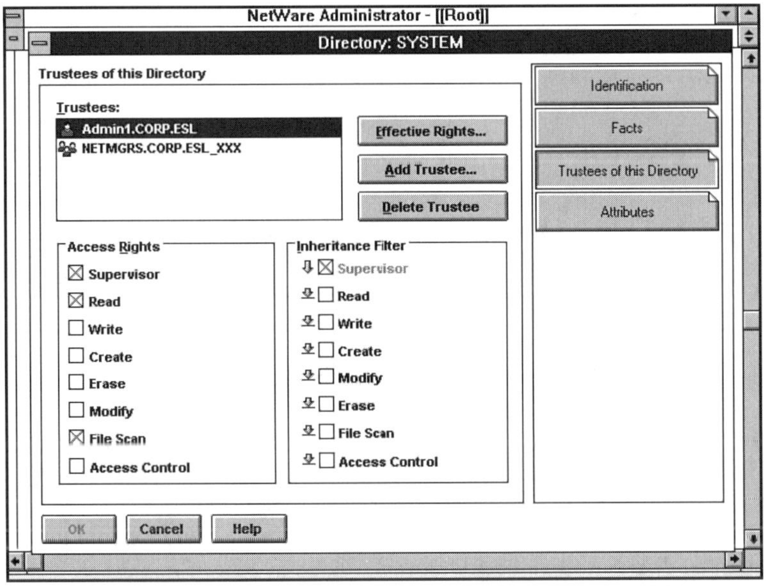

Figure 4.46
NetWare File System right assigned to a user NDS object.

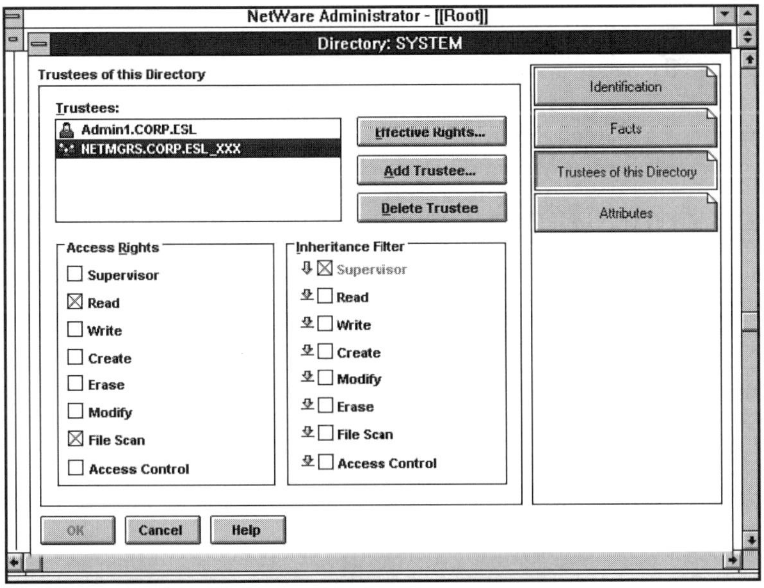

Figure 4.47
NetWare File System right assigned to a group NDS object.

You should exercise care when you assign a container object a right to another NDS object or a NetWare File System. All objects within a container inherit any rights assigned to that container object, because a container acts as a logical group of NDS objects.

For instance, if a Supervisor NetWare File System right is assigned to the [Root] object, all objects in the [Root] directory are assigned the Supervisor NetWare File System right. And because [Root] is the top-most container of an NDS tree, this includes all objects in the NDS tree.

Calculating Property Effective Rights

Calculating Property Effective rights is similar to calculating Object Effective rights. The same rules of inheritance apply.

You can deal with object property rights in terms of their All Property rights or Selective Property rights. Only All Property rights can be inherited. Selective Property rights cannot be inherited. Consider what would happen if a Selective Property were allowed to be inherited. A selected property might have no meaning for objects further down in the tree. For instance, intruder detection is a property of a container object, and if this property were inherited to an object (such as a user object that does not have an intruder detection property), it would not make sense. On the other hand, assigning rights to information inside objects might be convenient, regardless of the different types of properties NDS objects can have. This can be done by allowing the All Properties right to be inherited.

The All Properties right and the Selected Properties right each have a separate Inherited Rights Filter, so a right can be blocked at any level. Also, a right assigned to a Selected Property overrides the rights that can be inherited through the All Properties rights.

Case Study 1—Computing Property Effective Rights

Figure 4.48 shows a directory tree for organization IBL. Drew is made a trustee of Organization O=IBL and given the All Properties rights of Create, Read, Add/Delete Self. The All Properties IRFs for the containers are shown as follows:

IRF for O=IBL	[S C R W A]
IRF for OU=CORP	[C R W]
IRF for OU=MKTG	[S W A]

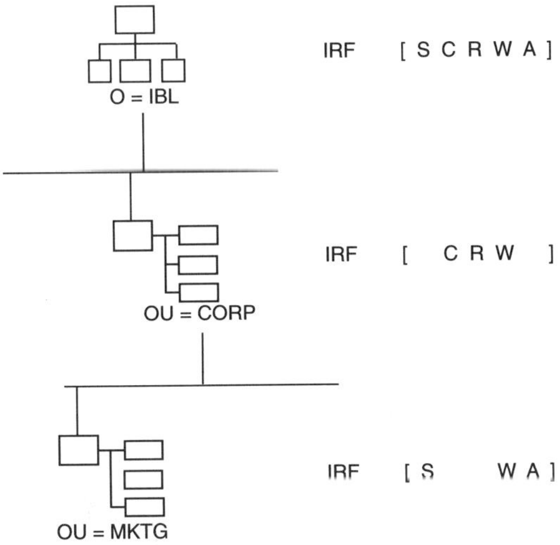

Figure 4.48
Property Effective Rights: NDS tree for case study 1.

Calculate Drew's Property Effective rights in containers O=IBL, OU=CORP and OU=MKTG. Assume that Drew does not inherit rights from any other source than the ones listed in the case study.

Figure 4.49 shows the completed worksheet containing the answers. The explanation for entries in the worksheet is presented next.

O = IBL		
	IRF	S C R W A
	Inherited Rights	None
	Trustee Assignment	C R A
	Effective Rights	C R A
OU = CORP		
	IRF	C R W
	Inherited Rights	C R
	Trustee Assignment	None
	Effective Rights	C R
OU = MKTG		
	IRF	S W A
	Inherited Rights	No Rights
	Trustee Assignment	None
	Effective Rights	No Rights

Figure 4.49
Property Effective Rights: Worksheet for case study 1.

Entries for O=IBL

According to the case study, the IRF is [S C R W A]. There are no rights inherited from above, and therefore the entry for Inherited rights is None. An explicit trustee assignment of [C R A] has been given to the user. The explicit trustee assignment overrides any other inherited rights, so the Effective rights for the user in container O=IBL are the same as the explicit trustee assignment. That is, the Property Effective rights of the user for O=IBL are [C R A].

Entries for OU=CORP

According to the case study, the IRF is [C R W]. The rights inherited from this are the Effective rights of the parent container masked with the IRF for this container as shown in listing 4.11.

Listing 4.11

```
IRF                            [    C R W   ]
Effective rights of parent     [    C R    A]

Inherited rights               [    C R     ]
```

The masking operation is a logical AND operation, which means that an entry needs to be in both of the rights for it to be in the final result.

The Inherited rights for OU=CORP are [C R]. Since no trustee assignment is made in OU=CORP, the Effective rights are the same as the Inherited rights. That is, Property Effective rights for OU=CORP are [C R].

Entries for OU=MKTG

According to the case study, the IRF is [S W A]. The rights inherited from this are the Effective rights of the parent container masked with the IRF for this container as shown in listing 4.12.

Listing 4.12

```
IRF                            [S     W A ]
Effective rights of parent     [  C R     ]

Inherited rights               [          ]
```

The Inherited rights for OU=MKTG are [ ], or No rights. Because no trustee assignment is made in OU=MKTG, the Effective rights are the same as the Inherited rights. That is, Property Effective rights for OU=MKTG are No rights.

Case Study 2—Computing Property Effective Rights

Figure 4.50 shows a directory tree for organization IBL. James is made a trustee of Organization O=IBL and given the All Properties rights of Create, Read, and Write. James is also made a trustee of organization unit OU=MKTG, and given the All Properties right of Write. The All Properties IRFs for the containers are shown below:

IRF for O=IBL	[S C R W A]
IRF for OU=CORP	[S C R W A]
IRF for OU=MKTG	[S R]

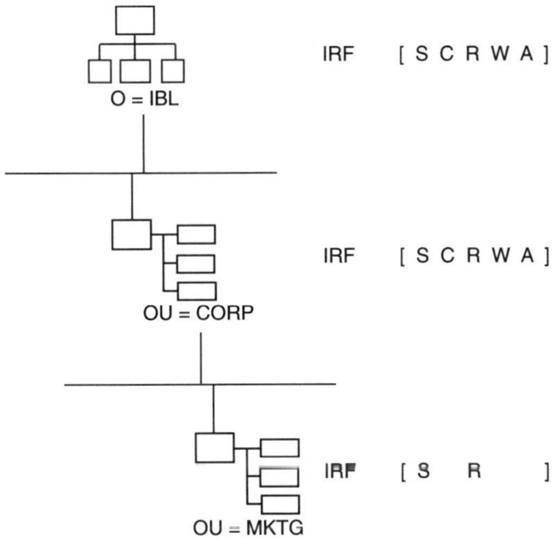

Figure 4.50
Property Effective Rights: NDS tree for case study 2.

Calculate James's Property Effective rights in containers O=IBL, OU=CORP, and OU=MKTG. Assume that James does not inherit rights from any other source than the ones listed in the case study.

Figure 4.51 shows the completed worksheet containing the answers. The explanations for entries in the worksheet are presented next.

O = IBL			
	IRF	S C R W A	
	Inherited Rights	None	
	Trustee Assignment	C R W	James
	Effective Rights	C R W (A)	James
OU = CORP			
	IRF	S C R W A	
	Inherited Rights	C R W (A)	
	Trustee Assignment	None	
	Effective Rights	C R W (A)	James
OU = MKTG			
	IRF	S R	
	Inherited Rights	(C) R	
	Trustee Assignment		
	Effective Rights	(C) R	James

Figure 4.51
Property Effective Rights: Worksheet for case study 2.

Entries for O=IBL

According to the case study, the IRF is [S C R W A]. There are no rights inherited from above, and therefore the entry for Inherited rights is None. An explicit trustee assignment of [C R W] has been given to the user. The explicit trustee assignment overrides any other Inherited rights, so the Effective rights for the user in container O=IBL are the same as the explicit trustee assignment. That is, the Property Effective rights of the user for O=IBL are [C R W (A)]. The [(A)] right is implied from the Write right.

Entries for OU=CORP

According to the case study, the IRF is [S C R W A]. The rights inherited from this are the Effective rights of the parent container masked with the IRF for this container as shown in listing 4.13.

Listing 4.13

```
IRF                          [S C R W  A  ]
Effective rights of parent   [  C R W (A) ]

Inherited rights             [  C R W (A) ]
```

The masking operation is a logical AND operation, which means that an entry needs to be in both of the rights for it to be in the final result.

The Inherited rights for OU=CORP are [C R W (A)]. Since no trustee assignment is made in OU=CORP, the Effective rights are the same as the Inherited rights. That is, Property Effective rights for OU=CORP are [C R W (A)].

Entries for OU=MKTG

According to the case study, the IRF is [S R]. The rights inherited from this are the Effective rights of the parent container masked with the IRF for this container as shown in listing 4.14.

Listing 4.14

```
IRF                          [S    R      ]
Effective rights of parent   [  C  R W (A)]

Inherited rights             [ (C) R      ]
```

The Inherited rights for OU=MKTG are [(C) R]. The [(C)] Inherited right is implied because of the presence of the Read right in the Inherited rights. Because no trustee assignment is made in OU=MKTG, the Effective rights are the same as the Inherited rights. That is, Property Effective rights for OU=MKTG are [(C) R].

Case Study 3—Computing Property Effective Rights

Figure 4.52 shows a directory tree for organization DCS. James is made a trustee of Organization O=DCS and given the All Properties rights of Create, Read, and Write. James is a member of the group ATEAM. ATEAM is given the All Properties right Write and Add/Delete Self to OU=SALES. The All Properties IRFs for the containers are shown as follows:

IRF for O=DCS	[S C R W A]
IRF for OU=SALES	[S C R W A]
IRF for OU=MKTG	[S R]

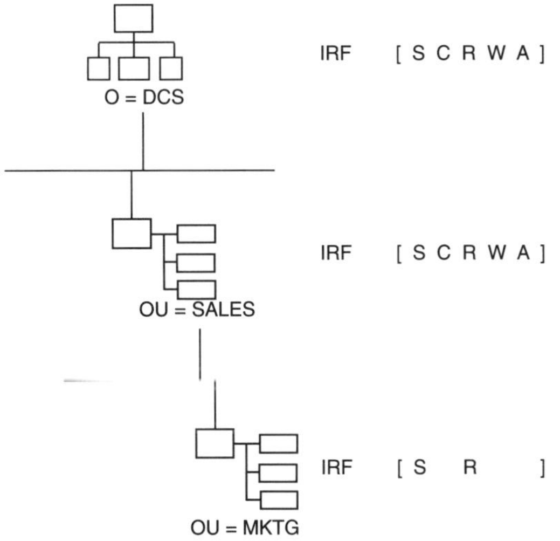

Figure 4.52
Property Effective Rights: NDS tree for case study 3.

Calculate James's Property Effective rights in containers O=DCS, OU=SALES, and OU=MKTG. Assume that James does not inherit rights from any other source than the ones listed in the case study.

Figure 4.53 shows the completed worksheet containing the answers. The explanations for entries in the worksheet are presented next.

O = DCS			
	IRF	S C R W A	
	Inherited Rights	None	
	Trustee Assignment	C R W	James
	Effective Rights	C R W	James
OU = SALES			
	IRF	S C R W A	
	Inherited Rights	C R W (A)	
	Trustee Assignment	W A	ATEAM
	Effective Rights	C R W A	James, Group ATEAM
OU = MKTG			
	IRF	S R	
	Inherited Rights	(C) R	James
	Trustee Assignment	W (A)	James
	Effective Rights	W (A)	James

Figure 4.53
Property Effective Rights: Worksheet for case study 3.

Entries for O=DCS

According to the case study, the IRF is [S C R W A]. There are no rights inherited from above, and therefore the entry for Inherited rights is None. An explicit trustee assignment of [C R W] has been given to the user. The explicit trustee assignment overrides any other Inherited rights, so the Effective rights for the user in container O=DCS are the same as the explicit trustee assignment. That is, the Property Effective rights of the user for O=DCS are [C R W (A)]. The [(A)] right is implied from the Write right.

Entries for OU=SALES

According to the case study, the IRF is [S C R W A]. The rights inherited from this are the Effective rights of the parent container masked with the IRF for this container as shown in listing 4.15.

Listing 4.15

```
IRF                           [S  C R W  A  ]
Effective rights of parent    [   C R W (A) ]

Inherited     rights          [   C R W (A) ]
```

The masking operation is a logical AND operation, which means that an entry needs to be in both of the rights for it to be in the final result.

The Inherited rights for OU=SALES are [C R W (A)]. A trustee assignment is made to group object SALES of Write and Add/Delete Self. This would override any inherited trustee assignments for group object ATEAM. But because no trustee assignments are inherited for group object ATEAM, there are no rights to override. You cannot override the Inherited rights of [C R W (A)], because these rights are for user object James and not group object ATEAM.

Since James is a member of group ATEAM, his rights to OU=SALES are the sum of the Inherited and Effective rights as shown in listing 4.16.

Listing 4.16

```
Inherited rights for user James    [   C R W (A)]
Trustee assignment for ATEAM       [         W  A ]

Effective rights for James         [   C R W  A ]
```

Property Effective rights of user object James for OU=SALES are [C R W A]. Notice that the Add/Delete to Self right is no longer an implied right [(A)], since it was explicitly assigned to group ATEAM. Also, the Write right is derived from both the Inherited rights and trustee assignment to group object ATEAM. If this right were removed from the Trustee Assignment, the Write right would still exist in the Effective rights because it would then be derived from the Inherited rights.

Entries for OU=MKTG

According to the case study, the IRF is [S R]. The rights inherited from this are the Effective rights of the parent container masked with the IRF for this container as shown in listing 4.17.

Listing 4.17

```
IRF                              [S      R       ]
Effective rights of parent       [    C  R W A   ]

Inherited rights                 [   (C) R       ]
```

The Inherited rights for OU=MKTG are [(C) R]. The actual right inherited is [R], but the [(C)] Inherited right is implied because of the presence of the Read right in the Inherited rights. Both of these rights are due to rights assigned to user James. Since an explicit trustee assignment is made in OU=MKTG to user James, the explicit trustee assignment of [W] overrides the Inherited rights. Property Effective rights for OU=MKTG are [W (A)] (see listing 4.18).

Listing 4.18

```
Inherited rights for James     [  (C)  R         ]
Trustee assignment for James   [           W (A) ]

Effective rights for James     [           W (A) ]
```

Comparing NetWare File System Security with NDS Security

The similarities are that both NDS and NetWare file system security make use of the concepts of trustees, trustee rights, inheritance, and Inherited Rights Filter. For a user to gain access to an object (NDS file/directory), the user must be made a trustee to an object and given appropriate rights. The rights flow down the tree and can be blocked by the IRF. The actual rights a user has at any level of the tree are called Effective rights.

The differences between NDS and NetWare file system security include the following:

- NDS rights are further sub-divided into Object rights and Property rights.
- In NDS rights, the IRF can block the Supervisor object right and the Property right. In the NetWare file system right the Supervisor file system right cannot be blocked.
- NDS rights do not flow to a NetWare file system right, except in the following case: Any user that has the Write property right to the ACL of the server object has the Supervisor right to the root of each of the server's volumes.

When a user object is created, no automatic file system rights are created except to the user's home directory, if one was specified at the time of creation. Figure 4.54 shows the rights to newly created user CN=KSS.O=IMF to the home directory USERS\KSS in volume CN=FS1_SYS.OU =SALES.O=ESL. Notice that the user has [S R W C E M F A] rights to his home directory; that is, the user has All Rights to his home directory.

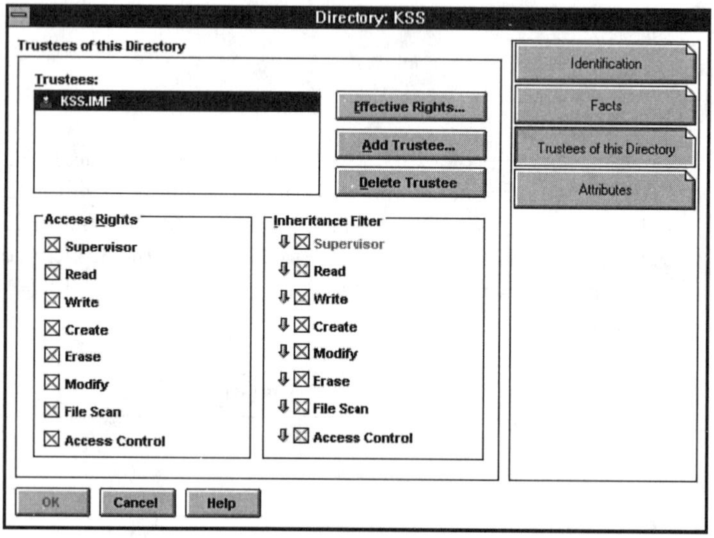

Figure 4.54
Right of user KSS in home directory.

In NetWare 3.x, the term *Inherited Rights Mask* (IRM) was used to describe the mechanism to block the flow of NetWare file system rights. In IntranetWare, the term *Inherited Rights Filter* (IRF) is used for both file system rights and NDS object rights.

Another minor distinction, though not documented in the Novell manuals, is that in NetWare 3.x the Supervisor file system rights were called Supervisory. They are now called Supervisor in IntranetWare.

As in NetWare 3.x, the file system supervisor right granted to a directory also grants Supervisor rights to files and directories below the directory.

One major conceptual difference between NetWare 3.x and IntranetWare file systems is the scope of the trustee. In NetWare 3.x, the trustee could only be a user account or a group account defined in the server's bindery. In IntranetWare, you can assign trustees to user objects and group objects in containers other than where the volume is installed. The trustee is not limited to the user and group objects—it can be any NDS object, such as another container object. If a container object is made a trustee of a file/directory, all objects within it (including, of course, user and group objects) inherit the trustee rights to the file or directory. When dealing with assigning file/directory rights it is easier to assign the rights using a container object, if the NDS containers and the leaf objects are properly designed to reflect usage of resources.

Any NDS object that has a Write right to the ACL property (Object Trustee property) of the NetWare server object, is also granted the Supervisor right to the root of each of the volumes hosted by the NetWare server. Because a Supervisor file/directory right cannot be blocked by an IRF, this should be a consideration in setting up Security rights.

You can grant the Write property right through the following:

- Write right to All Properties of the NetWare server object.
- Write right to the Selected Property ACL (Object Trustee) for the NetWare server object.
- Supervisor right to the All Properties right or ACL property (Selected Property) for the NetWare server object.
- Supervisor object right to the NetWare server object. This causes the object to have Supervisor right to the All Properties of the NetWare server object.
- Security equivalence to an object that has any of the rights listed above.

Directory and File Attribute rights in IntranetWare are a superset of the rights for NetWare 3.x. That is, IntranetWare directory and file attributes include all those for NetWare 3.x, and additionally, the rights listed in table 4.3.

Table 4.3
Additional IntranetWare Attributes

Attribute	File/ Directory	Abbreviation	Description
Migrate	File	M	Indicates that the file has migrated to near-line storage
Don't Migrate	File/ Directory	Dm	Prevents a file or the files in a directory from migrating
Compress	File	Co	Indicates if a file has been compressed
Don't Compress	File/ Directory	Dc	Prevents a file or the files in a directory from being compressed
Immediate Compress	File/ Directory	Ic	Specified file or files in a directory are marked for compression as soon as the OD can perform compression
Can't compress	File	Cc	Indicates that a file cannot be compressed because of limited space saving benefit

The attributes *Migrate* (M), *Compress* (Co), and *Can't Compress* (Cc) are status attributes and indicate the status of individual files only. The other attributes—*Don't Migrate* (Dm), *Don't Compress* (Dc), and *Immediate Compress* (Ic)—apply to both files and directories and specify actions that are to be performed or prevented from occurring.

The Data Migration feature is installed using INSTALL.NLM and requires a near-linestorage medium that acts as a secondary to the primary hard disk storage area.

The compression feature is enabled or disabled on a volume-by-volume basis during installation. It can be further controlled by a variety of SET parameters.

Default NDS Security

When the NDS tree is first installed, the *implicit* group [Public] is made a trustee of [Root] and given the Browse object right. The Browse object right is then inherited by all subcontainers under the NDS tree unless explicitly blocked by revoking rights from the Inherited Rights Filter. By definition, [Public] includes all user objects that are connected to an NDS tree, including those that are simply attached to a IntranetWare server and not logged (not authenticated) into the network (see fig. 4.55). You should avoid assigning excessive rights through [Public]. For example, if rights are assigned through [Public] to a NetWare file system, all users that attach to the network can access the file system *without logging in* to the network. You can run the DSREPAIR.NLM at the server to remove any [Public] trustee assignments to the NetWare file system.

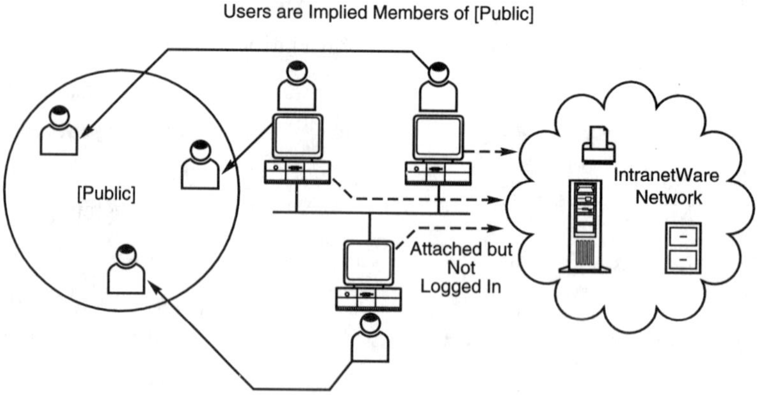

Figure 4.55
[Public] implicit group membership.

To run DSREPAIR for removing file system trustee assignments to [Public], follow these steps:

1. Type the following at server console:

   LOAD DSREPAIR

2. Select "1. Select Options"

3. Make sure that "5. Check file system for valid trustee IDs" is selected.

   Selected DSREPAIR options have an asterisk (*) next to them.

4. Select "8. Return to selection menu"

5. Select "2. Begin Repair"

6. Select "3. Exit"

You can assign rights explicitly, in which case they are called *explicit trustee assignment.* Another way to obtain rights is through *inheritance.* Rights assigned to a container of an NDS tree *flow down* to all objects in the container unless they are explicitly blocked. The rights that an NDS object inherits are called *inherited rights.* You use the Inherited Rights Filter (IRF) to block rights. The actual rights an NDS object inherits are the *logical AND* of the rights inherited from the parent of the NDS object and the IRF assigned to the NDS object. You can assign the IRF to any NDS object in the NDS tree besides the [Root] object. An explicit trustee assignment for an NDS object *overrides any inherited rights for that NDS object.* This new explicit trustee assignment flows down, until restricted by an IRF for an object, or until another explicit trustee assignment is made. You cannot set an IRF on an object for a particular trustee. The IRF that is set for an NDS object applies to all trustees of the NDS object.

You can grant property rights on a selected property basis, in which case the rights are called *Selected Property rights.* For example, a user object might have an explicit Read and Write right to the Login Script property, meaning that the user can read and modify the contents of his user login script. Granting the same property rights to all properties of an NDS object sometimes is desirable, such as assigning the right Read and Compare to all properties of an NDS object. The rights assigned in this manner are called *All Property rights.* All Property rights is a collective way to grant rights to all properties of an NDS object. The rights assigned through All Properties can be inherited, but the rights granted through Selected Properties cannot be inherited. The NDS security maintains separate Inherited Rights Filters for the following:

- Object rights
- All Properties rights
- Selected Property rights

Because object rights and All Properties rights can be inherited (or flow down), it makes sense that there are Inherited Rights Filters for them. But at first glance, it does not make sense that Selected Property rights has an IRF because it has been stated that Selected Property rights cannot be inherited. The reason that Selected Property rights have a separate filter is that the All Property rights apply to all the properties of an NDS object, and you might want to block out rights to a specific property. One way of doing this is to block out the rights by removing them from the Inherited Rights Filter for that specific property. Another way of modifying the property right for a specific property is to grant an explicit property right for that property. Explicit rights granted to a specific property override the All Property rights.

An example of the use of the mechanisms described so far are the default property rights assigned to user objects. A user is granted the Read and Compare All Properties to his or her user object. This allows the user to examine the property values set for the user object. The user is also granted the Read and Write selected property rights to the Login Script and Print Job Configuration properties. These selected property rights override the All Property rights of Read and Compare.

The NDS object rights are independent of the NDS property rights, except in one important case. A Supervisor object right to an NDS object gives the trustee the Supervisor property right of All Properties for that NDS object. The Supervisor property right of All Properties gives the trustee complete control over the object's properties, including any critical properties used to determine security rights for that object.

The ACL Property

A critical property that exists for all NDS objects is the Access Control List (ACL) property. The ACL property contains a list of all trustee assignments to that object. The ACL property is also called Object Trustees property in the NetWare Administrator (see fig. 4.56). For example, if a user object has a Supervisor object right granted for it to user CN=Admin.O=ESL, and a Read/ Write property right for property e-mail granted to CN=MailKeeper.O=ESL, then the ACL for the user object contains two entries in the ACL list:

1. Trustee CN=Admin.O=ESL granted [S] object right
2. Trustee CN=MailKeeper.O=ESL granted [R W] property right

Figure 4.56
Object Trustees (ACL) Selected Property.

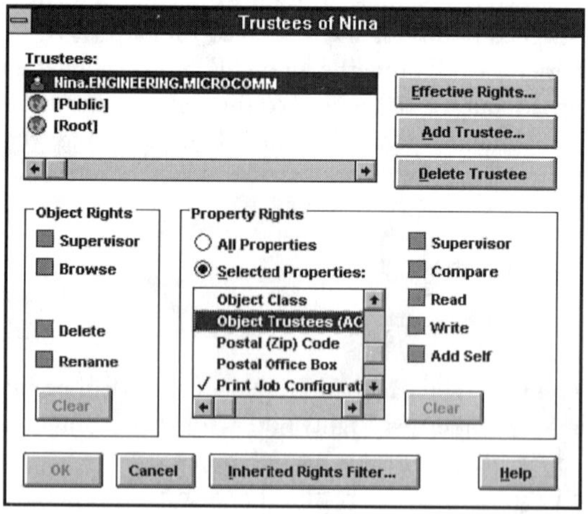

These two additional entries are a record of the trustee assignments given to the user object, and are in addition to any other entries that may have been granted to the user object, such as the trustee assignments to implement default rights for the user object.

The ACL property right lists only explicit trustee assignments. It does not, for instance, contain Inherited rights and Effective rights, which are computed based on considerations that are discussed later in this chapter. A conceptual view of the ACL property list is shown in figure 4.57. This figure shows that the volume object NW4KS_SYS has two trustee assignments (ACEs—Access Control Elements) in its ACL property. User object CN=Peter.OU=CORP.O=ESL has the object rights of Browse and Read, and container object OU=MKTG.O=ESL has the object right of Supervisor. The latter ACE implies that all objects under the container grouping OU=MKTG inherit the Supervisor rights to volume object NW4KS_SYS.

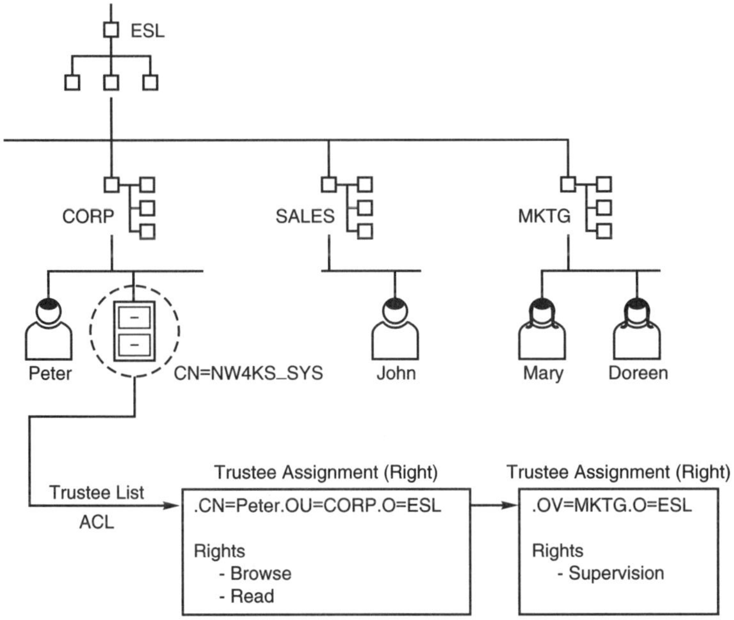

Figure 4.57
ACL and ACE.

If a user object has the Write property right to the ACL property right, the user can modify the ACL property. For instance, the user can modify the ACL property right and grant to himself the Supervisor object right.

Also, if a user has Supervisor object rights, the user automatically has Supervisor All Property rights to that object. The *Supervisor All Properties* right implies that the user has the Write property right to the ACL property right.

If a user has the Write property right to the ACL of a file server object, the user automatically has the Supervisor NetWare File System right to the root of all volumes attached to the server (see fig. 4.58). This is the only case where NDS security rights affect the NetWare file system security rights. Figure 4.58 shows that user CN=Dei.OU= CORP.O=ESL has the Write property right to server object CN=NW4KS.OU=CORP.O=ESL. The server NW4KS has two volumes attached to it whose volume object names are NW4KS_SYS and NW4KS_VOL1. User Dei is given Supervisor NetWare file system right to the root of these volumes. The Supervisor file system rights once assigned cannot be blocked.

Figure 4.58
Write property right and ACL of NetWare server object.

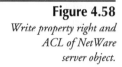

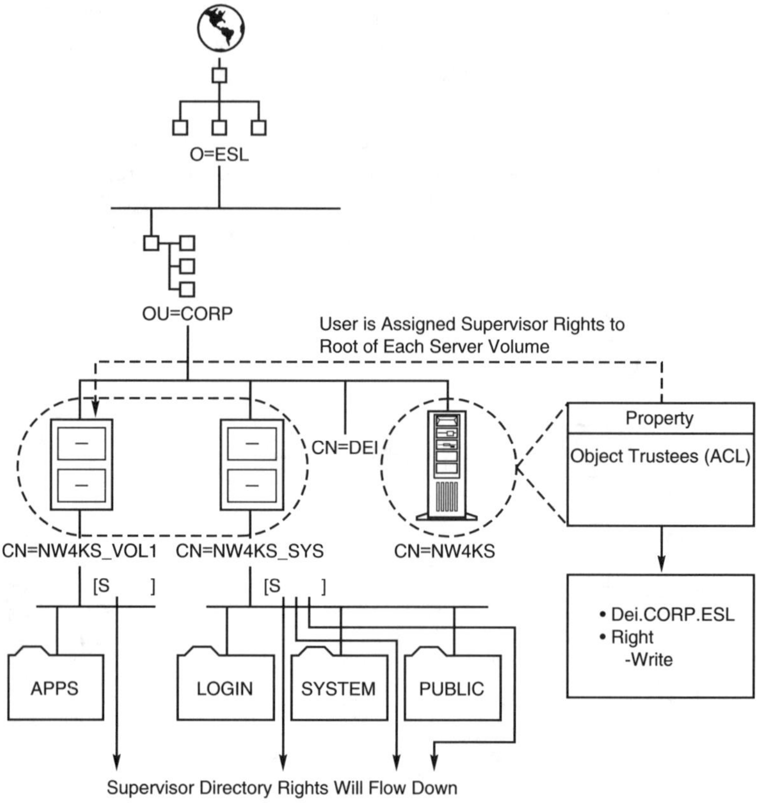

Figure 4.59 shows that the ACL for NetWare server NW4CS has been set so that Dei.CORP.ESL has the Write property right to this object. Figure 4.60 shows the Effective rights for Dei.CORP.ESL for the volume object NW4CS_SYS that is attached to the NetWare server NW4CS. Notice that figure 4.60 shows the Effective rights for user Dei to be *All rights,* because user Dei has Supervisor rights. When a Supervisor file system right is explicitly assigned, it cannot be blocked using an IRF or an explicit assignment further down the file system directory tree. Even though the Supervisor file system right assigned to a user through Write property right is not explicitly assigned, it cannot be overridden by an explicit assignment. Figure 4.61 shows that user Dei.CORP.ESL has been granted an explicit assignment of *No Rights* to the root directory of volume NW4KS_SYS. You can use the Effective Rights button on the screen in figure 4.61 to see the effect of these new trustee assignments. Figure 4.62 shows that the Effective rights of Dei.CORP.ESL to root of volume are still All rights.

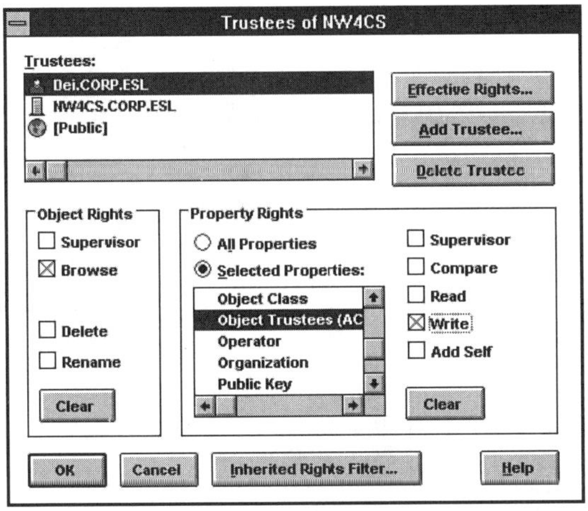

Figure 4.59
Write property right assigned to ACL of NetWare server object.

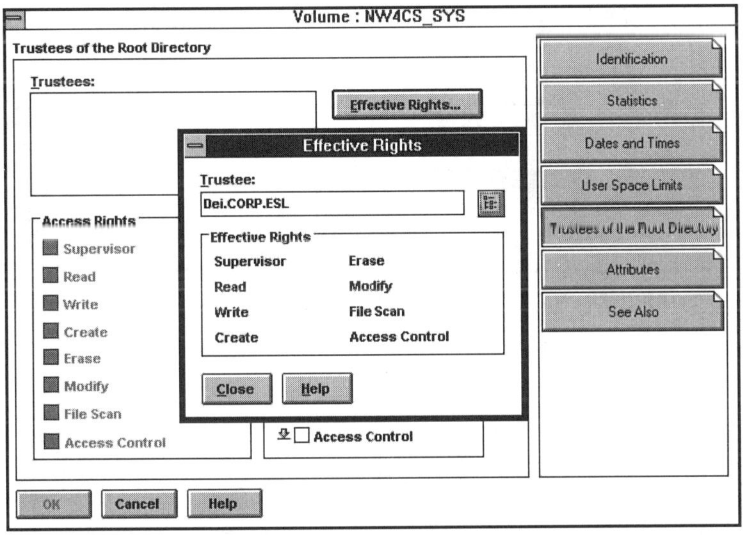

Figure 4.60
Effective rights of user to root of volume.

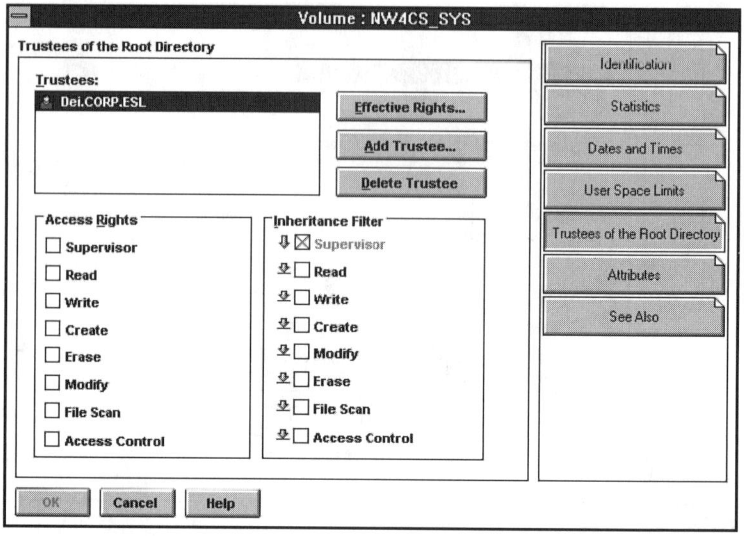

Figure 4.61
Explicit assignment of No Rights to root of volume.

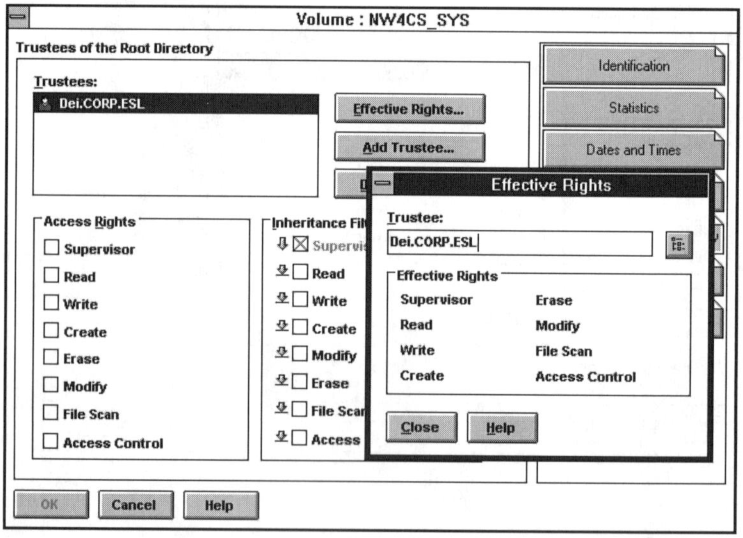

Figure 4.62
Effective Rights to root of volume not affected by explicit assignment.

If you want users to manage the server object and you do not want a user to inherit the Supervisor right to the NetWare file system through the Supervisor object right or the Supervisor All Properties right to the file server object, you can assign the user an alternate set of rights to the file server object. You can assign the user the [B D R] object right to the file server object and the [C R W A] All Properties right to the server object, except the ACL property.

You can assign the selected property right of [R C] to the ACL property of the server object, to prevent a user from inheriting the Write property through All Properties, or use the IRF for the ACL property to block the Write property right.

If you want a user to manage a NetWare server object and prevent the user from inheriting the Supervisor right to the NetWare file system, you can assign the following rights to the user:

- The [B D R] object right to the file server object
- The [C R W A] All Properties right to the server object
- The explicit [R C] (or [R] because [R] implies [C]) Selected Property right to the ACL property of the server object

Figure 4.63 shows that user Dei.CORP.ESL has been granted [B D R] object rights to NetWare server NW4CS. Notice that the Create right is not listed as it applies to container objects only. Figure 4.63 also shows that user Dei.CORP.ESL has been granted [C R W A] All Properties rights to NetWare server NW4CS. Figure 4.64 shows that an explicit Selected Properties trustee assignment of Read and Compare ([R C]) has been made to the Object Trustees (ACL) to override the All Properties assignment of [C R W A] that includes the Write property right.

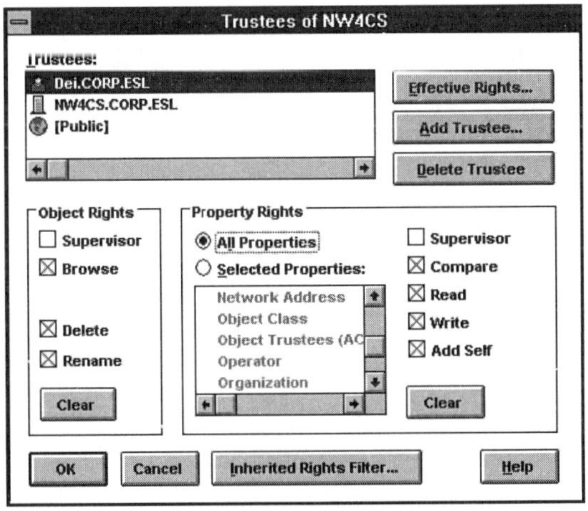

Figure 4.63
Restricted rights to manage server object.

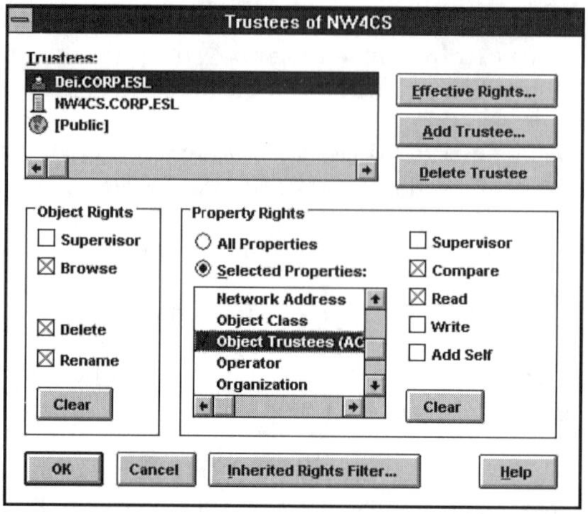

Figure 4.64
Restricting rights to ACL property of server object.

Security Equivalence

Another feature of IntranetWare security is security equivalence. Security equivalence is a property of a user object and is used to temporarily assign a user the same rights as another user. If a user is security equivalent to another user, called the *target* user in the discussion that follows, the user acquires the following:

- Explicit trustee assignments of the target user.
- Membership to groups of which the target user is a member.
- Organizational Roles that the target user occupies.
- Inherited rights from parent containers of the target user up to the [Root].
- All rights granted through [Public]. All attached users are implicit members of group [Public].

Security equivalencies to users, groups, and organizational role objects are called *explicit* security equivalencies. Security equivalencies through containers and [public] are called *implicit* security equivalencies.

In order to make a user object security equivalent, you need Write property right to the Security Equivalent property of the user object and the Write property right to the ACL of the target user object. Figure 4.65 shows the Security Equivalence property for a user. In figure 4.65, user Dei is security equivalent to the users:

```
CN=Jan.OU=CORP.O=ESL

CN=Lisa.O=ESL

CN=Nina.OU=ENG.O=MICROCONN
```

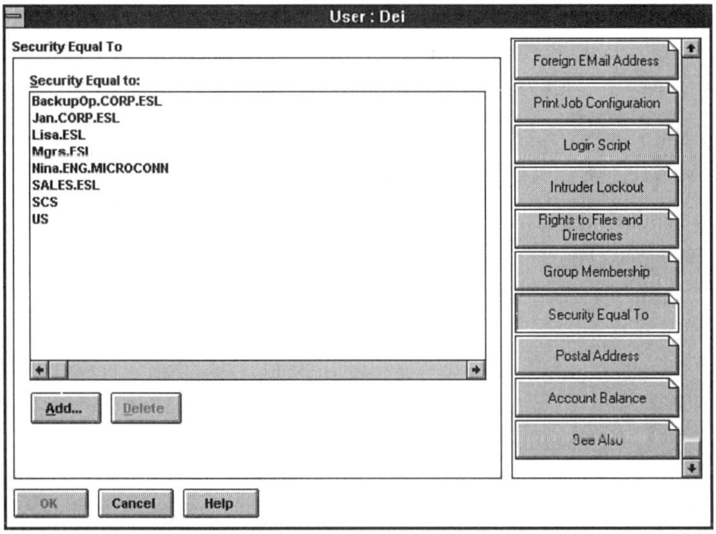

Figure 4.65
Security Equivalence property.

User Dei is also security equivalent to the group object CN=Mgrs.O=ESL, the organization unit OU=SALES.O=ESL, the organization O=SCS and the organization role object CN=BackupOp.OU= CORP.O=ESL. You can make the security equivalence to user objects, group objects, organizational role objects, and container objects such as organization units, organizations, and country objects. A user cannot be made security equivalent to [Root].

In general, Security Equivalence should be used on a temporary basis to quickly assign security rights. It is preferred that explicit trustee assignments be made for acquiring rights. Excessive use of security equivalencies can make tracing the source of rights difficult on networks with large NDS trees. Please note that in NetWare 3.x, to make a user a supervisor equivalent, you use the SYSCON utility to give him supervisor equivalency to the user Supervisor. In IntranetWare, you make a user a supervisor of an NDS tree branch by giving him Supervisor rights to the root container for that tree branch.

Default Rights Assignment

Proper assignment of rights is essential for implementing network security. Creating a secure network environment is one of the most potentially complex areas of IntranetWare network management. To aid in the implementation of NDS security, a default set of rights is assigned to key NDS objects. The default rights are designed in such a manner that you can use them to meet the most likely security configuration requirements for most organizations. The default rights make it possible to get a IntranetWare network running with the required security configuration with minimal effort.

You can further modify this default security configuration to meet any custom security requirements. The default rights are assigned during NDS installation, file server installation, and NDS object creation. These default assignments are considered next.

Default Rights Assigned to [Root]

The NDS database is created during installation. If you are installing the first IntranetWare server on the network, the NDS is installed as part of the server installation. NDS services can also be installed or removed by running the INSTALL.NLM at the server, and selecting:

- Maintenance/Selective Install from the INSTALL main menu
- Directory Options from the Installation Options menu

From Directory Services Option menu, you can select either:

- Install Directory Services onto this server
- Remove Directory Services from the server

When Novell Directory Services are first installed, the [Root] is given certain trustee assignments to simplify NDS administration. During NDS creation, the Admin user object is created. The Admin user object is given the Supervisor object right to the [Root]. Additionally, the group [public] is given Browse object rights to [Root].

Making trustee assignments to the [Root] causes the trustee rights to flow down the entire NDS tree. In other words, assignments made to [Root] have a global effect. The user object Admin gets the Supervisor object rights to all objects in the NDS tree. This allows the Admin user to administer all resources in the NDS tree. The NDS Supervisor right can be blocked from a tree branch (or any NDS leaf object) by removing the Supervisor right from the IRF for a tree branch or an NDS leaf object. This allows the creation of multiple levels of Administrators, where administrators have rights to manage parts of the NDS tree, but not the entire NDS tree.

Giving the group [Public] the Browse object right assignment, gives to all users Browse rights to the entire NDS tree. The group [Public] includes all users that are attached to the network. This includes even users that have not yet logged in. As soon as a user loads the VLM.EXE and makes a connection to a server, the user is automatically a member of group [Public]. Giving users the Browse right to the NDS tree allows users to navigate the NDS tree using the CX and NLIST commands that are found in the LOGIN directory of the server that the user initially attaches to. The CX command is particularly useful for changing current context and displaying a graphical NDS tree that shows the resources that are available. It should be emphasized that the Browse right gives a user the ability to list NDS objects in a container, and does not imply any other rights such as accessing information in the NDS object or the ability to create, delete or rename objects. You can remove the Browse right to [Root] for group [Public] after installation. If you do not have Browse rights to the NDS tree, you can still use the CX command to change your context, but the only objects you can see (using the CX /T/A command) are Bindery emulation objects.

The Browse rights are assigned to all users so that they can navigate the NDS tree and look for resources. In some secure environments, there may be concerns about users being able to "see" resource objects in the entire NDS tree. Here, you can remove the Browse trustee assignment from [Root]. A user can log in as a user object without having Browse rights to the user object. You can use the NAME CONTEXT configuration parameter in the NET.CFG file to place the user in the appropriate context, and lessen the need for a user to navigate the NDS tree.

If [Public] is removed as a trustee of [Root], and [Root] is made a trustee of [Root] and given the Browse object rights, only logged in users can browse the NDS tree. Other users can still log in to the NDS tree if they know their complete NDS name, or they know their login name and are initially placed in the same context as their default NetWare server.

Figure 4.66 shows the default rights for a newly installed NDS tree. This figure shows that Admin and [public] are trustees of [Root]. This figure also shows that Admin has Supervisor object rights to [Root]. Figure 4.67 shows that [Public] has Browse object rights to [Root].

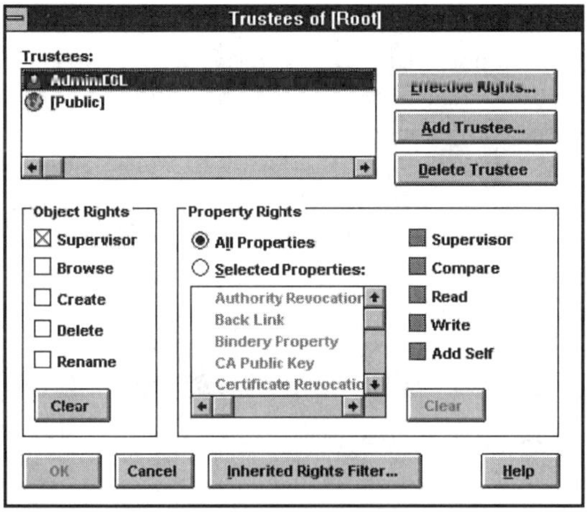

Figure 4.66
Default rights for Admin.

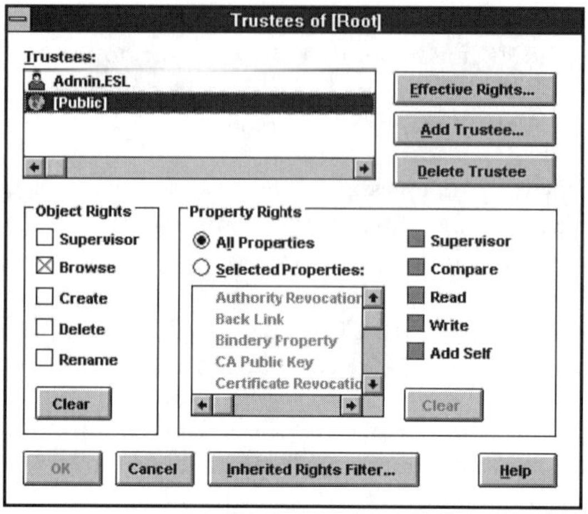

Figure 4.67
Default rights for [Public].

Default Rights Assigned for NetWare Server Object

When a IntranetWare server is installed it can be installed in a newly created NDS tree, or in a container in an existing NDS tree. The creator of the server object is automatically assigned the Supervisor object right. The creator of the server is the server object itself (see fig. 4.68). Figure 4.69 also lists [Public] as a trustee to the NetWare server object. This may seem puzzling at first, as excessive rights assigned to [Public] can potentially bypass NetWare security. The group [public] is given the Read property right to the Messaging Server property of the server object (see fig. 4.69). In pre-NetWare 4.1 servers, [Public] was given an explicit selective property assignment of [R C] to the Network Address property. The Network Address property contains the IPX address of the NetWare server (see fig. 4.70). The Network Address includes the Internal Network Number for the file server which is F0004101 in figure 4.70, the node address which is always 1 for a NetWare server on the internal logical network, and the socket number 451 (hexadecimal) at which NCP (NetWare Core Protocol) services are registered.

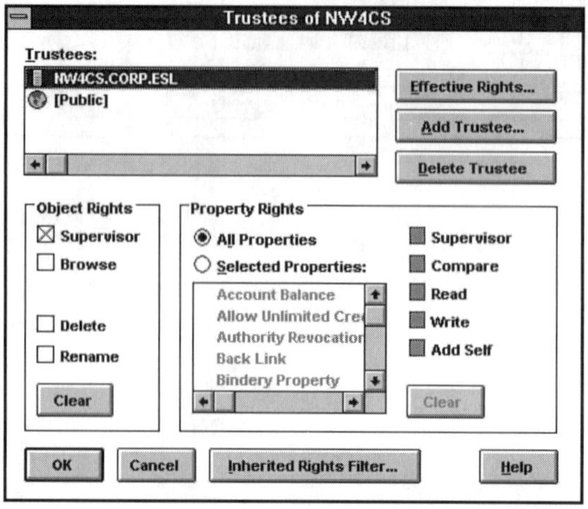

Figure 4.68
Default trustees for server object.

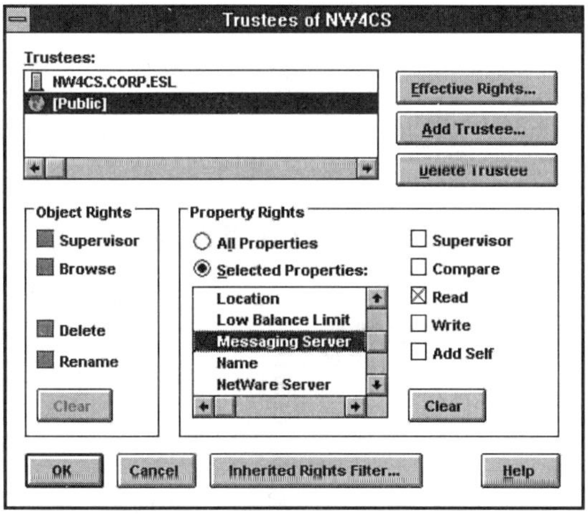

Figure 4.69
Default rights assigned to [Public] for server object.

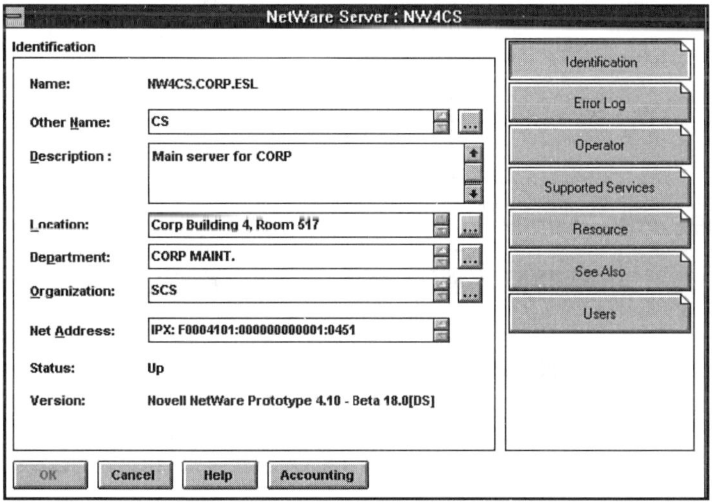

Figure 4.70
Network Address property for server object.

Any user, such as Admin, who has Supervisor Object right to the server object also has Supervisor File System rights to the volumes attached to the server. Such a user can perform file system administration for the server. If the Supervisor File System right is deemed to be excessive rights, then the user can be granted [B C D R] object rights to the server, and [C R W A] All Properties rights to the server object, except for the ACL property. The ACL property can be assigned [C R] Selected Property rights. It is important to safeguard users from having the Write property right to the NetWare server object's ACL property, because this would imply that the user has Supervisor File System rights to all volumes attached to the server.

The container in which the NetWare server object and its volumes are installed is automatically given certain default file system rights. This container is given Read and File Scan ([R F]) rights to directory SYS:PUBLIC and the Create ([C]) right to directory SYS:MAIL.

Figure 4.71 shows the trustees for directory PUBLIC. The trustee CORP.ESL is the organization unit under which the server was installed. Notice that the trustee CORP.ESL has a trustee assignment of [R F]. Figure 4.72 shows the trustees for directory MAIL. The container CORP.ESL is the organization unit under which the server was installed, and is listed as a trustee. The container CORP.ESL has a trustee assignment of [C].

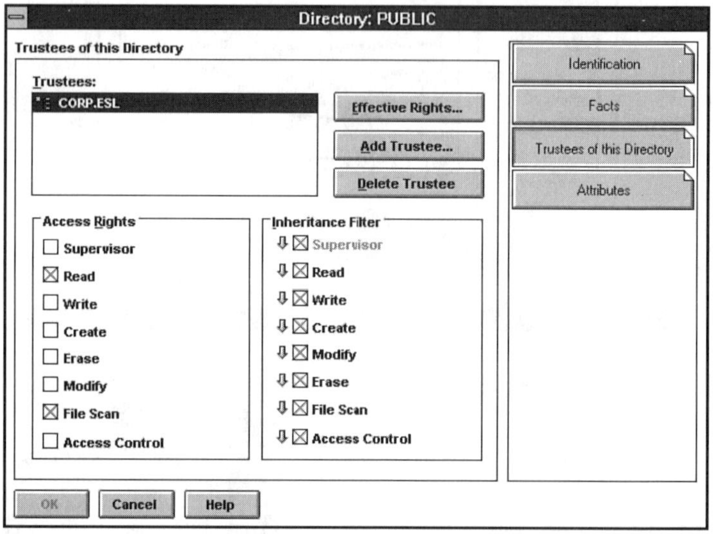

Figure 4.71
Default trustees for the PUBLIC directory.

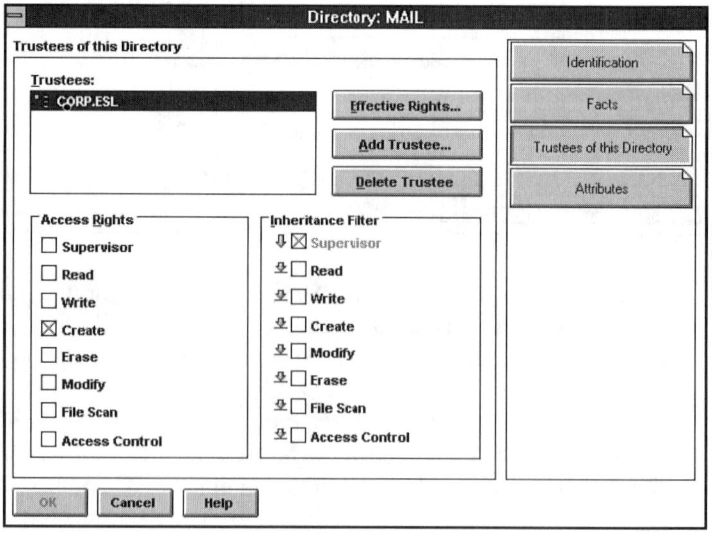

Figure 4.72
Default trustees for the MAIL directory.

The advantage of giving the file server's container object certain default rights is that all users in that container inherit those rights because container objects act as groups for assignment of rights. Because users that need access to the shared file system of a volume object are likely to be created in the same container as the volume object, assigning the container default rights simplifies file system administration. The container is given a default right of [R F] to PUBLIC, because users in the container need to map a search drive to PUBLIC, where the network utilities are kept. The MAIL directory is used in NetWare 3.x systems, and for this reason the default right of Create is given to MAIL, for bindery emulated users that are migrated from a bindery-based server.

If the volume object is moved to another container, the new container is not automatically granted rights to the PUBLIC and MAIL directories in the volume object. You must explicitly assign to the new container appropriate rights to the volume's PUBLIC and MAIL directories.

Another default trustee assignment that is made is that the [Root] has the Read property right to the Host Server property of the installed server's volume object. Figure 4.73 shows the trustees of the volume object NW4CS_SYS. [Root] is listed as a trustee and has the Read selected property right to the volume's Host Server property. This right allows all logged in users to determine the name of the host server to which this volume is attached.

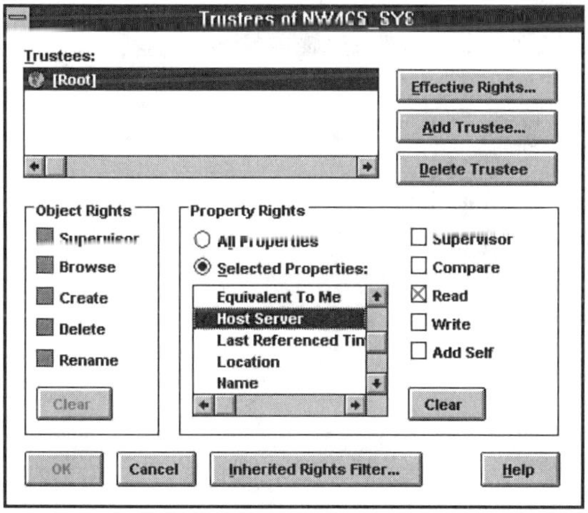

Figure 4.73
Default trustees for the volume object.

Default Rights Assigned to Containers

In a previous section, you learned that the [Root] container is given certain default rights for simplifying network administration. The organization and organization unit containers are given certain default rights when they are created. Both the organization and organization unit containers are given the Read property right to their Login Script property. Figures 4.74 and 4.75 show that the organization and organization containers are trustees of themselves and have a Read selected property to their Login Script property and Print Job Configuration.

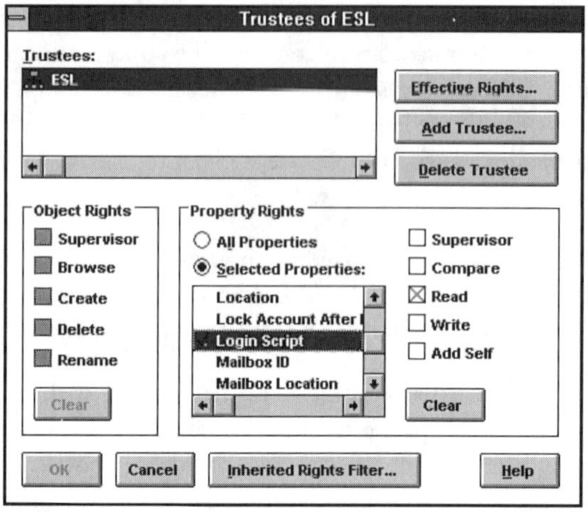

Figure 4.74
Default Login Script Selected Property rights for organization object.

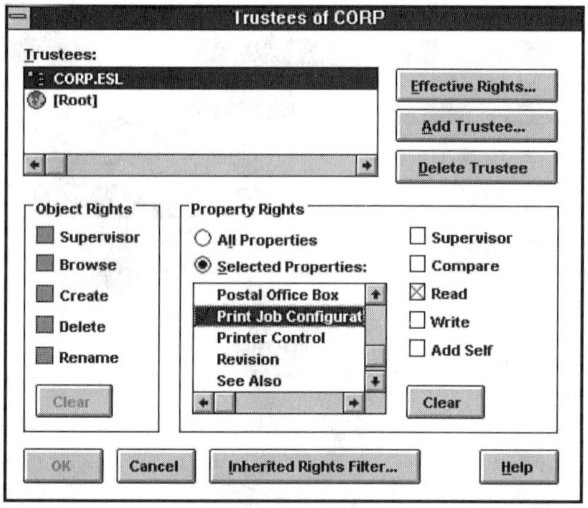

Figure 4.75
Default Print Job Configuration Selected Property rights for organization unit object.

The Country container object does not have any default trustee assignments.

The following are default rights for container objects:

- Organization and Organization Unit objects are given the [R] selected property right to their Login Script property and Print Job Configuration property.
- Country objects are given no default rights.

A container's login script property acts as the system login script for user objects directly in that container. Assigning a container the Read property right to the Login Script property ensures that users in that container can Read (and process) the system login script.

Using the Organization and Organization Unit objects as trustees is a very convenient way of assigning rights to other NDS objects and the NetWare File System. The rights assigned to these containers are inherited by all objects in that container and its subcontainers. Containers have a natural grouping which reflects the organizational structure or usage within an organization.

If all users in an organization need a specific right, it is easier to assign the *Organization* (O) as a trustee rather than assigning each of the *Organization Units* (OU) as trustees. In any case, you must ensure that you only assign the necessary rights to those users that need it.

If assigning rights to an Organization or Organization Unit leads to assigning rights to users who should not have these rights, you can assign rights using Group objects or Organizational Role objects. You should assign only users who need rights as members of these objects. Another advantage of using Group or Organizational Role objects is that the members of these group objects can be from different containers. You can only assign user objects as members of the Group or Organizational Role objects. For Group objects, membership is assigned by adding user objects to the Group Members property list. For Organizational Role objects, membership is assigned by adding user objects to the Occupant property list.

Both Group objects and Organizational Role objects can be used for assigning trustee rights. A reasonable question to ask is, what (if any) are the differences between them? Group objects are defined in the NetWare environment. Organizational Role objects have a formal definition in the X.500 specification from which NDS is derived. This makes it possible for third-party X.500 implementations to more easily access the information in the Organizational Role objects.

Organizational Role objects are more formal definitions of network responsibilities. For instance, you could have a job description (organizational role) for a Backup Operator. The occupants of this Organizational Role object could change, but the rights assigned the Organizational Role object are such that they are sufficient for performing the job description, and change only when the NDS tree is reorganized or the job description is changed.

Another distinction between these two types of group objects is that the Organizational Role has the additional properties of Telephone Number, Fax Number, and e-mail address, as per X.500 schema requirements for Organizational Role objects. The Group object does not have these additional properties.

Default Rights for User Objects

When a user object is created, the user is given a set of default rights to simplify the administration for the user object. Figures 4.76 and 4.77 show the default trustees of a newly created user. The trustees for user object Lisa are Lisa.ESL, [Public] and [Root]. The user object has three trustees:

- The user object
- [Public]
- [Root]

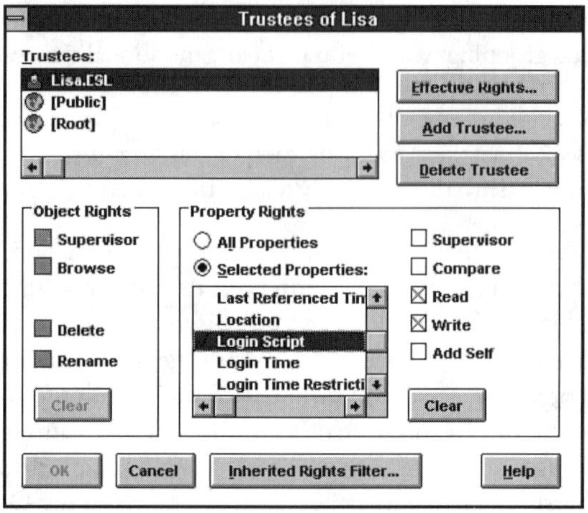

Figure 4.76
Default Login Script property right for user object.

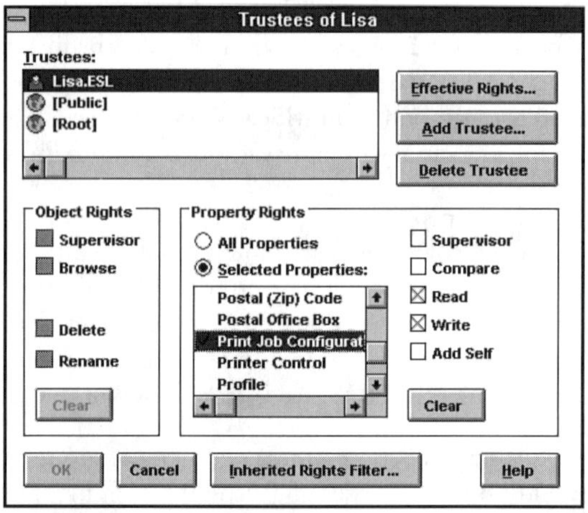

Figure 4.77
Default Print Job Configuration property right for user object.

The user object is given the Read and Write ([R W]) property right to its Login Script property and its Print Job Configuration property. Figure 4.76 shows that user Lisa has the default selected property right of Read and Write to her Login Script property. Similarly, the user also is given the Read and Write ([R W]) property rights to her Print Job Configuration property. Figure 4.77 shows the Print Job Configuration property right for the same user. If the user's home directory is created using NetWare utilities, such as NETADMIN and NetWare Administrator, the user is given [S R W C E M F A] File System rights to her home directory.

The [R W] property right for a user object allows the user object to modify his login scripts. If you wish to prevent the user from modifying his login script, you must assign the [R] right for the user login script. A user must, at a minimum, have the Read property right to his login script so that it can be processed.

If you do not wish a user to modify his print job configurations, you must revoke the Write property right from his Print Job Configuration property.

In addition to the Selected Property rights mentioned previously, the user is also given the Read ([R]) All Property rights of the user object's properties.

The [Public] group is given a default property right of Read to the user's default server. Figure 4.78 shows that user Lisa has been given the Read property right to the Default Server. This allows all users that are connected to the network to find out the default server name for that user. Figure 4.79 shows that the default server property for user Lisa is set to CN=NW4CS.OU=CORP.O=ESL. This property can be changed to another file server object. The Default Server is the NetWare server that the user object connects to when logging in to the network. It can be specified in the NET.CFG file using the DEFAULT SERVER parameter, or the *Preferred Server* (PS) option when loading the VLM Manager. The Default Server for a user is also used to store SEND messages for that user. The Default Server is the server used to synchronize your workstation's time when the SYSTIME utility is run without any parameters, and when you first connect to the network (unless explicitly disabled in NET.CFG).

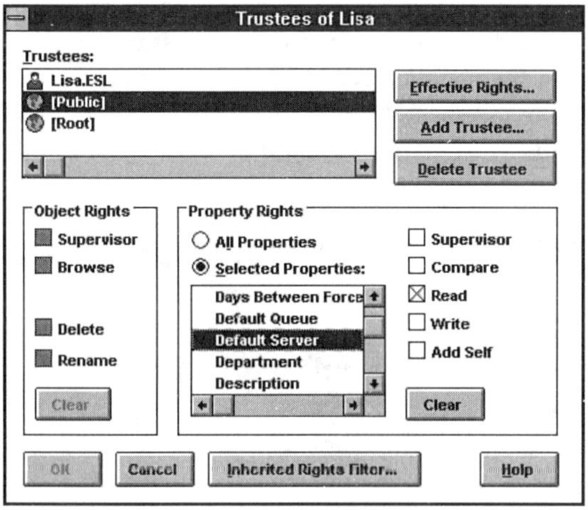

Figure 4.78
Default Server property right for trustee [Public] to user object.

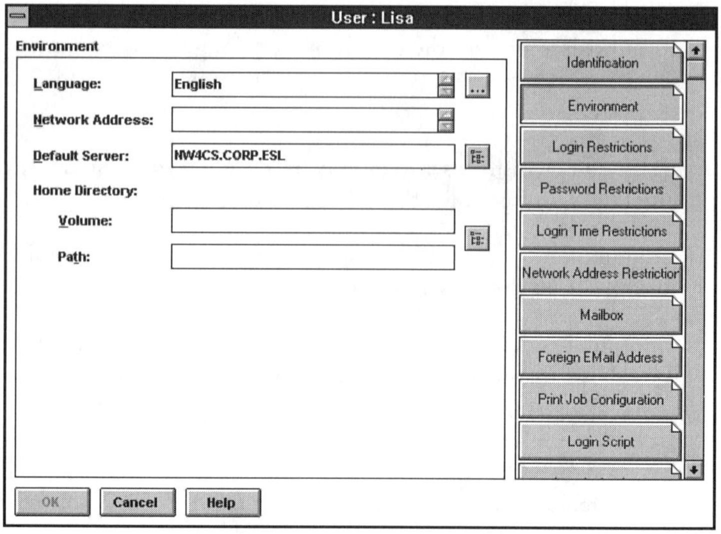

Figure 4.79
Default Server property for user object.

The [Root] is given the Read property right for the Group Membership property of a user object (see fig. 4.80). This Read property implies that all logged in users can find out which groups the user is a member of. The [Root] is also given the Read property right for the Network Address property of a user object (see fig. 4.81). This Read property implies that all logged in users can find out the workstation address a user is logged in from. The Network Address property shows a value for logged in users only. If a user is not currently logged in, the Network Address property is not defined. The user's Network Address property is the workstation's network address from which he is logged in. If IPX is used as the protocol transport, the Network Address consists of the network number (cable segment number), the node address (also called the MAC or hardware address), and the IPX socket number 400F (hexadecimal) that is used by the workstation networking software.

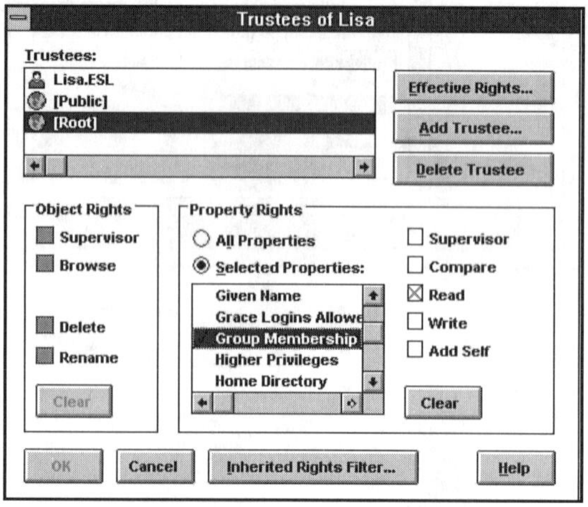

Figure 4.80
Default Group Membership property right to trustee [Root].

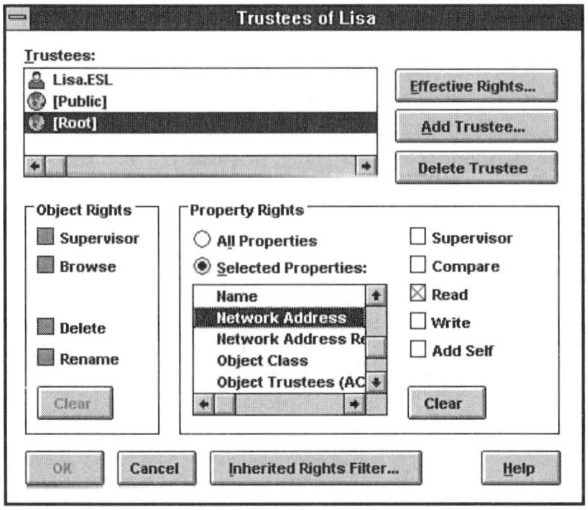

Figure 4.81
Default Network Address property right to trustee [Root].

The user object has the following default trustee assignments to it:

- The user object is given the Read and Write ([R W]) property right to its Login Script property and its Print Job Configuration property, and the [S R W C E M F A] file system rights to its home directory.
- [Public] is given the Read Selected Property right to the user's default server.
- [Root] is given the Read property right for the Group Membership property and the Network Address property of the user object.

Guidelines for Determining Excessive Rights

Occasionally you may discover that a user or group of users has excessive rights. Excessive rights are any rights that are above and beyond those required by users to complete their tasks. Excessive rights can also give users the ability to acquire additional rights or restrict rights of other users. To correct the problem of excessive rights you must be able to trace the origin of these rights. In an IntranetWare environment, this can be particularly challenging because of the many levels of NetWare security and the large number of sources rights can be acquired from. The following is a guideline for determining excessive rights:

1. Determine the explicit rights granted to the following objects:

    a. User objects

    b. Group and Organizational Role objects

    c. Containers between the user and the [Root]

    d. Security Equivalencies

2. Determine rights inherited through explicit trustee assignments to any of the objects listed in the previous item. Also, determine if a user inherits rights through group membership, container membership, or security equivalence.

3. Use the NetWare tools to determine Trustee Assignments and Effective Rights. For NDS rights you can use NETADMIN or NWADMIN. For File System Rights, you can use NWADMIN, NETADMIN, FILER, or the RIGHTS command.

Determining the Cause of Insufficient Rights

This is the opposite of the problemdiscussed in the previous section. Occasionally you may run into a situation where a user does not have sufficient rights to perform a task or has just lost these rights because of changes made to the NDS. In this case, you must consider the following:

1. Check to see if any explicit rights the user is supposed to have, have been granted. You might want to check if IRFs are blocking the user's rights. If they are, you can set the IRF to pass the desired rights or make an explicit trustee assignment.

2. Check to see if the user is a member of the group or organizational role objects that have been assigned the rights needed by the user.

3. If the user was given rights through security equivalence, check the user's security equivalence property to see if the security equivalencies exist.

4. Check the rights of the container through which the user inherits the rights. If a reorganization of the NDS tree has taken place, certain rights may not have been properly assigned to container objects.

Network Administration Strategies

The NDS tree can be potentially very big because it is used to represent network resources in an organization. For a small organization, the NDS tree can be managed by a single Administrator user. For larger organizations, it is more practical for the functions of network administration to be carried out by a number of users. In this case, the network administration tasks need to be divided among several network administrators. One way of doing this is to assign an Administrator per tree branch.

Figure 4.82 shows the NDS tree for organization O=ESL, with several Administrators for the department tree branches. Each of the tree branches within the organization units OU=CORP, OU=SALES, and OU=MKTG have administrators CN=Admin.OU=CORP.O=ESL,

CN=Admin.OU=ENG.O=ESL, and CN=Admin.OU=MKTG.O=ESL, respectively. Typically, these administrators have complete responsibility for managing their NDS tree branch, but no rights to manage another tree branch. The department administrators do not have rights to manage objects in the context O=ESL. Resources in context O=ESL are managed by user CN=Admin.O=ESL that is defined in the O=ESL context. The CN=Admin.O=ESL administrator can create new organization containers and manage rights to the [Root] object, but typically does not have rights to manage the tree branches for the individual departments.

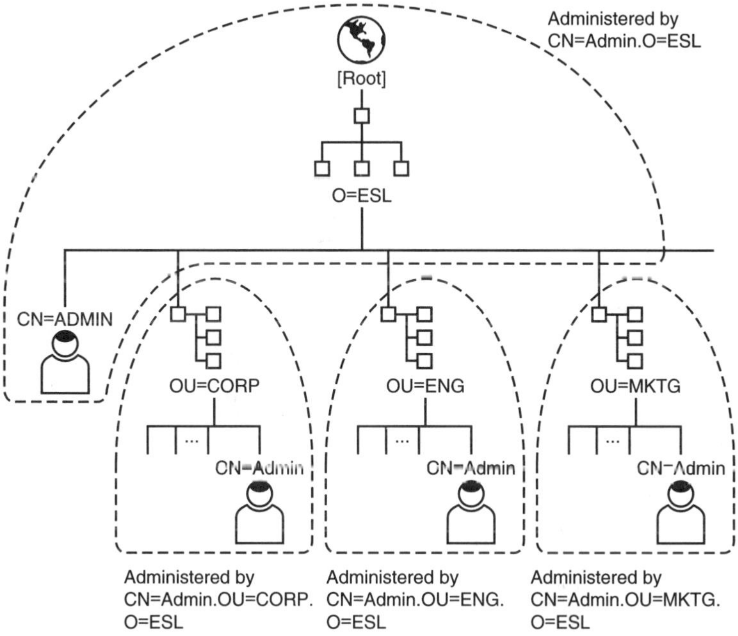

Figure 4.82
Administrators per NDS tree branch.

Assigning Administrators for each tree branch can be used to provide decentralized network management. It is possible for an organization to use this scheme effectively. You might even argue that because of decentralization, each department has jurisdiction over its network resources (its *turf*), and *turf wars* can be avoided. However, complete decentralization introduces another problem. Can the central MIS department (if one exists) trust the individual departments to manage their NDS tree properly? How much technical expertise and how many well-trained network administrators are there that can be trusted to manage their NDS tree branch? If there is a need to enforce global networking changes, how easy will it be to get the individual departments to comply, if you do not have any rights to the individual tree branches?

Because of the issues raised by some of these questions, many organizations consider it prudent not to lose control over individual tree branches. They have a special administrator account that has access rights for managing all of the tree branches. This user object may not be used for day-to-day administration tasks, but it exists as a *back-door* administrator user account, should the need arise to enforce a central network management policy. You should also enable auditing so that you can monitor attempts by individual departments to weaken the access rights of the special administrator account.

A second way to manage the NDS tree is to have one administrator account that manages the entire NDS tree and assistant network administrators who help the main network administrator. This is similar to the work group manager concept used in NetWare 3.x.

The procedures for implementing each of these network management approaches are discussed next.

Distributed Management—Single Administrator per NDS Tree Branch

As figure 4.82 indicates, in this approach you must block the rights of the original Administrator account CN=Admin.O=ESL. The general procedure for creating a separate Admin account for a department is shown below. The description is given in terms of creating a separate Administrator for OU=CORP.O=ESL (refer to figure 4.82). The administrator account for the OU=CORP.O=ESL tree branch is referred to by the name CN=Admin.OU=CORP. O=ESL. If you need to perform this procedure on your NDS tree, you probably have different names for the root of the tree branch and the Admin user accounts, and you have to make appropriate substitutions for these names.

1. Create an Admin account in the department container. In the case of figure 4.82, this is the user CN=Admin.OU=CORP.O=ESL.

2. Assign to the newly created Admin account the following rights:

   Object rights of [S B C D R] to OU=CORP.O=ESL

   All Property rights of [S C R W A] to OU=CORP.O=ESL

3. Revoke rights from the IRF for OU=CORP.O=ESL to block access rights for other network administrators outside the tree branch.

   The reason for doing this is to prevent CN=Admin.O=ESL from inheriting access rights to OU=CORP.

   As an example, you might want to set the IRF for object rights to [B] and IRF for All Properties for OU=CORP to [R]. Keeping the Browse right in the IRF for object rights allows users to see the objects in the CORP tree branch. The All Properties Read right allows other network administrators to read the properties of NDS objects in the tree branch, unless an object has a selected property right to override this.

4. Remove any trustee assignments to OU=CORP and any of its subcontainers for user CN=Admin.O=ESL.

5. Make sure that CN=Admin.OU=CORP.O =ESL has rights to itself. Also ensure that no other user such as CN=Admin.O=ESL has rights to CN=Admin.OU=CORP.O=ESL. If another user has access rights to CN=Admin.OU=CORP.O=ESL, they can restrict the right to this user.

6. Make sure that no other user is a security equivalent to the newly created Administrator and that there are no aliases to this user object.

Before revoking the Supervisor object right from the IRF for a container, you must have a user who has Supervisor object rights to that container. Otherwise, the system prevents you from revoking the Supervisor IRF right, and you get an error message that "you cannot filter the Supervisor object right because no object has explicit Supervisor object right to this object."

The NetWare utilities do not prevent you from deleting the only user object that has Supervisor object rights to the tree branch. You can, therefore, lose control of an NDS tree branch, if you inadvertently (or by design) delete the user object that has Supervisor object rights to the NDS tree branch. If you delete the only user object that has Supervisor object rights to the NDS tree branch, you have created a black hole in the NDS tree. A later section discusses the NDS Black Hole problem in more detail.

Central Management—Assistant Administrators

Because of the risk of losing control over a tree branch by either delegating responsibility to a department administrator or through inadvertent creation of a "black hole" in the NDS tree, you might want to use central network administration with work group managers that act as assistant administrators. You must implement security in such a manner that you can prevent loss of control over a tree branch. You can use the procedure that follows as a guideline. The description is given in terms of creating an assistant Administrator for OU=CORP.O=ESL (see fig. 4.83). The administrator account for the OU=CORP.O=ESL tree branch is referred to by the name CN=WMgr.OU=CORP.O=ESL. If you need to perform this procedure on your NDS tree, you probably have different names for the root of the tree branch and the Admin user accounts, and you have to make appropriate substitutions for these names.

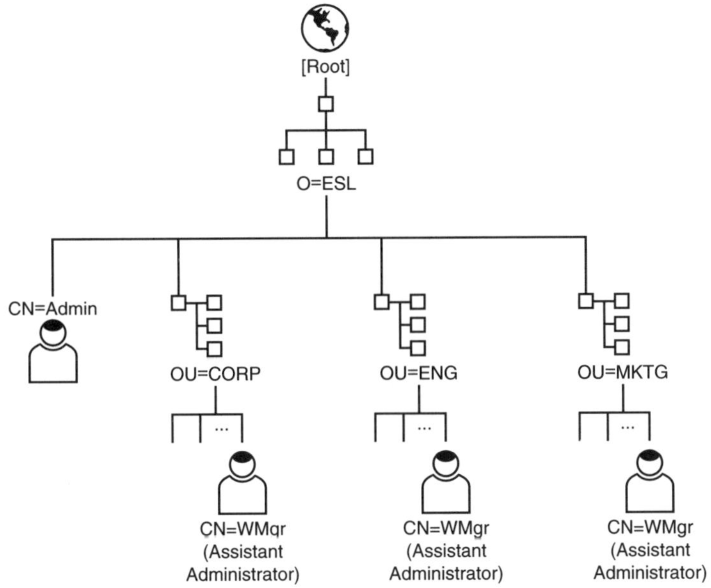

Figure 4.83
Creating a Workgroup Manager account.

1. Create a Workgroup Manager account, CN=WMgr, in the department container. In the case of figure 4.83, this is the user CN=WMgr.OU=CORP.O=ESL.

2. Assign to the newly created Workgroup Manager account the following rights:

   Object rights of [B C D R] to OU=CORP.O=ESL

   All Property rights of [C R W A] to OU=CORP.O=ESL

   Selected Property rights of [C R] to Object Trustees (ACL) Assigning the Selected Property rights of [C R] to the ACL property is important, otherwise the Workgroup Manager can inherit the Write property right for the ACL property through the All Properties rights, and this gives the Workgroup Manager the ability to modify the trustees for the CORP container, and even give himself the Supervisor object right to the CORP container.

3. Make sure that CN=Admin.O=ESL has an explicit Supervisor trustee assignment to manage OU=CORP. You can do this by assigning the following rights to CN=Admin.O=ESL:

   Object rights of [S B C D R] to OU=CORP.O=ESL

   All Property rights of [S C R W A] to OU=CORP.O=ESL

4. Make sure that CN=Admin.O=ESL has an explicit Supervisor trustee assignment to CN=WMgr.OU=CORP.O=ESL. This can be done by assigning the following rights to CN=Admin.O=ESL:

   Object rights of [S B C D R] to CN=WMgr.OU=CORP.O=ESL

   All Property rights of [S C R W A] to CN=WMgr.OU=CORP.O=ESL

5. Remove rights except from IRF for CN=WMgr.OU=CORP.O=ESL. This is to prevent the Workgroup Manager from inheriting excessive management rights. Set the IRF as follows:

   IRF for Object rights for CN=WMgr.OU= CORP.O=ESL set to [B]

   IRF for All Properties rights for CN=WMgr.OU=CORP.O=ESL set to [C R]

6. Restrict Workgroup Manager, CN= WMgr.OU=CORP.O=ESL, rights as follows:

   Object rights for CN=WMgr.OU=CORP.O =ESL set to [B]

   Selected Property right for CN=WMgr.OU =CORP.O=ESL set to [C R] for ACL property

   Selected Property right for CN=WMgr.OU= CORP.O=ESL set to [R W] for Login Script property

   Selected Property right for CN=WMgr.OU= CORP.O=ESL set to [R W] for Print Job Configuration property

The NDS Black Hole Problem

To study the black hole problem in NDS, you should be working on an experimental NDS tree. You can create an NDS tree branch as shown in figure 4.84. The name of the organization container is O=BLACK-HOLE. It is so named because you are about to create a black hole in the NDS tree and study the kinds of problems you can get into when you lose control over an NDS tree branch.

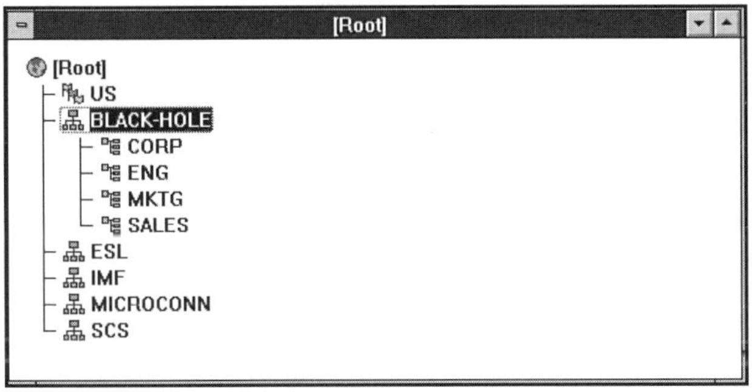

Figure 4.84
Experimental NDS Tree for studying the Black Hole problem.

To create a black hole in the NDS tree, use the steps that follow as a guideline:

1. Log in as the Administrator for the NDS tree.
2. Create an Admin account for O=BLACK HOLE. Create this Admin account in another container called O=TEST.
3. Give to CN=Admin.O=TEST [S B] object rights to the O=BLACK-HOLE container.
4. Set the Object rights Inherited rights Filter for O=BLACK-HOLE to [B]. This blocks all object rights except the Browse object right.
5. If you try to access the Trustees of this Object option from the NetWare Administrator, you are unable to access this option, as it is grayed out. This is because the IRF setting of [B] for O=BLACK-HOLE blocks out all but the Browse rights.

   You might want to log in as the newly created user Admin.TEST to see that you have Supervisor object rights to the O=BLACK-HOLE container. If you do this, make sure that the Admin.TEST has at least [R F] file system rights to the PUBLIC directory, so the user can access the NetWare tools.
6. Make sure that you are logged in as the original Admin user and delete the user account that has Supervisor rights to O=BLACK-HOLE. That is, delete the Admin.TEST user.
7. Now try to access the container object O=BLACK-HOLE, and try to create or delete NDS objects in it. Also, try to change the Trustee Assignments to the O=BLACK-HOLE container. You have created a black hole in the NDS tree, as that tree cannot be managed.

Solution to the NDS Black Hole Problem

The easiest solution is to prevent the black hole problem from occurring. One way is to make sure that a central network administrator has explicit Supervisor object rights to all the critical NDS tree branches.

Another solution based on using the SBACKUP program is outlined in the following steps:

1. On another IntranetWare server, create an NDS tree with the same tree name as the one that has the black hole.

2. Create the NDS objects with the same structure as the existing tree, but with the correct object rights set so you can access the tree branches. You can create the NDS tree structure for only the NDS tree branch that has the black hole problem, and the Admin user object that was deleted.

   Back up this NDS tree using SBACKUP.

3. Restore the backed up NDS tree, using SBACKUP, on the server that has the black hole problem.

   In the Restore Options for SBACKUP, set the following options:

   Overwrite existing parent: Yes

   Overwrite existing child: Yes

The SBACKUP writes over the existing NDS tree that has the black hole problem. The new set of NDS rights assigned to the tree branch with the black hole problem allows you to manage that tree branch.

The Danger of Giving a Workgroup Manager Write Property Rights to ACL of Container

A common problem in setting up a workgroup manager who acts as an assistant Administrator is the failure to revoke Write property rights from the ACL property of the container.

Consider a workgroup manager CN= WMgr. OU =CORP.O=ESL who has been given the following rights to manage the OU=CORP.O=ESL tree branch:

Object rights of [B C D R] to OU=CORP.O=ESL

All Property rights of [C R W A] to OU=CORP.O=ESL

Figure 4.85 shows the [B C D R] object rights and [C R W A] All Properties rights assigned for WMgr.CORP.ESL. Because the [C R W A] All Properties implies that the user WMgr.CORP.ESL has Write property right to the OU=CORP.O=ESL container's ACL property, the user WMgr.CORP.ESL can modify this ACL property.

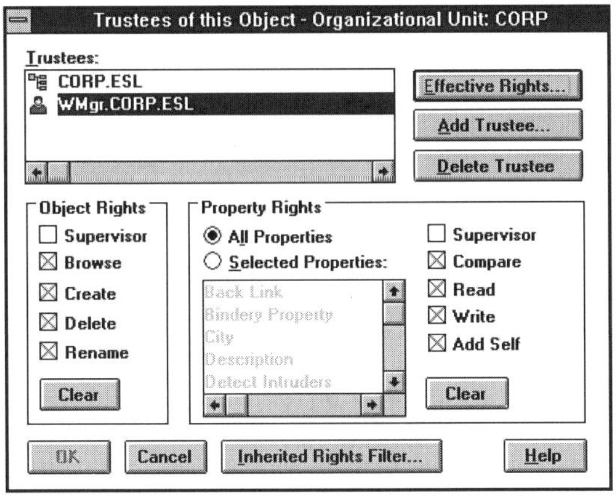

Figure 4.85
Workgroup Manager rights to container object.

Figure 4.86 shows that WMgr.CORP.ESL has acquired Supervisor object rights by selecting the Trustees of this Object for the CORP container, using the NetWare Administrator.

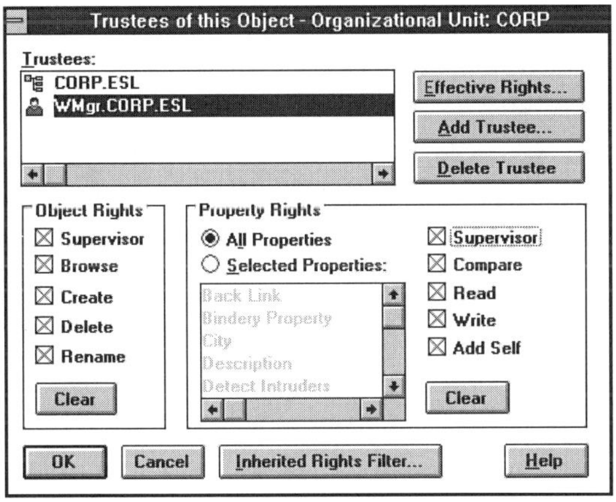

Figure 4.86
Workgroup Manager acquires Supervisor object rights because of Write property right to container.

To prevent the previous scenario from occurring, you should explicitly assign to the Workgroup Manager the Selected Property right of [C R] to the ACL property for the container.

Case Study: Implementing a NetWare Administrator Strategy

Consider the NDS tree in figure 4.87. It is proposed that the Admin.ESL user account manages the entire NDS tree for organization ESL. The department CORP has an Admin account Admin.CORP.ESL that has management jurisdiction over the CORP tree branch. The department SALES has a network Administrator whose name is James. James is relatively new to IntranetWare Administration, and it has been decided that the Admin.ESL retains control over OU=SALES, and James performs limited network administration and serves in the capacity of a Workgroup Manager for the SALES department.

Figure 4.87
NDS Tree for implementing a NetWare Administrator strategy.

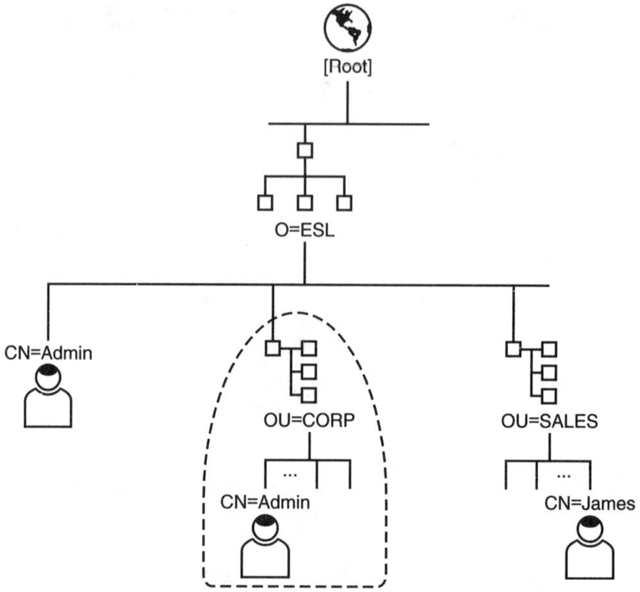

1. What should be Admin.CORP.ESL object rights and property rights to the OU=CORP container?

   Answer: The Admin.CORP.ESL should have the following object and property rights:

   Object rights of [S B C D R] to OU=CORP.O=ESL

   All Property rights of [S C R W A] to OU=CORP.O=ESL

   These rights allow Admin.CORP.ESL to manage the tree branch OU=CORP.

2. What should be the IRF settings on OU=CORP to revoke rights from Admn.ESL?

   Answer: The OU=CORP should have the following IRF settings:

   Object rights IRF set to [B]

   All Properties IRF set to [R]

   These IRF settings block Supervisor rights of Admin.ESL from flowing down to the CORP container.

3. Should any trustee assignments to the OU=CORP be removed for user Admin.ESL?

   Answer: Yes. If explicit trustee assignments for Admin.ESL are not removed, the user is able to manage the NDS tree. Explicit trustee assignments override any inherited rights restricted by IRF settings.

4. What trustee rights should Admin.CORP.ESL have to himself? What additional precautions should be taken for user Admin.CORP.ESL?

   Answer: The Admin.CORP.ESL should have [S] object rights to Admin.CORP.ESL.

   Additionally, you should ensure that user Admin.ESL does not have any trustee assignments to Admin.CORP.ESL.

5. User James.SALES.ESL needs to perform the following management tasks:

   - Create, Delete, Rename user accounts
   - Change property values for user accounts
   - Browse the SALES tree branch

   Additionally, James should not be able to change the trustee assignments to SALES.

   What minimal rights should be assigned to James?

   Answer: User James should have the following minimal rights:

   Object rights of [B C D R] to OU=SALES.O=ESL

   All Property rights of [C R W A] to OU=SALES.O=ESL

   Selected Property rights of [C R] for property Object Trustees (ACL) of container OU=SALES.O=ESL.

   Assigning the Selected Property rights of [C R] to the ACL property of the container is important, otherwise the Workgroup Manager can inherit the Write property right for the ACL property through the All Properties rights. This gives the Workgroup Manager the ability to modify the trustees for the SALES container, and even give himself the Supervisor object right to the SALES container.

6. What explicit trustee assignments should Admin.ESL have over OU=SALES?

   Answer: Admin.ESL should have the following explicit trustee assignments:

   Object rights of [S B C D R] to OU=SALES.O=ESL

   All Property rights of [S C R W A] to OU=SALES.O=ESL

7. What explicit trustee assignments should Admin.ESL have over James?

   Answer: Admin.ESL should have the following explicit trustee assignments over James:

   Object rights of [S B C D R] to James.SALES.ESL

   All Property rights of [S C R W A] to James.SALES.ESL

8. What rights should James have to himself to prevent him from assigning additional rights to himself?

   Answer: James should have the following explicit trustee assignments over himself:

   Object rights of [B] to James.SALES.ESL

   Selected Property right of [C R] for ACL property for James.SALES.ESL

   Selected Property right of [R W] for Login Script property for James.SALES.ESL

   Selected Property right of [R W] for Print Job Configuration property for James.SALES.ESL

9. What should be the IRF filter for James so that he does not inherit any rights to manage himself?

   Answer: James should have the following IRF settings on his user object to prevent himself from inheriting rights to manage himself:

   IRF for Object rights for James.SALES.ESL set to [B]

   IRF for All Properties rights for James.SALES.ESL set to [C R]

Rights Needed for Management Tasks

This section considers the rights that are needed to perform some common management tasks. The rights for the following management tasks are discussed:

- Printing on a network
- Mailing List Administration
- Using Directory Map objects
- Assigning Profile Login scripts
- Using alias user objects

Printing on a Network

Printing on a network does not require any special NDS rights. Access to printing functions is controlled by the users and operator properties of print-related objects. Access to a print queue object is provided through the print queue's Operators and Users property. Figure 4.88 shows that the creator of the queue and the Print Server object (if the Print Server object is linked to the queue) are automatically assigned to the Operators property list when a new queue object is created. Figure 4.89 shows the Users property of a Print Queue object. This figure shows that the container in which the print queue is defined, by default, becomes the print queue user. This means that all users defined in that container can print jobs to the queue. Also, the creator of the queue is assigned as a user of the Print Queue object. If the Print Queue object is moved to another container, its Users property is not automatically changed. In other words, the new container does not automatically get added to the Users property of the Print Queue object.

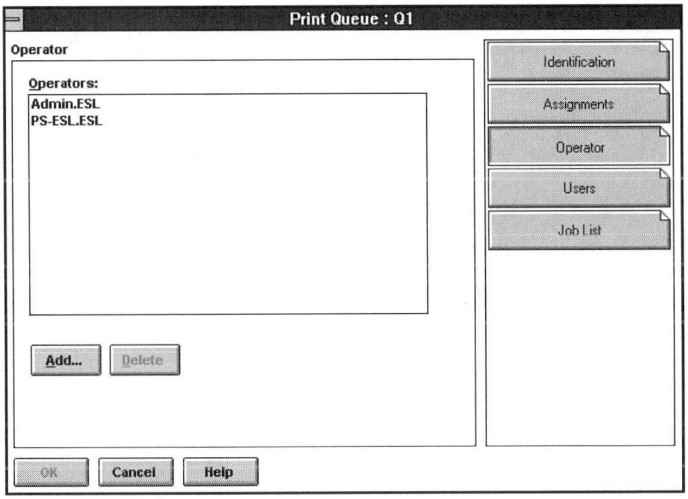

Figure 4.88
Default Operators property for Print Queue objects.

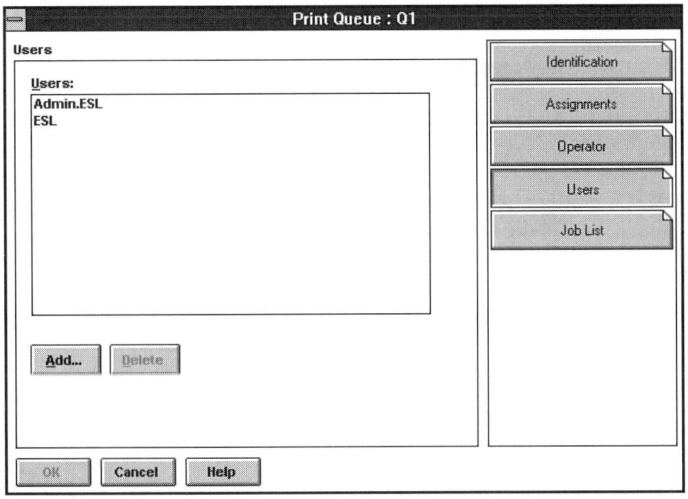

Figure 4.89
Default Users property for Print Queue object.

Figure 4.90 shows that the creator of the Print Server object is automatically assigned to the Operators property list of the Print Server object. Figure 4.91 shows the Users property of a Print Server object. This figure shows that the container in which the print queue is defined, by default, becomes the print server user. This means that all users defined in that container can print jobs to the queue. If the Print Server object is moved to another container, its Users property is not automatically changed. In other words, the new container does not automatically get added to the Users property of the Print Server object. The Print Server object has a password property, which if set, controls access to loading the print server at a server console. To load a print server at a server console no special NDS rights are needed. That is, the Print Server does not need to have any special rights to the file server object; and the file server object does not need to have any special file system rights to the Print Server object.

Figure 4.90
Default Operators property for Print Server object.

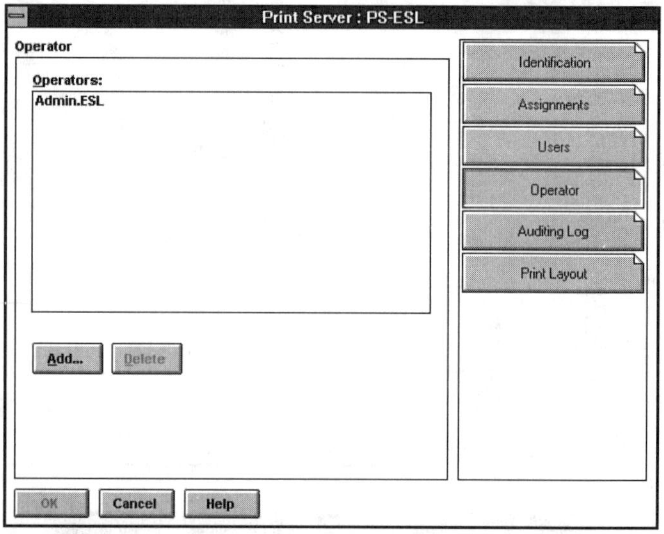

Figure 4.91
Default Users property for Print Server object.

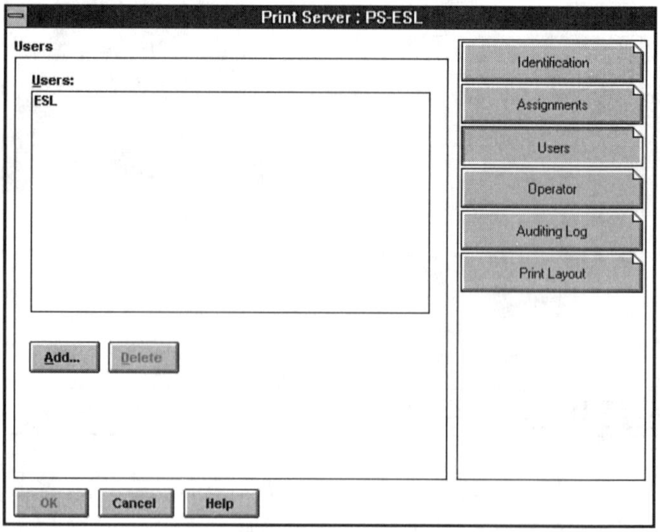

When the Print Queue, Printer, and Print Server objects are created, they are given a default set of NDS rights. These NDS rights are not required for printing. They are needed for managing the printing objects. Figure 4.92 shows the default trustees for a newly created Print Server object. The trustees of the Print Server object are the following:

- The creator of the Print Server object (Admin.ESL)
- The Print Server object (PS-ESL.ESL)
- [Public]
- [Root]

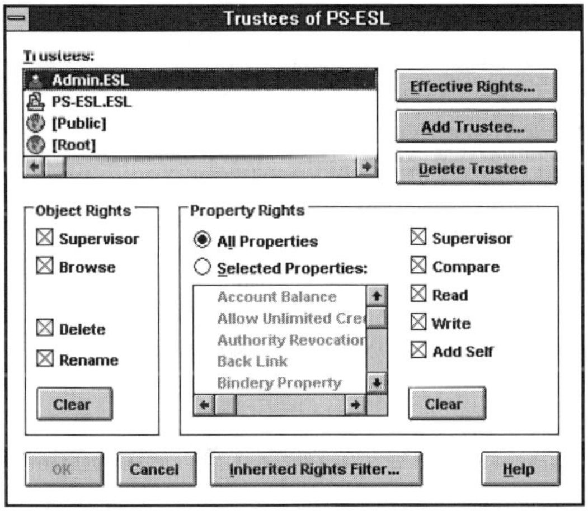

Figure 4.92
Default rights for creator of Print Server object.

Figure 4.92 also shows that the creator of the Print Server object has the object rights of [S B (C) D R] to the Print Server object, and the All Properties rights of [S C R W A] to the Print Server object.

Figure 4.93 shows that the Print Server object has the default object rights of Supervisor to the Print Server object.

Figure 4.93
Default rights for Print Server object.

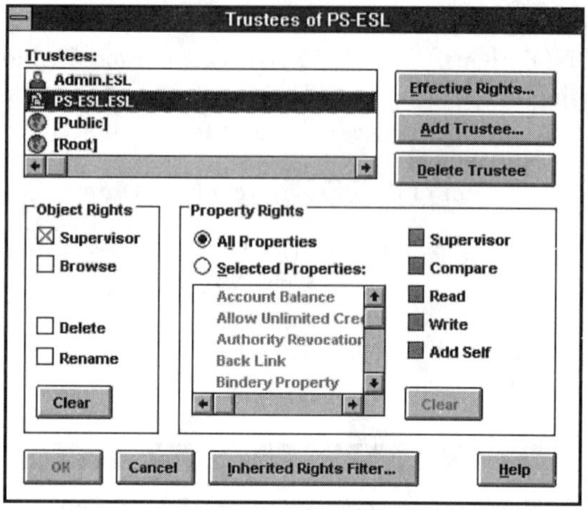

Figure 4.94 shows that [Public] has the default Selected Property rights of Read for the Network Address property of the Print Server object. This allows any user connected to the network (but not necessarily logged in) the ability to read the network address at which the Print Server object is installed. The Network Address property contains the IPX address of the NetWare server. The Network Address includes the Internal Network Number for the NetWare server on which the print server is running, and the node address (which is always 1 for the NetWare server on the internal network). The Network Address property value appears only if the print server is running.

Figure 4.94
Default rights for [Public] to Print Server object.

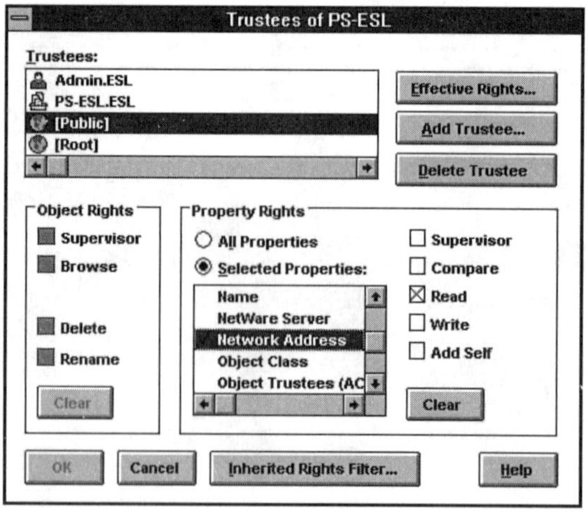

Figure 4.95 shows that [Root] has the default object rights of Browse to the print server object. This gives any user logged in to the network the ability to see the name of the print server object.

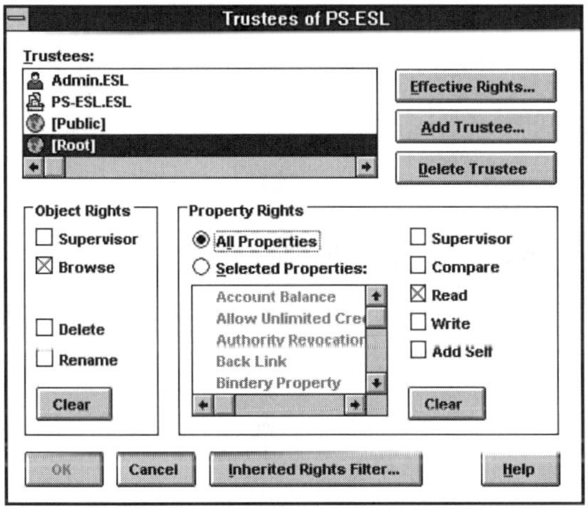

Figure 4.95
Default rights for [Root] to Print Server object.

The Print Server object has the following default trustee assignments:

- The creator of the Print Server object has [S B C D R] object rights and [S C R W A] All Properties rights to the print server object
- The Print Server object has [S] object rights to the Print Server object
- [Public] has the [R] Selected Property right for the Network Address property of the Print Server object
- [Root] has the [B] object rights to the Print Server object and [R] All Properties right to the Print Server object

Figure 4.96 shows the default trustees for a newly created Print Queue object. The trustees of the Print Queue object are

- The creator of the Print Queue object (Admin.ESL)
- [Root]

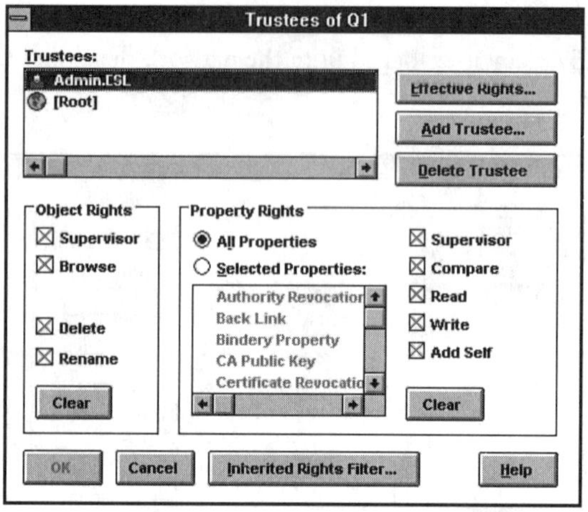

Figure 4.96
Default rights for creator of Print Queue object.

Figure 4.97 also shows that the creator of the Print Queue object has the object rights of [S B (C) D R] to the Print Queue object, and the All Properties rights of [S C R W A] to the Print Queue object.

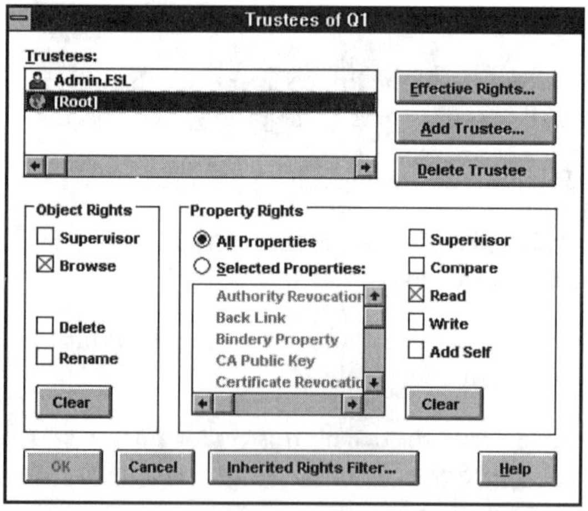

Figure 4.97
Default rights for [Root] to Print Queue object.

Figure 4.97 shows that [Root] has the default object rights of Browse to the print queue object and the default All Properties right of Read to the Print Queue object. This gives any user logged in to the network the ability to see the name of the Print Queue object and read its property values.

The Print Queue object has the following default trustee assignments:

- The creator of the Print Queue object has [S B C D R] object rights and [S C R W A] All Properties rights to the Print Queue object.
- [Root] has the [B] object rights and the [R] All Properties rights to the Print Queue object.

Figure 4.98 shows the default trustees for a properly configured Printer object. The trustees of the Printer object are the following:

- The creator of the Print Queue object (Admin.ESL)
- The Print Server object to which the Printer object is assigned
- [Root]

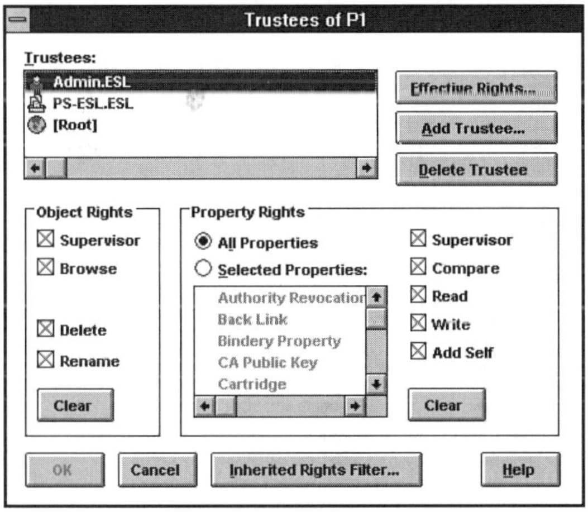

Figure 4.98
Default rights for creator of Printer object.

Please note that, if the Printer object is created by itself and is not yet assigned to a Print Server object, the Print Server object is not a trustee of the Printer object.

Figure 4.98 also shows that the creator of the Printer object has the object rights of [S B (C) D R] to the Printer object, and the All Properties rights of [S C R W A] to the Printer object. The printer object shown in figure 4.98 was created using the Quick Setup option of PCONSOLE, which correctly configures the Print objects.

Figure 4.99 shows that the Print Server object to which the printer is assigned has the default object rights of Browse to the Printer object and the default All Properties right of Read to the Printer object. This gives any user logged in to the network the ability to see the name of the Printer object and read its property values.

Figure 4.99
Default rights for Print Server object to which the Printer object is assigned.

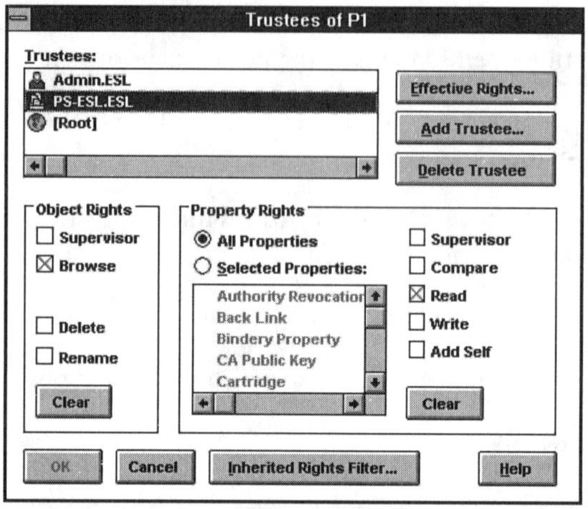

Figure 4.100 shows that [Root] has the default object rights of Browse to the Printer object and the default All Properties right of Read to the Printer object. This gives any user logged in to the network the ability to see the name of the Printer object and read its property values.

Figure 4.100
Default rights for [Root] to Printer object.

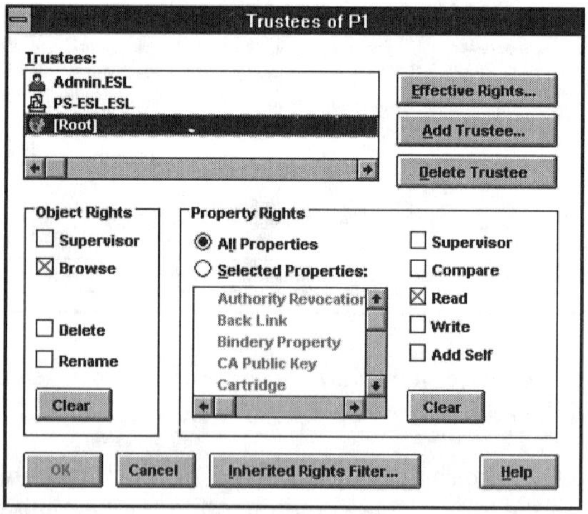

When a Printer object is created using NetWare Administrator (or PCONSOLE—but not using the Quick Setup option), the trustees assigned to it are the following:

- The creator of the Printer object
- [Root]

The Print Server object is not a trustee of the Printer object, because the printer has not been assigned to a print server. When the Printer object is assigned to the print server, the print server is made a trustee of the Printer object.

A properly configured Printer object has the following default trustee assignments:

- The creator of the Printer object has [S B C D R] object rights and [S C R W A] All Properties rights to the Printer object.
- The Print Server object to which the printer is assigned has the [B] object rights and the [R] All Properties rights to the Printer object.
- [Root] has the [B] object rights and the [R] All Properties rights to the Printer object.

Mailing List Administration

One of the properties of user objects, organization role objects, organization unit objects, and organization objects is the E-mail Address property. This property can be used to enter the electronic mail address for the object. The actual value of the E-mail Address depends on the type of e-mail system that is being used. Some organizations prefer to delegate the responsibility of maintaining properties such as E-mail Address, Telephone Number, FAX Number, and Postal Address to a special user called the Mailing List Administrator. The Mailing List Administrator should be able to modify these properties and should therefore have Read and Write property rights to the properties they manage. The Mailing List Administrator account can be implemented as a user object. If a more formal designation is needed for the Mailing List Administrator, it can also be implemented as an Organizational Role object.

The Mailing List Administrator should have the [R W] property rights for the following properties that the Mailing List Administrator manages:

- E-mail Address
- Telephone Number
- FAX Number
- Postal Address

The trustee rights assigned to the Mailing List Administrator must be assigned for each NDS object the Mailing Administrator manages. For a large organization, this can become a very laborious process. You might be tempted to give to the Mailing List Administrator rights for the users he manages through a group object or a container object, but you end up giving the Mailing Administrator more rights than he should have. Also, assigning the All Properties rights to the Mailing List Administrator would give the Write property right for the ACL property. If the Mailing List Administrator has the Write property to the ACL of an object, the Mailing List Administrator can modify the trustee assignments to the object.

Using Directory Map Objects

The Directory Map Object is used for simplifying the use of the MAP command, and for making the MAP command independent of changes to the location of the directory being mapped to. In order to use the Directory Map object, you must have the Read All Properties right to the Directory Map Object. When a Directory Map object is first created it does not have any default trustee assignment. You must explicitly assign the [R] All Properties right to the Directory Map object.

Listing 4.19 shows an attempt to map a Directory Map Object CN=DirMap.O=ESL by a user who does not have the Read All Properties right to the Directory Map Object.

Listing 4.19

```
F:\>MAP G: = .CN=DirMap.O=ESL
MAP-4.01-195: Directory [CN=DIRMAP.O=ESL] cannot be located.
```

If the user is assigned the [R] All Properties right to the CN=DirMap.O=ESL, the above command works correctly as shown:

```
F:\>MAP G: = .CN=DirMap.O=ESL
Drive G: = NW4KS_SYS.CORP: \DOC
```

In the previous example, the Directory Map Object, CN=DirMap.O=ESL, was set to point to the NW4KS_SYS:DOC directory. The user should have at least [R F] file system right to the directory being pointed to for the MAP command to work.

When a Directory Map object is first created it does not have any default trustee assignment. Before you can use the Directory Map object, you must have the [R] All Properties right to the Directory Map Object.

You might want to make the container in which the Directory Map object is defined a trustee to the Directory Map object and give to the container the [R] All Properties right. This gives all users in the container the [R] All Properties right to the Directory Map object, and allows them to use it. It is quite possible that future releases of IntranetWare may provide this as a default trustee assignment when a Directory Map object is created.

The Directory Map object has a property called Rights to Files and Directories. Assigning rights to a file system via this property does not cause these rights to be inherited by the users mapping to the Directory Map object.

Assigning Profile Login Scripts

The Profile object contains the profile login script. User objects have a property called the Profile, which can be set to point to a profile object. The profile login script is a way of implementing a common login script that is shared by any user that has their Profile property pointing to the same profile object. The profile login script is executed after the system login script (if one exists), but before the user's login script (if one exists). The system login script is the login script for the user's container. If the user's login script does not exist, and the NO_DEFAULT directive has not been specified in the system or profile login script, the default login script is run.

The following simple exercise demonstrates the rights needed to run a profile login script:

1. Create a container O=IBL, and a user object James in that container.
2. Create the profile object CProf in O=IBL and examine its default trustees. Notice that the profile object CN=CProf.O=IBL does not have any default trustees.
3. In the Profile Login script for the profile object CN=CProf.O=IBL, place the following login script statement:

   ```
   WRITE "Profile login script for CProf is executed"
   ```

4. Set the Profile property for user James to point to the CN=CProf.O=IBL object.
5. Log in as the user CN=James.O=IBL.

   Notice that the profile login script for the user James is not executed. The reason for this is that user James does not have [R] property rights to the profile object's Login Script property.

6. Log in as Admin.

   Make user CN=James.O=IBL a trustee of CN=CProf.O=IBL with the [R] Selected Property rights to the Login Script property.

7. Log in as the user CN=James.O=IBL, again.

   Notice that the profile login script for the user James is executed. The reason for this is that user James now has [R] property rights to the profile object's Login Script property.

When a profile object is created, it does not have any default trustees. A user who has his Profile property set to a profile object must be able to read the profile login script in order to execute it. This means that the user must have the Read property right to the profile object's Login Script property.

The Novell documentation says that if the user and the Profile object are in the same container, no additional rights to the Profile object are needed. If the container in which the profile login script was created was made a trustee of the profile object and given the Read property write to its Login Script, this would be true. As the exercise above indicates, this is not true for IntranetWare, and a user must have the Read property right to the profile login script, even if the user and the profile object are in the same container.

The following are the steps needed to set up a profile login script for a user:

1. Create the profile object and set its profile login script.

2. Set the Profile property of a user to point to the profile object.

3. Assign the user the [R] property rights to the profile object's Login Script property.

   If all users are in the same container, you can assign the container a trustee of the profile object and give it the [R] property rights to the profile object's Login Script property.

Typically, users who share a profile login script are in different containers. If they are in the same container, using the system login script for that container is usually sufficient. If the users are members of a group object or an organizational role object, you can make the group object or organizational role object a trustee of the profile object. Alternatively, you might want to individually assign users trustees of the profile object.

Using Alias User Objects

To understand the rights needed by alias users to execute their login scripts, consider the situation in Figure 4.101, which shows an NDS tree for organizations IBL and UNE.

Figure 4.101
Alias user object and login scripts.

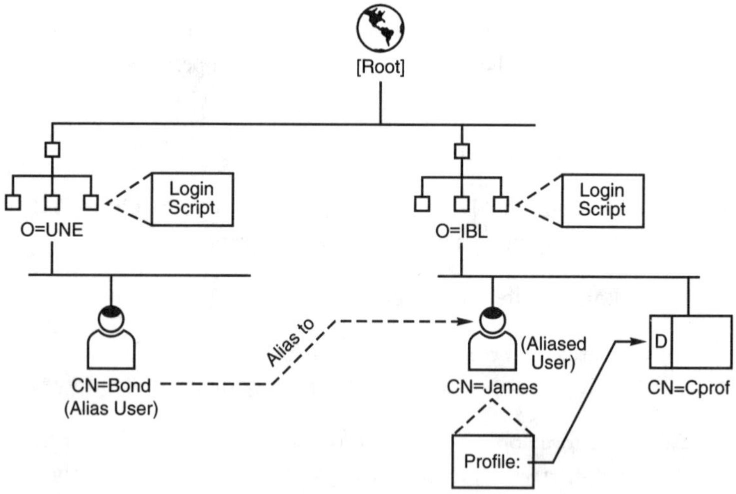

Organization IBL has a user James defined in the container O=IBL, and organization UNE has an alias object Bond that is an alias to CN=James.O=IBL. The user CN=Bond.O=UNE is the *alias* user, and the user CN=James.O=IBL is called the *aliased user.* The O=IBL has a system login script set that has the following login script statements:

```
WRITE "Executing login script for container IBL"
```

User CN=James.O=IBL has his Profile property set to the profile object CN=CProf.O=IBL. The profile login script has the following login statement:

```
WRITE "Executing profile login script CProf"
```

User CN=James.O=IBL has the following statements in his user login script:

```
WRITE "Executing login script for user James"
```

Additionally, user CN=James.O=IBL is a trustee of the profile object CN=CProf.O=IBL and has the [R] property right to the profile object's Login Script property. Since Bond is an alias to user James, Bond is automatically a trustee of CN=CProf.O=IBL with the same rights. The NetWare Administrator does not allow you to add the alias and the aliased user as trustees of the same object. (Try it, to verify this for your IntranetWare server.)

If you log in as user CN=James.O=IBL, you see messages similar to those in listing 4.20.

Listing 4.20

```
Executing login script for container IBL
Executing profile login script CProf
Executing login script for user James
```

If you log in as the alias user CN=Bond.O=UNE, you see messages similar to those in listing 4.21.

Listing 4.21

```
Executing profile login script CProf
Executing login script for user James
```

Notice that the login script for O=IBL container is not executed for the user CN=Bond.O=UNE. When an alias user logs in, it runs the container login script for the container the alias user is in, and not the container login script for the aliased user.

If you were to create a system login script for container O=UNE and place in it the statement:

```
WRITE "Executing login script for container UNE"
```

Then log in as the alias user CN=Bond.O=UNE, and you see messages similar to those in listing 4.22.

Listing 4.22

```
Executing profile login script CProf
Executing login script for user James
```

Notice that the login script for O= UNE container is not executed for the user CN=Bond.O=UNE, even though it has been set. In order for an alias user to execute the login script of the container it is defined in, the alias user must be granted the [R] property right to the Login Script property of its container. If this is done, logging in as alias user CN=Bond.O=UNE produces messages similar to those in listing 4.23, showing that the alias user's container login script is executed.

Listing 4.23

```
Executing login script for container UNE
Executing profile login script CProf
Executing login script for user James
```

It might seem a little strange that the alias user needs to be granted an explicit trustee assignment to the Login Script property of the container, especially because the container is made a trustee of itself and given the [R] Selected Property right to its Login Script property.

The reason for assigning the alias user an explicit trustee assignment to the Login Script property of the container is because the alias user is really a "phantom" user whose true existence is in the container that holds the aliased user, even though the aliased user does not execute the system login script of the aliased user. The aliased user needs to have [R] property rights to the alias' container's Login Script property.

If you assign the alias user the [R] property rights to its container, and then go back to re-examine the trustee assignments of the alias' container, you see that the aliased user is listed as a trustee, even though you initially made the alias user a trustee of the container.

Summary

In this chapter, you have learned the basics of IntranetWare security. NetWare security is layered. The first layer you must pass through is Login Authentication and Login Restriction. The second layer is NDS security. The last (third) layer is the NetWare File System security.

You were presented with a detailed explanation of how Login Authentication is done. Certain mathematical equations were presented, to show you how authentication works. You can use this as a reference, and to further your understanding.

You also learned about the default security assignments for many NDS objects such as [Root], container, user, and NetWare server objects. It is important to understand the default security assignments to NDS objects before attempting to change it to fine-tune NetWare security. The default rights are assigned to simplify network administration. If you change the default rights, you should make sure that the users can perform network tasks.

You were shown how to implement a network administration strategy by delegating network responsibility. This can be done using a distributed approach of assigning an Administrator per NDS tree branch or a centralized approach of having a central Admin account, and assigning assistant administrators that act as workgroup managers.

CHAPTER 5

Novell Directory Services Schema and X.500

The term "schema" describes the structure of a database and the rules of operation on the database. When applied to Novell Directory Services (NDS), it refers to the structure of the NDS database, the structure of the NDS objects, the properties of NDS objects, and so on. It describes the different types of object classes allowed and how these objects interrelate. Because NDS is based on X.500 and, over time, is expected to evolve to become even more like X.500, this chapter also discusses X.500, the terminology used in X.500, and its equivalent concept used in NDS.

The purpose of this chapter is to give you greater insight and knowledge about the structure of NDS. Detailed knowledge of X.500 is not essential to performing day-to-day IntranetWare administrative tasks.

Understanding the X.500 Standard

The X.500 is a set of *Open Systems Interconnection* (OSI) standards that describes the interconnection of information systems from different manufacturers, at different levels of complexity, under different management, and of different ages. The last criteria, *different ages,* implies that systems that comply with X.500 will be compatible with future evolution of the X.500 standards. This is important because it ensures that current X.500 systems will interoperate with future systems based on the evolving X.500 standard.

The information systems and their directory information are called the *Directory.* The information inside the Directory is called the *Directory Information Base* (DIB). In IntranetWare terms, the DIB is called the *Novell Directory Services* (NDS).

The Directory provides information on services such as OSI applications, OSI management processes, OSI layer entities, and telecommunication services. As in the case of NDS, however, the Directory can be used as a model to define directory services for other non-OSI systems.

The Directory provides a single, unified, name space directory for applications and users on the network. Figure 5.1 shows a simple usage model for the Directory. The *Directory user* refers to computer programs that act on behalf of end users or applications and request services to read or modify information in the DIB. The *Directory User Agent* (DUA) is the program that actually makes the request. In IntranetWare, the Directory Services for DOS workstations is implemented by the NDS.VLM.

Figure 5.1
A model of directory use.

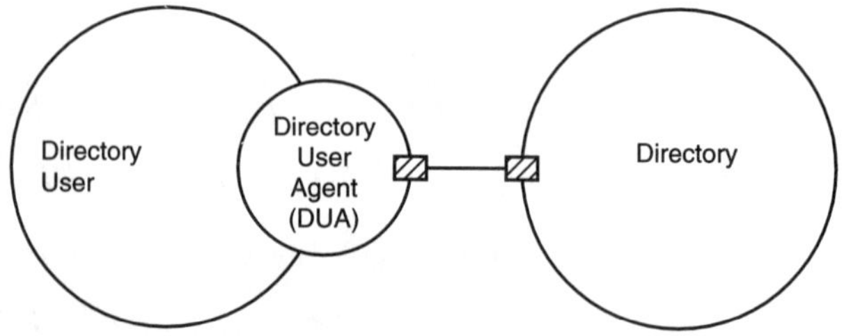

In the marketing literature of different organizations, the Directory is often cited as an example of a general-purpose database. This is not true, even though the Directory may be built using general-purpose database technology. The assumptions in X.500 Directory Services, and also NDS, are the following:

- Queries are more frequent than updates. This is true for a variety of directories such as the telephone directory published once every few months. The Directory is used for looking up information far more often than it gets updated.

- The updates are determined by the dynamics of people and organizations rather than the dynamics of networks.

- Updates to directories need not take place instantaneously. There may be transient conditions in which both new and old versions of the information may exist in the directory.
- Except for situations in which users have different access rights to the directory, the results of a directory query should be the same regardless of the location from which they are issued. This means that directory services such as NDS cannot be used for holding information, such as routing tables of a network, when the information queried depends on the location of the query.

X.500 is not just one standard, but a series of standards. Table 5.1 shows the names of the X.500 standard documents and their equivalent *International Organization of Standards/International Electrotechnical Commission* (ISO/IEC). This chapter covers the fundamental concepts behind CCITT X.500. For a more detailed discussion, you can refer to the standards listed in table 5.1.

Table 5.1
X.500 Recommendations

CCITT Recommendation	Equivalent ISO/IEC Standard
X.500	ISO 9594-1, Information processing system_Open Systems Interconnection. The Directory_Part 1. Overview of concepts, model and service.
X.501	ISO 9594-2, Information processing system_Open Systems Interconnection. The Directory_Part 2: Models.
X.509	ISO 9594-8, Information processing system_Open Systems Interconnection. The Directory_Part 8: Authentication framework.
X.511	ISO 9594-3, Information processing system_Open Systems Interconnection. The Directory_Part 3: Abstract service definition.
X.518	ISO 9594-4, Information processing system_Open Systems Interconnection. The Directory_Part 4: Procedures for distributed operation.
X.519	ISO 9594-5, Information processing system_Open Systems Interconnection. The Directory_Part 5: Protocol specifications.
X.520	ISO 9594-6, Information processing system_Open Systems Interconnection. The Directory_Part 6: Selected attribute types.
X.521	ISO 9594-7, Information processing system_Open Systems Interconnection. The Directory_Part 7: Selected object classes.

The Directory Information Base (DIB)

The DIB is the X.500 term for the NDS database. The DIB is composed of information on objects in the form of *directory entries.* A directory entry consists of *attributes.* The attributes have a *type* and one or more values. The directory entries in a DIB are arranged in the form of a tree (see fig. 5.2) called the *Directory Information Tree* (DIT). The DIT is the X.500 term for the NDS tree.

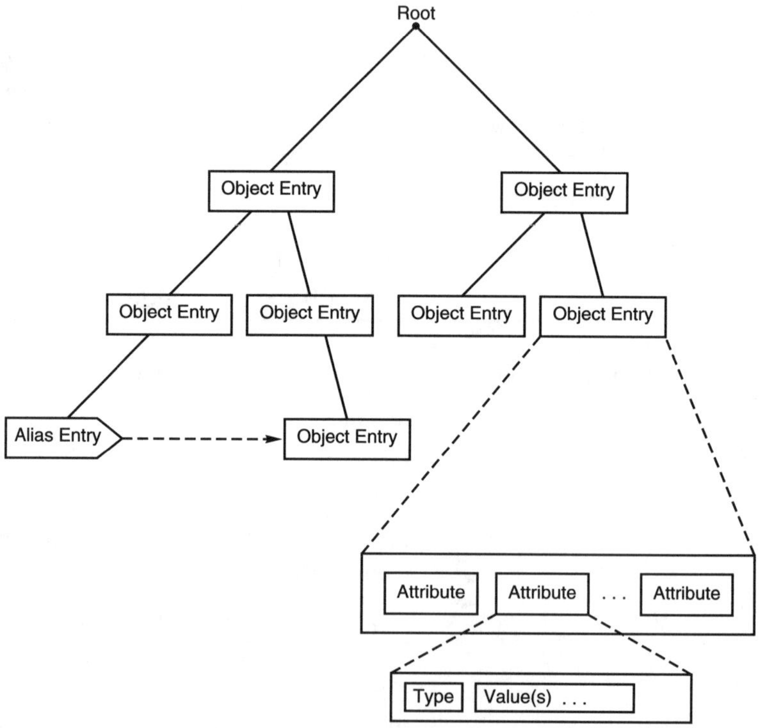

Figure 5.2
The Directory Information Tree.

Directory Names

Every directory entry has a *Distinguished Name* (DN) that uniquely and clearly identifies the entry and its location in the DIT. The Distinguished Name can consist of a combination of certain designated directory entry attributes. The Distinguished Name for a directory entry is made up of the Distinguished Name of its *superior* (immediate parent) and the *Relative Distinguished Name* (RDN) for the directory entry. Each directory entry has one or more "name" attribute values called *distinguished values* that serve to uniquely identify that directory entry from its siblings. The unordered collection of these values is called the Relative Distinguished Name. The RDN must distinguish a directory entry from its siblings. Most objects defined in NDS have only one attribute—the *Common Name* (CN)—that distinguishes the object from its siblings. The directory entries can be for object entries or alias entries (refer to figure 5.2). The object entries refer to the actual objects, and the alias entries provide an alternate name for the objects they point to.

Figure 5.3 shows a DIT. Notice how DNs for objects such as Bill are represented.

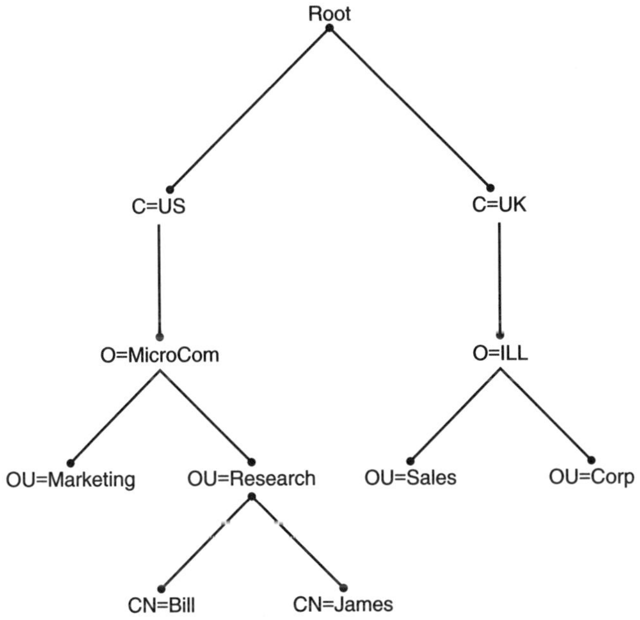

Figure 5.3
Distinguished Names in a DIT.

The X.500 standard does not define how the textual strings for Distinguished Names are to be represented, but it does define how Distinguished Names are exchanged between OSI systems. Typically, this is done using the *Abstract Syntax Notation 1* (ASN.1) that unambiguously transmits the Distinguished Names across the network. When dealing with implementations of NDS, you must have a textual representation of these distinguished names, which can differ between implementations.

Contrary to popular belief, Novell's syntax for complete names for the NDS is not the only way to represent Distinguished Names. This does not mean that Novell is not compliant with X.500, because the standard does not define the textual representation of the DN. In the X.500 standard document, the Distinguished Name for object Bill in figure 10.3 would be represented as the following:

```
{C= US, O=MicroCom, OU=Research, CN=Bill}
```

Compare this to the following NDS representation of the Distinguished Name for Bill:

```
.CN=Bill.OU=Research.O=MicroCom.C=US
```

From the preceding example, you can see that the term *Distinguished Name* is the X.500 term for *Complete Name* used in NDS.

Another interesting X.500 implementation that uses a different Distinguished Name syntax is *QUIPU*, developed at University College, London, and available as part of the *ISO Development Environment* (ISODE) release. ISODE can be obtained by contacting the following address:

University of Pennsylvania
Department of Computer and Information Science
Moore School
Attn: ISODE Distribution
200 South 33rd Street
Philadelphia, PA 19104-6319
U.S.A.
(215) 898-8560

QUIPU (pronounced *kwi-poo*) is named after the manner in which information was stored by the Inca of Peru. These people did not use writing; instead they used colored strings that they knotted to encode information. The strings were attached to a larger rope to form a device known as the Quipu. The Quipu could only be read by trained people and contained information about property locations and rights throughout the Incan empire.

The user Bill of figure 5.3 is named as follows in QUIPU:

```
@C=US@O=MicroCom@OU=Research@CN=Bill
```

Notice that in QUIPU, objects are written left to right, starting from the root of the DIT and moving down the tree to the object. This is in contrast to NDS in which objects, although written from left to right, are listed starting from the object and moving up the tree.

To move up one level from the current context, the syntax in NDS is as follows:

```
CN=KSS.OU=SCS.
```

To move up one level in QUIPU, the syntax is as follows:

```
..@OU=SCS.CN=KSS
```

The X.500 standard describes the existence of a *Locality* object that describes a location. Figure 5.4 shows a DIT that uses a Locality object. The NDS schema does implement the Locality object class; however, the administration tools do not offer it as a class that can be created. A special utility would have to be written to create the objects, but the NDS utilities can deal with a Locality object after it exists in the tree. The X.500 notation for the Distinguished Name for Janice is as follows:

```
{CN=US,  L=Berkeley, CN=Janice}
```

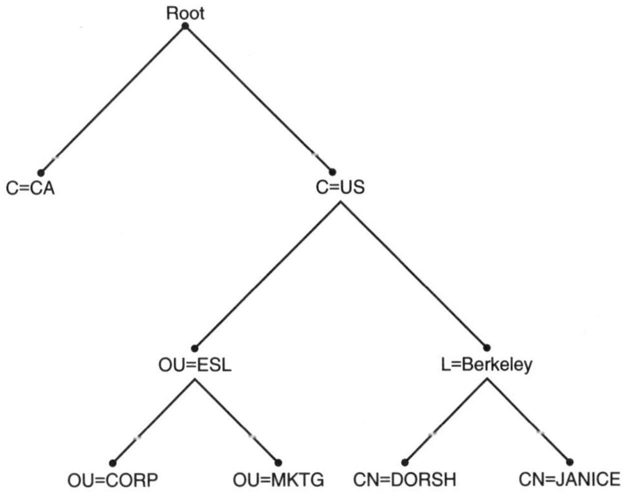

Figure 5.4
DIT using Locality object.

The Locality object acts as a container object and is meant to describe information for a person residing at a location such as a town, city, and so on. It could be used for organizing an electronic directory for locations that are similar to the paper telephone directories that exist in many parts of the world.

Understanding the Directory Schema for the NDS

The Directory enforces a set of rules on how the different types of directory entries are organized in the DIT and the types of operations that can be performed on them. These rules are called the *Directory schema* and help maintain consistency in the DIB.

The structure rules for how the different objects in the DIT are organized are described in an annex to the X.521 Recommendation and is shown in figure 5.5. This figure is interesting for a number of reasons. It shows the major classes of objects that can exist in the DIT and where they can occur in relationship to each other. Except for the Locality object, Application process, and Application entity, the rules for the DIT are the same as for the NDS tree. The Application process class is intended for OSI applications integrated with X.500. These are not currently implemented in NDS. The Locality object is not supported by IntranetWare utilities, although the NDS can support it.

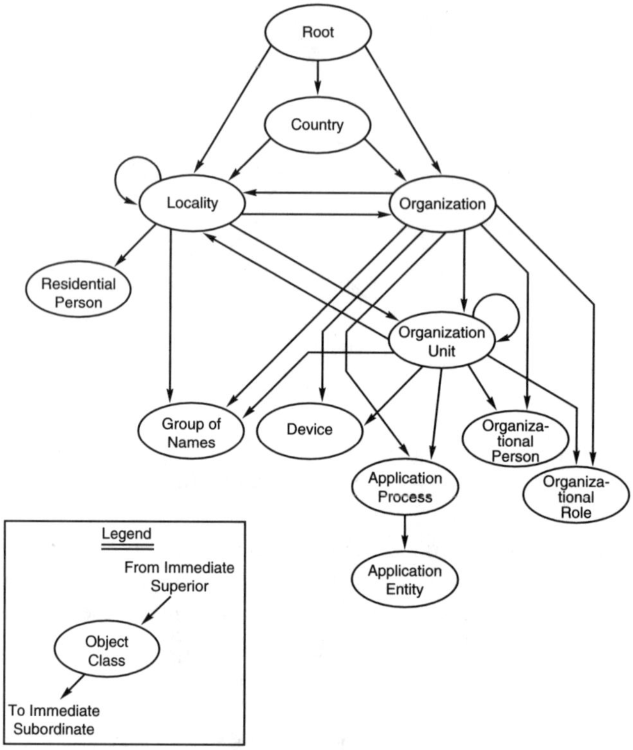

Figure 5.5
Objects in a DIT.

In figure 5.5, an arrow is drawn from a superior (parent) object class to its immediate subordinate (child). For example, an arrow is drawn from the root object class to the Country, Locality, and Organization object classes, respectively. This means that the Country, Locality, and Organization object classes can exist directly underneath the root of the DIT. In the NDS tree, only the Country and Organization classes can exist under the root. The Locality and Organizational Unit object classes have an arrow coming from themselves and going into themselves. This means that there can be several levels of the Locality and Organizational Unit object class in a DIT.

The NDS schema consists of the following three major components:

- Object classes
- Attribute types
- Attribute syntaxes

Object classes describe the different types of objects that can exist in the NDS. To describe the different object classes, you need to specify the structural rules for the object class, super class of the object class, mandatory attributes, and optional attributes.

The structural rules define the relationship of the object to other objects in the NDS tree. For example, you should know whether a certain object can appear in a specified container. In the example in figure 5.5, the Organizational Unit object can exist in an Organization or Locality container, but not directly underneath a Country or root object.

The *attribute type* is a particular piece of information in the object class. Examples of attribute types are Account Balance (occurs in a user object class), ACL (occurs in the Top object class), and Detect Intruder (occurs in the Organization and Organizational Unit object class).

An *attribute syntax* defines the type of data stored in an attribute type. An attribute type is made up of an attribute syntax (also called *property syntax*), and can have a constraint placed on it. Examples of attribute syntaxes are Counter, Integer, and Boolean. The attribute type Account Balance has the attribute syntax Counter; the attribute type Detect Intruder is made up of the attribute syntax Boolean; and the Common Name attribute type is made up of the attribute type Case Ignore String and can have 1 to 64 elements.

In general, an attribute syntax can consist of one or more data types with rules that express an ordering relationship between them. These rules are called *matching rules* and can be substring, equality, or ordering (less than, equal to, greater than). The set of attribute syntaxes is the only element of the NDS schema that is nonextensible. The other elements, object class and attribute types, can be extended by Directory Services APIs.

Table 5.2 shows constraints that can be placed on the attribute type.

Table 5.2
Constraints on Attribute Types

Constraint	Description
Hidden	The user cannot see or modify the attribute. The NDS name server is responsible for maintaining this attribute. Defined by DS_HIDDEN_ATTR in the NWDSDEFS.H file.
Non-removable	This attribute type cannot be deleted from the schema. For example, all attribute types that make up the base schema are flagged with this attribute to prevent an application from deleting attribute types from the base schema. Defined by DS_NONREMOVABLE_ATTR in the NWDSDEFS.H file.
Public Read	Anyone can read the attribute type. No object property rights are needed to read the attribute type. Also, the IRF cannot be used to prevent the reading of this attribute type. Defined by DS_PUBLIC_READ in the NWDSDEFS.H file.
Read Only	The user cannot modify the attribute. The NDS name server is responsible for maintaining this attribute. Defined by DS_READ_ONLY_ATTR in the NWDSDEFS.H file.

continues

Table 5.2, Continued
Constraints on Attribute Types

Constraint	Description
Single-valued	The attribute has a single value only. If an attribute does not have this constraint, it is a multi-valued attribute. For example, the attribute ACL does not have this attribute because it consists of multiple values. Defined by DS_SINGLE_VALUED_ATTR in the NWDSDEFS.H file.
Sized	The attribute has an upper and lower bound such as length of strings or values of integers. Defined by DS_SIZED_ATTR in the NWDSDEFS.H file.
String	The attribute is a string of characters. Primarily used for naming objects and text descriptions of objects. Defined by DS_STRING_ATTR in the NWDSDEFS.H file.
Server Read	Server class objects are given special read access to this attribute even though read right is not explicitly or implicitly given to the attribute. IRF cannot be used to block read right for server class objects. An example of an attribute type that uses this constraint is the Default Queue in the printer object. The NCP server can access the name of the default queue in the printer object regardless of any permission setting on the Default Queue property. Defined by DS_SERVER_READ in the NWDSDEFS.H file.
Sync Immediate	Modifications made to this attribute type are synchronized immediately rather than at the next synchronization interval. An example of an attribute type that uses this constraint is the CA (Certification Authority) Private Key and CA Public Key that describe the Certification Authority private and public keys for the object class partition. Defined by DS_SYNC_IMMEDIATE in the NWDSDEFS.H file.
Write Managed	You must have managed rights on the object that contains this attribute before you can change the attributes value. Defined by DS_WRITE_MANAGED in the NWDSDEFS.H file.
Suppress Synchronization	The information in this attribute is not synchronized to other replicas. Currently the only attribute type that uses this constraint in the NDS base class schema is the Reference attribute defined in the Top object class. The Reference class object is used for internal bookkeeping purposes. For example, if objects A, B, and C have privileges granted to object X (through the ACL attribute type), the Reference attribute of object X contains the object names A, B, and C. This makes it easy to find the objects that reference a given object. The Reference attribute is not synchronized to other replicas. Defined by DS_SF_PER_REPLICA in the NWDSDEFS.H file.

Class Inheritance in NDS

A very important attribute for directory entries (objects) is the *object class.* The value of the object class determines the type of the NDS object and the type of other attributes it can contain. NDS has a formal definition of all the different object classes that it can contain. The definition for NDS objects is based on class inheritance. *Class inheritance* uses a definition hierarchy similar to that used in object-oriented programming languages.

The structural rules for objects define the concept of an *immediate super class.* An *object class* can be defined as a sub-class of another object, with some additional refinements in terms of new attributes. Another way of saying this is that an object's definition is "derived" from its immediate superior class.

At the "top-most" level is an object called *Top.* Top is the super class of all objects. All NDS objects are directly or indirectly derived from Top. Figure 5.6 shows the derivation hierarchy of the different NDS object classes. Top is the only class that has no super class. When an object has a super class, the object's definition is said to be derived from this super class. This means that the object's attributes (properties) are those defined by the super class object plus any additional properties peculiar to that object. In other words, an object inherits some of its properties from its super class.

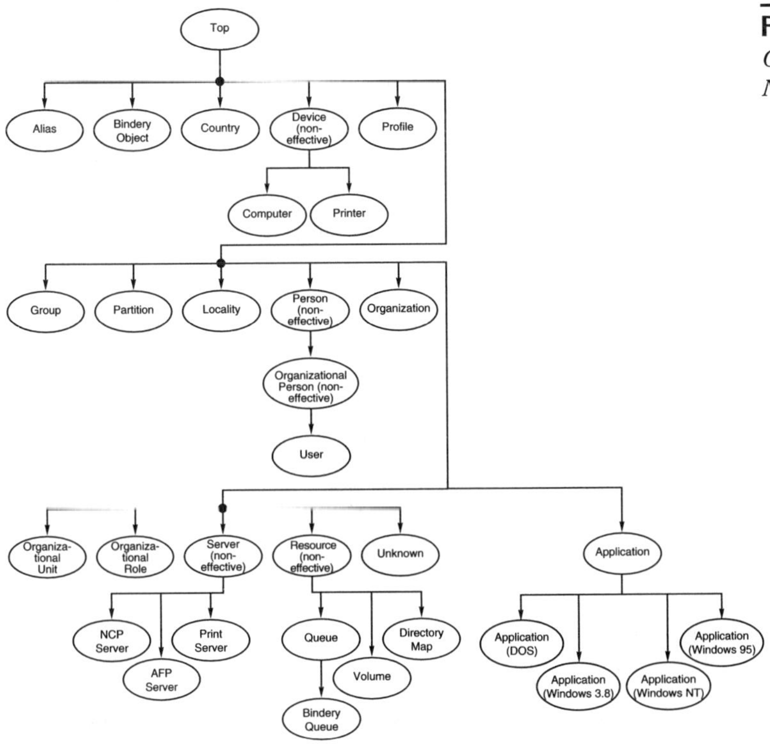

Figure 5.6
Overview of schema for NDS object classes.

The definition of the top object class can be expressed using the format of ASN.1 as shown in listing 5.1.

Listing 5.1

```
Top OBJECT-CLASS
MUST CONTAIN {Object Class}
MAY CONTAIN  { ACL,
Back Link,
Bindery Property,
Obituary,
Reference }

Revision
Authority Revocation
CA Private Key
CA Public Key
Certificate Revocation
Certificate Validity Interval
Cross Certificate Pair
Equivalent to Me
Last Referenced Time
```

ASN.1 is a standard that deals with rules of encoding and describing structural properties of application-level data. ASN.1 is part of the *International Organization of Standards* (ISO) recommendations for the presentation layer (layer 6) of the *Open Systems Interconnection* (OSI) reference model. It is the language used by protocol designers to describe upper-layer application protocols.

In the preceding definition of the Top object class, the clause MUST CONTAIN means that the properties listed in { } must have a value. The clause MAY CONTAIN means the properties listed in { } need not have values. In other words, the values of the properties listed in MAY CONTAIN are optional.

Other clauses that might be used in the definition are SUBCLASS OF, CONTAINMENT, and NAMED BY.

The SUBCLASS OF is used to indicate that the object is *derived from* another object. In the definition of the Top object class, no SUBCLASS OF clause exists because the Top class is not derived from any other object. The CONTAINMENT clause is used to describe the containers in which the defined object can be placed. For example, the CONTAINMENT clause for user objects is Organization and Organizational Unit objects. The user object cannot occur in any other container. The NAMED BY clause is used to indicate the object attributes used to name the object. Usually, the NAMED BY attribute contains attributes such as Common Name that are used for leaf objects. For container objects, attributes such as the Organization Name and Organizational Unit can be used.

The derivations of NDS objects from its super classes are defined in the following sections.

Defining Alias Objects

The derivation of the alias class is shown in figure 5.7. Listing 5.2 shows the formal definition of the alias object class.

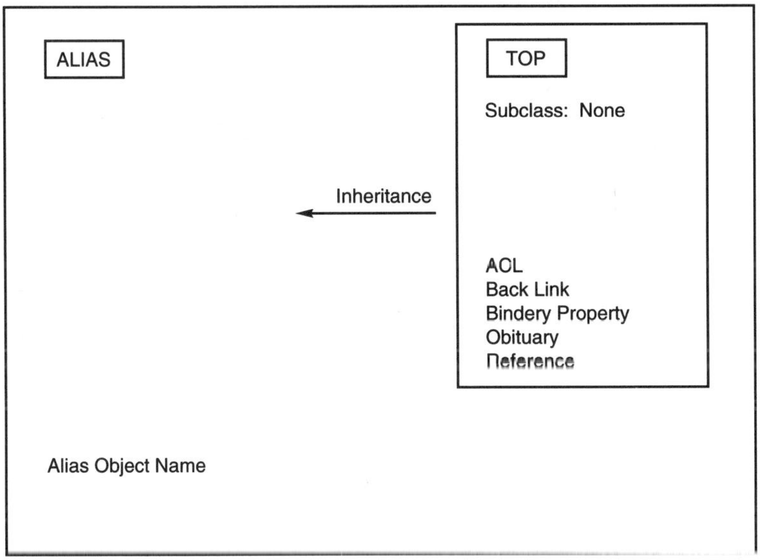

Figure 5.7
An alias object derived from the top class object.

Listing 5.2

```
Alias OBJECT-CLASS
SUBCLASS OF Top
MUST CONTAIN {AliasObjectName, // Called Name in NWADMIN
surName // Called Last Name in NWADMIN
}
MAY CONTAIN  { }
```

Figure 5.7 shows an example of derivation in which the alias object class is derived from the top super class. The only new attribute/property defined in the alias object class is the *aliasObjectName*; all other properties of the alias object class are inherited from the top super class.

Listing 5.3 presents a definition of the alias object.

Listing 5.3

```
alias OBJECT-CLASS
SUBCLASS OF Top
MUST CONTAIN {aliasObjectName}
```

The User Object

The user object class is actually derived from the super class *organizational person.* This means that the class has all information types defined in the Organizational Person super class as well as any additional attributes defined for the user class. The organizational person class is itself derived from the *person* class which is in turn derived from the top super class. This inheritance is shown in figure 5.8.

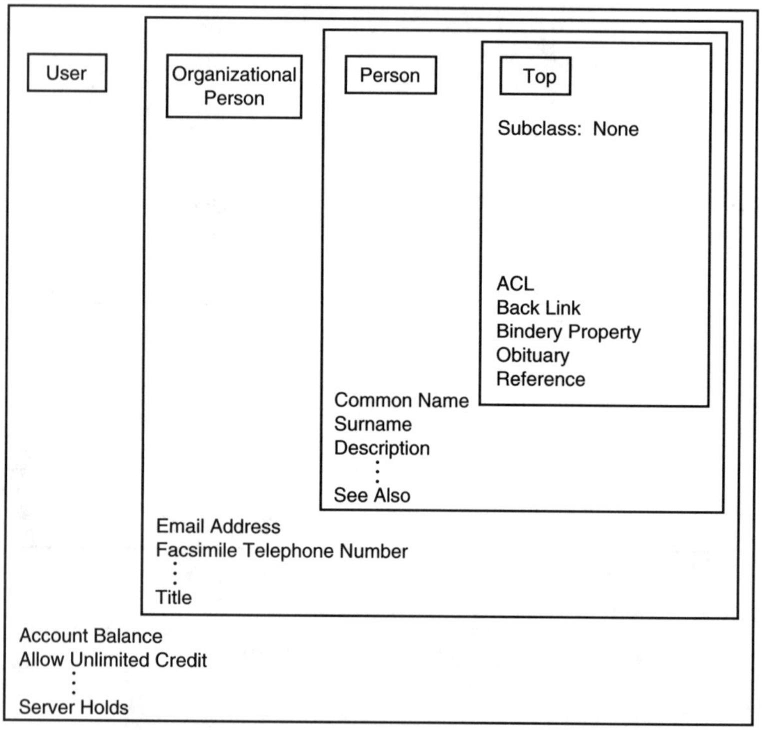

Figure 5.8
User object class derivation.

In formal terms the derivation of the user class is defined in listing 5.4.

Listing 5.4

```
Person OBJECT-CLASS
SUBCLASS OF Top
MUST CONTAIN { Common Name, // Called Name in NWADMIN
SurName // Called Last Name in NWADMIN
}
MAY CONTAIN  { Description, Telephone Number,
Full Name, See Also } Generational Qualifier, Given Name, Initials

Organizational Person OBJECT-CLASS
SUBCLASS OF Person
MAY CONTAIN {    EMail Address,
```

```
Facsimile Telephone Number,
Locality Name, //Mailbox ID
Mailbox Locality
Organizational Unit Name,
Physical Delivery Office Name,
Postal Address,
Postal Code,
Postal Office Box,
State or Province name,
Street Address,
Title }
CONTAINMENT {    Organization,
Organizational Unit }
NAMED BY        {    Common Name,
Organizational Unit }

User OBJECT CLASS
SUBCLASS OF Organizational Person
MAY CONTAIN {    Account Balance,
Allow Unlimited Credit,
Group Membership,
Higher Privileges, // Not implemented
Home Directory,
Language,
Last Login Time,
Locked By Intruder,
Login Allowed Time Map,
Login Disabled,
Login Expiration Time,
Login Grace Limit,
Login Grace Remaining,
Login Intruder Address,
Login Intruder Attempts,
Login Intruder Reset Time,
Login Maximum Simultaneous,
Login Script,
Login Time,
Message Server,
Minimum Account Balance,
Network Address,
Network Address Restriction,
Password Allow Change,
Password Expiration Interval,
Password Minimum Length,
Password Required,
Password Unique Required,
Passwords Used,
Print Job Configuration,
Printer Control,
Private Key,
Profile, Profile Membership
Public Key,
Security Equals, Security flags
Server Holds }
```

The X.500 standard defines two *subclasses* (derived classes) from the person class. These are the *residential person* and *organizational person.* The residential person object class is not defined in NDS. This is used in X.500 to define directory services similar to those found in telephone books. Refering to figure 5.5, you can see that the residential person occurs under the Locality object.

Objects belonging to object classes, such as person and organizational person, do not exist as objects in an NDS database. They are used for object derivation and construction only and are therefore called *non-effective classes.* Classes such as user, group, and so on can have their objects exist in an NDS tree. Such classes are called *effective classes.* Only an effective class can be used to create NDS objects. An object class used to create NDS objects is called the created object's *base class.* It therefore follows that only an effective class can be used as a base class for an object. Sometimes in object-oriented programming languages, the term *parent class* is the same as the base class. In NDS vocabulary, the term parent class is used for container objects that contain other objects, and is not used to describe the object derivation hierarchy.

The NDS base schema defines the following non-effective classes:

- Device
- Organizational Person
- Person
- Resource
- Server
- Top

The NDS base schema defines the following effective object classes:

- Alias
- AFP Server
- Bindery Object
- Bindery Queue
- Computer
- Country
- Directory Map
- Group

- Locality
- Partition
- NCP Server
- Organization
- Organization Role
- Organizational Unit
- Printer
- Print Server
- Profile
- Queue
- Unknown
- User
- Volume

The CONTAINMENT clause (see definition of Organizational Person) defines the container in which the object can have an existence. The NAMED BY clause defines the Relative Distinguished Name used to identify the object.

The Higher Privileges attribute in the user class definition is not currently implemented. It is meant to activate certain privileges on a temporary basis and then deactivate them. Users of Unix systems will readily recognize that the su (supervisor command) on a Unix system allows an already logged in user to assume *root* (supervisor) privileges after proper password authentication. The Higher Privileges attribute, if implemented, can provide a similar capability.

The Message Server attribute for the user object class is set to the server object that stores and forwards broadcast type messages.

The Bindery Object

The *Bindery object* is an effective-class object and is derived from Top (refer to figure 5.6). Its formal definition is in listing 5.5.

Listing 5.5

```
Bindery Object OBJECT-CLASS
SUBCLASS OF Top
MUST CONTAIN { Bindery Object Restriction,
Bindery Type,
Common Name }
MAY CONTAIN  { Any }

CONTAINMENT {Organization,
Organizational Unit}
NAMED BY { Bindery Type,
Common Name }
```

The Country Object

The *Country object* is an effective-class object and is derived from Top (refer to figure 5.6). Its formal definition is in listing 5.6.

Listing 5.6

```
Country OBJECT-CLASS
SUBCLASS OF Top
MUST CONTAIN { Country Name // C=
}
MAY CONTAIN  { Description }

CONTAINMENT { Root}
NAMED BY {Country Name }
```

The Computer and Printer Objects

The *Computer* and *Printer objects* are effective-class objects derived from the non-effective class object *Device*, which is in turn derived from the object class Top (refer to figure 5.6). Their formal definitions are in listing 5.7.

Listing 5.7

```
Device OBJECT-CLASS
SUBCLASS OF Top
MUST CONTAIN { Common Name // CN=}
MAY CONTAIN  { Description,
Locality name,  // L=
Network Address,
Organization,
Organizational Unit,
Owner,
Serial Number,
See Also }
```

```
CONTAINMENT {     Organization,
Organizational Unit}
NAMED BY {Common Name }

Computer OBJECT-CLASS
SUBCLASS OF Device
MAY CONTAIN  { Operator,
Server,
Status }

Printer OBJECT-CLASS
SUBCLASS OF Device
MAY CONTAIN  { Cartridge,
Default Queue,
Host Device,
Memory,
Network Address Restriction,
Notify,
Operator,
Page Description Language,
Printer Configuration,
Print Server,
Queue,
Status,
Supported Typefaces }
```

The Group Object

The *Group object* is an effective-class object and is derived from Top (refer to figure 5.6). Its formal definition is in listing 5.8.

Listing 5.8

```
Group OBJECT-CLASS
SUBCLASS OF Top
MUST CONTAIN { Common Name // CN=
}
MAY CONTAIN  { Description,
Full Name,
Group ID (GID),
Locality Name,
Member,
Organization,
Organizational Unit,
Owner,
Email Address,
Login Script,
MailBox ID,
MailBox Location,
Profile,
Profile membership,

See Also }
```

```
CONTAINMENT { Organization,
Organizational Unit}
NAMED BY {Common Name }

Email Address
Login Script
MailBox ID
MailBox Location
Profile
Profile membership
```

The Locality Object

The *Locality object* is an effective-class object and is derived from Top (refer to figure 5.6). Its formal definition is in listing 5.9.

Listing 5.9

```
Locality OBJECT-CLASS
SUBCLASS OF Top
MAY CONTAIN  { Description,
Locality Name,
State or Province Name,
Street Address,
See Also }

CONTAINMENT { Root,
Country,
Organization,
Organizational Unit}
NAMED BY {Locality Name,
State or Province Name }
```

The Organization Object

The *Organization object* is an effective-class object and is derived from Top (refer to figure 5.6). Its formal definition is in listing 5.10.

Listing 5.10

```
Organization OBJECT-CLASS
SUBCLASS OF Top
MUST CONTAIN { Organization } // O=
MAY CONTAIN  { Description,
Detect Intruder,
Email Address,
Telephone Number,
Facsimile Telephone Number,
Intruder Attempt Reset Interval,
Intruder Lockout Reset Interval,
```

```
Locality Name,
Lockout After Detection,
Login Script,
Login Intruder Limit,
NSS Domain,
Physical Delivery Office Name,
Postal Address,
Postal Code,
Postal Office Box,
Print Job Configuration,
Printer Control,
State or Province Name,
Street Address,
See Also }

CONTAINMENT { Root,
Country,
Locality }
NAMED BY { Organization } // O=
```

The Organizational Role Object

The *Organizational Role object* is an effective-class object and is derived from Top (refer to figure 5.6). Its formal definition is in listing 5.11.

Listing 5.11

```
Organizational role OBJECT-CLASS
SUBCLASS OF Top
MUST CONTAIN { Common Name } // CN=
MAY CONTAIN  { Description,
Email Address,
Telephone Number,
Facsimile Telephone Number,
Locality Name,
Organizational Unit,
Physical Delivery Office Name,
Postal Address,
Postal Code,
Postal Office Box,
Role Occupant,
State or Province Name,
Street Address,
See Also }

CONTAINMENT { Organization
Organizational Unit }
NAMED BY { Common Name } // CN=
```

The Organizational Unit Object

The *Organizational Unit object* is an effective-class object and is derived from Top (refer to figure 5.6). Its formal definition is in listing 5.12.

Listing 5.12

```
Organizational unit OBJECT-CLASS
SUBCLASS OF Top
MUST CONTAIN { Organizational Unit } // OU=
MAY CONTAIN  { Description,
Detect Intruder,
Email Address,
Telephone Number,
Facsimile Telephone Number,
Intruder Attempt Reset Interval,
Intruder Lockout Reset Interval,
Locality Name,
Lockout After Detection,
Login Script,
Login Intruder Limit,
NSS Domain,
Physical Delivery Office Name,
Postal Address,
Postal Code,
Postal Office Box,
Print Job Configuration,
Printer Control,
State or Province Name,
Street Address,
See Also }

CONTAINMENT { Organization,
Organizational Unit,
Locality }
NAMED BY { Organizational Unit } // OU=
```

The Partition Object

The *Partition object* is an effective-class object and is derived from Top (refer to figure 5.6). This object can only be created using the Partition Manager and PARTMGR tools. Its formal definition is in listing 5.13.

Listing 5.13

```
Country OBJECT-CLASS
SUBCLASS OF Top
MAY CONTAIN  { Authority Revocation,
CA Private Key,
CA Public Key,
Certificate Revocation,
```

```
Convergence,
Cross Certification Pair,
High Convergence Sync Interval,
Inherited ACL,
Low Convergence Reset Time,
Low Convergence Sync Time,
Partition Creation Time,
Received Up To,
Replica,
Synchronized Up To }
```

Because the Partition object does not occur in the NDS tree as it does in a normal NDS object, it cannot be referenced by NDS naming syntax. The Partition object does not have a NAMED BY or CONTAINMENT definition.

The Profile Object

The *Profile object* is an effective-class object and is derived from Top (refer to figure 5.6). Its formal definition is in listing 5.14.

Listing 5.14

```
Profile OBJECT-CLASS
SUBCLASS OF Top
MUST CONTAIN { Common Name,       // CN=
Login Script ]
MAY CONTAIN  { Description,
Locality Name, Full Name
Organization,
Organizational Unit,
See Also }

CONTAINMENT { Organization,
Organizational Unit }
NAMED BY { Common Name } // CN=
```

The Resource Object

The *Resource object* is a non-effective class object and is derived from Top (refer to figure 5.6). This object is used in the derivation of the effective class objects Print Queue/Bindery Queue, Directory Map, and Volume objects. Its formal definition is in listing 5.15.

Listing 5.15

```
Resource OBJECT-CLASS
SUBCLASS OF Top
MUST CONTAIN { Common Name }      // CN=
MAY CONTAIN  { Description,
Host Resource Name,
Locality Name,
```

```
Organization,
Organizational Unit,
See Also }
CONTAINMENT { Organization,
Organizational Unit }
NAMED BY { Common Name } // CN=
```

The Print Queue Object

The *Print Queue object* is an effective class object and is derived from the Resource non-effective class object. Its formal definition is in listing 5.16.

Listing 5.16

```
Print Queue OBJECT-CLASS
SUBCLASS OF Resource
MUST CONTAIN { Queue Directory }
MAY CONTAIN  { Device,
Host Server,
Network Address,
Operator,
Server,
User,
Volume }
```

The Bindery Queue Object

The *Bindery Queue object* is an effective class object and is derived from the Resource non-effective class object. Its formal definition is in listing 5.17.

Listing 5.17

```
Print Queue OBJECT-CLASS
SUBCLASS OF Print Queue
MUST CONTAIN { Bindery Type }
NAMED BY { Common Name, Bindery Type }
```

The Directory Map Object

The *Directory Map object* is an effective class object and is derived from the Resource non-effective class object. Its formal definition is in listing 5.18.

Listing 5.18

```
Directory Map OBJECT-CLASS
SUBCLASS OF Resource
MUST CONTAIN { Volume,
Path }
```

The Volume Object

The *Volume object* is an effective class object and is derived from the Resource non-effective class object. Its formal definition is in listing 5.19.

Listing 5.19

```
Volume OBJECT-CLASS
SUBCLASS OF Resource
MUST CONTAIN { Host Server }
Host Volume }
MAY CONTAIN { Status }
```

The Server Object

The *Server object* is a non-effective class object and is derived from Top (refer to figure 5.6). Its formal definition is in listing 5.20.

Listing 5.20

```
Server OBJECT-CLASS
SUBCLASS OF Top
MUST CONTAIN { Common Name } // CN=
MAY CONTAIN  { Description,
Account Balance,
Allow Unlimited Credit,
Full Name,
Host Device,
Locality Name,
Minimum Account Balance,
Network Address,
Organization,
Organizational Unit,
Private Key,
Public Key,
Resource,
Status,
User,
Version,
Security Equals
Security Flags
See Also }
CONTAINMENT { Organization,
Organizational Unit}
NAMED BY { Common Name } // CN=
```

The NCP Server Object

The *NCP Server* (or *IntranetWare Server*) object is an effective class object and is derived from the non-effective class Server. Its formal definition is in listing 5.21.

Listing 5.21

```
Server OBJECT-CLASS
SUBCLASS OF Server
MAY CONTAIN  {Operator,
DS Revision,
Messaging Server,
Supported Services }
```

The Print Server Object

The *Print Server object* is an effective class object and is derived from the non-effective class Server. Its formal definition is in listing 5.22.

Listing 5.22

```
Print Server OBJECT-CLASS
SUBCLASS OF Server
MAY CONTAIN  {Operators,
Printers,
SAP Name }
```

The AFP Server Object

The *AFP Server object* is an effective class object and is derived from the non-effective class Server. Its formal definition is in listing 5.23.

Listing 5.23

```
AFP Server OBJECT-CLASS
SUBCLASS OF Server
MAY CONTAIN  {Operator,
Supported Connections } Serial Number
```

The Unknown Object

The *Unknown object* is an effective-class object and is derived from Top (refer to figure 5.6). Its formal definition is in listing 5.24.

Listing 5.24

```
Unknown OBJECT-CLASS
SUBCLASS OF Top
MAY CONTAIN { Any }
```

The Template Object

The *Template object* is an effective-class object and is derived from Top (refer to figure 5.6). Its formal definition is in listing 5.25.

Listing 5.25

```
Template OBJECT-CLASS
SUBCLASS OF Top
MUST CONTAIN { Common Name } // CN=
MAY CONTAIN { Trustees Of New Object,
New Object's DS Rights,
New Object's FS Rights,
Setup Script,
Run Setup Script,
Members Of Template,
Volume Space Restrictions,
Set Password After Create,
Home Directory Rights,
Account Balance,
Allow Unlimited Credit,
Description,
EMail Address,
Facsimile Telephone Number,
Group Membership,
Higher Privileges,
Home Directory,
L,
Language,
Login Allowed Time Map,
Login Disabled,
Login Expiration Time,
Login Grace Limit,
Login Maximum Simultaneous,
Login Script,
Mailbox ID,
Mailbox Location,
Member,
Message Server,
Minimum Account Balance,
Network Address Restriction,
New Object's Self Rights,
OU,
Password Allow Change,
Password Expiration Interval,
Password Expiration Time,
Password Minimum Length,
Password Required,
Password Unique Required,
Physical Delivery Office Name,
Postal Address,
Postal Code,
```

```
Postal Office Box,
Profile,
S,
SA,
Security Equals,
Security Flags,
See Also,
Telephone Number,
Title }

CONTAINMENT { Organization,
Organizational Unit }
NAMED BY { Common Name } // CN=
```

The Application and DOS Application Objects

The *Application object* is a non-effective class object and is derived from Top (refer to figure 5.6). Its formal definition is in listing 5.26.

The *DOS Application object* is an effective-class object and is derived from the *Application* class (refer to figure 5.6). Its formal definition is in listing 5.27.

Listing 5.26

```
Application OBJECT-CLASS
SUBCLASS OF Top
MUST CONTAIN { App Path,
Description,
CN }
MAY CONTAIN { App Working Directory,
App Flags,
App Parameters,
App Blurb,
App Startup Script,
App Shutdown Script,
App Licensing,
App Drive Mappings,
App Printer Ports,
App Icon,
App Contacts,
See Also}

CONTAINMENT { Organization,
Organizational Unit }
NAMED BY { Common Name } // CN=
```

Listing 5.27

```
Application (DOS) OBJECT-CLASS
SUBCLASS OF Application
MUST CONTAIN { }
```

The Windows Application Object

The *Windows Application* object is an effective-class object and is derived from the *Application* class (refer to figure 10.6). Its formal definition is in listing 5.28.

Listing 5.28

```
Application (Windows 3.x) OBJECT-CLASS
SUBCLASS OF Application
MUST CONTAIN { }
```

The Windows 95 Application Object

The *Windows 95 Application object* is an effective-class object and is derived from the *Application* class (refer to figure 5.6). Its formal definition is in listing 5.29.

Listing 5.29

```
Application (Windows 95) OBJECT-CLASS
SUBCLASS OF Application
MUST CONTAIN { }
```

The Windows NT Application Object

The *Windows NT Application object* is an effective-class object and is derived from the *Application* class (refer to figure 5.6). Its formal definition is in listing 5.30.

Listing 5.30

```
Application (Windows NT) OBJECT-CLASS
SUBCLASS OF Application
MUST CONTAIN { }
```

Understanding Exotic Properties

When searching for properties (or attribute types) for NDS objects, you might see a number of *exotic* properties that have *intriguing names*, but are not documented in the online reference. With some of the property names, you can take an educated guess, but with others this is not always easy. For your reference, table 5.3 discusses some of these properties.

Table 5.3
Exotic NDS Properties

Property	Description
Authority Revocation	The *Authority Revocation* property is used in Partition non-effective object class. The Partition object class encapsulates information required for directory synchronization and connectivity for partitions of the directory. The Authority Revocation property is a time-stamped list of public keys that have been revoked. This attribute is used internally by NDS.
Back Link	*Back Link* is defined in the top super class. Because all NDS objects are inherited from the top super class, they all inherit the Back Link property. This property is used to define a list of servers that need to be notified of changes in the status of the object. The user cannot modify this property. It is used by name servers. Server class objects can read this property without being given an explicit trustee assignment to read this property. Inheritance masks also cannot be used to restrict the reading of this property by server class objects.
Bindery Object Restriction	*Bindery Object Restriction* is used in bindery objects and stores an error code that indicates the reason why the bindery object cannot be represented as a directory object.
Bindery Property	The *Bindery Property* is defined in super class Top and is used to emulate bindery properties that cannot be represented as NDS properties.
Bindery Type	*Bindery Type* is used in a Bindery Object or Bindery Queue to describe the type of the bindery object.
CA Private Key	*CA Private Key* is used in the Partition object class and contains the certification authority private key. User applications cannot access this key because it is hidden. This is used to validate public keys. The private key is encrypted using the certification authority's password.
CA Public Key	*CA Public Key* is used in the Partition object class and contains the certification authority public key and other certification information.
Cartridge	*Cartridge* is used in printer objects and contains a list of font cartridges present in the printer.
Certificate Revocation	*Certificate Revocation* is used in the Partition object class and contains a time-stamped list of public keys revoked by the certification authority.

Property	Description
Convergence	*Convergence* is defined for the Partition object class. It indicates the degree of effort a partition should make in attempting to keep replicas synchronized. A value of zero indicates *low convergence.* This means that updates should not be propagated immediately, but should wait for the next synchronization interval. A value of zero indicates that synchronization is done at low frequency to save on network resources. Partitions with low convergence should be synchronized at least once every 24 hours. A value of one indicates *high convergence.* This means that an immediate attempt should be made to propagate updates. If this attempt fails, synchronization should be done at the next synchronization interval. The default setting for this attribute is one, which means that high convergence is in effect.
High Convergence Sync Interval	*High Convergence Sync Interval* is defined for the Partition object class. It is the interval at which partition synchronization takes place if no directory events have caused synchronization to occur. When high synchronization is in effect, changes in partition information cause immediate synchronization to other replicas. If no changes take place in the High Convergence Sync Interval (default value 60 minutes), synchronization is started.
Low Convergence Sync Interval	*Low Convergence Sync Interval* is defined for the Partition object class. It is the interval (in seconds) of time that must elapse from one partition synchronization to the next. This has an effect only if Convergence is set to low (value of zero).
Low Convergence Reset Time	*Low Convergence Reset Time* is defined for the Partition object class. This property is used to store the time of day at which low convergence synchronization takes place. After this, the interval counter is reset. The next synchronization takes place only after the Low Synchronization Sync Interval time has passed. The Low Convergence Reset Time has an effect only if Convergence is set to low (value of zero).
Cross Certificate Pair	*Cross Certificate Pair* is defined for the Partition object class. It provides a pair of public keys that can be used to provide a simpler and shorter certification.
GID	*GID* is defined for the object class group. It is the group ID used by Unix clients.

continues

Table 5.3, Continued
Exotic NDS Properties

Property	Description
UID	*UID* is defined for the object class user. It is the user ID used by Unix clients.
Higher Privileges	*Higher Privileges* is defined for the user object class, but is not currently implemented. Its purpose is to enable a logged-in user to temporarily acquire a higher set of privileges. After a function is performed with the higher set of privileges, the higher privileges can be surrendered.
Message Server Message Server	*Message Server Message Server* is defined for the user object class. It contains the name of the server used to store and forward broadcast messages for the user.
Obituary	*Obituary* is defined in the Top super class, and is therefore a property of all NDS objects. This attribute is used internally by NDS for name resolution during directory operations, for example, renaming an object. When an object is renamed an obituary timestamp is recorded for the renamed object allowing it to be identified by its old name. Meanwhile, if changes are made to the renamed object in another partition, those changes refer to the older name of the object. Moreover, these changes are not immediately seen in the partition in which the renamed object resides. When changes to the object finally reach the partition in which the renamed object resides, it cannot find the original name of the object. The obituary attribute is then used to identify the object and implement the changes.
Object Class	*Object Class* is defined in the Top super class, and is therefore a property of all NDS objects. It is a list of all the super classes from which the object is derived.
Partition Creation Time	*Partition Creation Time* is defined for the partition object class and contains a timestamp identifying the "incarnation" of the replicas of a partition.
Received Up To	*Received Up To* is defined for the partition object class and contains a timestamp identifying the last time the replica received an update.
Reference	*Reference* is defined in the Top super class and is therefore a property of all NDS objects. It is used internally by NDS and contains a list of objects that reference an object. For example, if objects X, Y, Z have trustee assignments to U, then the Reference attribute of U lists objects X, Y, Z. This makes it easier for

Property	Description
	NDS to find all objects that reference object U. The Reference attribute type is not replicated, and refers to objects in the same partition. If an object outside of the current partition needs to be referenced, a backlink is used instead.
Replica	*Replica* is defined for the partition object class and contains the name servers that store replicas of the partition.
Synchronized Up To	*Synchronized Up To* is defined for the partition object class and contains the timestamp with which servers that have a copy of the partition's replica were synchronized.
Server Holds	*Server Holds* is defined for a user class object. This attribute is used when NetWare Accounting is active and describes the number of accounting charges pending while the server performs an operation. Before performing an operation, the server does the following: 1. Ensures that the user has sufficient balance. 2. Places the correct charges and user identification in Server Holds attribute. 3. After operation is complete, deducts the charges from the user balance.
Type Creator Map	*Type Creator Map* is used by user object class and identifies the user as a Macintosh file system client. It is used by NetWare for Macintosh to identify users who should be given type and creator descriptions when information on files is requested.
Unknown Base Class	*Unknown Base Class* is used to identify the class of an object before it was changed to an unknown class.

Summary

This chapter discussed the NDS schema and how it was derived from the X.500 schema. Because NDS is based on X.500 and, over time, has been expanded to become even more like X.500, this chapter also discussed X.500, the terminology used in X.500, and its equivalent concept used in NDS.

The components of the NDS schema are object classes, attribute types, and attribute syntaxes. The object class is defined in terms of attribute types and rules for building the object class. The attribute types are the properties that make up an object class and are defined in terms of attribute syntaxes. The attribute syntaxes are the different data types. The attribute syntax is the only non-extensible part of the NDS schema. New attribute types and object classes can be defined using the NDS APIs.

CHAPTER 6

Novell Directory Services Name Resolution

When an NDS object name is submitted to the NDS name service, it must be able to locate the network resource represented by the NDS object name. The NDS stores information on network resources in a distributed database. This means that portions of the NDS information may be kept on servers in different locations on the network. The NDS name service has to figure out which servers to contact to find information about the NDS object. Because a server may hold only a portion of the NDS tree, the request for the NDS object might have to be "bounced" around before the answer is found. One of the considerations in the NDS design is to have an optimal mechanism to resolve an NDS name. This chapter will give you a deeper understanding on the name resolution process.

Overview of Distributed Operations in NDS

Objects in the directory are organized in a hierarchical fashion, in the same manner that a file system organizes subdirectories and files. This object hierarchy is also called a *tree* or a *directory tree*. The tree can be divided into smaller pieces or subtrees called *partitions*. Each partition is named by the object at the root of the subtree. Thus, the partition describing the entire tree is called the [Root] partition. A copy of a partition is called a *replica*. Replicas are useful for providing an online backup of partition data and for minimizing the distance an NDS query has to travel to be satisfied. Replicas are kept synchronized, and the NDS query can be satisfied by a replica that is close to the source of the query.

IntranetWare supports multiple replicas of a partition that can be read-only or read-write.

Partitioning and replication enable distribution of the directory information among servers. This enables distribution of the work of the name service, as well as more convenient access to the data. Novell Directory Services, therefore, is a hierarchical, distributed, replicated name service. The job of a name service is to maintain information about objects and to locate the objects and the associated object information for clients.

Partitions are described in the NDS schema as a type of NDS object. A partition that represents a portion of the NDS tree can have a subordinate partition that represents a subtree linked to its parent tree. The parent partition (superior partition) is called a *partition root*. Objects that are partition roots have additional properties that are used by NDS for synchronization. One of these properties is the *replica pointer*, which contains the name and internal net address of the server where the replica is located for every replica of a partition. The replica pointers of a partition form a list of the locations of the replicas.

The commonly recognized replica types are Master, Read Write (sometimes called a *Secondary Replica*), and Read Only. Another less well-known replica type is that of the Subordinate Reference. The Subordinate Reference connects the tree. A *Subordinate Reference* (Sub Ref for short) is a complete copy of a partition root object. It exists on servers where the superior partition exists and the subordinate partition does not. Because a Sub Ref is a partition object and has a replica pointer property, it has a list of all the replica locations. From that list, the directory can locate a replica of objects in that partition. Consider the Subordinate Reference a pointer to the locations of subordinate replicas.

It is not a requirement that one server hold a copy of the entire object hierarchy. The directory tree can be both distributed and replicated. There has to be, therefore, a method of finding the physical location of objects. That method is called *tree walking*, or *resolving a name*.

What Is Tree Walking?

When an NDS client agent submits a request to resolve an NDS name, the request might not be received by the name server (IntranetWare server that has directory services installed) that has the information to fulfill the request. If the name server is not able to fulfill the request by consulting its NDS database, it must contact another name server that can fulfill the request. It is possible to have a situation in which several name servers may have to be contacted before finding the name server that can fulfill the request. To find the information, the name server searches through the hierarchy of partitions until the requested information is found. This process is called *tree walking* or *name resolution.*

Understanding Name Resolution

Tree walking or name resolution consists of resolving a name to the location of the object in the tree. This process performed by Directory Services is an essential part of the distributed, replicated name service of IntranetWare. It eliminates the necessity that clients be aware of the physical location of resources they use. Clients need only know the name of the resource or (using an NDS search utility like NLIST.EXE) the type of resource. The term *client* is used to describe anything that uses the services provided by the network or a server on the network. Users are the most common type of client in the networking environment.

The X.500 specification discusses three models for name resolution:

- Chaining
- Multicasting
- Referral

The Chaining Model for Name Resolution

The X.500 specification describes *chaining* as a mode of interaction that may be used by one *Directory System Agent* (DSA) to pass on a request to another DSA, when the former DSA has knowledge about naming contexts held by the latter.

Figure 6.1 shows the chaining method of name resolution. In this figure, the *Directory User Agent* (DUA) refers to the network entity submitting a request, such as resolving a name. In IntranetWare networks, the DUA corresponds to an NDS client, such as an IntranetWare workstation submitting a request for resolving an NDS name. The DSA is the network entity within which the *Directory Information Base* (DIB) is stored and managed. In IntranetWare networks, the DSA corresponds to IntranetWare servers that store and manage the NDS database. In figure 6.1, the numbers associated with the interaction lines show the order of interactions.

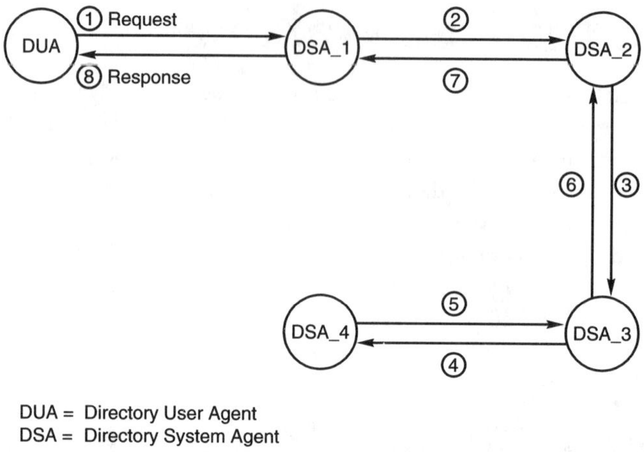

Figure 6.1
Chaining mode.

The DUA submits an object name and desires the address for the object. The original request goes to DSA_1, which cannot fulfill the request. DSA_1 contacts another DSA_2 that it thinks has the information. DSA_2 also cannot fulfill the request, and thus contacts DSA_3. This process continues until the object is finally located on DSA_4. In an IntranetWare network, the DSA_1, DSA_2, DSA_3, and DSA_4 directory system agents will be implemented in IntranetWare servers. DSA_4 returns the information on the physical location of the object back along the request chain until it is returned to the DUA client.

The Multicasting Model for Name Resolution

The X.500 specification describes multicasting as a mode of interaction that may be used by a DSA to chain an identical request in parallel or sequential manner to one or more DSAs when the former DSA does not have complete knowledge about naming contexts held by the latter.

Figure 6.2 shows the multicasting method of name resolution done in parallel. In this figure, the numbers associated with the interaction lines show the order of interactions. In figure 6.2, the DUA submits an object name and desires the address for the object. The original request goes to DSA_1, which cannot fulfill the request. DSA_1 submits an identical request simultaneously (in parallel) to DSA_2, DSA_3, and DSA_4. Each of these DSAs sends back a response. DSA_1 uses the response returned by the DSAs to fulfill the original request.

Figure 6.3 shows the multicasting method of name resolution done sequentially. In this figure, the numbers associated with the interaction lines show the order of interactions. In figure 6.3, the DUA submits an object name, and then waits for the address of the object. The original request goes to DSA_1, which cannot fulfill the request. DSA_1 submits the request to DSA_2 and waits for a response. If the response is negative, the request is submitted to DSA_3. If DSA_3's response indicates a success in finding an answer to the request, the result is returned by DSA_1, and there is no need to send the request to DSA_4.

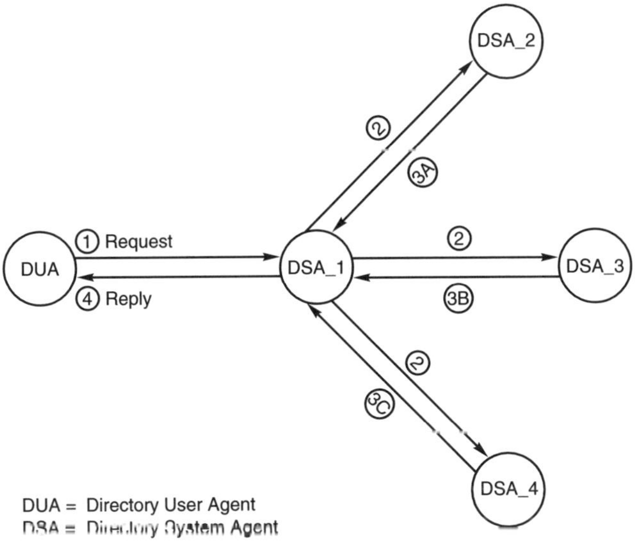

Figure 6.2
Multicasting mode done in parallel.

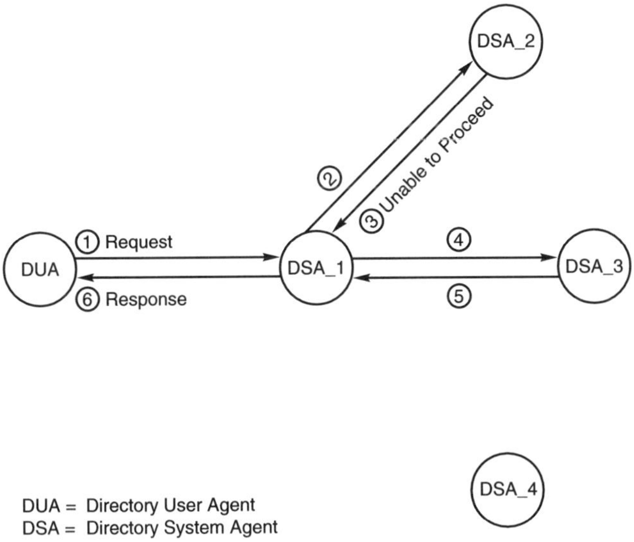

Figure 6.3
Multicasting mode done sequentially.

The Referral Model for Name Resolution

The X.500 specification describes *referral* as a mode of interaction in which a referral to another DSA is returned instead of the desired response. The referral contains a knowledge reference to another DSA. A knowledge reference associates the object name (DIT entry, DIT = Directory Information Tree) with the DSA (IntranetWare server) in which it is located. The referral is then used by the requesting agent, either a DSA or a DUA (IntranetWare client workstation), to query another DSA.

If the requesting agent is a DSA agent, it must use the knowledge reference in the referral to chain or multicast the original request to another DSA. Figure 6.4 shows a DSA handling a referral response, and figure 6.5 shows a DUA handling a referral response. In these figures, the numbers associated with the interaction lines show the order of interactions.

Figure 6.4
Referral mode—DSA makes requests.

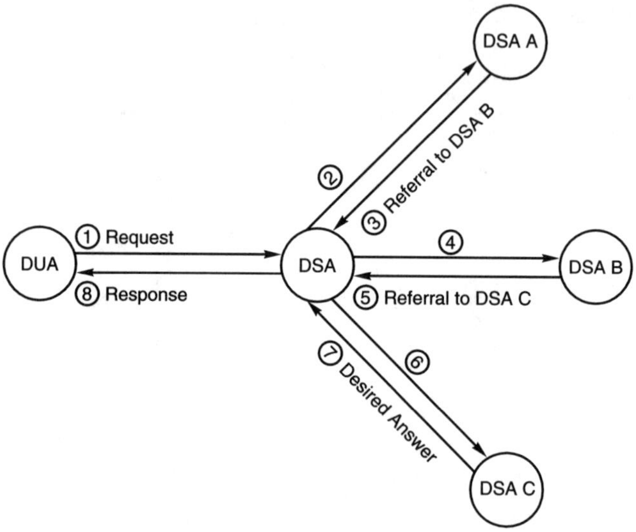

Figure 6.5
Referral mode—DUA makes requests.

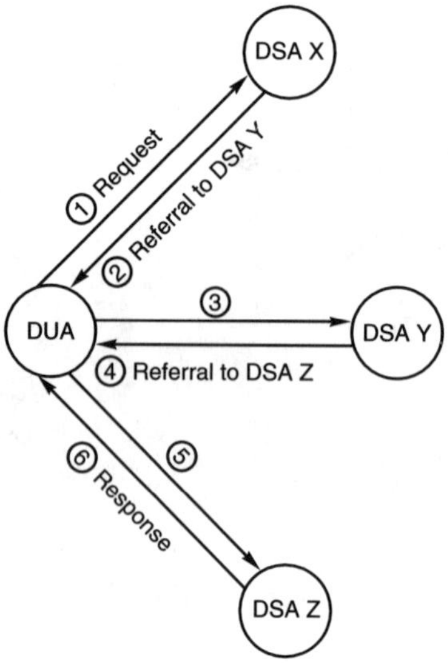

Tree Walking in IntranetWare

IntranetWare does not use chaining as a method of name resolution, but uses instead a sequential form of multicasting that may be combined with the referral mode. Figure 6.6 shows how IntranetWare might perform name resolution.

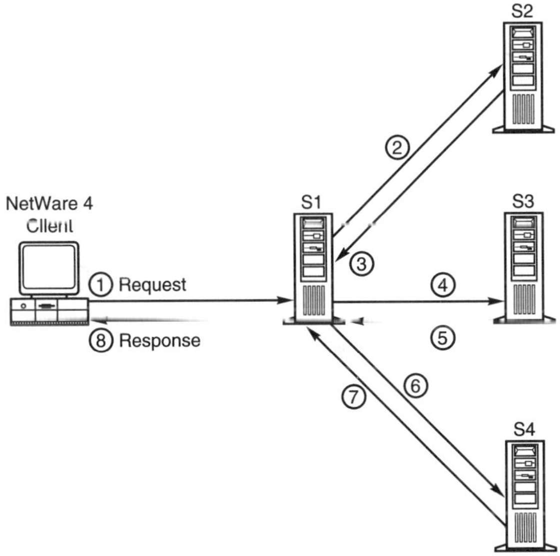

Figure 6.6
IntranetWare name resolution.

The client makes the original request for the object from the DSA, server S1. Unable to fulfill the request, S1 contacts the server S2. Server S2 returns its lack of success to S1, which then contacts server S3. This continues until the object is located on S4. The information as to the location of the object is then returned to the client. Once requested to walk the tree on behalf of the client, the server S1 DSA does not chain the request through the next server, but waits for each server in turn to reply to its request. Rather than appearing as part of a chain of requests, S1 looks like the hub in a wheel; it is in charge of locating the object. S1 returns to the client the physical location of the object requested.

Specific Examples of Tree Walking

Figure 6.7 shows the object hierarchy of a directory tree, which will be used to illustrate tree walking. Three partitions are in the EXAMPLE_TREE—[Root], DEPT_C.ESL, and DEPT_E.DEPT_C.ESL. The partition boundaries are indicated in figure 6.7 by a dashed line. Figure 6.8 shows the physical view of the same tree EXAMPLE_TREE. This figure shows what the actual object hierarchy looks like on each of the three servers. Server S1 has the Master replica of the partition [Root]. The partition object DEPT_C.ESL is a subordinate reference on S1. The Master replica of DEPT_C.ESL is located on server S2 with a subordinate reference of DEPT_E.DEPT_C.ESL. Server S3 has the Master replica of DEPT_E.DEPT_C.ESL. The external references on servers S2 and S3 are indicated by a dashed line.

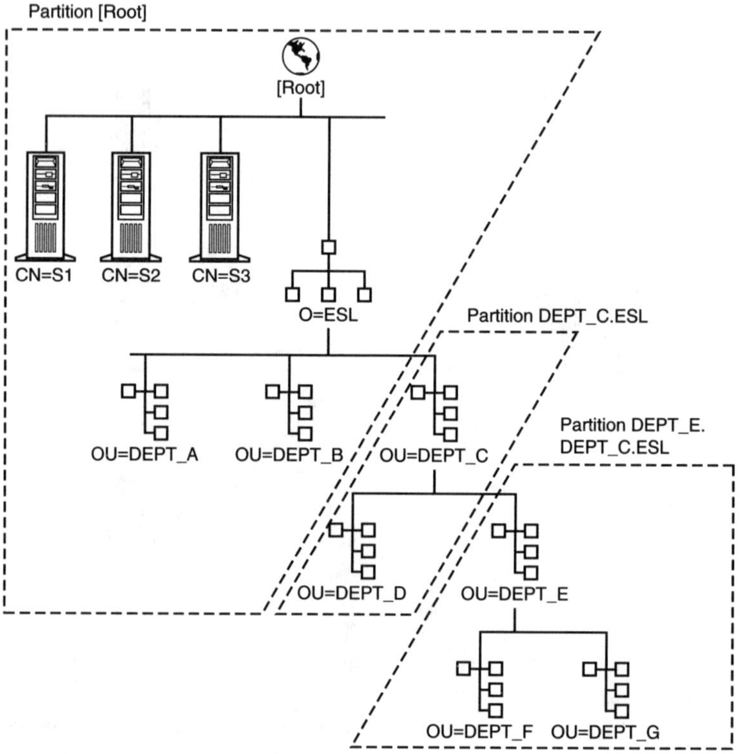

Figure 6.7
Object hierarchy of a directory tree.

This tree is set up for illustration purposes only. This is not a useful tree design for fault tolerance purposes because only one copy (replica) exists for each partition.

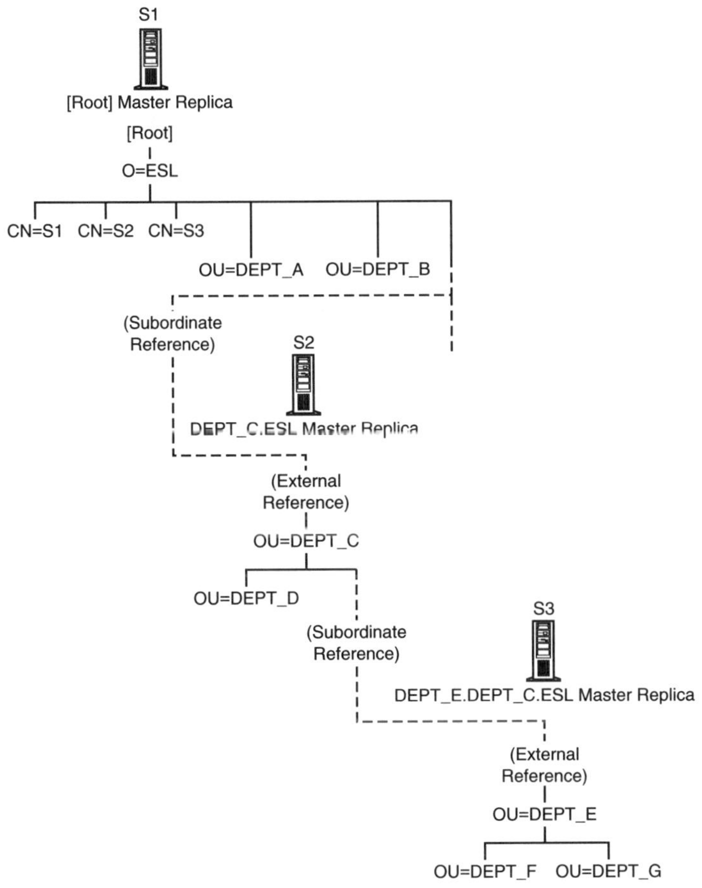

Figure 6.8
Replicas, Subordinate, and External References.

Object Found on Initial Server

In the first example, the client is attached to server S2 (shown in figure 6.9) and is asking for the location of object DEPT_D.DEPT_C.ESL. Figure 6.9 shows that server S2 has a copy of the object DEPT_D.DEPT_C.ESL (S2 holds a replica of partition DEPT_C.ESL, in which DEPT_D.DEPT_C.ESL is located). S2 returns the physical location of DEPT_D.DEPT_C.ESL to the client. The physical location is the network address of the DSA S2.ESL that holds the desired object.

Figure 6.9
Object found on initial server.

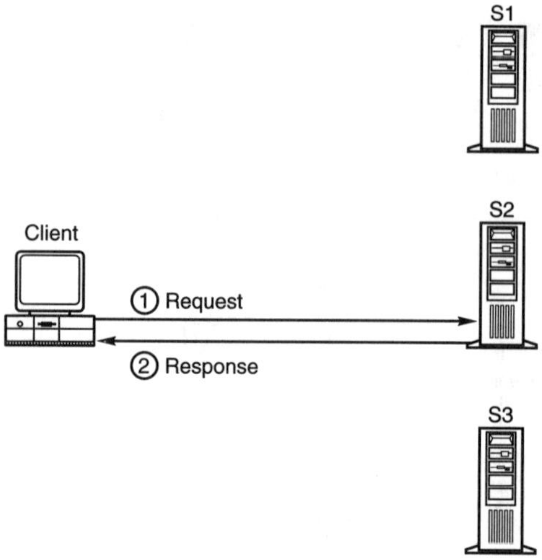

Object Not Found on Initial Server

In the second example, the client is attached to server S2, as shown in figure 6.10, and is asking for the location of object DEPT_F.DEPT_E.DEPT_C.ESL. S2 will check first to see if it has a copy of the object. Because that is not the case in this example, S2 must look on another server. These steps are followed:

1. From the replica pointer property of DEPT_E.DEPT_C.ESL (a Subordinate Reference) contained in partition object DEPT_C.ESL (see fig. 6.8), S2 finds the address of server S3.

2. S2 contacts server S3.

3. S3 verifies to S2 it has a copy of the desired object DEPT_F.DEPT_E.DEPT_C.ESL.

4. S2 returns to the client the physical location of DEPT_F.DEPT_E.DEPT_C.ESL. This is the network address of S3, the DSA that has a copy of the desired object.

5. The client connects to server S3 for access to the information associated with DEPT_F.DEPT_E.DEPT_C.ESL.

This example shows how NDS performs a referral mode operation to resolve the name.

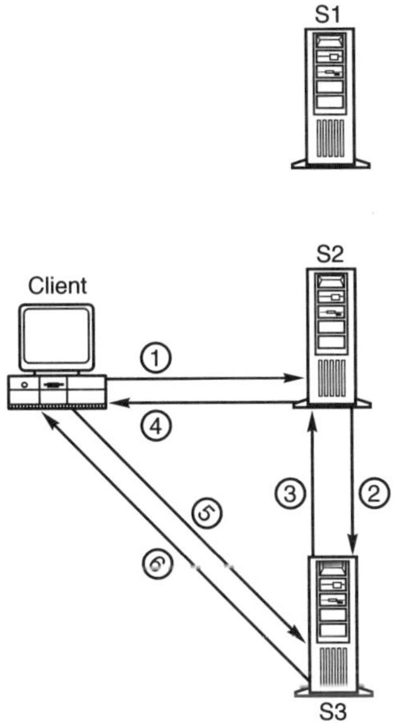

Figure 6.10
Object not found on initial server.

Walking Up the Tree

The previous example illustrates how the subordinate reference might be used to locate an object lower in the tree. The subordinate reference also is used in walking up the tree. Consider the example of the client request again going to server S2, and the object requested is [Root]. S2 does not have a copy of [Root], so it must walk the tree on behalf of the client. Remember that subordinate reference replicas reflect servers that hold the partition root object (parent or superior partition), but not the child (subordinate) partition. In this case, [Root] is the superior partition and DEPT_C.ESL is the child partition. Looking at the replica pointers of the partition DEPT_C.ESL, the subordinate reference replica type indicates there is a subordinate reference of DEPT_C.ESL—and therefore a replica of its parent partition—on server S1. Server S2 knows the location of a server (S1) that contains partitions higher in the tree. Server S2 is able to contact server S1 looking for the object [Root]. The physical location of the object [Root] then is returned to the client.

This is a simplistic example because there is only one replica of each partition. If a server does not have a replica of the object being requested by another server, it also returns additional addresses at which the object might be found.

As a user logs in to an IntranetWare directory tree, the name service needs to locate a writable copy of the user's object. This is necessary because two attributes—the "Last Login Time" and the "Network Address" attributes—are updated during the login process.

Name Resolution While Logging In to the Network

Clients log in to a network to use the services provided by the network. The login process makes use of name resolution. The process and end result of logging in are described in this section.

Logging In—Bindery-Based Servers

As the user of a bindery-based server logs in, the following happens:

1. User JOHN enters "login NW4CS/JOHN" as he logs in to the bindery-based server NW4CS from his DOS workstation using the utility LOGIN.EXE.

2. The NetWare shell locates the server NW4CS using the bindery of the server to which it attached during the bootup of the client workstation.

3. The utility first tries to log in to NW4CS without a password. If that fails, JOHN is prompted to enter his password.

4. If the password is correct, JOHN is considered logged in to the server NW4CS. His security equivalencies (any object on the server that has the same rights as JOHN) are calculated and stored in the connection table, along with his user name and his workstation's address.

5. LOGIN.EXE then executes John's login script.

If JOHN wishes to use the file system on the bindery-based server ATHENA, he uses the utility MAP.EXE and enters "map h:=ATHENA/sys:" on the command line. Steps 2, 3, and 4 also are executed by MAP.EXE. Notice that the only differences are the name of the utility used, and that the login script is not executed in the case of MAP.EXE. The end result is the same: the bindery-based server NW4CS and the bindery-based ATHENA know the identity and the rights (security equivalencies) of the user object JOHN. He now is able to use the services (file and print) provided by these two servers.

Conceptually, the process of logging in can be viewed as that of establishing an identity with the server. At the end of the login process, the server knows the name and the address of the client requesting services. The client's security equivalencies also have been established.

John's user name and password on the server NW4CS might be different than his user name and password on the server ATHENA. All the information about JOHN (login script, last login time, passwords used, security equivalencies, and so on) is stored independently on each of these servers.

Logging In—IntranetWare Servers

For the purposes of the following discussion, the IntranetWare servers being referred to form a single object hierarchy or tree. The name of the organization is ESL, and the name of the tree is ENET. The object hierarchy is shown in figure 6.11. This is a small tree with one user, Admin.ESL. Figure 6.12 shows the physical location of the data associated with the object hierarchy.

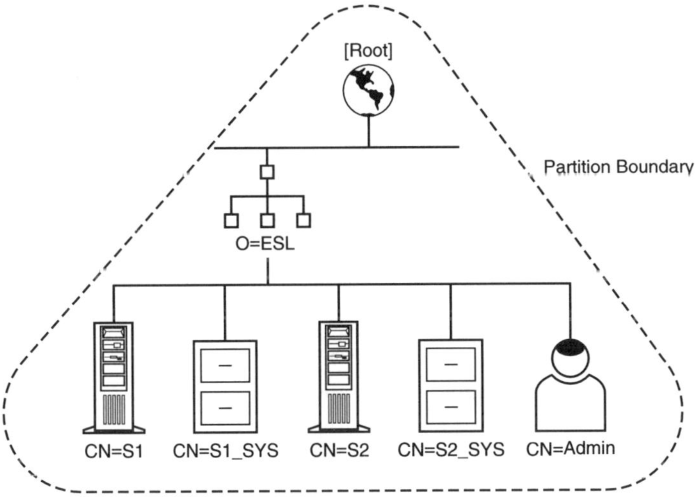

Figure 6.11
The logical view of the ENET tree.

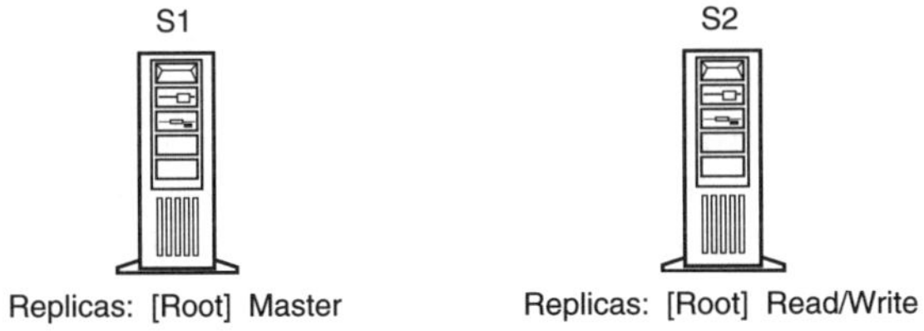

Figure 6.12
Replicas in the ENET tree.

When Admin.ESL logs in to the network, the following happens:

1. User Admin enters "login admin" on the command line as he logs in to the tree ENET from his DOS workstation using the utility LOGIN.EXE.

2. The NetWare Client locates the server S1, which first answers the broadcast for any server in the tree ENET during the bootup of the client workstation.

3. Using the name context (O=ESL) in the NET.CFG located at Admin's workstation, LOGIN.EXE uses Directory Services—the name service in IntranetWare—to locate the object Admin.ESL. Figure 6.12 shows that S1 has a copy of the object Admin.ESL.

4. Using the connection to S1, LOGIN.EXE tries to log in as "Admin.ESL" with no password. If that fails, Admin is prompted to enter his password.

5. If the password is correct, Admin is considered logged in to the tree, ESL. His network address is added as a property to the object Admin.ESL. His last login time and login time properties are updated to reflect the current login. Because an object's properties are modified during the login process, a writable replica of the object logging in must be available. These property modifications are synchronized to the replica on server S1.

   Having proved knowledge of the password, the authentication materials necessary for proving his identity to other servers in the tree are sent to the workstation.

6. The workstation now has all the pieces necessary to authenticate connections to any server in the ESL tree. LOGIN.EXE now authenticates the connection to S1. Admin's username and workstation address are stored in the connection table on the server S1. In addition, Admin's security equivalencies are calculated for use in the connection table.

7. The commands in the login script now can be executed.

If Admin.ESL wants to use the file system on S2, he enters "map h:=S2_SYS" at the command line. The utility MAP.EXE uses the directory to locate S2_SYS.ESL, connect to the server S2, and authenticate the connection to S2. Admin is not prompted for a password. The authentication process uses the material received during the login to generate the proof of identity to the server. Once again, the end result is the same. The identity of Admin.ESL has been proven to the server S2. The name, network address, and security equivalencies are stored in the connection table of S2.

On bindery-based servers, the process of establishing an identity with the server is called logging in to a server. In IntranetWare, the same process is called *authenticating* to a server. The end result of the process of authentication is the same as that of login in bindery-based servers: the client is identified to the server. The client's name and workstation address are stored in the server's connection table along with the client's security equivalencies, which were calculated by the name service (Directory Services, in the case of IntranetWare).

Differences in the process of logging between IntranetWare servers and bindery-based servers include the following:

- Users of IntranetWare do not need to be concerned with the physical location of resources. Directory Services provides this service through walking the tree, as described earlier.

- IntranetWare login is network-wide, not server-centric.

- After the initial login, users are not prompted for usernames and passwords (as long as they are using services in the same tree). The materials necessary to generate proof of identity to servers are stored on the client's workstation.

Using an Upgrade Tip

During the process of upgrading from 3.x and 2.x, it is possible to encounter the following:

- A user has bindery accounts on two servers.
- The two servers get upgraded into a IntranetWare Directory tree.
- The user now has two unique names in the tree.

For example, after the upgrade, John.Marketing.Apex and John.Engineering.Apex represent the same user. (John had user accounts on two servers upgraded into different contexts in the tree.) IntranetWare permits each user in the network of servers to be represented by the same object. During the upgrade process, however, some duplication of objects might exist. An administrator could remove duplicate entries when time permits.

A potential problem, however, during the period of time in which multiple objects exist for the same user is to make changes in reference to one object and have the results show up on the other object.

In this example, John logs in and does his work as the object John.Engineering.Apex. John needs rights to SYS:SYSTEM on the server Mktg1. Container Admin.Marketing.Apex maps a drive to SYS:SYSTEM on the server Mktg1 and enters on the command line: "RIGHTS . R F /NAME=John". The context of Container Admin is set to Marketing.Apex. John then tries to map a drive to SYS:SYSTEM on Mktg1 and receives the message that volume SYS: does not exist on Mktg1.

The problem here is that the object that was granted the file system rights is John.Marketing.Apex, because Container Admin entered "John" and the name was completed using the context, Marketing.Apex.

Container Admin.Marketing.Apex should enter "RIGHTS . R F /NAME=John.Engineering." on the command line. Also, the object John.Marketing.Apex should be deleted because it is not being used and is causing some confusion. The "." following Engineering is important here. It causes the name context to be shortened from "Marketing.Apex" to "Apex."

Using the Same Tree as a Different User

At any one time, a workstation supports a single login to a directory tree; this is because only one set of authentication information can be stored in the workstation. This authentication information is used for the background authentication.

It is sometimes desirable, however, to be able to log in to the same tree as more than one user. You can do that by using bindery emulation for the second login. As an example, Joe.Eng.ABC is logged in to the ABC_TREE. He needs to temporarily access an application on the server IS1, also in the ABC_TREE. Joe.Eng.ABC does not have any rights on IS1, but there is a well-known user object, IS_User, on the server IS1. IS_User has no password and limited file rights on the server.

Joe can use the IntranetWare LOGIN.EXE to gain IS_User's rights on the server IS1 by entering "login is1 /is_user /ns /b" on the command line. This is equivalent to ATTACH.EXE in 3.x and 2.x versions of NetWare. The "/ns" option tells LOGIN not to execute the login script. The "/b" option tells LOGIN to use bindery emulation.

Logging In to Multiple Trees

IntranetWare is the first release of NetWare 4 that includes the capability to log in to multiple NDS trees at the same time. This functionality is implemented through the 32-bit client and the GUI-based LOGIN utility included with it for DOS/Windows, Windows 95, and Windows NT.

In addition to the ability to log in to multiple trees, it is now possible (through the 16-bit and 32-bit Windows utilities) to administer and manage multiple trees.

Multiple tree logins can be made the same ways multiple server logins were made in NetWare 3.x; you can attach from within a login script, or you can use the GUI-based LOGIN utility to make the attachment later.

Under Windows 95 and Windows NT, you can also go to Explorer and browse multiple trees there. By right-clicking on the second tree, you can select the menu item Login to NDS Tree, which will launch the GUI Login utility. In order to maintain your current connections, however, you do need to check the options for "Clear current connections" and "Run scripts" on the *Connections* and *Scripts* tabs, respectively. If you clear your current connections, you will be disconnected from your currently logged-in tree. Similarly, if you run login scripts, you will likely lose printer mappings and captured printers that were assigned when you logged in to the first tree.

Using the NetWare Login Utility

Just prior to the release of IntranetWare, Novell introduced the 32-bit client for Windows 95 and, shortly later, for DOS/Windows. With IntranetWare, Novell introduced a new client for Windows NT, which is functionally identical to the other 32-bit clients.

IntranetWare ships with DOS-based, OS/2-based, and GUI-based LOGIN utilities. The DOS-based utility and OS/2-based utilities have not changed noticeably, but the GUI-based utility is new with the 32-bit clients and IntranetWare. Figure 6.13 shows the 32-bit GUI LOGIN utility, as it would be seen on Windows 3.x, Windows 95, and Windows NT.

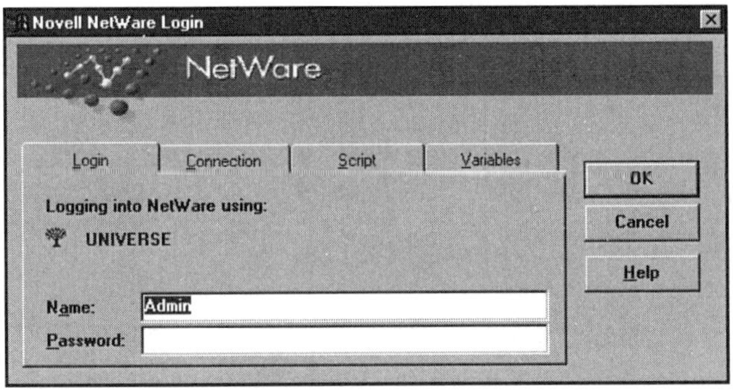

Figure 6.13
The GUI LOGIN utility.

The GUI LOGIN utility has 4 tabs of options as shown in figure 6.13. Each of the tabs, with the exception of the Login tab, can be disabled through the configuration options set in the Network applet in Control Panel. Novell did a very good job in making the interface consistent across platforms, which means that it doesn't matter if you use Windows 3.x, Windows 95, or Windows NT—you will find the configuration options in the same place in each operating environment.

The *Connection* tab, shown in figure 6.14, allows you to control how connections are made. This is the tab that enables you to disable clearing existing connections in order to make an attachment to additional NDS trees. This is also the tab in which you select whether the attachment is oriented at a particular tree or server, and whether the connection should be made as a bindery connection. You can also set the context you want to login to here, or you can enter it as part of the login name on the *Login* tab.

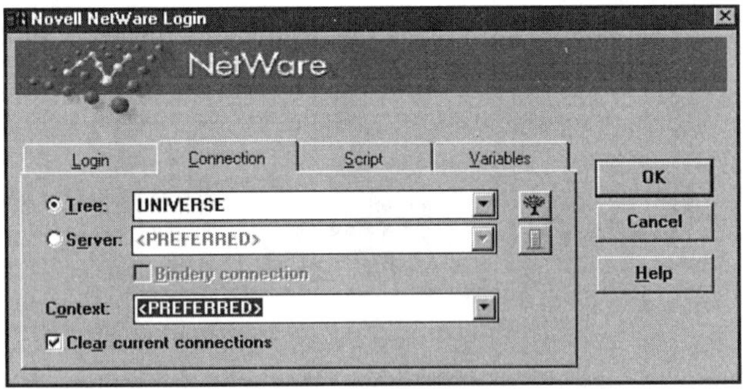

Figure 6.14
The Connection tab in the GUI LOGIN utility.

The next tab is the *Script* tab, shown in figure 6.15 The options on this tab enable you to bypass login scripts completely, or to leave the login script results window open in order to determine where a problem exists in a script. It is worth noting, however, that under certain types of error conditions, the login script results window will stay open regardless of the setting here. This tab also enables you to set a login script or profile script to run by name, rather than running the predetermined scripts for the user that is logging in.

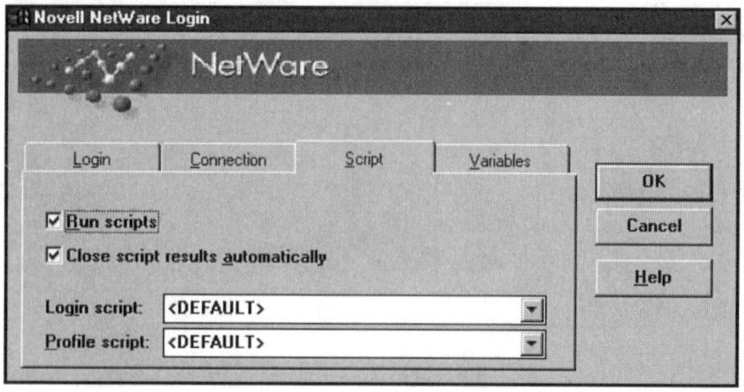

Figure 6.15
The Script tab in the GUI LOGIN utility.

Finally, the *Variables* tab, shown in figure 6.16, enables users to pass parameters to the GUI LOGIN program. With the DOS and OS/2 text-based LOGIN programs, you could specify additional parameters on the LOGIN script line and then perform specific actions in the login script based on the values of those parameters. The GUI LOGIN utility also allows parameters to be passed by selecting the *Variables* tab and entering the parameters in the appropriate boxes.

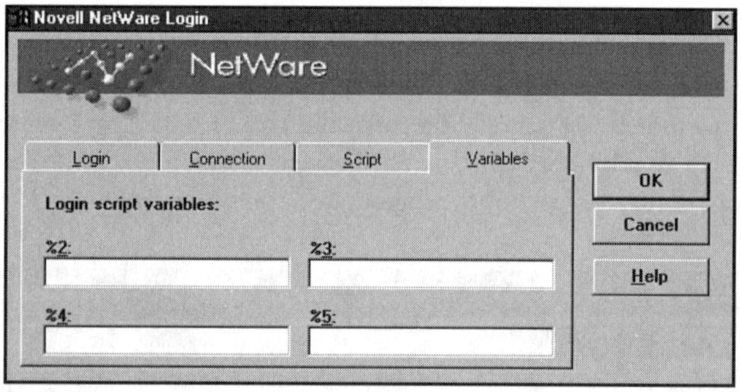

Figure 6.16
The Variables tab in the GUI LOGIN utility.

Understanding Server Objects

NCP Server is an object class defined in the base schema of IntranetWare. Objects whose base class is NCP Server represent the servers in the Directory Services hierarchy or tree. As each server is installed into a tree, an object is created in that object hierarchy that represents the server. Each server in the tree also is given a version property that describes the version of IntranetWare running on that server. "[DS]" is added to the end of the version string at the time of installation.

It is possible to add through the administrative utilities 3.x, 2.x, and even other IntranetWare servers as objects in the tree. Please note that while these servers appear in the tree as NCP server objects, they were not added through the installation process but rather through an administrative utility. These objects also have a version property. However, "[DS]" does not appear at the end of the version string on these servers.

It follows, therefore, that all IntranetWare servers installed into an object hierarchy or tree have "[DS]" appended to the version property. These servers can be thought of as all belonging to the same tree. Server objects that do not belong to the same tree ("non-tree" servers) are not important in the operation of the directory.

Server objects in the tree are very important to the operation of Directory Services. The names and addresses of the server objects are used to keep track of the physical location of the replicas. A property of partition objects (replica pointer) contains the name and address of the server on which the replica is located.

A server object can be moved to another location in the tree by using an administrative utility, such as NETADMIN.EXE or NWADMIN.EXE. The server's *Relative Distinguished Name* (RDN), or leaf portion of the name, can be changed only in the AUTOEXEC.NCF file located in SYS:SYSTEM on the server itself. The server's internal address can be modified in the same manner. In order for these changes to take place, the server must be downed and brought back up again. The server itself then takes care of notifying the directory hierarchy of the name and/or address change.

Servers in a IntranetWare tree should be thought of as part of a system of servers rather than as an isolated server. Although servers and links might go down, synchronization cannot complete until all the servers involved have been updated. In addition, partition and replication operations require that all the servers be contacted in order to successfully conclude. Hardware failure may necessitate removing a server from the system.

One very useful option of Novell Directory Services is the capability to have a server that contains no replicas. External references make this possible. Because a Read Write replica is required for bindery emulation, servers with no replicas will not be available for bindery emulation. It is also important to observe the following:

- The server does not need to hold a replica of its own object.
- Bindery emulation does not require that the server's bindery emulation context contain the server's own object.

Servers as Clients

Clients of the network are usually considered users accessing services from a workstation. IntranetWare adds another dimension to this model, as the servers themselves become clients of other servers in the tree. Servers use the same authentication protocol as the more traditional clients in identifying themselves to other servers. Because the object hierarchy is distributed as well as replicated, one server might need directory information held by another server in order to fulfill a request.

Rebuilding Replicas

Both the partition management utilities NWADMIN.EXE and PARTMGR.EXE have an option labeled "Rebuild Replicas." This option is necessary to correct a specific condition in Novell Directory Services. That condition occurs when the SET command is used on a server's console to set time back. This condition manifests itself with a certain error return from the server _0XFD6D or -659.

As modifications to the NDS objects are made by a client, a timestamp is issued by the server where the modification took place. This timestamp is part of the information maintained by each server for each replica located on the server. If a server "issues a timestamp" for a replica of a partition at a certain time (4/12/97 05:15:05, for example) and then the time on that server is set back to 4/10/96 10:14:12, no further modifications to that replica may be made until the server's time reaches and exceeds the previously issued timestamp (4/12/96 05:15:05). The reason is that issuing timestamps for a previous point in time might duplicate a timestamp that already had been issued.

The "Rebuild Replicas" option will correct this condition. This is a significant network operation. The Master replica re-timestamps every object in the replica being rebuilt. This means that a new timestamp is issued for every object and every property of every object in the entire partition. The Master replica then resends all the objects (with their new timestamps) to every replica.

During the time the Master replica is resynchronizing the objects in the replica, there is a period of time on the other replicas that the objects appear as having base class Unknown. These objects act as placeholders for the "real" object—the name and creation time of the object is known, but the property information has been deleted to be replaced with the data received from the Master. When the "real" object is received from the Master replica, the "real" object will take the place of the placeholder object.

This option also causes the partition creation time to increase. The *partition creation time* is a property of every partition object. It has two parts: the instance of the partition and the replica number where the instance was created. Remember that each replica is given a number when the replica is created. When a partition is initially created, the instance of the partition is 1 and the replica number is 1. If the "Rebuild Replicas" option were to be executed, the instance would be incremented to 2.

It is possible to change the replica type of a replica on a server through the partition management utilities. Replica 4 could be made the Master replica. If the "Rebuild Replicas" option were executed after this change in replica types, the instance of the partition would be 3 and the replica number 4.

Note that the replica number is used internally by Novell Directory Services. It is not visible to clients through the utilities, and is only useful for those interested in understanding the underlying technology of the product. Clients see the logical presentation of the tree as an object hierarchy, and need not be concerned with the internals, such as timestamps, partition creation time, replica number, and so on.

Summary

In this chapter, you learned how name resolution is performed according to X.500 specifications, and how IntranetWare implements name resolution. Novell Directory Services is a name service. One of the functions of this name service is to find the physical location of objects so that clients can be concerned with the names of objects rather than with their physical location. Resolving an object returns to the client the physical location of that object. This process relies on a property of partition objects called the replica pointer—a list of replica locations by server name and server address. Because the directory uses the name and address of servers to locate objects, the object representing the server is very important.

This chapter also described new features that permit a user to login to multiple NDS trees. This is a feature implemented through the use of Novell's 32-bit Client and is supported through the GUI utilities and the new GUI-based LOGIN utility.

Clients use the process of name resolution during the login as they identify themselves (authenticate) to servers in a directory tree.

CHAPTER 7

Novell Directory Services Partitions

This chapter presents the mechanisms used to store and manage the NDS database on the server. You are introduced to the concept of partitions and replicas and how they are used to improve fault tolerance of the NDS database. You learn about the different replica types, replica synchronization, and the rules for creating replicas on IntranetWare servers. You also learn about the IntranetWare tools that you can use to manage replicas and partitions.

Understanding NDS Partitions and Replicas

The NDS database that represents an NDS tree must physically reside on a storage volume. You need to consider two questions regarding where to keep this NDS database:

- Should the entire NDS database be centralized?
- Should you take subsets of the NDS database and distribute the database? If the database is distributed, what factors should determine its distribution?

Keeping the NDS database at a central location makes the NDS database unavailable to the entire network in the event of a failure in the network at the central location. For small LANs, centralization is not of much concern. For large networks that are separated by Wide Area Network links, a single NDS database becomes a single point-of-failure problem waiting to happen.

You should distribute the database in such a manner that a single failure does not disable the entire NDS service. The logical division (subset) of an NDS database is called a *partition.* The partition contains the resources and the organizational structure of a portion of the NDS tree. The partition does not contain any information on the file system structure of a network volume.

You can use NDS partitions to divide the NDS database logically. Because the NDS database has the logical structure of a tree, partitioning divides the NDS database into subtrees, with each partition storing NDS objects of that subtree. The partition is often described in terms of the object at the root of the partition, or the *Partition Root* object. The *partition root* of a partition is the top container (root) of the subtree that it represents. A partition's partition root defines the boundary of that partition.

Figure 7.1 shows an NDS tree logically divided into three partitions. The partition roots of the three partitions are [Root], OU=SALES, and OU=ENG. These Parent containers are the root of the subtree for their partition.

A partition is stored at an IntranetWare server's volume. In figure 7.1, the partition for [Root] is stored on the server FSC.CORP.ESL, the partition for OU=SALES is stored on the server FSS.SALES.ESL, and the partition for OU=ENG is stored on server FSE.ENG.ESL.

When talking about the location where a partition is stored, referring to the partition as being stored on a server is quite common, although a more accurate description is that the partition is stored on a server's volume. Partitioning allows the distribution of the NDS database across the network. One advantage of distributing the NDS database is that if a server goes down, only the NDS information stored in the partition being stored on the downed server is unavailable. You can minimize the risk of losing this NDS information by keeping duplicate copies of the partition at other locations.

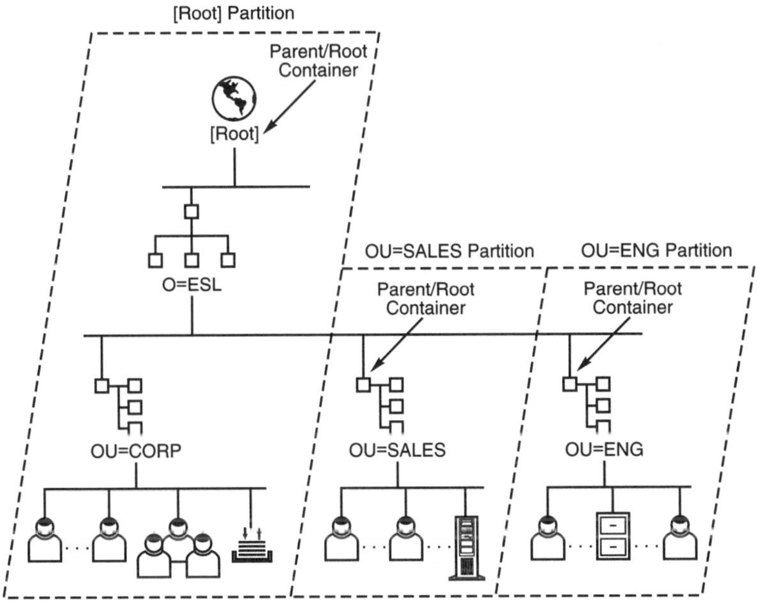

Figure 7.1
Logical division of a tree into partitions.

At the introduction of NetWare 4.0, Novell recommended that a partition contain no more than 500 objects. Later releases increase this limit to 100,000 objects per partition.

Partitions can help the NDS performance by doing the following:

- Dividing up the NDS database so the parts are where they are being used
- Reducing the need for NDS searches and lookups to be performed over slower Wide Area Links

Figure 7.2 shows an NDS database split into two partitions, where each partition resides on a server volume on LAN segments separated by a slow Wide Area Link. Here, most of the NDS lookups and searches are done against the local NDS partition, without having to go over the slow Wide Area Link.

A problem can arise with the example in figure 7.2. What if the storage volume or file server on which the NDS partition resides crashes? The portion of the NDS that the NDS partition implements becomes unavailable, and users cannot access those resources. You can use a technique called replication to solve this problem.

Replication consists of keeping a copy of an NDS partition at another location. A copy of a partition is called a *replica*. You keep a replica at a strategic location on another IntranetWare server. In figure 7.3, Location A keeps a copy of the NDS partition for Location B on its IntranetWare server, and Location B keeps a copy of the NDS partition for Location A on its IntranetWare server. If a user at Location A tries to access resources described by the NDS database in Location B, and if the remote server at Location B is temporarily unavailable or the Wide Area Link is down, the NDS queries for objects at the remote location serviced by the replica stored on the server at Location A.

Figure 7.2
NDS partitions across a Wide Area Link.

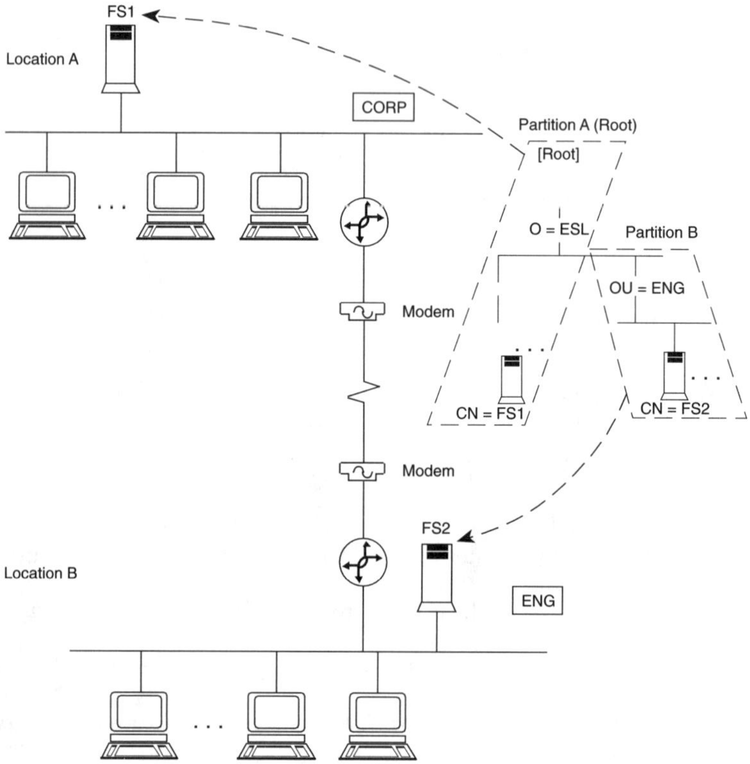

The preceding example illustrates how replicas provide fault tolerance for the NDS database by providing online backup copies of a partition, which eliminates any single point of failure for the NDS database and provides fault tolerance in the NDS database. Without replication, if a server that contains the NDS partition goes down, the NDS objects in that partition become unavailable. Because NDS objects provide the access to most network resources, these network resources also become unavailable.

You can establish an unlimited number of replicas for each partition. A large number of replicas for a partition, however, means that the synchronization overhead can be excessive when a replica is modified. If you want to be practical, you should limit the number of replicas to no more than 8 to 10 per partition. You also should limit the number of replicas on a particular server to 8. The first server on the network contains the [Root] partition and typically receives a replica of all new partitions that are installed. Making the [Root] server your fastest computer improves the performance of NDS operations carried out on the [Root] server. The context in which a server is placed in a partition has no bearing on the performance of NDS operations or the type of replicas it can contain. Servers anywhere in the NDS tree can contain any type of replica.

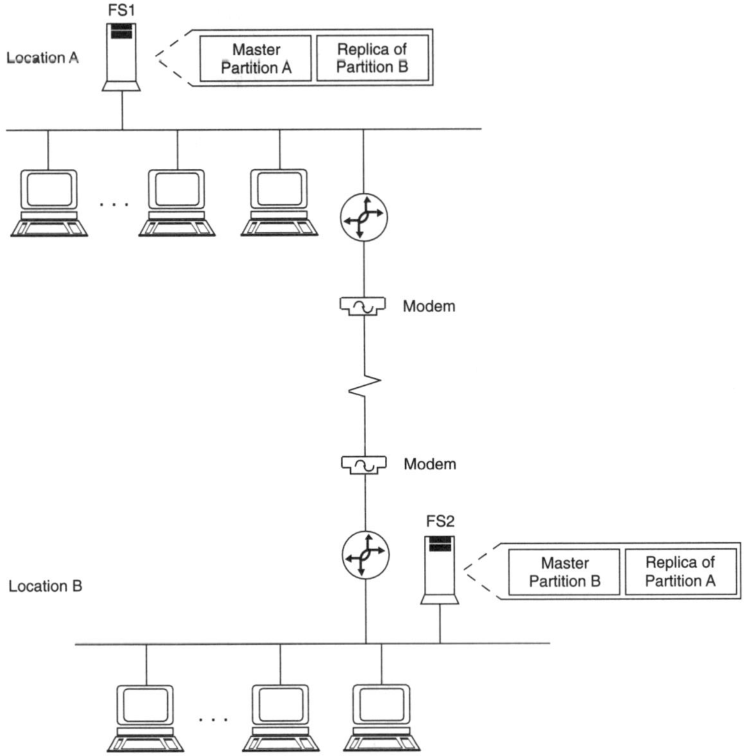

Figure 7.3
NDS replicas across a Wide Area Link.

Another advantage of using replicas is that the local replica can satisfy NDS queries for objects at remote locations, which makes it possible for a user logging in to a network to be authenticated by information in the local replica. If the NDS partition at the remote location changes from new objects added or old objects deleted, the NDS partitions can synchronize themselves by sending only the *new* information that has changed—a much more efficient way of doing NDS lookups and maintaining consistency of the NDS database.

Partitions represent logical portions of the NDS database that *can be copied*, and replicas are the physical parts of the NDS database that *are copied*.

Replicas thus provide the following advantages:

- Increased NDS fault tolerance and reduced risk of any single point of failure
- Fast access to NDS services across slow Wide Area Links
- Login access to the network, even when some IntranetWare servers are unavailable

Essentially, replication provides fault tolerance for the NDS, but does not provide fault tolerance for the file system.

Recognizing Types of NDS Partitions

Because a replica is a copy of the NDS partition, NDS makes the following distinctions for replicas:

- Master replica
- Read-Only replica
- Read-Write replica
- Subordinate Reference replica

Master Replica

The *Master replica* is the original partition that is created for representing a subset of the NDS database. The Master replica contains the authority for the objects defined on it. All other replicas must defer to information contained in the Master replica; that is, the Master replica, by definition, contains the most recent information, and there can be only one Master replica per partition. This replica is used by the NDS synchronization mechanism to update all other replicas. All other replicas are created from the Master replica.

A Master replica is created when an NDS partition is first created, and resides on the IntranetWare server on which the partition is created. The Master replica is the source used to create all other replicas for that partition, and for making updates to other replicas. If the partition has to be redefined, you can do so only by redefining the Master replica. A restructuring of the Master replica causes other replicas of the partition to be deleted automatically and new replicas of the Master partition to be created.

Figure 7.4 shows the Master replica for the [Root] partition. It shows that the replica stored on server CN=NW4CS.OU=CORP.O=ESL is of type Master. In this example, the [Root] partition contains only one Server object (CN=NW4CS.OU= CORP.O=ESL). When a partition contains only one Server object, there are no additional replicas for that partition unless you create one. If a new Server object is placed in the same partition as the server that contains the Master replica, the new Server object will have the option of copying a Read Write partition of the Master replica. Starting with NetWare 4.1, a Synchronization Up To field (see fig. 7.4) also is included that indicates the last time the replicas were synchronized. Additionally, you can use the screen in figure 7.4 and select the Send Updates button so that all other replicas are synchronized to the Master replica.

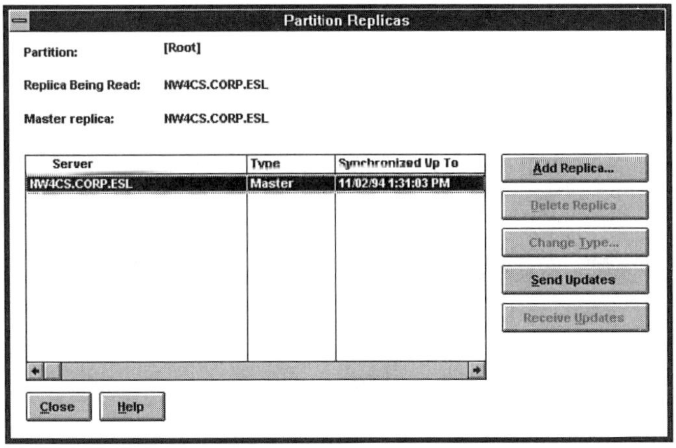

Figure 7.4
A Master replica.

Read-Only Replica

A *Read-Only replica* contains a copy of the Master replica that cannot be modified by ordinary users. The Read-Only replica can receive update information from the Master replica or the Read Write replica. The Read-Only replica cannot initiate changes on its own, however.

Read-Only replicas are similar to the concept of yellow pages on other directory systems and can be used for searching for information. The Read-Only replica is used as a database that can be queried against, but it cannot be used for logging into the network because that modifies the NDS tree. For instance, the Network Address property of the User object is altered to contain the station address of the workstation that the user is using. Also, the Last Login property of the User object is modified to contain the date and timestamp of the last login. The uses of Read-Only replicas are fairly limited, and these replicas are rarely found in production network environments.

Read-Write Replica

A *Read-Write replica* is a copy of the Master replica and can be used to update the NDS database and provide information to NDS queries. NDS objects in the Read-Write replica can be modified, deleted, or created. When these changes are made to a Read-Write replica, it generates update traffic to modify other Read-Write replicas and the Master replica. Changes made to the Read-Write replica result in directory synchronization network traffic that is sent to all replicas of the corresponding partition.

If the Master replica becomes corrupt, you can use the Read-Write replica to re-create it. Therefore, you should have several Read-Write replicas of a partition. You cannot use Read-Write replicas to split or merge a partition. Only the Master replica, because it has authority for the partition, can be used to restructure a partition. Examples of restructuring a partition are splitting a partition and merging partitions into a single partition.

Because the Read-Write replica is modifiable, it can, unlike the Read-Only replica, be used for logging in to the network.

Figure 7.5 shows the three replica types. The Master replica is on the CN=NW4CS. OU=CORP.O=ESL server, the Read-Write replica is on the CN=NW4KS. OU=CORP.O=ESL server, and the Read-Only replica is on the CN=NW4KS. OU=ENG.O=ESL server.

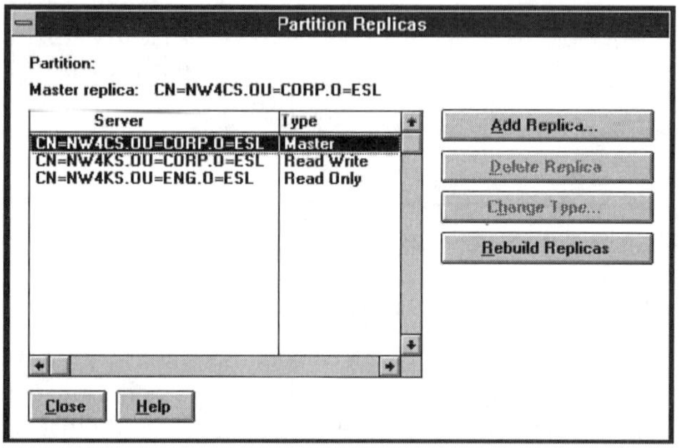

Figure 7.5
Master replica, Read-Write replica, and Read-Only replica.

Subordinate Reference Replica

The Subordinate Reference replica type is the only type of replica that an administrator cannot place; it is used by NDS for tree walking. Tree walking is the process NDS uses to locate objects in the tree. Subordinate Reference replicas are used by this process to link the tree together.

Subordinate Reference replicas are placed anywhere a partition exists and a child partition does not.

Replica List

The servers that hold the replica of a given partition are called the *replica list* for that partition. Figure 7.6 shows a replica list for a partition [Root]. This replica list consists of servers FSC.CORP.ESL, FSS.SALES.ESL, and FSE.ENG.ESL. Server FSC.CORP.ESL holds the Master partition for [Root], and servers FSS.SALES.ESL and FSE.ENG.ESL hold the Read-Write replica for the [Root] partition.

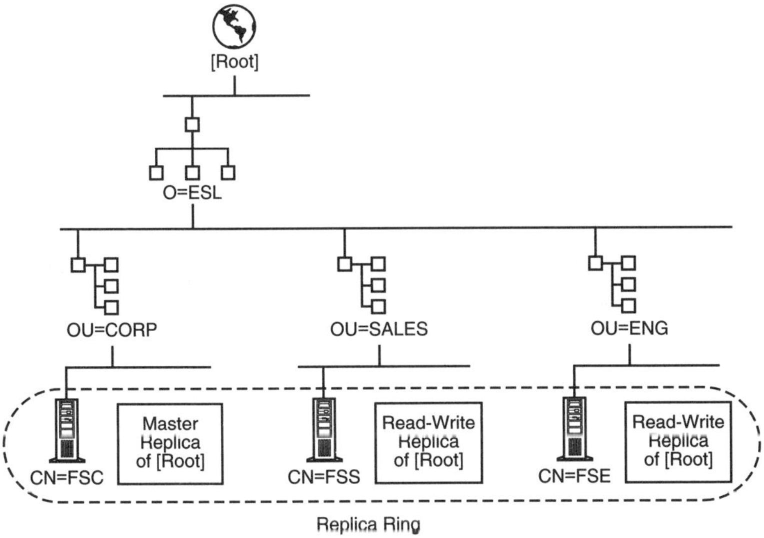

Figure 7.6
A Replica list.

Changes made to any replica, such as the Read-Write replica on server FSE.ENG.ESL, must be sent to the other servers (FSC.CORP.ESL and FSS.SALES.ESL) that make up the replica list for the [Root] partition. If a server is down when the changes are initiated, it cannot receive the changes. The members of a replica list will still initiate changes, regardless of the status of other members of the replica list. If a server that is down is brought up again, its replica is synchronized to the Master replica.

If the servers of the replica list are down during ordinary NDS changes, such as NDS object deletion, creation, or modification, they can be resynchronized when they are brought up again. However, if major changes such as partition splitting and merging are being attempted, all servers in a replica list should be online and reachable through the network for the changes to be successful.

If a server in a replica list must be taken down during a split/merge of the partition, you must perform the following precautionary tasks:

- If the server holds a Read-Write or Read-Only replica, you should delete this replica.
- If the server holds a Master replica, you should make this a Read-Write replica. Because the split/merge can be done only through a Master replica, you have to make another Read-Write replica the Master replica.

Designing Partitions

When designing partitions, you should be aware of the following rules for partitions and replicas:

- Partitions can be created only at the container level of the NDS tree.
- You do not have to have a replica of the entire NDS database at any location, because the NDS database is designed to be usable in partitions. The Master replica of a partition can be split into smaller partitions.
- An IntranetWare server can hold only one replica type of a partition. An attempt to store another replica of a partition on a server that already holds a replica of that partition will be denied (see fig. 7.7). Also, an IntranetWare server does not need to have a replica.
- There can be only one Master replica for a partition and any number of other replica types for the partition.

135: The master replica is already located on this server and another replica of this partition can not be created on server NW4KS.CORP. Error code: FD70.
Press <Enter> to continue.

Figure 7.7
Denial of an attempt to store more than one replica of a partition on a server.

Partitions should be created to organize the NDS database in logical manageable units that provide easy and efficient access. You should use replicas for partitions to increase the fault tolerance of an NDS database. Fault tolerance is important for preserving the integrity of a database, in case the server where a partition is maintained is not available.

You should take into account the following factors when designing partitions and replicas for improving fault tolerance and efficient access:

- Location of replicas
- Number of replicas
- Size of replicas
- Expensive/low-speed WAN links

Replicas should be located at strategic locations to improve fault tolerance and provide efficient access. To protect yourself from natural disasters that can plague a site (lightning or fire, for example), you should consider placing replicas on servers at different geographic locations (see fig. 7.8). This provides a high level of fault tolerance. Storing replicas at a single geographic location provides a relatively low degree of fault tolerance (see fig. 7.9). As a practical consideration, you also should back up the NDS database frequently—you can use SBACKUP to do this.

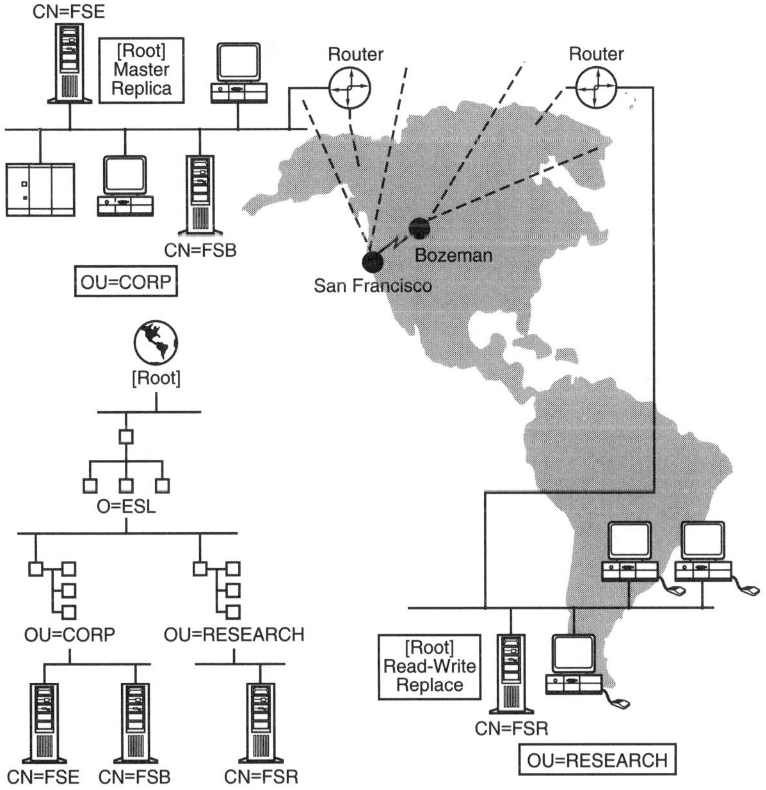

Figure 7.8
A high degree of fault tolerance.

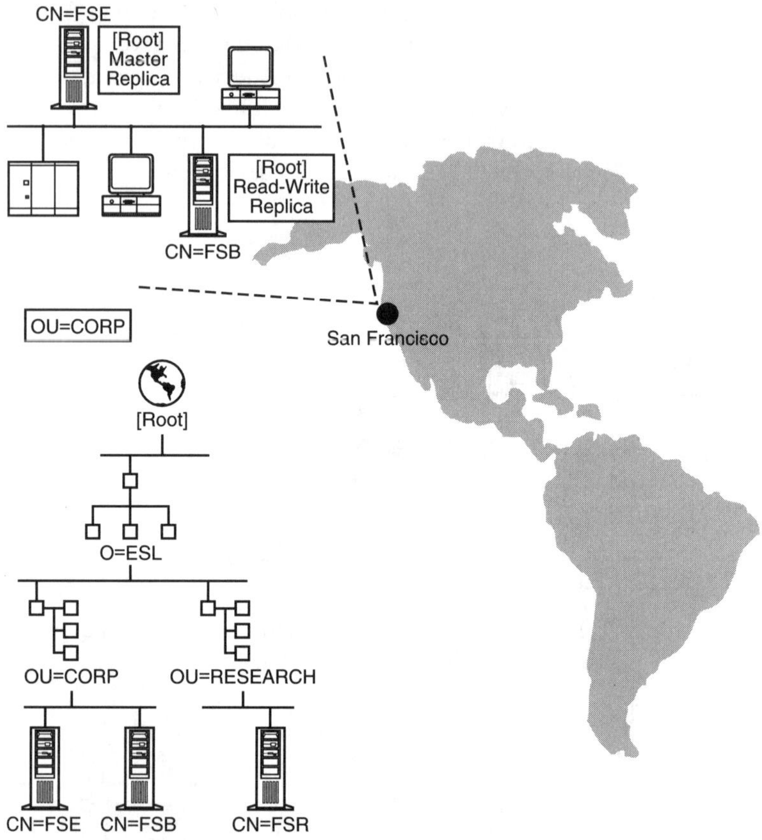

Figure 7.9
A low degree of fault tolerance.

If network resources are used for the most part by a certain group of users, those user objects and their resources should be kept in the same partition. Figure 7.10 shows a partition where users and the network resources they use are in the same partition. Figure 7.11 shows an example of a poor design, where users and their network resources are in different partitions. If the users and their network resources are in different partitions, additional traffic is generated to access these resources. If the replicas are separated by a slow and/or expensive wide area link, it further compounds the problem. If users need frequent access to a partition at a remote location, they should consider storing a replica of the partition on the user's local server to avoid traffic over the wide area link. Figure 7.12 shows a solution to the problem in figure 7.11, by keeping a Read-Write replica of the partition containing network resources local to the users who need to access them.

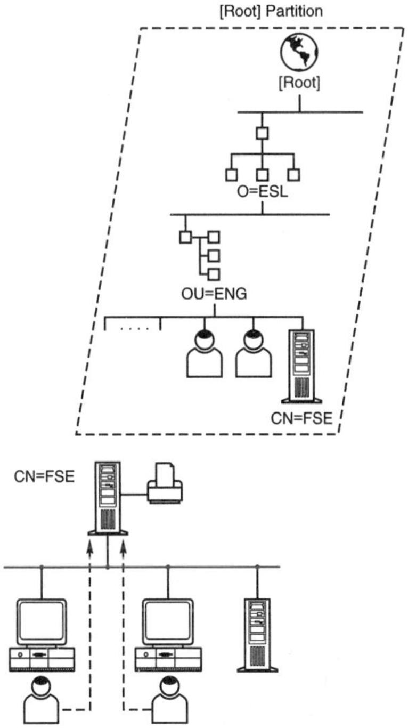

Figure 7.10
An example of a good design that has users and the network resources they use in the same partition.

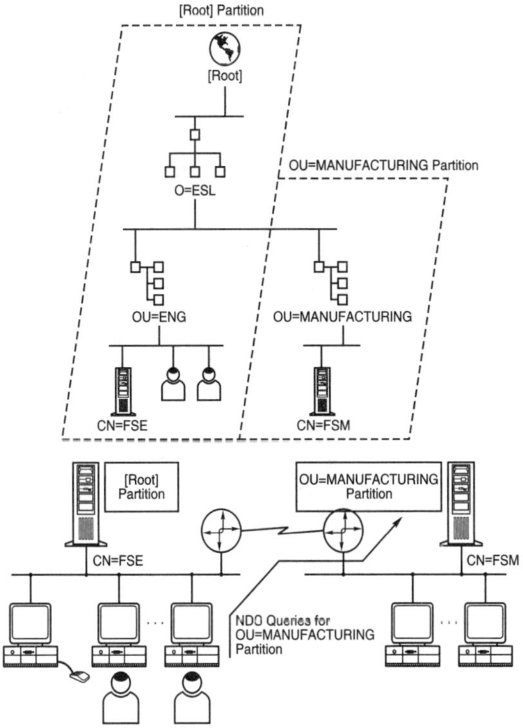

Figure 7.11
An example of a poor design that has users and the network resources they use in different partitions.

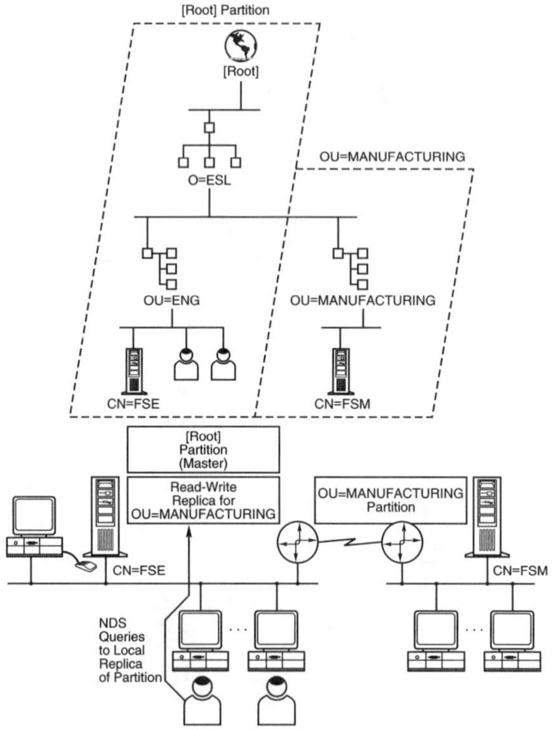

Figure 7.12
A solution to the problem of users accessing resources in a different partition.

As the number of replicas of a partition increases, so does the fault tolerance of that partition. This should be balanced against the fact that as the number of replicas increases, so does the amount of network traffic to keep the servers in the replica list properly synchronized. Each replica also takes up storage space on the server on which it resides. The average number of replicas on a server can be 4 to 5, but should not exceed 8.

You should consider carefully the locations where critical replicas should be kept. If Master replicas are on servers in disaster-prone cities, you should try to select another city that is relatively safe to keep a replica of this partition.

You should take into account the size of a replica before you decide to place it on a server. You should make sure that you have enough free disk space in the SYS volume. If you run out of space on the SYS volume, updates to NDS cannot be stored, and the integrity of the partitions stored on that server can be affected. Additionally, users will not be able to log in to the server.

Before you decide to store replicas at remote sites, you should take into account the speed and expense of the wide area link, and the anticipated NDS traffic across these links. You should know the type of wide area link you use. Is it a 9.6 Kbps dial-up link, an X.25 or Frame Relay link, a T1 (1.544 Mbps) or better link? If the link is too slow, you may be better off not keeping a replica at a remote location.

Understanding Replication

When you use the INSTALL.NLM program to install or upgrade a new IntranetWare server, you can create the server in an existing container or a new container. If you select a new container, this container is added to the NDS tree. The type of replicas that are placed on the installed server depends on whether the server is being installed in an existing or new container.

When a server is installed in the tree, the installation process follows a few rules to determine if a replica is placed on the server.

Unlike previous versions, IntranetWare does not put a server that is created in a new container in a separate partition; the existing partition is used, and a replica of that partition is placed on the newly installed server only if there are not three replicas of the partition located across the network (see fig. 7.13).

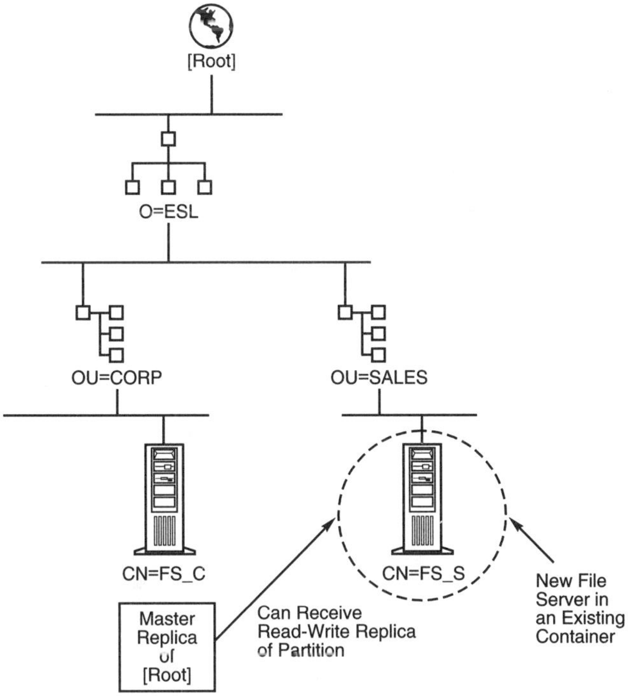

Figure 7.13
Installing a server onto the tree.

When the NDS tree is created, IntranetWare uses default rules for creating the replicas. These rules have been discussed previously in this chapter. The other rules are discussed in the context of an example. Consider the NDS tree in figure 7.14 that shows there are three partitions that cover the entire NDS tree.

Figure 7.14
An example of NDS partitions before splitting.

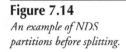

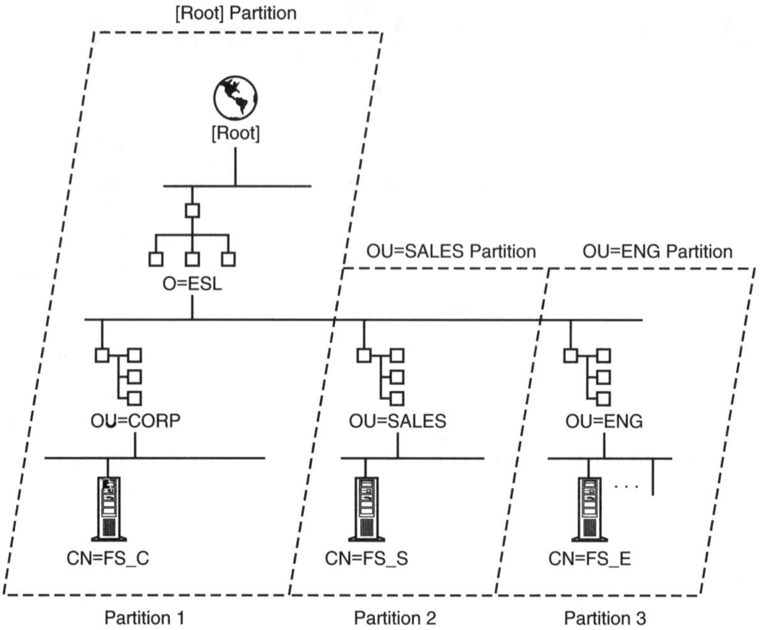

Partition 1 contains the [Root] partition, organization O=ESL, and organization unit OU=CORP. The Master replica is stored on the file server FS_C.CORP.ESL.

Partition 2 contains the OU=SALES organization unit. The Master replica for partition OU=SALES is stored on the file server FS_S.SALES.ESL.

Partition 3 contains the OU=ENG organization unit. The Master replica for partition OU=ENG is stored on the file server FS_E.ENG.ESL.

Additionally, assume the following:

- Server FS_C has a Read-Write replica of Partitions 2 and 3.
- Server FS_S has a Read-Write replica of Partition 1 and a Read-Only replica of Partition 3.
- Server FS_E has a Read-Write replica of Partitions 1 and 2.

Table 7.1 summarizes the replicas in each of the different partitions.

Table 7.1
Initial State of Replicas on Three Partitions

	Server for [Root]	Server for OU=SALES	Server for OU=ENG
Partition [Root]	Master	Read-Write	Read-Write
Partition OU=SALES	Read-Write	Master	Read-Write
Partition OU=ENG	Read-Write	Read-Only	Master

Now assume that the PARTMGR (or NDS Manager) is used to split Partition 1 into two partitions with roots at [Root] and OU=CORP. Table 7.2 shows the new distribution of replicas. This table shows that after splitting the original [Root] partition into two, any servers that had a replica of the old partition received a replica of the new partitions that is of the same type as the old replica. Server for [Root] originally contained the Master replica for [Root]. It now has Master replicas for [Root] and OU=CORP. Servers OU=SALES and OU=ENG contained a Read-Write replica of the original [Root] partition. They both now contain Read-Write replicas of [Root] and the new OU=CORP partition.

Table 7.2
Final State of Replicas on Four Partitions

	Server for [Root]	Server for OU=SALES	Server for OU=ENG
Partition [Root]	Master	Read-Write	Read-Write
Partition OU=CORP	Master	Read-Write	Read-Write
Partition OU=SALES	Read-Write	Master	Read-Write
Partition OU=ENG	Read-Write	Read-Only	Master

Understanding Replica Synchronization

To keep the replicas properly updated, a process called the *skulk* is used, which synchronizes the replicas with the updated information.

Any kind of global synchronization mechanism needs an accurate time reference that should be the same throughout the network. This ensures that the NDS operations would be timestamped accurately, regardless of where they were performed on the network. Timestamps are unique codes that identify when the event took place and the replica that originated the event.

All NDS events such as adding, deleting, and updating NDS objects must be performed consistently on all replicas of a partition. This is called *replica synchronization*, and takes place in the background between servers of a replica list. Replica synchronization is an automatic, user-transparent background process that is generally best left alone, even though administrators can fine-tune the timing parameters. It is not advised to adjust these timing parameters, as they might adversely affect the performance of the server and could lead to NDS corruption.

Accurate timestamps on NDS operations are essential to ensure that the NDS database is updated and synchronized correctly. The timestamps are used for ordering the directory events that occur. All servers should have the same time. Ideally, this time matches *Universal Coordinated Time* (UTC) time exactly, but this is not necessary for NDS operations to be done reliably, as long as a consistent time is kept across the network. Using UTC time is recommended primarily if the potential exists for two trees to be merged. To maintain the UTC time, an external time source is needed. The IntranetWare time synchronization mechanism allows for the use of external time sources.

The changes to NDS objects are done in the order in which the NDS modification requests are timestamped. If the timestamps on the modification requests do not have a common time reference, no guarantee can be made that the changes are made in the correct order. This will lead to inconsistencies in the NDS database.

NDS timestamps are based on a common network time that is maintained by time servers on the network. A common network time is important for replica synchronization. It ensures that NDS changes can be applied in the correct order. Timestamps also are used by NDS to set expiration times on temporary NDS entries.

Consider the case in which two servers, FSA and FSB, have a replica of a partition and are not properly synchronized. Assume that the time clock on FSA is 2 minutes ahead of the time clock on FSB. If an update is sent by FSA and the same update is sent by FSB 1 minute later, the update sent by FSB should be the one that is considered by other replicas as being the most recent. Because the clock in FSA is 2 minutes ahead of the clock in FSB, however, the FSA update will be registered by other servers as being the most recent.

In small networks, the server times will be apart by just a few seconds, and in very large complex networks they can be expected to be within 10 to 15 seconds from each other. This time differential between the server times is called the get caught interval. Any changes occurring in the get caught interval will be resolved in an unpredictable order. In real-life networks, most events occur outside the get caught interval, and users experiencing the situation just described is very unlikely.

When a user logs in, the Network Address and Last Login property of an object in a replica are modified. These login changes are sent out, by default, every 5 minutes (300 seconds). The timing of these changes can be modified through SET parameters, but as with other adjustments to NDS timing, it is not recommended that these timings be changed without a thorough understanding of the ramifications of making such changes.

Collecting updates and sending them at periodic intervals minimizes the network traffic. This is particularly true for network logins, which tend to occur at about the same time when the office day starts.

The server sending the update information keeps track of the time the information was sent. Other servers in the replica list keep track of the times the update was received. If the sender does not get back an acknowledgment, it waits a certain period of time before retrying the update. If a server in a replica list has not received an update within a certain time interval, it sends out a query asking for updates.

Managing Partitions and Replicas

As the needs of an organization change, networks must adapt to these changes and meet new requirements. The following are some of the changes you might have to make to adjust to new requirements:

1. Move replicas to other IntranetWare servers if the server needs to be replaced.
2. Split partitions that become too large.
3. Split/merge partitions to avoid excessive network traffic for directory operations.
4. Merge partitions to consolidate information and reduce synchronization overhead.

In addition, an administrator must monitor storage on the SYS volume in order to prevent NDS from synchronizing. In IntranetWare, it is generally a good idea to not permit users to store their data on the SYS volume. The only people that should be able to write to any directory on the SYS volume are the system administrators. Locating print queue directories on other volumes is also recommended in order to keep the risk of running out of space on the SYS volume to a minimum.

NDS partitions can be managed by one of the following:

- PARTMGR.EXE, a DOS-based text utility
- The Partition Manager option in the Legacy NetWare Administrator Tool
- The NDS Manager utility, which is covered in detail later in this chapter

The partition manager tools can be used to perform the following tasks on NDS partitions:

- Viewing existing NDS partitions
- Splitting partitions
- Merging partitions

Splitting a partition involves creating a new partition out of an existing partition. Merging a partition results in deleting old partitions.

Figure 7.15 shows an NDS partition using the Partition Manager GUI tool, and figure 7.16 shows the same partition using the PARTMGR tool.

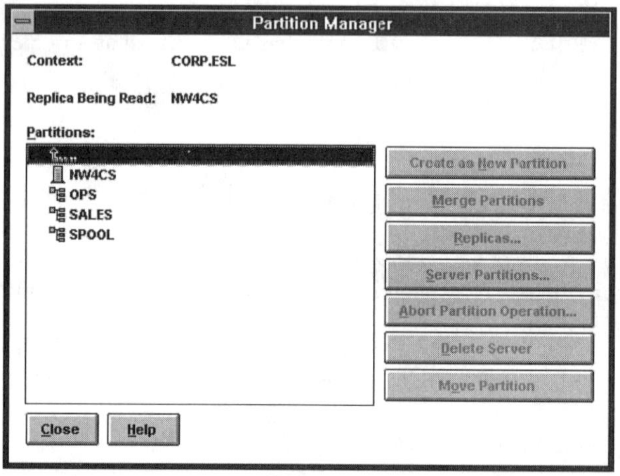

Figure 7.15
The Partition Manager used for viewing partitions.

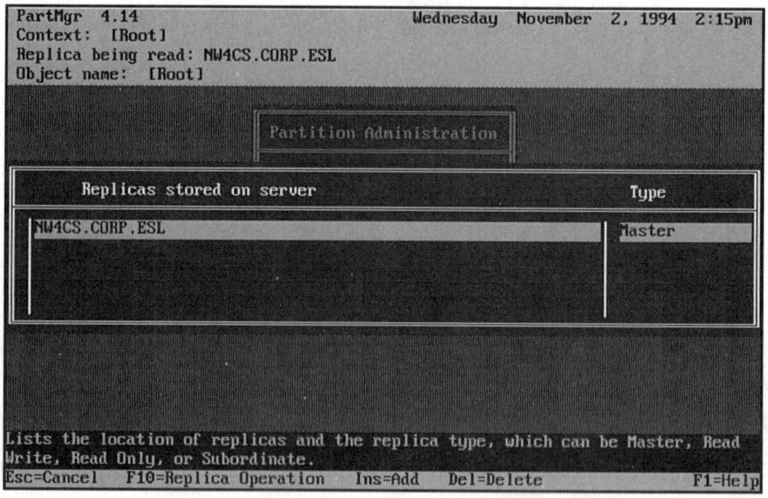

Figure 7.16
PARTMGR used for viewing partitions.

Viewing Replicas

You can display replica information in two ways:

- View replicas for a given partition.
- View replicas stored on a particular IntranetWare server.

You can use the Partition Manager and PARTMGR to view replicas of a partition.

To view replicas, you need the Write property right to the ACL property of the Server object on which the replicas reside.

Viewing Replicas for a Given Partition

The following is the general procedure for viewing replicas for both tools:

1. Select the container that is the root of the partition.
2. If you use Partition Manager, select the Replicas button. The list of replicas for that partition appears (see fig. 7.17).

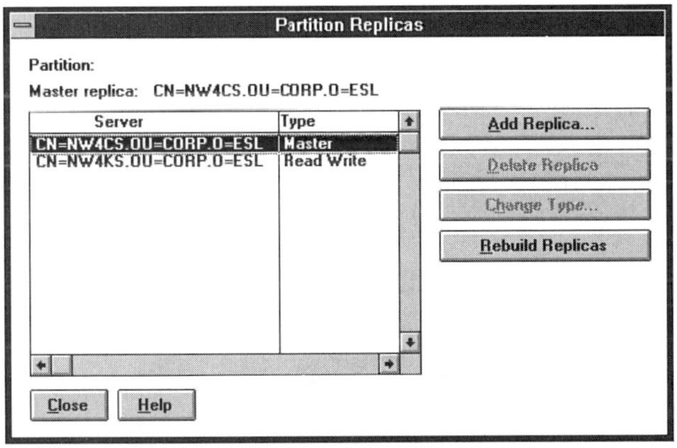

Figure 7.17
Viewing replicas for a partition using Partition Manager.

3. If you use PARTMGR, press F10 and select View/Edit replicas. A list of replicas for that partition appears (see fig. 7.18).
4. The list contains the servers on which a replica is stored and the replica type.

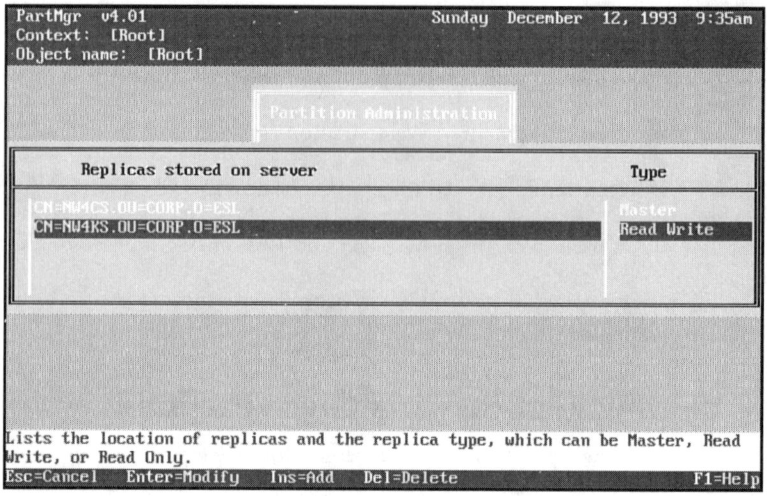

Figure 7.18
Viewing replicas for a partition using PARTMGR.

Viewing Replicas Stored on a Particular IntranetWare Server

To view replicas stored on an IntranetWare server:

1. Run the partition Manager or PARTMGR.
2. If you use Partition Manager, select the Server Partitions button and the list of replicas on that server appears (see fig. 7.19).

   If you use PARTMGR, press F10. You should see a list of replicas on that server (see fig. 7.20).

   The list contains the name of the replica and its replica type.

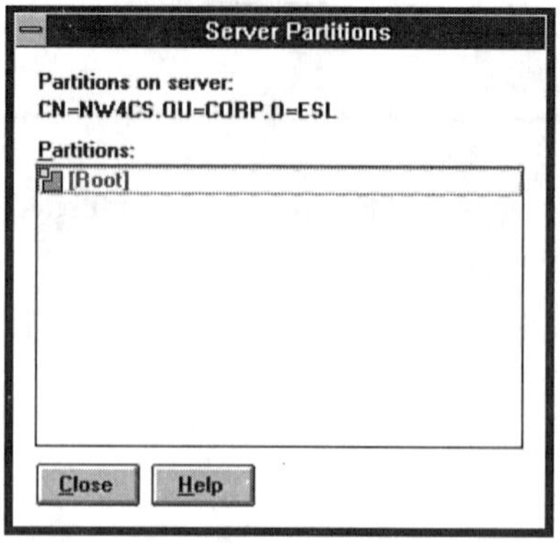

Figure 7.19
Viewing replicas on a server using Partition Manager.

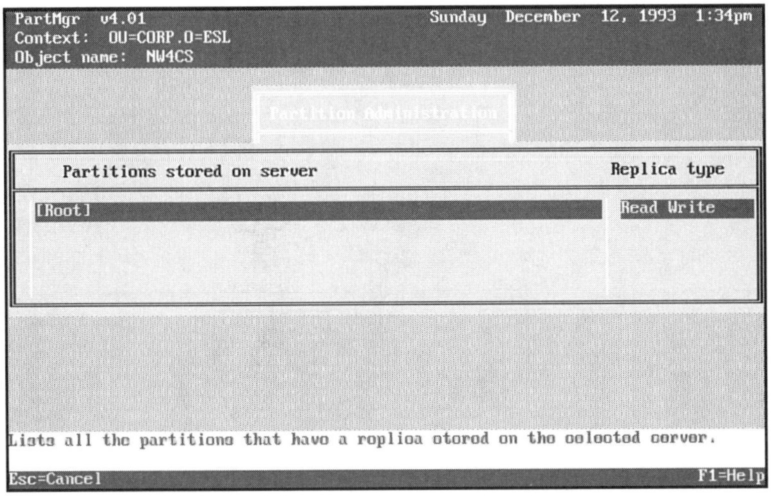

Figure 7.20
Viewing replicas on a server using PARTMGR.

Splitting Partitions or Creating New Partitions

When a partitioned tree becomes very large, splitting the partition might become necessary. You also should split a partition if a portion of the partition needs to reside at a different location. A classic example is when NDS objects in a subtree are used primarily at a remote location (that is, separated from the location where the partition now resides) by a slow wide area link. To minimize NDS traffic queries across a network, split the partition in two.

You can use any container in the NDS tree as the starting point for creating a new partition. This container becomes the first object in the NDS partition and is called the *root* or *parent container* of the partition.

To create a new partition, you need the Supervisor object right to the container that is being partitioned.

You can use NDS Manager or the PARTMGR utility to create the new partition. You can use these tools to make a selected container in the NDS tree of the root of a new partition. When you create the partition for the first time, a Master replica of the partition is placed on the current server.

When you split a partition, all servers that have a replica of the partition receive a copy of the replicas of the new partitions resulting from the split.

The procedure for splitting the partition is described in the context of the examples in figure 7.21, which shows an NDS tree for a LAN that has a single [Root] partition stored on the NW4CS server at site A. It has been decided that the SALES department has been relocated to a remote site B that is connected to site A with a slow wide area link. Because users in the sales department are now at site B, splitting the partition, creating a new partition whose root is OU=SALES, and keeping this partition on a server at site B is preferable.

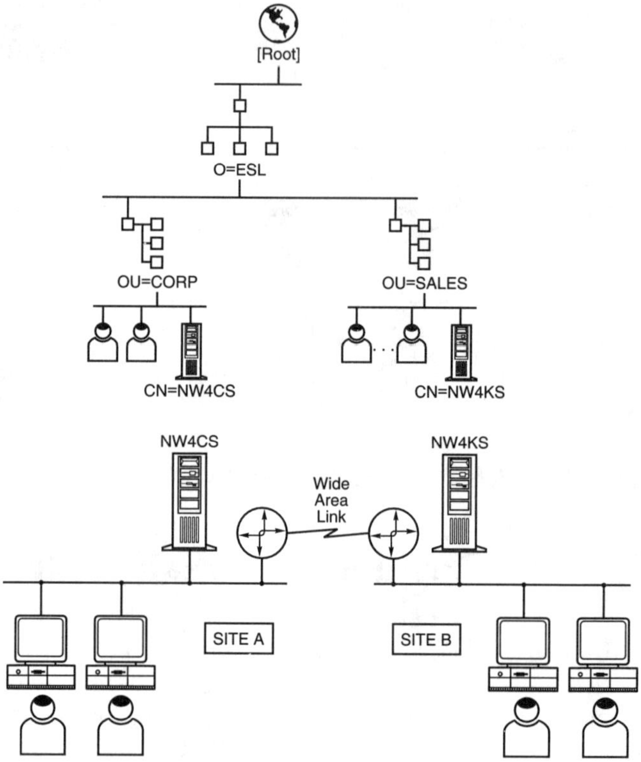

Figure 7.21
Case Study: Need for splitting a partition.

Creating (Splitting) a New Partition Using Partition Manager

When you start the Partition Manager, each container that is the root of a partition has a partition icon beside it (see fig. 7.22). Certain color codes are used to assist you in determining the meaning of the different objects. Containers at the root of a partition are red, IntranetWare servers that hold replicas are blue, and objects that are part of the [Root] partition are black.

To use the Partition Manager to create a new partition, perform the following steps:

1. Log in as Admin and start the Partition Manager from the Legacy NetWare Administrator utility.

2. Browse the NDS tree and highlight the container that should be the root of a new partition. Figure 7.23 shows that container OU=SALES is the root of a new partition.

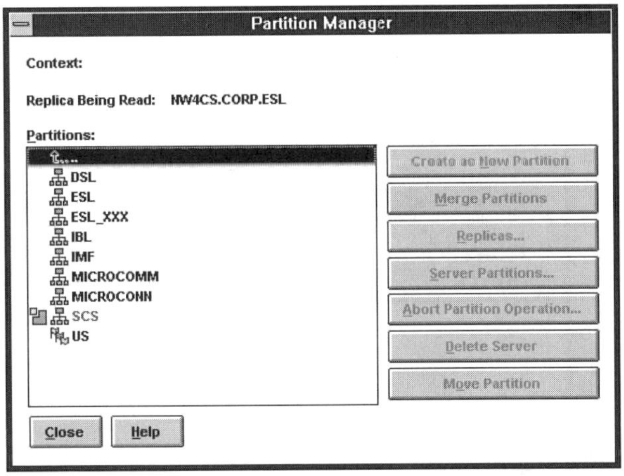

Figure 7.22
Containers that are roots of partitions.

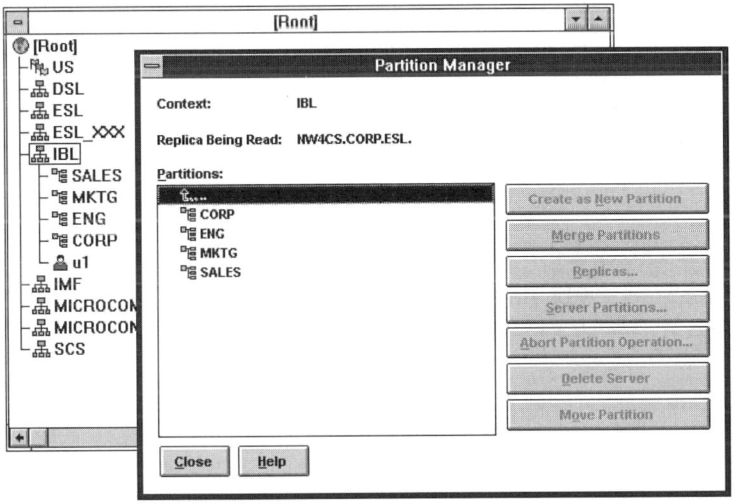

Figure 7.23
The container to become the root of a new partition.

Select the button Create as New Partition. When asked to verify whether you want to make this container the start of a new partition, select Yes. This can take from 1 to 10 minutes depending on the number of replicas, their size, and their location. When the operation is successful, you should see the partition icon next to the container that is the root of the newly created partition (see fig. 7.24).

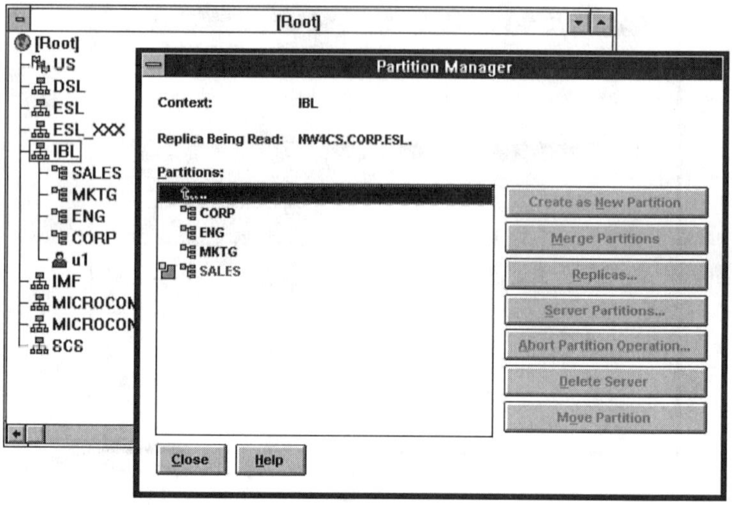

Figure 7.24
The container that is the root of a new partition.

To view the partition that you have created, select the container that you just partitioned and select Replicas. The complete name of the server on which you created the partition appears in the server column, and the type of replica appears in the Type column. Because you have just created the partition, the replica type should be Master. You can make additional replicas of this partition on other servers.

Creating (Splitting) a New Partition Using PARTMGR

To use the PARTMGR to create a new partition, perform the following steps:

1. Log in as Admin, and start the PARTMGR.
2. Select Manage Partitions.

   Those containers that are the root of a partition will have an object class of partition (see fig. 7.25).

3. Browse the NDS tree and highlight the container that should be the root of a new partition.
4. Press F10.

When asked to verify whether you want to make this container the start of a new partition, select Yes. This can take 1 to 10 minutes, depending on the number of replicas and their size and location.

When the operation is successful, you see that the name of the new partition is the same as the container name, but that the object class has changed to Partition (see fig. 7.26).

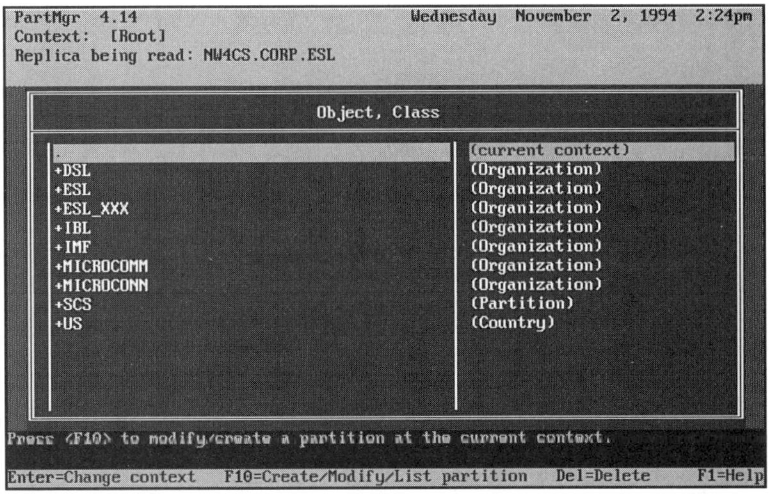

Figure 7.25
Object, Class container screen.

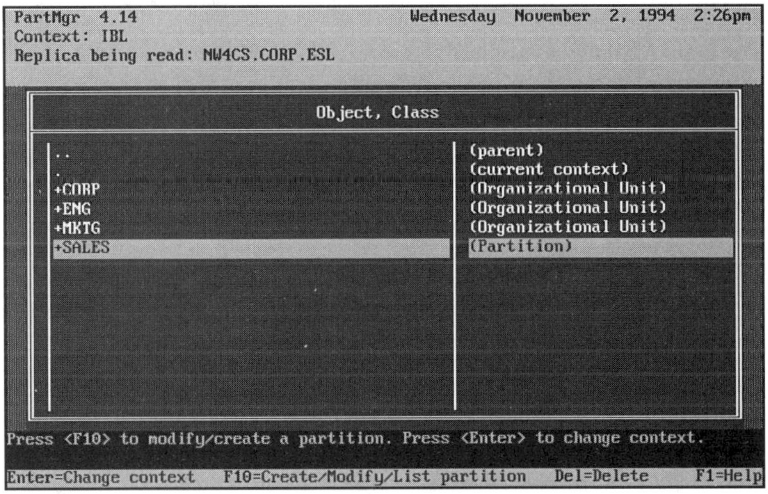

Figure 7.26
OU=SALES as the root of a new partition.

Merging Partitions

You may decide to merge partitions to consolidate resources. When merging partitions, a subordinate partition is merged with the parent partition.

In the example in figure 7.27, if you were to move the SALES department from site B to site A, you might want to merge the SALES partition into the [Root] partition. The partition OU=SALES is *subordinate* to the *parent* partition [Root]. To merge partitions, you need the Supervisor object right to the root of the parent partition. In the example in figure 7.27, you need the supervisor object right to [Root] to merge the OU=SALES partition into the [Root] partition.

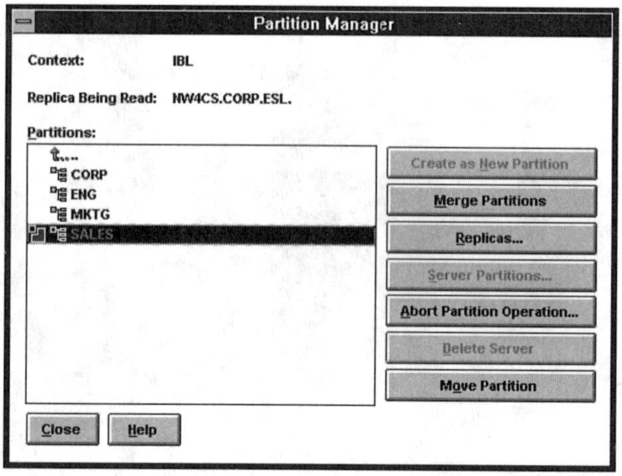

Figure 7.27
The container to be merged with the partition.

If you merge and split several partitions one after another, you might get a message that the partition is busy. You might have to wait a minute or longer for the replicas to synchronize.

For 20 servers in a single location, the synchronization can take 20 to 30 minutes. For 20 servers in multiple locations, the synchronization can take up to 60 minutes or longer.

The procedures shown in the next sections outline how to perform a merge operation.

Merging Using Partition Manager

To merge using Partition Manager, perform the following steps:

1. Log in as Admin and start the Partition Manager from the Legacy NetWare Administrator utility.

2. Browse the NDS tree and highlight the container that you want to merge with the parent partition (refer to figure 7.27).

3. Select the button Merge Partitions. When asked to verify that you want to merge the partition, select Yes. This usually takes from 1 to 60 minutes (or longer) depending on the number of replicas, their size, and their location.

   If you do not see the partition icon next to the partition that was merged disappear, you should go one level up the tree and browse that tree branch again. This will refresh the display.

Merging Using PARTMGR

To merge using PARTMGR, perform the following steps:

1. Log in as Admin.

2. Run PARTMGR.

3. Browse the NDS tree and highlight the container that you want to merge with the parent partition (see fig. 7.28).

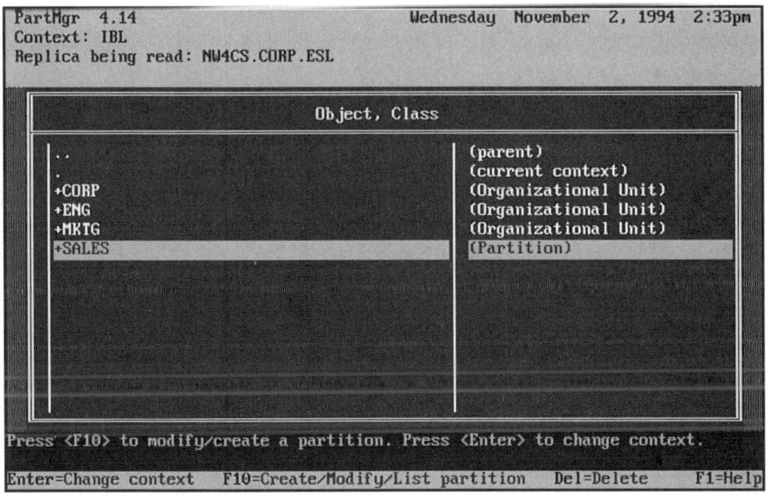

Figure 7.28
The container to be merged with PARTMGR.

4. Press F10.

   A list of operations that you can perform on the partition appears (see fig. 7.29).

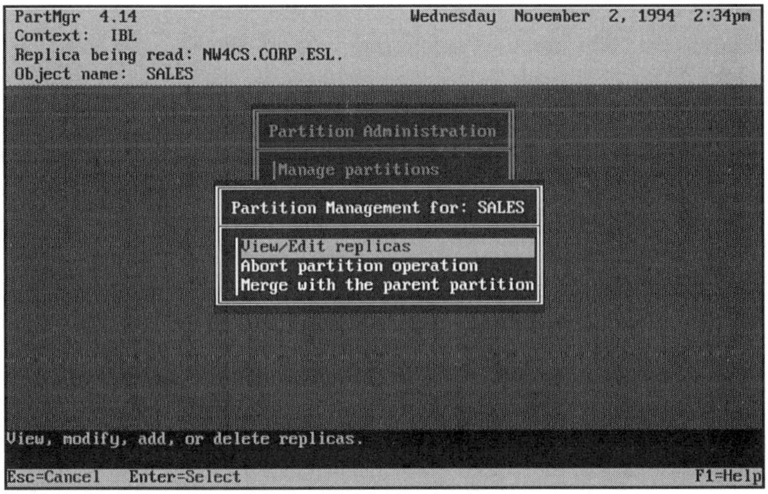

Figure 7.29
Operations that can be performed on the partition.

5. Select Merge with the parent partition.

6. You should see a message showing you the partition that is to be merged with the parent partition (see fig. 7.30). Select Yes to merge the partitions.

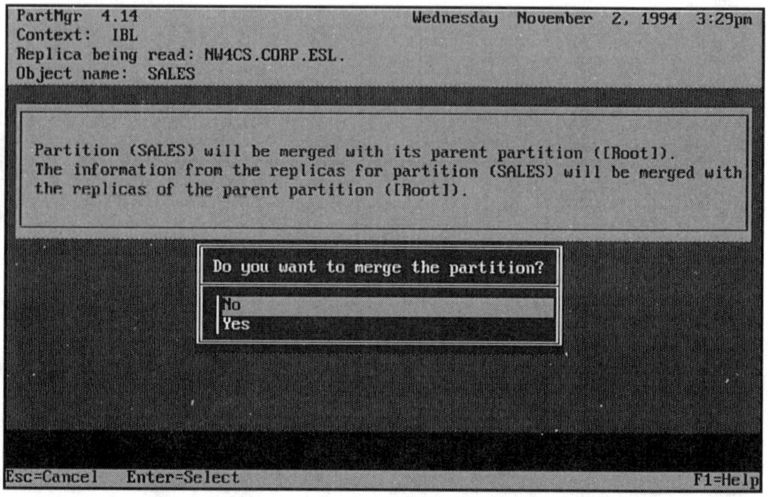

Figure 7.30
Message showing the name of the partition to be merged with the parent partition using PARTMGR.

Searching for Partitions

When the NDS tree is very large, finding all the partitions that are defined on the NDS tree is helpful. You can use the Legacy NetWare Administrator utility to do this.

To search for all partitions in the NDS tree, use the following as a guideline:

1. Start the Legacy NetWare Administrator utility.

2. Select Search... from the Object menu. You should see the search panel displayed. Set the fields in the Search dialog box as follows (see fig. 7.31):

   Start From: [Root] (or any container from which you want to start the search)

   Check the box Search Entire Subtree

   Search For: Partition

3. Select OK.

Figure 7.32 shows that three partitions were found: [Root], O=SCS, OU=SALES, and OU=ENG.

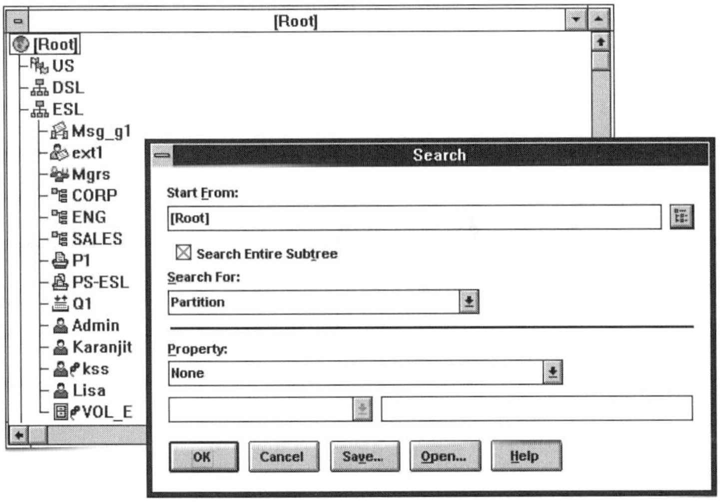

Figure 7.31
Search options for partitions.

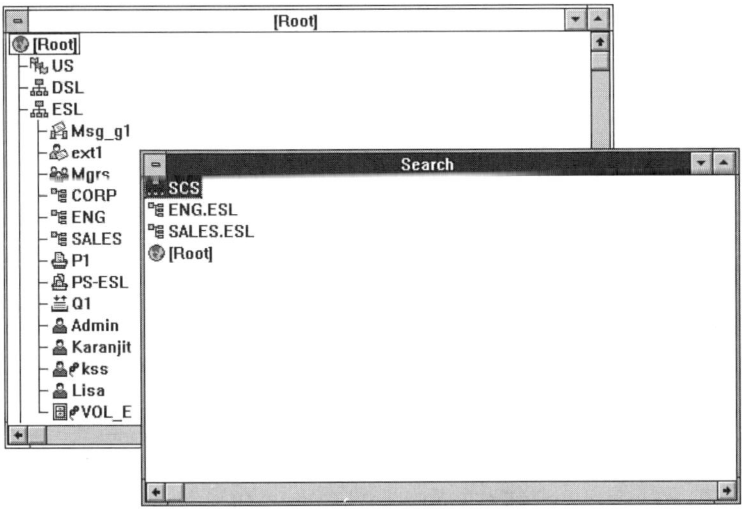

Figure 7.32
Partitions searched for in the NDS tree.

NetWare NDS Manager Services

Earlier in this chapter, a new utility was mentioned for performing NDS partitioning and replication operations—the *NDS Manager* utility. This new utility replaces the *Partition Manager* menu item in the legacy NetWare Administrator utility with a much more sophisticated set of tools that is much easier to use. There are versions of this utility for Windows 3, Windows 95, and Windows NT.

The main NDS Manager window, shown in figure 7.33, lists the replica information for each partition and provides status information for the partition in an organized manner that simplifies troubleshooting by graphically indicating where a problem might exist.

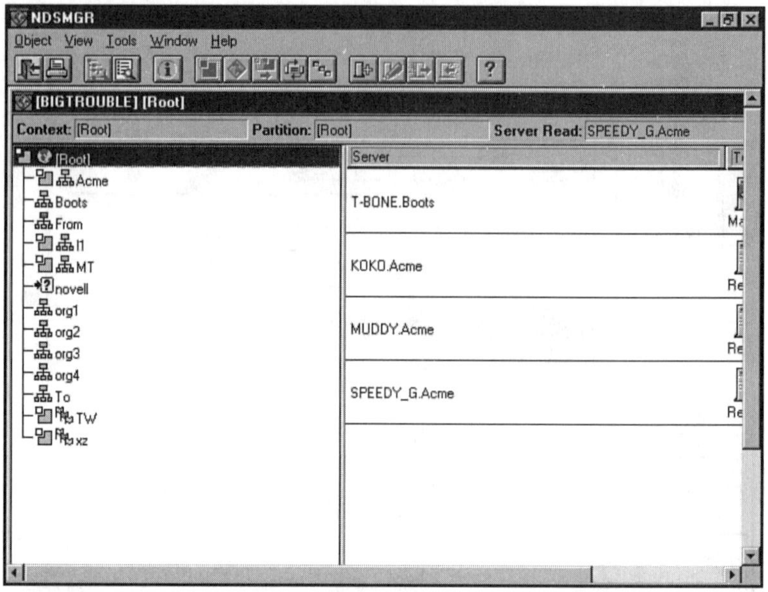

Figure 7.33
The NDS Manager main window.

Managing Partitions and Replicas with NDS Manager

As shown in figure 7.34, NDS Manager allows you to view partition information in a tree format in the left pane of the window, and it displays the replica list in the right pane.

Additionally, there is a second view, shown in figure 7.35, which displays the tree's partitions in a list format in the top half of the left pane, and in the bottom half of the left pane, it shows a list of the servers in the tree. You can select either a partition to view, which gives a list of the replicas of that partition by server in the upper right quadrant of the screen, or you can select a server and see a list of all the replicas stored on that server in the lower right quadrant of the screen.

Across the top of either view is a series of buttons on the button bar. They allow short access to the most useful functions of NDS Manager. The first two buttons let you exit from NDS Manager and print the information for the currently selected object. The next two buttons select which view of the two previously described views is displayed. The fifth button gives information on the selected object; if the selected object is a partition root, the information shown includes:

- The name of the selected object
- The name of the server that holds the master replica of the partition

- A count of the Read/Write, Read-Only, and Master Replicas
- The number of subordinate references this partition has
- The date and time of the last successful sync, as identified in the DSTRACE screen on the server with the message *ALL PROCESSED=Yes*
- The date and time of the last attempted sync

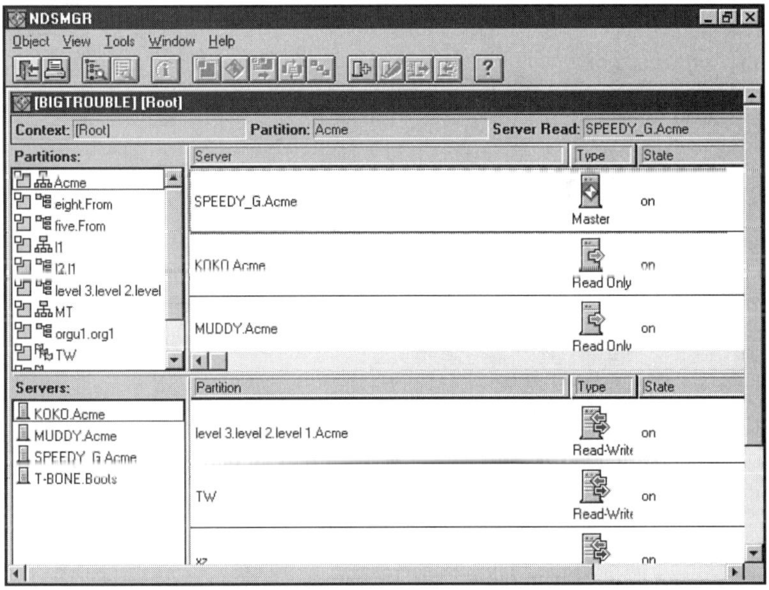

Figure 7.34
An Alternate view of the NDS Partitions and replicas.

If the selected object is a server object, the following information is displayed:

- The server's full NDS name
- The value of the server object's Full Name property
- The version of the server
- The version of DS.NLM, the Directory Services NLM, running on the server
- The time the server last synchronized its replica information with other servers in the tree
- The total number of replicas on the server
- The network address this server is known by in the other server's internal tables

The next sections covers buttons that perform operations on partitions.

Partition Operations Performed by NDS Manager

NDS Manager lets you perform the following partition operations with great ease using the buttons on the button bar:

- Create partitions (also known as a partition split operation)
- Merge partitions
- Move partitions
- Check partition synchronization
- Check partition continuity

Creating Partitions with NDS Manager

Creating a new partition with NDS Manager is simply a matter of pressing the Create Partition button. A confirmation box will pop up to verify that you want to create the partition, and if all of the preconditions (server availability, partition synchronization status, and so on) are met to allow a partition to be created, NDS Manager will create the partition for you.

Merging Partitions with NDS Manager

The inverse operation from creating a partition in NDS is merging two partitions together. This operation is commonly known as a *Partition Join* operation.

With NDS Manager, just as with the Create Partition operation, merging partitions is simply a matter of selecting the partition you want to merge into its parent, pressing the Merge Partition button, and telling the program to proceed if all the preconditions are met.

Moving Partitions with NDS Manager

The only way NDS allows you to move a container from one location in the tree to another is through Partition move operations. In order to move a container, you must first do a partition split, described in an earlier section, and then after NDS completes the operation, do a partition move operation.

As shown earlier, NDS Manager can do the partition split operation, and it can do the move operation as well. After the partition is created and NDS has completed the operation, press the Move Partition button, and put the NDS context to which the partition is to be moved in the To Context field. You also have the option to create an alias for the container in the old location so users' NET.CFG files do not need to be updated.

Checking Synchronization Status with NDS Manager

NDS Manager also provides an easy way to check the synchronization status for any partition in your tree or, optionally, all of the partitions viewed in the partition/server list view.

Checking synchronization status can give you an overall picture of the health of your NDS tree. Selecting the Check Synchronization button brings up a window that asks which partition or partitions you want to check, and then queries the servers in the tree about the state of synchronization.

Synchronization checks are based on a partition's All Processed status as it would be shown in the DSTRACE screen on the server. If a partition is not synchronized, you can press the Continuity button to get information on which server or servers are out of synchronization.

Checking Partition Continuity with NDS Manager

Partition continuity can be checked either when checking synchronization status for a partition, or (if you already know there is a problem with a particular partition) without going through that intermediate step.

The Partition Continuity window, shown in figure 7.35, summarizes the partition synchronization status for an entire partition across all of the servers involved in synchronization for that partition.

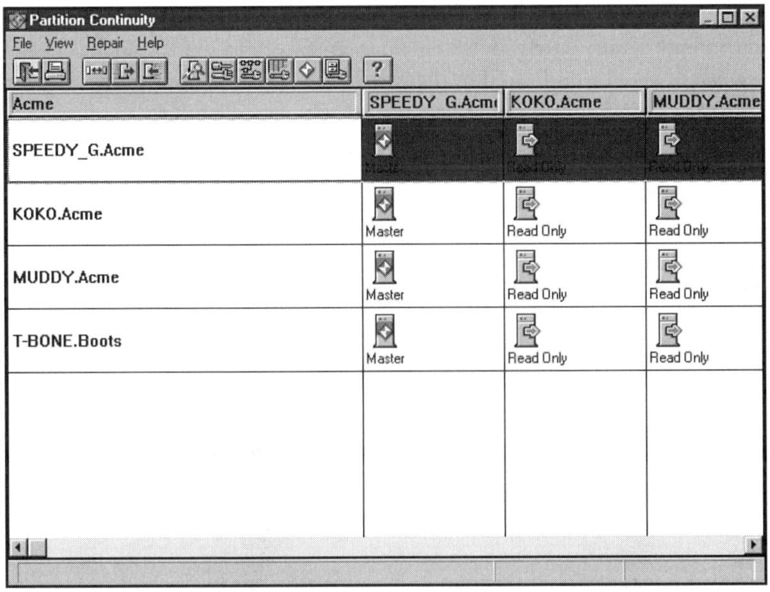

Figure 7.35
The Partition Continuity window.

The grid that is displayed when this option is selected shows the partition name in the leftmost heading in the window. The rows indicate the particular server being viewed, and the columns indicate how the server in a particular row sees the other servers involved in synchronization of the partition.

These lists are put together by querying each server in the replica list and getting that server's view of the replica list. This provides you with an instant picture of the replica lists on each server, where the errors are, and makes it possible to pinpoint a problem in which two servers might indicate, for example, that they each hold the master of the partition.

This window also provides a toolbar of its own that allows you to launch certain DSREPAIR operations. The options on the menu do not supersede DSREPAIR, but rather launch it remotely without requiring either direct access to the console or access using RCONSOLE.

Warning These repair options in NDS Manager do not replace DSREPAIR, but are dependent on DSREPAIR being available. If DSREPAIR is not available on a server that you are attempting to repair, you will get an error message indicating that DSREPAIR cannot be found.

The various repair options available permit you to perform commonly-used repair options of DSREPAIR. The first set of buttons is made up of the exit and print buttons.

The second group consists of options that have to do with transmitting data in the partition. They are, in order, Synchronize Immediately, Send Updates, and Receive Updates. The options all act on the selected server as indicated in the row of the partition continuity table. The Send Updates and Receive Updates functions can also be performed from the replica operations buttons from the main NDS Manager window.

The third group of buttons is made up of the actual repair options. You can verify remote server IDs, repair a replica, repair network addresses, repair the local database, reassign the master replica to a new server, or repair volume objects. Each of these options corresponds to a function in DSREPAIR—NDS Manager simply provides an easier-to-use interface for the options so you can centralize your repair efforts at a workstation rather than having to visit each server console directly or through RCONSOLE.

Replica Operations Performed by NDS Manager

In addition to the partition options described in the preceding section, NDS Manager can also perform options on replicas—the physical manifestations of a partition.

Replica operations consist of locating physical copies of logical partitions in the NDS tree. The operations that can be performed are:

- Add replica
- Change replica type
- Send updates
- Receive updates

Other Functionality in NDS Manager

NDS Manager is intended to provide management of NDS over the entire network. The preceding sections discussed the most commonly used options, which are presented in the button bar. All of the options available in buttons are also available in menu selections, but there are a few other options from the menus that are worth mentioning.

NDS Manager provides DS.NLM version verification and distribution from the Object menu. Selecting the NDS Version option provides one of two options, depending on whether a partition or a server is selected.

If a partition is selected, NDS Manager will present an option to view the versions of DS.NLM on the servers in the selected container, unless the preferences are set to have the program search the entire subtree for servers.

If a server is selected, NDS Manager will present an option to update the version of DS.NLM on the server or to use that server to distribute a version of DS.NLM to all of the servers in tree. The window that comes up allows you to select the source server and any target servers to which the update should be distributed. It will then distribute the update to the servers and reload DS.NLM to make the new version of DS.NLM active.

Note NDS Manager will not permit updates to cross versions of the NetWare operating system. If a tree consists of mixed versions of the NetWare operating system, the *NDS Update* menu item will only allow you to update DS.NLM on versions of NetWare the new DS.NLM is intended to be used with.

Another function that has been moved to NDS Manager is the ability to remove a server from the NDS tree. The Delete option is available under the Object menu if a server object is selected. This option permanently removes the selected server from the tree and removes all of the replicas that are stored on it from that server. A server holding a master replica of a partition will be prompted to select a new server to hold the master replica of the partition in question.

Lastly, under the Object menu, selecting the Partition submenu will provide an additional function not provided for in the button bar—aborting a partition operation in progress. When a partition operation has not completed its initial stages, it is possible to abort a partition split or merge operation.

Repairing NDS Partitions

If the Master replica becomes corrupt, it can propagate inaccurate information about the NDS partition. A corrupt Master replica also prevents you from performing partition restructuring, such as splitting and merging.

The causes of a corrupt Master replica can range from problems with the server's disk storage, the server being powered off unexpectedly, or the server crashing in the middle of an NDS operation, to simply having a bug in the NDS software.

You can use any of the following techniques to correct problems with replicas:

- Changing replica types
- Rebuilding a replica
- Using DSREPAIR.NLM

Changing Replica Types

If the Master replica is corrupt, you can replace it with a Read-Write replica. This is done by changing the replica type of a Read-Write replica to a Master replica. When this is done, the original Master replica (also, the corrupt Master replica, in this case) is downgraded to a Read-Write replica and is synchronized with the information in the new Master replica.

To change a replica type, you need the Supervisor object right to the root of the partition whose replica type is being changed. You can perform this task using the Partition Manager of PARTMGR.

Making a Read-Write Replica a Master Replica Using Partition Manager

You can use the following steps as a guideline for using Partition Manager to change a replica type:

1. Log in as Admin, and start the Partition Manager from the Legacy NetWare Administrator utility.

2. Browse the NDS tree and highlight the container whose replica type you want to change.

   You should see a list of servers and the replica types they have (see fig. 7.36).

3. Select the server that contains the replica type you want to change.

   Select the button Change Type.

   You should see a panel to change the replica type (see fig. 7.37).

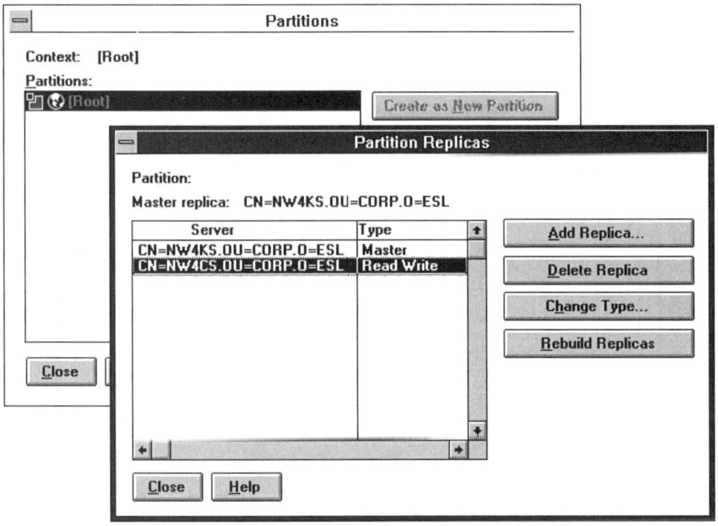

Figure 7.36
Replicas on the server using Partition Manager.

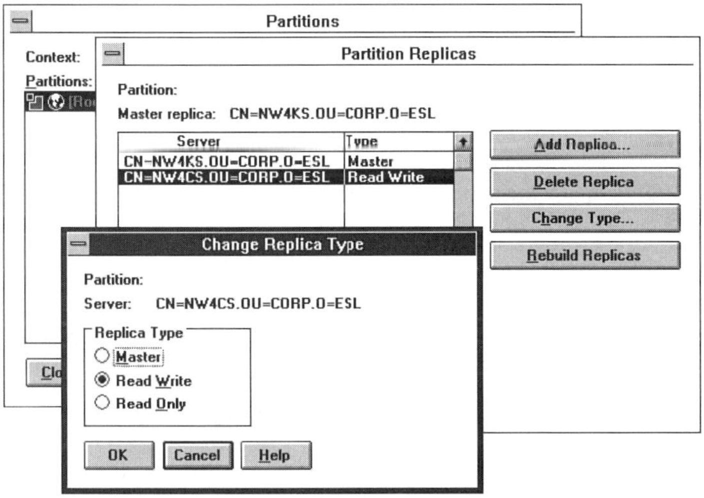

Figure 7.37
Change Replica Type options.

Select the Master replica type and select OK.

You should see a list of servers and the changes in the replica types (see fig. 7.38).

4. Select the Close buttons to exit the Partition Manager.

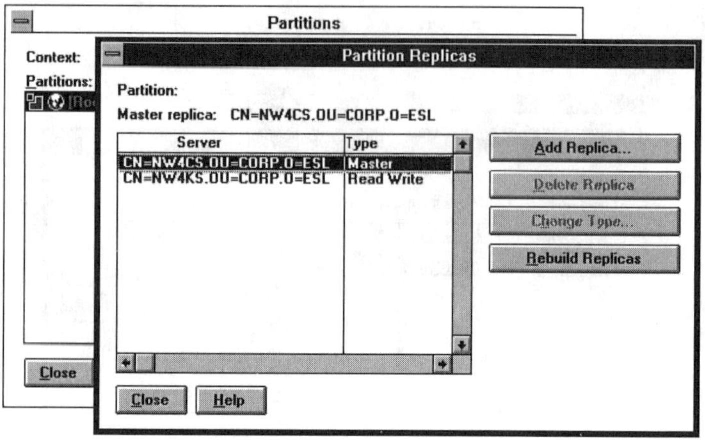

Figure 7.38
Replicas on the server.

Making a Read-Write Replica a Master Replica Using PARTMGR

You can use the following as a guideline for using PARTMGR to change a replica type:

1. Log in as Admin.
2. Run PARTMGR.
3. Browse the NDS tree, and highlight the container whose replica type you want to change.

   Press F10.

   Select View/Edit replicas.

   You should see a list of servers and their replica types (see fig. 7.39).
4. Highlight the server that contains the replica type you want to change, and press Enter.

   You should see an editable field for the current replica type. Press Enter to change.

   You should see the list of replica types to which you can change (see fig. 7.40).

   Highlight the Master option and press Enter.

   Press F10 to save your changes.

   You should see a list of servers and the changes in the replica types (see fig. 7.41).
5. Press Alt+F10 and exit PARTMGR.

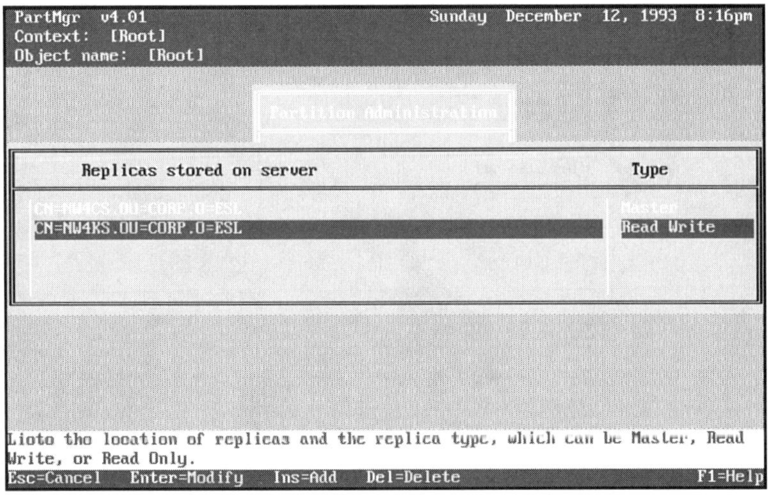

Figure 7.39
Replicas on the server using PARTMGR.

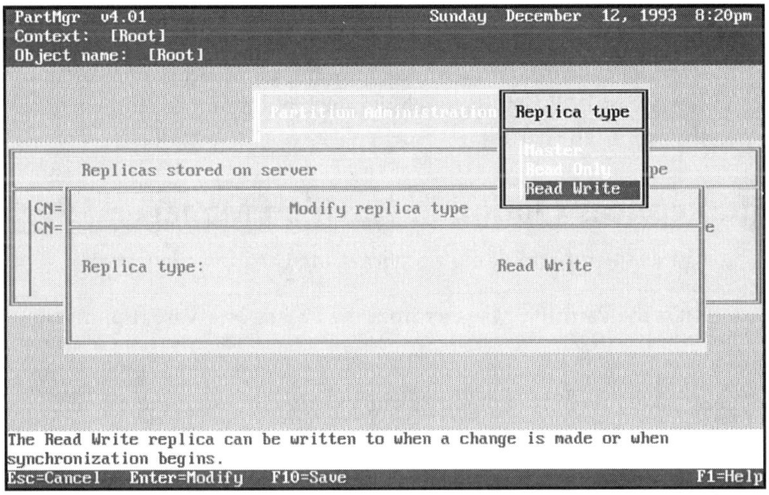

Figure 7.40
A list of replica type options.

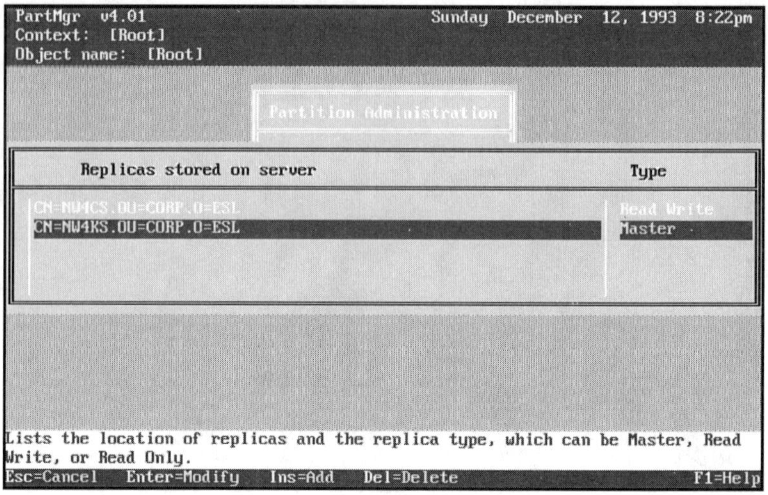

Figure 7.41
Changed replicas on the server.

Rebuilding a Replica

If the replicas on a partition are not synchronized with the Master replica, or become corrupt, you can use the Partition Manager or PARTMGR to rebuild the replicas. To do this, you need Supervisor object rights to the root of the partition whose replicas you are rebuilding.

Using the Rebuild Replicas Option in Partition Manager

Use the following steps as a guideline for rebuilding a replica using Partition Manager:

1. Log in as Admin and start the Partition Manager from the Legacy NetWare Administrator utility.
2. Browse the NDS tree, and highlight the container whose replicas you want to rebuild.
3. Select the Replicas button.
4. Highlight the Master replica; select the button Rebuild Replicas.

When asked if you want to replace another replica's data with data from this replica, answer Yes.

Rebuilding Replicas Using PARTMGR

Use the following steps as a guideline for rebuilding a replica using PARTMGR:

1. Log in as Admin.
2. Run PARTMGR.

3. Browse the NDS tree, and highlight the container whose replicas you want to rebuild.

   Press F10.

   Select Rebuild replicas.

   You should see a list of servers and their replica types.

4. Highlight the Master replica and press F10.

   Press Enter and select Yes to confirm your choice.

5. Press Alt+F10 and exit PARTMGR.

Using DSREPAIR.NLM

If the Master replica is corrupt or the server on which it resides is no longer available, you can run DSREPAIR at the server to re-create the Master replica from the information in the Read-Write replicas in the replica list. You must use caution when you use DSREPAIR and be sure to have only one Master replica in the ring.

The *NDS Manager* utility, previously discussed in this chapter, has hooks into DSREPAIR as well, enabling many of the operations discussed here to be done from a workstation. As previously discussed, DSREPAIR still needs to be available for those functions to be usable.

DSREPAIR selects a Read-Write replica to become a new Master, and the old Master replica is downgraded to a Read-Write replica.

To use DSREPAIR to repair a replica list with no Master replica, perform the following:

1. Run DSREPAIR at the server:

   ```
   LOAD DSREPAIR
   ```

   You should see DSREPAIR's main options screen (see fig. 7.42). The *Unattended repair* performs all possible operations that do not require operator assistance. If you are not sure of what the cause of the problem is with NDS, you should select this option.

   If you want to review the results of the repair operation, you can view the repair log file by selecting View/Edit repair log file.

   For more advanced options, such as manual control and global diagnostics, select Advanced options menu.

2. Figure 7.43 shows the results of performing an Unattended repair operation. As the repair operation proceeds you will see a status of the repair, and at the end you will see a summary of the repair operations (see fig. 7.43). In this case 41 errors were reported and repaired for the NDS.

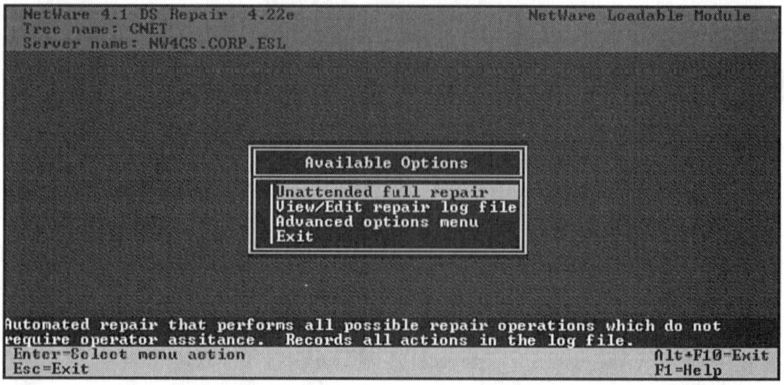

Figure 7.42
The DSREPAIR main options screen.

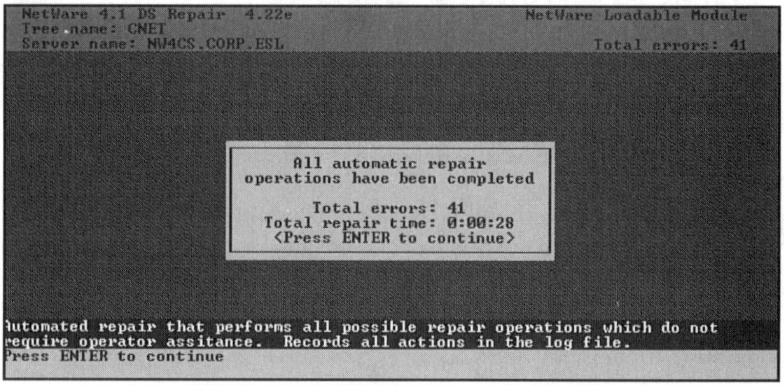

Figure 7.43
DSREPAIR's Unattended repair operation results.

3. Figure 7.44 shows the repair log file when the View/Edit repair log file was selected. This figure shows the start of the automatic repair process.

4. Figure 7.45 shows the options when the Advanced options menu is selected.

5. To perform operations on replicas, replica lists, and server objects, select Replica and partition operations. Figure 7.46 shows the list of replicas on the server on which DSREPAIR is being run.

6. To repair a replica, highlight it and press Enter. Figure 7.47 shows a list of operations that can be performed on the replica.

7. After performing the desired operation, exit DSREPAIR by pressing Alt+F10 or by pressing Esc a few times, and answering Yes when asked if you want to exit DSREPAIR.

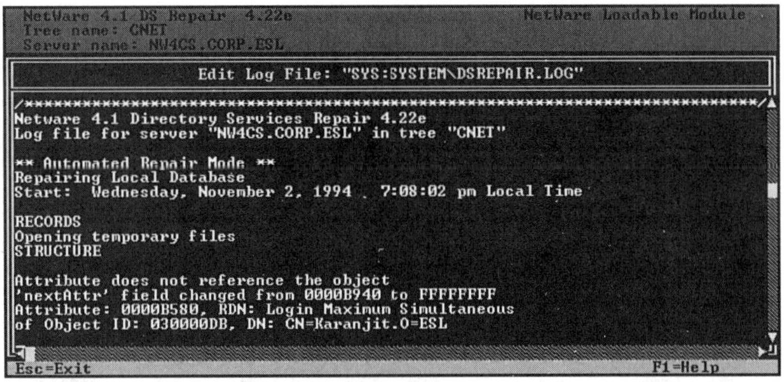

Figure 7.44
The DSREPAIR repair log file.

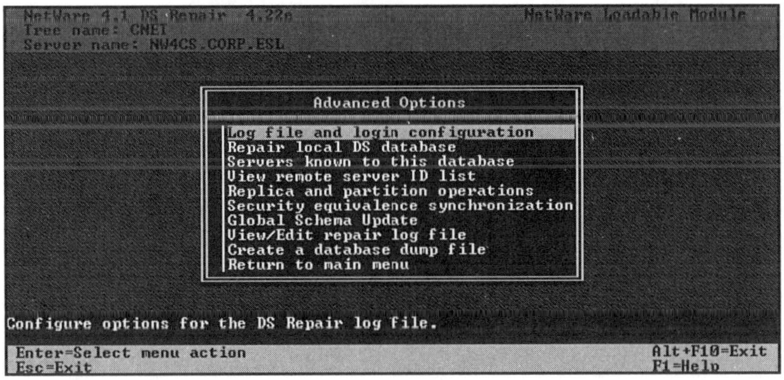

Figure 7.45
The DSREPAIR Advanced options menu.

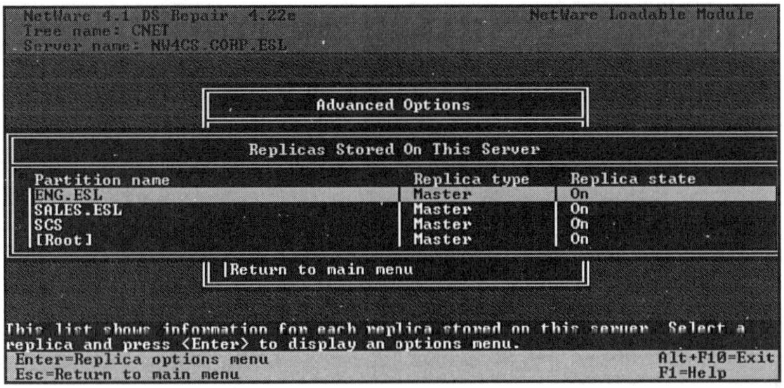

Figure 7.46
DSREPAIR—List of replicas on local server.

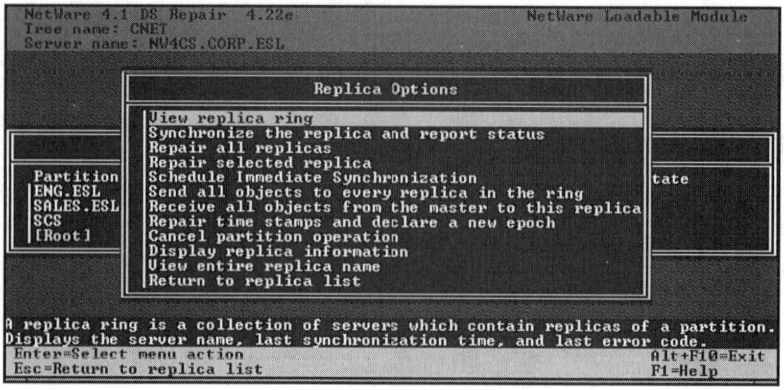

Figure 7.47
DSREPAIR—List of operations on selected replica.

Removing a Server Object from an NDS Tree

Occasionally, you might have to remove an IntranetWare server from the NDS tree. If you attempt to perform this on a server that is active, the error message shown in figure 7.48 appears. Because a Server object can contain replicas of partitions, you should use the Partition Manager or PARTMGR utility to delete it. If you do succeed in deleting an inactive server using NETADMIN or the NetWare Administrator, it can damage the replica list and cause serious problems.

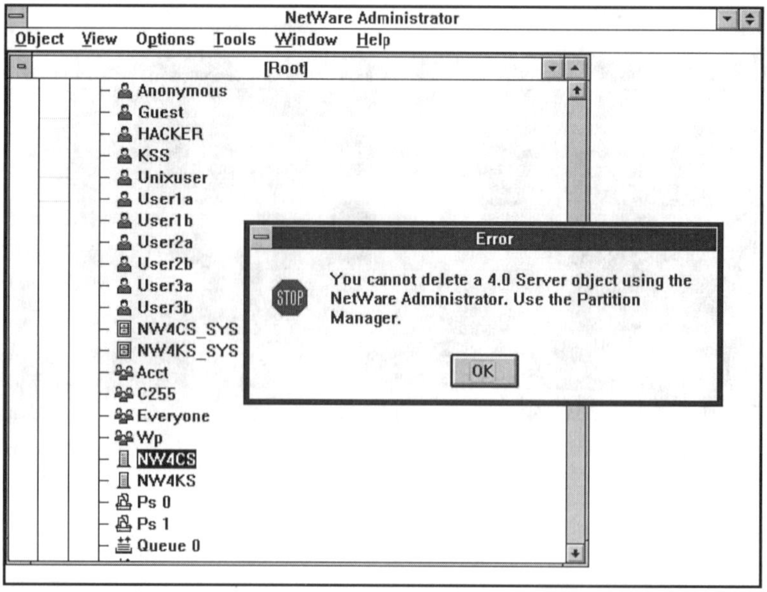

Figure 7.48
An attempt to remove the Server object from an NDS tree.

The procedures for deleting a Server object using the Partition Manager and PARTMGR are outlined next.

Deleting an IntranetWare Server Using the Partition Manager

To delete an IntranetWare server using the Partition Manager:

1. Log in as Admin.
2. Start the Partition Manager from the Tools menu of the Legacy NetWare Administrator utility.
3. Browse the NDS tree using the Partition Manager browse function and locate the Server object(s) that need to be deleted. Figure 7.49 shows the IntranetWare servers that hold partition replicas.
4. Highlight the Server object and select the Delete Server button.

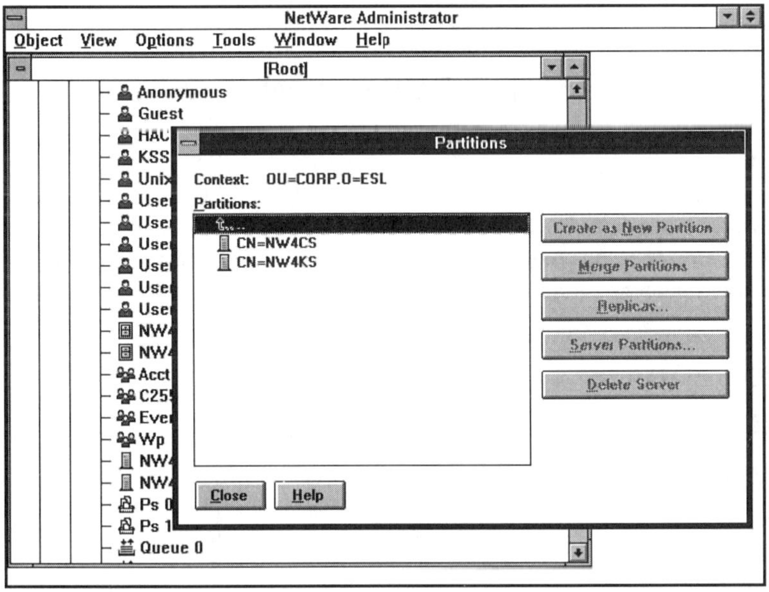

Figure 7.49
IntranetWare Server objects that hold replicas.

Deleting an IntranetWare Server Using the PARTMGR

To delete an IntranetWare server using the PARTMGR:

1. Log in as Admin.
2. Run the PARTMGR utility.

3. Browse the NDS tree and locate the Server object(s) that need to be deleted. Figure 7.50 shows the IntranetWare servers that hold partition replicas.

4. Highlight the Server object and press Del.

5. When asked if you want to delete the Server object, select Yes.

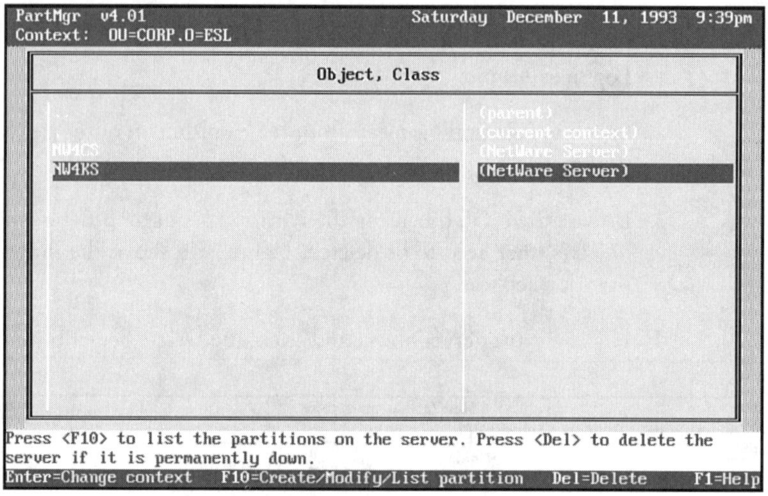

Figure 7.50
IntranetWare Server objects that hold replicas.

When you select the delete option for deleting the Server object using PARTMGR or Partition Manager, the replicas on the server are deleted first, and then the Server object is deleted. You should not bring the server down immediately after it has been deleted from the NDS tree. You should wait until all servers in the replica list are notified of the deleted server; you will then stop receiving replica updates.

Status of Server Volume Objects with Server Object ID Deleted

When the server is deleted from the NDS tree, the Volume objects for which the Server object is host are changed to object class Unknown. This prevents the volume from being accessed. You then can use the NetWare Administrator or NETADMIN to delete the Unknown objects.

Reinstalling the NDS Tree

If you run into a situation in which the NDS database is corrupted beyond repair, you might be left with no alternative other than to create a new NDS database. Fortunately, you can do this without losing the files and directories on the server's volumes. You will, however, lose trustee assignments to files and directories that you have added since the server was last installed. Trustee assignments are granted to NDS objects such as User objects, Group objects, and Container objects. As part of the process of reinstalling the NDS, you have to remove the existing NDS database first. When this takes place, the trustee assignments made to the objects in the NDS database are lost.

Before reinstalling the NDS tree, take the usual precautionary measure of backing up the files and directories on the server. The reinstalling of the NDS tree is a reliable process and you should not encounter any problems. The nature of computers and software being what they are, however, taking precautions that enable you to recover from the unexpected is prudent.

When you remove the directory services from a server, you also remove the Server object from the NDS tree, and *downgrade* the server's volumes to bindery volumes. The downgraded volumes and the servers are still available for access through bindery-based utilities. For example, RCONSOLE is a bindery-based utility, and you can use this to access the server's console, even though directory services are removed from the server.

If you remove the directory services from a server that has a Master replica or that has the only replica that has links to subordinate partitions, the subordinate partitions on other servers become invalid. For this reason, you should change the replica type of the Master replica to a Read Write replica, using the procedure outlined in this chapter. Then make replicas of any critical partitions on other servers.

To reinstall the directory service on a server, you need to have the Supervisor object right to the Server object and its associated Volume objects.

The following describes the procedure for reinstalling directory services on a server:

1. Ensure that all the servers' volumes are mounted.

   If all the servers' volumes are not mounted, you have to repeat the procedure for removing NDS from a server with the other volumes.

2. Run the INSTALL NLM at the server console:

   LOAD INSTALL

3. Make the following menu selections:

   Select Maintenance/Selective Install.

   Select Directory Options.

   Select Remove Directory Services from this Server.

4. When asked to confirm whether you want to remove directory services, select Yes.

5. Log in to the directory services, when prompted to do so, with the Admin password.

The server's volumes are downgraded, and a message appears informing you of the number of volumes that have been downgraded.

At this point, you are ready to reinstall NDS services on the server.

6. From the Directory Options of the INSTALL.NLM, select Install Directory Services onto this server.

7. You will be asked the name of the NDS tree. If you are connected to the rest of the network, INSTALL will remember the tree name that was used.

   You will be presented with a number of screens dealing with the context in which you want to install this server and the time services that will be installed on the server. Make the appropriate choices based on your NDS tree design. You may want to examine the AUTOEXEC.NCF file on the server to see the current configuration at the server. You can examine the AUTOEXEC.NCF options through the NCF Files Options in the Installation Options menu.

8. Run DSREPAIR on the server to update and fix the NDS database.

Instructions on running DSREPAIR were presented earlier in this chapter.

Summary

In this chapter, you learned about the mechanisms used to store and manage the NDS database on the server. You were introduced to the concept of partitions and replicas. Partitions enable you to manage a large NDS database using smaller manageable units. Replicas are copies of partitions and can be used to improve the fault tolerance of an NDS database. Placing replicas in strategic locations minimizes network traffic due to directory lookups. There are four types of replicas: Master, Read-Write, Read-Only, and Subordinate Reference. This chapter explained the differences between them and the reason for using each replica type.

This chapter also explored partition design and management issues and how replica synchronization works. Partitions can be managed by using the NDS Manager or PARTMGR.

CHAPTER 8

Novell Directory Services Time Synchronization

Time synchronization is important in IntranetWare-based networks because NDS operations and changes must occur in the proper sequence on the network.

The NDS database is distributed on the network. Time synchronization is implemented in IntranetWare to solve the problem of keeping a consistent view of the NDS database because portions of the NDS tree are kept on different servers that use separate hardware time clicks. When objects are added to the Directory, they are first added in a local copy of the database (replica). The changes in the NDS database are propagated throughout the network to other replicas. If the same object is modified in two different local copies of the database, or modified twice in the same local copy, the order in which the modifications were made must be preserved so that these changes can be performed on other replicas.

For example, deleting a user object, adding a new user object with the same name, and changing the user object has a different effect than changing it first, deleting it, and then adding the user object.

On a distributed network consisting of many servers, there is a tendency for server clocks and times to drift—even if they are initially set to the same time. The amount of drift depends on each machine and the accuracy of its time clock. A mechanism is needed to ensure that the server clocks are synchronized to within a predefined tolerance. This is called *time synchronization,* and it ensures that a common network-wide time exists throughout the network.

Although time synchronization is not part of the NDS schema, without it NDS would not work reliably. Time synchronization is implemented by the NetWare Loadable Module, TIMESYNC.NLM. This module must be run at each server and is loaded automatically when the Netware 4.x and IntranetWare servers are started.

Understanding Time Server Types

All NetWare 4.x and IntranetWare servers are required to synchronize their time to a common network time for NDS operations to be performed in a consistent manner; therefore, each NetWare 4.x IntranetWare server acts as a time server. Time servers fall into two categories: *time providers* and *time consumers.* Time providers act as sources of time (also called *time sources*).

When a NetWare 4.x or IntranetWare server is installed, you see the following time server types:

- Single Reference Time Servers (SRTS)
- Reference Time Servers (RTS)
- Primary Time Servers (PTS)
- Secondary Time Servers (STS)

Single Reference Time Servers

The SRTS is the default choice during a first time installation. The first installed NetWare 4.x or IntranetWare server can be designated as the SRTS. The SRTS is the authoritative time source on the network. All other servers synchronize their time to match the SRTS. Although the SRTS can be made to work for all kinds of networks, it is primarily recommended for small networks (see fig. 8.1). For larger networks, the SRTS acts as a single point of failure, and other mechanisms should be used. When SRTS is used, other types of time servers such as PTS or RTS cannot be used.

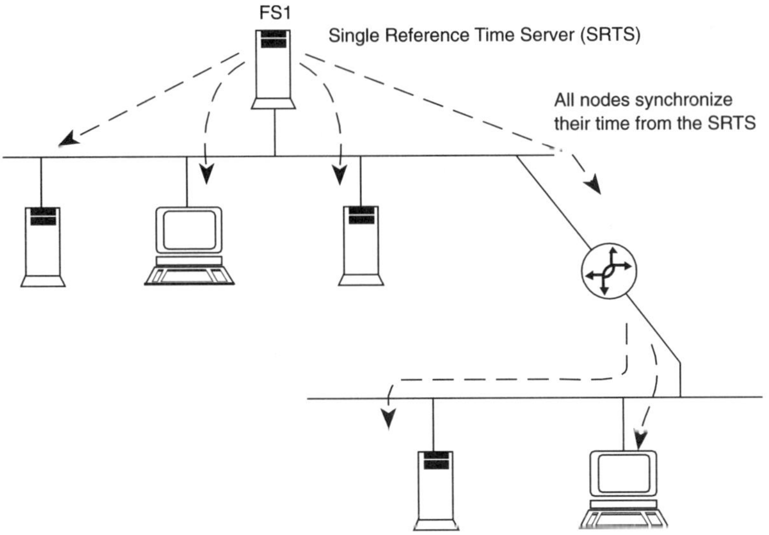

Figure 8.1
The Single Reference Time Server.

All servers on the network must be able to contact the SRTS because it is the only source of time.

Time synchronization can exist on a physical network even if a physical network is divided into separate logical directory trees. A physical network can contain several directory trees that do not normally share resources. Although each directory tree is treated as a separate logical network, they share a common network time because the time servers in the separate directory trees are reached through a physical connection. The default behavior is that you cannot have an SRTS for each directory tree if the servers in the directory trees can be reached through physical network connections. To override this default behavior of a common time synchronization across multiple directory trees, the SET TIMESYNC DIRECTORY TREE MODE parameter can be used. This parameter is discussed in table 8.2 later in this chapter.

For a small network that uses an SRTS, time synchronization is trivial or non-existent because all other servers synchronize their time to the SRTS. In larger networks, use of the SRTS poses a *single-point-of-failure* problem, and other types of time servers, such as Primary Time Servers and Reference Time Servers, can be used as sources of time. When more than one time source exists, a common network time is computed based on a voting process that occurs between the time providers.

Single Reference Time Servers, by definition, do not use another time provider to remain synchronized. A Single Reference Time Server is the sole authority for time on the network, and its time is used as the common network time.

Reference Time Servers

Reference Time Servers are used to provide an external time source. They are designed to be accurate and usually synchronize their time from a radio clock slaved to the Naval Observatory or some other equally accurate time source. Another way to design the RTS is by using a time synchronization NLM that contacts an accurate time source through a modem at regular intervals. An RTS can synchronize itself by an external time source, but it never adjusts its time from any other source on the network. For reliability, additional RTSs can be used, which should be strategically located at other points on the network (see fig. 8.2). Because there can be differences in the time provided by RTSs, a voting method is used to decide the reference time to be used on the network. All Reference Time Servers participate in this vote. If any Primary Time Servers exist, they too participate in the vote. The Primary Time Servers adjust their time to match the consensus reached as a result of the vote.

Figure 8.2
Reference Time Servers.

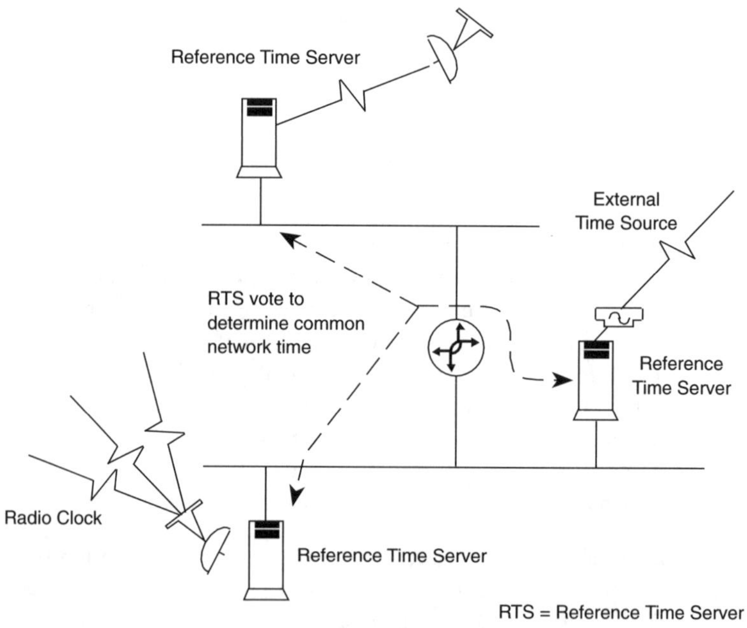

Use an RTS when you need to have a central point from which to control the accuracy of network time with respect to an external source. For large networks in which synchronization with an accurate external clock is needed, a backup RTS is recommended.

A Reference Time Server, by definition, does not initialize its clock with the common network time. It is used for the sole purpose of determining an accurate common network time.

Primary Time Servers

A *Primary Time Server* synchronizes its time by voting with at least one other PTS or RTS (see fig. 8.3). In other words, a PTS must have another PTS or another RTS to synchronize its time. The network might have several PTSs and RTSs, in which case, all the PTS and RTS time servers participate in the vote.

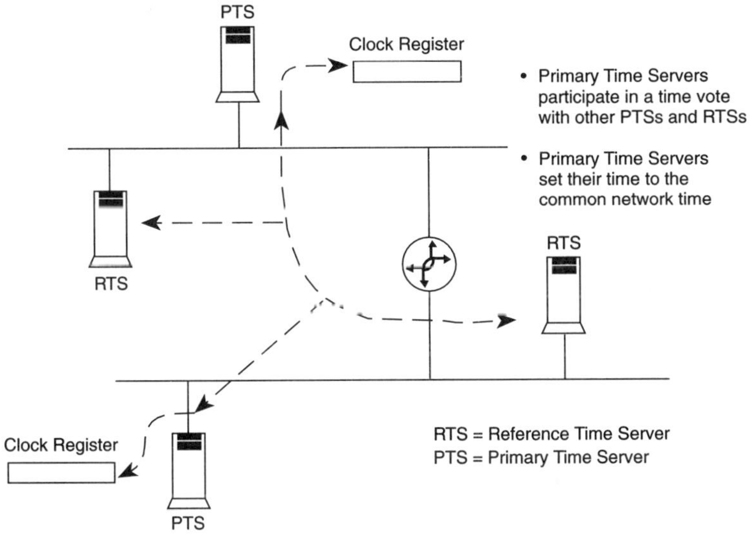

Figure 8.3
Primary Time Servers.

Unlike an RTS, a PTS adjusts its time to match the common network time (result of the vote). The RTS and PTS servers poll each other to determine each other's time before casting their votes. During the time PTSs are adjusting their clocks, the network time might drift slightly during the synchronization process. The other clients and servers take their time from the PTS. Having several PTSs on the network provides a measure of fault tolerance because as one PTS goes down, another PTS can be used to provide an alternate time source. It is recommended that you use one PTS for about every 125 to 150 secondary time servers. If greater fault tolerance is required, you can increase the number of PTSs.

The PTS provides time to other secondary time servers. You should, therefore, locate the PTS so that requests by secondary servers to synchronize their time from a PTS do not have to travel over expensive long-distance links. If the network consists of several locations, each location should have its own PTS.

Please note that Reference Time Servers and Primary Time Servers require another time provider with which they must be able to exchange timing information to remain synchronized. A Reference Time Server or Primary Time Server cannot claim to be synchronized unless it can contact other time provider(s), which are used to compute a common time used by the Primary Time Servers and Secondary Time Servers to initialize their time clocks.

Secondary Time Servers

Secondary Time Servers synchronize their time from a PTS, RTS, or SRTS (see fig. 8.4). Secondary Time Servers do not participate in the vote to obtain a common network time. If an SRTS is used, then all other servers must be Secondary Time Servers and must have a path to the SRTS. If an SRTS is not used, the STS can obtain its time through a PTS. To minimize network traffic and time synchronization delays, the STS should contact the nearest PTS, with a minimum of router hops and network segments between an STS and its time source.

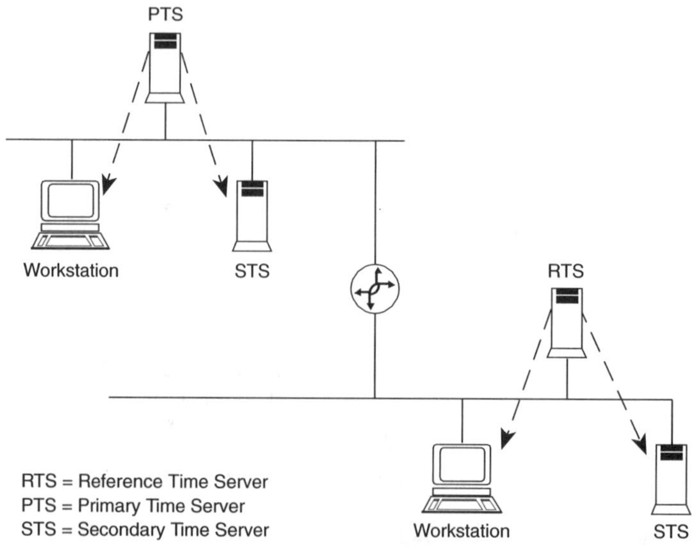

Figure 8.4
Secondary Time Servers.

Implementing Time Synchronization

The timestamps used for synchronization consist of the following two parts:

- The date and time measured in seconds since January 1, 1970
- An event counter that uniquely identifies all events occurring in the same second

To determine the network time, each NetWare 4.x or IntranetWare server keeps track of time zone information and daylight savings time information.

The time zone setting provides the following information:

- An abbreviation for the local time zone name
- Offset of the local time zone from *Universal Time Coordinated* (UTC)
- An abbreviation for the local time zone name to be used during daylight savings time

The city of Bozeman is in Montana in the United States; therefore, its time zone setting is set by the following command:

```
SET TIME ZONE= MST7MDT
```

The time zone without any daylight savings is represented by the characters preceding the start of the time zone offset, which can be any of the following characters: plus (+), minus (-), colon (:), or a digit (0–9). In the preceding example, the string *MST* represents the normal time for the city of Bozeman.

The characters following the time zone offset represent the daylight savings time abbreviation. The time zone offset in this example is seven hours from UTC. In general the time zone offset can be expressed as the following:

```
[+¦-]HH:MM:SS
```

It is customary to simplify the time zone offset and omit the plus sign or the MM:SS, if these fields are zero. For example, a time zone offset of +07:00:00 can be simplified to the single digit 7.

Locations west of zero degrees longitude have a positive time offset, and locations east of zero degrees longitude have a negative time offset. The following formula expresses the relationship between UTC, local time, time zone offset, and daylight savings time offset:

```
UTC = local time + time zone offset - daylight _savings time offset
```

In earlier versions of NetWare, the time zone setting was used by routines in the CLIB.NLM and did not directly affect server time. Starting with NetWare 4.x, the time zone string is used in determining the local time.

Table 8.1 shows the SET parameters that control the daylight savings time in IntranetWare.

Table 8.1
Daylight Savings Time SET Parameters in IntranetWare

SET Parameter	Description
SET Daylight Savings Time Offset	Is converted to seconds and added to the local time when daylight savings time begins for a location. The default value is +1:0:0.
SET Start of Daylight Savings Time	Specifies the rules for computing when daylight savings time commences.
SET End of Daylight Savings Time	Specifies the rules for computing when daylight savings time ends.

continues

Table 8.1, Continued
Daylight Savings Time SET Parameters in IntranetWare

SET Parameter	Description
SET Daylight Savings Time Status	Can have a value of OFF (default) or ON. Changing the value of this parameter does not change local time, but causes UTC to be computed based on the adjusted time offset.
SET New Time with Daylight Savings	Can have a value of OFF (default) or ON. Changing the value of this parameter changes local time based on daylight savings time, but does not change the UTC time.

The preferred method of setting daylight savings time status is to use the SET Start of Daylight Savings Time and SET End of Daylight Savings Time console commands.

These commands are stored in the AUTO-EXEC.NCF file during initial server installation.

Be careful when changing daylight savings time information using SET commands on a server. In particular, be careful not to inadvertently change the UTC time. This might happen if the SET Daylight Savings Time Status is used (see table 8.1). The SET New Time with Daylight Savings Time Status can be used to avoid the recalculation of UTC time and force local time to be recalculated instead.

The goal of time synchronization is to maintain the same UTC time on all NetWare 4.x or IntranetWare servers. Time synchronization deals only with UTC time, but changing UTC time does indirectly change local time to maintain the following time relationships discussed earlier:

```
UTC = local time + time zone offset - daylight _savings time offset
```

Changing the local time, time offset, or daylight savings time offset can cause the UTC time to be recalculated. When time synchronization is active, be cautious about changing local time information.

Time Synchronization Algorithm

Every server on which time synchronization is active shares a fundamental synchronization algorithm, as described in listing 8.1.

Listing 8.1

```
loop forever
// a polling loop or polling interval
begin
```

```
Find a time source (using SAP or direct data communication)
Exchange time information with the time source.
Adjust the time information to account for transmission delays.
Calculate the difference between the local UTC clock and that of
the time source.
Modify the tick rate to correct for difference during the next
sleep.
Go to sleep for the duration of the polling interval.
end loop
```

Each time-synchronized server performs the following three fundamental functions:

- Provides UTC time to any NLM or client workstation that requests it
- Provides status information indicating whether the UTC time is synchronized
- Adjusts its internal clock rate to correct for drift and maintain UTC synchronization

Each server determines if its internal UTC clock is within a maximum error interval, called the *synchronization radius*, of the common network time (the time sources agree to be the network time). If the server time is within the synchronization radius, it sets a synchronization flag in its status information to TRUE. This indicates to TIMESYNC.NLM that the server's internal UTC time can be exchanged as a time stamp with other servers on the network that also have their synchronization flags set. This condition provides a degree of assurance that the UTC time on the server does not differ from the time on other synchronized servers by more than a predictable error. Because time synchronization packets encounter delays and servers poll each other at intervals of time, there is no way to guarantee that the synchronization status on a server is correct at any given instant. Also, the maximum network delay experienced by time synchronization packets must be less than the time synchronization radius. If this is not so, the delays in sending time synchronization packets are excessive. Assuming a default time synchronization radius of two seconds and a signal speed through copper of *0.7× velocity of light in vacuum*, the maximum span of the network is as follows:

```
=2 × (0.7 × velocity of light in vacuum)
=2 secs × (0.7 × 300000000 meter/sec)
=420000000 meters = 420000 km
```

Such a network is large enough to span the Earth—and just about large enough to span the distance between the Earth and the moon!

This frequency at which time servers perform synchronization is controlled by the following SET parameter:

```
SET TIMESYNC POLLING INTERVAL = n
```

In the preceding parameter, *n* is in seconds and has a minimum value of 10 and a maximum value of 2,678,400 (31 days). Its default value is 600 seconds (ten minutes).

The type of time synchronization used on the network is identified during the NetWare 4.x and IntranetWare server installation. The actual time is stored as *Universal Time Coordinated* (UTC), which is the modern name for *Greenwich Mean Time* (GMT).

Because servers can reside in different time zones, the time zone must be selected accurately, and the local daylight savings time convention set correctly. For example, within the continental United States, certain areas do not use daylight savings time. The IntranetWare server is flexible enough to use whatever method is used locally. If necessary, even the Daylight Savings Time rules can be changed by programming them through SET commands on the NetWare 4.x and IntranetWare server. All the time synchronization parameters can be set by the server SET command.

Exchange of Time Information between Time Servers

Time servers poll each other to exchange their timestamps. Figure 8.5 shows how the time exchange might proceed between two servers. This figure shows two time servers attempting to synchronize. The first time server sends a packet containing its local clock reading, *t1*, to the second time server. The second time server notes the timestamp, *t2*, at which this initial packet arrives. The second time server takes a reading of its local time stamp, *t3*, and sends a packet containing *t2* and *t3* to the first time server. The first time server notes the timestamp, *t4*, when the second packet arrives.

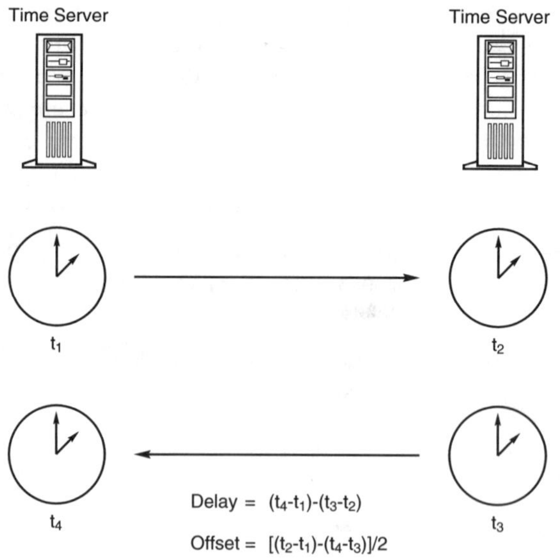

Figure 8.5
Time exchange between servers.

From the readings *t1*, *t2*, *t3*, and *t4*, the first time server can compute the transmission delay to the second server and the *time offset* between the two clocks. These values are calculated in listing 8.2.

Listing 8.2

```
Delay  = Time elapse between sending initial packet and receiving response  -
Time spent in processing packet at second server
Time elapse between sending initial packet and receiving response = t4-t1
Time sent in processing packet at second server = t3-t2
Delay = (t4-t1) - (t3-t2)
```

The time offset is computed as the difference between the time servers' initial readings (*t1* and *t2*) and their second readings (*t3* and *t4*). The resulting time offset value is split between the two time servers; that is, it is divided by two. The offset is computed as follows:

```
Offset = [ (t2-t1) - (t4-t3) ] / 2
```

The time server collects a number of offsets through the synchronization check mechanism previously described before applying a time correction to its clock. The set of offsets might be obtained through a series of synchronization checks with several other time servers. For example, if the server performed synchronization checks with four other time servers and obtained a time offset value of *O1*, *O2*, *O3*, and *O4* using the offset equation discussed earlier, then the set of time offsets is as follows:

```
{ 01, 02, 03, 04 }
```

The time server processes this set of offsets so obtained to compute the *probable clock error.* This process is called *offset filtering*. The probable clock error is computed as the average of the offsets. In the preceding example, probable clock error is computed as follows:

```
Probable Clock Error = ( 01 + 02 + 03 + 04 ) / 4
```

For primary time servers, the clock is corrected at half the probable clock error value. The sign of the correction value is reversed before it is applied because a clock that is ahead must be retarded, and a clock that is behind must be advanced. The following formula shows the corrected time as a function of old network time and the probable clock error.

```
Corrected time = Old Time - (Probable Clock Error) / 2
```

Role of the Clock

Intel-based NetWare 4.x and IntranetWare servers have two types of clocks: *hardware clocks* and *software clocks.* Hardware clocks are battery powered and maintained even when the computer is powered off. Software clocks are maintained by the operating system software and are initialized by the hardware clock during the computer boot process. The software maintains the time using the hardware-based timer interrupts, which occur every tick (1/18.26th of a second). After the boot process, the hardware clock is essentially ignored unless explicitly set by a server console command.

The hardware clocks on most computers are susceptible to errors. The term *clock jitter* describes a short-term variation; the term *wander* to describes long-term variation; and the term *clock drift* describes variations due to aging and ambient (temperature, humidity, and so on) conditions. The purpose of time synchronization is to correct these deviations among multiple clocks in remote locations to within the synchronization radius.

The software clock is maintained by the server in a data structure consisting of several registers and counters modified by the operating system Time Synchronization Services (TSS). The *Time Synchronization Services* control the clock by modifying three 64-bit registers and one 32-bit counter. The 64-bit register contains unsigned values. The most significant 32 bits contain the number of whole seconds, and the lower 32 bits contain the fractional seconds. A value of 1.5 seconds, for example, is represented by listing 8.3, a 64-bit value.

Listing 8.3

```
00000000000000000000000000000001  10000000000000000000000000000000
<—— msb 32 bit (seconds) ——> <-lsb 32 bit(fractional seconds) ->
```

The TIMESYNC.NLM

Time synchronization is implemented by the TIMESYNC.NLM, which can be configured using a number of console SET parameters or by placing configuration parameters in the TIMESYNC.CFG file kept in the SYS:SYSTEM directory. The TIMESYNC.CFG file is a text file and can be edited using any text editor. Alternatively, SERVMAN can be used to make changes in the SET parameters; save these changes in the TIMESYNC.CFG file.

Generally, it is better to make time synchronization changes in the TIMESYNC.CFG file rather than in the AUTOEXEC.NCF file or by using the SET commands at the server console. The TIMESYNC.CFG file is specially designed for time synchronization, whereas the AUTOEXEC.NCF file is used for general purpose server configuration. Also, TIMESYNC.CFG is processed earlier than AUTOEXEC.NCF. TIMESYNC.CFG is processed when the server boots up and TIMESYNC.NLM loads. TIMESYNC.NLM loads before the SYS: volume is mounted, after which AUTOEXEC.NCF is processed.

Using Time Synchronization Parameters

The following steps serve as a guide for using SERVMAN to configure time synchronization parameters:

1. Load SERVMAN from the server console.

2. Select Server Parameters from Available Options. You should see the Select a Parameter Category menu.

3. Select Time. You should see the Time parameters form showing the parameters that affect time synchronization. These time parameters are described in detail in table 8.2.

4. After making changes in the SET parameters, press Esc until you see the Update options menu.

5. Select Update TIMESYNC.CFG now to save parameters in the TIMESYNC.CFG file. Unless explicitly mentioned, the SET parameters in table 8.1 can be placed in the TIMESYNC.CFG file without the TIMESYNC keyword prefix.

6. To save parameter settings to a selected file (called *flushing to a file*), select Copy all parameters to file. Not only the SET TIMESYNC parameters are changed, but all SET commands are changed.

Table 8.2
SET TIMESYNC Parameters

TIMESYNC Parameter	Description
TIMESYNC ADD Time Source=*ts*	This is used to specify the time source, *ts*, to be contacted for obtaining the time. The time source name, *ts*, can be up to 48 characters long. You can use this to build a list of time servers that your server can contact to obtain its time. Normally, SAP is used to obtain the common network time. If this parameter is set, your server contacts the time servers in the order specified until it obtains the time. Only if none of the specified time servers are available will the SAP method be used (unless disabled by TIMESYNC Configured Sources Default parameter). By default this parameter is not set.
TIMESYNC Configuration File Default=pathname	This parameter is used to specify the default path for the configuration file. The default value is SYS:SYSTEM\TIMESYNC.CFG. You can use an alternate path name. You cannot specify this parameter in the TIMESYNC.CFG or AUTOEXEC. NCF file. You can only specify this parameter in the STARTUP.NCF file.
TIMESYNC Configured Sources Default=[ON|OFF]	This parameter is used to control whether your server uses SAP to obtain the time source or a preconfigured list of time servers (set by TIMESYNC ADD Time Source parameter). The default value is OFF, which means SAP will be used. To use a preconfigured list of time servers, set the value to

continues

Table 8.2, Continued
SET TIMESYNC Parameters

TIMESYNC Parameter	Description
	ON. If you set the value to ON, you must use the TIMESYNC ADD Time Source parameter to specify a list of time servers.
TIMESYNC Directory Tree Mode=[ON|OFF]	This parameter is used to specify the NDS tree scope of SAP broadcasts. If you set this parameter to ON, only SAP broadcasts from servers in your NDS tree are used for time synchronization. SAP broadcasts from servers that are not part of your NDS tree are ignored. The default value is ON, which enables you to maintain a tighter control for time synchronization in the NDS tree. If you set this parameter to OFF, SAP broad-casts from any server are used for time synchronization, regardless of the NDS tree to which it belongs.
TIMESYNC Hardware Clock Default=[ON|OFF]	This parameter is used to determine if the IntranetWare server uses an external time source or reads its internal time clock. If this parameter set to OFF, your server contacts an external time source (such as an atomic clock or radio clock) to obtain its time. The default is ON, which means that your server reads its internal clock. If this parameter is set to ON for Single or Reference time servers, these servers read their clocks. If this parameter is set to ON for Primary or Secondary time servers, these servers set their clocks based on the common network time.
TIMESYNC Polling Count Default=*n*	This parameter sets the number of time synchronization packets that will be exchanged during a polling cycle. The polling cycle is used for time synchronization. The default value is 3 and can range from 1 to 1,000. If you increase the value, the amount of synchronization traffic increases. Novell recommends that you do not increase this setting (unless you have a very good reason).
TIMESYNC Polling Interval Default=*t*	This parameter sets the amount of time, in seconds, that elapses between polling cycles. The default is 600 seconds (10 minutes), and the value can range from 10 to 2,678,400 seconds (31 days).

TIMESYNC Parameter	Description
	If you decrease this time parameter, your servers will be more closely synchronized, but the network time increases. If you want to decrease the network traffic due to polling cycles, you should increase this value. For slower WAN links, you might want to increase the polling interval.
TIMESYNC Remove Time Source=*ts*	This parameter is used to remove the specified time source from a list of configured time sources. It is primarily meant to be issued from the server console to make deletions in the list. This command is usually not added in the TIMESYNC. CFG or AUTOEXEC.NCF file.
TIMESYNC Reset =[ON|OFF]	This parameter resets the values changed by the TIMESYNC.CFG or SET TIMESYNC commands to their default values and removes the list of time sources. It does not alter the contents of the TIMESYNC.CFG or AUTOEXEC.NCF file. It only resets the current values of the parameters for the server. After the value is changed to ON, it executes the actions described and resets to OFF. The default value is OFF.
TIMESYNC Restart Flag =[ON|OFF]	This parameter is used to restart TIMESYNC.NLM with a new set of values from the TIMESYNC.CFG file without rebooting the server. After the value is changed to ON, it executes the actions described and resets to OFF. The default value is OFF.
TIMESYNC Service Advertising =[ON|OFF]	This is used by time providers *only*, not time consumers (secondary time servers), to determine the method by which the time source should advertise. This parameter has no effect on secondary time servers. The default value is ON, which means that time providers use SAP broadcasts for advertising time. If you set the TIMESYNC Configured Sources to ON, you should set the value of this parameter to OFF.
TIMESYNC Synchronization Radius Default=*t*	This parameter determines the "error" bounds for time synchronization. It determines how far apart the times on the servers can be before adjustment is necessary. If you set this parameter to a high value, you allow for larger differences between times on

continues

Table 8.2, Continued
SET TIMESYNC Parameters

TIMESYNC Parameter	Description
	servers. If the error margin is too large, it can reduce the integrity of NDS transactions being done in the correct sequence. If the radius is small, the servers are more closely synchronized but generate greater synchronization traffic. If the radius is made too small, time synchronization becomes difficult, if not impossible, to achieve. The value is measured in milliseconds and has a default of 2,000 milliseconds. It can range from 0 to 2,147,483,647 milliseconds.
TIMESYNC Time Adjustment =[+|-]*hh:mm:ss*[[*AT mm/ dd/ yy hh:mm:ss*	This parameter can be used to manually adjust time on a Single Reference or [AM|PM]] [CANCEL]] Primary time server. Use this command sparingly to correct network-wide time errors. Frequent use of this command can corrupt time synchronization on the network, and this causes inconsistencies in the order of events performed on the network. The AT option can be used to schedule a time adjustment on the specified day *mm/ dd/ yy* and time *hh:mm:ss*. To cancel a previously scheduled time adjustment, use CANCEL instead of AT. The maximum length of the value is 99 characters. The default date and time is six polling intervals or one hour from now, whichever is larger.
TIMESYNC Time Source = *ts*	This adds the name of the time source, ts, to the configured list of servers. When used without specifying a value, it displays a list of current time servers.
TIMESYNC Type = *type*	This is used to set the *type* of time server active on the file server. The *type* can have any of the following values: SINGLE, REFERENCE, PRIMARY, SECONDARY. SINGLE refers to Single Reference Time Servers; REFERENCE refers to Reference Time Servers; PRIMARY refers to Primary Time Servers; SECONDARY refers to Secondary Time Servers. The default value is SECONDARY.

TIMESYNC Parameter	Description
TIMESYNC Write Parameters =[ON|OFF]	When set to ON, this causes certain parameters (controlled by TIMESYNC Write Value parameter) to be written to the TIMESYNC.CFG file. The default is OFF.
TIMESYNC Write Value= *n*	The value of *n* controls the type of parameters Value written to the TIMESYNC.CFG file, if TIMESYNC Write Parameters is ON. If *n* is set to 1, only internal parameters from this file server are written to TIMESYNC.CFG. If *n* is set to 2, only external parameters from servers on the TIMESYNCTIME SOURCE list are written to TIMESYNC.CFG. If *n* is set to 3, both internal and external parameters from servers on the TIMESYNC TIME SOURCE list are written to TIMESYNC.CFG. The default value is 3.
Time Zone *sss* = *sssNddd*	This parameter determines the offset from UTC. refers to the standard time zone. Examples are PST, MST, CST, and EST. These are three letter abbreviations for U.S. Pacific Standard Time, U.S. Mountain Standard Time, U.S. Central Standard Time, and U.S. Eastern Standard Time, respectively. *N* refers to the number of hours offset from UTC. U.S. Pacific Coast is eight hours from UTC, and U.S. East Coast is five hours from UTC. The *ddd* indicates if daylight savings time is in effect. PDT = U.S. Pacific Daylight Savings Time. MDT = U.S. Mountain Daylight Savings Time. CDT = U.S. Central Daylight Savings Time. EDT = U.S. Eastern Daylight Savings Time.

Service Advertising Protocol versus Custom Time Synchronization

Time servers discover the existence of other time servers by using either of the following methods:

- Service Advertising Protocol (SAP)
- Direct communication (custom configuration)

The SAP is used by services, including time servers, to broadcast their existence across the network. For small networks, this is a very effective and simple way to discover services on the network, because it does not require extra configuration. On large networks, however, the SAP can use up large amounts of bandwidth. Use of the NLSP protocol (see Chapter 26, "Bridging, Switching, and Routing," on the CD.) to advertise services can eliminate the proliferating nature of SAP. Another solution is to use direct communication between time servers. The time servers are initialized with a list of other time sources using the following SET parameter:

```
SET TIMESYNC TIME SOURCE = time server
```

In addition, you must use the following SET commands (listing 8.4) to disable the use of SAP in conjunction with time servers.

Listing 8.4

```
SET TIMESYNC CONFIGURED SOURCES DEFAULT= ON
SET TIMESYNC SERVICE ADVERTISING = OFF (on time sources)
```

Custom configuration involves determining which servers on the network are time sources and which servers follow what time source. Each server is then given a configuration file (TIMESYNC.CFG) that lists the authorized time sources for that server and its parameters.

Secondary servers attempt to contact the time sources in the order listed and stop as soon as any time source is reached. It is even possible, at the risk of a greater time synchronization error, to have a secondary time server contact another time server. In most situations, the secondary servers can contact the other time source servers.

The following are some of the advantages of custom configuration:

- You have complete control of the time synchronization hierarchy.
- You can distribute time sources around the network based on the strategy of minimizing network traffic and improving reliability of time synchronization.
- You can increase the reliability of time synchronization by adding alternate time sources to be used in case of network failures.
- You can eliminate the excessive traffic caused by the use of SAP for finding out other time servers.

Custom configuration has the following disadvantages:

- Customization is more complex and requires careful planning, especially for large networks.
- If a new time source is added, the configuration files on other time servers have to be updated. The only way other time servers will discover the new time source is if they are explicitly told about it in their configuration files. Otherwise, the new time server will never be contacted.

In larger networks, a number of decisions need to be made concerning time synchronization. Some of the more important issues are included in the following list:

1. Which servers will be time sources (PTS, RTS) and which will be Secondary servers?
2. Will time synchronization use SAP exclusively to discover time servers, a configured sources list, or a combination of the two?

   To keep network design simple, you can decide to use either SAP or custom configuration. You can eliminate use of SAP for time synchronization by using the SET TIMESYNC SERVICE ADVERTISING = OFF and SET TIMESYNC CONFIGURED SOURCES DEFAULT = ON parameters in the TIMESYNC.CFG file.
3. If servers are to use a configured sources list, which servers will contact which time sources?
4. If more than one NDS tree is on the same network, will the trees be time synchronized independently or together?
5. Figure out how you will set the value of the polling interval, the polling count, and the synchronization radius. In most cases, the default values are adequate. You can consult the description of these parameters in table 8.2 and the discussion on determining network traffic due to synchronization, in the next section, to optimize these parameters.
6. Will there be more than one RTS? What external time sources will be used to synchronize the RTS?

Determining the Effects of Time Synchronization Traffic

The network traffic generated by time synchronization is determined by the size of the time synchronization packets and the number of time exchanges during each polling loop. The number of exchanges during each polling loop is determined by the following polling count parameter:

```
SET  TIMESYNC POLLING COUNT DEFAULT = n
```

The default value of this parameter is three—that is, it takes three time exchanges, each of which involve an NCP send/receive pair. Each NCP send/receive pair totals 332 bytes of data. Thus, the default three exchanges involve six packets—a total 996 bytes of data.

The frequency of polls is determined by the following SET parameter:

```
SET TIMESYNC POLLING INTERVAL DEFAULT=t
```

The default value of this parameter is 600 seconds (ten minutes), although when time synchronization is first started, polling occurs every ten seconds.

At the beginning of time synchronization, the time synchronization traffic is represented by the following equation:

```
= 996 Bytes/10 seconds = 996 Bytes × 8 Bits/Byte /_10
= 797 bits/sec
```

When time synchronization stabilizes, the default time synchronization traffic is as follows:

```
= 996 Bytes/600 seconds = 996 Bytes × 8 Bits/Byte _/600
= 8 bits/sec
```

As the number of *PTS* and *RTS* servers increases, the number of time synchronizations increases. If there are n time servers, the number of separate server exchanges is as given by the following:

```
N(N-1)/2
```

For a network with five time servers, the number of exchanges is computed as follows:

```
5(5-1)/2 = 10
```

For a network with ten time servers, the number of exchanges is computed as follows:

```
10(10-1)/2 = 45
```

Table 8.3 shows the traffic rates for different numbers of time servers. As the network grows and requires additional time servers, the amount of synchronization traffic grows. You can increase the polling interval to reduce the amount of time synchronization traffic as long as the server clocks do not drift beyond the synchronization radius during the polling interval. Increasing the polling interval might become necessary if the synchronization traffic is occurring over a slow WAN link. As you can see from table 8.3, on most networks the amount of synchronization traffic is small compared to traffic associated with network use.

Table 8.3
Estimates for Time Synchronization Traffic
Assuming a Default Poll Count of Three

Polling Interval (secs)	Number of Time Servers	Time Synchronization Traffic
10	2	797 bps
10	5	8.0 Kbps
10	10	35.9 bps
10	50	976.3 Kbps

Polling Interval (secs)	Number of Time Servers	Time Synchronization Traffic
10	100	3.94 Mbps
600	2	13 bps
600	5	130 bps
600	10	585 bps
600	50	15.9 Kbps
600	100	64.4 Kbps

Building a Time Synchronization Hierarchy

On large networks, it is useful to build a hierarchy of time servers. The time servers at the top level of this hierarchy are closely synchronized, and servers at lower levels are synchronized to servers on the next higher level. The hierarchical structure of the time servers is based on physical location of servers and synchronization traffic considerations and is independent of the hierarchical structure of the NDS tree.

As the number of levels in the time server hierarchy grows, the synchronization error between the top level and lower level time servers increases. In general, the time synchronization error between the top level and any lower level is directly proportional to the number of intervening levels.

The following are some suggestions to help you organize your time synchronization hierarchy:

1. Have Secondary servers synchronize to time sources such as the Primary, Reference, or Single Reference servers.

2. If Secondary servers must follow other Secondary servers, keep the depth of the tree as small as possible.

3. Minimize the number of time sources to keep network traffic low. The number of packet exchanges between N time servers is proportional to $N \times N$.

4. On large networks, use multiple time sources to reduce time synchronization network traffic. Use local time sources in separate geographic locations.

Repairing Time Synchronization

The best laid plans of network designers can sometimes go astray, and it is possible to lose time synchronization on the network. This can occur when links go down and the time servers are unable to contact each other to maintain proper time synchronization. The clock drift on most computers is such that they are accurate for a few hours without correction. If time synchronization is lost for a long period of time, it is possible for replicas on different servers to contain inconsistent views of the Directory tree. Timestamp problems can be repaired using the partition manager client utilities. These utilities assume that the master replica of the partition contains the most up-to-date information. The master replica of a partition is copied over to other replica types of the partition and overwrites these replicas. If the master replica does not contain the most recent information, more recent changes made to other replicas are lost.

If you can determine that some replica other than the master partition contains the most recent information, you must use the partition manager to change the most current replica to a master replica.

Several hidden parameters in TIMESYNC can be used for fine-tuning the synchronization algorithm. These parameters may be eliminated in future releases of TIMESYNC. Although they are still available, they might prove to be useful in debugging time synchronization activities.

You can enable time synchronization using the following command:

```
SET TIMESYNC DEBUG = 7
```

The preceding command displays time synchronization activity on the server console. To disable it, use the following command:

```
SET TIMESYNC DEBUG = 0
```

The TIMESYNC DEBUG parameter can be set to other values, in which each bit value in the number controls a group of messages or disables output altogether.

Information on decoding these message types is provided in listing 8.5.

Listing 8.5

```
TIMESYNC: Polled server NW4CS
Weight = 1, OFFSET.H = FFFFFFFF OFFSET.L = FFF03453
```

In the preceding message, the name of the polled server is NW4CS. The Weight value of 1 indicates that time synchronization exchange was successful. A value of 0 indicates that time synchronization did not take place because out-of-range data was detected. This might be because the time server is unreachable (not up or network link is down). The values for OFFSET.H and OFFSET.L are the calculated difference of the server's time from the polled server's time. The two values form a 64-bit signed number with an implied hexadecimal point separating the whole and fractional parts. In the preceding message, the OFFSET values form the number FFFFFFFF.FFF03453, which means that the server is a fraction ahead of NW4CS.

A reported Weight of 0 with nonzero offset values indicates that the synchronization data is out of range. For example, this might occur if one server is 10 years ahead of the other.

If a message of the preceding type does not appear at all, it implies that this time server does not know about any other time servers. This might be because the configured time source list is empty, or no SAP time source can be found, or both. If you disabled the use of SAP, the only possible cause is that the configured time source list is empty.

To examine the current setting of the time source list, use the following command on the server console:

```
SET TIMESYNC TIME SOURCE =
```

Consider another message type that appears as follows:

```
Uniform Adjustment Requested = -0.0E0F98DD
Server type = 2
```

This message shows the actual adjustment (Uniform Adjustment Requested) to be applied to the clock during the next polling period. The server type values reported have the following meanings:

```
2=Secondary Time Server
3=Primary Time Server
4=Reference Time Server
5=Single Reference Time Server
```

The time adjustment value is displayed as signed hexadecimal. In this case, the sign is a minus, so the time will be subtracted because the server is ahead of the polled server. The value 0.0E0F98DD corresponds to one tick. Generally, one-tick or half-tick errors are caused by random time behaviors and network delays between the two time servers. If an adjustment of +0.00000000 is seen, the time servers are in exact synchronization. You also might see this value stabilize at a small negative value, such as –.00000094, due to a small round-off error in the synchronization algorithm. An error of 0.00000094 corresponds to 34 nanoseconds, which is much smaller than the resolution of the time server clock.

Consider another message type that commonly appears as follows:

```
Adjustment smaller than Correction Floor was ignored.
```

This message means that the clock adjustment is so small that it is being ignored. The parameter that determines the "cut-off" value is set by the following command:

```
SET TIMESYNC CORRECTION FLOOR = t
```

The default value of this parameter is 1 millisecond and can be set to a value of t milliseconds. This value must always be less than the synchronization radius or synchronization does not occur. You can use this parameter to eliminate the correction for the one-tick jitter that sometimes occurs.

Another interesting undocumented time synchronization parameter is the following:

```
SET TIMESYNC IMMEDIATE SYNCHRONIZATION = ON
```

The preceding SET command awakens the synchronization process immediately and causes it to start a polling loop. After synchronization it automatically resets to OFF. You can use this to observe the effects of parameter setting changes immediately by forcing a time synchronization rather than waiting for time synchronization at the end of the polling interval.

If time servers fail to synchronize, check for obvious errors. The most common reason is that there are no reachable time sources. In this case, check the time source list or network connections. You can turn on the debug option by using the following command:

```
SET TIMESYNC DEBUG = 7
```

From the messages displayed, you can determine if the server is attempting to contact a time source. If the server's time is set far ahead, time synchronization might take a long time. The server's time does not move backwards. It could take two hours to lose two hours. Check the server's time and manually adjust the clock, if necessary.

When booting a new server, it might take several seconds before the new server learns about the other time servers. If using SAP, the SAP messages are received at the next SAP broadcast interval. Also, before exchanging time synchronization messages, a route request can be used to discover the address of the forwarding router. All this adds a few seconds of delays initially.

As long as one time source remains active, other time sources can be shut down and rebooted. A time server, upon joining the network, polls for and uses the network time. If only two time sources are on a network and these are booted for the first time, the time on the first server that polls is used as the initial value of the network time.

Occasionally, NDS might report the following error even though the SET TIME command reveals that the server times are synchronized:

```
Time_Not_Synchronized - Error 659 (FD6D)
```

This error actually occurs when NDS receives a timestamp older than information already in the Directory. This could happen if the server's time was set backwards, such as in the situation of losing the *Complementary Metal Oxide Semiconductor* (CMOS) battery or the server time being set incorrectly when the server was booted.

If the local time is misconfigured while time synchronization is active, the UTC time is also incorrect. The Time Synchronization mechanism attempts to adjust UTC time to correspond to the network time, which in turn changes local time. Time synchronization might therefore fight efforts to correct misconfigured local parameters. If the local time is badly misconfigured while time synchronization is active, you can reset time synchronization by using the following command:

```
SET TIMESYNC RESTART = ON
```

You also can bring the server down and up again. TIMESYNC.NLM is automatically loaded when the server is started. NetWare 4.01 does not ship with a separate TIMESYNC.NLM, so if you unload it using the UNLOAD command, you cannot load it without bringing the server down and up. You can contact Novell Technical Support to obtain a copy of TIMESYNC.NLM.

Summary

In this chapter, you learned about the importance of time synchronization on a distributed network consisting of many servers. Time synchronization is accomplished by running the TIMESYNC.NLM on each NetWare 4.x and IntranetWare server. You learned about the different time server types that can be used in NetWare 4.x and IntranetWare networks and when to use a particular time server type.

You also learned about the different SET parameters that can be used to affect time synchronization, and how the SAP and direct communication methods are used by time servers to find each other.

CHAPTER 9

NetWare Enhanced Security Services

The discipline of secure computing has gained a lot of attention over the years. Although security is seemingly high on the list of priorities for most people, factors of usability, performance, and information exchange appear to quickly diminish the importance of that security. System security is quite definitely a balancing game and as such it will require those in charge to perform a complete system analysis of security, usability, and performance before deciding upon a solution.

The goal of this chapter is to present one way to protect the information on your Novell network. The approach taken is that of configuring your network to run as a NetWare Enhanced Security network. Before examining this approach, this chapter begins with an overview of computer security.

Russell and Gangemi, in their text *Computer Security Basics,* define computer security as the following three aspects:

- **Secrecy.** Can be viewed as confidentiality. When examining your system for secrecy, you examine access controls (who is allowed to see what information), how those access controls are implemented (Mandatory vs. Discretionary), and possibly topics of data encryption.

- **Accuracy.** Demonstrates the integrity of the information you are storing. Accuracy allows you to be sure that when you receive information from the sender, the information is exactly what that sender had sent (has integrity), and that it is truly the user who sent you the information (non-repudiated).

- **Availability.** Availability is the assurance that your information will be made accessible to the intended user when that user requests it. Availability has become the prevention of what is known as denial of service attack. The usefulness of a system with high secrecy and accuracy becomes useless if an external user can exploit a bug that crashes your system repeatedly.

When you seek to solve a problem in system security, you must first identify the above areas that you wish to improve. The National Computer Security Center (NCSC) did just that when it wrote the *Trusted Computer Security Evaluation Criteria* (*Orange Book*). This book identifies certain areas that it decided needed to be addressed. In doing so it set forth a set of six models (C1, C2, B1, B2, B3, A1) that provide clear definitions and assurances for system security. For instance, the *Orange Book* does not deal with data encryption. It does, however, deal with access controls, auditing, identification and authentication, and assurances.

Novell has chosen to implement one of the NCSC models, C2. Because NetWare is a network server, Novell has implemented a model from the NCSC's network-based book, the *Trusted Network Interpretation* (*Red Book*). This model and implementation is discussed in the first section.

This chapter will give the reader an understanding of NetWare Enhanced Security (NES), which is Novell's implementation of the *Orange Book's* class C2 rating. At the time of this writing, Novell is in the final stages of having the NCSC evaluate NetWare 4.11 as a Class C2 network product. After years of work in preparing documentation, testing, and of course, building the product to meet the C2 specifications, NetWare 4.11 will be the only off-the-shelf, Class C2 evaluated network available.

This chapter has two sections. The first is a brief overview of C2 security and how it relates to Novell NetWare 4.11. The second section reviews installation issues of NetWare Enhanced Security (NES).

An Introduction to C2 Level Security

This section gives an overview of Class C2 security as it relates to Novell's NES network. It also defines some of the vocabulary used in network security, and gives refresher information to those already familiar with the industry. It is not written to teach, per se, but rather review basic computer security terminology.

It is assumed that the reader of this section is a security professional with an interest in designing a secure network around the NES server.

> **Note**
>
> You need not be a security guru to make your NetWare server an NES system. However, to create and maintain a full blown NES network is quite a different story. Network security administration is a tremendous job. It requires in-depth knowledge of security issues and a strong commitment to providing support to the network. This is not a job to be taken lightly.
>
> Other requirements, such as a site security plan, although not required by C2, are essential to maintaining security in a networked environment. You will need to reference your site security policy often when making decisions during the configuration of NES.

Note that an installation of the NES server only will be done, not of the NES client workstation. Client workstations are provided by third-party vendors and are not supported by Novell directly; consequently, vendors will provide their own installation requirements and instructions.

A Definition of Security: TCSEC

The *Trusted Computer System Evaluation Criteria* (TCSEC) is a document distributed by the Department of Defense in 1985. Known as the *Orange Book*, this document builds a definition of security for three purposes:

- To provide a standard for manufacturers on what to build in a secure system
- To provide a metric to measure security
- To provide the government with an easy way to make acquisition requests

The *Orange Book* begins by defining the "security relevant portions of a system" as the *Trusted Computing Base* (TCB). Essentially, this is any hardware, software, or firmware that is used in enforcing the security policy of the system. This may or may not be the entire operating system. This may or may not be all the pieces of hardware attached to that system. The TCB is the security perimeter around the system. The TCB is evaluated by the National Computer Security Center (NCSC).

The TCB must have privileges that extend to the hardware level that allow for switching control between trusted and untested software. For instance, on one of the clients in an NES environment, the TCB would allow for the use of a PC in a standard form (for example, running normal programs, or printing to an attached printer). However, when the system is talking to the trusted network, the TCB has full control and will disallow any user programs to gain access to the network.

The TCB will identify and authenticate the user using a user id and password combination. It can then associate that user with a subject (for example, process running a shell). It will use the security policy of the system to make decisions on whether the subject has access to an object. It will also record any subject events, according to the security policy, in the audit trail (see fig. 9.1).

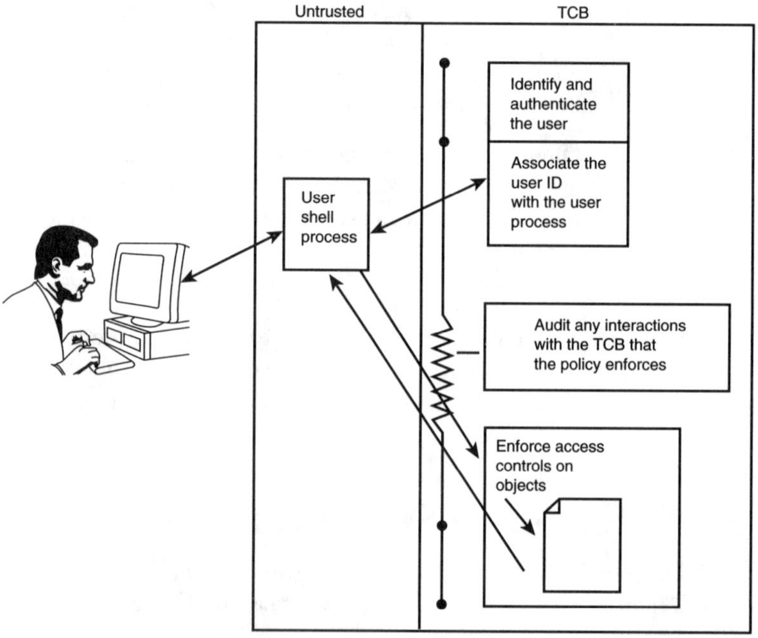

Figure 9.1
Overview of the TCB.

In the *Orange Book, subjects* can be thought of as user processes or devices that act upon objects. An *object* is a passive entity that is acted upon (for example, files, programs, printers, and so on).

TCSEC defines seven levels of trust: D, C1, C2, B1, B2, B3, and A1 (in an increasing order of trust). Because the *Orange Book* was written with system security in mind, rather than network security, this chapter does not go into any detail about these levels of trust. Instead, it examines the *Red Book,* which was written to deal with network security. This book expounds upon these levels of trust as applied to networks.

An Interpretation of a Definition of Security: TNI

The *Trusted Network Interpretation Of The Trusted Computer System Evaluation Criteria* (TNI) was put out by the Department of Defense in 1987 [NCSC-TG-005]. This is known to security professionals as the *Red Book* and, as the title suggests, gives an interpretation of TCSEC (the *Orange Book*) as it applies to computer networks.

The TNI extends the concept of a Trusted Computing Base (TCB) to what is referred to as a Network Trusted Computing Base (NTCB). Because a trusted network is essentially built on many component TCBs (for example, servers, clients, and so on), the term NTCB is used to describe the totality of this trust. Now, each of the components of the NTCB are not TCBs but rather an NTCB partition. The NTCB not only performs the functions of a TCB for each component, but it must also make sure interconnections are trusted. This means the network protocol must maintain its association with the user and allow for secure inter-component access (for example, you cannot run Lanalyzer on NES). Figure 9.2 illustrates these concepts.

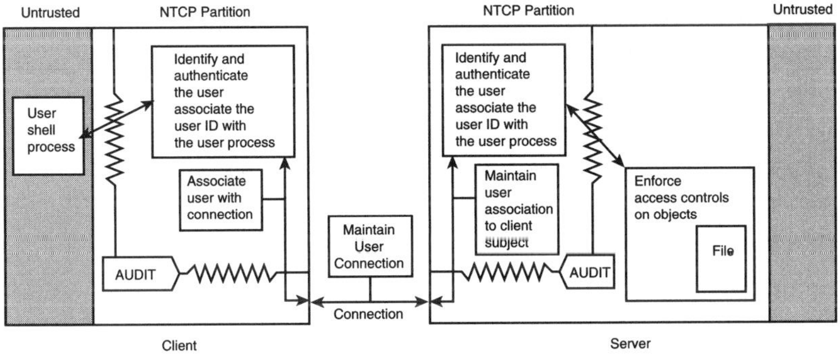

Figure 9.2
Overview of the NTCB.

NES allows users to be identified at all points within the network. The users' actions are controlled by what is known as the *security policy* of the system. This security policy is controlled by the *site security policy.* The actions of the user may also be audited by the network system, depending on the security policy.

Note

The *site security policy* is a set of rules the site (i.e. corporation) has implemented to monitor how its users are allowed to access information. Essentially, it details who is allowed access to what. Generally, portions of the site security policy are distributed to employees to inform them of their allowed network resources.

The *security policy* of the system is a set of protocols the system uses to implement your site security policy.

The seven levels of trust mentioned in the previous section are expanded upon in the TNI. For instance, each class addressed in the *Orange Book* is repeated in the *Red Book* and followed by an interpretation of the class and a rationale for that interpretation. The level of trust that you are concerned with is Class C2: Controlled Access Protection.

One of the advantages that the Novell NES network has is the evaluation was approached in a modular fashion. The NCSC and Novell allows for additional components to be evaluated and then plugged into the network. This is a tremendous advantage to third party developers wishing to build components for NES.

Understanding Class C2 Security

C2 is a class of network security that is defined in the *Orange Book* and interpreted in the *Red Book.* Class C2 is defined as:

> Network systems defined in this class enforce a more finely grained discretionary access control than (C1) network systems, making users individually accountable for their actions through login procedures, auditing of security-related events, and resource isolation.

Following is a summary of each area of the Class C2 definition as it applies to Novell's NetWare 4.11 NES server. Any and all quotes in the description of C2 are taken from the corresponding section of the *Red Book.*

Security Policy

The security policy of NetWare 4.11 is the set of rules explaining how NES protects its data. It defines how subjects (for example, users) interact with objects (for example, files, other servers, printers, and so on).

The *Orange Book* (and therefore the *Red Book*) examines two areas of the security policy of a system. They are Discretionary Access Controls and Object Reuse. Both of these areas are looked at in the following sections.

Discretionary Access Controls (DAC)

NES defines controlled access between all of its Novell Directory Services (NDS) objects (i.e. users, files, printers, and so on). Controlled access is defined in one of two contexts in the *Orange Book.* They are *Discretionary Access Controls* and *Mandatory Access Controls.*

Mandatory Access Control (MAC) is a powerful access control policy that uses a predefined set of access control rules to prevent users from accidentally (or willfully) sharing sensitive data to unauthorized users. It works on the premise that if you do not belong to the proper group(s) you simply cannot access that data. Unlike Discretionary Access Controls, you are not allowed to grant any users rights to the data. MAC is not a requirement for Class C2, and therefore not implemented in NES.

Discretionary Access Controls (DAC) are used in NES to allow owners of sensitive data to give other users access to their data. This form of sharing is not as secure as MAC, however, when implemented correctly it can be a very useful security policy.

DAC is generally implemented by the use of an *Access Control List* (ACL).The ACL allows users to specify access to objects that are shared. This access is granted to individual users, groups of users, or both. To state this simply, if you, an owner of an object, would like the User JANE and the Group R&D to Read your object, then you, the owner, have to assign rights to the User JANE and Group R&D to Read your object. The security administrator also has rights to grant access to objects.

Object Reuse

Object Reuse is a term used to describe the security of an object that has been released from privilege use. For example, if the System Administrator examines a file that contains a list of users and their phone numbers, the file gets read into memory. When the System Administrator finishes reading the file, he closes the object and the memory used to store the file gets released. This memory is now available to anyone on the system by simply allocating some new memory. If this memory is not cleared before it is given to another process, the sensitive information could be compromised. It is therefore important to have a good Object Reuse policy.

Object Reuse in NES requires that resources be cleared before being allocated to a program. This includes memory, disk space, password buffers, printer memory, terminal memory, and so on.

Accountability

Accountability defines who you are, what you are doing, and whether you can do it. C2 requires the following two areas of accountability:

- Identification and Authentication
- Auditing

Identification and Authentication

NES requires that a user identify himself or herself to the network. Identification is done in NES by providing a user name. Authentication is then established when the user provides a password. This user name identifies individual accountability. This individuality allows the system to check whether the user has access privileges to resources on the network. Individual accountability is required to enable the Discretionary Access Controls stated previously, and also to enable auditing, a requirement mentioned next.

Authentication can be established in many ways. Fingerprint scans, retinal examinations, challenge and response computers, and, of course, passwords. NES requires the use of passwords to Authenticate to the system. It is recommended that security policy of the system specify that the passwords be of a certain length, have certain non-alphanumeric characters (#,!,%,&, and so on), and have an expiration when the user will be forced to change the password.

Auditing

NES is required to have auditing capabilities, but it is up to the administrator to implement them on the network. C2 requires auditable actions to be associated with individual users. Other information found in the audit trail is: a date and time stamp, type of event, outcome of event, origin of event, and the involved objects.

Along with the requirement of auditing security-related events, it is also a requirement to protect the audited data from malicious or accidental tampering.

Assurance

Assurance comes from the confidence of NES Systems ability to implement the security policy of the NTCB correctly. The following list shows the two types of assurance:

- operational assurance
- life-cycle assurance

Operational Assurance

Operational assurance focuses on the basic architecture and features of the NTCB.

System Architecture

The architecture of NES allows for the security relevant functions to be separated from user programs. This is done by making the entire NES Server a NTCB partition in itself. No user programs can be run from the server, only evaluated NLMs. On the client side, the NTCB partition is separated by the design of the client. The user programs are separated from client NTCB partition that interacts with the Server NTCB partition.

The same system architecture prevents resources within the NTCB partition from being tampered with by users.

System Integrity

The system integrity tests ensure that the hardware and firmware of the system are working as intended. This is accomplished during the boot process of the system.

Life-Cycle Assurance

The design and development of NES is required to be maintained with formal standards. This insures that the hardware and software are not modified during the systems life-cycle.

Security Testing

NES is tested to assure that there are no obvious ways for users to bypass the security protection of the NTCB. This is done by "searching for obvious flaws that would allow violation of resource isolation, or that would permit unauthorized access to the audit or authentication data." The documentation of this testing is described in the next section.

Documentation

Documenting a Trusted System is a tremendous job. The range of documentation varies from user manuals to design and test documentation. The documentation required is grouped into four areas:

- Security Features Users Guide
- Trusted Facility Manual
- Test documentation
- Design documentation

As you can imagine, the first two are generally mapped to individual books. The latter two however, can consist of volumes.

Security Features Users Guide

The *Security Features Users Guide* is a manual that explains to users of NES about the security features of the system. The NetWare manual called, you guessed it, *Security Features Users Guide,* is Novell's implementation of this required document. This is part of the NetWare 4.11 Enhanced Security online distribution that can be found on the IntranetWare distribution CDs.

Trusted Facility Manual

Novell has provided the NCSC with a document entitled *Trusted Facility Manual.* This document is now being partially passed on to the user as *NetWare Enhanced Security Administration* (in the online distribution). The remainder of the original TFM describes auditing in detail.

Test Documentation

Novell provides the NCSC documentation of a test plan, test procedures, and test results of NES. Tens of thousands of tests have been developed and performed on NES. Security related tests are documented in the official test documentation. This documentation also includes a test plan that will ensure that all areas of NES are tested to adequately.

Design Documentation

This documentation explains how Novell has implemented its "philosophy of protection" within NES. It includes information on interfaces between NTCB modules and partitions. At the C2 level the design must be free from any "obvious flaws" as stated above.

If you desire to understand the architecture of NES, the design documentation is what you need to read. Novell's *Network Security Architecture and Design* documentation is a useful description of the NetWare 4.11 evaluated C2 product. This will give you information on services available within NES, including how the client-server design relates to the architecture, supported protocols in NES, the security policy of the network, and the NTCB. It is a must for anyone interested in understanding NES at its core level.

When submitted to the NCSC, NES is broken down into its NTCB partitions. Partitions, of course, are pieces of a whole network. For instance, a NetWare 4.11 trusted network is comprised of the following components:

- Servers
- Clients
- Interconnections
- Media

Each of these components contains an NTCB partition. Each of these NTCB partitions is responsible for maintaining the security policy for its area. When NetWare is first evaluated, it is evaluated with initial components. After the initial evaluation, additional components can then be evaluated and added to the C2 network. For instance, if Microsoft NT evaluated its workstation as part of a NetWare C2 network, the Microsoft NT station could be used as a client in Novell's NES environment. However, without this evaluation, Microsoft is not allowed to use their client in the C2 network. Instead, clients that were evaluated are allowed in.

A tremendous amount of work has gone into designing NetWare 4.11 as a C2 evaluated network server. There is also a tremendous amount of work required to create your own Class C2 network. If this is your desire, the next chapter will help you in installing your NES server. This is only a portion of the work required. If you do not have a site security plan, you should develop one before implementing NES. Also, make sure you have a trusted staff to support your C2 network. Depending on the size, this could require many knowledgeable individuals.

Installing a NetWare Enhanced Security Server

This section gives an overview of the process for setting up a NetWare Enhanced Security Server. Simply, this section describes topics you will need to examine when you do an NES installation. One chapter in a book could not possibly do justice to installing a C2 network. This would almost certainly be a mockery of security itself. However, this chapter will explain the installation process and cover specific security areas that the NetWare Enhanced Security Administration manual covers in greater detail. It would be wise to read this section before actually performing your NES installation. Doing this gives you a heads-up to all the areas you need to understand before you proceed with the installation. A knowledgeable system administrator with expertise in NetWare and security would be able to perform such an installation with just this chapter; however, this is assuming that a formal security policy that is NetWare-specific is already laid out. If anything else, this chapter will certainly bring a respect on the amount of information required in performing an NES installation.

Client Access to the Server

Novell does not provide a client for an NES network. Clients are provided by third-party manufacturers such as Cordant, and others. Remember that you cannot place any MS-DOS or MS-Windows client into an NES network; only certified clients that have been evaluated in a NES network are allowed. This does not include a standard MS-DOS, OS/2, MS-Windows 95, or MS-Windows NT Workstation/Server. Contact the Novell YES-certified program to get information on certified clients.

Overview of Installation

The process for installing a NetWare Enhanced Security Server can be divided into three sections:

1. NES hardware selection
2. Special NES installation issues
3. NES configuration issues

Essentially, you begin by making sure you use only hardware that is allowed by NES. After setting up the correct hardware, you perform a standard installation of NetWare 4.11, noting the special NES installation issues. After you install the server, the final step is to configure it with the NES configuration.

> **Note** Novell's 2.x, 3.x, 4.0, 4.01, and 4.10 servers are not evaluated to C2 level security. You may not upgrade these unevaluated versions of NetWare to NES. You must perform a complete installation.

Setting up an NES is not difficult. Creating a useful security plan is. Your C2 network security will only be as good as the plan that implements it. A security policy is a must for a real C2 system. Essentially, there is no real security where none is defined.

At the time of this writing, the NES network was still in evaluation. Novell provides regular updates on its web server (`www.novell.com`) and these should be checked to assure compliance with the C2 certification when met. Do not put your system online under the auspices of a C2 evaluated system until two factions have been met: Novell's evaluation is final, and all updates on the NES manuals have been complied with.

NES Hardware Selection

There are four types of components for trusted NetWare. They are:

- Servers
- Clients
- Interconnections
- Media

This section deals with the installation of an NES server and media. Clients are provided by third-party vendors and include their own installation manuals.

Novell has divided the NES server into the following components:

- **Machine-independent software.** This includes the NetWare core operating system, the installation software, the support NLM software, and the Administrative NLMs. All of this software must be run on a Novell YES-certified IBM PC compatible system (explained below).
- **Network hardware and software.** This includes a network card and device drivers for that card.
- **Storage hardware and software.** This is hard drives, tape drives, CD-ROM drives, and the respective device controller cards. It would also include the device drivers.
- **Platform hardware and BIOS.** This is the IBM PC compatible hardware, firmware, and BIOS that the NES Server runs on.
- **Printers.** This includes Novell YES-Certified printers and drivers.

Choosing the correct hardware, although a relatively simple exercise in attention to detail, is the foundation on which all of your security is based. If you choose hardware that is not on the YES-certified program, you will be introducing unknowns into your NTCB. This, of course, is not acceptable. For instance, choosing a NIC that is not on your list might allow for address spoofing.

Novell's YES-certified program maintains a standard in the quality and assurance of your hardware. You may receive a list of certified hardware from Novell. To do so, call Novell's fax back service at:

1-800-414-5227

1-801-861-2776 (international)

During the first call, you can order a catalog of documents. On this catalog is a list for NES certified NetWare. This is the item you should order. You may also find this list on Novell's Web Page, `www.novell.com`.

Media includes anything that connects the servers and clients together. NES is evaluated using 10BaseT (twisted pair). You may also use 10Base2 (thin Ethernet), and 10Base5 (thick Ethernet). Token-Ring and ARCNet are not evaluated. Media also includes hubs, routers, bridges, and repeaters. Contact Novell for components that have been YES-certified.

Special NES Installation Issues

The installation of Novell Enhanced Security Server is essentially a NetWare 4.11 Server installation with a few noted changes. After the basic installation, you are required to configure your NES server to meet Class C2 requirements. NetWare 4.11 provides Installation documentation. The following headings correspond to that documentation. Each heading notes any differences from the standard installation. You should perform standard NetWare 4.11 installation while noting the differences mentioned here. The following section is a summary of portions of the NetWare Enhanced Security Administration manual, provided with Novell's online documentation.

Setting Up Partitions and DOS

Follow the standard installation guidelines to create a DOS partition on the hard drive. This is used to boot to NetWare 4.11 and for storage of needed device drivers.

You must format the DOS partition. No pre-existing software should be on the partition. This could jeopardize the security of your server.

NES was evaluated with DOS version 6.11. However, you may use versions 5.0 and above and still comply with C2. You are not required to REMOVE DOS from server.

Server Boot Method

Booting a machine from diskette is allowed. However, you are still required to use DOS version 5.0 and above. There is no advantage to booting from diskette, because C2 requires a physically secured server.

Server Name

The name of the server is world readable. Do not give your server a name with any sensitive information within it.

SMP

Do not install SMP. NES does not support NetWare Symmetric Multi-Processing.

Device Drivers and LAN Drivers

Only install device drivers that are on the Novell YES-certified list. If your driver is not on that list, you may not use that device in the C2 configuration. Call Novell's Fax Back Program to find if your drivers are on the Novell YES-certified list. This is also true for LAN card drivers.

NetWare Volumes

NES does not allow for data migration. Do not enable this option. NES does not support HCSS, SFTIII, NetWare for Macintosh, and additional name spaces (MAC.NAM, OS2.NAM, NFS.NAM, FTAM.NAM). You may only use standard naming conventions and may not load any additional NLMs.

Networking Protocols

TCP/IP and AppleTalk have not been evaluated with NES Server. You may not load these protocols. You may only use the IPX/SPX combination.

Directory Services

Install your new server into its own tree or into a tree that has only evaluated C2 (or better) servers. Note that if you do install into an existing C2 tree, users may be able to log into your server before you enable auditing. To ensure that your server remains secure, either remove your server (physically) from the network, or disable logins, until you have completed the installation process.

Examine the Trustee Assignments for the NDS Tree

You do not want to allow [Public] browse rights to the [Root] of the NDS tree. Doing so would allow un-authenticated users the ability to view objects in your tree (i.e., user login names). This would allow unauthorized persons to attempt logins with known, valid login names.

STARTUP.NCF File

Make sure that the STARTUP.NCF file does not load any unevaluated NLMs.

AUTOEXEC.NCF File

Make sure that the AUTOEXEC.NCF file does not load any unevaluated NLMs.

Other Installation Options

Do not load any NLMs, or edit any configuration files to load NLMs that are not on the evaluated NLM list. For instance, the following are not allowed to be loaded on an NES Server.

- RCONSOLE (i.e., REMOTE.NLM or RSPX.NLM)
- Additional name space NLMs
- Upgrading NetWare 3.1x print services
- NetWare for Macintosh
- MHS
- INETCFG.NLM
- TCP/IP
- NetWare DHCP
- AppleTalk
- NetWare Server for OS/2
- SFT III

You are not required to remove DOS from memory after booting the server.

Conclusion

You should now have a standard NetWare 4.11 Server with a few minor differences in the installation. The next section will take you beyond the installation to additional setup requirements. Do not put your NetWare 4.11 server on the network yet. Wait until it is in the C2 evaluated configuration, after the next section.

NES Configuration Issues

This section describes how to configure your newly installed NetWare 4.11 Server. The following headings will direct you in setting up different portions of your server. Where exact installation specifications are not given, NCSC has left the particulars to the Site Security Policy.

Move Unevaluated NLMs to a Secure Directory

The following NLMs are evaluated to run on the NES Server. Any additional NLMs must be moved out of the SYS:\SYSTEM and SYS:\PUBLIC directories to a secure directory.

- **DOS files:**

  INSTALL.EXE, version 2.44

  MS-DOS 6.11 (5.0 or above may be used) utilities:

  IO.SYS

  MSDOS.SYS

  COMMAND.COM

  CHKDSK

  EDIT

  FDISK

  FORMAT

  SET

  SETUP

  SYS

- **Core operating system software:**

  DS.NLM, version 5.73

  DSLOADER.NLM, version 1.48

  SERVER.EXE, version 4.11

  TIMESYNC.NLM, version 4.15

- **Service NLM software:**

  NPRINTER.NLM, version 4.15

  PSERVER.NLM, version 4.15

  SMDR.NLM, version 4.10

  SMSDI.NLM, version 4.04e

TAPEDAI.DSK, version 4.14h

TSA410.NLM, version 4.14

TSANDS.NLM, version 4.13

- **Driver NLM software:**

CDROM.NLM, version 4.11u

ETHERTSM.NLM, version 3.11

IDEATA.HAM, version 1.21

NBI.NLM, version 1.44

NE2000.LAN, version 3.62

NWPALOAD.NLM, version 1.30

MSM.NLM, version 3.17

NWPA.NLM, version 2.31

SCSI154X.HAM, version 3.01i

SCSIPS2.HAM, version 1.22

Novell's standard NetWare distribution includes the following machine-dependent device drivers. Other machine-dependent drivers are permitted as described by Novell's YES-Certified program.

IDEHD.CDM, version 1.20

SCSI2TP.CDM, version 1.02n

SCSICD.CDM, version 1.05

SCSIHD.CDM, version 1.05

SCSIMO.CDM, version 1.05

- **Library NLM software:**

AFTER311.NLM, version 4.10a

CLIB.NLM, version 4.11

CLNNLM32.NLM, version 5.00b

DSAPI.NLM, version 5.00b

DSI.NLM, version 4.50

FPSM.NLM, version 4.11

LOCNLM32.NLM, version 5.00b

MATHLIB.NLM, version 4.20

MATHLIBC.NLM, version 4.20

NCPNLM32.NLM, version 5.00b

NETNLM32.NLM, version 5.00b

NIT.NLM, version 4.11

NLMLIB.NLM, version 4.11

NWSNUT.NLM, version 4.16

REQUESTR.NLM, version 4.11

SPXS.NLM, version 5.00o

STREAMS.NLM, version 4.10b

THREADS.NLM, version 4.11

TLI.NLM, version 4.10a

VREPAIR.NLM, 4.19

- **Administrative NLM software:**

  DSMERGE.NLM, version 1.63

  DSREPAIR.NLM, version 4.40

  INSTALL.NLM, version 2.24

  MONITOR.NLM, version 4.34

  SBACKUP.NLM, version 4.20

  SERVMAN.NLM, version 4.20

  VREPAIR.NLM, version 4.19

Configure Boot Files

A properly configured NES Server requires certain parameters to be set on it. Although some of the parameters are optional, setting them will increase the security of your system.

Miscellaneous Parameters

```
Allow Unencrypted Passwords = OFF
```

This must be set to OFF. NES Server will not support NetWare 2.x logins. Because NES does not support NetWare 2.x Servers, this should not be a problem.

```
Allow Audit Passwords = OFF
```

This parameter, when turned off, disallows passwords to be used in identifying auditors. It must be set to OFF for NES.

NCP Parameters

```
Reject NCP Packets with Bad Components = ON
```

This parameter, when set to on, will reject any NCP packets that fail component checking.

```
Reject NCP Packets with Bad Lengths = ON
```

This parameter, when set to on, will reject any NCP packets that fail boundary checking.

```
NCP Packet Signature Option = 3 (Optional)
```

Although not required for C2, setting this parameter to 3 will require both the server and the client to sign all NCP packets. Failure of the client to do so will fail the login.

Novell Directory Services

```
Check Equivalent to Me = ON (Optional)
```

Although not required for C2, setting this parameter to ON will force DSREPAIR to synchronize the Equivalence attribute and the Equivalent To Me attribute.

You do not have to set these yourself. These parameters are all included in a NetWare Configuration File named SECURE.NCF (in the SYS:/SYSTEM directory.) This file can be run as a batch file in NetWare. It will set all the required settings, but has the optional settings commented out. If you want the optional security features to be set, uncomment them in the SECURE.NCF file.

Your server has two configuration files that run automatically at startup. They are STARTUP.NCF and AUTOEXEC.NCF. Placing the following line in your STARTUP.NCF file will run the SECURE.NCF batch file:

```
SET Enable SECURE.NCF = ON
```

This will set all the required parameters for the C2 system.

Set Audit Configuration

Auditing capability is a requirement for C2 level security. The TNI does not address a specific audit configuration, however. This is up to your site security policy. You need to review your policy and implement auditing as required (see Chapter 10p, "Novell Directory Services Auditing"). By default, auditing is disabled. To use NetWare's AUDITCON program, you must have access to a trusted client.

Define USER_TEMPLATE

Defining a USER_TEMPLATE requires the use of NWADMIN (or equivalent.) This requires access to a trusted client.

You may set up your user template using either of two methods.

- You may use the user object named USER_TEMPLATE and specify default properties for it.
- You may also create a new template object class and then specify the default properties.

Whichever method you use, you will have to set up a template before you add any users to your system. This is imperative, because if a user is added to NDS without a template, it will be granted the default rights of its container. This could lead to undesired results.

Review NDS Rights

This section suggests some additional security precautions you may want to take when configuring your NES server. Manipulating the NDS requires the use of a trusted client.

The rights to objects in NDS is of critical importance. The NES Server cannot be allowed to reveal information about objects that is not intended to be revealed. You must understand NDS object rights thoroughly and make note of the following points.

Default Object Rights to NDS

This section explains the default object rights established in NES. Default object rights are NDS object and NDS object property rights that are assigned when a new object is created.

- **Rights to the [Root] object.** Novell advises, but does not require, that you turn off Scan rights to the [Root] NDS object.
- **Maximum Rights for NES.** The Maximum Rights objects are allowed to have in NES are shown Table 4.2 of the NetWare Enhanced security Administration Guide. These rights are the maximum EFFECTIVE rights, and as such they can be derived from assignment, inheritance, and security equivalence. Make sure a solid knowledge of how effective rights are computed is known before making assignments.

Use caution when assigning rights to a User Template object. If your template changes, all new users could be given undesirable rights.

Take care in naming containers and leaf objects. The names are public and therefore should not be given sensitive names.

Browse rights to the [Public] object will allow any user the ability to read the object names (i.e., login names) before they are logged in. Disable [Public] Browse rights.

Creating Container Objects

Container objects enable you to organize network resources and users within your network. As you add new container objects, take care to define a USER_TEMPLATE for that container.

Managing Groups of User Objects

You may have group objects containing other group objects, however, expansion of security equivalences are only one level.

Searching for Objects

You should use the search facility of NDS to identify potential problems with the security configurations. For instance, search for users who:

- Do not require a login password.
- Have a password shorter than the required length.
- Are security equivalent to Admin or other privileged accounts.

Moving Objects in the Directory Tree

Moving objects from container to container will change the objects rights if the new container has different rights from the original. This is due to the inherited rights feature of containers. Examine both containers' rights before the move to ensure no conflict in your site security policy.

Deleting Objects from the Directory Tree

Pay special attention to deleting an administrative account that might have the only supervisory rights to a tree. Deletion of this account could lead to loss of the ability to administer the tree. This is also true for any normal user account that has the only supervisory right to an object.

Changing Object Property Values

Be careful of the time required to implement a change of object property values when dealing with a distributed or replicated database. If a value is time critical, you may want to approach a change to it in another way.

User Account Administration

You can only use an evaluated NetWare Enhanced Security client workstation to perform account administration activities. This includes the specific tools and applications that are included in that workstation's evaluated configuration.

- **Configuring a USER_TEMPLATE object.** After you configure a USER_TEMPLATE object, review its contents to make sure that it addresses the required password restrictions and any other desired characteristics that you want to apply to all user accounts.

- **Required settings for USER_TEMPLATE.** Define the following NetWare Enhanced Security password restrictions for each USER_TEMPLATE.

  Select Password Required. For both NetWare Administrator and NETADMIN, this is found in the Password Restrictions menu.

  Define the Minimum Password Length as eight characters. For both NetWare Administrator and NETADMIN, this is found in the Password Restrictions menu.

  Select Account Disabled to prevent use of accounts before the initial password is defined. If you fail to set this option, then intruders may be able to take control of newly created accounts before you set a password for the account. For both NetWare Administrator and NETADMIN, this is found in the Login Restrictions menu.

- **Recommended settings for user templates.** You will want to set the Password Restrictions to match that of your site security policy. For an understanding of password management, examine the Department of Defense *Password Management Guidelines* [CSC-STD-002-85].

  In the User Template you may set the following options.

  - Allow User to Change Password
  - Force Periodic Password Changes
  - Require Unique Password

  Other account restrictions you may add to the user template are:

  - Login Time Restrictions
  - Network Address Restrictions
  - Print Job Configuration
  - Login Script
  - Group Membership
  - Postal Address

- **Adding a user account using NetWare Administrator.** When adding a new user account, make sure you select "Use User Template." Without using a USER_TEMPLATE, you will have to manually check each user created against the site security policy.

  Add a password to the account immediately.

  Set any Login, Network Address, or Time restrictions required by your site security policy.

  Set the per-user audit flag or the user's home directory to be audited if required by your site security policy.

- **Disabling a user account.** When disabling a user account, note that this will not immediately affect a currently logged in user. It will terminate a session within 30 minutes and prevent future logins. To remove a user immediately, you must delete the user object from NDS.

  - **Deleting a user account.** When deleting a user account, Novell recommends archiving the user's home directory and then deleting it.

- **Configuring intruder detection.** Intruder detection sets limits on the number of login attempts that can be made on an account before the account is disabled. The time the account is disabled is also configurable. Intruder detection is an optional security configuration. It is not required to maintain C2 compliance.

- **Detect Intruder = ON.** Sets intruder detection to on and allows the following options to be configured. Note that NES is NOT required to have Intruder Detection on to remain C2 compliant.

  - **Login Intruder Limit.** The Login Intruder Limit sets the number of failed login attempts before the account is disabled. It is recommended to be between three to six attempts.

  - **Intruder Attempt Reset Interval.** This is the time frame that the server waits before resetting the attempts to zero. If this is set to one hour, then the maximum attempts on the account can be the Login Intruder Limit per one hour.

  - **Intruder Lockout Reset Interval.** The Intruder Lockout Reset Value sets how long the server keeps the account disabled once the Login Limit is reached. How accessible the Network Administrator should be needs to be taken into consideration when setting this. Note that the Admin account is also affected by Intruder Detection. If someone attempts to break into your Admin account, you will be locked out. This is a good reason to rename Admin to something less well known. Also, you should have another account with all the Admin privileges in case your standard account is locked out.

Note, if you are completely locked out, you can go to the server console and type **ENABLE LOGINS**. This will allow for bindery emulation of the SUPERVISOR account on the respective server. You may then unlock the needed accounts.

Protecting Administrative Accounts

Administrative accounts need to maintain accountability to the user. There should not be a single ADMIN account used for all individuals. Each administrator should have his or her own account with the needed privileges. NetWare, by default, creates one ADMIN account and a bindery representation of that account (SUPERVISOR).

Safeguard your ADMIN account by creating a backdoor in case of Intruder Detection Lockout (discussed in the preceding section).

If an administrator is also a user, he or she should have two separate accounts. One administrative in purpose, the other, non-administrative (making a total of three accounts if the administrative account has a backup).

Review File System Rights

This section suggests some additional security precautions you may want to take when configuring your NES server. Manipulating the file system rights requires the use of a trusted client.

SYS:\LOGIN Directory

The SYS:\LOGIN directory is a public READ ONLY directory. Any programs copied into this directory will be world readable to even unauthenticated users. Use discretion when storing programs in this directory.

Fake Root Mappings

Mapping drives to a fake root is authorized in NES; however, this should not be done to implement any part of a site security policy. There is no assurance of a fake root mappings.

Making the File System Secure and Accessible

The following list shows how to secure your file system and make it accessible to the proper users. Examine each bullet and apply to your system.

- Do not use the directory and file attributes to protect information in directories and files. They are not addressed in the server component access control policy of the C2 evaluation.

- Ensure that non-administrative users are not allowed access to the contents of TCB files and directories.

- Never grant access to rights to the root directory of a volume. Only grant rights needed in individual directories on that volume.
- Do not grant any trustee rights to the SYS:\SYSTEM directory. This contains NES NLMs.
- Do not give any Write or Create rights to the SYS:\PUBLIC directory to any non-administrative accounts.
- To prevent users from giving other users access to their data, remove the Supervisor and Access Control rights of their home directories.
- Do not give any Write or Create rights to the SYS:\LOGIN directory. This would be an ideal place to store Trojan Horse applications.
- Audit files are stored in SYS:_NETWARE. This directory is only accessible by the NOS.
- Print Queues are stored in SYS:\QUEUES. Do not allow non-administrative trustees to this directory.
- Deleted, but not purged, files are stored in SYS:\DELETED.SAV. Do not allow administrative or non-administrative trustees to this directory.
- Novell's Online Documentation is stored in SYS:\DOC. User in need of this documentation should be given Read and File Scan rights.

Use the information in Chapter 4, "Novell Directory Services Security," to help you implement the remainder of your Site Security Policy.

Salvaging and Purging Deleted Files and Directories

To ensure that deleted files are unrecoverable, set the IRF of the file to be deleted to: Create, Read, and File Scan. This will disallow anyone from salvaging the deleted file (unless they have a Supervisor right to it). Then, run Purge immediately.

Configure Printer and Print Queues

This section on configuring the printer, print servers, and print queues begins with an overview of Network Printing in NES and then explains what is allowed in the NES environment. NES involves the following mechanisms to be configured properly.

NES printing is based upon NDS objects: queues, print server, and printers. NetWare 3.x printing is not supported. Workstation printing will be discussed in the client workstation manual and may or may not be supported.

Overview of Network Printing

Figure 9.3 shows the valid NES configurations for network printing.

Figure 9.3
NES Printing Configurations

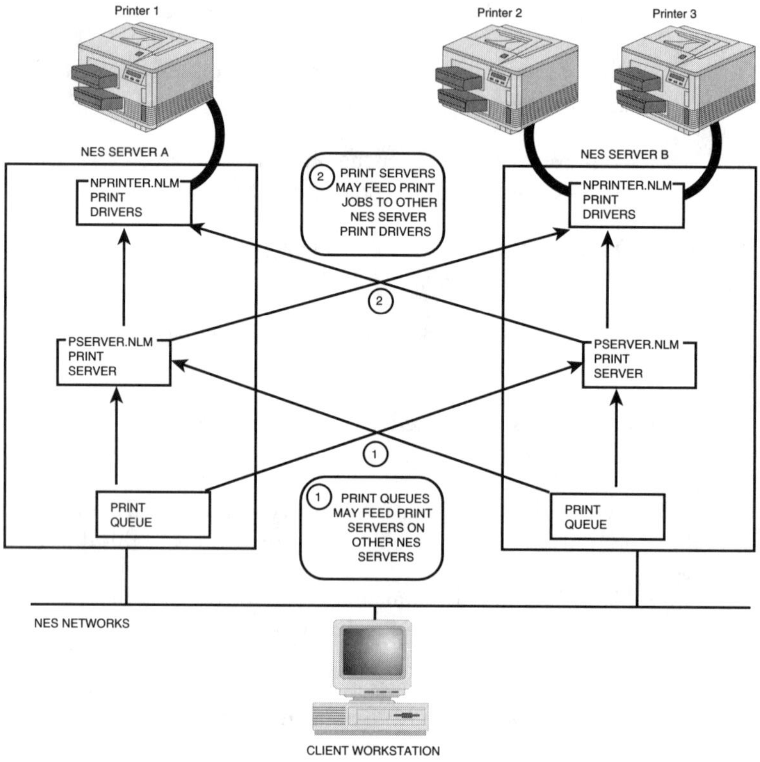

Only PSERVER.NLM and NPRINTER.NLM may be used with NES. Printers must be physically attached to an NES server.

Print Server Login

PSERVER.NLM may be configured to service print queues on different servers. In order for PSERVER to access a queue on a remote server, PSERVER must first log in to the remote server that holds the queue. Thus, the Print Server NDS object must be configured with a login password and PSERVER must be run with the password in order to log in to the remote server.

IPX Address Restrictions

When NPRINTER attaches to PSERVER, NPRINTER is checked to make sure it has an appropriate IPX network address. The connection is refused if the printer's IPX address is not a valid known printer IPX address.

Configuring Printing in the NetWare Enhanced Security Environment

If not all users are authorized to use the printers, you must set up a list of authorized users and make the print queue accessible to them. You must then remove the rights of all users to access the print queue.

The Security Features User Guide explains that users must select where to spool their output based on what other individuals are users of the print queue and have physical access to the printers.

Because submission of print jobs to programmable printers can be the same as loading a program in the printers' memories that could sabotage future printing, the ability to print should be restricted to users who have a genuine need to print. Also, jobs sent to the print queue should be considered world readable and thought should be given as to which queues users are assigned.

Creating Print Servers with Passwords

The creation of Print Server objects requires a password. This password is used for the Print Server to log into NDS. Without this password, a user could log into the network as a Print Server object.

Working with Printer Forms

Banner pages can be turned off by the user. Do not rely on them to show ownership to a printed document.

Additional Notes on Network Printing

The following are points of interest involved in NES network printing. Examine each and apply accordingly.

- Bindery queues are not supported in NetWare Enhanced Security systems.
- Auditing the print server is for accounting purposes only and does not generate an audit trail for NES.
- Mixing of NetWare 3.x (Bindery Mode) and NetWare 4.x is not supported in NetWare Enhanced Security systems.
- Only evaluated third-party print devices may be used in the NetWare Enhanced Security configuration.
- NetWare SFT III is not included in the server's NetWare Enhanced Security configuration.
- PUPGRADE.NLM is not included in the NetWare Enhanced Security configuration.

Summary

As you can see, there is a tremendous amount of attention to detail needed in creating and maintaining a C2 network. This introduction into the topic should be treated as such so that it may help you understand the resources needed to undertake such a project. You have been taken through an overview of C2 security as it relates to Novell's NetWare Enhanced Security Services.

You have also been taken through the outline of an NES Server installation. Although apparently straightforward, complexity is introduced in a properly written site security policy. Implementing a well-written policy is what C2 security is all about.

CHAPTER 10

Novell Directory Services Auditing

You are probably familiar with some of the tools that are available to IntranetWare administrators, such as NDS-based access control, which can be used to administer access to your organization's information assets. These tools enable you to configure your network environment in such a way that information access is restricted to those who have a "need to know" that information. These restrictions are generally defined in an organization's security policy, which describes what types of actions are permitted by what users in your environment. It isn't enough, however, to simply restrict rights and assume the security policy is being properly enforced. With much of today's information assets being spread out over different physical network servers, it is important for organizations to have the ability and tools to verify that their security policy is being properly enforced and maintained.

This problem is not new. In large computer operating systems, such as those that run on mainframes and minicomputers, it is common to have *auditing* capabilities that enable selected events, such as access of a specified file or directory, to be monitored. This information can be used to track security-relevant user actions on the network, examine how resources are being used and by whom, and so on. Additionally, some organizations might require that the roles of administrator and auditor be performed by different individuals to allow for independent verification of security implementation.

IntranetWare includes a powerful auditing feature that helps an administrator or independent auditor verify that a security policy is being adhered to. Although the audit information that is generated will be examined "after the fact," it is a useful tool to assist in the protection of information assets.

In this chapter, you learn about these powerful IntranetWare auditing features and capabilities. In particular, you will learn about the use of the AUDITCON utility for auditing; how events in the file system, NDS, and the client can be audited; how to customize the auditing environment; and how reports can be prepared from the audit log.

Examining the Need for Auditing

NetWare 3.x (and earlier versions) contained a feature called *accounting* that could be activated on a newly installed server using the SYSCON utility. After the accounting feature was activated, the system administrator could keep track of the number of blocks read from and written to, the services requested from the NetWare server, and the number of blocks of storage utilized by a user over a period of time. Although these statistics were interesting, their value to administrators tasked with protecting information assets was somewhat limited. What was often needed was a way to track the usage of individual files and directories. This would enable an administrator or auditor to verify that the security policy was being properly enforced.

For example, suppose security-relevant changes are taking place on the network, and the network administrator indicates he or she is not aware of how the changes are taking place. Standard network accounting does not report who has accessed system administrator tools such as NETADMIN or RCONSOLE. Even if the information were provided "after the fact," it would help an administrator or auditor discover or track down the breach in security.

Another deficiency with the accounting feature is that it could not determine the number of times an application was accessed over a particular period of time, which would enable the network administrator to determine if the number of licenses purchased for a particular application was appropriate. If an organization has purchased a 50-user license for an application when there are, at most, 20 users who use the application, it is better to implement a 20- or 25-user version.

NetWare 3.x accounting features remain in IntranetWare; however, IntranetWare also provides valuable security enhancements through its auditing capabilities. Auditing can be used to obtain information on individual files and directories and how they are accessed over a period of time. It can also be used to audit DS events such as changes in the NDS schema, or creation/deletion of user objects, and so on.

Auditing can be used to track the following:

- File/directory events
- Directory service events
- Server events
- Client events

As networks grow and become more complex, control over the network can become decentralized. As this happens, it is very difficult for management to determine if proper procedures are being followed to prevent security breaches or misuse of the network resources. Auditing, if properly implemented, can be used to determine who is performing security-sensitive tasks. Auditing can also be used to troubleshoot network-related problems, to determine if proper procedures are being followed, and if procedures are in accordance with the organization's network security policy.

Some examples of situations where auditing might help an organization protect its information assets are:

- Determining whether or not users have been granted sufficient system privileges to perform their duties. They might have access to too many network resources; this could occur if users are made security equivalents to other NDS objects temporarily and the security equivalencies are not removed; or, if a user's job responsibilities have changed. It is usually easy to tell when users don't have sufficient rights to complete a task; they complain!
- Discovering newly created files that are left unsecured. This can happen if new files and directories are created, but appropriate access restrictions are not placed.
- Keeping track of application software usage for determining if the application licenses are adequate.

Understanding the Function and Role of a Network Auditor

On most networks, administrators are all-powerful, in the sense that they can access all resources on the network without any restrictions. Such unrestricted power is necessary if the network administrator is to be able to effectively support the users.

However, this unlimited power also means that the network administrator can access information that could be considered sensitive and confidential without the owner's knowledge. Although it is hoped that the organization has confidence in the administrator's character, sensitive information exists on the network, and access to this information should be monitored by someone. From a practical and political standpoint, it may be desirable to have a separate auditor that can provide independent verification that administrative rights are being used correctly.

It should be noted that although it may seem auditing only benefits management, it also benefits the system administrator. In some organizations, a degree of mistrust exists between the network administrator and management. This mistrust is often fueled by the following facts:

- Management must rely on the network administrator for access to critical and confidential data within the company.
- The network administrator often has access to data that even top-level managers in an organization do not have.

Usually, network administrators are trustworthy and do not abuse the rights given to them. However, occasionally an administrator might be tempted to step over the line. With IntranetWare auditing, a check can be put into place to verify that management's trust has not been abused, intentionally or otherwise. If a security breach occurs, the audit logs can be examined to discover what happened. Without proper auditing, the network administrator might be automatically under suspicion if sensitive or confidential data is lost or compromised. If auditing is enabled, the network administrator can be cleared of any potential suspicion. Therefore, the auditing feature, if enabled, can be used for the administrator's protection as well as for management's.

Sensitive files can be audited for events that perform an operation on the files such as a read, write, and delete. Anytime a user, including the network administrator, accesses the audited file, that action is recorded in an NDS audit log. This NDS audit log can be used to discover accesses or modifications to the access rights and/or the contents of the audited file. The network administrator is very unlikely to misuse the access to classified files if he/she knows that the file is audited. Auditing cannot prevent a network administrator from accessing a file, but should such an access be performed, the event will be recorded in the audit log and can be discovered by the auditor. Knowledge of this capability might help keep the honest individual honest, so to speak.

As briefly discussed earlier, in some situations it doesn't make sense to have the same person perform both the network administrator duties and the auditor duties. The auditor may be from an outside firm, or it might be a particular user on the network. What makes the network auditor user special is that the auditor user has been given access rights to the Audit File Object (AFO) in NDS, which is needed to access the audit log created by the audit system. Because the only distinction between an ordinary user and an auditor user is access rights, the auditor's user account password must be guarded from non-auditor users, including the network administrator. Typically, the network administrator enables auditing and grants the auditor rights to the AFO. In IntranetWare, access to the audit logs is controlled by the access rights a user has to the AFO, which represents the audit file in NDS. After the auditor account has been set up, the user name and password is given to the auditor, and the auditor should immediately change the password to the user account without telling the network administrator what the new password is. Rights to the AFO's the auditor is responsible for can be revoked from the administrator to prevent the resetting or reconfiguring of auditing.

Controlling Access to Audit Files

Access to the audit files is determined by the NDS rights to the audit file object associated with the audit file. The audit system checks the user's rights whenever he/she attempts to access the audit data. If the user has the appropriate rights, he/she will be allowed access. This is the only access method allowed in NetWare's Enhanced Server configuration.

For compatibility with previous versions of NetWare, IntranetWare also supports a password access method. This option is enabled by setting Allow audit passwords to ON at the server console.

In the Enhanced Security Server configuration, IntranetWare is not permitted to password protect the auditing features. This is the default setting. This prevents users who are not specifically granted rights to audit the objects within the network from doing so.

IntranetWare allows organizations the flexibility of activating or deactivating various security features. Generally, traditional NetWare 3.x audit file passwords are not used in the NetWare 4.x environment.

Because passwords are no longer the primary authentication mechanism used to access audit logs, explicit rights to the audit file object must be granted to auditors. Also, if the security policy of your network dictates, the default rights of the network administrator to those AFOs must be revoked to allow for accountability of said administrator. Also, if the security policy of your network dictates, the default rights of the network administrator must be revoked to allow for accountability of the said administrator. To grant rights to a user, use the following instructions:

1. The Administrator enables auditing for the items to be audited. This includes enabling all volume, container, and client auditing required for the security policy. (These actions actually create the AFOs.) Note that the specific configuration options for each AFO do not need to be implemented yet, just the general enabling of auditing on each object.

2. Next, the administrator must assign explicit rights to the auditor(s). For instance you might want to assign a different auditor to each volume or container on your server. The needed rights are as follows. For a user assigned to administer auditing, the required rights would be:

R to AFO: Audit Policy

W to AFO: Audit Policy

R to AFO: Audit Contents

If you needed to create a user who would examine the audit files, then you would assign the following rights:

R to AFO: Audit Policy

R to AFO: Audit Contents

If you needed to grant rights to a specific volume, container, or external source, you would set the following:

W to AFO: Audit Contents

R to AFO: Audit Path

3. After rights are properly assigned, you may revoke the Administrators access rights to those Audit File Objects, being careful not to create a hole, in other words an Audit File Object with no user object that has supervisor object rights, in your NDS Tree.

This chapter explains the auditing tasks using the access control method only. If you are using the password access method you will have to select the Auditor volume/container login menu item before the Available audit options menu will appear.

In summary, the following precautions should be considered when implementing IntranetWare auditing:

- It might be advisable to create an auditor account apart from the network supervisor. The auditor may be independent of the network administrator.
- Auditor Account Security—The auditor should change the initial audit password assigned by the supervisor as soon as possible, and in the case of a separate auditor, rights to the audit object should be revoked for the network supervisor. The network supervisor should not have knowledge of the new auditor password.

Reviewing Auditing Features in IntranetWare

IntranetWare enables an organization's auditor(s) to verify that network security policy is being adequately enforced.

The auditor does not have to be a specially created user. Any existing user can be set up to perform the role of an auditor. Some organizations might prefer that the auditor be an outside contractor who is not part of the organization and can verify network security and procedures independently.

The network administrator must act in accord with management to implement auditing. The management of the organization company designates a particular user to be an auditor, and discusses with the auditor and/or administrator what the goals of the auditing process are. The network usage policy, if an organization has one, should be clarified at this point.

Management then informs the network administrator who the auditor is. The network administrator sets up the auditor's account. This includes the following:

- Creating a User object for the auditor and assigning appropriate file system and NDS rights. The auditor should have [R F] rights to SYS:PUBLIC where the AUDITCON tool is kept.
- Creating a home directory for the auditor to prepare and store audit reports.
- Creating the login environment and login script for the auditor. A search drive should be mapped to the directory containing the AUDITCON files. This is normally the SYS:PUBLIC directory.

After the auditor account has been prepared, it is necessary to set up the types of events that are to be audited. This should be specified in your organization's security policy.

It is possible to track several different types of events:

1. File system events such as changes and access to files and directories.
2. NDS events such as changes or access to specific NDS objects.
3. Server events such as bringing down a server, deleting bindery objects, and mounting/dismounting volumes.
4. Events occurring external to the server.

Auditing can be enabled at a volume, container, or external source. To audit file system events, auditing should be enabled at the volume level. For NDS events, auditing is enabled at the container level. For external sources, auditing is enabled at the client level. The AUDITCON tool is used to enable and maintain audit information.

When you enable auditing for a volume or container, you enable it for that container or volume only. In the case of containers, auditing is not automatically enabled for the subordinate containers of an audited container. If you want to enable auditing for the subordinate containers, you must do so as a separate task.

The auditor must then configure the auditing environment, by doing the following:

- Use AUDITCON to enable auditing for the appropriate volumes, containers, and clients. This will establish Audit File Objects in Directory Services so that rights may be granted. Before auditors can use AUDITCON to customize the auditing environment, they must have specific rights to the object to be audited. In the case of NDS-based access, the specific Audit Files are protected by NDS. Only a user with the correct access rights to the AFOs can access the audit logs.
- Change the auditor's user password assigned by the supervisor.
- Customize the auditing environment as per the guidelines specified in the security policy.

The auditor should take precautions not to leave his or her workstation unattended while logged into the network as an auditor. An unscrupulous user could then change the password of the logged in auditor and gain auditor access.

A common mistake is to enable auditing for too many events that are not of consequence to network security. This causes enormous audit reports to be generated, which often go unread. The auditor should be trained in the use of the AUDITCON features and functions.

Once the audit events have been identified, the auditor can generate audit reports and view the audit report on-screen, or print the audit report. These steps are described in detail in the following sections. The steps needed for auditing are shown in figure 10.1.

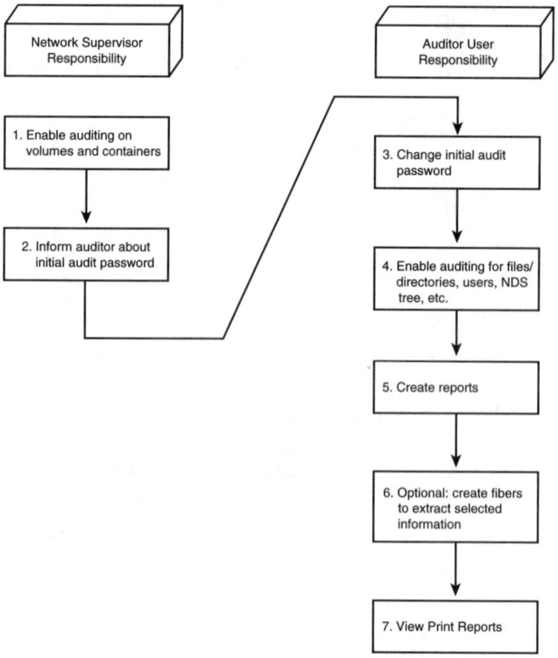

Figure 10.1
Setting up auditing tasks.

The auditor can do the following:

- Keep track of file system events
- Track events such as changes and access to NDS objects and trustee rights

Using the AUDITCON Tool

AUDITCON is the tool that the auditor uses to perform his or her audit functions. Figure 10.2 shows the main menu for AUDITCON; the last option listed is *Enable volume auditing.* Presence of this option in the main AUDITCON screen indicates that volume auditing has not been enabled for the currently selected volume. This option should be selected to enable auditing for the currently selected volume. The currently selected volume is displayed at the top of the screen.

Figure 10.2
The AUDITCON main screen when volume auditing has not been enabled.

When the Audit directory services option is selected (see fig. 10.3), you have a choice of enabling NDS audit for a selected container (option Audit directory tree). There is also an option to change the context for the session (option Change session context). The session context is displayed at the top of the screen.

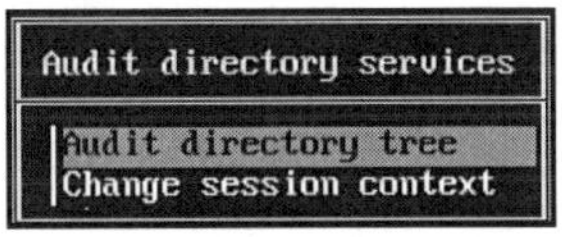

Figure 10.3
The Audit directory services screen.

The External Auditing option has been added to IntranetWare to enable the server to store auditing information from various network services and clients. This external data is generated by third-party software. It is beyond the scope of this book to completely explain the external auditing capabilities.

The Change current server option and Change current volume option enable you to select other servers and volumes for the purpose of enabling and configuring audit on them.

Enable volume auditing enables volume auditing for the currently selected volume. The currently selected volume is shown at the top of the auditcon main menu. After auditing is enabled on the currently selected volume, additional options are added to the main menu. These additional options enable the auditor to configure auditing for the currently selected volume.

Using the Audit Files

When an audit event occurs, the event information is recorded in a file named after the object that is being audited. All auditing files are stored in a secure directory that the server maintains. This directory is named _NETWARE. This directory cannot be viewed by standard clients or through standard NCP calls. This directory will exist at the root of the SYS volume and each additional volume being audited. The file naming convention is as follows.

Volume Audit Files are named NET$AUDT.CAF, NET$AUDT.[AO0-AOF]. The .CAF file is the Current Audit File and is the audit file that is being used to record audit data. The additional files are archived Audit files. These files contain the archived audit data for the volume where the audit files are stored. Other volume audit files are stored in the _NETWARE directory located on their respective volumes.

Container Audit Files are named ########.$AF, ########.[$O0-$OF]. The eight # signs represent the Object ID of the Container (that is, 0100000B9.$AF). The $AF file is the current Container Audit File and the $O0-F are archived container audit files. NDS auditing data is stored in the _NETWARE directory of the SYS volume.

External Audit Files have the same naming convention as the Container Audit Files. The eight-digit number, however, is the Object ID of the Audit Object File Object in DS used to represent the audited object. Remember the Audit Object File is what you assign specific rights to for the auditors.

If there are multiple auditors on the network, they should each be given a separate user account. This ensures that the auditing activities for each auditor are recorded using a unique user name.

The information in the Audit Files are kept in binary form. The auditor uses the binary audit files to generate an audit report. The audit report is displayed on the screen as text. This process creates a temporary file that is deleted upon exiting the view. If an auditor chooses to save the audit report onto the network, great care must be taken in deciding where he or she saves the audit report. This is because the audit report is saved as a text file that can be read by anyone who has rights to read files in the directory where it is stored.

Enabling Volume Auditing

One of the steps shown in figure 10.1 shows the network administrator how to enable auditing for a volume, directory services (container), or client, and grant rights to the auditor. Those steps required to enable volume auditing are described in this section. Screen captures are presented to help you review.

1. You must determine the volume to be audited. This decision is based on which volume is used for keeping sensitive data to be tracked, or the volume that contains program files whose usage needs to be monitored.

2. Log in to the network as a user that has the Supervisor Object right for the object to be audited and run AUDITCON.

3. From the main menu option, select Enable volume auditing.

   After enabling volume auditing, the main screen of AUDITCON will change (see fig. 10.4). The Enable volume auditing option will be missing from the Available audit options.

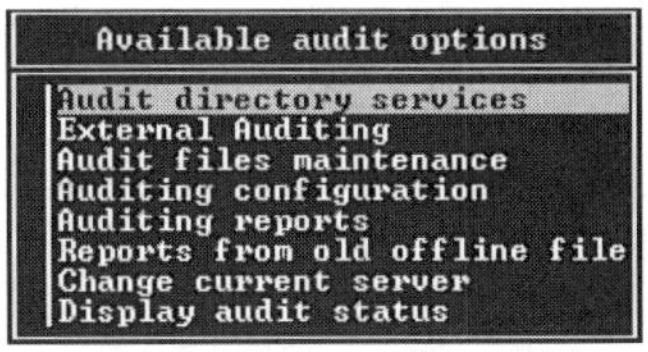

Figure 10.4
The AUDITCON main screen with volume auditing enabled.

   If you select the Display audit status option, you will see that the volume auditing has been enabled (see fig. 10.5).

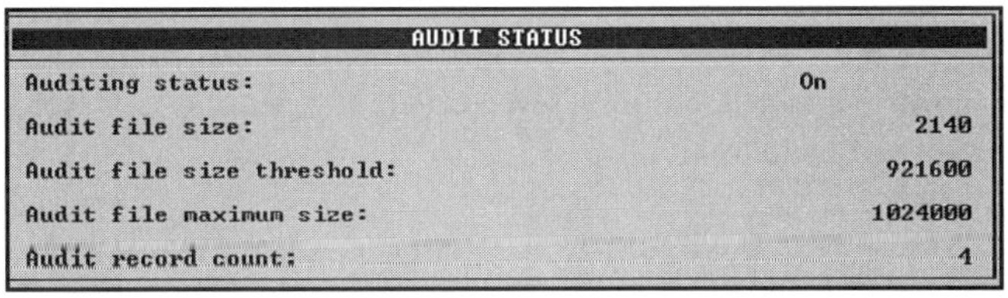

Figure 10.5
Display audit status when auditing is enabled.

4. Exit AUDITCON.

5. Notify the auditor that his user account has been set up and instruct the auditor to change his user account password immediately.

After the auditor password has been changed for the purpose of securing the auditor's user account, the auditing function can be performed. Some of the common auditing functions are outlined in the following sections.

Auditing Configuration Options

When auditing is enabled for the currently selected volume, the screen shown in figure 10.7 is displayed. From this screen, the auditor can select Auditing configuration, and the following options will be displayed (see fig. 10.6):

- Audit by event
- Audit by file/directory

- Audit by user
- Audit options configuration
- Disable volume auditing
- Display audit status
- User Restrictions

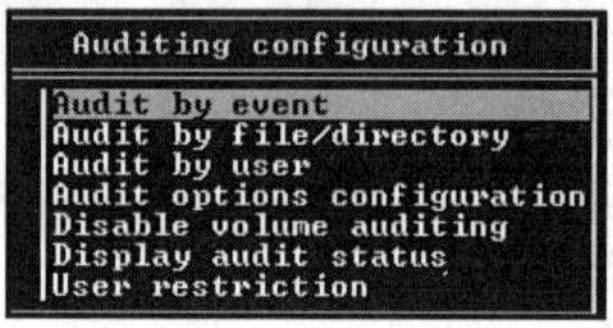

Figure 10.6
The AUDITCON Auditing configuration options menu.

The most commonly used configuration options are explained in the following sections.

Audit by Event

The Audit by event option allows you to select among seven different types of events (see fig. 10.7) to be audited. These events are as follows:

- Accounting events
- Extended Attribute events
- File events
- Message events
- QMS events
- Server events
- User events

Figure 10.7
The Audit by event option.

Audit by Accounting Events

The Audit by accounting events option enables you to monitor events associated with the accounting feature of IntranetWare, such as a getting account status, submitting account charges and holding an account.

Audit by Extended Attribute Events

The Audit by extended attribute events option enables you to monitor actions taken on files or directories that have extended file attributes. Examples of these events are read/write extended attribute and duplicate extended attribute.

Audit by File Events

The file events option audits file and directory operations such as open/read/write file, create file/directory, and delete file/directory. These events can be monitored on a global basis, by user or file, and by user and file. Global auditing means that the operations will cause the event to be logged, regardless of the user, file, or directory name on the audited volume. Auditing on a user or file basis means that the event will be recorded if it applies to an audited user or an audited file. Auditing on a user and file basis means that the event will be recorded if it applies to an audited user and an audited file or directory.

The "or" and "and" in these options act as the Boolean logical OR and AND operators. These options act as filters and control the amount of audit data that goes into the audit files.

Audit by Message Events

The Audit by message events option enables you to monitor events associated with broadcast messaging. These events include broadcast to console, get broadcast message, send broadcast message, and enable/disable broadcasts.

Audit by QMS Events

The Audit by QMS events option enables you to audit operations that affect the printer queues, such as creating and deleting of print queues.

Audit by Server Events

The Audit by server events option enables you to monitor events such as bringing down the server, restarting the server, or mounting a volume attached to the server. All server events are recorded globally.

Audit by User Events

Audit by user event enables you to monitor events associated with a user account. User events include user connection termination, user space restriction changes, disabling user accounts, and user logins and logouts.

Table 10.1 summarizes the Audit by Event types.

Table 10.1
Audit by Event Types

Event Type	Description
Accounting events	Audits events such as get account status, submit account charges, or submit account note.
Extended Attribute events	Audits operations that would get and set extended file attributes.
File events	Audits file and directory operations such as open/read/write file, create file/directory, and delete file/directory.
Message events	Audits events such as broadcasting to console, or disable/enable broadcast messages.
QMS events	Audits operations such as the creation and deletion of print queues.
Server events	Audits events such as bringing down the server, restarting the server, or mounting a volume.
User events	Audits user logins and logouts and trustee assignment changes, connection termination, user space restriction changes, disabling user accounts.

Audit by File/Directory

When this option is selected, you are presented with a list of files and directories (see fig. 10.8) in the current directory that can be audited. You can select any of the files and directories in the list to be audited. A column next to the file or directory contains the audit status (OFF or ON). If a file or directory is selected for auditing, an audit record is entered in the current audit file whenever an operation is performed on the selected file or directory.

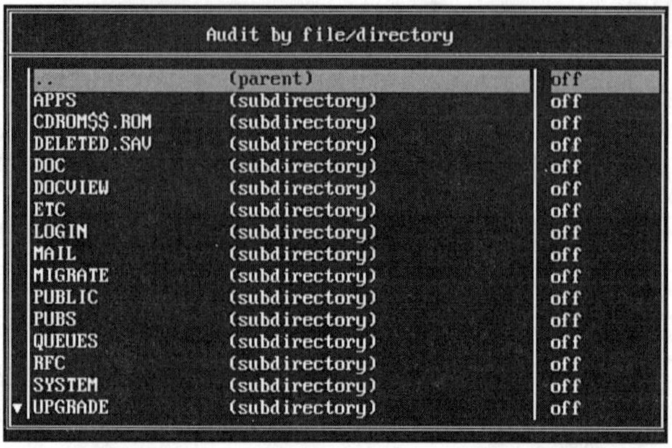

Figure 10.8
The Audit by file/directory option.

F10 can be used to toggle the audit status. A dot-dot (..) symbol indicates the parent directory, and can be used to "move up" one directory level. In general, pressing Enter when any directory is highlighted enables you to examine the contents of that directory.

Audit by User

Audit by user gives you a list of users who can be audited (see fig. 10.9). You can select any of the users whom you want to audit. A column next to the user name contains the audit status (OFF or ON) for that user. If a user is selected for auditing, an audit record is entered in the current audit file whenever that user performs an audited operation on the currently selected volume.

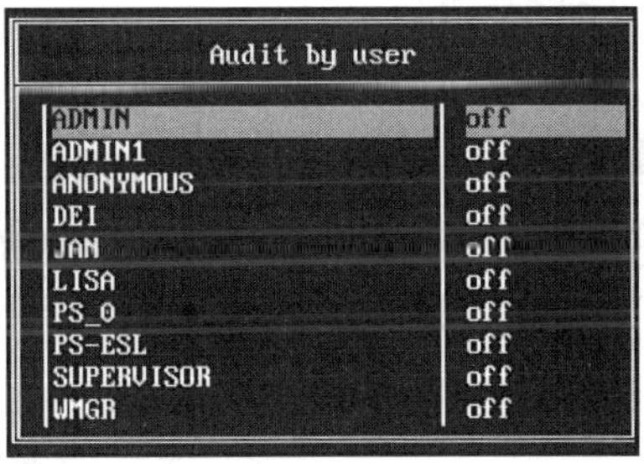

Figure 10.9
The Audit by user option.

The list of users in figure 10.9 are bindery emulation users. To audit other users outside the file server's bindery context you will have to use NDS Auditing. When you use volume auditing by user, it operates with bindery-emulated users only, and the events are stored in the current audit file. When you select NDS Auditing, any user can be audited regardless of the context in which the user is defined.

F10 can be used to toggle the audit status for the user.

Auditing Options for NDS

In the previous section you learned about the auditing options for a volume. At the volume level, the auditor can audit by user, events, or by files/directories.

At the NDS container, the auditor can audit by user or by NDS events. The general procedures for selecting the events to audit in a container are the following:

1. Run AUDITCON.
2. Select Audit directory services.
3. Select Audit directory tree.
4. Choose the container to be audited and press F10 to audit the container.

5. Select Audit configuration.
6. Select Audit by DS events or Audit by user.
7. After you complete your selections, press Esc to save your changes.

If you select Audit by DS events, you will see a list of NDS events that can be selected. When auditing is enabled for an NDS event, all occurrences of that event in the container will be logged. Figures 10.32 and 10.33, discussed later in this chapter, show the different types of DS Events that can be audited.

If you select Audit by user, a list of NDS objects is shown. You can select the User objects from this list or browse the NDS tree and select any other User object. You can use F10 to toggle the status of the user from audit off to AUDITED.

Audit Options Configuration

The Audit options configuration option can be selected from the Audit configuration menu (see fig. 10.10), and allows the auditor to configure auditing parameters. The auditing parameters are kept in the audit file header and they are also stored in an attribute of the Audit File Object.

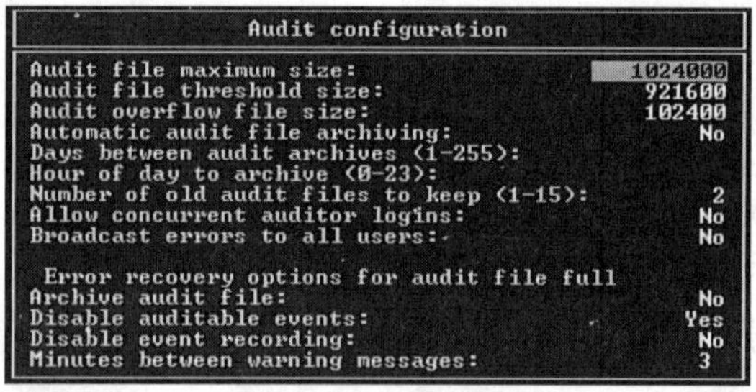

Figure 10.10
The Audit configuration option.

The following parameters can be changed:

- Audit file maximum size
- Audit file threshold size
- Audit overflow file size
- Automatic audit file archiving
- Days between audit archives
- Hour of day to archive
- Number of old auditor files to keep

- Allow concurrent auditor logins
- Broadcast errors to all users
- Error recovery options for audit file full
  - Archive audit file
  - Disable auditable events
  - Disable event recording
  - Minutes between warning messages

Audit File Maximum Size

The Audit File Maximum Size parameter allows you to enter the maximum audit data file size in bytes. The default file size is 1,024,000 bytes. When the file size is full, it must be reset or deleted. Certain recovery options such as disabling event recording can also be triggered when the audit log file fills up. If you want to increase the audit log file size, you should consult with the network administrator; this will affect available disk space on a volume.

Audit File Threshold Size

The Audit File Threshold Size parameter is used to specify a size of the audit log file. When the system reaches the audit file threshold, the system should start sending warning messages. The warning messages are sent at a default interval of three minutes, but can be changed by the Minutes between warning messages field. The default Audit file threshold size is set to about 90 percent of the Audit file maximum size.

Audit Overflow File Size

The Audit Overflow File Size is the size of the buffer saved on the volume that is used to store events from auditing when the audit file is in the overflow state. The buffer is created so that if the volume becomes full, auditing will still have space to write events.

Automatic Audit File Archiving

When set to Yes, the Automatic Audit File Archiving parameter can be used to automate the archiving of audit data files and audit history files. The automated archiving of these critical audit files can guard against human error in archiving these files. As you decide to keep more old audit files online, the disk space used to store these files increases.

Days between Audit Archives

If automatic archiving (also called auto-archiving) is enabled, you must set the number of days to wait before automatically archiving the file. The default parameter value is 7 days; it can range from 1 to 255 days.

If the parameter value is too large, the archive files can grow and may contain data that may not be of much use. If the parameter value is too small, too many small archives will be created. If examination of the audit data is done on a weekly or daily basis, the default value is sufficient.

Hour of Day to Archive

If auto-archiving is enabled, the Hour of Day to Archive is the time of day the automatic archiving is activated. The value can be from 0 to 23. A value of 0 represents midnight (default value).

Number of Old Auditor Files to Keep

If auto-archiving is enabled, the Number of Old Auditor Files to Keep is the maximum number of old archive files that are kept online. Auto-archiving closes the current audit files and archives the old files. When the maximum number of old files is reached, the oldest of the archived audit files is deleted. This parameter value ranges from 1 to 15 and has a default value of 2. Increasing the parameter value also increases the amount of disk space used.

Allow Concurrent Auditor Logins

The Allow Concurrent Auditor Logins parameter, when set to Yes, can be used to allow more than one auditor access to a volume or container. If this value is set to its default value of No, an attempt by a second auditor to log in to a volume or container that is already in use produces the error shown in figure 10.11. This parameter helps provide backward compatibility with previous versions of NetWare 4.

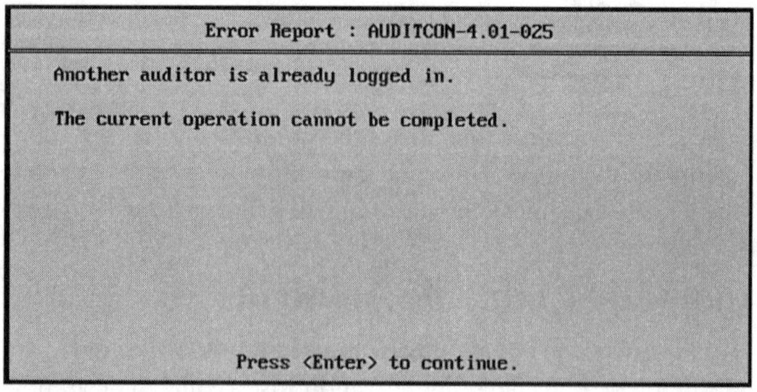

Figure 10.11
Audit error disallowing concurrent usage when Allow Concurrent Auditor Logins is set to No.

Broadcast Errors to All Users

The Broadcast Errors to All Users parameter sends a message to all attached workstations when the audit file reaches its threshold value defined in Audit file threshold size.

Force Dual-Level Audit Passwords

Note, this setting is only available when Allow Audit Passwords is set to ON.

The Force dual-level audit passwords parameter implements a second password that must be entered to save configuration or change audit file settings. This second password is in addition to entering the first password for volume or container login for auditing purposes. By default, the Force dual-level audit passwords field is set to No.

Error Recovery Options for Audit File Full

When the audit log is full, certain recovery options such as archive audit file, disabling auditable/audited events, or disabling event recording can be triggered. If the archive audit file is set to YES, the current audit file is archived when it gets full. This will occur as long as there is sufficient disk space.

If the Disable auditable/audited events field is set to Yes, the audit system will deny any request to perform an auditable/audited event when the audit file is full. Volume auditing disables auditable events. Container auditing disables audited events. The auditor will have to login to the network, at which point you can take actions such as deleting/saving the audit log file and resetting it. Before setting this option to Yes, the auditor should consult the network supervisor because it can cause a serious disruption to users on the network. Unless applications running at the client workstations are written in a robust manner, they can get locked if auditable events are disabled. This option must only be selected if the security requirements of maintaining a complete audit log are more important than the disruption of network applications. By default, the value of the Disable auditable events field is set to No.

Alternatively, if the audit log file is full, you can set the Disable event recording to Yes in order to stop the recording of any additional audit events. By default the value of this parameter is set to Yes.

The Minutes before warning messages is the time in minutes a warning message is sent to the server console (and also to attached workstations if Broadcast errors to all users is set to Yes) when the audit file size reaches the Audit file threshold size.

Auditing a Network User for a Specific Directory

It is sometimes useful to audit the actions a user can perform. Examples of these operations can be file creation/deletion/read or directory creation and deletion. The following steps outline how a network user can be audited for file read operations in a specific directory called SYS:PAYROLL.

1. Log in to the network as an auditor user and run AUDITCON.
2. Select Auditing configuration from the main menu.
3. From Auditing configuration (refer to figure 10.6), select Audit by event.
4. From the Audit by event menu, select Audit by file events. You should see a screen similar to that in figure 10.12.

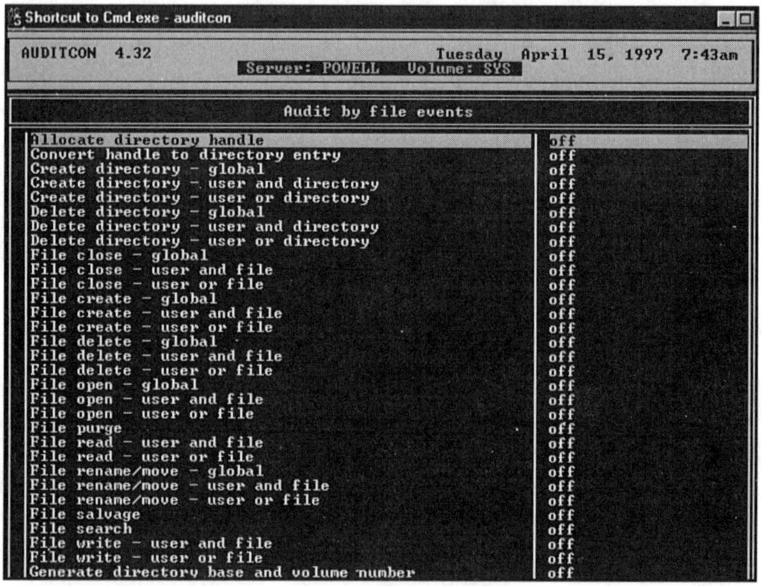

Figure 10.12
The Audit by file events screen.

The screen does not show all the operations that can be audited for files and directories on one screen. You can use the cursor keys or PgDn and PgUp to examine other entries. Using PgDn, you can see the other entries for operations that can be audited (see fig. 10.13). The second screen shows an entry for File read—user and file. This is the entry you must select for auditing a specified user for reading a file in a specified directory. It means that the system will track events that apply to an audited user and an audited file/directory.

5. Selecting File read-user and file can be done by pressing F10 (see fig. 10.14). Press Esc and answer Yes to save changes.

   Up to this point, you have only turned on auditing for a file event of the type File read-user and file. You must next specify the directory and the user to be audited.

6. Press Esc to go back to the Auditing configuration menu.

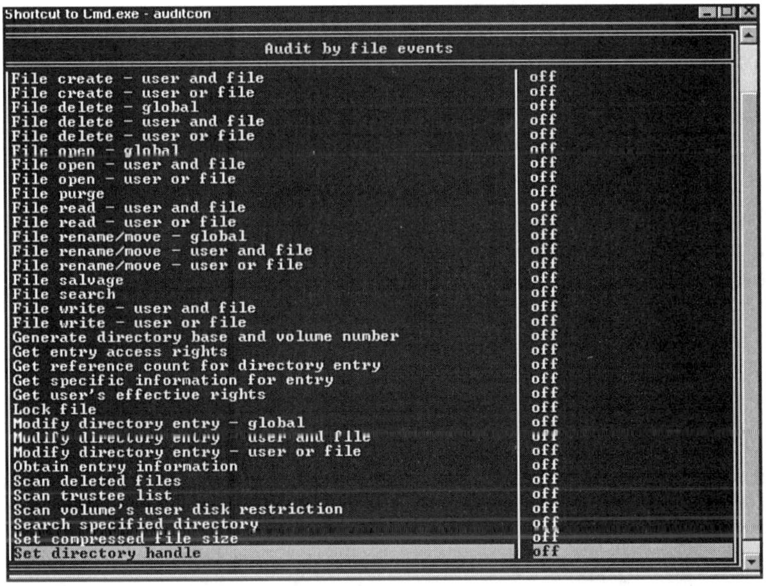

Figure 10.13
The Audit by file events screen—second screen.

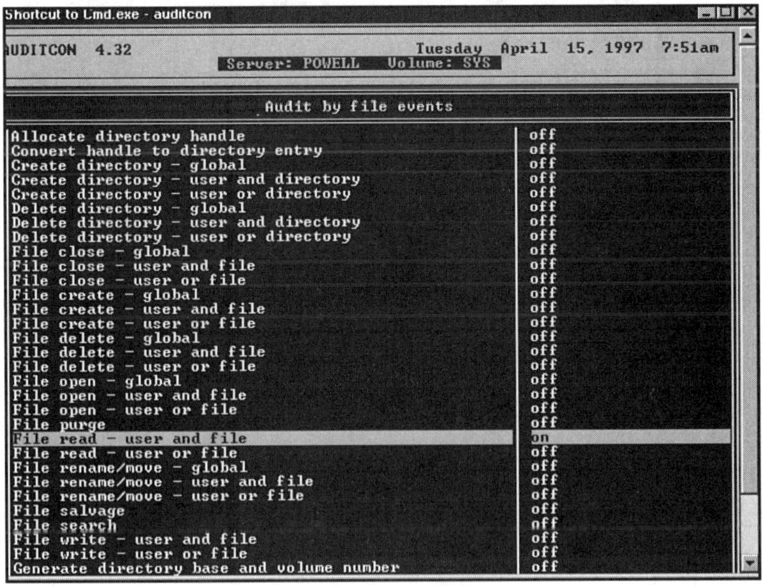

Figure 10.14
Auditing File read—user and file.

7. From the Auditing configuration menu select Audit by file/directory. You should see a screen similar to that in figure 10.15.

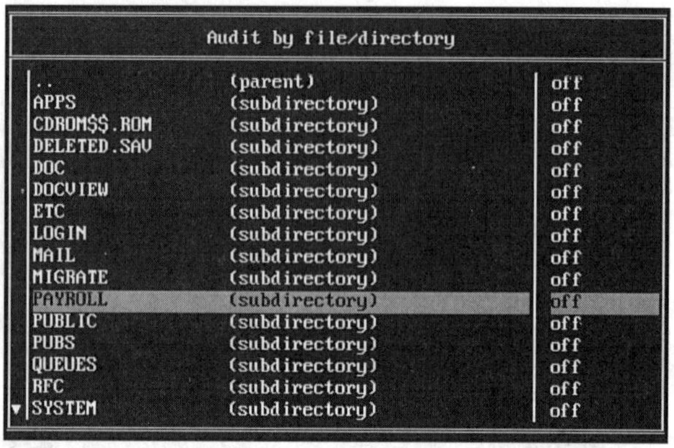

Figure 10.15
The Audit by file/directory selection.

8. Use the cursor keys and Enter to select the directory to be audited. Use F10 to toggle the audit status. Figure 10.16 shows the screen after selecting SYS:PAYROLL directory to be audited.

   Press Esc and answer Yes to save changes.

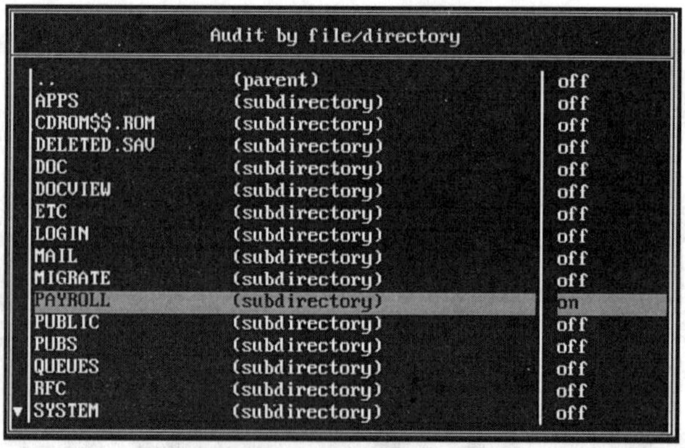

Figure 10.16
An audited directory.

9. Press Esc to go back to the Auditing configuration menu.

10. From the Auditing configuration menu, select Audit by user. You should see a screen similar to that in figure 10.17. Only users defined in the current bindery context are listed. If multiple bindery contexts exist (starting with NetWare 4.1), the bindery emulated users in the multiple bindery contexts are shown.

11. Use F10 to mark a user for auditing. Press Esc and answer Yes to save changes. Figure 10.18 shows the screen after selecting user HACKER to be audited.

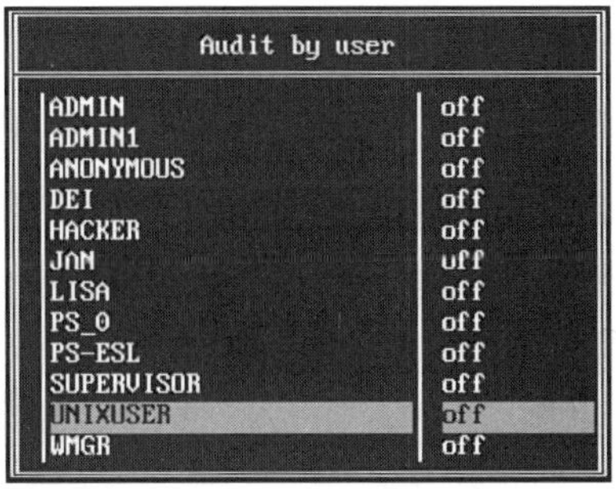

Figure 10.17
A user selection in the Audit by user screen.

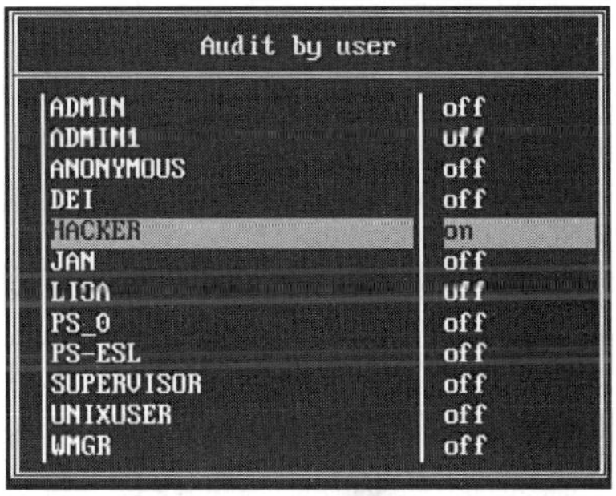

Figure 10.18
An audited user.

Auditing a Specific File

The auditor can flag files and directories to be audited. This is done by performing the steps that follow. The steps show how a particular file can be audited. An example of auditing a file could be to audit all attempts to access an application program-executable file such as NETADMIN.EXE to find out the frequency of access to this file. This knowledge could be used to determine all users who attempted to access this program file.

1. Log in to the network as an auditor user and run AUDITCON.

2. Select Auditing configuration from the main menu.

3. From the Auditing configuration menu (see fig. 10.19), select Audit by event.

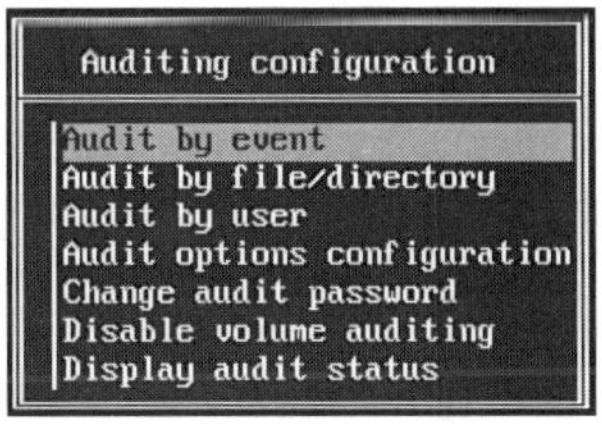

Figure 10.19
The AUDITCON Auditing configuration menu.

4. You can audit a specific file by selecting the option File open—user or file from the Audit by file events menu.

   Specifying File open-user or file means that you will track all occurrences of an event when it applies to an audited user or an audited file. In this case, you are interested in an audited file.

   Press Esc and answer Yes to save changes.

5. Press Esc to go back to the Auditing configuration menu.

6. From the Auditing configuration menu, select Audit by file/directory. You should see a screen similar to that shown in figure 10.15.

7. Use the cursor keys and Enter to select the directory to be audited. Use F10 to toggle audit. Figure 10.20 shows the screen after selecting SYS:PUBLIC\NETADMIN.EXE file to be audited.

   Press Esc and answer Yes to save changes.

8. Exit AUDITCON.

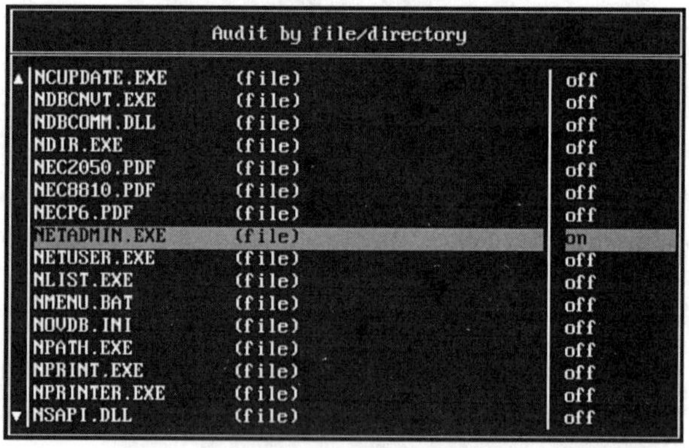

Figure 10.20
The audited file NETADMIN.EXE.

Auditing a Volume for Directory Creations and Deletions

There are situations when it is useful to audit operations such as creation and deletion of directories and subdirectories. It may also be useful to audit these events throughout the volume, regardless of the user performing the event. The following steps outline how this can be done:

1. Log in to the network as an auditor user and run AUDITCON.
2. Select Audit configuration from the main menu.
3. From the Audit configuration menu (refer to figure 10.19), select Audit by event. You should see the screen shown in figure 10.15.
4. You can audit creation or deletion of any directory by selecting the option Create directory—global and Delete directory—global from the Audit by file events menu.

   Specifying global mode means that you will track all occurrences of an event throughout the volume regardless of the user.

   Use F10 to toggle the audit status. Press Esc and answer Yes and save changes.

   Figure 10.21 shows the screen after making the previous selections.

6. Exit AUDITCON.

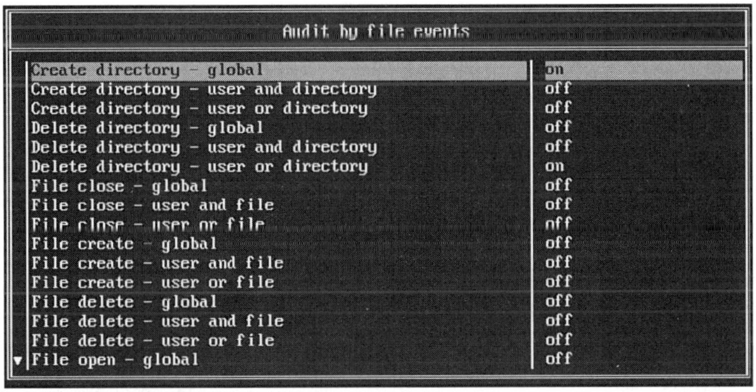

Figure 10.21
Audited create/delete directories.

Auditing NDS

AUDITCON can be used to keep track of NDS events. Examples of common NDS events are object creation/deletion and modifying a user object's telephone number. The auditor must have Browse object rights to the container that is audited. When auditing NDS events, you can audit any User object in the NDS tree for operations on that container. This is different from auditing files and directories where the user audit operations are done in bindery-emulation mode. This means that only users in the bindery contexts of the server can be audited. The following steps outline how to enable auditing on a container and also how a User object can be audited.

1. Log in to the network as an auditor user and run AUDITCON.
2. From the main menu of the AUDITCON utility, select Audit directory services.

3. From the Audit directory service menu, select Audit directory tree. You should see a screen similar to figure 10.22.

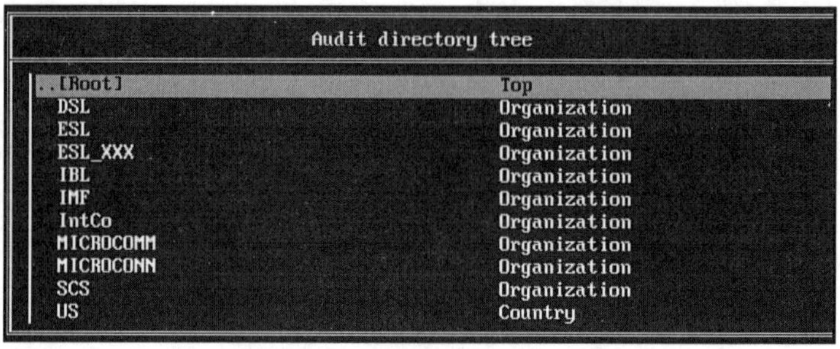

Figure 10.22
The Audit directory tree screen.

4. Highlight the container that should be audited. In our example, the O=ESL container is selected. Use F10 to toggle the audit status. You should see a screen similar to figure 10.23, showing the Available audit options.

Figure 10.23
Available audit options for a container when auditing is disabled.

The Admin user, or a user with Supervisor file system rights, must select the Enable container auditing option to enable auditing (see fig. 10.24).

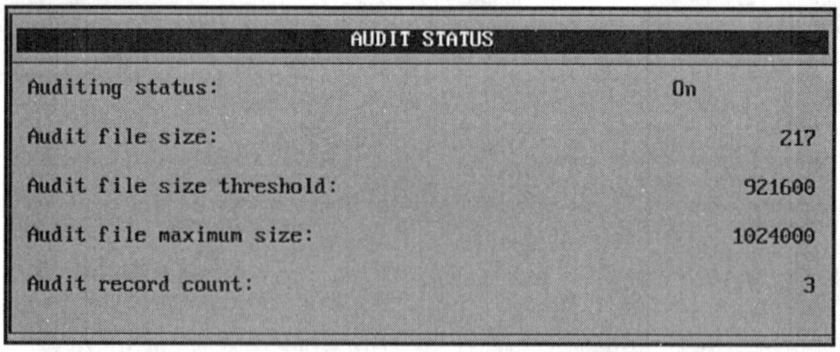

Figure 10.24
Display audit status for container when auditing is enabled.

5. The Available audit options menu will change for the audited container (see fig. 10.25).

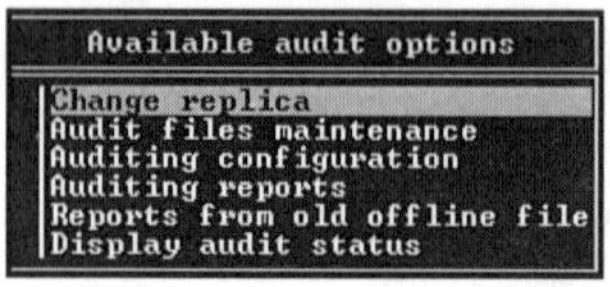

Figure 10.25
Available audit options for a container when auditing is enabled.

6. Select Auditing configuration. You should see the Auditing configuration options menu (see fig. 10.26).

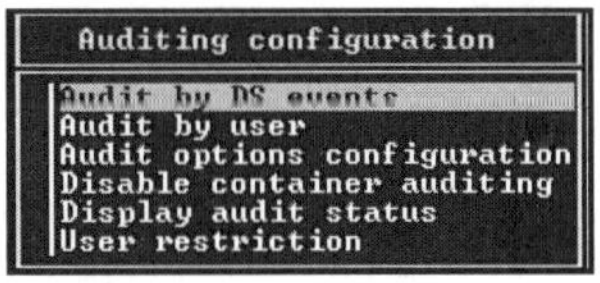

Figure 10.26
Auditing configuration for containers.

7. From Auditing configuration menu, select Audit by DS events. You should see the different types of events that can be audited (see fig. 10.27). You may have to use the cursor keys or PgDn and PgUp to see all of the DS events that can be audited. Figure 10.28 shows additional DS events.

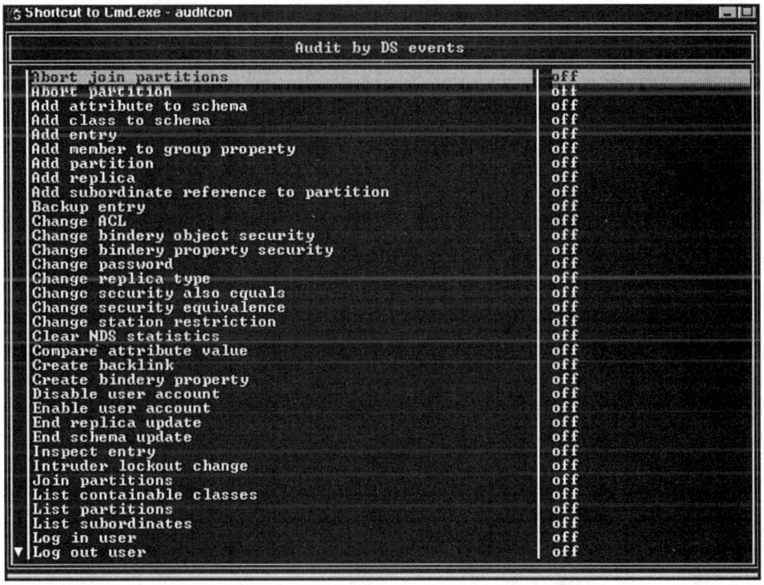

Figure 10.27
Audit by DS events.

11. To audit the following events, highlight each event and press F10 to toggle them to the AUDITED status. Figure 10.29 shows that these events have been enabled:

   - Change ACL
   - Change password
   - Log in user
   - Log out user

   Press Esc and answer Yes to save changes.

12. Exit AUDITCON.

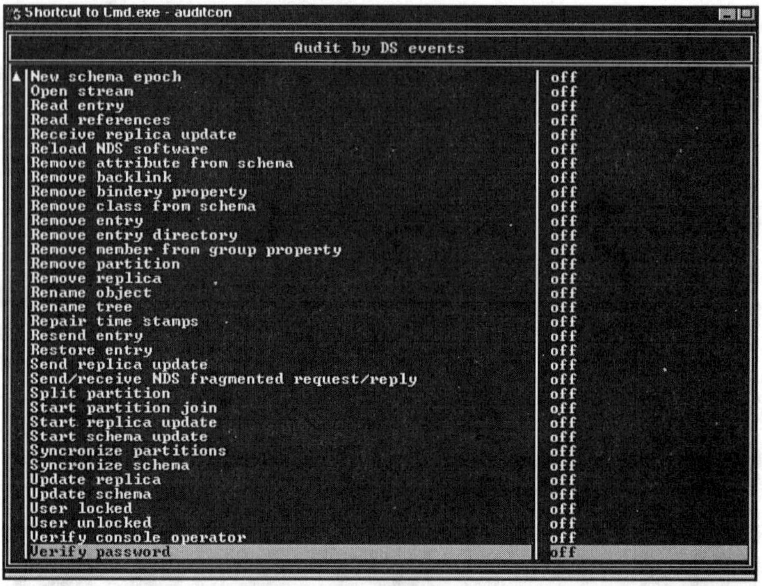

Figure 10.28
Audit by DS events—second screen.

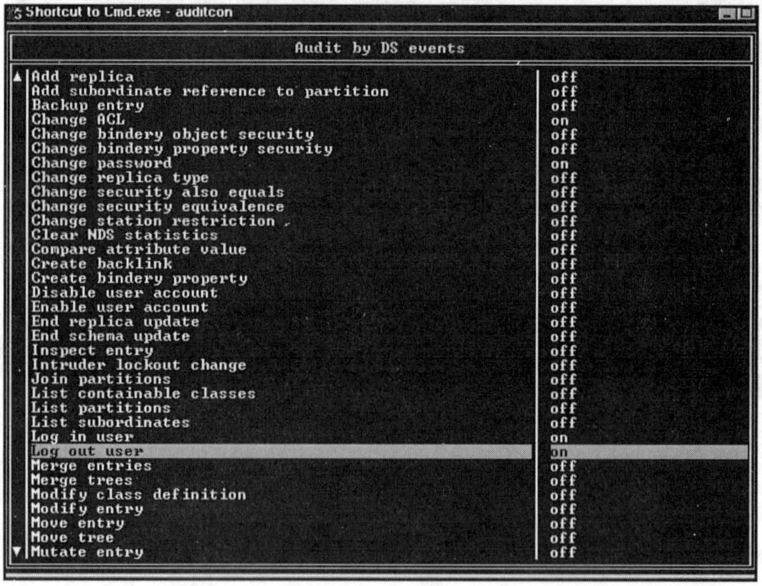

Figure 10.29
Audit By DS Events showing events that are audited.

Generating Audit Reports

The AUDITCON tool has the ability to view the contents of the current audit and archived audit files through a simple report-generation option. The reports are written to a text file, and can be printed or stored for long term archival. Because the report is a text file, you should exercise caution to make sure that ordinary users do not have access to this text file. For example, it is not a good idea to keep the report in the SYS:PUBLIC directory where users typically have Read and File Scan access rights. It is best to print the file, then delete and purge the report file from the network.

The report option also allows the setting of filters to view selected data. This is useful in situations where large amounts of audit data are generated.

Typical steps the auditor needs to perform to generate reports are as follows:

1. Create and apply a filter. An existing filter can be edited and modified also.

2. Generate the report in a DOS text file.

3. Print the report or view the audit report online.

The following steps guide you in generating an audit report.

1. Log in to the network as an auditor user and run AUDITCON.

2. From the main menu of the AUDITCON utility, select Auditing reports. You should see a screen similar to that in figure 10.30.

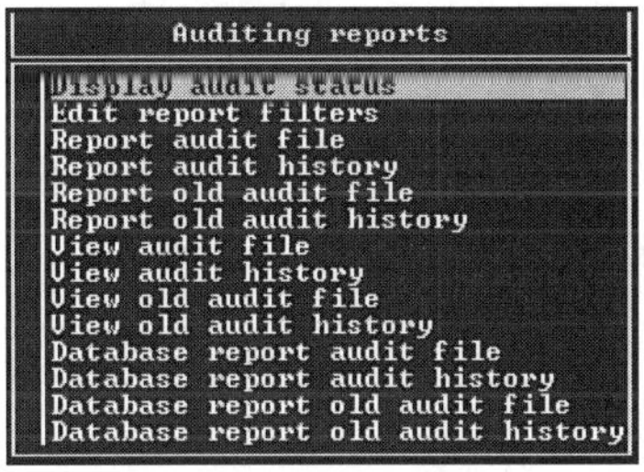

Figure 10.30
Auditing reports menu.

3. To view the current audit file, select View audit file from the Auditing reports menu.

4. You will be asked to select a filter. If a filter has not been defined, only the default filter _no_filter_ will be displayed (see fig. 10.31). Select this filter.

Figure 10.31
Auditing reports—Default filter _no_filter_.

5. To view a report, you can select View audit file from Auditing reports. Figure 10.32 shows an example report.

6. To view the history file, you can select View audit history from Auditing reports. Figure 10.33 shows a sample history report.

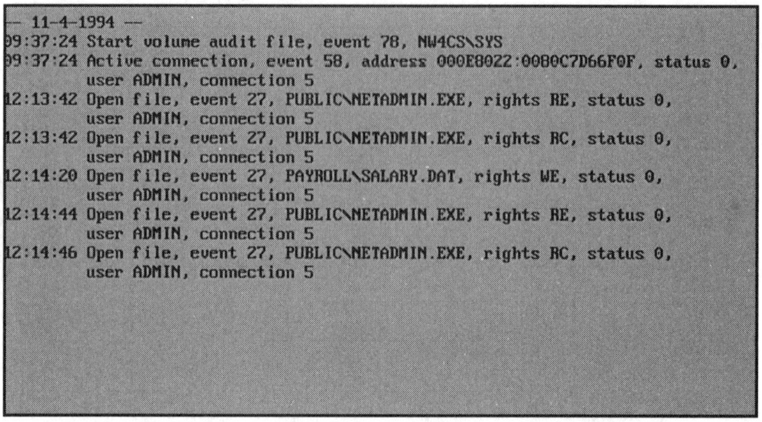

— 11-4-1994 —
09:37:24 Start volume audit file, event 78, NW4CS\SYS
09:37:24 Active connection, event 58, address 000E8022:0080C7D66F0F, status 0,
user ADMIN, connection 5
12:13:42 Open file, event 27, PUBLIC\NETADMIN.EXE, rights RE, status 0,
user ADMIN, connection 5
12:13:42 Open file, event 27, PUBLIC\NETADMIN.EXE, rights RC, status 0,
user ADMIN, connection 5
12:14:20 Open file, event 27, PAYROLL\SALARY.DAT, rights WE, status 0,
user ADMIN, connection 5
12:14:44 Open file, event 27, PUBLIC\NETADMIN.EXE, rights RE, status 0,
user ADMIN, connection 5
12:14:46 Open file, event 27, PUBLIC\NETADMIN.EXE, rights RC, status 0,
user ADMIN, connection 5

Figure 10.32
Audit reports—viewing audit report.

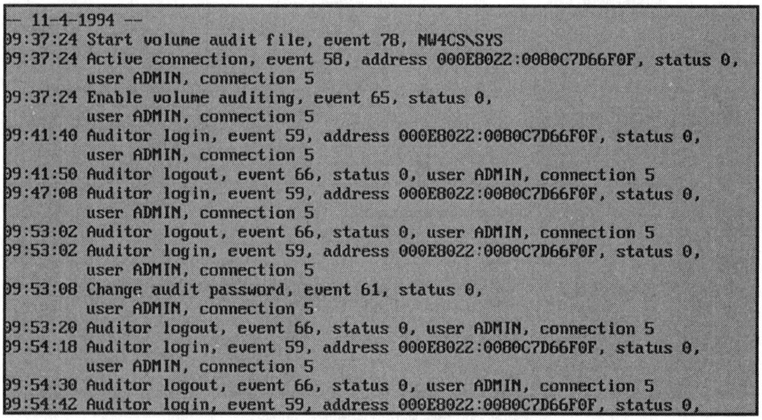

— 11-4-1994 —
09:37:24 Start volume audit file, event 78, NW4CS\SYS
09:37:24 Active connection, event 58, address 000E8022:0080C7D66F0F, status 0,
user ADMIN, connection 5
09:37:24 Enable volume auditing, event 65, status 0,
user ADMIN, connection 5
09:41:40 Auditor login, event 59, address 000E8022:0080C7D66F0F, status 0,
user ADMIN, connection 5
09:41:50 Auditor logout, event 66, status 0, user ADMIN, connection 5
09:47:08 Auditor login, event 59, address 000E8022:0080C7D66F0F, status 0,
user ADMIN, connection 5
09:53:02 Auditor logout, event 66, status 0, user ADMIN, connection 5
09:53:02 Auditor login, event 59, address 000E8022:0080C7D66F0F, status 0,
user ADMIN, connection 5
09:53:08 Change audit password, event 61, status 0,
user ADMIN, connection 5
09:53:20 Auditor logout, event 66, status 0, user ADMIN, connection 5
09:54:18 Auditor login, event 59, address 000E8022:0080C7D66F0F, status 0,
user ADMIN, connection 5
09:54:30 Auditor logout, event 66, status 0, user ADMIN, connection 5
09:54:42 Auditor login, event 59, address 000E8022:0080C7D66F0F, status 0,

Figure 10.33
Audit history reports—viewing audit history report.

7. To Save the Audit file, select Report audit file from the Auditing reports menu.

8. You will be asked to enter the file name for the report. You can accept the default name of AUDITDAT.TXT or choose another (see fig. 10.34). The auditor must have [RWCEM] rights to the current directory. These rights are needed because the auditor creates temporary files.

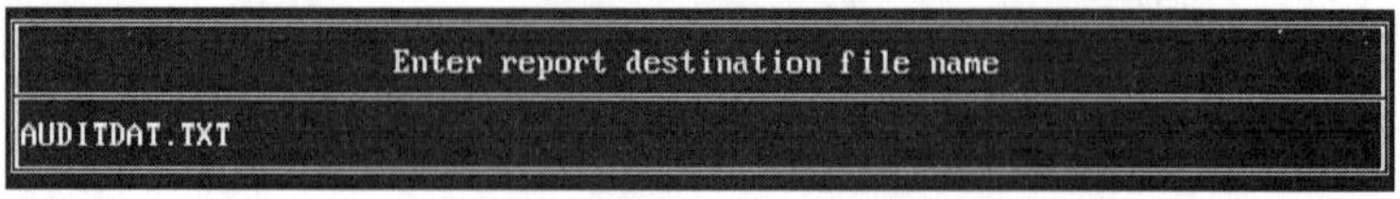

Figure 10.34
Auditing reports—enter file name.

9. You will be asked to select a filter. If a filter has not been defined, only the default filter _no_filter_ will be displayed (refer to figure 10.31). Select this filter.

10. Exit AUDITCON.

Creating a Report Filter

Because of the large amounts of audit data that can be generated, it is useful to know how filters can be created to select only the audit data of interest. After you create a filter, you can save it so that it can be reused later. When you create reports, you can select from a list of previously defined filters, and if necessary modify an existing filter and use it.

The following steps will guide you through creating a simple filter.

1. Log in to the network as an auditor user and run AUDITCON.

2. From the main menu of the AUDITCON utility, select Auditing reports. You should see a screen similar to the one in figure 10.30.

3. You can create new filters by selecting Edit report filters. When a list of filters appears, press Ins. You should see the Edit report filter menu (see fig. 10.35).

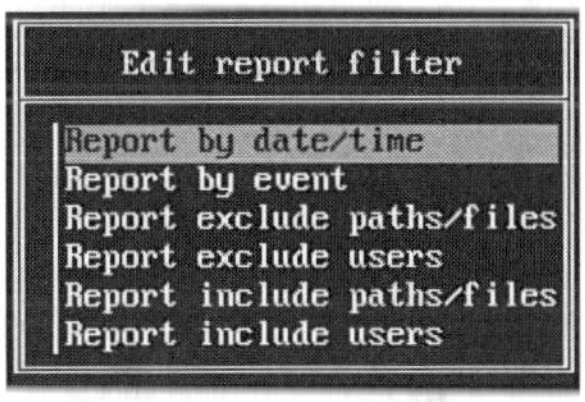

Figure 10.35
The Edit report filter menu.

You can set a filter using any of the following criteria:

- Date/Time
- Event
- Exclude/Include Paths and Files
- Exclude/Include Users

4. To select a report by its date and time, select Report By Date/Time and press Ins (see fig. 10.36). This enables you to select the start date/time and the end date/time for the audit events that are of interest. After you make your changes, press Esc.

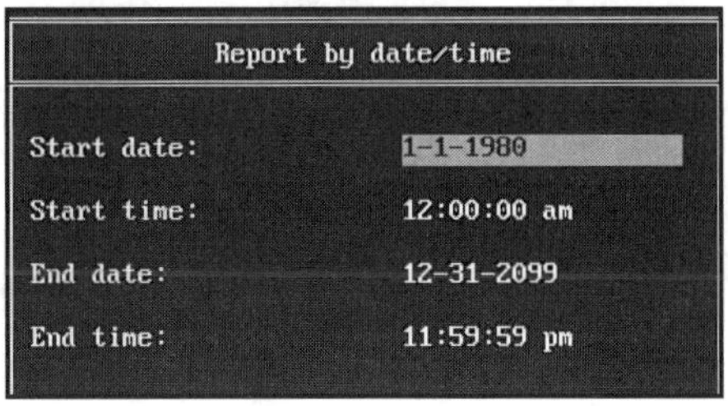

Figure 10.36
Edit report filter—date/time form.

Figure 10.37 shows a date/time filter set up from October 1, 1993, 12:00:00 p.m. to December 31, 2020, 11:59:59 p.m.

Press Esc to go back to the Edit report filter menu.

Figure 10.37

Edit report filter—date/ time filter.

```
-- 10-6-1993 --
19:12:38 Read File, event 42, PAYROLL\DATA\APR.PAY, length 67, offset 0,
         status 0, user HACKER, connection 3
19:12:38 Read File, event 42, PAYROLL\DATA\PAYROL.DAT, length 67, offset 0,
         status 0, user HACKER, connection 3
19:12:38 Read File, event 42, PAYROLL\DATA\SALARY.DAT, length 67, offset 0,
         status 0, user HACKER, connection 3
19:12:42 Read File, event 42, PAYROLL\DATA\APR.PAY, length 67, offset 0,
         status 0, user HACKER, connection 3
19:12:44 Read File, event 42, PAYROLL\DATA\PAYROL.DAT, length 67, offset 0,
         status 0, user HACKER, connection 3
19:12:46 Read File, event 42, PAYROLL\DATA\SALARY.DAT, length 67, offset 0,
         status 0, user HACKER, connection 3
19:13:06 Read File, event 42, PUBLIC\NETADMIN.EXE, length 1458, offset 0,
         status 0, user HACKER, connection 3
19:13:06 Read File, event 42, PUBLIC\NETADMIN.EXE, length 2560, offset 13824,
         status 0, user HACKER, connection 3
19:13:06 Read File, event 42, PUBLIC\NETADMIN.EXE, length 4096, offset 16384,
         status 0, user HACKER, connection 3
19:13:06 Read File, event 42, PUBLIC\NETADMIN.EXE, length 4096, offset 20480,
         status 0, user HACKER, connection 3
```

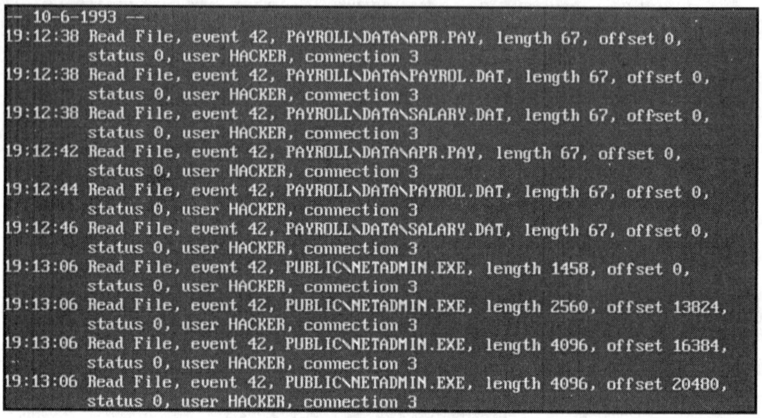

6. To select a report by file events select Report by event (see fig. 10.38). You should be able to set up a filter by file events, QMS events, server events, and user events.

Figure 10.38

Edit report filter—Report by event.

```
        Report by event

   Report by file events
   Report by QMS events
   Report by server events
   Report by user events
```

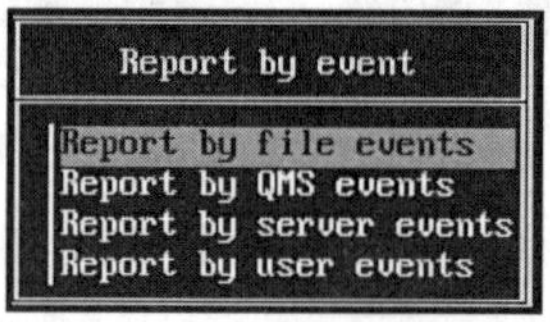

Figure 10.39 shows the Report by file events. There are two columns for each file event. These show the audit status and the report status. By default, an audited event is also reported. In figure 10.39, the File open—user or file and File read—user or file events are audited, and also reported. To toggle the report status, press F10.

Figure 10.39

Edit report filter—report by file events.

```
                    Report by file events

   Create directory - user or directory          off      off
   Delete directory - user or directory          on       on
   File close - modified file                    off      off
   File close - user or file                     off      off
   File create - user or file                    off      off
   File delete - user or file                    off      off
   File open - user or file                      on       on
   File read - user or file                      on       on
   File rename/move - user or file               off      off
   File salvage                                  off      off
   File write - user or file                     off      off
   Modify directory entry - user or file         off      off
```

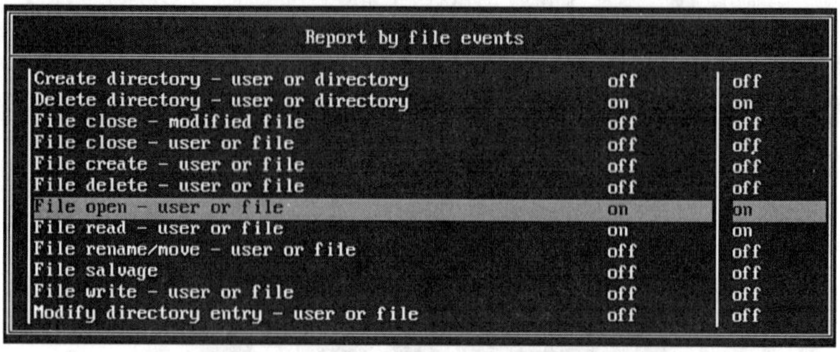

7. The Report exclude paths/files option and the Report include paths/files option can be selected to exclude or include information on specific files or directories.

8. The Report exclude users option and the Report include users option can be selected to exclude or include information on specific users. The Report exclude users list is by default empty, and the Report include users option contains the asterisk (*) entry indicating all users are included. You can use Ins and Del to insert and delete user names from this list.

   Figure 10.40 shows that auditing information for only the user HACKER will be presented.

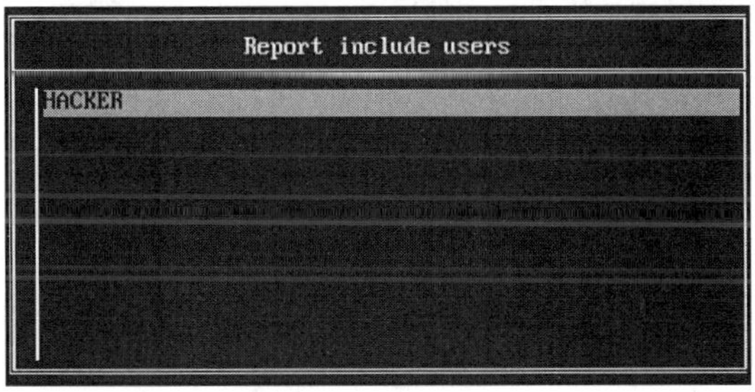

Figure 10.40
Edit report filter—Report include users.

9. After making the filter edits, press Esc twice. You will be presented with an option of saving the filter under a name (see fig. 10.41). Enter a suitable filter name and press Enter.

Figure 10.41
Edit report filter—Save filter changes.

10. You can test your filter by selecting View audit file from Auditing Reports, and selecting the newly defined filter.

Figure 10.42 shows an example of a report that uses a filter for looking at information for the user HACKER. Notice that the information is on user HACKER only. Also, in this filter the File open—user or file event has been filtered out, but the File read—user or file event has been retained in the filter.

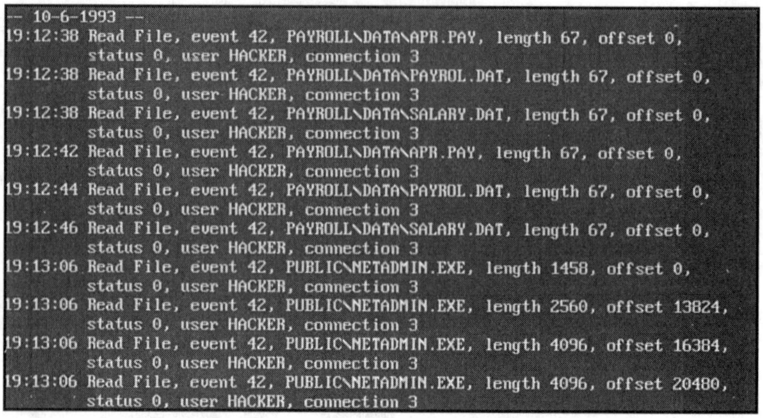

Figure 10.42

Edit report filter—using a filter on a report.

```
-- 10-6-1993 --
19:12:38 Read File, event 42, PAYROLL\DATA\APR.PAY, length 67, offset 0,
         status 0, user HACKER, connection 3
19:12:38 Read File, event 42, PAYROLL\DATA\PAYROL.DAT, length 67, offset 0,
         status 0, user HACKER, connection 3
19:12:38 Read File, event 42, PAYROLL\DATA\SALARY.DAT, length 67, offset 0,
         status 0, user HACKER, connection 3
19:12:42 Read File, event 42, PAYROLL\DATA\APR.PAY, length 67, offset 0,
         status 0, user HACKER, connection 3
19:12:44 Read File, event 42, PAYROLL\DATA\PAYROL.DAT, length 67, offset 0,
         status 0, user HACKER, connection 3
19:12:46 Read File, event 42, PAYROLL\DATA\SALARY.DAT, length 67, offset 0,
         status 0, user HACKER, connection 3
19:13:06 Read File, event 42, PUBLIC\NETADMIN.EXE, length 1458, offset 0,
         status 0, user HACKER, connection 3
19:13:06 Read File, event 42, PUBLIC\NETADMIN.EXE, length 2560, offset 13824,
         status 0, user HACKER, connection 3
19:13:06 Read File, event 42, PUBLIC\NETADMIN.EXE, length 4096, offset 16384,
         status 0, user HACKER, connection 3
19:13:06 Read File, event 42, PUBLIC\NETADMIN.EXE, length 4096, offset 20480,
         status 0, user HACKER, connection 3
```

Managing Audit Reports

The audit reports are generated as text files. Although the original audit files NET$AUDT.CAF and other audit files are not accessible to non-auditors, the text files can be read by any user who has Read rights to them. For this reason, it is best to print the audit report, then delete and purge the audit file. If an electronic text file of the report is desired, it can be downloaded onto a floppy disk, then deleted and purged from the network.

The following steps outline the procedure to print an audit report:

1. Log in to the network as an auditor user and run AUDITCON.

2. From the main menu of the AUDITCON utility, select Auditing reports.

3. Select Report audit file from the Auditing reports menu.

4. You will be asked to enter the file name for the report. Enter the full path name for the report.

5. Exit AUDITCON.

6. Print the Audit Report text file. You can use the NPRINT, NETUSER, PCONSOLE, or CAPTURE commands for printing. Alternatively, you can import the text file into a word processor and use the print function within the word processor.

7. Optionally, you can copy the report file onto a floppy disk.

8. Remember to delete and purge the report file from the network as soon as you are done using it unless it is stored in a secure place.

Maintaining Audit Files

AUDITCON has options to manage existing audit log files. These options are typically used when the audit log files get full. Using these options, the auditor can move existing audit log files to old audit log files, and reset audit log files.

The following steps outline how this can be accomplished:

1. Log in to the network as an auditor user and run AUDITCON.

2. From the main menu of the AUDITCON utility.

3. From the Available audit options menu, select Audit files maintenance. You should see the audit files maintenance menu (see fig. 10.43).

Figure 10.43
The Audit files maintenance menu.

The Copy old audit file option enables you to copy an old audit file. This file is copied as a compressed, non-readable file. You can specify the name and the destination of the file. The default name is AUDITOLD.DAT. If you want to copy this file in a readable report format, you can do this by activating the Auditing reports menu and selecting Report audit file.

The Delete old audit file option enables you to delete an old audit file. The current audit file is not affected.

The Display audit status option enables you to view the audit status such as audit status, audit file size, audit file threshold, the maximum audit file size, and the audit record count.

The Reset audit data file option moves current data in the audit file to the old audit data file. The audit data file is reset to zero records, and will continue gathering audit events based on the current configuration settings.

Auditing Guidelines

If you want to determine whether there is a security breach, you can audit the following:

- Changes to the ACL for an object (NDS event)
- File opens and reads of critical files

If you suspect security breaches by a particular user, you can audit the following:

- File opens/reads/writes by the user
- File opens/reads/writes to those files that you suspect the user is tampering with

If you suspect that there is a security breach at the file server, you can audit the following:

- NetWare server events
- Server volume mounts/dismounts
- Logins to the network
- Read/opens to RCONSOLE program for remote access

If you want to troubleshoot performance problems with an application, you can audit the following:

- File operations by the application that you suspect is slow
- File opens to the application program, to determine simultaneous use of the program

If you want to justify purchase of a higher license version of an application, you can audit the following events to determine if such a purchase is justified:

- Audit writes to the application's data and program files
- If the application prints to a queue, audit use of print queues

If you want to monitor usage of sensitive files, you can audit file opens/reads to that file.

Summary

In this chapter you learned about the auditing capabilities of IntranetWare. You learned about the reasons for using the auditing features of IntranetWare. Access to the audit data and configuration is controlled by NDS instead of passwords as in previous NetWare versions. The principal tool for auditing is AUDITCON. AUDITCON can be used for monitoring file system events, QMS events, server events, user events, and NDS events. The differences between these different types of events were described in this chapter. You also learned about the different parameters for audit configuration, such as setting audit file maximum size and specifying what recovery options to select in case the audit file is full.

This chapter also presented an outline of steps to be performed for setting up different auditing scenarios. Toward the end of the chapter you learned about report generation and filter creation for generating reports on selected events. Lastly, some auditing guidelines for different scenarios were discussed.

CHAPTER 11

NetWare Application Services

NetWare application services helps simplify the network administrator's job by enabling the administrator to manage network applications and user desktops from NetWare Administrator. Applications can be installed and managed centrally on the server by the administrator and access to these applications can be managed through Novell Directory Services (NDS). Objects for applications are created and managed through NetWare Administrator and NetWare Application Manager (NAM). Users launch the applications from NetWare Application Launcher (NAL) on their desktop.

This chapter describes application services and provides instruction for configuring applications through NetWare Application Manager by associating them with containers, groups, and users. Also described is the NetWare Application Launcher and its configuration. Instructions for replacing users' desktops with NetWare Application Launcher are included as well. There are many benefits of using application services and these benefits will be discussed throughout this chapter.

Exploring NetWare Application Manager (NAM)

NetWare Application Manager (NAM) is controlled through NetWare Administrator and enables the network administrator to manage application objects for DOS, Windows 3.1, Windows 95, and Windows NT applications. Applications can be installed centrally in the NetWare Tree to provide global access to users. Using NetWare Application Manager, the administrator can create Application Object icons that contain the executable path and the working directory for the application. These Application objects are used to establish drive mappings and printer capture statements as well as run pre-launch and post-termination scripts. The Application objects when associated with containers, provide access to the appli-cation to all users in the container. Objects can also be associated with groups and users through the NetWare Application Manager in NetWare Administrator. After these icons are associated with any of these objects, the applications are either launched automatically or are launched by the user, depending on the administrator's configuration in NetWare Application Manager. The NetWare Application Launcher (NAL) for associated objects, contains configuration options to enable the users to perform tasks such as exit the launcher or log in and out from the launcher. Configuring the launcher to enable these tasks is discussed later in this chapter.

NetWare Application Manager simplifies the administrator's job by enabling the administrator to centrally configure and manage the icons used to launch applications from the user's desktop. Application icons are dynamically added to the associated object's application launcher. This enables the administrator to create icons in NetWare Administrator and when associated with the containers, users, or groups, provides users with the icons to launch these applications from their desktop. This saves time because the administrator does not need to configure the user's desktop locally. The icons associated with the object are available dynamically through NetWare Application Launcher.

Because the NetWare Application Manager maps drives to the application, licensed connections normally taken up on other servers when drives are mapped through login scripts are not used until the application is launched, and are released when the user exits the application. This assists network administrators in maintaining licensed connections when the number of licensed connections is an issue. In addition, login scripts require less administration because drives are mapped and printers are captured through the application object. This might also decrease the amount of user support necessary for specific printer captures when running certain applications.

Creating Objects for DOS, Windows 3.x, Windows 95, and Windows NT Workstations using NetWare Application Manager version 1.0

The creation, configuration, and association of application objects to containers, groups, or users is performed with NetWare Application Manager through NetWare Administrator. The next portion of this chapter provides the steps performed when using NetWare Administrator to manage applications through NetWare Application Manager. Application objects for DOS, Windows 3.1, Windows 95, and Windows NT are created to run applications on their respective platforms. This section demonstrates the steps to create DOS and Windows application objects in NetWare Application Manager.

To create a DOS application object in the `.ou=AR.ou=ACCOUNTING.ou=US.o=IntCo` container, perform the following:

1. Login as Admin or equivalent user.

2. Launch NetWare Administrator.

3. Highlight the AR container and click on the Create a new object icon from the toolbar. This brings up the New Object dialog box (see fig. 11.1).

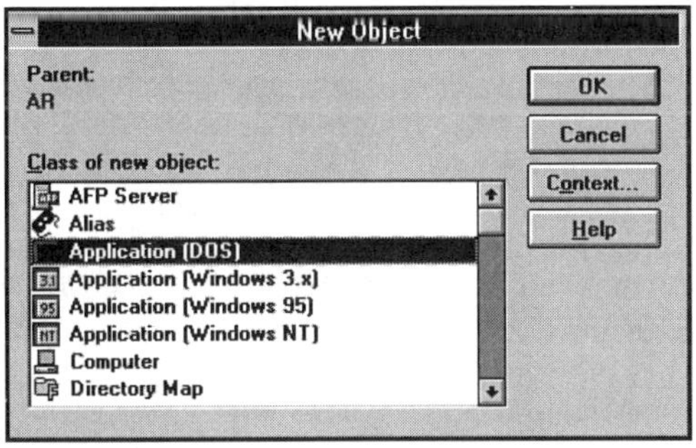

Figure 11.1
The New Object dialog box.

4. Select the Application [DOS] object from the object list.

Note

In step number five, it is important to note that when you are browsing the tree to locate an Available Object, the Context in which you are browsing will always be on the right side of the screen. You "navigate," or browse, on the right by clicking on the appropriate context and you select the object from the Available Objects list on the left side of the screen.

5. Click on the Browse button to browse for the NETADMIN.EXE file in the PUBLIC directory. Click on the scroll up arrow in the Browse Context to reveal the AP and AR containers. Double-click on the scroll up arrow from the Browse Context to reveal the ACCOUNTING and MARKETING containers. Double-click on the MARKETING container from the Browse Context to reveal the FS1_SYS Volume object. Double-click on the FS1_SYS Volume object to reveal the directory structure. Double-click on the PUBLIC directory from the Browse Context to reveal the files in the available objects list. Select the NETADMIN.EXE file under the Available Objects portion. Figure 11.2 shows the path information and name of the DOS Application Object for NETADMIN.

6. Click on the Create button to create the DOS Application object called NETADMIN.

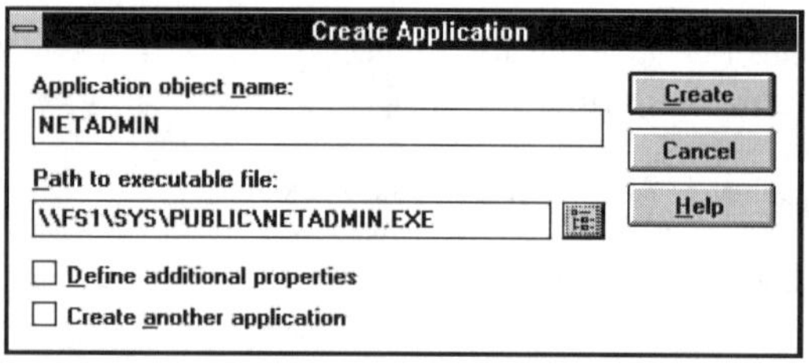

Figure 11.2
The Create Application dialog box for NETADMIN.

The next series of steps demonstrates how to create a Windows 3.1 application object in the `.ou=AR.ou=ACCOUNTING.ou=US.o=IntCo` container. To create the Windows 3.1 Application object for NetWare Administrator, perform the following steps:

1. Login as Admin or equivalent.

2. Highlight the AR container.

3. Select Object from the drop-down menu bar then click on the Create button. This reveals the object creation list (refer to figure 11.1).

4. Double-click on the Application(Windows 3.1) object.

5. Click on the Browse button and browse the tree to locate the NWADMN3X.EXE file for the NetWare Administrator utility. Perform the same steps as in step 5 of the previous list, except this time locate the NWADMN3X.EXE (instead of NETADMIN.EXE) name and path to executable in the create application box.

6. Change the Application object name to NetWare Administrator by typing it in the associated box (see fig. 11.3).

7. Click on the Create button to create the Application object for NetWare Administrator.

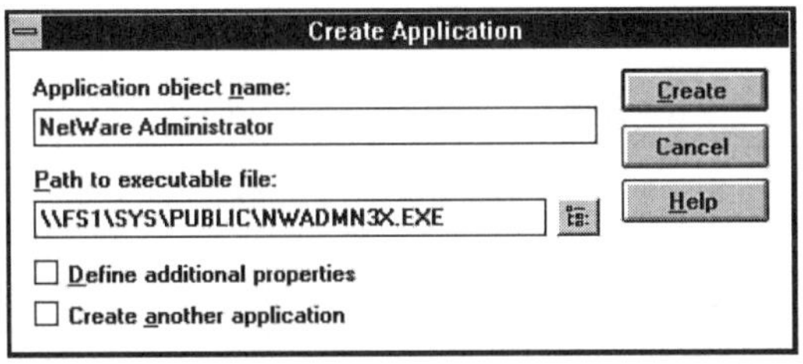

Figure 11.3
The Create Application dialog box for NetWare Administrator.

Defining Properties for Application Objects

The preceding steps demonstrated how to create the DOS and Windows 3.x application objects. Windows 95 and Windows NT objects are created in the same manner by selecting the appropriate Application object icon from the Object creation list. After the Application objects are created, additional properties must be defined for the objects. The following steps demonstrate how to configure the Windows 3.x Application object created in the previous section for the NetWare Administrator Application object.

1. Login as Admin or equivalent.

2. Launch NetWare Administrator.

3. Reveal the contents of the .AR.ACCOUNTING.US.IntCo container and double-click on the NetWare Administrator Application object to reveal an identification screen similar to figure 11.4.

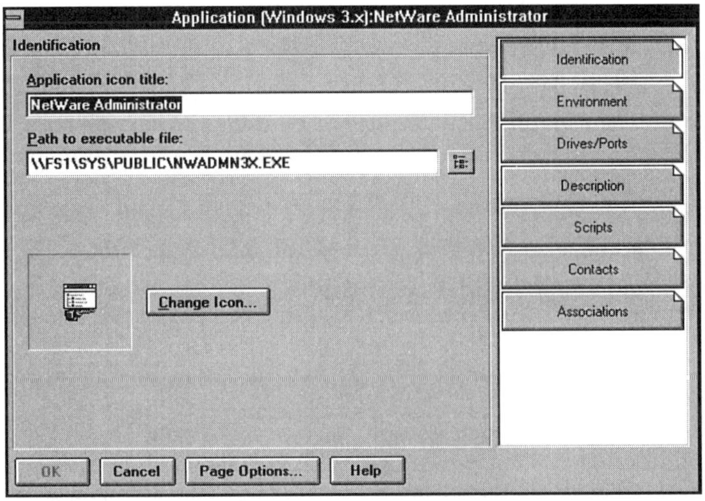

Figure 11.4
The identification property page for the NetWare Administrator application object.

4. Click on the Environment property button to reveal a screen similar to the one in figure 11.5. Place an X in the Clean up network resources check box to remove resources mapped by previously launched applications. Place an X next to the Run minimized check box to minimize the application when launched.

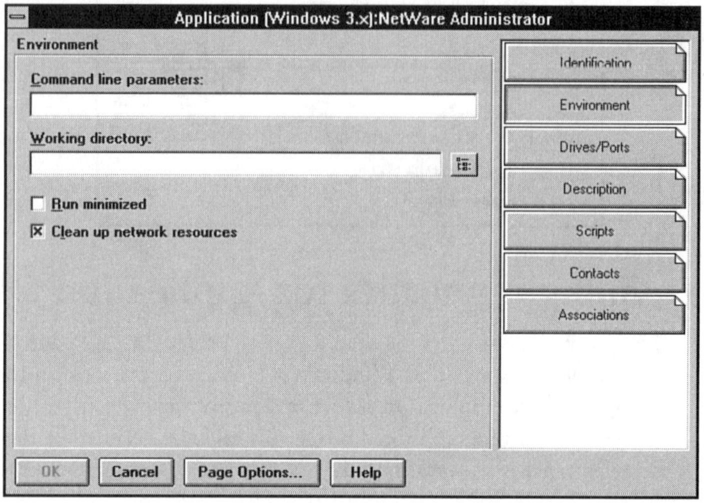

Figure 11.5
The Environment property page for the NetWare Administrator application object.

Table 11.1 provides information on each of the properties that can be defined for this Application object in NetWare Application Manager.

Table 11.1
Properties Defined for Objects in NetWare Application Manager

Property	Description
Identification	Identifies the Application object. Includes the icon title, path to the executable (which can be located by browsing), and change icon to change the icon seen in application launcher.
Environment	Contains information about the environment variables for the Application object.
Command line parameters	Contains parameters used to run the Application object.
Working directory	Contains the working directory path for the executable.
Run minimized	If selected, minimizes the application when the application executes.
Clean up network resources	If selected, cleans up previously mapped drives and printer capture statements created by applications launched prior to launching the new application.
Drives/Ports	Maps drives that might be necessary to execute the application or to create pointers to data directories when the application launches. Printer captures and flags can also be set with this option.

Property	Description
Option	Drive type options used when mapping drives with NetWare Application Manager. The following is a list of options for specifying the drive type. ■ **None.** Does not map a drive. ■ **Drive.** Allows a regular mapped drive pointer. ■ **Root.** Creates a map rooted drive pointer. ■ **Next.** Maps the next available drive pointer.
Drive	Allows a drive letter assignment to map a drive pointer.
Path	Allows administrators to browse for the executable file and path or can be typed in using the Universal Naming Convention (UNC).
Ports to be captured	Allows redirection of print jobs from the local workstation to the network. Used to set up printer captures when launching this application.
Port	Printer port used for redirection of local printing from LPT1 through LPT9 when capturing a printer.
Qucuc	Network print queue to be captured for redirection of print jobs for this application.
Capture flags	Sets capture flags for notification, banner, and form feed capture parameters. Can be set to override workstation capture settings.
Description	Description of the services provided by this application object. Can contain information about the application object including the application setup and cleanup. This screen is for information only.
Scripts	Using login script syntax, can map drives or run setup scripts necessary for the application.
Run before launching	Scripts that map drives and capture printers through setup scripts prior to launching the application.
Run after launching	Scripts run to remap previously mapped drives or delete drive mappings and redirect printing to a different queue after the application is exited.

continues

Table 11.1
Properties Defined for Objects in NetWare Application Manager

Property	Description
Contacts	Lists users to be contacted if there is a problem running the application. This information can be viewed by the user in the properties of the application object and displays the phone number of the contact if one is entered for the contact user's object.
Associations	Associates this application object with containers, groups, and users who will be provided access to these applications through NetWare Application Launcher.

5. Click on the Drives/Ports property button to assign drive mapping and printer capture statements to be used when launching the application. Refer to table 11.1 for information on parameters configured with this property button. Select a printer capture to .Q1.AR.ACCOUNTING.US.IntCo, capturing LPT1 with capture flags of no form feed, no banner, and no notify. Figure 11.6 demonstrates the capture statement and maps drive G: to the user's home directory.

   The next set of commands demonstrates the steps performed when assigning printing options.

   a. Click on the arrow under the Port icon to reveal the LPT ports.

   b. Click on Browse to locate the print queue in the AR container and select Q1.

   c. Click on the Set… button and place an X next to each capture flag option.

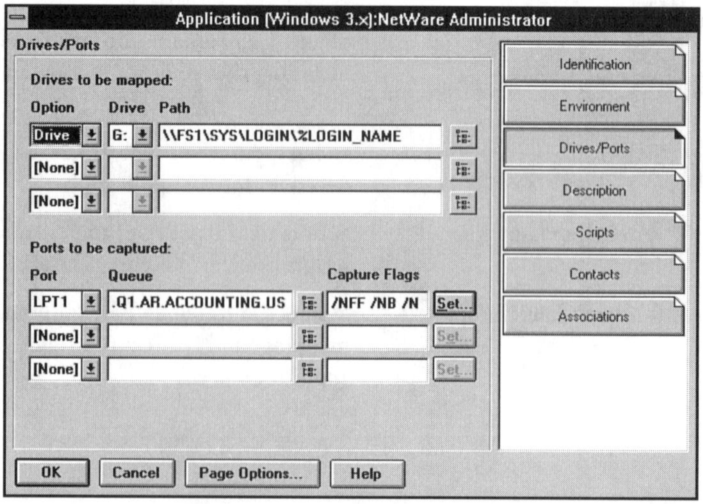

Figure 11.6
The Drives/Ports property page for the NetWare Administrator application object.

6. Click on the Description property option and enter a brief description of the application object in the box provided. Figure 11.7 shows a description for the NetWare Administrator application object. This description will appear in the application launcher properties for this application object. Figure 11.8 shows the description property shown from NetWare Application Launcher.

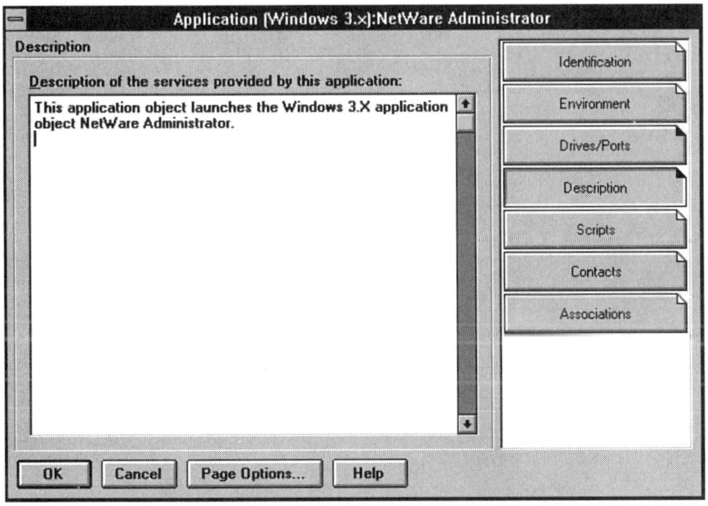

Figure 11.7
The Description property page for the NetWare Administrator Application object.

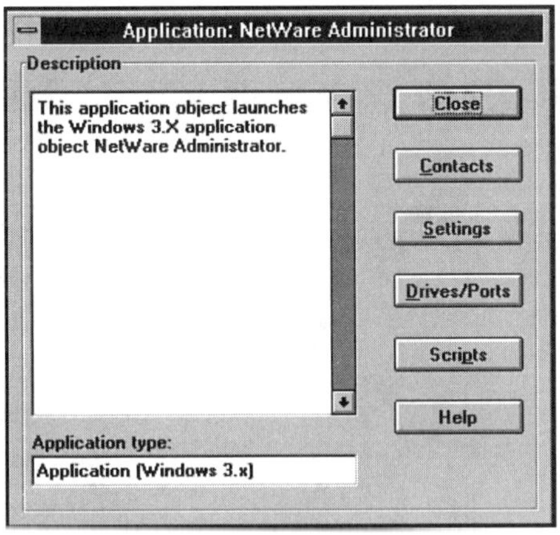

Figure 11.8
The description information shown in file properties for NetWare Administrator in NetWare Application Launcher.

7. Click on the Scripts property option to create pre-launch scripts and post-termination scripts. Use login script syntax to create drive mappings before the application runs. Type in the login script syntax, the appropriate commands to delete drive mappings or remap drives and redirect printing to a different queue when the application terminates. Figure 11.9 shows pre-launch and post-termination scripts for the NetWare Administrator Application object.

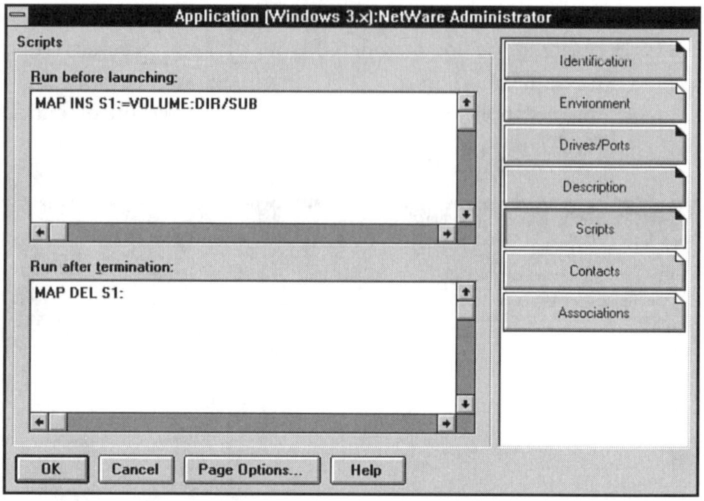

Figure 11.9 *The Scripts property page for the NetWare Administrator application object.*

8. Click on the Contacts property button to add users who should be contacted if problems occur with this application. Click on the Add… button to add the user to the list of contacts. The Delete button removes the user from the contact list. Figure 11.10 shows contact information for the NetWare Administrator Application icon. This information will be available through the file properties option for this icon in NetWare Application Launcher. If the contact's User object has a phone number defined for it, the phone number will appear in the contacts information in application launcher (see fig. 11.11).

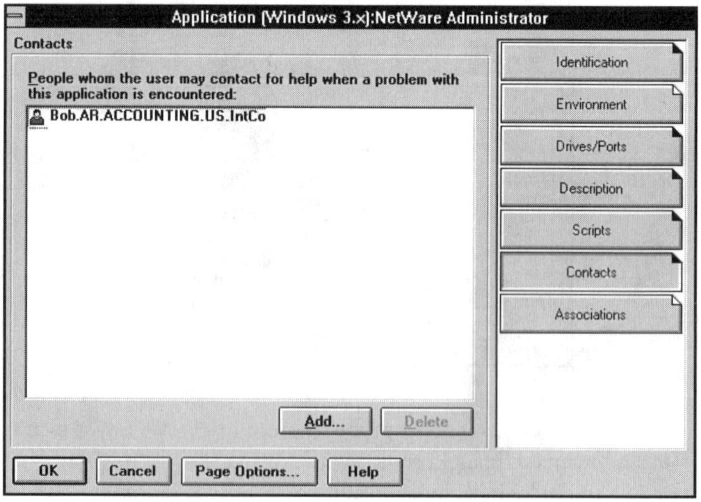

Figure 11.10 *The Contacts property page for the NetWare Administrator application object.*

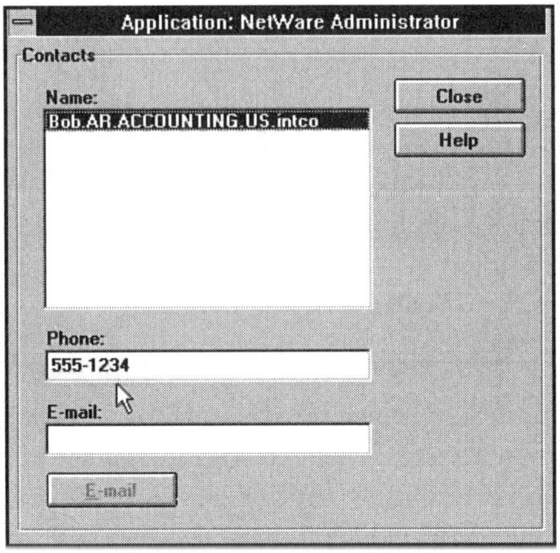

Figure 11.11
The contacts information shown in file properties for NetWare Administrator in NetWare Application Launcher.

9. Click on the Associations property button and add the users, groups, or containers that will be allowed to launch this application. To allow all users in a container access to this application, add the container object to the associations list. Browse and select the AR container as the container to be associated with this object. The context for the AR container is .AR.ACCOUNTING.US.IntCo container for this exercise (see fig. 11.12).

10. Click on OK to save the application configuration.

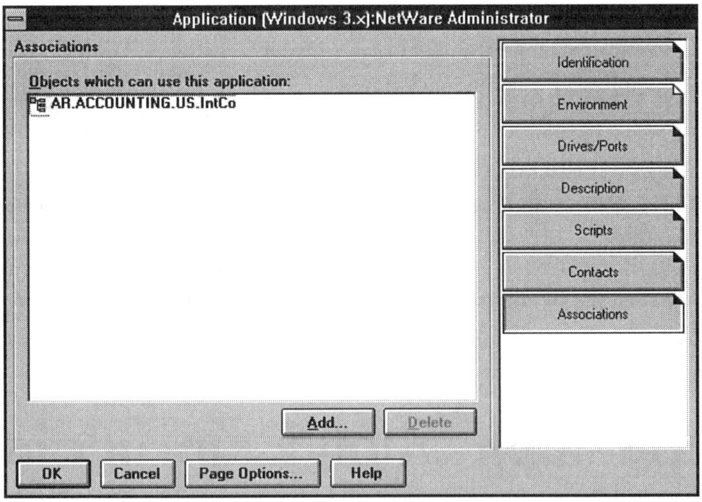

Figure 11.12
The Associations property page for the NetWare Administrator application object.

The steps you just performed in NetWare Administrator are repeated when creating the DOS, Windows 95, and Windows NT Application objects. Enter the appropriate configuration information for each new object and associate them to the users, groups, or containers requiring access to these objects running from the appropriate platform. In the last numbered list, the objects were configured in NetWare Application Manager using NetWare Administrator. Users who were associated with the Application object will dynamically receive access to the applications through the associated icons when they launch the NetWare Application Launcher. The administrator does not need to change the desktop on the local PC for users for the icons to be available. NetWare Application Manager and NetWare Application Launcher work dynamically together by managing the application objects in the NDS. Users' desktops will be updated and the icons refreshed as soon as the object is created and configured and the user is assigned authority to use it by being associated with the object.

The beginning of this chapter discussed the capability of using NetWare Application Manager to create and manage networked Application objects for users to launch from their workstations. NetWare Application Manager can also be used to create and manage application objects for applications installed on local machines. Running applications from the server can increase traffic and seem to run more slowly when launched from the server. Administrators might find that installing applications on the local workstations can help solve these problems; however, it increases the amount of administration time because the administrator must visit each workstation to upgrade the local applications. Applications can be installed or upgraded using NetWare Application Manager and NetWare Application Launcher by creating and configuring application objects used for the installation. The path to the setup executable or image is placed on the network, and is then launched by the user using NetWare Application Launcher. This type of installation requires preliminary installation of the application installation files or image on the server. Administrators can have the Application object launch automatically in NetWare Application Launcher, mentioned later in this chapter, or it can be launched by the user. By configuring the application object appropriately, administrators need not be present during local installations of applications. Administrators can install several local applications in this manner such as desktop applications including Microsoft Office, as well as operating systems, such as Windows 3.1x and Windows 95.

NetWare Application Manager can also be used to configure the application icons for locally installed applications to be launched from NetWare Application Launcher. Administrators can include the path to the executable on the local workstation when configuring the path to the executable for the application, and run locally installed applications from the launcher. Because local applications are not maintained by the NDS, the path to the executable must be entered manually instead of browsing the tree to locate it.

Configuring the Application Launcher in NetWare Administrator

NetWare Application Manager is one of the components used in NetWare Application Services to set up icons and configure them to be used with NetWare Application Launcher, another component of application services. NetWare Application Launcher is loaded at the workstation and is used to launch the applications created in NetWare Application Manager. Launcher configuration settings for containers, groups, and users are managed through

NetWare Administrator. After the application objects are created, configured, and associated to the objects who will receive access to them, the network administrator can configure how these applications are launched and can enable users to perform tasks from the NetWare Application Launcher such as logging or exiting the launcher.

The launcher configuration is managed in NetWare Administrator in the Application and Launcher Configuration property buttons for the object associated with the application. For example, if an application has been associated with a container, the launcher configuration will be performed in the details screen for the container in the Application and Launcher Configuration properties buttons. This section discusses the application settings and launcher configuration for NetWare Application Launcher. Instructions for configuring how applications launch and the launcher configurations are also included in this section. This section will also discuss container launcher configuration and user launcher configurations.

Container Launcher Configuration

This section will discuss container launcher configurations for the Application and Launcher Configuration properties for the Application object created earlier for NetWare Administrator. The Application object for NetWare Administrator was created using NetWare Application Manager and was associated with the .AR.ACCOUNTING.US.IntCo container. This exercise takes you through the steps of configuring the Application and Launcher Configuration properties for the AR container. The Application and Launcher Configuration property buttons are added to the property buttons of the AR container because an Application object has been associated with the container (see fig. 11.13). Application objects can also be associated with groups and users.

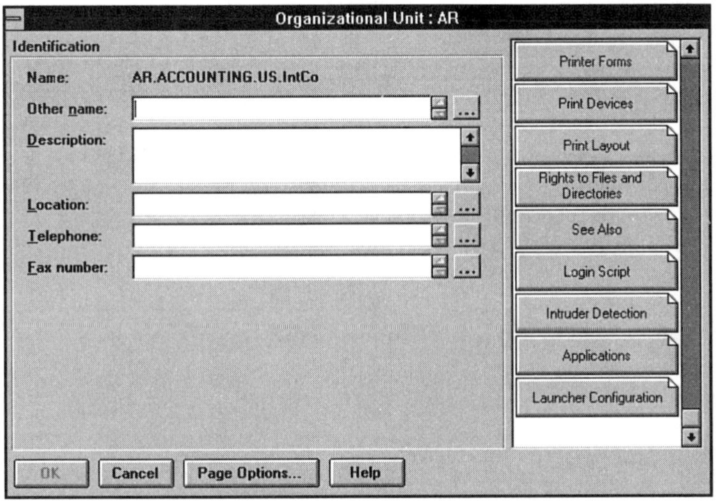

Figure 11.13
Details for the AR container.

To configure the Application and Launcher Configuration property buttons for the AR container, perform the following steps:

1. Login as Admin or equivalent.
2. Highlight the AR container and click the right mouse button then choose Details from the list of options.
3. Select the Applications property button. This reveals a screen similar to the one in figure 11.14. The two applications we associated earlier are listed in the Launched by user portion of the screen because they have been associated with the container. Users in the AR container double-click on the icons from NetWare Application Launcher to launch the applications on this list.

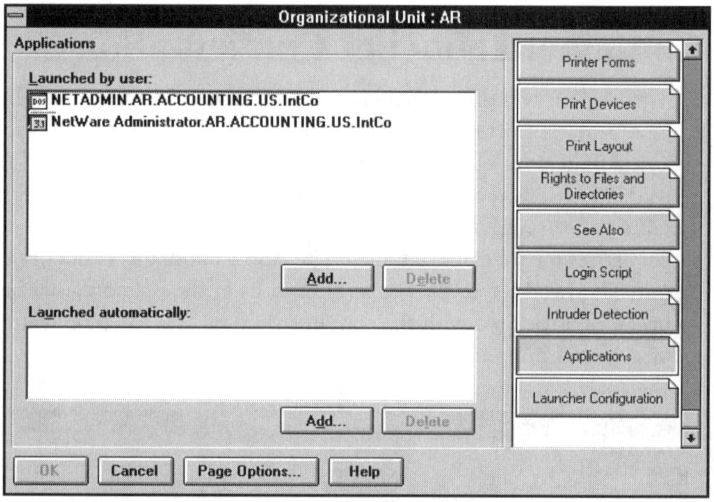

Figure 11.14
The Applications property page for the AR container.

Applications launched automatically are added to the Launch automatically list in NetWare Application Manager. To add Launched automatically to the list, click on the Add… button and browse for the Application object. For this exercise, the user will be allowed to launch the applications.

4. Click on the Launcher Configuration property button to configure the tasks to be enabled by the launcher (see fig. 11.15). Make changes to the launcher configuration using the information in table 11.2.

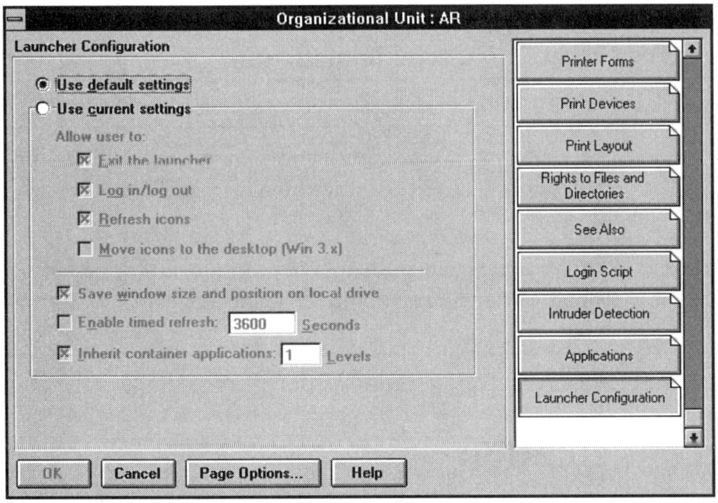

Figure 11.15
The Launcher Configuration property page for the AR container.

5. Click on OK to modify the launcher configurations.

The following table includes information on each of the properties in the launcher configuration.

Table 11.2
Properties in the Launcher Configuration

Property	Description
Use Default Settings	Identifies the default settings for the launcher.
Use Current Settings	Allows settings other than the defaults.
Exit the Launcher	Enables the user to exit the NetWare Application Launcher by clicking on File then Exit from the drop-down menu. The default is ON.
Log in/Log out	Enables the user to log in using NetWare Application Launcher. The default is ON.
Refresh Icons	Enables users to refresh the NetWare Application Launcher manually. Application objects that were associated to the container, group, or user since NAL was launched will be added to NAL when refreshed. The default is ON.
Move Icons to the Desktop	This is for Windows 3.1x only and enables the user to move icons from NAL to their desktop. The default is OFF.
Save Window Size and position on local drive	Keeps window size and position on the user's desktop. The default is ON.

continues

Table 11.2, Continued
Properties in the Launcher Configuration

Property	Description
Enable Timed Refresh	This parameter is in seconds and determines how often the workstation will ask the server to deliver new application objects.
Inherit Container Applications Levels	This number enables the user object to inherit its parent container's application object. The default is ON and 1 level.

User Launcher Configuration

If an application has been associated with a container, the users in the container will automatically be associated to the Application object. Administrators can configure the user launcher configuration to accept the container defaults, or they can customize the user configuration to include options for the user that differ from the ones that would be inherited from the container. Launcher configurations are modified for the user in the Launcher Configuration property page for the user object in details.

Figure 11.16 shows the launcher configuration screen for a user. If Use parent container settings is selected, this user's launcher configuration will use the same configuration as the parent container.

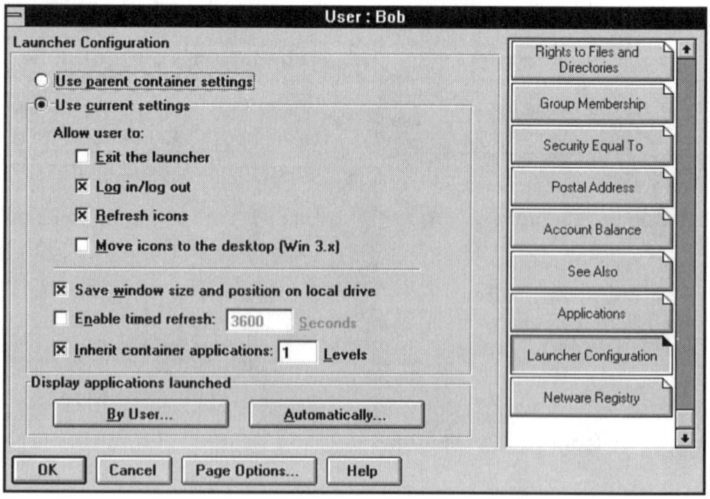

Figure 11.16
User Launcher Configuration for the user Bob in the ACCOUNTING container.

To customize the launcher configuration for the user .BOB.AR.ACCOUNTING.US.IntCo to enable a different configuration, perform the following steps:

1. Login as Admin or equivalent.
2. Launch NetWare Administrator.
3. Highlight the .AR.ACCOUNTING.US.Intco container and double-click on it to reveal its contents.
4. Select Details on the User object Bob by clicking the right mouse button and selecting Details with the user Bob highlighted, or by double-clicking on the User object for Bob.
5. Double-click on the Launcher Configuration property button to reveal a screen similar to figure 11.16. Use Table 11.2 for guidelines to use when changing user launcher configurations.
6. Select the Use current settings radio button.
7. Modify the options to be unique for the user Bob by removing the X next to Exit the launcher.

   Click on the By User… button to display the Application Objects dialog box that lists the applications that Bob will launch from the Application Launcher (see fig. 11.17). These applications are configured with the Applications property button for the container. The Automatically… button displays the applications launched automatically when NetWare Application Launcher is executed.

Figure 11.17
Launcher Configuration: Application Objects Launched by User.

8. Click on OK to save changes to Bob's launcher configuration.

Users must have access rights to all of the applications and printer captures configured in NetWare Application Manager in order for the applications to map drives, capture printers, and launch using NetWare Application launcher. Make sure you have assigned the appropriate trustee and NDS rights for running the scripts, executing the applications, and capturing printers prior to allowing the user to use NetWare Application Launcher when launching applications.

Installing the Application Launcher

The NetWare Application Manager is installed in an IntranetWare installation; however, manual installation can be performed if the Snap-in is not available when creating objects in NetWare Administrator. To perform a manual installation of NAL and NAM, perform the following steps:

1. Login as Admin or equivalent.
2. Copy APPSNAP.DLL, APPSNAP.HLP, and APPRES16.DLL to PUBLIC.
3. Edit the NWADMIN.INI in the windows directory and add the following to the [Snapin Object Dlls] section:

   ```
   [Snapin Object Dlls]
   SNAPINCP = Z:\PUBLIC\APPSNAP.DLL
   ```

   SNAPINCP is a unique name assigned by the administrator for the Snapin and the DLL file is located in the PUBLIC directory in this example. You would include the name and the location to which you copied the application files in your INI file.
4. Run NetWare Administrator to modify the schema. You will be prompted to update the tree's schema if the extensions do not already exist.

To install NetWare Application Launcher on the workstation, perform the following steps:

For a Windows 3.1 workstation:

1. Copy NAL.EXE and NALW31.EXE to the PUBLIC directory or to a directory to which users have access if running from the network. These files can also be copied to the local drive.
2. Copy NALRES.DLL, NALBMP.DLL, and NAL.HLP to PUBLIC or other accessible directory if using the network. Copy them to the local drive if launching locally.
3. Copy WIN16.DLL to a directory called NALLIB below the directory when it contains NAL.EXE. For example, PUBLIC\NALLIB.
4. Add NAL.EXE to the startup window to launch in startup, if desired.

For a Windows 95 workstation:

1. Copy NAL.EXE and NALW95.EXE to an accessible network directory or to the local drive.
2. Copy NALRES32.DLL, NALBMP32.DLL, and NAL.HLP to PUBLIC or other accessible network directory or to the local drive.
3. Add NAL.EXE to the startup folder if launching on startup is desired.

Exploring NetWare Application Launcher

NetWare Application Launcher works with Client32 to provide users the ability to launch applications that have been configured by the administrator using NetWare Application Manager in NetWare Administrator. When the user runs the NetWare Application Launcher, the icons that have been associated with the user will appear in the NetWare-delivered Applications dialog box (see fig. 11.18). The user runs the application by clicking on the application icon in NetWare Application Launcher. The properties for the application were configured by the administrator in NetWare Application Manager, so users do not need to map drives or capture printers because this has been performed by the application object configuration.

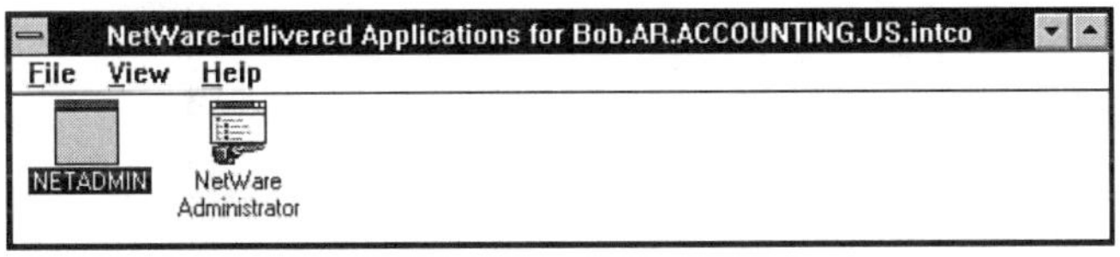

Figure 11.18
The NetWare Application Launcher-NetWare delivered Applications for user Bob.IntCo.

When the user clicks on File in the drop-down menu bar in NetWare Application Launcher, the user sees the options that were configured in the Launcher Configuration for the user or container object. Figure 11.19 shows the options for the launcher configuration for the user .Bob.ACCOUNTING.AR.US.IntCo. Notice that the option to Exit the launcher is grayed out. This was configured in the launcher configuration property for Bob and the option to exit the launcher was removed. (Refer to figure 11.16.) Because the launcher configuration did not include the option to exit the launcher, Bob cannot exit out of the NetWare Application Launcher window to go to DOS. The options that appear are enabled through the launcher configuration for the user object Bob.

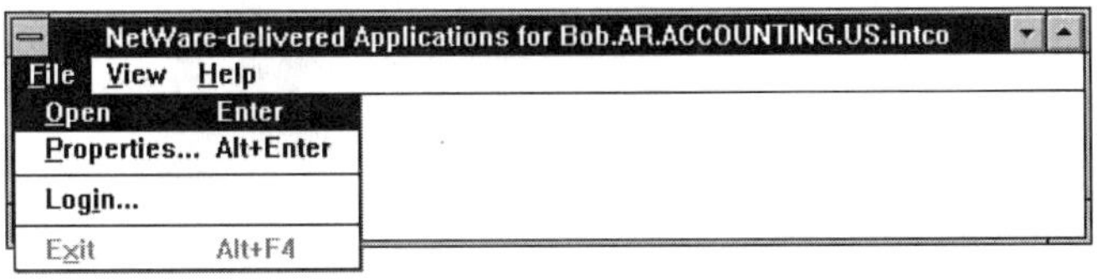

Figure 11.19
Options Available in the NetWare-delivered Applications for Bob.

Properties of applications are viewed by the user in NetWare Application Launcher by clicking on File in the drop-down menu, then by clicking on Properties… with the icon highlighted. Users cannot change these properties, they can only view them. Figure 11.20 shows the setting information for the NetWare Administrator Application icon as seen in NetWare Application Launcher. The Application object was configured in NetWare Administrator and the information seen in figure 11.20 was included in figure 11.4 in the identification property screen where the object name and path to executable file were entered. The command line parameter information, working directory, run minimized, and clean up network resources were configured with the environment property. (Refer to figure 11.5.)

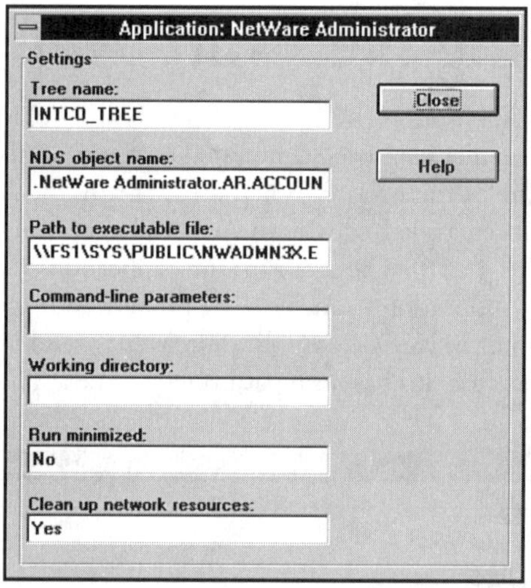

Figure 11.20
The Settings property screen seen through NetWare-delivered Applications in NetWare Application Launcher.

Figure 11.21 shows the information configured in the Drives/Ports property for this object (refer to figure 11.6). Figure 11.22 shows the information configured in the Scripts property page shown in figure 11.9.

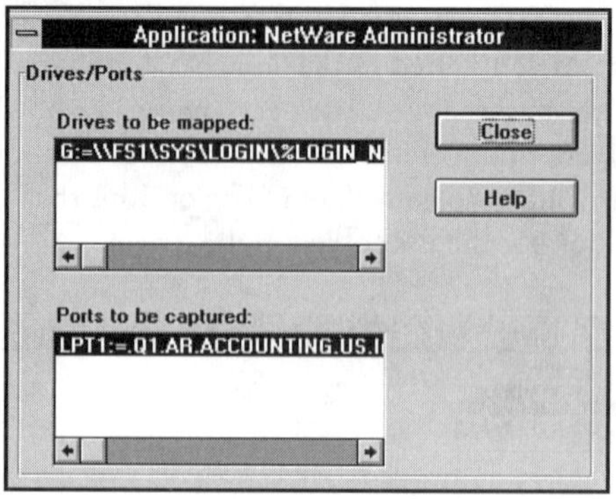

Figure 11.21
The Drives/Ports property screen seen through NetWare-delivered Applications in NetWare Application Launcher.

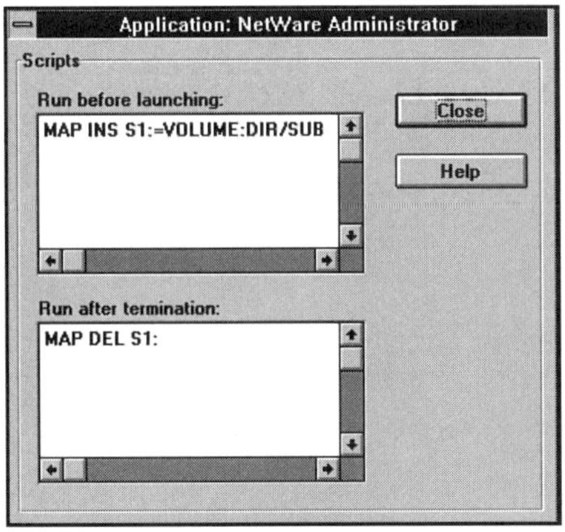

Figure 11.22
The Scripts property screen seen through NetWare-delivered Applications in NetWare Application Launcher.

Replacing PROGMAN.EXE and EXPLORER.EXE with NAL

Users' desktops can be replaced by NetWare Application Launcher to help make administrators jobs easier. For users who do not understand windows and tend to delete or lose icons, confusion can be reduced by replacing the desktop with NetWare Application Launcher. The desktop for both Windows 3.1 and Windows 95 can be replaced by NetWare Application Launcher. When replaced with NAL, desktop icons that users do not need or shouldn't have (such as games), are no longer available. Only the icons associated with the user in NetWare Application Manager will appear on the desktop with NetWare Application Launcher.

Follow these steps to replace the desktop on a Windows 3.1 machine:

1. Copy the NALW31.EXE, NALRES.DLL, NALBMP.DLL, and NAL.HLP files to a local directory.

2. Copy the WIN16.DLL file to the WINDOWS\SYSTEM directory.

3. Edit the SYSTEM.INI file in the WINDOWS directory and replace the PROGMAN.EXE shell in the [BOOT] section with NALW31.EXE. For example, the original SYSTEM.INI file contains:

   ```
   [Boot]
   shell=progman.exe
   ```

   Replace the PROGMAN.EXE with NALW31.EXE:

   ```
   [Boot]
   shell=c:\path\nalw31.exe
   ```

   The path should be included to ensure the correct path for the executable.

4. Save changes and run windows. NetWare Application Launcher is now the desktop and users can only perform the functions to run applications allowed by the administrator through launcher configuration.

To replace the EXPLORER.EXE in Windows 95:

1. Copy the NALW95.EXE, NALRES32.DLL, NALBMP32.DLL, and NAL.HLP files to the local drive.

2. Edit the SYSTEM.INI file and in the boot section:

   ```
   [Boot]
   shell=explorer.exe
   ```

   Replace the EXPLORER.EXE with:

   ```
   [Boot]
   shell=c:\path\nalw95.exe
   ```

Launching Applications with NetWare Application Launcher

Users who access NetWare Application Launcher must have access to the NAL executable files. These files can be stored on the network in the PUBLIC directory for users to use when logged in or can be copied to the local workstation to be launched locally as previously discussed. The files necessary to launch NetWare Application Launcher for Windows 3.1 are NAL.EXE and NALW31.EXE. Other necessary files were discussed previously. The files necessary to launch NetWare Application Launcher from Windows 95 are NAL.EXE and NALW95.EXE. The additional files were also mentioned earlier in the installation section.

When the user launches the NALW31.EXE or NALW95.EXE files to launch NetWare Application Launcher, the NetWare-delivered Applications for the user box appears on the screen with the associated icons for that user similar to figure 11.18. The user can launch the application by clicking on the appropriate icon.

If the NAL executable files are located on the local workstation, the user does not need to be logged in to run the application launcher. This provides the user with access to his/her Application icons in the event that the network is down. If the applications are installed locally, the user can run the applications even if the network is down, as long as the icons have been configured to run the application from the local workstation. However, the user would still be required to make sure his/her data is transferred to the network if it is to be backed up by the administrator.

Benefits of NetWare Application Manager and NetWare Application Launcher

Throughout this chapter, some of the benefits of using NetWare Application Manager and NetWare Application Launcher have been listed. These benefits include the most important benefit of simplifying the network administrator's management responsibilities. NetWare

Application Manager and NetWare Application Launcher enable administrators to configure Application icons that will map drives, capture printers, run scripts, and so on. When the user double-clicks on an icon in NetWare Application Launcher. Icons can be added, removed, reconfigured, and so forth from the administrator's desk, eliminating the need for the administrator to visit every workstation on the network to configure them. NetWare Application Manager and NetWare Application Launcher are dynamic, so changes made to the objects appear in NetWare Application launcher on the desktop without the administrator updating them locally by visiting the machine. Network applications can be installed on the server and launched by users with NetWare Application Launcher without the administrator installing icons at the desktop by visiting the workstation to add the icons. Local applications can also be installed or upgraded using NetWare Application Manager and NetWare Application Launcher. Client software and operating systems can also be installed in the same manner centrally from the network.

Because resources across servers do not need drives mapped through login scripts, licensed connections on servers on which resources would have been mapped with login scripts are freed up because the application maps the drives when the application launches. Licensed connections on other servers mapped through NetWare Application Launcher are released when the application is no longer in use. Users can be required to stay within NetWare Application Launcher if the option to exit the launcher is not permitted. Users cannot delete or lose Application icons that are included in the NetWare Application Launcher. NetWare Application Launcher configuration is tied to objects in the tree and follows the associated user whenever the user logs in. This eliminates the problem of users not having access to their unique network application objects when using someone else's machine.

Summary

This chapter introduced you to NetWare Application Services. These services include NetWare Application Manager, a GUI utility managed with NetWare Administrator by administrators; and NetWare Application Launcher, launched at the workstation, used to launch applications. This section described NetWare Application Manager and NetWare Application Launcher and demonstrated the steps used when creating and configuring objects for DOS and Windows 3.1. The types of objects for different operating systems were discussed. The properties used to define application objects were also discussed. This chapter demonstrated the way in which NetWare Application Manager configuration parameters are included in the properties of the icon in NetWare Application Launcher. Steps to install NetWare Application Manager and NetWare Application Launcher were discussed in this chapter. Finally, the benefits of using NetWare Application Manager and NetWare Application Launcher were discussed throughout.

CHAPTER 12

IntranetWare Developer Services

Computer software development in the years gone by has undergone changes that are more evolutionary than revolutionary. As such, the way software is developed has likewise changed. Early programmers typically wrote in assembler code. Assembler code is difficult to read, write, understand, and dramatically more difficult to maintain. Such programmers were often called systems programmers, and wrote in assembler code to interact with the operating system that was available. Debugging assembler code was considered an art form because the tools used were primitive or nearly nonexistent; and furthermore, developers not only created the software that made up their profession, but they had to create the tools they needed to manipulate and maintain their programs. As time marched onward, the concept of connecting computers into a network of cooperative computing resources was born.

Some of those systems programmers were able to expand on the concept of programs running on a single piece of hardware, and the idea of network computing was created. As with the original systems programming, network programming was started by a few ambitious individuals with a vision.

The goal of this chapter is to alert you whether or not you are a systems programmer, networking software developer, the serious LAN or network administrator, or the sophisticated end user, to the tools and development needs for computer networking in the future. I do not intend to go into great depth about each of the different programming styles for each of the development environments being discussed here in this chapter of the reference. These are the main tools that are available for developing software which will be useful in implementing a heterogenous networking computing environment. You should research each of these possibilities to their fullest and leverage more from your network of computing resources.

At end of the chapter, you will see the content of the Novell programs for assisting developers in their creation of all types of software. These programs include Novell's Net2000 Application Programming Interfaces and the DeveloperNet 2000 program. This chapter will also cover Novell's most recent release of the Software Development Kit (SDK) including all of the SDK's components. The development tools included with these SDKs will enable a developer or system administrator to create applications and utilities for the Novell IntranetWare operating system. Several popular third party tools that aid developers in using network services will also be addressed.

Net2000

The Net2000 Application Programming Interface (API) is designed to enable software developers to take advantage of network infrastructures and services. Because this includes programs which may be written in languages or with tools such as C, C++, NetBasic from HiTechSoft, Java, Microsoft's Visual Basic C and C++, and Delphi, a lesson in programming styles, tips, and tricks would be incredibly broad in its scope and cannot be completely described in one chapter. This chapter describes the development environment for IntranetWare that enables the developer to quickly create and use any of these tools for the creation, maintenance, and ultimately the migration or implementation to newer and more powerful networked computing environments.

Novell's Net2000 initiative creates a group of networking standards which encompass the major development environments, allowing the addition of networked services, including a directory infrastructure or service for the management, maintenance, and performance in an Intranet, Internet, or Extranet environment. Net2000 currently encompasses the following four major development environments:

- Java Development in an IntranetWare Environment
- NetBasic Scripting

- Rapid Application Development Environments
- Traditional C/C++ Development Environments

By offering the developer a choice of programming interfaces and tools, Novell makes the networking infrastructure in the form of Novell's Directory Service to be available to the majority of software developers. Novell's Net2000 initiative helps software developers enhance and extend the basic functionality of each of these development approaches by making the network an easy to program extension of the software being developed.

Java Development in an IntranetWare Environment

The computer industry has suffered as a result of the way that developers were forced to create their software for one specific platform. Many independent software vendors were compelled to make unpopular choices about the platforms that would support their software applications. These choices often left new and innovative platform vendors without the customer base that was necessary to achieve the critical marketing mass required for those innovative platforms in which to become consumed as a mainstream commodity. Although somewhat true, the portability promised by the C language and the Unix operating system did not produce the expected result the proliferation of extensions to the C language and the Unix operating system made this dream difficult to achieve.

The Java programming language was created out of the need to simplify programming scopes to provide a more heterogenous software development environment. Java finds it's roots at Sun Microsystems during the fall of 1995. Java is an object-oriented programming language that focuses on the information being consumed rather than manipulating the programming language to get the desired consumption of information from a program. Java also carries little or none of the less desirable baggage that comes with the C and C++ languages. In development support organizations, pointers and pointer manipulations that come with C and C++ programming languages cause near 80 percent of that organization's support queries. The Java language has no pointers, eliminating one of the major sources of troubles involved with creating programs.

Another source for difficulty in the C and C++ languages is memory management. *Memory management* (the allocation and release of memory after it is no longer needed) is handled automatically in Java, releasing the programmer from most of the concerns of managing memory. The advantages of the Java programming language give it great potential to create platform independent applications capable of taking great advantage of networking services and resources. These programs can have security, multi-threading for multi-processor execution, exception services, and login heuristics built into them without too much extra work by the developer.

How Java Works in an IntranetWare Environment

In most operating system environments, including IntranetWare, Java source code is compiled into a platform independent executable binary pseudo-code called byte-code. Byte-code arrives at one of two mechanisms designed to translate it into the assembler code which executes on the hosting platform. The first execution mechanism to be available is a translator called the Java Virtual Machine (JVM). The Java Virtual Machine is an important part of the Java Development Kit (JDK), and is available from JavaSoft™. The JVM is the most difficult portion of the JDK to port to a specific platform because it has all of the operating system dependent portions of the Java execution environment. Novell's port of the JVM is available for the IntranetWare environment. The Java Virtual Machine converts the byte-code into the system calls which execute the Java code natively. This allows for the support of Java executing Applications which run natively on an IntranetWare based machine.

The second execution platform, a Just in Time (JIT) compiler, was released from Novell in November of 1996 with the Java Development Kit for IntranetWare. This JIT enables Java applications, applets, servlets, and netlets to run much faster than under the interpretive JVM. Both of these execution platforms ultimately transform the byte-code into executable assembler code which in turn executes on the IntranetWare platform. Java Applets, are Java classes which execute in a Java Application. Java Netlets are classes that execute as network agents performing work on the network, and Java Servlets are Java classes which execute on a server as an agent for the a specific server.

The Java Advantages

The Java language and its executing environment offer significant advantages to the developer. The first is that it is object-oriented. Object-oriented programming offers the developer the freedom to concentrate on developing the task at hand and to commit less concentration to the tools that the developer needs to execute a procedure. Object-oriented programming gives the developer the ability to reuse methods or procedures that simplify the entire programming task.

Java also removes some of the more difficult issues that accompany a language as flexible and complex as C or C++, the first and most important of which is pointers. There are no pointers in Java, which eliminates approximately 80 percent of the most typical bugs that manifest in C or C++ programs. Pointers and pointer arithmetic offer the developer an excellent opportunity to attempt to access illegal memory pages within the operating system and thus cause a page fault that results in an abnormal termination of the server or an abend. Memory leaks and garbage collection are easier to do in the C and C++ environments. Such leaks occur much less frequently in the Java development environment because the JVM or JIT compiler handles the allotment and reclamation of memory for objects that are used in a Java application.

Java offers a high degree of security because of the Security Manager (a part of the JVM or JIT Compiler) and does not allow a malicious developer's applet, netlet, or servlet the opportunity to take over the machine's resources. This prevents developers from causing potential damage to a client, server, or network regardless of whether or not that damage was a planned thing or an accidental function of an application.

What Does Java on IntranetWare Gain for Me?

If you've been involved with the computing and networking environment, you might remember a time when Windows was first available, as well as the NetWare OS. Many people began to use their NetWare to launch Windows from their NetWare server. For small environments, this was not extremely troubling. In larger environments, networking bandwidth could quickly get consumed causing networks to perform slowly.

Consider how the indiscriminate launching of Java executables could result in a similar reduction of network bandwidth. It quickly becomes obvious that one of the best ways to implement Java executables is to distribute the application logic across the network with the pieces that make sense running on the IntranetWare JVM or a JIT compiler run there, and the pieces which should run on the client workstation run there, minimizing the impact on the network. An example of this would be to run a database query on the machine where the database exists, rather than run the database information across the network to be acted on by the client-side Java application.

NetBasic Scripting

Novell's server products have often been criticized for their lack of an easy application development environment. IntranetWare's NetBasic changes the Novell server development environment dramatically. NetBasic was developed by HiTechSoft, using their ManageWare Network Management Language development environment. NetBasic can use Microsoft's Visual Basic as a development environment. The NetBasic components to be added as custom tools to the Visual Basic development environment. This enables the Visual Basic developers, who make up a majority of software developers to easily add networking services and resources to their applications.

The NetBasic Scripting Engine

The IntranetWare NetBasic Scripting Engine is a series of Novell supplied NLMs which support the NetBasic scripts. This enables Visual Basic developers to create scripts that help to maintain and manage intranets using Novell's IntranetWare. The NetBasic interpreter, which is one of those NLMs, can run scripts and other NLM's through the L-CGI interface on the NetWare Web Server. This enables these applications to generate dynamic web pages for viewing through web browsers, management tools, database interactions, and a wide variety of other applications. This is useful to help webmasters maintain their web page hierarchies. Hypertext Markup Language (HTML) is the language that is used to generate web pages.

These HTML documents, or web pages can be one of two varieties, dynamically generated, or static. Because the information contained in web pages often changes, dynamically generated HTML codes are much easier to maintain and have more accurate content than static pages. Using the NetBasic libraries or components allow a developer to create dynamic web pages that either update or consume network information. Such information could be in the form of Novell Directory Service (NDS) that can be used to enforce user authentication to HTML documents. Any of the other components that make up the NetBasic development environment could be used to create easier to maintain web pages. These components will be listed later in this chapter. The following example uses NetBasic to add a new user and their user attributes to NDS.

```
#include "HTML.H"
' **********
' Required include file
' **********
#define GRAPHICS_DIR "/cgi/ndsobj/images/"
' **********
' The web page heading
' **********
#define NDS_HEADING  "Add NDS User"
#define URL_PFX      "/netbasic/"

Sub Main
' **********
' Main routine
' **********
' **********
' All DOC calls are for HTML code
' All NDS calls are to do some work in NDS
' **********
DOC:Heading(NDS_HEADING)
DOC:Body(DOC_WHITE,DOC_BLACK)
CENTERON()
DOC:Print:H2(NDS_HEADING)
DOC:Hr(2,50)
CENTEROFF()

CurrSess = NDS:Session:Login("admin","adminpassword")
Error = Err
If (Error != 0)
   DOC:Print("Error (",Error,") Logging into NDS"); NewLine
   Return
EndIf
' **********
' Setup the correct context first, this MUST be done or this does not work!
' **********
NDS:Context:Path:Change("[Root]")
' **********
' UserID is username (change to suit your needs)
' Organization name is org (change to suit your needs)
```

```
' **********
userObject=".CN=username.O=org"
' **********
' Returns 1 if call is successful 0 if not
' **********
Success = NDS:Search("[Root]",2,False,"CN","=","username")

if (Success = 1)
   Print("Object .username.org already exists.  Removing object");newline
   NDS:Delete(".username.org")
EndIf

Success = NDS:Add:User(userObject,"UserName")
If (!Success)
   Print("Error adding User Object") ; Newline
   Return
Else
   Print("User added OK") ; Newline
EndIf
' **********
' Now we can add a bunch of attributes, for example;
' User's first name is FirstName
' Last name is LastName
' **********
Success = NDS:Attribute:Value:Add(userObject,"Full Name","FirstName LastName")
If (!Success)
   Print("Error adding Full Name") ; Newline
EndIf
Success = NDS:Attribute:Value:Add(userObject,"Given Name","FirstName")
If (!Success)
   Print("Error adding Full Name") ; Newline
EndIf
' **********
' The user's location is Location
' **********
Success = NDS:Attribute:Value:Add(userObject,"L","Location")
If (!Success)
   Print("Error adding Locality") ; Newline
EndIf
' **********
' Telephone number
' **********
Success = NDS:Attribute:Value:Add(userObject,"Telephone Number","123-5678")
If (!Success)
   Print("Error adding Telephone Number") ; Newline
EndIf
' **********
' Login and password restrictions
' **********
Success = NDS:Attribute:Value:Add(userObject,"Login Disabled",1)
If (!Success)
   Print("Error Disabling account") ; Newline
```

```
EndIf
Success = NDS:Attribute:Value:Add(userObject,"Login Maximum Simultaneous",2)
If (!Success)
   Print("Error adding Login Maximum Simultaneous") ; Newline
EndIf
Success = NDS:Attribute:Value:Add(userObject,"Password Allow Change",1)
If (!Success)
   Print("Error adding Password Allow Change") ; Newline
EndIf
Success = NDS:Attribute:Value:Add(userObject,"Password Required",1)
If (!Success)
   Print("Error adding Password Required") ; Newline
EndIf
Success = NDS:Attribute:Value:Add(userObject,"Password Minimum Length",5)
If (!Success)
   Print("Error adding Password Minimum Length") ; Newline
EndIf
Success = NDS:Attribute:Value:Add(userObject,"Password Expiration Inter-
val",4320000)
If (!Success)
   Print("Error adding Password Minimum Length") ; Newline
EndIf
Success = NDS:Attribute:Value:Add(userObject,"Password Expiration
Time",DATE:Utf()+4320000)
If (!Success)
   Print("Error adding Password Minimum Length") ; Newline
EndIf
' **********
' Here we add their home directory, HOME on volume SYS
' **********
Success = NDS:Attribute:Value:Add(userObject,"Home
➥Directory","[N]0,[V]CN=HOME_SYS.O=org,[P]\netbasic")
If (!Success)
   Print("Error is ",err); newline
   Print("Error adding Home Directory") ; Newline
EndIf
' **********
' Login Script
' **********
Success = NDS:Attribute:Value:Add(userObject,"Login
➥Script","Testing"+chr(10)+"Second Line")
If (!Success)
   Print("Error is ",err); newline
   Print("Error adding Login Script") ; Newline
EndIf

Success = NDS:Session:Logout
End Sub
```

Because the scripting components are designed to be modular and reusable, this NDS authentication code can be reused in many different ways. One can use this sample NetBasic source code to create or modify applications to consume or manipulate user information. Such code would simply execute this code fragment to add a user that is not in NDS yet, or use portions of this code to add or change attributes to a specific user. Web pages could use this source code to use NDS to consume or manipulate user attributes. Many examples of NetBasic source code are available for free from the Novell and HiTechSoft web sites, `http://developernet.novell.com/`, and `http://www.hitechsoft.com/` respectively.

Network Management Extensions

An important component of the NetBasic architecture is the Net2000 Network Management Extensions (NMX). The NMX engine is a set of rules that enable developer to build IntranetWare NLMs and NetBasic components that can be registered on an IntranetWare server. These NLMs and components are executed by the NMX engine and gain memory protection from the NMX NLM. NMX compliant NLMs and components can then be used by NetBasic scripts executing on that server. These NetBasic scripts can execute from the server's console, or from web pages that are hosted on the server. The Net2000 NMX compliant components which are currently available include:

- **Oracle Database Connectivity.** This component enables the script to connect to an Oracle database, execute queries, update information, and have complete access to the Oracle Database.
- **Btrieve Database Connectivity.** This component enables a script to automatically load the Btrieve NLM and to connect to a Btrieve Database and support 80 different database commands, including open, close, get, getnext, getequal and many others.
- **dBASE Database Connectivity.** This component enables a developer to create NetBasic scripts that can access, query, and update dBASE DBMS's.
- **SNMP Management.** This component enables a developer to instrument his or her application to report all types of alarms to a management console or agent any place on the network.
- **FTP Component.** This component enables a developer to include the standard Internet file transfer protocol requests over a network, further enhancing the capability for a script to manipulate information in a network environment.
- **American Power UPS and Excide Electronics Components.** These two parts of the NMX component library enables a developer to query either type of UPS to monitor and act on information from a power supply.

Note

> Check the web site `http://www.hitechsoft.com/` for further information on new NMX components. This same web site can also be used to download NMX components, and updates to those components.

NMX components have several important features which should be understood by developers seeking to take full advantage of their development efforts by making it easy to create network aware applications and tools. These features and their associated benefits include:

- **Memory Management.** NMX compliant components have the advantage of having the capability to be loaded and unloaded in the script on demand, thus removing the need to have those components taking up server memory at all times, waiting for its time to execute. Being able to be dynamically loaded and unloaded on demand reduces the overall server memory requirements, further expanding the capabilities of the server without having to add additional memory to accommodate the extra services.
- **NMX Components are interchangeable.** Each of the components listed, and those which are to be available in the future will be able to work together in a script, enabling, for example, NDS authentication to be used with web services, with a database, and other functions to create a new level of services available to the developer, end user, or administrator.
- **NMX API's are available and expandable.** NMX components are built using C, C++, NetBasic Integrated Development Environment (IDE), Novell's NLM Software Development Kit, or Visual Basic. To be considered an NMX Compliant component, the software libraries must adhere to NetBasic's development guidelines using the NMX APIs.

NetBasic Library Routines

NetBasic scripts are a collection of library components and the logic to complete tasks that can use those components. These library components have been written by HiTechSoft, Novell. Additionally, custom libraries can be written by developers who need to create other modules for their applications. Such modules can be used for data conversion, managing and maintaining network services, user interfaces, server interaction, and more.

The way a library routine is called from a NetBasic script is the library name, listed in uppercase characters, followed by the specific component's name. The component portion is often organized in a hierarchal format, ending the line of a script with the actual arguments submitted to the library routine delimited by "("and")", character literals are delimited by double quotes, and values are represented by their number. An example library call would be:

```
DOC:Heading("This is a header")
```

This line of NetBasic source code would call the Heading routine from the web authoring or DOC library with the argument,"This is a header." The NetBasic interpreting NLM upon being passed this code would dynamically generate HTML code and return it to the web server. The output from the web server would look like:

```
<H1>This is a header</H1>
```

The preceding HTML code fragment is a correct header tag for a HTML document.

Table 12.1 shows the different libraries and their corresponding functional descriptions as provided by Novell in IntranetWare.

Table 12.1
NetBasic Components provided with IntranetWare

Basic System Libraries	
COM	Controls communications (reading and writing involving a serial port).
DATE	Reports System Time and Date.
DIR	Directory operations on the server volumes.
FIO	File I/O Operations, such as open, read, write, and close.
INI	Manipulates an INI file.
KEY	Gets Keyboard input.
LPT	Manipulates a printer being managed by this server.
NDS	Consumes and manipulates Novell Directory Services.
NET	Consumes and manipulates other Novell networking services, such as NCPs, Bindery Services, Broadcast system wide messages, manage printing or faxing queues, file and directory rights, and trustee information.
PORT	Communications with a specific server port.
RPC	Calls and runs an external program such as another NetBasic script.
SYS	Miscellaneous system calls, such as load and unload NLMs, get and set server attributes, and so on.
Data Manipulation Libraries	
BTR	Btrieve database access and manipulation.
MATH	Math functions such as sin, cos, tan, square root, absolute value, and more.
ORA	Oracle database access and manipulation.
STR	Consumes and manipulates character strings.

continues

Table 12.1, Continued
NetBasic Components provided with IntranetWare

HTML and Web Libraries	
DOC	Generates and manipulates HTML tags and content for dynamically created web pages. Generates FORMS for submission through Common Gateway Interfaces (CGI). Publishes images onto web pages.
User Interface Libraries	
WIN	Makes server based C Worthy screen interface calls.

Rapid Application Development Environments

The great majority of developers today create their applications using advanced Rapid Application Development tools, or RAD. To accommodate this developer community, Novell's Net2000 initiative supports the most popular Rapid Application Development standard desktop development interfaces. Those include Microsoft's Visual Basic versions 3 and 4, Borland's Delphi, and PowerBuilder. Each of these popular development environments have a standard desktop interface. As a result, Microsoft's OLE Controls (OCX and ActiveX), Visual Basic Controls (VBX), and the Delphi Controls (VCL) are now all available as standard desktop development interfaces linking Net2000 into each of those development environments. These interfaces into their respective RAD environments allow the developers in each environment to create application and utility programs which can utilize the defacto industry standard for directory and network services, but allows them to easily enhance existing applications to perform the same thing. Such enhancements allow the capability to authenticate a user to the network, software licensing and metering, network management, security, storage management, accessing or consuming information from the directory, as well as many other services. A developer can create, delete, or modify the information that makes up a network's infrastructure.

How Does RAD with IntranetWare Work?

In order to use these components, you must first have installed and have in working order, the RAD environment of your choice. After that has been accomplished, you may add the Net2000 component that corresponds with the RAD environment you are using. Insert the Net2000 CD into the workstation's CD-ROM player and execute the net2000.exe file which is found on the root directory of the CD. If you've downloaded the Net2000 software from Novell's DeveloperNet web site, `http://developer.novell.com/`, you simply execute the net2000.exe file from the directory where you expanded the Net2000 software. From the resulting Setup Window, you must select the components for your RAD environment that you want to install. After a successful installation of the Net2000 components, select those components you want to use by choosing the Custom Controls selection from the Tools menu. You may now program as you would with any application being developed or modified in your RAD environment of choice. Debugging is performed using the same RAD tools that come with the RAD environment.

C and C++ Development Environments

Most of the development that has taken place for the NetWare environment has been in the C language, and its object oriented cousin, C++. Most traditional NLMs for the IntranetWare environment have been written in C. There are no real technical reasons for not developing NLMs in other languages, and we may see more and more NLM development being done in object oriented languages such as Java or C++.

One of the most significant issues surrounding NLM development under the C language is that the IntranetWare operating system has been designed to be very fast and extremely efficient. As such, cleaning up resources after being used, or garbage collection prior to a program's termination is an extremely important point to keep in mind while developing NLMs for the IntranetWare environment.

The most common C/C++ development environments, including the link editors are:

- Watcom C/C++ Version 10.0 with Novell's NLMLink
- Borland Delphi C/C++ with Apiary's Developer Suite
- Borland C/C++ 4.51 with Base Technology's NlinkPro
- Visual C/C++ 4.0
- PowerBuilder 5.0

NLM coding requires initialization code, that is compiled into the NLM, and is usually called, PRELUDE.OBJ. Both Novell and the major compiler vendors supply this initialization code. That code sets up the NLM when it starts execution. After satisfying the initialization code requirement, you must setup a procedure to unload the needed resources used for your NLM. This is a critical step and must receive important consideration because this is the main source of memory leaks which can eventually stop the server from processing because a lack of usable resources. Several Novell DeveloperNotes have been created to outline this important task and are worth a read. Finally, you create a main program that is the actual body of execution and performs most of the work.

Other considerations include making your code re-entrant and multithreaded. This enables you to support multiuser and multi-processor environments which are normal in the IntranetWare environment. This re-entrant and multithreaded style can also be referenced in Novell DeveloperNotes.

Enhanced CLIB

IntranetWare has dramatically enhanced the C Libraries to improve performance, maintainability, and use less server memory. In order to do this, the C Libraries, CLIB was reengineered to be modular. As a result, it is not necessary to replace the entire library when a problem is found. This improves the time needed to generate bug fixes to the CLIB and, because all of CLIB need not be loaded in memory at once, reduce the memory requirements for running CLIB by 80 percent, a dramatic change in the way the Novell C library routines are implemented.

The libraries now include the following six NLM modules:

- **CLIB.NLM.** CLIB is an ANSI compliant runtime interface that provides backward compatibility with older versions of CLIB, insuring that NLMs written to prior versions of NetWare will run properly.
- **FPSM.NLM.** FPSM provides support for floating point routines.
- **THREADS.NLM.** THREADS support the threading capabilities in an IntranetWare environment.
- **REQUESTR.NLM.** REQUESTR provides the standard networking requester functions and routines.
- **NLMLIB.NLM.** NLMLIB provides POSIX and some basic NLM runtime support.
- **NIT.NLM.** NIT is for backward compatibility with the older NetWare interface tools.

Remote and Source Level Debugging

One of the most important tools available to the developer is the debugger. The *debugger* is an important tool that is used to test, troubleshoot, and verify fixes to NLMs running in an IntranetWare server. Novell's Net2000 initiative includes a new debugger, *RDEBUG,* which is different from the NLMDebug or the standard Novell Internal Debugger, for helping with the burden testing and debugging software.

RDEBUG is a remote and a source level debugger for the C and C++ environments. RDEBUG includes all of the important features expected from a professional debugging tool. These features include:

- Setting
  - Breakpoints
  - Watchpoints
  - Passpoints
  - Hardware Breakpoints

- Displaying
    - Memory locations
    - Source
    - Source and Assembly Code in one view
    - Registers
    - Variables
    - Any routine in the trace or call stack
    - Procedures
    - Math Registers
- Stepping
    - Single Stepping
    - Step Over
    - Step Into
- Jumping to a procedure
- Modifying
    - Variables
    - Math Registers
    - Registers
    - 128 Bits Integers

RDEBUG consists of two parts: an NLM that runs on the server being debugged and the Windows 3.X, Windows 95, or Windows /NT client, which provides the menus, dialog boxes, and controls used to manage the debugging session.

RDEBUG also enables the software engineer to toggle between both the Novell Internal Debugger and RDEBUG at the same time. In this manner, RDEBUG can stop the server at any given moment to observe the state of the server software and hardware. RDEBUG enables the engineer to create and execute a batch file containing debugger commands to execute. This saves time in the more complex debugging sessions.

RDEBUG must connect to the server from a client. This is accomplished in one of two ways. The first and most commonly used way is to make a serial connection to the server. The second mechanism is to use an NET2000 network card and utilize TCP/IP to communicate via UDP to the server over Ethernet. The second method can be helpful in trying to debug a server over large distances using the corporate intranet or the Internet.

To use RDEBUG, the following three files or groups of files must be present:

- The source code of the NLM being debugged
- The NLM executable that is being debugged or tested
- The symbols file (.SYM) that contains all of the procedural references being used by the NLM

Additionally, the NLM must be compiled with the debugging switches turned on. These switches are specific to the compiler and will retain extra debugging information to enable RDEBUG to keep better track of what is happening with the software while it executes.

To begin debugging, the engineer starts the Novell Internal Debugger and then starts the RDEBUG server NLM from the Internal Debugger. The workstation then takes control of the debugging session and has control over the target server, and the executing NLM. At this point, the engineer can load or unload any NLM. After control is passed to an NLM, the debugger, by default, stops in the startup routine for the NLM to enable the engineer to set break, watch, and pass points to control execution. At this point, the debugging session begins, and it is up to the engineer to supply the intuition to actually debug or learn what the software is executing.

Internet/Intranet Web Services

IntranetWare provides a series of NLMs which allow for HTML or web pages to be served to a requesting client. The HTML documents are sent from a requesting client that sends such a request via the HyperText Transport Protocol (HTTP). IntranetWare's web serving NLMs receive this request over TCP/IP and reply with the HTML document which has been requested. HTML documents can be one of two types, dynamically generated, or static. Dynamically generated web pages are the result of a program running either on the server, or on another networked platform that executes a program and returns the results of that program to the web server for delivery to the originating client. Such programs are called *Common Gateway Interfaces.*

Common Gateway Interfaces (CGIs)

IntranetWare's Web server, Web Server 2.51, fully supports Common Gateway Interfaces, or CGI's. IntranetWares CGI support includes both CGI 1.0 and 2.0 revisions. CGIs enable programs to be executed in its own memory space on the server, or on a remote server that might function to perform such things as generating a dynamically built HyperText Markup

Language (HTML) page, to update a database record, or any one of a number of processes outside of the world of HTML code and HyperText Transfer Protocol (HTTP). In such a manner, you can create dynamic HTML documents, which can enhance the usability of web page content or allow for external programming to be a part of a web page interface.

The CGI specification was originally written for a Unix environment an example of a general purpose operating system. Such an environment has much more work happening at one time and requires additional features that are not needed in a special purpose operating system such as IntranetWare. The implementation for IntranetWare has to have some differences in order to accomplish the same end serving files or accessing services on the network. These differences require two different implementations for CGIs in an IntranetWare environment, the Local and Remote Common Gateway Interfaces.

Local Common Gateway Interfaces (L-CGIs)

The Local Common Gateway Interfaces (L-CGI) was written to permit programs that can execute locally on the same IntranetWare server as the web server. These can be NLMs, Java applets, netlets, servlets, or NetBasic scripts. L-CGI programs utilize a STREAMS based communication mechanism to communicate within the server in a very efficient and, therefore, fast manner. Such requests are submitted through an HTML interface to the web server NLMs on the server. The NMLs look up the routine to start in the http.srm file (located in the SYS volume) WEB/CONFIG directory for the web server in question. The routine begins by getting started or loaded and passes any arguments that the HTML interface gets from the client workstation. This routine then executes and passes the results back to the web server in the form of a dynamically built HTML document. This HTML information is then displayed by the client in a browser window.

Remote Common Gateway Interfaces (R-CGIs)

Remote Common Gateway Interfaces (R-CGI) enables programs to run in an environment that is external to the IntranetWare environment. These cases would include: a Unix bourne shell script, Java executables, C programs, Fortran, or any Unix program executing over TCP/IP and using sockets to communicate with another application platform that would supports sockets such as a Unix platform. The IntranetWare server's R-CGI mechanism connects to and allows the execution of programs running on UnixWare, Solaris, SunOS, and most flavors of Unix, as well as any operating system platform which also supports sockets.

How to Write a CGI for IntranetWare

L-CGI and R-CGI sample source code ship with the IntranetWare Web Server. After the installation of the Web server, you can find the examples for creating L-CGI programs as well as sample source code and the Makefiles for creating and maintaining the R-CGI programs. These examples are in the "samples" directory under the main directory for your web server. Typically, this is "SYS:\WEB."

To use the sample source code you must first compile this sample source code into a Unix executable and placing it on the remote Unix file system. You must then enable it to run as a service under the inetd daemon on the Unix-based machine. This enables the IntranetWare Web Server to establish communications with that Unix machine, permitting that Unix machine to run executables on behalf of the Web server. HTML code is then passed as arguments to the program running on the remote Unix machine. Those arguments include the name of the executable that will run on the Unix machine along with any other arguments needed to run that executable. After executing on the Unix machine, the output of the program is HTML code that is returned to the IntranetWare Web Server. It is then sent back to the requesting client via the HyperText Transport Protocol (HTTP).

Server Side Includes

A developer can also encode dynamic information into HTML documents by using a Server Side Include (SSI). SSIs, which are shipped with IntranetWare, are a set of more commonly used routines that can dynamically generate HTML code when the HTML page is accessed. This includes page hit counters, text inclusion from a file, the date and time, and many others. Samples of each SSI, which has been implemented for the IntranetWare web server, are listed in the SYS volume under the WEB/SAMPLES directory. The IntranetWare Web Server supports Extended Server Side Includes. Server Side Include files are maintained separately from their associated HTML documents and must end with the SSI extension. The directory in which the SSI files are maintained must have SSI processing enabled in the Web Manager directories options.

The following list includes the commands supported by the NetWare Web Server:

- **Append.** Instructs the Web server to append information to a specific text file.
- **Break.** Truncates the document.
- **Calc.** Performs mathematical calculations.
- **Config.** Instructs the Web server how to display the last modified date or the file size information. This command is used in conjunction with the flastmod command or the fsize command.
- **Count.** Instructs the Web server to print the number of times the document has been accessed.
- **Echo.** Instructs the Web server to display information defined by a set of environment variables in the document.
- **Flastmod.** Instructs the Web server to display the date on which a specific file was last modified in the document.

- **Fsize.** Instructs the Web server to display the size of the file or another file in the document.
- **Goto.** Instructs the Web server to jump to a specific location in the document.
- **If command.** Instructs the Web server to perform an operation based on a condition.
- **Include.** Instructs the Web server to include a specified file to the document.
- **Label.** Identifies the location to which an if… goto command or a goto command jumps.

An example of an SSI command script included with the NetWare Web Server follows:

```
<HTML>
<head>
<title>SSI Date Demo</title>
</head>
<BODY background="/images/blue_pap.gif" text="#000000">
The current date and time is <!--#echo var="DATE_LOCAL"--><p>
<hr>
<! Standard trailer.  Note use of ESSI variable substitution to insert document
name in hyperlink below. >
<! Hyperlink points to a BASIC script that displays raw HTML rather than trans-
lated HTML. >
<a href="/scripts/convert.bas?docs<!--#echo var="DOCUMENT_URI"-->">
<it>See how this page is written.</it></a>
<p>
Copyright &#169; 1995 Novell, Inc.  All Rights Reserved.
</BODY>
</HTML>
```

As you can see, this script simply gets the date and time from the server and displays it as a web document. This script could easily be included in a web page HTML document to provide the date and time, or potentially the count for the number of hits on the page or other functions.

Practical Extraction and Reporting Language Interpreter

The IntranetWare Web Server includes support for interpreting programs written in the Practical Extraction and Reporting Language (PERL) 4.0 with support for the 5.0 revision coming out with the Web Server 3.0 product. PERL is a very common Internet language that has been available for Unix and other operating systems for several years. The PERL implementation that ships with IntranetWare is missing only a few libraries that are Unix specific, but is otherwise a full implementation of PERL. The PERL scripts are executed by an NLM that is loaded with the Web server starts and can be considered an L-CGI. Examples of PERL scripts come with the IntranetWare Web Server and when the server is installed, they are stored on the SYS volume under the WEB\SCRIPTS\PERL directory.

BASIC Interpreter

Support for the Basic language extends further than the NetBasic scripting language. IntranetWare includes a Basic Interpreter for executing basic scripts which have been written for the Dartmouth implementation of the Basic language. This interpreter is also an NLM that loads when the web server is loaded. This NLM is called BASIC and is automatically loaded with the Web server. It can be accessed through a HTML document. Examples of Basic script are stored on the SYS volume under the WEB\SCRIPTS directory.

DeveloperNet

Novell has created a program to assist, empower, and encourage developers to take advantage of the networking infrastructure IntranetWare and Novell Directory Service provides. The program also helps developers get the technical support that they need as well as help to provide marketing for the developed products which result from this program. All developers of networking applications and services are encouraged to join and benefit from the help Novell extends to their developer community. This program is called DeveloperNet.

There are three levels of participation in DeveloperNet:

- Free
- Base
- Advanced DeveloperNet Subscriptions

Free DeveloperNet Subscription

The lowest level of participation, free subscription, includes the capability to download the latest Novell SDK that is updated quarterly, and offers no support options. It also offers discounts on Computer Based Training (CBT), discounts from the Novell Press on documentation, and educational discounts for developer classes, a subscription to the quarterly *E-Mail* magazine, DeveloperNet Connections, and DeveloperNet co-marketing opportunities.

Base DeveloperNet Subscription

The second level of participation, is called the Base Subscription. It includes everything that is offered with the free subscription as well as a quarterly update of the Novell SDK on CD-ROM. It includes Novell's Developer Notes monthly journal for networking developers. It also includes all of Novell's software products on the Novell Software Connection Library, (NSCŁ), the DeveloperNet Essentials CD which now includes Sun Microsystems' Java Workshop, a Developer Notes subscription, the Power Partner CD which is a marketing CD distributed monthly by Novell, Novell's Research Anthology, and one standard incident from Novell Developer Support organization. The Base DeveloperNet Subscription costs $345.00 annually.

Advanced DeveloperNet Subscription

The highest level of participation Advanced Subscription, includes all of the items mentioned for the base subscription, as well as access to additional software licenses for testing purposes, access to additional copies of Novell's software, Novell's Application Notes, and two more additional standard incidents from Novell Developer Support organization. Novell recognizes the opportunity to have the primary relationship with regard to co-marketing of your software product. The Advanced DeveloperNet Subscription costs $995.00 annually.

Novell's Software Development Kits

DeveloperNet includes all of Novell's Software Development Kits in one neat package called Novell's SDK. The latest revision of this Software Development Kit as of this writing is revision 10. This free kit is available for downloading from the Internet at `http://developer.novell.com/`. You must first subscribe as a developer on the web page or you can call 1-800-RED-WORD (1-800-733-9673). After you have subscribed, you will be given a user ID and a password, this is needed in order to get into the developer section of the web page hierarchy. You can then begin downloading each of the SDKs you will need for your software project.

The latest, Novell SDK, is at revision level 10 and includes the following developer kits.

- Telephony SDK
- GroupWise SDK
- NEST SDK
- Novell Licensing Services
- Novell Application Manager SDK
- Novell ManageWise SDK

Telephony SDK

Novell's Telephony Services offer the developer the exciting opportunity to add the networking services for including telephone equipment to their application software. This API set is called "TSAPI." The SDK for Telephony includes support for network managed control of PBX hardware, and managing calls for a telemarketing system or problem tracking system for technical support markets. The TSAPI also includes support for Caller ID, Teleconferencing, Forwarding, Transfers, and many other features. By allowing control of both incoming and outgoing calls, these features enable an organization to take additional advantage of their investment in telephone equipment. The details of Novell's Telephony SDK are available in the Novell SDK and can be downloaded by subscribing to DeveloperNet with Novell Developer Services.

GroupWise SDK

Novell's award winning Groupware product, GroupWise 5, is a full-featured implementation of a messaging system. The Groupware product includes the capability to track outgoing messages, the capability to create customized messages, work flows to enforce custom business logic, task assignment, appointment and calendaring, and document management. It is clearly the leader in the world of advanced messaging and is closely connected in a technical manner to IntranetWare. There are two GroupWise SDKs, one for 4.1 and one for the newest version of GroupWise, revision 5. Each allows the developer to create applications that can work with the GroupWise message store to perform multiple operations on that message store.

GroupWise API Gateway

The GroupWise API Gateway is a separate product for developer wanting to take advantage of GroupWise's capability to be flexible and the glue to create a complete Groupware solution. The GroupWise API Getaway enables a developer to create a new gateway to either allow a different messaging system to coexist with GroupWise, help migrate their end users from a different messaging system, or to act as a go-between to send and receive messages through any of the other GroupWise gateways to a third messaging system that cannot be reached without GroupWise's other gateway functions, such as Web Access, Pager, Telephone Access, or other Gateways.

Using the GroupWise SDK in conjunction with the GroupWise API Gateway, a developer can create a single cohesive messaging system out of several different heterogenous messaging systems. Developers can also create a new market by adding enhancements to existing GroupWise systems. This would enable the developer to take advantage of new technologies such as web browsers, Personal Data Assistants, Data Wrist Watches, paging services, and many other emerging technologies. With the current explosion of Groupware products, this is an exciting area for software developers to enter into markets and create new ones. The API Gateway is accessible through the OLE languages such as Delphi, Visual Basic, and from object oriented languages such as C++.

GroupWise Custom 3rd Party Objects

The GroupWise Custom 3rd Party Objects (C3POs), can be used to extend the basic functionality of GroupWise. To do this, C3POs allow new data types, such as Uniform Resource Locaters (URLs), Voice Mail messages, and other items to be added to the GroupWise message store, to become represented in the Universal Message Box as different icons. Additionally, these C3POs can have different behaviors built into them so that when they are selected, they perform a certain function, such as launching a web browser, or playing a voice mail through the client computer's speakers. C3POs, like the API Gateway, can be accessed through Visual Basic, Delphi, or C++. The details of the Novell GroupWise SDK and the GroupWise API Gateway are available within the Novell SDK and can be downloaded by subscribing to DeveloperNet with Novell Developer Services.

NEST SDK

Developers can embed networking smarts into a wide variety of devices by using the Novell Embedded Systems Technology (NEST). NEST contains all the tools needed to build and test network enabled devices such as smart houses that can automatically turn on and off appliances like a furnace, air conditioner, lights, or a garage door. Power and utility companies are already developing and deploying network smart meters to reduce their costs to read those meters for billing purposes by utilizing the NEST SDK. NEST is being used by printer, fax, and copier companies to create smart peripherals that dramatically reduce the administrative overhead involved with maintaining networked peripherals. Cable companies are using the NEST SDK to create set top computers that replace cable switching boxes with the capability to download content and explore the Internet from the home. Such smart devices can be controlled and managed via NDS and SNMP. NEST is implemented in ANSI-C for portability purposes.

NEST has been implemented to be modular. This enables developers to use only the parts of NEST that they need in order to implement their smart device. NEST is also designed to be both operating system and processor independent, making this SDK one of the more flexible SDKs available for device manufacturers. The details of NEST and the modules that come with NEST are available within the Novell SDK and can be downloaded by subscribing to DeveloperNet with Novell Developer Services.

Novell Licensing Services

Novell Licensing Services are available for the first time as a part of IntranetWare. These extensions enable the developer to embed code within their application that is capable of initializing and consuming licensing services in IntranetWare.

The following are the four main reasons for Novell's implementing a Licensing API:

- To provide vendors with a mechanism by which they can track shrink-wrap software in their network to insure that they honor their license agreements with their ISVs.
- Be extendable so that additional licensing philosophies can be added or modified in the future.
- Integration with Novell's network management products to help to troubleshoot if necessary, or to ease the management burden associated with the software product being licensed.
- Finally, to provide the first in a series of steps to ensure that future licensing require ments can be accommodated, and to help in the maintenance of the licensed software.

Such services include the capability to restrict the concurrent number of applications used at one time on the network, and allowing application developers to enforce the number of application licenses they have sold to their customer base. The mechanism by which this is enforced in the IntranetWare environment is via a certificate that outlines the number of concurrent licenses available, and a sub-system that allows for the addition or modification of that certificate by an administrator with appropriate rights. This certificate is an object that resides within the NDS tree and includes information such as Software being licensed, the owner of the license, the current active users, as well as other information. The details of the LSAPI are available within the Novell SDK and can be downloaded by subscribing to DeveloperNet with Novell Developer Services.

Novell Application Manager SDK

Novell Directory Services offers not only a replicated, scalable, fault tolerant source of network wide information, but it is also extensible. An example of such an extension would be a new class and the corresponding subclasses of objects in NDS, the Application object class.

One of the most time-intensive tasks an administrator must undertake is to make sure that the business critical applications their end users require to do the day-to-day business tasks are available and run properly from each and every desktop in their organization. For the administrator, this type of tasks can be very time-consuming and nearly impossible in very large environments. To ease this burden, the Application object in NDS enables an administrator to create, modify, and delete applications. This includes subclass information such as drive mappings, captured printing ports, initiation and termination scripts, contact information, general comments, as well as other object information that can be administrated via one program, NWadmin.

Additionally, the newest version of the NetWare Application Launcher enables the administrator to specify several servers that can launch the application. This permits both fault tolerance and load balancing on a group of servers. The object information and the information that dictates the behavior of this extension to the X.500 based NDS exist in the NDS snap-in, appsnap.dll. The source code for the snap-in and examples that show how the NetWare Application Manager and the client portion, (the NetWare Application Launcher) are a part of the NetWare Application Manager SDK. This information can be obtained by subscribing to Novell's DeveloperNet with Novell's Developer Services.

Novell ManageWise SDK

As a network grows, the mathematical likelihood of a problem occurring is directly related to the size and complexity of your network. Additionally, a problem can grow in size or significance without detection until it manifests itself in a dramatic manner. One of the keys to preventing dramatic displays of dysfunction is to proactively monitor your network and all of the devices on your network to detect problems areas before those problems become significant.

The ManageWise SDK enables developers to instrument new devices by using the MIB compiler. This instrumentation ensures the new device is not only seen from the ManageWise console, but configured and managed as well. Like NDS, it permits centralized management of devices one location takes care of the network. The software developer can also take advantage of the ManageWise SDK to instrument an application as well. By creating the necessary alarms in the application, the developer can alert the administrator to conditions that require attention, or take action on the part of the administrator. Inventory control can also be a part of a ManageWise enabled application by allowing the administrator to keep track of which workstations are using which software.

The details of the Novell ManageWise SDK and example code is available within the Novell SDK and can be downloaded by subscribing to DeveloperNet with Novell Developer Services.

Support Policy for DeveloperNet Subscribers

There are many support plans available for the developer. These plans range from on-site developer support, to pay-per-incident fees which range from $100 to $400 depending on the urgency of the call into the Developer Support Organization.

Yes Certification

The Novell SDK includes the tools to test your applications or devices so they can be certified at Novell's Labs. These testing tools include load testing as well as functionality testing to insure to your customers that your products whether they be software, hardware, or both work properly with Novell's products. Novell will allow the developer to use the "Yes" logo for IntranetWare, GroupWise, ManageWise, and Telephony products provided that they have passed testing at Novell's labs. The "Yes" logo can be used on marketing literature as well as on the product's packaging, insuring your products work well with Novell's products. This also delivers an amount of confidence in your products to your prospective customers. You can get more complete information on the "Yes" trademarking program by contacting Novell at 1-800-453-1267, or directing your web browser at `http://yes.novell.com/`.

Summary

This chapter provided a brief overview of development under the IntranetWare environment. To go into the details and the depth required to completely inform the developer of each and every tip or trick would require an entire volume that would surpass the size of this reference book. This chapter lists the development options available to not only the developer of software applications or NLMs, but provides the network administrator with the information. This information covered how to develop some needed tools and how to scope out the required work needed to be done in order to add tools the administrator could use to further ease their networked workload. Development can be somewhat non-trivial for creating NLMs, however using the NetBasic scripting language, Java, or any of the Rapid Application Development environments can help the less experienced developer or administrator that help them create some useful tools. At Novell, great efforts are being made to reduce the amount of work that must be done to manage and administrate an organization's network. In specialized environments, there might be a need for additional tools that are not currently supplied by Novell or by any of it's partners. A Systems Integrator, Reseller, LAN Administrator, Developer, or even a sophisticated power end user, you can take advantage of any of these development environments. Using these resources, you can make the tools to ensure that your most valuable organizational asset, your data, is both secure and easy to use by those authorized to use it.

A proper development project usually has several phases that include the statement of need, the initial requirements documentation, detailed requirements document, the pseudo-code to outline the project's needed components, the coding, testing, and test implementation. A good development philosophy eliminates the number of troubles you must deal with during your project and ensure that the tools or networked applications you intend to create meet the needs which brought about the development process in the first place.

Partnering with Novell's DeveloperNet program as outlined earlier in this chapter ensures that you have the tools necessary to create and deploy the networked utilities or applications you intend to create. It is also a great place to start to fill in the blanks from this chapter with a large amount of development information, tips, and tricks.

CHAPTER 13

IntranetWare Web Services

As the Internet and intranets become more and more prevalent parts of modern corporate networks, IntranetWare has been promoted as an ideal platform for serving web-based documents. After all, IntranetWare is the platform of choice for providing file and print services, and serving web documents is little more than another form of file service.

IntranetWare now includes the current release of the Novell Web Server. This chapter looks at the features and benefits of using version 3 of Novell Web Server. Novell Web Server 3 is a free download from Novell's Web site at `http://www.novell.com/intranetware`*. Look for the product information on Novell Web Server. After filling out a short customer information form, the web server software can be downloaded free of charge.*

Note

As of this writing, Novell Web Server 3 is supported on the IntranetWare platform running NetWare 4.11 or later. Novell does not support running this product on NetWare 4.10. Administrators wanting to run the product need to determine which updates are required to run Novell Web Server 3. As of this writing, the TCP/IP update in TCPN03.EXE and the CLIB module updates in LIBUPC.EXE are required. Both of these updates can be found in the IntranetWare Service Pack 2 file, named IWSP2.EXE on the Novell FTP site.

Installing Novell Web Server 3

Installation of Novell Web Server 3 is a very simple process. From the INSTALL. NLM main menu, select Product Options, then Install Product not Listed. The INSTALL. NLM will prompt for a path, and will install automatically after the path is entered. There are a few places where the installation process provides information; those informational breaks provide information about what you might see if you are upgrading from Novell Web Server 2.x, and where to find the new INDEX.HTM file that would have been the default for a new installation. The installation of Novell Web Server 3 takes less than 5 minutes, during which it installs a set of HTML files that includes documentation, script examples, sample pages, the HTTP server modules, and the WEBMGR utility.

Exploring Web Services

Novell Web Server 3 includes the features of previous releases, and adds new features to provide a complete platform for hosting web services utilizing the latest technologies. The new features of Novell Web Server 3 include the following:

- Fault tolerance support
- Symmetric multiprocessing support
- Enhanced document security
- Improved performance
- Oracle database connectivity
- Virtual directories and multihoming

Fault Tolerance Support

NetWare SFT-III is the industry standard platform for providing fault-tolerance network services. Novell Web Server 3 can run on an SFT-III server pair, providing a completely mirrored system for running web services. In the event of a hardware failure on one server in the pair, the secondary server can take over the functions of the primary server.

Symmetric Multiprocessing Support

Novell first introduced symmetric multiprocessing (SMP) through OEM partners with NetWare 4.1. IntranetWare includes support for SMP right out of the box. High-traffic sites may see a performance benefit in running on a multiprocessing server, and Novell Web Server 3 fully supports these capabilities.

Although it is possible to see a benefit in running a web server on a multiprocessor platform, the real benefit to running on such a platform is realized when CGI applications are provided through SMP aware NLMs running on the server.

Another note of importance is that currently, the SFT-III and SMP features of IntranetWare cannot be used concurrently. The system administrator may choose to use one or the other—or neither—but both SMP and SFT-III cannot be used at this time. Selection of either of these platforms depends on the needs for the web server. If high-performance is the overriding factor and the CGI applications are running as NLMs, NetBASIC scripts, or PERL scripts, the SMP implementation is the better choice. If high availability is the more important factor, then implementation on the SFT-III platform should be considered.

Enhanced Document Security

In this version of Novell Web Server, Novell has introduced support for the Secure Sockets Layer (SSL). Novell Web Server 3 provides support for versions 2.0 and 3.0 of the SSL specification, providing secure web browsing capabilities through any SSL-aware web browser.

SSL uses public key/private key cryptography similar to what NDS uses between a client and a server for authentication. This means that when using a properly configured server and a web browser that supports SSL, it is possible to have a completely secure conversation between the browser and the web server.

In Novell Web Server 3, Novell introduces a new utility specifically used for managing the certificates used by SSL. This utility, called KEYMGR, runs at the server as an NLM, as shown in figure 13.1.

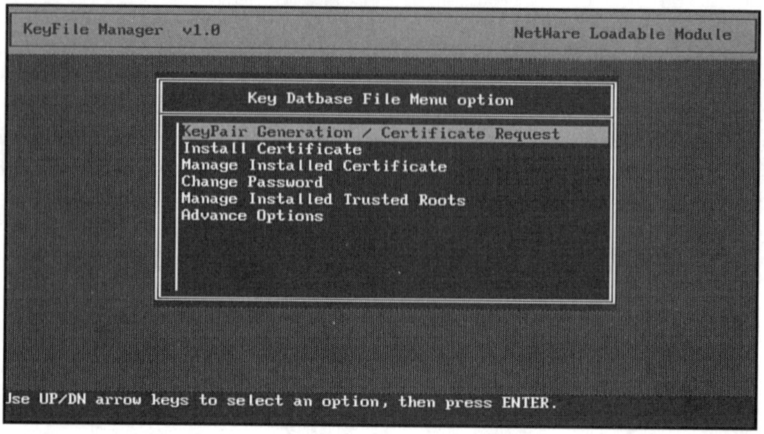

Figure 13.1
The KEYMGR utility.

As can be seen in figure 13.1, there are several options in the KEYMGR utility for managing certificates on the web server. Although each server can have only a single key database file, that database file can contain as many certificates as the site needs. This enables sites using the multihoming features of Novell Web Server 3 to use SSL for each of the virtual hosts and to maintain a separate certificate for each name the web server uses.

Novell includes the procedure for acquiring a certificate through VeriSign in the documentation supplied with Web Server 3. The process involves the following steps:

- Creating the key database file
- Generating the certificate signing request
- Requesting a certificate
- Installing a certificate
- Setting the location of the key database file
- Enabling and configuring SSL

The following sections talk about each of these steps in more detail.

Creating the Key Database File

SSL uses a public key/private key cryptosystem to sign information that is passed from a web server to a client that is running an SSL-enabled web browser. In order to maintain these certificates, the Novell Web Server needs a key file that contains all of the certificates used on the hosts that particular web server runs. This information is maintained in a password protected database file known as the *key database file*. The *Key Manager* (KEYMGR.NLM) utility is used to create and maintain that database file.

Creation of the key database file takes place the first time you run the KEYMGR utility. It asks for the path and name, excluding the extension, of the key database file and also asks for a password of eight characters or less to create the key database file.

> **Warning** It is important to remember the key database file's password, because that password will be required to perform any and all management of the certificates in the database. This password is also required when modifying security settings in the web manager utility or when restarting the web server from the console prompt. Loss of this password requires that SSL be disabled, a new key database be generated, and that new certificate requests be generated for all of the virtual hosts running on the web server.

Generating the Certificate Signing Request

After the key database is created, a certificate signing request can be generated. The *certificate signing request* is a text file that can be sent to the Certificate Authority, or CA, for validation. To generate the request, select the KeyPair Generation/Certificate Request menu item in KEYMGR. KEYMGR will ask for the identification of the Certificate Authority, if the certificate request is for a new certificate, and if the request is for a renewal.

After the first set of prompts is filled in, press <Esc>, and the KEYMGR utility will prompt for several pieces of information:

- **The certificate name.** This is the name that identifies the certificate.
- **The common name.** This should be the hostname of the URL for the server. For example, if the server's URL is *http://www.proref.com*, the common name would be *www.proref.com*.
- **The organization.** This value is the full legal name of the company requesting the certificate. Note that this is not necessarily the NDS "Organization" level object name, but rather the legal name of the company.
- **The organizational unit.** This value is the name of the department or division requesting the certificate. As with the organization, this is not related to any object in the NDS tree.
- **City.** The city in which the organization is located.
- **State or province.** The state or province in which the organization is located.
- **Country.** The country in which the organization is located. This will be a two-character ISO value.
- **The requestor's name.**

- **The requestor's e-mail address.**
- **The requestor's telephone number.**

When this information is all entered and verified, a certificate request is generated. The process of generating the request might take several minutes. When completed, the request is put in the same directory as the key database file. The request is an ASCII file that is similar to that shown in listing 13.1.

Listing 13.1: A sample certificate request file

```
Webmaster: jimh@fiber.net
Phone : 801-555-1212
Server : www.proref.com

Common-Name : www.proref.com
Organization Unit : Web Server Division
Organization : Professional Reference
Locality : Salt Lake City
State : UT
Country : US

——BEGIN NEW CERTIFICATE REQUEST——
MIIBRjCB8QIBADCBizELMAkGA1UEBhMCVVMxCzAJBgNVBAgTAlVUMRcwFQYDVQQH
Ew5TYWx0IExha2UgQ2l0eTEfMB0GA1UEChMWUHJvZmVzc2lvbmFsIFJlZmVyZW5j
ZTEcMBoGA1UECxMTV2ViIFNlcnZlciBEaXZpc2lvbjEXMBUGA1UEAxMOd3d3LnBy
b3JlZi5jb20wXDANBgkqhkiG9w0BAQEFAANLADBIAkEA2F5geohxGWYqW7elXM0l
h9ozyoyaZ+1PfGOloPqAA4Z/RjEZc3L/Q6RzuQO363ggzsY2WJlzkS8M8cEql5dq
+wIDAQABoAAwDQYJKoZIhvcNAQEEBQADQQB74JrO7kyAXotk9DITx0R4EYbvoX32
gCGMm18873SDtkBy/VvuP7c+Bf1QssJPAHh19ddsv1FHwXsikHY/TtcY
——END NEW CERTIFICATE REQUEST——
```

This sample shows the entire request file; the only part that needs to be sent in is the part from where the certificate request begins, denoted with the text "——BEGIN NEW CERTIFICATE REQUEST——", and ending with the line that reads "——END NEW CERTIFICATE REQUEST——."

Installing a Certificate

After the request for the certificate is processed by the CA, a reply message is sent back with the actual certificate. The format of the certificate file is similar to the request, except that it contains the actual certificate to be installed on the server.

When the certificate file is received, use the KEYMGR utility to install it. Enter the path and filename of the web server's key database file and the password for the key database file, and then select Install Certificate from the main menu. The KEYMGR utility asks whether the certificate is a part of a chain—this tells the utility whether there is one or more certificates in the certificate file. It also asks if the certificate should be installed, or if it should be verified only, and if the certificate comes from a trusted root. It also asks for the path and filename of the certificate to install.

After the certificate is installed, the information about the certificate that was sent in will be displayed in order to verify that the installed certificate is for the requested server. When this is verified, it is time to set the location of the key database file in the Web Manager utility (WEBMGR) in order to configure SSL for use on the web server.

Setting the Location of the Key Database File

At this stage, configuration using the KEYMGR utility is complete; all further configuration is done from the WEBMGR utility. This is done by selecting the web server to be configured, and then selecting the Set Key Database File option from the Options menu in WEBMGR. After this is set, enter the password for the key database file to save and restart the web server.

Enabling and Configuring SSL

Now it is time to enable and configure SSL. To do this, select the virtual host to be modified and click the Enable SSL checkbox for the host. If the default ports need to be changed, change them as well; the default for the HTTP server is port 80; for SSL, the default port is 443. Normally, these ports should not need to be changed; however, it may be necessary to do so, depending on how the server is being used.

After these steps are complete, select the Security Options button, the certificate to be used on this virtual host, and the version or versions of SSL to be supported by this host. Novell Web Server 3 supports use of either SSL 2.0, SSL 3.0, or both versions. By default the server is configured to use both.

Another checkbox of importance is the Require Client Certificate checkbox. This configures the server so that it requires any attaching web browser to present its own certificate to the server in order to establish an SSL session with the server.

Improved Performance

The previous version of Novell Web Server—version 2.5—was a fairly capable performer. Version 3 improves the performance even further, delivering a measured performance of 700 connections per second with 128 clients. Novell has also reengineered how the web server NLM uses resources, making it more efficient in releasing control to other NLMs, meaning that this performance increase does not cost in terms of performance for other NLMs running on the server.

Oracle Database Connectivity

Also new to version 3 is connectivity to Oracle databases. Novell provides this through the CGI interface provided through NetBasic, a NetWare-based BASIC scripting language.

Virtual Directories and Multihoming

In previous versions of the Novell Web Server, all of your documents had to be located on the server running the web server NLM. Virtual directories enable you to put the documents on any NetWare server on your network and still access them as if they were on the server running the NLM.

Multihoming is a feature that enables a web server to host sites under multiple names. An example of this in use is a content provider that enables its customers to use their own domain name to access their site. All of the names point to the same server, and the web server treats them as separate entities, even though they are all being hosted on the same physical machine.

Multihoming is configured through the WEBMGR utility, shown in figure 13.2. After a web server has been selected, another server can be created using the menu, and an entirely new directory structure is created, along with all of the necessary configuration files. When this is done, the HTTP NLM is restarted, and it recognizes requests to both the original server and the second virtual server. Novell Web Server 3 has no inherent limitation as to the number of virtual hosts it can support.

Figure 13.2
The WEBMGR Utility.

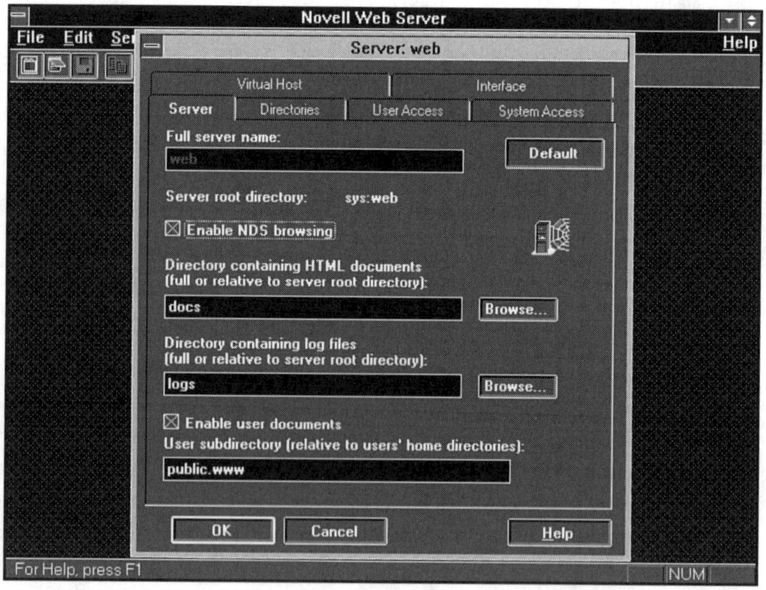

Web Features Support

Web servers can provide other services as well, such as file transfer capabilities and DNS lookup. IntranetWare includes components to provide all of these services in order to provide a rounded solution for hosting a web site.

Domain Name Services (DNS)

One component of NetWare/IP, which is also included with IntranetWare, is Domain Name Services (DNS). DNS is the service that enables a station to associate a name—such as www.novell.com—with an IP address. All traffic on the Internet uses IP addresses to determine where packets are coming from and where they're going. Names such as www.novell.com provide a human-readable address that is associated with an IP address. DNS is the service that provides the translation between IP address and the host name.

For more information on DNS, see Chapter 22, "NetWare/IP Connectivity Services."

Netscape Browser

One would wonder what good a Web Server product would be without some way to access the documents being served. Fortunately, Novell has established a working relationship with Netscape Communications, which has resulted in an agreement to bundle an equal number of Netscape Navigator licenses to the user count for each IntranetWare package.

File Transfer Protocol

Although a web server's primary content is viewed in Hypertext Markup Lanuguage, or HTML, it also provides access to file transfers through the use of standard File Transfer Protocol, or FTP. IntranetWare includes not only the Web Server product, but also includes FTP Services for IntranetWare on CD number 4.

A component of using FTP is the use of anonymous and registered user transfers. Novell's FTP server supports both methods of authorization for access to downloadable files. Figure 13.3 shows an example of using Netscape to download files through an FTP connection.

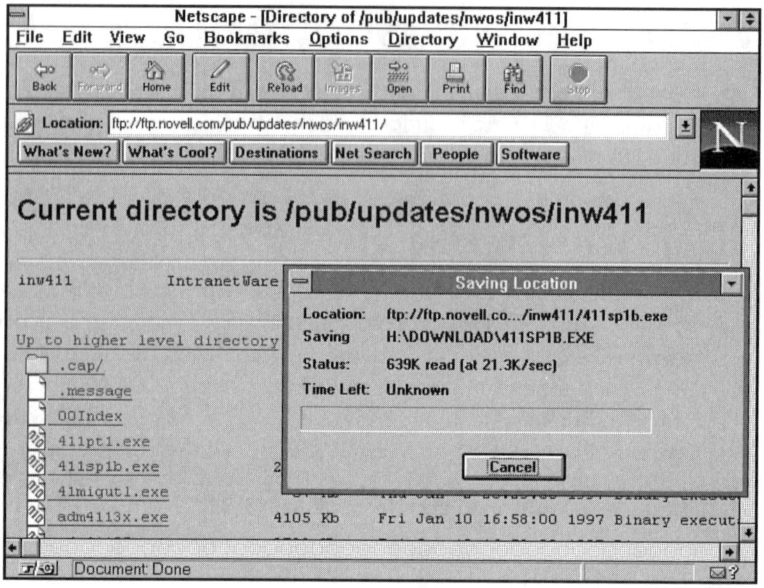

Figure 13.3
Using Netscape for performing file transfers with FTP.

Previous versions of Novell's FTP product did not work with the Web Server product. The version included with IntranetWare on CD number 4 does support the web server. Standard user access requires only that NFS name space be applied to the volumes the registered user is authorized to access. Anonymous users, however, have to be handled differently because the anonymous user account allows any text as a valid password. Here is how to configure the system for anonymous access.

The first step in making the FTP server product function with the Web Server product—after the FTP server product is installed—is to ensure that anonymous FTP access is enabled. To do this, go to the server console and load UNICON. Select Manage Services, FTP Admin, Set Parameter, and verify that the anonymous user access is set to YES and that the home directory value is filled in.

Next, it is necessary to ensure that NFS name space is applied to the volume the anonymous user's home directory is located on. At the server console, type **VOLUMES** and check which name spaces are applied to the volume. If NFS is not listed, do the following:

1. Type **LOAD NFS.NAM** at the server console.

2. Type **ADD NAME SPACE NFS TO VOLUME <volume>**, replacing *<volume>* with the name of the volume the anonymous user's home directory is located on.

Next, verify that the anonymous user's home directory is owned by the anonymous user, and that the file access is set properly for the anonymous user. To do this, follow these steps:

1. LOAD UNICON if it is not already loaded.

2. Select the File Operations menu option.
3. Select View/Set File Permissions.
4. Walk through the file system and select the anonymous user's home directory.
5. Set the owner for the directory to "anonymous."
6. Set the owner NFS access for the directory to the values appropriate for the environment. Typically, this will be read-only access.

Using the IPX/IP Gateway

Another piece of supporting software included with IntranetWare is the IPX/IP Gateway, also known as Novell Internet Access Server, or NIAS.

Any administrator who has had to administer TCP/IP addresses—even through the use of a dynamic address allocation tool like BOOTP or DHCP—knows how difficult it is to keep track of the information used for address administration. NIAS provides a simple alterative, enabling you to use IPX/SPX from the workstation, which the NIAS NLMs translate to TCP/IP so stations can communicate with sites on the Internet. This is accomplished by replacing the standard TCP/IP implementation of WINSOCK.DLL with a version that uses IPX/SPX instead. The gateway then does a protocol conversion and automatically creates a TCP/IP socket connection from the server to the desired host.

After the NIAS product has been installed on the server using INSTALL.NLM and started, installation of the client software can be done. The default installation for the client software—which supports Windows 3.1 and Windows 95—is in the SYS:PUBLIC\CLIENT directory structure, under the WIN3.1 or the WIN95 directory, depending on which version of Windows is being run.

Access Control

Another feature of the IPX/IP gateway included with NIAS is the capability to restrict access to the Internet based on host address, time, or a specific TCP/IP port number. Because the access control information is stored in NDS, administration is done through NWADMIN.

To use NWADMIN to configure access control, the user interface of NWADMIN needs to be extended through a snapin. To add this extension to NWADMIN, add a line that reads:

```
ipxgw3x.dll=ipxgw3x.dll
```

into the Snapin Object DLLs section of NWADMIN.INI.

After this is done, start NWADMIN and select a container, group, or user object in the tree. Right-click on the object and select Details, and then select the IPX/IP Gateway Service Restrictions page in the object.

From this page, restrictions can be configured. The precedence of the restrictions start with user, then group, and finally container restrictions. For example, if you disallow access to the URL *http://www.mcp.com* for a container, all objects in that container and below have that restriction unless either a group a user is in has a different restriction for that same URL, or unless an explicit exception is made for a specific user.

Publishing for the Intranet and Internet

Information can be published on the Internet through many different means; there are two basic types of web pages: *static* pages and *dynamic* pages.

Static Pages

Static web pages are created using the Hypertext Markup Language, or HTML. HTML is nothing more than a combination of ASCII text and special formatting commands to make a browser format the text in a particular way. It also includes commands for the placement of graphics and other objects, such as sound files, animations, and downloadable files. The main index page in Novell Web Server 3 is an example of a static page, and is shown in figure 13.4.

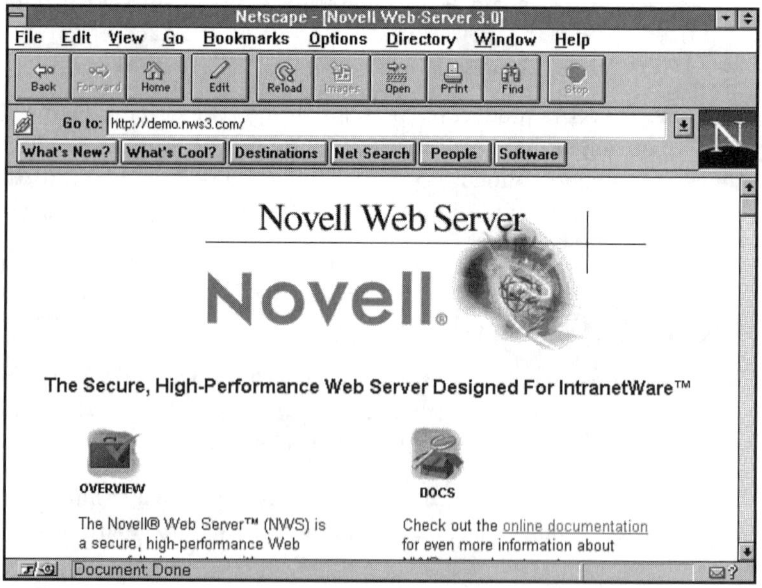

Figure 13.4
A Static Web page.

Server Side Includes

Server side includes, or SSI, enable a static page to have dynamic components. SSI is implemented on the Novell Web Server through the use of specially-formatted HTML comments that the server interprets and fills in with text values. The web server NLM will take care of interpreting these comments as long as they are properly formatted by the web page designer.

SSI has one other requirement, however; the document file must have the extension SSI instead of HTM or HTML. Otherwise, the web server will not interpret the embedded SSI commands and will leave blank spaces in the document.

Dynamic Pages

Dynamic pages can be created a number of ways; however, the creation of dynamic pages is ultimately handled the same way no matter what language is used—a program dynamically looks up or generates data, and then the program generates HTML-formatted documents on the fly and serves them to the client through the web server.

LCGI and RCGI APIs

One method for developing dynamic pages is through what is referred to as a Common Gateway Interface, or CGI application.

CGI programs are usually written in C and run as executables on the platform the web server is running on, or they can run on a remote machine if the application has some way to get back to the web server when a request comes in for a dynamically created document.

The Novell Web Server product supports both local CGI, or LCGI and remote CGI, or RCGI.

LCGI is implemented through an API set for writing NLMs that run on the server. Anything that can be done through an NLM running on the server can be served to a dynamically generated HTML document by that NLM. Novell's NDS Browser, shown in figure 13.5, is an example of an LCGI program that generates web pages.

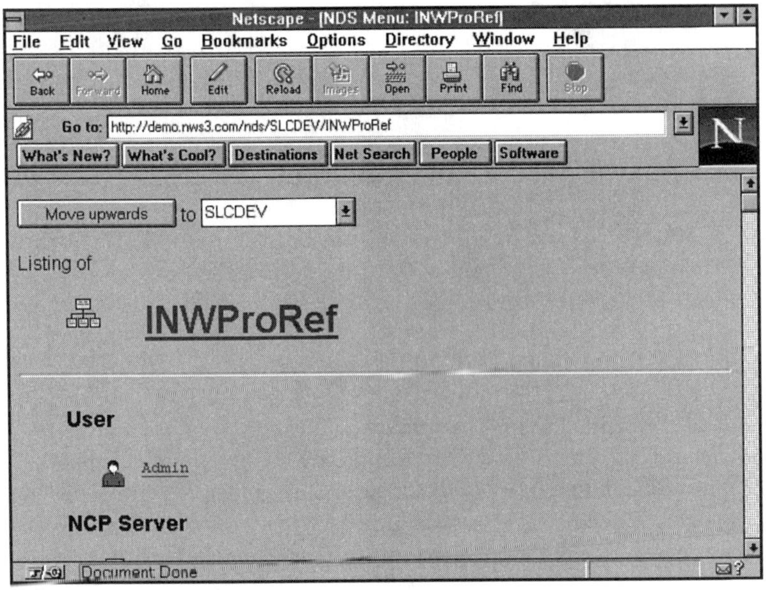

Figure 13.5
The NDS Browser LCGI application.

One of the drawbacks of writing NLMs, however, is that they can cause a server abend. Novell provides another alternative to writing an NLM to provide CGI, though—the RCGI interface. This consists of an NLM that runs on the IntranetWare server and a daemon that runs on a Unix host. The RCGI application then is written to run on the Unix host and serves the dynamic page to the web server remotely.

NetBasic

An alternative for those who either do not program in C or who do not desire to write NLMs or work through setting up a second machine running Unix for an RCGI NLM is provided through High Technology Software Corporation's NetBasic NLM. NetBasic, as included with IntranetWare, includes NLMs to perform HTML document functions, such as creating HTML tags. Figure 13.6 shows a list of some of the functions available through NetBasic.

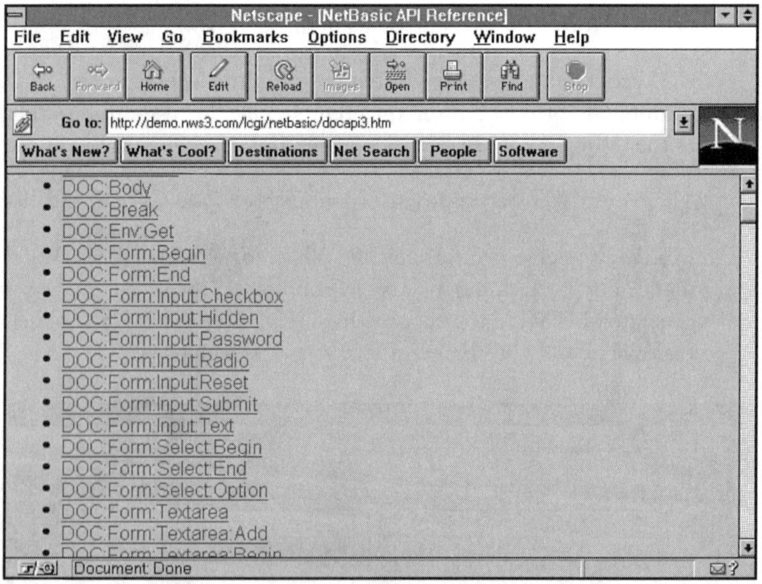

Figure 13.6
Document functions in NetBasic.

NetBasic is an NLM-based BASIC language interpreter that can be used to manipulate NetWare much as you could through an NLM, but without the development time or effort in debugging problems that may cause server abends.

PERL

The Practical Extraction and Reporting Language, commonly known as *PERL* is another method for generating dynamic documents. There are many ready-to-run web server applications written in PERL, and for the most part, they should not require much—if any—modification to run on the Novell Web Server. Version 3 of the web server software supports the use of PERL 5, which is new to the product—previous versions limited programmers to PERL 4.

Java Support

Perhaps the hottest technology being used for dynamic web page generation today is Java. Figure 13.7 shows the sample clock Java applet included with Novell Web Server 3.

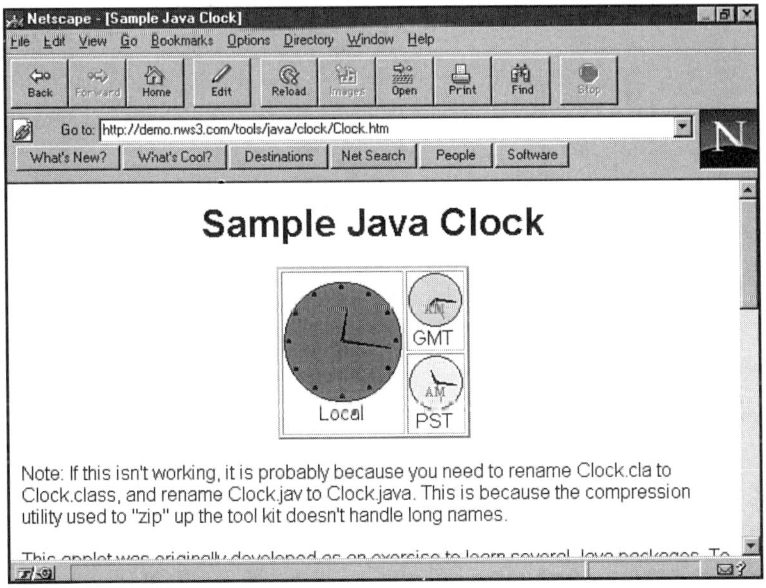

Figure 13.7
The Clock Java applet.

Java is a platform-independent, object-oriented programming language that interfaces with the web browser to produce dynamic graphics and animation. Novell includes with the Web Server product several samples of Java including the clock applet shown previously in figure 13.7, a page hit counter, and a web performance monitor.

Summary

In this chapter, we looked at using IntranetWare as a Web Server platform and the services included that make this a very well-rounded platform for hosting these services. Support for SSL 2.0 and 3.0 permits administrators the ability to use secure client/server connections between a web browser and the web server, providing a high degree of security in communications. We also discussed how to allow anonymous FTP access for file downloads from the web server. With the IPX/IP gateway and support for both static and dynamic web pages, this platform provides a robust solution for the Internet and intranets of today and tomorrow.

PART PART PART PART PART PART PART PART PART

II

The NetWare Network Environment

CHAPTER 14

Using the Enterprise Tools NetSync and DSMERGE

A large enterprise may have a mix of NetWare 3.x and 4.x servers. NetWare 3.x servers use the bindery to represent their network resource information, such as user, group, and print objects. The bindery contains only information pertaining to the NetWare server on which it is stored. You are required manage a separate bindery for every NetWare 3.x server on the network. IntranetWare, on the other hand, enables you to represent network resources in a global database, called NDS. This enables you to use the global NDS to manage many IntranetWare servers using a single database. Many organizations are upgrading their NetWare 3.x servers to IntranetWare to help reduce the cost of managing a large network. This migration might involve a transition phase during which the NetWare-based LAN runs a mix of NetWare 3.x and 4.x servers.

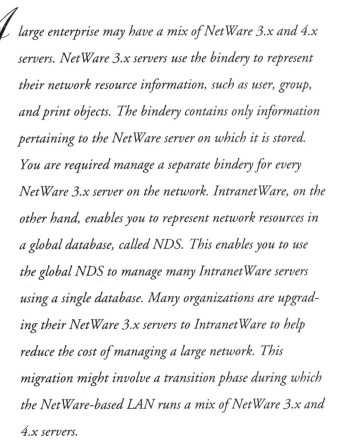

Novell has created a set of NLMs called NetSync. *NetSync* enables many of the NetWare 3.x server administration tasks to be performed from the NetWare Directory Services (NDS) by using IntranetWare tools such as the NetWare Administrator and NETADMIN. NetWare Administrator is available for Windows 3.x and Windows 95.

Another helpful tool for managing an IntranetWare network is DSMERGE. DSMERGE is an NLM that runs on the server and enables you to merge two separate NDS trees into a single tree.

This chapter discusses the NetSync and DSMERGE enterprise tools.

The NetSync Enterprise Tool

NetSync enables you to use the NDS to manage NetWare 3.x servers. You must have at least one IntranetWare server to provide the NDS services needed to supported NetSync. You use the IntranetWare tools NETADMIN or NWADMIN (NetWare Administrator) to manage NetWare 3.x servers, such as to create user and group accounts. NetSync consists of the NETSYNC3 and NETSYNC4 NLMs, which run on NetWare 3.x and IntranetWare servers, respectively. These NLMs enable you to use the NDS representations of bindery object data on a IntranetWare server to synchronize the NetWare 3.x bindery.

Overview of Bindery Objects and Bindery Context in IntranetWare

The IntranetWare server has the capability to enable you to view the objects in any NDS container as bindery objects, called bindery emulation. The container of NDS objects is called the bindery context. By default, the IntranetWare server's bindery context is set to the container in which the IntranetWare server object is created during the server installation. Beginning in NetWare 4.1, you can use the SET BINDERY CONTEXT console command to set the bindery context to include up to 16 containers. The bindery-based tools will see the NDS objects in these containers as a single container that can be emulated as a NetWare 3.x bindery. In earlier versions of IntranetWare, you could set the bindery context to only a single container, which forced NetWare administrators to place into a single container all objects that bindery-based clients needed to see. You now have greater flexibility when you place objects in separate containers and still be able to view these objects as belonging to a single bindery. This is possible because multiple containers are allowed to be included in the bindery context.

IntranetWare searches the Bindery context's containers in the order in which they are specified in the bindery context. If more than one object has the same Common Name (CN), only the object in the first bindery context is visible; the remaining bindery objects in other containers remain hidden by the first occurrence of the object that has the same name.

In general, you should avoid objects having the same name in containers that are to be included in the bindery context. Consider two users in the Corporate and Engineering departments, respectively, of the organization Kinetics: Karen Smith and Kim Smith. Assume that the organization uses the login name convention of first name initial plus last name. These users are in different departments, so you could assign both of them a login name of KSmith. For example, you could use the user object CN=KSmith.OU=CORP.O=KINETICS to describe user Karen Smith and CN=KSmith.OU=ENG.O=KINETICS to describe user Kim Smith. No conflict would occur if Kim and Karen were to log in using an NDS-based client, because they are in different containers. Now, you might wonder what would happen if the bindery context for the NetWare server used by Karen and Kim were set as follows:

```
SET BINDERY CONTEXT = OU=CORP.O=KINETICS;OU=ENG.O=KINETICS
```

If user Kim Smith uses login name KSmith from the bindery-based client, the server first searches the container OU=CORP.O=KINETICS for the object KSmith. It finds the KSmith user object in the container OU=CORP.O=KINETICS, and user Kim attempts to log in as KSmith. The object that the server finds, however, is for user Karen Smith, not user Kim Smith. User Kim attempts to log in using her own password, because she thinks that the server is asking her to log in under her user name. The server rejects the login if user Kim's password differs from user Karen's. In the unlikely event that user Kim and Karen have the same password, user Kim logs in to user Karen's account, but does not find the files and directories she expects in her home directory. In either case, the situation can create chaos to user and administrator.

NetSync depends on the bindery context set on the IntranetWare server, and you must not change this bindery context. The default bindery context set for IntranetWare is the container in which the server is installed. However, you can set the bindery context for NetSync to any context, including a context that does not contain an IntranetWare server.

The following shows the general format of the SET BINDERY CONTEXT command:

```
SET BINDERY CONTEXT=NDS container {; NDS container}
```

You can issue this command using a set command typed at the server console, but Network Administrators generally place the bindery context setting in the AUTOEXEC.NCF file to ensure that the bindery context is set whenever the server is started.

Bindery emulation enables workstation clients that use the older shell-type clients (NETX.EXE or NETX.COM) to access the IntranetWare server. The IntranetWare server appears to the clients as a bindery-based NetWare 3.x server, and the NDS objects in the containers in the bindery context appear as bindery objects. Bindery emulation also is important for NLMs that have been written to access bindery files. For example, the earlier version of the Norton Antivirus NLM requires that you log in as the bindery user SUPERVISOR when you make configuration changes. Other applications that depend on bindery-based objects are the following:

- Old UnixWare clients
- Old Windows NT and OS/2 clients
- Old DOS clients logged on to an NDS tree and making an attachment to another NDS tree

- Host access via NetWare for SAA
- Users using the DOS MAP command to access a directory in another NDS tree

When you specify the bindery context, you can choose to use a leading period in the container name or not. Here is an example of not using a leading period in the container name:

```
SET BINDERY CONTEXT=OU=CORP.O=ESL;.O=ESL
```

Here is an example of using a leading period in the container name:

```
SET BINDERY CONTEXT=.OU=CORP.O=ESL;O=ESL
```

Because the Bindery context parameter is set using a SET command, you also can use the SERVMAN.NLM or MONITOR.NLM to change the Bindery context parameter.

The NetSync Cluster

A NetSync cluster consists of one IntranetWare server and as many as 12 attached NetWare 3.x servers (see fig. 14.1). The NetWare 3.x servers attach to the IntranetWare server in the bindery emulation mode.

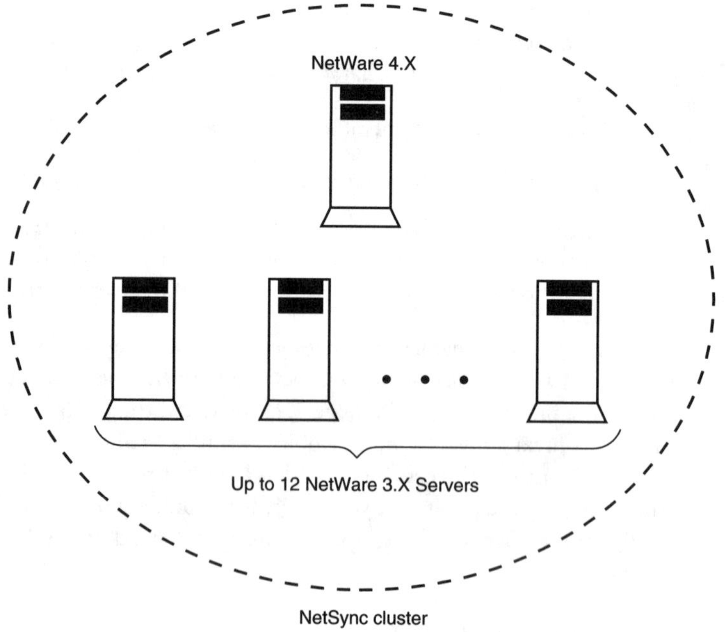

Figure 14.1
A NetSync cluster.

Whenever you update a user in the bindery context of the IntranetWare server, that user is synchronized with all NetWare 3.x servers in the NetSync cluster. If you create a new user in the bindery context of the IntranetWare server, that user exists as a bindery user on all NetWare 3.x servers that are part of the NetSync cluster and attached to the IntranetWare server. Similarly, if you change a property of the user, such as the user's last name, that change is replicated to all the NetWare 3.x servers in the NetSync cluster. A practical benefit of this is that you do not have to update or create the user on each NetWare 3.x server.

The updated bindery on each NetWare 3.x server is a superset of all the individual binderies that would be contained at each NetWare 3.x server if you were not using NetSync, and therefore is called the super-bindery. Any NetWare 3.x user can access any other NetWare 3.x server that is part of the same NetSync cluster.

After you create a NetSync cluster, you must use IntranetWare administrative utilities, such as NETADMIN or NWADMIN, to make all user and group account changes. You should not use SYSCON for these tasks, because the syncronization used by NetSync is one-way. Changes made using SYSCON on an individual NetWare 3.x server will result in the bindery objects on the servers being out of synchronization with each other. NetSync uses the NETSYNC3.NLM that runs on each NetWare 3.x server and the NETSYNC4.NLM that runs on the IntranetWare server to achieve synchronization of the NetSync cluster.

The IntranetWare server acts as a repository for bindery objects to be copied to the NetWare 3.x server from its bindery context. The NETSYNC4.NLM continuously monitors changes to objects in the IntranetWare server's bindery context. Any changes you make to the bindery objects in the IntranetWare server's bindery context are downloaded to all the Binderies on the NetWare 3.x servers in the NetSync cluster (see fig. 14.2).

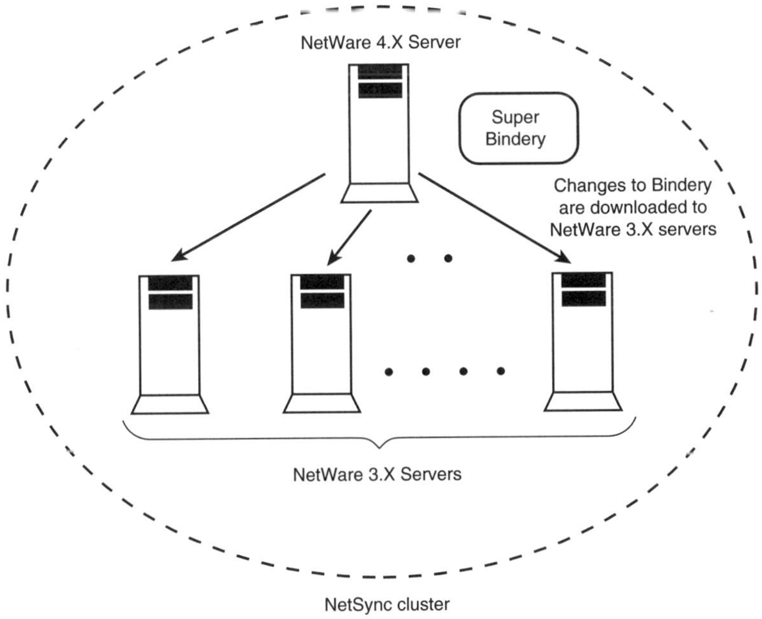

Figure 14.2
NetSync synchronization.

If you do not want to manage the NetWare 3.x servers from a central IntranetWare server, you should not join the NetWare 3.x server as part of the NetSync cluster. For example, if you plan to have a separate network supervisor for each NetWare 3.x server and to use SYSCON to manage users and group accounts separately, you should not make the NetWare 3.x server a part of a NetSync cluster. Also, if you have only IntranetWare servers on your network, or intend to migrate all your NetWare 3.x servers to IntranetWare at the same time, creating a NetSync cluster would be pointless.

Understanding Bindery Synchronization

Synchronization of the binderies in the NetSync cluster takes place from the IntranetWare server bindery context to the NetWare 3.x binderies (refer to figure 14.2). Changes are made to the objects in the IntranetWare bindery context first and these are automatically copied as part of the bindery synchronization to the NetWare 3.x binderies. These updates from the IntranetWare bindery context to the NetWare 3.x binderies are automatic and the IntranetWare bindery context is monitored continuously for changes.

If a NetWare 3.x server that is part of a NetSync cluster is down when the IntranetWare server sends out an update, the NetWare 3.x server's bindery will be out of synchronization. When you bring the NetWare 3.x online again, the IntranetWare server detects this event, and downloads its bindery context to the NetWare 3.x server to synchronize the NetWare 3.x server's bindery.

Ordinarily, the only time a NetWare 3.x server's bindery is copied to the IntranetWare bindery context is when you first make the NetWare 3.x server part of the NetSync cluster. If you use SYSCON and inadvertently make changes to the user and groups on a NetWare 3.x server that is part of a NetSync cluster, these changes are not copied to the other binderies in the NetSync cluster, which causes the binderies to be out of synchronization. In this case, you must make an explicit copy of the changed object on the NetWare 3.x server to the IntranetWare bindery context.

After a NetWare 3.x server joins a NetSync cluster, you must use the NETADMIN or NetWare Administrator in the IntranetWare server to make all changes to users, groups, and print services on the NetWare 3.x servers. Changes that you make using these utilities are automatically sent to all servers in the NetSync cluster. Remember, one of the benefits of joining a NetSync cluster is central administration of the NetWare 3.x servers. If you do not want central administration, and prefer to use SYSCON to manage users and groups, you should use NetSync.

SYSCON must still be used for managing accounting charge rates on each NetWare 3.x server, because accounting charges represent service and disk block usage, and are always for a specific server. By definition, the account charges are local to a server, and synchronizing this information across the servers in the NetSync cluster makes little sense.

Figures 14.3 and 14.4 illustrate bindery synchronization by showing the bindery objects on NetWare servers before and after joining a cluster, respectively.

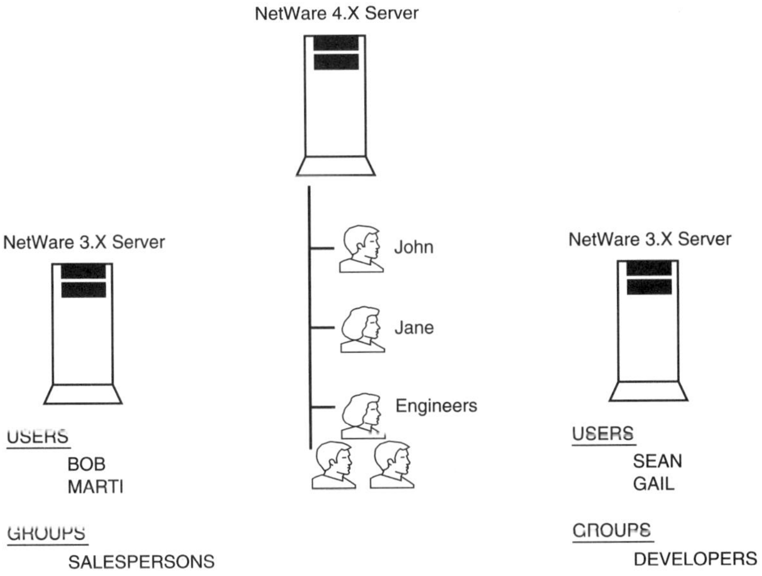

Figure 14.3
Bindery objects before joining a NetSync cluster.

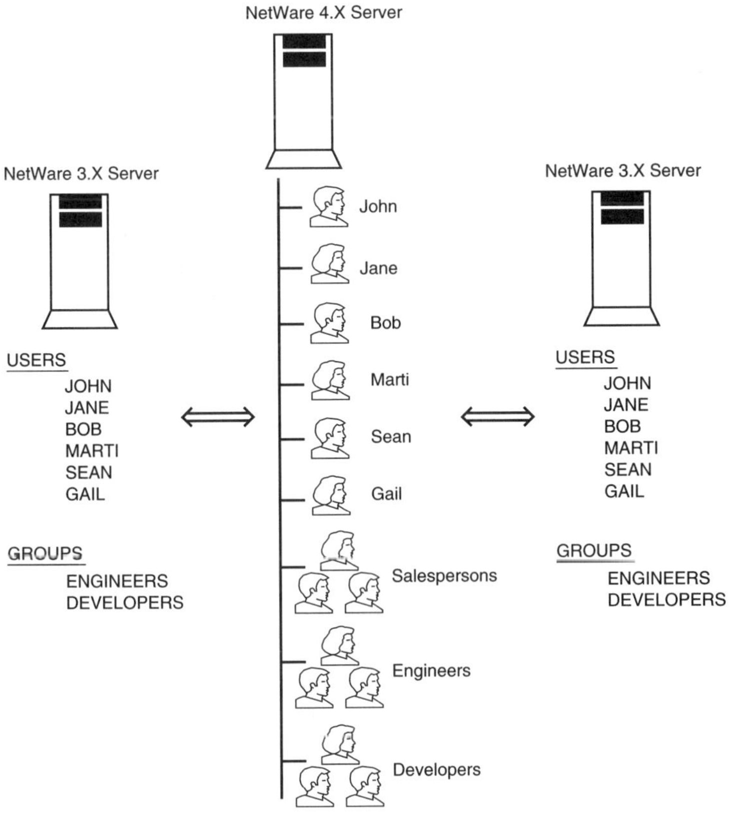

Figure 14.4
Bindery objects after joining a NetSync cluster.

Table 14.1 summarizes the items that NetSync does or does not synchronize.

Table 14.1
NetSync and Processing of Items for Synchronization

Item	Synchronized Status	Description
Users	Yes	Bindery-based users are combined into the IntranetWare server's bindery context.
User passwords	Yes	Passwords are the only pieces of information in NetSync that are synchronized in both directions. You can change passwords on any NetWare 3.x or IntranetWare server in the NetSync cluster. This change is propagated throughout the cluster. The reason for this is that if users have accounts on more than one server, they will typically maintain the same password on all servers. If you use NetWare 3.x SETPASS or LOGIN is used to change passwords, the utilities will ask you if you want to synchronize password changes to all attached servers. However, Passwords are synchronized even if you answer "No" to this question.
User login scripts	Yes	Login scripts are transferred into the NDS as Login script properties of the user object. NetSync synchronizes NetWare 3.x users' login scripts kept in the MAIL directory to the NDS login script property on the IntranetWare server. Changes made to the NDS user's login script on the IntranetWare server are synchronized to the login script files (in the MAIL directory) on all NetWare 3.x servers. You also can specify that NetSync create a login script file in the user's MAIL directory on the IntranetWare server. In this situation, the user login script will be synchronized in three places: the NDS login script property on the IntranetWare server, the user's 3.x MAIL directory, and the user's 4.x MAIL directory. Keeping a synchronized login script in the MAIL directory on the IntranetWare server enables NetWare 3.x

Item	Synchronized Status	Description
		users to log in to the NetWare 3.x using bindery emulation and execute the same login script that is on the NetWare 3.x server. If you have multiple IntranetWare servers in the same bindery context and you want to keep the login script in SYS:SYSTEM\MAIL synchronized with the NDS login script on all the servers, you must run NETSYNC4 on each IntranetWare server.
User GUEST	Yes	The user GUEST becomes an NDS user object.
Groups	Yes	All bindery-based groups become NDS groups.
Group EVERYONE	Yes	An NDS group EVERYONE is created. All users in the IntranetWare server's bindery context are added to this group. Any file and directory rights assigned to group EVERYONE on a NetWare 3.x server are synchronized (combined) and apply to all users in the NetSync cluster.
NetWare Name	Yes	NetWare Name Service profile login scripts are common Service (NNS) Profiles login scripts for a group of servers running NNS. These profile login scripts are converted to NDS profile objects.
Account Balances	Yes	Bindery-based user account balances become NDS properties of their respective user objects.
PRINTCON database	Yes	PRINTCON job configuration templates created on NetWare 3.x servers become properties of NDS objects.
PRINTDEF database	Yes	The PRINTDEF database on NetWare 3.x server becomes the property of the container object that is in the IntranetWare server bindery context.
User SUPERVISOR	No	The user SUPERVISOR remains as a separate object on each NetWare 3.x server in the NetSync cluster. This is for security reasons, because the SUPERVISOR account is used to control critical functions and tasks on each NetWare 3.x server.

continues

Table 14.1, Continued
NetSync and Processing of Items for Synchronization

Item	Synchronized Status	Description
Accounting	No	The accounting charge rates are server-based. For this reason, accounting charges are not synchronized. Accounting charge rates apply to the server on which accounting has been installed and configured. For example, when a user uses disk blocks on a NetWare 3.x server, the user's account balance is diminished on that 3.x server only, and not on the synchronized user definitions on other servers in the NetSync cluster. NetWare 3.x accounting is managed through SYSCON, and IntranetWare accounting is managed through NETADMIN or NetWare Administrator.
File system	No	File system rights continue to be server-based. The file system trustee rights apply to individual files and directories on the server. Synchronizing them would lead to situations that would give excessive rights or rights to nonexistent directories on servers. If you want users on a server to be assigned rights on other servers, you must perform this step manually.
Home directories	No	Home directories are not synchronized, as they are specific to users on a file server. When a user is created in the IntranetWare bindery context and synchronized with the NetWare 3.x servers, NetSync does not create a home directory for that user on each NetWare 3.1x server. Also, when users are copied from the NetWare 3.x server into the IntranetWare bindery context, no home directories are created on the IntranetWare server. If you need home directories on other than the original server, you must manually create them and grant appropriate trustee assignments.
Illegal characters	No	Any object names that include characters that are illegal in bindery names are not synchronized. The only legal characters in bindery names are letters A–Z, numbers 0–9, hyphens, and underscores. NDS object names, on the

Item	Synchronized Status	Description
		other hand, can be up to 64 characters long and permit and allow a wider range of permissible characters.
System login	No	System login scripts are not synchronized. These login scripts are specific to server, and therefore should not be synchronized.

Understanding NetSync Synchronization Problems

A NetWare 3.x server that is down cannot receive synchronization information sent by the IntranetWare server, which causes the NetWare 3.x server to be out of synchronization with the NetSync cluster. When you bring the NetWare 3.x server back up, the super-bindery on the IntranetWare server is downloaded to the NetWare 3.x server, which resynchronizes the NetWare 3.x server.

In general, you should avoid deleting or renaming objects unless all servers in the NetSync cluster are online. If you delete or rename user or group objects in the IntranetWare bindery context while the NetWare 3.x servers are down, these servers will be out of synchronization. When you bring the downed NetWare 3.x servers online again, the deleted objects are not cleared after the connection is re-established. If you manually upload the NetWare 3.x's bindery to the IntranetWare server then the deleted objects are re-created. You must then manually remove the objects you deleted from the NetSync cluster. Remember that if you add a new object to the super-bindery, that object is synchronized to all the NetWare 3.x servers in the cluster even if one of the NetWare 3.x servers was down when the change happened.

If the IntranetWare Server Goes Down

If the IntranetWare host in the NetSync cluster goes down while you are uploading the binderies of one or more NetWare 3.x servers to the IntranetWare server, you should restart the synchronization after the IntranetWare server comes back up.

If a NetWare 3.x or 4.x server runs out of disk space during bindery synchronization information, an error message appears on each server. You should add more disk space or make room for the bindery objects, then reload NETSYNC3.NLM or NETSYNC4.NLM, as appropriate.

Effect of Unloading NetSync

If you unload NETSYNC4 from the IntranetWare server, the NETSYNC3 NLMs on the NetWare 3.x servers in the NetSync cluster are automatically unloaded. Before you can reload NETSYNC3 on the NetWare 3.x servers, you must first load NETSYNC4 on the IntranetWare server.

The REMAPID.NLM is used for password synchronization. It must always be loaded on the NetWare 3.x server. If you unload it, you must assign new passwords to all bindery users in the system.

Understanding Super-Clusters

If multiple IntranetWare servers are in the same bindery context and are all running NetSync, all NetWare 3.x servers attached to these hosts are synchronized with the same super-bindery.

Consider the example in figure 14.5, in which three IntranetWare servers are in the same bindery context. If all three IntranetWare servers are running NetSync and each of them has 12 NetWare 3.1x servers attached, then all 36 NetWare 3.x servers will upload their binderies to the 4.x bindery context, and this super-bindery will then be downloaded to the 36 NetWare 3.x servers. The IntranetWare and 3.x servers form a NetSync super-cluster.

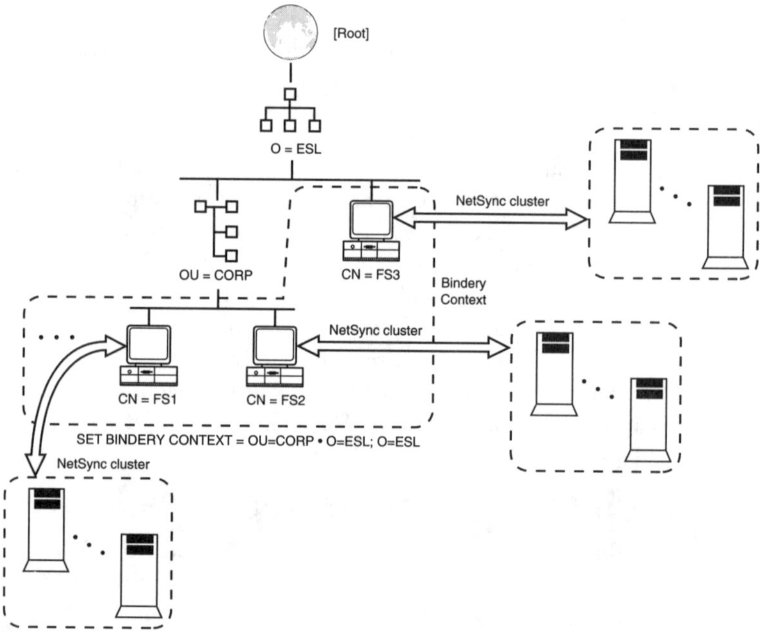

Figure 14.5
Three IntranetWare servers in same bindery context.

There is no limit to the number of IntranetWare servers in any bindery context, but as the number of IntranetWare and 3.x servers increase, so too does the processing overhead on the servers. The NetSync NLMs are CPU- and memory-intensive processes. As the size of the super-cluster increases, more objects need to be synchronized, and thus, synchronization traffic also increases.

Understanding the NetSync Modules

NetSync consists of three primary NLMs (see fig. 14.6):

- NETSYNC4 that runs on IntranetWare servers
- NETSYNC3 that runs on NetWare 3.x servers
- REMAPID that runs on NetWare 3.x servers and is used for password synchronization

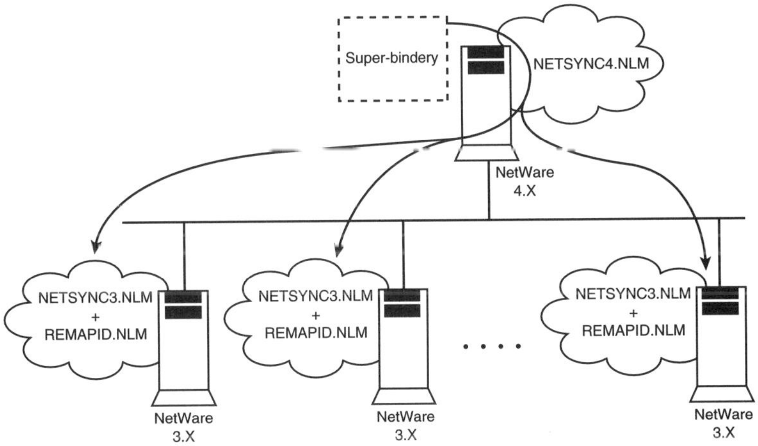

Figure 14.6
NetSync NLMs.

The NETSYNC4.NLM runs on a IntranetWare server and enables you to control the NetSync cluster. You can use NETSYNC4 to authenticate NetWare 3.x servers and copy necessary files to the 3.x servers. After you synchronize NetWare 3.x servers to the bindery on the IntranetWare server, NETSYNC4 monitors the super-bindery for changes and downloads updated bindery information to all NetWare 3.x servers in the NetSync cluster. For the NetSync cluster to work, NETSYNC4 should run continuously. Therefore, you should place the following command in the IntranetWare server's AUTOEXEC.NCF file:

```
LOAD NETSYNC4
```

The NETSYNC3.NLM runs on each NetWare 3.x server that is part of the NetSync cluster. When NETSYNC3 joins the cluster, it uploads the 3.x server's bindery information to the IntranetWare server's bindery context. The NetWare 3.x server then establishes a connection to the IntranetWare server to receive updates to its bindery. In addition to synchronizing the server bindery, NETSYNC3 converts the 3.x PRINTDEF and PRINTCON databases to a IntranetWare-compatible database format, and it can move NetWare 3.x print servers and their associated queues and printers to the IntranetWare server. NETSYNC4 and NETSYNC3 log their activity in the SYS:SYSTEM\NETSYNC working directory on their respective servers, under the file name NETSYNC.LOG. The log file is in ASCII format and contains the messages that NETSYNC3 displays on the server console, which describe the occurrence of events such as uploads and downloads of bindery information. NetSync creates the

SYS:ETC\NETSYNC directories during its installation. The default log file maximum size is 0.5 MB. If you do not clear the NETSYNC.LOG file before it reaches its maximum size, NetSync automatically closes it and renames it to NETSYNC.OLD, then creates a new NETSYNC.LOG. You can have only two NETSYNC files, NETSYNC.LOG and NETSYNC.OLD, at any time; NetSync automatically deletes older NetSync log files.

You should run NETSYNC3 continuously so that the NetWare 3.x server can receive updates. However, NETSYNC3 can receive updates only if NETSYNC4 is loaded on the IntranetWare server. You must, therefore, first load NETSYNC4 on the IntranetWare server, then load NETSYNC3 on the NetWare 3.x server. You should add the following command to the NetWare 3.x server's AUTOEXEC.NCF file:

```
LOAD NETSYNC3
```

NetSync automatically loads the REMAPID.NLM when you load NETSYNC3.NLM. REMAPID performs password synchronization for the bindery objects, and you should leave it loaded even if you unload the NETSYNC3 module.

When you install NETSYNC3 on a NetWare 3.x server, NetSync also loads certain support NLMs: CLIB, STREAMS, NWPSRV3X, NWSNUT, AFTER311, A3112, and PBURST. The latest versions of these NLMs replace older versions on all NetWare 3.x servers in the NetSync cluster.

Preparing to Install NetSync

Before you can install and configure NetSync, you must review the names of NDS objects in the bindery context and the NetWare 3.x binderies to avoid name conflicts. Specifically, you must ensure that you have no duplicate NDS or bindery object names. If you do have duplicate names, be aware that any existing NDS object name takes precedence over any bindery object that has the same name.

Duplicate names arise because the binderies on NetWare 3.x servers are separate. After synchronization, NetSync creates a super-bindery object that contains the objects in all the binderies in the NetSync cluster. Objects that have identical names cause name collisions and unintended results.

Duplicate object name conflicts can arise in any of the following situations:

- Objects of the same type
- Objects of different types
- Objects in a bindery context path
- Object names that contain diacritic characters

Duplicate Names Caused by Objects of the Same Type

Consider this scenario: Two user accounts named Mark are on two NetWare 3.x servers that are to become part of the same NetSync cluster. The user account Mark might refer to the same person or different persons.

The user account on the first NetWare 3.x server to be synchronized takes precedence over user accounts that have the same name on NetWare 3.x servers to be synchronized later. This means that NetSync copies the properties of the user account Mark on the first NetWare 3.x server to be synchronized intact to the first container in the IntranetWare bindery context. When NetSync encounters the second user Mark on a different server, it scans this user for properties that did not exist for the first user Mark. If a property value is defined for the first user Mark, NetSync discards the property value for the second user Mark. If a property value did not exist for the first user Mark, NetSync adds the second user Mark's property. Essentially, NetSync merges the two user accounts that have the same name, giving precedence to the first user it encounters in the synchronization process.

If the two Marks refer to the same person, you would want the synchronization behavior just described. If the two Marks do refer to different persons, however, the resulting merged user account will be useless to both users. To prevent such an occurrence, you must change the login names so that they are distinct before you run NetSync. For example, you could make the first user name MProphet and the second user name MSmith.

Duplicate Names Caused by Objects of Different Types

If the objects that are to be synchronized have identical names and are of different type, NetSync will convert only the first object it uploads to an NDS object.

Consider a potential situation in which you have a user named Ops and a group named Ops on different NetWare 3.x servers. If NetSync first synchronizes the NetWare 3.x server that has user name Ops, it converts this user name to the NDS user object Ops. When NetSync synchronizes the NetWare 3.x server that has the group Ops, it does not convert the group Ops to an NDS group object.

Duplicate Names for Objects in a Bindery Path

Beginning in NetWare 4.1, the bindery context can include as many as 16 containers. NetSync copies the NetWare 3.x bindery objects into the first container listed in the bindery context path. Then it synchronizes all objects from all containers in a bindery context path with each NetWare 3.x server. If duplicate names exist for objects in the containers specified in the bindery context, a situation can occur as described in the following paragraphs.

Consider the situation in which the bindery context of an IntranetWare server is set to the following:

```
OU=CORP.O=ESL;OU=MKTG.O=ESL
```

Assume that a user object Phylos exists on a NetWare 3.x that is part of a NetSync cluster. When this NetWare 3.x server initially joins the NetSync cluster, NetSync synchronizes the user object Phylos into the super-bindery on the IntranetWare server. NetSync creates the NDS object Phylos in the first container of the context path; in this case, OU=CORP.O=ESL.

If an NDS object that has the name Phylos already exists in the container OU=CORP.O=ESL, the existing NDS object takes precedence. If the existing NDS object is a user object, NetSync merges the properties of the NetWare 3.x user object Phylos with the NDS user object Phylos.

If the container OU=CORP.O=ESL contains no user object Phylos, NetSync creates a user object in this container for the NetWare 3.x user Phylos. Another user object Phylos might exist in the container further down the bindery context path, in the container OU=MKTG.O=ESL. The second user object in container OU=MKTG.O=ESL is hidden (or eclipsed) by the first user object Phylos and will not appear in the super-bindery.

Duplicate Names Caused by Object Names Containing Diacritic Characters

The NetWare 3.x utilities convert diacritic characters (such as umlaut, accents, cedilla, tilde, circumflex, and so on) to uppercase letters. IntranetWare does not perform such a conversion. Therefore, you can end up with two user names in the super-bindery—one that contains the diacritic characters and one that contains the translated characters. NetSync tries to solve this problem by matching approximately the two user names and assuming that they refer to the same user. Novell recommends the following precautions to ensure consistent behavior of foreign language characters in user names:

- Use the same code page in the IntranetWare server's LCONFIG.SYS file (done through INSTALL.NLM), and in each NetWare client's CONFIG.SYS file (done through the COUNTRY= statement)
- If you use the IntranetWare LOGIN and SETPASS utilities, you should use the following syntax:

```
LOGIN servername/username /b
LOGIN username /b
SETPASS servername/username /b
SETPASS username /b
```

If you use the IntranetWare LOGIN utility to log in to attach to a NetWare 3.x server, you must use the LOGIN /NS command, equivalent to the ATTACH command in NetWare 3.x. You should be aware, however, that if you use the LOGIN /NS command, this attachment does not show up as a connection if you view it from NetWare 3.x utilities—unless you map a drive to the NetWare 3.x server.

Dealing with NetWare Name Service (NNS)

NNS performs its own synchronization of user accounts in a NNS domain, but NNS's synchronization is not compatible with the NetSync synchronization. Therefore, you must migrate all NetWare 3.x servers running NNS to NetSync at the same time. In fact, if you load NETSYNC3 on a NetWare 3.x server running NNS, NetSync automatically deactivates and uninstalls NNS, because the NETSYNC3 NLM checks for the presence of NNS on the server and removes it from the server.

During the NetSync installation, NetSync converts NNS profiles to NDS profile objects and converts the default profile property in NNS to the profile property of the profile object in the NDS. This ensures that users who had default profiles in NNS still have them after you convert from NNS to NetSync. Because the NetWare 3.x LOGIN utility does not understand profile login scripts, when you install NetSync, NetSync copies the IntranetWare LOGIN utility to each NetWare 3.x server, which enables NetSync users to use profile login scripts, even if they were not doing so with NNS. If you plan to use profile login scripts for NetWare 3.x users, you must use NETADMIN or NetWare Administrator to change the profile login script on the IntranetWare server. Login scripts execute in the following order: first system login script specific to each 3.x server, profile login script, and then user login script.

Installing NetSync

Before you can install NetSync, you must have at least one IntranetWare server, and no more than 12 NetWare 3.x servers per IntranetWare server. You also should keep in mind that NetSync is memory- and CPU-intensive on the IntranetWare server, and CPU-intensive on the NetWare 3.x servers. Novell recommends that when you run NetSync, you should not let the cache buffer count drop below 200 or server utilization rise above 80 percent.

The IntranetWare NetSync files are copied into SYS:SYSTEM directory during the IntranetWare server installation. After you install NetSync on a NetWare 3.x server, NetSync files exist in the SYS:SYSTEM\NETSYNC directory on the NetWare 3.x.

Before you begin the NetSync installation, you should perform the following tasks:

- Scan objects in the bindery context and each NetWare 3.x server that is to be part of the NetSync cluster to ensure that no unintended duplicate names exist.
- Ensure that the bindery context on the IntranetWare server is set to the proper containers.
- Do not change the bindery context when NetSync is running.
- Ensure that you have a valid user account and rights to the SYS:SYSTEM directory on all servers to be part of the NetSync cluster.

The following is an outline of the steps to install NetSync:

1. You must load NETSYNC4 on the IntranetWare server before you load NETSYNC3 on the NetWare 3.1x servers.

   Run the following command at the IntranetWare server console:

   ```
   LOAD NETSYNC4
   ```

   NETSYNC4 autoloads the following NLMs: CLIB, STREAMS, NWPSRV, NWSNUT, and DSAPI.

   The SYS:SYSTEM\NETSYNC directory, which contains NetSync log files and NetWare 3.x NetSync files, is automatically created during NetWare 4.1 server installation.

2. When NETSYNC4 first loads, a screen similar to figure 14.7 should inform you that you must authorize at least one NetWare 3.x Server before you can use NetSync.

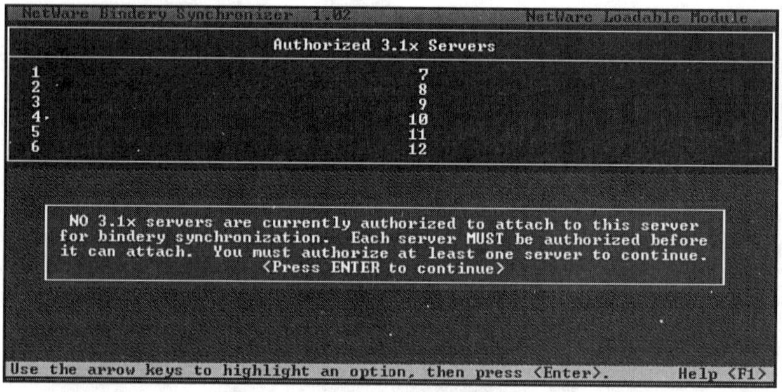

Figure 14.7
NETSYNC4 initial screen.

3. Press Enter. You should see the Authorized 3.1x Servers menu (see fig. 14.8). You must authorize each NetWare 3.x server that will be part of the NetSync cluster. The authorization enables a NetWare 3.x server to attach to the IntranetWare host.

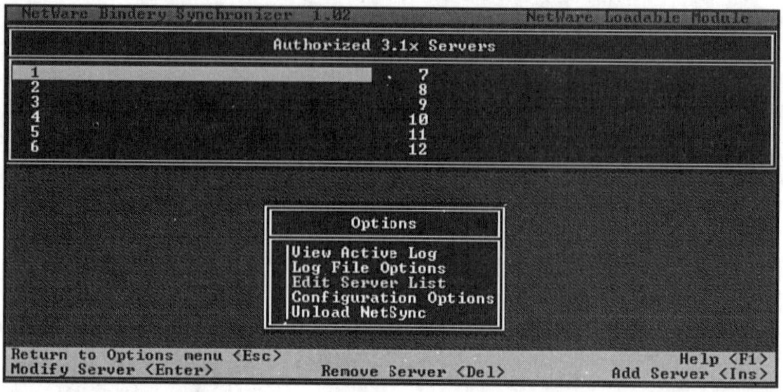

Figure 14.8
The NETSYNC4 Authorized 3.1x Servers menu.

4. From the Authorized 3.1x server menus, highlight the number of the NetWare 3.x server you want to authorize.

   Press Enter or Insert. You should see the Authorized Server Information form (see fig. 14.9).

   NetWare 3.x servers in the NetSync cluster are numbered from 1 to 12. If this is the first time you use NETSYNC4, the number 1 is highlighted.

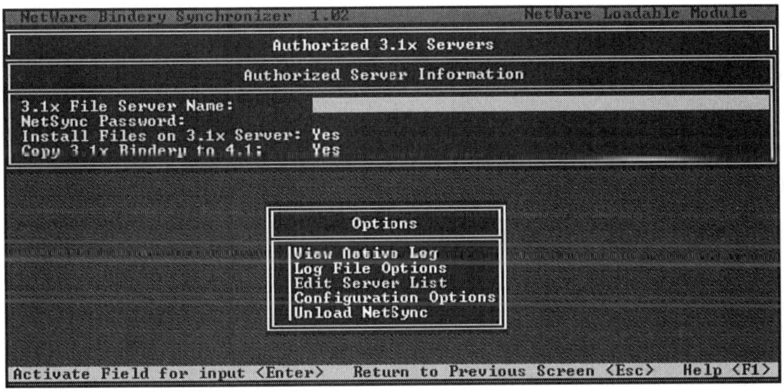

Figure 14.9
The NETSYNC4 Authorized Server Information form.

5. You should use the Authorized Server Information to add NetWare 3.x servers to the cluster. The fields in this form have the following meanings:

   - **3.1x File Server Name.** This is the name of the NetWare 3.1x server whose bindery you want to synchronize with the IntranetWare host.
   - **NetSync Password.** The NetSync password appears only when you authorize a NetWare 3.1x server. When you re-edit the server information, you do not see the password option. You must not confuse the NetSync password with the user password or Admin password. You should avoid using privileged account passwords to prevent these passwords from being compromised if they are accidentally discovered. The NetSync password is used only for NetSync authorization purposes. You use it to initially authorize the each NetWare 3.x server to initially attach to the IntranetWare server's NetSync cluster. After you set the password, NetSync remembers it. You can specify a different NetSync password for each NetWare 3.x server. But you must use the same password to authorize the NetWare 3.x server to attach to the 4.x server. If you should forget the password, you must remove the NetWare 3.x server from the "Authorized 3.1x Servers" list and use a new password to reauthorize it.
   - **Install Files on 3.1x Server.** To copy NetSync files to the NetWare 3.x server, set this field to Yes. This option appears only when you initially authorize a NetWare 3.x server, not when you re-edit the server information. The default value is Yes, so that you can copy all the necessary NetSync files to a newly

authorized NetWare 3.x server, to the SYS:SYSTEM\NETSYNC directory on the NetWare 3.x server.

- **Copy 3.1x Bindery to 4.1.** This option enables you to upload bindery data from the NetWare 3.x server to the IntranetWare server. The initial default value is Yes, so that the NetWare 3.x server can synchronize itself to the super-bindery. If you re-edit the server information, the default is No, because the NetWare 3.x server is assumed to be synchronized. Answer No for the server authorization if you run NNS and already copied the domain information to the IntranetWare server when you authorized another NNS server. If you want to discard the authorized server's user and group bindery objects, but still be part of the NetSync cluster, you should answer No.

After you enter the necessary information, press Esc and answer Yes to the question `Is this information correct?`.

6. You will be informed that a user name that has Read, Write, Modify, and Erase rights to the SYS:SYSTEM directory on the NetWare 3.x server is needed before NetSync can copy the files to the NetWare 3.x server's SYS:SYSTEM directory (see fig. 14.10).

   Press Enter to continue.

   You can enter the SUPERVISOR names, but any other user that has "RWE" rights is fine.

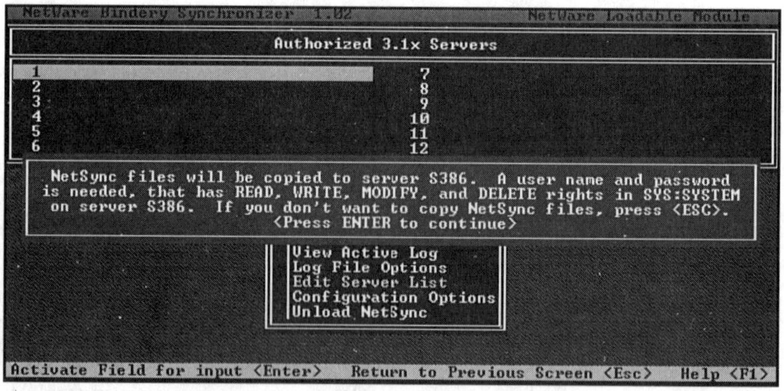

Figure 14.10
The NETSYNC4 Authorized Server Information.

7. You are prompted for the user's password. Enter this password.

8. You are asked if you want to include the command to load NetSync in the AUTOEXEC.NCF file of the NetWare 3.x server. Answer Yes.

9. If the files copy successfully, the message shown in figure 14.11 should appear, letting you know that the NetSync files have been successfully copied to the NetWare 3.x server.

   Press Enter to continue.

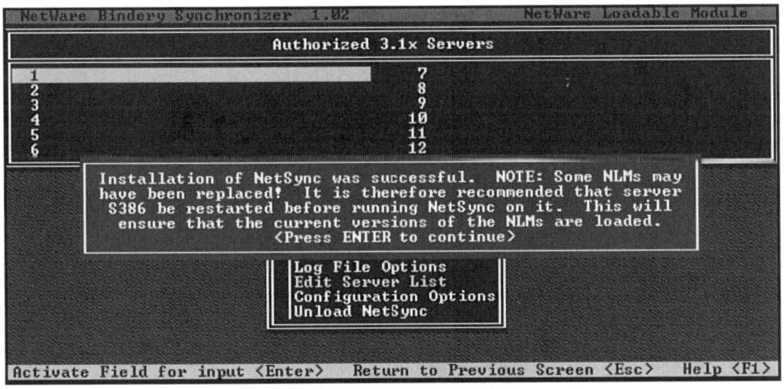

Figure 14.11
Message indicating successful copy of NetSync files to a NetWare 3.x server.

10. The name of the NetWare 3.x server that was authorized appears in the Authorized 3.1x Servers screen (see fig. 14.12).

    You might see any of the symbols *, @, or ! against a server name. The asterisk (*) means that you are currently attached to this server. The @ symbol means that the server is currently receiving downloaded bindery information from the IntranetWare host. The exclamation (!) symbol means that the server is currently uploading information to the IntranetWare host.

    Press Esc to return to the options menu.

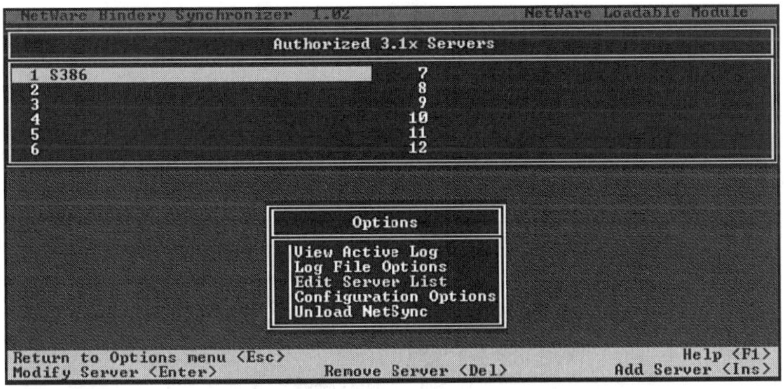

Figure 14.12
Name of authorized NetWare 3.x server displayed.

11. You can repeat steps 4 through 10 to authorize additional NetWare 3.x servers to be part of this NetSync cluster.
12. After you authorize at least one NetWare 3.x server, you can access the Options menu. The Options menu appears whenever you load NETSYNC4, as long as you have authorized at least one NetWare 3.x server.
13. You must now load NETSYNC3 on each NetWare 3.x server to be included in the NetSync cluster. Before you do this, make sure that NETSYNC4 is already loaded on the IntranetWare server.

Before you load NETSYNC3, be sure to unload any of the following NLMs if they are running:

PSERVER.NLM, CLIB, STREAMS, NWPSRV3X, NWSNUT, AFTER311, A3112, and PBURST (for NetWare 3.11 only)

During the installation, newer versions of these NLMs needed by NETSYNC3 are copied to the NetWare 3.x server. If these NLMs are already in memory, newer IntranetWare versions of these NLMs do not load. You must, therefore, unload these NLMs. You can use the console MODULES command to find out which NLMs are loaded.

14. Load NETSYNC3 on the NetWare 3.x server that should join the NetSync cluster:

    ```
    LOAD NETSYNC3
    ```

    The NETSYNC3.NLM autoloads REMAPID.NLM, and the following NLMs:

    CLIB, STREAMS, NWPSRV3X, NWSNUT, AFTER311, A3112, and PBURST (NetWare 3.11 only)

15. If this is the first time you load NETSYNC3 on this server, you are asked to enter the name of the IntranetWare host to which you want to synchronize this NetWare 3.x server (see fig. 14.13).

    Enter the name of the IntranetWare server, then enter the NetSync password.

    NetSync uploads NetWare 3.x bindery information to the IntranetWare bindery context. If other NetWare 3.x servers exist in the NetSync cluster, NetSync downloads this information from the IntranetWare bindery context to the NetWare 3.x servers in the NetSync cluster.

    The Options menu appears after the bindery synchronization (see fig. 14.13).

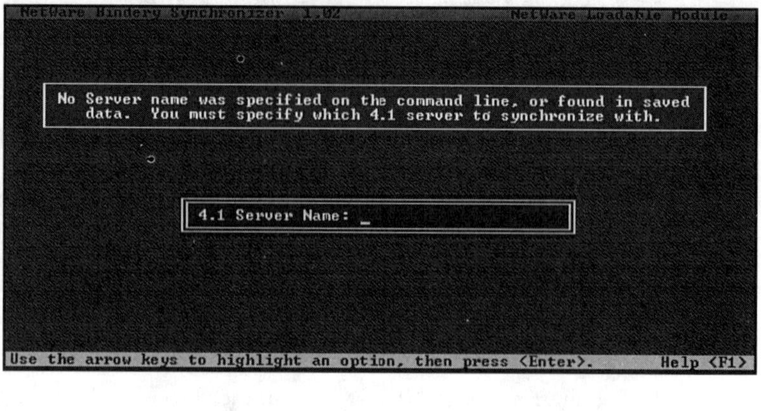

Figure 14.13
NETSYNC3 initial screen asking name of 4.x with which to synchronize.

16. You can optionally configure the NetSync environment on the NetWare 3.x server by selecting the options in figure 14.14.

17. You can verify that all information is synchronized. You can also examine the NetSync log files by selecting the View Active Log option from the Options menu.

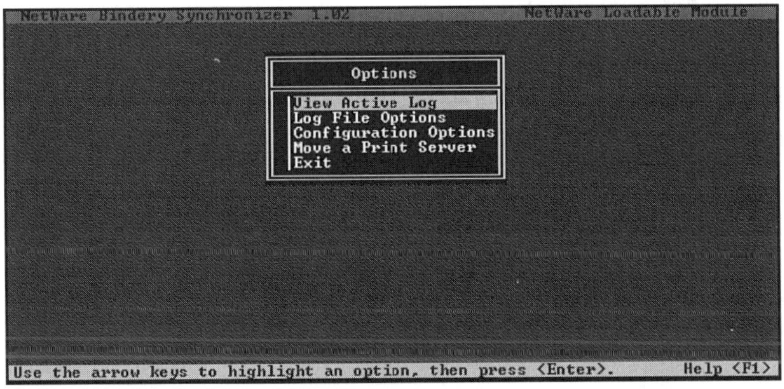

Figure 14.14
The NETSYNC3 Options menu.

Installing NetSync on NetWare 3.x from Disk

You can install NetSync on NetWare 3.x servers from disk. This involves creating the installation disks and then using the Product Options from the INSTALL.NLM menus to install. The steps to perform these tasks are outlined, as follows:

1. Log in to a IntranetWare server as a user who has at least Read and File Scan rights to SYS:SYSTEM.

2. Change to the SYS:SYSTEM\NETSYNC directory.

3. Run the MAKEDISK batch file to create the installation disks.

   ```
   MAKEDISK A:
   ```

4. Insert blank formatted disks in drive A:, as prompted.

5. From a NetWare 3.x server, load the INSTALL NLM:

   ```
   LOAD INSTALL
   ```

6. Select Product Options. A list of currently installed products installed via this option should appear, for example, NetWare NFS, NetWare for SAA, NetWare Communications Server, and so forth.

   Press Ins to add a new product.

7. When prompted to insert the installation disk in drive A:, insert the NetSync installation disks you prepared in steps 3 and 4.

   The INSTALL.NLM invokes the installation script on the disks and proceeds with the installation.

8. Exit INSTALL.NLM after installation is complete.

NetSync Maintenance

After NetSync is running, you might have to do some maintenance tasks and monitor NetSync's performance of the bindery synchronization. You can use the Options menu of the NETSYNC4 and NETSYNC3 NLMs to do the maintenance tasks, including the following (see fig. 14.15):

- View Active Log
- Log File Options
- Edit Server List
- Configuration Options
- Unload NetSync

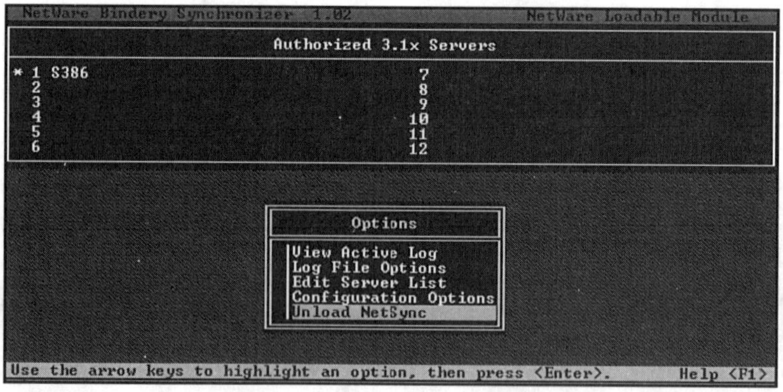

Figure 14.15
NETSYNC4 Options menu.

These options are shown in figure 14.15 for NETSYNC4 on an IntranetWare server.

You use the Edit Server List options to add NetWare 3.x servers to the NetSync cluster or to edit information on the servers. Adding a new NetWare 3.x to a NetSync cluster is described in the NetSync installation section earlier in this chapter.

You use the View Activity Log option to view a log of the bindery synchronization events. Figure 14.16 shows a typical activity log that appears when you select this option.

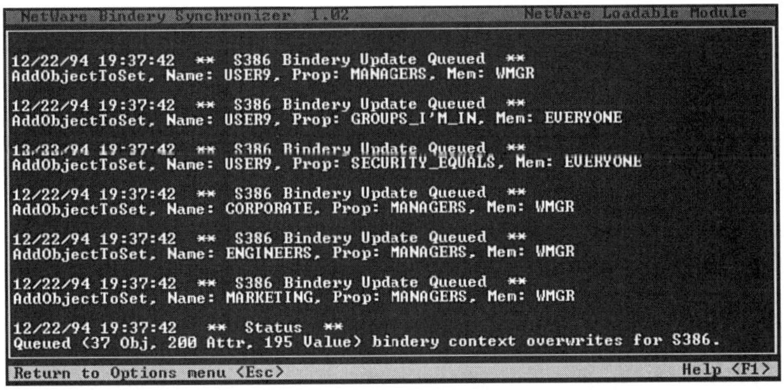

Figure 14.16
The NETSYNC4 Activity Log.

This activity log consists of the contents of the file SYS:SYSTEM\NETSYNC\NETSYNC.LOG. Each entry in the log shows a date and time for the occurrence of each event. A brief description of the event enclosed in asterisks (**) is given. The second line in each log entry shows the NetSync function called and the parameters to this function. The NetSync log file includes synchronization events such as the following:

- Additions, deletions, or changes to users or groups
- Password changes
- Logins and logouts of NetSync servers
- Login script changes
- Success or failure of local modification attempts
- Items that are queued to be sent to other servers

The Log File Options are shown in figure 14.17. The View Log File History option shows the entire contents of the NETSYNC.LOG file, which differs from the View Activity Log option, which shows only the events currently occurring.

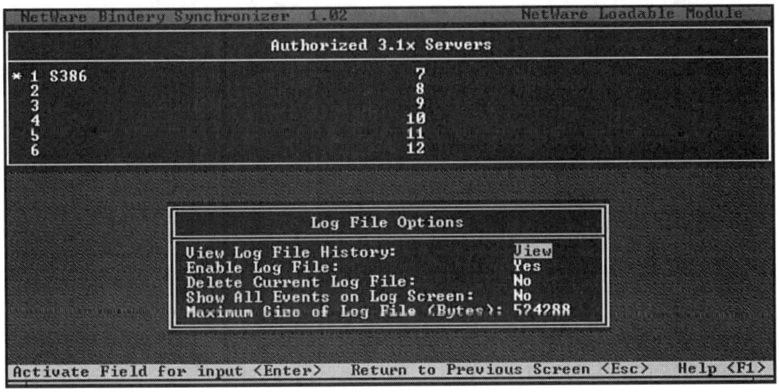

Figure 14.17
NETSYNC4 Log File Options.

When you set the Enable Log File option to Yes (refer to figure 14.17), synchronization events are logged. If you set it to No, logging of these events is disabled.

When you set the Delete Current Log File option to Yes (refer to figure 14.17), the current log file is deleted, and a new log file is started. If you do not want to delete the current log file, set this field to No.

When you set the Show All Events on Log Screen to Yes (refer to figure 14.17), all bindery synchronization events are logged, which can result in a very large log. If you only want to report major bindery synchronization events, set this field to No.

The Maximum Size of Log File shows the maximum size of the NETSYNC.LOG file in bytes (refer to figure 14.17). You use this field to control the amount of data in the log file. After the file reaches the maximum size, the file is renamed with an OLD extension, and a new log file is begun. If an existing NETSYNC.LOG files exists, it will be deleted first before the current log file is renamed. Because the system can have two log files at any time, you should have free disk space greater than or equal to twice the value of this field. The default value is 524,288 bytes.

Figure 14.18 shows the Configuration Options of the NETSYNC4 main menu. If you set the Delete NetSync Configuration Data option to Yes, the system default values for the NetSync configuration parameters are used.

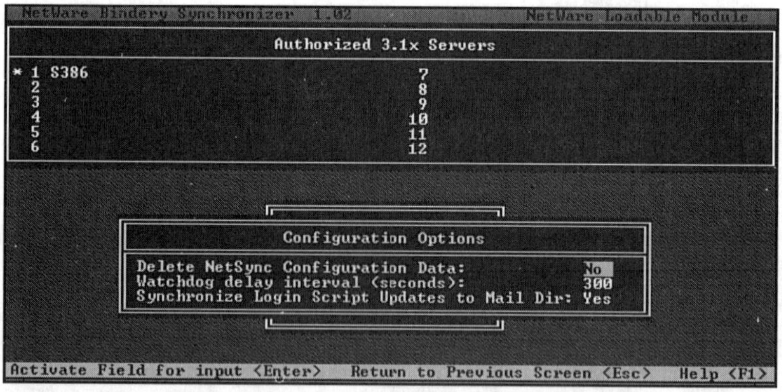

Figure 14.18
NETSYNC4 Configuration Options.

The Watchdog delay interval (refer to figure 14.18) enables you to control the frequency with which the NETSYNC4.NLM checks for whether the NetWare 3.x servers in the NetSync cluster are online. The default value is 300 seconds; you can set the interval from 30 seconds to 18 hours. If a NetWare 3.x server does not respond within the specified interval, NETSYNC4 retries a several more times, and if it still receives no response, it terminates the connection to the NetWare 3.x server.

If you set the Synchronize Login Script Updates to Mail Dir (refer to figure 14.18) to Yes, the NDS login script changes are sent to the login scripts in the IntranetWare server's SYS:MAIL directory, which enables users to log in to the IntranetWare server in the bindery mode and execute the same updated login scripts that are synchronized to the NDS login script for the user. If you have users who log in as NDS users and as bindery users, you should set this option to Yes, so that the users' login environment is similar on both the NetWare 3.x and IntranetWare servers. If you do not have users who log into the servers in the bindery mode, you should set the option to No to avoid the overhead of login script synchronization.

Removing a NetWare 3.x Server from a Cluster

On occasion, you might want to remove a NetWare 3.x server from a NetSync cluster. For instance, if you want to upgrade a NetWare 3.x server to a IntranetWare server, you would first remove it from the NetSync cluster.

You can use the NETSYNC4 NLM to remove a NetWare 3.x server from a NetSync cluster, by deleting the server name from the list of Authorized Servers, which automatically removes the NetWare 3.x server from the NetSync cluster. You can remove the servers only one at a time.

You can use the following procedure to remove a NetWare 3.x server from a NetSync cluster:

1. Make sure that NETSYNC4 is running on the IntranetWare server.
2. Select Edit Server List from NETSYNC4's Options menu.
3. Highlight the NetWare 3.x server you want to delete and press Del.

Uploading a NetWare 3.x Server's Bindery to the IntranetWare Server

If you use SYSCON on the NetWare 3.x server to modify user properties other than the user password, you force the server bindery out of synchronization with the super-bindery. The NetWare 3.x bindery could also be forced out of synchronization if you ran a program on the NetWare server that modified the bindery.

In this case, you must manually upload the changes to the IntranetWare server, so that the all the servers in the NetSync cluster can synchronize the changes.

You must perform this synchronization from NETSYNC4. The following is an outline of these steps:

1. Make sure that NETSYNC4 is running.
2. Select Edit Server List from NETSYNC4's Options menu.
3. Highlight the NetWare 3.x server whose bindery you want to upload and press Enter. The Authorized Server Information screen appears (see fig. 14.19).

4. Set the Copy 3.1x Bindery to 4.1 field in the Authorized Server Information form to Yes.
5. Press Esc. You are asked to verify whether the information is correct. The NetWare 3.x server bindery information is copied to the IntranetWare server. Only new information is added. Duplicate information is ignored. Then the NetSync syncronization process will syncronize the changes to the other NetWare 3.x servers in the NetSync cluster.

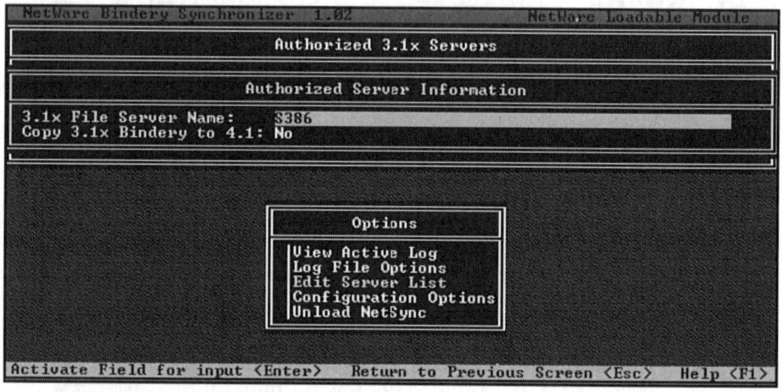

Figure 14.19
The NETSYNC4 Authorized Server Information screen.

Deleting NetSync Configuration Information

If you lose the NetSync password, or want to move the NetWare 3.x server to a different NetSync cluster, or the NetWare 3.x server is not going to run NetSync any more, you must delete the NetSync configuration information.

On an IntranetWare server, the NetSync configuration data includes the names of the NetWare 3.x servers in the NetSync cluster, associated passwords, and the NetSync password.

On a NetWare 3.x server, the NetSync configuration data includes the name of the IntranetWare host and the NetSync password.

The procedure for deleting the NetSync configuration data for a NetWare 3.x server is outlined in the following steps:

1. From NETSYNC3's Options menu, select Configuration Options.
2. Select Delete NetSync Configuration Data.
3. Enter **Yes**.

Observing the Effects of Super-Bindery Synchronization

The NDS user and group objects in the bindery context form a super-bindery. These objects are the aggregation of all user and group objects from the NetWare 3.x servers in the NetSync cluster. Any changes you make to objects in the bindery context on the IntranetWare server are synchronized to all NetWare 3.x servers in the NetSync cluster, which enables you to manage the servers in the NetSync cluster from a central location.

Although NetWare 3.x servers have no directory service capability, they can benefit from directory services if they join a NetSync cluster. If you add a new user object to the super-bindery, the system replicates it to all the servers in the NetSync cluster. You must still assign appropriate file system rights, such as rights to individual home directories, however, for the new users in their respective servers.

Any NetWare 3.x server can join the NetSync cluster, within the limit of 12 NetWare 3.x servers per IntranetWare server. This limit owes to performance reasons. The NetSync NLMs are memory- and CPU-intensive. As more NetWare 3.x servers join a cluster, the amount of synchronization can increase and adversely impact the performance of the servers.

You must also take into account the number of objects in the super-bindery on the IntranetWare server. Although no limit exists for the number of objects you can have in a container, experience suggests that you should limit a single container to 3,000 objects. Novell recommends a more liberal limit of 10,000 objects. Remember, as the number of objects increase in a container, using NWADMIN95, NWADMIN3x, or NETADMIN to scroll through the lists of objects to find the object you want can become tedious.

The following is a guided tour of observing the effects of bindery synchronization when you make changes to the super-bindery.

Figures 14.20 and 14.21 show the objects in the containers OU=CORP.O=ESL and O=ESL. The bindery context of the IntranetWare server is set to OU=CORP.O=ESL;O=ESL. Figures 14.22 and 14.23 show the group and user objects you see when you use SYSCON on a NetWare 3.x server synchronized to the super-bindery on the IntranetWare server.

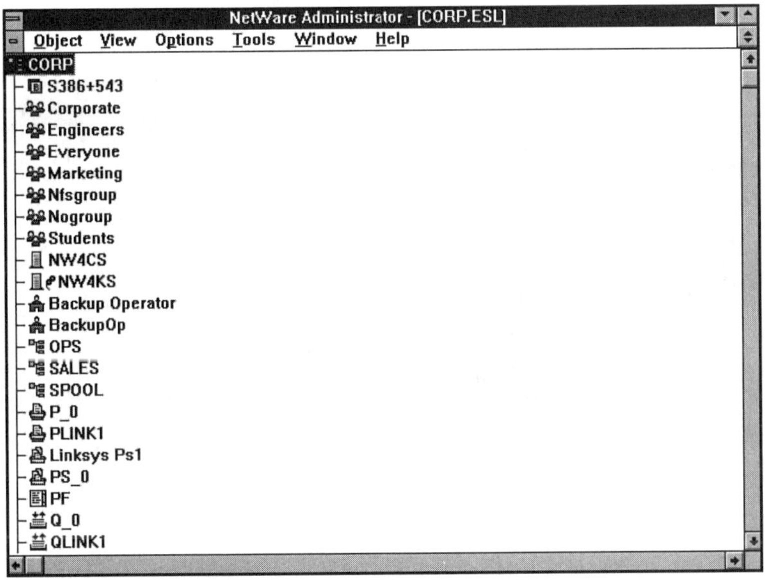

Figure 14.20
Objects in container OU=CORP.O=ESL.

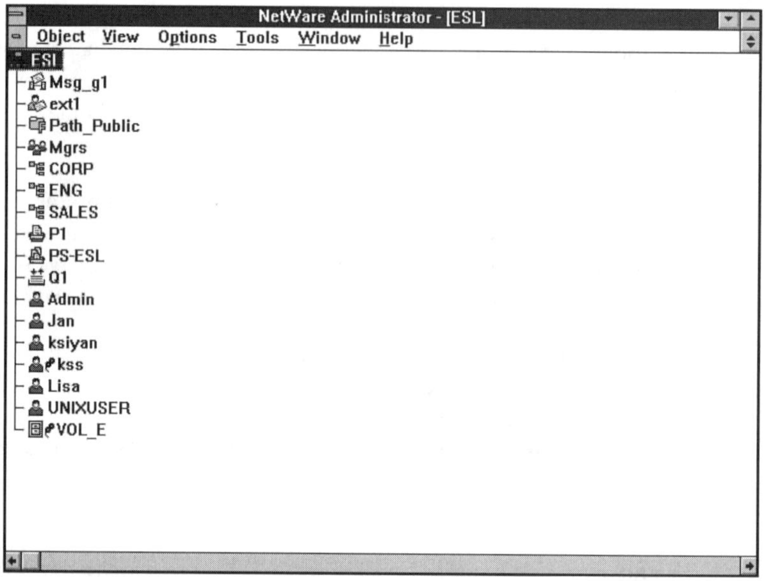

Figure 14.21
Objects in container O=ESL.

The group objects Corporate, Engineers, Everyone, Marketing, Nfsgroup, Nogroup, and Students (refer to figure 14.20) existed originally on the NetWare 3.x server (see fig. 14.22). When the NetWare 3.x server joined the NetSync cluster, these bindery objects were uploaded to the super-bindery as corresponding NDS group objects. The bindery group MGRS (see fig. 14.22) originally existed in the container O=ESL (refer to figure 14.21) prior to bindery synchronization. Because O=ESL is in the bindery context, the NDS group object Mgrs was synchronized to the NetWare 3.x server when the NetWare 3.x server joined the NetSync cluster.

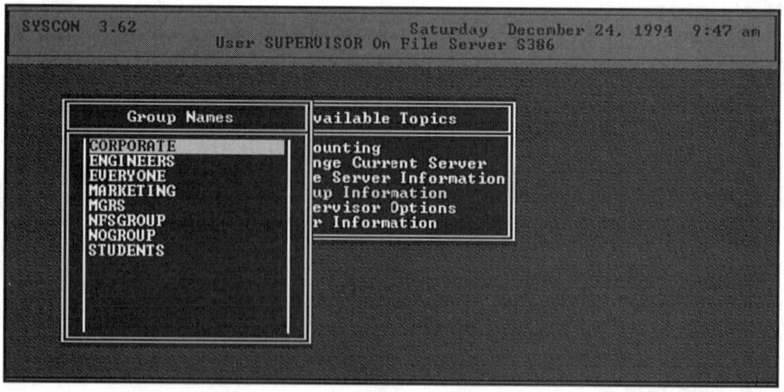

Figure 14.22
Group objects on NetWare 3.x server.

The users ADMIN, JAN, DEI, KSS, and LISA (see fig. 14.23) originally existed in the bindery context on the IntranetWare server (refer to figures 14.20 and 14.21). These IntranetWare users were synchronized to the NetWare 3.x server as bindery user objects. Figure 14.24 shows additional user objects in the OU=CORP.O=ESL container that are not shown in figure 14.21. The NDS users Anonymous, Guest, HACKER, Nobody, Test, User1, User10, User11,

User12, User13, User14, User2, User3, User4, User5, User6, User7, and User8 were transferred from the NetWare 3.x bindery to the bindery context on the IntranetWare server.

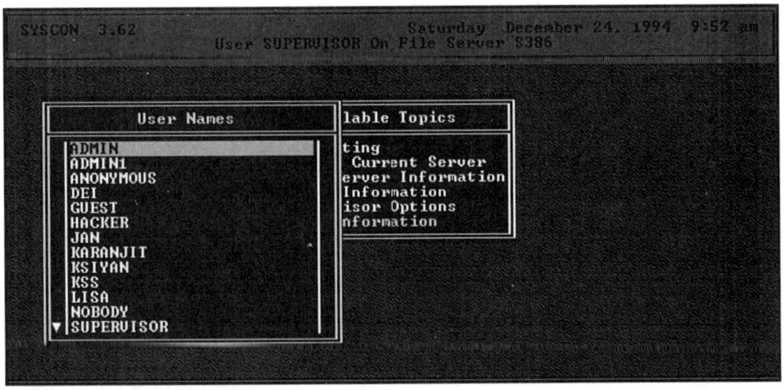

Figure 14.23
User objects on NetWare 3.x server.

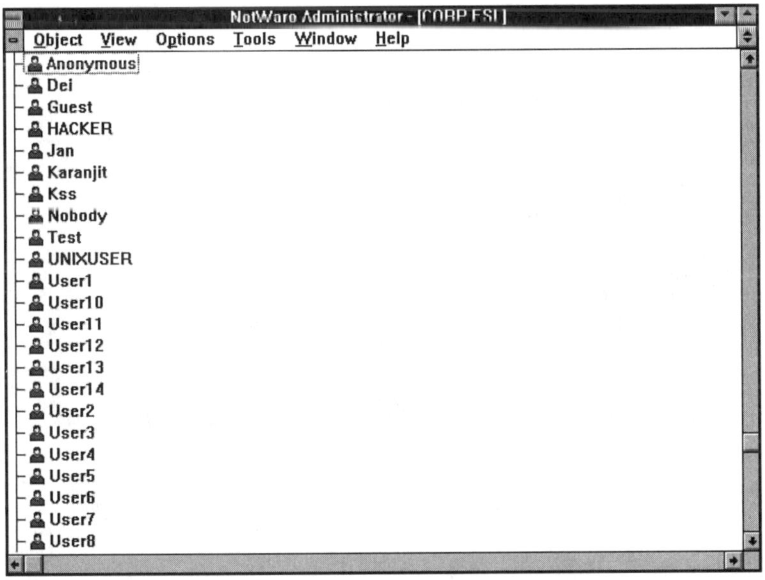

Figure 14.24
Additional user objects in OU=CORP.O=ESL.

Now consider what would happen if you created a new user object Newuser in the bindery context container OU=CORP.O=ESL. Figure 14.25 shows this new user object being created on the IntranetWare server. Figure 14.26 shows the list of users on SYSCON a few seconds after creating the user Newuser. The Newuser object appears in the list of users on the NetWare 3.x server. Figure 14.27 shows the full name property of this user on the NetWare 3.x server. The full name property for the NDS user Newuser (see fig. 14.25) is preserved during synchronization.

Figure 14.25
Newuser object created in OU=CORP.O=ESL.

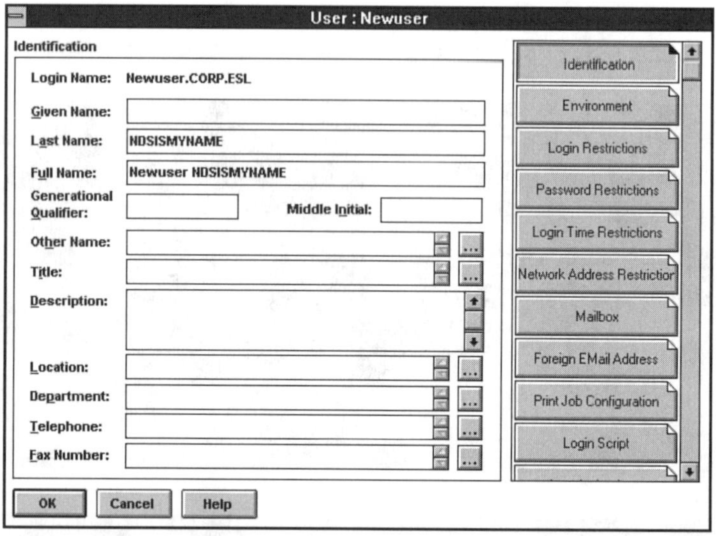

Figure 14.26
Newuser object synchronized to NetWare 3.x server.

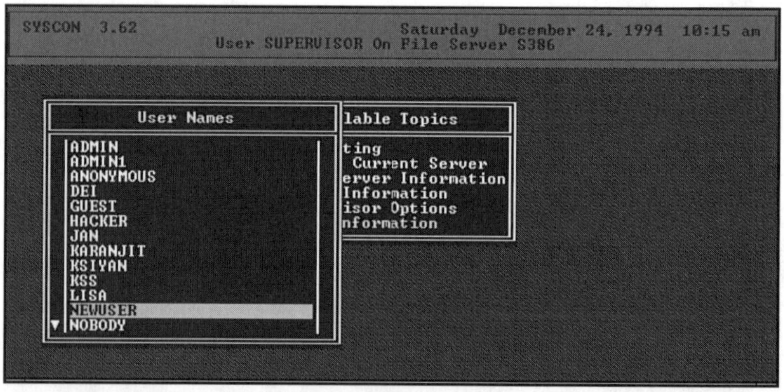

Figure 14.27
Full name property of user synchronized to NetWare 3.x server.

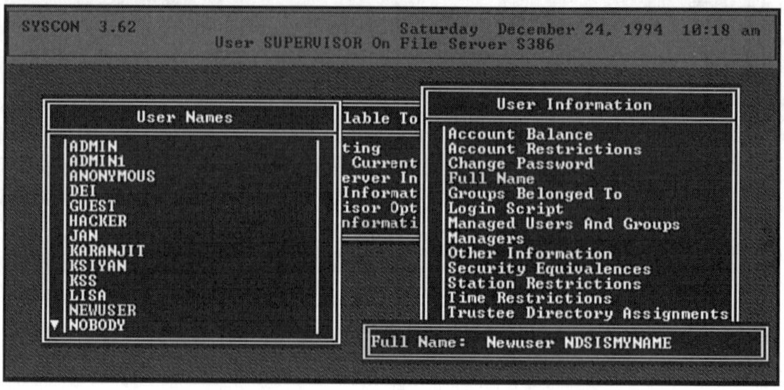

Creating Home Directories for Synchronized Users

When you create a user in the super-bindery on the IntranetWare server, the system replicates it to all the NetWare 3.x servers in the NetSync cluster. However, it does not create the home directory for this user on each of the NetWare 3.x servers in the NetSync cluster. You must perform this as a separate step. You can create the home directories by logging into the NetWare 3.x servers and then creating the home directories and assigning suitable file system rights to the user.

Alternatively, you can use the NDS tools, such as NWUSER, on the central IntranetWare server, to create the home directories. Before you can do so, you must have an NDS object which represents the NetWare 3.x servers and its volumes in the NDS tree. Creating these NDS objects for the NetWare 3.x server and volume objects is described in the next section. After you create the NDS object for the NetWare 3.x server, you can create the home directory by selecting the volume object from NWADMIN. Figure 14.28 shows the directories under the NetWare 3.x volume object S386_SYS for the server S386. Figure 14.29 shows the creation of the home directory. To obtain the screen shown in figure 14.29, you would highlight the USERS directory, press the mouse right-button, select Create, enter the directory name you want to create, and then press Enter.

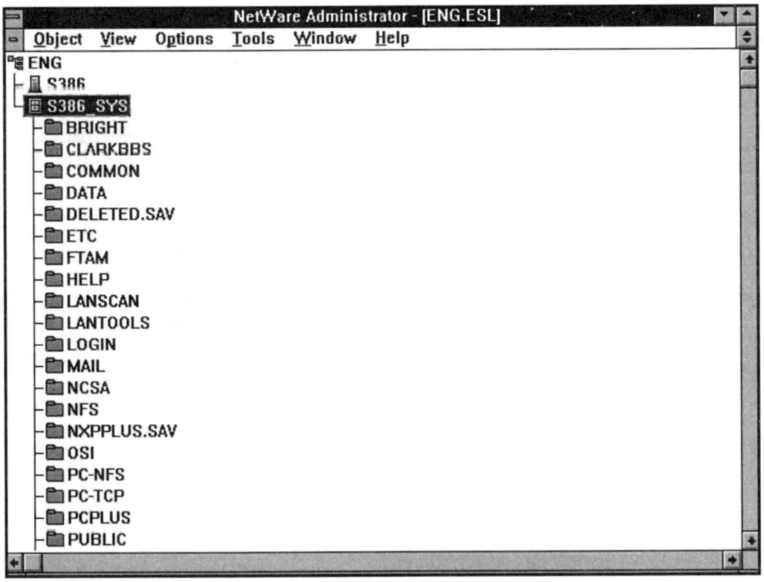

Figure 14.28
Directories under NetWare 3.x Volume object.

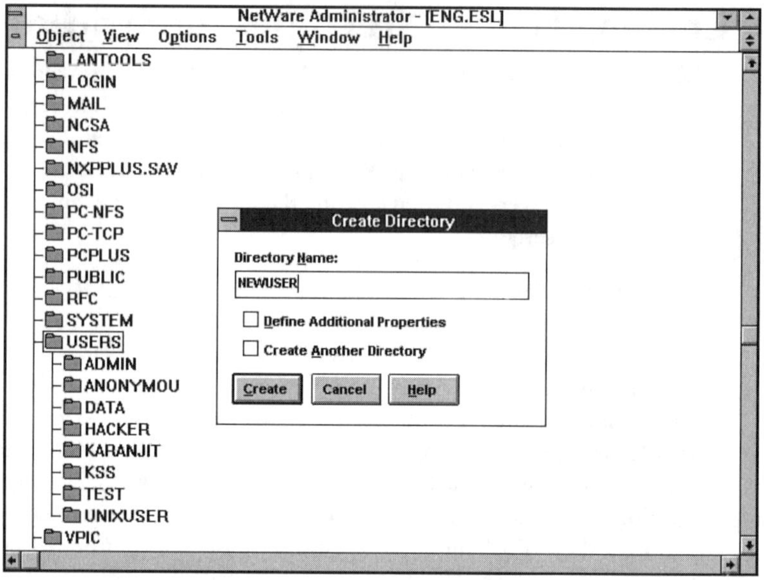

Figure 14.29
Creation of home directory for a NetWare 3.x user from the IntranetWare NWADMIN.

You can use NWADMIN to assign trustee rights to the user's home directories. Figure 14.30 shows trustee rights of Read, Write, Create, Erase, Modify, File Scan, and Access Control being assigned to user NEWUSER for the home directory SYS:USERS\NEWUSER.

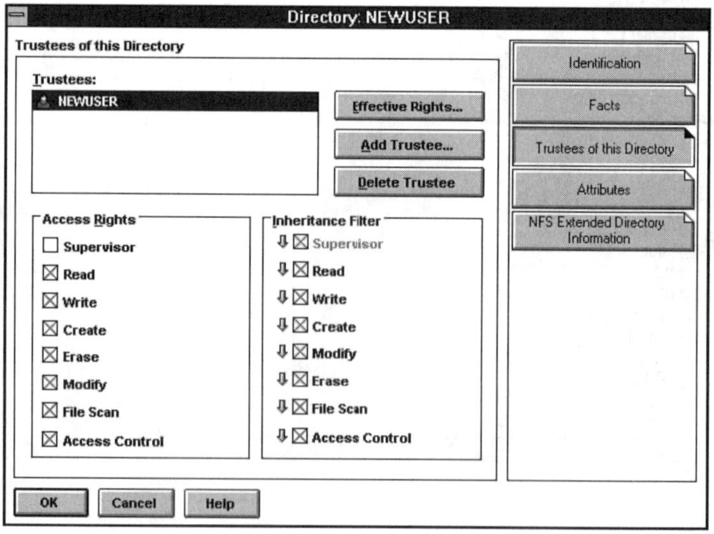

Figure 14.30
Assigning trustee rights to home directory for NetWare 3.x user NEWUSER using NWADMIN.

Figure 14.31 shows the directory trustee assignments of user NEWUSER on the NetWare 3.x server as you would see it if you were to use SYSCON. From this figure, you can verify that the rights changed using NWADMIN are indeed changed on the NetWare 3.x server, and you can verify this by using SYSCON to confirm these changes.

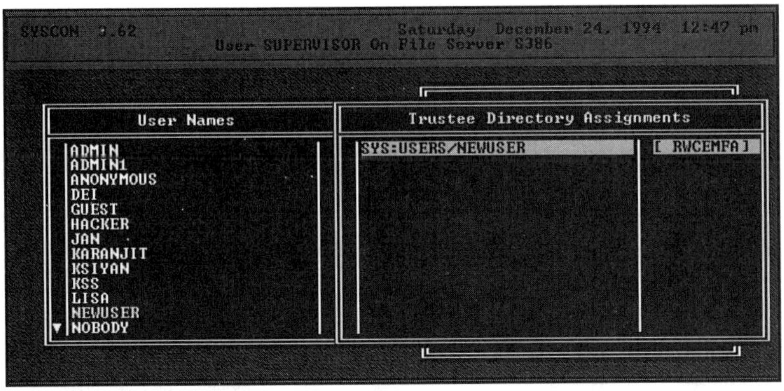

Figure 14.31
Viewing trustee rights to home directory for NetWare 3.x user using SYSCON.

Creating NDS Objects for NetWare 3.x

IntranetWare enables you to create NDS objects that correspond to NetWare 3.x servers within the NDS tree. You can define these NDS objects anywhere in the NDS tree. As long as you assign an NDS name that matches the name of the NetWare 3.x server, you can perform limited server management functions.

The following is a guided tour of how you can create the NDS representation of a NetWare 3.x server and perform management functions.

1. Log into the NDS tree as a user with Browse and Create object rights in the container where you plan to create the NDS object.

2. Run NETADMIN, NWADMIN3x, or NWADMIN95, and select the container where you want to create the NDS object.

   For the purpose of this tour, assume that you want to create the server objects in the container OU=ENG.O=ESL. Also, assume that you are using the NWADMIN tool. The steps for using NETADMIN are very similar.

3. With the container highlighted, select the Create function.

4. When the New Object dialog box appears, select the NetWare Server object, then choose the OK button.

5. When the Create NetWare Server dialog box appears, enter the name of the NetWare 3.x, then choose the Create button.

6. If you are prompted for a login name, enter the login name and password for a valid user who has supervisor privileges to the NetWare 3.x server.

7. Highlight the newly created server object and examine its properties (see fig. 14.32).

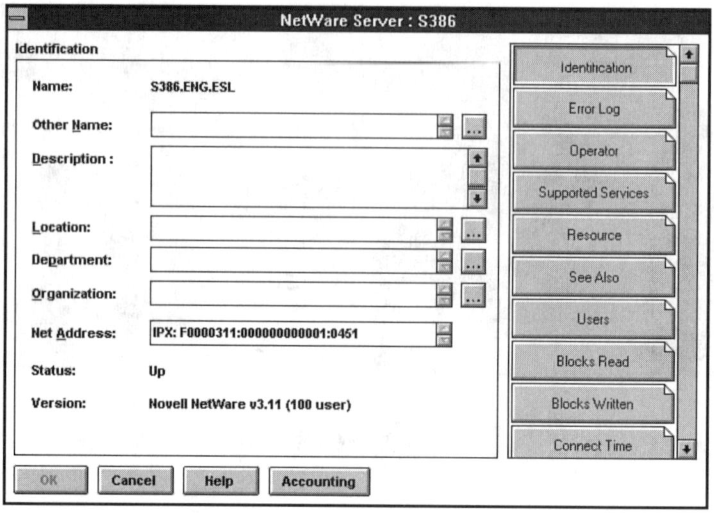

Figure 14.32
Properties of the NetWare 3.x server object.

You can examine the name of the server, the network address, and the version number of the server. Figure 14.32 shows that the name of the server is S386.ENG.ESL; its IPX network address is F0000311: 000000000001:0451; and its version number is Novell NetWare 3.11 (100 user).

You also can examine other properties of the NetWare server, such as error log, operators, and accounting information such as blocks read, blocks written, connect time, disk storage, service requests, and so on.

You can use the NDS tools to install or remove accounting functions for the NetWare 3.x server. These functions are described in Chapter 29, "Managing IntranetWare Users," on the CD.

8. Next, you should create the volume NDS objects for the NetWare 3.x server, while still logged on as a user who has Browse and Create object trustee rights to the NDS container in which you want to create the volume objects.

   Highlight the container in which to create the volume object.

9. With the container highlighted, select Create.

10. When the New Object dialog box appears, select the Volume object, then choose the OK button.

11. When the Create Volume dialog box appears, enter the following information:

    - **Volume Name.** This is the NDS name of the volume. It does not have to match the physical volume name on the NetWare server.

- **Host Server**. This is the name of the NetWare server to which the volume is connected. Here you must enter the name of the server in the NDS tree. For NetWare 3.x, you enter the server name.

- **Physical Volume**. This is the physical name of the volume as seen from the host server. You can select the down arrow to the right of this field to select the physical volume names on the server.

A sample Create Volume dialog box is shown in figure 14.33. Click on the Create button to create the Volume object.

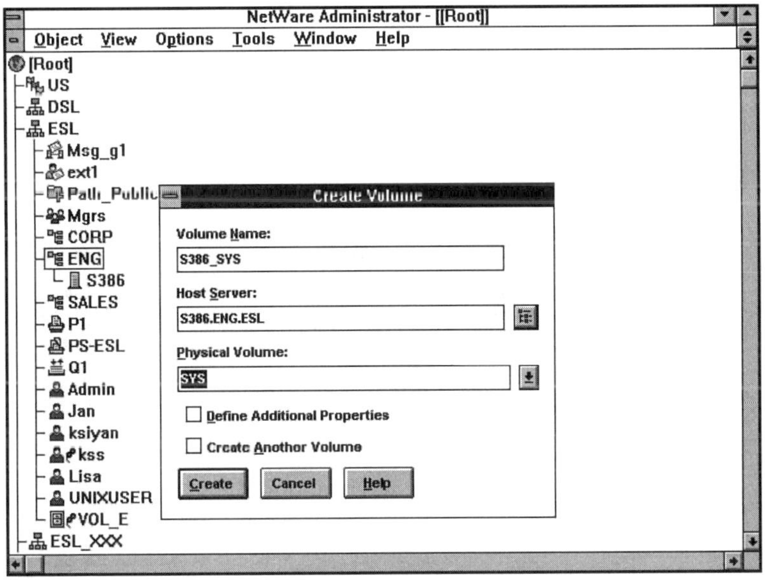

Figure 14.33
The Create Volume dialog box for a NetWare 3.x volume.

You can now manage the NetWare 3.x Volume object as any other NDS Volume object. Specifically, you can see the file system directory structure for the volume, create and delete file system directories, assign trustee rights to the file system, and view volume statistics.

Figure 14.34 shows the detail property screen for the NetWare 3.x NDS Volume object. Figure 14.35 shows the statistics for the volume that shows a graphical display of disk space and directory usage. In the example shown in the figure, the disk space is 85% full with only 9 MB available. If you were to use the PURGE command, 7,872 KB of space would become available. The volume block size is 4,096 bytes and 71% of the allocated directory entries are in use. This screen also shows the name spaces installed on the volume. In this example, the volume S386_SYS has DOS, NFS, and FTAM name spaces.

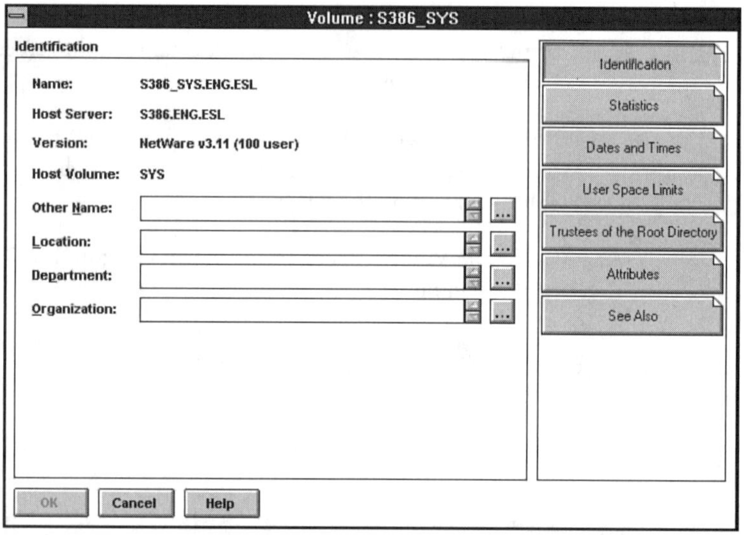

Figure 14.34
Volume properties for a NetWare 3.x volume.

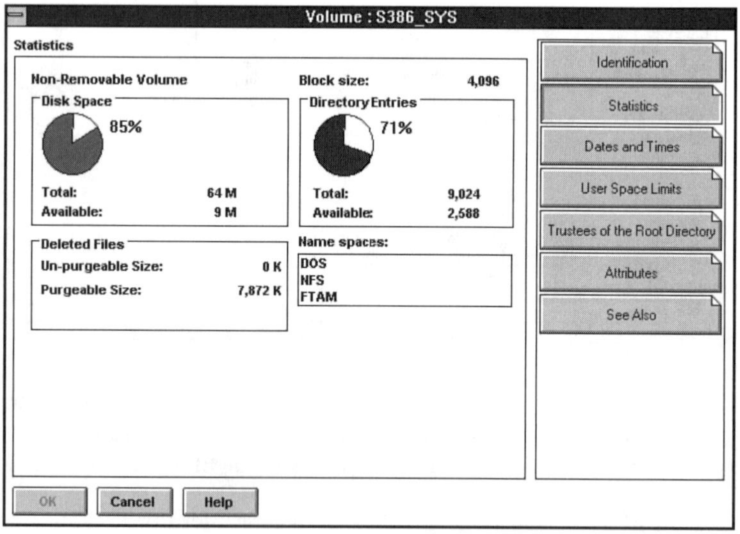

Figure 14.35
Volume statistics of a NetWare 3.x volume.

Figure 14.36 shows the user space limits report obtained by clicking on the User Space Limits button in the Detail Properties Screen for the volume object (refer to figure 14.33). User HACKER has a space limit of 1,024 bytes and has used 20 KB. You also can see the amount of disk space used by each user on the NetWare 3.x server.

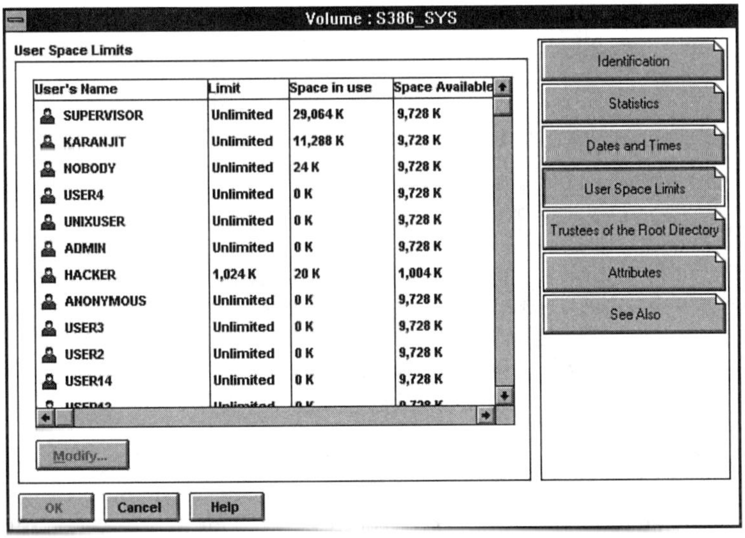

Figure 14.36
User space limit restrictions on a NetWare 3.x volume.

Using NetSync to Synchronize Printing Functions

During NetSync installation on the NetWare 3.x servers, all IntranetWare workstation print utilities are copied to the NetWare 3.x servers that join the NetSync cluster. The print utilities copied during installation are CAPTURE, NPRINT, NPRINTER (.NLM and .EXE), PCONSOLE, PRINTCON, PRINTDEF, PSC, PSERVER.NLM, and PUPGRADE.NLM and all the support files needed for these utilities. After NetSync installation on the NetWare 3.x server, you should replace the use of the NetWare 3.x RPRINTER.EXE in NetWare 3.x workstations with the equivalent NPRINTER.EXE utility. Replacing RPRINTER with NPRINTER can improve the printing performance on remote printers.

If you are running the NetWare 3.x PSERVER.NLM on NetWare 3.x servers, you should unload them and run the IntranetWare PSERVER.NLM that was installed as part of the NetSync installation onto the NetWare 3.x server. When the IntranetWare PSERVER loads, it automatically loads the IntranetWare NPRINTER.NLM.

The IntranetWare print utilities can operate in a bindery mode, and their behavior in the NetWare 3.x server enviroment is similar to what you can expect from the NetWare 3.x counterpart. The print job configurations and print databases created with PRINTCON and PRINTDEF are converted by NetSync to a IntranetWare format and copied to the IntranetWare print databases.

To simplify administration of the NetWare 3.x print servers, you can merge them into a single print server object in the NDS. Doing so also causes the NetWare 3.x printers to be placed in the NDS where you can manage them from the single IntranetWare print server.

When you run NETSYNC3 on a NetWare 3.x server, you must confirm that you will use the IntranetWare print databases and utilities. If you do not confirm this change, NETSYNC3 unloads itself.

The following sections discuss additional details for print synchronization.

Using IntranetWare Print Databases

After you convert the NetWare 3.x print database to the IntranetWare print database format, the original information is retained in the conversion process; only the format is changed. The IntranetWare utilities that are copied to the NetWare 3.x servers in the cluster need the IntranetWare print database format. The IntranetWare utilities cannot use the NetWare 3.x print databases directly because they have an incompatible format.

To avoid conflicts, the NetWare 3.x PRINTCON and PRINTDEF utilities are deleted during the NetSync synchronization. Even though the NetWare 3.x print databases cannot be accessed by the IntranetWare utilities, they are retained as a backup and for third-party utilities that might yet need them. If you do not need these NetWare 3.x print databases for backup or third-party utilities, you should delete them.

The IntranetWare server acts as a focal point of all changes that you need to synchronize. You should, therefore, make changes to the IntranetWare print databases from the NetWare 4.1 server. These changes are then synchronized to the NetWare 3.x servers. If you make changes to the NetWare 3.x server print database directly, these changes are not synchronized with other servers in the NetSync cluster.

Synchronizing Print Servers

If you have a complex printing environment under NetWare 3.x, you can simplify it by moving it to an IntranetWare environment. NetSync does much of the necessary synchronization, but you still might need to do some manual configuration.

You can use NetSync to move the NetWare 3.x print servers to the IntranetWare NDS so that you can administer these print servers from a central location. You can merge the print resources of all the NetWare 3.x servers in the NetSync cluster (up to 12 NetWare 3.x servers). As a result of this merging, configuration information for the NetWare 3.x print servers and their associated printers and queues is transferred to a single IntranetWare print server NDS object.

During the print server merging operation, NetSync does not distinguish between a NetWare 3.x PSERVER.NLM running on a server and a PSERVER.EXE running on a dedicated workstation. It merges both types of print servers into the IntranetWare print server object. Under IntranetWare, PSERVER.EXE and RPRINTER.EXE do not exist; they are replaced by NPRINTER.EXE at the workstation. NPRINTER.NLM running on the NetWare server handles remote printers attached to IntranetWare servers. NPRINTER.NLM has no equivalent in the NetWare 3.x printing environment.

The first NetWare 3.x print server you merge retains the configuration information it had in the NetWare 3.x bindery, including printer numbers. When NetSync merges additional NetWare 3.x print servers, the printer numbers might conflict with printer numbers already assigned to the IntranetWare print server. When print number conflicts arise, NetSync assigns new numbers to the new printers. You do not need to merge all NetWare 3.x print servers to the same IntranetWare server. You can, for instance, merge seven NetWare 3.x print servers to the print server PS-CORP running on an IntranetWare server and merge five other NetWare 3.x print servers to PS-ENG on another IntranetWare server.

When you merge NetWare 3.x servers to an IntranetWare server, keep in mind that the maximum number of printers you can use within a single IntranetWare print server object is 255, which is considerably larger than the NetWare 3.x print server's limit of 16 printers per print server. You must administer NetWare 3.x print servers that you do not merge, using the PCONSOLE utility on the NetWare 3.x server.

The following is a guided tour to performing the print merge administration tasks.

1. Log in to the IntranetWare server as a user who has Browse and Create object trustee rights to the server's bindery context containers.

2. To merge the print servers on the NetWare 3.x server, you must have access to the NetWare 3.x server console. You can do this by physically going to the NetWare 3.x server or by using RCONSOLE for remote console access.

   From the NETSYNC3 menu running on the NetWare 3.x server, select the Move a Print Server option. You should see a list of print servers that are available for merging (see fig. 14.37). If only one print server is available, NetSync asks you to confirm the name of the print server.

Figure 14.37
List of NetWare 3.x print servers available for merging.

3. After you select the print server name, you must enter the name of the IntranetWare print server to which to merge the NetWare 3.x print server (see fig. 14.38).

Figure 14.38
IntranetWare print server to which to merge.

   The selected print server is now merged to the IntranetWare printing environment.

To examine the changes that have taken place, you can view the activity log on the NetWare 3.x (see fig. 14.39) and IntranetWare servers (see 14.40).

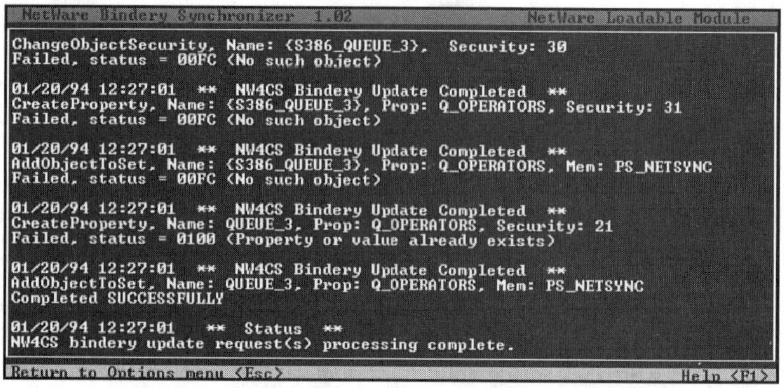

Figure 14.39
Activity log for NETSYNC3 showing the print server merger.

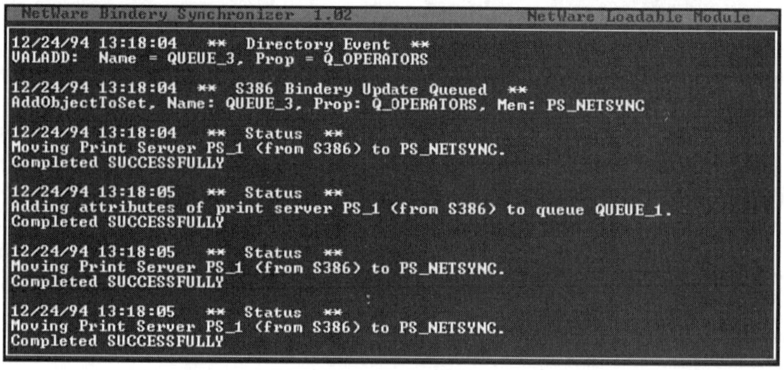

Figure 14.40
Activity log for NETSYNC4 showing the print server merger.

You also can use PCONSOLE, NWADMIN3x, or NWADMIN95 to examine the printing environment. Figure 14.41 shows the queues imported using PCONSOLE. Four queues named {S386_QUEUE_0}, {S386_QUEUE_1}, {S386_QUEUE_2}, and {S386_QUEUE_3} are imported. These queues were connected to the merged NetWare 3.x print server and were named QUEUE_0, QUEUE_1, QUEUE_2, and QUEUE_3.

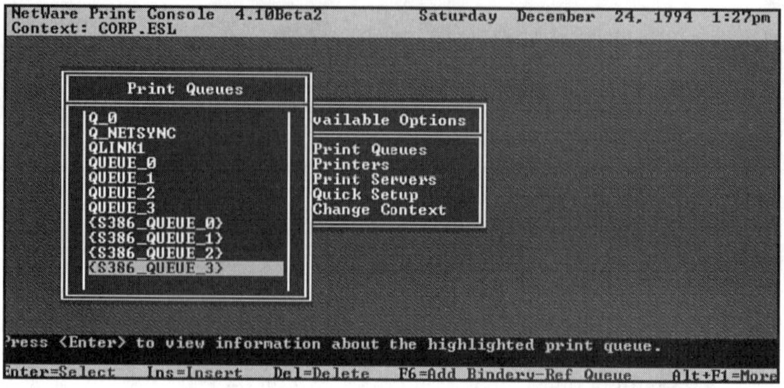

Figure 14.41
Viewing queues imported from NetWare 3.x using PCONSOLE.

Figure 14.42 shows the print server PS_NETSYNC's assignment property. The PS_NETSYNC was the name of the IntranetWare print server to which the NetWare 3.x print server was merged. The printer P_NETSYNC.CORP.ESL was already defined on the IntranetWare server. The printers "Serial Printer.CORP.ESL" and "unixprinter.CORP.ESL" were imported from NetWare 3.x as a result of the merger.

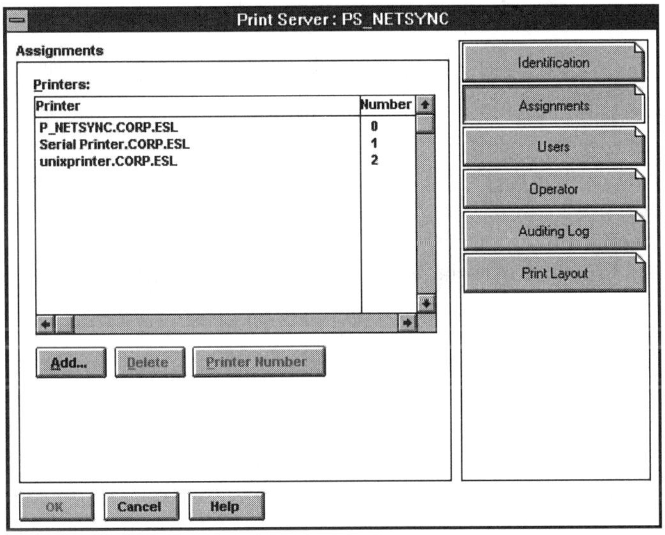

Figure 14.42
Viewing changes to the IntranetWare print server assignments using NWADMIN3x.

To examine the print server, printer, and print queue associations, click on the Print Layout button from the detail properties of the print server object. Figure 14.43 shows the new associations. From this figure you can see the following:

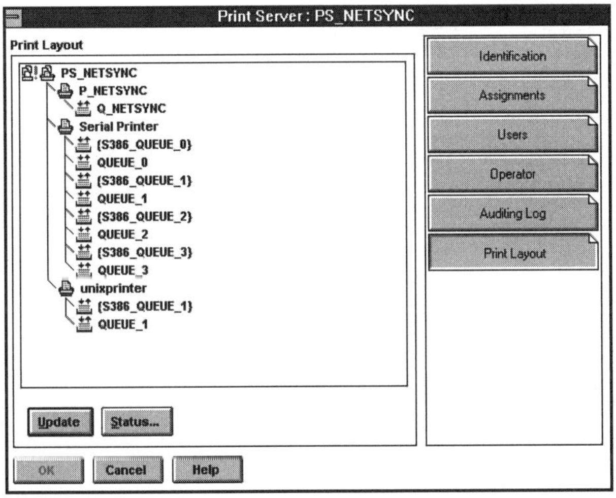

Figure 14.43
Viewing changed IntranetWare Print Layout using NWADMIN.

- The queue Q_NETSYNC is assigned to the printer P_NETSYNC.
- The queues {S386_QUEUE_0}, QUEUE_0, {S386_QUEUE_1}, QUEUE_1, {S386_QUEUE_2}, QUEUE_2, {S386_QUEUE_3}, and QUEUE_3 are assigned to Serial Printer.
- The queues {S386_QUEUE_1}, QUEUE_1 are assigned to the printer unixprinter.
- The printers P_NETSYNC, Serial Printer, and unixprinter are assigned to the print server PS_NETSYNC.

To complete the print configuration, you must make sure that the printers are connected as indicated in the IntranetWare printing environment. NetSync does not know about the physical printer configuration, nor to which device or printer port the printer should be connected. You also must load the PSERVER NLM and specify the merged print server to activate the IntranetWare printing environment. Because IntranetWare print server functions are more efficient than NetWare 3.x print server functions, NetWare 3.x users might notice an improvement in speed and performance over the NetWare 3.x printing environment.

Some print environments use third-party direct network attached print devices. These devices connect to a printer and then to the network, or are installed in a port at the printer or placed in a slot inside the printer itself. These print devices emulate a NetWare 3.x print server and are designed to search in the NetWare 3.x bindery for network printing information. Therefore, you should not move the queue server configurations used by these print devices unless you plan to reconfigure these print devices to the IntranetWare environment. The third-party print devices can work with the IntranetWare printing environment if you are using the bindery emulation mode at the IntranetWare print server.

Merging NDS Trees

Ideally, when you design the NDS tree for an organization, you should agree on a top-level design of the NDS tree so that you can add departments within the organization as subcontainers to the tree. This means that the organization should have a high level of coordination and agreement between the departments on the top-level structure of the NDS tree. Few large organizations have this level of coherence and agreement on the top level NDS design. Losing the main objectives in political turf-war issues is very easy. Using DSMERGE enables independent design of departmental networks, which later can be merged into one NDS tree. You can have multiple NDS trees, but the only way to access resources in the separate NDS tree is to have run a multi-tree aware client to login to the NDS trees, or to use bindery emulation—a process that circumvents the many advantages of NDS.

Understanding the DSMERGE Tool

You can use the DSMERGE NLM to merge the roots of two separate NDS trees. The [Root] objects of the separate NDS trees are merged. The container objects and their leaf objects can maintain separate identities within the newly merged tree. When discussing merging of NDS trees, two types of NDS trees are defined: a source NDS tree and a target NDS tree. The source NDS tree is merged into the target NDS tree. The root of the target NDS tree becomes the new root of the consolidated tree. Objects in the source NDS tree are moved to the target NDS tree. In actual practice, this movement is accomplished by deleting the [Root] of the source NDS tree and making its immediate child containers separate partitions to the [Root] of the target NDS tree. The source NDS tree becomes a branch or branches of the target NDS tree. This means that the objects in the source NDS tree become part of the target NDS tree. The target [Root] object becomes the new root for objects that are moved from the source tree.

The DSMERGE tool does not change NDS names of objects or context within the containers. Therefore, the complete names for objects in the consolidated tree are the same as the names before the trees are merged.

You must decide which NDS tree is the source tree and which NDS tree is the target tree. Because the source NDS tree is merged with the target NDS tree, it is usually the smaller of the two NDS trees. However, this need not be the case. Sometimes political factors intervene and decide who merges with whom. Merging a smaller tree with a larger tree is faster than merging a larger tree with a smaller tree. After the merge, the target tree name is retained; the source target tree name is lost.

The objects that were subordinate to the local Root object become subordinate to the target Root object.

Before you can merge the two NDS trees, you must have Supervisor object rights to the roots of both NDS trees. You are asked to supply NDS login names and passwords for both trees at the beginning of the merge process.

DSMERGE enables you to merge the roots of only two separate NDS trees. The top-level containers are immediately placed beneath the [Root]. Container objects and leaf objects maintain their identity under the newly merged root, meaning complete names of objects in the source and target trees should not change in the merged tree. You must make sure that containers at the top level in the source and target trees have unique names. If you have two containers in the top level of both trees that have the same names, you cannot merge the trees; DSMERGE asks you to change the name of the source organization object that conflicts with the target organization name. You can use NWADMIN3.x, NWADMIN95, or NETADMIN to rename the source organization object.

Figure 14.44 shows examples of the source and target trees that are used in the tree merging process. The O=KINETICS tree branch is merged into the target NDS tree. The consolidated NDS tree has the [Root] of the target tree with O=KINETICS added as a tree branch directly under [Root]. The organization O=SCS in the source NDS tree has the same name as the organization O=SCS in the target NDS tree. During the merge, DSMERGE will detect the duplicate name and ask you to rename the source organization name O=SCS. In the example in figure 14.44, O=SCS is renamed to O=KSCS in the consolidated tree. If you do not want to change the name, your only choice is to move the duplicate name container O=SCS under another tree level. It is possible to have duplicate Organizational Unit (OU) objects as seen by the OU=CORP in figure 14.44 that exist in containers O=ESL and O=KINETICS. The problem with duplicate names exists for objects that are immediately below the [Root] objects. These objects are the Country (C) and Organization (O) container objects.

Figure 14.44
NDS tree merger example.

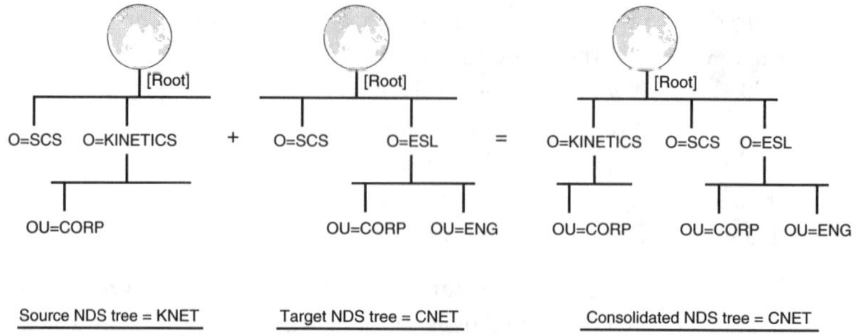

Preparing for DSMERGE

Before you can merge the NDS trees, you must prepare both source and target trees. Merging is a single transaction and, according to Novell, is not subject to catastrophic failure caused by power outages or hardware failure. You should, however, back up the NDS database in the source and target trees. You can use SBACKUP to perform the NDS backup.

The following is a list of preparation tasks that you should perform before you merge two NDS trees:

- Ensure that you have unique names for organization and country objects under [Root]. You can resolve duplicate names during the tree merge operation or by using NETADMIN, NWADMIN3.x, or NWADMIN95 in a separate step.
- Obtain login names and passwords for a user account in each tree that has Supervisor object rights to the [Root] of the NDS tree.
- Back up each NDS tree. You can use SBACKUP or a third-party backup utility to perform the backup.
- Establish time synchronization in each NDS tree.
- Change time synchronization at each server so that all servers in the source and target trees have one SINGLE REFERENCE or REFERENCE server for a time source.
- If both NDS trees have the same name, rename one of them so that the NDS tree names are unique.
- Locate the servers on which DSMERGE should run. These are servers that have a master replica of the [Root] partition for the source tree.
- Run DSREPAIR on source and target NDS trees to clean up any NDS database problems.

The more important issues listed previously are discussed in the following sections.

Time Synchronization before Merging

Before NDS can work correctly, only Reference or one Single Reference time server should exist in a tree. After the merge, the tree should contain only one Reference or one Single Reference time server. If the source and target trees each have a Single Reference time server or a Reference time server, then after the merge, the consolidated tree has too many Single Reference or Reference time servers. To avoid this, you must change the time server types so that you have a maximum of one Single Reference and one Reference time server in both the trees, to ensure that the consolidated tree contains only one Reference or one Single Reference time server. For additional information on time synchronization, see Chapter 8, "Novell Directory Services Time Synchronization."

You can use the server console SET TIME SERVER TYPE command to change the time server type or SERVMAN.NLM to change this parameter. You also can edit the TIMESYNC.CFG file.

If you make time synchronization changes on a server, you should bring the server down and restart it. You can use the following console command line to force time synchronization:

```
SET TIMESYNC RESTART FLAG = ON
```

The preceding flag activates the TIMESYNC.NLM, after which the flag value is set to OFF. After you establish the time synchronization, you see messages similar to listing 14.1.

Listing 14.1

```
NW4CS: SET TIMESYNC RESTART FLAG = ON
TIMESYNC Restart Flag action was SUCCESSFUL.

12-24-94: 5:12:33 pm: TIMESYNC-4.10-138
Time Synchronization has been established.
NW4CS:
```

Wait until all the servers report that they have established time synchronization. On a large network, this can take as long as an hour or more.

Renaming an NDS Tree

The source and target trees should have different tree names. The tree name of the target tree becomes the name of the consolidated tree. If the source and target trees have the same name, you should change one of the tree names. You should change the tree name of the source tree, because this is the one that disappears because of the merger.

You use DSMERGE to change the name of a tree. To find out the NetWare server on which you must run DSMERGE, you use the NDS Manager to find the server that has a replica of the [Root] partition. The following is an outline of the procedure to change the name of a tree.

1. Log in to the source NDS tree with Supervisor object rights to [Root].

2. You can use the NDS Manger from the NetWare Administrator or use the PARTMGR.EXE DOS-based tool.

   The steps that follow assume that you are using the NDS Manager.

3. Run NetWare Administrator and change the context to [Root]. If you do not change your context to [Root] at this point, you must do so from within NDS Manager. Either method is fine.

   To change context to [Root] from the NetWare Administrator:

   - Select the View menu
   - Select Set Context...
   - Enter the new context [Root]

4. Run NDS Manager from the NetWare Administrator:

   - Select the Tools menu
   - Select NDS Manager

   If you have changed your context to [Root], you are examining the [Root] partition; otherwise, you must change your context to [Root] from within NDS Manager. From the NDS manager screen for the [Root] partition, you should see a screen similar to figure 14.45. This screen shows the replicas of the [Root] partition, and the server that contains the master partition. Note the name of this server. You must run DSMERGE on the server that has the master replica of the [Root] partition.

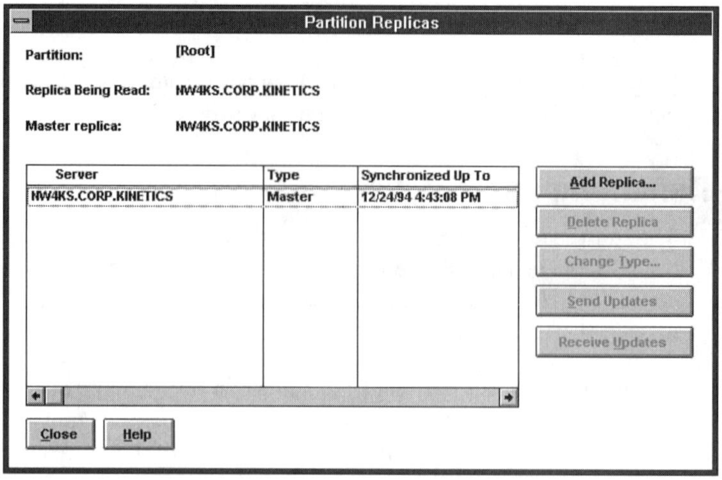

Figure 14.45
Replicas of [Root] partition.

5. Exit NDS Manager.

6. Run the DSMERGE.NLM on the server that you noted in step 4.

```
LOAD DSMERGE
```

7. You should see the DSMERGE Available Options screen (see fig. 14.46).

   Select the Rename this tree option.

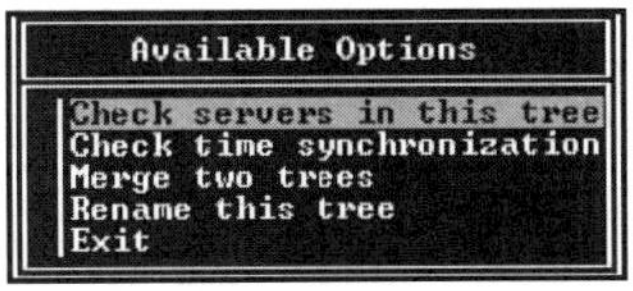

Figure 14.46
DSMERGE Available Options.

8. The Rename Tree Information dialog box appears (see fig. 14.47). Enter the administrator name, the administrator password, and the new name of the tree. The administrator name and password should be for a user that has Supervisor object rights to the [Root] of the tree to be renamed.

Figure 14.47
The DSEMERGE Rename Tree Information dialog box.

9. After you finish making entries in the Rename Tree Information dialog box, press F10 to rename the tree.

   A warning message appears (see fig. 14.48), advising you of the serious consequences of changing a tree name, and the fact that you might need to change the Preferred Tree statement in the NET.CFG file of NetWare workstations. Because you do want to change the tree name, press Enter to continue.

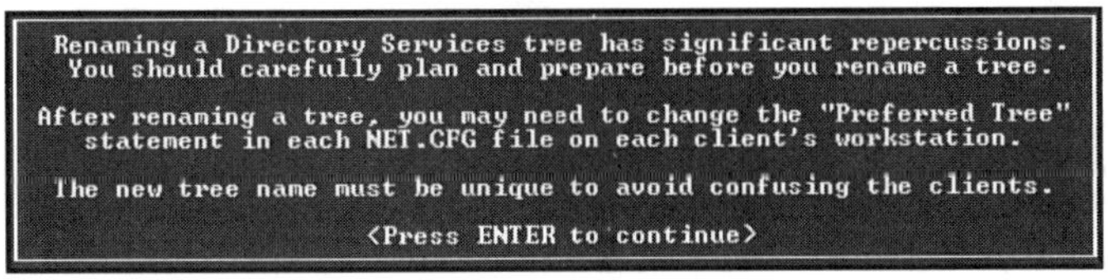

Renaming a Directory Services tree has significant repercussions.
You should carefully plan and prepare before you rename a tree.
After renaming a tree, you may need to change the "Preferred Tree" statement in each NET.CFG file on each client's workstation.
The new tree name must be unique to avoid confusing the clients.
<Press ENTER to continue>

Figure 14.48
DSMERGE warning message about consequences of changing tree name.

   You are prompted to confirm renaming of the tree. Select Yes.

   You see status messages as DSMERGE collects information about servers in the tree and updates all the servers in the tree. On a large network that has slow WAN links, this process can take a long time. If the tree renaming is successful, a message appears that informs you of a successful operation. Press Enter.

You are returned to the Available Options menu of the DSMERGE screen. However, this time you should see the changed tree name at the top of the screen.

Understanding DSMERGE Options

Figure 14.46 shows the DSMERGE options. You can use these options to perform a number of useful checks and operations.

You use the Check servers in this tree option to verify that each server in the tree has the correct name. This option requires that the server on which you run DSMERGE has a replica of the [Root] partition; this replica need not be a master replica. If you select this option, DSMERGE verifies the status of servers in the tree and reports a list of the servers and their status. Figure 14.49 shows a sample screen report for a tree that has only one server.

Figure 14.49
Status of servers in the tree.

You use the Check time synchronization option to check each server in the tree for proper time synchronization. This option requires that the server on which you run DSMERGE has a replica of the Root partition; this replica need not be a master replica. If you select this option, DSMERGE verifies the status of time synchronization and time sources on all servers in the tree. Figure 14.50 shows a sample screen report for a tree that has only one server.

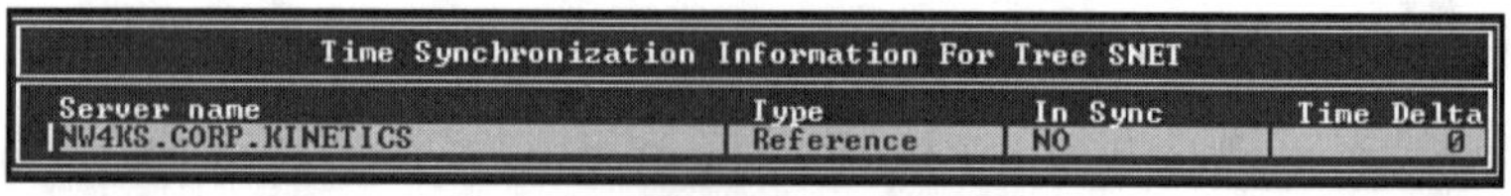

Figure 14.50
Time synchronization status of servers in the tree.

The Rename this tree option was discussed in the previous section. You use the Merge two trees option for merging the NDS tree, as described in the next section.

Using DSMERGE to Merge NDS Trees

You must load DSMERGE on a server that contains the master replica. You can use NDS Manager to find the name of this server. If you do not know the server where the master replica is stored, you are prompted with the correct server name when you attempt an operation that requires the master replica.

When you merge many trees, operation is faster if you designate the tree that has fewer objects as the source tree. Each tree that you add to the target tree has its own NDS partition. You might want to use NDS Manager if you want to combine separate partitions into a single NDS partition.

After the merge, the source tree name no longer exists. You must, therefore, update the Preferred Tree statement in the NET.CFG file on NetWare workstations. If you want to minimize the number of NET.CFG files to update, designate the tree with the most clients as the target tree. This is because the final tree retains the name of the target tree. You can also rename the tree after the merge operation so that the consolidated tree name is referenced in the majority of the NetWare workstations NET.CFG file.

To perform the NDS tree merge operations, you must have Supervisor object rights to the [Root] of the source and target trees, and the servers in the tree should be synchronized to the same time source. The following is an outline of the tree merge operation.

1. Load DSMERGE on the server that has the master replica of the source tree.

   LOAD DSMERGE

2. Select the Merge two trees menu option from the Available Options menu.

3. You should see the Merge Trees Information dialog box (see fig. 14.51).

   Enter the values for the fields in the dialog box, and press F10 to start the merge. The meanings of these fields are explained next in their order of appearance in figure 14.51.

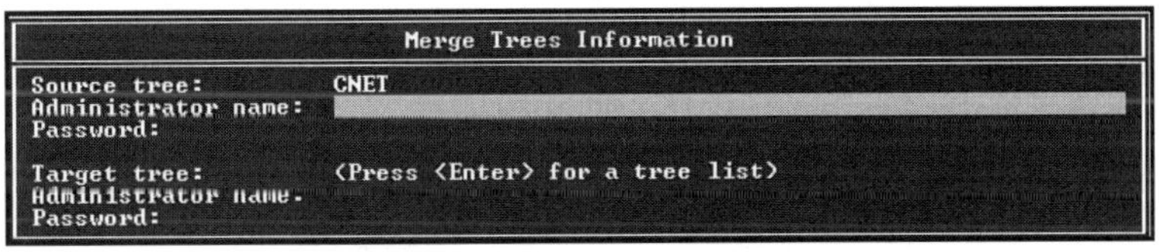

Figure 14.51
The DSMERGE Merge Trees Information dialog box.

- **Source tree.** This is the name of the tree on the source server.
- **Administrator name.** This is the name of the user with Supervisor object rights to the [Root] of the NDS source tree. You should enter the complete NDS name of the user (example: .CN=CORP.O=KINETICS or .CORP.KINETICS).
- **Password.** Enter the password of the user account for the source tree that was entered in the previous Administrator name field.
- **Target tree.** This is the name of the NDS tree into which the source NDS tree is to be merged. This name becomes the name of the consolidated tree.
- **Administrator name.** This is the name of the user with Supervisor object rights to the [Root] of the NDS target tree. You should enter the complete NDS name of the user (example: .CN=CORP.O=KINETICS or .CORP.KINETICS).
- **Password.** Enter the password of the user account for the target tree that was entered in the previous Administrator name field.

4. After you enter the information in the Merge Trees Information box, press F10 to start the merge. A message screen informs you of the different phases of the merge process. DSMERGE has four merge phases. You can back out of the merge process at any time during the first three phases (check, preparation, and merge phases), but after you reach the completion phase, the changes become permanent. The different DSMERGE phases are explained in the following list:

   - **Check phase.** This checks the source and target NDS trees for problems that could prevent a successful merge.
   - **Preparation phase.** This prepares the source NDS tree for merging. The preparation consists of creating a separate partition for each organization and country object and deletion of all replicas of the [Root] partition except the master replica.
   - **Merge phase.** This phase modifies the source NDS tree so that the master replica of the [Root] of the source tree changes to a read/write replica of the [Root].
   - **Completion phase.** The merging is complete. At this point the process is not reversible. DSMERGE waits for NDS synchronization to complete, and all servers to recognize the new replica of the [Root].

   Press F10 to start the execution of the DSMERGE phases.

5. After you move past the check phase, a dialog box appears, asking you to confirm that you want to merge the NDS trees.

   Select Yes to continue.

   If the time is not synchronized, or you need to repair the NDS database, the merging process does not continue. You must synchronize the servers and repair any problems in the NDS database before you can complete the tree merging.

6. As the merge process continues, the server addresses are collected and processed. When the merge process completes, you will see a message informing you of this fact.

Organizing the New Tree

After you complete the tree merging, you must examine the consolidated tree for the following items:

- Examine object and property rights in the consolidated tree. If you had a user Admin in the source and target trees, you also have two Admins in the consolidated tree. You might only need one Admin, in which case, for security reasons, you must decide which Admin user to retain.
- Execute the DSMERGE option Run Verify Servers in Tree to confirm that all tree names were changed correctly.

- Examine the new partitions that are created in the merge process. If there are many small partitions in the new tree, you might want to join/merge them together.
- Examine the number and types of replicas you have. You might want to create new replicas, or place replicas in a location that will allow efficient fault tolerance and access to network resources.
- Ensure that the server's time synchronization is consistent with the consolidated tree.
- Update the NetWare workstations that reference the source tree's name in the PREFERRED TREE statements in the NET.CFG.

Summary

Large enterprises transitioning from NetWare 3.x to IntranetWare often have a mix of NetWare 3.x and IntranetWare servers. NetWare 3.x servers do not have any central management capability. By using NetSyncbindery, it is possible to manage NetWare servers from the NDS of an IntranetWare host. Users, groups, and print environments of a NetWare 3.x server can be managed from the IntranetWare NDS. This is accomplished by using the NetSync tool.

Another helpful tool for managing an IntranetWare enterprise network is DSMERGE. You use DSMERGE to merge two separate NDS trees into a single NDS tree.

CHAPTER 15

Supporting DOS, Windows 3.1x, and Windows 95 Workstations

The IntranetWare Client for DOS/Windows 3.1x and the IntranetWare Client for Windows 95 bring the proven NLM technology of the IntranetWare file server to the workstation. Users can improve the performance of their network connection and extend the life of their hardware investment by updating to the improved 32-bit workstation software. The 32-bit architecture, known as Client 32, combines the best technologies of previous client architectures and can increase network performance with its improved design and features. Workstations that have been slow or have not had an adequate amount of RAM with the older NETX or the NetWare DOS Requester (VLMs) should be able to do their work efficiently with the 32-bit client. Administrators can manage the workstation more easily with improved installation and configuration options.

In this chapter, you learn about the new client architecture and how to manage networked workstations by performing the following tasks:

- Install the IntranetWare Client for DOS/Windows
- Use Auto Client Upgrade to update workstation
- Install and use the IntranetWare Client for Windows 95

This chapter includes hints that will help you avoid common problems and understand implementation issues. A knowledge of the networking architecture will enable you to be better equipped when managing and configuring workstations on the network. The following section examines the architecture of the IntranetWare Client for DOS/Windows and its software components.

IntranetWare Client for DOS/Windows Architecture

IntranetWare Client for DOS/Windows represents the next step in the evolution of the client software. The best of Novell's previous client architectures, NETX and VLMs, were leveraged in creating the DOS/Windows Client. More importantly, the IntranetWare Client for DOS/Windows was modeled after the proven NLM technology of the IntranetWare file server. It offers 16-bit desktop users full 32-bit access to IntranetWare services, including Novell Directory Services (NDS). Built on the same code-base as the IntranetWare Client for Windows 95, the IntranetWare Client for DOS/Windows provides increased speed through 32-bit access. Users also benefit from Client 32 features such as full automatic reconnection to all network files and resources, access to multiple Directory trees, and improved local file caching routines.

The IntranetWare Client for DOS/Windows works with workstations running MS-DOS 5.0 or above and Windows 3.1 or above, including Windows for Workgroups. Besides supporting connections to IntranetWare (4.11), the Client also supports connections to NetWare 2.2, 3.1x, and 4.1 servers.

Architecture Overview

The IntranetWare Client for DOS/Windows is designed to take full advantage of the 32-bit capabilities of Intel's 386, 486, and Pentium microprocessors. Unlike the 286 microprocessor, which addresses memory in 16-bit, these newer microprocessors address memory in 32-bit, making it possible to run 32-bit programs. Because 32-bit processors can move data in bigger chunks, a program that is optimized for 32-bit processors can be smaller and execute much faster than the same program written to run on 16-bit computers. The IntranetWare Client uses 32-bit NetWare Loadable Modules (NLMs) and 32-bit Open Data-link Interface (ODI) LAN drivers to take advantage of the advanced microprocessors.

Earlier Novell clients, NETX and VLMs, operate in 16-bit real mode, which requires conventional memory. In a typical DOS configuration, all DOS-based software must run in a fixed amount of conventional memory (640KB) or in the Upper Memory Blocks (UMBs) between 640 and 1024KB (1MB). As a result, the NETX and VLM clients had to contend with other DOS based applications and utilities for available conventional/UMB memory. In multiple-protocol configurations, network connectivity can take up quite a bit of this memory, leaving precious little memory for applications.

The IntranetWare Client provides a 32-bit protected-mode environment for DOS/Windows clients. When Client 32 loads, it switches the CPU to *protected mode*. In this mode, all of the computer's extended memory (beyond 1MB) is addressable as one continuous range of addresses. This flat memory model makes memory allocation and management more efficient and flexible.

Figure 15.1 shows the basic architecture of the client.

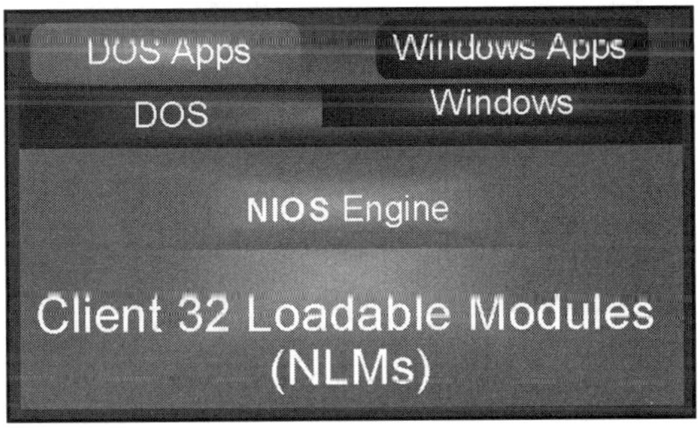

Figure 15.1
Client architecture.

Because it utilizes extended memory, the IntranetWare Client requires a memory manager such as HIMEM.SYS to make extended memory available for loading the IntranetWare Client modules. The resulting memory environment can accommodate client-based NLMs and LAN drivers, enabling them to be loaded and unloaded in extended memory as needed, just like NLMs and LAN drivers on IntranetWare servers. Because the majority of the Client modules are loaded in extended memory, the IntranetWare Client requires a mere 4KB of conventional or UMB memory.

Detailed Architecture

The IntranetWare Client architecture is comprised of three main components that make up the 32-bit client environment:

- The NetWare I/O Subsystem (NIOS.EXE)
- Communications protocols and LAN drivers (LSLC32.NLM, CMSM.NLM, CNE2000.LAN, IPX.NLM, TCPIP.NLM, SNMP.NLM, and so on)
- The Client Requester (CLIENT32.NLM)

NIOS

NIOS is the main component of the IntranetWare client around which all the other Client components revolve. NIOS serves as the client management layer between the client operating system and the 32-bit Client services provided by IntranetWare (see fig. 15.2).

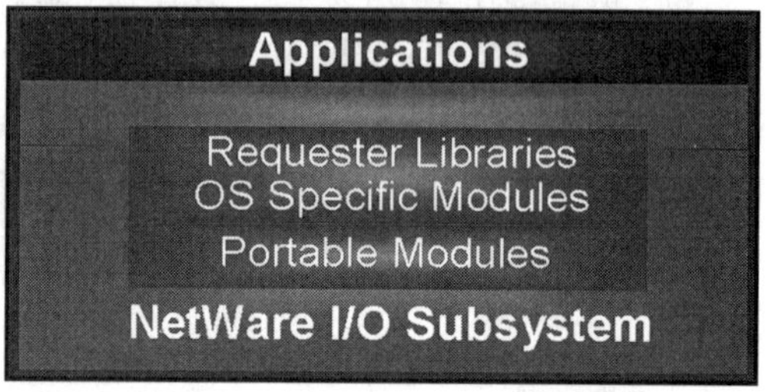

Figure 15.2
Architecture of the NetWare I/O Subsystem (NIOS).

NIOS is the first Client component that is loaded. It is essentially a DOS-extender program that creates a protected mode, flat memory environment for loading the other Client modules and drivers.

After you load NIOS.EXE, you will not be able to unload it unless you reboot the workstation. However, after NIOS is loaded, it makes the NetWare client environment flexible and dynamic. You can load and unload the other Client modules and drivers at any time. The other modules are not .EXEs but are implemented as client NLMs and are loaded with the LOAD command from the STARTNET.BAT file. The following is a standard STARTNET.BAT file:

```
SET NWLANGUAGE=ENGLISH
 C:\NOVELL\CLIENT32\NIOS.EXE
 LOAD C:\NOVELL\CLIENT32\LSLC32.NLM
 LOAD C:\NOVELL\CLIENT32\CMSM.NLM
 LOAD C:\NOVELL\CLIENT32\ETHERTSM.NLM
 LOAD C:\NOVELL\CLIENT32\CNE2000.LAN FRAME=ETHERNET_802.2 INT=3 PORT=300 RETRIES=5
 LOAD C:\NOVELL\CLIENT32\CNE2000.LAN FRAME=ETHERNET_II INT=3 PORT=300 RETRIES=5
 LOAD C:\NOVELL\CLIENT32\TCPIP.NLM
 LOAD C:\NOVELL\CLIENT32\IPX.NLM
 LOAD C:\NOVELL\CLIENT32\CLIENT32.NLM
```

Note

> If needed, you can load the LAN driver for multiple frame types and bind IPX to each of them. In the STARTNET.BAT file listed above, the CNE2000.LAN driver is loaded twice to bind the board to the two frame types needed for IPX and TCP/IP communications.

The following shows a STARTNET.BAT file if a 16-bit LAN Driver is used:

```
SET NWLANGUAGE=ENGLISH
C:\NOVELL\CLIENT32\NIOS.EXE
```

```
C:\NOVELL\CLIENT32\N16ODI.COM
C:\NOVELL\CLIENT32\NESL.COM
C:\NOVELL\CLIENT32\NE2000.COM
LOAD C:\NOVELL\CLIENT32\LSLC32.NLM
LOAD C:\NOVELL\CLIENT32\PC32MLID.NLM
LOAD C:\NOVELL\CLIENT32\IPX.NLM
LOAD C:\NOVELL\CLIENT32\CLIENT32.NLM
```

Most of the IntranetWare Client software loads in extended memory. The Client uses only about 4KB of memory as a Client manager in either UMBs or conventional memory. Having only a 4KB real-mode footprint for the network connectivity software frees up conventional memory for DOS-based applications as shown in figure 15.3. This is especially beneficial for workstations that load multiple frame types and protocols.

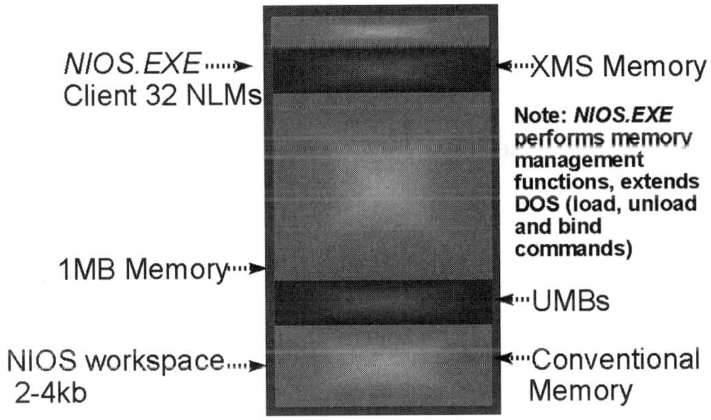

Figure 15.3
Standard memory usage on a workstation.

Note

> Network performance can be improved by adding additional RAM to a workstation. The additional RAM can be used by the IntranetWare Client's local file cache and other features that decrease network traffic and improve network client performance.

LAN Driver Communications and Protocols

The IntranetWare Client for DOS/Windows uses the *ODI* (Open Data-link Interface) architecture to communicate to the network. The Client's Link Support Layer, IPX, and TCP/IP components have been rewritten as client NLMs. This way, the IntranetWare Client components can take advantage of the flat memory model that NIOS provides.

The following modules comprise the LAN driver communications and LAN drivers portions of the client:

- LSLC32.NLM (Link Support Layer).
- CMSM.NLM.

- ETHERTSM.NLM (or TOKENTSM.NLM or FDDI.NLM if using Token-Ring or Fast Ethernet topologies). Note that Arcnet is not supported with the IntranetWare Client for DOS/Windows.
- CNE2000.LAN (or other LAN driver that matches the LAN card in your machine).

For best results, use 32-bit LAN drivers whenever possible. If you are running an adapter that does not have a 32-bit .LAN driver, you can continue to run the .COM driver for that card. The installation will read and keep your existing settings if a 32-bit matching LAN driver is not found. Because these are NLM files, they are loaded using the **LOAD** command. Configuration settings such as frame type, interrupt, I/O port, and retries are specified in the **LOAD** command of the STARTNET.BAT (refer back to the standard STARTNET.BAT listing).

Tip

> If you are running a 16-bit driver with your LAN card, you need to make configuration settings in the NET.CFG file instead of on the LAN Driver load line in the STARTNET.BAT. The 16-bit driver will look for configuration in the NET.CFG. You will also notice that the 16-bit version of LSL, LSL.COM, is loaded in place of LSLC32.NLM.

Many 32-bit ODI LAN drivers are provided with the IntranetWare Client for DOS/Windows. If your card is not supported by the included LAN drivers, a LAN driver might be available from your LAN adapter manufacturer. You can also use many of the 32-bit *.LAN drivers included with the NetWare 4.1 and the IntranetWare 4.11 operating systems. This is possible because the new client architecture uses NIOS.EXE, a derivative of SERVER.EXE.

The IntranetWare Client for DOS/Windows supports both IPX/SPX and TCP/IP protocols equally. The IPX, TCP/IP, and NetWare/IP protocol stacks have been ported to NLM format (IPX.NLM, TCPIP.NLM, and NWIP.NLM) for use with the Client. The TCP/IP stack includes support for DHCP (Dynamic Host Configuration Protocol), while NetWare/IP 2.2 includes support for BootP+ (Novell's implementation of DHCP).

The Client protocols are optimized for performance with built-in support for Packet Burst and Large Internet Packets (LIP). These packet transfer methods provide enhanced network performance in both local and wide area networks. In addition to the protocol modules, other optional modules, such as SNMP.NLM, are implemented as NLMs as well.

The Client Requester

The IntranetWare Client Requester (CLIENT32.NLM) replaces the NETX shell or the NetWare DOS Requester (VLMs). The Client Requester provides the internal tables and services necessary to track network resources, file caching, and automatic reconnection levels.

As with the VLMs, the IntranetWare Client Requester works with a set of subcomponents, or modules. However, as opposed to the old client architecture, the modules are all contained within the CLIENT32.NLM file instead of as separate files. Table 15.1 lists the modules contained within CLIENT32.NLM.

Table 15.1
CLIENT32.NLM Modules

Module	Name	Description
CONNMAN	Connection Manager	Used by the Client to keep track of the connection tables and to store other connection information.
TASKMAN	Task Manager	Keeps track of each task in the system, whether these are WINDOWS, WIN16, or WIN32 applications or activities.
FILEDIR	File and Directory	Handles all file system functions.
PRINT	Printing	Set up network printing capabilities for the client.
SESSMUX	Session Multiplexor	Currently supports only NCP (NetWare Core Protocol) sessions attaching and accessing IntranetWare servers.
NCP	NetWare Core Protocol	A child module that ties to the Session Multiplexor.
NSMUX	Name Service Multiplexor	Coordinates activities between the child modules, or processes, that you load.
NDS	Novell Directory Services	A child module to the Name Service Multiplexor module. Provides the name resolution and authentication processes for Directory Services connectivity.
BINDERY	Bindery Services	A child module to the Name Services Multiplexor. It provides the name resolution and authentication processes for Bindery connectivity.
MOCKNW	Mock NetWare	Catches raw NCPs sent from applications and redirects them to the Client functions in order to take advantage of the Client's caching and automatic reconnection settings.
POLYPROC	Poly-procedure	Contains a set of generic miscellaneous routines that didn't specifically fit in any of the other Client32.NLM modules.
NETX	DOS Interrupt 21h redirector	Used to redirect all Interrupt 21h (NETX) function calls to Client functions.

continues

Table 15.1, Continued
CLIENT32.NLM Modules

Module	Name	Description
VLMMAP	VLM Mapper	Used to redirect all DOS Requester (VLM) function calls to Client functions. The VLMMAP module is used to support applications and utilities that are written to NETX and DOS Requester APIs.

The IntranetWare Client is fully backward-compatible with the NETX shell and the VLMs, so existing NetWare-aware applications should run with no modification with the IntranetWare Client for DOS/Windows. This compatibility is accomplished through the NETX and VLMMAP modules that are a part of CLIENT32.NLM.

This section has shown the architecture for the IntranetWare Client for DOS/Windows. This advanced architecture allows for 32-bit networking of DOS and Windows 3.1x workstations via 32-bit network protocols, 32-bit LAN drivers, and 32-bit network components. The next section demonstrates how the IntranetWare Client for DOS/Windows is installed with the Windows GUI SETUP.EXE and the DOS C-Worthy INSTALL.EXE.

Installing IntranetWare Client for DOS/Windows

The IntranetWare Client for DOS/Windows features an improved installation process, including both DOS-based and Windows-based installation programs. The features of the DOS and Windows installations are very similar except that the DOS INSTALL.EXE allows for shared Windows installation and includes the Auto Client Upgrade (ACU) functionality that will be discussed in the next section. If you need these features then the DOS install should be used. The ACU can perform the client installation on your machines without user intervention via the ACU login script. This section details the installation choices and lists modifications to the workstation's DOS and Windows configuration files.

Note

Before you begin, ensure that you are installing that latest client software by downloading the latest files from **`http://support.novell.com/client/home`**.

Also, ensure that your workstations meet the following hardware and software requirements:

- A 386 processor or higher
- MS DOS 5.x or PC DOS 5.x or above
- Windows 3.1 or Windows for Workgroups 3.11 (optional)
- A VGA or better graphics board and monitor
- A minimum of 4MB of memory (plan on at least 8MB if you run Windows)
- An XMS memory manager (HIMEM.SYS or equivalent)

If you want the client installation program to update a shared Windows directory on the network, you must run the DOS-based INSTALL.EXE.

Because installation from a network drive is the most common method of installation, that method is covered in this section. Usually the client files are placed in a subdirectory of public. For example, ServerName/Volume:Public/DOSWIN.

To start the installation process, go into the Windows' Program Manager and select Run from the File drop-down menu. In the Command Line box, type the full directory path up to and including the Client SETUP.EXE file (for example, I:\PUBLIC\DOSWIN\SETUP.EXE). Then click the OK button.

The initial screen for the NetWare Client 32 Installation program is displayed. Click on Continue. After reading the license agreement screen, click on Yes to proceed. The File Locations screen is then displayed (see fig. 15.4).

Figure 15.4 shows the File Locations screen.

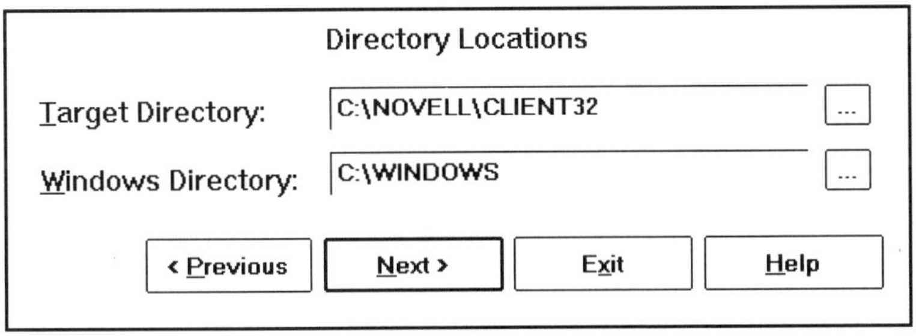

Figure 15.4
Specify your file's destination directory.

The default directory for the IntranetWare Client for DOS/Windows files is C:\NOVELL\CLIENT32. The installation program looks for Windows files in C:\WINDOWS. If Windows files are in a different location specify the location of the Windows files. The "..." button can be used to browse and locate the Windows directory. Then click on the Next button to continue.

During the Windows installation procedure, you next see the ODI Driver Selection and Configuration screen (see fig. 15.5). This allows you to choose the LAN driver that matches your network board.

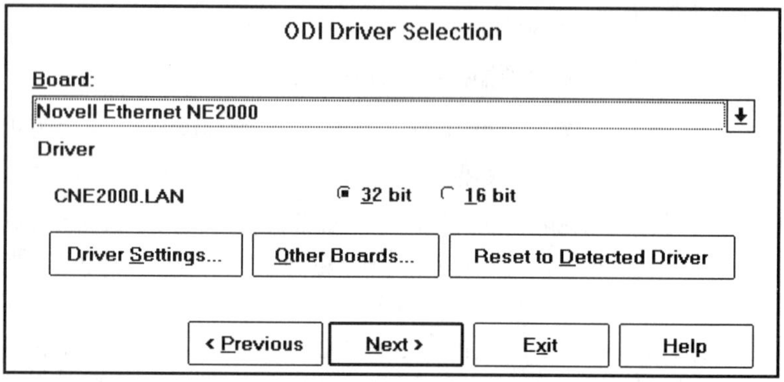

Figure 15.5
The network board/LAN driver Selection and Configuration screen.

Note

This part of the installation is slightly different when running the DOS-based INSTALL.EXE. The next section, DOS Install, provides details about the differences.

If you are already running on a network, the installation detects this and selects an appropriate LAN driver for the currently installed network card. The installation program also queries the loaded NIOS or LSL to find out which NET.CFG or STARTNET.BAT file was used when loading the previous client software. After this is determined, the install program checks that file for pertinent information on network board settings, TCP/IP and NetWare/IP information, and information about SNMP or TSA configurations. This information is then used to build the new NET.CFG and/or STARTNET.BAT file that is placed in the target directory, along with the new Client software.

If the workstation is not currently attached to the network, the installation program looks in the following three locations on the local hard drive for an existing NET.CFG or STARTNET.BAT files:

- The current target directory
- NOVELL\CLIENT32
- NWCLIENT

If existing parameters are not found, you will need to type in the LAN driver configuration information as prompted during the installation process.

If the install detected your existing LAN card, in the Board entry box, you will see a selection matching the network board you have installed. Under the Driver section of the window is the LAN driver for that board. Client 32 supports the C-code 32-bit .LAN drivers that come with the client software, some Assembly-based 32-bit .LAN drivers that ship with IntranetWare, and the 16-bit .COM drivers that ship with the Client or that work with the VLM software.

The installation program will try to match a 32-bit driver if you are not already using one. If it cannot find a 32-bit driver match in its list of certified LAN drivers, the installation program will retain your existing 16-bit driver or prompt you to load a driver from another location (such as drive A).

Note

> The install uses LAN driver vendor supplied files to read valid settings that your driver can use. 32-bit .LAN drivers use an .LDI file and 16-bit .COM drivers use an .INS file. If not present, these files can be obtained from the board manufacturer.

If the board and driver you need are not listed, but you have the driver files, click on the Board entry box and select User Supplied Driver from the list. Follow the prompts to install the driver and then click on the Next button to go to the next screen.

The installation program next displays the Additional Options window (see fig. 15.6), where you specify whether to install the following components:

- TCP/IP and/or NetWare/IP
- Simple Network Management Protocol (SNMP) and a Host MIB
- A Target Service Agent (TSA) for NetWare's Storage Management Services (SMS)

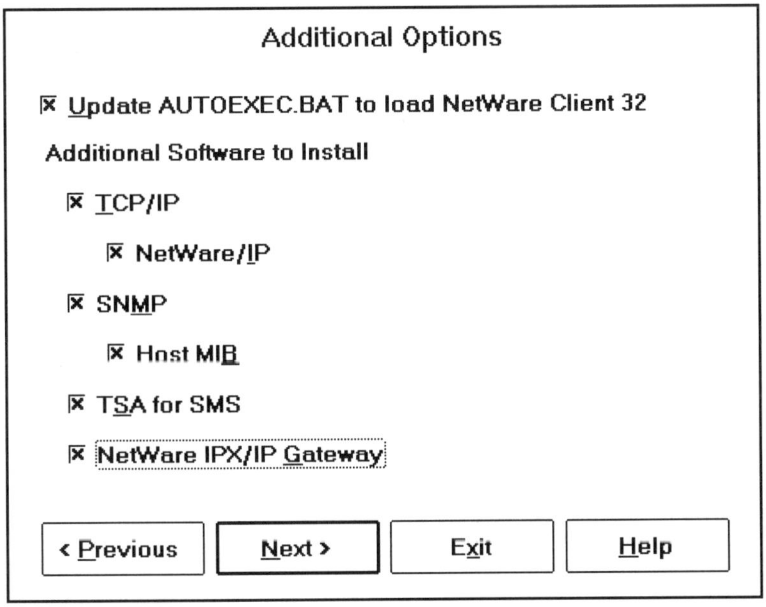

Figure 15.6
The Additional Options window.

The first choice on this screen lets you decide whether you want the AUTOEXEC.BAT file to load the Client. Most users select to have the client software load during the boot process, giving them immediate access to network resources. If you decide to load the Client from the AUTOEXEC.BAT file, the following two lines will be added to the file:

```
PATH C:\NOVELL\CLIENT32\;%PATH%
@CALL C:\NOVELL\CLIENT32\STARTNET
```

The call to the STARTNET.BAT file is placed at the bottom of the AUTOEXEC.BAT file unless ":WIN" is found and then the call is placed just before the call to start Windows. The @CALL command, which can be use to load any program from the AUTOEXEC.BAT, can be manually moved anywhere within the AUTOEXEC.BAT file.

The next option as shown in figure 15.6 is for TCP/IP Configuration. If your workstation was already set up for TCP/IP connectivity, the TCP/IP box will already be selected. With this option selected, you will see the TCP/IP Configuration window when you click on Next to proceed (see fig.15.7). Here you need to fill in the information about Client IP address, router address, subnetwork mask, and DNS domain name.

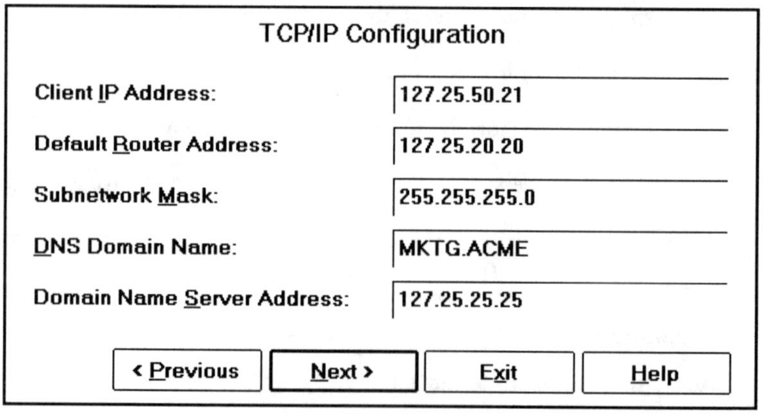

Figure 15.7
The TCP/IP Configuration window.

If the workstation's TCP/IP parameters are dynamically determined by DHCP, BOOTP, or RARP, leave the screen blank and move on. If you put spaces in the address slots, the installation program won't pull the information into its proper places. Simply proceed to the next screen.

If your TCP/IP information is contained in an existing NET.CFG file in the current Target Directory, in C:\NOVELL\CLIENT32, or in C:\NWCLIENT, the installation program will read the TCP/IP settings and place them into the TCP/IP Configuration window for you. However, if your TCP/IP settings are in a NET.CFG file in some other directory, you will have to type in the TCP/IP information manually.

Note If you change the TCP/IP configuration in INSTALL, the BIND statements in the TCP/IP section of the NET.CFG file are not updated. You'll need to make the changes manually.

If you have selected to install support for TCP/IP you could have also selected to install support for NetWare/IP(NWIP). You will see the NetWare/IP Configuration window after you have completed the information in the TCP/IP window and clicked on the Next button. Enter the NetWare/IP Domain Name, the IP address of the Preferred DSS, and the Nearest NWIP Server address for workstation access. Click on the Next button to proceed to the next optional component that you have chosen, or if you haven't selected other components, the actual installation portion of the install process will begin.

If you have selected to install support for configuring SNMP, you will see the SNMP Configuration window, as shown in figure 15.8.

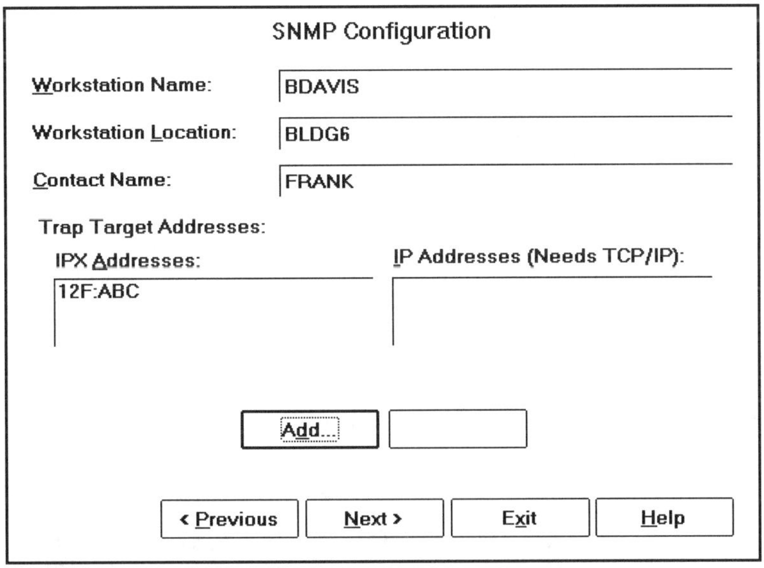

Figure 15.8
The SNMP Configuration window.

Fill in the Workstation Name field, which identifies the computer; the Workstation Location field, which describes the location of the computer; and the Contact Name field, which is generally the network administrator's name. You also need to fill in the network addresses of the SNMP management consoles for the Trap Target Addresses. If the SNMP console is running on IPX, type in the IPX addresses needed in the IPX window. If the console is running on IP, type in the appropriate addresses in the IP field.

If you have selected to install support for host resources for the MIB (Management Information Base), the next window allows you to add local devices, such as a printer or modem, to that database. Click on the Add button, type in the information that you want to include, and click on OK. Then in the Directory Level to Search from Root entry, type the number of directories away from the root directory you want the SNMP agent to scan for installed software. You can also designate Additional Search Paths if needed. Click on Add, type in the directory that you want SNMP to inventory, and click OK. Click on the Next button to proceed to the next optional component that you have chosen, or if you haven't selected other components the copy portion of the install process will begin.

If you selected support for the Target Service Agent (TSA) for Storage Management Services (SMS), you will see the TSA for SMS Configuration screen, as shown in the figure 15.9.

Figure 15.9
Setting up TSA for SMS support.

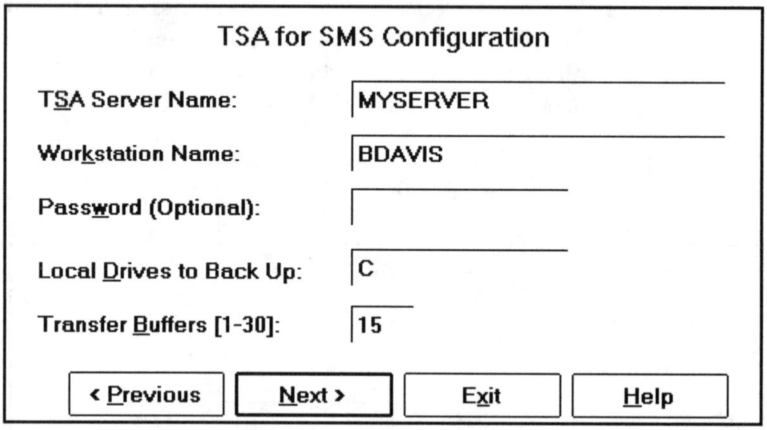

First select the file server that is running the TSASMS.NLM for SBACKUP or equivalent backup software. Next, enter a name for your workstation. This can be any name that identifies your workstation.

Note The workstation name used for workstation backup must be different from all other workstation names on the network. It's best to keep the name simple, yet unique.

The next field allows you to (optionally) set up a password for SBACKUP access. Be sure to coordinate any passwords you set here with the network administrator so that he or she will know the password needed to access the workstation when running the SBACKUP procedure.

The *Local Drives to Back Up* field lets you specify the local hard disk drives you want to back up. Click in this field or press Enter to see a list of local disk drives that you can select. Only enter the drive letter(s), no colons or slashes, separated by spaces or commas.

The *Transfer Buffers* entry can be set from 1 to 30 buffers. Each buffer matches the size of the network protocol you are using. If you want to speed up file transfers, set this number between 5 and 10.

After you have finished configuring the additional options that you selected, the installation program begins copying the files to install the IntranetWare Client software to the workstation. Figure 15.10 shows the screen displayed while file are copied.

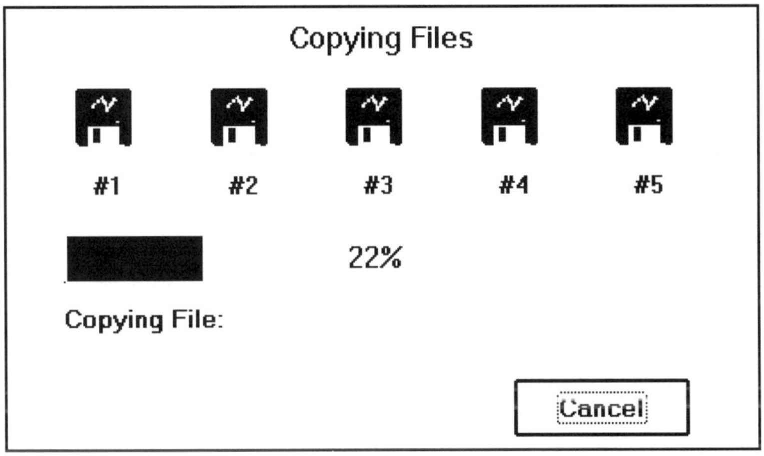

Figure 15.10
The Windows Installation copy files screen.

After the process is completed, you can either reboot your computer so that the new client installation will take effect, or you can return to Windows or to DOS, and reboot later.

The DOS Install

With the C-Worthy based DOS installation program there are a few differences from the Windows setup program. For example, the initial DOS install screen is shown in figure 15.11.

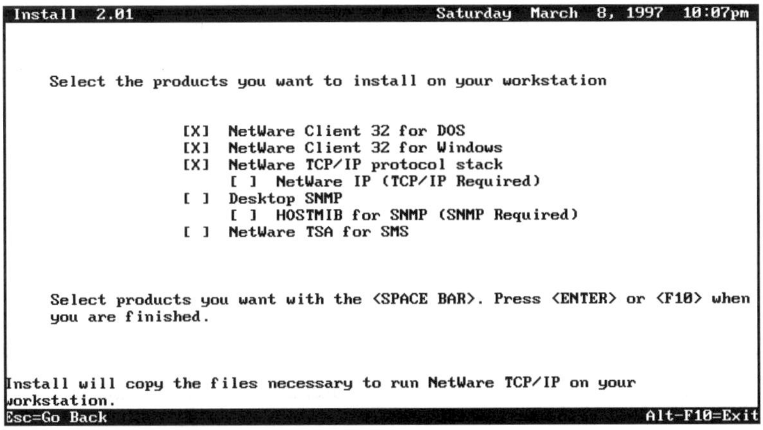

Figure 15.11
The initial DOS install screen.

Most of the additional options are the same ones you see in the Windows installation program. One difference, however, is that installing the Windows files is selected by default, but you can select to not install Windows components if you are not running Windows on your workstation. If you do select to install Windows components, you can customize the Windows support by selecting country codes and shared Windows support.

The *COUNTRY=CountryName* parameter in the CONFIG.SYS files is used to determine which Unicode file to copy to your workstation. The Unicode files are used by the Windows help and utilities files for language support. If no COUNTRY=CountryName parameter is specified in the CONFIG.SYS file, the Client defaults to ENGLISH. For DOS utilities, language support is handled by the NWLanguage variable in the STARTNET.BAT file.

Network administrators who have set up a shared Windows directory using the SETUP/A option when they installed Windows on a file server can install the IntranetWare Client for DOS/Windows to that shared directory. You must have rights to create files and directories in the path specified. The setup for a shared copy of Windows only needs to be run once. After the shared Windows directory has been prepared by the network administrator, the user can run SETUP.EXE/N to copy the necessary personal files to a personal Windows directory on the network. For example, user Dave could select F:\USERS\DAVE\WINDOWS as the location for those Windows files that are not shared. After Windows support has been installed, you are prompted for parameters for other additional options you may have selected. Follow the prompts as directed.

Another difference between the DOS-based and Windows-based installs is that the DOS Install program selects the LAN driver last, whereas the Windows Setup program performs this function first. However, the functionality of auto-detecting boards and drivers is the same for both versions. The Install program looks for an installed network board and automatically selects a 32-bit .LAN driver for the board if it finds one in its list of certified drivers. After a driver has been selected and configured, the Install program displays the Installation Configuration Summary screen shown in figure 15.12.

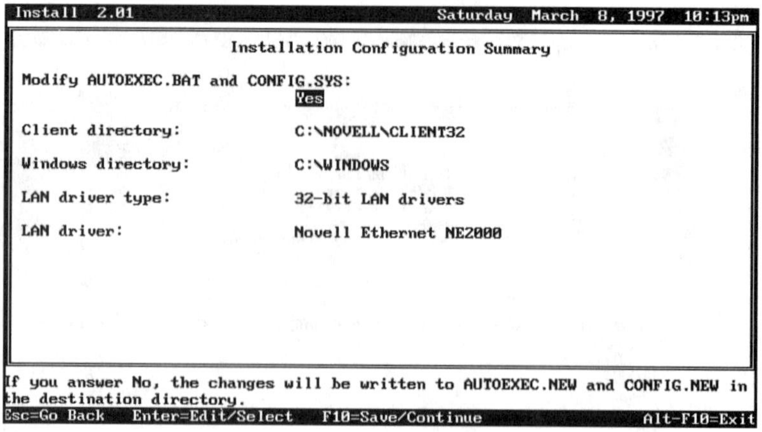

Figure 15.12
The Installation Configuration Summary screen.

The first line in the Installation Configuration Summary screen, Modify AUTOEXEC.BAT and CONFIG.SYS, is set to Yes by default. If you keep the default setting, the INSTALL program adds the following two lines to the AUTOEXEC.BAT file:

```
PATH C:\NOVELL\CLIENT32\;%PATH%
@CALL C:\NOVELL\CLIENT32\STARTNET
```

The AUTOEXEC.BAT calls the STARTNET.BAT file to load the client software. INSTALL then checks the CONFIG.SYS file to ensure that the Files = 35 and Buffers = 20 are set to at least these minimums.

The summary screen also shows the other selections you made. You can change these settings now or press F10 and the INSTALL will continue and copy the Client files to the designated directories. When the file copy is completed, INSTALL prompts you to reboot the workstation.

The client is now installed on the workstation. The following section covers the Automatic Client Upgrade process for installation.

Automatic Client Upgrade (ACU)

In the past, when Novell has released updates to the client software, network administrators have had to physically go to each workstation and manually upgrade the client software. Novell has developed an *Automatic Client Upgrade* (ACU) process that enables administrators to set up the installation so that client updates occur automatically when users log in.

To accomplish the ACU, administrators place instructions in a login script. These instructions automatically upgrade the client workstations during the next log in, without requiring any manual intervention from the user or the administrator. Automatic Client Upgrade is the name of a process, rather than a specific utility. The process involves the following new utilities:

- **NWDETECT.EXE.** NWDETECT.EXE begins the ACU process by looking for a client version stamp in the NET.CFG file and detecting whether there is a difference between the client version stamp parameters within the login script and those within the NET.CFG file.
- **NWSTAMP.EXE.** NWSTAMP.EXE updates (or creates for the first time) the Install Stamp in the NET.CFG file.
- **NWLOG.EXE.** NWLOG.EXE creates a log file of all upgraded nodes in a subdirectory specified by the network administrator. The log file lists the date, time, username, IPX external network number, node address, and, optionally, any text defined by the network supervisor.
- **REBOOT.COM.** REBOOT.COM is an executable file that automatically reboots the workstation.

Overview of the ACU Process

The basic process by which the client software is automatically updated with ACU is simple. Before you perform the actual ACU process, however, you need to complete a few preliminary tasks, as follows:

1. Decide which of login script to use (container, profile, and so on).
2. Install the NetWare Client 32 files onto a network server.
3. Copy the ACU utilities to the Client 32 parent directory.

Note For easier access to the ACU utilities, copy the executables from the \ADMIN\DOS_ACU subdirectory to the parent directory into which you copied the IntranetWare Client files.

4. Create a directory for the ACU log files. For example, create a LOG subdirectory under the DOSWIN32 directory in PUBLIC. Grant all users Create and Write rights to this subdirectory, which will be used for log files produced by NWLOG.EXE.
5. Review the settings in the INSTALL.CFG file and change the InstallType setting from BASIC to AUTO, as follows:

   ```
   [Setup]
        InstallType=AUTO
   ```

   This setting allows the installation program to run in unattended mode, which does not require the user to answer any prompts. Any other desired configuration changes in INSTALL.CFG should also be made at this time.
6. Insert the ACU commands into the login script (see the following section).
7. Test the ACU on a small set of users or in a lab environment.

An ACU Example

This example assumes that you are running an IntranetWare container login script and that you are upgrading your VLMs workstations to the IntranetWare Client for DOS/Windows.

Install the NetWare Client 32 for DOS/Windows 3.1x files to a network server. The files could be placed in the SYS:PUBLIC\CLIENT\DOSWIN32 subdirectory on the server. Copy the ACU utilities and message files to this directory and create the \LOG subdirectory as instructed.

In a text editor, bring up the INSTALL.CFG file and, under the [Setup] heading, change the InstallType= setting to AUTO. Then, using the NWADMIN utility, access the container login script and insert the following lines at the beginning of the script:

```
MAP I:=MYSERVER/SYS:PUBLIC\CLIENT\DOSWIN32
#I:NWDETECT Novell_Client32 4.1.0
IF ERROR_LEVEL = "1" THEN
     #I:INSTALL
          IF ERROR_LEVEL = "0" THEN
               #I:NWSTAMP Novell_Client32 4.1.0
               #I:NWLOG /F I:\PUBLIC\CLIENT\DOSWIN32\LOG\UPDATE.LOG
               #I:REBOOT
          END
END
MAP DEL I:
```

During login, the container login script maps drive I to the SYS:PUBLIC\CLIENT\DOSWIN32 subdirectory. The NWDETECT.EXE utility then runs and looks in the workstation's NET.CFG file for an Install Stamp. In this case no Install Stamp exists, so NWDETECT returns an exit code of "1". This tells the script to keep processing because the workstation has not been upgraded.

Next, the INSTALL.EXE program is run. When the installation completes successfully, the INSTALL.EXE returns an exit code of "0". If the install does not complete successfully, an exit code of "1" is returned and the log file will not show this workstation as being updated.

The NWSTAMP.EXE utility runs next. Because no Install Stamp existed in the NET.CFG file, it creates one with the values indicated on the command line:

```
Install Stamp
     Name=Novell_Client32
     Major Version=4
     Minor Version=1
     Revision Version=0
```

The workstation is now set up with an updated Install Stamp so that the ACU process will be bypassed during subsequent logins. When a new version of the IntranetWare Client for DOS/Windows is available, the version stamp will be compared and the new version can be automatically installed.

Then the NWLOG.EXE utility runs. NWLOG.EXE appends the date and time of the update, the username, and the network and node address to the UPDATE.LOG file in the \LOG subdirectory of SYS:PUBLIC\CLIENT\DOSWIN32. Finally, the REBOOT.COM utility reboots the workstation so that the new client software can be loaded.

When the workstation reboots and the container login script runs, NWDETECT finds the Install Stamp in the NET.CFG file and detects a match for the four parameters. It returns an exit code of "0", which causes the login script to bypass the ACU instructions and proceed with the rest of the login script.

Most users will not need to modify INSTALL.CFG except for the ACU-specific settings under the [SETUP] heading. The only necessary modification is to change the InstallType= setting from BASIC to AUTO under the [SETUP] heading. You can use a text editor to do this.

The [SETUP] section of the INSTALL.CFG file is shown below, as it should appear with the InstallType set to AUTO:

```
[Setup]
InstallType = AUTO
TargetPath = *AUTO
InstallWindows = AUTO
WindowsUserPath = C:\WINDOWS
UpdateDOSSystemFiles = True
OverwriteStartnetBat = True
DoInstallIfLowSpace = True
CopyAllUnicodeFiles = False
OverwriteNewerFiles = False
OverwriteNewerINIFiles = False
OverwriteReadOnlyFiles = False
OverwriteReadOnlySYSFiles = False
Use32BitDrivers = True
UpdateRequester = False
```

In this section you have learned how to set up an Automatic Client Upgrade. By using the Automatic Client Upgrade functionality of the IntranetWare Client for DOS/Windows, you can easily deploy new client technology to all network desktops. The next section introduces the IntranetWare Client for Windows 95 and shows you how it works.

The IntranetWare Client for Windows 95

The IntranetWare Client for Windows 95 uses the same architecture and components as the IntranetWare Clients for DOS and Windows 3.1x. This section focuses on the specific installation and usage differences in Windows 95.

Installing IntranetWare Client for Windows 95

The installation process for the IntranetWare Client for Windows 95 is very simple. Just run the SETUP.EXE that comes with the client. The first screen you see enables you to view the readme file, the help file, or continue. You might also see a check box on the initial screen that indicates that ODI will be the default LAN driver type. If you uncheck this box then NDIS will be your default LAN driver type. The selection box will not be on the screen if ODI has already been selected as your default LAN driver type. The client supports both Novell's ODI specification and Microsoft's NDIS specification for LAN drivers. Because Windows 95 was only designed to handle one driver specification you might have difficulties getting connected to the network. For example, if you selected to use NDIS but the NDIS driver didn't work, you would need to reinstall and select ODI as the default LAN driver type. Conversely, you would need to delete the ODI drivers from the Windows\INF directory if they were not functioning properly. If your machine is hanging on boot up, you can disable networking components from loading by editing the Windows 95 MSDOS.SYS file and changing the parameter for loading of network components.

Note If the installation is not successful, run the UNC32.EXE that is available on Novell's technical support web site at **`http://support.novell.com/client/home`**. This uninstall program removes the client load commands from the startup process and from the Windows 95 registry.

When the client is installed, the registry is stamped with the version of the client that was installed. This version key is in the following location:

```
MyComputer\HKEY_LOCAL_MACHINE\Network\Novell\SystemConfig\Install\ClientVersion
```

Notice Level, Major Version, Minor Version, and Revision. Novell uses the first three values to update the client software. The Revision level is available for network administrators to use in the Automatic Client Upgrade (ACU) process. The ACU is built into the SETUP.EXE program of the Windows 95 client. If the location you are installing from includes an ADMIN.CFG and/or a NWSETUP.INI file, the settings in these files will be made available to all workstations that install from that area. These files allow specifying Preferred Tree, Preferred Server, and the other advanced parameters. Notice in the following samples from the ADMIN.CFG and NWSETUP.INI files that administrators can customize individual parameters and version information that is stamped in the registry.

```
ADMIN.CFG
     NETWARE DOS REQUESTER
          PREFERRED TREE=ACME

NWSETUP.INI
     [ClientVersion]
     Version=2.1.1.0
     [AcuOptions]
     DisplayFirstScreen=NO
     DisplayLastScreen=NO
```

In addition to the setup configuration provided by Novell, network administrators can also install the IntranetWare Client as they are installing Windows 95. This Microsoft process is called *MSBATCH*. The MSBATCH process is somewhat complicated, but if hundreds of workstation installs are planned, administrators can save time by installing both the client and Windows 95 simultaneously. A limitation of the MSBATCH install method is that it can only install NDIS drivers and not ODI drivers.

Using IntranetWare Client for Windows 95

The IntranetWare Client for Windows 95 uses the Windows 95 built-in interfaces of My Computer, Explorer, and Network Neighborhood. You can browse network drive mappings, log in to a file server, map network drives, and modify client settings through these interfaces. To set up printing, for example, simply set up a new printer icon in the Printer folder and select a network print queue.

A new feature with this client is the ability to set directory and file rights without using NWADMIN. Simply select the network file and click the right mouse button to display the following dialog box (see fig. 15.13).

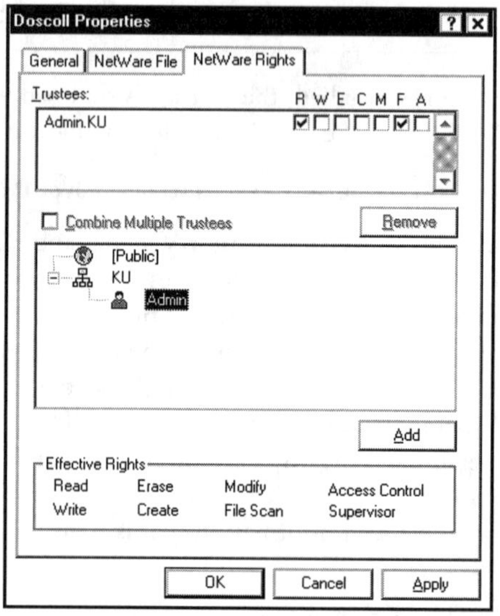

Figure 15.13
Setting trustee rights on a file.

From this interface you can browse the NDS tree and select individual users, groups, or containers to grant rights to a directory or file.

You can use the Network Neighborhood to browse for all network resources. Both Novell and Microsoft networking resources can be accessed through this interface. You are prompted to log in to any network resources that you are not already logged in to as you browse the network using Network Neighborhood. Microsoft resources are available if you have loaded *Microsoft's Server Message Block* (SMB) peer-to-peer client. The IntranetWare Client for Windows 95 coexists with the Microsoft client allowing for access to both sets of resources.

Microsoft also offers a *File and Printer Sharing for NetWare Networks* (FPNW). FPNW does not work with the IntranetWare Client for Windows 95. The CLIENT32.NLM component of the IntranetWare Client determines which level of NCPs to use for communication with the file server. If the file server is 3.12 or above, advanced CASE 87 NCPs are used for communication. If the file server is older than 3.12, CASE 22 NCPs are used. Windows 95 workstations can load a service, called File and Printer Sharing for NetWare Networks (FPNW), that works like an IntranetWare file server by allowing for sharing of file and print functions. FPNW will not work with workstations running the IntranetWare Client. If this is the case, FPNW incorrectly reports back to the IntranetWare Client that it is a 3.12 file server. The Client then attempts to use CASE 87 NCPs, which the FPNW service does not understand because it is an implementation that uses CASE 22 NCPs. As of this writing, a revised FPNW is not available.

Users can modify all client settings by clicking on the Network icon in the Control Panel folder. The dialog box shown in figure 15.14 appears.

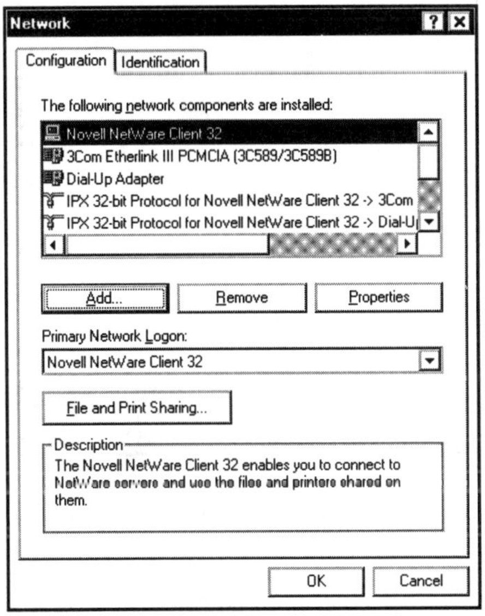

Figure 15.14
Windows 95 Network Control Panel.

Notice that Novell leverages the Microsoft TCP/IP stack rather than providing one of their own. From this screen, a user simply selects IntranetWare Client component and clicks on the Configure button. From here, a user can configure their client network setting.

Figure 15.15 shows the Client 32 tab, which has the following options:

- **Preferred server.** Determines the server the Client will attempt to attach to first upon login.
- **Preferred tree.** Establishes the default tree used at login.
- **Name context.** Sets the context for the user object so that they can simply enter their username when logging in.
- **First network drive.** The first drive that can be mapped to network resources.

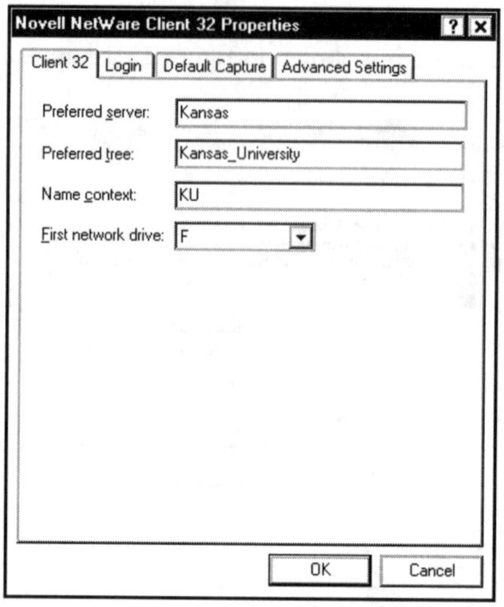

Figure 15.15
The Client 32 tab.

The Login tab is shown in figure 15.16. The following options are available:

- **Display Connection Page.** Users can specify if they would like to log in to a server by default or a tree. Server login is required with NetWare 3.x or if bindery emulation is required. By deselecting the check box at the top of the 'Display' pages user will not see tab page and associated options when the login prompt appears.

- **Display Script Page.** Use the Script boxes to specify the path to a login script other than the default scripts in NetWare or IntranetWare. The login script results window may stay open after login even if the Close script results automatically option is selected. This is because the results windows does not close if an error occurred in the login script.

- **Display Variable Page.** This option could be used for legacy DOS applications that still run under Windows 95 and need environment variables set.

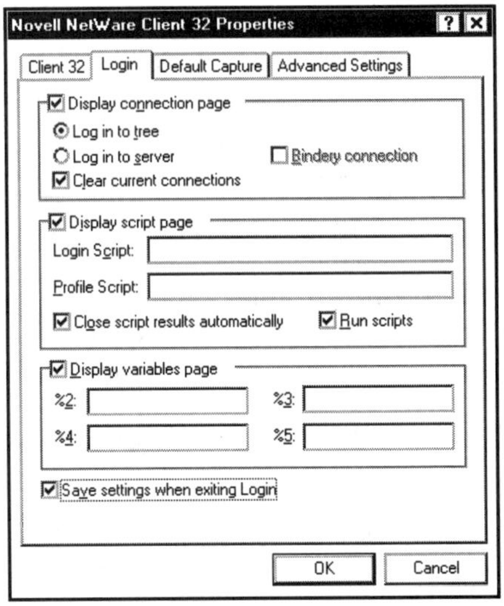

Figure 15.16
The Login tab.

Figure 15.17 shows the Default Capture tab. With this tab, you can set the following options:

- **Output Settings.** Enables users to specify number of copies and other print settings. The settings on this page will only be used if you are using a CAPTURE statement to establish your print environment. Windows 95 printing is usually created and configured in the 'Printer' folder.
- **Banner Settings.** Establishes the name printed on the banner page.
- **Other Settings.** Sets print options used when capturing a port.

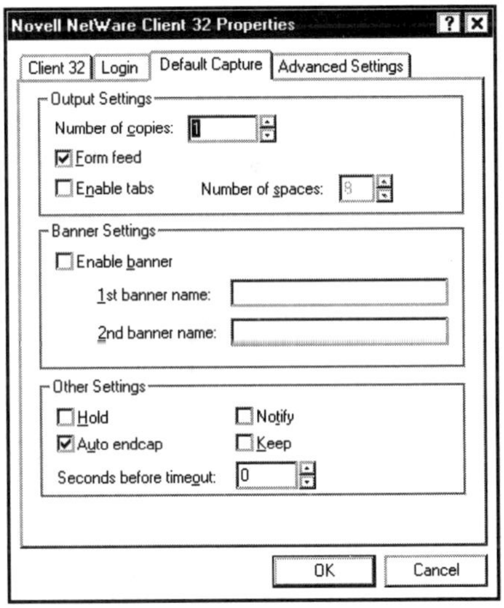

Figure 15.17
The Default Capture tab.

> **Note** Print capture settings made on this tab page are only valid for legacy capture statements. For example, a capture statement made in a login script. Most printing is done from the Windows 95 Printers interface as described earlier.

The Advanced Settings tab is shown if figure 15.18. The following options are available:

- **Connection.** Default values for all Advances Settings is usually sufficient. Only make changes as necessary. The client has several dynamic parameters and self tunes for optimal operation. Connection settings such as NetWare Protocol can be set here.
- **Environment, NETX Compatibility.** Select values for NWLanguage and other environment settings.
- **File System.** Database modifications or specific changes for Read Only Compatibility can be set here.
- **Packet Management.** Large Internet Pact and other packet settings.
- **Performance, Cache.** Increase performance by increasing cache size and other cache parameters.
- **Printing.** Specify Print Tail and other print settings.
- **Troubleshooting.** Set the size of the error Log File and other options.
- **WAN.** Configure the level of WAN performance by modifying settings such as Minimum Time To Net.

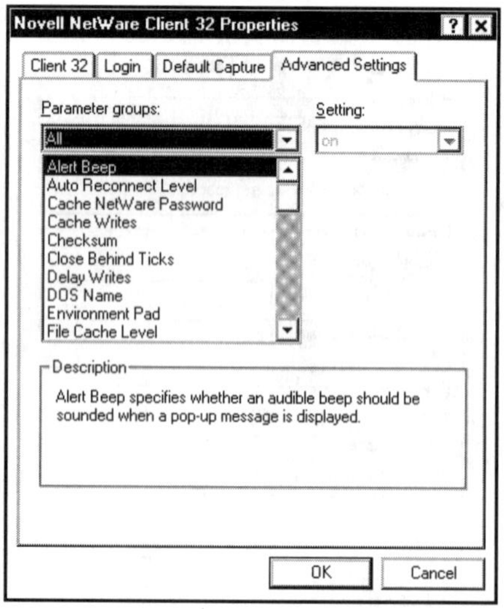

Figure 15.18
The Advanced Settings tab.

The Advanced Settings can also be viewed by category. For example, if you are trying to adjust the performance of your workstation, you would select the Performance option from the drop list and modify those parameters.

Tip

> If you installed an earlier versions of Novell IntranetWare Client for Windows 95, you might have had problems with data corruption on CC:Mail or database products. This was caused by the advanced setting called Opportunistic Locking. This setting should be set to Off. The setting was completely removed from newer versions of the client.

Summary

In this chapter you learned the architecture of the IntranetWare Client for DOS/Windows and Windows 95. The 32-bit networking provided by these clients makes them superior to the previous NETX and VLM clients. You have also learned how to install the IntranetWare Clients and automatically upgrade workstation software with the Automatic Client Upgrade process. The IntranetWare Clients include many features such as client-side caching, Large Internet Packet support, and a 32-bit version of the NetWare Administrator for Windows 95. With the IntranetWare clients, users can seamlessly interface with and manage their network the desktop of their choice.

CHAPTER 16

Supporting Non-DOS Workstations

NetWare has long provided services for DOS/Windows clients. Other clients such as OS/2, Unix, Windows NT, and Windows 95 are becoming more important. Therefore, Novell has aggressively pursued the goal of enabling IntranetWare to provide services to a variety of computer environments.

Currently, IntranetWare provides connectivity for Macintosh, OS/2, Unix, and Windows 95/NT computers. This connectivity is provided through a variety of protocol and file-support options that can be installed on the server or the client.

By adding AppleTalk protocol support for connectivity, Apple Filing Protocol support for file access, and AppleTalk Print Service Protocol support for printing on your IntranetWare server, you enable your Macintosh users to access files on a NetWare server and print to NetWare printers as though the resources were installed on a standard Macintosh network. By installing IntranetWare Client for Macintosh on your Macintosh clients, you enable them to access resources on NetWare networks using IP and IPX, in addition to servers running their native AppleTalk protocol.

By adding IntranetWare Client for OS/2 to OS/2 clients you enable transparent access to NetWare resources using NDS and Novell's IPX/SPX protocols, or IBM's TCP/IP to reach NetWare/IP enabled IntranetWare servers.

Unix workstations are also supported using Novell's Unix Print Services and NFS Services as well as through the many NetWare server connectivity options available on the Unix servers.

Windows NT users can also be integrated into the IntranetWare network by adding Microsoft's Gateway Services for NetWare onto the NT server, and through the addition of the Novell's IntranetWare Client for NT.

This chapter discusses the support IntranetWare provides for Macintosh, OS/2 and Unix workstations, and for Windows NT users.

Macintosh

Every Macintosh station comes with a built-in LocalTalk adapter that communicates at speeds up to 254 KB per second. If you want higher communication speeds, Token-Ring or Ethernet NICs can be used on Macintosh stations equipped with expansion slots. The native protocol used by Macintosh workstations is AppleTalk. For an IntranetWare server to coexist with Macintosh workstations running their native AppleTalk protocols, the IntranetWare server must support AppleTalk protocols as well.

Figure 16.1 shows that the IntranetWare server runs a dual protocol stack that consists of the native NCP/SPX/IPX stack and the AppleTalk protocol stack. The Service Protocol Gateway (SPG) translates Apple File Protocol requests issued by Macintosh workstations to NCP requests at the server. The SPG then translates the NCP responses of the IntranetWare server to AFP responses before they are relayed to the requesting workstation. This procedure creates the illusion that the IntranetWare server is a Macintosh server.

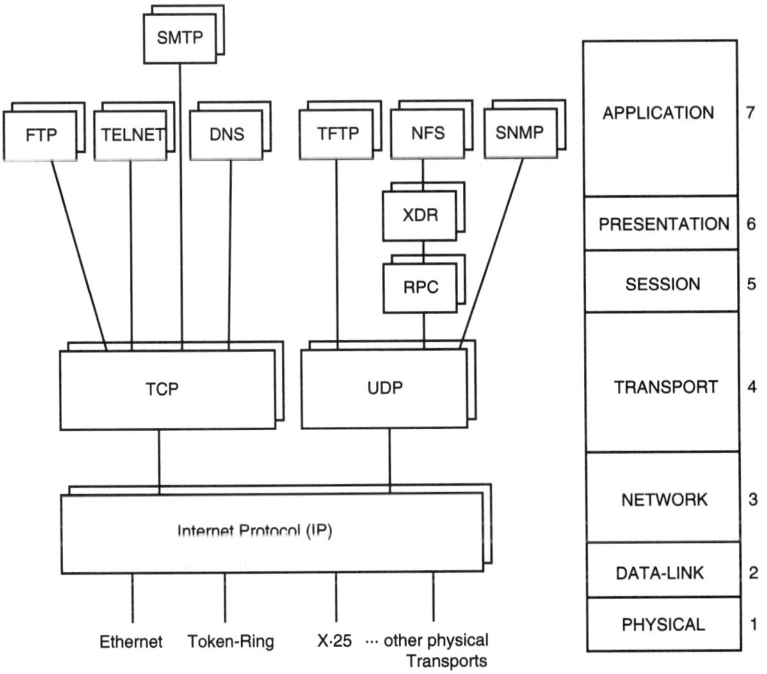

Figure 16.1
A Macintosh workstation. (Graphic courtesy of Learning Group International.)

The AppleTalk protocol stack is implemented as an NLM on NetWare 3.x/4.x. The client software that runs on Macintosh workstations is their native AppleShare. Macintosh workstations see the NetWare servers as AppleShare servers. This enables Macintosh users to use the familiar AppleShare interface; for instance, they can use the Chooser program to select the NetWare server.

From the Macintosh workstation's perspective, the IntranetWare server looks just like an AppleShare server, and the Macintosh user can use the familiar Chooser program to log in to the IntranetWare server and access the NetWare volumes.

Most of the complexity of setting up Macintosh stations on a NetWare network is at the server. The discussion that follows is for configuring the IntranetWare server to act as an AppleShare server.

Configuring IntranetWare Servers as AppleTalk Servers

Configuring an IntranetWare server to act as an AppleTalk server consists of the following steps. When the IntranetWare server is installed, the MACINTOSH name space and AppleTalk NLMs are loaded by default, but configuration of the AppleTalk protocol stack and file/printer services is still required.

1. On the system console, load INSTALL. Then select Product Options.
2. Select Choose an Item or Product listed above. Then scroll down the list to Install NetWare for Macintosh. The files are copied to the server.
3. A screen appears asking which drives you want MAC name space added to, and whether the AppleTalk File and Print Services should be added to the AUTOEXEC.NCF file. You can also select whether or not to install the Macintosh client support files into the SYS: volume. To install the client support files, the volume must have the MAC name space added.
4. A screen for NetWare for Macintosh configuration appears. This screen provides links to the configuration modules for the AppleTalk Stack, File Services, Print Services, and HFS CD-ROM services (INETCFG.NLM, AFSCON.NLM, AFPSCON.NLM, and HFCDCON.NLM respectively). Each of these configuration tools can be loaded manually from the system console.
5. From the Configuration menu, select Configure AppleTalk Stack. This starts the INETCFG utility. Select Protocols to enable and disable the protocol and configure routing parameters. Then select Bindings, press Insert and select the AppleTalk protocol to be bound to a board. A list of available boards is displayed. Exit back to the NetWare for Macintosh Configuration menu.
6. Next select Configure File Services. This starts the AFP Configuration Console (AFPCON.NLM). Use this console to configure general server information, user information, and other file service performance parameters. Exit back to the NetWare for Macintosh Configuration menu.
7. Select Configure Print Services. This starts the Print Services Console (ATPSCON.NLM). This configures printer models, print servers, print queues, log options, and other management parameters. Exit to the NetWare for Macintosh Configuration menu.
8. AppleTalk is now configured on the IntranetWare server. You should verify that the AUTOEXEC.NCF file contains the lines 'load AFP' and 'load ATPS' and any other required parameters. These parameters are explained in greater detail in the sections that follow. The STARTUP.NCF file should already contain the line 'load MAC' (this can be moved to the AUTOEXEC.NCF file). You can verify this by pressing Esc until you get back to the main INSTALL menu, and then selecting NCF Files Options.
9. You can get back to the NetWare for Macintosh Configuration menu at any time by loading INSTALL, selecting Product Options, then selecting View/Configure/Remove Installed Products. Select NW-MAC from the list of displayed products.

AUTOEXEC.NCF File Parameters for AppleTalk

The following listing shows a typical AUTOEXEC.NCF file containing additional parameters that can be required for an AppleTalk network. When installing and configuring the AppleTalk protocol, if you elect to have network configuration commands moved from the AUTOEXEC.NCF, then not all of the commands shown appear in your AUTOEXEC.NCF file. The same parameters still need to be configured through the INETCFG.NLM. A description of the configurable parameters follow in listing 16.1.

Listing 16.1

```
load appletlk net=50001 zone={"Admin"}

load  ne2000 int=2  port=300  frame=ethenet_snap name=EtherNet1
load  dl2000  int=3  port=200  name=LocalTalk1

bind  appletlk EtherNet1 net=1-4 zone={"Admin", "Dept1"}
bind  appletlk  LocalTalk1  net=6  zone={"Dept2"}

load afp
load atps
```

The APPLETLK.NLM contains the AppleTalk protocols and the AppleTalk router. The AFP.NLM and ATPS.NLM implement the Apple Filing Protocol and the Apple Print Services (see fig. 16.2). The AppleTalk routing in figure 16.2 is performed at the level of the Datagram Delivery Protocol (DDP) by the Routing Table Maintenance Protocol (RTMP).

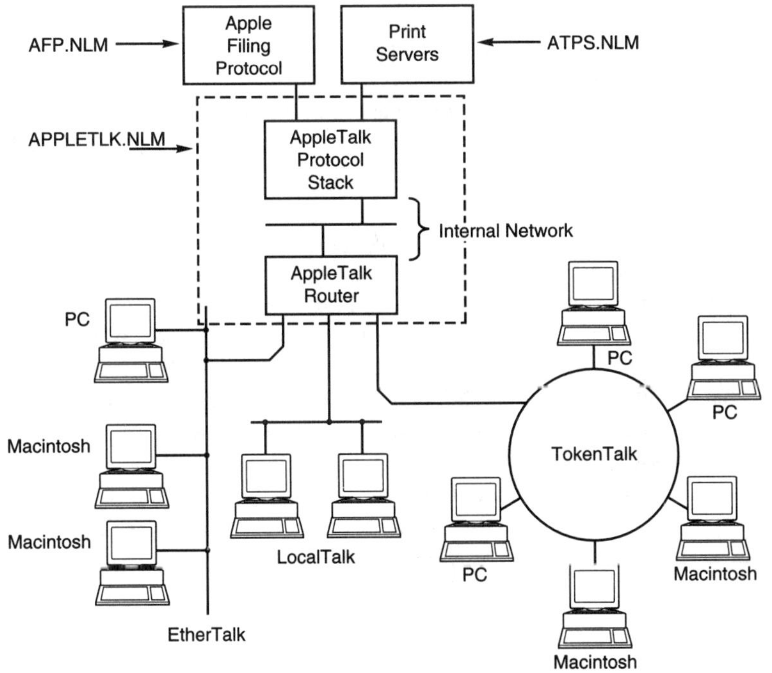

Figure 16.2
AppleTalk modules and Internal Routing.

When the LOAD APPLETLK command is issued, the AppleTalk routing and communication protocols (ASP, ATP, DDP) are loaded.

The LOAD NE2000 and LOAD DL2000 commands load the drivers for Ethernet and LocalTalk respectively. This configuration is for a network of the type shown in figure 16.3 that has an Ethernet and LocalTalk board installed in the server. The Ethernet network must use the SNAP protocol for encapsulating upper-layer AppleTalk protocols, and, therefore, the FRAME=ETHERNET_SNAP parameter must be specified when the driver is loaded. Because the DL2000 driver uses the standard LocalTalk Link Access Protocol (LLAP), no frame parameter is required.

Figure 16.3
An example of an AppleTalk network.

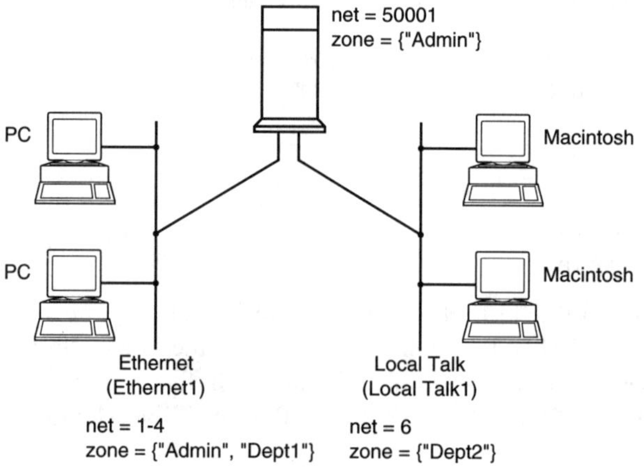

The BIND statements specify the binding of the AppleTalk protocols to the NIC drivers. The NET=1-4 may look peculiar but is used to refer to the fact that Extended network addressing is being used to support Extended Networks. Extended Networks were defined at the time AppleTalk Phase 2 protocols were defined to overcome the shortcomings of AppleTalk Phase 1 protocols. AppleTalk Phase 1 protocols could not have more than 254 node addresses per physical network segment. This was due to the fact that the network address field in LLAP is 8 bits long. Modern networks, such as Ethernet and Token-Ring, can easily have more than 254 node addresses on a physical network segment. To support these networks, a network range was defined. The actual node address consisted of network number and a node number pair. Each network number could have associated with it 254 node addresses. Thus, a network range of NET=1-4 can have 4 ′ 254 = 1,016 node addresses. LocalTalk networks are unchanged in AppleTalk Phase 2. Thus, you see the NET=6, which is a single network number. This is semantically equivalent to using a NET=6-6 network range. The network range is a pair of numbers that must be between 1 and 65,279. Physical segments cannot have overlapping numbers, otherwise the AppleTalk router would get confused. All AppleTalk routers connected to the same physical network must have the same network-number range. This is similar to the rule for connecting IPX routers to the same physical network.

The BIND parameters specify a zone parameter. Zones are a logical grouping of devices on an AppleTalk network that make it easier to locate devices through the Chooser panel. Searches for resources on a network are always done in the context of the currently selected zone. The user is free to pick other zones through the Chooser panel. Normally, the current zone is the same as the default zone. The default zone can be changed by the user through the Macintosh Control Panel.

The LOAD AFP and LOAD ATPS commands load the AppleTalk Filing Protocol and Print Service protocols.

One of the areas of potential confusion experienced by network administrators for Macintosh networks is the assignment of zone names. The following discussion will clarify some of these issues.

Zones are used to narrow the search for resources on the network. A user belonging to the "Engineering" department, for example, normally needs to see only those resources belonging to his department and should not be presented with resources for other departments. Occasionally, a user may need to access network resources belonging to another department, in which case, a facility exists to make the selection. In this discussion, departments of an organization are used to logically divide the network. Other logical groupings are possible such as grouping by physical location for "Building1," "Building2," and so on. These logical divisions have a name assigned to them called the zone name.

In the example of the AUTOEXEC.NCF file, several zone names are used. The first is the zone name used with the LOAD APPLETLK command. This zone name refers to the internal AppleTalk network within the server. This internal network number must have a network number and a zone name assigned to it. It is treated as a non-extended Phase 2 network and, therefore, has a single network number assigned to it. It is a good idea to choose network numbers with a high value for internal network numbering to distinguish between other network numbers. The internal network is contained within the AppleTalk module (refer to figure 16.2) and does not have any physical components. When the internal AppleTalk receives a file request for the AppleTalk server, it routes it as it would any other packet. Because the AppleTalk server is in the same module as the AppleTalk router, the packet is sent directly through the internal network to the server. The AppleTalk server with the given zone name and its print services will show up in the list for the zone name to which they belong. Zone names are represented as quoted (") strings. They can be 32 characters long and can even include spaces.

Zone names also must be specified in the BIND command. For extended networks, multiple zone names (up to 255) are possible. This is seen in the BIND NE2000 example. For non-extended networks (Phase 1 networks), a single zone name must be used as seen in the BIND DL2000 example. In extended networks, the first zone name listed becomes the default zone. If there are several routers connected to the same physical network segment, they must agree about the zone name or zone list assigned to it. Because the default zone is the first zone name, the zone list for each router must begin with the same zone name.

For complex networks, the number of possible zones in the zone list can become quite large. Because there is a limit of 82 characters for the BIND command, it is not always possible to list all the zone names on the command line. To solve this problem, the -z option can be used when the AppleTalk protocol stack is loaded:

```
LOAD APPLETLK  NET=5001 -Z
```

The -z option causes the LOAD APPLETLK command to look for the file ATZONES.CFG in the SYS:SYSTEM directory. This file can be created by a text editor and is a list of the network range and zone list pairs. An example of an ATZONES.CFG file is shown in listing 16.2.

Listing 16.2

```
net=50002 zone={"Control"}
net=50003 zone={"Control"}
net=50004 zone={"Control"}

net=10-15 zone={"Control", "Building1", "Building2"}
net=16-20 zone={
"Building3",
"Building4",
"Building5"
}

net=21-25 zone={"Manufacturing", "Marketing }
```

Essentially, the ATZONES.CFG file contains a mapping between net numbers and associated zone names.

Typically, a user selects the zone name as top-level organizer for accessing the network resources in the Chooser panel. After a zone name is selected, the user clicks on the service icon. This causes the Macintosh station to send Name Binding Protocol (NBP) broadcasts for the service in the selected zone. Any intervening routers will re-broadcast the NBP request to the appropriate networks. The routers directly connected to the selected zone broadcast the NBP request to all nodes in that zone. The nodes that provide the service send an NBP reply packet containing their names. These names are then displayed in the Chooser panel.

Zone names are maintained by the AppleTalk network routers. After a router discovers a new router through the RTMP protocol, it sends a Zone Information Protocol (ZIP) request to that router querying it for its zone information. The zone information is cached by all the routers, and as long as the router has a good entry in the RTMP table, another zone query is not issued. Routers are not automatically informed about changes in zone configuration. This becomes a problem if the zone name is deleted; it will show up as a valid zone name in the Chooser for Macintosh computers, even though it does not exist. The only way to update zone information in the list is to force the RTMP tables to change. This can be done by isolating a network segment and waiting for the RTMP protocol to detect the change. This procedure can take between 10 to 20 minutes, or longer, in a large AppleTalk Internet. The other approach is to reset all routers by bringing them down and up again.

IntranetWare Client for Macintosh OS

IntranetWare Client for Macintosh OS gives Macintosh OS-based workstations access to NetWare resources using Novell Directory Services. IntranetWare Client for Macintosh OS enables Macintosh OS users to locate NetWare file and print services in a Novell Directory Services tree, regardless of whether AppleTalk and NetWare for Macintosh are running on the servers on which the services are located. The MACINTOSH client can use IP, IPX, or AppleTalk protocols either individually or simultaneously.

In addition, it lets network supervisors manage Macintosh OS clients the way they administer Windows, DOS, and other clients. IntranetWare Client for Macintosh OS also eliminates the need for NetWare for Macintosh on the server, but is still compatible with NetWare for Macintosh so network managers can upgrade their clients over time. Macintosh OS users can drag and drop NDS objects that are frequently used to the desktop, and log into multiple NDS trees simultaneously. A remote console utility is also included that allows remote management of an IntranetWare server from a Macintosh OS workstation.

IntranetWare Client for Macintosh OS requires the following hardware and software:

- A Macintosh OS-based workstation with a 68030 or better processor
- 5 MB of available memory
- System 7.1 or later
- NetWare 4.1 or later

Installing IntranetWare Client for Macintosh

Installing the IntranetWare Client for Macintosh OS consists of performing the following steps:

1. Install the IntranetWare Client for Macintosh OS software to the Macintosh OS-based workstation.
2. Install MACFILE.NLM on the IntranetWare server.

There are several ways to load the IntranetWare Client for Macintosh OS software onto the Macintosh workstations.

- For Macintosh workstations with CD-ROM drives, the software can be loaded directly from the IntranetWare CD-ROM onto the Macintosh workstation.
- Macintosh workstations without CD-ROM drives can install the software from an IntranetWare server running NetWare for Macintosh. The client files must be extracted and uncompressed onto a volume on the IntranetWare server that has the Macintosh Name Space loaded on it. Log the Macintosh workstation into the IntranetWare server and click on the Installer icon.

Installing the Client Software on a Macintosh Workstation with a CD-ROM

To install IntranetWare Client for Macintosh OS, follow these steps after closing all open applications:

1. Insert the CD-ROM and double-click on the Macintosh OS Clients Installer icon, or go to the \PRODUCTS\NWCMAC\ENGLISH and double-click on the NW Client Installer icon.

2. Click the Install button at the bottom of the NW Client Installer window. An alert warns you that the workstation will restart after the installation is complete.

3. Click the Yes button. (To prevent the installation from taking place, select the No button.)

4. When the software has been installed, click the Restart button to restart the workstation.

Installing From an IntranetWare Server

Macintosh OS workstations can also load the IntranetWare Client for Macintosh OS directly from an IntranetWare server running NetWare for Macintosh. The files must be copied onto a volume on the server that has the Macintosh Name Space loaded on it. The Client software files are available on the IntranetWare CD-ROM in the \PRODUCTS\NWCMAC\ENGLISH directory.

1. On the system console, load INSTALL.

2. Select Product Options, then select an item or product listed above.

3. Select Install NetWare Client for Macintosh OS. This copies the installer file for the Macintosh OS files into the /PUBLIC/CLIENT/MAC/ENGLISH directory.

4. From the Macintosh OS, log into the IntranetWare server. Follow the previous directions starting at step 1 for installing the software from a CD-ROM drive on the Macintosh workstation. Browse for the Installer icon on the IntranetWare server instead of on the workstation's CD-ROM drive.

Installing MACFILE.NLM on the IntranetWare Server

IntranetWare Client for Macintosh OS includes one NLM, MACFILE.NLM, that you should install on the server. When you install the NetWare Client for Macintosh OS files to the IntranetWare server using INSTALL, MACFILE.NLM is automatically loaded into the AUTOEXEC.NCF. You may also manually add the NLM by typing:

```
load MACFILE
```

on the system console. When you install MACFILE.NLM, additional support files are also installed on the server.

You may also install and load MACFILE.NLM remotely from the Macintosh OS workstation. Because you install MACFILE.NLM and the other server components on the SYS volume of a server, you must have sufficient rights to copy files to the SYS volume.

To install the server components from the Macintosh Client workstation to the server, follow these steps:

1. After the client components have been installed, locate the NetWare Directory Services Tree icon in the upper-right corner of the workstation screen, and choose the Login option in the Directory Services menu.

2. Enter the requested information in the dialog that appears, including your name, password, context, and the name of the tree that contains the server in which you want to install the server components. The Tree and Context information might already be entered by default. Select the More Options button, if all of the items do not appear.

3. After you are logged into the Directory tree, you need to mount a NetWare server SYS volume on your workstation desktop so you can install the server components. The NetWare Client Utilities Folder is installed at the root of the workstation's startup volume.

   To mount a volume, open the NetWare Directory Browser application in the NetWare Client Utilities Folder on the workstation. Then, locate the volume's icon in the Items pane of the NetWare Directory Browser window and double-click on it.

   If you do not see any volumes, make sure you are at the correct context and you have the NCP Server and Volume object types selected in the Show Types pane of the Browser window.

4. After the SYS volume is mounted, locate the SERVER folder contained in the Macintosh Client folder, extracted from MACCLT.SEA.

5. Copy the SERVER folder to the SYS volume of the server.

6. Go to the server console or use the IntranetWare Client for Macintosh OS Remote Console utility to complete the server component installation.

   If you choose to use the server console, go directly to step 7. If you choose to use the Remote Console utility, you must install and configure additional client and server components. To do this, continue reading this step.

   Remote Console is the Macintosh version of the DOS RCONSOLE utility. Remote Console also requires RSPX.NLM and REMOTE.NLM to be loaded on the IntranetWare server to function. Remote Console is not installed on the Macintosh workstation when you perform an Easy Install. To install Remote Console, double-click the NW Client Installer icon. Click on the Custom button. Highlight the Remote Console Install option in the list of install packages. Click on the Install button.

7. At the server console (or Remote Console window), type the following command:

   ```
   LOAD INSTALL
   ```

8. Choose the Product Options option in the Installation Options menu.

9. Choose the Install a Product Not Listed option in the Other Installation Actions menu.

10. Press F3 and enter the path to which you copied the server files. If the SERVER folder was copied to the root of the SYS volume on a NetWare 4.1 server, the path would be:

    ```
    SYS:SERVER\INSTALL
    ```

11. From the Install NetWare Client for Macintosh OS menu, select the Easy Install option. The Easy Installation Summary screen appears.

12. Press Esc to close the summary.

13. Select the Proceed with the Installation option.

14. Upon completion of the installation, the Other Installation Actions menu appears. Press Esc twice and choose Yes from the Exit Install menu.

15. At the server console, type the following command:

    ```
    LOAD MACFILE
    ```

When you are finished installing the server software, you can delete the Server folder you copied to the server in step 5, or you can keep that folder on the server and use it to install the IntranetWare Client for Macintosh OS server software on other IntranetWare servers.

IntranetWare Client for OS/2

Novell's IntranetWare Client for OS/2 packages the features of the previously available OS/2 LAN Requestor with several new features. It now provides NDS support for global WIN-OS/2 and DOS sessions so that NDS aware applications can be run in WIN-OS/2 sessions. Several performance enhancements were added, and 32-bit IPX/SPX calls have been provided so that true 32-bit NetWare aware applications can be written for the OS/2 platform.

The IntranetWare Client for OS/2 is a group of OS/2 ODI drivers that load in the OS/2 workstations CONFIG.SYS file and allow the OS/2 workstation to connect to a NetWare 2.x, 3.x, 4.x, and IntranetWare server. The components of an OS/2 IntranetWare Client workstation resemble the ODI architecture discussed for DOS workstations because OS/2 NIC drivers are based on the ODI specification. The Link Support Layer provides a logical network interface for the protocol stacks to bind to. In addition to IPX/SPX support, Novell Named Pipes and Novell NetBIOS are also supported. The IntranetWare Client ODI drivers can coexist on the OS/2 workstation with NDIS applications and IBM's TCP/IP stack. Using the

ODINSUP and LANSUP drivers provided with the IntranetWare Client, or using IBM's ODI2NDI.OS2, the IntranetWare Client can share a single NIC with NDIS and TCP/IP applications.

The IntranetWare Client for OS/2 supports OS/2 version 3.0 Warp, 2.11, and 2.10. In addition, there are several other product dependencies that may require additional configuration of the IntranetWare client. If IBM's Extended Services, LAN Server, or LAN Requester have been installed, refer to the IntranetWare Client documentation for additional configuration details.

Installing IntranetWare Client for OS/2

During installation of the IntranetWare Client on the OS/2 workstation, a Novell folder is added to the desktop that contains icons for the Install utility, Network Printer, NetWare Tools, documentation, and the NetWare Target Service Agent for Backup (TSA). The installation makes changes to the OS/2 CONFIG.SYS file to load the required ODI drivers. Minor manual changes to the CONFIG.SYS might also be required.

A NET.CFG file is not created. In most instances where the default NIC and protocol settings are adequate, a NET.CFG file is not required. If advanced configuration of the NIC or network is required, the NET.CFG must be manually created as described in the following section, "NET.CFG for OS/2 IntranetWare Workstations." The NET.CFG is similar, but not identical to a DOS workstation NET.CFG file.

Installing the IntranetWare Client for OS/2 involves two main tasks. Install the IntranetWare Client for OS/2 on the OS/2 workstation, then install the IntranetWare utilities for OS/2 on the IntranetWare file server. These steps are explained in detail in the following sections. You can also add the Remote Initial Program Load capability for diskless workstations if desired.

To install the IntranetWare Client, the associated drivers for link support, and the SPX/IPX protocols, run the INSTALL program located on the REQUESTER disk. Install the IntranetWare OS/2 components in the C:\NETWARE directory on the OS/2 workstation hard disk.

To install the IntranetWare Client, follow these steps:

1. Boot the workstation with OS/2 and select either OS/2 window or OS/2 full-screen from the Group-Main window.

2. Insert the REQUESTER disk in drive A and type the following at the OS/2 prompt:

   ```
   A:INSTALL
   ```

3. Follow the instructions to select the installation directory. The default is C:\NETWARE. The installation program guides you through the process.

4. Edit the CONFIG.SYS file to enable the network driver for the NIC in the OS/2 workstation. You usually must remove the REM (remark) comment that precedes the DEVICE= statement for the NIC driver. You should also remove the CONNECTIONS parameter from the SET AUTOSTART= statement

Listing 16.3 shows the CONFIG.SYS file for an OS/2 IntranetWare workstation. The CONFIG.SYS statements are grouped for easy identification. Most of the CONFIG.SYS commands deal with OS/2 configuration. Toward the end of the CONFIG.SYS are the IntranetWare Client components (also called the NetWare Requester). Before the NetWare requester component (NWREQ.SYS) is activated, a number of support components, such as link support, NIC driver, and protocol stack, must be activated. A number of statements dealing with other protocols such as SPX, Named Pipes, and NetBIOS are commented out. If these components are needed for the OS/2 workstation, the REM that precedes them must be removed.

Listing 16.3

```
IFS=C:\OS2\HPFS.IFS  /CACHE:512 /CRECL:4 /AUTOCHECK:C
PROTSHELL=C:\OS2\PMSHELL.EXE
SET USER_INI=C:\OS2\OS2.INI
SET SYSTEM_INI=C:\OS2\OS2SYS.INI
SET OS2_SHELL=C:\OS2\CMD.EXE
SET AUTOSTART=PROGRAMS,TASKLIST,FOLDERS,CONNECTIONS
SET RUNWORKPLACE=C:\OS2\PMSHELL.EXE
SET COMSPEC=C:\OS2\CMD.EXE
LIBPATH=.;C:\OS2\DLL;C:\OS2\MDOS;C:\;C:\OS2\APPS\DLL;C:\NETWARE;
SET PATH=C:\OS2;C:\OS2\SYSTEM;C:\OS2\MDOS\WINOS2;C:\OS2\INSTALL;C:\
;C:\OS2\MDOS;C:\OS2\APPS;L:\OS2;P:\OS2;C:\NETWARE;
SET DPATH=C:\OS2;C:\OS2\SYSTEM;C:\OS2\MDOS\WINOS2;C:\OS2\INSTALL;C:\
;C:\OS2\BITMAP;C:\OS2\MDOS;C:\OS2\APPS;C:\NETWARE;P:\OS2;
SET PROMPT=$i[$p]
SET HELP=C:\OS2\HELP;C:\OS2\HELP\TUTORIAL;
SET GLOSSARY=C:\OS2\HELP\GLOSS;
SET IPF_KEYS=SBCS
PRIORITY_DISK_IO=YES
FILES=20
DEVICE=C:\OS2\TESTCFG.SYS
DEVICE=C:\OS2\DOS.SYS
DEVICE=C:\OS2\PMDD.SYS
BUFFERS=30
IOPL=YES
DISKCACHE=64,LW
MAXWAIT=3
MEMMAN=SWAP,PROTECT
SWAPPATH=C:\OS2\SYSTEM 2048 2048
BREAK=OFF
THREADS=256
PRINTMONBUFSIZE=134,134,134
COUNTRY=001,C:\OS2\SYSTEM\COUNTRY.SYS
SET KEYS=ON
REM SET DELDIR=C:\DELETE,512;D:\DELETE,512;
```

```
BASEDEV=PRINT01.SYS
BASEDEV=IBM1FLPY.ADD
BASEDEV=OS2DASD.DMD
SET EPMPATH=C:\OS2\APPS
SET FAXPM=C:\OS2\APPS
DEVICE=C:\OS2\APPS\SASYNCDA.SYS
PROTECTONLY=NO
SHELL=C:\OS2\MDOS\COMMAND.COM C:\OS2\MDOS /P
FCBS=16,8
RMSIZE=640
DEVICE=C:\OS2\MDOS\VEMM.SYS
DOS=LOW,NOUMB
DEVICE=C:\OS2\MDOS\VDPX.SYS
DEVICE=C:\OS2\MDOS\VXMS.SYS /UMB
DEVICE=C:\OS2\MDOS\VDPMI.SYS
DEVICE=C:\OS2\MDOS\VWIN.SYS
DEVICE=C:\OS2\MDOS\VCDROM.SYS
REM DEVICE=C:\OS2\PCMCIA.SYS
REM DEVICE=C:\OS2\MDOS\VPCMCIA.SYS
BASEDEV=OS2CDROM.DMD /Q
IFS=C:\OS2\CDFS.IFS /Q
BASEDEV=OS2SCSI.DMD
BASEDEV=NECCDS1.FLT
BASEDEV=AHA154X.ADD
DEVICE=C:\OS2\MDOS\VMOUSE.SYS
DEVICE=C:\OS2\POINTDD.SYS
DEVICE=C:\OS2\MOUSE.SYS SERIAL=COM2
DEVICE=C:\OS2\COM.SYS
DEVICE=C:\OS2\MDOS\VCOM.SYS
CODEPAGE=437,850
DEVINFO=KBD,US,C:\OS2\KEYBOARD.DCP
DEVINFO=SCR,VGA,C:\OS2\VIOTBL.DCP
SET VIDEO_DEVICES=VIO_VGA
SET VIO_VGA=DEVICE(BVHVGA)
DEVICE=C:\OS2\MDOS\VSVGA.SYS

REM - NetWare Requester statements BEGIN -
DEVICE=C:\NETWARE\LSL.SYS
RUN=C:\NETWARE\DDAEMON.EXE
DEVICE=C:\NETWARE\NE2000.SYS
DEVICE=C:\NETWARE\IPX.SYS
DEVICE=C:\NETWARE\SPX.SYS
RUN=C:\NETWARE\SPDAEMON.EXE
rem DEVICE=C:\NETWARE\NMPIPE.SYS
rem DEVICE=C:\NETWARE\NPSERVER.SYS
rem RUN=C:\NETWARE\NPDAEMON.EXE NP_COMPUTERNAME
DEVICE=C:\NETWARE\NWREQ.SYS
IFS=C:\NETWARE\NWIFS.IFS
RUN=C:\NETWARE\NWDAEMON.EXE
rem DEVICE=C:\NETWARE\NETBIOS.SYS
rem RUN=C:\NETWARE\NBDAEMON.EXE
DEVICE=C:\NETWARE\VIPX.SYS
DEVICE=C:\NETWARE\VSHELL.SYS
REM - NetWare Requester statements END -
```

The NetWare Requester components and protocol stacks are all implemented as device drivers. For example, IPX is implemented by the IPX.SYS device driver, SPX by the SPX.SYS device driver, Named Pipes by the NMPIPE.SYS device driver, and NetBIOS by the NETBIOS.SYS device driver. This contrasts with DOS workstations that implement these components by Terminate-and-Stay Resident (TSR) programs.

OS/2 NetWare Utilities

OS/2 IntranetWare workstations cannot use the DOS NetWare utilities installed during the server installation. Novell has written OS/2 versions of utilities, such as SYSCON, FCONSOLE, FILER, and SESSION. These utilities are on disks labeled OS2UTIL-1, OS2UTIL-2, and so on. The utilities must be installed on the server for OS/2 IntranetWare workstations to use them. This must be accomplished as a separate step.

To install the OS/2 NetWare utilities from an OS/2 workstation, complete the following steps:

1. Boot up the workstation with OS/2 and select either OS/2 window or OS/2 full screen from the Group-Main window.

2. Insert the OS2UTIL-1 disk in drive A or insert the IntranetWare CD-ROM into the CD-ROM drive and use the LOGIN program to log in as SUPERVISOR to the IntranetWare server (serverName):

   ```
   A:\LOGIN\LOGIN serverName/SUPERVISOR
   ```

   (Replace *serverName* with the name of the server.)

3. Change to the drive that contains the OS2UTIL-1 disk or the appropriate directory on the CD and type the following command:

   ```
   SERVINST serverName
   ```

4. Follow the instructions until the OS/2 NetWare utilities are installed.

The utilities can also be loaded from the IntranetWare server console, or from a DOS/Windows workstation using RCONSOLE logged into the server. To do this, perform the following steps:

1. Load INSTALL on the system console.

2. Select Product Options, then Install a Product Listed Above.

3. From the list displayed, select Install NetWare Client for Macintosh OS. This option installs the client utilities for both Macintosh and OS/2 client workstations.

After the OS/2 NetWare utilities are installed, the OS/2 utilities are located in the directories indicated in the preceding list. The separate directories SYS:LOGIN/OS2, SYS:PUBLIC/OS2, and SYS:SYSTEM/OS2 are created to avoid name conflicts with DOS utilities.

When the OS/2 IntranetWare client workstation logs in to a IntranetWare server that has the NetWare utilities installed, drive L is mapped to the SYS:LOGIN/OS2 directory. This enables you to invoke the OS/2 LOGIN program in that directory. SYSCON must be used to modify the user's login script to include drive mappings to SYS:PUBLIC/OS2.

To invoke the OS/2 LOGIN program, when attached to a IntranetWare server without the OS/2 NetWare utilities installed, you must copy the OS/2 LOGIN program onto the OS/2 workstation's hard disk.

NET.CFG for OS/2 IntranetWare Workstations

To configure the NetWare Requester for non-default settings, you must use the NET.CFG configuration file. The NET.CFG file for OS/2 is similar to that used for DOS workstations, but some differences exist. The main section headings for the OS/2 NET.CFG file are left-justified, and the entries under each heading are indented by a space or a tab.

The BUFFERS parameter can be changed in the LINK SUPPORT section. The general form of the BUFFERS parameter is as follows:

```
BUFFERS bufferNumber [bufferSize]
```

The BUFFERS parameter changes the number (*bufferNumber*) and size (*bufferSize*) of communication buffers.

The *bufferSize*, which is optional, has a default value of 1,130 bytes. The total amount of buffer space for LSL buffers must not exceed 64 KB:

bufferNumber × *bufferSize* <= 64 KB

The protocolName in PROTOCOL STACK can be IPX or SPX. Each of the protocol stacks, IPX and SPX, has a different set of parameters. Tables 16.1 and 16.2 describe the parameters for IPX and SPX.

Table 16.1
OS/2 IPX Parameters for Protocol Stack

Parameter	Meaning
socket count	Specifies the maximum number of sockets (count) that IPX can have open at a workstation. The number of sockets can be from 9 to 128. The default value is 32.
router mem size	Specifies the memory size in bytes in the router memory pool allocated for routing. Default value is 450.
bind name	Specifies the NIC driver that is bound to the IPX protocol name stack. Primarily used for workstations with several NICs.

Table 16.2
OS/2 SPX Parameters for Protocol Stack

Parameter	Meaning
sessions count	Specifies number of SPX connections (count) to be supported. Acceptable values are between 8 and 256 with a default of 16.
abort timeout val	Specifies the number of milliseconds (val) SPX must wait for an acknowledgment before terminating a connection. Minimum value is 10 milliseconds, and the default is 30,000 milliseconds (30 seconds).
verify timeout val	Specifies the number of milliseconds (val) SPX must wait between packet transmissions before asking for an acknowledgment that the connection is still intact. Minimum value is 10 milliseconds, and the default is 3,000 milliseconds (3 seconds).
listen timeout val	Specifies the number of milliseconds (val) SPX waits for a packet timeout from the connection. Minimum value is 10 milliseconds and the default is 6,000 milliseconds (6 seconds). If no packet arrives in the specified time, SPX includes a request for immediate acknowledgment in every packet sent. If no acknowledgment is received, SPX uses the abort timeout value.
retry count val	Specifies the number of times (val) the workstation attempts to resend a packet. Acceptable values are from 1 to 255 with a default of 20.

An example is listing 16.4.

Listing 16.4

```
PROTOCOL STACK IPX

socket 128     ; Increase socket count to max of 128
bind trxnet    ; Bind IPX to Novell RX-Net driver

PROTOCOL STACK SPX

sessions 19   ; SPX session to 19
abort timeout 450000    ; Abort time out to 45 secs.
verify timeout 20000    ; Verify time out to 40 secs.
listen timeout 15000    ; Listen timeout to 15 secs.
retry count 10    ; Reduce retries to 10
```

The NETWARE REQUESTER Section

The OS/2 NetWare requester can be configured in the NETWARE REQUESTER section of the NET.CFG file. The parameters that can be controlled are described in table 16.3.

Table 16.3
OS/2 NetWare Requester Parameters

Parameter	Meaning
cache buffers cnt	Specifies number of buffers (cnt) at workstation to be used to cache data from open files. Acceptable values range from 0 to 128, with a default of 8.
sessions cnt	Specifies number of file server connections (cnt) that the requester supports. Acceptable values range from 8 to 20 with a default of 8. (Each connection uses at least 3 IPX sockets.)
request retries cnt	Specifies number of times (cnt) the requester tries to resend a request following a communication error. Minimum value is 5 and the default value is 20.
preferred server sn	Specifies the server name (sn) to attach to when the NetWare requester loads.

An example is listing 16.5.

Listing 16.5

```
NETWARE REQUESTER

sessions 15               ; Set to 15 sessions
cache buffers 20          ; 20 read/write buffers
request retries 5         ; Reduce retries to 5
preferred server KSS      ; Attach to server with name KSS
```

The NETWARE NETBIOS Section

The NETWARE NETBIOS section of the NET.CFG file is used only if the NetBIOS protocol stack is loaded (DEVICE=NETBIOS.SYS in CONFIG.SYS). Configuration of NetBIOS protocol includes name management, session creation, and session management. Table 16.4 describes the NetBIOS parameters.

Table 16.4
OS/2 NetWare NetBIOS Parameters

Parameter	Meaning
names cnt	Specifies the number of names cnt the workstation can have in its name table. The values can range from 4 to 128 with a default of 26.

continues

Table 16.4, Continued
OS/2 NetWare NetBIOS Parameters

Parameter	Meaning
sessions cnt	Specifies the number of NetBIOS sessions cnt the workstation can have. The values can range from 4 to 128 with a default of 32.
commands numb	Specifies the number of outstanding NetBIOS commands that can be waiting for completion at the workstation. The values range from 4 to 128 with a default of 12.
sessions cnt	Specifies the number of NetBIOS sessions cnt the workstation can have. The values range from 4 to 128 with a default of 32.
retry delay numb	Specifies delay in milliseconds numb. If no response is received to a NetBIOS connection request or a packet transmission, it waits for the specified amount of time before trying again. The default value is 500.
retry count numb	Specifies the number of times numb NetBIOS tries to establish a connection or send data, if there is no response the first time. The default value is 20.
Internet [on|off]	The Internet parameter determines the behavior of the claim-name packet. NetBIOS requires all stations to have a unique logical name. Claim-name packets establish a unique NetBIOS name. When set to ON, NetBIOS broadcasts claim-name packets to all stations on the Internet to establish the uniqueness of the claim-name packet. When Internet is OFF, NetBIOS sends name-claim packets to stations on the local network only. It ignores responses from outside the local network.
broadcast count N	Specifies the number of times N. NetBIOS broadcasts a claim for a name. Minimum value is 1. Default value is 4 if Internet is ON, or 2 if Internet is OFF.
broadcast delay N	Specifies delay in milliseconds N. NetBIOS waits for the delay N specified time between a query and claim broadcasts. Value can be from 100 to 65,535. Default values are 2,000 if Internet is ON or 1,000 if Internet is OFF.
abort timeout N	Specifies timeout value in milliseconds N. If no acknowledgment is received in the timeout interval, NetBIOS terminates the connection. Minimum value is 500. Default value is 30,000.
verify timeout N	Specifies the timeout in milliseconds N. NetBIOS waits for at least the specified value before sending a "probe" packet to the remote station to confirm the connection. Value can be from 100 to 65,535. Default value is 3,000.

Parameter	Meaning
listen timeout N	Specifies timeout in milliseconds N. NetBIOS waits for the specified time for a packet from a remote station. It then sends a "probe" packet to verify its connection. Value can be from 200 to 65,535. Default value is 6,000.

An example of the NETBIOS Protocol section is shown in listing 16.6.

Listing 16.6

```
PROTOCOL NETBIOS

names 28         ; Name table size 28
sessions 20      ; NetBIOS sessions
internet off     ; Turn claim-name packets off across
internet
```

The LINK DRIVER *driverName* Section

The *driverName* in the LINK DRIVER section heading must be replaced with the OS/2 network *driver name.* All parameters included in the LINK DRIVER section heading apply to driverName. These parameters are as follows:

- DMA
- INT
- MEM
- PORT
- NODE ADDRESS
- SLOT
- FRAME
- PROTOCOL

These parameters have the same meaning and syntax as described for ODI LINK DRIVER parameters. Refer to the section on ODI drivers to see how to use these parameters. The only difference is the SLOT parameter. SLOT has an additional option—the "?" parameter. The SLOT ? parameter tells the OS/2 NetWare requester to find the first board corresponding to the board designated in the LINK DRIVER *driverName.*

If OS/2 IntranetWare stations are used with IBM Source Routing bridges, the source routing driver must be enabled by placing the following statement in the OS/2 CONFIG.SYS file:

```
DEVICE=C:\NETWARE\ROUTE.SYS
```

The router parameters can be configured through the PROTOCOL ROUTER main-section in the OS/2 NET.CFG file. The general syntax of the parameters for this section is in listing 16.7.

Listing 16.7

```
PROTOCOL ROUTE
source route def gbr mbr nodes n board n
```

The parameters for the source route are DEF, GBE, MBR, NODES N, and BOARD N. These parameters have the same meaning as the corresponding DOS ODI source routing parameters. For details about these parameters, consult Chapter 15, "Supporting DOS, Windows 3.1x, and Windows 95 Workstations."

For example, to enable DEF, GEBR, and MBR at the OS/2 NetWare station, place listing 16.8 in the NET.CFG file.

Listing 16.8

```
protocol route
source route def gbr mbr
```

The NetWare SPOOLER Section

The NetWare spooler controls print jobs initiated at the workstation.

The NetWare SPOOLER section takes the general syntax presented in listing 16.9.

Listing 16.9

```
netware spooler
form n
copies n
[keep ¦ no keep]
size n
[tabs ¦ no tabs]
file s
name s
[banner ¦ no banner]
[form feed ¦ no form feed]
maxsetup n
maxreset n
```

Table 16.5 explains each of the parameters of the NetWare SPOOLER syntax.

Table 16.5
OS/2 NetWare SPOOLER Parameters

Parameter	Value
form n	Specifies the form number n to be used for printing. Default is form 0.
copies n	Specifies the number n of copies to be printed. Default is 1 copy.
[keep|no keep]	Specifies that printing should continue keep even if capture is interrupted. Default is keep.
space n	Specifies the number n of spaces in a tab. Default is 8.
[tabs|no tabs]	Spooler expands tab to the number of spaces specified in the space n parameter. Default is tab.
file s	Specifies the file name s to be printed in the banner.
name s	Specifies the user name s to be printed in the banner.
[banner|no banner]	Enables/disables printing of banner.
[form feed|no form feed]	Enables/disables form feed at end of job.
maxsetup n	Specifies the maximum number of characters n setup string that is sent to the printer.
maxrest n	Specifies the maximum number of characters n in the reset string that is sent to the printer.

Unix Workstations

For many years, Unix has been the most widely used operating system for servers providing Internet services. Only recently have applications been developed that allow servers running operating systems like Microsoft Windows/NT and Novell's NetWare to provide Internet services. The majority of the WWW, FTP, Gopher, and other Internet servers are still running some version of Unix. Most Unix operating systems now include Internet services as part of their base distribution.

Unix currently runs on a wide variety of proprietary RISC processors, as well as Intel's x86 family of processors. Traditionally, Unix has supported only the TCP/IP networking protocol, providing several common tools for exchanging files and data, and for sharing file systems, printers, and other network resources.

Most people are now familiar with Web servers used for viewing and downloading information and files. A File Transfer Protocol (FTP) utility is also included and widely used for exchanging files, although Telnet and X-Windows have allowed users to log on and use remote Unix servers. Network File System (NFS) (developed by Sun Microsystems) became the standard means for Unix systems to share file systems. Unix systems used LPR/LPD protocols over NFS to enable access to printer resources. NFS and the LPR/LPD protocol uses even extended to the PC desktop as PC-based workstations required access to those same Unix-based file systems and printers.

As the numbers of NetWare servers on the networks increased, most Unix vendors included connectivity options for users on the Unix system to access resources on the NetWare servers, and to allow clients on the NetWare servers to access resources on the Unix system. Several IPX to IP gateway products evolved, allowing clients running only the IPX protocol to access resources on IP-based servers, and even to access the Internet, without adding TCP/IP to the client. Most also included a means for accessing the NetWare server's file systems and printers. Although these utilities differ from vendor to vendor, they are all very full-featured and are usually included with the Unix operating system, although some must be purchased separately.

Novell has also added new features and functionality to integrate more fully into the total network environment and communicate and share resources with Unix servers and users. IntranetWare now offers several of the services traditionally found only on Unix servers. IntranetWare now includes a WWW Server, an FTP server, NFS File and Printer sharing services, a Domain Name Server, a Dynamic Host Configuration Protocol (DHCP) server, as well as other Unix integration tools.

NetWare NFS Services 2.1

NetWare NFS Services 2.1 provides transparent, bidirectional access to file and print services between Unix systems and IntranetWare servers using the NFS protocol. This product enables NetWare and Unix clients to use familiar commands and interfaces to access all files and printers on the network, regardless of where they reside. It also enables Unix system administrators to use the X Window System or Telnet to manage IntranetWare servers remotely, and lets Unix and File Transfer Protocol (FTP) clients transfer files to and from IntranetWare servers using their native FTP commands and interface. NetWare NFS Services also provides an FTP server that enables any LAN or Internet client running an FTP client and using valid NetWare access to transfer files to and from any NetWare server.

NetWare NFS Services runs as a set of NetWare Loadable Modules on NetWare 4.x and IntranetWare servers. It requires no additional hardware or software on either the PC or Unix client workstations while providing full resource sharing for users in both the NetWare 4 and Unix environments. NetWare NFS Services provides centralized NetWare and Unix account administration through UNICON and is fully integrated with Novell Directory Services (NDS), the Unix Domain Name System (DNS), and Network Information Service (NIS). For example, changes made to Unix user accounts through UNICON are automatically updated in NDS, DNS, and NIS directory trees.

NetWare Unix Print Services 2.1

NetWare Unix Print Services 2.1 provides a bidirectional printing solution between Unix systems and the NetWare 4 environment. It provides print-sharing services for NetWare and Unix users, allowing companies to leverage valuable network resources. NetWare Unix Print Services lets Unix users use their native commands (lpr and lpd) to spool their print jobs to any NetWare printer, and lets NetWare users print to Unix-attached printers using their familiar drop-down menu or command sets.

Additional features include a File Transfer Protocol (FTP) server and remote management of IntranetWare servers through Novell's XCONSOLE utility. Because NetWare Unix Print Services takes advantage of Novell Directory Services, it provides centralized administration of Unix and IntranetWare user accounts, therefore eliminating the need to manage IntranetWare and Unix user accounts separately.

NetWare Unix Print Services is implemented as a set of NetWare Loadable Modules without requiring any additional hardware or software on Unix and PC workstations.

Unix Products for Integrating IntranetWare Servers

SCO's UnixWare product was originally developed to integrate fully with NetWare server environment. Although the product no longer belongs to Novell, it still includes a substantial set of NetWare connectivity features.

Even though we highlight the SCO UnixWare features, it is important to point out that other leading Unix vendors like SUN and the Solaris product and Calderra's LINUX operating system among others that include some very similar utilities and features. The next sections highlight some of the available products for integrating UnixWare servers into your IntranetWare environment.

SCO Gateway for NetWare

The SCO Gateway for NetWare allows SCO Unix systems to mount volumes from a NetWare file server. It also allows print requests from a SCO Unix system to be printed to NetWare servers.

SCO NetWare Unix Client File System (NUCFS)

The NetWare Unix Client file system (NUCFS) is a UnixWare network file system that provides NetWare file services to a UnixWare platform, giving UnixWare system users direct and transparent access to NetWare files and directories on remote NetWare servers. The NUCFS file system distributes UnixWare file service requests which reference file services on a remote NetWare server platform to the NetWare network operating system.

UnixWare 2.1 as a NetWare Client

UnixWare provides built-in services for both IPX/SPX and TCP/IP networks. This enables SCO UnixWare 2.1 users to receive and distribute information throughout an organization that has one or both of these networking environments. The standard installation procedures enables SCO UnixWare 2.1 Application Servers to connect immediately to an existing NetWare environment, allowing them to share e-mail, data, and printers with NetWare. This enables NetWare clients to access line-of-business applications running on the SCO UnixWare 2.1 Application Server using the network services and data located on a NetWare server.

NetWare Integration with SCO UnixWare 2.1 provides graphical login, single network login, and authentication for easy connection to multiple servers.

NetWare Unix Client (NUC)

The NetWare Unix Client (NUC) enables SCO UnixWare 2.1 to be a client to NetWare servers (3.x and 4.x). The NUC permits UnixWare users to access a NetWare file system as if it was mounted on a UnixWare system. It also supports the ability to print on a NetWare printer from a UnixWare system. The NUC provides NetWare Core Protocol (NCP) connectivity from a SCO UnixWare 2.1 client to NetWare servers. NUC features are enhanced over those supported on other NetWare client stations (DOS, MAC, OS/2, Windows) by the multi-user, multitasking, and multiprocessor capabilities of UnixWare. Each user on the local UnixWare system can access remote resources on many different servers simultaneously. NUC maps UnixWare services into NetWare, providing a transparent interface between the UnixWare operating system and the NetWare operating system, giving the user access to directories, files, and printers on remote NetWare servers. Local Unix operating system service semantics are preserved without compromising NetWare security.

Remote Backup on IntranetWare Servers

A UnixWare Target Service Agent (TSA) permits a UnixWare system to participate as a client of NetWare's Storage Management Services (SMS). The TSA supports remote backup and restore of UnixWare files as well as of NetWare files.

UNIXWARE 2.1 as a NetWare Services Provider

The NetWare Services (NWS) provides Novell's NetWare 4.1 File, Print, and Directory services on the UnixWare 2.1 platform. The features and components that are included with this technology include:

- Novell Directory Services 4.1 (NDS)
- NetWare 4.1 File Services
- NetWare 4.1 Print Services
- Graphical Administration

- Integrated backup and restore
- Hybrid user management
- User Licensing

Windows NT

Windows NT is a 32-bit multitasking operating system which has a GUI interface based on the latest releases of Microsoft's Windows family products.

Support for Windows NT is available from both Microsoft and Novell. Before installing any of the client software, you should check with Microsoft and Novell to see if any patches to the Windows NT clients are required. You can obtain the requesters from Microsoft and Novell. They are also available on CompuServe and the Internet (`host ftp.microsoft.com` or `ftp.novell.com`). The client software kits contain detailed instructions on installing the software and you should consult these as there could be last minute changes that are usually documented in these sources.

Microsoft Support for IntranetWare

Microsoft's NetWare client software, called the Client for Netware Networks (CNN) uses an IPX-compatible protocol implemented by Microsoft called NWLink. The NWLink protocol module in Windows NT contains Microsoft's implementation of IPX, SPX. With CNN, you can configure the Windows NT clients to use packet burst provided the NetWare server supports it.

You can use CNN to connect to NetWare 2.x, 3.x, 4.x, and IntranetWare servers running bindery emulation. At the moment, CNN does not include support for NetWare Directory services (NDS) that require extended NCP services. You can use tools such as FILER, SYSCON, MAP to access and configure network services, as well as the native Microsoft graphical interfaces provided by the Explorer and Network Neighborhood interfaces. Using these tools you can browse and connect to Novell servers and map network drives that use them.

Windows NT also provides a Gateway Service for NetWare (GSNW) that provides a gateway that can be implemented on a Windows NT server that enables users connected to the Windows NT machine to access resources on an IntranetWare server. The GSNW acts as a NetWare NCP (NetWare Core Protocol) blocks to be translated into Server Message Blocks (SMBs) that Microsoft clients use and understand. Remote users connected to the NT server using NT's Remote Access Service (RAS) can also access the IntranetWare servers resources.

The Windows NT machine that acts as a gateway logs in to the NetWare server on behalf of the Windows NT users (see fig. 16.4). The Windows NT gateway machine logs in to the NetWare server as a user that is defined on the NetWare server.

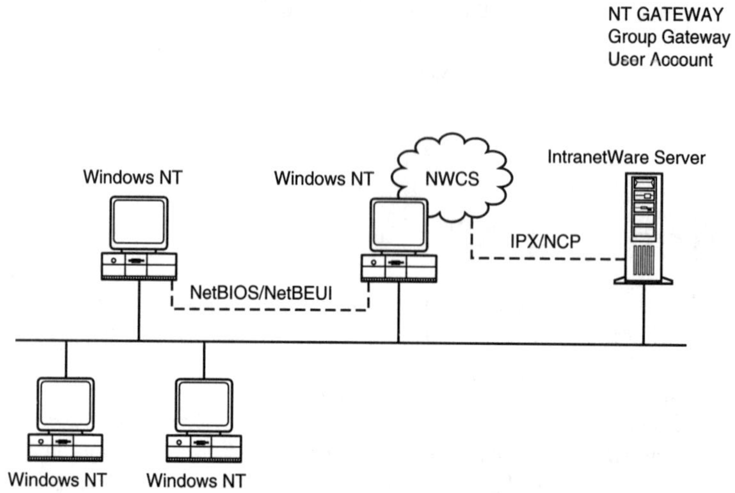

Figure 16.4
The GSNW Gateway.

To enable the GSNW gateway, you must have Microsoft Client for NetWare Networks installed. Next, you can use the following steps as a guideline to enable the IntranetWare gateway:

1. Open Control panel and activate (click using mouse button) the GSNW icon.
2. Click on the Gateway button.
3. Fill in the name and password of the NetWare user account on the screen.
4. Fill in the share names using Microsoft's Universal Naming Convention (UNC). For example, if you are sharing volume SYS on server KSS, the UNC share name will be as follows:

   ```
   \\KSS\SYS
   ```

5. Windows NT or Windows Clients can map to this share name using their native NetBEUI/NetBIOS protocols and access services on the NetWare server.

IntranetWare Client for Windows NT

Novell developed the IntranetWare Client for NT to take full advantage of IntranetWare's directory services (NDS), use Novell's enhanced performance NCPs for communication with the server, and integrate into the NT environment and security scheme. The IntranetWare Client includes a full 32-bit implementation of Novell's IPX/SPX protocol stack, Novell's Application Launcher (NAL) and a 32-bit implementation of the NWADMIN administration tool.

An NT server can connect to an IntranetWare server using either the Microsoft NWLINK IPX/SPX-compatible protocol module running over NT's native NDIS drivers, or with the IntranetWare Client's IPX/SPX protocol module running over either the NT NDIS drivers or Novell's ODI drivers.

The IntranetWare client can be used to connect to NetWare 2.x, 3.x, 4.x, and IntranetWare servers, using either bindery emulation or full NDS login support. Login script processing has now been added.

The IntranetWare Client has been performance optimized to take advantage of Novell's latest performance-oriented NCPs, and is integrated with the Windows NT Cache manager for resource caching. The IntranetWare Client also supports packet burst protocol, an NCP that increases the performance of large file reads and writes over a wide area network.

The IntranetWare Client for NT extends the NT access profiles from residing only on the local workstation to the IntranetWare server as well. When users log in from a location other than the local workstation, Windows NT loads the user's profiles from the IntranetWare server and configures the desktop according to the information contained in the profile. This enables users to see the same familiar desktop regardless of their login location.

Beame & Whiteside's MultiConnect for Windows NT

Beame & Whiteside offer MultiConnect for Windows NT that enables NetWare clients to access Windows NT servers. This product runs on Windows NT and causes it to appear as a bindery-based NetWare server to NetWare clients. In other words, it emulates NetWare services on a Windows NT machine (see fig. 16.5). The MultiConnect implements IPX/SPX/NCP protocols on the Windows NT machine.

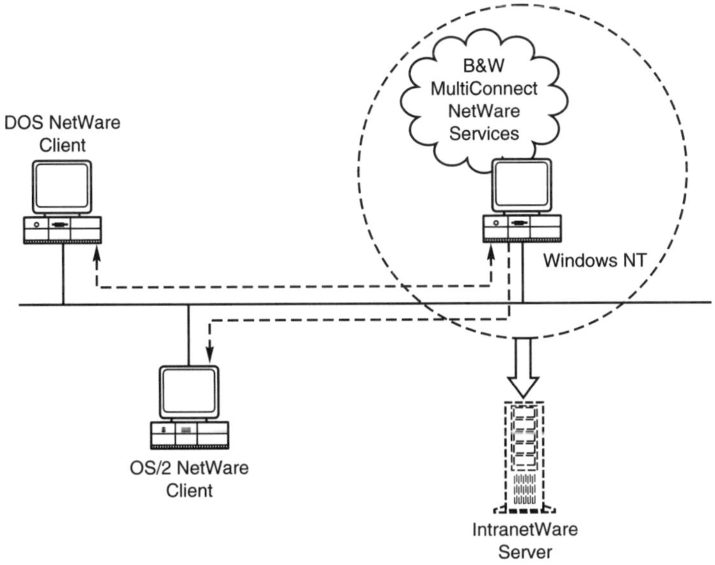

Figure 16.5
MultiConnect for Windows NT.

Summary

This chapter discussed IntranetWare's extensive support for Macintosh, OS/2, Unix, and Windows NT client workstations. It introduced you to the many different options available for connecting these clients to an IntranetWare server, and sharing data between them by either modifying the IntranetWare server, or by adding client-side support on the workstations.

Almost all operating systems now offer options for connecting to an IntranetWare network. Some of these options have also been presented in this chapter.

CHAPTER 17

Performance Tuning in IntranetWare Servers

Several factors affect network performance. In this chapter, you learn what these factors are and how you can improve the performance of your network. Some of the decisions that affect network performance can be made before installing a network, whereas others can be made only after installation. Decisions made prior to network installation include the choice of server machine platforms, network adapters, disk subsystems, and so on. To fine-tune the network after installation, you must monitor how well the network is performing. Some of these tools, such as MONITOR NLM for IntranetWare, are provided by Novell. Third-party tools such as the Frye Utilities perform similar functions.

Future versions of IntranetWare are expected to improve on network management and performance monitoring functions. Protocol analyzers such as LANalyzer are powerful tools for improving network performance. The purpose of such monitoring tools is to analyze current performance, checking for bottlenecks. When you discover the bottlenecks, you can take steps toward eliminating them.

Understanding the Factors Affecting Network Performance

Because the network is made up of hardware and software components, the factors that affect network performance are hardware-related and software-related.

This section enables you to have better understanding of the hardware and software performance factors. There is a strong relationship between hardware and software factors, and both must be considered together to evaluate the performance of a network. This chapter first examines the hardware performance factors, and then the software factors.

Hardware Components Affecting Server Performance

The following major hardware-related factors affect network performance:

- Disk subsystem: speed and storage capacity
- Network adapters: speed, bus width, and network access technology
- Server bus characteristics
- Speed of server and workstation computers

The hardware-related factors are not confined to any single piece of equipment, such as the server machine, but also include the type of network adapters in the server and the workstation, and the network access speed and method (CSMA/CD, Token Access, and so on). One of the most important hardware elements in the server computer, its disk subsystem, and the type of network adapter inside the server. In IntranetWare LANs, the server computer plays a central role; any improvements on the server hardware directly affect network performance.

Sometimes, installing a faster computer as the server does not necessarily improve performance. Understanding this point is important because the performance of the entire network is limited by its slowest component. If the LAN's physical layer is the slowest component of the network, for example, replacing the server machine or disk subsystem with a faster component does not improve performance in general.

Some of the tools described here can help you determine which component is the cause of the bottleneck. Generally there are no cut-and-dry formulas for determining performance bottlenecks. Most experienced network managers use a combination of knowledge of their network, knowledge of underlying technology, and good common sense and intuition to detect and isolate performance-related problems. Some promising technology exists in the area of expert systems to better solve these problems. But expert systems are only as good as the people programming them; they can help guide you to a solution to the problem but cannot necessarily solve the problem for you.

Disk Subsystem

The most important function an IntranetWare server performs is to provide file services. Because the server files are stored on the server disk, a fast disk subsystem results in faster file services and, from a user's perspective, a faster network. The disk subsystem is responsible for filling and emptying the contents of the operating system cache to satisfy network requests for data retrieval and storage. The operating system cache should be large enough to satisfy most network read retrieval requests from cache. The disk subsystem should be fast enough to keep the operating system cache full of needed data.

The data-transfer rate between the CPU and the disk is determined by the disk, the disk controller, and the bus interfaces. The older PC AT disks that used MFM encoding are among the slowest hard disks. Today, most disks use a higher level of RLL encoding, enabling them to pack more data per sector, which means that the disk has to rotate smaller distances (requiring less time) to deliver the same amount of data. This translates to faster data-transfer rates.

The types of disks that give the best performance in the marketplace today are disks based on Integrated Device Electronics (IDE) and Small Computers Systems Interface (SCSI).

The IDE disks replace the older AT-style disks and provide a higher performance interface between the computer and the disk, enabling them to be faster than the AT-style disks. IDE implements most of its logic on the electronics contained on the drive itself. However, IDE uses the computer's CPU to perform many of its tasks. It is limited to drives per controller, has a data transfer rate of 2 to 3 MB/sec, and has a maximum file size limit of 528 MB owing to PC BIOS limits. Some of the more recent IDE drives perform close to SCSI speeds, if only one drive is used. If two drives are used, IDE usually performs at less than SCSI speed owing to the fact that the device electronic controls have to be shared by two drives.

The disk manufacturers seem to have voted on the SCSI interface as the best technique for providing high-capacity, high-speed disks. The most recent version of SCSI interface, called the SCSI-II interface, has some performance improvements over the older SCSI-I interface.

SCSI devices can transfer data at rates up to 40 MB/sec (320 Mbps), which is well over the speed of Ethernet (10 Mbps), Token-Ring (16 Mbps), ARCnet PLUS (20 Mbps), and FDDI (100 Mbps). In actual practice, these devices achieve smaller data-transfer rates if used with the ISA-style bus because the ISA bus currently is limited to transfer rates of 4 to 8 Mbps. Therefore, for best performance, use SCSI devices with either PCI or EISA bus that can support higher data rates.

SCSI-I uses an 8-bit bus and has a data rate of 5 MB/sec. There can be seven devices per master device (the SCSI controller) that are daisy-chained on the SCSI bus. Also, only one command can be pending for a SCSI device.

SCSI-II supports the SCSI-I command set and uses parity checking on the bus to detect errors. It also supports a bus disconnect feature where a SCSI device releases the bus while performing a command. This makes the SCSI bus available for other devices. SCSI-II overcomes the SCSI-I limitation of one command per SCSI device. With SCSI-II, multiple commands can be issued to a SCSI-II compatible device that are kept in the Tag Command Queue (TCQ). Because the device holds commands in a queue, it can execute them in sequence as each command finishes, and does not have to wait for the next command from the SCSI controller as in the case of SCSI-I. This leads to a dramatic improvement in performance. Other performance improvement features of SCSI-II are double the bus clock speed of SCSI-I, and double bus width (16 bits). The current classifications that are used in the industry for classifying SCSI features are shown in table 17.1.

Table 17.1
SCSI Classifications

Bus Width Classification	Data Transfer (bits)	Rate (MB/sec)	Command Queuing
SCSI-I	8	5	Single command only
SCSI-II	8, 16, 32	5, 10, 20	Supports Tag Command Queuing
Fast SCSI-II	8	10	Supports Tag Command Queuing
Fast and Wide SCSI-II	16	20	Supports Tag Command Queuing
Fast and 32-bit Wide SCSI-II	32 (most devices do not support 32 bits)	40	Supports Tag Command Queuing

Another type of disk subsystem is called RAID. It has the potential of providing a high degree of reliability through a fault-tolerant architecture. Redundant Array of Inexpensive Disks (RAID) enables data to be distributed across multiple inexpensive disks, so that if any one disk were to fail, data can be recovered based on information on the other active disks.

Network Adapters

In a networking environment, the network adapters determine the data-transfer rate through the network media. Not all adapters for a network technology are created equal. There are many manufacturers of Ethernet adapters, for example; although they all comply with the

Ethernet standard of 10 Mbps, they have different effective data rates. Network adapters from 3COM are quite popular, but there are at least two types of adapters for IBM PCs: 3COM EtherLink and 3COM EtherLink Plus. The 3COM EtherLink Plus is a higher-performance card, and is therefore more expensive. It has more packet buffers and faster circuitry. Ideally, all stations on a network should have high-performance cards to obtain the maximum possible data-transfer rate. If cost is a major factor, at least the server computer and external routers should have a high-performance card. Using a high-performance network adapter for the server can dramatically improve the network performance.

The following factors affect the performance of a network adapter:

- Media access scheme
- Raw bit rate
- Onboard processor
- NIC-to-host transfer

The *media access scheme* refers to the arbitration mechanism, inherent in baseband LANs, that limits how the messages are placed on the media. Examples of this are CSMA/CD, used in Ethernet and IEEE 802.3, and Token Access, used in IBM Token-Ring (IEEE 802.5). Token Access gives a deterministic performance even under heavy network loads, whereas CSMA/CD is susceptible to reduced throughput because of collisions under heavy loads. Under light loads, on the other hand, the CSMA/CD access method is simpler and faster than Token Access.

The *raw bit rate* is the maximum bit rate possible on a given medium. The effective bit rate (taking into account protocol, overhead, and queue and processing delays) is much less. The raw bit rate represents an upper limit for the medium.

Effective use of an onboard processor can speed up a network adapter. If the firmware for the NIC is poorly written, however, it can have just the opposite effect as that seen in the earlier IBM PC Broadband LAN adapters. Some vendors implement upper-layer protocol processing on the NIC card itself for better overall throughput. An example of such an NIC is Federal Technologies' EXOS series board that has onboard TCP/IP processing.

Data arriving on the network adapter needs to be transferred into the host computer's memory. The NIC connection to the host channel can be implemented using shared memory, DMA, or I/O ports. NICs may use any of these methods or a combination of them. Observations have shown that shared memory is the fastest, followed by I/O ports, with DMA the slowest. Avoid NICs that use DMA exclusively for transferring data, as these probably are slow NICs. Some cards use a combination of shared memory and DMA, which gives them a certain level of parallelism that can improve their performance.

The data width of the bus interface has a dramatic effect on NIC-to-host transfer speeds. Current data widths are 8, 16, or 32 bits. The wider the data width, the faster the data transfer. EISA and PCI NICs are faster than ISA NICs. It is a good strategy to use an EISA or PCI machine with an EISA or PCI adapter at the server because network traffic is concentrated at this point.

Try to avoid mixing network adapters from different vendors on one LAN. Although all vendors claim to follow a standard, important implementation differences that can affect the performance of a network may exist between them. Some Ethernet vendors implement the random-time backoff algorithm differently, for example, so that in case of Ethernet bus contention and collision, they will timeout before network adapters from other vendors. In practical terms, this means that these network adapters access the LAN bus before network adapters from other vendors. Another way to look at this is to see these network adapters as "poor citizens" on the network. One way to handle these network adapters is to isolate them in their separate LAN segment, where they have minimum impact on other stations on the network.

Another property of most PC LANs, and LANs based on the IEEE standards, is that the bigger (in geographical size) they are, the smaller their network utilization is. This factor is often overlooked during the design of backbone LANs to span large distances. Network administrators are surprised by the drop in network utilization, and hence data throughput, as LAN size increases. The reason for this is a bit technical but very interesting, and is explained next.

Network utilization is defined as the percentage of time spent in transferring data, not including the time spent in packet processing and transmission delays. One can estimate the maximum utilization achievable by assuming that under the best possible conditions, there will be zero processing delay and queue delay, but you cannot avoid the transmission delay due to the finite propagation speed of the signal.

The data *transmit time* (Tx) is the time it takes to deliver data to the LAN media for a given transmission rate. The *transmission delay* (Td) is caused by the finite propagation speed of signals in the LAN media. Under the highest possible data-transfer rate, the messages are sent one after another with minimal delays. The message consists of a channel-use time of Tx and a propagation delay (nonuse) time of Td. The actual utilization (U) is the fraction of useful time spent transmitting data. You can make this determination by using the following formula:

$$U = Tx / (Tx + Td)$$

$$= 1 / (1 + Td/Tx)$$

$$U = 1 / (1 + a)$$

in which a = Td/Tx.

If the LAN data rate for transmitting a packet of size P bits is D bps, then

$$Tx = P/D \text{ seconds}$$

If the propagation velocity of signal in media is V meters/sec and the size of the LAN is L meters, then

$$Td = L/V \text{ seconds}$$

Studies show that the average packet size for most LAN applications is small (about 128 bytes). Using this, you can compute the network utilization of the 10BASE-T LAN.

In the 10BASE-T LAN of figure 17.1, the maximum length of the LAN will be 200 meters, not including the backplane. The backplane CSMA/CD bus in the 10BASE-T concentrator has a length of about 0.5 meters. Using the formulas for 10BASE-T LAN, and assuming a signal propagation speed of 0.7 times speed of light in vacuum, you can make the following calculation:

P (Packet size) = 128 × 8 bits = 1024 bits

D (Data Transfer Rate) = 10 Mbps (fixed for Ethernet)

L (Length of LAN) = 200.5 meters

V (Signal Propagation speed) = 0.7 × speed of light in vacuum = 0.7 × 3 × 100,000,000 = 2.1 × 100,000,000

Tx = *P*/*D* = 1024/10 Mbps = 102.4 micro-seconds

Td = *L*/ *V* = 200.5 / (2.1 × 100,000,000) = 0.95 microseconds

a = *Td*/ *Tx* = 0.95/102.4 = 0.0093

U (10BASE-T) = 1 / (1 + a) = 1 / (1 + 0.0093) = 99 percent

Figure 17.1 also shows a larger LAN, such as an IEEE 802.3 10BASE-5 LAN that has a maximum size of 2800 meters. Repeating the calculations with the 10BASE-5 parameters gives the following result:

P (Packet size) = 128 8 bits = 1024 bits

D (Data Transfer Rate) = 10 Mbps (fixed for Ethernet)

L (Length of LAN) = 2800 meters

V (Signal Propagation speed) = 2.1 ′ 100,000,000 meters/sec

Tx = *P*/*D* = 1024/10 Mbps = 102.4 micro-seconds

Td = *L*/ *V* = 2800/(2.1 ′ 100,000,000) = 13.3 microseconds

a = *Td*/ *Tx* = 13.3/102.4 = 0.13

U (10BASE-5) = 1/(1 + a) = 1/(1 + 0.13) = 88.4 percent

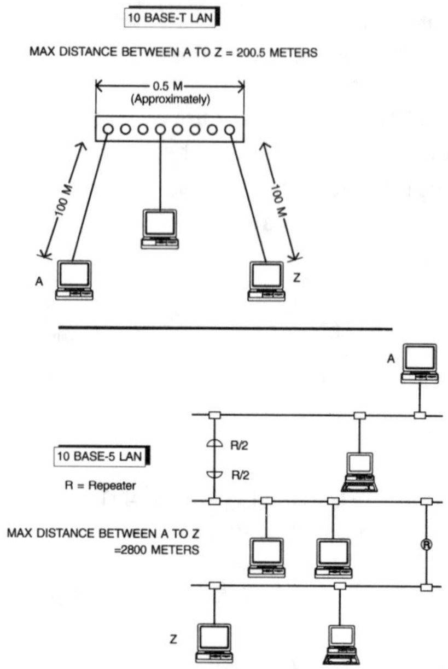

Figure 17.1
A larger 10BASE-T LAN.

A drop in performance of about 10 percent is noted between 10BASE-T (99%) and 10BASE-5 (88.4%). These calculations do not include processing and queuing delays at the network adapters. Actual network utilization is much less if these additional delays are taken into account; nevertheless, it explains why connecting a 10BASE-T LAN to a 10BASE-5 by means of a repeater results in a drop in performance for the 10BASE-T stations. One solution to this problem is to connect the 10BASE-T LANs to the 10BASE-5 through bridges, so that the CSMA/CD mechanism is partitioned into separate domains (see fig. 17.2).

For faster network performance, you might want to consider EtherSwitches, Fast Ethernet, ATM, and Virtual LANs.

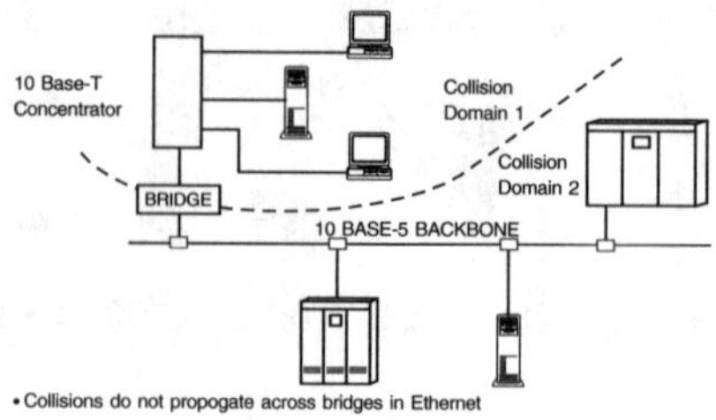

Figure 17.2
Partitioned CSMA/CD mechanism.

Server Bus Characteristics

The server bus reliability and performance has an effect on server performance. For instance, if you are using a high-performance Fast and Wide SCSI-II interface with a slow ISA bus, the

ISA bus speed could be a bottleneck in I/O operations. Some of the parameters to consider in evaluating the server bus requirements are:

- Data integrity
- Reliability
- Performance
- Compatibility with existing hardware and software
- Industry acceptance
- Flexible architecture that allows for growth and increased functionality

Data integrity and reliability implies that the data should be transferred reliably over the server bus without errors. A bus should implement at least a parity scheme to detect single bit errors. Errors can be caused by faulty electronics, electrical interference, particle bombardments, and radiation from other devices. If such errors are detected, the receiving device on the server bus can request that the corrupt data be re-sent.

Performance can be increased by using a bus with a wide data path and by using bus mastering. Bus mastering is a technique that enables a device to gain control of the bus and transfer data. This enables I/O to be performed without processor intervention and overhead.

Common server buses on Intel based servers are:

- ISA
- EISA
- PCI

The *Industry Standard Architecture* (ISA) bus is used in old AT designs and has a data path width of 16 bits. It transfers data at 10 MB/sec and does not use bus mastering or bus parity.

The *Extended Industry Standard Architecture* (EISA) uses software configuration to automatically configure EISA boards, and uses a 32-bit wide bus. It can be used to support the older ISA bus cards. It uses full bus mastering but does not have bus parity. It can transfer data up to 66 MB/sec.

The *Peripheral Component Interconnect* (PCI) is a redesign of the system bus by Intel. It is a 64-bit wide bus and has auto configuration capability and full mastering and bus parity. It can transfer data from 132 to 264 MB/sec. It can accommodate fast video transfers needed with client operating systems that have a graphical interface.

CPU Speed of Server

A fast server computer executes the IntranetWare operating system code faster and gives better performance. Server CPU performance is often rated in *Millions of Instructions Per Second* (MIPS).

The overall performance of the server system speed can be measured for IntranetWare servers, and this number can be used as a speed index to fine-tune the server's performance.

When IntranetWare loads, using the SERVER.EXE program, it performs a system speed test. The purpose of this speed test is to inform the network administrator of the server's operating speed. Some Intel 80386-based machines come with selectable speeds; during system startup time they may be operating at speeds as low as 6 MHz or 8 MHz. A low speed is an indication that the server is not operating at its maximum clock speed and that server performance will be affected accordingly. Actually, the speed rating is a function of more than the CPU clock speed. It is a measure of the following factors:

- CPU type
- CPU clock speed
- Memory speed
- Memory wait states
- Speed and size of CPU cache
- Overall system design

Because of the preceding factors, the speed rating is a good indication of the server's overall performance. A higher rating indicates a faster system. Table 17.2 shows the speed ratings of different server machines. From this table, you can see that the Compaq 386S, which has an 80386SX CPU at 16 MHz, has a speed rating of 98, whereas an 80386 CPU running at the same 16 MHz clock has a speed rating of 121 because of its wider data bus. Properly designed 80486 machines can have speed ratings of over 600. The speed rating also indicates that computers requiring memory wait states should be avoided as server machines.

Table 17.2
Speed Index Rating

Computer	Chip	Clock speed	Wait state	Rating
Compaq	386S	80386SX	1	98
Novell	386AE	80386	1	121
Compaq	386/25	80386	0	242
AT Clone	486/25	804860	0	686

The server speed test is a simple loop that runs for approximately 0.16 seconds and counts the number of times a given piece of code can be executed in less than 2/100ths of a second. A larger number of iterations indicates a faster machine. The flowchart in figure 17.3 shows the speed test. Before the speed test begins, the floppy drive is shut off. (Some computers automatically switch to a slower speed when the system floppy is accessed, which affects the speed rating.) The piece of code executed checks the timer to see whether three clock ticks (0.16 seconds) have elapsed. This operation involves a number of instructions that move data from CPU registers and memory. A faster CPU and faster memory increment the counter to a larger value in the same amount of time. The counter is divided by 1,000; the result is displayed as the speed index. A speed rating of 242 means that the counter was incremented 242,000 times in three clock ticks.

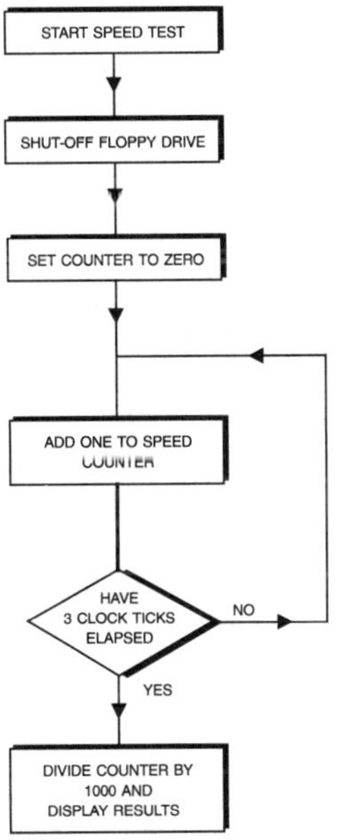

Figure 17.3
The speed test.

When running database NLMs or other application NLMs on the IntranetWare server that use numerical computations, it is important to have a floating point coprocessor on the server. For Intel 80486 and higher, the Floating Point Processor (FPU) is built into the microprocessor chip. For file services, the IO bus speed is more critical than CPU speed. But for application NLMs, the CPU and the FPU speed can also be critical. For memory intensive NLMs the memory transfer burst rates can also be significant. Intel 80486 processors can do 160 MB/sec burst transfers to memory. Pentium processors can do 528 MB/sec burst transfers to memory.

For faster server CPU performance, you may wish to consider other alternatives to Intel processors, such as Symmetrical Multi-Processing (SMP) machines or NetWare for Unix running on SMP and RISC platforms.

Software Aspects Affecting Server Performance

The software factors that determine network performance focus primarily on the Network Operating System. Because the bulk of the NOS runs on the server computer, software performance usually is concerned with fine-tuning the NOS operation on the server.

Aspects that affect server performance are as follows:

- Server memory management
- Server file caching, directory caching, and hashing
- Elevator seeking
- Tuning server parameters

Server Memory IntranetWare

Server memory is allocated in IntranetWare on a dynamic basis, depending on the situation at hand. IntanetWare does the best job it can to allocate memory so that overall system performance is improved. It occasionally needs some help from the network administrators through use of SET parameter commands, which are examined in greater detail later.

IntanetWare uses a 4 GB segment for program code and data (called the *flat memory* model). Because the segment size is larger than the RAM available on most machines, we don't have the performance hits that we had in previous versions of NetWare that used smaller segment sizes.

In IntranetWare there is one global pool that is used by the OS and the application NLMs. When memory is released by a process, it is returned to this global pool. IntranetWare memory allocation is consequently simpler and faster.

Another fact to keep in mind is that servers configured with larger amounts of memory are more likely to experience failures in memory. The probability of failure in memory increases linearly with the amount of memory. Consider that the probability of failure in a 1 MB over a period of 1 month is p. Then the number of failures in M megabytes over T months is as follows:

$$F = M \times T \times p$$

The value of p is typically 0.00033 for most memory chips on the market, and therefore the expected number of failures of 16 MB of RAM over a period of 60 months (5 years) is as follows:

$$16 \times 60 \times 0.00033 = 0.32$$

Many IntranetWare servers are typically configured with 16 MB of RAM and seldom experience any memory problem, because the expected failure is only 0.32. Consider a server configured with 64 MB or 128 MB of RAM. Using the previous formula, the failure rates work out as follows:

Failures over 60 months for 64 MB of RAM
$= 64 \times 60 \times 0.00033$

$= 1.3$

Failures over 60 months for 128 MB of RAM
$= 128 \times 60 \times 0.00$

$= 2.6$

You can see from the previous calculations that one can expect at least one failure in server memory for memory sizes greater than 64 MB over a period of 5 years. When a single bit memory failure occurs, the parity check on memory on most Intel based machines will detect the error and generate a Non-Maskable Interrupt (NMI). The NMI causes most operating systems, including IntranetWare, to crash. This is unacceptable in mission-critical applications. A solution to this is to use special servers that use Error Correcting Checks (ECC) that can detect and correct memory problems dynamically without user intervention, or use SFT III or some specialized fault-tolerant server architecture (NetFRAME, Pyramid, and so on).

Caching and Hashing

Memory that remains after allocating space for the IntranetWare operating system kernel, data tables, and NLM processes and applications is used for file caching. File caching is an attempt to substitute fast RAM for the slower disk storage. The difference in speed between RAM and most disks is in the order of 100 to 1. Substituting the use of RAM wherever possible can result in a file access 10 to 100 times faster than disk access. If disk speeds were the same as RAM speeds, there would be no need for file caching. As long as disks are slower than RAM, file caching can be used to improve file access.

In file caching, server RAM is used to keep the most frequently used disk blocks. Disk blocks ahead of the one currently being read may be perfected in server RAM, in anticipation of subsequent disk-block needs. These techniques can improve server performance on server reads. For server file writes, the disk block is written out first to cache and then to the server disk by a background process controlled by the SET parameter value of `DIRTY DISK CACHE DELAY TIME`.

Normally, a copy of the server directory is kept on the server disk. Many file operations require the reading of the disk's directory entries. These operations can be accelerated if the directory is maintained in RAM. (This is called *directory caching.*) To further accelerate access to the desired directory entry, a directory hashing function can be used to localize the search for a directory entry.

Elevator Seeking

IntranetWare uses elevator seeking to minimize excessive arm movements of the disk when satisfying multiple Read/Write requests from several workstations. If the I/O operations were performed in the order in which they arrive, disk requests arriving in random order could lead to excessive disk arm movements, called *disk thrashing*. One way to avoid this problem, sort the disk operations by the track number of the disk blocks being accessed, rather than by their order of arrival. The disk arm needs to make fewer sweeps to handle the disk requests. This is called elevator seeking.

Elevator seeking not only results in faster I/O operations but also reduces wear and tear on the disk.

File Server Performance Characteristics

An interesting study on file server performance was done by IBM using Comprehensive LAN Application-performance Report Engine (CLARE) at the IBM LAN Systems Performance Laboratory in Boca Raton, Florida. The CLARE application benchmark is an alternative to other popular approaches in performance benchmarking and system measurement. The benchmarks are designed to be more realistic, using the unique I/O patterns of applications such as WordPerfect, Lotus 1-2-3, cc:Mail, FoxBASE+, and File Copy (DOS COPY).

Systematic measurements of server performance yielded a graph similar to that in figure 17.4. This graph shows the transactions per second versus number of active server users. The transactions per second are measured at the server and are not the individual transaction rates at each workstation.

The number of *transactions per second* indicates how many units of work were done per second. A transaction is any arbitrary unit of work. The problem in many benchmarks is defining the unit of work that is being measured. For example, it could be a user loading a spreadsheet, processing it, and saving it to the server's file system. Given a definition of a transaction that involves network file I/O, it follows the performance characteristics shown in figure 17.4.

Figure 17.4
General file server performance characteristics.

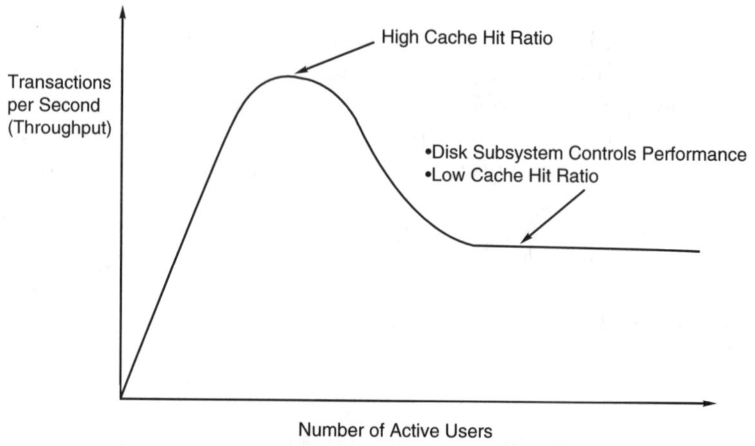

The graph shows that initially, as the number of active users increases, the transactions increase at a constant rate. This is because the server has enough capacity to be able to satisfy immediate demands placed on it. It also represents the fact that the server is able to satisfy I/O requests directly from the cache. As the number of users increase, they will issue requests to perform transactions on their behalf, and the server is able to do so because it has the capacity to perform them without any bottlenecks. The initial slope of the curve, which is a constant, is dependent on how quickly the transactions are processed at the server, which in turn depends on how quickly the network and LAN adapter is able to transfer data between the workstation and the server. The peak of the curve represents the maximum transfer rate that the server configuration can sustain for a specific transaction type and network adapter. Figure 17.5 shows the file server performance with different network adapters. Using a faster network adapter increases the initial slope and the peak. With a faster network adapter, user requests are delivered more quickly to the server; therefore, more transactions can be processed per second.

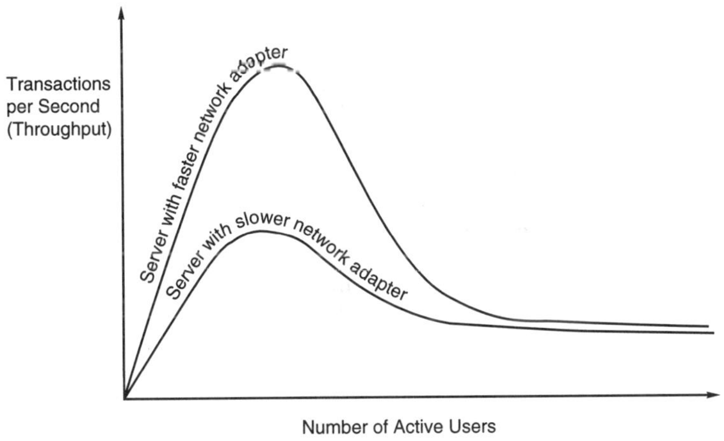

Figure 17.5
File server performance with different network adapters.

Beyond a certain number of active users, the curve begins to flatten out and the curve begins to slope downward as the transactions per second drop. This is caused by an increased amount of I/O activity that starts breaking down the "caching engine" at the server. As the number of active users increases, the users need an additional data space in the cache to satisfy their requirements. If the user's request cannot be satisfied from the cache, it must be satisfied directly from the disk. This increases the time for a transaction, which in turn reduces the rate at which transactions can be performed. Users will experience long delays in their network requests.

As additional users are added beyond the peak, the ratio of requested data to the servers cache size increases. This ratio (U) can be defined as follows:

$$U = T/C$$

in which

T = Total requested data by active users

C = Server data cache size

As the value of *U* becomes greater than 1, the disk cache loses its effectiveness. Furthermore, as active users increase, the portion of the cache used to store write-data increases. Write-data must be written to disk ("flushed") to free up space in the available cache. Thus the cache size is reduced by the amount of write-cache data in the disk at any time. The previous equation should be written as

$$U = T / (C - W)$$

in which

T = Total requested data by active users

C = Server data cache size

W = Total write-data in the server cache

You can use the previous formula to work out an interesting case study.

Assume a cache size of 6 MB on a server, and that an active user submits a transaction that needs 200 KB of read-cache data and 2 KB of write-data in the server's cache constantly. How many active users (*N*) will cause the server cache size to saturate?

Cache will saturate when $U = 1$

From the case study,

$T = N\,'\,200$ KB

in which N is the number of active users.

$C = 6$ MB $= 6000$ KB

$W = N \times 2$

Plugging the previous values in

$$U = T / (C - W)$$

results in

$$1 = N \times 200 / (6000 - N \times 2)$$

Solving this equation

$$6000 - N \times 2 = N \times 200$$

$$N \times (200 + 2) = 6000$$

$$N = 6000 / (202) = 29.7$$

Rounding this result, you get a value of 30 users as the number that will cause the server cache to saturate. In this simplified case study, it is assumed that the server cache requirements are the same for each user. In real life, you will have to estimate a user's cache requirements based on that individual's activity. Another assumption made in this case study is that the user constantly ties up the cache with a certain amount of data. In real-life, many users need the cache only occasionally, and there are periods of time when they do not have any data in the server cache.

Performance can be improved by adding a faster disk subsystem that does not allow the write-cache data (W) in the server cache to build up. A faster disk I/O subsystem will flush the write-cache data quickly, and this will give a flattened peak in the server performance curve (see fig. 17.6), which means that the peak performance will be sustained over a longer period of time.

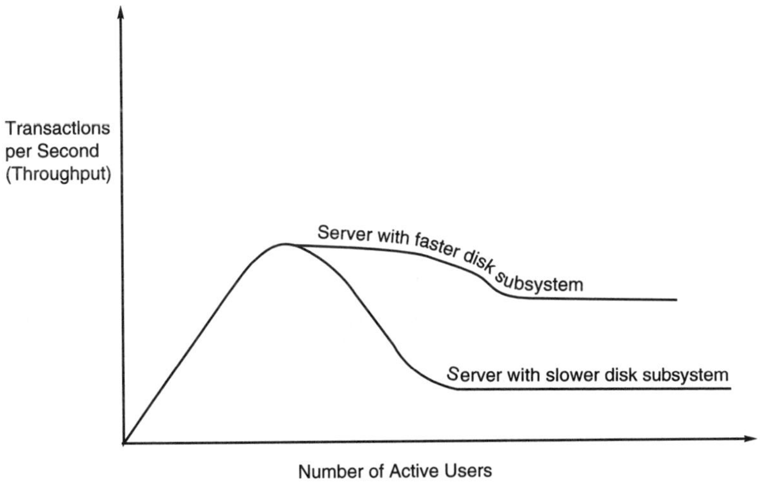

Figure 17.6
File server performance with different disk subsystems.

Tuning IntranetWare Performance

IntranetWare does a good job of monitoring the server's resources, and changes parameters automatically to try to improve server performance. For most system resources, the parameters specify minimum and maximum limits as well as a wait-time limit that specifies how rapidly a resource is allocated. The wait-time limit parameters smooth out peak load demands for system resources so that the operating system does not overreact to a transient demand situation.

These parameters also can be controlled or viewed through the SET command. When you type **SET** at the DOS prompt, IntranetWare lists the following configuration categories and asks which category you want to view:

1. Communications
2. Memory
3. File caching
4. Directory caching
5. File system
6. Locks
7. Transaction tracking
8. Disk
9. Time
10. NCP
11. Miscellaneous
12. Error Handling
13. Directory Services

From a performance point of view, many of these parameters are closely associated. The SET commands for memory, file caching, and directory caching affect the server's memory performance. The SET command controls the file system, locks, and transaction tracking categories, for example, affect file system performance. Because of this interrelationship, the SET commands are grouped and discussed here as follows:

- Memory performance tuning
- File system performance tuning
- Communications performance tuning
- Operating system processes tuning
- Threshold and warning parameters

To change a SET parameter value, the general command is as follows:

```
SET parameter description=New parameter value
```

To view a parameter's current setting, use:

```
SET parameter description
```

Certain parameters cannot be set at the console prompt or in the AUTOEXEC.NCF file. They can be set only in the STARTUP.NCF file. A list of these parameters follows:

```
AUTO REGISTER MEMORY ABOVE 16 MEGABYTES
AUTO TTS BACKOUT FLAG
CACHE BUFFER SIZE
MAXIMUM PHYSICAL RECEIVE PACKET SIZE
MAXIMUM SUBDIRECTORY TREE DEPTH
MINIMUM PACKET RECEIVE BUFFERS
```

Later in this chapter, using the MONITOR.NLM to configure the set parameters and save them for reuse later is discussed.

Memory Performance Tuning for IntranetWare

IntranetWare uses only one memory pool, compared to the five memory pools that NetWare 3 used. After a NetWare 3 server has been running for a long time, the server can run of memory because some management routines don't release memory back to the operating system. IntranetWare 4 solves this problem by using one memory pool. This allows IntranetWare to operate more efficiently because memory management operations are reduced. IntranetWare's memory allocation routines increases its performance by eliminating certain conditions that often lead to server slowdowns.

AUTO REGISTER MEMORY ABOVE 16 MEGABYTES = [ON | OFF]

EISA machines can support more than 16 MB of RAM. Under certain circumstances, you might have to use this parameter to allow IntranetWare to handle extra memory correctly. Setting this parameter in the STARTUP.NCF file allows IntranetWare to register this memory when it first comes up. This parameter cannot be set at the console prompt or in the AUTOEXEC. NCF file. IntranetWare needs to know all the memory available when it first boots up. The default value is ON. If you are using a board that can address only 24 bits of RAM, you may have to set this value to OFF, or you may have corrupted lower memory because 24 bits can address only 16 MB. Any higher address value maps to lower memory.

MINIMUM FILE CACHE BUFFERS = *n*

File caching can be used to improve the performance of file I/O operations. IntranetWare uses memory remaining after allocation of the operating system and NLMs for file caching. In IntranetWare, you can set aside a certain amount of memory for file caching. The file-cache memory also acts as a memory reserve. The server draws on this memory reserve for its needs. The problem with this is that the file-cache memory can be severely depleted, which can seriously affect server performance. A certain amount of memory should always be reserved for file caching (this parameter can be used to set the minimum amount reserved for file caching).

If file I/O seems slow, or long delays and timeouts occur for network operations, the file cache may have fallen below the minimum value necessary for acceptable server performance. If such is the case, the value of this parameter should be increased. The default value for this parameter is 20, which also is the minimum value. The number should be increased gradually to a maximum of 2,000 (the file-cache buffer's usage using MONITOR NLM). Using an extremely high value for this parameter could result in wasted memory that could impact other critical data structures that need memory. The IntranetWare server should give warning if the file-cache buffer reserve falls below the minimum level.

GARBAGE COLLECTION INTERVAL = *n*

Garbage collection is the process of cleaning up the fragmented memory on the server. Memory returned to file cache (such as unloading an NLM) can become fragmented. The garbage collection process makes this memory available to new processes. Garbage collection interval refers to the maximum time between the activation of consecutive garbage collections. This can range from 1 minute to 1 hour, and has a default value of 15 minutes.

MINIMUM FREE MEMORY FOR GARBAGE COLLECTION = *n*

This parameter specifies the minimum number of allocated bytes that need to be free before garbage collection can occur. The system will not perform garbage collection until at least the specified number of bytes can be made free. Set this value low if you want garbage collection to occur and do not care if only a small amount of memory is made free at each garbage collection. You may wish to do this if you are short on memory at the server. Set this value high if you have plenty of RAM and do not need garbage collection to occur frequently. The parameter can be set from 1,000 to 1,000,000 bytes. The default is 8,000.

NUMBER OF FREES FOR GARBAGE COLLECTION = *n*

When an NLM wants to allocate memory, it makes a call to the malloc() function. When an NLM releases memory, it makes a call to the free() function. IntranetWare keeps track of the total number of times NLMs make a "free" request. This parameter sets a limit to the minimum number of frees needed before garbage collection can take place. The parameter value can range from 100 to 100,100 frees, and has a default value of 5,000.

Tuning Server File System Performance for IntranetWare

File caching enables faster access of frequently used files by keeping the disk blocks in fast RAM for read and write operations. Write operations are performed in a delayed fashion, with the writes being done first to RAM. A background process writes these disk buffers (dirty buffers) to the disk during less critical moments but within the time specified by the Dirty Disk Cache Delay Time parameter.

File caching affects both memory and file system performance. The minimum file-cache buffers parameter, discussed in the section on memory performance tuning, affects both memory performance and file system performance.

Directory caching also plays an important role in file system performance, because it enables fast access to frequently used directories. Directory tables are kept in directory buffers in RAM, and the server uses a "least recently" algorithm to keep the directory entries in memory. When the server starts, IntranetWare starts with a *minimum directory cache buffers* (default is 20). When the minimum directory cache buffer is used up, the server must wait for a directory cache allocation wait time (default 2.2 seconds) before allocating another buffer. Under periods of sustained directory access, the number of directory entries could increase to the *maximum directory cache buffers* (default 400). As directory cache buffers increase, the number of buffers available for file caching decreases. Hence, a trade-off is made between directory caching and file caching; they must be carefully balanced for optimum performance.

The following are SET parameters for file system performance.

READ AHEAD ENABLED = [ON | OFF]

IntranetWare contains heuristics to determine if the network I/O pattern issued by a workstation is sequential or random. If the READ AHEAD ENABLED parameter is set to ON and the server determines that a file is being accessed sequentially, it will read the next disk block when the workstation crosses the mid-point of the current block being processed. This feature has tremendous benefits for applications that access network file data sequentially. An example of this is database sort where records are accessed sequentially. The default for this parameter is ON. There is no need to normally turn this parameter OFF. One possible reason would be to measure the difference in performance with read-ahead and without read-ahead. Another possible reason would be if you suspect that the IntranetWare heuristics is incorrectly classifying the network I/O pattern as sequential when it is in fact random. Turning this parameter OFF will avoid waste of file cache buffer space used for reading ahead file blocks that are never used.

READ-AHEAD LRU SITTING TIME THRESHOLD = *n*

Read-ahead occurs in the background and is a low priority process. If the LRU sitting time for a cache block is below this parameter, it indicates that the server is busy performing file I/O. In this case, read ahead will not be performed. The default for this parameter is 10 seconds and it can range from 0 seconds to 1 hour. To disable the behavior described below you can set the parameter to 0.

MAXIMUM CONCURRENT DISK CACHE WRITES = *n*

Unlike DOS, IntranetWare can perform several disk writes concurrently. One reason for this is that IntranetWare does not rely on the single-threaded BIOS on the machine to perform I/O. The disk drivers for IntranetWare allow multi-threaded or concurrent I/O. To speed up disk I/O operations, a number of requests can be placed on the elevator mechanism. The elevator mechanism enables the disk head to move in continuous sweeps across the disk, which are more efficient than the random back-and-forth movements. This mechanism can be used to set the number of write requests (*n*) that can be queued on the disk elevator for a single sweep across the disk surface. A high value for this parameter makes write requests more efficient; a lower number makes read requests more efficient. One way to decide how to set this parameter is to monitor the number of dirty cache buffers using MONITOR. If this number says that a majority of the buffers (70 percent or more) are dirty buffers, the writes are more predominant than reads. In this case, you can improve performance by increasing this parameter. The value ranges from 10 to 4,000, with a default of 50.

DIRTY DISK CACHE DELAY TIME = *n*

To improve disk I/O, the server performs delayed writes by writing first to RAM and then from RAM to disk during idle times. IntranetWare enables you to control how long this wait period should be. If there are many small requests, buffering the writes in RAM before writing them out to the disk is more efficient. This is especially true if the write requests are contiguous sectors on the disk because these can be combined as a smaller number of disk writes. A disk-cache delay time that is too small is the same as disabling the delayed write mechanism. Without delayed writes, server performance could suffer. The default value of 3.3 seconds is long enough for a typical mix of disk I/O operations that take place on the server. The value can be as small as 0.1 seconds, but not more than 10 seconds. An extremely high value can make the server file system more vulnerable in the event of a server crash because many disk I/O operations would be in RAM and not committed to the disk.

MINIMUM FILE-CACHE BUFFER REPORT THRESHOLD = *n*

IntranetWare issues a warning if the number of file-cache buffers falls below a certain threshold. The first warning that the number of cache buffers is getting too low is issued when the following condition is met: Current number of cache buffers + minimum file-cache buffers <= minimum file-cache buffer report threshold. Suppose that the minimum file-cache buffers parameter is set to 20, and the minimum file-cache buffer report threshold is set to 30; when the current number of cache buffers is 50, the previously described condition is met and a warning message is issued. If the number of cache buffers continues to fall to the minimum file-cache buffers, the warning `Cache memory allocator exceeded minimum cache buffer left limit` is issued on the server console. The default value of the threshold is 20, which means that if the minimum file-cache buffer is set to its default of 20, the first warning is issued when the cache number falls to 40. The minimum value of this parameter is 0; it cannot exceed 2,000.

MINIMUM FILE DELETE WAIT TIME = *n*

When a file is deleted, it is not purged immediately from the volume. This parameter controls the minimum amount of time a file should remain on the volume before being purged. Files that have been deleted will not be purged for at least this time, even if the volume is full and the user is unable to create new files. The parameter value ranges from zero to seven days, with a default of 1 minute, 5.9 seconds.

FILE DELETE WAIT TIME = *n*

When a file is deleted, it is not purged immediately from the volume. This parameter controls the amount of time a file should remain on the volume before being purged. Files that have been deleted will not be purged at this time. After this time, the server is free to purge these files. The server keeps at least 1/32 of its disk space free, and starts purging files (starting with the oldest file) to meet this criteria. The parameter value ranges from zero seconds to seven days, with a default of 5 minutes, 29.6 seconds. A small value for this parameter could slow down the server if many deletions are being made. A large value could adversely impact availability of disk space if the server disks were almost full.

MINIMUM DIRECTORY-CACHE BUFFERS = *n*

In IntranetWare, directories are cached in RAM for fast directory searches and directory updates. The directories are kept in directory-cache buffers, whose minimum number is controlled by this parameter. This number must be high enough to perform most directory searches quickly. If the number is set too high, the unused portion is not available for file caching and other server operations. If the server responds slowly to directory searches, especially when it is first booted, monitor this number through the MONITOR NLM. The delay could be caused because the minimum directory-cache buffers parameter is set too low and the server spends time allocating new directory buffers. The value ranges from 10 to 8,000, with a default of 20.

MAXIMUM DIRECTORY-CACHE BUFFERS = *n*

As the number of directory entries and files increases, the server allocates more directory-cache buffers to hold the directories. To prevent the situation from getting out of hand with all available space being used for directory caching, the server enables you to set a limit on the maximum number of directory-cache buffers. If the file server continues to respond slowly, this parameter can be increased after consulting the MONITOR NLM on the directory-cache usage. If the MONITOR NLM reports a shortage of available RAM, and if this parameter is too high, the parameter value should be reduced. Because the server does not release memory automatically if this parameter value is reduced, it must be restarted to free up the unused memory. The parameter value ranges from 20 to 20,000, with a default of 500.

DIRECTORY-CACHE BUFFER NONREFERENCED DELAY = *n*

Only a finite amount of space is in the directory-cache buffers. As new directory entries are loaded into RAM, the older ones can be overwritten. Overwriting older directories too quickly can be a waste, especially if the older directory entries are needed again. This parameter controls the amount of time a directory entry should remain in RAM in the nonreferenced state before it can be overwritten by another directory entry. A higher value indicates that the directory entry is more likely to be cached in memory when needed. This not only speeds up directory access, but also increases the number of directory-cache buffers because directory entries are held longer in the cache. A lower value can slow down directory access because they can be overwritten by new directory entries and will not be in RAM when needed. The parameter value ranges from 1 second to 5 minutes, with a default of 5.5 seconds.

DIRTY DIRECTORY-CACHE DELAY TIME = *n*

Directory entries that are modified in RAM need to be written out to disk to keep the directory on the server disk synchronized with changes in the file system. This parameter controls how long a directory entry can remain in RAM before it must be written to disk. Keeping this parameter high results in faster directory writes but also increases the chance of directory tables getting out of synch with those on disk in the event of a crash. A low value for this parameter reduces the possibility of directory tables becoming corrupt, but the more frequent writes can reduce the performance. The parameter value ranges from zero seconds to 10 seconds, with a default of 0.5 seconds. A zero setting disables the cache delay. Directory entries must be written immediately to disk, which causes slower directory writes.

MAXIMUM CONCURRENT DIRECTORY-CACHE WRITES = *n*

To speed up directory operations, several requests can be placed on the elevator mechanism. The elevator mechanism allows the disk head to move in continuous sweeps across the disk, which are more efficient than the random back-and-forth movements for disk I/O. This parameter controls the number of directory writes that can be queued on the elevator. A high value makes write requests more efficient; a lower number makes read requests more efficient. The parameter value ranges from 5 to 500, with a default of 10.

DIRECTORY-CACHE ALLOCATION WAIT TIME = *n*

IntranetWare does not respond immediately to a demand for new cache buffers. It waits for a period of time before satisfying this demand. This period of time, which is set by this parameter, is used to smooth out peak transient requests that may cause allocation of more directory-cache buffers than are needed. If the wait time is too low, the server will seem too eager to satisfy transient loads and may allocate more directory-cache buffers than are needed. If the server delays too long to satisfy the request, it will seem sluggish and seem to adapt slowly to user needs. The parameter value ranges from 0.5 second to 2 minutes, with a default of 2.2 seconds.

NCP FILE COMMIT = [ON | OFF]

This parameter controls the behavior of an NCP FILE COMMIT request by a client. If this parameter is set to ON, an NCP FILE COMMIT request causes all pending writes to be written immediately to disk. If the parameter is set to OFF, the cache manager flushes the pending writes to disk later. The default value for this parameter is ON. Changing this parameter to OFF can lead to small speed improvements, at the risk of a small chance of data corruption should the server crash before the disk writes are done.

TURBO FAT RE-USE WAIT TIME = *n*

Turbo FATs (indexed tables) are used for indexed files (files with more than 64 entries) and take time to build. If a number of indexed file operations are being performed, releasing the turbo FATs when they may be used again does not make sense. On the other hand, not releasing turbo FATs after their use consumes RAM space that could be used by IntranetWare. This parameter can be used to set the period of time turbo FAT buffers should remain in memory after an indexed file is closed. After the wait time value, the turbo FAT buffer can be reused for another indexed file. If applications perform random accesses and close many large files, this parameter value should be increased to avoid the overhead of rebuilding the turbo FAT index. If you want memory to be released for other operating system resources, this parameter can be increased. The parameter value ranges from 0.3 seconds to 1 hour, 5 minutes, 54.6 seconds, with a default of 5 minutes, 29.6 seconds.

ENABLE DISK READ AFTER WRITE VERIFY = [ON | OFF]

This enables and disables the hot-fix mechanism, which performs a read after a write, and compares the block read with that in memory. You should leave this parameter set to its default value of ON. If disk mirroring or duplexing is used and you are ensured of disk reliability, turning this parameter OFF can lead to faster disk writes.

ALLOW DELETION OF ACTIVE DIRECTORIES = [ON | OFF]

If this parameter is ON, a user with sufficient file system rights can delete a directory that another user has in use. A directory is considered to be in use if the user has a drive mapping to it and is performing operations in the directory, such as copying in to or out of the directory. The default for this parameter is ON.

Transaction Tracking System (TTS) Parameters

The following group of parameters places limits on the TTS system. TTS is the ability to ensure that either all operations defined in a transaction are done or none are.

AUTO TTS BACKOUT FLAG = [ON | OFF]

In IntranetWare, the TTS feature is built into the operating system. In the event of a server crash, files that have been flagged transactional can be restored to a previous consistent state. Setting this parameter to ON causes the server to back out any incomplete transactions automatically at start-up time. The default value is OFF, which means that the user is prompted with the message `Incomplete transaction(s) found. Do you wish to back them out?` This parameter can be set only in the STARTUP.NCF file, not at the console prompt or AUTOEXEC.BAT file.

TTS ABORT DUMP FLAG = [ON | OFF]

The TTS feature enables incomplete writes to a transactional file to be backed out in the event of a server crash. With this parameter set to ON, IntranetWare creates a file called TTS$LOG.ERR on the SYS volume, to back out incomplete writes for transactional files. The default value is OFF, which means that the information to perform the backout is not saved. The result is faster writes and less reliability.

MAXIMUM TRANSACTIONS = *n*

Because IntranetWare is multitasking, the transaction operations can occur simultaneously. IntranetWare enables you to set the number of transactions that can be performed simultaneously on the server. Decrease this value if few transactions are used on the server. The parameter value ranges from 100 to 10,000, with a default of 10,000.

TTS UNWRITTEN CACHE WAIT TIME= *n*

Transactional data is held in RAM to be written out later. IntranetWare enables you to control the amount of time transactional data can be held in memory. If a transactional block is held in memory after this time, other write requests are held up until the transactional data is written. The default value of 1 minute, 5.9 seconds is adequate for most purposes. Increasing this value can result in small speed improvements if the TTS feature is used extensively by applications. The parameter value ranges from 11 seconds to 10 minutes, 59.1 seconds.

TTS BACKOUT FILE TRUNCATION WAIT TIME = *n*

The TTS backout file holds backout information for files, so that the files can be backed out if the server crashes. IntranetWare clears the backout file when the file is not in use. IntranetWare enables you to determine how long an allocated block remains available for the TTS backout file when these files are not being used. The parameter value ranges from 1 minute, 5.1 seconds to 1 day, 2 hours, 21 minutes, 51.3 seconds, with a default of 59 minutes, 19.2 seconds. The default value works well in most situations.

File and Record Locking Parameters

The following group of parameters control how the operating system responds to file and record locks.

MAXIMUM RECORD LOCKS PER CONNECTION = *n*

IntranetWare enables any station to issue record locks. Every record lock consumes server resources. IntranetWare enables you to limit the number of record locks any workstation can issue, to prevent any one station from consuming too many resources. The number of locks can be monitored also through the MONITOR NLM. The parameter should be increased if an application fails while locking records. The parameter should be decreased if the workstation is consuming too many server resources. The parameter value ranges from 10 to 100,000, with a default value of 500.

MAXIMUM FILE LOCKS PER CONNECTION = *n*

IntranetWare enables any workstation to issue file locks. IntranetWare enables you to limit the number of file locks any workstation can issue, to prevent any one station from consuming too many resources. The number of locks can be monitored also through the MONITOR NLM. The parameter should be increased if an application fails while locking records. The parameter can be decreased if the workstation is consuming too many server resources. The parameter value ranges from 10 to 1,000, with a default value of 250.

MAXIMUM RECORD LOCKS = *n*

IntranetWare enables you to set a system-wide global parameter that sets a limit on the total number (n) of record locks IntranetWare can process simultaneously. The purpose of this parameter is to prevent too many record locks from consuming too many server resources. Increase this number if applications are failing and receiving messages about insufficient record locks. The parameter value ranges from 100 to 20,000, with a default value of 20,000.

MAXIMUM FILE LOCKS = *n*

IntranetWare enables you to set a system-wide global parameter that sets a limit on the total number (n) of file locks IntranetWare can process simultaneously. The purpose of this parameter is to prevent too many file locks from consuming too many server resources. Increase this number if applications are failing and receiving messages about insufficient file locks. The parameter value ranges from 100 to 10,000, with a default value of 100,000.

Tuning File-Compression Performance

This group of parameters is used to control file compression in IntranetWare. File compression occurs after a user has accessed a file and certain conditions, set by SET parameters, have taken place.

COMPRESSION DAILY CHECK STARTING HOUR = *n*

This parameter controls when the file compression process starts. The value can range from 0 (midnight) to 24, and has a default value of 0. A value of 24 represents 11:00 PM. You can flag a file for immediate compression by setting the *Immediate Compression* (Ic) flag. The Ic flag is reset automatically after compression has taken place. Otherwise, a file is compressed after a certain minimum time interval (DAYS UNTOUCHED BEFORE COMPRESSION) has elapsed.

COMPRESSION DAILY CHECK STOP HOUR = *n*

This parameter controls when the automatic file compression process stops. The value can range from 0 (midnight) to 24 (11:00 pm), and has a default value of 6. You might want to control this parameter if you have an automatic backup that runs during the hours that the automatic file compression process is active.

MINIMUM COMPRESSION PERCENTAGE GAIN = *n*

This parameter controls the minimum percentage savings that must occur on a file before compression can proceed. If the file compression process determines that the savings are less than that specified by this parameter, the file will not be compressed. An example of this is if you already have files compressed using a utility such as PKZIP. The percentage you can gain by compressing such files is typically low (about 1 percent). Trying to compress these files is wasteful of CPU time as the savings are small. The parameter can be set to a value from 0 to 50 percent. The default is 20 percent.

ENABLE FILE COMPRESSION = [ON | OFF]

When set to OFF, this parameter prevents the server from performing file compression. The default value is set when you first install the file server.

MAXIMUM CONCURRENT COMPRESSIONS= *n*

This parameter controls the number of compressions the server can perform simultaneously. A high setting speeds up compression but takes CPU time away from other processes, and may result in a degradation of server performance for network file I/O. The parameter can range from 1 to 8 and has a default value of 2.

CONVERT COMPRESSED TO UNCOMPRESSED OPTION = *n*

This parameter controls the disposition of a file that has been uncompressed. The parameter can range from 0 to 2 and has a default value of 1. The meaning of the parameter values are described next.

Parameter Value	Description
0	Always leave the file uncompressed.
1	If the compressed file is read only once within the time period described by the DAYS UNTOUCHED BEFORE COMPRESSION parameter, leave the file compressed. On any future access of this file within this time period, leave the file uncompressed.
2	Always leave the file uncompressed.

If you wish to conserve disk space, set the value to 0. If you wish to leave the file uncompressed after it has been accessed just once, set the parameter to 2.

DECOMPRESS PERCENT DISK SPACE FREE TO ALLOW COMMIT = *n*

This represents the percentage of disk space that must be free before IntranetWare will attempt to uncompress the file permanently. Set this value high if you are concerned that you have many compressed files which, if uncompressed, could fill up the hard drive. The parameter can range from 0 to 75 percent and has a default value of 10 percent.

DECOMPRESS FREE SPACE WARNING INTERVAL = *n*

This parameter sets the number of seconds between warning messages that tell you when there is not enough disk space to uncompress a file. The parameter can range from 0 seconds to 29 days, 15 hours, 50 minutes, 3.8 seconds. The default value is 31 minutes, 18.5 seconds.

DELETED FILES COMPRESSION OPTION = *n*

This parameter controls the disposition of files that have been deleted. The parameter can range from 0 to 2 and has a default value of 1. The meaning of the parameter values are described next.

Parameter Value	Description
0	Do not compress deleted files
1	Compress the next day
2	Compress immediately

Choose a value of 2 if you do not want to recover a deleted file immediately, or if you want to conserve disk space. Choose a value of 0 if the network users tend to salvage deleted files soon after they have been deleted.

DAYS UNTOUCHED BEFORE COMPRESSION = *n*

This parameter sets the time period before automatic compression occurs for files that have not been accessed. The parameter value can range from 0 (compress the same day) to 100,000 days and has a default value of 7 days. The setting may be overridden by the Ic attribute on a file or directory. Set this parameter to the average number of days files remain active.

Tuning Communications Performance

The communications parameters control characteristics of communication buffers. Communication buffers are areas in the server RAM dedicated for holding packets. The packets remain in memory before they are processed by the File Service Processes (FSPs).

The following sections describe how these SET parameters can affect the communications performance of a server.

MAXIMUM PHYSICAL RECEIVE PACKET SIZE = *n*

The size of a packet that can betransmitted is determined by the network's physical access mechanism and driver limitations. On the server side, IntranetWare enables you to define the maximum size (*n*) of a packet that can be processed by the file server. When a workstation makes a connection to the server, the packet size is negotiated, based on the settings of the network driver being used at the workstation. This parameter value needs to be large enough to accommodate the maximum packet size used by a workstation. The parameter value ranges from 618 to 24,682 bytes, with a default of 4,202 bytes. Generally, a large packet size can speed communications but consumes more RAM. The parameter can be set only in the STARTUP.NCF file.

MAXIMUM PACKET RECEIVE BUFFERS = *n*

The server needs to keep a certain number of packet buffers in RAM to avoid being overrun by data. Normally, the server allocates receive buffers dynamically, based on its needs. IntranetWare enables you to set an upper limit on the number of packet receive buffers (*n*) the operating system can allocate. The MONITOR NLM can be used to monitor current usage of this parameter. If this parameter is close to the maximum value, increase the value until you have at least one packet receive buffer per workstation. For OS/2 and MS Windows, increase this value, based on the number of simultaneously running network applications at the workstations. Allow for at least one buffer per application. The MONITOR NLM can be used also to monitor the No ECB available count errors. If these errors are being reported, increase this parameter in increments of 10. For EISA and Micro Channel server machines, increase this parameter to allow for five to 10 packet receive buffers per EISA/PCI network board. If the number of file service processes reported by MONITOR NLM is close to its maximum, you can increase the parameter maximum number of service processes to reduce the need for more packet receive buffers. The parameter value ranges from 50 to 4,294,967,295, with a default of 100.

MINIMUM PACKET RECEIVE BUFFERS = *n*

IntranetWare enables you to set a minimum number of packet receive buffers (*n*) at the server. The MONITOR NLM can be used to monitor current packet receive buffers. The default value is 50. Too few receive buffers will cause the server to respond sluggishly when it first comes up. If No ECB available count errors are reported through the MONITOR NLM after the server boots, increase this parameter. For EISA and PCI server machines, increase this parameter to allow for at least five packet receive buffers per EISA/PCI network board. The parameter value ranges from 10 to 294,967,295.

REPLY TO GET NEAREST SERVER = [ON | OFF]

This parameter determines if the file server will respond to Get Nearest Server SAP requests. These requests are generated by workstations when they first log in to the network. If you are using diskless workstations you might want to limit the diskless workstation requests to one physical server. You can do this by turning this parameter OFF on other servers on the segment. Another reason for using this parameter is to hide certain servers on the network for security reasons. You can still log in to servers that have this parameter set OFF by explicitly specifying the name of the server.

NEW PACKET RECEIVE BUFFER WAIT TIME = *n*

IntranetWare enables you to set a waiting period before a request for a new packet receive buffer is satisfied. The reason for this wait is to smooth out peak demands for receive buffers and to allocate receive buffers for sustained loads only. Otherwise, you could end up with more receive buffers than are needed for optimal performance. However, if the parameter is set to too high a value, the server will be slow to respond to sustained needs for additional packet receive buffers. If the parameter is set too low, the server may be too quick to respond to transient demands for additional receive buffers and may end up allocating more receive buffers than are necessary. Novell recommends that this parameter not be changed for EISA bus master boards on the server. The parameter can range from 0.1 to 20 seconds, and has a default value of 0.1 second.

DELAY BETWEEN WATCHDOG PACKETS = *n*

This is the time interval (*n*) between watchdog packets sent from the server to the workstation after there is no response to the first watchdog packet. The watchdog packet is sent to see whether the workstation is still "alive" on the network. If this parameter is set too low, this could generate excessive network traffic because the watchdog packet is sent to every station attached to the server. The parameter value ranges from 9.9 seconds to 10 minutes, 26.2 seconds, with a default of 4 minutes, 56.6 seconds. Normally, the default value is adequate for most networks. For workstations and servers connected by wide area networks, the parameter value can be increased to avoid extra overhead and to account for extra delays. On a wide area network, the setting of this parameter can be critical. Setting the delay too low causes a second watchdog packet to be sent without waiting to receive a response from the first. The delay between watchdog packets must be set greater than the round-trip delay to the workstation.

DELAY BEFORE FIRST WATCHDOG PACKET = *n*

The server sends watchdog packets to a station that has been quiet for some time. IntranetWare enables you to set how long a server should wait before polling a station that has been inactive; then a watchdog packet is sent as a probe to see whether the station is still alive. The parameter value ranges from 15.7 seconds to 14 days, 4 min. 56.6 seconds.

NUMBER OF WATCHDOG PACKETS = *n*

The server sends repeated watchdog packets if the workstation does not respond to a poll from the first watchdog packet. In a heavily congested network, the workstation response to a watchdog packet or the server watchdog packet can get lost. The server gives the workstation a few more chances (*n*) before declaring it dead and clearing the connection. The parameter ranges from 5 to 100, with a default value of 10. Setting a low delay between watchdog packets when the number of watchdog packets is high can cause excessive network traffic and affect the network performance.

Tuning Operating System Processes in IntranetWare

A number of parameters deal with tuning the process scheduling time in the IntranetWare operating system. These SET parameters for operating system processes are described in the following sections.

PSEUDO PREEMPTION COUNT = *n*

IntranetWare uses nonpreemptive scheduling. Processes must relinquish control voluntarily. This parameter forces certain NLMs to relinquish control if they have made this number of reads and writes. The parameter value should be set along the guidelines that come with the NLMs you run. The values range from 1 to 4,294,967,295 with a default of 10. Setting this parameter to a value higher than the default enables each thread to perform more I/O before it is forced to relinquish control.

GLOBAL PSEUDO PREEMPTION TIME = [ON | OFF]

If set to ON, this parameter causes all threads to use pseudo preemption. The default value is OFF.

WORKER THREAD EXECUTE IN A ROW COUNT = *n*

This parameter places restrictions on the operating system scheduler. The parameter value represents the number of times the scheduler can consecutively schedule new work before allowing other threads to do their work. The parameter value ranges from 1 to 20 and has a default value of 10. By setting this value high, you enable the OS to handle more requests at the cost of slowing down existing requests. Set this value to low if you want to force the server to finish existing work in a thread before dispatching new work.

UPGRADE LOW PRIORITY THREADS = [ON | OFF]

If you set this parameter to ON, low priority threads, such as file compression threads, will be upgraded to regular priority. The file server will display a warning message on the server console telling you to adjust this parameter if an ill-behaved NLM freezes a low-priority thread. The default for this parameter is OFF.

MINIMUM SERVICE PROCESSES = *n*

In IntranetWare file service processes are created on demand. IntranetWare enables you to set a lower limit on the number of file service processes (*n*) it can create. This number also can be monitored by the MONITOR NLM. Increase this parameter if the server is always near its maximum. The parameter ranges from 10 to 500, with a default value of 10.

MAXIMUM SERVICE PROCESSES = *n*

In IntranetWare file service processes are created on demand. IntranetWare enables you to set an upper limit on the number of file service processes (*n*) it can create. This number also can be monitored by the MONITOR NLM. Increase this parameter if the server is always near its maximum. The parameter ranges from 5 to 1,000, with a default value of 50.

NEW SERVICE PROCESS WAIT TIME = *n*

IntranetWare creates file service processes on demand. Under transient peak loads, too many file service processes can be created. IntranetWare enables you to smooth out transient demands for file service processes by setting up a waiting period. The parameter ranges from 0.3 seconds to 20 seconds, with a default value of 2.2 seconds. This parameter prevents IntranetWare from reacting too quickly to peak loads and from allocating too many file service processes.

MAXIMUM OUTSTANDING NCP SEARCHES = *n*

Directory searches for existing files are common on a NetWare server because of the flexibility of NetWare's search-mode feature. Normally, only one NCP search operation is permitted per workstation connection. If your applications support it, multiple NCP searches can speed up the application. This parameter enables you to set a limit on the maximum number of NetWare Core Protocol (NCP) searches that can be outstanding at any time. The parameter ranges from 10 to 1,000, with a default value of 51.

Threshold and Warning Parameters

IntranetWare has many parameters that generate warning messages when their threshold values are crossed. These parameters do not affect the performance of the system directly but are important for status alert messages and system operation. These SET threshold and warning parameters and their descriptions follow.

CONSOLE DISPLAY WATCHDOG LOGOUTS = [ON | OFF]

The watchdog process clears inactive connections with workstations. Normally it does this silently. If you want a report of when the connection is cleared on the server console, set this parameter ON. The default value is OFF.

IMMEDIATE PURGE OF DELETED FILES = [ON | OFF]

IntranetWare enables deleted files to be salvaged by the SALVAGE utility. When this parameter is set to ON, all files are immediately purged on deletion; that is, the salvage file feature is disabled. The default value (OFF) permits deleted files to be salvaged.

VOLUME LOW WARN ALL USERS = [ON | OFF]

IntranetWare enables users to be informed when a volume is almost full. The default value is ON; users are alerted when the volume is almost full.

VOLUME LOW WARNING THRESHOLD = *n*

IntranetWare enables you to set how many free disk blocks (*n*) remain on a volume before it issues a warning. To estimate this number, you must divide the desired free-space threshold by the disk-block size. The value for this parameter can range from 0 to 100,000 blocks, with a default value of 256.

VOLUME LOW WARNING RESET THRESHOLD = *n*

The VOLUME LOW WARNING THRESHOLD issues the first warning that disk space is low. IntranetWare enables you to set the number of disk blocks that must be freed (*n*) before a second warning is issued. This parameter is used to prevent repeated warning messages being sent if free space hovers around the threshold set by `VOLUME LOW WARNING THRESHOLD`. When the first warning `VOLUME LOW WARN ALL USERS` is issued, and users reduce disk space just below the threshold, having a warning message may not be desirable if disk-space utilization rises above the threshold. Actually, this process could repeat several times—dipping below the threshold and then rising again—and the repeated warning messages could be a source of great annoyance to the user. The value for this parameter can range from zero to 100,000 blocks, with a default value of 256.

MAXIMUM PERCENT OF VOLUME USED BY DIRECTORY = *n*

IntranetWare enables you to set an upper limit on the percentage (*n*) of a volume that may be used as directory space. This percentage value ranges from 5 to 85, with a default value of 13.

MAXIMUM PERCENT OF VOLUME SPACE ALLOWED FOR EXTENDED ATTRIBUTES = *n*

IntranetWare supports multiple file-name spaces such as Macintosh, NFS, OS/2, and FTAM. These names spaces require extended attribute support. NetWare enables you to set and limit the percentage (*n*) of a volume that may be used for extended attribute storage. When the volume is being mounted, the setting becomes effective. This percentage value ranges from 5 to 50, with a default value of 10.

MAXIMUM EXTENDED ATTRIBUTES PER FILE OR PATH = *n*

IntranetWare enables you to set an upper limit on the number of extended attributes (*n*) that can be assigned to a file or path. This parameter setting affects all server volumes. The parameter value ranges from 4 to 512, with a default value of 16.

MAXIMUM SUBDIRECTORY TREE DEPTH = *n*

IntranetWare enables you to set the number of directory levels supported by the IntranetWare file system. The default value of this parameter is 25, even though some DOS applications cannot support more than 10 levels. The parameter value ranges from 10 to 100. This parameter can be set from the STARTUP.NCF file only. It cannot be set from the console prompt.

ALLOW UNENCRYPTED PASSWORDS = [ON | OFF]

When set to OFF, this parameter enables users to use encrypted passwords only. The OFF setting is used if all file servers are IntranetWare. If servers on the network are below NetWare 3.x, this parameter can be set to OFF to avoid login problems. If the servers are NetWare 2.12 and above, the IntranetWare utilities can be copied to these servers and password encryption can be enabled by keeping this parameter value OFF. For NetWare servers below 2.12 (such as NetWare 2.0a), this parameter should be set to ON.

DISPLAY SPURIOUS INTERRUPT ALERTS = [ON | OFF]

IntranetWare enables you to be alerted about spurious interrupts. Spurious interrupts, caused by IRQ conflicts between devices on the server, generate the message `Spurious hardware interrupt <number> detected`. The default setting is ON because spurious interrupts need to be resolved for the proper functioning of the server. A value of OFF is provided as a convenience (to turn off the messages while waiting for a resolution of the problem)

DISPLAY LOST INTERRUPT ALERTS = [ON | OFF]

IntranetWare enables you to be alerted about lost interrupts. This message is generated when a driver or adapter generates an interrupt request and then drops the request before the CPU can respond to it. This generates the message `Interrupt controller detected a lost hardware interrupt`. The default setting is ON because lost interrupts can degrade server performance. A value of OFF is provided as a convenience (to turn off the messages while waiting for a resolution of the problem). This usually indicates a driver or board problem.

DISPLAY DISK DEVICE ALERTS = [ON | OFF]

IntranetWare enables you to be alerted to disk events such as a hard disk added, activated, deactivated, mounted, or dismounted. The default setting is OFF. Setting the parameter to ON during disk testing and debugging can yield information that might be helpful.

DISPLAY RELINQUISH CONTROL ALERTS = [ON | OFF]

IntranetWare enables you to be alerted when an NLM uses the server CPU continuously for more than 0.4 seconds, without relinquishing control to other processes. This parameter is meant for software developers during the testing phase of their NLM product. Its default value is OFF.

DISPLAY OLD API NAMES = [ON | OFF]

Some of the API names were changed in NetWare 3.1x, and resource tracking was added for better monitoring and control of NLMs and their use of system resources. Also, resource tracking forces NLMs to release all their resources when they are unloaded. The default value of this parameter is OFF. Set this parameter to ON to monitor whether old APIs are being used. If older APIs are being used, contact the vendor of the software to get a more compatible version of the API.

HALT SYSTEM ON INVALID PARAMETERS = [ON | OFF]

Setting this parameter to ON causes the server to stop when an invalid parameter or condition is detected in executing the operating system or NLM code. This parameter can be set in the STARTUP.NCF or AUTOEXEC.NCF file. You may wish to set this parameter to ON when debugging new NCF files or new NLMs. Normally, you should set this value to OFF to enable the server to boot despite anomalous conditions. The default for this parameter is OFF.

SERVER LOG FILE OVERFLOW SIZE = *n*

This value controls the maximum size that the server log file (SYS$ERR.LOG) can achieve. The size can be set between 65,536 and 4,294,967,295 bytes. The default value is 4,194,304 bytes.

SERVER LOG FILE STATE = *n*

This setting controls the action to be taken if the server log file exceeds the overflow size set by the preceding parameter. The parameter values have the following meaning:

Parameter Value	Meaning
0	Take no action
1	Delete the log file (default)
2	Rename the log file

VOLUME LOG FILE OVERFLOW SIZE = *n*

This value controls the maximum size that the volume log file (VOL$ERR.LOG) can achieve. The size can be set between 65,536 and 4,294,967,295 bytes. The default value is 4,194,304 bytes.

VOLUME LOG FILE STATE = *n*

This setting controls the action to be taken if the volume log file exceeds the overflow size set by the preceding parameter. The parameter values have the following meaning:

Parameter Value	Meaning
0	Take no action
1	Delete the log file (default)
2	Rename the log file

VOLUME TTS LOG FILE OVERFLOW SIZE = *n*

This value controls the maximum size that the TTS log file (TTS$ERR.LOG) can achieve. The size can be set between 65,536 and 4,294,967,295 bytes. The default value is 4,194,304 bytes.

VOLUME TTS LOG FILESTATE = *n*

This setting controls the action to be taken if the TTS log file exceeds the overflow size set by the preceding parameter. The parameter values have the following meaning:

Parameter Value	Meaning
0	Take no action
1	Delete the log file (default)
2	Rename the log file

Monitoring Tools

Several monitoring tools are available. Some are among the IntranetWare products; others, such as the Frye Utilities, must be purchased through the product vendor.

Console MONITOR NLM for IntranetWare

MONITOR is one of the most useful utilities for monitoring server performance. This section will briefly describe the MONITOR NLM for IntranetWare.

The MONITOR NLM can be activated using the LOAD command. The MONITOR command has a few optional parameters, as shown in table 17.3.

Table 17.3
Monitor Options

Monitor Option	Description
/L or L	Locks the server console.
/NS or N	Disables the "snake" screensaver, which is otherwise activated after 10 minutes of inactivity.
/NH	Disables the Help screens for MONITOR. Note: Although this switch is included in the Novell documentation, it does not work with MONITOR version 4.01.

The MONITOR NLM can be used for monitoring:

- Server utilization
- Status of cache memory
- Network connections (licensed and attached connections) and their status
- Disk drive information
- File lock status
- LAN driver information
- NLMs loaded at server
- Memory usage
- Mounted volumes
- Scheduling information
- Resource utilization

Additionally, the MONITOR NLM can be used to lock the server console.

The most important screens are displayed and discussed in this section. Menu selections to reach a particular screen from the MONITOR NLM are described by the following convention:

MONITOR -> Selection 1 -> Selection 2

This convention shows that from the MONITOR main menu, you select the Select 1 option and then the Select 2 option.

Understanding General Server Statistics

The main MONITOR screen (see figs. 17.7 and 17.8) shows a number of general statistics for the server and the network. The screen in figure 17.8 is obtained by pressing the Tab key to show additional statistics.

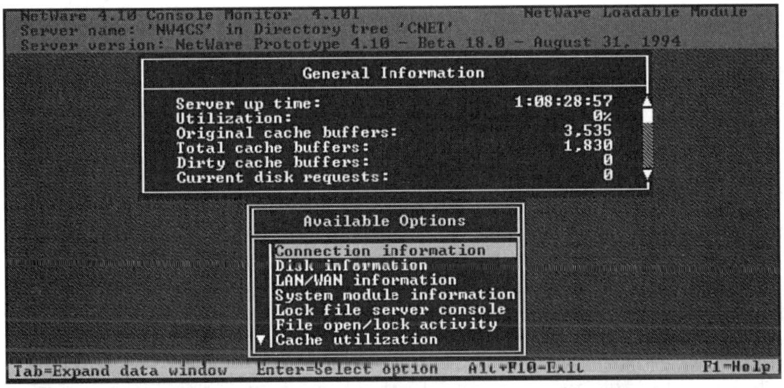

Figure 17.7
General MONITOR statistics.

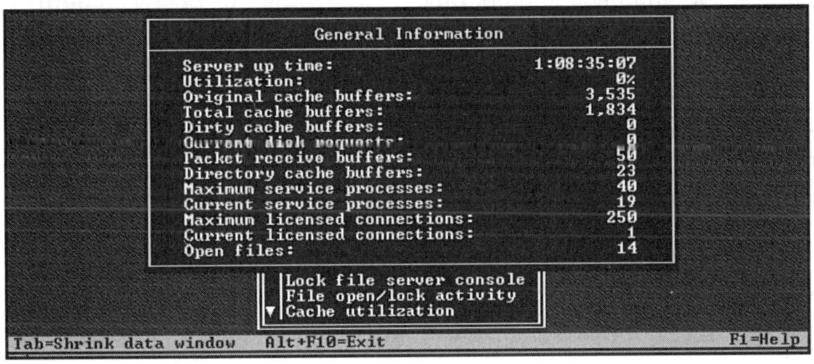

Figure 17.8
Expanded General MONITOR statistics.

The Server Up Time field on the MONITOR (refer to figures 17.7 and 17.8) shows how long the server has been up since the last time it was started. The Utilization field in MONITOR shows the CPU utilization of the server. This is expressed as the percentage of time the server is busy.

The Original Cache Buffers field in the MONITOR screen shows the total number of cache buffers that were available when the server was first started.

Original Cache Buffers = (M–N–D) / B

in which

M = Total server memory

N = Memory used by IntranetWare kernel

D = Memory used by DOS on server

B = Block size

The Original Cache Buffer's value as reported by the screen in figure 17.8 is 3,543. Assuming a block size of 4 KB (4,096 bytes), the initial memory allocated for cache buffers is 3,543* (4,096 = 14,512,128 bytes). The server in figure 17.7 had a total memory of 16 MB (16,777,216 bytes). This means that the memory used by the IntranetWare OS kernel and DOS is 16 MB – 14,512,128 bytes = 2,265,088 bytes, or 2.2 MB.

The Total Cache Buffers field in the MONITOR screen is the number of buffers currently available. As NLMs are loaded, this number decreases. The number in figure 17.7 is 2,063 buffers. This means that Original Cache Buffers – Total Cache Buffers = 3,543 – 2,063 = 1,480 cache buffers are used by additional NLMs. On the server in figure 17.7, the additional NLMs were MONITOR, SERVMAN, and TCP/IP NLMs.

The Dirty Cache Buffers field in the MONITOR screen is the number of buffers that contain file data that is yet to be written to the disk. These buffers are called dirty because the information in them is not synchronized to the disk. The SET Dirty Disk Cache Delay Time parameter can be used to control the minimum amount of time the server waits before synchronizing a dirty disk cache buffer to disk. It has a default value of 3.3 seconds and can range from 0 to 10 seconds. For applications where data integrity is very important, you can set this parameter to 0, to avoid dirty disk blocks not being synchronized to disk. If Dirty Cache Buffers is consistently high, it indicates a high level of write I/O activity where the background process that writes file cache buffers to disk is unable to keep up with the I/O activity.

The Current Disk Requests field in the MONITOR screen indicates the number of disk I/O requests that are in queue waiting to be serviced. If Current Disk Requests is consistently high, it indicates a high level of I/O activity. Using a faster disk controller/disk combination, or splitting the I/O activity across several volumes or servers, will generally improve I/O response times.

The Packet Receive Buffers field in the MONITOR screen is the number of communication buffers at the server that can process workstation requests. This parameter is in the range controlled by the SET Minimum Packet Receive Buffers and the SET Maximum Packet Receive Buffers parameters.

The Directory Cache Buffers field in the MONITOR screen is the number of buffers reserved for directory caching. In IntranetWare, portions of the directory entry tables are cached to improve directory search response times.

The Service Processes field in the MONITOR screen is the number of processes dedicated by the IntranetWare operating system to handle station requests. During peak server activity, when workstation requests exceed the number of service processes that have been assigned, additional service processes are assigned. After assigned, the memory allocated to the service processes is not reduced, unless the server is restarted. You can control the rate at which new service processes are allocated by the SET New Process Service Wait Time that delays the request for a new service process. This parameter can range from 0.3 to 20 seconds and has a default value of 2.2 seconds. The SET Maximum Service Processes parameter limits the growth of the number of processes that handle packets, and can be set to a value between 5 and 100. It has a default value of 40.

The Licensed Connections field on the MONITOR screen is the number of licensed connections to the server. This number reflects the number of users that are using resources on this server. This value is different from the "Active Connections" that can be displayed by selecting the Connection Information option on the MONITOR screen. The Active Connections includes the licensed connections and any other network devices (usually workstations) that are attached to the server but are not making use of server resources.

The Open Files field in the MONITOR screen is the number of files that are currently open at the server. IntranetWare can support 100,000 open files. To view file names that are opened by a particular user, you must select the Connection Information option, highlight the user name, and press Enter.

MONITOR Connection Information

The MONITOR connection information screen is shown in figure 17.9. This screen can be reached through:

MONITOR -> Connection Information

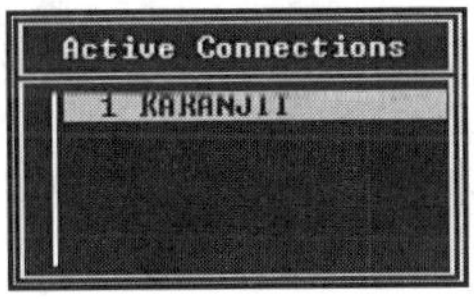

Figure 17.9
The MONITOR connection information screen.

Users who are logged out are indicated by NOT-LOGGED-IN. They show up in the connection information list because the shell at the workstation is still attached to the server.

If a displayed user is selected, information on that user is displayed as shown in figure 17.9. The top half of the screen in figure 17.9 displays statistics on the user; the bottom half (not shown) indicates the files opened by the user (see fig. 17.10). The statistics for the user indicate the following:

- **Connection time.** Measured in days, hours, and minutes.
- **Network Address.** This address consists of three parts: network number (cable segment number), node address, and socket address. The socket address for the workstation shell is 4003 (hex); this is the software address of the workstation shell process.
- **Requests.** The total number of NCP requests generated by the workstation connection is displayed.

- **Kilobytes Read.** Measure of amount of information read. If enabled through accounting services, a user can be charged for this service.
- **Kilobytes Written.** Measure of amount of information written. If enabled through accounting services, a user can be charged for this service.
- **Status.** A user status can be Normal, which means the user is logged in; Waiting, which means the station is waiting for a file to be unlocked; or Not-logged-in, which means the shell attached to the server by the user is not logged in.
- **Semaphores.** Displays the number of semaphores used by the station. Semaphores can be used to arbitrate access to resources (NICs, areas of RAM, bus), and also to limit the number of workstations that can use a shared application.
- **Logical Record Locks.** Displays the number of logical locks used by a connection. A logical lock is implemented by assigning a logical name to a resource and locking that name. Other applications check for a lock on the name before accessing the resource. A logical record is enforced by applications. (This is different from physical locks that are enforced by the network operating system and can lock a range of bytes on a file. If another user attempts to access a range of bytes that is physically locked, the user receives an `Access Denied` error message.)

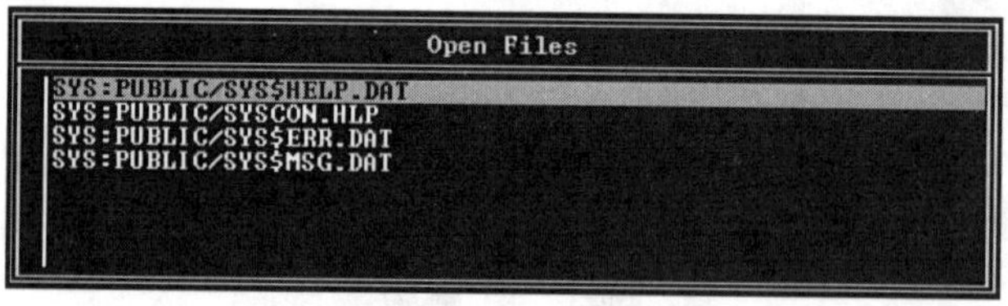

Figure 17.10 *MONITOR user information.*

The physical locks for an open file can be displayed by selecting an open file and pressing Enter. Figure 17.11 shows the headings for the physical locks. The Start and End columns indicate the byte offset at which the lock begins and ends. The Physical Record Locks column indicates one of the four types of record locks defined in table 17.4.

Figure 17.11 *MONITOR physical record locks for user connection.*

Table 17.4
Types of Physical Locks

Physical Lock	Description
Locked Exclusive	Locked so that no one else can read or write to the specified range of bytes
Locked Shareable	Locked so that reads are allowed but only one station can write
Locked	Logged for future locking
TTS Holding Lock	Unlocked by application but still locked by TTS because transactions are not complete

MONITOR Disk Information

You can see the Disk information on the server by using MONITOR or SERVMAN. The information shown by these tools complement each other, and in some cases the same information is shown in the MONITOR and SERVMAN NLMs.

You can optimize server disk utilization by enabling sub-allocation, compression, and data migration (if you have the hardware support). To improve response times for the server disk, you can use high performance disk and disk controllers. Many high performance servers use SCSI controllers that come with custom disk drivers that are optimized to take advantage of the special hardware features of the disk controllers. Use of a 32-bit bus and bus mastering technique, such as that used in EISA and PCI adapters, can further improve data transfer rates for the server disk.

To view disk information using MONITOR, select Disk Information from the Available Options screen. Highlight a system disk driver and press Enter. You should see a screen similar to figure 17.12. The top half of the screen shows the driver information.

The driver information includes the following:

- **Driver.** This is the driver name.
- **Disk Size.** Size in megabytes of all partitions on the disk.
- **Partitions.** Number of partitions defined on the hard disk.
- **Mirror Status.** The values are Mirrored, which indicates that disk mirroring is in place; Not Mirrored, which indicates that disks are being used independently; and Remirroring, which indicates that data is being transferred between disks so that they can be mirrored.
- **Hot Fix Status.** Normal indicates that hot fix is enabled. Not-hot-fix indicates that hot fix has been disabled or has failed.

- **Partition Blocks.** Total space in disk blocks on the server disk.
- **Disk Blocks.** Number of blocks from the total partition blocks that can be used for data.
- **Redirection Blocks.** Number of blocks reserved for the Hot Fix Area.
- **Redirected Blocks.** Number of bad blocks found and redirected by hot fix.
- **Reserved Block.** Used for hot-fix tables.

The DOS partition on a server disk is counted as a partition. shows the Mirror Status and the Hot Fix Status of the disk. The Partition Blocks field shows the total number of 4 KB disk blocks that are available. A certain number of redirection blocks—shown in the Redirection Blocks field—are reserved for hot fix, and the actual number of 4 KB data blocks—shown in the Data Blocks field—that are available is the difference between the values in the Partition Blocks and Redirection Blocks fields.

Partition Blocks = Data Blocks + Redirection Blocks

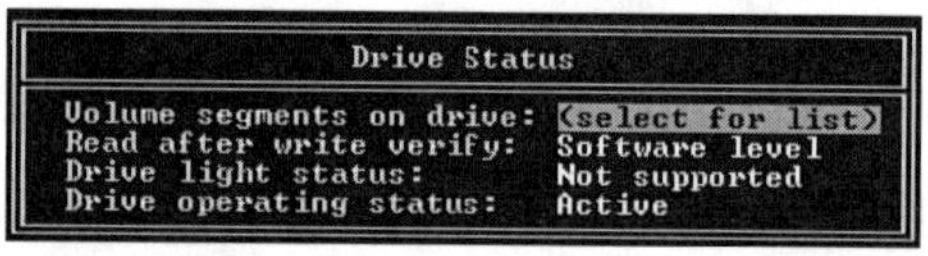

Figure 17.12
Disk Information using MONITOR.

The Redirection Blocks field indicates the number of blocks that were relocated because of hot-fix errors. If this number increases rapidly, it usually indicates a rapidly deteriorating disk. You should reformat the disk and perform surface analysis, or replace the disk.

The Reserved Blocks field represents the number of redirection blocks reserved for system use. When the following condition holds, hot-fix on the volume has failed.

Redirected Blocks + Reserved Blocks = Redirection Blocks

The lower half of the screen indicates the following information:

- **Volume Segments On Drive.** A volume can be made up of many disk partitions or disks; they are listed if this field is selected.
- **Read-After-Write Verify.** Normally set to Software Level Verify, because Hot Fix performs Read-After-Write Verify. Some disk controllers can perform this test, in which case Hardware Level Verify may be selected. The Disable Verify disables the Read-After-Write Verify. This option should be selected only for benchmark tests. Under normal operation, always have some form of Read-After-Write Verify check.

- **Drive Light Status.** Can be used to physically flash the drive-light status indicator at regular intervals, so that you can identify the physical disk. This option may not be supported for some disk drivers/drive types.

- **Drive Operating Status.** Used to manually deactivate/activate disk; used primarily for testing disk drives.

The Volume Segments On Drive field shows the volume segments that make up the logical volume. An IntranetWare volume can consist of 32 volume segments. The Read After Write Verify field indicates if the read-after-write feature is supported by the volume. Figure 17.12 shows that the read-after-write feature is hardware-supported for the volume. The Drive Light Status field indicates the current drive-light flash status. If a parameter is not supported by the hardware, a value of Not Supported is displayed. The Drive Operating Status field indicates if the drive is Active or Deactivated. For removable disks, two other parameters—Removable Drive Mount Status and Removable Drive Lock Status—are displayed. These indicate if the removable drive is currently mounted or if the drive is locked.

MONITOR LAN Information

The MONITOR LAN information screen is shown in figure 17.13. This screen can be reached through:

MONITOR -> LAN Information -> Select a LAN driver

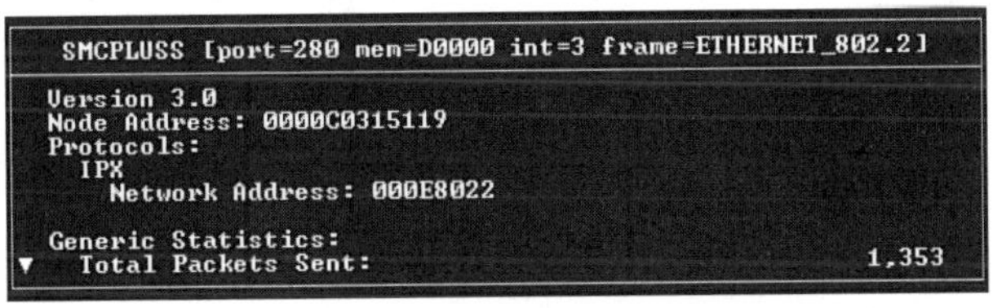

Figure 17.13
MONITOR LAN driver information.

Figure 17.13 displays the LAN driver information for the selected LAN driver. The bottom half of the screen shows a window titled with the name of the LAN driver selected. The LAN driver information indicates the version number, node address of the NIC in the server, protocols bound to the LAN driver, and the network address of the cabling segment on which the LAN driver is working.

Figure 17.14 shows more of the Generic Statistics information. The statistical information for a LAN driver cannot fit on-screen, but you can use the cursor or PgDn keys to see the rest of the information.

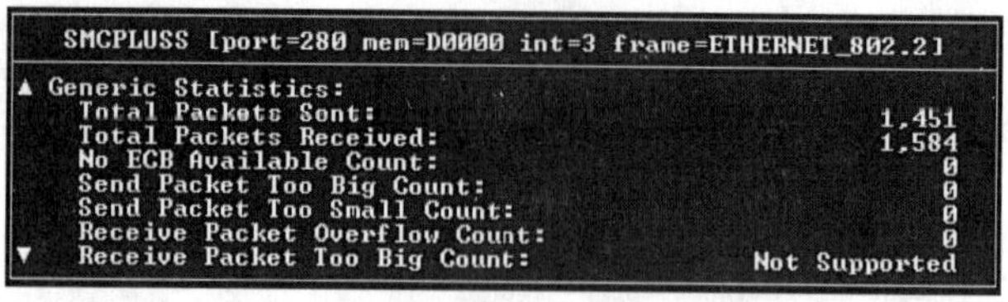

Figure 17.14
MONITOR LAN Generic Statistics.

Generic Statistics information, available for all LAN drivers, is described in table 17.5.

Table 17.5
MONITOR Generic Statistics for LAN Drivers

Parameter	Description
Total Packets Sent	Total packets sent through this LAN driver; indicates which driver is handling most of the traffic, and how much traffic.
Total Packets Received	Total packets received by this LAN driver; indicates which driver is handling most of the traffic, and how much traffic.
No ECB Available Count	A counter that increments when a packet receive buffer is not available for an incoming packet. Server allocates packet receive buffers on demand until the MAXIMUM PACKET RECEIVE BUFFERS is reached (see the earlier section in this chapter on SET parameters).
Send Packet Too Big Count	A counter that increments when server transmits a packet too big for the NIC to handle; indicates an incorrect setting of MAXIMUM PHYSICAL RECEIVE PACKET SIZE or a problem with the server software or NIC driver.
Send Packet Too Small Count	A counter that increments when server transmits a packet too small for the NIC to handle; indicates a problem with the server software or NIC driver.
Receive Packet Overflow Count	A counter that increments when server receives a packet too big to store in a cache buffer; indicates a problem with workstation software in negotiating a proper packet size; could also be a problem with NIC driver or card at sender.

Parameter	Description
Receive Packet Too Big Count	A counter that increments when server receives a packet too big for the NIC to handle; indicates an incorrect setting of MAXIMUM PHYSICAL RECEIVE PACKET SIZE or a problem with sender software or NIC driver.
Receive Packet Too Small Count	A counter that increments when the server is too small, the counter receives a "packet too small" message for the NIC to handle; indicates problem with sender software or NIC driver.
Send Packet Miscellaneous Errors	A catch-all error counter that increments when an error occurs during transmission of a packet that does not fit any other category. A large value could indicate problems with network hardware.
Receive Packet Miscellaneous Errors	A catch-all error counter that increments when an error occurs during reception of a packet that does not fit any other category. A large value could indicate problems with network hardware.
Send Packet Retry Count Hardware	A counter that increments when server retries sending a packet because of an error; indicates a problem with cabling or NIC hardware, or a problem with long delays across a Wide Area Network. Try increasing the retry count using the LOAD driver command.
Checksum Errors	A counter that increments when a data error is detected by the CRC checksum at the end of the MAC frame (packet); indicates a problem with NIC hardware, noise, or cabling.
Hardware Receive Mismatch Count	A counter that increments when the packet length indicated by the length field in a packet does not match the size of the packet received by the NIC; indicates a problem with NIC or NIC driver.

In addition to Generic Statistics, Custom Statistics specific to the NIC hardware are being used. These are reported by the driver for that NIC and are different for different network hardware. Figure 17.15 shows the custom statistics for an Ethernet NIC. Among other statistics, a variety of custom statistics deal with collision count. This is in keeping with the operation of Ethernet.

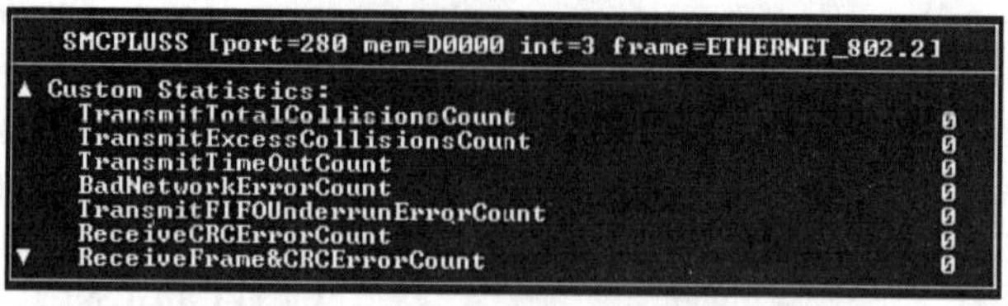

Figure 17.15
MONITOR LAN Custom Statistics.

MONITOR System Module Information

The MONITOR System Module List screen is shown in figure 17.16. This screen can be reached through:

MONITOR -> System Module Information

Figure 17.16 shows the System Module Information for the Novell Directory Services. To see this figure, select System Module Information from Available Options in MONITOR. Highlight the desired system module, and press Enter. The top part of the screen indicates the module size in RAM and the file name under which the system module was loaded. The bottom half of the screen shows the resource tags for that system module. A resource tag is a mechanism introduced in NetWare 3.10 to keep track of system resources. It also enables IntranetWare to ensure that all tagged resources are released when the system module is unloaded. Because the system modules can be written by third-party vendors over whom Novell has little control, this is a useful addition to the IntranetWare operating system, enabling it to release resources when a module unloads. From figure 17.16, you can see that the name of the Novell Directory Services is DS.NLM and it uses 562,709 bytes. You can also see a list of resource tags used by the NLM. When an NLM makes use of resources, it can register the name of the resource and other information on the resource as a set of resource tags. This enables the server to monitor and track how these resources are used. Figure 17.17 shows that the Alloc memory tag uses 45,136 bytes of memory. To view the memory used by a resource tag, highlight the resource and press Enter. This displays the tag name (Tag), the name of the parent module this resource belongs to (Module), the type of resource (Resource), and the amount of memory used by the resource (In Use).

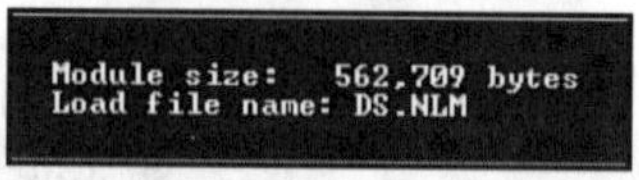

Figure 17.16
System Module information for DS.NLM.

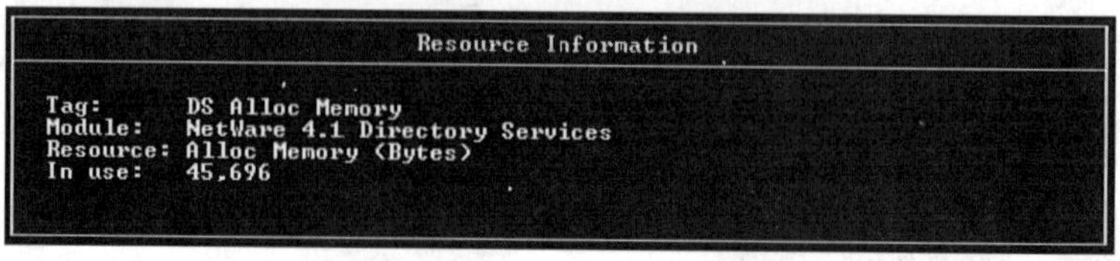

Figure 17.17
Memory used by resource tag in MONITOR.

MONITOR File Open/Lock Activity

The MONITOR File Open/Lock Activity screen is shown in figure 17.18. This screen can be reached through:

MONITOR -> File Open/Lock Activity -> Select path name of a file

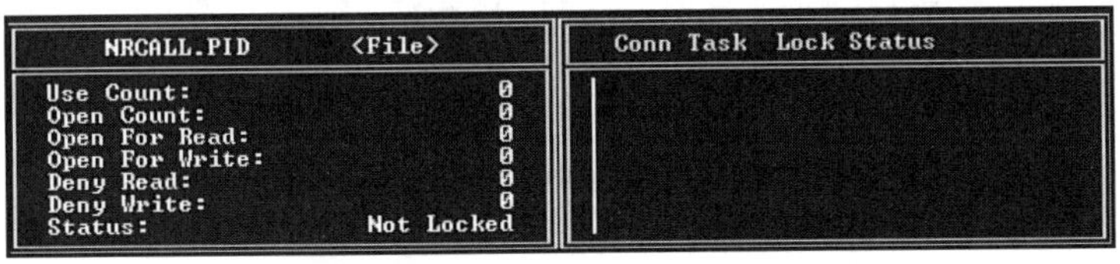

Figure 17.18
MONITOR File Open/Lock activity.

Use Count is the number of connections that have the file opened or locked. Open Count defines the number of connections that currently open the file; Open Read indicates the number of connections reading from the file; and Open Write, the number of connections writing to the file. The following relationship holds true at all times:

Open Count = Open Read + Open Write

The Deny Read and Deny Write fields indicate whether the file lock for the open operation is exclusive or shared. Deny Read indicates the number of connections that have opened the file, but denies even the read operation (exclusive file lock). Deny Write indicates the number of connections that have opened the file, but denies writes to other stations (shared read).

The Status field indicates whether the file is Locked or Unlocked. The Conn column indicates a list of connections using that field. The Task is an internal number used by the client for the application using the file. The lock status can have the values of Exclusive, Shareable, TTS Holding Lock, Logged, or Not Logged. The Exclusive lock means that no one else can read or write to the record; Shareable means that others may read but not write to the record. TTS Holding Lock means that the file was unlocked by an application, but because the transactions are not complete, the TTS has the file locked. Logged means that a set of records is being prepared for locking, to avoid a deadly-embrace situation. Not-Logged, the normal condition, indicates that no locks are pending.

Examining Cache Utilization

IntranetWare improves the performance of disk reads and writes by allocating an area of server RAM called the *file cache*, and by reading disk blocks into the file cache area. Subsequent reads of the same disk block can be satisfied from the file cache. Reads from the file cache are much faster than reading directly from the disk. Similarly, writes are done to the cache and returned as being completed. A background process called the *lazy cache write process*, flushes the written blocks to server disk. When a read request is satisfied from the file cache, it is called a *cache hit*. *Cache utilization* can be defined as the percentage of cache hits.

To observe cache utilization, select Cache Utilization from Available Options in MONITOR (see fig. 17.19). The parameters for cache utilization are described in table 17.6.

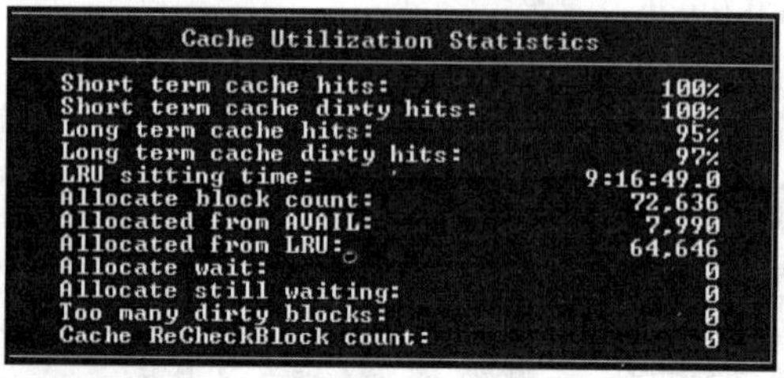

Figure 17.19
Cache Utilization using MONITOR.

Table 17.6
Cache Utilization Parameters

Cache Parameter	Description
Short Term Cache Hits	This indicates the percentage of disk cache requests that were satisfied with cache blocks that were already in the file cache over the last one second.
Short Term Cache Dirty Hits	This indicates the percentage of disk cache requests that were satisfied with cache blocks already in the file cache, but the disk block was dirty (not yet flushed to disk), over the last one second.
Long Term Cache Hits	This indicates the percentage of disk cache requests that were satisfied with cache blocks that were already in the file cache. Long Term means longer than a second.
Long Term Cache Dirty Hits	This indicates the percentage of disk cache requests that were satisfied with cache blocks that were already in the file cache, but the disk block was dirty (not yet flushed to disk). This parameter indicates how often a request was made for a block that was just recently written to the cache. Blocks written to the cache are written to the disk in a time interval controlled by the SET the Dirty Disk Cache Delay Time, whose default value is 3.3 seconds. Long Term means longer than a second.
LRU Sitting Time	This indicates the time since the oldest block in the LRU list was last referenced.
Allocate Block Count	This indicates the number of disk cache block requests that have been made since the server was started.
Allocated From AVAIL	This indicates the number of disk cache block requests that were satisfied from the AVAIL list, which consists of blocks that are not currently used.

Cache Parameter	Description
Allocated from LRU	This indicates the number of disk cache block requests that were satisfied from the LRU list, which consists of blocks that are Least Recently Used (oldest blocks not referenced).
Allocate Wait	This indicates the number of times a cache block request had to wait because there were no available cache blocks.
Allocate Still Waiting	This indicates the number of times a cache block request had to wait behind another cache block request in the queue that was still waiting because there were no available cache blocks. This indicates the number of times the queue size for memory allocation requests was more than 1.
Too Many Dirty Blocks	This indicates the number of times a write request was delayed because there were too many dirty blocks.
Cache ReCheckBlock Count	This indicates the number of times disk cache requests had to be retried, because the target block was being used.

Processor Utilization Option

Selecting Processor Utilization gives a screen similar to that shown in figure 17.20, which lists the Available Processes and Interrupts. The list includes active processes (or threads) as well as all available hardware interrupts. To select multiple processes for observation, mark them with the F5 key and press Enter. Alternatively, you can select all the processes by pressing F3. Figure 17.21 shows the processor utilization for processes selected using F3.

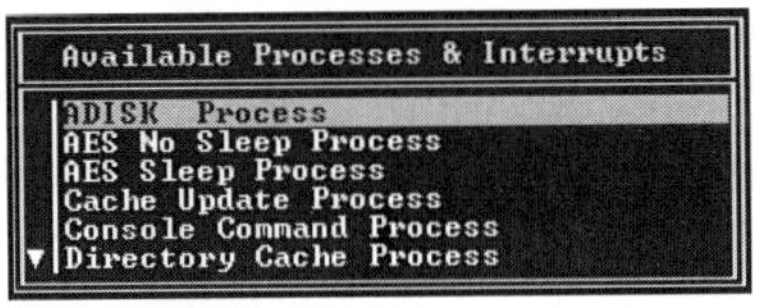

Figure 17.20
Available processes and interrupts.

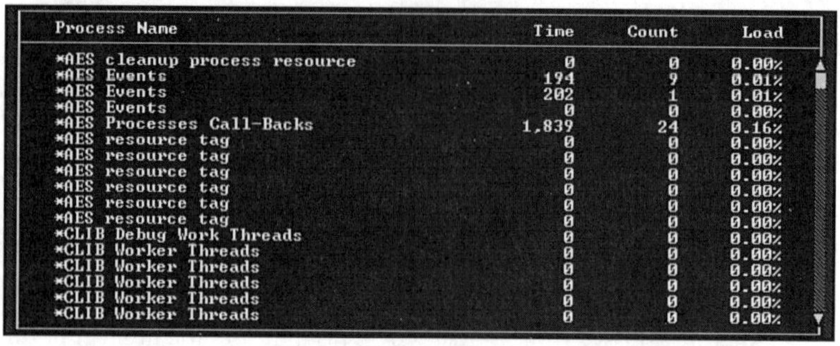

Figure 17.21
Processor Utilization for all processes.

The screen in figure 17.22, for example, shows the process activity for seven processes marked with the F5 key. The Time column indicates the amount of time the CPU spent executing the code in the context of that process. For interrupts, this is the amount of time spent in the Interrupt Service Routine (ISR) associated with that interrupt. The Count column represents the number of times the process ran during a sample period. For interrupts, this number indicates the number of interrupts serviced during a sample period. The Load column gives the percentage of time the CPU spent in this process or interrupt.

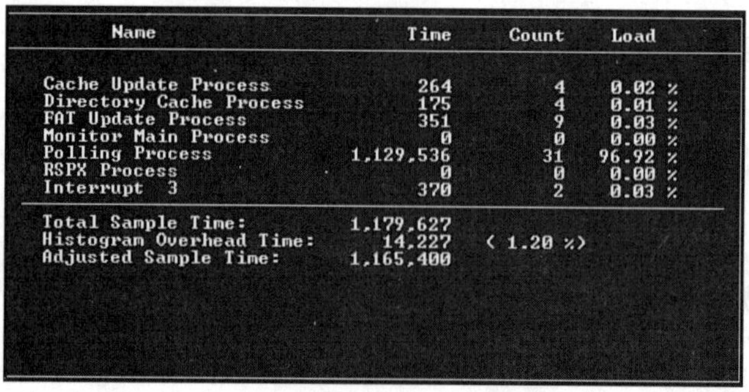

Name Time Count Load
Cache Update Process 264 4 0.02 %
Directory Cache Process 175 4 0.01 %
FAT Update Process 351 9 0.03 %
Monitor Main Process 0 0 0.00 %
Polling Process 1,129,536 31 96.92 %
RSPX Process 0 0 0.00 %
Interrupt 3 370 2 0.03 %
Total Sample Time: 1,179,627
Histogram Overhead Time: 14,227 (1.20 %)
Adjusted Sample Time: 1,165,400

Figure 17.22
Process activity.

At the bottom of the screen, an overhead summary displays the total sample time, the amount of time spent generating the utilization information (along with the percentage), and the adjusted sample time—the amount of time available for all the processes and interrupts to use. All the process and interrupt statistics are relative to the adjusted sample time.

Note that the utilization information is generated only when MONITOR is in this screen. When you enter this screen, MONITOR turns on the statistics-generation engine in IntranetWare. When you leave this screen, MONITOR turns off the statistics-generation engine, and the operating system returns to its normal mode of operation.

When the server is idle, the CPU will spend most of the time in the Polling Process and the STREAMS Q Runner Process if STREAMS is loaded. This can be used as an indication of low CPU utilization. Server Processes are used to service workstation requests. If other processes or interrupts have an unusually high percentage of the CPU's time, it may indicate bad hardware, drivers, or NLMs, or simply a busy server.

As you can see from figure 17.23, most CPU time is allocated to the Polling Process. Because there was no other activity on the system on which this measurement was taken, most of the time was spent in the Polling Process. The NIC setting on the server was set to Interrupt 3; as packets are processed by the NIC, Interrupt 3 shows activity. Whenever packets were transferred between workstation and server, the Interrupt 3 activity jumped up, as figure 17.23 shows. Interrupt 0 also shows a high level of activity because this interrupt is the timer interrupt on Intel processor-based servers.

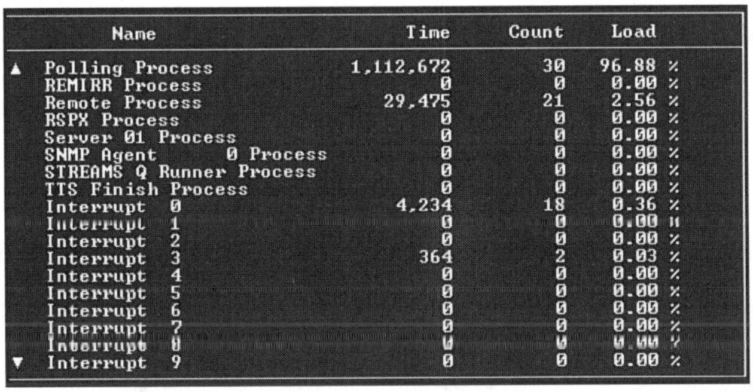

Name	Time	Count	Load
Polling Process	1,112,672	30	96.88 %
REMIRR Process	0	0	0.00 %
Remote Process	29,475	21	2.56 %
RSPX Process	0	0	0.00 %
Server 01 Process	0	0	0.00 %
SNMP Agent 0 Process	0	0	0.00 %
STREAMS Q Runner Process	0	0	0.00 %
TTS Finish Process	0	0	0.00 %
Interrupt 0	4,234	18	0.36 %
Interrupt 1	0	0	0.00 %
Interrupt 2	0	0	0.00 %
Interrupt 3	364	2	0.03 %
Interrupt 4	0	0	0.00 %
Interrupt 5	0	0	0.00 %
Interrupt 6	0	0	0.00 %
Interrupt 7	0	0	0.00 %
Interrupt 8	0	0	0.00 %
Interrupt 9	0	0	0.00 %

Figure 17.23
Polling Process time and increase in Interrupt 3 activity.

MONITOR Resource Utilization

The MONITOR Resource Utilization screen is shown in figure 17.24. This screen can be reached through:

MONITOR -> Resource Utilization -> Select a resource

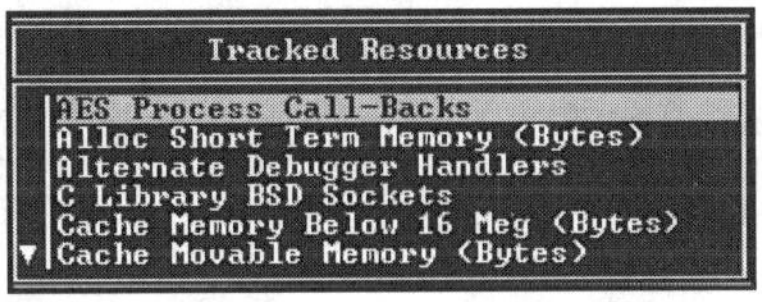

Tracked Resources

AES Process Call-Backs
Alloc Short Term Memory (Bytes)
Alternate Debugger Handlers
C Library BSD Sockets
Cache Memory Below 16 Meg (Bytes)
Cache Movable Memory (Bytes)

Figure 17.24
MONITOR tracked resources.

The server tracks resources such as the Alloc Memory Pool by forcing procedures to use a resource tag when doing an allocation. The top part of the screen contains server memory statistics. The individual fields are as follows:

- **Allocated Memory Pool.** Memory used by NLMs. As an NLM needs memory for data, it is allocated from the Cache buffer pool. This memory is returned to the Cache buffer memory pools when the NLM unloads.

- **Cache Buffers.** The amount of memory in the cache buffer pool. This memory currently is being used for file caching. The amount of memory in this area should be greater than that in any other area.

- **Cache Movable Memory.** Memory allocated directly from the cache buffer pool. When freed, this memory will be returned to the cache buffer pool. It differs from Cache Non-Movable Memory in that the memory manager may move the location of these memory blocks to optimize memory usage. Volume tables and hash tables typically use this memory.

- **Cache Non-Movable Memory.** Memory allocated for OS and other NLM programs to store their code and data.

- **Code and data memory.** Memory allocated directly from the cache buffer pool. When freed, this memory will be returned to the cache buffer pool. Used when large pieces of memory are needed.

- **Total Server Work Memory.** This is the sum of all the memory pools.

The lower left side of the screen shows the resource types that are tracked by the server (see fig. 17.25). If you highlight a tracked resource and press Enter, you can see the resource tags for that resource type. Figure 17.26 shows the resource tags for the SNMP Abstract Object resource type. If you highlight a resource tag and press Enter, you can see the Tag name, Module name (NLM name), Resource type the resource tag belongs to, and the amount of the resource type that has been allocated (in use) by the resource tag (see fig. 17.27).

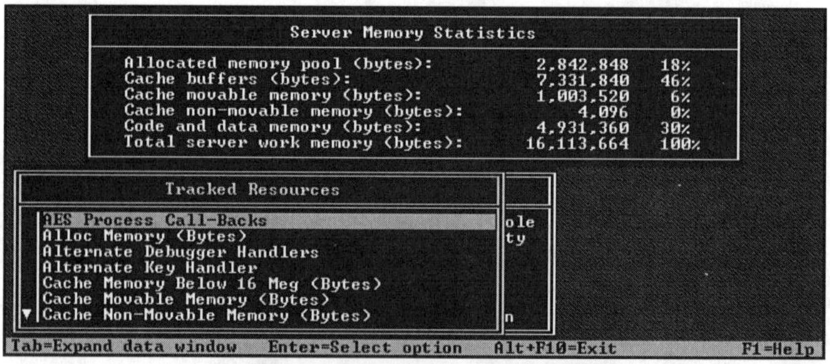

Figure 17.25
Resources tracked by the server.

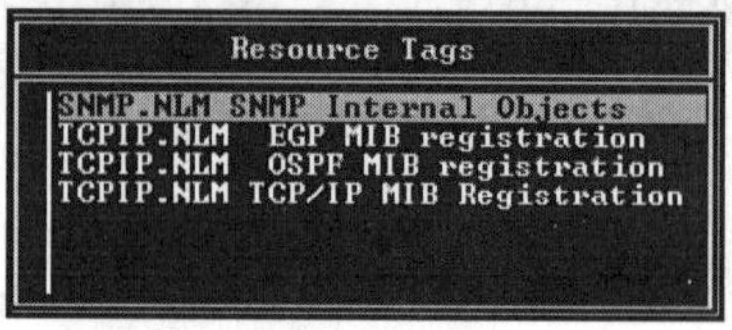

Figure 17.26
Resource tags for a tracked resource type.

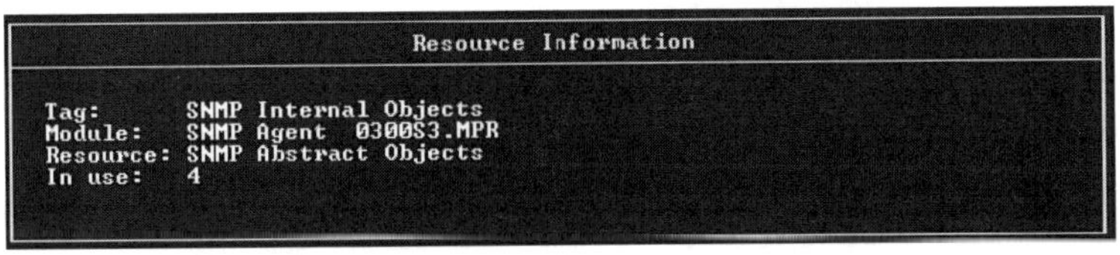

Figure 17.27
Resource tags details.

Notice that the resources under the tracked resource processes are NLMs. This is to be expected because the NLMs act as processes. Selecting a specific resource tag gives more information on that resource.

Examining Memory Utilization

IntranetWare manages memory in 4 KB page sizes. The memory for NLMs is allocated from a common file cache pool and released to this common pool when the NLM is unloaded. An NLM can also issue the system free() call to release memory that it has dynamically allocated.

The memory needed by an NLM is the memory for itself, plus any other NLMs it depends on. Because common NLMs, such as CLIB, STREAMS, and TLI, can be shared by a number of NLMs, the overall system memory requirements are reduced. The memory used by an NLM is approximately the same as the size of the NLM file. Certain NLMs allocate additional memory when they are running, and this must be factored into the estimated memory usage for that NLM.

When you select Memory Utilization from Available Options in MONITOR, and use the Tab key to expand the data window, the top part of the screen shows the allocated memory information for all modules (see fig. 17.28).

Figure 17.28
Allocated Memory Information for all Modules using MONITOR.

The 4 KB Cache Pages field shows the number of cache pages in the memory allocation pool. This pool is the set of pages from which memory is allocated.

The Cache Page Blocks field represents the memory that has already been allocated and is in the allocated memory pool.

The Percent In Use field is the percentage of memory in the allocated memory pool (Cache Page Blocks) that is in use, and the Percent Free field is 100 minus the Percent In Use value.

The Memory Blocks In Use field is the number of pieces of memory that have been allocated and are currently in use.

The Memory Bytes In Use field is the number of bytes of memory that have been allocated and are currently in use.

The Memory Blocks Free field is the number of pieces of memory that have been freed and are available for reuse.

The Memory Bytes Free field is the number of bytes of memory that have been freed and are available for reuse.

To see memory allocation for an individual system module, highlight the module and press Enter. The lower part of the screen displays the memory allocated for that module. Figure 17.29 shows the memory utilization for the Novell Directory Services. The description of these parameters is the same as that discussed for all the system modules, except that the values refer to the individual system module rather than all the system modules.

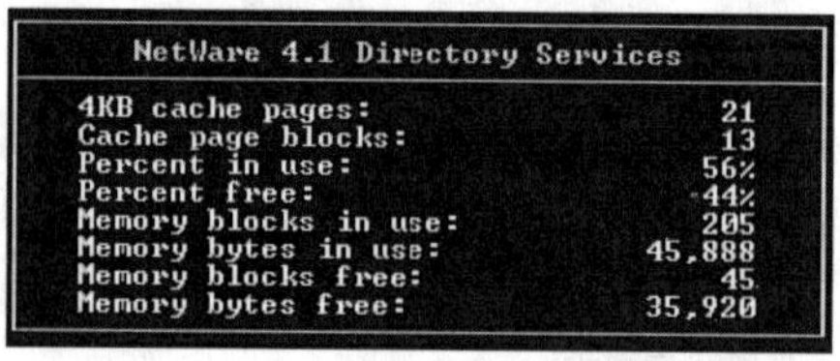

Figure 17.29
Allocated Memory Information for Novell Directory Services using MONITOR.

You can perform garbage collection from the screen in figure 17.29. Garbage collection looks for whole pages in the free area of the allocated memory pool and returns them to the system. To perform garbage collection for the selected module, press F3, and to perform garbage collection for the entire system, press F5.

Examining Scheduling Information

The general MONITOR and SERVMAN statistics show the overall processor utilization (see figs. 17.7 and 17.30). IntranetWare can be used to see processor utilization on a per process basis. This enables you to determine where most of the processor time is being spent. Under continuous heavy processor loads, it is usually just a few processes that contribute to most of the processor load. You can use MONITOR to quickly identify which processes use most of the processor cycles. You may then decide to load these applications on separate servers dedicated to running them.

You can also see process utilization when you select Scheduling Information from Available Options (see fig. 17.31).

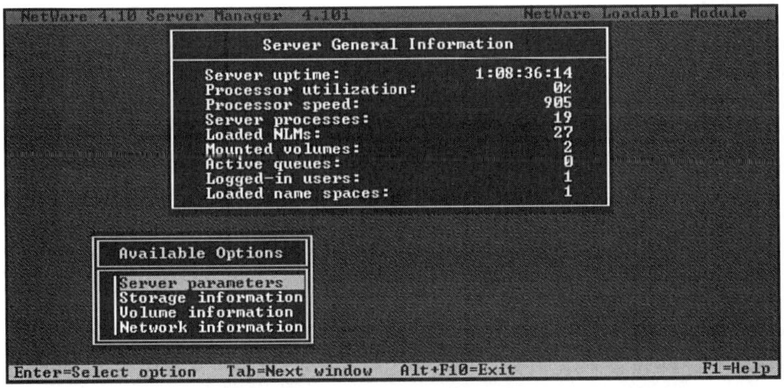

Figure 17.30
General SERVMAN statistics.

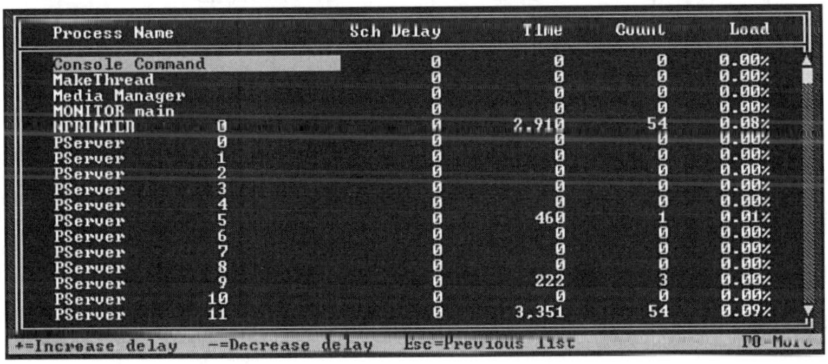

Figure 17.31
Scheduling Information for processes.

In figure 17.21, process utilization information is sampled, processed, and displayed in 1 second; in figure 17.31, information is sampled, processed, and displayed every 2 seconds.

The Name column displays the name of the process being displayed. The Time column indicates the time the CPU spent executing code in that process or interrupt service routine. The Count column shows the number of times the process or interrupt service routine ran during the sample period. The Load column indicates the percentage of time the CPU spent in this process or interrupt service routine. If you scroll through the screen, you will see an overhead summary at the bottom. The summary includes Total Sample Time, Histogram Overhead Time, and Adjusted Sample Time. All statistics are displayed relative to the Adjusted Sample Time, which is the difference between the Total Adjusted Time and Histogram Overhead Time values. The statistics collection is turned ON only when the screens in figures 17.7 and 17.31 are displayed, and turned OFF when you exit these screens.

If the server is idle, it spends most of its time in the idle loop process. This indicates a low server utilization.

The Scheduling Information displays only processes whose scheduling delay can be adjusted. You can use the + or – key to increase or decrease the scheduling delay of the highlighted process. If the server CPU utilization for a process is too high, you can reduce it by increasing the scheduling delay.

Another way to change the scheduling delay is to use SCHDELAY.

The general syntax for this NLM is

```
LOAD SCHDELAY [processName = number]
```

in which *processName* is the name of the process and number is the amount of delay.

Loading SCHDELAY without any parameters shows the list of processes that are running and their current delay. For example, to increase the delay of the Media Manager process to 5, the command would be as follows:

```
LOAD SCHDELAY MEDIA MANAGER=5
```

To change the delay for a particular process to 0 (no delay), use the command:

```
LOAD SCHDELAY processName = 0
```

To change the delay for all processes to 0 (no delay), use the command:

```
LOAD SCHDELAY ALL PROCESSES = 0
```

SERVMAN NLM for IntranetWare

The SERVMAN NLM can be activated using the LOAD command.

The SERVMAN NLM can be used for

- Viewing and configuring IntranetWare OS parameters
- Viewing and Updating SET parameters in STARTUP.NCF and AUTOEXEC.NCF
- Viewing network adapter, device, and partition information
- Viewing volume information
- Configuring IPX/SPX parameters
- Viewing network information

Additionally, the main screen in SERVMAN.NLM (refer to figure 17.30) also shows a number of general statistics for the server and the network. The parameters that are displayed on the screen give an overview of the network and server status.

The Server up time field on the MONITOR (refer to figures 17.7 and 17.8) and the SERVMAN screen (refer to figure 17.30) show how long the server has been up since the last time it was started. The Processor Utilization field in SERVMAN shows the CPU utilization of the server. This is expressed as the percentage of time the server is busy.

The Service Processes field in the MONITOR and SERVMAN screen is the number of processes dedicated by the IntranetWare OS to handle station requests. During peak server activity, when workstation requests exceed the number of service processes that have been assigned, additional service processes are assigned. Once assigned, the memory allocated to the service processes is not reduced, unless the server is restarted. You can control the rate at which new service processes are allocated by the SET New Process Service Wait Time that delays the request for a new service process. This parameter can range from 0.3 to 20 seconds and has a default value of 2.2 seconds. The SET Maximum Service Processes parameter limits the growth of the number of processes that handle packets, and can be set to a value between 5 and 100. It has a default value of 40.

The Licensed Connections field on the MONITOR screen, and the Users logged in field on the SERVMAN screen, is the number of licensed connections to the server. This number reflects the number of users that are using resources on this server. This value is different from the "Active Connections" that can be displayed by selecting the "Connection Information" option on the MONITOR screen. The Active Connections includes the licensed connections and any other network devices (usually workstations) that are attached to the server but are not making use of server resources.

The SERVMAN General Information reports other information (refer to figure 17.30) such as Processor Speed, which is an index that indicates how fast the processor is. The Mounted volumes field indicates the number of server volumes that are mounted, including any CD-ROM volumes that may be mounted. The Active queues field refers to the number of print queues that are active on the server. The Name spaces loaded field shows the number of name spaces that are supported. This value should be at least 1, because the DOS name space is always supported.

Viewing Storage Information in SERVMAN

To view storage information using SERVMAN, select Storage Information from Available Options (see fig. 17.32). If you select an adapter you will see information on the top half of the screen for the selected object (see fig. 17.33). In figure 17.32, adapter objects in the Storage objects menu are not indented. Device, Magazines, and Changer objects are indented once, and Partition objects are indented twice.

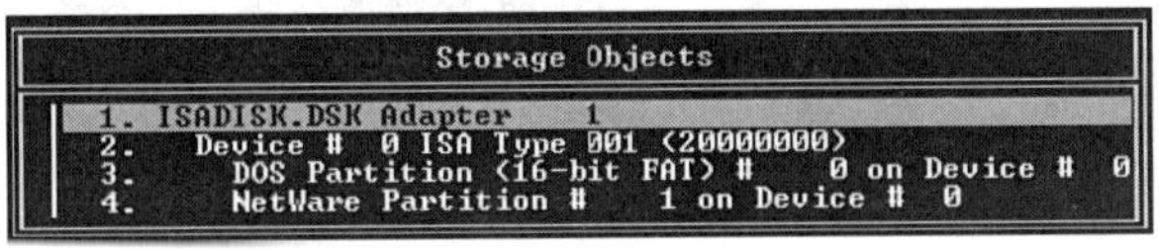

Figure 17.32
Disk controller adapter information using SERVMAN.

The disk controller adapter information in figure 17.33 shows the system name of the adapter, its system number (internal number used by system to identify the adapter), driver name, and number of devices on the adapter. The hardware settings for the adapter are also displayed. For instance, figure 17.33 shows that the adapter uses a port of 1F0 (hex), port length of 8 bytes, interrupt value of E (hex).

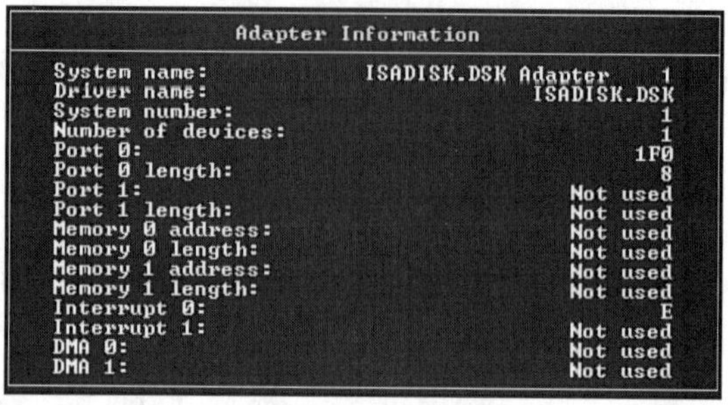

Figure 17.33
Adapter Information using SERVMAN.

Selecting option 2 (`Device # 0 ISA Type 001`) shows information about the device attached to the adapter (see fig. 17.34). The device information shows the heads, cylinders, sectors per track, block size, and disk capacity of the device attached to the adapter. It also shows the device type of the attached device and the adapter number to which the device is attached.

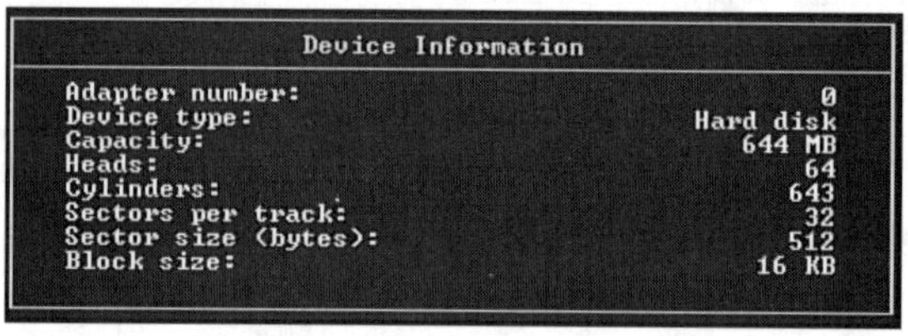

Figure 17.34
Device information using SERVMAN.

Selecting option 4 (`NetWare Partition # 1 on Device # 0`) shows information about a NetWare partition on the device. Figure 17.35 shows the NetWare partition type (101) as recorded in the partition manager table, the partition size in blocks, total number of hot fix blocks available, used hot fix blocks, mirror status and condition, number of mirrors, and partition offset in blocks.

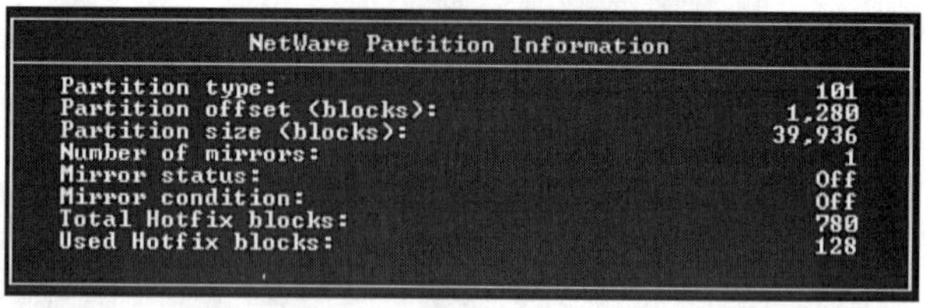

Figure 17.35
Partition information using SERVMAN.

Viewing Volume Information in SERVMAN

To view volume information using SERVMAN, select Volume Information from Available Options. You will see a list of volumes. If you select a specific volume, you will see information on the top half of the screen for the selected volume object. Figure 17.36 shows information about the selected volume object SYS:.

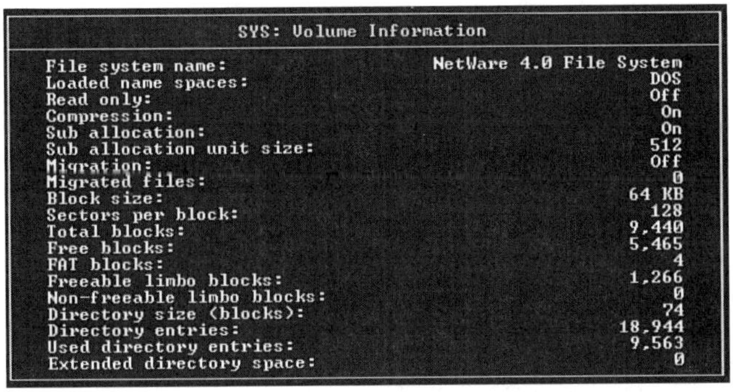

Figure 17.36
Volume information using SERVMAN.

The Volume information in SERVMAN includes information such as file system name, name spaces that are loaded, status of compression, suballocation, migration, number of migrated files, volume block size, sectors per block, total blocks, free blocks, directory size in blocks, directory slots, used directory slots and read-only status (ON for CD-ROM volumes), freeable limbo blocks and non-freeable limbo blocks. For most of these parameters, their meaning is self-evident and contained in the name of the parameter. However, a few of the parameter names do not easily reveal their meaning and are discussed next.

Limbo blocks refers to disk blocks that are in a state of "limbo" in which they are not usable. Freeable limbo blocks refers to the number of blocks that would be usable if they could be freed. Examples of these freeable limbo blocks are blocks holding deleted files. To regain these blocks, you can use the PURGE command. Non-freeable limbo blocks refers to the number of blocks that are not in use by the system and are not freeable by ordinary means. These blocks indicate potential problems with the server volume. You may be able to free some of these blocks by running VREPAIR. Use of VREPAIR is described at the end of this chapter.

Managing Cache Utilization

To observe cache utilization, you would select Cache Utilization from Available Options in MONITOR (refer to figure 17.19). The parameters for cache utilization are described in table 17.6.

If the Long Term Cache Hits falls below 90 percent, you can improve performance by adding more server RAM. Meanwhile, you can make more RAM available to the system by unloading NLMs that are not needed. You can also remove DOS (used to boot the server machine) by using the REMOVE DOS command. However, this typically frees up only 104 KB of server RAM.

You can also improve cache utilization by making the cache buffer size and the volume block size the same. IntranetWare requires that the cache block size be equal to the smallest volume block size. If you are using volumes with different volume block sizes, you cannot make the cache buffer and volume block size the same.

Novell makes the following recommendations for the SET parameters for improving speeds of disk reads and writes. These changes can be made by the SET command or by the SERVMAN.NLM.

Increase Concurrent Writes to improve speed of disk writes. This can be done by changing the Maximum Concurrent Disk Cache Writes to 100. The default value is 50 and can be set to a value from 10 to 4,000.

SET MAXIMUM CONCURRENT DISK CACHE WRITES= 100

To change disk and directory caching for faster writes, set the Dirty Disk Cache Delay Time to 7 seconds, Maximum Concurrent Directory Cache Writes to 25, and Dirty Directory Cache Delay Time to 2 seconds. See listing 17.1.

Listing 17.1

```
SET DIRTY DISK CACHE DELAY TIME= 7 SECONDS
SET MAXIMUM CONCURRENT DIRECTORY CACHE WRITES= 5
SET DIRTY DIRECTORY CACHE DELAY TIME= 2 SECONDS
```

To change disk and directory caching for faster reads, set the Maximum Concurrent Disk Cache Writes to 10, Maximum Concurrent Directory Cache Writes to 5, and Dirty Directory Cache Buffer NonReferenced Delay to 60 seconds. See listing 17.2.

Listing 17.2

```
SET MAXIMUM CONCURRENT DISK CACHE WRITES= 10
SET MAXIMUM CONCURRENT DIRECTORY CACHE WRITES= 5
SET DIRTY CACHE BUFFER NONREFERENCED DELAY= 60 SECONDS
```

The Dirty Disk Cache Delay Time has a default value of 3.3 seconds and can range from 0.1 to 10 seconds. This is the minimum amount of time the system waits before writing a dirty file cache buffer to server disk.

The Maximum Concurrent Directory Cache Writes has a default value of 10 and can range from 5 to 50. This is the maximum number of simultaneous writes of the directory cache buffers.

The Dirty Directory Cache Delay Time has a default value of 0.5 seconds and can range from 0 to 10 seconds. This is the minimum time the system waits before flushing a dirty cache buffer to disk.

The Dirty Cache Buffer NonReferenced Delay Directory Cache Delay has a default value of 5.5 seconds and can range from 1 second to 5 minutes. This is the time to wait after a directory cache buffer was referenced before reusing it.

Understanding the Disk Read Ahead Mechanism

IntranetWare implements a disk Read Ahead mechanism. For files that are sequentially accessed, it is an advantage to read the next few blocks after the current block is being read, and cache them in memory, because subsequent sequential reads will find these blocks in cache. IntranetWare has built-in heuristics to determine if a file is being accessed sequentially or randomly. If IntranetWare determines that the file is being read sequentially it begins to stage data beyond the current block that is being read in cache.

Using a large volume block size is an advantage, as larger amounts of read-ahead data can be cached, and a disk read can often be processed in a single rotation of the disk. For example, if the volume block size is 64 KB, a 64 KB data block can be read in a single read. If the volume block size is 4 KB, the server has to perform 16 read operations to read the same 64 KB of data.

Whenever a file on the server is open, IntranetWare begins tracking the patterns in which data blocks in the file are read. If IntranetWare determines that the file is being accessed sequentially, it activates an internal read-ahead process. When the workstation requester accesses data beyond the midpoint of the current block, the next block of data is read into cache. For a 64 KB data block, the requester has to reach the 32 KB midpoint mark, and the next sequential data block is read.

IntranetWare keeps a watchful eye on the pattern of data access even after it has determined that a file is being accessed sequentially. If the access to a file changes from sequential access to random access, IntranetWare detects this, and deactivates the Read Ahead process. IntranetWare does not use read-ahead for randomly accessed files because read-ahead can introduce an extra overhead, where data that is read ahead of its time is not likely to be used.

Read-ahead requests are placed in a queue and processed in the background at a lower priority than normal read and write requests. Because read-ahead requests are processed in the background, they do not significantly impact the normal I/O operations. The "scheduling mechanism" in IntranetWare ensures that under peak-load conditions, fewer read-ahead requests are performed in comparison with normal reads and writes.

Controlling Turbo FAT Reuse Time

IntranetWare uses the Turbo FAT feature to improve access to large randomly accessed files. Normally files are accessed by the File Allocation Table (FAT). The FAT is shared by all files on a NetWare volume, and is cached in server RAM to provide faster access to its contents. The FAT contains a chain of pointers to data blocks for files. When a file needs to be accessed, the server finds the start of the chain in the Directory Entry Table (DET), and follows the chain in the FAT table.

For files that have more than 64 FAT entries and that are randomly accessed, IntranetWare builds a special FAT table for that file in the server RAM. This special table is called the Turbo FAT table (also called Index table), and contains an index of blocks for that specific file only. This makes it possible to very quickly find data blocks for the indexed file.

The system has built-in heuristics to determine if a file is accessed randomly, and only uses Turbo FATs for files that are randomly accessed files. Files that are accessed sequentially do not have Turbo FATs built for them.

When an indexed file is closed, its Turbo FAT is not immediately released, in case that file is to be reused again. This delay is controlled by the SET Turbo FAT Re-Use Wait Time parameter that has a default value of 5 minutes 29.6 seconds. Indexed files that are reused within this SET parameter value will find their Turbo FATs in RAM and be able to reuse it. If the indexed file is used after this time, the Turbo FAT will have to be rebuilt again. You can increase the value of this parameter, if you expect that there will be longer delays in the reuse of a file.

Understanding Disk Request Prioritization in IntranetWare

In earlier versions of NetWare, it was possible to run into certain rare situations where read requests would be ignored. This situation would occur in situations involving a large number of Write requests. Write requests are written to cache buffers and a background process flushes the dirty cache buffers to disk. If the number of dirty write cache buffers increased beyond a certain threshold, the server would switch the task of flushing the dirty disk buffers from the background to the foreground mode, so that it could quickly recover the use of the dirty cache buffers. When the server switched to foreground writes, it did so to the exclusion of processing other tasks. If a high priority read request occurred when the server was performing foreground writes of dirty cache buffers, it would get ignored.

To prevent the previous problem from occurring in IntranetWare, disk requests are prioritized into four queues:

- Critical events
- Read requests
- Write requests
- Read-ahead requests

The priority of these queues is in the order in which they are listed, with Critical events being at the highest priority and Read Ahead requests at the lowest priority. The four queues are often called disk elevators by Novell.

Critical events are those that must be guaranteed to be completed. Examples of critical events are file commits and TTS log writes.

Read requests are the next priority, because they are generated by foreground client tasks that depend on the results of the read (read of directory or a file). Read requests also constitute the bulk of the work done at a server.

Write requests are at the next priority, because most write requests can be performed in the background (write requests are typically written to the cache and await the lazy-cache write process that flushes them to disk). When a client makes a write request, it expects the request to be performed, but very often the subsequent actions the client performs do not depend on the results of the write request. Even if the client needs to access the data that was immediately written, the dirty cache buffer can be read, as it holds the most current data. When this occurs, the number of writes to the server disk can be occurred. You can monitor the occurrence of this event through MONITOR's cache utilization statistics Long Term Cache Dirty Hits and Short Term Cache Dirty Hits fields.

Read-ahead requests are performed at the lowest priority, as they can generally improve the performance of sequential reads, but are not critical to the operation of the server.

IntranetWare does not require that the higher priority queue requests always be fulfilled before a lower priority queue can be fulfilled. Instead, IntranetWare takes a percentage of requests from each request queue and services them in the order of their priorities. The higher the priority of the queue, the greater the percentage of requests serviced from that queue. This mechanism guarantees that requests from each queue are processed, regardless of the fact that there may be a large number of requests in a high priority queue.

Protocol Analyzers

Protocol analyzers are another tool that can be used to monitor performance of networks. A protocol analyzer tool called LANalyzer enables the monitoring of a variety of statistics on the network. LANalyzer is a hardware/software package that can be installed in an IBM-compatible PC with a hard drive. The hardware consists of a special Ethernet or Token-Ring board that can operate in promiscuous mode—it can capture and store all packets, even those not directly addressed to the LANalyzer. Special digital processing techniques are used on the network boards to obtain timing and collision information that would not be possible with ordinary network boards.

Figure 17.37 shows LANalyzer in the process of collecting traffic on a NetWare Ethernet LAN. As it captures packets and stores them in a trace buffer, LANalyzer also reports conditions on the network such as local collisions, remote collisions, CRC/Alignment errors, and illegal packet lengths. LANalyzer uses the concept of traffic channels to classify traffic. A channel is a user-definable category of network traffic. If a packet satisfies the user-defined criteria, it is counted by that channel and saved into the trace buffer. A packet may satisfy more than one channel and therefore be counted more than once. Only one copy of the packet will be saved, however. The bar graph window in figure 17.37 corresponds to the Rate column. The musical symbol represents an alarm that sounds if the rate exceeds a certain threshold indicated by the position of the musical symbol.

Figure 17.37
Novell LANalyzer capturing traffic.

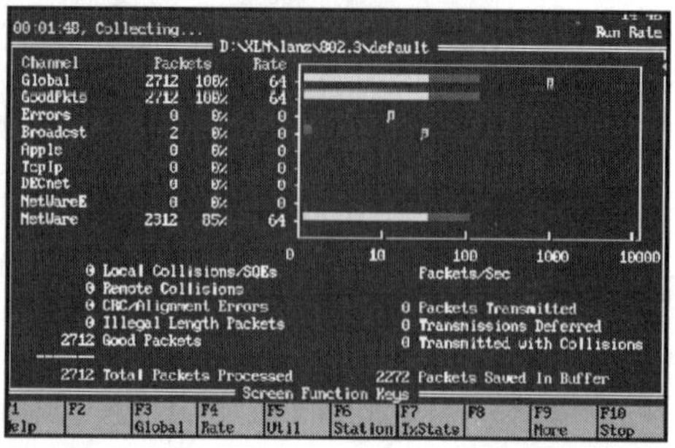

In addition to capturing and decoding packets, LANalyzer comes with several preconfigured applications designed for NetWare LANs. The applications listed in figure 17.38 are for a NetWare Ethernet LAN.

Figure 17.38
Novell LANalyzer IntranetWare-specific applications.

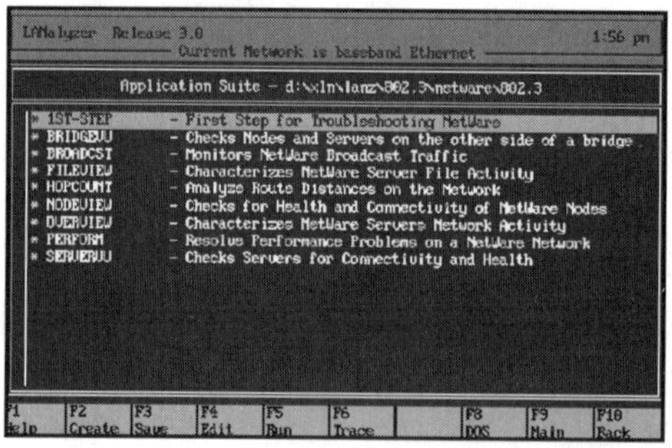

Besides providing trace decodes of IntranetWare protocols, LANalyzer also can be used for decoding the following classes of protocols:

AppleTalk I & II	SMB
DECnetSNA	
IntranetWare	TCP/IP
NetWare Lite	Vines
NFS	XNS
OSI	

Protocol analysis tools such as LANalyzer or The Sniffer from Network General can be quite expensive. Fortunately, relatively inexpensive software-based protocol analysis tools also are available. These tools, which use the network board inside a workstation, consist of software that can capture and decode network traffic. One such tool is LANWATCH, from FTP Software (508- 685-4000); another is LANdecoder, from Triticom (612-937-0772); another is

LANalyzer for Windows, from Novell. The original hardware-based LANalyzer was, at one time, manufactured by Novell. Novell currently sells a Windows-based version called LANalyzer for Windows.

Figures 17.39, 17.40, and 17.41 show NetWare traffic captured using LANWATCH, LANdecoder, and LANalyzer for Windows.

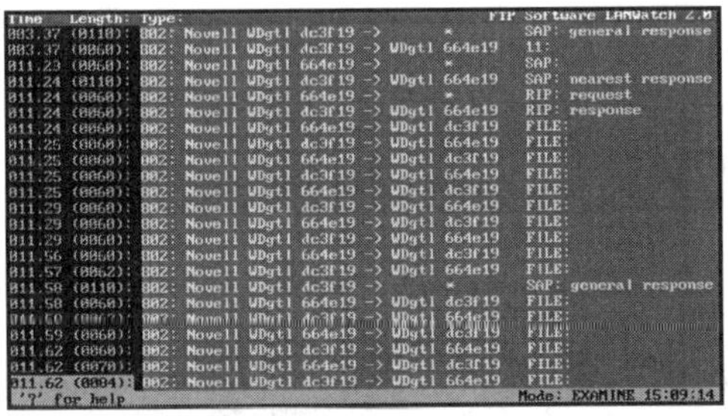

Figure 17.39
FTP Software's LANWATCH decode.

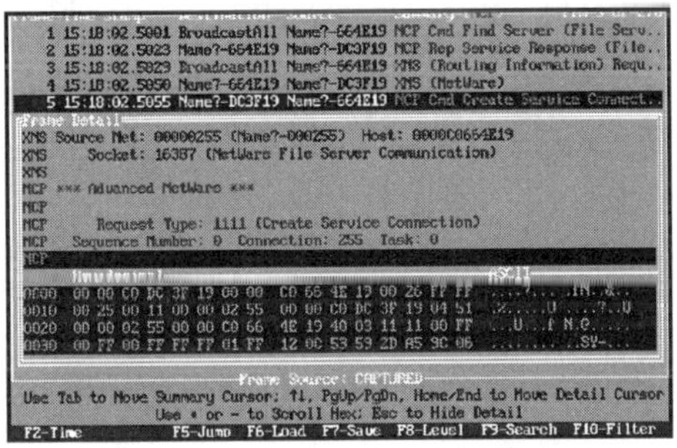

Figure 17.40
Triticom's LANdecoder.

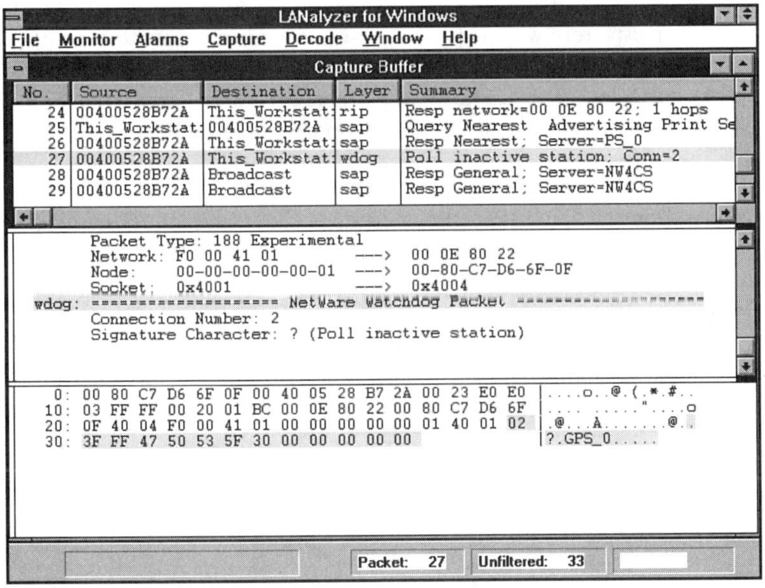

Figure 17.41
LANalyzer for Windows.

Understanding How FSPs Affect Server Performance

The number of File Service Processes (FSPs) is vital for good server performance. An FSP is a process that handles file service requests (NCP requests) from workstations. For optimum performance, there need to be as many FSPs as there are simultaneous file service requests.

In IntranetWare, the number of FSPs is increased on demand, in keeping with the flexible nature of IntranetWare's memory and resource-allocation architecture.

Managing Complex IntranetWare Networks

One of the main problems of managing complex IntranetWare-based networks is server management. IntranetWare servers are available in licenses of 20, 50, 100, or 1,000 users. Long before a server reaches the license limit, it may become necessary to add additional servers.

You may want to add additional servers for the following reasons:

- To increase server processing power available to users
- To prevent network traffic from becoming a bottleneck at a single server
- To increase remote file system storage capacity on the network
- To split application usage across servers for better performance

The server must process file requests from workstations. IntranetWare has a more flexible technique for managing the number of FSPs, and uses dynamic memory management to create more FSPs if needed. As the number of users increases, the probability of file service requests waiting in a queue to be processed increases. You can increase the number of FSPs and CPU power by adding servers.

The nature of server-based computing is such that the majority of file service requests are directed to the server. If you have a single server, this server and the NIC in the server can become overloaded. Introducing a second server can reduce the amount of network traffic directed to a single server (see fig. 17.42). Cost-conscious organizations often add a second NIC card on a single server and divide the LAN into two LANs interconnected by a server (see fig. 17.43). This scheme also increases effective NIC bandwidth at the server. The second approach does not, however, add more processing power for the server.

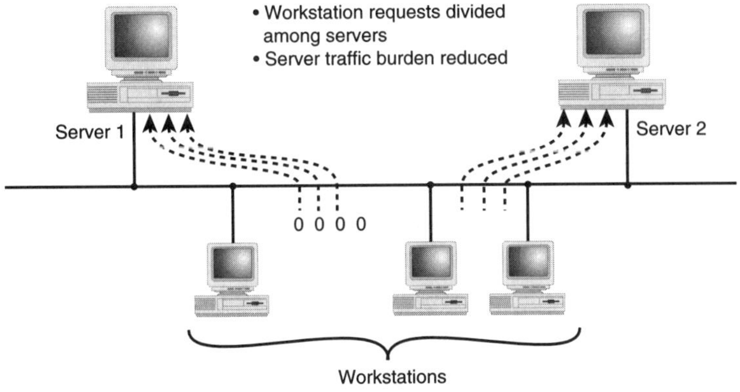

Figure 17.42
Reducing network traffic with multiple servers.

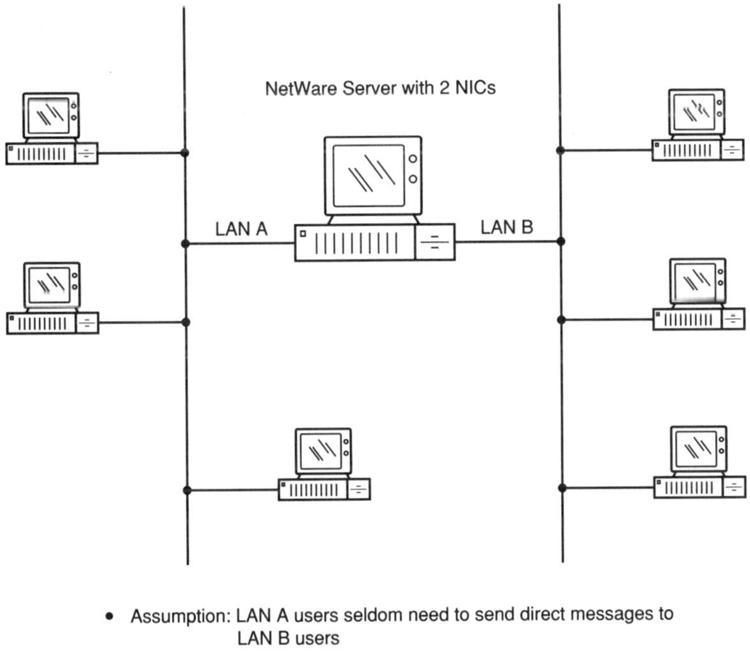

Figure 17.43
Reducing network traffic with multiple NICs.

If the disk storage on the server is not sufficient to support the users, you can add a second disk or a second server with additional storage capacity.

You can use a server to run a variety of network applications. Some applications, primarily those that are database-intensive, place great demands on processing power and server disk storage. These applications are best placed on their own server platform so that they have the dedicated resources of their own server without impacting other applications.

Figure 17.44 shows a LAN with a number of servers. This LAN contains five file servers, six database servers, and a communications server. A user can log in to a number of these file servers to access the resources. IntranetWare limits the number of servers to which a user can attach to no more than eight.

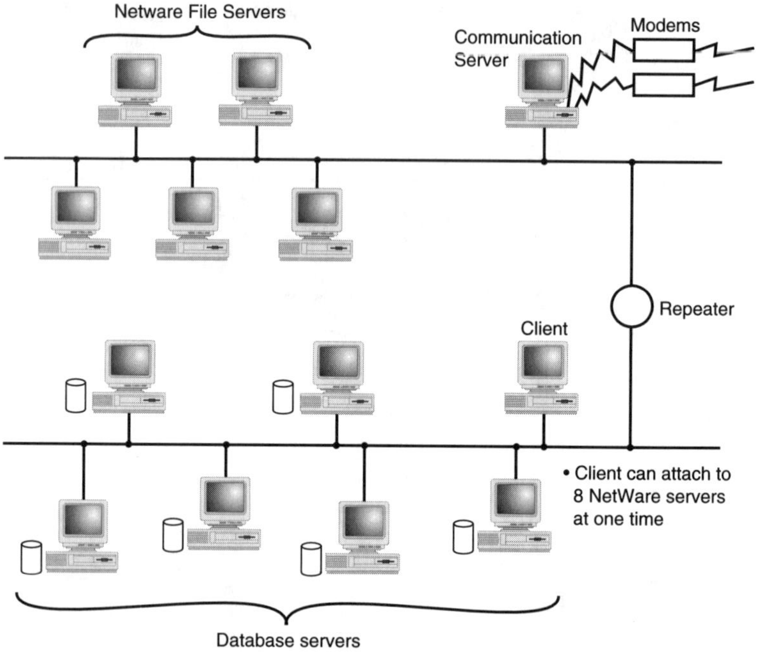

Figure 17.44
Multiserver configuration.

Summary

In this chapter, you learned about the factors that affect network performance. These factors can be hardware-based and software-based. The most important factors in each category were discussed.

Some of the monitoring and performance tools discussed in this chapter are the MONITOR NLM, SERVMAN NLM, LANalyzers, LANWATCH, and LANDecoder. These tools can be used to fine-tune the network after installation, and to monitor how well the network is performing.

You also learned about the importance of the File Service Process and learned about key aspects of managing complex networks.

CHAPTER 18

Managing User Sessions

The network environment is where the user lives and breathes on the network, and therefore must be configured with a great amount of planning and attention to detail. This chapter discusses the different types of startup files for the individual DOS workstation and the network environment. Network startup files are called login scripts.

The following sections discuss the login script commands and script variables that make up the network startup files. Recommendations are presented on how to organize the login scripts to keep them simple and understandable. You also learn about the menu system in IntranetWare.

Understanding Login Scripts

After the user logs in successfully, a network login script is processed, which sets up the network environment for the user. The login script file is kept on the server and plays a role similar to the AUTOEXEC.BAT file for a stand-alone PC. Each instruction in the login script is executed one line at a time.

When a user logs in to a server, login scripts associated for that user are executed. First, the container login script is executed if it exists. The next login script executed is the profile login script if it exists. The last login script executed is the user login script. If the user login script does not exist, then the default login script will execute. It is important to remember you have the NO_DEFAULT command for container or profile login scripts. If you have set the user's environment for the network with the other two types of login scripts then a user login script is not necessary. You will need to use NO_DEFAULT in the last login script processed. In a large network, maintaining user login scripts is a time-consuming task. It is more efficient to maintain container and profile login scripts than user login scripts.

After the last login script is executed, control is returned to the client workstation's OS, and the user's network environment is considered to be set.

The system login script does not exist in IntranetWare.

The commands in the login script files are interpreted by the LOGIN utility, including the MAP command. The MAP command is in the SYS:PUBLIC directory. The first time you execute the MAP command in the login script, you do not have a search drive mapping to the SYS:PUBLIC directory. The MAP commands, however, still work regardless of the absence of a search path to the SYS:PUBLIC directory. The reason for this is that the MAP command is interpreted and not invoked as an external program.

If you want to invoke external utilities, you must precede them with the # character. To invoke the utility NVER, for example, use the following command in the login script file:

```
#NVER
```

Another item in the login script file is the use of variables. These are called login script identifier variables and are examined later in this chapter. These variables evaluate to character strings, which then can be used in commands, such as WRITE Good %GREETING_TIME, %LOGIN_NAME. This statement, for example, may produce the following message:

```
Good Morning, ADMIN .
```

The %GREETING_TIME evaluates to Morning, and %LOGIN_NAME evaluates to the user's login name, in this case, ADMIN . When you use these variables in a string, such as Good %GREETING_TIME, %LOGIN_NAME, the script variables must be in uppercase letters to evaluate correctly.

Complex Login Script Files

One of the more powerful commands that can be used in a login script is the IF ... THEN conditional statement. This type of statement has the following general form:

```
IF expression THEN BEGIN
statements
ELSE
statements
END
```

or

```
IF expression THEN statement
```

The IF statement in the login script file gives you the power to conditionally execute statements; that is, the IF statement executes statements only if a certain condition is true. It can be used to customize a login script. The login script, however, might become too complicated when you use the IF ... THEN statement. Listing 18.1 is an example of a complicated login script.

The following system login script resembles a BASIC program more than a simple login script. Its only redeeming feature, besides the fact that it may work for a specific environment, is that it uses almost every type of script variable and login statement.

Listing 18.1

```
MAP DISPLAY OFF
BREAK OFF
FIRE PHASERS 3 TIMES
WRITE ""
WRITE "Good %GREETING_TIME, %LOGIN_NAME"
WRITE ""
WRITE "You have logged in to file server %FILE_SERVER"
WRITE "from station %NETWORK_ADDRESS:%P_STATION."
WRITE ""
WRITE "Your connection number is %STATION and you are"
WRITE "using shell %SHELL_TYPE on machine %SMACHINE."
WRITE "Your internal userid is %USER_ID"
WRITE ""
WRITE "Today is %DAY_OF_WEEK %MONTH_NAME, %DAY %YEAR"
IF MEMBER OF "NONCIVILIAN" THEN
WRITE "System time is %HOUR24:%MINUTE:%SECOND"
ELSE
WRITE "System time is %HOUR:%MINUTE:%SECOND %AM_PM"
END

IF MONTH = "1" AND DAY = "1" THEN BEGIN
WRITE "Happy new year %YEAR, %FULL_NAME"
END

IF SHORT_YEAR = "00" THEN WRITE "Have a nice new century!"
```

continues

Listing 18.1, Continued

```
IF NDAY_OF_WEEK = "6" THEN
WRITE "Have a good weekend!"

IF NDAY_OF_WEEK > "1" AND NDAY_OF_WEEK < "7" THEN
FDISPLAY SYS:MESSAGES/DAILY.MSG

ELSE
DISPLAY SYS:MESSAGES/WEEKEND.MSG
END

IF MEMBER OF "ENGINEERING" THEN BEGIN
IF DAY_OF_WEEK="TUESDAY" THEN
WRITE "STAFF MEETING AT 3:00 PM"
IF DAY_OF_WEEK="FRIDAY" THEN BEGIN
WRITE "STATUS MEETING AT 3:30 PM."
WRITE "BE THERE OR BE SQUARED!"
END
END

MAP INS S1:=SYS:PUBLIC
MAP INS S2:=SYS:PUBLIC/%MACHINE/%OS/%OS_VERSION

IF MEMBER OF "PAYROLL" THEN BEGIN
IF DAY_OF_WEEK="MONDAY" THEN
WRITE "STAFF MEETING AT 1:00 PM IN CONF.RM. 303"
IF DAY_OF_WEEK="FRIDAY" THEN
WRITE "REVIEW MEETING AT 11:00 AM."
END

ATTACH LAKSHMI/%LOGIN_NAME
MAP L:=LAKSHMI/SYS:USERS/%LOGIN_NAME
END

COMSPEC=S2:COMMAND.COM

IF MEMBER OF "ACCOUNTING" THEN
MAP INS S16:=SYS:APPS/AMRIT
END

IF MEMBER OF "WPUSERS" THEN
MAP INS S16:=SYS:APPS/WP
END

IF MEMBER OF "PAYROLL" OR MEMBER OF "ACCOUNTING" THEN BEGIN
MAP INS S16:=SYS:APPS/ADP
MAP *2:=SYS:PAYROLL
END

IF LOGIN_NAME = "SUPERVISOR" THEN BEGIN
MAP *1:=SYS:USERS/SUPER
MAP *2:=SYS:SYSTEM
```

```
MAP INS S2:=*2:
MAP INS S3:=SYS:SYSTEM/NMUTILS
END

IF MEMBER OF "ACCOUNTING"
#CAPTURE Q=ACCT_LASERQ NB TI=25

IF MEMBER OF "ENGINEERING" THEN BEGIN
#CAPTURE Q=ENG_LASERQ NB NT TI=15
IF ERROR_LEVEL <> "0" THEN BEGIN
SEND "ERROR IN CAPTURE" TO TOM
#EMAIL TOM "ERROR IN CAPTURE FOR %LOGIN_NAME"
END
END

IF <EDITOR>="BRIEF" THEN
MAP INS S16:=SYS:APPS/BRIEF
END

DOS SET X = "1"
ALOOP:
SET X = X 1 "1"
WRITE "VICTORY PARADE!"
IF <X> IS LESS THAN 7 THEN GOTO ALOOP

DRIVE *2:
DOS VERIFY ON
SET PROMPT = "$P$G"
MAP DISPLAY ON
MAP
EXIT "MENU *1:TOPAPPS"
```

Recommendations for Organizing Script Files

You can organize login script files in a way that avoids most of the preceding complexity and yet provides a flexible mechanism that can be adapted as new needs arise. Simplicity is the key to your login scripts. If you can set the user's network environment without having to create a user login script, you will have less maintenance for login scripts. Login scripts work the same for DOS, Windows, Windows 95, and OS/2. All the commands that apply to DOS may not function in OS/2. This is important to remember for container or profile login scripts when users have different client operating systems. You can use additional login scripts if you need to bypass the traditional login scripts described previously. External login scripts are a good way of testing to see if a login script will work—before storing it in the NDS. Techniques for implementing an external login script include the following:

- Using the LOGIN /S option to call an ASCII text file when first logging in
- Using the INCLUDE command to call a login script of another object or an ASCII text file

The LOGIN /S option is used to specify an alternate login script file when logging in. This option bypasses the other login scripts in favor of the script file specified. Use this option when testing a new login script or when an existing login script does not work. The syntax is as follows:

```
LOGIN [server/][username] /S <login script file>
```

Listing 18.2 shows you a sample login script.

Listing 18.2

```
WRITE "Begin Alternate Login Script "
MAP INS S1:=SYS:PUBLIC
MAP F:=.PARTAIN_SYS:
WRITE "Alternate Login Script Executed OK..."
WRITE "End Alternate Login Script "
```

Listing 18.3 shows you a sample session in which this file is used as an alternate to the standard login scripts.

Listing 18.3

```
F:\>LOGIN .ADMIN.DEP /S C:\NRP\INTRANET\MYFILE.TXT
Your current context is DEP
Your current tree is: NRP
You are attached to server PARTAIN.
Begin Alternate Login Script
S1: = Z:. [PARTAIN_SYS: \PUBLIC]
Drive F: = PARTAIN_SYS: \
Alternate Login Script Executed OK...
End Alternate Login Script

F:\>
```

The INCLUDE statement can run either an external login script file or the login script of another object. If you want to run the login script of another object, you must have Browse object rights and Read rights to the object's Login Script property.

Figure 18.1 shows a login script for user Dorothy that uses the INCLUDE command to both run an external login script file and to run the login script of another object. Figure 18.2 shows the login script of the User object the INCLUDE statement references.

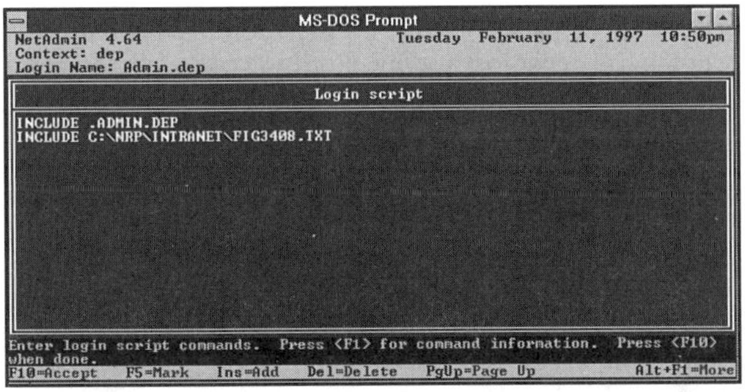

Figure 18.1
Viewing the login script for the user Dorothy.

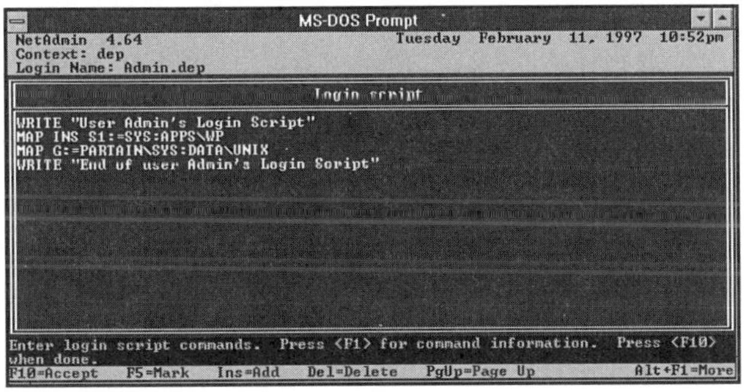

Figure 18.2
Viewing the login script for the user Admin.

Listing 18.4 displays the results when user Dorothy logs in.

Note

The user Dorothy had to be given Read rights to the Login Script property for the User object Admin.

Listing 18.4

```
F:\>LOGIN .dorothy.dep
Your current context is DEP
Your current tree is: DEP
You are attached to server PARTAIN.
S1: = Z:. [PARTAIN_SYS.: \PUBLIC]
S1: = Y:. [PARTAIN_SYS.: \APPS\DB]
ADMIN Login Script
S1: = X:. [PARTAIN_SYS.: \APPS\WP]
Drive G: = PARTAIN_SYS.: \DATA\Unix
End of Admin Login Script
Begin Alternate Login Script
S1: = W:. [PARTAIN_SYS.: \PUBLIC]
Drive F: = PARTAIN_SYS.: \
Alternate Login Script Executed OK...
End Alternate Login Script

F:\>
```

Note in the previous listing that the drive mappings that occurred prior to the start of ADMIN's Login Script are from the container login script. Both the container login script and the alternate login script contain duplicate assignments of a search drive to SYS:PUBLIC.

Login Scripts in IntranetWare

IntranetWare supports the following four types of login scripts:

- Container
- Profile
- User
- Default

The container login script is a property of the organization or organization unit container objects. The profile login script is a property of the profile leaf object. The user login script is a property of the user object. The default login script does not exist as an object or a property; it is contained in the LOGIN.EXE utility used for logging in to the network. Because login scripts are properties of objects, NDS tools such as the NETADMIN or the NetWare Administrator can be used for creating and modifying login scripts.

Each of these different login scripts is discussed in the following sections.

Container Login Script

The container login script is a property of the organization and organization unit container objects. Any object located under this container has the capability to use the container login script. This means that the container login script is a convenient way to specify the commands that should be executed for all users belonging to a container object. Container objects are given Read rights to their own Login Script property.

The container login script is executed for only the immediate users in that container. In figure 18.3, the container login script for organization O=DEP applies only to users defined in that container. It does not apply to users in container OU=TEST_DEP.O=DEP. The container OU=TEST_DEP has its own container login script, and this applies to users in this container. The container OU=SALES.O=DEP in figure 18.3 does not have a container login script. This means that for users in this container, no container login script exists. If a container does not have a container login script, it does not inherit the container login script from a parent container.

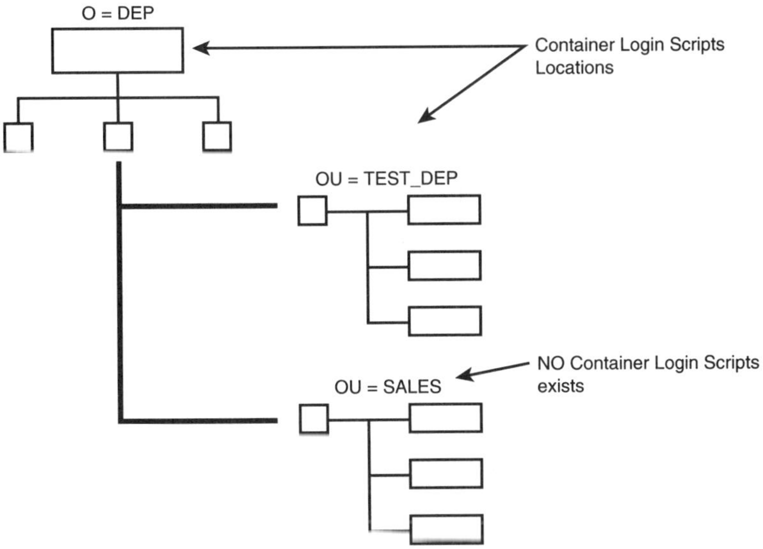

Figure 18.3
The scope of container login scripts.

The container login script is the first type of login script executed and can be used to set up the general environment for all users in that container.

To create a container login script, you must highlight the container object using NETADMIN or the NetWare Administration tool (NWADMIN), and select its login script property for modification.

Profile Login Script

The *profile login script* was designed to serve as a login script to meet the needs of a group. The profile login script (see fig. 18.4) serves the purpose of providing a common environment for many users performing similar tasks on the network. A profile login script is a property of the profile object.

Typical uses for the profile login script are for drive mappings, messages, setting environmental variables, and other mechanisms needed by a group. Any user, in any container, can be assigned a profile login script. If the profile assigned is not in that user's container, you must ensure that the user has Browse object trustee rights and Read property rights to the Profile object's login script property.

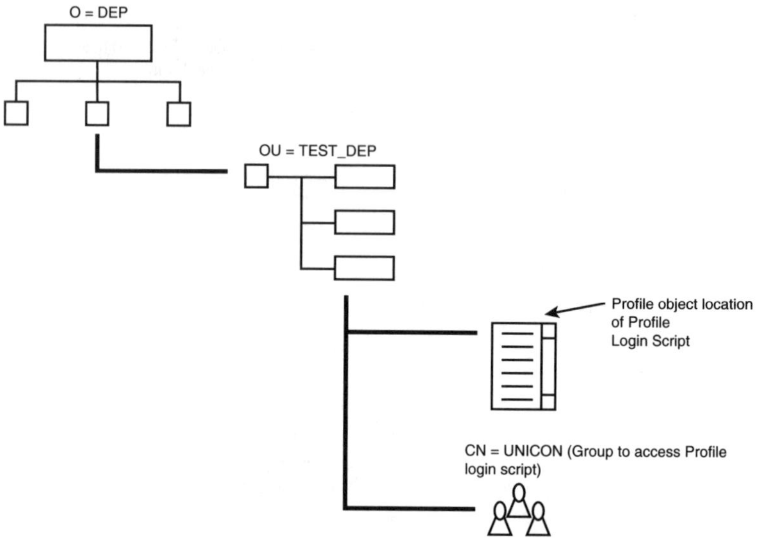

Figure 18.4
Profile login script.

The user must have the Browse object trustee right to the Profile object. This right is assigned by default to the object [Public] at the [Root], and might have been blocked by an IRF or an assignment that overrides the right. The Read rights to the profile's Login Script property is not automatically assigned. You must take action to ensure users assigned to a profile have sufficient rights to read its login script.

User Login Script

Every user object has a login script property (see fig. 18.5). The value for the login script property can be a sequence of login script commands. The same type of login script commands used for the container and profile login scripts can be used for user login scripts.

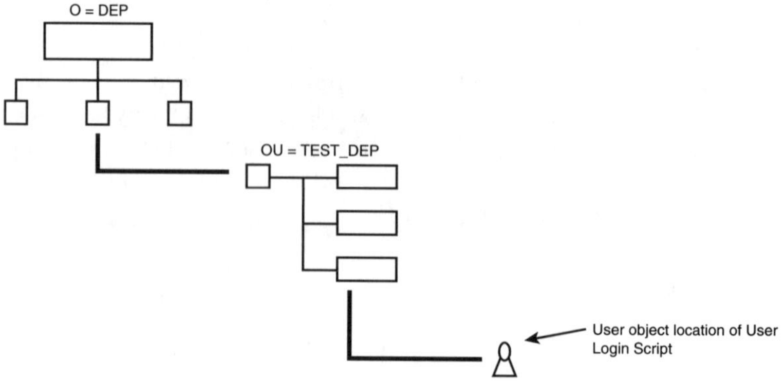

Figure 18.5
User login script.

The user login script is executed after the profile login script (if any).

The user login script can be used to customize a user's login environment. The other login scripts (container and profile) are used to share common login script commands with other users. A user may have special needs not addressed by these "group" login scripts. In that case, the user login script can further customize the user's environment.

It is possible for the login script commands from one login script to override commands of an another. Commands issued in the user login script, for example, occur last. As a result, you may have one drive mapping overwrite an earlier drive map assignment. For this reason, carefully plan the sequence of events in your login scripts.

Default Login Script

The default login script for IntranetWare, unlike the other login script types, cannot be modified. The default login script is fixed and is part of the login program, LOGIN.EXE. The default login script provides a minimum user environment in case a user logs in and does not have a user login script. This is certainly true the first time the user ADMIN logs in to the network after IntranetWare is installed. After IntranetWare is installed; the container, profile, and user login scripts will have to be created. The ADMIN user can at least perform some basic administration without having to create drive mappings.

After a user login script is created for a user, the default login script does not execute for that user. In some situations, all the login script needs of a user can be met by the container login script or the profile login script. In this case, a user login script is not necessary. Because the user login script has not been set, however, the default login script executes in addition to any container and profile login scripts. One of the default actions the default login script performs is to set up a search drive mapping to SYS:PUBLIC. If the container or profile login script already maps a search drive to SYS:PUBLIC, a second search drive mapping to SYS:PUBLIC is created unless the user login script property is set, or a NO_DEFAULT login directive exists in the container or profile login script.

The text of the default login script is shown in listing 18.5:

Listing 18.5

```
MAP DISPLAY OFF
MAP ERRORS OFF
MAP *1:=%FILE_SERVER/SYS:;*1:=%FILE_SERVER/SYS:%LOGIN_NAME
IF "%1"="SUPERVISOR" ¦¦ "%1"="ADMIN" THEN MAP *1:=%FILE_SERVER/SYS:SYSTEM
MAP INS S1:=%FILE_SERVER/SYS:PUBLIC; INS S2:=%FILE_SERVER/SYS:PUBLIC/%MACHINE/%OS/
%OS_VERSION
MAP DISPLAY ON
MAP
```

As you study this default login script, you can see the MAP command in the login script looks similar to the MAP.EXE command. Certain login script MAP command variables such as MAP DISPLAY ON and MAP DISPLAY OFF cannot be executed with MAP.EXE from the DOS prompt.

The commands in the login script files are interpreted by the LOGIN utility. One of the most important commands, the MAP command, is identical to the MAP.EXE command-line utility. The MAP command is in the SYS:PUBLIC directory, and the first time you execute the MAP command in the login script, you do not have a search drive mapping to the SYS:PUBLIC directory. Yet somehow the MAP commands still work, regardless of the absence of a search path to the SYS:PUBLIC directory. This is because the MAP command in the login script is interpreted and not invoked as an external program.

The NO_DEFAULT Directive

The NO_DEFAULT directive in the container or profile login script can explicitly disable the execution of the default login script (see fig. 18.6). This is useful if you want to override the default mappings created when the user login script property is not set, but do not want to set the user login property because the login scripts of the container and/or profile login script are sufficient to set up the required user environment.

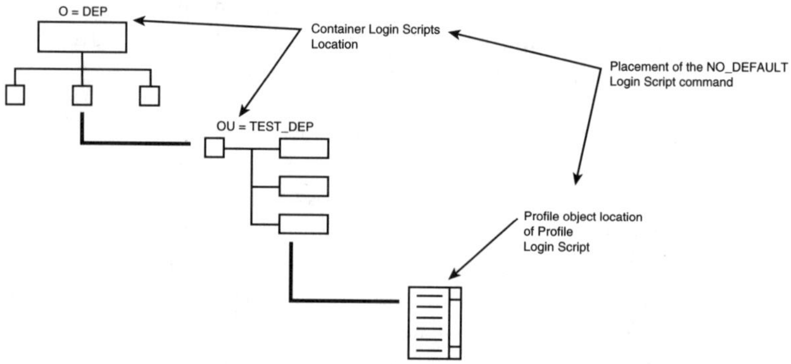

Figure 18.6
The NO_DEFAULT login script command.

Login Script Execution Order

The order of execution for the login script types is illustrated in figure 18.7 and in the following list. These steps are executed when the user logs in to an IntranetWare network.

1. If a user's container has the container login script property set, the container login script is executed for that user.

2. If a user's profile login script property is set to a profile object, the profile login script for that profile object is executed for that user.

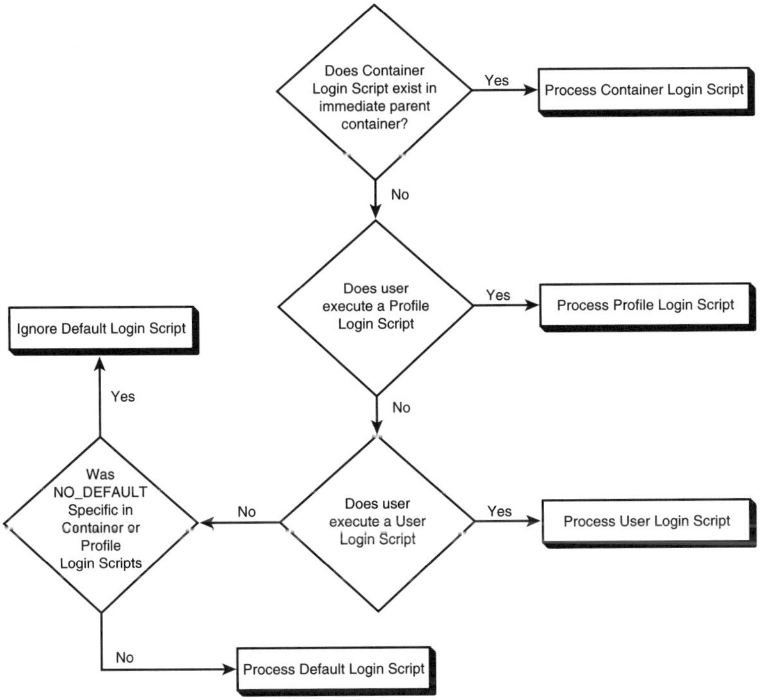

Figure 18.7
Login script order.

3. If a user's user login script property is set, the user login script for that user object is executed.

4. If a user's user login script property is not set, the default is executed unless the NO_DEFAULT login script command is included in the container or profile login script.

Some examples may help illustrate the preceding rules. Figure 18.8 shows an example of the NDS tree for organization O=DEP that has a container login script.

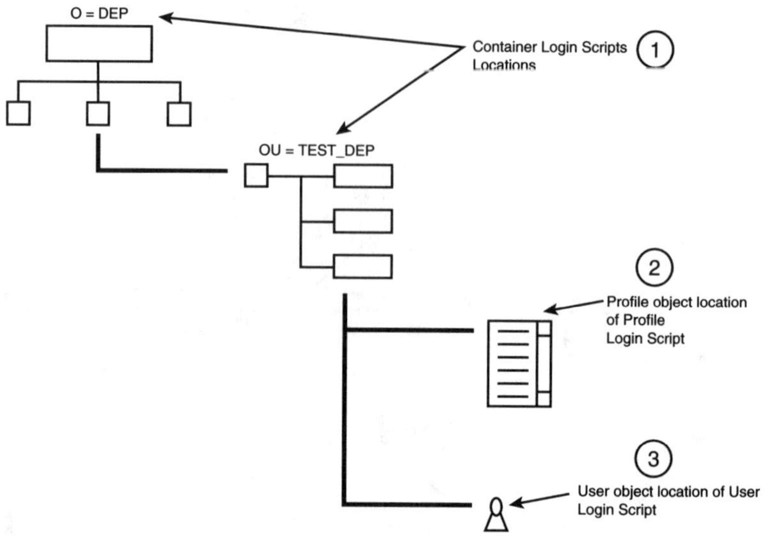

Figure 18.8
Example of login script execution.

When to Use the EXIT Command

Avoid using the EXIT command in all but the last line in the individual login script because the EXIT command terminates the processing of the login script, and this might not be what you want to do.

If used in the container login script file, the EXIT command stops the processing of the container login script and returns control to the DOS prompt. The other login scripts are bypassed.

The EXIT command sometimes can be placed in the individual login script file to serve as a convenient means of escaping to the DOS prompt. For properly designed script files, however, this should not be necessary.

Understanding Login Script Commands

The following commands can be used in login scripts:

(Execution of external commands)

ATTACH

BREAK

DOS BREAK

CLS

COMSPEC

FIRE PHASERS

GOTO

IF ... THEN ... ELSE

INCLUDE

LASTLOGINTIME

CONTEXT	MAP
DISPLAY	PAUSE
FDISPLAY	PCCOMPATIBLE
DOS SET or SET	REMARK or REM
DOS VERIFY	SHIFT
DRIVE	WRITE
EXIT	NOSWAP and SWAP

The following sections discuss these commands.

The # Character

When placed before an external command, the # character provides external program execution. The following is the general syntax of the command:

```
# [path]filename parameters
```

The *[path]filename* statement specifies the full path name of the external command. The # character must be the first character in the command line. Under DOS, you can execute any EXE and COM file. To execute a DOS batch file or a DOS internal command, you must invoke the command-line processor by using the following command:

```
#COMMAND /C batch or internal
```

In the preceding command, *batch or internal* is replaced by the name of a batch file or an internal command. To clear the screen from the login script, you can use the DOS DIR internal command, as shown in the following command:

```
#COMMAND /C DIR
```

When executing an external command, you must make sure that the proper drive mappings and search drives have been set. This is because the external command executes within the IntranetWare network environment set up at the time of execution. You must have sufficient network rights in the directory in which the program is located—minimum rights should be [R F].

When the external command is executed, the login program is still resident in RAM and is not released until termination of the login script processing. Therefore, do not load TSRs during login processing because it leaves a hole in memory (where the login program was) when login script processing terminates.

The ATTACH Command

The ATTACH command enables users to attach to servers using bindery services. The servers can be a NetWare 2, NetWare 3, or NetWare 4 server performing bindery emulation. You can attach to a maximum of eight file servers. This command enables you to attach to other file servers without interrupting the current execution of the login script. The general syntax of the command is as follows:

```
ATTACH [fileserver[/username[;password]]]
```

If the fileserver, username, and password are not specified, you are prompted for them.

You need to be careful about including password information in the login script file. Anyone with Read access to the login script file can read the password, which compromises the security of your network.

The BREAK Command

The BREAK ON command enables you to terminate the execution of your login script. The general syntax of the command is as follows:

```
BREAK [ON ¦ OFF]
```

If the command is set to BREAK ON, the command enables you to terminate the processing of your login script by pressing Ctrl+C or Ctrl+Break. The default value is OFF.

The BREAK command is different from the DOS BREAK command, explained next.

The DOS BREAK Command

If DOS BREAK is set to ON, it enables Ctrl+Break checking for DOS. With Ctrl+Break checking enabled, whenever a program sends a request to DOS, it can be terminated by pressing Ctrl+Break. This command is equivalent to the BREAK command available under MS-DOS.

The CLS Command

CLS will clear the users screen of any information previously displayed during the running of a login script. The general syntax is the following:

```
CLS
```

The COMSPEC Command

COMSPEC specifies the directory that DOS should use to load the command-line processor COMMAND.COM. The general syntax is the following:

```
COMSPEC=[path]COMMAND.COM
```

You can use a command-line processor other than COMMAND.COM, but such implementations are rare. The COMSPEC command directly sets the COMSPEC DOS environment variable.

When a large program loads, it can overwrite the transient portion of DOS. When this program exits, the transient portion of COMMAND.COM needs to be restored. DOS uses the COMSPEC environment variable to obtain a copy of COMMAND.COM. If the COMMAND.COM in memory and the one indicated by COMSPEC are for different versions of DOS, the client workstation crashes with an `Invalid COMMAND.COM` message. On a network, chances are that users may be using different versions of DOS, and therefore, COMSPEC may be pointing to an incorrect version of DOS. The COMSPEC variable should be set to the correct directory. This can be done by using the commands in listing 18.6.

Listing 18.6

```
MAP S2:=SYS:PUBLIC/%MACHINE/%OS/%OS_VERSION
COMSPEC=S2:COMMAND.COM
```

In the first command, for example, you can use the following command for MS-DOS 6:

```
SYS:PUBLIC/IBM_PC/MSDOS/V6.00
```

Another technique that can be used for users who boot from the hard disk is to set COMSPEC as follows:

```
COMSPEC=C:\COMMAND.COM
```

The preceding command takes care of different versions of DOS on the workstation's hard disk.

OS/2 users should not set their COMSPEC variable as indicated earlier. In case a login script needs to be shared by OS/2 users and users using the Virtual DOS Machine (VDM), the OS/2 users should reset their value of the COMSPEC variable.

The CONTEXT Command

This command is used to set a user's current context in the Directory tree. This is similar to the CX command-line utility. As with CX, you can use periods to move up toward the root of the Directory tree. CONTEXT does not support all functions of the CX command. The following is the general syntax:

```
CONTEXT context
```

To set your context to OU=LAB.OU=INVE.O=ETC, you can use the following login command:

```
CONTEXT OU=LAB.OU=INVE.O=ETC
```

or

```
CONTEXT LAB.INVE.ETC
```

To move up two levels in the Directory tree you would use the following:

```
CONTEXT ..
```

The DISPLAY Command

This command shows the contents of the specified file on the client workstation screen. The exact characters are displayed, including any control codes for printer and word processing formats. The following is the general syntax:

```
DISPLAY [pathname]file
```

The [pathname]file statement is the name of the file whose contents are displayed.

The FDISPLAY Command

The FDISPLAY command shows the contents of the specified text file on the client workstation screen. The text is formatted and filtered so that only the text is displayed. The general syntax is the following:

```
FDISPLAY [pathname]file
```

The [pathname]file statement is the name of the file whose contents are displayed.

The DOS SET or SET Command

This command can be used to set a DOS environment variable from within a login script. The general syntax is as follows:

```
[option] [DOS] SET name = "value"
```

The [option] parameter can be replaced by an optional keyword, such as TEMP, TEMPORARY, or LOCAL, to signify that the variable is set only during the login script processing and does not affect the DOS environment. Replace name with the name of the environment variable and value with its actual value. The value must always be enclosed in quotation marks (" ").

Listing 18.7 shows examples of the use of the SET command.

Listing 18.7

```
SET PROMPT = "$P$G" (For setting DOS prompt)
SET FNAME =         (For removing the definition of the environment variable)
SET Y = "1"
SET Y = <Y> 1 1
SET UDIR = "*1:\\USERS\\%LOGIN_NAME"
```

If you want to use the backslash character (\) in a string value, you must specify two backslashes, as shown in the following example:

```
SET FILENAME = "F:\\PUBLIC\\TEMP\\KSSFILE"
```

The reason for providing two backslashes is that the single backslash character indicates special character codes, as shown in the following list:

- **\r.** Indicates a carriage return.
- **\n.** Specifies a new line.
- **\".** Embeds quotation marks in string.
- **\7.** Generates a beep sound (bell).

The DOS VERIFY Command

When set to ON, the DOS VERIFY command verifies that the data copied to a local drive can be written without errors. The default is OFF, and the general syntax is the following:

```
DOS VERIFY [ON¦OFF]
```

The NCOPY command automatically does a read-after-write verify check and can be used to copy files. If you want to use the MS-DOS COPY command, you should have the following command in your login script for added reliability when copying files:

```
DOS VERIFY ON
```

The DRIVE Command

The DRIVE command can be used to specify which network drive is the default drive. The general syntax is as follows:

```
DRIVE [driveletter: ¦ *n:]
```

Replace the driveletter statement with a drive letter, and *n with the network drive number, such as *1, *2, and so on. The first network drive *1 is the default drive, but you can change this by specifying the new default drive in the DRIVE command.

The EXIT Command

Normally, execution of the login scripts terminates at the end of processing the individual user login script. The EXIT command can be used to prematurely terminate the login script processing or to specify the command to be executed upon termination. The general syntax is the following:

```
EXIT [filename]
```

Replace the filename statement with the program name and arguments of any command to be executed after the login script terminates. If an error message about limitations in the size of the command string that can be executed is displayed, you can try to minimize the characters in the command string by leaving out file extensions.

The following are examples of the use of the EXIT command:

`EXIT`	Terminates login processing.
`EXIT MENU`	Executes the MENU utility upon termination.
`EXIT "F:USEREXEC.BAT"`	Executes USEREXEC.BAT in the default drive upon termination.

The FIRE PHASERS Command

The FIRE PHASERS command produces sound effects. It does not work from the DOS command line.The general syntax is as follows:

```
FIRE PHASERS n TIMES
```

Replace *n* with a number from 1 to 9. Some examples of this command follow:

```
FIRE PHASERS 4 TIMES
```

```
FIRE PHASERS %NDAY_OF_WEEK TIMES
```

The GOTO Command

Use the GOTO command to repeat processing of portions of the login script. The following is the general syntax:

```
GOTO label
```

You can replace the label with an identifier, but it must be specified in the current login script. The example in listing 18.8 shows how to use the command.

Listing 18.8

```
SET X = "1"
REM The line below shows how labels can be defined.
LOOP:
REM The indentation shown below is for purposes
REM of clarity and readability of the login script.
REM It is not a requirement.

REM Placing <> around X tells the login processor
REM that this is an environment variable whose value
REM needs to be evaluated.
SET X = <X> + "1"

REM Do whatever login script processing
REM that needs to be repeated, here.

REM Place a condition for terminating the loop, otherwise
REM you will repeat this loop indefinitely!
IF <X> <= "10" THEN GOTO LOOP
```

Set BREAK ON in the login script before experimenting with loops just in case you want to break out of a loop you create unintentionally.

The IF ... THEN ... ELSE Command

This statement enables you to execute certain commands conditionally. The general syntax is shown in listing 18.9.

Listing 18.9

```
IF conditional(s) [AND¦OR¦NOR] conditional(s) THEN
command
ELSE
command
END
```

If the command is a series of statements, you must include the BEGIN command on the previous line.

In the syntax, the conditional(s) statements can be generated by using the following operators:

The following operators are equivalent to Equal:

=

==

EQUAL

EQUALS

The following operators are equivalent to Not Equal:

!=

<>

Not equal

Does not equal

Not equal to

The following are used as greater-than and less-than relational operators:

>	Is greater than
<	Is less than
>=	Is greater than or equal to
<=	Is less than or equal to

The INCLUDE Command

The INCLUDE command can run either an external login script file or the login script of another object.

For an external login script file the INCLUDE command indicates a level of indirection for processing login scripts. The content of the file specified in the INCLUDE statement is to be processed next, after which processing returns to the statement following the INCLUDE command. The general syntax is as follows:

```
INCLUDE [pathname]filename
```

The [pathname]filename statement is the location of the file to be processed.

You can nest INCLUDE commands up to any level limited only by the memory available for processing. As a practical matter, do not use more than two levels of nesting, or your login script will be difficult to figure out by others. You must have a minimum of [R F] rights to the INCLUDE file.

In IntranetWare, you can specify an NDS object that has a login script property. This type of INCLUDE statement has the following form:

```
INCLUDE objectname
```

The [pathname]filename statement is the location of the file to be processed, and objectname is the name of the object whose login script you want to use. Container objects, profile objects, and user objects can have login scripts associated with them. To run the login script of another object, you must have Browse object rights and Read rights to the object's Login Script property. For example to execute the login script for the container OU=CORP.O=SCS, use the following command:

```
INCLUDE OU=CORP.O=SCS
```

The LASTLOGINTIME Command

This command displays the last time the user logged in; it is used for informational purposes only.

The MACHINE Command

This command can be used to set the value of the MACHINE login script variable. The MACHINE value also can be changed from the NET.CFG file. The general syntax of the command is as follows:

```
MACHINE = machinename
```

The *machinename* statement is replaced by a name that can be up to 15 characters long. If a machine name is longer than 15 characters, it is truncated to conform to this limit. For example, to specify that a machine name is NECULTRA, use the following command:

```
MACHINE=NECULTRA
```

The NO_DEFAULT Command

If you do not want to create a user login script and do not want the default login script to run, you can use the NO_DEFAULT command. Using NO_DEFAULT disables the execution of the default login script, which normally runs if the user login script is not set.

The NOSWAP and SWAP Commands

LOGIN.EXE is normally in conventional memory when an external command is executed through the #. If insufficient memory is available, LOGIN.EXE is swapped out to high memory, if available, or to the local hard disk. If you want to disable this swapping action, use the NOSWAP login command. In this case, if LOGIN.EXE cannot be held in conventional memory and run the external command, execution of the external command fails.

You can revert to the default behavior by using the SWAP command.

The MAP Command

The MAP command has the same syntax and meaning as the MAP command found in the SYS:PUBLIC directory, with only a few extensions. Use the following extensions to the MAP command for login script processing:

```
MAP DISPLAY [ON¦OFF]
```

```
MAP ERRORS [ON¦OFF]
```

The MAP DISPLAY ON command shows the drive mappings when you log in. This is the default setting. To disable the MAP processing messages, use MAP DISPLAY OFF.

MAP ERRORS ON displays error messages that occur, for example, if the path to which you are mapping does not exist (not locatable). The default setting is ON. To disable the display of MAP errors, you can use MAP ERRORS OFF. Leave the MAP ERRORS command to its default setting of ON.

The PAUSE or WAIT Command

This command pauses the execution of the login script. Its general syntax is the following:

```
PAUSE
```

or

```
WAIT
```

This command can be used to pause the execution of the login script so that the messages do not scroll by before you have time to read them.

The PCCOMPATIBLE or COMPATIBLE Command

This command indicates that the client workstation PC is IBM PC-compatible. Its general syntax is as follows:

```
PCCOMPATIBLE
```

or

```
COMPATIBLE
```

If your machine is IBM PC-compatible, but you changed the long machine or short machine name by using the LONG MACHINE TYPE= or SHORT MACHINE TYPE= statements in the NET.CFG (older SHELL.CFG) file, you must use the PCCOMPATIBLE command to indicate to the shell that your machine is IBM PC-compatible. If you do not do this, graphic NetWare utilities, such as SYSCON and FILER, which use the C-Worthy library routines, do not work correctly.

The REMARK or REM Command

This command places comments in the login script file for enhancing the readability of the login script. You can use REMARK or enter remarks with REM, *, or ;. The general syntax is the following:

```
REM [text]
```

or

```
* text
```

or

```
; text
```

The SCRIPT_SERVER Command

The SCRIPT_SERVER command enables users to designate a NetWare 3.x or 2.x server from which their bindery-based user login scripts can be read. This has no effect on NDS users. The syntax is as follows:

```
SCRIPT_SERVER <file server name>
```

The *file server name* can be any valid NetWare 3.x or older file server.

The SET TIME [ON | OFF] Command

The command SET TIME ON in the login script synchronizes client workstation time to the server to which it is first attached. This is the default behavior.

The command SET TIME OFF disables synchronization of client workstation time to the server to which it was first attached.

The SHIFT Command

The SHIFT command can be used to pass variables after the LOGIN servername/username command. These variables are referred to as %0, %1, %2, and so on.

In the LOGIN command, you might have typed something such as the following:

```
LOGIN WE_SERVE/LYDIA PUBS GRAPHIC
```

The following shows how the variables of the general syntax are replaced with statements in the preceding command:

%0= WE_SERVE

%1= LYDIA

%2= PUBS

%3= GRAPHIC

The %0 variable is always assigned to the file server being logged in to, even if the file server name is not explicitly specified in the LOGIN command. The %1 variable always is mapped to the user's login name. The %2 variable and other variables are mapped to the additional arguments on the LOGIN command line.

The SHIFT command shifts the variable assignments. Its general syntax is as follows:

```
SHIFT [n]
```

The *n* variable can be a positive number for the number of variables you want to shift to the right, or it can be a negative number for shifting to the left. If *n* is left out, the default value of 1 is assumed.

The primary use of the SHIFT command is to sequence through the parameters specified in the command line. The following loop, for example, can be used to assign %2 to each of the parameters specified in the LOGIN command line after the user name:

```
LOOP:
IF "%2" = "VAL1" THEN Command
IF "%2" = "VAL2" THEN Command
IF "%2" = "VAL3" THEN Command

SHIFT 1
IF "%2" <> "" THEN GOTO LOOP
```

The preceding loop checks each parameter against a specific value and, if a match is found, performs the action specified. The SHIFT 1 command causes the %2 variable to be assigned to the next parameter to the right until no more parameters are left to process. When no more parameters are left, the conditional expression in the IF statement evaluates to false, and execution proceeds to the statement following the IF statement.

The WRITE Command

The WRITE command displays a text message on-screen. Its general syntax is the following:

```
WRITE text
```

You can use the semicolon (;) to concatenate text strings. The following two WRITE commands, for example, result in the same output as shown in listing 18.10.

Listing 18.10

```
WRITE Good ; GREETING_TIME; , %LOGIN_NAME

WRITE Good %GREETING_TIME, %LOGIN_NAME
```

Login Script Identifier Variables

This chapter makes many references to login variables. The login script variable is used to identify, in symbolic format, a network resource that varies. Many examples of login script variables are used throughout the chapter. Table 18.1 gives a formal definition of each of these script variables.

An important part of the login script language is the identifier variable. Identifier variables are categorized by their various functions. Categories include the following:

- Date
- Time
- User-Related
- Network
- Workstation
- DOS Environment
- NDS Objects

Identifier variables should be all uppercase to ensure they are interpreted as a variable. When you use an identifier variable inside quotation marks (" ") or in a MAP command, the identifier variable should be preceded with a percent sign (%).

Table 18.1
Identifier Variables

Variable	Description
**n*	Used to assign the next drive letter, starting with the letter assigned in your NET.CFG file as the FIRST NETWORK DRIVE. *1 is usually drive F, *2 would be G, and so on.
<>	Enables you to use any DOS environment variable as a string.
ACCESS_SERVER	Displays TRUE if access server is functional. Displays FALSE if not functional.
AM_PM	Displays the time as day or night, using a.m. or p.m.
DAY	Displays the day from 01 to 31.
DAY_OF_WEEK	Displays the day of the week.
ERROR_LEVEL	Displays the number of errors. If 0, no errors are found.
FILE_SERVER	Displays the name of the file server.
FULL_NAME	Displays the full name of bindery-based users.
GREETING_TIME	Displays the time of day as morning, afternoon, or evening.
HOUR	Displays the time of day in hours, from 1 to 12.
HOUR24	Displays the hour in 24-hour time, from 00 to 23.
LAST_NAME	User's surname.
LOGIN_CONTEXT	Context where user is located in the tree.
LOGIN_NAME	Displays the user's login name.
MACHINE	Displays the machine for which the shell was written, such as IBMPC.
MEMBER OF *group*	Displays TRUE if the user is a member of a specified group. Displays FALSE if the user is not a member of the specified group.
MINUTE	Displays the minute from 00 to 59.
MONTH	Displays the month from 01 to 12.
MONTH_NAME	Displays the name of the month.
NDAY_OF_WEEK	Displays the numeric value of the weekday.

continues

Table 18.1, Continued
Identifier Variables

Variable	Description
NETWARE_REQUESTER	Version of the VLM requester, or the NetWare Client for OS/2.
NETWORK_ADDRESS	Displays the network number of the cabling system in eight hexadecimal digits.
NOT MEMBER OF *group*	Group to which the user is not assigned.
OS	Displays the client workstation's operating system, such as MS-DOS.
OS_VERSION	Displays the DOS version of the client workstation.
P_STATION	Displays the station address or node address in 12 hexadecimal digits.
PASSWORD_EXIRES	Number of days before user password expires.
REQUESTER_CONTEXT	The current context at the time the LOGIN.EXE process was started.
SECOND	Displays the seconds from 00 to 59.
SHELL_TYPE	Version of the client workstation's DOS shell. Supports VLM as well as NetWare 3 and older shells.
SHORT_YEAR	Displays the year in short format, such as 97, 98, and so on.
SMACHINE	Displays the name of the machine in short format, such as IBM.
STATION	Displays the connection number.
USER_ID	Displays the ID number of each user.
YEAR	Displays the year in full format, such as 1997, 1998, and so on.

In addition to the list summarized in table 18.1, you can use any NDS property as a variable. If the property name contains spaces, the property name must be enclosed in quotation marks.

Examining Menus in IntranetWare

With IntranetWare you have the capability to set up an intranet using a graphical user interface. Therefore, the idea of a text-based menu system might seem dated. The text-based menu system can still perform many functions useful for system administrators or end users. It can provide a user interface to command-line utilities or text-based utilities. IntranetWare comes with its own menu generation facility. The menuing program is a runtime version of the Saber Menu system licensed from Saber Software Corporation. The menus you can create with this system are fast and do not allow users to break out of them. The NMENU.BAT implements the IntranetWare menus. It invokes other utilities for the menu system such as MENUEXE.EXE and MENURSET.EXE.

One of the improvements in the NMENU utility is the requirement of less memory, which allows programs that need more memory to be run.

A scripting language is used to create the ASCII source file for the menu system. The source (.SRC extension) file is then compiled by the MENUMAKE utility to produce a data file (DAT extension). The NMENU batch file sets up the environment and runs MENUEXE.EXE. The data file is used with NMENU.BAT.

Figure 18.9 depicts the steps to perform these operations.

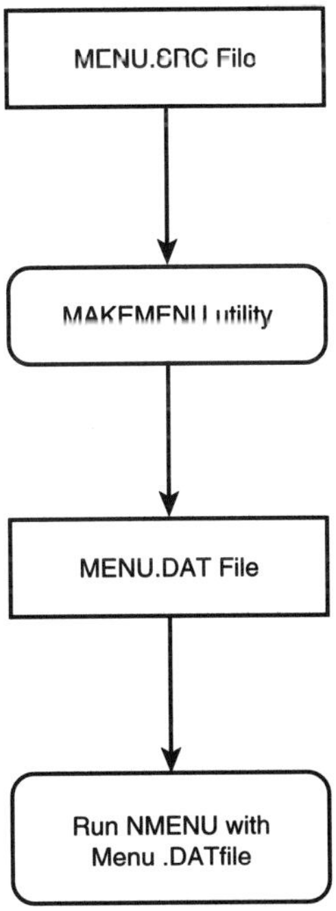

Figure 18.9
IntranetWare Menu compilation steps.

Older menu script files (.MNU extension) used with the scripting language of the NetWare versions 3.11 and earlier Menu utility can be converted to the IntranetWare menu script language by using a conversion tool called MENUCNVT.EXE. NetWare versions 3.12 and later do not require conversion. Figure 18.10 shows the conversion process.

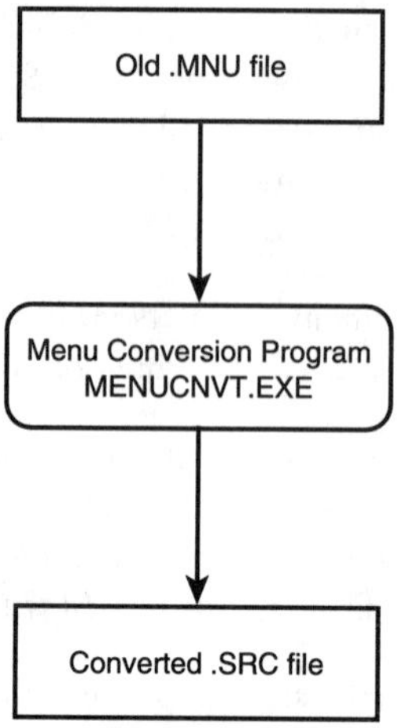

Figure 18.10
IntranetWare Menu conversion process.

If the older Novell Menu script file is named MAIN.MNU, then to convert, compile, and run the menu using the IntranetWare menu system, you can perform the following steps:

1. MENUCNVT MAIN.MNU (produces a MAIN.SRC file).
2. Examine MAIN.SRC file and edit as necessary.
3. MENUMAKE MAIN.SRC (produces a MAIN.DAT file).
4. NMENU MAIN.DAT.

Menu Temporary Files

When the Novell Menus are executed using the following command:

```
NMENU compiledfile
```

in which compiledfile contains the compiled menu description, a number of temporary files are created. These default files are created in the current directory unless special environment variables are set. To create these temporary files, the user needs the following permissions:

- Read (R)
- Write (W)
- Create (C)
- Erase (E)

- Modify (M)
- File Scan (F)

These rights are in the user's home directory and local hard disk, so these commands can be run from the home directory or local hard disk. If the machine is turned off or stops while running the NMENU program, temporary files are left behind. Some administrators may prefer to define a common directory in which these temporary files are kept because it makes it easy for the administrator to clean up old temporary files. To set NMENU to use a specific directory for holding NMENU temporary files, you can set the S_FILEDIR environment variable. For instance, to set the NMENU to use Z:\MENUDAT as a temporary directory, you can use the following command in the client workstation's AUTOEXEC.BAT file.

```
SET S_FILEDIR=Z:\MENUDAT
```

Alternatively, you can set the following command in a login script file, such as the system, profile, or user login script file:

```
SET S_FILEDIR="Z:\MENUDAT"
```

A problem with using a common directory for holding temporary files is the temporary file names are based on the user name. As long as the user names are unique, the temporary files are unique per user, and the IntranetWare menus work just fine. But, what if a user logs in more than one time using the same user name and uses the IntranetWare menus? This is possible unless the number of concurrent connections restriction is kept to one. In this case, the IntranetWare menu tries to create a separate set of temporary files with names that already exist. The resulting name collisions causes the IntranetWare menu not to work as expected. The solution to this is to have IntranetWare menus create temporary files based on station connection number, which is unique per user session. Therefore, if a user logs in using the same user account, each user session has a different connection number, and a different set of temporary files for IntranetWare menus.

The S_FILE environment variable can be used to determine how temporary files are to be named. This can be used to change temporary files to use the station connection number using the following command in a login script:

```
SET S_FILE="%STATION"
```

To set the IntranetWare menus to use the user's home directory for temporary files, use the following command in a login script:

```
SET S_FILEDIR="SYS:USERS/%LOGIN_NAME"
```

Example Menu Script

Listing 18.11 shows you a simple menu with two submenus:

Listing 18.11

```
MENU 1,Main Menu
ITEM ^1Lotus 1-2-3 {BATCH CHDIR SHOW}
EXEC 123
ITEM ^2WordPerfect {BATCH CHDIR SHOW}
EXEC WP
ITEM ^3Print Menu
SHOW 2
ITEM ^4DOS Menu
SHOW 3
ITEM ^XExit to DOS Prompt
EXEC exit
ITEM ^LExit and Logout
EXEC logout

MENU 2,Print Menu
ITEM Print Console
EXEC pconsole
ITEM Print Job Configuration
EXEC printcon
ITEM Print Management
EXEC netuser

MENU 3,DOS Menu
ITEM View Contents of Home Directory {PAUSE}
EXEC NDIR F:
ITEM Execute DOS Shell {CHDIR}
EXEC prompt Type 'EXIT' to Return $_$P$G
EXEC command.com
EXEC prompt $p$g
```

Figure 18.11 shows what the main menu looks like when it is run.

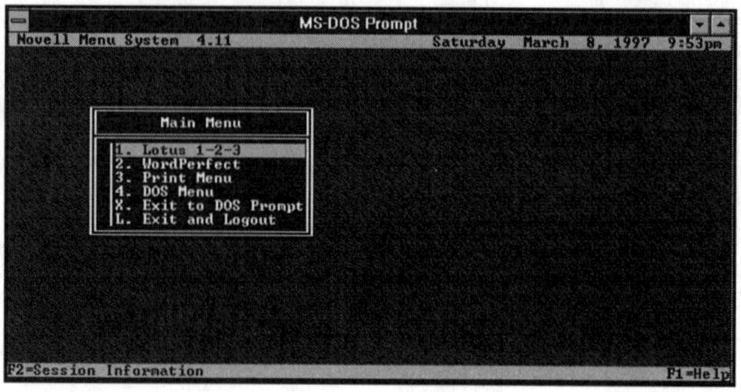

Figure 18.11
A sample menu file.

The name of the menu is called the menu title and is defined by the MENU command. Each option in the menu item is defined by the ITEM statement. The names of the programs to be executed when an option is selected are defined by the EXEC statement.

You examine the details of the menu script next.

Menu Parts

A NetWare menu can consist of four components. The components are specified in the Menu source file and are given in the following list:

- A main menu that has a title and at least one option
- Commands to be executed when an option is selected
- Submenus displayed when an option is selected
- Prompts for user input

The first two items in the preceding list are necessary. The remaining parts, the submenus and prompted user input, are optional.

Menu Commands

As you saw earlier, the principle menu commands are MENU, ITEM, and EXEC. The MENU and ITEM commands are used for organizing the structure and appearance of the menu. The EXEC command is used to control the execution of commands when a particular item is selected. In general, menu commands can be divided into the following two categories:

- Organizational commands
- Control commands

These two categories of commands are discussed in greater detail in the following sections.

Organizational Commands

Organizational commands are responsible for the overall organization and contents of the menu; they also determine the appearance of the menu on-screen. Currently, only two commands are defined for this category, which are the following:

- MENU
- ITEM

Every menu and submenu is defined by a MENU command. The parameters for the MENU command are a menu number and the title of the menu. Its general syntax is the following:

```
MENU menuNumber,menuTitle
```

The menuNumber is unique per menu, and it can be any number between 1 and 255. No special ordering relationship exists between the menu numbers and the menus displayed. The only requirement is that they be unique. No spaces should be between the menuNumber, the comma, and the menuTitle. The menuTitle is a string of characters that should not exceed 40 characters and is displayed at the top of the menu. It is used to identify the title of the menu.

For example, if a menu is given a number of five and a title of Available Options, its menu command appears as follows:

```
MENU 5,Available Options
```

The preceding command defines the start of the menu Available Options identified by the menu number five.

The ITEM organizational command defines the option displayed for a menu. The items are listed in the order in which you want them to appear in the menu. An option consists of a text string parameter to the ITEM command. The general syntax of the ITEM command is as follows:

```
ITEM  itemText { itemOption itemOption ... }
```

or

```
ITEM  ^tagchar itemText { itemOption itemOption ... }
```

In the first format for the ITEM command, every itemText is preceded by a letter automatically assigned by the MENU utility. The letters are from A to Z, with the first ITEM command assigned A, the next B, and so on. These letters or item tags serve as a short-cut to selecting the option. Pressing the letter key corresponding to an option causes that menu item to be selected. The item tags do not determine the order in which the menu is displayed. The display order is determined by the order in which the items are listed. The itemText is the text string that you want displayed for the menu option. The itemOptions are placed within { } braces, and can consist of zero or more item options that further qualify the menu option. The itemOption statement is discussed in greater detail in the following section. An example of the syntax for the first format is the following:

```
ITEM    NetAdmin Tool { }
```

The itemText is NetAdmin Tool; no itemOptions are specified, and therefore the { } braces are empty. If the braces { } are empty, they can be omitted, as in the following example:

```
ITEM Display Context
        EXEC CX
```

If this were the first ITEM listed under a MENU command, it would have a tag character of A; if this were the second item, its tag character would be B, and so on.

The second format for the command is similar to the first format. The difference is that ^tagchar can precede the itemText. The caret (^) character followed by a single character, the tagchar, allows this character to override the default letter assignment for that item. For example, if you want to use digits 1 to 6 to designate the menu options, use the following command:

```
ITEM  ^1First Option { }
ITEM  ^2Second Option { }
ITEM  ^3Third Option { }
ITEM  ^4Fourth Option { }
ITEM  ^5Fifth Option { }
ITEM  ^6Sixth Option { }
```

The item options are displayed in the order in which they are listed. The MENU utility makes no attempt to sort them based on any tag characters specified. It is possible to mix ITEM statements with tag characters and the ITEM statements without tag characters as in listing 18.12.

Listing 18.12

```
MENU 01, NLIST and NDIR Menu
ITEM    Show all objects  {PAUSE}
EXEC NLIST * /D /S /CO "[Root]"
ITEM    NLIST Help
EXEC NLIST /? ALL
ITEM    Change Context    {PAUSE}
EXEC CX %
ITEM    ^XEXIT
EXEC EXIT
ITEM    ^LExit and Logout
EXEC LOGOUT
```

ITEM Options

The itemOptions, placed in the { } braces in the ITEM command, further qualify how the commands associated with the ITEM are executed. The following example shows the ITEM command and the commands executed when an item is selected:

```
ITEM Menu Option Text { }
command 1
command 2
         :
command N
```

The commands executed when the ITEM is selected are listed immediately following the ITEM. These commands are preceded by one of the following key words: EXEC, LOAD, SHOW, GETO, GETR, and GETP, and are discussed in greater detail in the next section.

The itemOption that can be placed in { } can be any of the following:

- BATCH
- CHDIR
- SHOW
- PAUSE

The BATCH item option is used to free up additional memory when running an application. The IntranetWare menu utilities NMENU/MENUEXE take up almost 32 KB of RAM. For applications that take up a large amount of memory, it is desirable to use as much RAM as possible for the application. By using the BATCH option, the commands associated with the Menu are written in a temporary batch file. The menu utilities are removed from memory, and the batch file runs. The last command in the batch file re-invokes the menu utilities. To run the NETADMIN utility using a batch file, use the following:

```
ITEM NetAdmin Utility {BATCH}
EXEC NETADMIN
```

The CHDIR item option is used to restore the default directory to the one that existed prior to executing the command. Some programs give you the option of changing the default directory or changing the default directory when they are run. After exiting these programs, you may be placed in a default directory different from the one in use prior to executing the program. It is often desirable to have the same default directory when a program is accepted from NMENU batch file. For example, to keep the same default directory for a program called TELNET, throughout the execution of the NMENU.BAT, you can use the following:

```
ITEM Remote login via TELNET {CHDIR}
EXEC TELNET
```

The different item options can be combined. For example, to execute FILER as a batch file and to retain the same default directory, you can use the following:

```
ITEM Filer Utility {BATCH CHDIR}
EXEC FILER
```

The order in which the item options are placed inside { } is not significant. Therefore, the preceding statements are equivalent to the following:

```
ITEM Filer Utility {CHDIR BATCH}
EXEC FILER
```

The SHOW item option displays the name of the DOS command executed from the MENU.DAT file on the upper-left hand corner of the screen as it executes. This is particularly useful if the DOS command that is executing is passed a parameter, which also is displayed as the command executes. An example of this usage is shown in the following command:

```
ITEM Directory Contents Listing {SHOW}
EXEC DIR %
```

The PAUSE option causes the message `Press any key to continue` at the end of executing the command(s). This gives the user an opportunity to read the screen before proceeding to the next step. The menu does not proceed to the next step unless the user presses a key. Listing 18.13 is an example of using the PAUSE option.

Listing 18.13

```
ITEM Search for files that have "SCS (C)opyright"  {PAUSE}
EXEC GREP  "SCS (C)opyright"  *.*
```

Table 18.2 summarizes the ITEM different options discussed earlier.

Table 18.2
ITEM Options

Item Option	Description	Example
BATCH	Frees up RAM occupied by MENU utility (32 KB) when a program runs.	ITEM Application X {BATCH}
CHDIR	Restores default directory to that which existed prior to running the commands associated with the menu item.	ITEM Application X {CHDIR}
SHOW	Shows DOS commands on upper-left corner of screen as they execute.	ITEM Application X {SHOW}
PAUSE	Pauses display and waits for user to press a key, at end of executing a command.	ITEM Application X {PAUSE}

Menu Control Commands

The MENU and ITEM commands discussed in the preceding section are used to determine the contents of a menu or submenu and the manner in which options should be displayed or run. The actual commands processed occur after the ITEM command. These commands are called control commands, and are used to execute applications from within the MENU.DAT file, to load menu definitions kept in separate files, to show submenus, and to obtain user input. Six control commands that begin with key words are the following:

- EXEC
- LOAD
- SHOW

- GETO
- GETR
- GETP

The first three of the preceding control commands (EXEC, LOAD, and SHOW) deal with executing programs and loading and displaying submenus. The last three of these commands (GETO, GETR, and GETP) solicit input from the user, which can then be used as parameters for commands and programs executed.

The EXEC Control Command

The EXEC (or EXECUTE) command is used to run an application. The command that is run can be an EXE, COM, BAT, an internal DOS command, or any of the following:

- DOS
- EXIT
- LOGOUT

An example of using the EXEC command for a DOS internal command is shown in listing 18.14.

Listing 18.14

```
ITEM        ^DShow Directory listing {SHOW}
EXEC DIR
```

The following is an example of using the EXEC command for a NetWare .EXE program file:

```
ITEM    ^UNetwork User {BATCH}
EXEC NETUSER
```

The EXEC DOS command runs a second copy of the command shell. For DOS, this is the COMMAND.COM command processor. When a second copy of the command shell runs, the user is presented with a command prompt and can type in any DOS or application command. The files NMENU.BAT, MENUEXE.EXE, <file>. DAT and the previous copy of the command shell are still loaded, so you are limited by the remaining memory available for your DOS application. The following is an example of the use of the EXEC DOS command:

```
ITEM  Exit to DOS { }
EXEC DOS
```

To return to the IntranetWare menu, you must type the **EXIT** command at the command prompt. This terminates the second shell and returns to the menu.

If you want to give users the option of exiting the menu program completely and going to the DOS prompt, you can use the EXEC EXIT command. This command terminates the menu, which causes the system to remove the program from memory. Control is returned to the command shell and the command prompt. An example of the use of the EXEC EXIT command is as follows:

```
ITEM  Exit NMENU { }
EXEC EXIT
```

It could be possible to have a completely menu-driven interface for the user while the user is on the network. In this type of environment the user must be able to logout. To accomplish this, a special EXEC LOGOUT command has been defined. When the EXEC LOGOUT option is used, it logs the user out of the network and simultaneously terminates the menu.

An example of the use of the EXEC LOGOUT command is as follows:

```
ITEM  Exit IntranetWare  Menus and logout { }
EXEC LOGOUT
```

Table 18.3 summarizes the different EXEC commands that can be used.

Table 18.3
EXEC Command Summary

EXEC type	Description
EXEC command	Replace command with a DOS internal/external command, EXE or COM program file, or a DOS batch file.
EXEC DOS	Starts a secondary shell and gives user access to the command prompt through the secondary shell.
EXEC EXIT	Terminates the Menu (NMENU) utility and returns control to the command shell and the command prompt.
EXEC LOGOUT	Terminates the Menu (NMENU) utility and logs user out of the network. Provides a secure option to exit the Novell Menus.

The SHOW Control Command

A menu is defined using the MENU command in which you must define the menu number and title. There can be many such menu commands in a single file. The first menu command in a complied file (produced by running MENUMAKE), that is passed as a parameter to the NMENU command, becomes the first menu displayed. This is the main menu. All other menus in the file are displayed by using the SHOW command. The syntax of the SHOW command is as follows:

```
SHOW menuNumber
```

The menuNumber should be replaced with a number that represents the menu number defined in the MENU statement for the submenu that should be displayed. A single menu file can have up to 255 submenus or menu commands (menu definitions).

The submenu displayed is cascaded in relationship to the previous menu. Its position on-screen is determined automatically by the menu utility.

Figure 18.12 shows the SHOW commands in a menu script file. The two SHOW commands, SHOW 3 and SHOW 8, refer to the indicated submenus in the script file.

Figure 18.12
SHOW commands in a menu script file.

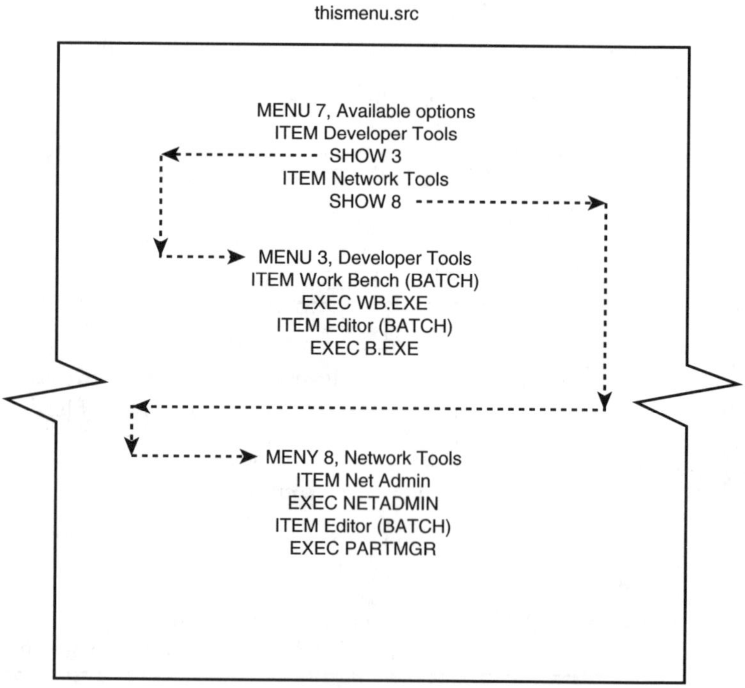
thismenu.src
MENU 7, Available options
ITEM Developer Tools
SHOW 3
ITEM Network Tools
SHOW 8
MENU 3, Developer Tools
ITEM Work Bench (BATCH)
EXEC WB.EXE
ITEM Editor (BATCH)
EXEC B.EXE
MENY 8, Network Tools
ITEM Net Admin
EXEC NETADMIN
ITEM Editor (BATCH)
EXEC PARTMGR

The LOAD Control Command

You are limited to 12 choices per menu. To gain additional choices, you can divide your menu into smaller menus. One menu called from another is referred to as a *submenu.* The first menu you define in your source menu file is the *main menu.* You can call a submenu from the main menu, and then another submenu from the first submenu, and so forth. The submenu *depth* cannot exceed 11 (the main menu plus 10 submenus). Although this seems like a severe limitation, bear in mind that each menu choice can call a submenu. Each submenu can have 12 choices, each of which in turn can call a submenu. The limit of 11 limits the depth of the menu structure, not the breadth. You can have a total of 255 menu screens altogether. Submenus can be defined in the source menu file or from an external file. The syntax of the LOAD command is as follows:

```
LOAD menuName
```

The menuName should be replaced by the file name of the compiled menu file. When the LOAD command is executed, the original menu system is left running, but a second menu is added to the screen.

Figure 18.13 shows the use of the LOAD command. It shows how a large menu can be broken into smaller menus. In this figure, three menus MENU1, MENU2, and MENU3 are shown defined in separate files MENU1.DAT, MENU2.DAT, and MENU3.DAT.

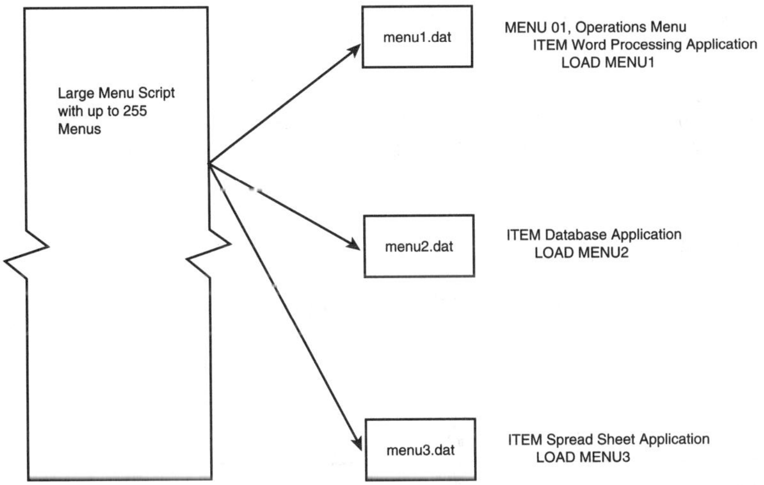
Large Menu Script with up to 255 Menus
menu1.dat
MENU 01, Operations Menu
ITEM Word Processing Application
LOAD MENU1
menu2.dat
ITEM Database Application
LOAD MENU2
menu3.dat
ITEM Spread Sheet Application
LOAD MENU3

Figure 18.13
Use of menu LOAD command.

The GETx Commands

The three forms of the GETx commands are GETO, GETR, and GETP. Like the other control commands, GETx commands are listed after an ITEM command and are executed when the menu item is selected. Listing 18.15 is an example of some of the GETx commands.

Listing 18.15

```
ITEM   ^LDirectory Listing
GETO  Enter directory name: {} 45,, {}
EXEC  DIR
```

The GETO Command

The GETO command is used for obtaining an optional input from the user. The "O" in GETO stands for "optional." When the GETO command is executed, as shown in the preceding example, a dialog box is displayed. The message text in the dialog box, the width of the user input, the initial value of the user input, and so on are passed as parameters to the GETO command.

With the GETO, GETR, and GETP commands the Enter key signals that you have completed the information. If you press F10 without completing the user input, it signals that you want to continue with the menu execution.

The user has the choice of making an entry or not making an entry (optional GET). In either case, when the user presses the F10 key, execution continues. If the user makes an entry, the entered value is passed as a parameter to the command that follows. In the preceding example, the command that follows is the EXEC DIR command. In this example, if a user makes the entry F:\SYSTEM, the following EXEC command executes:

```
EXEC DIR F:\SYSTEM
```

The preceding command displays the contents of the directory F:\SYSTEM. If the user does not make any entry, but just presses F10, the EXEC command that executes is as follows:

```
EXEC DIR
```

The preceding command displays the contents of the current directory.

The % character can be used as a place holder for a single user input. The preceding example of the use of the GETO command can be alternatively expressed using the % placeholder as shown in listing 18.16.

Listing 18.16

```
ITEM   ^LDirectory Listing

GETO  Enter directory name: {} 45,, {}

EXEC  DIR %
```

The GETR Command

The GETR command works similarly to the GETO command just described. The big difference is that the GETR command requires users to enter information. Just pressing F10 (or Enter if GETR is in its own dialog box), does not cause the GETR command to continue execution. The menu display pauses and does not continue until a valid input is entered.

Listing 18.17 is an example of the use of GETR.

Listing 18.17

```
ITEM  User Command
GETR Enter a user command: {}80,,{}
EXEC %
```

The preceding example passes the user typed string as a command to be executed by the EXEC command.

The GETP Command

The GETP command works similarly to the other GETx commands described earlier. The special feature of GETP is that it assigns a variable to the user input. This variable can then be used in other commands. Listing 18.18 is an example of the use of GETP.

Listing 18.18

```
ITEM    Network Copy {PAUSE SHOW}
GETP    Source: {} 60,, {}
GETP    Destination: {} 60,,{}
EXEC    NCOPY  %1 %2
```

The first GETP parameter assigns the user input to the variable %1, and the second GETP command assigns its user input to %2. These parameters are used in the EXEC NCOPY command as the source and destination, respectively. Table 18.4 summarizes the different GETx commands.

Table 18.4
GETx Commands

Command	Description
GETO	Used to obtain optional user input.
GETR	Used to obtain required user input.
GETP	Used to obtain user input assigned to variables %1, %2, and so on.

Comparing GETP, GETR, and GETO Command User Input Processing

Whereas the GETR and GETO commands append the input they receive to the next EXEC command, the GETP command parses the input and breaks it down into words assigned to parameter variables %1, %2, %3, and so on.

Thus if the user input is as follows:

```
MONTHS  12 YEARS 25
```

the parameter variables have the following values:

```
%1 = MONTHS
%2 = 12
%3 = YEARS
%4 = 25
```

These parameter variables can be used in the next EXEC command, as in the following example:

```
EXEC CalcInt  %3=%4  TYPE %1=%2
```

Given the previously discussed parameter values, the above EXEC command evaluates to the following:

```
EXEC CalcInt YEARS=25 TYPE MONTHS=12
```

As you can see, the GETP enables you greater control over how you can use the user typed-in values.

GETx Parameter Options

In the examples of the GETx commands in the preceding section, you saw the use of the { } braces and the commas (,) as part of the syntax of the GETx command. This syntax is part of a general syntax that gives you options to control the width of the user input and the initial value displayed for the user. You also can modify the user input by prefixing or appending special text string values to the user input. The syntax of these parameters is as follows:

```
GETx  promptString, {prependString} _length,prefillString,{appendString}
```

or

```
GETx promptString, {prependString} _length,prefillString,SECURE {appendString}
```

The x in GETx is O, R, or P for the different types of GET commands. The promptString is the text displayed for the GET command and is meant as an aid to the user to enter the appropriate value. The prependString placed inside the { } is a string attached to the beginning of the data the user enters. If there is no value that you want to prefix to the entered data, you must enter the empty string inside { }. Listing 18.19 is an example of the use of the prefix string.

Listing 18.19

```
ITEM    ZIP code for Montana Residents
GETR    {MT }5,,{}
EXEC    RecZip %
```

In the preceding example, the prefix string "MT" is prefixed to the supplied user input. The RecZip represents a custom application that processes user-supplied data.

Please note that the difference between the { } braces with no space between them and the { } braces with a space between them. The former represents a null or empty string and means that no value will be prefixed to the user data. The latter represents a blank character prefixed to the user data. These comments also apply to the {appendString} in the GETx command syntax.

The length specifies the size of the user input field. It is the number of characters the user can enter for the GET command. The length field is mandatory and can have a maximum value of 80 characters. Listing 18.20 is an example of a maximum length field of 80 being used.

Listing 18.20

```
ITEM  Address Information
GETR  Enter your street address {}80,,{}
EXEC  RecData %
```

The RecData in the EXEC command in the preceding example is meant as an example of a custom application (RecData) that can process the user supplied information.

The prefill String is the initial value placed in the user's response field. It is used as the default value that the user can accept, if the user chooses not to enter a different value. The prefillString is optional. The prefillString is separated from the length field by a comma (,) and no spaces. If no prefill string is used, it can be omitted as shown in listing 18.21.

Listing 18.21

```
ITEM Get user information
GETO Enter your company name:{}50,,{}
EXEC RecData  %
```

Listing 18.22 shows a prefillstring being used.

Listing 18.22

```
ITEM Get user information
GETO Enter your company name:{}50,IBM,{}
EXEC RecData  %
```

In the preceding example, the Enter your company name: field in the dialog box for the GETO command has an initial value of IBM. The user can accept this value or override it with a different value. The user-supplied value is used as a parameter to a custom application called RecData.

The SECURE keyword is optional. If present, it must occur between the prefillString parameter and the {appendString} parameter. If the SECURE keyword exists as part of the GET command syntax, it means that the typed-in user data is not displayed (hidden). This is useful if the user wants to enter a password, security code, or some other confidential data. Listing 18.23 is an example of the use of the SECURE keyword.

Listing 18.23

```
ITEM    Security Information
GETR    Enter Personal Identification Number(PIN): {}4,,SECURE{}
EXEC    ValidPIN %
```

The ValidPIN in the EXEC command signifies a custom application—one that, perhaps, validates the user-supplied PIN data.

The appendString placed inside the { } is a string attached to the end (appended) of the data the user enters. If there is no value that you want to append to the entered data, you must enter the empty string inside { }. Listing 18.24 is an example of the use of the appendString.

Listing 18.24

```
ITEM  Security Information
GETR  Enter Personal Identification Number(PIN): {}4,,SECURE{KXVZ}
EXEC  ProcPIN
```

In the preceding example, the appendString "KXVZ" is appended to the supplied user input. The ProcPIN represents a custom application that processes the user supplied data. In this example, the appendString is used as a special security code sent in conjunction with the user-supplied data to the processing program ProcPIN.

If several GET commands are listed under an ITEM command, the GET fields are grouped in the order of occurrence with 10 GETs per dialog box. In other words, there can be a maximum of 10 GET command prompts per dialog box. If you want to override this default behavior and have a GET command appear in its own dialog box, you must use the caret (^) at the beginning of the prompt text for the GET command. The following example shows how each of the GET commands can appear in its own dialog box:

```
ITEM  Enter User Information
GETP  ^User Name:{}50,,{}
GETP  ^Address:{}80,,{}
GETP  ^Password:{}30,,SECURE{}
EXEC  ProcUser %1 %2 %3
```

The ProcUser represents a custom application that processes the user-supplied input.

The following listing shows another use of the GET commands that prompts users for options. The user is prompted for the source and destination directories. These are used as parameters %1 and %2 in the NCOPY command as shown in listing 18.25.

Listing 18.25

```
ITEM    Network Copy {PAUSE SHOW}
GETP    Source: {} 60,, {}
GETP    Destination: {} 60,,{}
EXEC    NCOPY %1 %2
```

In listing 18.26, the user is asked for a password. The user's response is not displayed because of the SECURE option.

Listing 18.26

```
ITEM    Authenticate User
GETR    User ID:  {} 10,guest,{}
GETR    Password: {} 25,,SECURE{}
```

In listing 18.27, the user is asked for the directory path for which a listing should be displayed. If one is not specified, the DIR command is executed without an argument.

Listing 18.27

```
ITEM    Directory Listing
GETO    Directory Path: {  } 40,,{}
EXEC    dir
```

No more than 100 GET commands are allowed per ITEM command. Also, the GETO and GETR commands must be entered between the ITEM and the EXEC line associated with them.

The general syntax of the GETx command is as follows:

```
GETx promptString,{prependString}length,
_prefillString,[SECURE]{appendString}
```

The [ ] brackets around SECURE imply that SECURE is optional; it is not part of the syntax for GETx.

Table 18.5 summarizes the different GET parameters discussed in this chapter.

Table 18.5
GET Parameters

GETx Parameter	Description
promptString	Message that must be displayed to the user.
prependString	User-entered data is prefixed with the prependString placed in the first set of { }.
length	Maximum number of characters for the user field. Its maximum value is 80 characters.
prefillString	Used as the default response, in case the user does not enter a value.
SECURE	User typed-in information is not displayed. Used for secure data such as passwords and codes.
appendString	User-entered data is appended with the appendString placed in the first set of { }.

NMENU Limitations

The following list outlines the menu limitations:

- Up to 255 submenus or menu commands (menu definitions) can be in a single menu file.
- Maximum number of characters for the user field is 80.
- Maximum number of characters on a line in the menu script is 80. Longer lines can continue to the next line by ending the preceding line with the line continuation character +.
- No more than 100 GET commands are allowed per ITEM command.
- If several GET commands are listed under an ITEM command, the GET fields are grouped in the order of occurrence with 10 GETs per dialog box.
- The Novell Menus can have no more than one main menu and 10 submenus (using the SHOW command) on the screen at any time. This means that the maximum level of submenu nesting cannot exceed 10.
- You cannot mix EXEC and SHOW submenu commands under an ITEM option. Therefore, the following example is illegal:

```
ITEM Telmail option

        EXEC MAP T:=FS1/SYS:INET/BIN

        SHOW 06
```

Summary

In this chapter, you learned the different types of startup scripts necessary to set up an IntranetWare user environment. Login scripts and the menu system are two tools at your disposal. These are familiar to you if you are experienced in older versions of NetWare. The changes to the types of login scripts and the menuing system for IntranetWare were discussed in this chapter. These are not the only tools for setting the user environment in IntranetWare. To make your intranet an interesting place for your users, you should be familiar with all IntranetWare utilities.

CHAPTER 19

The IntranetWare File System

IntranetWare is a network-centric operating system. This concept is different from NetWare versions 3.1x and earlier operating systems as these are server-centric. IntranetWare views the file server as an object in the network. The file server remains the location for storage of the NetWare 4.11 operating system as well as the files and directories that comprise IntranetWare.

The IntranetWare file server provides a remote file storage system accessible by NetWare clients. Because many users share this remote-access file system, the following points are important:

- *The file server's remote file system must be well-organized and easy to maintain.*
- *Users must share the server's file system without violating system security or another user's privacy.*

- Access to the file system must be intuitive and consistent with the workstation operating system used by the client.
- Access to the file system must be nearly as fast as access to a workstation's local hard disk.

IntranetWare combines all of the previously mentioned features. The IntranetWare system and utilities are organized into standard directories, such as LOGIN, SYSTEM, and PUBLIC. Users can be assigned a home directory to store their personal files. If a directory contains system programs used for network administration, access to these programs can be restricted. Access to the network files is simple and intuitive; you can access the server files by using the workstation's operating system commands. And because most networks operate at speeds of megabits per second, access to the server's file system is fast. You can read and write to a network file about as fast as you can read and write to a local disk.

Looking at Directory Organization

A high-performance disk subsystem has a dramatic effect on the file server's overall performance. Many types of disk subsystems exist. A knowledge of disk subsystem features helps you to choose the correct disk to improve a server's performance.

The user sees a logical view of the server disk. This logical view must be consistent with the workstation operating system used by the client. For example, a user of a Macintosh station sees the remote file system by using the FINDER interface, and a user of a DOS workstation sees the file system as a number of remote drives designated by letters, such as F, G, H, and so on.

Disk Subsystems

Disk systems are internal or external. The computer's chassis houses the internal disk; you can access internal disks only by removing the chassis, which involves powering down the computer. External disk systems exist outside the computer. A host bus adapter in the computer acts as a bus interface for the external disk. External disks are more convenient for the network administrator because you do not have to turn off the computer to access an external disk.

A good disk subsystem for a server has the following characteristics:

- Large capacity
- High-data, throughput-fast disks, and system bus
- Low cost
- Reliability

Choose a disk subsystem based on how well it satisfies the preceding criteria.

Because the server is a repository for programs and data shared by many network users, it should have as large a disk system as is practical based on drive cost and drive support. A fast disk system improves server performance as long as other factors, such as LAN speed and server system bus, are not bottlenecks. The type of system bus must be considered carefully if fast disk performance is required because the data has to travel through the system bus.

Reliability is one of the most important criterion of the server's disk subsystem. If the disk subsystem fails, the file server may be unusable. The result may be the loss of critical data on the server. To avoid this, proper backups must be made.

IDE and EIDE Disk Subsystems

IDE and EIDE drives contain the drive controllers on the physical drive. IDE is known as Integrated Drive Electronics and EIDE stands for Enhanced Integrated Drive Electronics. EIDE allows the use of more physical drives than IDE and it has a comparable data throughput of Fast SCSI-II drives. You can connect up to four physical drives on a EIDE controller. EIDE also allows physical drives a capacity of over 8 GB. At first, EIDE might seem to offer an inexpensive disk subsystem for a file server, however the EIDE is not very well-suited for multitasking as required for IntranetWare. If you use IDE or EIDE as a disk subsystem you can use the IDE.DSK NLM or NWPA drivers (.CDM and .HAM extensions).

ESDI Disk Subsystems

Maxtor developed the Enhanced Small Devices Interface (ESDI) in 1983, and a number of disk drive manufacturers have adopted it since then. The I/O interface used for many minicomputer environments is the foundation of the ESDI. ESDI drives were popular for file server disk subsystems before SCSI became the defacto standard. The following information is helpful if you have servers on your network using an ESDI disk subsystem.

ESDI drives use 2,7 or 3,9 RLL encoding that enables them to compress more sectors per track. The number of sectors per track can be 26, 53, or a higher number. Because ESDI drives can use different RLL encoding, make sure that you buy a matched disk controller and disk—that is, buy them from the same source.

Many ESDI controllers implement track buffering. When a request for a single sector is made, the entire track is read and cached in fast RAM on the disk controller. This is done in anticipation of subsequent sector requests from the same track. ESDI track buffering works only for read operations, not write operations.

Track buffering does not replace NetWare's file caching mechanism, but instead, complements it. NetWare's file caching mechanism provides cache buffering for both read and write operations, which improves the file system's overall performance.

SCSI Disk Subsystems

The Small Computer Systems Interface (SCSI), pronounced "scuzzy," is a bus interface for peripheral devices. SCSI enables devices such as disk drives and tape drives to be connected to an external I/O bus. Developed by Adaptec, SCSI became an American National Standards Institute (ANSI) standard in 1982. Apple's Macintosh PLUS and later models made the SCSI popular. These machines are equipped with a SCSI port that enables you to plug in disk drives and tape units externally.

The SCSI architecture is based on the block-multiplexor I/O channel interface of IBM mainframes and can transfer data at rates up to 32 Mbps.

Because the SCSI is a bus interface, I/O devices are connected serially—or daisy chained—to the bus. Up to eight such devices can be connected to the bus. SCSI products integrate the device controller with the SCSI adapter. The bus interfaces with the computer through a card known as a host bus adapter or HBA. Many SCSI controllers can perform a function known as bus mastering. This allows the SCSI device to directly control the computer's data bus. This eliminates the intervention of the CPU and data is placed directly into the computer's main memory.

The SCSI bus must be terminated on the last device attached to the bus. Termination can be an external terminator or it can be terminated with the setup utility of the HBA. This last method is known as passive termination. Depending on the hardware configuration of your server, you may have several types of SCSI devices. CD-ROMs and tape drives should be on a separate controller from your SCSI hard disks.

SCSI technology has improved in the past several years to provide the faster rate of reading and writing data. Fast SCSI and SCSI II are two of these new SCSI technologies. RAID (Redundant Array of Inexpensive Disks) technology is usually built upon SCSI technology. RAID requires a special HBA. IntranetWare sees a RAID disk array as one drive even though there several physical disks in the array. If a physical disk fails in the disk array, the data on the failed disk is rebuilt on the other disks in the array. Some RAID systems allow for "hot swap," if a disk fails in the array you can replace it without having to take down the server.

Logical View of Disk Subsystem

The NetWare 4.11 operating system portion of IntranetWare contains several enhancements for file storage. Disk block suballocation, File compression, Data Migration, and Read-ahead are features IntranetWare uses to improve the disk subsystems performance.

The IntranetWare operating system presents a logical view of the file server's disk. An IntranetWare client sees the server's disk as being organized into volumes, directories, and files. Internally, IntranetWare manages the disk as a sequence of disk blocks of fixed size. Block sizes for IntranetWare can be 4, 8, 16, 32, and 64 KB. When installing IntranetWare, if you choose the simple installation, the install program will make the determination which block size to use for a volume. Normally, the default block size is 64 KB. This block size might be too large for your needs, and you may want to use the custom installation to set your block size. The anticipated average size of the files stored on a volume can help determine the block size. Because IntranetWare manages the disk as a sequence of blocks, IntranetWare remains independent of the physical disk structure, such as number of sectors per track, number of cylinders, and number of disk platters (surface area).

IntranetWare has the capability to do what is known as *Disk block suballocation.* In NetWare versions 3.1x and earlier, the smallest unit in which NetWare can store data is a block. For example, if you had a file with a size of 6 KB that you wanted to store on a NetWare volume with a block size of 4 KB, the file would occupy 2 blocks. So a 6 KB file would, in fact, use 8 KB of physical disk space. Disk block suballocation in IntranetWare would still write the file to 2 blocks, but it will recognize there is still 2 KB available in one block. This means after you stored your 6 KB file on a volume, you could store another 6 KB file on the volume.This would use a total of 3 blocks for both files versus the 4 blocks used in NetWare versions 3.1x and earlier. Disk block suballocation unit is 512 bytes each. Disk block suballocation can be disabled for any volume. Disk block suballocation does utilize more of your server's memory when it is enabled (the default).

IntranetWare also has the capability to do file compression automatically. After a file has been stored on a volume for a set period of time, the IntranetWare operating system will compress the file using an algorithm similar to Stac Technologies STACKER program for data compression. You can set a number of parameters for file compression, including:

- The time of day to compress data
- The number of days before compressing a file
- The amount of available disk space before uncompressing a file
- The amount of disk space needed before compressing a file

Data migration is a feature that will automatically move files from the file server's disk subsystem to another type of media such as a writeable CD-ROM. IntranetWare migrates data based on two factors: age of the file, and when the volume has reached a predetermined percentage of its capacity. The network administrator sets the parameters of time a file has been stored on a volume, and the percentage of the volume's capacity.

Files migrated off the volume still appear on the directory listings. The file is flagged with an attribute of "M" for Migrated. When a user tries to access this file, IntranetWare will restore it to the volume from the media to where it was migrated. If the media device is off-line, IntranetWare will display a console message indicating the device is not mounted.

Read-ahead gives IntranetWare the ability to read the block of a file into the file cache buffers. This feature works only when the access of the file is in sequential blocks. *Read-ahead* is a CPU intensive operation and is assigned a low priority by the operating system.To use the server's disk, unused drive letters (usually F to Z) are mapped to directories on the server. After this logical association is made, you can treat the server directories as extensions to the local disk subsystem. Access to the server's remote file system can be made with the workstation operating system commands by using a network drive letter.

Volumes

A server's disk is organized into volumes. Volumes are a logical division of the space available on a server's disk.

In IntranetWare, a server supports 64 volumes that have, in theory, a maximum size of 32 Terabytes. Because this is greater than the size of disks available today, you do not need to partition a large disk into logical volumes in IntranetWare. An entire physical disk can be assigned to a single volume.

With IntranetWare, it is possible to span a logical volume across several server disks. A volume consists of up to 32 volume segments. Each volume segment can be a disk partition or an entire disk. The volume segments are defined by using the Disk Options in the INSTALL NLM.

To perform volume spanning, you must follow these steps:

1. After you load INSTALL.NLM, select the following choices:

   Installation Options

   Volume Options (Configure/Mount/Dismount Volumes)

2. After a list of volumes appears, press Ins to add a new volume. If you have more than one hard disk that potentially can be used for volume spanning, a list of these partitions appears.

3. Enter on free space to make a volume assignment From the Volume Disk Segment List, select the disk to be used as a volume segment. Enter on a new segment (Status N) to modify a segment's size.

   If you want to use a smaller value, you can compute the new block size by using the formula:

   Disk blocks = (Amount of space to be allocated in MB ´ 1024) / Block size in KB

   If you want to use only 25 MB for a volume configured with 4 KB blocks, the number of disk blocks for Initial Segment Size is:

   Disk blocks = 25 ´ 1024 / 4 = 6400 blocks

   The block size must be the same for all volume segments.

4. In the Volume Information menu, enter the Volume Name and Volume Block Size.

   The Initial Segment Size field holds the total number of blocks available for that volume segment.

5. Press F10, and save the volume definition.

The Volume Definition Table stores the details of volume name, size, and segments. Every volume contains a Volume Definition Table in its partition.

An advantage is that multiple simultaneous I/O operations can be done on the volume in parallel because the volume now has a number of separate disks and disk controllers that provide concurrent access to it. This also means that requests to access a volume do not have to be queued up as long as they refer to an area of the volume on a separate disk, because the requests can be processed by the separate disk controllers and drives.

The disadvantage to volume spanning is if any of the disks comprising a volume fails, the entire volume fails. It is recommended you use disk mirroring to avoid this problem; and when mirroring disk subsystems, the disks should be duplexed. *Duplexing* is a method of disk mirroring that requires a redundant disk controller but this approach can be expensive when very large disks are involved.

By default the first volume in an IntranetWare server always is named SYS:. This volume contains the NetWare operating system files and the files and directories required for IntranetWare. Other volumes can have names consisting from two to 15 characters. It is recommended to keep volume names simple and easy to remember. For instance, the first volume created after SYS: can be labeled VOL1:, as an example the next one VOL2:, and so on.

Larger block sizes provide more efficient file access for large files because fewer blocks must be accessed for a given file. Larger disk blocks also require fewer entries in the File Allocation Tables (FATs) and, therefore, less RAM to keep track of them. Smaller size disk blocks use more RAM for their FAT tables.

If you have a volume intended for large database files, you can configure it for larger block sizes to provide more efficient file access. After you select a block size, you cannot change it without destroying the data on the volume.

Directories and Files

A volume can be further divided into directories and files. IntranetWare supports a hierarchical file structure. Figure 19.1 illustrates the hierarchy of dividing a volume into directories and files. For DOS workstations, the files and directories follow the 8.3 naming rule which is, eight characters, a period, and a 3-character extension. For Windows 95, Windows NT, and OS/2 support for long file names is available in IntranetWare with LONG.NAM. This will allow users of these operating systems to store files on IntranetWare file server volumes.

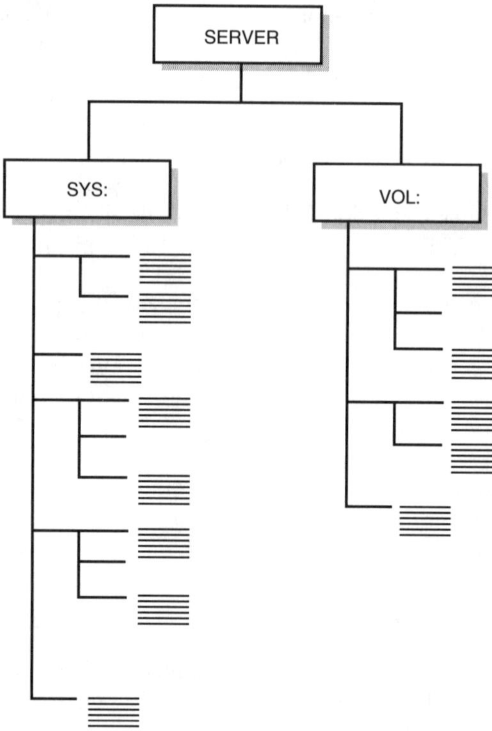

Figure 19.1
Logical organization of a server's file system.

To specify a file on a particular server, the full path name of the file is used. Use the following syntax:

```
[serverName/]volName:dir1{/dir2}/fileName
```

The directory separator delimiter character is / or \. Listing 19.1 shows examples of IntranetWare path names.

Listing 19.1

```
KSS/SYS:PUBLIC/SCRIPTS/STUDENTS.SCR
SYS:APPS\README.DOC
VOL1:BRIGHT/DOC\MANUAL.DOC
```

In the first example, the path name includes the file server name KSS. The server name is separated from the rest of the path name by either the / or \ character. This example uses /. The volume name is SYS:. The first directory is PUBLIC, and the subdirectory name is SCRIPTS. The file name is STUDENTS.SCR.

In example two, the optional server name is left out. This implies that the name of the default server is used. The directory APPS that contains the file README.DOC is under the volume name SYS:.

In example three, the optional server name is left out. The volume name is VOL1:. The directory name is BRIGHT. BRIGHT has a subdirectory named DOC, which contains the file MANUAL.DOC. In example 3, both / and \ are used as directory separators. As a matter of style, one or the other character should be used consistently.

Using Volume Object Names

In IntranetWare, a Volume Object Name is created at the time of creating the physical volume name during server installation (see fig. 19.2). Every physical volume name has an NDS object name counterpart. The Volume Object Name for a physical volume is its NDS object name. The Volume object is placed in the same context as the file server object, and its name is derived from the file server using the following rule: The default volume object name is a concatenation of the file server object name, the underscore character (_), and the physical object name.

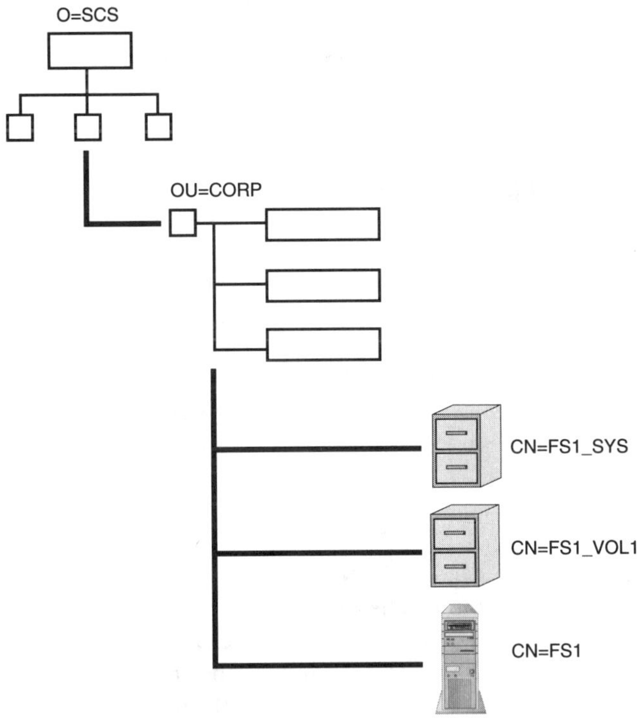

Figure 19.2
Volume object naming.

Therefore, for a volume that has the physical name PhysicalVolumeName that is attached to the server whose name is ServerName, the Volume object name is ServerName_PhysicalVolumeName.

Examples of the application of this rule are shown next:

Physical Volume Name	Server Name	Volume Object Name
SYS:	FS1	FS1_SYS
VOL1:	LTREE1	LTREE1_VOL1
CORP_VOL:	FS_CORP	FS_CORP_CORP_VOL
APP$ENG!VOL	KSS_FS	KSS_FS_APP$ENG!VOL

The Volume object contains properties such as the Host Server Name and the Host Volume Name that refer to the server object and the volume's physical name. Though the Volume objects are created in the context in which the File Server object is placed, they can be moved to a different context. However, it is advisable to keep the Volume objects in their default context (same as server context), because it is most likely to be used by User objects defined in this context, and to avoid confusion about the location of Volume objects.

Because Volume object names refer to the Volume object in the NDS tree, you can use the NDS syntax to refer to its name. To refer to the Volume object name FS1_SYS in the context OU=CORP.O=SCS, you can use any of the following in listing 19.2:

Listing 19.2

```
.CN=FS1_SYS.OU=CORP.O=SCS
.FS1_SYS.CORP.SCS
FS1_SYS  (if current context isOU=CORP.O=SCS)
```

Using NDS Syntax to Access IntranetWare Files

You can refer to a file on an IntranetWare server using the NetWare 3.1x file naming syntax. In this case, bindery emulation is used to resolve the file name. The syntax for NetWare 3.1x is:

```
<server name>\<volume name>:<directory>\<sub-directory>\file name
```

Because an IntranetWare volume is a leaf object in the NDS tree, the directories' and files' path names can use the NDS syntax to refer to the volume name (see fig. 19.3). This figure shows the path name for sub-directories ENG and CORP that are in the COMMON sub-directory in the Volume object FSDEV_SYS. The Volume object is in the context OU=CORP.O=LGROUP. If the current context is O=LGROUP, the partial NDS name of

```
FSDEV_SYS.CORP.LGROUP
```

or

```
CN=FSDEV_SYS.OU=CORP.O=LGROUP
```

can be used to refer to the Volume object. To refer to the subdirectory CORP or ENG, the volume object name must be prefixed with the file directory path COMMON/CORP or COMMON/ENG. The Volume object name and the directory path are separated by the colon (:) delimiter. Therefore, the CORP and ENG directories can be referred to by the syntax in listing 19.3, if current context is O=LGROUP.

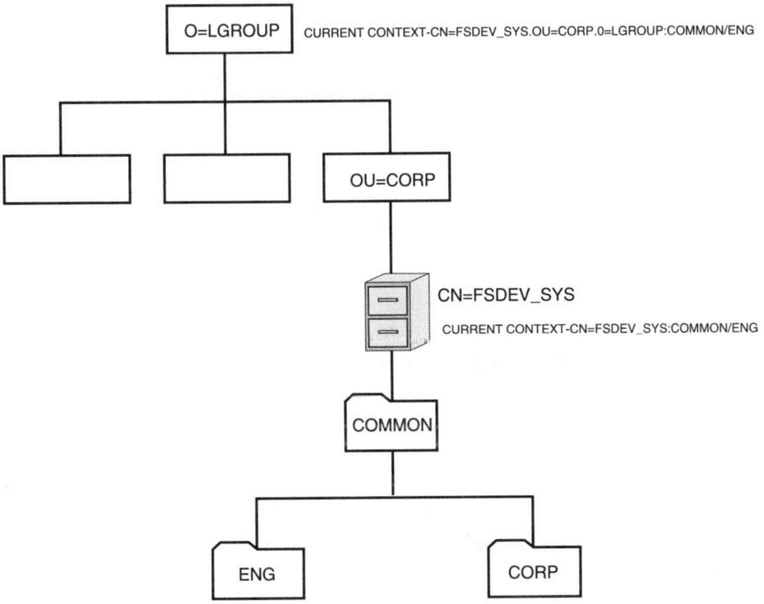

Figure 19.3
NDS syntax for file names.

Listing 19.3

```
FSDEV_SYS.CORP.LGROUP:COMMON/CORP
CN=FSDEV_SYS.OU=CORP.O=LGROUP:COMMON/ENG
```

If the current context is OU=CORP.O=LGROUP, the partial NDS name of

```
FSDEV_SYS
```

or

```
CN=FSDEV_SYS
```

can be used to refer to the Volume object. To refer to the subdirectory CORP or ENG, the Volume object name must be prefixed with the file directory path COMMON/CORP or COMMON/ENG. Therefore, the CORP and ENG directories can be referred to by the following syntax, if current context is OU=CORP.O=LGROUP

```
FSDEV_SYS:COMMON\CORP
CN=FSDEV_SYS:COMMON/ENG
```

Notice that either the backslash (\) or forward slash (/) characters can be used to separate file directory names.

Instead of using partial names for the Volume object, as in the previous examples, you can also use complete names. Examples of complete name syntax for referring to the file directory are shown here. Notice, that complete names as shown in listing 19.4 must have a leading period (.).

Listing 19.4

```
.FSDEV_SYS.CORP.LGROUP:COMMON/CORP
.CN=FSDEV_SYS.OU=CORP.O=LGROUP:COMMON/ENG
```

The first example uses typeless distinguished names for the Volume object, and the second example uses distinguished names with attribute type designators (CN, OU, O).

What is often confusing to beginners about the syntax examples in figure 19.3, is the normal convention of naming files is to start from the top of the file directory tree, and enumerate the directories separated by the delimiters backslash (\) or forward slash (/), all the way down to the file or directory. The NDS naming convention, on the other hand, is the complete opposite. In NDS naming, you start with the bottom of the tree, and list the object names separated by the delimiter period (.) all the way up to the [Root] object. The [Root] object is not listed, because an NDS tree can have only one root.

When you name file directories using the NDS syntax, you are combining the NDS and File naming conventions. Figure 19.4 shows graphically that these two conventions can be thought of as going up the hill to list the NDS path name. At the peak, you list the colon (:) separator. The colon character is listed at the peak of the hill, and marks the switch-over to the file naming convention. The file naming convention lists the file directories starting with the root directory and goes down the hill to the file or directory.

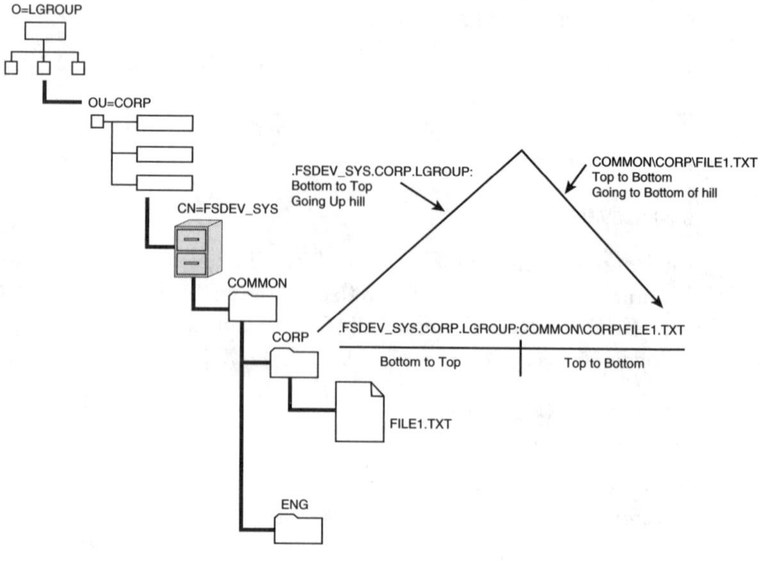

Figure 19.4
Combining NDS syntax and file naming syntax.

In summary, when combining NDS syntax for volume names with NetWare file system directory syntax remember that

- Path names in NDS syntax are listed from bottom to top
- Path names in NetWare file system are listed from top to bottom

Drive Mappings

To use the IntranetWare server's file system, the user assigns a network drive to a directory on the server. The process of assigning a workstation drive letter to a server directory is called mapping a network drive. Figure 19.5 shows the available drive letters. Drive letters A through E are usually reserved for local drives. Drives F through Z are assigned as network drives. IntranetWare does not support IPX.COM or NETX.EXE for Client workstations. You must use the client VLM software or the NetWare Client 32 software for workstations, and the LASTDRIVE=Z must be in the CONFIG.SYS file of the workstation.

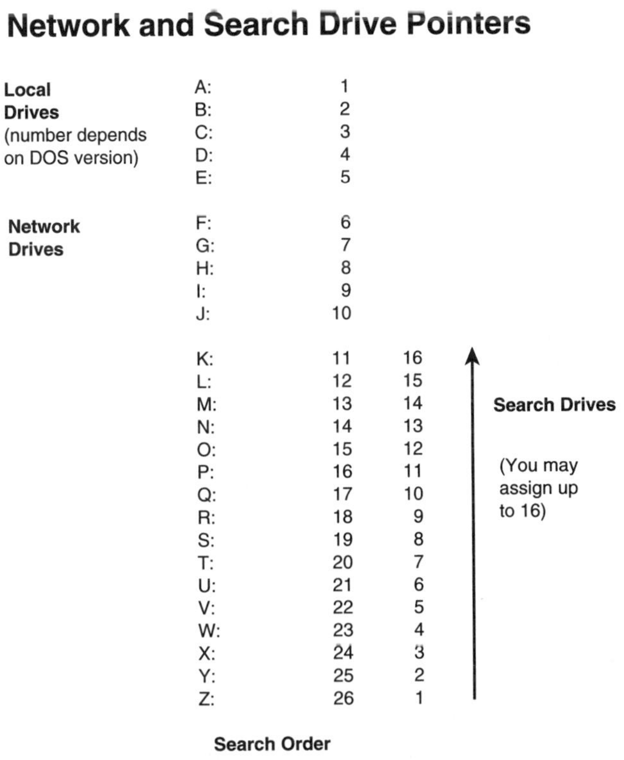

Network and Search Drive Pointers
Local Drives (number depends on DOS version)
A: 1
B: 2
C: 3
D: 4
E: 5
Network Drives
F: 6
G: 7
H: 8
I: 9
J: 10
K: 11 16
L: 12 15
M: 13 14
N: 14 13
O: 15 12
P: 16 11
Q: 17 10
R: 18 9
S: 19 8
T: 20 7
U: 21 6
V: 22 5
W: 23 4
X: 24 3
Y: 25 2
Z: 26 1
Search Drives
(You may assign up to 16)
Search Order

Figure 19.5
Search drives.

Figure 19.6 shows drive mappings to the file system on the server. Use the MAP command to set up the drive mappings. The syntax of the MAP command is as follows:

```
MAP [INS ¦ DEL ¦ ROOT] driveName:
_ [ = networkDirectory]
```

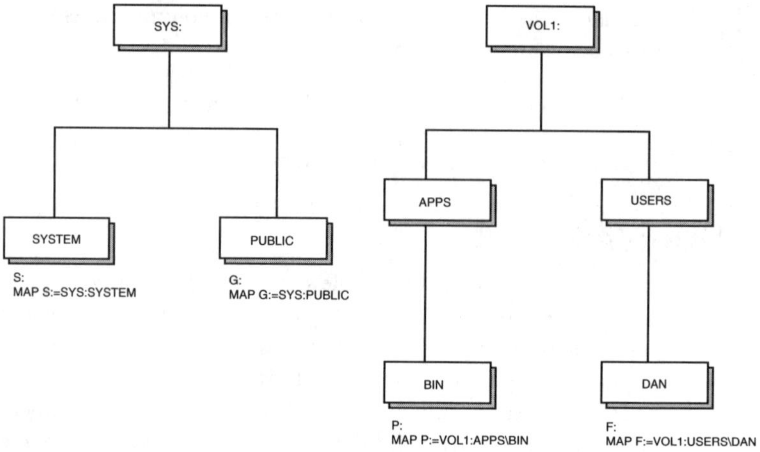

Figure 19.6
Drive mappings to file server's file system.

DriveName is a drive letter or a search drive (see next section). The [= networkDirectory] means that the assigned network directory is optional if the DEL option is used.

Examples of how to use the MAP command are as follows:

```
MAP F: = PARTAIN_SYS:PUBLIC
MAP ROOT G: = KSS/VOL1:DEVELOP/BIN
MAP DEL F:
```

Example one maps drive F to SYS:PUBLIC on the default server. You can make a drive mapping to a volume with either its NDS volume object name or with the physical name of the volume.

Example two maps drive G to VOL1:DEVELOP/BIN on server KSS. In addition, G is a root drive mapping (ROOT or R) to the network directory KSS/VOL1:DEVELOP/BIN. When a map drive letter is a root to a network directory, the network directory acts as a fake root of the file system. Because the root directory is the top-level directory, you cannot move up higher in the volume directory structure by using the following DOS command:

```
CD ..
```

When you use the map command, a root drive mapping is displayed with the backslash (\) four spaces past the last directory of the root drive map.

This fake root helps protect the security of the network directory and should not be considered a replacement for security. You also can use the fake root to install single-user applications on the IntranetWare server. Some single-user applications are required to be installed in a directory off the root of a drive. Normally, these applications are not network aware. A fake root enables you to install a single-user application in a subdirectory on a file server volume. To legally install a single-user application on the server, you must have a license for every user of the application on the network.

Example three deletes (DEL) the drive mapping for F. If you delete a drive mapping, the [= networkDirectory] is omitted.

You cannot map to a network directory unless you have access rights to that directory. If you attempt to map to a network directory for which you do not have access rights, the error message `DIRECTORY XXX NOT LOCATABLE` appears.

In IntranetWare the CD command alters the drive mapping, so you should use it with care. Consider what would happen if you used the following command from the local C: drive prompt:

```
C:\> CD SYS:COMMON\DATA
```

This would map your C: drive to SYS:COMMON\DATA. You would then lose access to your C: drive. You can regain access to the local drive C: by typing:

```
MAP DEL C:
```

The MAP NEXT or MAP N command assigns the next available drive as a network drive. Consider the following example, in which only network drive F: has been assigned:

```
MAP  F: = PARTAIN_VOL1:USERS\RSMALL
MAP  F: = SYS:USERS\JOHN
```

Then, using the following MAP NEXT commands

```
MAP NEXT PARTAIN_VOL1:USERS\RSMALL\DATA
MAP N PARTAIN_VOL1:APPS
MAP NEXT PARTAIN_VOL1:DATA
```

Assign network drive G to PARTAIN_VOL1:USERS\RSMALL\DATA , network drive H: to PARTAIN_VOL1:APPS and network drive I: to PARTAIN_VOL1:DATA. The second form of the MAP command shows that the letter "N" is an abbreviation for option "NEXT."

When the MAP NEXT command executes, it reports the network drive that has been assigned. Therefore, MAP NEXT is a convenient way to provide network drive mappings, using a simpler syntax, when it does not matter which network drive is assigned, as long as it is not a network drive that is already in use.

IntranetWare provides for an NP option in the MAP command. The MAP NP option allows a local or search drive mapping to be overridden without prompting the user. Its general syntax is

```
MAP NP  [Option] Drive: = DirectoryPath
```

Thus, to override the local drive mapping D:, you can use

```
MAP NP D: = SYS:USERS/KSS/BIN
```

To override a search drive mapping for search drive S3:, that might already exist, use:

```
MAP NP S3: = SYS:USERS/DORSH/BIN
```

The MAP CHANGE option can be used in IntranetWare to toggle between a search drive and a network drive.

Consider a network administrator who has just installed an application in a network drive J: that is mapped to PARTAIN_SYS:. The network administrator now wants to test the application by placing it in the search drive. In that case, the administrator can issue the command.

```
MAP CHANGE J:
```

or the abbreviated form

```
MAP C J:
```

If the next available search drive is S10:, you should see the following displayed as a result of executing any of the previous MAP CHANGE commands:

```
S10: = J:. [PARTAIN_SYS: \]
```

If you want to remove the search drive and make it a regular drive, you can use the MAP CHANGE to toggle back to the network drive:

```
MAP C S10:
```

Throughout the preceding operations, the drive J: is still mapped to PARTAIN_SYS:. Even when J: is mapped as a search drive, the association between J: and its orginal drive mapping is maintained.

Search Drives

In DOS, the PATH command specifies the order that directories are searched if a program file is not found in the current directory. The directories specified in the PATH command are stored in a DOS environment variable of the same name (PATH). IntranetWare uses the environment variable PATH to store search drives.

You cannot include IntranetWare directories as part of the original DOS PATH command by using the IntranetWare syntax for a directory. For example, a DOS station has the following setting for the PATH environment variable before logging into an IntranetWare server:

```
PATH=C:\;C:\DOS;C:\WINDOWS;C:\NOVELL\CLIENT32
```

DOS cannot process the IntranetWare syntax in the PATH environment variable because DOS only recognizes one-letter drives. To solve this problem, IntranetWare uses search drive mappings to specify network volumes and directories as part of the search path.

Figure 19.5 shows search drives. Sixteen search drives exist, and they are labeled SEARCH1 to SEARCH16. You can abbreviate SEARCH by using S. The first search drive, therefore, is abbreviated as S1, and the sixteenth search drive is abbreviated as S16. Use the MAP command to make search drive assignments. Search drives specify the order that directories, including network directories, are searched. This is similar to the way the DOS PATH command operates, except search drives enable you to work with network directories.

In the following example, therefore, if you want to include the network directory SYS:PUBLIC\UTIL as part of the search path, you can use the following MAP commands:

```
MAP S1:=SYS:PUBLIC\UTIL
```

or

```
MAP INS S1:=SYS:PUBLIC\UTIL
```

The first MAP command maps search drive 1 (S1) to the network directory SYS:PUBLIC\UTIL, and this directory is searched first. The second MAP command inserts (INS) SYS:PUBLIC\UTIL as the first search drive. If the first search drive was assigned previously, the INS option pushes it down the list to become the second search drive. Figure 19.7 illustrates this "push-down" effect. This figure shows the search drives before and after the user issues the MAP INS command.

Search Drive	Drive Assign.	Search Directory
S1	Z:	SYS:PUBLIC
S2	Y:	SYS:SYSTEM

(+) MAP INS S1:=PUBLIC\UTIL (=)

Search Drive	Drive Assign.	Search Directory
S1	Z:	SYS:PUBLIC\UTIL
S2	Y:	SYS:PUBLIC
S3	X:	SYS:SYSTEM

Figure 19.7
The push-down effect of the MAP INS command.

When the user issues the MAP S1:=SYS:PUBLIC\UTIL command to map search drive 1, the DOS PATH environment variable changes also. It assigns an unused drive letter starting with Z to the network directory, and inserts Z in the DOS PATH environment variable. Therefore, the DOS PATH environment variable before the MAP S1:=SYS:PUBLIC\UTIL command looks like this:

```
PATH=C:\WP51;C:\BIN;C:\BC\BIN;C:\WC386\BIN
```

After using the MAP command, the DOS PATH environment variable looks like this:

```
PATH=Z:.;C:\WP51;C:\BIN;C:\BC\BIN;C:\WC386\BIN
```

DOS recognizes the single letter Z as another directory letter, and it searches drive Z as it does any local drive. The period (.) stands for the current directory, and when used in the PATH environment variable, it indicates that the current directory Z, mapped to SYS:PUBLIC\UTIL, is to be searched.

IntranetWare assigns search drive letters beginning with Z and moving backward through the alphabet to K. Figure 19.5 illustrates that search drive 1 uses Z, and search drive 16 uses K. The reverse order of letter assignment for search drives minimizes conflicts between the applications and search drives.

Search drive mappings affect only the user's current network session. When a user issues a MAP command to map to a network directory, the mapping is only for the user who issues the command. The workstation's operating system shell holds the drive mappings only for a session. When the user logs out of a server by using the LOGOUT command, the drive mappings disappear from the drive map table. To make the drive mappings permanent, the user must automate the execution of the MAP commands. One way to do this is with a login script. MAP commands used to build a network search path can be placed in a login script file. A login script defines a user's network environment. Login scripts are discussed in detail in Chapter 18, "Managing User Sessions."

Another way to automate drive maps is to use the NetWare User's Tools in Windows 3.1 or Windows 95. You can create permanent drive mappings for Windows. Each time Windows is started or after the user has logged onto the network in Windows 95 the permanent drive mappings are automatically set.

If an attempt is made to map a search drive that does not exist, the next logical search drive is assigned as a search drive. Consider the following example in which an IntranetWare session has three search drive mappings as shown:

```
MAP INS S1:=SYS:PUBLIC
MAP INS S2:=SYS:PUBLIC\BIN
MAP INS S3:=SYS:APPS\BIN
```

Any other search drive that is not used will exhibit the same behavior, when used in the MAP command. Thus, if the only search drives that exist are described by the MAP commands that follow:

```
MAP INS S1:=SYS:PUBLIC
MAP INS S2:=SYS:PUBLIC\BIN
MAP INS S3:=SYS:APPS\BIN
```

Then, using search drive S16: that does not exist, in the following MAP command:

```
MAP S16:=SYS:APPS\WP
```

will map search drive S4: to SYS:APPS\WP.

If you reassign a search drive map to an existing search drive number, the previous search drive map pointer will become a regular map drive pointer. Information is still available to you; however, it is no longer in the path environment. You will have to change to the drive pointer in order to access the information stored this location.

Network Drive Assignments

The best way to learn about network drive assignments is to experiment with them. This section gives you hands-on experience with drive mappings.

To follow the exercises listed in this section, you must have access to the user ADMIN and a User object.

1. Log in as ADMIN or use a valid user account.

2. Type:

   MAP

The MAP command examines the current drive mappings. The response to this command looks like the following output. The details depend on the way your login script is set up.

```
Drives A,B,C,D,E map to a local disk.
Drive F: = PARTAIN_SYS: \SYSTEM
Drive G: = PARTAIN_VOL1: \DANNY
Drive H: = PARTAIN_SYS: \PUBLIC\WIN95
Drive I: = PARTAIN_VOL1: \
      --    Search Drives    --
S1: = Z:. [PARTAIN_SYS: \PUBLIC]
S2: = Y:. [PARTAIN_SYS: \]
S3: = C:\NOVELL\CLIENT32\
S4: = C:\CPS
S5: = C:\WINDOWS
S6: = C:\CCMOBILE
S7: = C:\CPQDOS
S8: = C:\
S9: = C:\DOS
S10: = C:\MOUSE
```

3. Issue a MAP command to map drive I to SYS:PUBLIC:

   MAP I:=SYS:PUBLIC

   To verify that your mapping has been successful, type:

   MAP

4. Try to map to a directory that does not exist.

   MAP J:=SYS:DEVELOP

   The message returned is:

   ```
   MAP-4.13-195: Directory [J:=SYS:DEVELOP] cannot be located.
   ```

5. Map to a directory for which you do not have access rights. To perform this step you must create a directory called SYS:DEVELOP/BIN using a user object such as ADMIN, and then log in as a User object that does not have access rights. Type:

   MAP J:=SYS:DEVELOP/BIN

   If you do not have access to this directory, you will get an error message that states the directory cannot be located.

You also can log in as a ADMIN, assign Read and File scan access rights of SYS:DEVELOP to the User object you are working with, and then map drive J to the directory SYS:DEVELOP while logged in as the User object:

MAP J:=SYS:DEVELOP/BIN

This time the mapping is successful.

6. To delete the drive J mapping, type:

```
MAP DEL J:
```

7. To map drive J to the same directory as I, type:

```
MAP J:=I:
```

Use the MAP command to verify this mapping.

8. You do not need to use the IntranetWare network directory syntax to specify the volume name to map to a network directory. Try the following:

```
MAP H:=F:\PUBLIC
```

The preceding command maps H to the same volume as F, starting from the root, and going down to the PUBLIC directory.

9. You can experiment with search drives in the next few sections.

To note the current search drives, type:

```
MAP
```

The following response appears:

```
Drives A,B,C,D,E map to a local disk.
Drive F: = PARTAIN_SYS: \
Drive H: = PARTAIN_SYS: \PUBLIC\
Drive I: = PARTAIN_SYS: \PUBLIC\
Drive J: = PARTAIN_SYS: \PUBLIC\
      -----    Search Drives    -----
S1: = Z:. [PARTAIN_SYS: \PUBLIC]
S2: = Y:. [PARTAIN_SYS: \]
S3: = C:\NOVELL\CLIENT32\
S4: = C:\CPS
S5: = C:\WINDOWS
S6: = C:\CCMOBILE
S7: = C:\CPQDOS
S8: = C:\
S9: = C:\DOS
S10: = C:\MOUSE
```

In the preceding example, search drive 1 is mapped to PARTAIN_SYS: \PUBLIC .

To display the current DOS search path, type:

```
PATH
```

The following response appears:

```
PATH=Z:.;Y:.;C:\NOVELL\CLIENT32;C:\CPS;C:\WINDOWS;C:\
CCMOBILE;C:\CPQDOS;C:\;C:\DOS;C:\MOUSE
```

Notice that the PATH command is consistent with the current search drive mappings.

10. Insert SYS:DOC as the first search drive. Type:

```
MAP INS S1:=SYS:DOC
```

To examine the changed drive mappings, type:

```
MAP
```

The following response appears:

```
Drives A,B,C,D,E map to a local disk.
Drive F: = PARTAIN_SYS: \
Drive H: = PARTAIN_SYS: \PUBLIC\
Drive I: = PARTAIN_SYS: \PUBLIC\
Drive J: = PARTAIN_SYS: \PUBLIC\
-----    Search Drives    -----
S1: = X:. [PARTAIN_SYS: \DOC]
S2: = Z:. [PARTAIN_SYS: \PUBLIC]
S3: = Y:. [PARTAIN_SYS: \PUBLIC]
S4: = C:\NOVELL\CLIENT32\
S5: = C:\NWCLIENT\
S6: = C:\CPS
S7: = C:\WINDOWS
S8: = C:\CCMOBILE
S9: = C:\CPQDOS
S10: = C:\
S11: = C:\DOS
S12: = C:\MOUSE
```

Compare the search drive mappings with those in step 9.

To examine the DOS PATH environment variable type:

```
PATH
```

The following results appear:

```
PATH= X:.;Z:.;Y:.;C:\NOVELL\CLIENT32;C:\CPS;C:\WINDOWS;C:\
CCMOBILE;C:\CPQDOS;C:\;C:\DOS;C:\MOUSE
```

Compare the DOS PATH environment variable with that in step 9. Notice that the DOS PATH environment variable reflects the changed search drive mappings.

11. Delete the first search drive mapping by typing:

    ```
    MAP DEL S1:
    ```

    To examine the new search drive mappings and the DOS PATH environment variable, use the commands outlined in step 10. These should have the same values, as in step 9.

12. Try to delete a drive that does not exist by typing:

    ```
    MAP DEL S16:
    ```

    The message returned is:

    ```
    MAP-4.13-195: Directory [DEL S16:] cannot be located.
    ```

13. Add a search drive at the end.

    You probably have fewer than 16 search drive mappings for your current log-in session. If you do, type the following command:

    ```
    MAP  S16:=SYS:DOCS
    ```

    To examine the search drive mappings, type:

    ```
    MAP
    ```

    ```
    S5:= W:. [PARTAIN_SYS:DOCS \]
    ```

    Notice that you did not create search drive 16, but you did create a search drive with a number one greater than the last search drive. When you want to create a search drive, but do not know the number of the last search drive, use the MAP S16: command. This command automatically assigns the next available number to the new search drive.

14. The MAP command also can be applied to a local directory:

    ```
    MAP  S16:=C:\
    ```

    To examine the new search drive mappings and the DOS PATH environment variable, use the MAP and PATH commands. Notice that directory C:\ is now in the search drive list and the DOS PATH environment variable.

15. To map drive H to SYS:PUBLIC, type:

    ```
    MAP H:=SYS:PUBLIC
    ```

    Make H the current drive, and use the DOS change directory command to go one level up to the root SYS:.

    ```
    H:CD ..
    ```

    Type the MAP command to find out the current search drive mappings.

The change directory command changes the drive mapping of Drive H.

16. Repeat step 15 with a fake root MAP command. For instance, to map Drive H to SYS:PUBLIC with a fake root, type:

    ```
    MAP ROOT H:=SYS:PUBLIC
    ```

    Make sure that H is the current drive, and use the DOS change directory command to move up one level to the root SYS:.

    ```
    H:CD ..
    ```

    Now use the MAP command to find out the current search drive mappings. Unlike step 15, the change directory command does not go above the fake root.

17. If you inadvertently wipe out the DOS PATH environment variable, the search drives also are deleted.

    To delete the DOS PATH, type:

    ```
    F:
    CD \
    SET PATH=
    ```

    Unless your current directory is SYS:PUBLIC, which stores the MAP command, type **MAP**. The following message appears:

    ```
    Bad command or file name
    ```

    To change to the SYS:PUBLIC directory that holds the MAP.EXE (command program file) type:

    ```
    CD \PUBLIC
    ```

    Next, type **MAP**. Note that the search drive mappings also have been wiped out.

Using Directory Map Objects

In the preceding exercise you see how time consuming it can be to make drive mappings. The degree of difficulty is compounded by multiple servers and partitions in your network. In the NDS you have an object you can create called a Directory Map Object. This is a predefined pointer to a volume or directory located on your network. A Directory Map Object can be placed in a container object to allow all user objects in the container access to the Directory Map Object. You can create as many Directory Map Objects as you need to facilitate drive mappings. The Directory Map Object name should be short and simple, but recognizable to users accessing it. For instance, the application program Word is located in the following directory structure:

```
SERVER3\SYS:APPS\MSOFFICE\WINWORD
```

To make a map drive to this location the user would have to type the following:

```
MAP I:= SERVER3\SYS:APPS\MSOFFICE\WINWORD
```

or

```
MAP I:= SERVER3_SYS:APPS\ MSOFFICE\WINWORD
```

In the predefined Directory Map object called WORD the user only has to type:

```
MAP I:=WORD
```

The Directory Map object can also be accessed from NWUSER to create drive mappings in Windows or Windows 95. You have the option to make this a permanent drive map so each time you begin in a Windows environment the mapping will be set automatically. Figure 19.8 shows an example of using a Directory Map object.

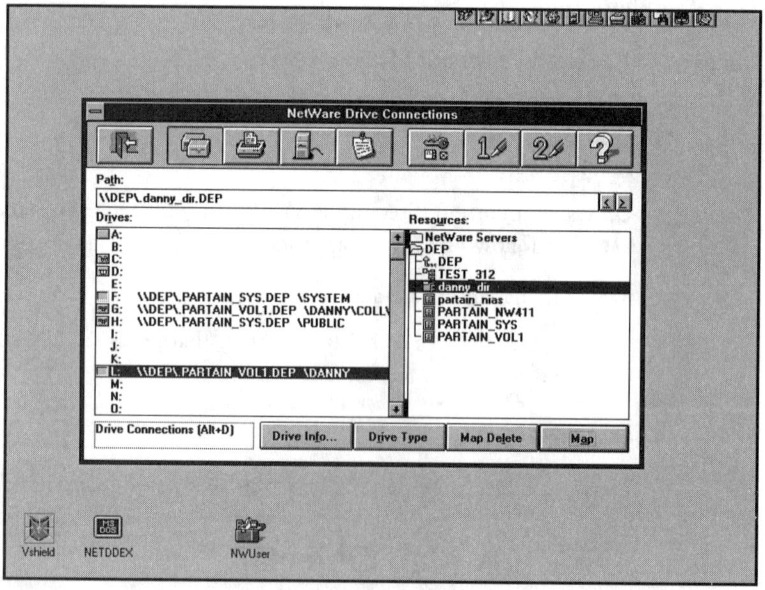

Figure 19.8
Using the Directory Map object in NWUSER to create a drive map.

The Directory Map object can be updated or changed as the need arises. You can use either NETADMIN or the NetWare Administrator (NWADMIN) in DOS or Windows. For Windows 95 or Windows NT, you can use NWADMIN95. Figure 19.9 shows the available properties for a Directory Map object.

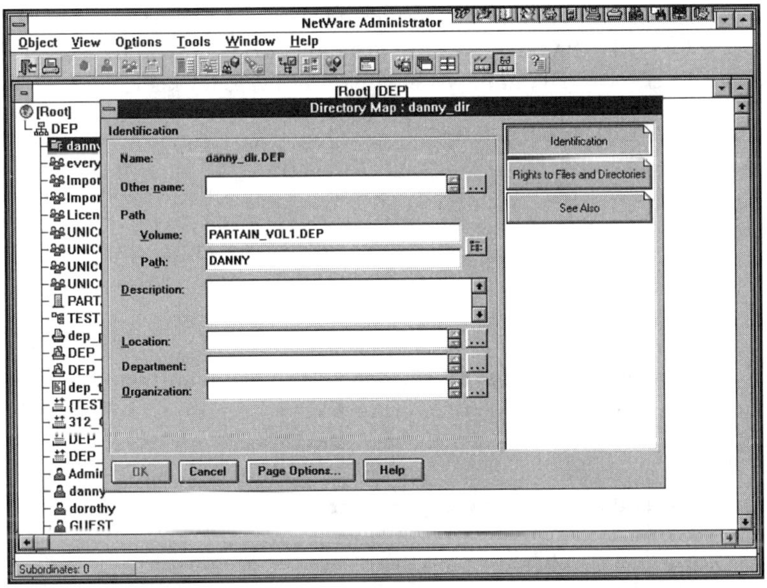

Figure 19.9
Directory Map object properties in Windows 3.1.

Figures 19.10 and 19.11 show other examples of the use of Directory Map objects.

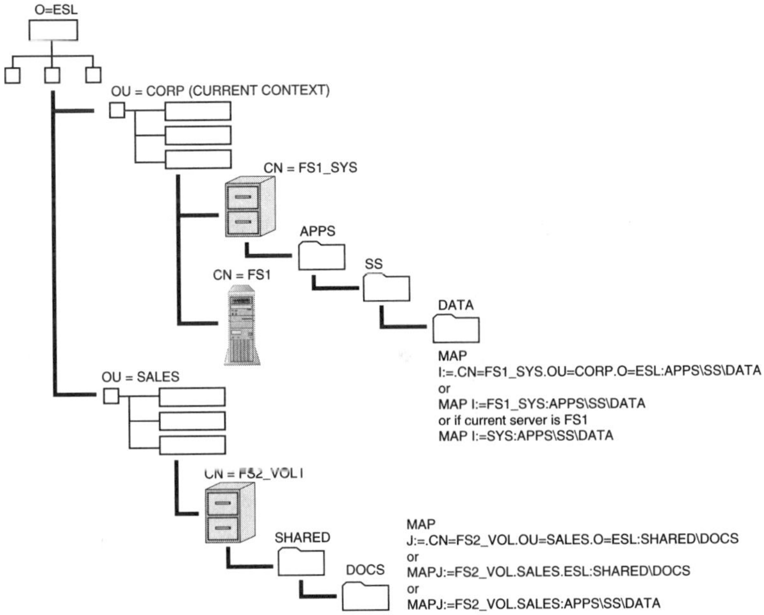

Figure 19.10
Network drive mappings to directories on different volumes.

Figure 19.10 shows directory mappings to different Volume objects. Assume that the current context in the NDS tree is OU=CORP.O=ESL. A drive mapping of I: to the APPS\SS\DATA directory for the Volume object FS1_SYS can be written in any of the following forms:

```
MAP I: = .CN=FS1_SYS.OU=CORP.O=ESL:APPS\SS\DATA
```

or

```
MAP I: = FS1_SYS:APPS\SS\DATA
```

or

```
MAP I: = SYS:APPS\SS\DATA
```

The first form of the MAP command uses a distinguished name for the Volume object with attribute type designators (CN, OU, O). The second form refers to the relative distinguished name of the Volume object, and because the Volume object is in the current context, the common name of the Volume object can be used. The third form uses the physical name of the Volume object and can be used if the user initially connects to the file server FS1.

In the tree branch under the container OU=SALES, a drive mapping of J: to the SHARED\DOCS directory for the Volume object FS2_VOL can be written in any of the following forms:

```
MAP J: = .FS2_VOL.SALES.ESL:SHARED/DOCS
```

or

```
MAP J: = .CN=FS2_VOL.OU=SALES.O=ESL:SHARED/DOCS
```

or

```
MAP J: = FS2_VOL.SALES.:SHARED/DOCS
```

The first form refers to the typeless distinguished name of the Volume object. The second form of the MAP command uses a typeful distinguished name for the Volume object with attribute type designators (CN, OU, O). The third form uses the relative distinguished name of the Volume object (relative to the current context O=ESL).

The mappings shown in figure 19.10 can be simplified using Directory Map objects as shown in figure 19.11. In figure 19.11, two Directory Map objects CN=Path_Docs and CN=Path_Data are created. The Directory Map object CN=Path_Docs contains a mapping to the SHARED\DOC directory for Volume object CN=FS2_VOL.OU=SALES.O=ESL, and the Directory Map object Path_Data contains a mapping to the APPS\SS\DATA directory for Volume object CN=FS1_SYS.OU=CORP.O=ESL. The drive mappings of I: and J: in the example in figure 19.10 can now be expressed in terms of the Directory Map objects.

```
MAP I: = .CN=Path_Data.OU=CORP.O=ESL
```

or

```
MAP I: = .Path_Data.CORP.ESL
```

or

```
MAP I: = Path_Data
```

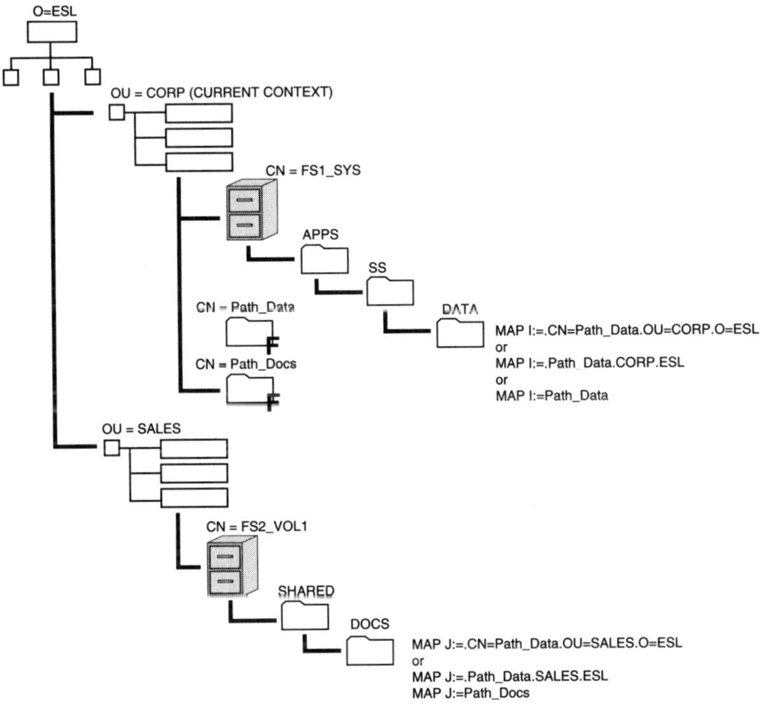

Figure 19.11
Network drive mappings using directory map objects.

The first form of the MAP command uses a typeful distinguished name with attribute types (CN, OU, O) for the Directory Map object. The second form uses a typeless distinguished name, and the third form uses the name for the Directory Map object. Because the Directory Map object is in the current context, the common name of the Directory Map object can be used.

The drive mappings for J:, using Directory Name object are the following:

```
MAP J: = .Path_Docs.CORP.ESL
```

or

```
MAP J: = .CN=Path_Docs.OU=CORP.O=ESL
```

or

```
MAP J: = Path_Docs
```

The first form of the MAP command uses the typeless distinguished name of the Directory Map object. The second form of the MAP command uses the typeful distinguished name for the Directory Map object. The third form uses a common name for the Directory Map object.

Because the Directory Map object is in the current context, the common name of the Directory Map object can be used.

Alternate Name Space Support

IntranetWare supports alternate file systems, such as the Macintosh file system. These alternate file systems also are called *alternate name spaces*. Macintosh workstations see the IntranetWare file systems in terms of folders. A Macintosh file has two components—a data fork and a resource fork. A data fork holds the data portion of the file and the resource fork contains file attributes, such as the icon used to display the file and access rights to a file.

In addition to the Macintosh name space, IntranetWare supports Windows 95 and Windows NT name space, OS/2 name space, NFS name space, and FTAM name space. These name spaces have longer file and directory names (typically 254 characters). If OS/2 uses the FAT file system (a DOS-compatible file system), the OS/2 name space is not needed. The OS/2 name space must be installed if the High Performance File System (HPFS) is used.

To add name space support, load the name space module in the STARTUP.NCF file and use the ADD NAME SPACE command in the AUTOEXEC.NCF file.

For example, to add name space support for a Windows 95 file system, perform the following steps:

1. Load the disk driver and add the following line in STARTUP.NCF:

   ```
   LOAD LONG
   ```

2. After you mount the volume to which you want to add the name space, type the following line in AUTOEXEC.NCF:

   ```
   ADD NAME SPACE LONG TO VOLUME SYS
   ```

   To add name space support for a volume other than SYS, replace SYS with the volume name. To examine current name-space modules use the command:

   ```
   ADD NAME SPACE
   ```

   To add name space support for MACINTOSH, NFS, or FTAM, replace LONG with MACINTOSH, NFS, or FTAM.

Organizing a Directory

Upon its installation on the file server, IntranetWare creates a standard volume (SYS:) and directory structure to store its program and system files. To install applications and user's data on the server, you can augment the volume and directory structure. This section examines how the standard volume and directory structure can be augmented.

Default Directory Organization

During installation, IntranetWare creates a standard directory structure shown in figure 19.12. The SYSTEM, PUBLIC, LOGIN, WEB, NETBASIC, ETC, and MAIL directories are created on volume SYS:

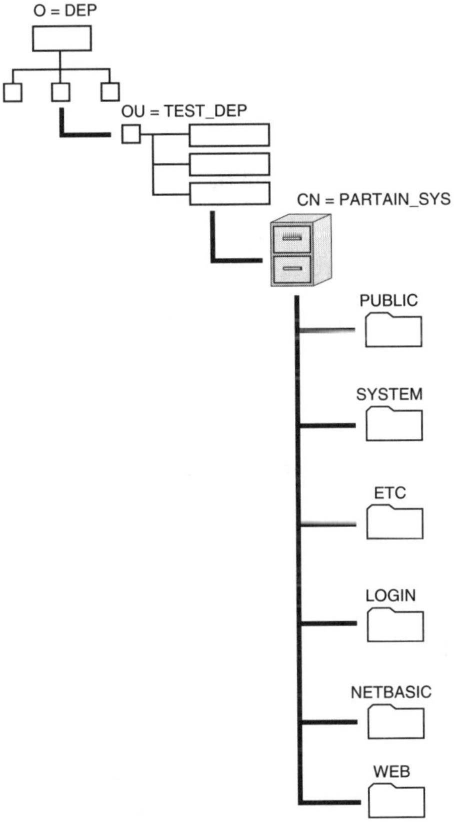

Figure 19.12
An IntranetWare server's SYS: volume structure as installed.

In the sections that follow, you learn about the kinds of files in each of these directories.

LOGIN Directory

The LOGIN directory contains the IntranetWare utilities LOGIN.EXE, NLIST.EXE, and CX.EXE. The LOGIN directory also holds the operating system boot images created by the DOSGEN program for diskless workstations.

The default access rights to the SYS:LOGIN directory prevent modification of programs in this directory. You must make sure that these default access rights are not changed. Otherwise, the LOGIN directory can become a place through which a virus can spread.

PUBLIC Directory

The PUBLIC directory contains the IntranetWare utilities that are most commonly used. IntranetWare has added some very exciting and useful utilities for network managers and users. Many of the functions of IntranetWare are now included in graphically based programs for Windows and Windows 95. In the PUBLIC directory are a number of BAT files. Each one is for a NetWare version 3.1x or earlier utility. If a user tries to invoke an old NetWare command the batch file will run instead. It tells the user the command no longer exists in IntranetWare and which utility they should use. Care must be exercised to limit access to SYS:PUBLIC so that IntranetWare utilities may be run but not modified.

For a description of the utilities in the PUBLIC directory, refer to the IntranetWare on-line documentation. A description of these utilities is beyond the scope of this book, but the more important files in SYS:PUBLIC are listed in table 19.1 for your ready reference.

Table 19.1
Important Files in SYS:PUBLIC

File Name	Description
ATOTAL.EXE	Generates an accounting summary of server resource usage.
AUDITCON.EXE	This enables a user to audit the file system and NDS events on the network.
CAPTURE.EXE	Redirects local printer output to a network printer. Used for single-user applications that print to the local printer only. The ENDCAP command from NetWare 3.1x has been consolidated with using the /EC switch.
COLORPAL.EXE	Selects the color palettes to be used with IntranetWare graphic utilities.
CX.EXE	This allows you to change your context in an NDS directory tree.
FILER.EXE	Manages files and directory rights, rights filter, and attributes. In addition the functions of SALVAGE, PURGE, VOLINFO from NetWare 3.1x has been consolidated into FILER for IntranetWare.
FLAG.EXE	Sets file attributes. The functions of FLAGDIR and SMODE NetWare 3.1x commands have been consolidated into the FLAG command.
LOGIN.EXE	Authenticates users' request to log in to the server and executes the login. The ATTACH command from NetWare 3.1x has been consolidated with using the /NS switch.
LOGOUT.EXE	Logs out from the server.

File Name	Description
MAKEUSER.EXE	Adds or deletes users from directives in a script file.
MAP.EXE	Assigns drive letters to network directories.
MIGWIN3X.EXE	NetWare 3.1x to IntranetWare file migration utility.
NALW31.EXE/	The NetWare Application Launcher allows users to mangage NALW95.EXE and access network applications as NDS Directory objects. This is a Windows-based utility.
NMENU.BAT	Runs compiled menu script files.
NETADMIN.EXE	This utility is a DOS-based program for NDS management. This program does not contain all the functions of NWADMIN. EXENCOPY.EXE Copies network files. More efficient than DOS COPY commands.
NETUSER.EXE	The functions of SESSION from NetWare 3.1x and other user configuration utilities for DOS.
NDIR.EXE	The functions of CHKDIR, CHKVOL, NDIR, LISTDIR, VERSION commands from NetWare 3.1x have been consolidated into NDIR. Use the NDIR /? to view the functions of NDIR for IntranetWare.
NDSMGR16.EXE	This is a 16-bit version of NDS Manager, for creating and managing partitions.
NLIST.EXE	This utility lets users view information about servers, users, groups, files, volumes, and queues. The functions of SLIST and USERLIST commands from NetWare 3.1x have been consolidated into NLIST.
NPRINTER.EXE	Installs remote printing services for the Print Server.
NVER.EXE	Lists NetWare operating system version on server.
NWADMIN.EXE	The NetWare Administrator utility for Windows. This utility enables users to create and manage NDS objects. It also incorporates the functions of PCONSOLE,PARTMGR, NETADMIN, and FILER.
NWIPMAP.EXE	This is the map command utility for systems using NetWare/IP.
NWUSER.EXE	This Windows utility enables users to manage their network environment for printing, drive mappings and NDS Directory access.
PCONSOLE.EXE	Configures and manages shared printers and queues.

continues

Table 19.1, Continued
Important Files in SYS:PUBLIC

File Name	Description
PRINTCON.EXE	Creates and modifies print job configurations.
PRINTDEF.EXE	Configures form and printer device driver information.
PSTAT.EXE	Displays printer status.
PSC.EXE	Controls/displays status of network printers.
PURGE.EXE	Removes files erased in the current login session.
REMOVE.EXE	Removes a user or group from the list of trustees for a path.
RENDIR.EXE	Renames a directory.
RIGHTS.EXE	Displays effective rights of a user for directories and files.
RPRINTER.EXE	Sets up a remote non-dedicated printer.
SEND.EXE	Sends a message to other stations.
SETPASS.EXE	Sets or changes user passwords.
SETTTS.EXE	Sets transaction tracking level.
SYSTIME.EXE	Displays server time and synchronizes workstation time to server time.
UIMPORT.EXE	This utility allows you import bindery data into an NDS database.WEBMGR.EXE This is the utility to manage and configure your WEB Server for IntranetWare
WHOAMI.EXE	Displays information about your connection.

The PUBLIC directory for IntranetWare contains the following subdirectories:

NLS	Contains the national language support for public utilities.
WIN95	Contains programs and files for IntranetWare support in Windows 95.
OS2	Contains programs and files for IntranetWare support in OS/2.
NALLIB	Contains programs to support the NetWare Application Launcher or NAL.
CLIENT	Contains programs and files to install for client workstations.
PERL	Contains PERL script files for IntranetWare.

SYSTEM Directory

The SYSTEM directory contains the IntranetWare operating system files and system programs. Access to SYS:SYSTEM must be limited to system administrators and special management utilities that may need to access SYS:SYSTEM. IntranetWare has several major enhancements for the network operating system. IntranetWare now supports multiple processors, and has eliminated the need for separate protocol support for Macintosh clients.

For a description of the utilities in the SYSTEM directory, refer to the IntranetWare on-line documentation. Table 19.2 lists the more important SYS:SYSTEM files for your reference.

Table 19.2
Important Files in SYS:SYSTEM for NetWare 3.x

File Name	Description
AUTOEXEC.NCF	Contains system configuration information.
BROUTER.EXE	Routes Btrieve record manager requests.
BSTART.NCF	Loads Btrieve NLM from the server console—a NetWare Command File.
BSTOP.NCF	Unloads Btrieve NLM—a NetWare Command File.
BTRIEVE.NLM	Provides Btrieve Record Management service.
CDROM.NLM	This enables you to mount a CD-ROM drive on a server as a read only volume.
CLIB.NLM	Supports utilities requiring C library routines and functions.
CONLOG.NLM	This enables you to capture console messages from modules and store them to a data file. The default file is CONSOLE.LOG.
DHCPCFG.NLM	This lets you manage NetWare Dynamic Host Configuration Protocol services.
DSMERGE.NLM	This enables you to merge and rename NDS trees.
DSREPAIR.NLM	This utility repairs the NDS database.
EDIT.NLM	Text editor NLM that can run from server console.
HCSS.NLM	This utility will let you view and change a list of High Capacity Storage System settings.
INETCFG.NLM	This enables you to configure internetworking for IPX, TCP/IP and Appletalk protocols.
INSTALL.NLM	Installs and configures 3.x NOS.

continues

Table 19.2, Continued
Important Files in SYS:SYSTEM for NetWare 3.x

File Name	Description
IPCONFIG.NLM	NLM for configuring IP addressing.
IPXCON.NLM	This utility lets you monitor and troubleshoot IPX routers and IPX network segments.
IPXS.NLM	STREAMS interface to IPX protocols.
KEYB.NLM	This utility sets the keyboard language on a server.
MAC.NAM	Macintosh file system Name Space support NLM.
MATHLIB.NLM	Math library routine interface for the Intel 80387 coprocessor.
MATHLIBC.NLM	Math library routine emulation of the Intel 80387 coprocessor. Used if coprocessor does not exist.
MONITOR.NLM	Monitors server resources.
MPDRIVER.	This enables processors on a multiprocessor server running NetWare SMP software.
NETSYNC3.NLM	This utility is loaded on a NetWare 3.1x server to make it a part of a NetSync managed network.
NETSYNC4.NLM	This utility is loaded on a NetWare 4.11 server to manage NetWare 3.1x servers in NetSync managed network.
NPRINTER.NLM	This enables a printer connected to a server to be a network printer.
NUT.NLM	This is required for NetWare 3.11 NLM's using the NUT library.
NWIPCFG.NLM	This utility is used to configure and manage NetWare/IP software on the server.PSERVER.NLM. Loads printer server on file server.
RCONSOLE.NLM	This is the remote console utility, the functions of ACONSOLE have been consolidated into this program.
REMOTE.NLM	Monitors server console remotely in Remote Management Facility.
ROUTE.NLM	Supports source routing for IBM Token-Ring bridges.
RPL.NLM	This utility enables the remote rebooting of IBM PC-compatible diskless workstations.

File Name	Description
RS232.NLM	Support for remote console connection over an asynchronous link.
RSETUP.EXE	Creates custom server boot disk to support remote server control.
RSPX.NLM	Supports remote management of server console.
RTDM.NLM	This enables data migration at the server console.
SBACKUP.NLM	This utility backs ups and restores data you specify on a server or workstation.
SNMP.NLM	SNMP Agent on server.
SPXS.NLM	SPX protocol for STREAMS.
STREAMS.NLM	Implements STREAMS protocol. Used as a common transport interface for multiple transport protocols.
SYS$LOG.ERR	System error message log file.
TCPIP.NLM	Implements TCP/IP protocols on NetWare 3.x server.
TCPCON.NLM	This utility lets you monitor TCP/IP segments on the network
TIMESYNC.	This utility controls time synchronization.
TLI.NLM	Transport Layer Interface NLM. Common transport interface.
TCPCFG.NLM	Configures TCP/IP.UNICON.NLM. This utility lets you manage the DNS and DSS for NetWare/IP.
UNISTART.NCF	This NCF file loads the support NLMs into memory for the Web Server.
UNISTOP.NCF	This NCF unloads the support NLMs from memory for the Web Server.
UPGRADE.EXE	Upgrades from NetWare 2.x to NetWare 3.x.
UPS.NLM	Implements the software link between server and UPS (Uninterrupted Power Supply) device.
VREPAIR.NLM	Repairs minor volume problems.
WEBINST.NLM	This utility lets you set up and configure your Web Server.
WSUPDATE.EXE	Updates shell files from the file server.

MAIL Directory

The MAIL directory is used by First Mail and Groupwise to install Email services for users. The MAIL directory can be used for bindery emulation purposes. NetWare Message Handling Services and the First Mail program are not shipped with IntranetWare but can be downloaded from `www.novell.com`.

DOC and DOCVIEW Directories

These two directories are created when the Novell Online Documentation is installed on a server volume. The DOC directory contains all the IntranetWare manuals in electronic data form. To access the IntranetWare manuals, the DynaText program is installed in the DOCVIEW directory either for Windows or Macintosh.

ETC Directory

This directory contains configuration files for setting up an intranet using TCP/IP protocol support with IntranetWare. In the past, this directory was mostly a curiosity to most NetWare administrators who used IPX protocol. For IntranetWare it is an essential directory for intranet services. This directory stores the configuration files for DNS, Web Server, NetWare/IP, and INETCONFIG. It still has a subdirectory /SAMPLES containing sample files that can be customized.

QUEUES Directory

This is an optional directory that can exist at the root of any IntranetWare server volume, and contains the print queue associated with an NDS print queue object. It is created with set up print services for IntranetWare. This directory can be placed on any IntranetWare volume. The advantage to this is you are no longer in danger of running out of space on the SYS: volume because of large print jobs placed in print queues.

WEB Directory

This directory contains the files and subdirectories to support the Web Server for IntranetWare. Files included are for CGI, HTML, PERL, NETBASIC, and JAVA programming languages. Also this directory contains the necessary files to view the NDS in your Web browser.

NETBASIC Directory

Included with IntranetWare is NetBASIC from HiTecSoft Corp., for supporting Web Server. The NETBASIC directory is created upon installation and contains BAS files for Web Server. When you load NETBASIC.NLM at the server console you then can type **SHELL** and with BAS utility files are able to perform several DOS like commands at the server console such DIR and COPY.

Applications Directories

In the previous section, you learned about the standard directory structure required for IntranetWare during installation. When you want to install applications, you need to consider the following:

- Create an efficient applications directory structure.
- Provide a balance of server and network resources.
- Protect the applications directories.

You must define your directories to keep these applications separate from the IntranetWare operating system files. This separation results in easier maintenance and upgrades of IntranetWare and application programs.

Directory Organization for Applications on the Server

The placement of applications on your network should be carefully planned. With the addition of the NetWare Application Launcher (NAL) for IntranetWare, you can control users' ability to access applications by associating the application to the user in the NDS. How the directories for applications are placed in the NDS tree becomes very important. Applications should be in the same container as the users who will require access to them. This means applications should be placed on volumes of servers in the same NDS container as the users. Placing applications in other containers across WAN links can cause a slow response from the network, especially if the WAN link is slow.

Depending on your resources, it would be optimal to have an application server. If this resource was not practical or unavailable, you could have a volume on a server just for applications. Again, if this is not practical, you could have a directory on a volume just for applications. As a minimum, you should have at least the last option mentioned. As an example VOL1:APPS directory. The subdirectories of the APPS directory would be for the installed applications directories. An old NetWare principal of making your directory structure not too deep and not too wide still applies. The depth of the directory structure should be 4 to 5 levels.

The applications directory structure should be designed to accommodate all your users no matter what operating system the user's workstation has. The directory structure should be flexible to accommodate future applications with a minimum impact on the network. The server should have sufficient disk space to support current applications and future upgrades or additional applications. Protect the application files with proper access control to the applications directories.

Data created from applications should be stored in a separate directory structure from applications. To optimize the performance of your server, store your data files on a separate volume from the applications. This helps control access to the data and helps to protect it.

User's Home Directory Organization

A user's home directory on the server disk stores a user's personal files. Users usually have unrestricted access to their home directories. The disadvantage to this is users can install personal applications or store non-essential files in their home directories. This can waste network resources. The network administrator should establish guidelines for the user as to what should and should not be placed in users' home directories. A few years ago, a version of a game called DOOM was popular with many network users because it was network-aware. Several users could play the game at the same time on a network. Because the game was resource intensive, three to four players could crash a network. The home directory acts as an extension of the local disk space for the user.

The placement of a user's home directory whenever possible should be in a directory called USER or HOME. The subdirectories of this directory are the users' home directories. The user's home directory can be located on any volume on your server. The option to create a user's home directory and the location of it are given to you at the time you create a user. Placing users' home directories on a volume other than SYS: on a server would help protect your server and network.

The previous sections of this chapter have discussed the placement of files and directories on your network. By now it should be clear the SYS: volume should be used for operating and managing IntranetWare. Access control should be placed on users for IntranetWare's utilities and programs. Dedicating the SYS: volume to the operation of IntranetWare helps to provide a stable and secure network environment.

DOS Directories

The final directory covered in this chapter is the DOS directories. A DOS environment variable required by the NetWare 4.11 portion of IntranetWare is called COMSPEC. This environment variable is set up when you install the workstation client software. This helps to insure the client workstation will always have the ability to locate a copy of COMMAND.COM upon exiting an application in a network environment.

Where COMSPEC is set to point to the location to find COMMAND.COM can be either of several locations. First, it can point to the root of the C:\ drive or to the C:\DOS directory of the client workstation. However, if the situation becomes such that the network cannot locate the client workstation's local drive then the first case becomes unusable. Placing a copy of the COMMAND.COM in a subdirectory of the SYS:PUBLIC directory offers a better solution.

The subdirectories for the COMMAND.COM files should be for every type and version of DOS you would have on your client workstations. The types of DOS can be IBM-DOS, MS-DOS, DR-DOS, and COMPAQ-DOS. The versions should be at least the minimum required by IntranetWare for client workstations. You do not need the complete DOS operating system files stored on the SYS: volume. As a minimum, all you need is COMMAND.COM. It would be simpler if all the client workstations had the same type and version of DOS. In most networks, this is not the case.

The structure of the DOS directories should look like the following example:

```
SERVER/SYS:PUBLIC\MSDOS\V6.20
```

As the previous example shows, the subdirectory in PUBLIC is the type of DOS. The type DOS subdirectory contains the subdirectories for the versions of this DOS.

Because many versions of DOS can be used by users on the network, the recommended directory structure is shown to store DOS programs in figure 19.13 for DOS programs. To support this directory structure, IntranetWare defines a number of login script variables. These script variables are used to specify directories in the login script and are mapped into values as shown in figure 19.13. The script variable %OS can map into values MSDOS or COMPAQ; the script variable %VERSION can map into version numbers such as V6.0, V3.31, V5.0. Depending on the DOS version and operating system, the appropriate network directory can be specified by using the generic script variables.

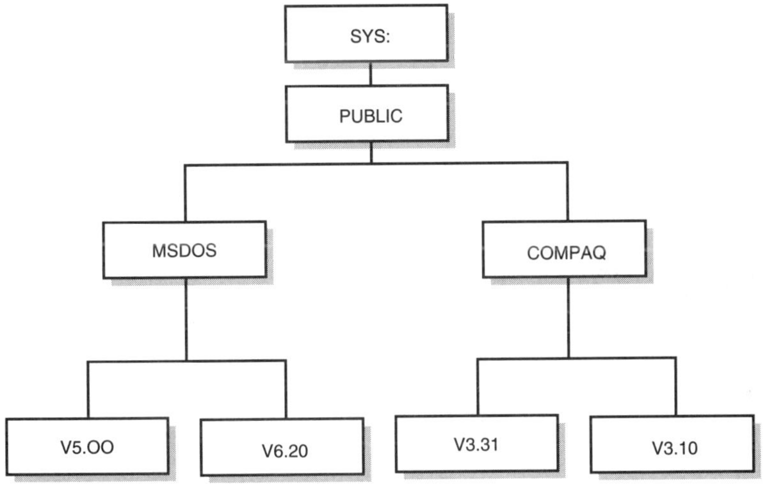

Figure 19.13
DOS directory structure on a server.

File System Performance

Several factors can improve a disk subsystem's performance. These factors include optimum selection of disk block size, file caching, directory hashing and caching, and the use of Turbo FATs.

Disk Block Size

In IntranetWare, you have the option to select a disk block size different from the default. You select this block size at the time you define a volume by using INSTALL.NLM. The disk block size values that are legal in IntranetWare are 4, 8, 16, 32, and 64 KB. When installing IntranetWare, you can either do simple installation or custom installation. Selecting custom installation will let you specify the block you want for a volume.

In a database consisting of a small number of very large data files, a large disk block size is best. Database operations typically are executed in a local region of a data file. If the disk block size is large, fewer blocks must be fetched compared to a volume that has a smaller disk block size. In addition, the fewer the disk blocks you have in a volume, the smaller the size of the FAT to keep track of them in RAM.

Memory for File Caching and Directory Caching and Hashing

The cache memory in IntranetWare allocates memory to many functions. *Cache memory* is used by the FAT, the Turbo FAT, NLMs, suballocation tables, and directory cache. When cache memory is used for file caching, file services can be up to 100 times faster than if the file were read directly from the hard disk. The directory cache is used to store the DET or Directory Entry Table.

In IntranetWare, the SET command controls some of the parameters that affect file and directory caching.

Turbo FAT Index

If a file uses more than 64 blocks, then IntranetWare creates a special FAT index called a *Turbo FAT index* to group all the FAT entries for the file together. This method of indexing allows the file to be accessed quickly.

Disk Space Management

Because users share disk space on the server, you can limit disk space per user. To limit disk space for a user on a volume, you can use the NetWare Administrator in Windows. From the NDS tree, select a volume and then select User Space Limits. You can also use NETADMIN for DOS.

One reason to restrict disk space is to prevent a user from using an inordinate amount of disk space. Suppose that a user runs an application that has a software bug. This bug causes it to go in a loop while it writes to a data file. The data file can become large enough to consume all available disk space on the server and to prevent others from using the server's disk. In IntranetWare, the SET command can be used to monitor volume usage.

IntranetWare SET Command for Volume Utilization

You can use the SET VOLUME command to set thresholds and warnings for volume utilization. These commands are as follows:

```
SET VOLUME LOW WARN ALL USERS
SET VOLUME LOW WARNING THRESHOLD
SET VOLUME LOW WARNING RESET THRESHOLD
```

The SET VOLUME LOW WARN ALL USERS command warns all users that the volume is almost full. The values can be set to either ON or OFF, but ON is the default. Some network managers turn this value to OFF so that the beginning network user is not confused by unfamiliar system messages.

Example:

```
SET VOLUME LOW WARN ALL USERS=OFF
```

The SET VOLUME LOW WARNING THRESHOLD command controls how many free disk blocks remain on a volume before IntranetWare issues a warning. To estimate this number, you must divide the desired free space threshold by the disk block size. The value for this parameter ranges from 0 to 100,000 blocks, with a default value of 256.

If you want to set the threshold to 1 MB, for a nondefault disk block size of 8 KB, for example, the number of free blocks is estimated by:

Free blocks = Free disk space/Disk block size

= 1 MB/ 8 KB = 128

The SET command would be as follows:

```
SET VOLUME LOW WARNING THRESHOLD=128
```

For a disk block size of 4 KB (default), the free block count will be 1 MB/ 4 KB = 256 (the default value).

The SET VOLUME LOW WARNING RESET THRESHOLD command determines how many disk blocks must be freed up before a second warning is issued. This parameter prevents repeated warning messages from being sent if the free space hovers around the limit established by SET VOLUME LOW WARNING THRESHOLD. When the first warning is issued (SET VOLUME LOW WARN ALL USERS), and the users reduce disk space to just below the threshold, you might not want another warning message to appear if the disk space utilization soon rises above the threshold again. This process of dipping below the threshold and then rising again can occur repeatedly, and a repeated warning message is very annoying to the user. The value for this parameter ranges from 0 to 100,000 blocks, with a default value of 256.

To set this threshold value to 256 blocks (1 MB for 4 KB size blocks), the command is as follows:

```
SET VOLUME LOW WARNING RESET THRESHOLD=256
```

These SET values can be recorded in the STARTUP.NCF file.

Rights Access

After a user successfully logs in to the server, NetWare 4.11 operating system portion of IntranetWare controls access to directories and files on the server.

Trustee Rights

In IntranetWare, users are assigned rights to perform operations such as Read, Write, Create, and Erase in files in a directory. The user entrusted with these rights is called a Trustee, and the actual rights assigned are called Trustee Assignments.

A user can be given a trustee assignment explicitly. In other words, the trustee assignment can be given on an individual-user basis. To set individual rights for a large number of users, however, is very tedious and difficult to maintain. In addition, many users have similar needs; they access the same directories and files on the server. For instance, all engineers in the engineering department need access to the same directories. To help with the management and administration of users with similar needs, IntranetWare uses groups.

A group is a collection of network users that have the same access privileges to directories and files on the server. For instance, all engineers are members of a group called ENGINEERS. The group ENGINEERS can be given a trustee assignment in a manner similar to that for individual users. The difference is that all members of the group automatically inherit the trustee assignments for that group (see fig. 19.14). If new members are added to the engineering department, they are made members of the group ENGINEERS. If engineers leave the department, they are removed from the group ENGINEERS. This automatically removes the privileges for the user as a member of the group ENGINEERS.

Users can be members of more than one group. The total rights for a user is the sum of all the rights inherited by virtue of membership to all groups. For example, a user has Read and Write trustee assignments to directory SYS:COMMON/DATA. This trustee assignment is made because of the user's membership in one group. The user also has Read, Create, and Erase trustee assignments to the same directory because of membership in a second group. The user has trustee assignment of Read, Write, Create, Erase to SYS:COMMON/DATA. This is because the user is a member of both groups.

Groups are created using either NETADMIN or the NetWare Administrator program in Windows or Windows 95. Users are assigned to groups with the same utilities.

Figure 19.14
Trustee assignment on a group basis.

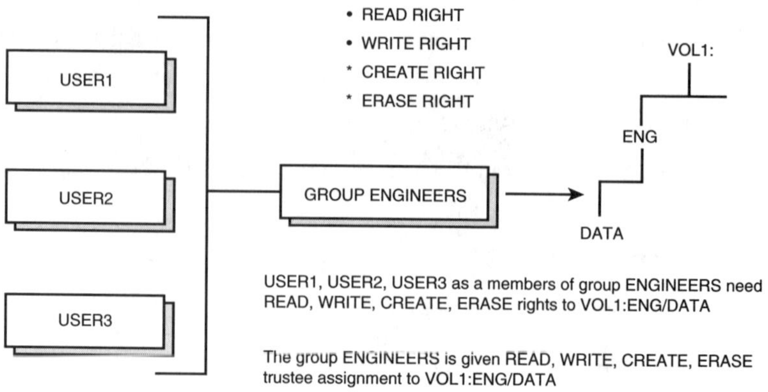
• READ RIGHT
• WRITE RIGHT
* CREATE RIGHT
* ERASE RIGHT
VOL1:
ENG
DATA
USER1
USER2
USER3
GROUP ENGINEERS
USER1, USER2, USER3 as a members of group ENGINEERS need READ, WRITE, CREATE, ERASE rights to VOL1:ENG/DATA
The group ENGINEERS is given READ, WRITE, CREATE, ERASE trustee assignment to VOL1:ENG/DATA

Directory Rights and File Rights

Table 19.3 shows the IntranetWare directory rights.

Table 19.3
IntranetWare Directory Trustee Rights

Name	Description
S	Supervisor rights.
R	Read rights to open files in a directory, read contents, and execute.
W	Write rights to open and write (modify) contents of files.
C	Create rights to create files and subdirectories in a directory.
E	Erase rights to delete a directory, its files, and its subdirectories.
M	Modify rights to change directory and file attributes and rename.
F	File scan rights to view names of subdirectories and files.
A	Access Control rights to other users, modify trustee rights, or the IRF.

The Read and Write rights in Table 19.3 enable the user to read and write files in a directory. The user needs both of these rights to perform updates on files in a directory. Reading and writing also imply that the user has a right to open files in a directory.

The User needs the Create and Erase rights to create and remove files and subdirectories. Modify rights can be used to change file attributes. Without Modify rights, you cannot use IntranetWare commands, such as FLAG, to change file attributes.

The File Scan right enables a user to view names of files and subdirectories. If you do not want a user to see file names in a directory, you can remove the File Scan right. With this right removed, the user can issue DIR or NDIR, but cannot see the name of files in the directory.

The Access Control right enables other users to modify trustee rights and the Inherited Rights Filter (IRF). In IntranetWare, the IRM has been changed to the Inherited Rights Filter (IRF). They serve the same purpose for files and directories. The functionality of the IRF has been extended to include NDS objects. The IRF is discussed later in this chapter. This means that a user who has Access Control rights to a directory can use a NetWare utility, such as FILER, to assign rights to other users for this directory. Access Control rights must be assigned only to trusted users.

Table 19.4 shows file level rights for IntranetWare. In IntranetWare, Trustee Assignments can be made at the file level. NetWare 4.11 operating system portion of IntranetWare gives you control over files in a directory. In most situations, such a high level of control is not needed, but this control is nice to have if you do encounter a situation that requires it. Trustee rights for files are similar to those for directories, except that the scope of these rights is limited to an individual file. File trustee rights use the same symbols as directory trustee rights. The Create right for a file gives the user the right to salvage a file after it has been deleted. This is different from the Create right for a directory, which enables you to create files and subdirectories in a directory.

In IntranetWare, you can use FILER, NETADMIN, the NetWare Administrator (NWADMIN), and the RIGHTS command to determine Trustee Assignments.

Table 19.4
IntranetWare File Trustee Rights

Name	Description
S	Supervisor's right to all rights to the file.
R	Read rights to open a file, read contents, and execute the program.
W	Write rights to open and write (modify) contents of a file.
C	Create rights to salvage a file after the file has been deleted.
E	Erase rights to delete a file.
M	Modify rights to change a file's attributes and rename the file.
F	File Scan rights to view name of a file and its full path name.
A	Access Control rights to modify file's trustee assignments and IRF.

Examples of Controlling Rights in IntranetWare

The following examples illustrate the control of file system rights using the command-line utility RIGHTS in IntranetWare.

The RIGHTS command allows you to:

- View/set the rights of a directory or file
- View trustee assignments to a specified directory
- See inherited rights
- View and set the inherited rights filter

The examples that follow show the control of file system rights.

To view the rights for user KSS in SYS:USERS/KSS directory, the command is as follows:

```
RIGHTS SYS:USERS/KSS
```

To list trustees, use the /T option. For example, to view the trustee assignments for a specified directory such as SYS:USERS/KSS, use the command:

```
RIGHTS SYS:PUBLIC  /T
```

Listing 19.5 shows a sample display output.

Listing 19.5

```
NW4CS\SYS:\PUBLIC
User trustees:
CN=KSS.OU=CORP.O=SCS                    [ R    F ]
-----
Group trustees:
CN=Everyone.OU=CORP.O=ESL                    [ R    F ]
-----
Other trustees:
OU=CORP.O=ESL                           [ R    F ]
```

Please note that group Everyone is not a pre-defined group under IntranetWare. It appears in the above example because the server was upgraded from NetWare 3.x to 4.x.

The output of the previous RIGHTS command shows that a user, a group object and a container object have rights to NW4CS\SYS:\PUBLIC. The user object CN=KSS.OU=CORP.O=SCS, the group object CN=Everyone.OU=CORP.O=ESL, and the container object OU=CORP.O=ESL all have Read and File Scan rights to NW4CS\SYS:\PUBLIC.

Because the container object OU=CORP.O=ESL has Read and File Scan rights to NW4CS\SYS:\PUBLIC, all user objects in the container OU=CORP.O=ESL have the same Read and File scan rights to NW4CS\SYS:\PUBLIC.

Notice that the /T option lists all trustees that have been given an explicit trustee assignment to SYS:PUBLIC. Whereas NWADMIN and NETADMIN can also display this information, using the previous RIGHTS command is simpler (and usually faster).

You can grant and revoke rights using the /NAME= option. The general syntax of RIGHTS using the /NAME= option is as follows:

```
RIGHTS  directory_file_name  [+¦-]rights  /NAME=objectname
```

To set the rights for user KSS in SYS:USERS/KSS directory so that the user has all rights except Supervisor rights, type:

```
RIGHTS SYS:USERS/KSS  CRWEMFA /NAME=.KSS.CORP.SCS
```

To remove the Erase and Create rights for user KSS in SYS:USERS/KSS directory, type:

```
RIGHTS SYS:USERS/KSS  -C-E  /NAME=.KSS.CORP.SCS
```

You can use RIGHTS to assign rights to more than one user using a single RIGHTS command. Consider two user objects KSS in contexts CORP.ESL and CORP.SCS. To assign both users all rights, except Supervisor right, to the current directory, the command shown in listing 19.6 could be used.

Listing 19.6

```
RIGHTS . ALL /NAME=.CN=KSS.OU=CORP.O=ESL,.CN=KSS.OU=CORP.SCS
NW4CS\SYS:USERS
Directories                                 Rights
--------------------
KSS                                         [ RWCEMFA]
```

Rights for one directory were changed for .CN=KSS.OU=CORP.O=SCS as shown in listing 19.7.

Listing 19.7

```
W4CS\SYS:USERS
Directories                     Rights
--------------
KSS                             [ RWCEMFA]
```

Rights for one directory were changed for .CN=KSS.OU=CORP.O=ESL

Notice that the period (.) can be used for the current directory name. Also, that ALL means all rights except Supervisor rights. The /NAME= option enables you to list a number of NDS names.

To remove all rights (except Supervisor, if given) for the two user objects KSS in contexts CORP.ESL and CORP.SCS, you can use the command shown in listing 19.8.

Listing 19.8

```
RIGHTS . -ALL /NAME=.CN=KSS.OU=CORP.O=ESL,.CN=KSS.OU=CORP.SCS
NW4CS\SYS:USERS
Directories                                 Rights
--------------------
KSS                                         [        ]
```

Rights for one directory were changed for .CN=KSS.OU=CORP.O=SCS, as shown in listing 19.9.

Listing 19.9

```
NW4CS\SYS:USERS
Directories                                 Rights
--------------------
KSS                                         [        ]
```

Rights for one directory were changed for .CN=KSS.OU=CORP.O=ESL

All rights have been removed for the two user objects.

Table 19.5 shows the rights letter codes that can be used with the RIGHTS command.

Table 19.5
Rights Letter Codes in the RIGHTS Command

Rights Letter Codes	Description
ALL	Grant all rights except supervisor
N	Revoke all rights
S	Supervisor right
C	Create right
R	Read right
W	Write right
E	Erase right
M	Modify right
F	File scan right
A	Access Control right
+	Adds the right to existing rights
-	Removes a right from existing rights

When you precede the /NAME= with the keyword REM, the names listed in the /NAME parameter are removed as trustees to the file or directory. This is different from removing trustee rights. Removing trustee rights can remove rights, including all rights but the user is still listed as a trustee.

To remove user .KSS.CORP.ESL as a trustee of SYS:USERS/KSS, you can use the command shown in listing 19.10.

Listing 19.10

```
NW4CS\SYS:USERS\KSS
User .KSS.CORP.ESL is no longer a trustee of the specified directory.
Trustee .KSS.CORP.ESL was removed from one directory.
```

Inherited Rights Filter

In NetWare versions 3.1x and earlier, the Inherited Rights Mask (IRM) is the filter that blocks the inheritance of rights from parent directories. NetWare versions 3.1x and earlier assign an IRM to each subdirectory and file. In IntranetWare the IRM has been replaced with the *Inherited Rights Filter.* The Inherited Rights Filter can be used with files and directories as well as with objects in the NDS. For files and directories the IRF controls the rights a trustee can inherit from a parent directory. The default for the directories IRF is to allow all rights [SRWCEMFA] to be inherited from the parent. The IRF can allow or revoke rights; it cannot be used to grant or add rights in a directory. A right must exist in the parent directory before it can be allowed by the IRF. The same principal applies for revoking rights with the IRF. When a user has a trustee assignment to a directory or file, then the IRF does not apply.

You can use the IntranetWare utilities FILER, NETADMIN, NetWare Administrator, or the command-line utility RIGHTS to modify the IRF.

Controlling IRF with the RIGHTS Command

You can use the /F option to examine or change the Inherited Rights Filter. To see the current IRF for SYS:USERS/KSS, use the command shown in listing 19.11.

Listing 19.11

```
RIGHTS SYS:USERS/KSS  /F
NW4CS\SYS:USERS
Directories                             Rights
-----------------------------------
KSS                                     [SRWCEMFA]
```

You can precede a right with a + or – to add or remove that right from the IRF. You can remove all rights from the IRF, except the Supervisor right.

To remove the Write right from the IRF for SYS:USERS/KSS, use the command shown in listing 19.12.

Listing 19.12

```
RIGHTS SYS:USERS/KSS  -W   /F

NW4CS\SYS:USERS
Directories                             Rights
-----------------------------------
KSS                                     [SR CEMFA]
```

To set the IRF for SYS:USERS/KSS to [SR   F], use the command shown in listing 19.13.

Listing 19.13

```
RIGHTS SYS:USERS/KSS   SRF    /F

NW4CS\SYS:USERS
Directories                               Rights
-----------------------------------
KSS                                      [SR     F ]
```

In IntranetWare, the /I option of the RIGHTS command allows you to see how the inherited rights contribute to effective rights.

To see your rights that have been inherited for SYS:PUBLIC for the user KSS defined in container OU=CORP.O=SCS, use the command shown in listing 19.14.

Listing 19.14

```
RIGHTS SYS:PUBLIC  /NAME=.KSS.CORP.SCS  /I
Name= .KSS.CORP.SCS
Path Rights
-------------------------------------------------
NW4CS\SYS:

Inherited Rights Filter:  [                      ]

Inherits from above:      [                      ]

Effective Rights =        [                      ]

NW4CS\SYS:\PUBLIC

Inherited Rights Filter:  [SRWCEMFA]

Inherits from above:      [                      ]
KSS.CORP.SCS              [ R                F   ]

Effective Rights =        [ R            F   ]
```

The /I option enables you to see inherited rights. It shows you the sequence of steps as to how rights are computed.

Effective Rights

Figure 19.15 illustrates how effective rights can be determined from Trustee Assignments and the Inherited Rights Filter by applying some rules of combination. These rules of combination are illustrated in figures 19.16 and 19.17 for directories and files. In the computation examples of rights, the term IRM is used.

At first glance, the rules of combination look complex, but after you study a few examples, you can appreciate the logic behind them. The examples that follow determine effective rights for directories.

Trustee Assignments
+
Inherited Rights Filter
=
Effective Rights

Figure 19.15
Effective Rights and Inherited Rights Filter.

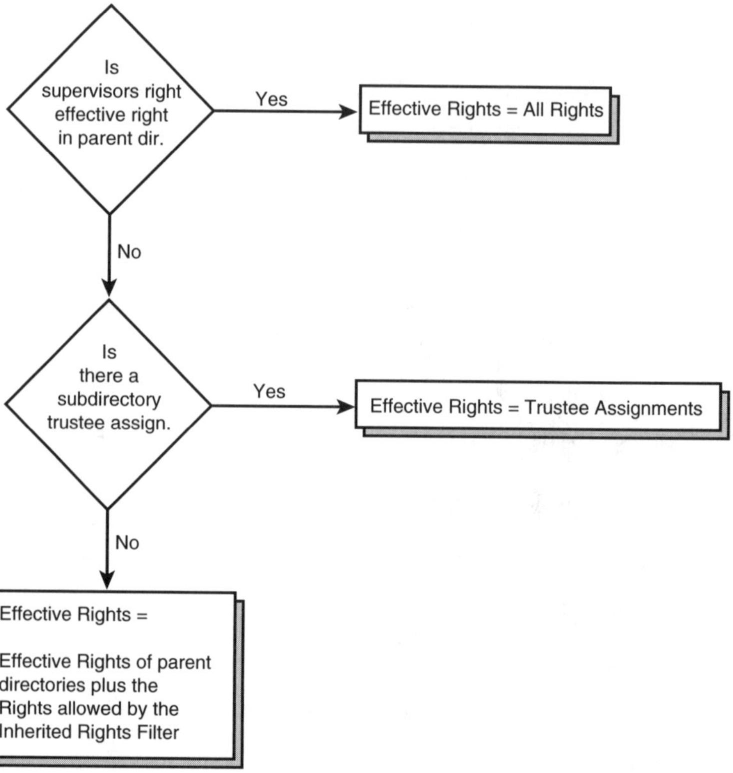
Is supervisors right effective right in parent dir.
Yes
Effective Rights = All Rights
No
Is there a subdirectory trustee assign.
Yes
Effective Rights = Trustee Assignments
No
Effective Rights =
Effective Rights of parent directories plus the Rights allowed by the Inherited Rights Filter

Figure 19.16
Effective Rights for directories.

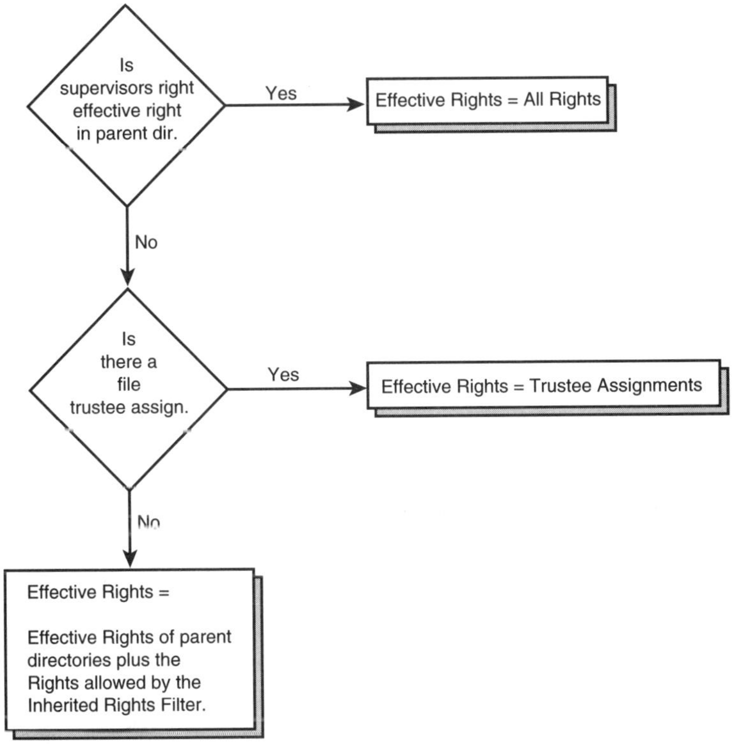

Figure 19.17
Effective Rights for files.

Example 1: If no explicit Trustee Assignment has been granted to a subdirectory, the effective rights for the subdirectory are determined by the subdirectory's Inherited Rights Filter and the parent directory's effective rights. The effective rights of SUBDATA1 and the logical AND operation are shown in figure 19.18.

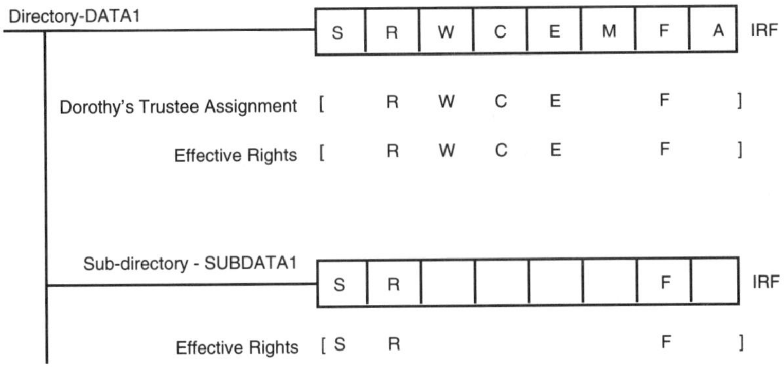

Figure 19.18
No explicit trustee assignment in sub-directory.

Example 2: If explicit Trustee Assignment has been granted to a subdirectory, the effective rights for the subdirectory are the same as the explicit Trustee Assignment regardless of the subdirectory's Inherited Rights Filter. In other words, an explicit TA overrides any IRF setting. The effective rights to subdirectory SUBDATA2 are shown in figure 19.19.

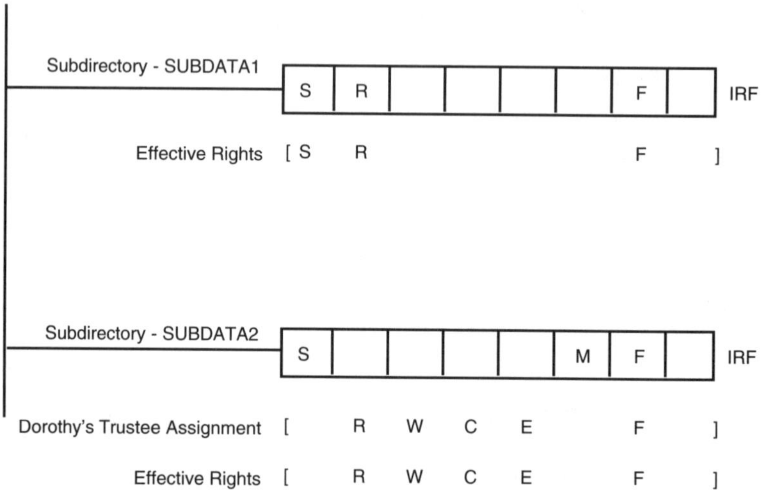

Figure 19.19
Trustee rights in subdirectory.

Example 3: If Supervisory Rights are granted to the parent directory, the user has all rights for the subdirectories and files regardless of a subdirectory's Trustee Assignment and Inherited Rights Filter (see fig. 19.20). (You must be careful when you assign Supervisors right.)

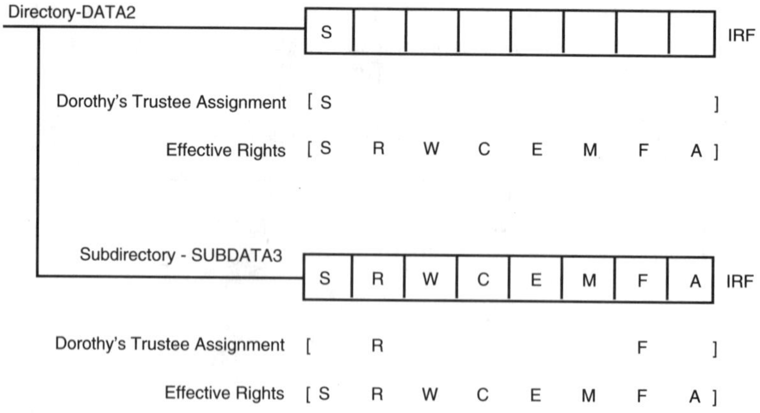

Figure 19.20
Supervisors right in a parent directory.

You can examine the effective rights by using the IntranetWare utility FILER or the command-line utility RIGHTS.

To view the effective rights for the current directory for the user issuing the command, type:

```
RIGHTS
```

To view the effective rights of user ATHENA for directory SYS:USERS, type:

```
RIGHTS SYS:USERS/ATHENA
```

The rules of combination are designed so that effective rights flow down subdirectories. If no explicit Trustee Assignment is made, the effective rights are modified by the IRF. When an explicit Trustee Assignment is made, a new set of effective rights flows down to the subdirectories.

Attribute Security

Individual files or directories can be assigned attributes that override a user's effective rights (see fig. 19.21). The user has Read, File Scan, Create, Erase, and Write effective rights to VOL1:COMMON/DATA. But the file is flagged with a Delete Inhibit attribute that prevents the file from being deleted even though the user has the Erase effective right for the directory.

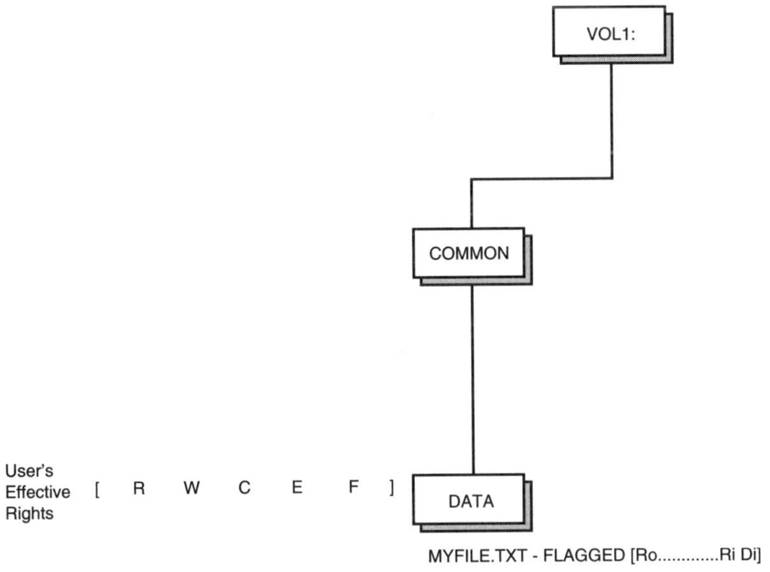

Figure 19.21
File Attribute Security.

The FLAG command can be used for setting attributes of files and directories.

Tables 19.6 and 19.7 show IntranetWare directory and file attributes.

Table 19.6
Directory Attributes for IntranetWare

Directory Attribute	Meaning
All	Specifies *all* the attributes as a group.
Di	The *Delete Inhibit* attribute prevents the directory from being erased.
Dc	The *Don't Compress* attribute prevents the directory from being compressed, even if compression set for the volume.
Dm	The *Don't Migrate* attribute prevents a directory from being migrated, even if migrate is set for the volume.
H	The *Hidden* attribute hides a directory from a DOS DIR command.
Ic	The *Immediate Compress* attribute sets the directory to be compressed as the operating system can.
N	The *Normal* attribute specifies no attributes.
P	The *Purge* attribute purges all files in directory when deleted.
Ri	The *Rename Inhibit* attribute prevents a directory from being renamed.
Sy	The *System* attribute similar to H; used for system directories.

The Data Migration feature is installed using INSTALL.NLM and requires a near-line-storage media that acts as a secondary to the primary hard disk storage area.

The compression feature is enabled or disabled on a volume-by-volume basis during installation. It can be further controlled by a variety of SET parameters.

Table 19.7
File Attributes for IntranetWare

File Attribute	Meaning
A	The *Archive Needed* attribute is automatically assigned to files modified after backups.
Cc	The *Can't Compress* attribute indicates that a file cannot be compressed because of limited space-saving benefit.
Co	The *Compressed* attribute indicates that a file has been compressed.

File Attribute	Meaning
Ci	The *Copy Inhibit* attribute restricts copy rights for Macintosh users.
Di	The *Delete Inhibit* attribute prevents file from being erased.
Dc	The *Don't Compress* attribute prevents a file or the files in a directory from being compressed.
Dm	The *Don't Migrate* attribute prevents a file or the files in a directory from migrating.
Ds	The *Don't Suballoacate* attribute prevents files from the using block suballocation feature on a volume.
X	The *Execute Only* attribute prevents files from being copied; is permanent.
H	The *Hidden* attribute hides a file from a DOS DIR scan.
Ic	The *Immediate Compress* attribute specifies file or files in a Compress directory are marked for compression as soon as the operating system can perform compression.
M	The *Migrate* attribute indicates the file has migrated to near-line storage.
N	The *Normal* attribute has no file attributes set.
P	The *Purge* attribute purges a file when deleted.
Ro	The *Read only* attribute cannot write to, erase, or rename files.
Rw	The *Read Write* attribute is the default setting for a file.
R	The *Rename Inhibit* attribute prevents a file from being renamed.
S	The *Sharable* attribute file can be used by more than one user.
Sy	The *System* attribute is similar to H; used for system files.
T	The *Transactional* attribute protects against incomplete operations on files.

FILER

Many workstation utilities from NetWare versions 3.1x and earlier are consolidated in the NetWare 4.11 operating system portion of IntranetWare. FILER now includes the functions of the older version of Filer plus the functions of previous utilities: SALVAGE, PURGE, and VOLINFO.

FILER can be used to perform many of the file, directory, and volume related tasks.

Some of the tasks that can be performed using FILER are the following:

- View file contents and directories
- View/set directory and file rights
- View/set directory and file attributes
- View/set the Inherited Rights Filter
- Copy, move, and delete files
- Delete entire subdirectory structure (including non-empty subdirectories)
- Purge and salvage files and directories

Figure 19.22 shows the main menu for FILER when the command FILER is run at a workstation.

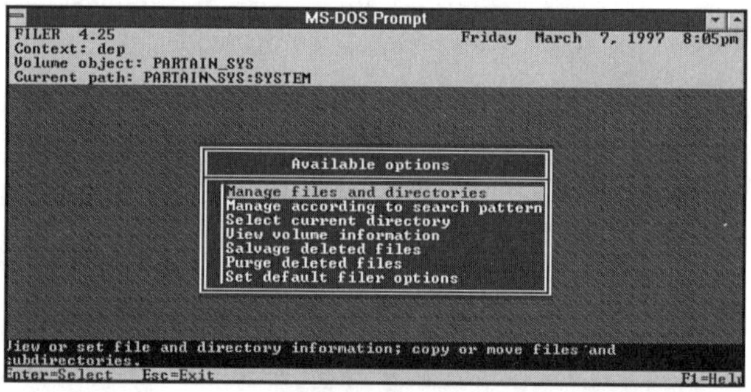

Figure 19.22
IntranetWare FILER Main Menu.

The Manage files and directories option in the main menu shows you a list of directories and files in the current directory (see fig. 19.23).

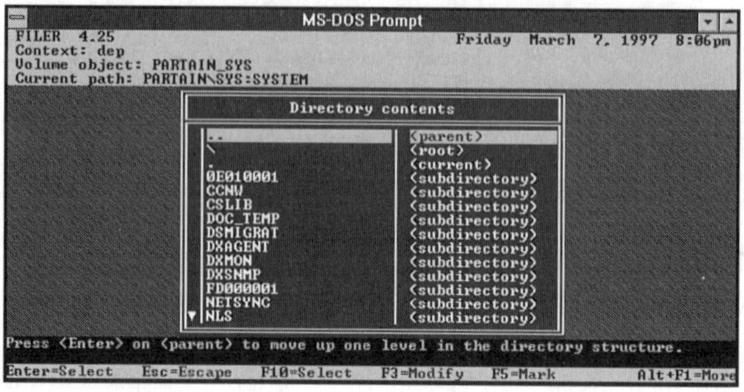

Figure 19.23
FILER Directory Content.

The Manage according to search pattern option in the main menu gives you the ability to set search patterns for the files and directories to view (see fig. 19.24).

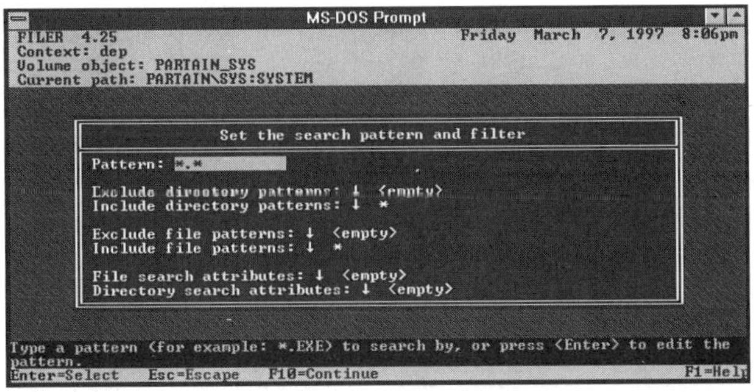

Figure 19.24
FILER managing according to search patterns.

The Select current directory option in the main menu gives you the ability to set the current directory (see fig. 19.25). The current path is displayed on the top of the screen.

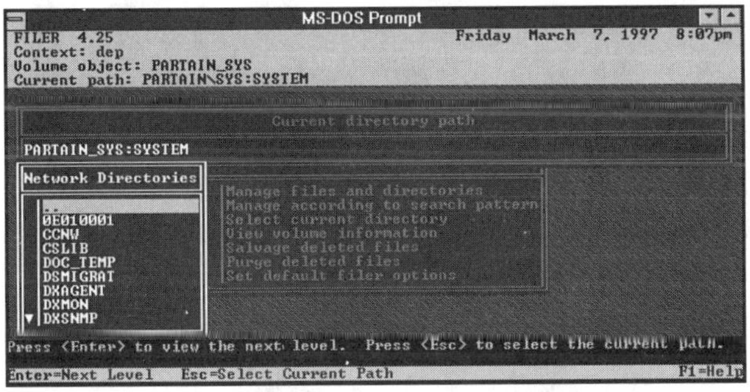

Figure 19.25
FILER Select Current Directory.

The View volume information option in the main menu gives you the ability to view statistics, features, date and time information for a volume (see fig. 19.26). The volume information is shown in figures 19.27, 19.28, and 19.29.

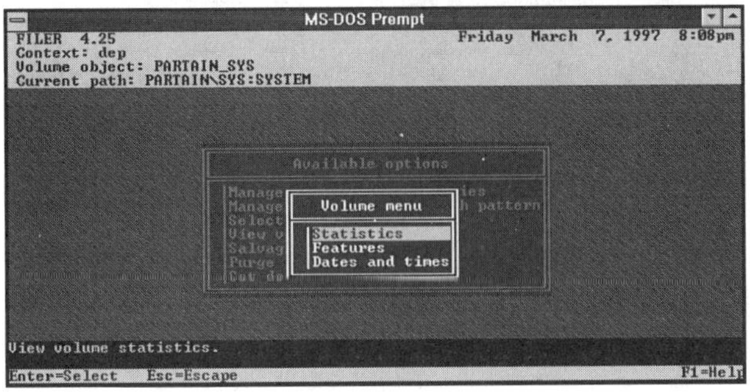

Figure 19.26
FILER View volume information.

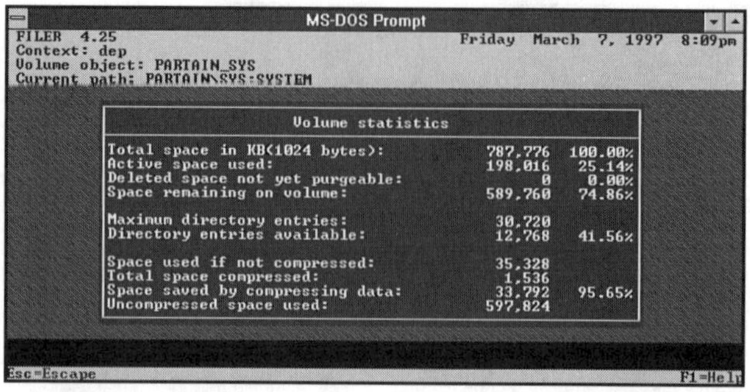

Figure 19.27
FILER Volume Statistics.

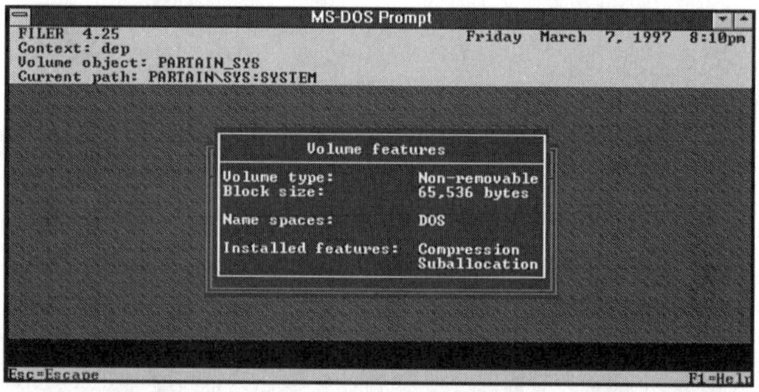

Figure 19.28
FILER Volume Features.

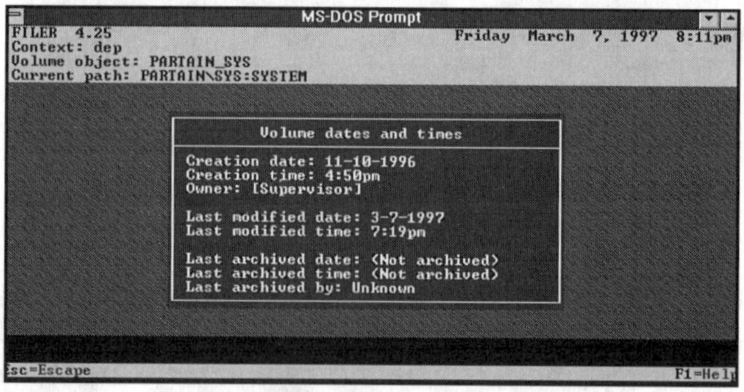

Figure 19.29
FILER Volume Date and Times.

FILER restores files that have been deleted. FILER enables the recovery of files that have been deleted but whose disk space has not been reallocated for other purposes.

The FILER utility can be used to change a user's rights to a file or a directory. FILER enables you to set a Trustee Assignment to a directory (or file) and to modify the IRF.

When you select Salvage deleted files from Filer's Available options menu the Salvage menu is displayed with the following selections:

- **View/Recover Deleted Files.** This option enables you to view files in the current directory. You can then recover or purge these files.

- **Salvage From Deleted Directories.** This option recovers erased files from directories that do not exist.
- **Set Salvage Options.** This option enables you to change the way files are displayed on the screen. For example, you can display files sorted by deletion date, file size, file name, or owner name.

Recovered files are placed in the directory from which they were deleted. But if the directory has been deleted, the recovered files are placed in a hidden directory in the root of a volume called DELETED.SAV. IntranetWare currently does not track deleted directories, but it does track files by date and time. Because of this, you can have several versions of a file with the same name. If the file being recovered to a directory already exists, FILER prompts you to rename the file being salvaged.

If you select View/Recover Deleted Files, the default pattern (*) shows all files. When you highlight a file for recovery and press Enter, information appears that tells you when the file was deleted, when it was last modified, who the owner of the file was, and who deleted it. To restore a file, choose Yes when the question Recover This File? appears.

To purge a file, highlight the file and press Del. Figure 19.30 shows the purge screen.

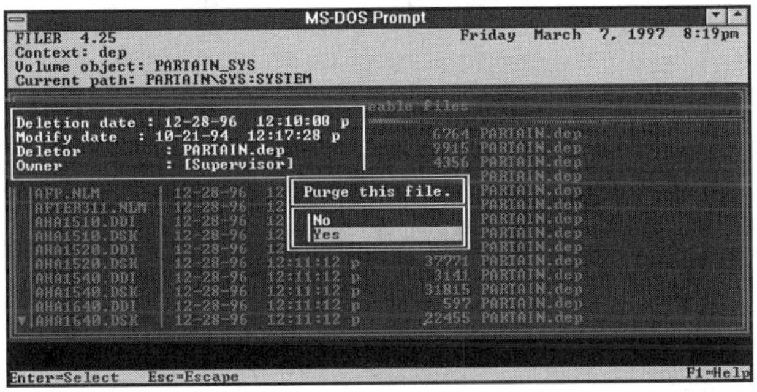

Figure 19.30
The IntranetWare Filer purge screen.

The files to be viewed can be sorted by a number of options shown in figure 19.31. Use Salvage Sort Options in the SALVAGE option menu to determine these options.

The Set default filer options option in the main menu gives you the ability to confirm deletions, copy operations, and overwrites (see fig. 19.32). It also allows you to specify if file attributes should be preserved, and if you should be notified if you are going to lose file attribute information when copying from one name space to another. IntranetWare allows the implementation of sparse files. *Sparse files* are common in database applications when a file may currently contain only a few of the total records that the file can contain. Because the valuable data is a small portion of the overall file size, a sparse representation of a file that occupies much less space can be designed. You can specify if the files should be copied in their sparse format or not. You can also specify if the compressed files should be copied in the compressed state or not.

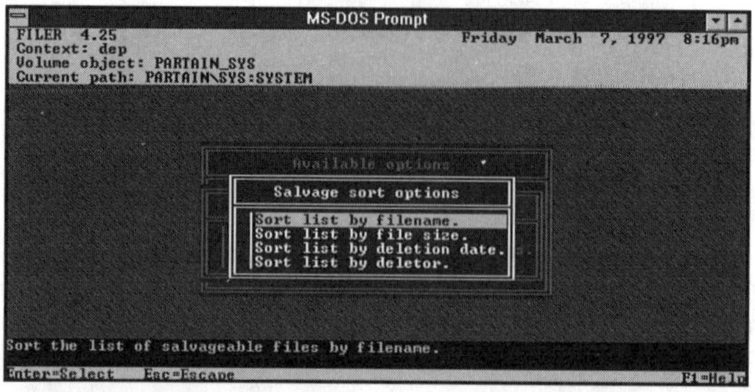

Figure 19.31
The IntranetWare Filer's Salvage Sort Options.

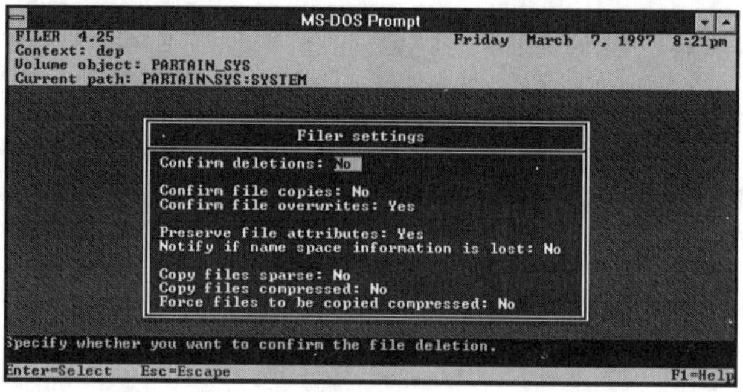

Figure 19.32
Filer settings.

Summary

In this chapter, you have learned about the organization of the IntranetWare file system. The IntranetWare file system resides on physical hard disks at the file server and is, therefore, affected by the performance of the server hard disk. You learned the characteristics of common server hard disks such as IDE, ESDI, and SCSI. This chapter also covered the use of the IntranetWare file system through network drives. Drive mappings and search drives were discussed, as well as the file security system.

CHAPTER 20

Printing with IntranetWare

In this chapter, you learn the fundamental concepts behind IntranetWare printing. You learn about the IntranetWare printing model, how to install print servers and remote printers. You also are shown how to use IntranetWare printing utilities. As in previous chapters, some of the more important and intricate steps of network printing are covered in several examples.

The first part of this chapter covers general printing concepts that apply to IntranetWare. Printing has changed very little since NetWare 3.x, and it remains basically the same in IntranetWare. However, the entire NetWare printing paradigm will shift in future releases of IntranetWare as Novell Distributed Print Services (NDPS) is introduced. NDPS is discussed later in the chapter.

Network Printing Basics

Sharing printers on a network is one of the key benefits of networking technology, but it also presents many problems. Most printers were not designed to handle print requests from more than one attached user, although network-ready printers are available today from many printer manufacturers. Making a printer available on a network presents four problems:

- **The difficulty of establishing a connection between network stations and the printer.**

  Most laser printers available today come with the option of attaching a network interface instead of, or in addition to, the standard parallel port. This enables the printer to be connected directly to the network and not just to a particular computer. Most laser printers come with the option of an Ethernet 10Base-T connection.

  If no network port is available, the printer can be connected to a network workstation or server, which can act as a bridge between printer and network. This creates the physical link between, but because the printer and the network communicate using different protocols, software must be used to translate network messages into a format that the printer can recognize.

  Print server software provided with NetWare converts network messages into a language understandable by the printer. The software also provides a buffer, to compensate for the difference in speed of the network and the printer.

- **The inability of printers to handle concurrent print job submissions.**

  With a printer being on a network, the likelihood of the printer receiving multiple print job submissions at the same time is high. This creates a problem for printers, because they are dumb output devices incapable of deciphering between the end of one print job and the beginning of another.

  Intelligent print server software creates separate buffers for each print job submission. Each queued print job is then submitted one at a time to the printer. The print queue must be stored on the computer acting as the print server, whether it be a workstation or server.

- **The lack of a standard page description language.**

  Printers use page description languages (PDLs) to allow the software to control the characteristics of the text and images to be created by the printer. Unfortunately, there is no standard printing language, and different printers support different PDLs. Different applications used by users on a network might have different printer PDL requirements, and most printers do not support multiple configurations.

  Newer network printers are offering support for multiple PDLs. And most importantly, some of these printers have the capability to automatically detect the type of print job being submitted and use the correct PDL.

- **The inability of printers to communicate their status over the network.**

  Most printers can only receive data and print it out. They don't have the capability to communicate their status back to network users. This means that a user doesn't know if there is a problem with the printer unless the print job fails to come out of the printer. The print server software has the capability to poll the printer, and different printers have different levels of capabilities in how they can respond. Newer, more intelligent printers have the capability to report to the print server that it is out of paper, low on toner, etc. These messages can then be directed to those trying to use the printer, or also to those in charge of maintaining it.

The good news is that all of these issues are currently being addressed by printer manufacturers. New network-ready printers address these problems with the following capabilities:

- The capability to connect directly to the network and to accept print jobs at network speeds.
- The capability to communicate with other stations on the network and to accept print jobs from remote stations.
- The capability to deal with concurrent print jobs successfully.
- The capability to work with popular PDLs without printer reconfiguration.
- The capability to diagnose printing problems and report them to the network administrator.

In addition, network-ready printers include high-speed print engines, built-in intelligence, increased capacity, and paper handling features. They are more robust, and built to handle high-output demanded by network users.

Understanding IntranetWare Printing

IntranetWare supports several different configurations to allow users on the network to print to network-attached printers. The print server configurations that currently are available in IntranetWare are as follows:

- **Print server NLM.** The printer is physically attached to one of the printer ports on the file server. The print server NLM then enables the printer to be accessed and printed to by users on the network.

  The disadvantages of this method is that there are only a small number of printer ports on a file server, limiting most connections to two printers. Additionally, the printers must be located within a printer cable's length from the file server. Most printer cables are six feet long, which limits your choices.

- **Dedicated print server at workstation.** The printer is physically attached to a workstation on the network. A print server application is then run on the workstation, which enables network users to print to it. This workstation cannot be used for anything else while it is running the print server application—it must be dedicated.

  The advantage of this method is that the printers can be placed near the users who need them. One apparent disadvantage is that a dedicated workstation is required, but older hardware can be used that many companies already have lying around unused.

- **Nondedicated print server at workstation.** The printer is attached to a user's workstation on the network. The workstation loads a TSR application, which makes the printer available to the rest of the network, but which also enables the user to continue using the workstation.

  This is the least popular method because both printing performance and the performance of the workstation is negatively impacted. In addition, loading the TSR on the workstation consumes memory and has been known to make some systems unstable. For these reasons, this method is only used for small networks.

After one of these methods is implemented and printing resources are made available on the network, the next step is knowing how to send a print job to a printer that sits on the network rather than at the other end of your workstation's parallel port.

IntranetWare printing requests can be made from the workstation in several ways:

- Using NPRINT
- Using PRINTCON
- Using CAPTURE and ENDCAP
- NetWare-aware applications
- NETUSER

Figure 20.1 shows some of these methods.

In each of these methods, the data to be printed is directed from the workstation to a queue on the connected server. A print server process services the queue and directs the print job to a local printer or a remote printer (see fig. 20.2).

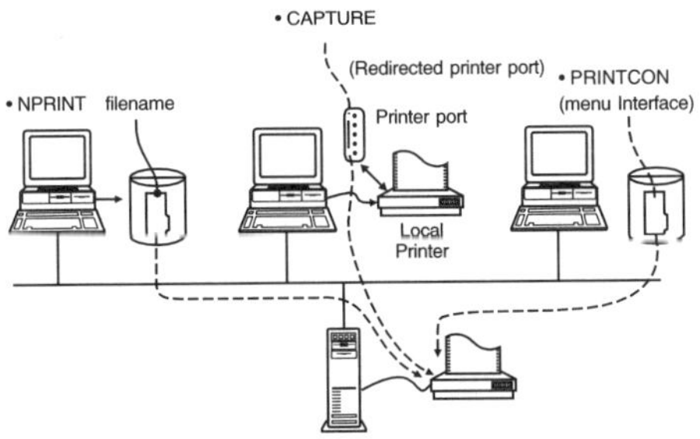

Figure 20.1
Common methods of printing from workstations.

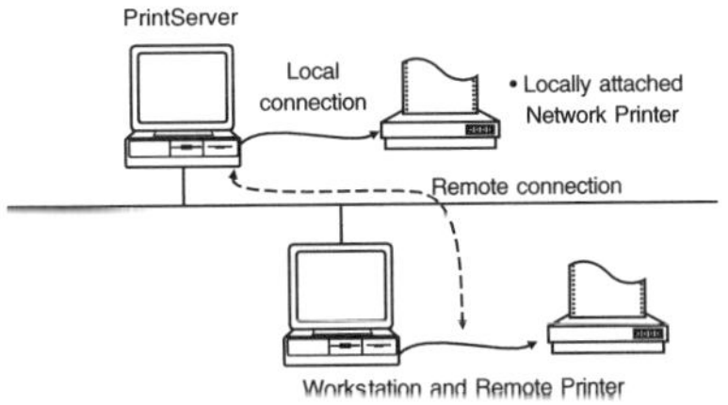

Figure 20.2
Network printers can be local or remote.

Using Local and Network Printers

Figure 20.3 shows a network that has a combination of local and network printers. Local printers can be used only by the workstations to which they are attached. Network printers can be shared by more than one user on the network.

After a print job leaves a workstation, it is stored temporarily in a print queue at the file server, and then is sent to the print server. If the print server is on a different machine than the file server, the print job is sent from the queue on the file server across the network to the printer. Figure 20.4 illustrates this concept.

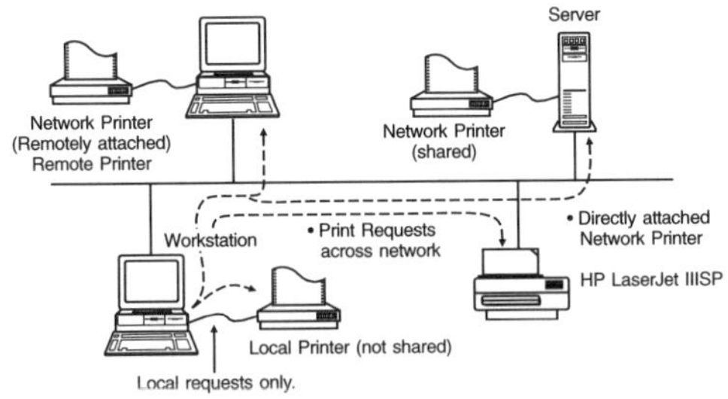

Figure 20.3
Local and network printers.

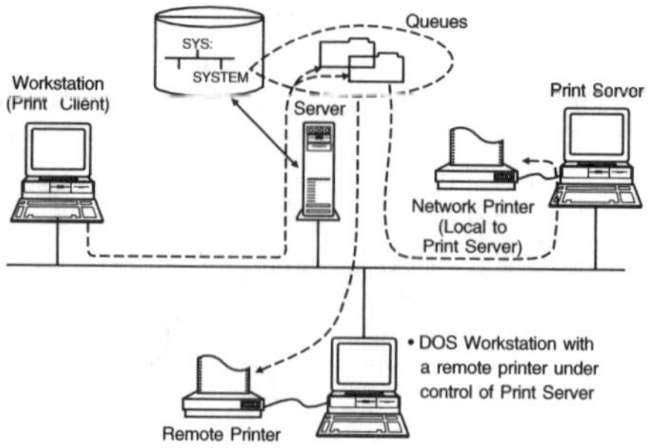

Figure 20.4
Routing print jobs from a print queue to a printer through a print server.

Print Queues

Every print job sent to a network printer is sent to a print queue on the file server first. The queue stores the print job temporarily until the network printer is ready.

The print queues are created as subdirectories on the file server. In IntranetWare print queues can be stored on any server writeable volume in the QUEUES directory. The print jobs are stored as files in the print queue subdirectory. After the print job is completed, the file containing the print job is removed.

Print queues must be created by using the PCONSOLE utility, and they must be created before defining a print server. The important concept to remember is that print queues are serviced by print servers; a logical association or assignment exists between a print queue and printers defined by the print server. The print server also can be considered a queue server because it prints jobs in the queue.

For the sake of simplicity and ease of management, it often is best to keep this logical association between a queue and a printer on a one-to-one basis, as shown in figure 20.5. Other types of logical associations, such as many-to-one, one-to-many, or many-to-many, also are possible. These are illustrated in figures 20.6 and 20.7.

Figure 20.5
One-to-one queue-to-printer assignment.

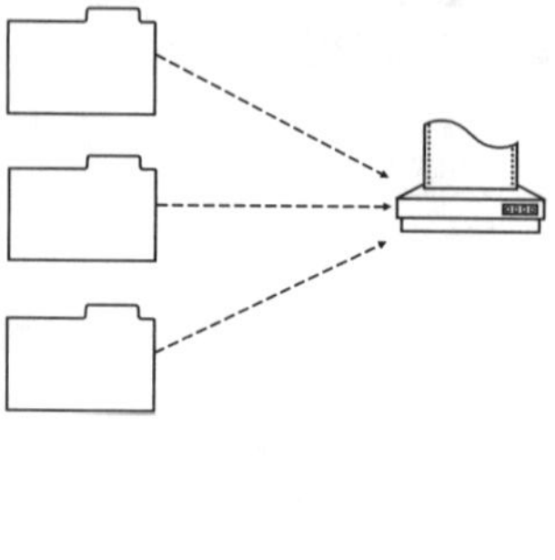

Figure 20.6
Many-to-one queue-to-printer assignment.

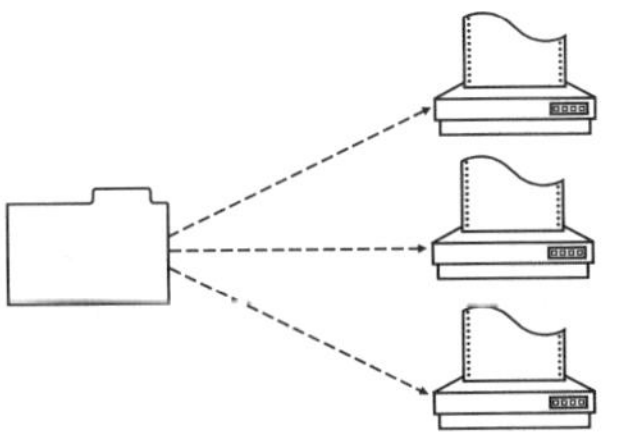

Figure 20.7
One-to-many queue-to-printer assignment.

In complex logical associations, you might need to use the queue priority feature. When a printer is assigned to a queue through PCONSOLE, you can select a priority number from 1 to 10 that determines the order in which the queue is serviced. Figure 20.8 shows a many-to-one printer setup in which queues are assigned at different priorities. The higher priority queue is serviced first, and the lower priority queues are serviced only when no print jobs are in the higher priority queues.

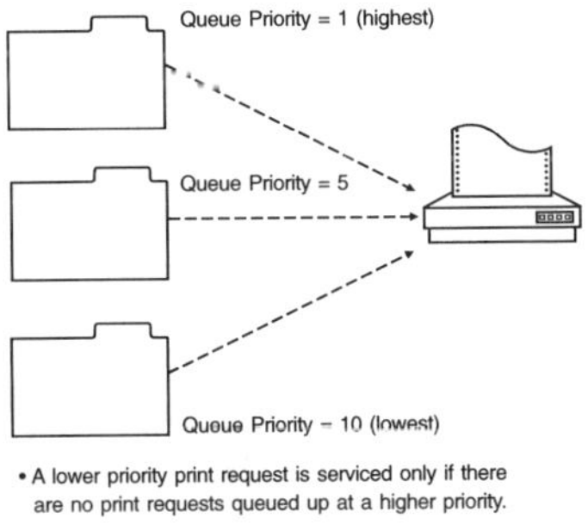

Figure 20.8
Queue priorities.

It is best to keep a one-to-one logical association between print queues and printers; that is, one print queue is serviced by one printer. Print queues and print servers should be given names that make it easy to identify this logical association. Also, the names selected must be indicative of the type of print jobs associated with print queues and print servers.

IntranetWare Print Services

You have to explicitly add print services to IntranetWare before you can enable network printing. The primary tools to add print services are:

- NetWare Administrator Tool
- PCONSOLE

To enable printing in IntranetWare you need:

- Printers

- Print queues
- Print servers

Administrators of NetWare 3.x networks will recognize that these are the same concepts that were used with NetWare 3.x. The big difference here is that these components are objects in the NDS tree. The objects model physical and logical concepts. Thus the Printer object corresponds to the printer device attached to the network (directly or via a server or workstation). In IntranetWare you can submit a job to the Printer object. This is done by specifying the NDS name of the Printer object when printing a job. The Printer object contains a logical association with the Print Queue and Print Server object so that the job ends up being processed by the appropriate print server and ends up in the correct network queue.

Figure 20.9 shows the physical components of network printing and figure 20.10 shows the logical components as part of the NDS tree. Figure 20.10 shows that print jobs submitted by the workstation are processed by the print server and are stored in a queue on some storage volume, and then printed to a network printer. These physical print components are represented as objects in the NDS tree in figure 20.9. The print jobs are submitted by the user objects User A and User B, to the printer object HP_PRINTER. Printer jobs can also be submitted to the Print Queue object HP_QUEUE, which is the traditional way printing is done in NetWare 3.x.

Figure 20.9
Physical components of network printing.

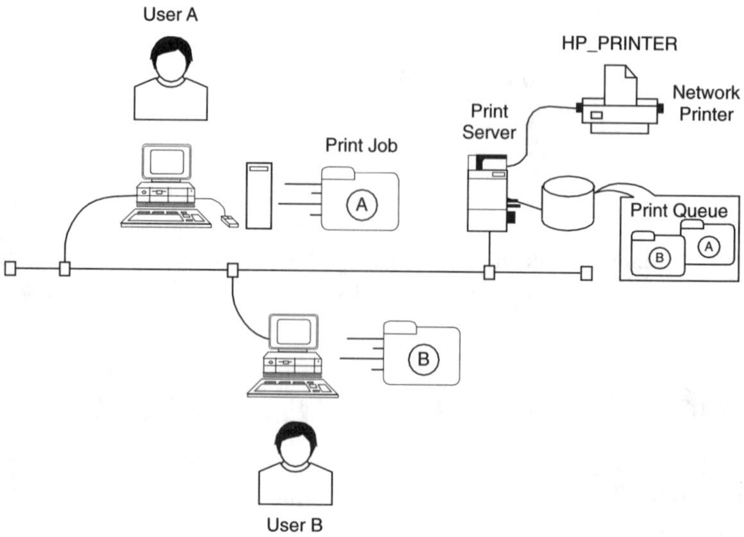

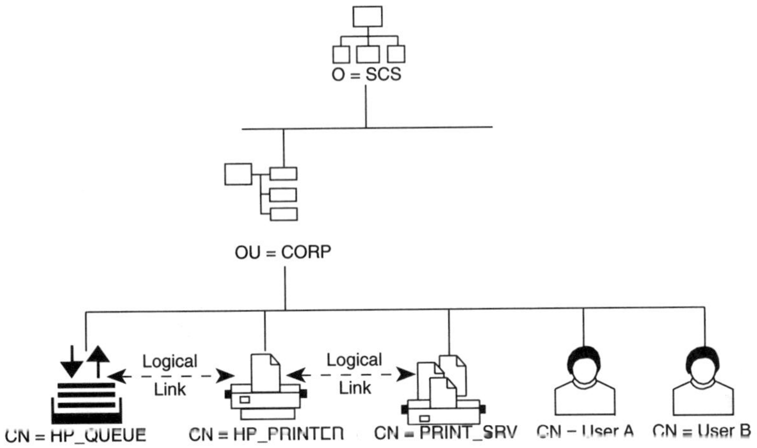

Figure 20.10
Logical (NDS) components of network printing.

If an application does not understand the network printer objects or print queue objects, the CAPTURE command can be used to redirect (map) a local printer to a printer object or print queue object. The CAPTURE command for IntranetWare contains appropriate options to support this mode of operation.

Print Queue Object

The Print Queue object is a logical representation of the physical print queue. The physical print queue is a directory on a storage volume where the print jobs are kept while they are waiting to be printed. The Print Queue object can be created using the NetWare Administrator or the PCONSOLE utility. The print queue object should be placed in the context it is most likely to be used. One of the properties of a print queue object is the physical location of the queue. This queue is always located on a storage volume that must be specified at the time of creating the print queue object. The print queue is placed in a subdirectory of the QUEUES directory. If the QUEUES directory does not exist at the time of creating the queue, it is automatically created.

Printer Object

The Printer object is a logical representation of the physical printer. The physical printer can be directly connected to the network (if it has a network interface), or to a workstation or a file server. The Printer object can be created using the NetWare Administrator or the PCONSOLE utility. The Printer object should be placed in the context it is most likely to be used.

Figure 20.11 shows some of the configuration properties for the printer object. This shows the printer type (LPT1, Serial, AppleTalk, Unix, AIO, XNP). The option types besides LPT1 and Serial are for direct network connection. The Banner Type can be Text or PostScript. The Service Interval shows how often the print server checks the print queue for print jobs assigned to this printer. This can be a value from 1 to 15 seconds (default). The Buffer Size represents how large each a segment of print data sent to the printer can be. The buffer size can range from 1 to 20 KB and has a default value of 3 KB. The Network Address Restrictions show the network address the printer can use. The Service Mode for Forms property is the policy for changing forms.

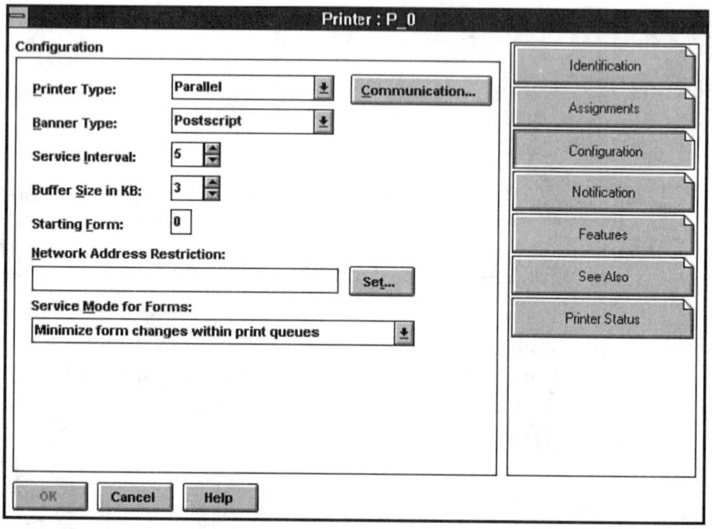

Figure 20.11
Configuration properties for the Printer object.

The Print Server and PSERVER.NLM

The Print Server object describes the print server. The Print Server object is activated by the PSERVER.NLM and can therefore run on NetWare servers only. This program takes the Print Server object name as a parameter when it is loaded.

```
LOAD PSERVER  PrintServerObjectName
```

The above command can be run on any NetWare server that is in the NDS tree. The PrintServerObjectName is replaced by the complete name of the Print Server object. Thus to activate the Print Server object CN=PS-CORP.OU =CORP.O=SCS, you would have to run the following on the NetWare servers the PSERVER.NLM as shown:

```
LOAD PSERVER .CN=PS-CORP.OU=CORP.O=SCS
```

The PSERVER.NLM is the only type of print server that exists. The PSERVER.EXE of NetWare 3.x is no longer supported in IntranetWare.

The PSERVER.NLM can support up to 256 printers. Up to 5 of the 256 printers can be attached to the server where PSERVER.NLM is run (local printers). The remaining 251 printers can be attached anywhere else on the network (remote printer). These remote printers can be on other NetWare servers, workstations or directly attached to the network.

Figure 20.12 shows the types of printers used with a print server and figure 20.13 shows the operation of the PSERVER.NLM. The PSERVER.NLM monitors the queue and the printer, and directs print jobs in the network print queue to the appropriate network printer.

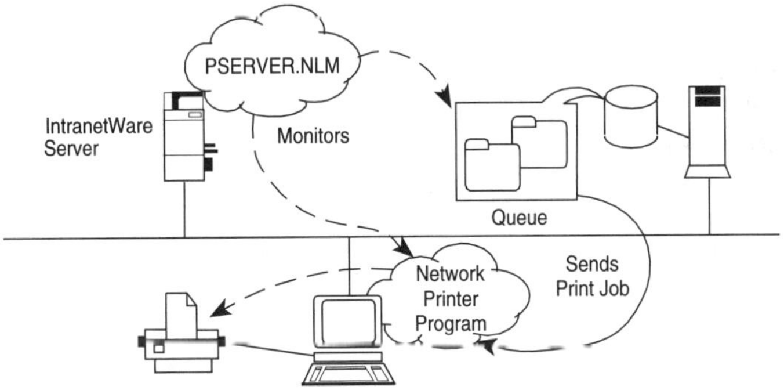

Figure 20.12
Types of printers used with Print Server.

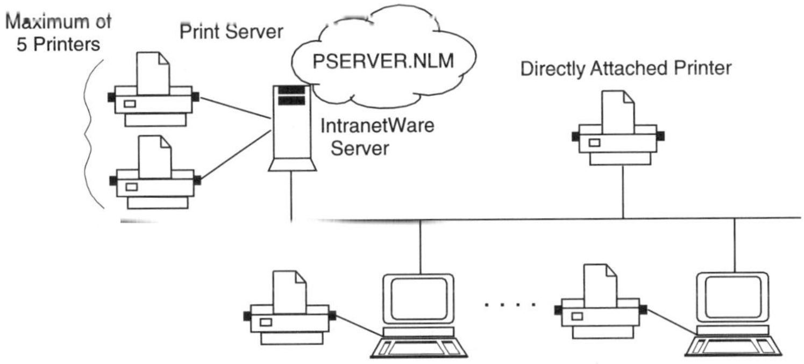

Figure 20.13
Print Server operation.

Print Server Object

The Print Server object is a logical representation of the print server program (PSERVER. NLM) running at a server. The Print Server object can be created using the NetWare Administrator or the PCONSOLE utility. The Printer object should be placed in the context it is most likely to be used.

Figure 20.14 shows the properties of the Printer object. Besides the Name property (Common Name), the only property that is set on this screen is the Advertising Name. Server programs in the NetWare environment, such as the PSERVER.NLM that activates a print server from the description in the Print Server object, advertise their existence using the Service Advertising Protocol (SAP). The other properties such as Other Names, Description, Location, Department and Organization are not set when the queue is initially created via PCONSOLE. It is a good practice to set these values to a meaningful description of the queue object. The Network Address property is only set when the print server is running. The print server in figure 20.14 is running. This is shown by the status fields and the Version property that reports the version number of the PSERVER.NLM that is running. The Network Address property shows that the print server is at F0000055:000000000001:8060. The F0000055 is the internal network number of the NetWare server on which the PSERVER is running and 000000000001 is its node address. The number 8060 is the IPX/SPX socket number associated with the print server process.

You can unload the print server by selecting the Unload button (see fig. 20.14). The print server can also be unloaded directly from the NetWare console on which it was loaded or through the PCONSOLE program. The print server password is used to secure access to the print server object and can be changed via the Change Password button.

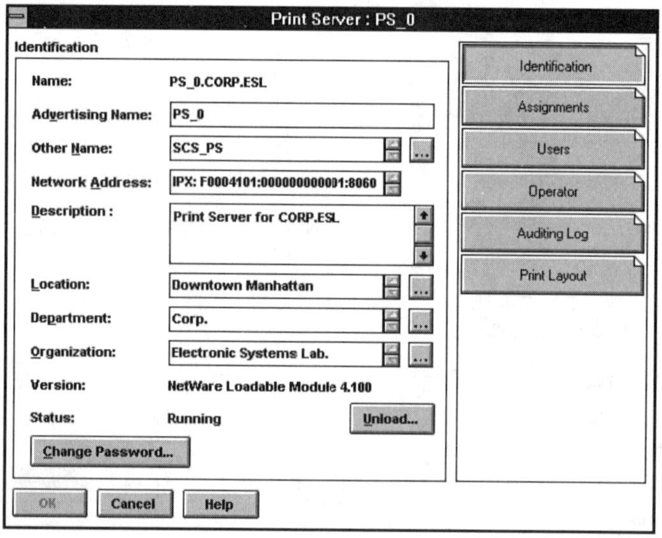

Figure 20.14
Print Server object properties.

Loading of Printer Definition

When the PSERVER.NLM loads, it activates the Printer objects defined in the specified print server object's printers property list. If the printer is defined local to the PSERVER.NLM, a program called NPRINTER.NLM is autoloaded to activate any attached local printers (see fig. 20.15). For this reason, printers attached locally to the NetWare Server on which PSERVER.NLM is run are called Autoload printers. In figure 20.15, you can see that the printer, P_0, was loaded successfully, but the second printer (printer 1) failed to load because, it too was trying to use interrupt line 7 that was already in use by the first printer. If the second printer was defined on a different port from LPT1, this problem would not exist.

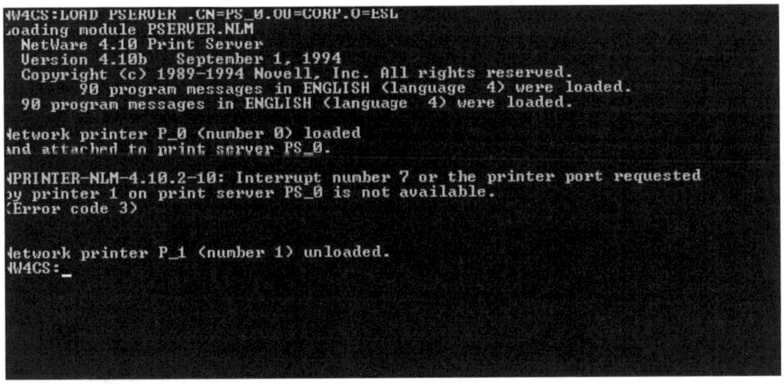

Figure 20.15
Load PSERVER.NLM console messages.

Printers that are attached to other NetWare servers or workstations are called remote printers. These must have the NPRINTER program manually loaded on them. For NetWare servers the NPRINTER program is NPRINTER.NLM and for workstations it is NPRINTER.EXE. Because the NPRINTER program has to be manually loaded, for remote printers they are referred to as Manual load printers.

The NPRINTER Program

The syntax for loading the NPRINTER program is

```
NPRINTER [PrintServerObjectName]   [PrinterObjectName]
```

or

```
LOAD NPRINTER PrintServerObjectName  PrinterObjectName
```

The first form is used for DOS and OS/2 workstations and the second form is used for loading the printer definition on a NetWare server. Multiple printers can be serviced at the NetWare server by running the LOAD NPRINTER command several times and specifying a different printer number each time.

The PrintServerObjectName refers to the print server object to which the printer is assigned. Since a print server object could have more than one printer object assigned to it, the second parameter, PrinterObjectName, further qualifies the statement by specifying the actual printer object name. You can also load the printer definition directly by leaving out the print server object name. Thus, to load printer object CN=HP_PRINTER.O=SCS at a workstation as a remote printer, you can use:

```
NPRINTER   .CN=HP_PRINTER.O=SCS
```

If NPRINTER is used without any options, it runs as a menu utility.

To unload the NPRINTER.EXE, use the command:

```
NPRINTER /U
```

To see the status of a printer, use the command

```
NPRINTER /S
```

Listing 20.1 shows the output produced by running NPRINTER /S on a workstation that had NPRINTER loaded in a prior step.

Listing 20.1

```
NetWare Network Printer Driver v4.01.
Copyright 1988 - 1993, Novell, Inc.  All Rights Reserved.

Print server:             PS-CORP
Printer name:             HP_PRINTER
Printer number:           1
Printer port:             Unknown
Using IRQ:                None (Polled Mode)
TSR status:               Shared Mode
NPRINTER status:          Waiting for Print Job
Printer status:           Out of Paper
```

Figure 20.16 shows a summary of the different types of NPRINTER programs that are possible.

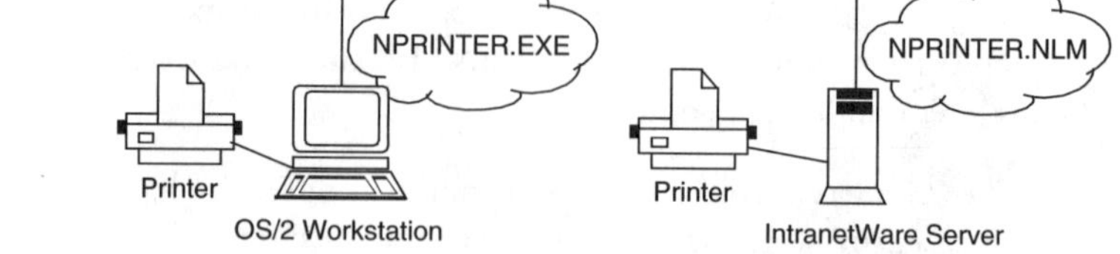

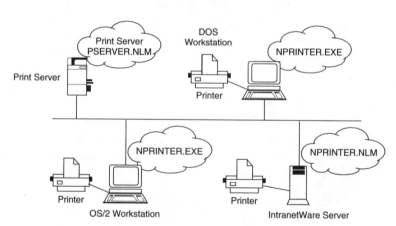

Figure 20.16
Different NPRINTER types.

Interactions between Print Queue, Print Server, and Printer Objects

When configuring network Printing objects, certain critical properties for each of these objects need to be set up. You saw the use of some of these critical properties in the earlier discussion on Print Queue, Printer, and Print Server objects.

Figure 20.17 shows the important or critical properties for the Print Queue, Printer, and Print Server objects. The print queue is assigned to the Print Queues property of the Printer object, and the Printer object is assigned to the Printers property of the Print Server object. This assignment allows a link to be made between the different printing objects, regardless of their context. That is, the network print configuration objects (Printer Queue, Print, and Print Server objects) can be placed in the same context or different context. You should, however, try to create them in contexts that they are most likely to be used.

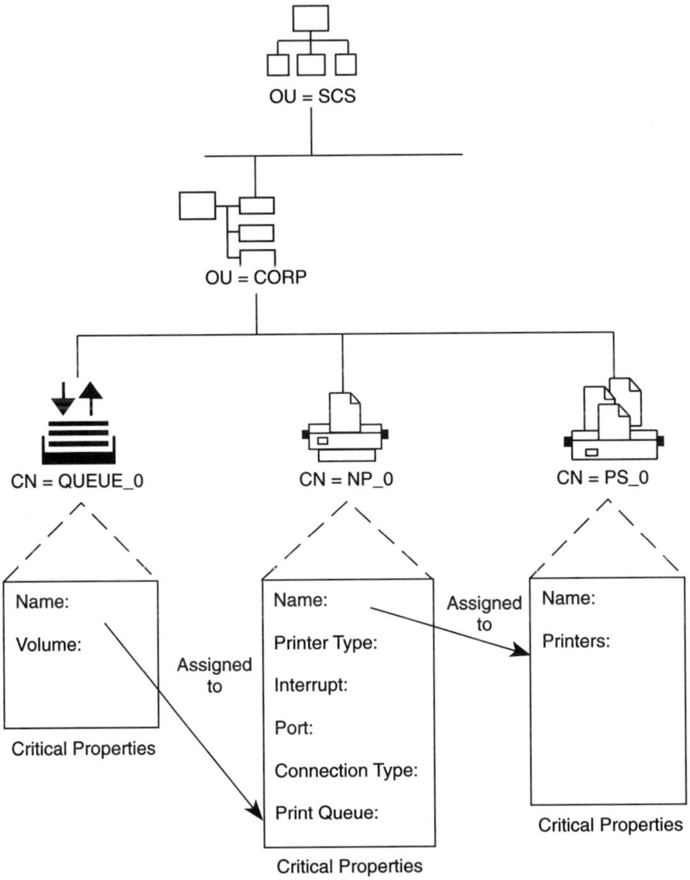

Figure 20.17
Setting of Critical Properties for Print objects.

The diagram in figure 20.16 shows a one-to-one correspondence between the Print Queue, Printer, and Print Server object. This is the simplest and most often used setup. More complex, many-to-one assignments can be made. Figure 20.18 shows that multiple queues can be assigned to a single printer object, and multiple printer objects can be assigned to a single print server object.

Figure 20.18
Many-to-one relationship between Print objects.

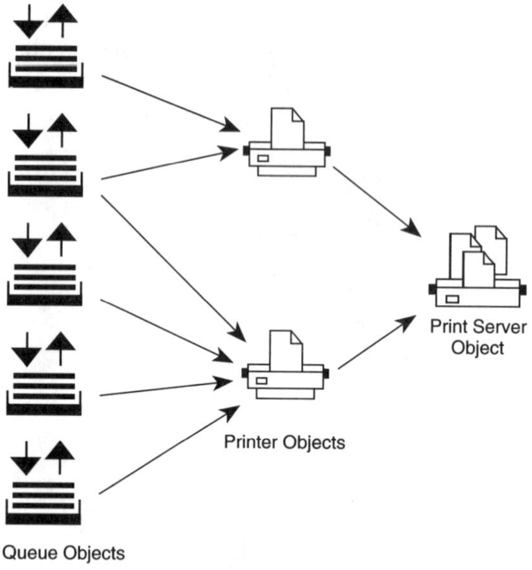

To create the print configuration objects, you should have the Create object right to the container where these objects will be placed. The quickest way to create these objects is to use the Quick Setup option under PCONSOLE. If you do not have the Create object right, this option will not be shown on the PCONSOLE menu.

By default, the creator of the Print objects is made a trustee and given all object rights and property rights to that object. Figure 20.19 shows the trustee rights to object PS_0. The creator of the object is Admin.ESL. This user has all rights to Object Rights (Supervisor, Browse, Delete, Rename) and the All Properties rights (Supervisor, Compare, Read, Write, and Add Self).

Figure 20.19
Trustee right of owner to Print Server object.

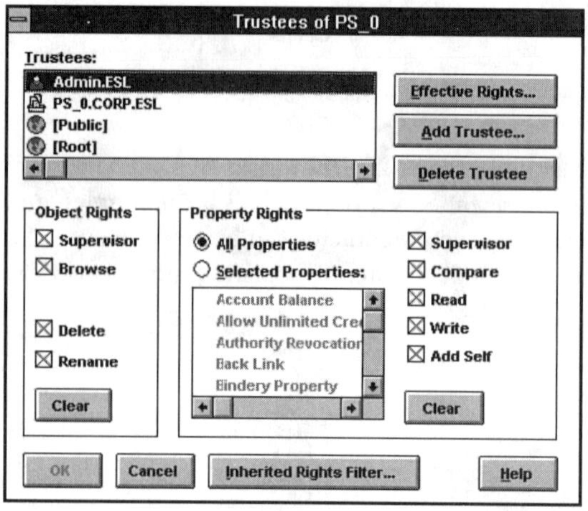

Configuring Network Print Services

As mentioned earlier, the primary tools for configuring network services are PCONSOLE and Network Administrator. But only PCONSOLE has the Quick Setup option. The other options in PCONSOLE are the same as in the PCONSOLE for NetWare 3.x, with the exception that they have been modified to work with NDS objects.

If you use the NetWare Administrator tool to create Print objects, you have to make sure that their critical properties are defined, and the logical links between them are properly defined.

The NETADMIN.EXE program cannot be used to create Print objects. You cannot use this tool to view or edit properties of Print objects.

The PCONSOLE Utility

You will now be given a guided tour on implement network printing by using the PCONSOLE utility by creating Print Queues, Printer, and Print Server objects, and configuring them.

1. Log in as an Admin user and run PCONSOLE. You can log in as another user as long as you have create, delete, and browse privileges to the container where you are creating the print objects. Should you wish to rename any print objects you create, you may also wish to have Rename object rights to leaf objects in the container.

2. Select Change Context from PCONSOLE and change your context to the container where you wish to place the print objects. In this guided tour the container name is OU=CORP.O=ESL_XXX. If you are practicing using PCONSOLE, you might wish to create an organization with a similar name. Substitute any characters for *XXX*, so you can experiment with different organization trees. You can always delete these trees at a later point.

   You can see your context reported on the top half of the PCONSOLE screen.

3. Select Print Queues from Available Options. You should see a list of Print Queue objects defined in the OU=CORP.O=ESL_XXX context. The list should initially be empty unless you have already created Print Queue objects in this container.

4. Press Ins to create a Queue object. You should see a screen asking you to enter the new queue name.

5. Enter the name of the print queue object as QUEUE_1. (You can choose any other name, but for the purpose of this exercise, it will be referred to as QUEUE_1.) You should see a screen asking you to enter the queue's volume. The queue has to be placed on a Volume object. It is created as a subdirectory (with the name of the Print Queue ID) under the QUEUES directory.

6. ACTION: Enter the name of a Volume object. For the purpose of this exercise the volume name is referred to as CORP_VOL. You can use the Volume object name on your IntranetWare server, or create an alias in your current context to the server volume, name it CORP_VOL and use this name.

   You can also press Ins and browse through the NDS directory tree, searching for the volume to place the queue on.

   After you enter the volume name to used with the Print Queue object, you should see the newly created Print Queue object in the Print Queues list.

7. Your next step is to create a Printer object. Return to the main PCONSOLE menu by pressing Esc.

   Select the Printers option from Available Options.

   You should see a list of Printer objects defined in the OU=CORP.O=ESL_XXX context. The list should initially be empty.

8. Press Ins to create a Printer object. You should see a screen asking you to enter the new printer name.

9. Enter the name of the Print Queue object as PRINTER_1. (You can choose any other name, but for the purpose of this exercise, it will be referred to as PRINTER_1.)

   You should see the newly created Printer object in the Printers list.

10. Select the Printer object you have created from the Printers list. You should see a screen on the printer configuration.

11. Assuming that you have a parallel printer, configure the printer as follows. If you have a serial printer, use one of the COMx ports.

Printer Type:	Parallel
Configuration:	Port: LPT1
Location:	Manual Load or Autoload
Interrupt:	7
Address restriction:	No
Print Queues Assigned:	Assign QUEUE_1 to this printer

   When you assign the Queue object that you created earlier, you will select the Print queues assigned: (list) field from the Printer Configuration screen. You will see a Print Queue list. Press Ins and select the name of the Queue object. You can also browse the directory tree, looking for Queue objects, by selecting on the ".." (parent) entry.

The priority column displays the priority for jobs in queue. You can select the queue name entry to change its priority from 1 (highest) to 10 (lowest).

The state column displays codes that have the following meaning:

A = Printer is actively servicing the queue.

C = Printer is configured to service this queue.

D = This is the default print queue.

In the print configuration screen, you can also select the Notification field to select the users/groups that should be notified when a print job has been completed. The default Notification list contains the Print job owner value.

12. Press Esc a few times, and save printer configuration changes when asked to do so.

    Return to the main Available Options menu.

13. The last step is to create a Print Server object.

    Select the Print Servers option from Available Options.

    You should see a list of Print Server objects defined in the OU=CORP.O=ESL_XXX context. The list should initially be empty.

14. Press Ins to create a Printer object. You should see a screen asking you to enter the new print server name.

15. Enter the name of the print server as PSRV_1 (or any other print server name). You will see a message that you should wait while the Print Server object is being created. You should see the newly created Printer object in the Print Servers list.

16. Your next step is to configure the Print Server object. Select the Print Server object you have created from the Print Servers list. You should see a list of Print Server Information options.

17. Select the Printers option from the Print Server Information list. You should see a list of Serviced Printers. Initially the list should be empty.

    Press Ins. You should see a list of Printer objects that can be assigned to the print server.

18. Select the Printer object you created earlier (PRINTER_1) and assign it to the print server. You should see a list of serviced Printer objects that are assigned to the print server.

    You can assign up to 256 printer objects to a Print Server object. If you need to assign more than 256 printers, define another Print Server object.

19. Return to the main Available Options menu by pressing Esc a few times. You have created a Print Queue, Printer, and Print Server object and configured them properly.

The next step is to load the print server (PSERVER.NLM) on a server.

The LOAD PSERVER Command

The PSERVER command syntax is as follows:

```
LOAD PSERVER PrintServerObject
```

To load the PSERVER.NLM for the print server object CN=PSRV_1.OU=CORP.O=ESL_XXX that you created in the previous section, use the command:

```
LOAD PSERVER     .CN=PSRV_1.OU=CORP.O=ESL_XXX
```

When the PSERVER.NLM loads, you should see a list of Available Options for the PSERVER.NLM (see fig. 20.20). Selecting Printer Status should show the list of printers that are defined for the print server object (see fig. 20.21). Selecting any of the printers listed shows the printer status (see fig. 20.22). Selecting Print Server Information from Available Options shows the print server information and status (see fig. 20.23).

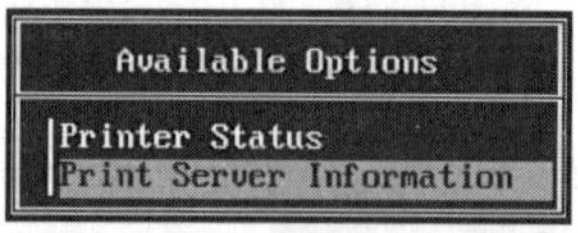

Figure 20.20
PSERVER Main Screen.

Figure 20.21
PSERVER Printer List.

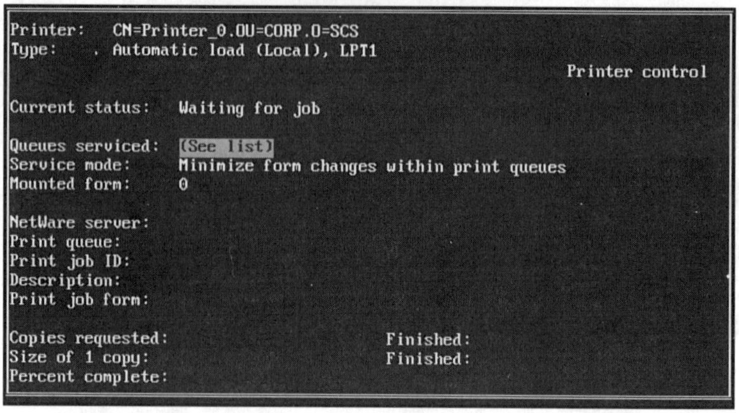

Figure 20.22
PSERVER Printer Status.

You can change the Current Status field in the Print Server Information (see fig. 20.23) from Running to Unload to unload the print server immediately. If you want to wait until all print jobs are finished before unloading the print server, you can set Current status filed to Unload after active print jobs.

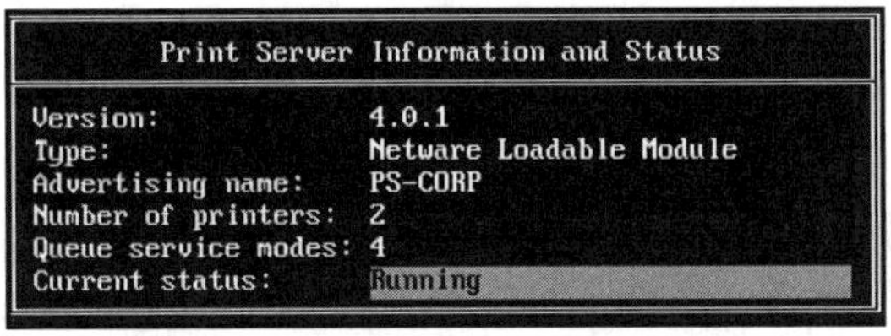

Figure 20.23
PSERVER Print Server Information and Status.

Quick Setup Configuration

The Quick Setup information option in PCONSOLE can be used to create in a single step a Print Queue, Printer, and Print Server object that have all of their critical properties defined. The Print objects are created to have the proper logical links between themselves. This means that the Print queue object is assigned to the Printer object's Print Queues list property, and the Printer object is assigned to the Print Server object's Printers list property.

The Print objects that are created have default names of Q1 for Print Queue object, P1 for Printer object and PS-container for the Print Server object. The container in the print server name PS-container is the name of the container in which the print server is defined. At the time of creation of these objects, you can change the default names to any other names (as long as they do not conflict with leaf names of other objects in the container).

Quick Setup will also make assumptions about the printer properties. For the Printer object it defines the following property values.

Printer type:	Parallel
Location:	Auto Load (Local)
Interrupt:	None (polled mode)
Port:	LPT1

These values can be modified during Quick Setup, but they should match your physical printer configuration.

You will now be presented with a guide tour on using the Quick Setup Option of PCONSOLE.

1. Login as an Admin user and run PCONSOLE.
2. If your context is not OU=CORP .O =ESL_XXX where XXX is replaced by your group identity, select Change Context and change your context to where you want to create the print objects.

3. Select Quick Setup from Available Options.

   If your context is a container, such as [Root], where Print objects cannot be created, you will not see the quick Setup option in the Available Options menu.

   After selecting the Quick Setup option, you should see the Print Services Quick Setup screen (see fig. 20.24).

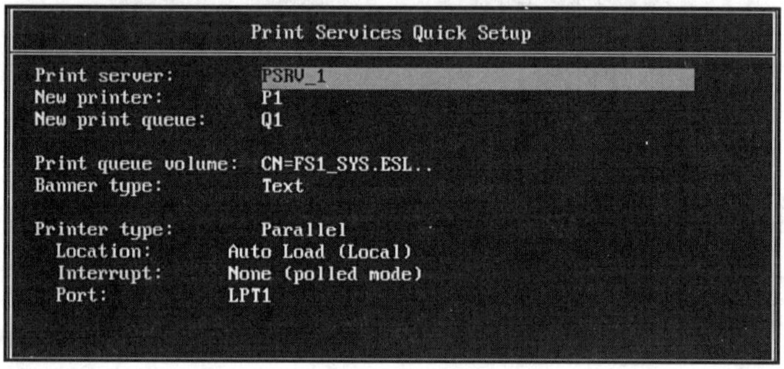

Figure 20.24
Print Services Quick Setup screen.

4. Change the names of these objects to whatever names you want to use.

5. Change printer configuration to match your needs.

   The printer location to Auto Load (Local) means local printer, and a value of Manual Load means remote printer.

6. Press F10 to save changes. The Printer objects will be created after a short wait.

Network-Direct Print Servers

IntranetWare provides network users with several printing services, including increased printer support, increased network print performance, and graphical print management tools. IntranetWare also supports existing "network-direct" printers and hardware queue servers produced by various manufacturers. These devices either connect to a printer and then to the network, or are installed on a port at the printer. Some of the companies that manufacture such devices include Castelle, Compaq, Eagle, Hewlett-Packard, Intel, and Lexmark.

In many cases, these devices offer a fast, effective, low-cost printing solution in IntranetWare. These print devices are typically shipped with their own installation utilities. The manufacturers' utilities configure the device to recognize network print components and to communicate with the network. To effectively use network-direct print servers in an IntranetWare environment, you will need to know the manufacturer's procedures for installing the specific device that you are using.

Most network-direct print servers can be configured to run in one of the following modes:

- Queue server mode
- Remote printer mode

Queue Server Mode

In queue server mode, the hardware print server directly accesses the print queue using NCP (NetWare Core Protocol) calls. Under most circumstances, this mode will place the least load on an IntranetWare server. In IntranetWare, there are minimal performance differences between the two printing modes.

The only limitation posed by Queue server mode is that the original queues, printers, and the print server object definitions must all exist in the same bindery context. Aliases to these print queues and printers can exist in other contexts so that VLM users can capture to a queue in their local context.

Setting up a network-direct print server in queue server mode is fairly simple and straightforward. Use PCONSOLE or NWADMIN to create your printing services. To do this you must create one or more queues to be services by the printer. Then you must create a Printer object for the printer, configure the Printer object as Other/Unknown, and assign it the queues previously created. Create the Print Server object to service the printer and assign the printer to the Print Server object.

You must now run the printer configuration software provided by the network-direct print server's manufacturer. Select the printer to be configured, choose to configure it as a queue server, assign it a name, and select the file server where the queues will reside.

Remote Printer Mode

In remote printer mode, the device functions in a way similar to a workstation running NPRINTER.EXE. Devices configured for remote printer mode are controlled by an IntranetWare print server.

Devices running in this mode under IntranetWare run considerably faster than they did under NetWare 3.x. This increased speed and flexibility offered with IntranetWare makes remote printer mode a very effective way of providing network printing with these devices.

In order to run these devices in remote printer mode under IntranetWare, be sure you have loaded PSERVER.NLM at the NetWare server console. The only limitation is that the Print Server object must be defined in the server's bindery context. All other Printing objects, including Print Queues and Printers, can be in any context.

To set up a network-direct print server in remote printer mode is also fairly simple and straightforward. You must use PCONSOLE or NWADMIN to create your printing services. To do this you need to create one or more queues to be serviced by the printer. Create a

Printer object for the printer, and configure the Printer object as Other/Unknown. Assign it the queues previously created. Create the Print Server object to service the printer and assign the printer to the Print Server object. You can use an existing PSERVER for this. Simply assign to it the printer to be serviced.

Load the PSERVER.NLM at the server console, or reload it to reinitialize the print server with the new changes. Then run the printer configuration software provided by the network-direct print server's manufacturer. At this point you must select the printer to be configured, configure it as a remote printer, select the print server to service the printer, and select which printer number it is.

Sending a Print Job

After the network printing is set up, print jobs can be submitted using:

- NETUSER
- CAPTURE
- NPRINT
- PCONSOLE

The NETUSER is a menu-driven tool that can be used to perform common network related tasks such as network printing, messaging, drive mappings, attaching to other servers. This is a new tool that was first introduced with NetWare 4.0.

The NPRINT and CAPTURE are commands that take a number of options and can be used for sending a print job to network printer.

These printing tools will be briefly examined next.

Printing Using NETUSER

Figure 20.25 shows that one of the options available to NETUSER is Printing. Selecting the Printing option shows you a list of available printer ports local to your workstation. You can select any of these ports for network redirection. After selecting a port, you are given a choice of examining Print Jobs or redirecting the selected port by using Change Printers (see fig. 20.26). You cannot examine print jobs on a printer port that has not been captured (redirected to a network printer).

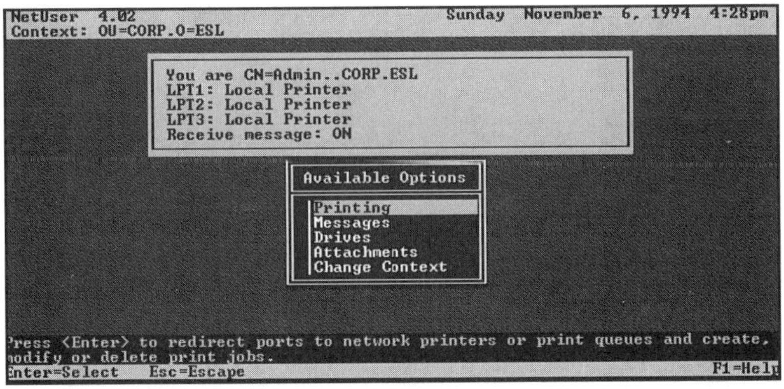

Figure 20.25
NETUSER options.

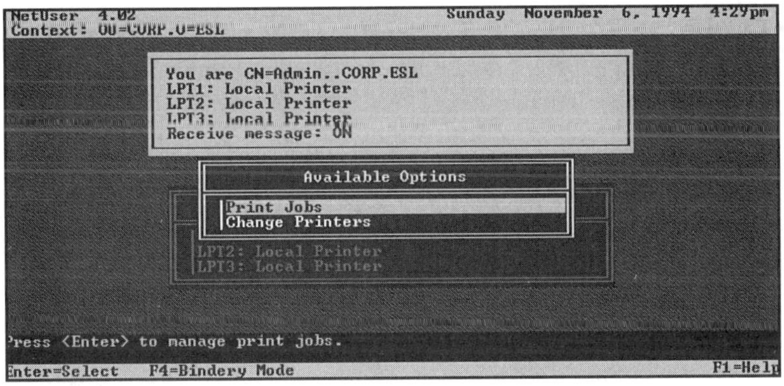

Figure 20.26
Available Printer Ports.

After selecting Change Printers, you are given a list of printers and queues in the current context. If no printers or queues are shown, you can use Ins to browse the NDS tree. Figure 20.27 shows that a queue Queue_0 and a printer Printer_0 NDS objects were found in the context OU=CORP.O=SCS. You can select either the Printer_0 or the Queue_0 object to direct the network print jobs. After redirecting a local printer, the Available Ports menu in NETUSER will show the queue name to which the port is redirected. You can now select the Print Jobs option to send a print job to the network queue. From this point on the procedure for sending print jobs is similar to that for PCONSOLE. That is, you can press Ins and browse directories for files to print.

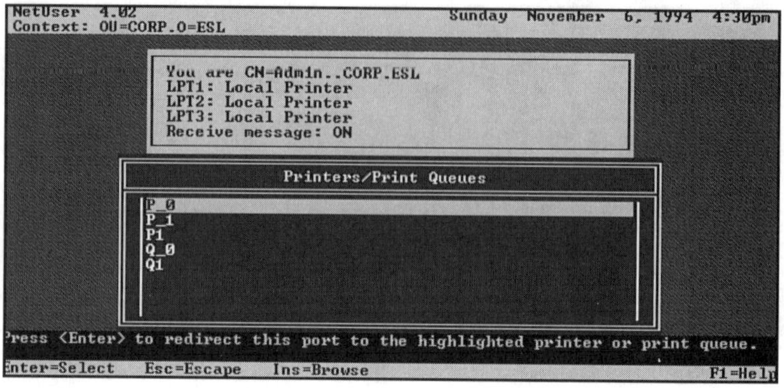

Figure 20.27
Printers/Print Queues.

Printing Using CAPTURE

The CAPTURE command is used to redirect a local printer port to a network queue or network printer. Table 20.1 shows the CAPTURE options. Option abbreviations are shown in bold. Therefore, the option EndCap can be abbreviated as EC.

Table 20.1
CAPTURE Options

Option	Description
SHow	Shows current status of local printer ports. Used as an option by itself.
Printer=name	Specifies network printer to which redirected print jobs should be sent. If name is a complete NDS name with embedded blanks, quotes can be used.
Local=n	Redirects local LPT port n.
Queue=name	Indicates queue object to which print job should be sent.
EndCap	Ends redirection to local ports.
EndCap ALL	Ends redirection of all local printer ports.
CReate=path	Sends print job to file path.
Keep	Retains print job in queue, if workstation fails.
Job=jc	Specifies print job configuration to use. No need to specify other options.
No**B**anner	Suppresses printing of banner page.
Banner=name	Prints banner page. Limit is 12 characters for banner name. Appears in lower half of page.

Option	Description
NAMe=name	Default is name of file being printed. Indicates text in upper part of banner page. Limit is a 12-character name.
Form=n	Specifies form number or name that is to be used for print job.
Copies=n	Specifies number of copies for print job (1–255).
Tabs=n	Number of spaces to use for a tab character.
No **T**abs	Suppresses tab expansion to space characters.
TImeout=n	Number of seconds to wait before closing job.
Form Feed	Generates a form feed character at end of print job.
No **F**orm **F**eed	Suppresses form feed character at end of job.
AUtoendcap	Captured data should be closed and sent to printer on exiting application
No**A**utoendcap	Captured data should not be closed and sent to printer on exiting application.
NOTIfy	Specifies that user receive notification of print job completion.
No**NOTI**fy	Specifies that user not receive notification of print job completion.
/?	Help.
/? ALL	Displays all help screens.
Verbose	Provides detailed information on command as it is executed.

The Printer=name option can be used to specify the network Printer object name to which to send print jobs.

The ENDCAP command is no longer used with IntranetWare. Instead CAPTURE has a new EndCap option to stop printer redirection. To stop the capture of local printer port LPT1:, you can use:

```
CAPTURE EndCap
```

or

```
CAPTURE  EC
```

To stop printer redirection for all local printers, you can use the EndCap ALL option in one of two ways:

```
CAPTURE EndCap ALL
```

or

```
CAPTURE EC ALL
```

Printing Using NPRINT

To print a job using NPRINT, use the following syntax:

```
NPRINT    filename    [option]
```

The *option* can be replaced by any of the options in table 20.2.

Table 20.2
NPRINT Options

Option	Description
Server=name	Specifies a non-NDS server (bindery server) whose bindery contains the print queue definition.
Printer=name	Specifies network printer to which redirected print jobs should be sent. If name is a complete NDS name with embedded blanks, quotes can be used.
Local=n	Redirects local LPT port n.
Queue=name	Indicates queue object to which print job should be sent.
Job=jc	Specifies print job configuration to use. No need to specify other options.
No**B**anner	Suppresses printing of banner page.
Banner=name	Prints banner page. Limit is 12 character for banner name. Appears in lower half of page.
NAMe=name	Default is name of file being printed. Indicates text in upper part of banner page. Limit is a 12 character name.
Form=n	Specifies form number or name that is to be used for print job.
Copies=n	Specifies number of copies for print job (1–255).
Tabs=n	Number of spaces to use for a tab character.
No **T**abs	Suppresses tab expansion to space characters.
Form **F**eed	Generates a form feed character at end of print job.
No **F**orm **F**eed	Suppresses form feed character at end of job.
NOTIfy	Specifies that user receive notification of print job completion.
No**NOTI**fy	Specifies that user not receive notification of print job completion.

Option	Description
/?	Help.
/? ALL	Displays all help screens.
Verbose	Provides detailed information on command as it is executed.

Printing Using PCONSOLE

To print using PCONSOLE, select the Print Queues option from Available Options in PCONSOLE. If the print queue you want to print to is not displayed, use Change Context to change context to the container that has the queue object.

After selecting the Queue name from the Print Queues list you will see a menu on Print Queue Information. Select Print Jobs option. You should see the jobs in the current queue. Press Ins, enter a directory name to print from and press Enter. Select the files that you wish to print. You will be given a choice of Print Job Configurations to use for printing. If no print job configurations have been defined for the current container, you can select the (Defaults) print job configuration.

Network Printing Tools

Table 20.3 shows the list of network printing tools that are available for IntranetWare. The PCONSOLE, PSERVER, NPRINTER, and NWADMIN (Network Administrator) have been discussed so far. The PRINTCON and PRINTDEF tools will be discussed briefly.

Table 20.3
Network Printing Tools

Program	Extension	Executed On	Used For
PCONSOLE	EXE	Workstation	Creating and configuring Print Servers, Print Queues, and Printer objects.
PRINTCON	EXE	Workstation	Creating and configuring print job configurations.
PRINTDEF	EXE	Workstation	Defining print forms, importing/ exporting print device definitions.
PSERVER	NLM	Server	Activating the Print Server object.
NPRINTER	EXE	Workstation	Allowing network printer attached to a station to be shared.

continues

Table 20.3, Continued
Network Printing Tools

Program	Extension	Executed On	Used For
NPRINTER	NLM	Server	Allowing network printer attached to a server not running PSERVER.NLM to be shared.
NWADMIN	EXE	Workstation	GUI utility to perform printer management functions.
PSC	EXE	Workstation	Command-line utility to control and see status of printers and print servers.

IntranetWare offers PRINTCON and for PRINTDEF print job configuration. The print job configurations can be used as the Job Configuration parameter in CAPTURE and NPRINT to simplify the options by aggregating them under a print job configuration template. It is also used when submitting jobs to a queue using the Print Job option in NETUSER and PCONSOLE.

The PRINTCON Utility

Figure 20.28 shows the main menu for PRINTCON. The Edit Print Job Configuration is used to create new print job configurations. The Select Default Print Job Configuration allows you to select the print job configuration that will be used as a default. The Change Current Object allows you to change the container object or user object for which the print job configuration will be defined.

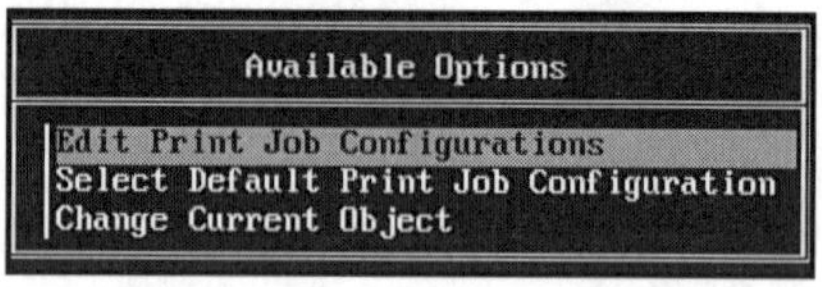

Figure 20.28
PRINTCON Main Menu.

Print job configurations are stored as the Print Job Configuration property of an organization, organization unit or user object. If stored in a container, all users within the container can use the print job configuration. If the print job configuration is stored as a property of a user object, only that user can make use of the print job configuration.

The PRINTCON can operate in the directory mode (default) or the bindery mode. F4 can be used to toggle between these two modes. This allows the IntranetWare PRINTCON to be used with NetWare 3.x bindery. In NetWare 3.x, print job configurations are stored in the bindery.

The PRINTDEF Utility

Figure 20.29 shows the main menu for PRINTDEF. The Print Devices option is used to modify printer definitions for print devices. The Print Forms option allows you to create and modify printer form definitions. The Change Current Context allows you to change the container object for which the form definition will be defined.

Print device definitions and forms are stored in the Print Devices and Print Forms property of the container object. If stored in a container, all users and print job configurations within the container can use the print device definition.

Figure 20.29
PRINTDEF Main Menu.

The PRINTDEF can operate in the directory mode (default) or the bindery mode. F4 can be used to toggle between these two modes. This allows the NetWare 4.x PRINTDEF to be used with NetWare 3.x bindery. In NetWare 3.x print device definitions are stored in the bindery.

A Look Forward at NDPS

If you have a history with NetWare, you realize that printing hasn't changed much since NetWare 3.x. The tools have changed, but the architecture has remained the same. However, this will all change with Novell Distributed Print Services (NDPS). NDPS isn't included in the current shipping version of IntranetWare, but it deserves mention here because IntranetWare II promises to incorporate it. Novell plans to release NDPS as an independent software release in mid July of 1997, and it will be incorporated in the Moab release, also dubbed IntranetWare 2, in early '98.

NDPS is the best thing to happen to network printing—it addresses all the problems mentioned at the beginning of this chapter. It is a complete re-architecture of the current printing model and was created by Novell in conjunction with Hewlett-Packard and Xerox. The benefits and features of NDPS include:

- **Full authentication.** Offers greater security by registering the printer as an NDS printer object. By being represented as a printer object in Novell's NDS database, the printer takes advantage of security benefits without sacrificing the ease of printing.
- **Intelligently conceived defaults.** Reduces or eliminates user intervention during installation to achieve satisfactory printing results with little effort.
- **Print drivers are automatically installed.** Users no longer need to worry whether their workstation is running the correct print drivers for the printers they want to use.

- **Plug-and-Print.** Offers maximum printing convenience. A printer simply needs to be connected to the network for users to begin sending print jobs to it.
- **Smart detection of environment configuration.** Includes the types of printers available, eliminates the need for users to configure their workstation with drivers for specific printers and other devices.

As shown in figure 20.30, print queue, print server, and print spooling functions are combined into one entity under the NDPS architecture—a printer agent. Each printer incorporated in an NDPS environment must have an associated printer agent. The agent software runs on the NetWare file server, and is controlled by an NDPS Manager NLM. The configuration options available from this NLM can be accessed from the server console or through NWAdmin.

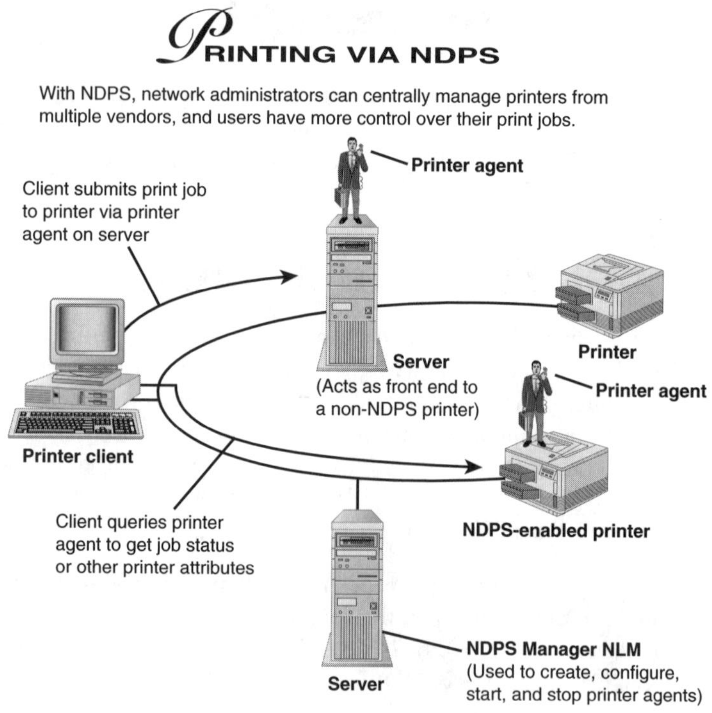
PRINTING VIA NDPS
With NDPS, network administrators can centrally manage printers from multiple vendors, and users have more control over their print jobs.
Printer agent
Client submits print job to printer via printer agent on server
Printer
Server
(Acts as front end to a non-NDPS printer)
Printer agent
Printer client
Client queries printer agent to get job status or other printer attributes
NDPS-enabled printer
NDPS Manager NLM
(Used to create, configure, start, and stop printer agents)
Server

Figure 20.30
The printer agent can reside either on the file server or be embedded in the printer.

Printers supporting bi-directional communications can (through the agent) report on print job and printer status. For example, a bi-directional printer can send a message to a user explaining that a paper tray is empty, that toner is low, or that there is a paper jam. Printer configuration information, such as memory and font configuration, can also be provided.

Many printer manufacturers have shown support for NDPS by agreeing to create NDPS-aware printers, which will have the agents built right into the printer. With these printers, you'll only need to plug them into the network to make them available to users. Network administrators can control access to the printer by denying specific users or groups access to the printer object.

Even though NDPS-aware printers will be slow to hit the streets, the tools that will enable NDPS to work with existing printers are the same tools that will offer backward compatibility down the road. This makes NDPS usable when it is first released, and it makes your existing printers usable when NDPS-aware printers enter the market.

Will NDPS make queue-based printing obsolete, along with the information presented in this chapter? Not soon enough, because previous versions of NetWare will be around for a long time. But as the technology seeps into the mainstream, it will change the way users look at printing on a network, and more importantly, how they administer it.

Summary

In this chapter, you have learned how to use and set up NetWare's printing mechanisms. NetWare supports a variety of printing methods to suit the needs of different printing applications. NetWare-aware applications designed to make use of the NetWare printer function Application Programming Interfaces (APIs) require very little configuration support. Applications that do not work as intimately with the NetWare printing mechanisms, however, require additional support.

Most of the printing chores can be done by using the PCONSOLE utility. A detailed guided tour of how to use PCONSOLE in IntranetWare is presented in this chapter, along with examples on using many of NetWare's command-line utilities for printer support. A brief look at NDPS was also covered, as was a discussion of how it affects printing in future releases of NetWare.

CHAPTER 21

Implementing NLSP

IntranetWare servers typically rely on the Routing Information Protocol (RIP) to route IPX packets. RIP is an example of a distance-vector protocol. RIP has the following problems:

- *Excessive broadcast traffic*
- *Does not scale well as the size of the network increases*
- *Does not stabilize rapidly when route changes*

Many modern routing protocols use the link state algorithm, which offers a number of advantages over RIP. RIP relies on broadcast traffic sent at frequent intervals. Novell's Service Advertising Protocol (SAP) also exchanges service information with other IntranetWare servers at frequent intervals.

On wide area networks (WANs) that have limited bandwidth, using broadcast traffic can be expensive. Novell, therefore, has developed the *NetWare Link Services Protocol* (NLSP), which can exchange routing and service information much more efficiently. You can use NLSP to replace the traditional RIP and SAP protocols for exchanging routing and service information. NLSP uses a link state algorithm that requires that information be sent only if changes occur in routing and service information.

Overview of NLSP

NLSP is derived from IS-IS (Intermediate System-to-Intermediate System) protocols that were specified for OSI-based networks. The protocol was developed by Radia Perlman, who also did much of the development work for IS-IS protocols.

NLSP routers exchange connection status information about neighbor routers, throughput, maximum packet size (MTU size), route path costs, and network numbers learned through RIP. If the NLSP routers connect with networks that use RIP and SAP between routers and servers, the routers also keep track of services and external (RIP-based) routes. The route and service information is transmitted in packets, called *Link State Packets* (LSPs). NLSP routers use LSPs to build and maintain a logical map of the entire network, and transmit LSPs only if a change occurs in a route or service information on the network.

If you configure the routers to use NLSP, they use NLSP, rather than RIP and SAP, to exchange routing information between themselves. Workstations continue to use RIP and SAP to determine routing and service information. To migrate to NLSP service, you need configure only the IntranetWare servers and routers. You do not need to install any special software on the IntranetWare workstations.

For additional details on NLSP theory, see Chapter 26, "Bridging, Switching, and Routing," on the CD.

Reasons to Use NLSP

The following section outlines some of the reasons to use NLSP. The following are the primary benefits of using NLSP:

- Efficient routing
- Reduced routing and service traffic on the network
- Scaling to larger IPX networks
- Reduced overhead over WAN links

- Faster data transfer
- Compatibility with IPX RIP and SAP
- Improved network management
- Configurable link-cost assignment
- Load balancing

These benefits are described in the following sections.

Efficient Routing

RIP routers use a distance-vector algorithm, and store distance information (hops, time) to adjacent routers. NLSP routers use a link-state algorithm. The link-state algorithm provides NLSP routers with the capability to store a complete logical map of the entire network. This map lets NLSP routers make more intelligent routing decisions than RIP-based routers, or, in practical terms, makes NLSP routers determine with greater ease the most efficient route to a destination. When changes occur on the network, the NLSP routers can quickly determine these changes and update their routing tables to reflect the network status. This is called *rapid convergence.*

Because NLSP is likely to select the most efficient route, using NLSP results in a more efficient use of network bandwidth, which is very important in large networks that have complex topologies and in which routing information needs to be transmitted over low-speed or expensive links.

Reduced Routing and Service Traffic on the Network

RIP routers, by default, broadcast their entire routing table and service database every 60 seconds, even if no change occurs in the route information. As the number of networks increases, the size of the routing messages also increases. An increase in the number of networks causes the number of routers also to increase. Each router contributes to the network routing traffic.

NLSP routers, on the other hand, do not broadcast their routing tables at periodic intervals. NLSP routers transmit information only if a change occurs to a route or service. NLSP routers broadcast changes in the routing and service information throughout the network. If the network interface supports multicast transmission, NLSP can use multicast to send changes to NLSP routers only. With multicasting, non-NLSP stations do not receive the NLSP link-state packets.

Scaling to Larger IPX Networks

NLSP gives you the ability to build and operate larger IPX networks than RIP makes possible. When you use RIP, IPX packets can travel through no more than 15 routers, but when you use NLSP, the packets can travel through as many as 127 NLSP routers.

NLSP routers use Djikstra's Open Shortest Path First algorithm to compute the shortest path. In general, this algorithm is more CPU-intensive than the distance-vector algorithm, which RIP uses. The computation of the route path cost is more CPU-intensive in NLSP than in RIP. However, the NLSP routers do not have to compute route path costs unless a change occurs in route or service information. On the other hand, RIP routers must compute route path costs whenever they receive a RIP broadcast, so must do so more frequently than NLSP.

Tests that Novell has performed on large networks indicate that the NLSP algorithms provide good performance and use a nominal amount of CPU. In a large network, you can expect NLSP to use up to 400 KB of server memory. This figure does not exclude the IPX protocol stack's memory image.

The packet size of the underlying network limits the number of NLSP routers connected to any LAN segment. An Ethernet LAN segment can have as many as 230 NLSP routers (router and server devices). Because token ring and FDDI networks have a larger packet size than Ethernet LANs, the number of routers limit is higher for these networks.

NLSP can coexist with other routing protocols, such as RIP, OSPF and IS-IS, and can even run on the same network or same router as the other routing protocols. Because NLSP information stricture is distinct from other routing protocols, it does not interfere with other routing protocols that run on the same network.

Reduced Overhead over WAN Links

Both SAP and RIP broadcast traffic can consume substantial bandwidth on a network. By default, both RIP and SAP propagate information in distance vector update messages every 60 seconds. For networks that have a limited bandwidth, such as low speed WAN links, the SAP and RIP network traffic easily can saturate the network. NLSP also can distribute routing and service information, but NLSP broadcasts that contain this information are sent only when a change occurs in a service or route, or every two hours—whichever occurs first. Additionally, NLSP uses a reliable delivery mechanism for transmitting and updating service information across a WAN connection, which eliminates the need for retransmissions that can consume network bandwidth.

If few changes occur in the routing and service information, NLSP reduces the advertising overhead to 1/120 of what SAP generates. Novell estimates that a typical network running NLSP can expect a 90 to 99 percent reduction in service advertising overhead.

Faster Data Transfer

NLSP uses compression to reduce network traffic and increase the data transfer rate. NLSP compresses the IPX packet headers and encodes the service information it carries in an efficient manner, which reduces the size of the packet and the overhead represented by the IPX header. These improvements are especially noticeable over low speed WAN links.

Compatibility with IPX RIP and SAP

NLSP routers can coexist and interoperate with traditional RIP and SAP services. NLSP can encapsulate and propagate the routing and service information it receives from RIP/SAP devices and networks to other networks that need this service. This interoperability provides a migration path to NLSP.

Improved Network Management

SNMP managers can use the SNMP agents that run on NLSP routers to access the *Management Information Base* (MIB) variables defined on the routers.

An SNMP manager, such as HP's OpenView, Novell's NMS, SUN's SunNet Manager and IBM's NetView, can access the information on NLSP routers. Some SNMP managers have already integrated the NLSP, IPX RIP, and SAP MIB variables. The NetWare IPX Router Upgrade software provides MIB variables in ASN.1 format so that you can use a MIB compiler to convert them into a format for your SNMP manager.

Because NLSP routers contain a topological map of the network, the SNMP managers can display a map of the entire IPX network from a single NLSP router.

Configurable Link-Cost Assignment

You can configure the route path cost of each link to the NLSP router. You can use the INET-CFG.NLM utility to set the cost of a link. You can base the cost of a link on parameters such as delay, hop, bandwidth, and so forth. The NLSP router uses the route path cost to determine the most efficient path for each outgoing packet, which makes it possible for you to designate that NLSP should route traffic through a preferred and less-costly link.

Load Balancing

If NLSP routers determine that two or more paths to a destination have the same link cost, the router distributes the traffic evenly among them, unlike RIP routers, which select only one route and ignore the rest, even if several routes have equal costs.

NLSP, therefore, is more efficient than RIP, because it automatically distributes network traffic across several network interfaces, called *load balancing*, and increases the data throughput for the network traffic.

You use the INETCFG.NLM utility for load balancing. You can use INETCFG.NLM to specify up to eight equal-cost paths. Alternatively, you can configure a router to use a single path.

Using the IPXRTR.NLM

The IPXRTR.NLM implements the IPX protocol with NLSP routing and full RIP/SAP functionality for network-level operations. You can use the IPXRTR.NLM to activate or disable RIP, SAP, and NLSP on any network interface within the same server or router. Therefore, you can use RIP and SAP on one interface, and NLSP on another. An interface also can use NLSP as the active routing protocol while processing RIP and SAP broadcasts from network nodes that use RIP and SAP.

You can use IPXTR to distribute network traffic to the server across several NICs attached to the server, called *load sharing* or *path splitting*. You can perform load sharing by using IPXRTR to bind IPX to several NICs at the server that connects to the same LAN, because doing so enables IntranetWare workstations on that LAN to use any of the server NICs during server access.

Migrating to an NLSP Network

This section outlines the steps you need to follow to migrate to an IPX network. You can configure NLSP on networks that range from a small LAN to a large enterprise-wide network. For large networks, you should perform the migration in phases in which you convert LAN segments to NLSP one at a time, which lets you solve any unexpected problems on a smaller scale, and provides you with the experience and confidence to manage NLSP services.

Selecting a Network Segment to Convert to NLSP

When you make your first NLSP conversion, try to select a network that has no more than 10 servers that run NetWare 3.x, 4.x, or IntranetWare, and no third-party routers that connect the LAN to other networks. You also might be interested in measuring existing network traffic due to SAP and RIP and comparing it with the network traffic when you convert to NLSP. You can use any of the following NetWare or IntranetWare software to examine server and network utilization:

- Use the `TRACK ON` server console command to note the frequency of incoming and outgoing RIP and SAP traffic on the server.
- Use a protocol analyzer, such as the LANalyzer, to record the percentage of network utilization that broadcast traffic consumes.
- If your IPX network has a large number of NetWare 3.x servers, load MONITOR on one of the servers on which you intend to install NLSP software. Note the CPU utilization for the server, which shows the percentage of time the CPU is busy. On a large network of NetWare 3.x servers, CPU utilization can exceed 95 percent during RIP and SAP broadcasts. You can compare this utilization to the CPU utilization after migration.

Steps for Migrating Servers to NLSP

The following is an outline of the steps for migrating the servers on the LAN:

1. Install and configure IntranetWare IPX Router Upgrade software on the IntranetWare server. This product and support documentation is available through the NetWire electronic bulletin board.
2. After you migrate the servers, use the methods outlined in the previous section to reexamine server and network performance.
3. Compare the network and server utilization with those you observed before you migrated the servers.
4. To migrate other parts of your IPX internetwork, you need to develop a migration strategy, outlined in the next section.

Developing an NLSP Migration Strategy

Your migration strategy must include a determination of the network size, which involves determining the number of internal and external network numbers in use on the network. The internal network numbers generally correspond to NetWare 3.x, NetWare 4.x and IntranetWare servers. You must then find out the version numbers of the servers and routing that exist on your network.

You can determine the size of your network by using the following NetWare or IntranetWare server console:

```
DISPLAY NETWORKS
```

The internal network number of each NetWare or IntranetWare server and the external network number of each network segment reachable from the NetWare or IntranetWare server should appear on-screen. The total number of network numbers should also appear at the end of the list.

Novell characterizes networks that have fewer than 400 network numbers as small networks. These networks are relatively easy to migrate, especially if they do not have third-party routers that do not support NLSP. In such networks, you can install the NLSP software on the servers in any order. Many major router vendors, such as Cisco and Wellfleet, provide upgrades that enable their routers to use NLSP.

Novell characterizes networks that have more than 400 network numbers as large networks. You should partition large networks into routing areas for efficiency and better performance. The next section covers partitioning the routing area.

During migration, do not disable RIP and SAP on any interface that has devices that depend on these services. You can disable these services after you install NLSP software on every system using RIP and SAP.

Partitioning an IPX Internet into Routing Areas

If your IPX network has more than 400 network numbers, Novell recommends that you partition your network into routing areas.

You use routing areas to establish a routing hierarchy within an IPX internetwork (see fig. 21.1). Routers that connect such a network are called *hierarchical routers.* Routers within a routing area are called *level 1 routers.* Using hierarchical routing allows routers to make routing decisions that involve two nodes in the same routing area to be made independent of other routing areas.

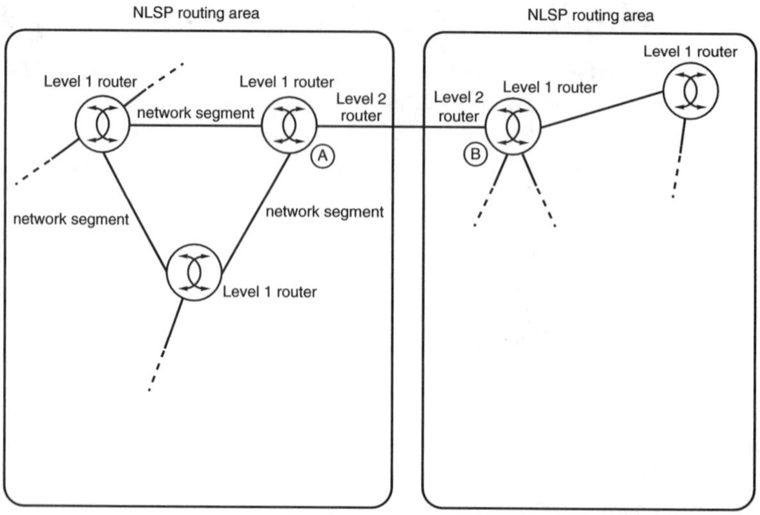

Figure 21.1
NLSP routing areas.

The routing tables for routers within a routing area need to know routing information only for networks within the routing area. Keeping routing tables small produces more efficient routing decisions and reduces the CPU power necessary for computing the topological map when changes occur in routing information. Using routing areas permits better scaling as the number of network segments, servers, and routers increase. You can treat each routing area as a separate, more manageable internetwork, which can lead to simpler network administration.

Routers that join adjacent routing areas are called *level 2 routing areas.* In figure 21.1, routers A and B act as both level 1 and level 2 routers.

Identifying a Routing Area

In IPX networks that do not use routing areas, the IPX network number (sometimes called the network address) identifies the network. When you use routing areas, you must identify the network numbers that belong to the same routing area. You can identify the network numbers by treating the 32-bit IPX network number as if it consists of two parts: the routing area number and the network number in the routing area, which is represented symbolically by the following:

```
N = <a, n>
```

Figure 21.2 shows the logical division of the 32-bit IPX network number. To show this logical division, you can use a 32-bit mask. Therefore, the following 32-bit numbers can completely describe a routing area:

- Network number
- Network mask

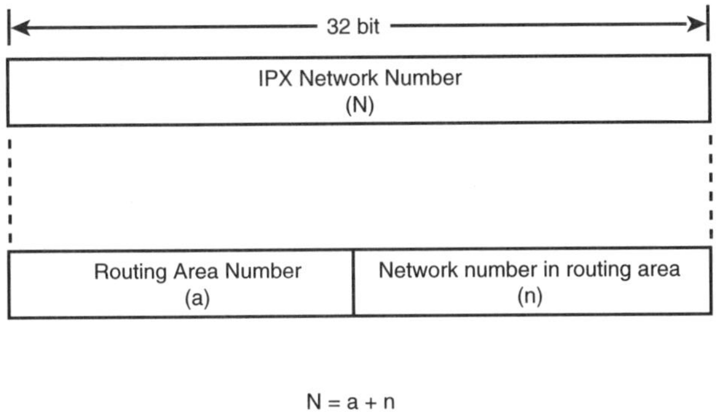

Figure 21.2
Logical division of the 32-bit IPX network number.

The 1s in the network mask correspond to the routing area and the 0s in the network mask correspond to the network number within that routing area. Consider the following description of a network number in a routing area:

Network number = D1127001

Network mask = FFFFF000

In this example, D1127 is the routing area number, and 001 is the network number within the routing area.

The default values for the network number and mask are 00000000. These default values are selected to ensure compatibility with future versions of NLSP. Zero values mean that all NLSP routers operate in a single routing area.

Network Number Assignments and the Novell Network Registry

The network numbers in a routing area must have a common routing area prefix. In the example in the previous section, in which the network number was D1127001 and the network mask was FFFFF000, the network numbers in the routing area all have a common prefix of D1127, which implies that you should assign a contiguous block of network numbers to a routing area.

If organizations, each with their own enterprise network, use an IPX router to connect to each other, they must assign a unique network number to each of their network segments. Novell offers the Novell Network Registry, which ensures that each organization has a unique network number (or range of network numbers) assigned to it. The Novell Network Registry service assigns and tracks IPX network numbers and organization names, so participating organizations can share data between interconnected IPX networks without name and address conflicts.

The Novell Network Registry assigns a contiguous block of IPX network numbers that are unique to an organization. The size of the contiguous network number block depends on the number of IPX network segments and servers in your IPX internetwork, including any additional LANs or servers you anticipate installing over the next two years.

You can contact the Novell Network Registry at 1-408-577-7506 or send Internet e-mail to `registry@novell.com`, or through e-mail. The MHS e-mail address is `registry@novell`. You must ask for a publication titled *The Novell Network Registry*.

Using RIP to Partition Routing Areas

Although NLSP supports hierarchical routing, initial releases of NLSP do not support interarea (level 2) routing. You can, however, create routing areas by using RIP on the network interfaces used to link the areas (see fig. 21.3).

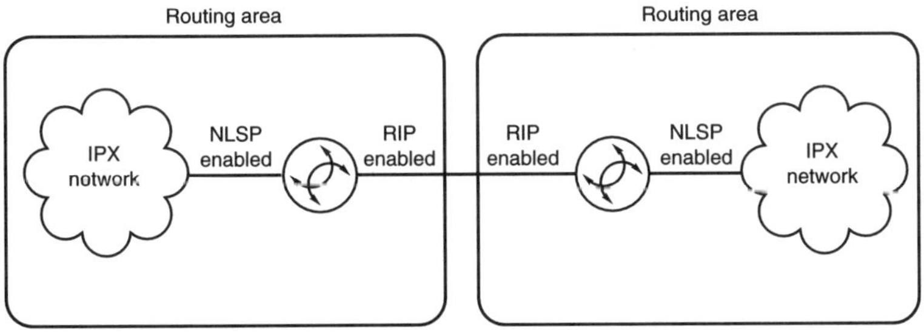

Figure 21.3
Using RIP to link routing areas.

If you use a NetWare or IntranetWare server as a router, you would enable NLSP routing by using the following command at the server:

```
LOAD IPXRTR ROUTING=NLSP
```

When RIP is enabled, and you use the TRACK ON command to observe RIP and SAP messages, the "Router tracking screen" appears. However, when NLSP is enabled, separate RIP Tracking and SAP Tracking screens appear when you use the TRACK ON command.

If you use NetWare 4.x or IntranetWare you should use the INETCFG.NLM to complete the NLSP configuration. The following is an outline of these steps:

1. Run INETCFG.

   LOAD INETCFG.

   If this is the first time you load INETCFG, you should transfer the LOAD and BIND statements in the AUTOEXEC.NCF to the INITSYS.NCF and the NETINFO.CFG files in the SYS:ETC directory so that INETCFG.NLM can manage them.

   Listing 21.1 is a sample SYS:ETC\ INITSYS.NCF file that you can invoke from the AUTOEXEC.NCF.

Listing 21.1

```
#! -- WARNING -- WARNING -- WARNING -- WARNING -- WARNING -- WARNING --
#! This file was created by the Internetworking Configuration Console.
#! It is intended to be modified ONLY by the configurator (INETCFG.NLM).
#! Tampering with this file may cause severe malfunctioning of the system.
#! The configurator will check for tampering and abort if it is detected.
#! -- -- -- -- -- -- -- -- -- -- -- -- -- -- -- -- -- -- -- -- -- -- -- --
load snmp config=Sys:Etc
initialize system
```

The INITIALIZE SYSTEM command uses the statements in the SYS:ETC\NETINFO.CFG file to perform the network load driver and bindings. A sample SYS:ETC\NETINFO.CFG file is shown in listing 21.2.

Listing 21.2

```
#!VERSION=2.2
#!
#! -- WARNING -- WARNING -- WARNING -- WARNING -- WARNING -- WARNING --
#! This file was created by the Internetworking Configuration Console.
#! It is intended to be modified ONLY by the configurator (INETCFG.NLM).
#! Tampering with this file may cause severe malfunctioning of the system.
#! The configurator will check for tampering and abort if it is detected.
#! -- -- -- -- -- -- -- -- -- -- -- -- -- -- -- -- -- -- -- -- -- -- --
#!
#!SERVERTYPE=NORMAL
#!SERVERNAME=NW4CS
#!
#!BEGINGENLOAD
LOAD SNMP
#!END
#!
#!BEGINTSMLOAD
#!END
#!
#!BEGINBOARD DRVR=NE2000 NAME=NE2000_1 STATUS=ENABLED NUMPORTS=1 DRVRTYPE=LAN
VARIABLEPORTS=NO_PORTPARAM=CHANNEL INT=F PORT=300
#Transferred from AUTOEXEC.NCF
#!BEGINPORT NAME=NE2000_1 NUMBER=1 STATUS=ENABLED FRAMES=YES NUMLINKS=1
MEDIA=EtherTsm WANFRAME=UNCONFIGURED
#Transferred from AUTOEXEC.NCF
#!REFCOUNT=2
LOAD NE2000 NAME=NE2000_1_E83 FRAME=ETHERNET_802.3 INT=F PORT=300
#!REFCOUNT=2
LOAD NE2000 NAME=NE2000_1_E82 FRAME=ETHERNET_802.2 INT=F PORT=300
#!REFCOUNT=2
LOAD NE2000 NAME=NE2000_1_EII FRAME=ETHERNET_II INT=F PORT=300
#!END
#!END
#!
#!BEGINPROTO PROTO=TCPIP STATUS=ENABLED
LOAD TCPIP
#Transferred from AUTOEXEC.NCF
#!BEGINBIND STATUS=ENABLED
BIND IP NE2000_1_EII MASK=FF.FF.FF.0 ADDRESS=199.245.180.10
#199.245.180.10
#!END
#!END
#!
#!BEGINPROTO PROTO=IPX STATUS=ENABLED
SET Reply To Get Nearest Server=ON
#
LOAD IPXRTR ROUTING=NLSP CFGDIR=SYS:ETC SEQ=3
#
LOAD IPXRTRNM SEQ=3
#
```

```
LOAD SPXCONFG Q=1 A=540 V=108 W=54 R=10 S=1000 I=1200
#
SET IPX NetBIOS Replication Option=2
#
#!BEGINBIND STATUS=ENABLED
BIND IPX NE2000_1_E82 NET=E8022
#E8022
#!END
#!BEGINBIND STATUS=ENABLED
BIND IPX NE2000_1_E83 NET=E8023
#E8023
#!END
#!END
```

If you use INETCFG.NLM, you should modify only the previously listed files. If you try to manually modify these files, you can cause severe malfunctioning of the system.

A result of running the INETCFG.NLM program is that it removes from the AUTOEXEC.NCF file all references to the LOAD and BIND statements. The INETCFG.NLM program adds a command to load the CONLOG.NLM for recording console messages, and a command to run the SYS:ETC\INITSYS.NCF file. A sample AUTOEXEC.NCF file is shown in listing 21.3.

Listing 21.3

```
set Time Zone = MST7MDT
set Daylight Savings Time Offset = 1:00:00
set Start Of Daylight Savings Time = (APRIL SUNDAY FIRST  2:00:00 AM)
set End Of Daylight Savings Time = (OCTOBER SUNDAY LAST  2:00:00 AM)
set Default Time Server Type = SINGLE
set Bindery Context = OU=CORP.O=ESL;O=ESL
file server name NW4CS
ipx internal net F0004101
load conlog  maximum=100
; Network driver LOADs and BINDs are initiated via
; INITSYS.NCF. The actual LOAD and BIND commands
; are contained in INITSYS.NCF and NETINFO.CFG.
; These files are in SYS:ETC.
sys:etc\initsys.ncf
#load NE2000.LAN INT=F PORT=300 FRAME=Ethernet_802.3  NAME=NE2000_1_E83
#bind IPX to NE2000_1_E83 net=E8023
#load NE2000.LAN INT=F PORT=300 FRAME=Ethernet_802.2  NAME=NE2000_1_E82
#bind IPX to NE2000_1_E82 net=E8022
#LOAD TCPIP
#LOAD NE2000 INT=F PORT=300 FRAME=Ethernet_II  NAME=NE2000_1_EII
#BIND IP NE2000_1_EII ADDR=199.245.180.10 MASK=ff.ff.ff.0
SET NDS trace to file = On
SET NDS trace to screen = 80
load pserver .cn=ps_0.ou=corp.o=esl
mount all
```

2. Select Protocols from the Internetworking configuration menu. You should see a list of protocols and their configuration status (see fig. 21.4).

3. Select IPX. The IPX configuration parameters should appear (see fig. 21.5).

Figure 21.4
Protocol Configuration status.

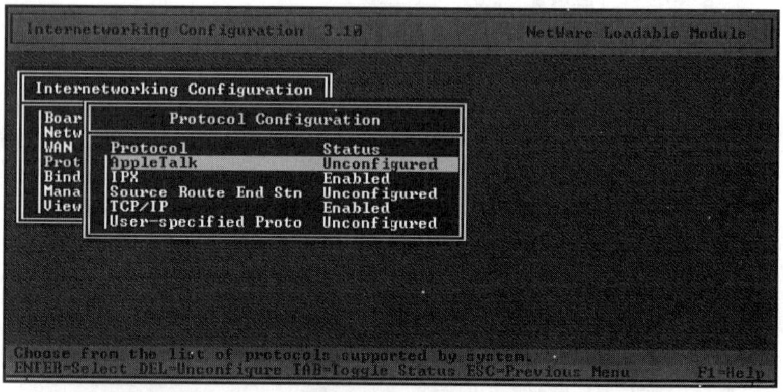

Figure 21.5
Protocol Configuration parameters.

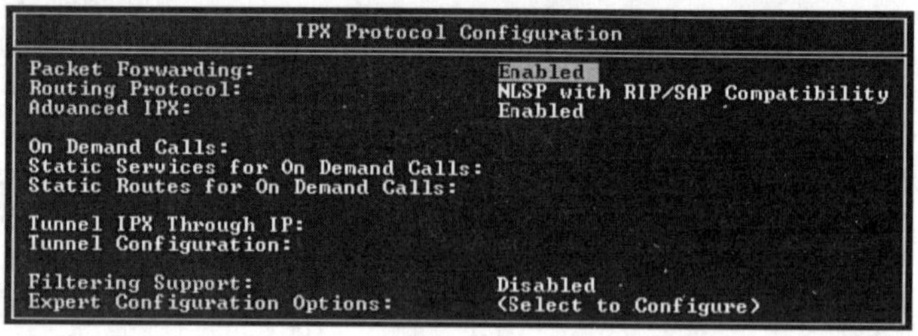

4. Set the Routing Protocol parameter to NLSP with RIP Compatibility.

5. Save your changes.

6. If you use RIP to link the routing areas, turn off NLSP and turn on RIP and SAP on the network interface that links the areas, using the following BIND IPX statement:

```
BIND IPX boardname NET=network_number RIP=YES _SAP=YES NLSP=NO
```

If you use NetWare 4.1, complete the following steps:

6a. Load INETCFG.

6b. Select Bindings.

6c. Select the network interface that links the areas.

6d. Select Expert Bind Options, then choose RIP Bind Options.

Set the RIP State parameter to On.

6e. Return to the Expert Bind Options window, then select SAP Bind Options.

Set the SAP State parameter to On.

6f. Return to the Expert Bind Options window, then select NLSP Bind Options.

Set the NLSP State parameter to Off.

6g. Save your changes.

Even though NLSP is disabled on the interface at the area boundary, each router still imports the routes and services from the connected network into its own routing area.

7. Changes made using the INETCFG.NLM are not effective immediately. You can restart the server, or use the REINITIALIZE SYSTEM console command.

Filtering between Routing Areas

Sometimes preventing RIP and SAP traffic on one network to cross over to another network is desirable. You might want to do so to prevent users on a network segment from gaining access to the services on another network. You can use service filters or routing filters to restrict access to services and network segments on another network. You cannot filter routes or services within a routing area, but you can use IPX filtering to filter routes and services between areas at the area boundaries.

If you use route and service filters, you must configure all NLSP routers connected to the same LAN within the same area. If you use NLSP routers, all NLSP routers in the same area share the same link state information. To reduce the amount of NLSP traffic for NLSP routers connected to a common LAN, a single router, called the designated router, imports routes and services for that LAN. You must, therefore, configure the inbound route or service filter on all NLSP routers, or at least the designated router, before the filter can be effective.

Identifying Routing Areas

When you identify routing areas for a large network, you need to decide what constitutes the core backbone structure of the network. The core backbone, then, becomes the principal means of connecting the different routing areas.

If you have more than one RIP connection between a backbone router and a single routing area, the routers duplicate the same routing and service information from the backbone into the routing area through each router connection, which is a situation you want to avoid.

If you partition routing areas across WAN links, you can end up with SAP/RIP traffic across the WAN link, which can consume a significant amount of network bandwidth. You should run NLSP over the WAN links to avoid the network traffic overhead of RIP and SAP.

Define only one routing area per LAN. Typically a LAN is built using a broadcast-based technology. Nodes and router connections to a broadcast-based LAN constitute a logical area. Also, if NLSP routers on the LAN automatically share a common area prefix, they become neighbors to form a single routing area.

The following are examples of identifying routing areas.

Identifying Routing Areas for a Corporate WAN Backbone

Figure 21.6 shows an example of a network that has four IntranetWare LANs joined by a network backbone. The network backbone consists of routers and WAN links. Figure 21.6 illustrates one possible WAN backbone. The positioning of the routers in the backbone depends on the amount of network traffic between the different LANs. In figure 21.6, the routers WR2, WR3, and WR4 are connected to each other in anticipation of the high volume of traffic between these routing areas. Also, if any one of the WAN links between routers WR2, WR3, and WR4 go down, the interconnected LANs can be reached through the other WAN links. Figure 21.7 illustrates another possible WAN backbone structure that does not involve additional links. Only three WAN links are in this backbone, as opposed to four WAN links in figure 21.6. Because this type of backbone has fewer WAN links, it is less expensive, and also does not provide the extra level of redundancy of the backbone in figure 21.6.

Figure 21.6
Routing areas on a backbone network.

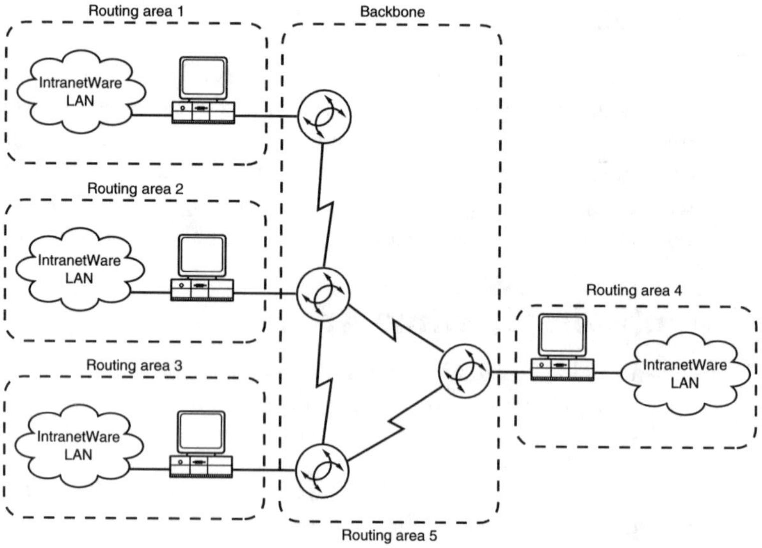

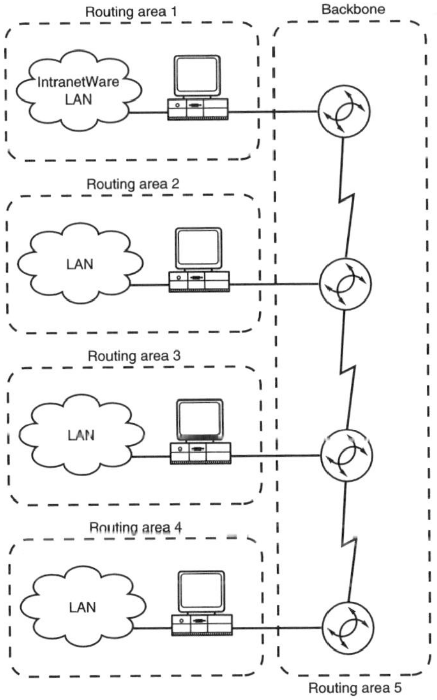

Figure 21.7
A simplified network backbone.

You could partition the network shown in figure 21.6 into the five routing areas labeled 1 to 5. The network backbone that joins the routing areas corresponding to the LANs forms its own separate routing area. Treating each LAN as a separate routing area is convenient, because it enables you to treat the LAN as an autonomous network. An autonomous network has its own administration, free to select any routing protocol within its autonomous network.

You should enable NLSP routing on the WAN links. Using RIP and SAP on the WAN link can consume a substantial portion of the WAN link bandwidth. On the network interface that joins the backbone router to the LAN, you can use NLSP or RIP/SAP. If you want to gradually migrate from a RIP/SAP environment to an NLSP environment, you can convert the backbone to use NLSP and then convert the LAN routing areas to NLSP. If you use older devices and applications on the LAN that rely on SAP and RIP, you might need to continue to use RIP and SAP on the LANs. If you use NLSP on the backbone network, the RIP/SAP traffic does not traverse the backbone.

If you use an earlier version of NLSP that does not support hierarchical routing, you need to use RIP/SAP to join the routing areas, which means that the interface between the backbone router and routing areas use RIP and SAP, even though the backbone and the LANs use NLSP.

Identifying Routing Areas in the Presence of a Transit LAN

A *transit LAN* is defined as a high-speed LAN, such as a high-speed token ring or a Fiber Distributed Data Interface (FDDI) ring, that serves as a backbone for all internetwork traffic. Because it acts as a backbone, a transit LAN can link several routing areas. Figure 21.8 shows an FDDI transit LAN in which routing areas 1 and 2 are autonomous LANs. Routing area 3 is a WAN backbone routing area that can join other sites. Four *feeder routers,* also called *branch office routers,* are used to link several branch office LANs to the transit LAN.

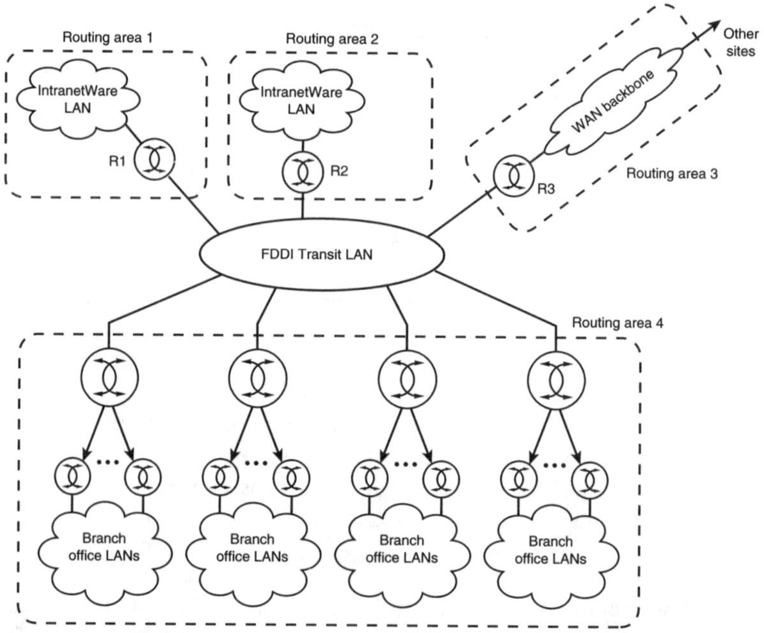

Figure 21.8
Routing areas in a transit LAN.

If you use an earlier version of NLSP that does not support hierarchical routing (nonhierarchical NLSP), you must use RIP/SAP to join the routing areas. For later versions of NLSP that support hierarchical routing, you can use NLSP to join the routing areas.

For nonhierarchical NLSP, RIP/SAP routing is enabled on the network interface between routers R1 and R2 that connect routing areas 1 and 2 to the transit LAN. NLSP routing can be enabled on the network interface between routers R1, R2, and routing areas 1 and 2.

If you use nonhierarchical NLSP, backbone router R3 has to use RIP/SAP to connect to the FDDI transit LAN. NLSP routing is used on the network interface between the backbone router, R3, and the WAN backbone network. Use of NLSP routing on this interface allows the routing and service information received from the transit LAN to be converted to LSPs.

Because the backbone router is running NLSP on the interface to the backbone network, it incorporates the route and service information it receives from the LAN routers into its LSPs. The backbone router passes these LSPs to the backbone network.

In routing area 4, the feeder routers, branch office routers, and branch office LANs use NLSP routing. NLSP routing is enabled on all the network interfaces of these routers. The feeder routers use NLSP to exchange information amongst themselves and RIP/SAP with the three other routers on the transit LAN.

Migration to NLSP with Different NetWare Versions

NetWare 3.x, 4.x, and IntranetWare servers support NLSP. NLSP support is bundled with current release of IntranetWare. If you have earlier versions of NetWare 3.x, you might need to download the NetWare IPX Router Upgrade from NetWire or Novell's FTP server at `ftp.novell.com`. A quick way to check if your server has NLSP support is to run the following command from the server console:

```
LOAD IPXRTR
```

If the IPXRTR.NLM loads, you have NLSP support on your server; otherwise, you do not have NLSP support on your server.

NetWare 2.x (and earlier versions) do not have NLSP support. These older servers can only use RIP and SAP for route and service information. If you have not upgraded these older servers, and still plan to run NLSP, you can still interoperate with these servers, because NLSP software can receive and broadcast RIP and SAP packets.

On an IPX network that runs NLSP and has NetWare 2.x servers, NLSP automatically detects NetWare 2.x servers and updates them with RIP and SAP broadcasts. So, to limit RIP and SAP broadcasts through the network, you should place all the NetWare 2.x servers on a single LAN.

Migration to NLSP with Devices That Require RIP and SAP

A number of devices, applications, and operating system platforms require SAP and RIP. If such devices are connected to your network, you must consider the dependence of these devices on SAP and RIP. Fortunately, NLSP can operate in a SAP/RIP compatibility mode, which makes it possible to use these devices on an NLSP-based network.

Novell's MultiProtocol Router versions 2.0, 2.1, and 2.11 support RIP-based IPX routing. The servers or dedicated routers running the 2.x versions of MPR can use RIP and SAP and still operate with NLSP. NLSP converts the SAP/RIP information to NLSP's link state packets.

If UnixWare clients use the internal Unix NetWare client rather than the DOS NetWare client, you must enable RIP and SAP explicitly on the server network interface that is on the same network segment as the UnixWare client (see fig. 21.9). Similarly, if an OS/2 client runs a Named Pipe application, you also must enable RIP and SAP explicitly on the server's network interface (see fig. 21.9). You can enable SAP and RIP by adding the RIP=YES and SAP=YES parameters on the BIND console command. This assumes that you use the NetWare IPX Router Upgrade on the connected system; that is, you have loaded the IPXRTR NLM. The following is an example of the BIND command that enables RIP and SAP on the network interface:

```
BIND IPX boardname NET=network_number RIP=YES _SAP=YES
```

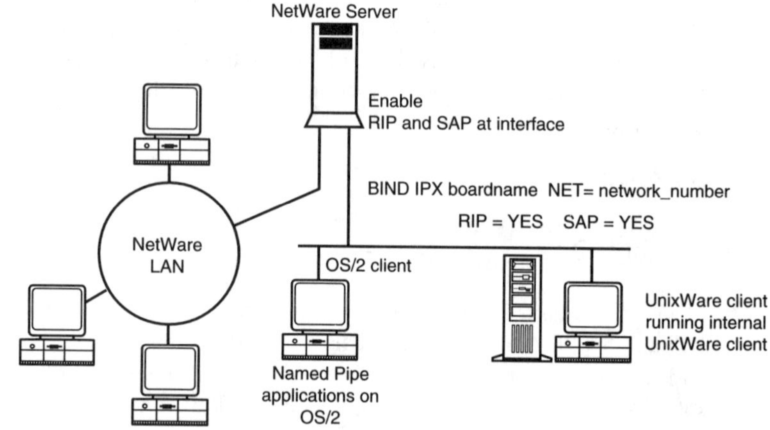

Figure 21.9
UnixWare and OS/2 clients on an NetWare LAN.

If you have installed NLSP software on a server that runs NetWare/IP, you must enable RIP and SAP and disable NLSP on the interface to which IPX is bound (see fig. 21.10). You can enable SAP and RIP and disable NLSP by adding the RIP=YES, SAP=YES, and NLSP=NO parameters for the BIND console command. This assumes that you used the NetWare IPX Router Upgrade on the connected system; that is, you have loaded the IPXRTR NLM. The following is an example of the BIND command that enables RIP and SAP, but disables NLSP:

```
BIND IPX boardname NET=network_number NLSP=NO _RIP=YES SAP=YES
```

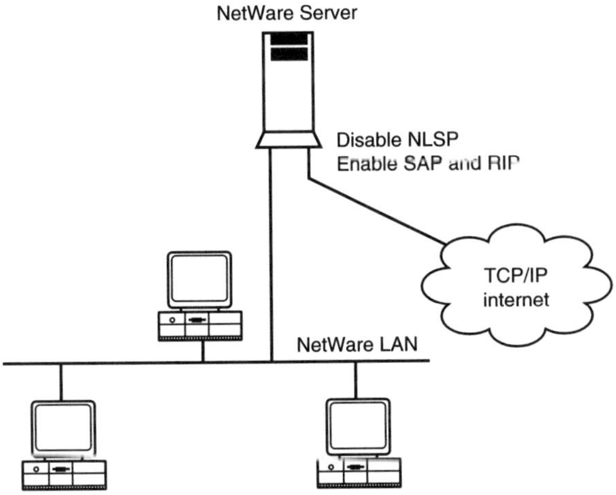

Figure 21.10
NetWare/IP and NLSP on the server.

Summary

NetWare and IntranetWare servers typically rely on the Routing Information Protocol to route IPX packets and the SAP protocol to discover IntranetWare-related services on the network. Use of RIP and SAP can lead to excessive network traffic. On a low speed WAN link, SAP and RIP network traffic can consume a substantial portion of the network bandwidth. Moreover, RIP, because it is a distance-vector protocol, does not scale well with increase in size of network, and does not stabilize rapidly with changes in network routes.

To solve these problems, Novell has designed a link state protocol called NLSP that can be used for exchanging routing information and transmitting IntranetWare service information. NLSP can be used to replace the traditional RIP and SAP protocols that are used for exchanging routing and service information. NLSP makes use of the link state algorithm that requires that information be sent only when there are changes in routing and service information.

This chapter discussed how NLSP is implemented on an IntranetWare server, and describes different migration strategies to help you migrate your network to use the more efficient NLSP services.

CHAPTER 22

NetWare/IP Connectivity Services

The communication between a NetWare workstation and a NetWare server takes place using the IPX network layer (OSI layer 3) protocol. When NetWare was originally designed, Novell developed IPX based on the Internet Datagram Protocol (IDP) found in the Xerox Network System (XNS) network protocols used in Xerox networks. In the mid-1980s, TCP/IP, which originated as a protocol used on the old ARPANET, became a de facto standard not only in universities and research organizations, but also in the commercial sector. Although TCP/IP has traditionally been used in Unix networks, it is not limited to running on Unix networks. Today, TCP/IP is available on all major computer/operating-system platforms ranging from microcomputers to mainframes. This chapter examines how a product called NetWare/IP can be used to provide access to NCP services using TCP/IP. This chapter also introduces the Dynamic Host Configuration Protocol (DHCP) used for dynamically assigning and administering TCP/IP addresses.

Understanding the Need for NetWare/IP

Novell began supporting TCP/IP at the NetWare server in 1988 using technology it obtained through the purchase of Excelan of San Jose. Today, every NetWare 3.1x and 4.x server ships with a TCPIP.NLM that implements the TCP/IP protocol at the server. The TCPIP.NLM can be used to convert a NetWare server to an IP router and provide transport services for TCP/IP applications that can run at the server. The NetWare *Network File System* (NFS) product is an example of TCP/IP applications that run at the NetWare server. The NetWare NFS product implements NFS server, *File Transfer Protocol* (FTP) server, Unix-to-NetWare, and NetWare-to-Unix print gateways. NetWare NFS is now included with IntranetWare.

Until the development of NetWare/IP there was no way to send NCP requests to a NetWare server using TCP/IP. The LAN Workplace products or third-party products from FTP Software, Chameleon, Beam & Whiteside, and so on can be used to talk to TCP/IP applications such as FTP, NFS, and print gateways at the server, but they cannot be used to obtain NCP services from a NetWare server.

NetWare/IP allows the native IPX protocol service to be replaced by the TCP/IP transport services (see fig. 22.1). Many organizations have a mix of TCP/IP and IPX protocols running on their networks. Typically, TCP/IP is used by engineering workstations and large machines, and IPX is used by NetWare workstations and servers. Network managers have to support and understand both types of protocols. With NetWare/IP, IPX can be replaced by TCP/IP. This allows an organization to support only one protocol: the de facto TCP/IP.

Figure 22.1
Use of TCP/IP in NetWare/IP.

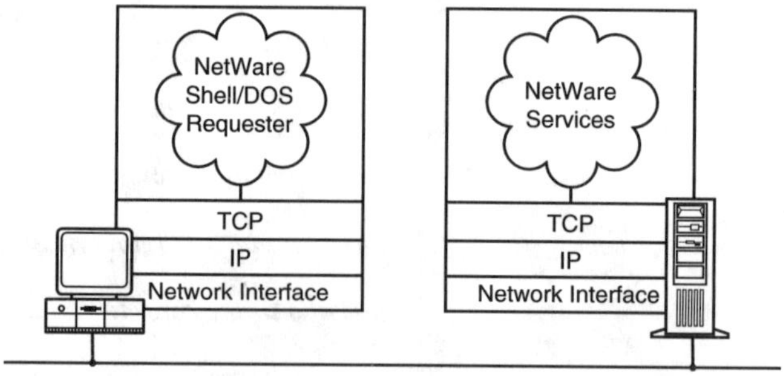

NetWare/IP consists of a set of NLMs and client software that allows NetWare 3.1x and 4.x servers to use TCP/IP as their transport protocol for communicating with NetWare workstations. The NetWare workstations can be configured to use TCP/IP exclusively, or they can use TCP/IP in addition to the native IPX protocol.

NetWare/IP is now distributed as part of IntranetWare. NetWare/IP 2.2C is included in the package and is still backward-compatible with NetWare 3.1x and 4.x servers. The NetWare/IP product comes with the DOS TCP/IP transport stack (TCPIP.EXE) from the LAN Workplace for DOS products.

Some of the benefits of NetWare/IP include the following:

- Network managers have the option of running IP-only networks. This is valuable for those organizations that standardized on TCP/IP as their protocol of choice. Routers on such networks can be configured to handle the IP packet only.
- Existing NetWare 3.1x and 4.x applications can continue to run and use TCP/IP as their transport protocol. These applications that use the standard NetWare APIs can run unmodified on a NetWare/IP node.
- Cost in managing network protocols is reduced because the network engineers who troubleshoot and configure network nodes have to understand and configure only one protocol—TCP/IP.
- NetWare/IPX and NetWare/IP networks can coexist. NetWare/IP has a feature called the NetWare/IP gateway that can be used to transparently connect native NetWare IPX networks with NetWare/IP networks. This gateway allows NetWare IPX clients to access NetWare/IP servers, and also allows NetWare/IP clients to access NetWare servers on the IPX network.
- The NetWare/IP gateway enables you to gradually convert NetWare clients to use NetWare/IP while allowing the network to function.
- NetWare/IP includes an application called XCONSOLE. This runs as an NLM at the server, and allows an X Windows terminal to act as a console from which NetWare/IP can be managed. Unix workstations or terminals that have X Windows can manage a NetWare/IP server. These Unix users have a choice of Windows manager such as MOTIF, OpenLook, or TWM.

Configurations Using NetWare/IP

Examples of network configurations that use NetWare/IP can clarify how NetWare/IP can be used. The following sections give some examples.

IP Backbone with IPX Islands

Consider an organization that standardized on using TCP/IP on its backbone network. A good reason for doing this, besides the fact that TCP/IP is now a de facto standard, is that the organization also has connectivity to the Internet, which is predominantly based on TCP/IP. It is also possible for such an organization to have a policy in which IPX can be used on local networks as long as the backbone only uses TCP/IP. Reasons for using TCP/IP exclusively on the backbone include the reduced costs of configuring backbone devices and of training personnel to administer the backbone. Another reason to use TCP/IP on the backbone is that TCP/IP has been proven to work efficiently on a WAN that has long delays in transmission and a variability in the delay. Local departments within the organization may, however, prefer the ease of configuration of IPX networks that do not require an explicit IPX network address assignment per workstation. Also managers of NetWare LANs are traditionally unfamiliar with the configuration requirements of TCP/IP networks. Because of this, it may be preferable for departmental networks to continue using IPX for accessing NetWare servers.

Figure 22.2 shows a campus network that has an IP backbone used to connect departmental networks. The departmental LANs run IPX to access NetWare servers. These departmental LANs can be joined to the IP backbone using the NetWare/IP gateway. This network configuration allows local departments to continue using IPX while IP is used on the backbone. The users in a department can continue using IPX locally and access servers in other departments using the IP backbone and the NetWare/IP servers configured as IPX-to-IP gateways.

Figure 22.2
IP Backbone with IPX islands.

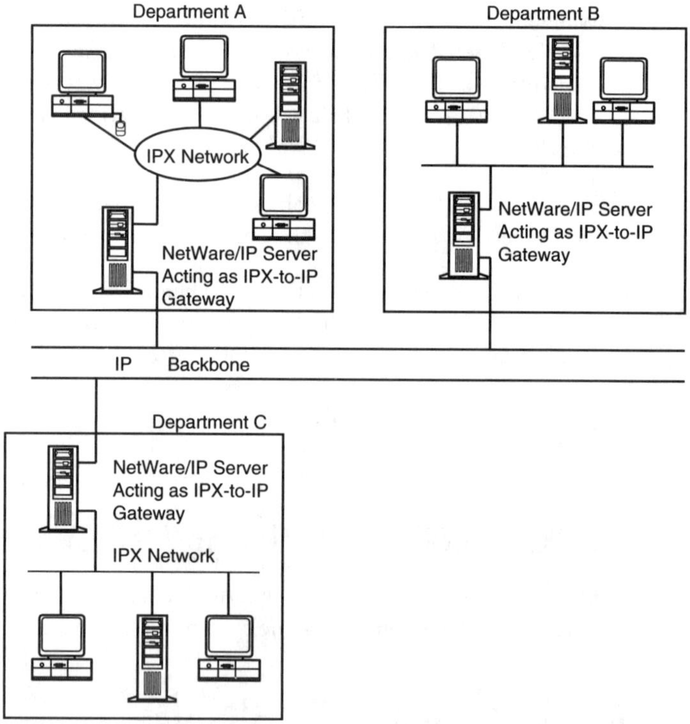

This configuration also gives the organization the option of gradually converting the local NetWare IPX environment to one based on using IP entirely. After all the servers in a department are converted to NetWare/IP servers, the workstations can be configured to use TCP/IP as their transport protocol. The NetWare/IP server configured as an IPX-to-IP gateway can then be configured as an IP router instead. Alternatively, you can replace the IPX-to-IP gateway function with a dedicated IP router.

An IP-Only Network

Figure 22.3 shows a network that uses IP only. This configuration can be used by a department that has many locations scattered over long distances. NetWare/IP allows each NetWare server and workstation to use the TCP/IP protocols, which work equally well on LAN and WAN links. The NetWare workstations at each location have access to all NetWare servers on the local network and other locations.

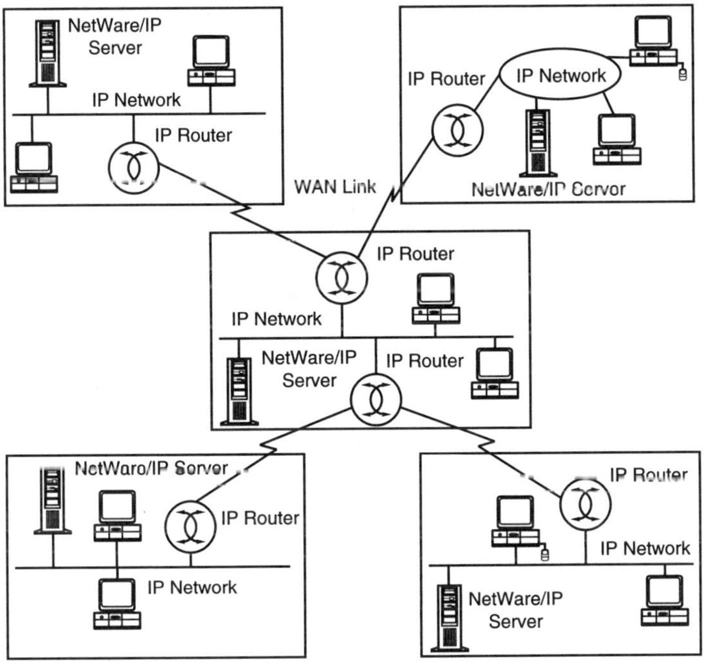

Figure 22.3
An IP-only NetWare network.

The networks in figure 22.3 also can support non-NetWare workstations and servers that also use TCP/IP protocols. This allows the entire enterprise to be based on a single TCP/IP protocol.

Examining NetWare/IP

NetWare/IP has the following components:

- **NetWare/IP server.** This is a series of NLMs that run on a NetWare 3.1x or 4.x server. These NLMs enable NetWare applications that previously used IPX to use TCP/IP as their transport protocol.

- **NetWare/IP client.** This allows a network workstation configured with an NIC to use TCP/IP protocols instead of (or in addition to) the IPX protocol. The NetWare client must be configured to use ODI drivers. The NetWare client support includes a TCP/IP stack implemented by TCPIP.EXE. Additional modules needed are NWIP.EXE, used for emulating the IPX Far Call interface, and a shell (NETX.EXE) or DOS Requester. If the VLMs are used, the NETX.VLM can be used to access bindery-based servers. To access NetWare 4.x servers, the DOS Requester VLMs are needed.

- **Domain Name System (DNS) server.** A NetWare server can be set up as a DNS server. The DNS server provides a distributed name look-up service that resolves symbolic names of hosts to their IP addresses. NetWare/IP clients use the DNS to look up the name of their nearest *Domain SAP Servers* (DSS).

- **Domain SAP/RIP Servers (DSS).** These are used as repositories of SAP/RIP information on the network. *Service Advertising Protocol* (SAP) is used in NetWare networks by NetWare services to advertise themselves to the rest of the network. *Routing Information Protocol* (RIP) is used to exchange IPX routing information. Using DSS, it is possible to partition networks into domains called NetWare/IP domains so that NetWare/IP clients and servers know of services in their NetWare/IP domain only.

Novell estimates, based on an internal study, that NetWare/IP provides comparable performance to NetWare IPX-based networks. On the average, the throughput of NetWare/IP is eight percent less than using IPX for the network transport. Most applications will not notice a performance loss.

Understanding NetWare/IP Domains

NetWare/IP domains should not be confused with DNS domains used in IP networks as a general purpose name look-up service for host names. Whereas DNS can be used by a mix of NetWare workstations, NetWare servers, and Unix-based machines, DSS is used only in NetWare networks. DSS and DNS servers can coexist on a network without any conflict.

Figure 22.4 shows an IP network for three separate departments of the hypothetical organization SCS. These department networks can be in different locations and are connected using IP routers. Department A has server NWS1 and workstation WS1; Department B has server NWS2 and workstation WS2; and Department C has server NWS3 and client WS3.

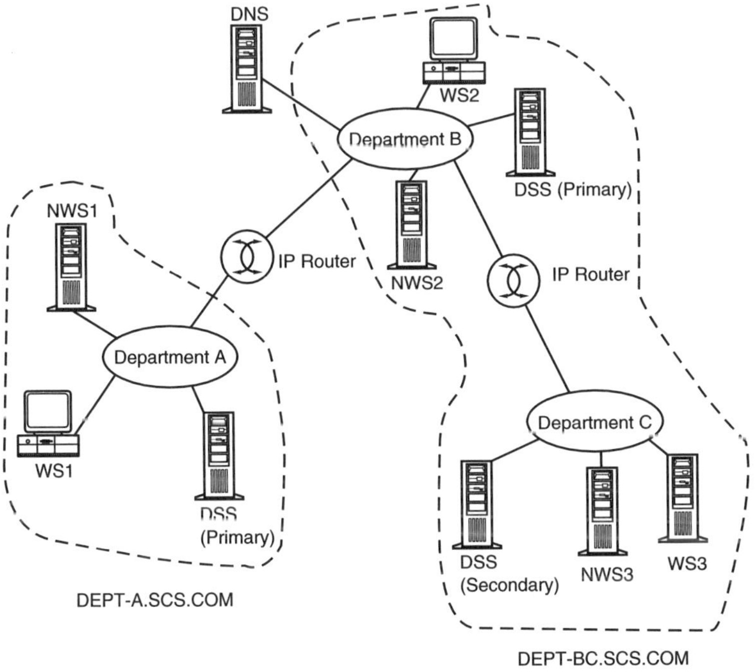

Figure 22.4
NetWare/IP domains.

You can have one logical NetWare/IP domain encompassing the entire network or break the network into several logical domains.

The NetWare/IP domain must have at least one Domain SAP/RIP Server, called the *primary DSS server*. The DSS server acts as a repository for all SAP/RIP information. It broadcasts SAP/RIP information at periodic intervals to workstations and servers within the NetWare/IP domain. By performing this action, it emulates the requirements for SAP/RIP broadcasts for an IPX network. NetWare/IP nodes learn of services on a NetWare network from the DSS. NetWare/IP servers communicate with the DSS periodically to obtain and update SAP/RIP updates. When a NetWare/IP client uses commands such as SLIST (NetWare 3.x), NLIST SERVER (NetWare 4.x), or DISPLAY SERVERS (console command) that require SAP information, the NetWare/IP server responds with information obtained from a DSS server.

It is not necessary for a DSS server to also be a NetWare/IP server. In other words, the DSS server does not have to be running NWIP.NLM, the component that implements the NetWare/IP server. The NLM needed for implementing DSS is DSS.NLM.

The primary DSS server supports all NetWare/IP nodes (clients and servers) in its NetWare/IP domain. The NetWare/IP nodes use DNS to find the name of the nearest DSS for obtaining SAP/RIP information.

You might decide to divide the IP network into several logical NetWare/IP domains. Reasons for doing this include the following:

- To limit the amount of SAP/RIP information that must be maintained by DSS servers for a domain
- To reduce the processing overhead on a DSS server

You also can increase efficiency by spreading the processing load across multiple DSS servers deployed throughout the network.

Figure 22.4 shows a network divided into two NetWare/IP domains. One NetWare/IP domain encompasses the Department A network, and the other NetWare/IP domain encompasses the Department B and Department C networks. The NetWare/IP domains are shown with the following names:

- DEPT-A.SCS.COM (Department A network)
- DEPT-BC.SCS.COM (Department B and Department C networks)

The choice of names for the NetWare/IP domain such as DEPT-A or DEPT-BC is arbitrary. Use a convention that meets the needs of your organization. Novell documentation suggests Department B and Department C networks NWIP.SCS.COM and NWIP2.SCS.COM as names for the NetWare/IP domain.

The NetWare/IP domain DEPT-A.SCS.COM has a single primary DSS. The NetWare/IP domain DEPT-BC.SCS.COM has a primary DSS and a secondary DSS. The secondary DSS is located in the department C network. This makes it possible for the department C network to obtain SAP/RIP information by contacting a local DSS server rather than going across a router (and potentially slow and expensive WAN links) to obtain SAP/RIP information from the primary DSS server for domain DEPT-BC.SCS.COM.

If a NetWare/IP client in a NetWare/IP domain needs access to a server in another domain, you can use the NWIPMAP.EXE utility that comes with NetWare/IP to create a drive mapping to the server. In the example in figure 22.4, if WS1 needs to access the PUBLIC directory on server NWS2 in domain DEPT-BC.SCS.COM, it can do so by creating a drive mapping H: to the PUBLIC directory of S2 as follows:

```
NWIPMAP H: = S2/SYS:PUBLIC@DEPT-BC.NOVELL.COM
```

Figure 22.4 shows a DNS server outside the NetWare/IP domains. This emphasizes the point that NetWare/IP domains are used for NetWare-based networks, and DNS servers can be used by NetWare and non-NetWare nodes (UNIX, VMS, MVS, and so on).

NetWare/IP Workstation Components

Figure 22.5 shows the NetWare workstation architecture that uses IPX only, and figure 22.6 shows the workstation architecture that uses TCP/IP to access NetWare services.

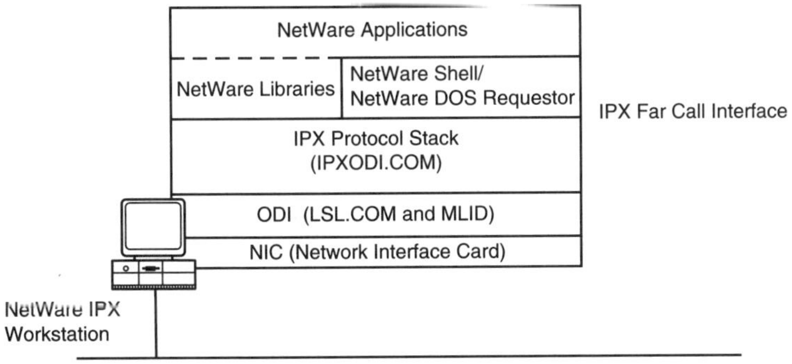

Figure 22.5
NetWare IPX client.

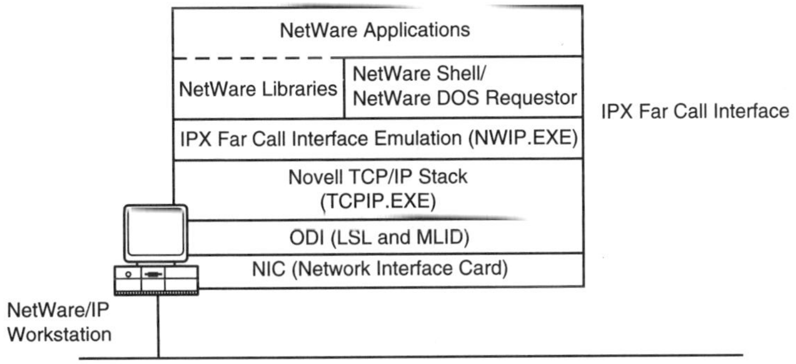

Figure 22.6
NetWare/IP client.

In figure 22.5, the bottom layer consists of the NIC hardware that represents layers 2 and 1 of the OSI model. The ODI interface is implemented by the Link Support Layer (LSL.COM), which communicates with the Multiple Link Interface Driver (MLID) for the NIC. The MLID communicates with the NIC hardware and with the Link Support Layer. The Link Support Layer provides a universal interface to the network adapter that allows a single protocol stack to establish communications with multiple NICs or multiple protocol stacks to communicate with a single NIC. For more details on the ODI interface see Chapter 24, "IntranetWare Protocols," on the CD.

The IPXODI.COM implements the SPX/IPX protocols and provides the end-to-end transport protocols used by NetWare workstations. The IPXODI.COM exports an Application Binary Interface (ABI) called the IPX Far Call Interface that is backward-compatible with earlier versions of IPX.

The NetWare libraries can be used by applications to access the transport protocols directly. The NetWare shell and the DOS Requester are special purpose applications that provide file and print redirection.

The IPX Far Call Interface mechanism is needed for future and existing applications to run over TCP/IP. It also ensures backward-compatibility with earlier versions of IPX.

Comparing figure 22.6 with figure 22.5 shows that the IPXODI.COM is replaced with TCPIP.EXE. The TCPIP.EXE TSR implements the TCP/IP protocol stack. The TCP/IP protocol stack contains a transport layer (OSI layer 4) protocol called User Datagram Protocol (UDP). UDP is a simpler transport protocol than TCP and is more efficient for broadcasts and the request/reply nature of IP traffic.

Simple replacement of IPXODI.COM with TCPIP.EXE, however, is not sufficient to connect to a NetWare server because the ABI used by TCPIP.EXE is different from that used by the shell/DOS Requester and other NetWare applications for using IPXODI.COM. The goal is to leave the existing applications unmodified and yet be able to use TCPIP.EXE, which uses a different ABI. Remember that IPXODI.COM exports the IPX Far Call Interface used by existing NetWare applications. A new module called NWIP.EXE interfaces with TCPIP.EXE and is used to export the IPX Far Call Interface. This allows existing NetWare applications to use the IPX Far Call Interface. NWIP.EXE translates this into the ABI used by TCPIP.EXE. This architecture allows future NetWare applications to work transparently with TCP/IP as long as they use the IPX Far Call Interface ABI. You can use the NETX.EXE or the NetWare DOS Requester with TCPIP.EXE.

The only limitation to the NetWare/IP architecture is applications that use IPX-based NetBIOS. NetBIOS applications use the IPX broadcast mechanism. If TCP/IP is used as the transport protocol, these broadcasts are confined to the local IP subnet because IP routers do not forward non-directed UDP/IP broadcasts to other IP networks.

The memory used by TCPIP.EXE and NWIP.EXE is 17.2 KB and 15.1 KB, respectively.

The TCPIP.EXE used in NetWare/IP is the same protocol stack used in the LAN WorkPlace for DOS product. Novell claims the following advantages/features in using this TCP/IP implementation:

- Support for 64 TCP and 32 UDP sockets
- IP support for up to four ODI interfaces
- Support for up to three default routers on each interface
- Duplicate IP Address prevention because of the Address Resolution Protocol (ARP) mechanism detecting this problem
- Support for network interfaces that use ODI Drivers for Ethernet, Token-Ring, FDDI, ARCnet, SLIP, PPP, and IBM Broadband
- IP configuration options through a choice of DHCP, BOOTP, RARP, or ASCII text file
- Troubleshooting utilities and support for SNMP

- Support for NetBIOS over TCP/IP using the enhanced "B-node" implementation of RFCs 1001 and 1002
- Support for the BSD Socket interface and WinSock interface

The Domain Name System

NetWare/IP contains the file NAMED.NLM that implements the *Domain Name System* (DNS). DNS is a distributed name-to-IP address database used on many TCP/IP-based networks including the Internet. When a workstation issues a TCP/IP command such as the following:

```
ftp ftp.novell.com
```

The name of the host ftp.novell.com needs to be resolved to the IP address of the host. The IP address is then used by the TCP/IP protocols to interact with the host. Users in general find the symbolic host name easier to remember than the IP address (32-bit number) of the host. The function of DNS is to translate the symbolic host name to an IP address number that can be used by the protocol software. The term *host* refers to any machine that implements a TCP/IP stack. The resolution of the host name to its equivalent IP address is performed by DNS protocols. These protocols and mechanisms are described in RFCs 1034, 1035, 1101, and 1183.

The IP address is a four-byte (32-bit) number assigned to every interface used by the IP protocol. If a NetWare server has two network interfaces to which IP is bound, a different IP address must be assigned to each of the boards. Most workstations have a single NIC, and if IP is used over this interface, a unique IP address must be assigned for the network interface.

The 32-bit IP address is usually written in a special format called the dotted decimal notation. In this notation, each of the four bytes that make up the IP address is expressed as a decimal number. The largest number contained in a byte is 255, and the smallest 0. Therefore, each of the bytes in the dotted decimal notation is a number between 0 and 255, inclusive.

The following is an example of an IP address in a dotted decimal notation:

```
144.19.74.201
```

The decimal number 144 corresponds to the most significant byte (left-most byte) of the 32-bit IP address, and the number 201 corresponds to the least significant byte (right-most byte) of the IP address. The dotted decimal number notation is much simpler to read than the 32-bit number translated as one decimal number. For example, the IP address also can be represented as the single decimal number: 2417183433.

DNS is implemented as a distributed database for looking up name-to-IP address correspondence. Another way of performing the name look up is to keep the name-to-IP address information in a static file. On Unix systems, this static file is the /ETC/HOSTS file. On NetWare servers, this static file is kept in the SYS:ETC/HOSTS file.

A sample host file format is shown next:

```
# Local network host addresses
#ident "@(#)hosts 1.1 - 88/05/17"
#
127.0.0.1        local localhost
144.19.74.1      sparc1 sp1
144.19.74.2      sparc2 sp2
144.19.74.3      sparc3 sp3
144.19.74.4      sparc4 sp4
144.19.74.5      sparc5 sp5
144.19.74.6      sparc6 sp6
144.19.74.7      sparc7 sp7
144.19.75.1      sparc8 sp8
144.19.75.2      sparc9 sp9
144.19.75.3      sparc10 sp10
144.19.75.4      sparc11 sp11
144.19.75.5      sparc12 sp12
144.19.75.6      sparc13 sp13
144.19.75.7      sparc14 sp14
144.19.74.101    cdos
144.19.74.102    server1 s386 nw
144.19.74.103    spws sparcsrv sps ss
144.19.74.201    sparcc1 spc1
144.19.74.202    sparcc2 spc2
```

The IP address 127.0.0.1 is a special address called the loopback address. Packets sent to this address never reach the network cable. The loopback address can be used for diagnostic purposes to verify that the internal code path through the TCP/IP protocols is working. It also can be used by client applications to communicate with software programs running on the same machine.

Each <IP Address, Host name> pair is expressed on a single line using the style shown in the host file. The multiple host names for the host are alias names. The protocol software, if configured to perform name resolution using this static host file, looks up the information for resolving a name. Consider the following command:

```
telnet sp14
```

The protocol software uses the following entry in the host file to resolve the name sp14:

```
144.19.75.7     sparc14 sp14
```

The name sp14 is an alias for the host name sparc14. The corresponding IP address is 144.19.75.7. The protocol software resolves the name sp14 to 144.19.75.7. The preceding command then becomes the following:

```
telnet 144.19.75.7
```

A number of problems exist with the static host file approach. As the number of hosts on a network becomes large. It becomes increasingly difficult to keep this file up to date. Also, many organizations have more than one network Administrator. It is difficult for these

Administrators to coordinate with each other every time host files need to be changed. Even keeping this information in a large central static file becomes quickly unmanageable as the number of entries in this file becomes large.

The DNS system was developed to overcome the problems of name resolution on a large IP network. It provides a distributed database of names and IP addresses. The names could be host names or names of mail exchanger hosts. It also has provisions for keeping text descriptions of host names and for providing name resolution for other protocol families besides TCP/IP (such as Chaos net, XNS, and so on). It is, however, used predominantly for resolving host names for the TCP/IP protocols.

Part of the scheme used in DNS refers to the use of hierarchical names, in which names are organized into a hierarchical tree. At the top of the tree is the root domain named by the period symbol (.). Because all names have this common root, the period is omitted when specifying the hierarchical name in most TCP/IP applications. Below the root domain are top-level domains (see fig. 22.7). These reflect how names are organized. Table 22.1 shows examples of top level domains.

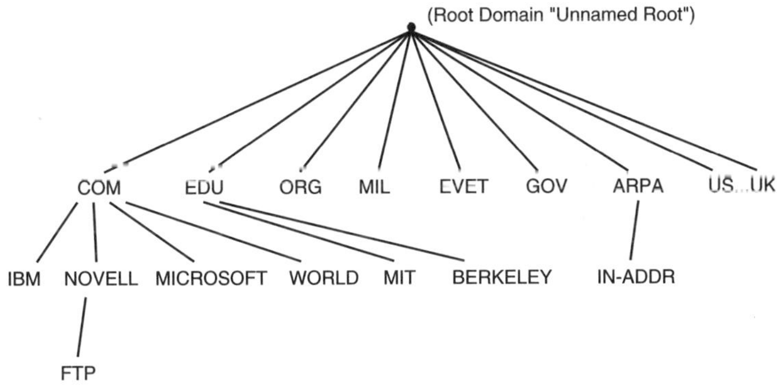

Figure 22.7
Hierarchical names in DNS.

Table 22.1
Top-Level Domains

Top Level Domain	Description
COM	Commercial organization
EDU	Education institution. Universities, schools, and so on
MIL	Military
GOV	Government (United States)
NET	Network provider
ORG	Organization

continues

Table 22.1, Continued
Top-Level Domains

Top Level Domain	Description
ARPA	ARPANET; now historical; still used for inverse address mapping
US	Country USA
CA	Country Canada
UK	Country United Kingdom
DE	Country Germany
SE	Country Sweden
FR	Country France
IN	Country India
CN	Country China
JA	Country Japan

The two-letter designations are assigned to the country as per the CCITT standards. These are the same country designations used for specifying country objects in NetWare Directory Services. Below the top level domains are middle level domains. A number of middle level names can exist. Each name is separated from each other by use of the period (which can never occur as part of the name of a domain). The length of a complete domain name such as the following:

```
world.std.com
```

cannot exceed 255 characters. In the name "world.std.com," the name of the host is as follows:

```
world
```

The following name is in the domain:

```
std.com
```

If another host is in the same domain whose name is "sparky," its Fully Qualified Name (FQN) is as follows:

```
sparky.std.com
```

Many of the middle-level names refer to names of organizations. An organization is free to define subdomains within the organization. If it does this, it should provide appropriate name services to resolve names in these subdomains. For example, consider the organization SCS that has the following domain name:

```
scs.com
```

If this organization has separate networks for its Corporate, Marketing, and Research arms, it can define three separate subdomains named CORP, MKTG, RESCH, and provide a DNS server or a number of DNS servers to resolve names on its networks. The domains in this case are as follows:

```
corp.scs.com
mktg.scs.com
resch.scs.com
```

Although a DNS server is not required for each domain, it is common to have one or more for each domain being served. Figure 22.7 shows several DNS servers for the root domain. These servers would know about names of the top-level domains such as COM, EDU, MIL, ORG, NET, and so on. Several DNS servers can be used for a domain to perform load balancing, avoid unnecessary network traffic, and for reliability in case the primary DNS server was not available. The COM domain would have one or more DNS servers that knows the names of all commercial organizations in the COM domain. Within the COM domain, a subdomain such as IBM.COM has its own DNS servers for that domain. Hosts within a domain query the local DNS server for the domain to resolve names. For example, the host WORLD.STD.COM queries the DNS server for the domain STD.COM to find out the IP address of the host FTP.NOVELL.COM or the IP address of ATHENA.SCS.ORG. When this query is resolved, the results are usually cached locally for a configurable period of time.

The DNS servers for a domain need to resolve names of hosts in their domains. They do not need to know about hosts in subdomains if DNS servers are defined for subdomains. Secondary DNS servers in a domain must know the IP address of the primary server in the domain it can contact for resolving a name query. A DNS server must also know the IP address of the parent DNS server.

The Relationship between DNS Domains and NetWare/IP Domains

A NetWare/IP domain is defined as a collection of NetWare/IP servers and clients that receive SAP/RIP information provided by one or more DSS servers in that domain. A NetWare network can be partitioned into multiple NetWare/IP domains. A NetWare/IP domain must exist in the context of a DNS domain. A NetWare/IP domain is created by creating a DNS subdomain with the following properties:

- The DNS subdomain must be a subdomain of an existing DNS domain.
- The DNS subdomain cannot have subdomains.

After creating the NetWare/IP domain, you must configure NetWare/IP nodes that belong to this domain with the NetWare/IP domain name.

The organization SCS has a registered domain SCS.ORG. This organization has two existing DNS subdomains for two separate networks for the Engineering and Marketing department as follows:

```
ENG.SCS.ORG
MKTG.SCS.ORG
```

SCS decides to have a NetWare/IP domain cover the entire Engineering network and two NetWare/IP domains for the Marketing network. To create these NetWare/IP domains, you must first create DNS subdomains. For the DNS domain ENG.SCS.ORG, you can create a NetWare/IP domain called the following:

```
NWIP.ENG.SCS.ORG
```

For the Marketing network, you must create two NetWare/IP domains. Therefore, you must first create two DNS subdomains of MKTG.SCS.ORG. You can do this by creating the following domains:

```
NWIP1.MKTG.SCS.ORG
NWIP2.MKTG.SCS.ORG
```

After creating these DNS subdomains, you must configure the NetWare/IP nodes and DSS servers that are in the NetWare/IP domain with the names of these subdomains.

Examining the DSS Server

To provide SAP/RIP information to a NetWare/IP network, you must have at least one DSS server in a NetWare/IP domain. The DSS server holds a database of SAP/RIP information for a NetWare/IP domain. The information in the DSS server can be replicated on multiple DSS servers to improve performance across WAN links and to increase reliability. This section helps you understand how the DSS server updates its information and how this information is disseminated to other NetWare/IP nodes. It also covers the issue of DSS database replication for improved reliability.

Updating DSS Servers

In a IPX-based NetWare server, NetWare services such as File, Print, and Database services advertise their existence using the SAP protocol. These services send SAP broadcast packets every 60 seconds. (The actual value is configurable, but 60 seconds is the default.) The broadcast packets are sent out over every network interface to which IPX is bound.

In NetWare/IP networks, NetWare services also advertise themselves using SAP. These SAP packets are sent directly to the DSS servers using UDP/IP packets.

When a NetWare server boots, it sends a SAP broadcast advertising its existence. If the server is configured as a NetWare/IP server, it also sends a SAP packet directly to the nearest DSS server using the UDP/IP protocol. The NetWare/IP server sends this information to the DSS server every five minutes (the value is configurable). If the DSS server does not receive the SAP refresh information, it times out the information.

Disseminating DSS Information

In an IPX-based network, NetWare servers listen for SAP packets and cache this information. They then create temporary bindery entries that list the services seen by the server. NetWare IPX clients and applications locate these services by looking up the bindery information stored on the server.

NetWare/IP servers also keep a list of available services in the NetWare bindery. They do this by periodically requesting a download of this information from the DSS server. The download occurs at a configurable time interval whose default value is five minutes.

Replicating the DSS Database

To increase the reliability and availability of the DSS information, you can have several secondary DSS servers in a NetWare/IP domain. If the primary DSS server is unavailable or too busy to respond to requests by NetWare/IP servers, the secondary server can be used to provide the desired information.

To provide consistency of the DSS information, the DSS database is replicated to all the DSS servers in the NetWare/IP domain. In a large network consisting of slow WAN links, performance can be improved by avoiding sending requests for DSS information across the WAN links. This can be achieved by installing a local DSS server on each network so that NetWare/IP nodes can query the local DSS server instead of querying a remote DSS server separated by the slow WAN link. The primary DSS server holds the master copy of the DSS server, and the secondary DSS servers hold a Read/Write replica.

SAP/RIP information can be received by DSS servers at different times. This can result in the DSS servers not having the same information. To keep the DSS servers synchronized, the secondary DSS servers contact the primary DSS server at periodic intervals to synchronize their information. If the DSS databases are out of synchronization, the synchronization process commences. If at any time, connectivity between primary and secondary DSS servers is lost, the secondary DSS server periodically attempts to establish a connection and initiate synchronization. If the secondary DSS server is activated after being down, it attempts to synchronize with the primary DSS when it comes up.

To ensure that synchronization is done correctly, each DSS server maintains a database version number for the information stored on it at any time. The database version number is changed whenever the database is changed by new information. The database version numbers help the DSS servers determine if the database is out of synchronization. During synchronization, the secondary DSS server uploads to the primary DSS any new records received since the last synchronization. It also downloads any records not in its database. Only changed, deleted, or new records are exchanged, not the entire database.

Understanding NetWare/IP Installation

The amount of memory needed to run a NetWare/IP server depends on the components loaded at the NetWare server, and the number of NetWare/IP servers configured in its NetWare/IP domain. If *N* is the number of NetWare/IP servers, the server memory requirements can be calculated using the formulas in table 22.2. The amount of disk space needed on the NetWare server is about 2 MB on the SYS: volume.

Table 22.2
Memory Requirements on a NetWare/IP Server

Type of NetWare Services	Memory Requirements(Bytes)
NetWare/IP	*N* * 380 + 75000
DSS on NetWare 3.1x	*N* * 440 + 450000
DSS on NetWare 4.x	*N* * 440 + 710000

N = Number of NetWare/IP Servers in a NetWare/IP Domain

NetWare/IP at the workstation requires approximately 2 MB of free disk space for DOS and 3.2 MB of free disk space for Windows. The TCPIP.EXE requires 17.2 KB of RAM, and the NWIP.EXE requires 15.1 KB of RAM. Using memory managers, these components can be loaded in upper memory.

Installing NetWare/IP

You must log in as SUPERVISOR (NetWare 3.1x) or Admin (NetWare 4.x). If installing on a NetWare 4.x server, you must have the bindery context set using the following server console command:

```
SET BINDERY CONTEXT = context
```

The bindery context is normally set in the AUTOEXEC.NCF file. To view the current server bindery context, use the following command:

```
SET BINDERY CONTEXT
```

You can install the NetWare/IP from a DOS workstation or the NetWare server.

Installing NetWare/IP from a DOS Workstation

To install from a DOS workstation, you must have REMOTE and RSPX running at the server. This can be done using the following commands:

```
LOAD REMOTE password
LOAD RSPX
```

The steps for installing are as follows:

1. Log in with Supervisor (NetWare 3.1x) or Admin (NetWare 4.x) access to the server.
2. Create a directory called NWIP1 on one of the NetWare volumes.
3. Use NCOPY to copy the disk or CD-ROM directory labeled NWIP1 to the NWIP1 directory on the server as follows:

   `NCOPY A: SYS:NWIP1 /S /E`

4. Run RCONSOLE.
5. Select the server to install NetWare/IP.
6. Enter the password used when loading REMOTE on the server.
7. Proceed with instructions in the following section.

Installing NetWare/IP from a Server

The steps for installing are as follows:

1. At the server console, run the INSTALL program by issuing the following command:

   `LOAD INSTALL`

- Select Product Options and press Enter. The screen shown in figure 22.8 appears.
- Select Choose an Item Listed Above and press Enter.
- Select Install NetWare/IP and press Enter.

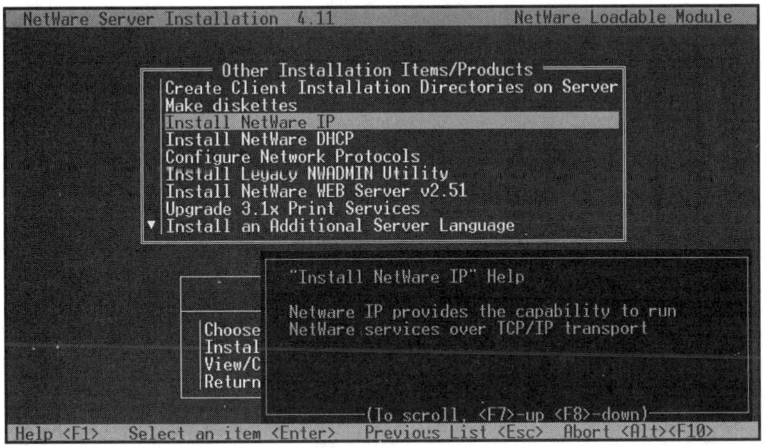

Figure 22.8
The Product Options Screen.

2. When prompted to insert the disk, enter the disk or alternate location for the source files.

   Press F3 to specify a different source on the server, or use F4 to specify a path on a remote workstation (most PCs map the CD-ROM to drive E:).

3. You are informed about a README file. Press Esc to continue.

4. Select No when asked if you want to exit installation. Select Yes if you want to read the README file and start the installation again.

5. If TCP/IP was not already configured and loaded on the server, you will be prompted with this message:

```
TCP/IP is not configured. Switch to the system console using <Alt>-<Esc> keys
and configure TCP/IP. Then switch back to the Install screen to continue
<Press ESCAPE to Continue>
```

6. You will not be allowed to continue until TCP/IP is configured. Switch to the system console and perform the commands shown in listing 22.1

Listing 22.1

```
LOAD LANDriver NAME=IPNET FRAME=ETHERNET_II (for Ethernet)
LOAD LANDriver NAME=IPNET FRAME=TOKEN-RING_SNAP (for Token Ring)
BIND IP TO IPNET ADDR=IPAddress MASK=Subnet mask
```

7. The INSTALL program begins copying system files to the server and displays several status messages.

8. When prompted, enter the local host name. The default is the name of the server. Accept the default.

9. The INSTALL program finishes copying files to the server. When the installation completes, an informative message appears (see figure 22.9).

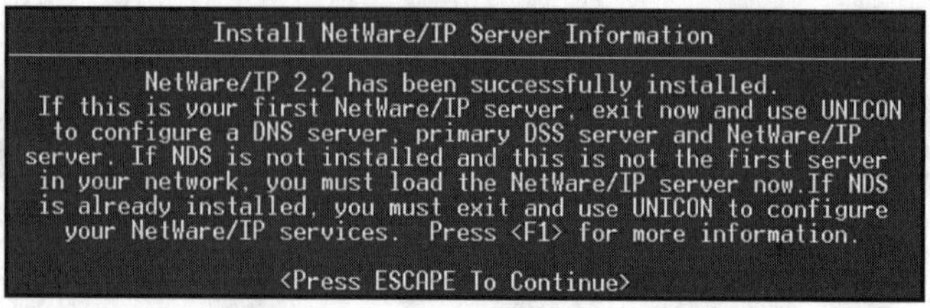

Install NetWare/IP Server Information
NetWare/IP 2.2 has been successfully installed.
If this is your first NetWare/IP server, exit now and use UNICON
to configure a DNS server, primary DSS server and NetWare/IP
server. If NDS is not installed and this is not the first server
in your network, you must load the NetWare/IP server now.If NDS
is already installed, you must exit and use UNICON to configure
your NetWare/IP services. Press <F1> for more information.
<Press ESCAPE To Continue>

Figure 22.9
The information screen displayed when installation completes.

10. After pressing Esc, the message, `Do you want to configure the NetWare/IP Server?` is shown.

    At this point you may either answer NO, and then use UNICON to configure the NetWare/IP and DNS Servers, or you can answer YES, which invokes NWIPCFG.NLM.

You should answer YES, and then enter the NetWare/IP Configuration Console (NWIPCFG.NLM). See the following section, "Configuring NetWare/IP," for instructions on initializing the NetWare/IP Server with this utility. This utility or UNICON may be used at any later time to reconfigure the server.

11. When initial configuration using the NetWare/IP Configuration Console (NWIPCFG.NLM) is complete, exit the utility. A message appears, warning that the NetWare/IP Server has not yet been started. Press Esc to exit the utility, and continue the installation process.

12. INSTALL then starts NDS and prompts for the ADMIN password. Enter the password for the user Admin. UNICON user groups and NDS user accounts are then automatically created. Several status messages appear.

13. The message `Product Initialization Complete  <Press ESC to Continue>` appears. Press Esc.

14. A screen appears with the notice, `*****IMPORTANT***After your server is installed, make sure that the line UNISTART.NCF is at the end of the autoexec.ncf file.`

15. Press Esc twice to return to the Installation Options Menu.

16. Select NCF files options, then Edit Autoexec.NCF to make sure it contains the line UNISTART.NCF at the end of the file.

    Also insure that the TCP/IP and NetWare/IP configuration parameters are entered correctly. Insure that the TCP/IP commands issued in Step 6 above are entered here as well, so that TCP/IP is properly loaded whenever the server is restarted.

18. Exit INSTALL and down the server.

19. Restart the server.

Proceed to the following sections on configuring NetWare/IP software.

Configuring NetWare/IP

After you install NetWare/IP, it must be configured before it can be used.

During the installation of NetWare/IP, the NetWare/IP Configuration Console (NWIPCFG.NLM) is started. The Configuration Console provides menus to configure NetWare/IP and DNS client parameters. NetWare/IP also installs a configuration tool called UNICON (UNICON.NLM) that contains all of the same menus used in the Configuration Console and several others, including those used for creation of DSS and DNS services. Either utility can be used for DNS and NetWare/IP parameters, but only UNICON provides menus to create DSS services, and create and administer a DNS server.

The NetWare/IP Configuration Console (see fig. 22.10) provides the menus to Configure DNS Client parameters only. If the DNS Server is installed on the server, then UNICON must be used to configure and administer the DNS server parameters.

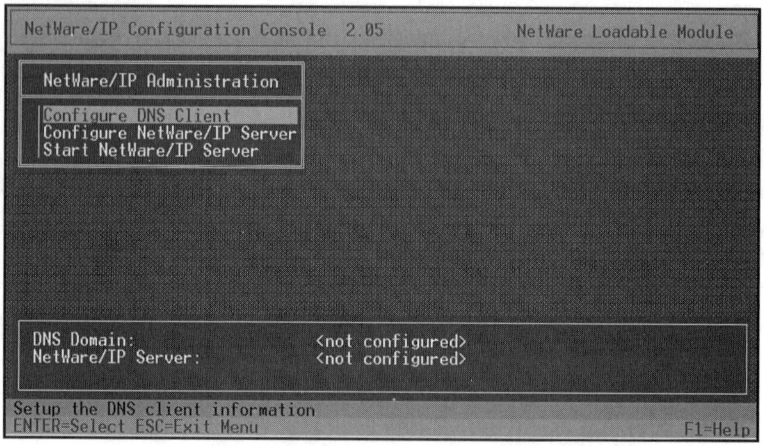

Figure 22.10
The NetWare/IP Configuration Console.

NetWare/IP Configuration Console menus are provided to Configure DNS Client, Configure NetWare/IP Server, and Start NetWare/IP Server.

1. Select Configure DNS Client. The DNS Client Access screen appears (see fig. 22.11).

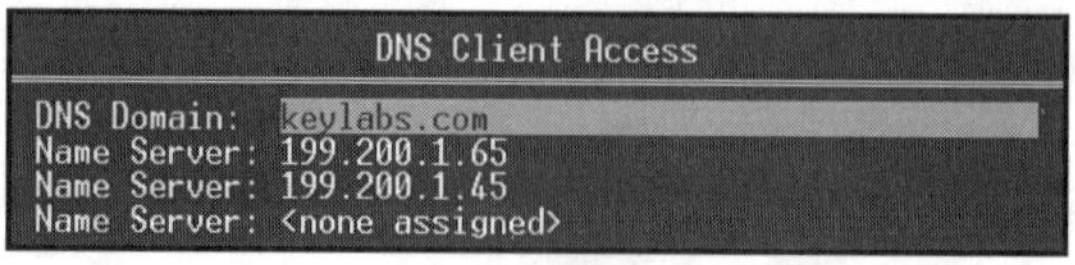

Figure 22.11
The DNS Client Configuration screen.

2. Enter the server's DNS Domain Name and enter the IP addresses of up to three DNS servers. See the section named "The Relationship between DNS Domains and NetWare/IP Domains" earlier in the chapter. Do not enter the NetWare/IP domain name here.

3. Exit the Configure DNS Client menu by pressing Esc.

4. On the main menu, select Configure NetWare/IP Server. The NetWare/IP Server Configuration screen appears (see figure 22.12).

5. On this form, enter the NetWare/IP Domain Name.

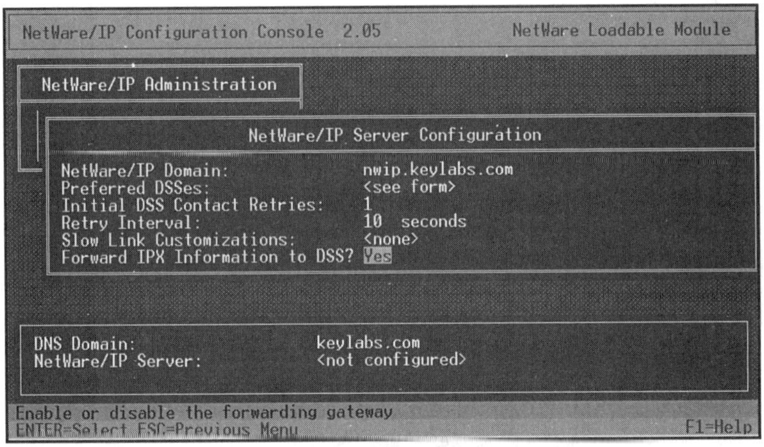

Figure 22.12
The NetWare/IP Server Configuration screen.

6. Select PREFERRED DSSes <see form> and press Enter.
7. Enter up to five DSS server names or IP addresses in the fields provided. Press Esc.
8. Enter the remaining parameters.

Note

> The Forward IPX Information to DSS entry is particularly important. If IPX is bound to any network adapters in the server, then the server appears to be configured as an IPX forwarding gateway (a gateway between a TCP/IP and an IPX network segment). You must either enable this selection, or remove IPX from the network adapter bindings. After NetWare/IP is installed, IPX is no longer required on that network segment and should be removed. Refer to the section, "Disabling the IPX/IP Gateway," later in this chapter.

9. After all NetWare/IP parameters are entered, press Esc to return to the main menu.
10. If the DSS servers selected as the preferred DSS servers are available on the network, then select Start NetWare/IP Server.

    If they are not, or if the NetWare/IP server will also be set up as a DSS server, then exit the Configuration Console without starting the NetWare/IP server, start UNICON and initialize the required DSS services. See the following sections for UNICON usage information.

Using UNICON

You can start UNICON by typing the following command at the server console:

```
LOAD UNICON
```

If asked to log in, specify the server name on which you want to perform NetWare/IP configuration. You must also specify the Admin or Supervisor account name and password.

Figure 22.13 shows the main UNICON screen. You can use the options on this screen to perform most NetWare/IP configuration tasks.

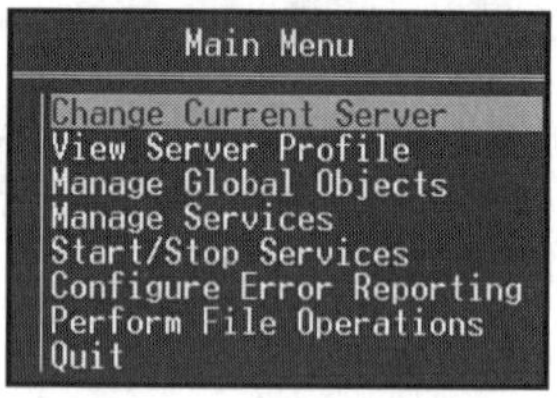

Figure 22.13
The Main UNICON screen.

The *Change Current Server* option is used to log in to other NetWare servers for performing NetWare/IP configuration.

The View Server Profile screen (see fig. 22.14) is used to display the server's currently assigned network parameters. It is for display only so values cannot be edited with this option.

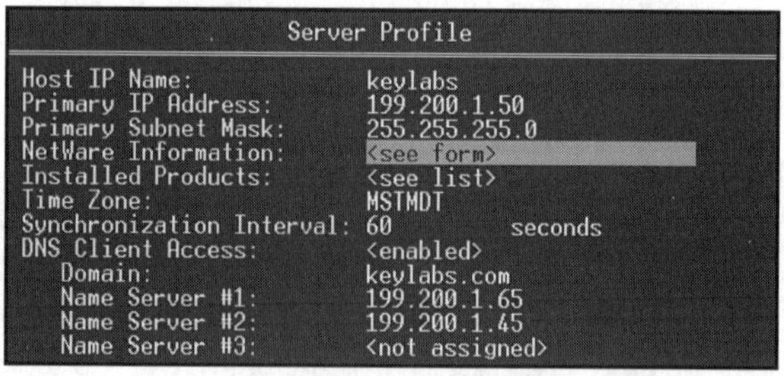

Figure 22.14
The Server Profile screen.

The server's IP host name, IP address, and subnet mask are displayed along with the Time Zone, DNS domain name, and DNS server addresses. Selecting NetWare Information displays the server's NetWare Operating System version, current NDS Context, and NDS tree. Selecting Installed Products pops up a list of currently installed software products.

The Manage Global Objects option displays a list of the global objects managed by UNICON. Depending on the products installed, the following options are listed:

- Configure Server Profile
- Manage Groups

- Manage Users
- Manage Hosts

Using these options, you can set the server's synchronization interval, DNS client access, and create/modify/delete user and group lists and host entries.

The *Manage Services* option is used to configure DNS server and Host information and NetWare/IP domains. Selecting DNS allows you to Initialize the DNS Master database, manage the Master and Replica Databases, and link to the existing DNS hierarchy. Selecting NetWare/IP allows you to configure NetWare/IP parameters, create and configure primary/secondary DSS services, and browse DSS databases.

The *Start/Stop Services* option starts services not running, and stops services that are running. Press Enter to display running services. Highlight a service and press Delete to stop any of these services. Press Insert to display a list of services available to be started.

The *Configure Error Reporting* option is used to set the error reporting level for messages reported to the Product Kernel screen or the AUDIT.LOG file. It also can be used to specify the maximum size of the AUDIT.LOG file. Setting the error levels can be useful for troubleshooting NetWare/IP configuration.

The *Perform File Operations* option is used to copy files through FTP, edit files, and view/set file permissions.

Configuring DNS Server

The DNS server must be configured before a NetWare/IP server or DSS server can be activated. You can configure DNS servers in the following two ways:

- Configure DNS server to run on a NetWare server.
- Configure DNS server to run on another operating system. An example choice is to use Berkeley Internet Domain Service (BIND) available on Unix or DOS (from FTP Software, Inc.).

Configuring DNS on a NetWare Server and Creating NetWare/IP Domains

The DNS server must contain IP Address and Host name mappings. You can enter these names directly into the DNS database. Each entry in the DNS database is called a *resource record.*

You must first create the DNS Master Database. You can do this by performing the following steps:

Note

> If this is the initial configuration of DNS, check the file SYS:/ETC/DBSOURCE and make sure there are no unnecessary host entries. In some distributions of NetWare/IP, this file contains several sample entries that should be commented out.

1. Load UNICON.
2. Select Manage Services.
3. Select DNS. The screen in figure 22.15 appears.

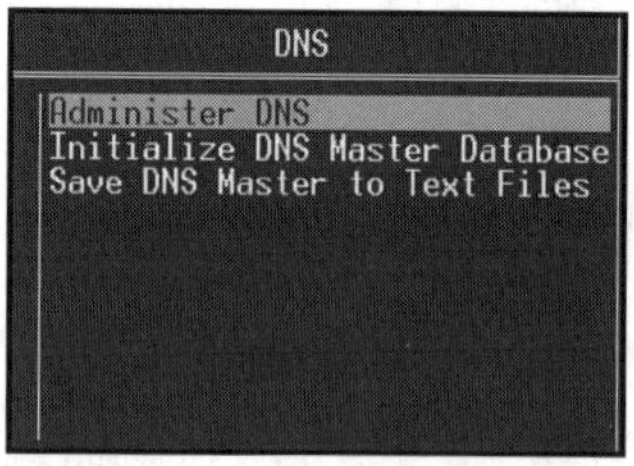

Figure 22.15
The Manage Services - DNS screen.

4. Select Initialize DNS Master Database. The prompt shown in figure 22.16 appears.

Figure 22.16
The prompt for the Domain Name to be served.

5. Enter the Fully Qualified Name (FQN) for the DNS domain and press Esc. The following is an example:

   ```
   SCS.COM
   ```

6. Wait a few seconds for the `Please Wait` message to disappear, and press Esc.
7. You are asked, "Do you want DNS service for specific subnetworks." If you implement subnetworking on your network enter YES, otherwise enter NO.
8. You are asked if you want to initialize the DNS database. Select Yes. This initializes the DNS database from the text files located in the SYS:/ETC/DBSOURCE directory.
9. You see a status message similar to the one in figure 22.17. Press Esc to continue.

Figure 22.17
The DNS database creation status messages.

At this point, you have created the database for the domain name and started the DNS server. The database initially contains just the hostname record for the NetWare/IP server.

10. Press Esc a few times to get back to the main UNICON menu.

You can now enter hosts information for DSS servers in the domain that you just created by performing the following steps:

1. Select Manage Global Objects.
2. Select Manage Hosts.
3. Select Hosts. You should see a list of DSS server and other hosts in the DNS database (see fig. 22.18).

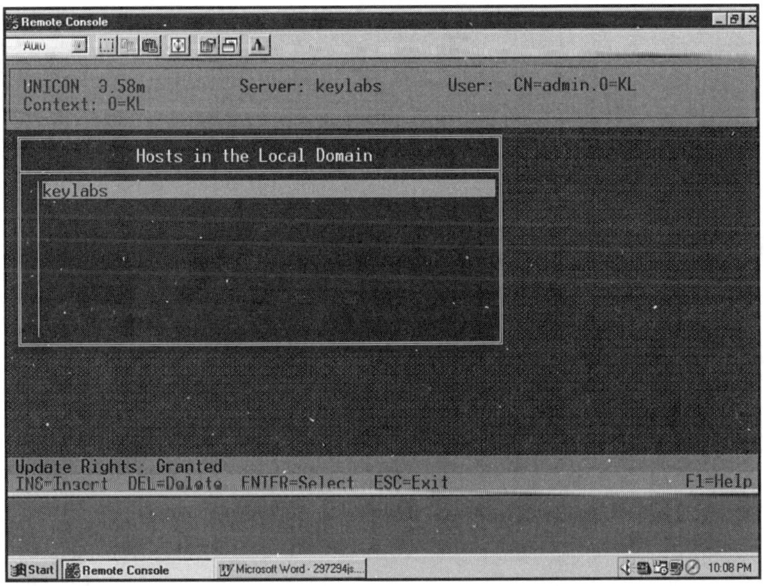

Figure 22.18
The Hosts in local domain screen.

You can display or modify information about a specific DSS server or other hosts by highlighting a host and pressing Enter (see fig. 22.19).

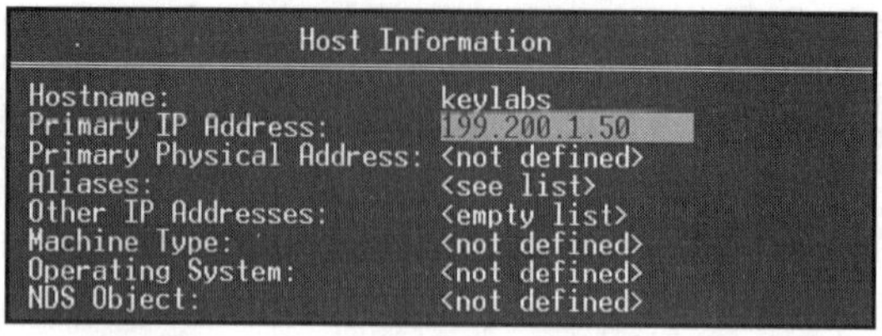

Figure 22.19
The Host Information screen.

4. To add additional secondary DSS servers' host names, press Ins on the screen in figure 22.18 and enter the new host name.

5. Go to the Manage Services menu option. (Press Esc if you have just performed step 2.)

6. Select DNS, then select Administer DNS. The screen in figure 22.20 appears.

Figure 22.20
The DNS Server Administration screen.

7. Select Manage Master Database. The screen in figure 22.21 appears.

Figure 22.21
The Manage Master Database Screen.

8. Select Delegate Subzone Authority. The screen in fig. 22.22 appears.

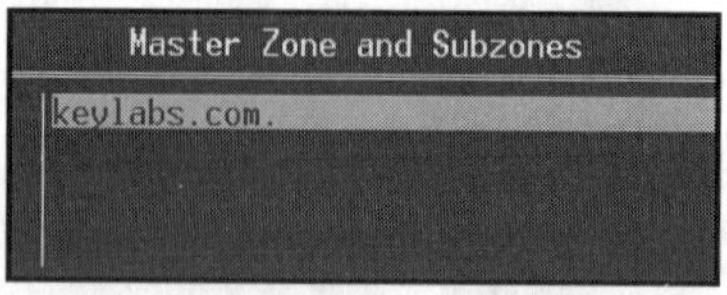

Figure 22.22
The Master Zone and Subzones screen.

9. The list shows the master domain you have just created. You need to add a DNS subdomain for the NetWare/IP domain. To do this press Insert and enter the name of the NetWare/IP domain. If the master domain zone name was keylabs.com., you can enter the NetWare/IP domain as follows:

   ```
   .NWIP.KEYLABS.COM
   ```

   and then Press Enter.

10. A list of available hosts is displayed (see fig. 22.23). Highlight the host that will be the Primary DSS server for the NetWare/IP domain you have just created and press Enter.

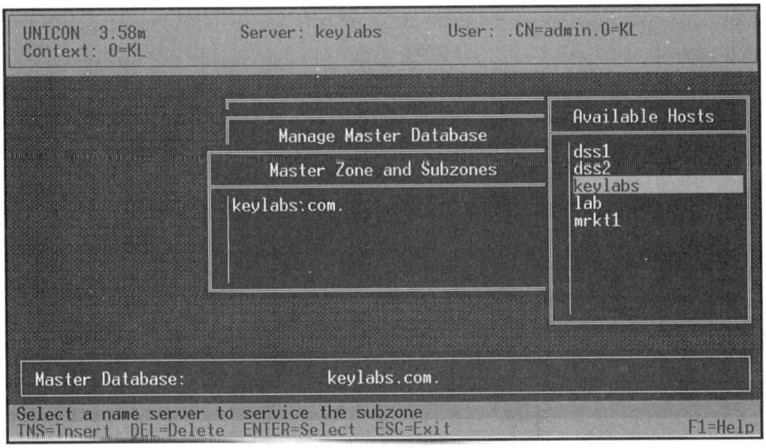

Figure 22.23
A screen showing hosts available to be Name Servers.

11. To add secondary DSS servers to the NetWare/IP domain, Highlight the Subzone (subdomain) you have just created and press Enter. A list of configured Name Server Hosts is displayed. Press Insert and the list of servers again appears (refer to fig. 22.23). Select the desired host to be the secondary DSS.

12. Repeat step 11 to add additional DSS servers to the NetWare/IP domain.

13. After creating a NetWare/IP subdomain (also DNS subdomain), you must inform the DNS server for the parent domain about the new DNS subdomain you just created. The parent DNS server can be on another node administered by someone else. You have to request the DNS administrator for the parent domain to add your subdomain to the parent's database. In the example in this guided tour, the parent DNS server is on the same server as the DSS server, and figure 22.24 shows that the master domain KEYLABS.COM. knows about the subdomain (sub-zone) NWIP.KEYLABS.COM.

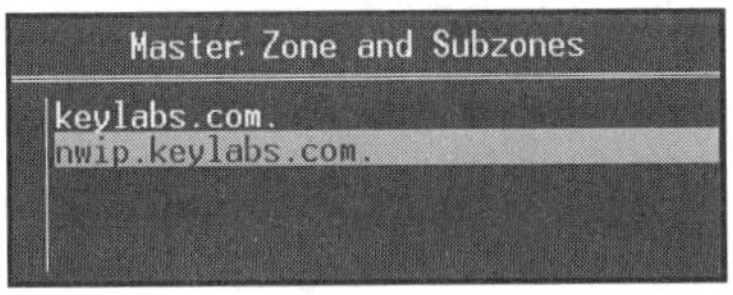

Figure 22.24
The master domain knows about the new NetWare/IP domain.

When a new domain record is added to the parent DNS server, the NetWare DNS server automatically links into the DNS hierarchy by using the information stored in SYS:ETC\DNS\ROOT.DB.

14. Anytime you add records in the DNS database, you must restart the DNS service, so that it can initialize its cache with the new information.

To restart the DNS service, you must stop it and then start it again. The following steps outline how you can accomplish this:

1. Go to the main menu of UNICON.
2. Select Start/Stop Services.
3. If the DNS service appears in the list of Running Services (see fig. 22.25), highlight it and press Delete. Answer Yes to the query verifying if you want to stop the service.

Figure 22.25
List of running services.

4. To start the DNS service again, press Insert on the list of running services. You should see a list of available services that you can run (see fig. 22.26). Highlight DNS Server and press Enter. This activates the DNS Service, and it appears in the list of Running Services.

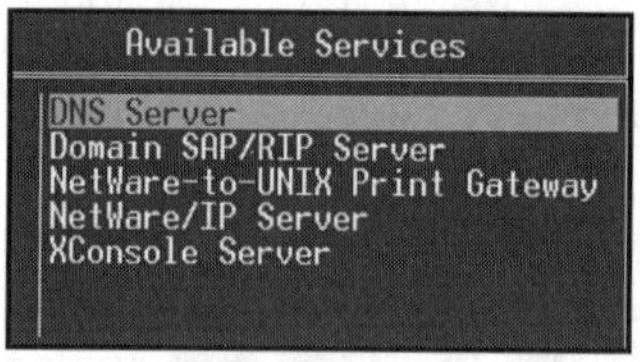

Figure 22.26
List of Available Services to run.

Creating a Replica of the DNS Database

For reliability, you may want to create one or more replicas of the DNS database on other servers. The following steps outline how you can do this:

1. LOAD UNICON.
2. Select Manage Services (refer to figure 22.13).
3. Select DNS Server.
4. Select Administer DNS (refer to figure 22.15).
5. Select Manage Replica Database (refer to figure 22.20). You should see a list of replica databases that initially is empty.
6. Press Insert to create a replica of the DNS database on the server. A form for importing database information appears (see fig. 22.27).

Figure 22.27
The Replica Database Information form.

The *Domain field* specifies the name of the domain for which this replica has a copy.

The *Name Server field* contains the IP address of the DNS master nameserver. Three nameserver fields are provided to enter IP addresses of additional DNS nameservers.

7. After filling in the form, press Esc. If asked to save your changes, answer Yes.

Configuring DNS Servers on Non-NetWare Platforms

If you are using a non-NetWare platform as a DNS server for a domain, you need to consult the documentation for DNS services for that operating system.

On Unix systems, DNS is implemented by BIND. On BSD derived Unix, this is implemented by running the following program:

```
named
```

On SVR4 Unix, the following is implemented by the program:

```
in.named
```

DOS-based implementation of BIND is available from FTP Software, Inc. It runs as a TSR called NAMED.

BIND uses a file called /etc/named.boot that contains a list of other files for holding the zone records for the DNS database. FTP Software's BIND uses the file name NAMED.BOO.

The DNS zone files are text files and have a special format. You can refer to the DNS RFCs referenced earlier for information on the syntax of these text records, or consult your operating system's implementation.

If you are using non-NetWare DNS servers for the master domain, you must add a record in its database for the new subdomains that you created for NetWare/IP. This usually involves using a text editor and adding a record to the zone data file for the DNS server. If you created a primary DSS named nw4cs.scs.com (IP address 144.19.73.102) and a secondary DSS named ucs.scs.com (IP address 144.19.74.103) for the NetWare/IP domain nwip.scs.com, add the records shown in listing 22.2 to the zone data file for non-NetWare DNS.

Listing 22.2

```
# Domain/Host      Class     RR Type     Data

nwip.scs.com.      IN         NS          nw4cs.scs.com.# Primary DSS
nwip.scs.com.      IN         NS          ucs.scs.com.     # Secondary DSS
nw4cs.scs.com.     IN         A           144.19.74.102    # Host record
ucs.scs.com.       IN         A           144.19.74.103    # Host record
```

On most DNS implementations, you must restart the DNS service before the changes are registered.

Configuring DSS Server

After the DNS server is configured, you can configure the DSS server. This involves configuring the primary and secondary DSS servers and starting the DSS service.

Configuring Primary and Secondary DSS Servers

The following steps outline the DSS configuration procedure:

1. LOAD UNICON.
2. Select Manage Services.
3. Select NetWare/IP.
4. Select Configure Primary DSS. The Primary DSS Configuration form appears (see fig. 22.28).

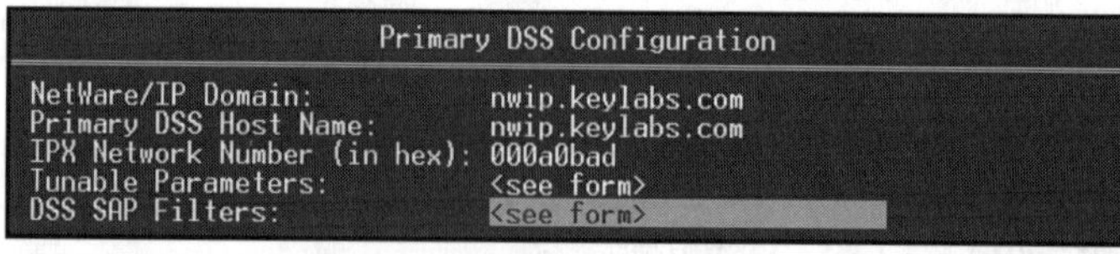

Figure 22.28
The Primary DSS Configuration form.

The Primary DSS Configuration form contains the following fields:

- The *NetWare/IP Domain* field contains the name of the NetWare/IP domain. All NetWare/ IP nodes (clients and servers) are members of this NetWare/IP domain. The NetWare/IP Domain, for example, can be the following:

  ```
  nwip.scs.com.
  ```

- The *Primary DSS Host Name* field contains the fully qualified name of the primary DSS host. For example, it can have a name such as the following:

  ```
  nw4cs.SCS.COM.
  ```

- The *IPX Network Number (in hex)* field contains the IPX network number assigned to the DSS service. This number must be different from the IPX internal network numbers assigned to NetWare 3.x and 4.x servers and from network numbers assigned to any IPX interface.

- Selecting the *Tunable Parameters* field brings up a form for tuning DSS parameters (see fig. 22.29).

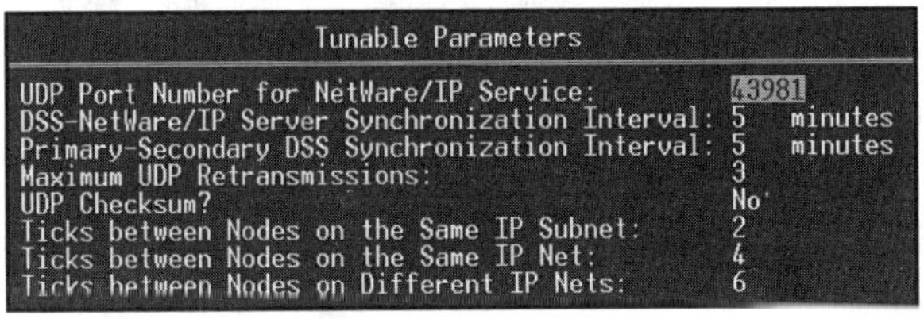

```
Tunable Parameters

UDP Port Number for NetWare/IP Service:           43981
DSS-NetWare/IP Server Synchronization Interval:   5   minutes
Primary-Secondary DSS Synchronization Interval:   5   minutes
Maximum UDP Retransmissions:                      3
UDP Checksum?                                     No
Ticks between Nodes on the Same IP Subnet:        2
Ticks between Nodes on the Same IP Net:           4
Ticks between Nodes on Different IP Nets:         6
```

Figure 22.29
The Tunable DSS Parameters form.

The Tunable DSS Parameters form contains the following fields:

- The *UDP Port Number for NetWare/IP Service* field can be used to specify the UDP port number used by the NetWare/IP service. The default value is 43981. Two successive port numbers are assigned. The first port number 43981 (default) is used for packet transmission. The second port number 43982 (default) is used for SAP/RIP queries.

- The *DSS-NetWare/IP Server Synchronization Interval* field can be used to specify how often a NetWare/IP server queries DSS for updated information. The value can range from 1 to 60 minutes with a default of 5 minutes.

- *Primary-Secondary DSS Synchronization Interval* field can be used to specify how often a Secondary DSS Server queries the Primary DSS Server for updates. The default is 5 minutes with a range of 1 to 240 minutes.

- The *Maximum UDP Retransmissions* field can be used to specify how many times a packet should be present if no acknowledgment is received for the packet. The value can range from 1 to 48 minutes with a default of three minutes.

- The *UDP Checksum?* field determines whether the UDP packet uses the checksum field (set to Yes or No). The default value is No. LANs have a reliable transmission rate, and a value of No gives maximum performance. If you suspect that the physical network transport is unreliable, you may want to set the value to Yes. If set to Yes, UDP checksums are performed over the data packet. Checksum errors cause a packet to be rejected and retransmitted.

- The *Ticks between Nodes on the Same IP Subnet* field controls how long it takes in ticks (1/18 second) for a packet to travel one-way between two nodes on the same IP subnet.

- The *Ticks between Nodes on the Same IP Net* field controls how long it takes in ticks (1/18 second) for a packet to travel one-way between two nodes on the same IP network.

- The *Ticks between Nodes on the Different IP Nets* field controls how long it takes in ticks (1/18 second) for a packet to travel one-way between two nodes on different IP networks.
- The *DSS SAP Filters* field from the Primary DSS Configuration screen brings up the screen shown in figure 22.30.

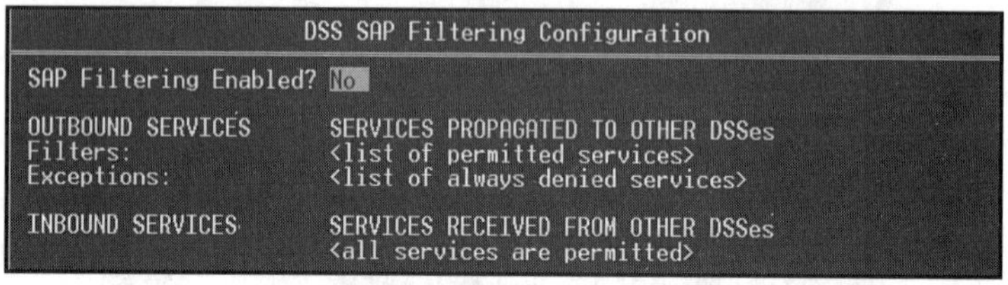

Figure 22.30
The DSS SAP Filter Configuration form.

Use this form to configure DSS SAP filtering for the entire NetWare/IP network. You can control which SAPs get propagated to other DSSes. Only outbound filtering is supported.

Filters displays a list to configure services that will propagate to other DSSes.

Exceptions displays a list of services which are not allowed to propagate.

If any of the DSS tunable parameters are changed, you must stop and restart all DSS servers for the domain. You should also unload NWIP.EXE and reload it at each workstation.

5. After configuring the primary DSS, press Esc. If asked to verify that you want to set up this host as a primary DSS server, answer Yes.
6. The next step is to configure any optional secondary DSS servers.

To configure Secondary DSS servers, make the following selections:

1. Select Managing Services.
2. Select NetWare/IP.
3. Select Configure Secondary DSS. A secondary DSS server form with the following fields appears:

   Field NetWare/IP Domain field contains the name of the NetWare/IP domain to which the secondary DSS belongs.

   Field DSS Primary Host field specifies the name or IP address of the primary DSS server.

After the DSS servers are configured, you must start them by performing the following steps:

1. Go to the main menu of UNICON.
2. Select Start/Stop Services.
3. If the DSS server appears in the list of Running Services, highlight it and press Del. Answer Yes to the query confirming that you want to stop the service.
4. To start the DSS service again, press Ins on the list of Running Services. A list of available services that you can run appears. Highlight DSS Server and press Enter. This activates the DSS Service, and it appears in the list of Running Services. Starting the DSS server also starts the DNS server (if the DNS server is not running).

Changing DNS Servers Associated with DSS Servers

UNICON provides a Server Profile Form that can be used to change DNS server names accessed by DSS servers.

To access the Server Profile form, perform the following steps:

1. Load UNICON.
2. Select Manage Global Objects.
3. Select Configure Server Profile. The form shown in figure 22.31 appears.

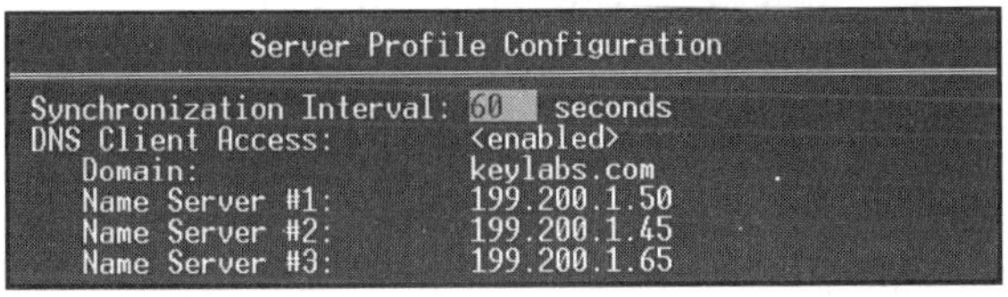

Figure 22.31
The Server Profile Configuration form.

The Server Profile Configuration form contains the following fields:

- The *Synchronization Interval* field is the number of seconds at which the NetWare/IP server checks the SYS:ETC\NFSUSERS, SYS:NFSGROUP, and SYS:NWPARAM for changes. The first two files are used by the NetWare NFS product. The parameter ranges from 1 to 1,000 seconds and has a default value of 60 seconds.
- The *DNS Client Access* field informs you if DNS is enabled or disabled.
- The *Domain* field in the DNS Client Access group displays the DNS name configured during installation. You can enter a different value to change the domain name.
- The *Name Server #1* field in the DNS Access group can be set to the IP address of the first DNS server to contact for name resolution.

- The *Name Server #2* field in the DNS Access group can be set to the IP address of the second DNS server to contact for name resolution if the other DNS servers fail to respond with the desired answer.

- The *Name Server #3* field in the DNS Access group can be set to the IP address of the third DNS server to contact for name resolution if the other DNS servers fail to respond with the desired answer.

Configuring the NetWare/IP Servers

After the DNS and DSS servers are configured, the next step is to configure the NetWare/IP servers.

The following is an outline of the steps needed to configure NetWare/IP:

1. Load UNICON.

2. Select Manage Services.

3. Select NetWare/IP.

4. Select Configure NetWare/IP Server.

   The NetWare/IP configuration form appears. This is the same menu described in the preceding section, "Configuring NetWare/IP" (refer to figure 22.12).

5. Press Esc after you finish making changes and answer Yes to use this server as a NetWare/IP server. The status box at the bottom of the screen changes to indicate that the NetWare/IP server is configured.

You must start the NetWare/IP service. Before starting the NetWare/IP server, you must make sure that DNS and DSS are setup. To start the NetWare/IP Server, follow these steps:

1. Go to the main menu of UNICON.

2. Select Start/Stop Services.

3. If the NetWare/IP server appears in the list of Running Services, highlight it and press Del. Answer Yes to the query verifying that you want to stop the service.

4. To start the NetWare/IP server again, press Ins on the list of Running Services. A list of available services that you can run appears. Highlight NetWare/IP Server and press Enter. This activates the NetWare/IP Server, and it appears in the list of Running Services.

Disabling the NetWare/IP Gateway

If the IPX protocol is bound to a network interface, the NetWare/IP server acts as an IPX-to-IP gateway. If you are on a purely IP-based network, you do not need the NetWare/IP gateway. You can disable this by unbinding IPX from the network interface. You can do this from the server console by typing the following command:

```
UNBIND IPX FROM network_board
```

Alternatively, you can comment out the BIND command in the AUTOEXEC.NCF files. You also can "comment out" the LOAD statement for the network drivers that use frame types used for IPX only.

Changes to AUTOEXEC.NCF & UNISTART.NCF

The NetWare/IP installation at the server adds a command called UNISTART.NCF at the end of the AUTOEXEC.NCF file. The UNISTART.NCF file contains the commands to start DNS, DSS, and NetWare/IP services. The following is an example of the contents of the UNISTART.NCF file:

```
load NETDIR
load RPCSTUB
load TCP_ND
load NETDB
load TIRPC
load dispatch
load NAMED
load NISBIND
load NISSERV
load DSS
load NWIP.NLM
```

Installing and Configuring NetWare/IP Clients

The last phase in NetWare/IP installation is installing and configuring the NetWare/IP client. Before running the NetWare/IP client, you must do the following:

1. Set the CONFIG.SYS files to the following:

   FILES=40 (or higher)

   BUFFERS=20 (or higher)

2. Do not use the DOS APPEND command. To cancel any APPEND commands, you can use the following:

   ```
   APPEND ;
   ```

3. Disable the SHARE command, if it is in effect.

4. If you plan to run LAN WorkPlace or LAN WorkGroup, install these products before installing the NetWare/IP client. NetWare/IP is compatible with these products, but has files that include additional functionality.

Installing NetWare/IP Client

To install the NetWare/IP client software, perform the following steps:

1. Insert the disk labeled WSDOS_1 in drive A: and type the following command:

   INSTALL

   The INSTALL screen appears (see fig. 22.32).

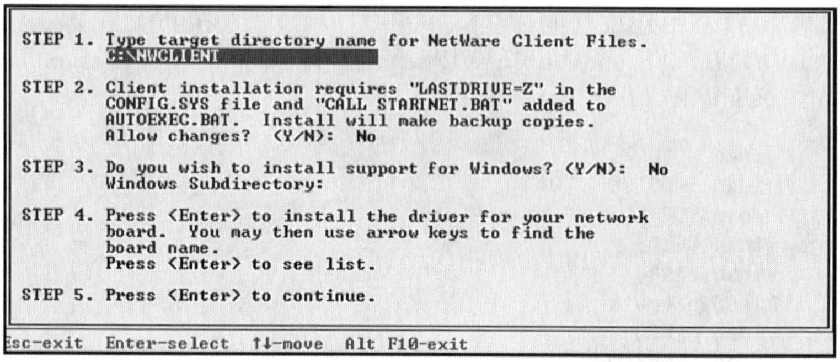

STEP 1. Type target directory name for NetWare Client Files.
C:\NWCLIENT
STEP 2. Client installation requires "LASTDRIVE=Z" in the CONFIG.SYS file and "CALL STARTNET.BAT" added to AUTOEXEC.BAT. Install will make backup copies.
Allow changes? (Y/N): No
STEP 3. Do you wish to install support for Windows? (Y/N): No
Windows Subdirectory:
STEP 4. Press <Enter> to install the driver for your network board. You may then use arrow keys to find the board name.
Press <Enter> to see list.
STEP 5. Press <Enter> to continue.
Esc-exit Enter-select ↑↓-move Alt F10-exit

Figure 22.32
NetWare/IP Client INSTALL screen.

2. For STEP 1, type in the directory that contains NetWare/IP files. The default directory is C:\NWCLIENT.

3. For STEP 2, enter Y to have the INSTALL program modify the CONFIG.SYS and AUTOEXEC.BAT files. Enter N if you want to change these files manually.

4. For STEP 3, enter Y to install MS-Windows support; otherwise, enter N. If you entered Y, enter the pathname where MS Windows is installed.

5. In STEP 4, select the driver for your interface board.

   If you already have a driver loaded, INSTALL recognizes it. You can install the latest version of this driver or continue with the next step.

6. In STEP 5, continue with the installation by pressing Enter. The second form showing the remainder of the steps appears (see fig. 22.33).

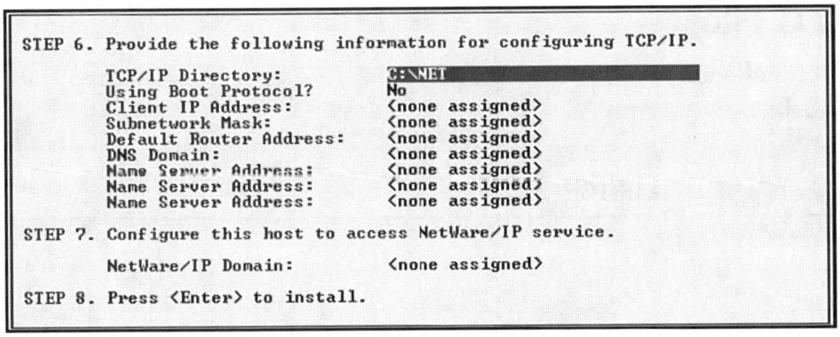

Figure 22.33
Rest of NetWare/IP INSTALL screen.

7. In STEP 6, enter the NetWare/IP client information in each field.

8. In STEP 7, enter the name of the NetWare/IP domain to which this NetWare/IP client belongs. Figure 22.34 shows some sample values.

9. In STEP 8, press Enter to continue with installation. Follow instructions to enter appropriate disks.

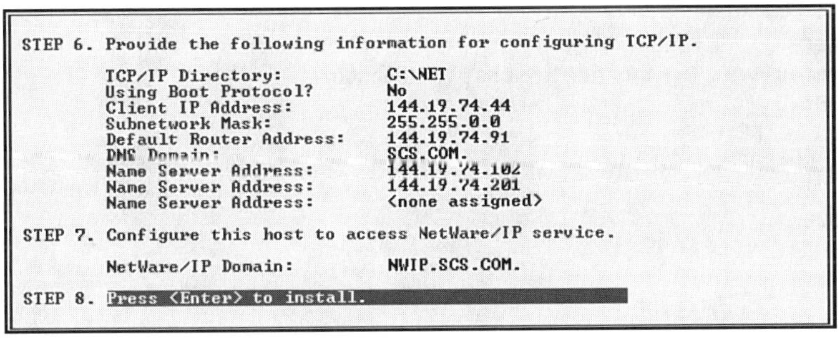

STEP 6. Provide the following information for configuring TCP/IP.
TCP/IP Directory: C:\NET
Using Boot Protocol? No
Client IP Address: 144.19.74.44
Subnetwork Mask: 255.255.0.0
Default Router Address: 144.19.74.91
DNS Domain: SCS.COM.
Name Server Address: 144.19.74.102
Name Server Address: 144.19.74.201
Name Server Address: <none assigned>
STEP 7. Configure this host to access NetWare/IP service.
NetWare/IP Domain: NWIP.SCS.COM.
STEP 8. Press <Enter> to install.

Figure 22.34
NetWare/IP Client Configuration values.

Checking Frame Types

The NetWare/IP client uses any of the following frame types for TCP/IP:

- Ethernet: ETHERNET_II or ETHERNET_SNAP
- Token-Ring: TOKEN-RING_SNAP
- FDDI: FDDI_SNAP
- ARCnet: NOVELL_RX-NET
- PCN or PCN II: IBM_PCN2_SNAP

Checking NET.CFG File

The NetWare/IP client installation modifies the NET.CFG file. Listing 22.3 is an example of the modified NET.CFG file.

Listing 22.3

```
#Link Driver CEODI
Link Driver CEODI
    FRAME Ethernet_802.2
    FRAME Ethernet_802.3
    FRAME Ethernet_II
    INT          5
    PORT         300
    MEM        d0000
    SOCKET         1
    IOWORDSIZE      16
    SOCKETSERVICES     Y
    CARDSERVICES     Y
Protocol IPX
    bind 1
;    bind 2
NetWare DOS Requester
    PB BUFFERS=4; Default is 3. 4 provides best throughput
    FIRST NETWORK DRIVE = F
    PREFERRED SERVER =  KEYLABS
    NAME CONTEXT = "OU=CORP.O=ESL"
Link Support
    Buffers     8 1500
    MemPool     4096
Protocol TCPIP
    PATH TCP_CFG          C:\NET\TCP
    ip_address     144.19.74.44
    ip_netmask     255.255.0.0
    ip_router     144.19.74.91
NWIP
    NWIP_DOMAIN_NAME     NWIP.KEYLABS.COM.
    NSQ_BROADCAST     ON
```

The new sections added are the Protocol TCPIP and the NWIP. These contain the IP address interface and the NetWare/IP domain information.

Checking STARTNET.BAT File

The STARTNET.BAT file contains a line to load NWIP.EXE, the IPX Far Call Interface module.

Listing 22.4 is a sample STARTNET.BAT.

Listing 22.4

```
C:\NET\bin\yesno "Load Networking Software? [y/n]"
@ECHO OFF
if errorlevel 1 goto nonet
C:
CD \NWCLIENT
SET NWLANGUAGE=ENGLISH
LSL
CEODI
C:\NET\BIN\TCPIP
NWIP
if errorlevel -1 goto err_loading_nwip
VLM
CD \
:err_loading_nwip
:nonet
```

Dynamic Host Configuration Protocol (DHCP)

IntranetWare also includes a Dynamic Host Configuration Protocol (DHCP) Server to assist administrators using NetWare/IP on their networks. This following material introduces DHCP and Novell's DHCP Server.

The Need for DHCP

TCP/IP requires that all devices obtain an IP address. Traditionally, these were permanently assigned by writing them into a *hosts* file contained on each device, which also allowed administrators to assign easy to remember *hostnames* and *aliases* for network users to substitute for the clunky IP addresses. An example of a hosts file follows.

```
# A typical /etc/hosts file from a UNIX system would have entries in it
# that describe itself and any other systems it needs to connect to

127.0.0.0          loopback

#SERVERS
192.168.5.150          engnrg_tst     localhost
192.168.5.192          slc_legal
192.168.3.10           slc_finance     gateway
```

This still made it difficult to find and contact remote systems that had no entry in the *hosts* files, and to compensate for changes in the network, such as new users and relocatable devices like laptops. It also provided no built-in means to detect or protect against address duplication, which creates havoc on the network, and provided no tools to reclaim addresses that became available as connections were no longer needed.

Domain Name Services (DNS) was then developed to make it easier to find and contact remote systems. It created a hierarchical series of distributed administered databases (similar to *hosts* files) that could be searched for a system's IP address by using a combination of the *hostname* and a *domain name.*

The *Bootstrap Protocol* (BOOTP) soon followed, allowing IP addresses to be configured remotely and eliminating the need for physically going to each workstation and manually installing addresses. With BOOTP, a centrally located file statically (permanently) maps and distributes IP addresses to devices as they boot based on their MAC address.

The *Dynamic Host Configuration Protocol* (DHCP) is an extension to BOOTP that dynamically (temporarily) assigns IP addresses to devices when they boot and make a DHCP request. DHCP provides a pool of IP addresses that are 'leased' for a specified period rather than having a single address permanently assigned. In this way, a smaller number of IP addresses can serve a larger number of devices because not every device will be using its address at the same time, and unused addresses are reclaimed and returned to the pool for future use by others. DHCP also protects against address duplication by checking the network for the existence of any address it is assigning prior to actually allowing any device to use it.

DHCP also greatly simplifies administration of the network by allowing the central distribution of other network information that would normally require manually changing the parameters on each client. Information such as default gateways and routers, network mask, DNS, and NETBIOS parameters and more can be centrally changed and distributed from the DHCP server while it provides the IP address to the client.

The Standards that Define DHCP

DHCP is an ongoing series of Request For Comments (RFCs) that have described DHCP and BOOTP, and then gradually added new features and interoperability for servers and clients on several different operating systems. There have been recent updates to almost every applicable RFC, and future updates to RFC 1533 will add support for NetWare/IP-based DHCP servers and clients. The current RFCs that describe DHCP are listed below and are freely available on the Internet from InterNIC and several other sites.

RFC 1541 "Dynamic Host Configuration Protocol"

R. Droms, 10/27/1993 (Obsoletes RFC 1531)

RFC 1542 "Clarifications and Extensions for the Bootstrap Protocol"

W. Wimer, 10/27/1993 (Obsoletes RFC 1532)

RFC 1533 "DHCP Options and BOOTP Vendor Extensions"

S. Alexander, R. Droms, 10/08/1993 (Obsoletes RFC 1497)

RFC 1534 "Interoperation Between DHCP and BOOTP"

R. Droms, 10/08/1993

Key features currently being developed include automated registration of DHCP clients with DNS (requiring extensive updates to the DNS RFCs as well), and development of an Inter-server communication protocol for coordination of multiple DHCP servers. Work is also moving quickly toward a specification for DHCP for IP version 6 (DHCPv6 for IPv6), which is currently available as an Internet Draft. The current DHCP specification is based on IPv4.

The current RFCs define the DHCP protocol to provide the following information to a client:

- Standard TCP/IP Parameters such as:
  - Clients IP Address
  - Subnet Mask Options
  - Hostname of Client
  - Routers/Gateways Addresses and Options
  - IP Forwarding Enable and Options
  - Source Routing Options
  - Several IP and TCP Layer Options
- NIS Parameters
- Diskless Client Information
  - Boot File / Root Path
  - Swap Servers
- DNS Parameters
- LPR/LPD Servers
- Time Servers
- Vendor Specific Information
  - NETBIOS Parameters
  - X Windows Parameters

This is not a complete list. For more detail, refer to the appropriate RFC.

NetWare/IP Specific Parameters

NetWare/IP servers and clients require additional network parameters at boot time to operate correctly. NetWare/IP clients want to know the address of the Primary and Preferred DSS Servers, the IP addresses of up to five nearest NetWare/IP servers, and some other items. Many of these parameters are optional for most NetWare/IP clients, so NetWare/IP clients can still obtain IP addresses from standard DHCP servers running on other platforms (like Windows NT and Unix that are not "NetWare/IP aware") when a Novell DHCP Server is not available on the network.

Packet Format

The minimum IP packet size for a DHCP packet is 576 bytes with 512 bytes of actual DHCP information. There are 236 bytes of DHCP header information that define the hardware type (i.e. 10Mb Ethernet is a '1'), address length (Ethernet is 6 bytes), source and destination addresses, and several other flags. This is followed by a marker called a "magic cookie" (the hex values 63, 82, 53, 63) and at least 312 bytes of DHCP data that describe several optional and vendor specific parameters. A diagram of a DHCP packet follows in figure 22.35.

Figure 22.35
Diagram of a DHCP packet.

```
 0.................1.................2.................3........
........:
 0 1 2 3 4 5 6 7 0 1 2 3 4 5 6 7 0 1 2 3 4 5 6 7 0 1 2 3 4 5 6 7
:
 +-+-+-+-+-+-+-+-+-+-+-+-+-+-+-+-+-+-+-+-+-+-+-+-+ :
 I     op  (1)        I      htype  (1)    I        hlen  (1)     I   ho
ps (1)     I
+-------------+-------------+-------------+----------
-----:
 I                         xid (4)
                            I
+---------------------------+-----------------------
-------:
 I           secs  (2)                     I            flags (2
)                   I
+---------------------------+-----------------------
-------:
 I                        ciaddr (4)
                        I
+---------------------------------------------------
-------:
 I                        yiaddr (4)
                        I
+---------------------------------------------------
-------:
 I                        siaddr (4)
                        I
+---------------------------------------------------
-------:
 I                        giaddr (4)
                        I
+---------------------------------------------------
-------:
 I
                           I
 I                        chaddr (16)
                     I
 I
                           I
 I
                           I
 I
+---------------------------------------------------
-------
 I
                           I
 I                        sname  (64)
                        I
+---------------------------------------------------
-------:
 I
                           I
 I                        file      (128)
                        I
+---------------------------------------------------
-------:
 I
                           I
 I                        options (312)
                        I
+---------------------------------------------------
-------:
```

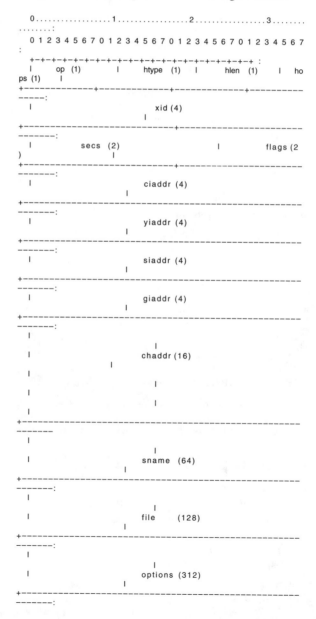

The following identifies the byte offset, field length, and a description of the fields identified in the previous diagram.

```
Byte
Offset        Field Name      Length     Description
(HEX)

00             OP              1          Message type / Op code
01             HTYPE           1          Hardware address type (i.e. 1 = 10Mb
➥Ethernet)
02             HLEN            1          Hardware address length (i.e. Ethernet MAC
➥address
                                          is 6 bytes long)
03             HOPS            1          # of hops; (primarily used by relay agents -
                                          clients set to zero)
04             XID             4          Transaction identifier
08             SECS            2          Seconds since client started to boot
0A             FLAGS           2          Miscellaneous flags
0C             CIADDR          4          Client IP address; (client fills in
➥requested IP address
                                          when requesting verification of previously
➥used parameters;
                                          otherwise 0.0.0.0)
10             YIADDR          4          'Your' client IP address (Clients IP address
➥for anything other
                                          than a DHCPREQUEST verifying previously used
➥parameters)
14             SIADDR          4          P Address of next DHCP server to use
18             GIADDR          4          Relay Agent IP address (Used when booting
➥via relay-agents)
1C             CHADDR          16         Client hardware address
2C             SNAME           64         Server host name (Optional)
6C             FILE            128        Boot file name
EC             COOKIE          4          The Magic Cookie (marker bytes 63 82 53 63)
F0             OPTIONS         312        Optional and vendor specific options
224            END
```

The main message types defined in byte 0 are:

- **DHCPDISCOVER.** The client broadcasts this message to locate any available DHCP servers on the network. (Client sends CLIENT ID.)
- **DHCPOFFER.** All DHCP servers respond with this to a client's DHCPDISCOVER request. It offers the client limited configuration information. (Server sends SERVER ID, LEASE TIME, T1, T2, MASK, ROUTER, DNS SERVER & DOMAIN NAME.)
- **DHCPREQUEST.** The client broadcasts this message to all DHCP servers requesting the offered parameters from one DHCP server, and implicitly declining the offers from the others. (The client sends CLIENT ID, ACCEPTED SERVER ID, REQUESTED IP ADDRESS, PARAMETER LIST.)

- **DHCPACK.** The selected DHCP server sends this message to the client with the committed network address and other configuration parameters. The client then verifies the received parameters will work, and if it finds a problem (i.e. duplicate address) it sends a DHCPDECLINE back to the server. (Server sends SERVER ID, LEASE TIME, T1, T2, MASK, ROUTER, IP, DNS.)
- **DHCPNAK.** This message is sent from the DHCP server to refuse the client's request for configuration parameters; as when the client requests an address already in use.
- **DHCPDECLINE.** This message is sent by the client to the DHCP server to indicate that the parameters it received were somehow invalid. The client does an ARP with the newly received parameters to insure they are valid and sends this response if not.
- **DHCPRELEASE.** This message is sent by client to server to indicate that it is releasing its address and canceling the rest of its lease.

Address Assignment Message Sequence

The following shows the typical message sequence for a successful address assignment. It is important to note that Client A is sending broadcasts to all DHCP servers on the network. Therefore, all valid servers respond with an offer (directly to the client; not a broadcast). The client then responds with another broadcast message to all servers (a DHCPREQUEST) which contains the ID of the server it has selected to continue negotiating with. Only the selected server (Server B in the example below) responds with a DHCPACK, which contains address and lease parameters.

```
SERVER A                CLIENT A
                        ← DHCPDISCOVER
DHCPOFFER →
                        ← DHCPREQUEST

SERVER B
                        ← DHCPDISCOVER
DHCPOFFER →
                        ← DHCPREQUEST
DHCPACK →

SERVER C
                        ← DHCPDISCOVER
DHCPOFFER →
                        ← DHCPREQUEST
```

Denied Request

The following shows a typical message sequence that occurs when the selected DHCP Server denies service to the client. This would occur if the IP address requested during the DHCPREQUEST was already assigned by the server.

```
SERVER  B                                CLIENT A
                                      ← DHCPDISCOVER
DHCPOFFER →
                                      ← DHCPREQUEST
DHCNACK →
```

At this point the client is responsible for renegotiating the DHCP request.

Declined Request

The following shows the message sequence that is displayed when the DHCP client declines the DHCP parameters. This would occur if the IP address just assigned by the selected server in the DHCPACK is found in use on the network, or some other parameter is found to be invalid. (The client does an ARP with the new address prior to using it to detect conflicts.)

```
SERVER B                                  CLIENT A
                                      ← DHCPDISCOVER
DHCPOFFER →
                                      ← DHCPREQUEST
DHCACK →
                                      ← DHCPDECLINE
```

At this point, the client is responsible for renegotiating the DHCP request.

IntranetWare DHCP Server

IntranetWare's DHCP Server does not provide all of the vendor specific options and services described in RFC 1533, but provides most of the main functionality described in that RFC, along with several NetWare/IP extensions. RFC 1533 defines the mechanism that vendors use to specify and implement vendor specific options for DHCP.

Specifically, IntranetWare's DHCP Server provides client configuration of the following parameters:

- **Standard TCP/IP Parameters**
  - Client IP Address and Subnet Mask
  - Router Addresses—Up to three
  - DNS Domain Name and up to 3 Server Addresses
  - NETBIOS Name Servers, Scope, and Node Type
  - Lease Time, Renew (T1) and Rebind (T2) Times
- **NetWare/IP Parameters**
  - NetWare/IP Domain Name
  - Preferred DSS Server addresses—Up to five

- Nearest NetWare/IP Servers—Up to five
- Auto-Retry Options

IntranetWare's DHCP Server provides backward compatibility to BOOTP clients. The DHCP Server honors requests from BOOTP clients and assigns them a permanent address in the DHCPTAB. The DHCP Server makes Novell's BOOTPD.NLM obsolete, and does not run on the same system as BOOTPD.NLM.

The DHCP Server also provides an EXCLUDED NODES LIST. DHCP and BOOTP requests received from workstations with physical (MAC) addresses listed in the EXCLUDED NODES LIST will be denied requests for IP addresses.

What Comprises the DHCP Server

IntranetWare includes an update to Novell's previously released DHCP Server 2.0 that consists of three NLMs that the administrator needs to be concerned about (DHCPSRVR.NLM, DHCPIO.NLM and DHCPCFG.NLM) as well as some updates to other system modules.

The DHCP Server NLMs do not require NetWare/IP to operate, originally being released on Novell's TCP/IP stack provided by TCPIP.NLM. In addition, the DHCP Server operate on other NetWare platforms all the way back to NetWare 3.12. There are certain restrictions that apply for installing DHCP Server 2.0 on versions other than IntranetWare. These are clearly outlined in the README files included with the DHCP install files.

NetWare/IP Client with NT and Unix DHCP Servers

NetWare/IP workstations set-up as DHCP Clients may not always have their DHCP requests serviced from an IntranetWare DHCP Server. In those situations, the NetWare/IP Client will still be able to obtain whatever standard network parameters were available from other DHCP servers on the network. The Client will not receive any NetWare/IP specific parameters, but will still be able to participate on the network.

Because DHCP servers can assign IP addresses across multiple subnets, a server is not required for each subnet. If the DHCP server on the primary subnetwork is not available, then a DHCP server on another subnetwork can fulfill the DHCP requests. DHCP requests will work through routers as long as the router supports BOOTP/DHCP relay agents as described in RFC 951.

Windows 95/NT and Unix DHCP Clients with IntranetWare DHCP Server

The IntranetWare DHCP Server honors valid DHCP requests from any DHCP Client, not just NetWare/IP Clients. Most TCP/IP based Clients have DHCP functionality built-in. The IntranetWare DHCP Server passes all of the parameters it is configured to pass, and the

DHCP client uses them as it wants. If it doesn't need the parameters specified by the NetWare/IP option codes, then it ignores them, or it might convert them in some way. Those details are left up to the DHCP client.

The current TCP/IP implementations used by Microsoft in Windows 95 and NT versions 3.51/4.0 all support DHCP to obtain their network parameters. The IntranetWare DHCP Server supports the Microsoft DHCP client implementation, as well as those from most other TCP/IP vendors.

Installing DHCP Server on IntranetWare

To install a DHCP Server, perform the following steps:

1. Load INSTALL.NLM.
2. Go to PRODUCT OPTIONS. The screen shown in figure 22.36 appears.
3. Select Choose an Item or Product Listed Above.

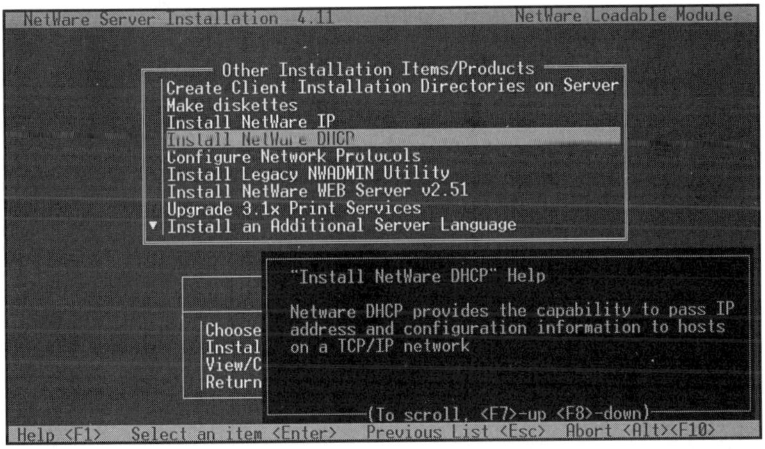

Figure 22.36
The Product Options screen.

4. Select Install NetWare DHCP.
5. Select the proper path from which to install.
6. Select Install Product.
7. Select the desired NetWare server from the list displayed.
8. Answer YES to 'Start Installation?'
9. After prompt appears indicating 'Installation was successful', press Enter to return to the Product Installation menu.

10. Select EXIT.

11. Exit INSTALL.NLM.

12. The server should then be brought down and restarted to load any updated NLMs and system modules.

Starting the DHCP Server

Following are the main steps required to get the DHCP server running after it has been installed. The steps are explained in more detail in the following sections.

1. After the server is restarted, load DHCPCFG.NLM from the console. This is the configuration tool for the DHCP server. You must run DHCPCFG.NLM to initialize the DHCP server prior to proceeding to the next step.

   After the desired DHCP parameters are configured, exit DHCPCFG. See the following section for instructions on using DHCPCFG.NLM to configure and administer the DHCP server.

2. On the console, load DHCPSRVR.NLM. This automatically loads DHCPIO.NLM and other required system modules.

Note In certain circumstances (outlined in the next section), DHCPIO.NLM should explicitly (manually) be loaded so that additional startup options can be used. In most configurations, this is not required.

   These lines should be added to the AUTOEXEC.NCF file so the DHCP Server restarts each time the system is rebooted.

3. The DHCP server should now be dispensing addresses on your network.

Configuring/Administering DHCPCFG.NLM

For first-time configuration of the DHCP Server, perform the following steps. Detailed descriptions of these steps follows.

1. Load DHCPCFG.NLM by typing LOAD DHCPCFG on the system console. The screen shown in figure 22.37 appears.

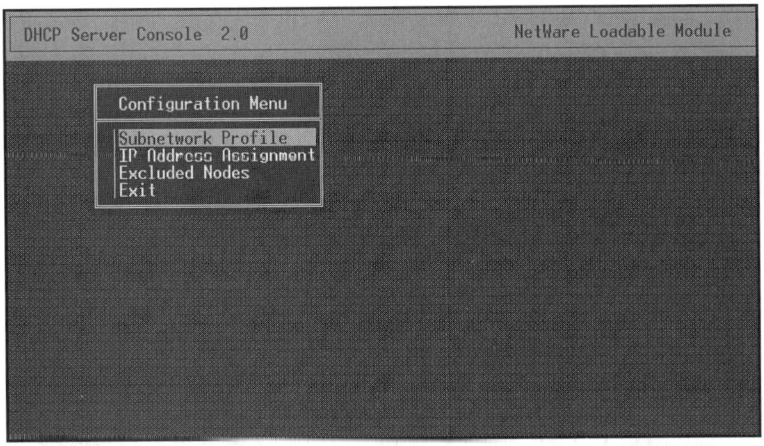

Figure 22.37
The DHCP Server Console screen with the Configuration Menu.

2. Select Subnetwork Profile. Make any necessary changes to the profiles to describe your subnetworks. You must have at least one profile.

3. If a workstation has an established IP address or you want to assign a specific address to a particular workstation, use IP ADDRESS ASSIGNMENT to assign IP addresses to these workstations.

4. If there is any workstation to which you don't want to assign IP address automatically, you can configure it in EXCLUDED NODES.

The Main DHCP Configuration Menu contains the following choices:

- **Subnetwork Profile.** Lets you define settings for each network or subnetwork supported by your workgroup server.
- **IP Address Assignment.** Displays all currently configured workstations and lets you add and delete workstation IP address assignments. Use this selection to configure workstations that have established IP addresses.
- **Excluded Nodes.** When a node on this list requests an IP address from the DHCP server, the request is ignored.
- **Exit.** Returns you to the NetWare console prompt.

Subnetwork Profile Menus

Use the Subnetwork Profile menu to supply the information for a subnetwork profile.

Select Subnetwork Profile. This displays the known and available subnetworks. The default subnetwork that is bound to the TCPIP NLM is displayed, as well as any additional subnetwork profiles that have been defined.

Highlight the desired profile and press Enter. The form shown in figure 22.38 appears. Press Insert to add an additional profile.

Fields containing values that are bound to LAN adapters such as SUBNET ADDRESS and SUBNET MASK cannot be edited via the DHCPCFG.NLM. They must be edited in the original place they are defined (i.e. AUTOXEC.NCF via INSTALL.NLM or INETCFG.NLM).

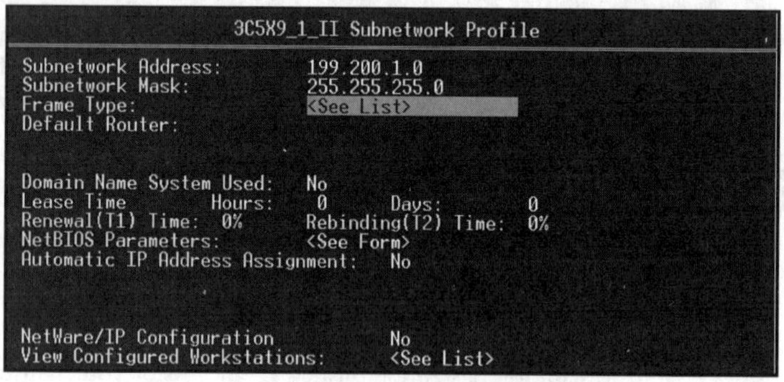

Figure 22.38
The Subnetwork Profile form.

Several fields are displayed, some with default values filled in. Some are for viewing and others prompt the user for input. Additional fields might be presented, based on the responses provided in the following fields.

- **Subnet Address.** Displays the values derived from LAN adapters bindings.
- **Subnetwork Mask.** Use this list to select the subnetwork mask for your network. If your network does not support subnetworks, you must still enter the default subnetwork mask.
- **Frame Type.** Displays a list of available frame types. The frame type is determined by LAN card bindings in INETCFG.
- **Default Router.** Use this field to enter the IP address of the default router for the subnetwork. The router must be on the same subnetwork as the workstation you are configuring. If your network does not have a router, leave the field blank and press Enter.
- **Domain Name System Used.** Use this field to indicate whether to set up Domain Name System (DNS) configuration parameters for this subnetwork. Selecting Yes causes an additional menu to pop up. See the "Additional Fields to Subnetwork Profile Menus" section that follows.
- **Lease Time.** When a DHCP client requests an IP address, the DHCP server leases the address to the client for the duration from this field. If the lease time is not configured, default is 3 days. The maximum time that can be configured is 10,000 days and 23 hours.

If the client has not contacted its initial DHCP server (T1 or Renew Time) or any other server (T2 or Rebind Time) by the end of the lease time, it then surrenders its IP address and the IP transport must be reloaded.

- **Renewal (T1) Time.** The client maintains two times, Renewal(T1) Time and Rebinding(T2) Time, that specify the times at which the client tries to extend its address lease on its network.

  T1 is the time at which the client enters the RENEWING state and attempts to contact the DHCP server that originally issued the client's network address. If T1 is not configured, it defaults to 50 percent of the lease duration.

- **Rebind (T2) Time.** T2 is the time at which the client enters the RENEWING state and attempts to contact any DHCP server. If T2 is not configured, it defaults to 87 percent of the lease duration.

- **NetBIOS Parameters.** Indicates whether to configure NetBIOS over TCP/IP information for this subnetwork. Press Enter to display an additional menu with fields for NETBIOS Name Server addresses, Node Type, and Scope.

- **Automatic IP Address Assignment.** If you select YES, workstations without IP addresses are automatically assigned an available address when the DHCP and BOOTP requests are received. This address is assigned permanently to BOOTP clients and assigned for the lease time duration if it is a DHCP client. Both are recorded and you can subsequently view the workstation's name, IP address, and physical address by selecting the View Configured Workstations field.

  Selecting YES displays additional fields to indicate which IP addresses to use for new workstations.

  If you select YES, you must use the IP Address Assignment selection on the Configuration Menu to create entries for every system within the address range you designate that has a pre-assigned (static) IP address. These are usually Unix systems or other Name Servers on the network that require addresses that cannot change.

  If you select NO, you must manually assign an address to every workstation on the subnetwork using the IP Address Assignment selection on the Configuration Menu. Select YES or NO and press Enter.

- **NetWare/IP Configuration.** Indicates whether the DHCP server also dispenses NetWare/IP parameters to NetWare/IP clients on the subnetwork. Selecting YES displays an additional menu to fill in NetWare IP specific parameters. See the section "Additional Fields to Subnetwork Profile Menus" that follows. Selecting NO indicates that only standard TCP/IP parameters (and possibly NETBIOS if enabled) are dispensed.

- **View Configured Workstations.** This screen lists the names, physical addresses, and IP addresses for all configured workstations on this subnetwork. If no workstations are configured, the list is blank.

The list includes both workstations that you configured manually (using the IP AD DRESS ASSIGNMENT selection on the Configuration Menu), and workstations that received their IP addresses automatically. The list is for viewing only. To both view and change (add, modify, or delete) configured workstations, use the IP Address Assignment selection on the Configuration Menu.

Additional Fields to Subnetwork Profile Menus

As fields are filled in on the Subnetwork Profile Menu, additional fields are presented for input. Following are descriptions of those additional fields:

- **Domain Name System Used.** When this option is switched from NO to YES an additional menu to appears with these fields (see fig. 22.39).

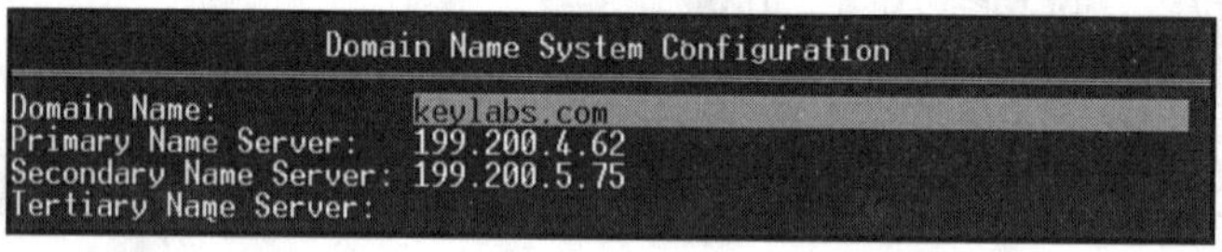

Figure 22.39
The DNS Client Configuration screen.

- **Domain Name.** Enter the Domain Name as it appears to the Domain Name System.
- **Primary, Secondary, Tertiary Name Servers.** Use this field to enter the IP address of the primary DNS name server for this subnetwork. Enter the address in dotted notation (for example, 122.43.12.8). You must include the address for a primary name server address when you enable DNS services. Additional name servers (secondary and tertiary) are optional.
- **NETBIOS PARAMETERS.** To enter NETBIOS parameters highlight <SEE FORM> and press Enter. An additional menu appears with these fields (see fig. 22.40).

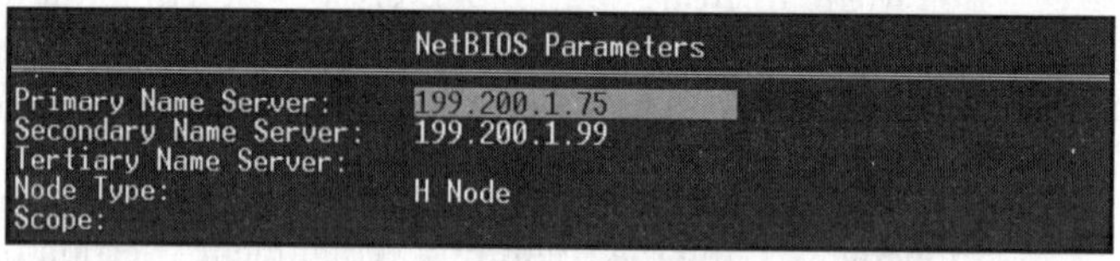

Figure 22.40
The NetBIOS Parameters form.

- **Primary, Secondary, and Tertiary Name Servers.** NetBIOS over TCP/IP Name Server Option. You can fill in up to three NetBIOS name servers in order of preference. Enter the IP address here for the NetBIOS Name Servers.
- **Node Type.** NetBIOS over TCP/IP Node Type option. This allows the administrator to configure the NetBIOS over TCP/IP client types. There are four different node types: B-Node, P-Node, M-Node, and H-Node.

- **Scope.** The NetBIOS scope option specifies the NetBIOS over TCP/IP scope parameter for the client. A "NetBIOS Scope" is the population of computers across which a registered NetBIOS name is known.
- **Automatic IP Address Assignment.** Changing this field from NO to YES causes these additional fields to be displayed (see fig. 22.41).

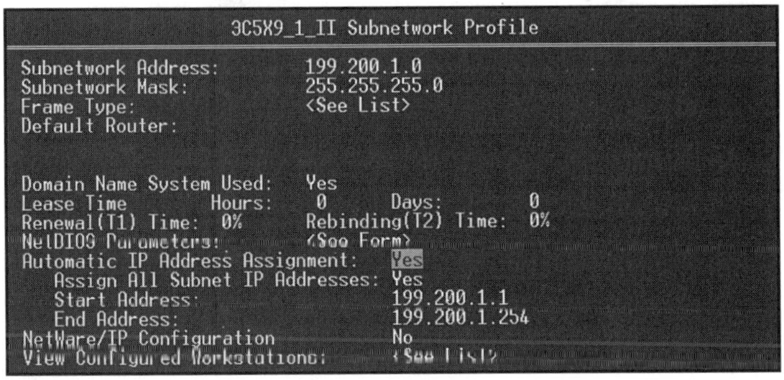

Figure 22.41
Display of extra IP Address Assignments fields.

- **Assign All Subnet IP Addresses.** Use this field to specify whether all or only some of the IP addresses on this subnetwork are available to be assigned dynamically by the DHCP server.

  Select Yes if all the addresses in the subnet can be assigned to workstations. When you select Yes, the Start Address and End Address fields are automatically filled in with full range of subnet addresses that are available for automatic assignment.

  If you select Yes, you must use the IP ADDRESS ASSIGNMENT selection on the Configuration Menu to identify every system on the subnetwork that has a static (pre-assigned) IP address. Typically, these are Unix hosts or other NetWare/IP servers running as Name Servers.

  Select No if you do not want the full range of addresses in the subnet available for dynamic assignment. When you select No, you must fill in the START ADDRESS and END ADDRESS fields to specify the range of subnet addresses available for automatic assignment. All addresses outside the range are reserved for static or manual assignment. Use the IP Address Assignment selection on the Configuration Menu to assign these addresses.

- **Start Address.** The first address of the range of IP addresses being made available for automatic assignment.
- **End Address.** The last address of the range of IP addresses being made available for automatic assignment.
- **NetWare/IP Configuration.** Changing this field from NO to YES causes an additional menu to appear with the following fields (see fig. 22.42).

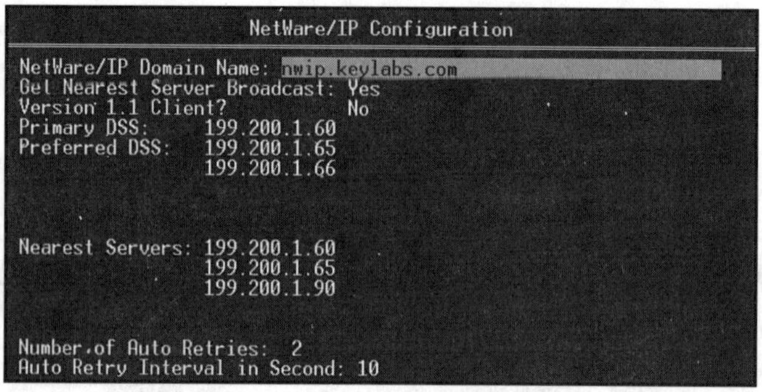

Figure 22.42
The NetWare/IP Configuration form.

- **NetWare/IP Domain Name.** Use this field to identify the name of the NetWare/IP domain to which the workstations using this profile belong. You must include a domain name when you set up NetWare/IP support.

  Enter the fully qualified name using dotted notation. For example, enter NWIP.MYCOMPANY.COM. You can enter the name in uppercase or lowercase letters.

- **Get Nearest Server Broadcast.** Use this field to specify whether the NetWare/IP client will use nearest server query (NSQ) broadcasts to locate the nearest server.

- **Version 1.1 Client.** Defines whether the client supports NetWare/IP Version 1.1 compatibility. A Client only needs this compatibility if it contacts NetWare/IP Version 1.1 servers.

- **Primary DSS.** This field identifies the Primary Domain SAP/RIP Service (DSS) Server for this NetWare/IP domain. NetWare/IP uses this parameter when configuring a secondary DSS server. Enter the IP address of the desired Primary Server.

- **Preferred DSS.** Identifies the preferred Domain SAP/RIP Service (DSS) servers. NetWare/IP clients use DSS servers to locate and access services on the network. You can identify up to five preferred DSS servers. Identify each server by IP address. Identifying preferred DSS servers is optional. If none are identified, a Client will query a DNS server at startup to locate a DSS server. Preferred servers allow the Client to skip this process and start up faster.

- **Nearest Servers.** Identifies up to five of the nearest NetWare/IP servers. A Client requiring access to a NetWare/IP server attempts to connect with the nearest servers first. Identify each server by IP address. Identifying nearest servers is optional. If none are identified, the Client will query a DSS server at startup to find the nearest server. The nearest servers field allows the Client to skip this process and start up faster.

- **Number Of Auto Retries.** Defines the number of times the NetWare/IP Client attempts to communicate with a given DSS server at startup.
- **Auto-retry Interval in Seconds.** Defines the time interval in seconds between attempts to communicate with a given DSS server at startup. The default is 10 seconds. Values from 5 to 60 are valid.

IP Address Assignment Menus

The screen shown in figure 22.43 lists all workstations to which IP addresses have been assigned. Each time a workstation starts, it sends a message requesting (BOOTP or DHCP request) its IP address to a DHCP server. The DHCP server consults this list first to determine the IP address, if it is not configured in this list, DHCP server will get an address from the pool. Entries to this list are made manually by the administrator, or are entered automatically during workstation initial startup. If no workstations are listed, none have been configured.

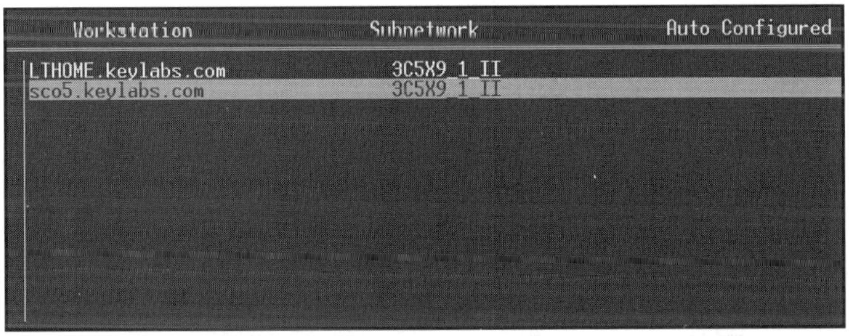

Figure 22.43
The configured workstations screen.

Use this screen to monitor and manage IP address assignment for the workstations. After an IP address is assigned here, it cannot be assigned automatically to any other workstation. This prevents a workstation's established IP address from being assigned to a different workstation.

To add a new workstation, press Insert. The screen in figure 22.44 appears. Add only workstations to which you want to assign a specific IP address. To modify information about a workstation, select the workstation and press Enter.

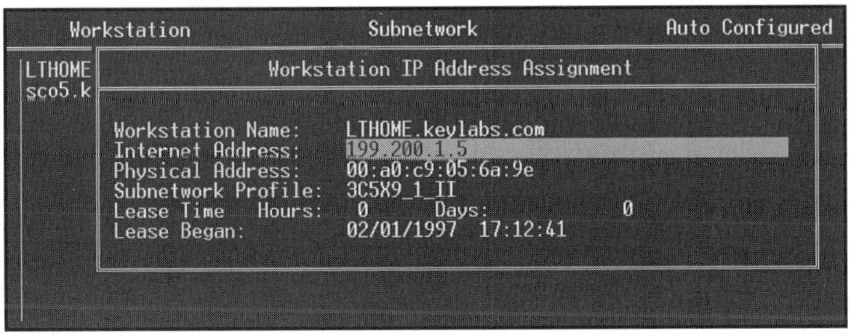

Figure 22.44
The Workstation IP Address Assignment screen.

To delete a workstation, select the workstation and press Delete.

To rename a workstation, select the workstation and press F3.

Use this form to enter the setup information for a workstation that already has an established IP address.

Before you can configure these workstations, you must use the Subnetwork Profile selection on the Configuration Menu to create a subnetwork profile for the subnetwork where the workstations are located.

If you are entering information for a workstation with an established IP address that falls within an automatic address assignment range, enter its IP address and physical address. You must create an entry for all such workstations so that their established addresses are not assigned to different workstations. Typically, these systems are UNIX hosts or other NetWare/IP servers.

Type the IP and physical addresses in the fields provided; then press Esc to create the workstation entry.

Excluded Nodes Menus

The screen shown in figure 22.45 lists all the DHCP and BOOTP excluded nodes. When a node on this list requests an IP address assignment from the DHCP server, the request is ignored. Use this screen to view, add, and delete nodes.

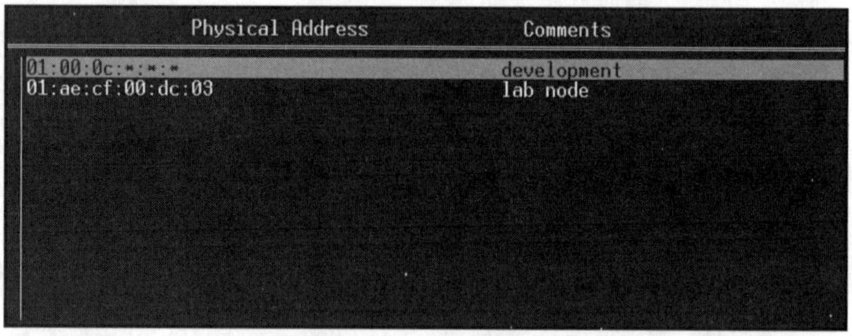

Figure 22.45
The excluded nodes list.

To add (exclude) a node, press Insert. You must then enter the physical address of the node to be excluded. This would be the six byte hexadecimal MAC address of the NIC.

You can also exclude a group of nodes by using the asterisk (*) as a wildcard character in the physical address. The first three bytes of the physical address identify the manufacturer; and the last three actually identify the node. To exclude all nodes with network interface cards from a particular manufacturer, you might enter the following:

```
00:00:1c:*:*:*
```

To delete a node, press Delete.

DHCPIO.NLM Options

Although DHCPIO.NLM usually loads automatically when DHCPSRVR.NLM is loaded and runs without any additional startup options, there are some instances when it needs to be started in CONFIGURE WORKSTATION ADDRESS ASSIGNMENT MODE. This mode allows DHCPIO to handle some special cases dealing with clients that move from one subnet to another (like laptops).

The syntax is:

```
DHCPIO -mMODE
```

An example using one of the modes defined below would be:

```
LOAD DHCPIO.NLM -mDeleteDuplicate.
```

This would need to be manually loaded from the server console or added to the AUTOEXEC.NCF file prior to loading DHCPSRVR.NLM.

DHCPIO looks at the physical (MAC) address of the client making the DHCP requests prior to assigning IP addresses. These modes know how DHCPIO reacts to requests from the same MAC address on several different subnets. The following modes are recognized:

- **DeleteDuplicate.** When a Client moves from subnet A to subnet B, the original address on subnet A is deleted when the new address on subnet B is assigned.
- **YesDuplicate.** When a Client moves from subnet to subnet, assign a new address in every subnet. Do not delete duplicate assignments to the same MAC address.
- **NoDuplicate.** If a Client moves from subnet A to subnet B before the address is deleted (for BOOTP Clients) or expired (DHCP Clients), the request will be dropped.

Related Files

The following list shows related files:

- **/ETC/DHCPTAB.** This text file is created by the DHCP Server. It contains all of the parameters it has assigned to BOOTP and DHCP clients. It is for viewing only and should not be edited in any way. Changes must be made through the DHCPCFG.NLM.
- **/ETC/DHNORESP.** This text file lists all of the nodes configured in the EXCLUDED NODES LIST. It is for viewing only and should not be edited in any way. Changes must be made through the DHCPCFG.NLM.
- **/ETC/DHCP.LOG.** This text file contains all of the console messages printed by the DHCP server. This includes Server start/stop messages as well as errors and comments generated during client address configuration. This is a running log of all messages and can grow rather long. Periodically, it should be reviewed for possible problems like excessive requests from particular clients or failed requests from other subnets or routers. The file can be saved and deleted to clear it. The server will create the file when needed.

Summary

This chapter covered the essential concepts needed to design, install, and configure NetWare/IP-based networks. It also covered the use and configuration of the Dynamic Host Configuration Protocol on NetWare/IP based servers.

NetWare/IP solves a very important problem. It allows network designers to use the TCP/IP protocol for transport services on a NetWare network. This enables large networks currently based on TCP/IP to use this protocol for all their network services, and DHCP can greatly simplify the administration of host IP addresses on these large networks.

NetWare/IP also can be used as a gateway to link IPX networks with a backbone network based on TCP/IP only.

INDEX

Symbols

A

B

C

D

E

J - K

L

M

N

O

P

Q

R

S

T

U

X - Y - Z

REGISTRATION CARD

Novell IntranetWare Professional Reference

Name ______________________________ Title ______________________

Company ____________________________ Type of business ______________

Address ____

City/State/ZIP ____

Have you used these types of books before? ☐ yes ☐ no

If yes, which ones? ____

____

How many computer books do you purchase each year? ☐ 1–5 ☐ 6 or more

How did you learn about this book? ______________________________

Where did you purchase this book? ______________________________

Which applications do you currently use? __________________________

____

Which computer magazines do you subscribe to? ____________________

____

What trade shows do you attend? ________________________________

____

Comments: ____

____

____

Would you like to be placed on our preferred mailing list? ☐ yes ☐ no

☐ **I would like to see my name in print!** You may use my name and quote me in future New Riders products and promotions. My daytime phone number is: ______________________

New Riders Publishing 201 West 103rd Street ◆ Indianapolis, Indiana 46290 USA

Fax to **317-817-7448**

Fold Here

NO POSTAGE
NECESSARY
IF MAILED
IN THE
UNITED STATES

BUSINESS REPLY MAIL

FIRST-CLASS MAIL PERMIT NO. 9918 INDIANAPOLIS IN

POSTAGE WILL BE PAID BY THE ADDRESSEE

NEW RIDERS PUBLISHING
201 W 103RD ST
INDIANAPOLIS IN 46290-9058

Getting Started with the CD-ROM

This page provides instructions for getting started with the CD-ROM.

Windows 95/NT Installation

Insert the CD-ROM into your CD-ROM drive. If autoplay is enabled on your machine, the CD-ROM setup program starts automatically the first time you insert the disc.

If setup does not run automatically, perform these steps:

1. From the Start menu, choose Programs, Windows Explorer.
2. Select your CD-ROM drive under My Computer.
3. Double-click SETUP.EXE in the Contents list.
4. Follow the on-screen instructions that appear
5. Setup adds an icon named CD-ROM Contents to a program group for this book. To explore the CD-ROM, double-click on the CD-ROM Contents icon.

Windows 3.1 Installation

1. Insert the CD-ROM into your CD-ROM drive.
2. From File Manager or Program Manager, choose Run from the File Menu.
3. Type ***<drive>*:\SETUP** and press Enter, (where *<drive>* is the drive letter of your CD-ROM). For example, if your CD-ROM is Drive D, type **D:\SETUP** and press Enter.
4. Follow the on-screen instructions that appear.

How to Contact New Riders Publishing

If you have a question or comment about this product, there are several ways to contact New Riders Publishing. For the quickest response, please send e-mail to `support@mcp.com`.

If you prefer, you can fax New Riders at 1-317-817-7448.

New Riders' mailing address is as follows:

New Riders Publishing
Attn: Julie Fairweather, Publishing Manager
201 W. 103rd Street
Indianapolis, IN 46290

You can also contact us through the Macmillan Computer Publishing CompuServe forum at `GO NEWRIDERS`. Our World Wide Web address is `http://www.mcp.com/newriders`.

MACMILLAN COMPUTER PUBLISHING USA

A VIACOM COMPANY

Technical Support:

If you cannot get the CD/Disk to install properly, or you need assistance with a particular situation in the book, please feel free to check out the Knowledge Base on our Web site at **http://www.superlibrary.com/general/support**. We have answers to our most Frequently Asked Questions listed there. If you do not find your specific question answered, please contact Macmillan Technical Support at **(317) 581-3833**. We can also be reached by e-mail at **support@mcp.com**.